THE VERSE REVOLUTIONARIES:
EZRA POUND, H.D.
AND THE IMAGISTS

THE VERSE REVOLUTIONARIES:

Ezra Pound, H.D. and The Imagists

Helen Carr

JONATHAN CAPE
LONDON

Published by Jonathan Cape 2009

2 4 6 8 10 9 7 5 3 1

Copyright © Helen Carr 2009

First published in Great Britain in 2009 by
Jonathan Cape

Random House
20 Vauxhall Bridge Road
London SW1V 2SA

www.rbooks.co.uk

Addresses for companies within The Random House Group Limited
can be found at: www.randomhouse.co.uk/offices.htm

The Random House Group Limited Reg. No. 954009

A CIP catalogue record for this book is available from the British Library

ISBN 9780224040303

The Random House Group Limited supports The Forest Stewardship Council
(FSC), the leading international forest certification organisation. All our titles that
are printed on Greenpeace approved FSC certified paper carry the FSC logo.
Our paper procurement policy can be found at www.rbooks.co.uk/environment

Mixed Sources
Product group from well-managed
forests and other controlled sources
www.fsc.org Cert no. TT-COC-2139
© 1996 Forest Stewardship Council

Typeset in Ehrhardt by Palimpsest Book Production Limited,
Grangemouth, Stirlingshire

Printed and bound in Great Britain by
Clays Ltd, St Ives plc

To Tony, and in memory of Ben Pimlott

CONTENTS

LIST OF ILLUSTRATIONS

SECOND SECTION

PROLOGUE

ONE afternoon in 1912, Ezra Pound, flamboyant poet and polemicist, already viewed by literary London with mingled amusement and alarm, met his fellow-American Hilda Doolittle in the British Museum tea-room. They had both been working in the Reading Room. Pound already had eight – admittedly slim – books to his credit: Doolittle had published nothing but a few children's stories, though she had been writing poetry for some years. She had given him one of her recent poems to read. 'But . . . this is poetry,' Pound exclaimed. He scrawled 'H.D. Imagiste' at the bottom, and took it off to post to *Poetry*, Harriet Monroe's Chicago-based avant-garde magazine.[1] The imagist movement was born.

That, at any rate, is H.D.'s version of the origin of imagism, though according to her future husband, Richard Aldington, the first poet to be published with the imagist label attached, it was in the Fuller tea-shop in Kensington that Pound first named the pair of them imagists. According to Pound himself, he thought up the term one evening, apparently in solitude, and tea-less. But they all three agree that imagism was named by Pound some time in 1912: indeed this is one of the few elements in the contentious and hotly disputed story of the imagist movement on which there is general agreement. Where it came from, whose ideas it represented, what indeed imagism meant, who was or was not an imagist were all fiercely debated questions for most of the movement's existence, as they have been in literary history since.

All these are questions which I try to answer in this book. The advent of the imagists, one of the most turbulent and colourful poetic group-ings of the twentieth century, marked the beginning of Anglo-American modernism, three decades of extraordinary creativity in which appeared the most important works of such writers as T.S. Eliot, Virginia Woolf, Wallace Stevens, W.B. Yeats, James Joyce, D.H. Lawrence, William Carlos

Williams and many more. There were earlier works which would now be identified as modernist, Gertrude Stein's 1909 *Three Lives* for example, but it was with the imagists that it became apparent that a new movement was launched. As Eliot was to say, appropriately rein-voking the imagist habit of turning anything they admired into French, the imagist movement was modern poetry's *point de repère*.[2] Yet what was the imagists' significance for this richly productive period of radical and self-conscious experiment? A disparate, stormy group, who had dispersed before the 1920s began, there is no doubt that they achieved a *succès de scandale*. Their poetry – pared-down, elliptical, fragmentary, vivid, with unexpected images and juxtapositions – exerted a powerful influence on modernist writers, both poets and novelists, and their ideas and the debates they provoked played a vital role in the transformation of American and British cultural life that occurred at the time of the First World War.

The story of the imagists themselves is full of rich drama, involving passion, betrayal, sexual jealousy, literary envy, bereavement, shell-shock, class antagonisms, friendship, adultery, cruelty, bullying and pique. Three years before imagism was named by Pound, many of its ideas and practices were being tentatively explored by a group of young poets who met in the Tour Eiffel restaurant in Soho, led by the pugnacious T.E. Hulme. Of these, only the American Pound and the English F.S. Flint would go on to form part of the later imagist group, Hulme having given up poetry, though his ideas would still be influential, while two of the others, Joseph Campbell and Desmond FitzGerald, were by then more interested in a different kind of revolution, the fight for Irish inde-pendence. The new recruits included, besides H.D. and Aldington, two more Americans, Amy Lowell, rich, charismatic and determined, and the moody, super-sensitive John Gould Fletcher. The English D.H Lawrence would contribute to the anthologies, though always insisting he was not an imagist, but their way of writing undeniably had an impact on his poetry. There had been a possibility that Ford Madox Ford would join them, and though he did not, he plays a not insignificant role in this story; and while W.B. Yeats allegedly described imagist poetry as the 'devil's metres', he was also a potent presence for many of them.[3] Indeed the relative importance of the influence of Yeats, Ford and Hulme is one of the most disputed aspects of the story. Most contentious of all, however, is what one might describe as the third stage of imagism, when Pound's role as impresario was taken over by Amy Lowell. Pound insisted that imagism became hopelessly diluted 'Amygism' after that, and would have nothing to do with the later anthologies. He incorporated his version of imagism into his next movement, Vorticism, which he launched with the painter and writer Wyndham Lewis and the sculptor Gaudier-Brzeska, and found a new poetic ally in T.S. Eliot. Yet it was Lowell's promotion of imagism that had most impact in America. The Vorticists were aggressively masculine, described indeed as 'masculomaniacs' by the art critic, John Cournos; imagism after Pound was very much led by women.

Like the Russian Bolsheviks in 1917 – the year incidentally of the fourth and final annual imagist anthology – the imagists, those 'verse revolutionaries' as Aldington dubbed them, sometimes portrayed themselves as sweeping away the debris of a moribund system and effecting a clean break with their predecessors.[4] Yet for all their attacks on Victorianism they did not so much repudiate the past as create a new story about the traditions they had inherited. Indeed, their insistence that they were upholding the best standards of the greatest writers has caused some critics to accuse them of being an anti-avant-garde, poetic Young Fogeys at heart. The truth was more complex than either position; they certainly wrote in a strikingly new way, a modern *dolce stil nuovo*, but there were many continuities, as well as much that they took over, and others at the time were changing in similar or related ways. As F.S. Flint was to insist, 'Imagism, like all other literary movements, was a general movement, a product and impulse of the time'.[5] It came out of a period of social and intellectual unrest, when the inequalities of a class-ridden and patriarchal society were under fire, and ideas of progress and the superiority of Western modernity increasingly questioned. London was full of people intent on changing the world: socialists, suffragettes, anarchists, proponents of free love, theosophists, Russian émigrés, Irish nationalists, Nietzscheans, Ibsenites, protopsychoanalysts. The imagists wanted to change the world too, though they were by no means agreed on how or in what way; as a group they were not just from different countries but from very different class backgrounds, from those of working-class origin like Flint and Lawrence, to an American patrician like Lowell, a heterogeneous *mélange* perhaps only possible in a great metropolis like London. Meeting in what was already a multicultural city, at the hub of a great empire, they were acutely conscious that there were other ways of being and thinking than those of Victorian Britain. Dissatisfaction with the mechanised modern world, disenchantment with Western rationality, greater knowledge of other cultures, paradoxically the fruit of Western imperialism, had already led modernist painters to a new appreciation of non-Western art. The imagists too drew widely on other cultures, particularly the Japanese and Chinese. Working with translations, discovering themselves, as Paul Ricoeur has put it, by the detour of the other, would be crucial.

There have been books of literary criticism on the imagists before, as well as biographies of a good number of the figures involved in this story and a torrent of critical work on the movement's central figures, on much of which I draw. This, however, is a group biography, an attempt to get beyond the partisan rewriting of history in which so many of its members later participated, to unpick the story of how they came together, what they gained from each other in the heady excitement of those early days, and what fissures eventually broke up the movement and their friendships in the dark days of the Great War. When Aldington asked himself in his memoir, *Life for Life's Sake*, what the imagists achieved between 1912 and 1917, he had a variety of answers, but what he points out with most satisfaction is that 'they livened things up a lot': it is to that lively tale I now turn.[6]

PART I

AMERICAN BEGINNINGS

I

POUND and H.D. were the first of the imagists to meet. They were introduced at a Hallowe'en party in Philadelphia, in 1901. Pound had been
sixteen the day before; H.D. was fifteen. She was still at school; he was,
precociously, a first-year undergraduate, with, as H.D. later remembered,
flaming 'Gozzoli bronze-gold' curls.[1] Pound was wearing an extravagant,
eye-catching green robe, bought for him, in Tunis she thought, by his
Aunt Frank on his first transatlantic visit. 'Immensely sophisticated,'
H.D. recalled, 'immensely superior, immensely rough-and-ready, a
product not like any of the brothers and brothers' friends – and boys
we danced with (and he danced badly) . . . was he showing off?'[2] Yet
when H.D. told him about a friend's sister, who was suffering from
'stupid nerve-specialists', he offered to give her the coat, because he
hoped it might 'cheer her up'.[3] H.D. was intrigued by this contradictory figure, his exhibitionism, his flashiness, his exotic cosmopolitanism,
his lack of Philadelphian propriety, his impulsive generosity. What Pound
thought of H.D. on that occasion is not recorded, though possibly his
kindness to H.D.'s friend had something to do with his being taken with
H.D.'s beauty. But it was 1905 before their relationship developed.

Both Pound and H.D. lived on the outskirts of Philadelphia, Pound
in Wyncote, a suburb to the north, H.D. just outside Philadelphia to
the west, in Upper Darby. The outskirts were where the respectable
Philadelphian bourgeoisie lived. For all the civilised elegance
of Philadelphia's ordered avenues, the middle classes, largely Anglo-Saxon
Protestants, had for some decades gradually drifted to the margins of
the city. Some of the Philadelphian aristocracy – twenty-odd families
– remained in the best areas of the centre. Also in the centre, though
naturally in the less good areas, were the long-established black inhabitants, as well as the continental immigrants, Catholic or Jewish, who

had poured in during the last century. H.D.'s family had specific reasons for living where they did, for her father, a distinguished astronomer, was Professor of Astronomy and Mathematics at the University of Pennsylvania, and Director of its Flowers Observatory, based in Upper Darby. But neither H.D. nor Pound was native to Philadelphia, and neither found it congenial. That story of the Hallowe'en party, which H.D. told in 1933 when she was beginning analysis with Freud, undoubtedly carries more than one level of meaning. The friend's sister, one might note, was suffering, not from 'nerves', but from 'stupid nerve-specialists'. In 1901, the most renowned nerve specialist in the States, Silas Weir Mitchell, practised in Philadelphia. Mitchell, whose famous rest-cure was first developed in 1873, is probably best known nowadays through his patient Charlotte Perkins Gilman, who recorded her account of his methods in her nightmarish story, 'The Yellow Wallpaper'. He treated unhappy, disturbed or disturbing young women with enforced bed-rest, large amounts of food, and the complete absence of intellectual stimulation. As those who have read Gilman's story will know, writing was regarded as particularly undesirable; passivity, dependence and conformity were the rest-cure's aims. For H.D., who had come to Freud for help with her writing block, Silas Weir Mitchell must have hovered in her mind as a symbol of all she had found stifling and inhibiting in Philadelphia. H.D.'s relationship with the bizarrely colourful, oddly foreign Pound, deeply though it hurt her, was to make possible her escape from what Henry James described as the 'charming pink and drab heritage' of Philadelphia.[4] Pound, she would later say, was the scorpion sting that set her free.

H.D.'s family had moved to Upper Darby when she was nine, from Bethlehem on the north-east border of Pennsylvania. Her parents, like so many late nineteenth-century bourgeois couples, lived lives shaped by a strict division of gender roles, and as she grew up, H.D. saw in them a cleavage of the world into male and female whose irreconcilability was to haunt her for decades. It was at the heart of the problems she brought to Freud in the early 1930s. Charles Doolittle, H.D.'s father, was born in 1843, and was ten years older than her mother, his second wife: his first had borne him two sons, but died giving birth to a daughter, who also died. As early as H.D. could remember, he was a venerable, bearded, distant figure, much preoccupied with his research, a brooding, forbidding presence at the dinner table. He came from what seemed to her the faraway country of Indiana. His ancestors, she told Freud, were Puritans; they had exterminated Indians and burnt witches. He had enlisted in the Civil War at seventeen, claiming to be eighteen; he had seen, and inflicted, pain and death. He spent every clear night at his telescope, no matter what the temperature; some nights his beard froze to the glass. H.D. was the fourth of six living children from the two families, and the only surviving girl (her mother's first baby had also been a girl, who died). She was her father's favourite child, though that to her was a burden rather than a reassurance; and to her pain her mother's favourite was her older brother Gilbert.

Bethlehem, her first home, was her mother's birthplace. It had been founded in 1741 by a group of Moravian Brethren, escaping persecution in Europe. They were one of several such sects to be accepted by the tolerant Pennsylvanian Quakers (others included the Amish, the Mennonites, the Schwenkfelders and the Dunkers). The Moravians claimed to be the earliest Protestants, having seceded from the Church of Rome in 1467, though their German Reformed neighbours in Pennsylvania accused them of popish practices. Unusually among Nonconformist Protestants, their rituals were aesthetically satisfying and dense with symbolism. Like the Quakers, Moravians were pacifists, and had a gentle and tolerant way of life. They were cultured, valued learning and had a particularly strong musical tradition; Bethlehem is still famous today for its annual Bach Festival, founded by H.D.'s maternal uncle Frederick. Unlike her father's ancestors, the Moravians had good relations with their Native American neighbours, and one of the most sympathetic accounts of Native American culture to be published before the twentieth century was written by the Moravian Brethren missionary John Heckewelder, an account that inspired Longfellow's *Hiawatha* and Cooper's portrayal of the Delaware Indians. (A Native American chief, said to be the model for Cooper's Chingachgook, is buried in 'God's Acre', the original Moravian cemetery in Bethlehem.) H.D.'s mother was artistic; before her marriage, she had begun to train as a painter, and had taught painting and music. But, though her paintings hung in the house, she had ceased to paint when she married. She still played the piano, though she had given up singing. She occupied herself with the children of the two marriages, and with domestic and religious affairs.

Pound's family were not quite of the same class as H.D.'s – one of several reasons for her parents' alarm when they feared he might become a prospective son-in-law, or worse. To be more exact, Pound's father was not the same class: his mother, Isabel, whose family were related to the Wadsworths of Henry Wadsworth Longfellow fame, and who had

smart New York relations, was not so different from the Doolittles. If
Isabel had come slightly down in the world, she made up for that in
intense gentility, and awed her neighbours with her 'high society' voice.[5]
Pound's father Homer, unpretentious, earnest, a little slow, 'the naïvest
man who ever possessed sound sense', as Pound described him, came
from a more mixed and rackety background.[6] 'Mrs Pound,' H.D. wrote,
'was a beautiful woman, well-bred, somewhat affected in manner. One
was inclined to be embarrassed and baffled by her little witticisms, her
epigrams, as one so often was by Ezra's. Mr Pound was hearty, informal,
very kind.'[7]

In his youth Pound identified, the evidence suggests, with his mother's
family, particularly with his dashing Aunt Frank who had him to stay
regularly in the metropolitan delights of New York, and took him for
exciting European tours. In later life, however, when he came to denounce
the bourgeois propriety so dear to his mother, his sympathies moved
more to his father's side, or at least his own colourful reconstruction of
his father's family history. Yet even as an adolescent and in his early
twenties, he would tell his father of problems or scrapes, rather than
his more demanding and easily shocked mother. In 1920, when he left
England, having buried one version of himself in *Hugh Selwyn
Mauberley*'s elegant 'E.P. Ode pour l'Election de Son Sepulcre', he
wrote a quite different burlesque prose account of his origins, entitled
Indiscretions, in which the phrase in that ode, 'born/In a half savage
country', is expanded to 60 pages. Pound's grandfather Thaddeus had
indeed been born in a log cabin, of a Quaker family that had been in
the States for over a century, though not perhaps two, as *Indiscretions*
claimed. He married one Sarah Loomis, whose family Pound with
dubious evidence claims to have been horse-thieves. It was doubtless
part of his rejection of the bourgeois side of his descent that he finally,
after considerable wavering, settled on Loomis for his middle name
rather than his mother's surname Weston. Thaddeus moved to
Wisconsin, and Pound's father was the first white child to be born there,
being looked after by a Chippewa nurse, and learning Chippewa before
English. Thaddeus was always a hero to Pound. He rose to become a
senator, and would have been a member of the cabinet had it not been
that by then he had left his wife and was living with another woman,
this time 'without sanction of clergy'.[8] He was a highly successful entrepreneur, and salvaged his stolid and unworldly son's career at various
stages. It was he who obtained Homer the job as land-assessor in the
frontier town of Hailey, Idaho, partly in order to have his own rights to

silver mines there safeguarded, a task in which Homer singularly failed. Isabel Pound, and her mother even more so, were appalled by the 'half-savage' behaviour of the settlers, and they headed home when young Pound (the Infant Gargantua as he named himself in *Indiscretions*) was eighteen months old. They lived in New York for a few years, until Homer was offered a job at the Government Assessor's office in Philadelphia, and they moved first to West Philadelphia and then north to Wyncote, to a comfortably big house, paid for by Thaddeus. The young Pound, much doted on by his parents throughout his life, had four free bedrooms at his disposal, and moved between them, getting into practice for the itinerant life.

Homer's employment was for many years precarious: government employees had no employment rights and were liable to be sacked without a second thought with every change in policy or administration. The family kept a maid (black, of course) but they were much less well off than many of their neighbours. Homer, however, held on to his job, and rose to become second in command, though never, according to his son, well paid. In *Indiscretions*, Pound's first memory of life past the age of three is of visits with his father to the Mint, which was then housed in an imposing building built to resemble the Parthenon. Later H.D. went with Pound to see Homer at work and was amazed by the 'stacks of gold bars': looking back, she wondered how much Pound's later obsession with economics could be traced back to his father's work: 'I don't mean that Ezra wanted the gold for himself. He wanted to change the world with it.'[9] Pound's memories of these mounds of gold, each bar too heavy to lift (one of Homer's favourite jokes was inviting visitors to help themselves), combined with his experience of his own and his fellow-writers' financial struggles, perhaps lay behind his dogmatic embrace in the inter-war years of Major Douglas's ill-conceived Social Credit theory. If Social Credit were implemented, it would, he believed, produce plenty for everyone – resources would be properly distributed and prevented from falling into the hands of greedy speculators and the malign banking profession.

Pound, as H.D. knew, all his life made global assumptions based on his personal experience. In *Indiscretions* he asserted that his family history was a miniature of that of the whole United States. His later vision in the *Cantos* of an America with an ordered, cultured, beauty-conscious past which had degenerated into a utilitarian, morally grubby and money-centred present surely had its primary model in his home city. In the late eighteenth century, Philadelphia had been politically and culturally the leading city of America. The Declaration of Independence was signed there; hence the city's honorary title as 'Birthplace of the Nation', and its choice for the first centennial celebrations in 1876. Philadelphia was capital of the young United States from 1790 to 1800. Before the American Revolution it had already become the centre of the book trade, of publishing, and of cultural life. The University of Pennsylvania had been established in 1740, the American Philosophical Society founded there by Benjamin Franklin in 1743, and the Philadelphia Academy of Fine Arts in 1805. But during the nineteenth century Philadelphia lost its cultural supremacy to Boston. It produced no important writers; during Pound's and H.D.'s youth its most acclaimed author was none other than the nerve specialist Silas Weir Mitchell, who had a second and apparently equally remunerative career as a popular novelist and poet. When Henry James visited the University of Pennsylvania in 1905, it was Dr Silas Weir Mitchell, as the pre-eminent local man of letters, who showed him round. (Silas Weir Mitchell has a mention in Sir Paul Harvey's 1932 *Oxford Companion to English Literature*, a compilation which forbears to acknowledge the existence of either Pound or H.D., though Pound – if he ever looked at it – would have welcomed its warm account of Mussolini's Fascists.) The University of Pennsylvania in Pound's day had less than 15 per cent humanities students, the vast majority studying medicine, economics or science, and even the humanities courses (to Pound's lasting outrage) were primarily based on the accumulation of scholarly facts, not on any kind of philosophical or cultural value. All American universities were increasingly moving away from the arts, but the average in 1910 was one-third classical to two-thirds vocational: the University of Pennsylvania was an extreme example.

Politically, Philadelphia's reputation was very different from its early days. Penn's City of Brotherly Love, founded on his tolerant ideals, had become a place of intolerance and prejudice. During the nineteenth century racism and xenophobia grew along with the immigrant population; the city that had welcomed religious exiles now burnt down Catholic and black churches. In the years in which H.D. and Pound grew up, the city was managed by Republicans well known for their corruption; indeed in an era when the widespread corruption of American cities was being exposed by muckraking journalists, Philadelphian city politicians were regarded as the most corrupt of all. But what the city of Philadelphia had maintained was its role as a financial centre. In 1770 it had already become the third most important business centre in the British Empire; it became the birthplace of

American banking (anathema to the later Pound), and possessed its first stock exchange. The Philadelphia Commercial Exchange was opened in 1868, the Maritime Exchange in 1875, and the Philadelphia Bourse in 1891. It was wealth that allowed the upper and middle classes of the city in their domestic life to remain complacently and oppressively respectable, perhaps why the most famous of the muckrakers, Lincoln Steffens, in his book *The Shame of the Cities*, described Philadelphia as both 'corrupt and contented'.[10] There was more artistic life, particularly in the visual arts, than Pound ever gave the city credit for, but, for Pound, Philadelphia typified the victory of commercialism over art, and the worst of provincial philistinism.

Henry James – whose attitude to America had much in common with Pound's – had a deeply equivocal response to Philadelphia on his 1905 visit there, and his interpretation of the city undoubtedly influenced Pound's later view. According to the account in *The American Scene*, the book which for Pound was the 'triumph of the author's long practice . . . A book no "serious American" will neglect',[11] James was at first rather taken with the place, delighted that for once he had come to an American city that, as he put it, 'didn't *bristle*', a city where, as he looked out of his 'ample, tranquil window', the 'note of the perpetual perpendicular' was absent. Philadelphian high society – the twenty-odd best families mentioned earlier – was intricately interrelated, 'every individual was as many times over cousin, uncle, aunt, niece, and so through the list, as poor human nature is susceptible of being'. He felt he was sure to discover that Philadelphia would be, 'of all goodly villages, the very goodliest, probably, in the world; the very largest, and flattest, and smoothest, the most rounded and complete'. But to his dismay, he found that 'parallel' to this 'most genial and delightful' elite society, 'beside it and beneath it, behind it and before it, enclosing it as in a frame of fire in which it still had the secret of keeping cool' was 'a proportionate City . . . organized all for plunder and rapine, the gross satisfaction of official appetite, organized for eternal iniquity and impunity'. In no other place than Philadelphia, he says, except perhaps at Jefferson's house, Mount Vernon, 'does our historic past so enjoy the felicity of an "important" concrete illustration', especially in the 'amplitude and decency', 'serenity and symmetry' of Independence Hall, where the Declaration was signed. But in the Philadelphian penitentiary he found a mirror-image of the genial club patronised by the best families, this time a club whose members' faces show them all to be of 'full-blown basenesses'.

This reading of the American fall into the rank and mercenary abyss would become centrally important to Pound after he left the country, but in his youth he, like H.D., was much more aware of the boredom than of the baseness of Philadelphia, of its smooth surface rather than its murky depths, of what James refers to as its 'immeasurable bourgeois blankness', its 'afternoon blandness . . . the little marble steps and lintels and cornices and copings, all the so clear, so placed accents in the good prose text of the mildly purple houses, which seemed to wear them, as all the others did, up and down the streets, in the manner of nice white stockings, neckties, collars, cuffs'. The word 'drab' appears over a dozen times in the chapter on Philadelphia. According to James, Philadelphia was not vulgar, but its keynote was drabness. According to the Philadelphians, as will become apparent, Pound, by 1908, was a vulgar, strident, if poetic, aberration in its bland, commendably drab, prose text.

II

POUND suggests in *Indiscretions*, just after he has described a scene with his grandfather when he was three, that 'the serpent appeared early in his garden'.[12] Perhaps the expulsion from Eden came when he started school, which followed the move to Philadelphia. The evidence seems to point to Pound's increasing misery at his educational establishments, mitigated only partially at times by his excited involvement in his work, and the occasional kind teacher. On the whole, he was laughed at, bullied and friendless. Isabel had taught him before he went to school, encouraging him to speak in a formal, polysyllabic style that bemused and disconcerted his fellows, who called him the 'Professor'.[13] No doubt Isabel had also communicated her 'high society' voice, which in the States then meant as English-sounding as possible. (According to Brigit Patmore, when Pound arrived in England he had 'no American accent – or just the slightest,'[14] and though Ford Madox Ford, never in any case a reliable witness, commented on his 'Philadelphian' accent, it was to say it was quite 'comprehensible if disconcerting'.)[15] Pound was too light and small while growing up to fare well at most sports, which might have eased his way.[16] He was all his life devoid of conventional social skills: how much that was a result rather than a cause of his school experience one can only guess, but certainly the rapid movement from idolised son to class butt must have been traumatic for him.

At his first school Pound had one teacher to whom he was devoted, Miss Ridpath, but otherwise he found the teaching of his early years uncongenial. Photographs of him at this stage show a vulnerable, tight-drawn face, the mouth clammed miserably shut, most notably in a photograph taken while he was at Cheltenhan Military Academy, the boarding-school to which he went at the age of eleven, where, the smallest in a crowd of uniformed schoolboys, for the most part confident, broad-faced, and slightly brutal-looking, a pale young Pound in round glasses and uncomfortable collar stares bleakly and blankly out. Pound's cultivation of masks in his early poetry was perhaps a continuation of this earlier face-masking. At Cheltenham, where he stayed until four-teen, he hated the drilling, and felt his failure at sport acutely. He did, however, play tennis, and assured his parents – his letters home were always firmly cheerful – that he was a success at fencing, though according to William Carlos Williams a few years later, his fencing was appalling, not to say dangerous. Pound continued to fence, later prac-tising with W. B. Yeats during his London years, even challenging a startled poet (Lascelles Abercrombie) to a duel, and he also remained enthusiastic about tennis. It is perhaps significant that neither tennis nor fencing is a team sport. Pound's relations with the staff appear to have been no better than with his fellow-pupils – one letter home says, 'things are going a little better and I only got two demerits this week'.[17] He left Cheltenham in mysterious circumstances – there were, it appears, unconfirmed rumours of a homosexual incident. As a slight, pretty boy in an all-male school, it seems possible.[18]

While Pound was at Cheltenham he had made the transatlantic visit with Aunt Frank and his mother from which he returned with the exotic green coat, visiting England, Belgium, Germany, France, Italy, Spain and Tangiers in this American version of the Grand Tour.[19] As H.D. bears witness, he managed in his three months abroad to acquire a veneer of cosmopolitanism, sufficient at any rate to impress an untravelled schoolgirl. By the time he entered the University of Pennsylvania in 1901, two years younger than most of his year, he appears to have learnt to meet rejection head-on by cultivating a high-profile isolation. When H.D. tried to find out what was held against him, no one could define quite what made him so unacceptable:

'What is it?' They would never answer directly. They would say, 'He is so eccentric.' 'What is it?' 'He is impossible; he told Professor Schelling that Bernard Shaw was more important than Shakespeare.' 'What is it?' 'He makes himself conspicuous; he wore lurid, bright socks that the older students ruled out for freshmen. The sophomores threw him in the lily pond. They called him "Lily" Pound.'[20]

Other practical jokes were played on him, which he affected not to notice. Humphrey Carpenter suggests he was simply unaware that he was being teased, simultaneously too naïve and taking himself too seri-ously to grasp such a possibility. Appealing though this interpretation is, and though it fits with the brash, self-confident persona Pound would cultivate, it doesn't tally with the pain and self-doubt that often emerges in his early poetry. William Carlos Williams, whom Pound met in his second year, at last making a friend among his fellow-students, wrote home to his mother:

If he ever gets blue nobody knows it, so he is just the man for me. But not one person in a thousand likes him, and a great many people detest him and why? Because he is so darned full of conceits and affectations. He is really a brilliant talker and thinker but delights in making himself just exactly what he is not: a laughing boor. His friends must be all patience in order to find him out and even then you must not let him know it, for he will immediately put on some artificial mood and be really unbearable. It is too bad, for he loves to be liked, but there is some quality in him which makes him too proud to try to please people.[21]

In H.D.'s quasi-autobiographical novel *Her*, the Pound figure, George Lowndes, also at times transforms disturbingly into a boorish (indeed boar-like) joker:

the sea-green eyes that became sea-grey, that she saw as wide and far and full of odd sea-colour, became . . . small and piglike. George being funny is piglike. His eyes are too small in his face. His teeth are beautiful but when he is being funny he unnerves one.[22]

Perhaps his cultivation of the figure of the 'laughing boor' is what led Pound in 1906 to think of writing a Ph.D. thesis on the role of the *gracioso* or buffoon in Lope de Vega's plays: had he completed it, there might have been some interesting insights into Pound's own psyche. This persona was to emerge again after Pound left England in 1920, as Ole Ez, and later Grampaw, writer of jokey, misspelt, cryptic and frequently offensive letters, but the laughing boor was only part of the self-protective system which Pound was beginning to construct, an emotional armour and armoury which was to last him by and large until his fall into despair and silence in the early 1960s.

As the young Williams was aware, Pound attempted to block, increasingly successfully, any entry into his feelings – sometimes even, one suspects, by himself. Failure would be ignored; uncertainty not countenanced; changes of mind not admitted, instead emerging as attacks on such demented souls as still held the discarded point of view. His conversations with his male friends would always be on literature, the arts, politics – never his emotional life; and even in his love affairs he treated his women more as pupils than as confidantes. Whilst the intensity of those affairs had the appearance of intimacy, he was always, it appears, holding something back – in the early days not least the fact that he was having equally intense quasi-intimacies with other women. Not to give himself completely was his lifelong pattern; for decades he balanced his relationships with Dorothy Pound and Olga Rudge and other devotees. Of the hundreds of thousands of words of prose he poured out over the years, only the tiniest handful admit openly anything of his inner self. In his poetry, which deals obsessively with isolation, loneliness, exile and loss, those emotions are distanced through historical or mythological personae; as he said in an early poem significantly entitled 'Masks', by 'old disguisings'.[23] The construction of this carapace needs more than his painful school experience to explain it. It may also have been related to his relationship with his mother, of whom he was undoubtedly both deeply fond and deeply wary; he was in 1918 to refer to 'the maternal or abysmal relation'.[24] In any case, emotional vulnerability was scarcely regarded, either in Philadelphia or London, as a manly trait.

In these early days the armour was by no means securely in place, and Williams was certainly right, one would guess, in thinking that Pound 'love[d] to be liked'. Pound had a great hunger for admiration and emotional support, and, luckily for him, his isolation in his university years was mitigated by a series of significant relationships. The first, possibly one of the most deeply felt of his life, was with William Brooke Smith, a young art student whom he met at about the time he began university. Pound later referred to Smith as his 'first friend', and spoke of his memories '*eius mihi caritate primus*', 'of him who first was dear to me'.[25] Smith was, it seems, the only male friend to whom Pound risked revealing his emotions: their friendship had a tenderness which none of his later relationships matched. William Brooke Smith was a year and a half older than Pound, and a painter. When they first met, probably in 1901 or early 1902, Smith was studying ceramics at what was later known as the Philadelphia College of Art, then the School of Industrial Art. Philadelphia had been one of the centres, though less important than either Boston or New York, of the American arts and crafts movement, which had reached the United States during the 1870s, when, in the post-Civil War boom, the country was rapidly becoming more industrial, and the educated East Coast bourgeoisie in particular feared the emergence of a new America devoted exclusively to the profit motive, where quantity would always be more important than quality, and where tradition and beauty would have no place. No single event had done more to introduce the movement than the 1876 Centennial Exhibition in Philadelphia itself, one of whose most spectacular exhibits was a cast-iron Japanese pagoda, a fusing of Eastern and Western art that the later Pound would have admired. The School of Industrial Art was founded that same year, the first of many such colleges that were created to put into practice John Ruskin's belief that artisans should have the spirit and training of artists.[26]

Through Smith, Pound learnt much about the world of the arts that passed many Penn students by. He was introduced to the Pre-Raphaelites and the aesthetic movement, and Noel Stock suggests it was to this friendship that Pound 'owed the threads and echoes from Pater's *Appreciations* and Wilde's *Intentions* which appear later in his work'.[27] It seems to have been through Smith that Pound first discovered the English poets of the 1890s (by 1902, Noel Stock says, he was reading poetry by Arthur Symons, Ernest Dowson and Fiona Macleod), Maeterlinck, the best known of the Symbolists in the States at this time, and the translations of Andrew Lang. Smith was in addition an enthusiast for the works of Shaw, and it was probably from him that Pound learnt to admire Ibsen. These iconoclastic dramatists were certainly important in giving Pound the beginnings of a critical distance from Philadelphian bourgeois mores, the sense of an intellectual world out there, on his side against the conventions. But emotionally and artistically the introduction to Pater, the Pre-Raphaelites and their successors was for some years to be much the most significant to him in his rejection of the American doctrine of progress and its materialistic present. In particular, Pater's radical apostasy from Victorian values played a vital role in enabling him to escape Philadelphian conformity. Pater's contribution to the aesthetic movement is sometimes presented as more style than the seismic shift it actually was, though Oscar Wilde, for one, understood how truly revolutionary and disturbing Pater was, how deeply subversive of all that Victorian society stood for: morality, duty, earnestness. Pater's is a post-Christian doctrine. In a world without a divine plan, without recompense in another existence, all we have is the brief span of human life; as one of his most famous passages puts it:

Not the fruit of experience, but experience itself, is the end. A counted number of pulses only are given to us of a variegated, dramatic life . . . While all melts under our feet, we may well catch at any exquisite passion . . . we have an interval, and then our place knows us no more. Some spend this interval in listlessness, some in high passions, some, the wisest, . . . in art and song . . . For art comes to you proposing frankly to give nothing but the highest quality to your moments as they pass, and simply for those moments' sake.[28]

Not all the aesthetes could cope with this radicalism, which is perhaps why so many turned to Catholicism, absinthe or the occult. Yet, though Pater might write in the wake of the death of the Christian God, he reinvokes the pagan gods and goddesses and a sensuous humanism. He does not offer an empty universe, but one of multiple pulsing energies whose centre is human subjectivity. It is not easy to be sure how thoroughly Pound read Pater, for he was not a great prose reader, but what is certain is that many of Pater's attitudes and phrases suffuse his writing as a young man, and in his early and not so early comments on poetry, Pater's passionate aestheticism and celebration of the visionary moment are central to his thought.[29] The heritage of Paterian aesthetics was to be vitally important for the imagist movement as a whole, even when the imagist poets, particularly Pound, repudiated him. The imagist poem in its brief intensity would be in itself, one could argue, an attempt to record 'the highest quality of [our] moments as they pass'.

Smith lived in one of the grand Philadelphian mansions; his aunt, who had taken him in after his parents died, was married to a rich lawyer and city politician, at the time Sheriff of Philadelphia. After Smith left college in 1905, he set up a studio as a designer in their house, and Pound visited him frequently. He took Smith one day to meet H.D. in Upper Darby. She knew Smith was Pound's best friend of the time, and in *End to Torment* she gives a brief but evocative picture of the young painter:

Ezra had brought him to see me. He was an art student, tall, graceful, dark, with a 'butterfly bow' tie, such as is seen in the early Yeats portraits. Ezra read me a letter he wrote . . . The letter was poetic, effusive . . . The boy was consumptive. His sister had just died.[30]

Smith was on his way to visit his sister's grave, in the cemetery where he himself would be buried in 1908. In spite of ill health, he was passionate about his work as an artist. Designing was essentially a way of earning money. Smith's heart was in his painting. He succeeded in selling a few pictures, but, not unnaturally at this stage, scarcely a sufficient number to live on, and his rich relations did not approve of subsidising an artist's life. His friends were other young artists, notably Morton Schamberg and Charles Sheeler, who later made reputations as modernist painters and photographers, Sheeler becoming one of the outstanding American modernist artists.

Only three of the 'poetic, effusive' letters from Smith have survived, one undated, and two from 1907. No letters are extant from Pound to Smith. The undated letter makes it clear that Smith was already suffering from the consumption from which he would die:

My very dear Boy: –

Thank you so much for the beautiful verses. You understand just what I have been thinking, and just the cry that is in my soul, so I don't have to say any more than my joy in the knowledge that it is so.

I have been busy, trying to do some work each day, but I tire myself out so soon and get fatigued so early in the game . . . My dear, I wish you were here to-night. I would put out every light and I would not speak, but you would give me peace. Peace and rest.

Good night.

Toujours W.

That Pound could have been associated with peace and rest by any of his acquaintance now seems remarkable; Pound clearly showed a different face to Will. Another letter dated April 1907, written only a year before Smith's death, yet full of fervour, gives a particular insight into the aesthetic passion that Smith communicated to the young Pound. He begins by apologising for a criticism that he has made of Pound's poetry which he fears Pound misunderstands:

I didn't mean that lack of color was lack of loveliness, for you know me to love the quiet, still things best, and the days of fading flower and falling leaf best of all, So don't think that because I said as I did, I fail to see what you write. These days of awakening life and throbbing pulses . . . have perhaps made me wish to see everything through a golden veil, rather than through a violet mist. The whole world of jade and sapphire is calling to me, and with God in his heaven surely there is a song of joy and gladness. I can't sing the song, so you must, because you are part of me . . .

Goodby. You are very dear to me.[31]

James Wilhelm, who identified these letters, has pointed out the Browning reference here ('God in his heaven'), and the vigorous

Browning was, as is well known, a potent influence on the young Pound. Yet the actual language (fading, falling, golden veil, violet mist, jade, sapphire) is more like the poetry of the 1890s than Browning, and these letters show Smith's deeply Paterian desire for intensity of feeling and response.

One question that Brooke Smith's letters inevitably raise for the present-day reader is how far this friendship was a homoerotic one. Pater and Wilde among other of the aesthetes are associated with homo-erotic attachments, and the closeness that Brooke Smith's letter suggests between himself and Pound could be read in those terms. The young Pound, it has to be said, appears to have delighted in raising the gravest doubts about his inclinations with his dandified airs and outfits. When he was sacked in 1907 from Wabash College in Crawfordsville, Pound told H.D.: 'They say in Wyncote I am bi-sexual and given to unnatural lust'.[32] He had clearly raised doubts in his home town, though in fact the scandal imagined by the people of Crawfordsville only amounted to accusations of the most mundane heterosexual impropriety. In Wilhelm's final footnote to the article in which he published these letters he writes, referring to the rumours about Pound's departure from Cheltenham that I mentioned earlier, 'One should not mistake effusive Edwardian mannerisms for direct sexual contact'.[33] Wilhelm is right, of course, that one must not read 1907 language as if it were written today: modern definitions of homosexuality were only emerging at that period, and even more slowly in the States than in Europe. Whitman was trau-matised, or claimed to be, by J.A. Symonds' homosexual interpretation of his poetry. There were no American sexologists like Edward Carpenter or Havelock Ellis. According to Silas Weir Mitchell's biographer (appro-priately enough named Ernest Earnest), on the one occasion when Mitchell began to read a book about Freud, he was scandalised, exclaiming with horror, 'Where did this thing come from?' He threw the book straight on the fire – straight in the sense of immediately, that is to say, not, as it happened, very accurately, and his provident – or prurient – nephew was later able to rescue it. As Earnest comments: 'American mores made it almost impossible for psychiatrists to study the part that sex plays in the psyche'.[34] Earnest slightly overstates the case: in Massachusetts, particularly at the radical Clark University, some psychologists were already putting forward theories of the unconscious and of childhood sexuality. But they had to be circumspect; as late as 1913, one well-known psychologist, Morton Prince, was threatened with arrest by the Boston police for writing psychoanalytic articles that dealt with sex.[35] Yet, four years before that, only two years after Smith wrote his letter, Freud came to the USA to lecture at Clark, and his lectures were reported, even if in bowdlerised form, in the highly respectable *Boston Evening Transcript*.

Ever since the Wilde trial, however, the late Victorian idealisation of sublimated male love as a spiritual and creative experience had become suspect. This was a time of transition, and Smith's language is hard to gauge. Smith certainly moved in circles where close male-bonding was valued. Sheeler and Schamberg lived together and were largely inseparable until Schamberg's sudden death in October 1918. Pound and Smith's relationship was different, of course, if only because Pound by 1904 had already embarked on a series of heterosexual relationships. Wilhelm is probably right that it was an emotional relationship, a meeting of minds, rather than a physical one, since this was, after all, Philadelphia, and Pound, at any rate, still quite prudish. Smith was certainly at times too advanced for him – later Pound recounted his horror when Smith showed him the edition of Wilde's *Salomé* illustrated by Beardsley: he was so disturbed he cut the pictures out. If the story about the homosexual incident at Cheltenhan Military Academy is true, the most likely explanation is probably that advances were made to a frightened small Pound, and that he demanded of his parents that he be taken away; if he had been expelled for 'impure' behaviour the assiduous combers of Poundiana would doubtless have discovered it. Yet none of his letters to women suggests an intimacy of comparable depth to that with Brooke Smith; indeed, with the exception of those in 1910 to 1912 to his patron, Margaret Cravens, though chatty, and full of advice on books and art, they give very little away of Pound's inner life at all.

Pound wrote of Smith in 1921: 'How in Christ's name he came to be in Phila. – and to know what he did know at the age of 17–25 – I don't know. At any rate, thirteen years are gone; I haven't replaced him and shan't and no longer hope to.'[36] Smith was clearly an exceptional young man, and as Wilhelm suggests might have made a name for himself as an artist as his friends Sheeler and Schamberg were to do. Yet as a student at a college devoted to the arts and crafts movement, Smith would necessarily have learnt about the Pre-Raphaelites, at any rate as artists and craftsmen, as well as about the work of Beardsley. As a member of the sophisticated Arts Club associated with the art schools, as the friend of those who were to be leading artists, he moved in circles where new 'advanced' ideas were being discussed. It is typical of Pound that he wants to praise the individual not the milieu, and that he refuses to credit a Philadelphian educational establishment with any kind of enlightenment. In that once again he was judging by his own experience. All his life he continued to inveigh against the way literature was taught at places like the University of Pennsylvania, where the study of literary texts in whatever language was essentially historical and philological, based on the system at German universities, and introduced to Penn only fifteen years earlier as the 'best modern method', in Yeats' ironic phrase, by Professor Felix Schelling. Schelling – the professor to whom Pound had announced Shaw's superiority to Shakespeare – was a prominent Shakespearean, but a learned scholar rather than a literary critic: his department had earlier produced the weighty Variorum Shakespeare. Schelling, for his part, remembered Pound solely as 'a remarkably idle student'. 'I recall saying to him,' he claimed in after years, 'Mr Pound, you are either a humbug or a genius.' There is no uncertainty about which of these terms he thought in 1903 best described Pound.[37]

III

POUND later claimed that he first decided to be a poet when he was fifteen, that is, about the time he met Smith, and it may well have been this early friendship that led him to his discovery of his vocation. Certainly the white cravat and aesthetic garb that Pound took to wearing early in his university career, to the consternation of his more conservatively attired fellow-students, could well have been the product of his admiration for Smith. If his association with the Yeatsian art student did not influence his decision to *be* a poet – though it most likely did – it certainly encouraged him to *act* the poet, which he continued to do through all his London years. Pound became an artist in the tradition of dandy and showman established by Whistler, Wilde and Beardsley, outrageous but highly effective self-promoters. When Amy Lowell met him in 1913, she wrote to a friend: 'I imagine that never, since the days of Wilde, have such garments been seen in the streets of London. He arrays himself like the traditional "poet" of the theatre.'[38] But Pound's friendship with Smith undoubtedly played a crucial role in his early poetic career, opening up his horizons, enabling him to discover at an early age the heady world of aesthetic passion, and giving him his first close association with a fellow-artist.

Pound's second friendship with an artist, this time a fellow-poet, was with William Carlos Williams, who came to the University of Pennsylvania in 1902. Word had got round that Pound was a literary type, and he was introduced to Williams as such. This was a very different kind of relationship from that with Smith, much more combative and wary. Though companionship was essential to Pound, friendship in the sense of an equal relationship was not something that came easily to him. He found the role of disciple (in the early days) or of guru and leader (increasingly) more congenial. In his relationship with Smith,

admiring disciplehood seems to have played an important part; with
Williams, Pound, although two years younger, did his best to conde-
scend, though not entirely successfully. Williams was taken with Pound,
it is true; 'it just took one look and I knew it was it'. Before and after
meeting Pound was, he said, like 'BC and AD', a compliment that oddly
highlights how different they were.[39] For the forward-looking Williams
perhaps the analogy of historical progress came naturally, but it was a
curiously inappropriate simile to apply to meeting Pound, for whom AD
was certainly not necessarily better than BC. Williams claimed later that
as a student Pound was 'completely indifferent' to the present, and
'absorbed, completely absorbed' in 'the romantic times' of the past.[40]
He never took Pound as seriously as Pound took himself; the real strength
of the relationship, at any rate in those early years, seems to have lain
in their sheer disregard for each other's estimation of their work,
combined with appreciation of their shared interest in writing. Pound,
Williams wrote, 'was not impressed' by the poetry he showed him. 'He
was impressed with his own poetry; but then, I was impressed with my
own poetry, too, so we got on pretty well.'[41] Williams was writing imitation Keats and Pound imitation Pre-Raphaelite poetry, and they found
identifying each other's weaknesses easy.

Williams' family had come to the States when he was a baby. His
father was English, his mother Caribbean Spanish, of part Jewish
descent. Williams' home culture was in many ways European rather
than American; he sometimes spoke Spanish at home, and had spent a
year in a school in Geneva, and then in Paris. ('I knew French which
impressed Pound,' Williams wrote later, 'and he thought I knew more
Spanish than I did. I never let on.')[42] His father was an advertising
manager for a cologne manufacturer, never well off, but a man of culture.
His mother, like H.D.'s, had wanted to be a painter, but also gave up
that ambition on marriage. Williams studied dentistry, and later medicine, and, unlike Pound, was a hard worker, with little leisure outside
his medical courses: he was pleased to have found someone with more
time than himself for books and with enthusiasm for talking about them.
Unlike Pound again, indeed to Pound's amazement and disgust, Williams
was to remain in the States, a central figure in non-expatriate American
modernism. Williams and Pound sturdily continued for some years to
pour scorn on the other's work, particularly their respective first books.
But they came to admire each other's poetry: Pound helped Williams
to get his second book, *The Tempers*, published in London in 1913
(though he was only prepared to admit to liking two of the poems), and

was to ask Williams to contribute to the 1914 *Des Imagistes* anthology.[43]
The imagist movement was to have a profound influence on Williams,
whose poems were often more imagist than Pound's own. Their sometimes cantankerous, always uneasy friendship was to last throughout
their lives.

One of the curious things about Pound in those years was that he
somehow made sure that Smith and Williams never met, in spite of the
fact that Williams was acutely interested in the visual arts, and spent
his Sundays – apart from church – painting. One of Williams' other
close friends at university was Charles Delmuth, later well known as an
artist: Williams met Charles Sheeler in New York after Schamberg's
death, in about 1919 or 1920, and they became lifelong friends, with
Williams writing about Sheeler's work, which like his own focused on
American urban modernity – all that Pound rejected. Yet it was only in
the 1920s that Pound mentioned his friendship with Smith to Williams.
Even in his Philadelphian days Pound's life was already sprouting
compartments. The university was, for the most part, at any rate in his
first two years, the scene of ignominy and hostility; his friendship with
Smith, happiness and acceptance. Perhaps he didn't want to risk letting
the two worlds make contact. But it is an indication of the limitations
of his friendship with Williams. Williams was to claim Pound in his
autobiography as one of his own few 'intimate' male friends, but he also
clearly reveals the complex mixture of emotions they aroused in each
other:

He was the livest, most intelligent and unexplainable thing I'd ever seen, and the
most fun – except for his often painful self-consciousness and his coughing laugh.
As an occasional companion over the years he was delightful, but one did not want
to see him often or for any length of time. Usually I got fed to the gills with him
after a few days. He, too, with me, I have no doubt . . . He was often brilliant but
an ass. But I never (so long as I kept away) got tired of him, or, for a fact, ceased
to love him . . . What I could never tolerate in Pound or seek for myself was the
'side' that went with all his posturings as a poet.[44]

Pound may have made a splash in his 'posturings' as a poet at the
University of Pennsylvania, but academically he had two undistinguished
years. He moved on to complete his undergraduate degree at the smaller,
private Hamilton College in New York State. Hamilton had been attended
by the Reverend Carlos Tracy Chester, until 1901 the minister at their
local Presbyterian church, and now a family friend: he later organised

the publication of some of Pound's earliest prose in the Philadelphian *Book News Monthly*, where he was co-editor, and Pound would dedicate to him his third book of poetry, *Exultations*. The actual decision to move appears to have been mainly that of the seventeen-year-old Pound, made on the grounds that Hamilton would offer him a range of European languages unavailable to him on his course at the University of Pennsylvania, where taking on extra languages at the third year was not permitted. It was Pound himself who visited Hamilton in June 1903 and arranged to enter the following academic year. His mother (and possibly very briefly Pound himself) had hopes that he would make it to the lucrative diplomatic service, and that prospect may have been what persuaded his parents to pay the much greater cost of Hamilton. In addition, they perhaps hoped he would work harder in a smaller place, and away from Smith.

After his June visit Pound had been full of enthusiasm for this new move; he was, he told his father, 'delighted with about everything'. Yet in the autumn, his beginnings at Hamilton were not propitious. Having written to explain to his father how vital it was, in spite of the cost, to join a fraternity 'or be out in the cold',[45] he was not accepted by a single one, and remained one of the few non-fraternised outcasts, a humiliating and lonely position in the private college system. After some months he admitted to his father ('You needn't tell mother I'm feeling this way about things') that he was 'tired of the place', with no one congenial to share with ('all the fellows fit to room with are in the frats'). He even suggested a return to the University of Pennsylvania.[46] Yet he stayed on at Hamilton, in spite of his loneliness. He did not wish to give up his aim of proficiency in several modern languages, and perhaps even more significantly loved the work and thrived on the kindness and friendship of several of the professors. At Pennsylvania the languages he had worked on were Latin and German, and some Middle English. At Hamilton he added French, Italian, Spanish and Provençal, all of which he studied with a distinguished young Romance scholar, William Pierce Shepard. He also learnt a little Greek, though his Greek was to remain rudimentary, and Anglo-Saxon, to which he took greatly, sending his mother home lists of Anglo-Saxon works that she should read. Hamilton was not so 'modern' as the University of Pennsylvania, and therefore not so determined to prove that the humanities could boast as many facts as a science subject; philology was less important, and enthusiasm more.

Pound was especially drawn to medieval Romance literature, which

the Pre-Raphaelites' romantic recreation of the Middle Ages predis-
posed him to admire. Dante Gabriel Rossetti had led him to Dante and
the early Tuscan poets, but it was Shepard who enabled him to read
them in the original, and was undoubtedly the Hamilton professor from
whom Pound learnt most. He was a withdrawn, ascetic man (Mrs Pound
described him as a 'smokedried skeleton'), but although in general
absorbed in his work and unsociable, he made something of an exception for Pound, who reported home pleasant visits to 'Bill' out of school
hours.[47] The teacher with whom Pound became most friendly, however,
was Joseph Darling Ibbotson. Ibbotson, known by the students as 'Bib',
taught English Literature, Anglo-Saxon and Hebrew. Pound does not
seem actually to have learnt Hebrew, though 'Bible Study', presumably
with Ibbotson, was one of several subjects in which he gained a distinction. He did a course on the 'Literary and dramatic study of the Book
of Job', which was perhaps the foundation of his continuing admiration
for, and possibly unconscious emulation of, the Old Testament prophets.
A letter home to his mother in March 1905 is much more cheerful than
any of the previous year:

Yesterday was quite a day. Two decent classes & two of tomorrows jobs done in
a.m.

P.m. about two hundred pages of french on Raimon de Miravel troubadour of
Provence.

Evening. Called on Bill [Shepard] he was pleased with what I had been about
during week & is willing to give me some Dante which is not catalogued next
term . . . Going on my homeward way at 10 pm I noticed Bibs lights ablaze &
knowing that he is still mostly college boy despite his family & professorship
I dropped in & we smoked & ate & talked an hour or two longer. All these calls
were very pleasant. Today we have been hearing wonders about medical
missions.[48]

Were the medical missions just a sop to his pious mother? At this stage
Pound himself still went to chapel, as he would duly report home,
though more than once, as here, mentioning his attendance rather as a
conciliatory afterthought. In another letter, after an excited account of
a translation he had just done, he adds enigmatically 'Prex [the principal, Dr Stryker] preached a philological sermon this morning'.[49] Pound
was later to date the beginning of his move away from institutionalised

religion to 1901, though he continued going to church for several years after that. Undoubtedly his meeting with Brooke Smith and his 'advanced ideas' in 1901 played a significant part in his ceasing to be an orthodox believer, though Pound blamed the arrival of a new and hearty minister, a writer of bad verses for the papers, for this apostasy. Till then he had been, he said, an earnest Christian, brought up to be a regular church-goer by Homer and Isabel, themselves conscientious and devout Presbyterians. They appear to have belonged to the liberal branch of the American Presbyterian Church, which was relatively undogmatic, able to accommodate, for example, evolutionary theory. According to the historian Francis Prucha, American Presbyterianism's chief belief was in the American way of life. Hence its liberal tolerance did not extend to Catholicism, although Emersonian Transcendentalism was quite acceptable. Pound had gone as a schoolboy with his parents to the Italian Presbyterian Mission in Philadelphia, for which Homer was a tireless worker, striving to transform easygoing Roman Catholic immigrants into strenuous American Protestant citizens.

Pound was later to blame his Presbyterian beginnings for his own unremitting missionary spirit, as he saw his compulsion to persuade all whom he met that their greater happiness lay in recognising that his views were right. During Pound's absence at Hamilton, his parents were spending increasing time on the downtown Philadelphian missions, and both Homer and Isabel were clearly disturbed by their son's growing enthusiasm for writers who purveyed the kind of backward Romish superstitions from which they wrestled to save the Italian immigrants. Pound's obsession with the medieval past was very much at variance with American liberal Presbyterianism, whose progressive theology was already known, ironically in terms of their son's future, as 'modernist'. Isabel wrote to him, one deduces from Pound's reply (Pound rarely saved his parents' letters, unlike their hoarding of every scrap of his), urging him to attend to the moral and intellectual virtues of modern American culture, including modernist theologians and the Emersonians. Emerson was a great favourite of Pound's mother, but Pound was bitterly opposed to his call for a specifically American poet who rejected the European past. Pound responded vigorously:

The joy I get from the mediaevalians [?] is this. You current eventers think you *so* god darn smarter than anybody else that is a comfort to go back to some quiet old cuss of the dark, so called quiet centuries, & find written down the sum & substance of whats worth while in your present day frothiness . . .

But for the love of right mercy & justice don't try to show off modern literature & brain quality

Oh yes. 'E'merson to make one think! (mainly to detect his limitations)

But find me a phenomenon of any importance in the lives of men & nations that you cannot measure with the rod of Dante's alegory . . . until you can show me men of today who shall excel certain men some time dead, I shall continue to study Dante and the Hebrew prophets.[50]

In many ways this reads much like the arguments Pound would be having in his first years in London, defending his love of past writers against the claims of the present. Though from this letter it hardly sounds as if he were as yet giving up his Christian faith, however robustly Pound rebuffed his mother, he must have felt troubled by the problem of reconciling his admiration for the Catholic Middle Ages, both on the one hand the passionate amours of the troubadours and on the other the paradisal visions of Dante, with a Protestant faith whose chief dogmatic requirements were to uphold conventional morality and oppose Roman Catholicism. Pound might have learnt from Smith of the strong precedent among the nineties poets for conversion to Catholicism, but such a move would have been considerably more unacceptable than agnosticism among the Philadelphian middle classes. Yet if Homer and Isabel feared that Pound would go over to Rome, they were mistaken. By the time Pound got far enough away conceivably to contemplate such a thing, the personal, and indeed cultural moment had gone. As Yeats was later famously to describe the end of the 1890s:

Then in 1900 everybody got down off his stilts: henceforth nobody drank absinthe with his black coffee; nobody went mad; nobody committed suicide; nobody joined the Catholic Church; or if they did I have forgotten.[51]

Pound became neither a Catholic nor a decadent. For all his later admiration for 'Latin Order' as a principle, he would scarcely have been happy submitting to church discipline. He, like Yeats, like H.D., like many he was to meet in London, was to be drawn to more esoteric yet inclusive beliefs, reinventing rather than either simply accepting or rejecting Christianity.

In the meantime, for Pound, as for many before him, part of the attraction of the aesthetic doctrines he absorbed at this stage was that

they helped loosen the grip of conventional Christianity without necessarily shedding the religious spirit altogether. For all the ultimately
secular and sceptical basis to Pater's thought, aestheticism was not called
'the Religion of Beauty' for nothing. Aestheticism made it possible to
escape Christian dogma without giving up a sense of the spiritual or
the ineffable; it made it possible to hold on to parts of Christian
symbolism or tradition whilst discarding its dogmatic imperatives. In
the Provençal poets, with their quasi-heretical cult of love, which Pound
believed, following Pater, was partly a revival of pre-Christian traditions,
he found a religion to his liking. Like the works of Dante, Provençal
French was not generally on the Hamilton timetable, and Shepard had
in this case too agreed to a request from Pound for special tuition.
Provençal literature occupied a special place for Pater; these poets, whom
he praised in his essay on 'Aesthetic Poetry', in *The Renaissance* and
elsewhere, he argued had emerged at the 'exquisite' moment when the
Renaissance was born within the Middle Ages:

Here and there, under rare and happy conditions, in pointed architecture, in the
doctrines of romantic love, in the poetry of Provence, the rude strength of the middle
ages turns to sweetness, and the taste for sweetness generated there becomes the seed
of the classical revival in it, prompting it constantly to seek after the springs of perfect
sweetness in the hellenic world.[52]

This combination of 'rude strength' and 'sweetness' must have
appealed to Pound. It is certainly the version of the Provençal poet that
he himself was to present – vigorous yet tender, spirited yet spiritual,
fighters as well as melodious poets. But what must have attracted him
even more in his state of defiant social outcast and lonely aesthete was
Pater's further description of the Provençal poets as ardent rebels against
their society, heretical, beauty-loving spirits, tinged with paganism,
fighting against a moralistic, oppressive authority. Pater identified them
as 'antinomians', a description, incidentally, that has been persuasively
attached to Pound, in theological terms an antinomian being one who
insists that God speaks directly to him or herself, and refuses to bend
to church dictates.[53] Pound's belief that he, as a poet, was, like the troubadours, a follower of 'a strange rival religion' in opposition to the
modern world and its values began in those early years and remained
deep.

For the next seven years, most of Pound's poetry was to consist of
translations, pastiches, recreations and reinventions of the poetry that

he had found through the Pre-Raphaelites and the aesthetes, and that Shepard had enabled him to read. The method he used with Shepard in studying these poets was to write translations of their work in verse that replicated their complex rhyme schemes, a poetic strategy that he would in one way or another employ frequently in his later career, finding a form that, if it did not replicate, echoed the original. Pound gave a warm tribute to Shepard at the beginning of his 1910 book on what Pater would have called 'medieval Renaissance poetry', *The Spirit of Romance*: 'My thanks are due to Dr Wm. P. Shepard of Hamilton College, whose refined and sympathetic scholarship first led me to some knowledge of French, Italian, Spanish and Provençal'.[54] The importance to his imagination of these poets was to remain to the end; the late *Cantos* are still threaded with them.

IV

POUND made another important relationship while at Hamilton, though
not this time within the college itself, but one which also played a part
in his move away from American Presbyterianism. Whilst staying in
New York with Aunt Frank, probably in the late summer of 1904, he
met a concert pianist, Katherine Ruth Heyman. Heyman, known to
Pound and her friends as Kitty, was a fine musician and international
performer. Her main home was in London, but she visited the States
regularly. She was another of Pound's early friends who was of Jewish
descent, though Pound may never have known this, as she routinely
denied it, preferring to emphasise the double-barrelled Anglo-Saxon
credentials of her middle name, Willoughby-Benchley, inherited from
her mother.[55] Pound wrote home about her, with the arrogance that no
doubt contributed much to his isolation at college, saying that it was 'a
comfort to find a person with brains & sense, once in a while.'[56] Later
he described her as his 'second' friend, saying in 1916, 'My first friend
was a painter, male, now dead. 2nd. a Pyanist, naturally 15 [it was actually 11] years plus agée que moi'.[57] Williams is ignored in this account;
by 'friend' in this context Pound clearly means a deeper bond than he
felt his relationship with Williams to be.

Kitty was a deeply moral woman, and Pound apparently was not
given, as he perhaps archly hints here, the traditional services of an
older woman to a young inexperienced lover. Humphrey Carpenter's
suggestion that she was in many ways a mother figure – and perhaps a
less demanding one than Isabel – is persuasive. All the same, in poems
Pound presented her not just as a muse but as his 'Lady' in Provençal,
courtly love fashion, even, in one that he dedicated to her, comparing
her to Dante's Beatrice, leading him to higher things.[58] She gave him a
diamond ring, charging him to keep it for life: he gave it to at least two

of his fiancées, including H.D., within the next few years. But like Smith, Heyman was important not just in herself but for the books and ideas to which she introduced him. Kitty undoubtedly helped his appreciation of music, significant in itself, but she was also a student of the occult, and through her Pound was first introduced to the world of theosophical and mystical writings so compellingly attractive to many intellectuals and artists of the period. Theosophy, the most prevalent form of occultism at that time, was a set of beliefs which can be traced back as far as Pythagoras in the West, but which also drew on Eastern religions, combining belief in the possibility of a direct mystical apprehension of spiritual reality, in the esoteric meanings of certain sacred texts, in reincarnation, and in the oneness of all things; in 1875 the Theosophical Society was founded by Madame Blavatsky and Henry Steele Olcott in New York, though there were numerous splits and dissensions among its followers, theosophy being as prone to sectarianism as any orthodox religion.

From today's standpoint, it is easy to dismiss the occult as a pastime for cranks and simpletons, an earlier version of New Age gullibility, and literary critics have tended to downplay its appeal to turn of the century and modernist writers. But if Pater, Morris and Rossetti were all engaged on a critique of Western modernity and its values, so were those who turned to the occult and theosophy. The Pre-Raphaelites and Pater returned to – or rather reinvented – the European past as an alternative to a mechanical present, but the occult went beyond Europe, though it often also included Europe's own suppressed heresies and pagan traditions, so valued by Pater. Turn of the century occultism was the continuation of a countercultural evocation of non-Western thought and religion, and of magical, mystic and pagan traditions, which from the Romantics onwards constituted one powerful element in the critique of both institutional Christianity and Western scientific rationalism, and was to remain a significant strand in modernism. Denis Saurat once described the occult as a 'strange and monstrous alliance' of 'all the conquered religions: Gnostic beliefs, Neo-Platonism, hermeticism, Manicheanism, Mithraism, Zoroastrianism'.[59] The occult was the return of what Western military might and rationality had repressed: it registered the deepest of doubts about Western progress. The Theosophical Society declared itself committed to a universal brotherhood of humanity, open to any race, colour, class, caste or sex, astonishing for its day amidst the hegemony of white supremacy. Its members didn't always live up to this, but it was one reason so many radicals, feminists and socialists were attracted to it. In political terms, Elizabeth Butler

Cullingford has argued, Madame Blavatsky's theosophy 'set itself resolutely against British imperialism',[60] and while Pound was never a theosophist in any formal way, and Yeats only briefly so, both thought in terms close to theosophy; their shared enthusiasm for non-Western beliefs and dislike of the British Empire would come together, as will become apparent, in their support of the Bengali poet Rabindranath Tagore. Madame Blavatsky may have been in some ways a charlatan (and a bully, Yeats thought) but the loss of faith in Western superiority to which her work spoke was very real. As the painter Wassily Kandinsky said in a book which was later to influence Pound powerfully, *Concerning the Spiritual in Art*, theosophy, like the modernist interest in the primitive, was a reassessment of those 'nations whom we, from the height of our knowledge, have been accustomed to regard with pity and scorn'.[61]

The occult mysticism to which Heyman introduced Pound, or at least the version of it which he evolved for himself (and its *au choix*, pick-and-mix quality was an essential part of its appeal) was to fuse with the aesthetic faith he had learnt from Smith. It was one more stage in escaping American Presbyterianism without betraying the religious sensibility which his upbringing had so deeply implanted, one more move away from the American belief in progress, and it would eventually play a central part in his development into a modernist. Heyman herself was later to write a book that would bring together occultism and modernist music, *The Relation of Archaic to Ultramodern Music*, which she published in 1921, and in which, incidentally, she also discusses the poetry of both Pound and H.D. with some insight.[62] Perhaps partly through her influence, music always remained important to Pound, though Williams, H.D. and Yeats were all dismissive of Pound's musical talents. According to Williams, himself an accomplished violinist,

[Pound] could never learn to play the piano, though his mother tried to teach him. But he 'played' for all that. At home, I remember my mother's astonishment when he sat down at the keyboard and let fly for us – seriously. Everything, you might say, resulted except music. He took mastership at one leap; played Liszt, Chopin – or anyone else you could name – up and down the scales, coherently to his own mind, any old sequence. It was part of his confidence in himself.[63]

Yet Pound was later to be a music critic, composer (though admittedly not widely performed), tireless promoter of new experimental music and supporter of the revival of Vivaldi and the baroque. Most of all, though, there was the musicality of his verse, perhaps his single most striking lyric gift, and his understanding of the part music played in poetry. Pound's mother was an able pianist herself, and loved going to concerts. Kitty may have been a musical connection of hers; she was already known to Pound's parents when he met her, for in an early letter Pound sends her remembrances to his father. His parents were, however, as H.D. later recalled in a letter to Bryher – from 1919 her companion, sometime lover and always friend – alarmed by this friendship with an '"older woman" (Homer Pound speaking) "whose influence on Son was not for the best, but (apologetically) once you heard her music, you could understand Son's feelings"'.[64] Whether they feared that she was tampering with his virtue or his faith isn't clear.

Notwithstanding meeting these sympathetic spirits, whom he regrettably referred to as 'the few white folks . . . up here', Pound wrote home that autumn that he still felt in 'absolute isolation from all humanity'.[65] But the next semester, in early 1905, he found a way to socialise, discovering for the first time that whilst he might be a failure in acquiring the companionship of equals, as the charismatic leader of a band of eager disciples he was a success. A number of admiring freshmen came to his rooms every Tuesday. Perhaps he had already heard of the London writers' penchant for this kind of weekly gathering. Pound's meetings started by chance when he found a group of students struggling with Emerson's essay 'Self-Reliance' as an assignment, and launched into a spontaneous tutorial. Whatever his strictures on Emerson to his mother, it is hard not to see 'Self-Reliance' as a very Poundian piece, and no doubt he applied himself to expounding its upbeat exhortations with verve. But he was still cold-shouldered by his peers. He managed to find a room-mate in the second year, but only by sharing with one of the freshmen. Those in his own year avoided him. In the 1930s, one of the professors, John Brown, recollected that:

[Pound] was always walking about the campus, and of the hundreds of times I have seen him passing my house, he was always walking alone . . . He lacked companionship, understanding, appreciation. He was lonely and out of his element . . . And there were tales of a more than quiet dislike of this brilliant boy, proud and conscious of his own superiority, tales of his being hazed and his room torn up by college mates in search of sport.[66]

No wonder Pound was later to describe his time at Hamilton as 'hell'.[67]

Pound spent much of his enforced isolation working and reading, but he was also writing poetry, a considerable amount of it transla-

tions. He would wake up his room-mate, Claudius Hands, at all hours
of the night, and insist on reading his latest effusion to him – and
then melodramatically tear it up.[68] In his second year there, he had a
poem included in the *Hamilton Literary Magazine*. This was not his
first poem to be published: his local paper, the *Jenkintown Times-
Chronicle*, had in 1896 published a truly terrible limerick he had written,
on the presidential elections, an early indication of his interest in politics, with the author given as 'Aged 11 years. E. L. Pound, Wyncote'.
Before this poem was found, Noel Stock suggested that he was the
author of a dialect poem (equally dire) entitled 'Ezra on the Strike',
published anonymously in the same newspaper in 1902. Stock had
been told by Carl Gatter, who bought the family house when Pound's
parents finally left it, that Pound had said to him that he was first
published in the *Times-Chronicle*. Stock was at that stage unable to find
any verses signed by Pound (possibly he didn't think of looking as
early as 1896), but hopefully alighted on this. 'Ezra on the Strike',
which praised Theodore Roosevelt for putting down a big coal-miners'
strike, certainly fits with Pound's political views as they emerge from
his exchanges with Williams a year or two later. David Frail has argued
that both Williams and Pound shared some of the attitudes of
Roosevelt's supporters in the early years of the century; opposed both
to union power and business monopolies, their philosophy was individualist and they believed change was best brought about by strenuous exhortation. Essentially these assumptions – that big organisations
were bad, that individuals (at least the right individuals) were good,
and that hectoring repetition was the best political tool – were to remain
fundamental to Pound's political outlook. But does that mean he wrote
'Ezra on the Strike'? It would have been an extraordinary beginning
to a poetic career in which he scarcely ever spoke as himself to have
put his own name in the title of a poem. It could, Stock admits, have
been written by the Reverend William Barnes Lower, who published
a number of such dialect poems in the *Times-Chronicle*, sometimes
signed and sometimes not.[69] Lower was none other than the new and
hearty minister who had arrived at Pound's church in 1901, and for
whom Pound later expressed such distaste. Since Pound dutifully
continued going to church when at home, Lower would have known
him well. It seems more likely that this poem is Lower's mocking of
the young Ezra's views, doubtless freely and frequently given,
presenting him as a hillbilly farmer, not so unlike the pose Pound was
to take himself, at any rate in his letters, from the 1920s onwards.

Pound's dislike of Lower may have been aroused by more than his approach to religion.

The poem published at Hamilton was very different, and rather more characteristic of Pound's early verse. It was, he wrote to his father, a translation of the earliest Provençal poem, from the tenth century, a poem of the dawn. Pound was always attracted by the Provençal genre of dawn poems, which perhaps exemplified most quintessentially to him the quality of freshness, of opening possibilities that he found in Provençal poetry. Pound's translation is a somewhat stiff little piece, but already his inventive ear is at work, with two iambic pentameters followed by a much freer-moving line:

> Phoebus shineth ere his splendour flieth
> Aurora drives faint light athwart the land
> And the drowsy watcher crieth,
>
> 'ARISE'[70]

The watchman is warning a pair of lovers (who are not directly mentioned in the poem) that they must prepare to part for 'the white dawn' is coming. When Pound used a variation on this poem as the introduction to his 1918 poem 'Langue d'Oc', Harriet Monroe, of whom more later, would not publish it, because the poem, more accomplished but also more explicit than the earlier version, was clearly celebrating the pleasures of adulterous love. Luckily Hamilton read the original poem quite innocently. If Pound felt a certain glee, he does not report it.

Pound was also writing poems influenced by more recent writers. Although he had probably not yet come across Yeats he was already attracted by what he knew of the Celtic movement (he would say disparagingly in 1915 that in 'America ten or twelve years ago, one . . . was drunk with "Celticism"'), and especially admired Fiona Macleod, about whom, he told his mother in the autumn of 1904, he had found an excellent article in the *Fortnightly Review*.[71] One of the earliest of Pound's poems, 'Motif', later published in *A Lume Spento*, written just before or as he was starting Hamilton, has touches of this now largely forgotten poet.[72] ('Fiona Macleod', alias William Sharp, was not exactly a pseudonym, more an invention: Sharp claimed she existed and he was simply passing on her verses and tales to the world.) 'Motif' is a poem about a 'wee wind' searching for the speaker and searched for by him 'thru still forests' and 'o'er silent waters' – not an exciting poem in itself, but interesting in what it shows of Pound's early desire to be a

poet, for in Fiona Macleod's work the wind represents poetic inspiration. Hugh Witemeyer has argued that '"her" [i.e. Fiona Macleod's]
imagery of wind, dreams and roses greatly resembles the dominant
imagery' of Pound's first two books, but by then Yeats' own influence
played its part.[73] Pound did not embrace Celtic imagery as an alternative poetic world to his Provençal poets: what interested him were the
likenesses he found between them. One of the discoveries he made while
at Hamilton was of the poetry of Ossian, James Macpherson's eighteenth-century reinvention of the early Celtic poet, whose fame had
spread like wildfire across Europe. Even in Goethe's bestselling novel
of sensibility, *The Sorrows of Young Werther*, the hero, just before he
dies, quotes the words that Ossian spoke just before *he* died. Pound,
perhaps appropriately enough, read Ossian first in German, with great
excitement. He was in 1915 to date the 'romantic awakening', as he
described the beginnings of Romanticism, back to Ossian, without
betraying any indication that he was aware the work was generally considered a fake.[74] Even if he knew, James Macpherson's inspired pastiche
was so close to his own poetic method that he could hardly have been
unsympathetic.

Pound finished at Hamilton in June 1906, collecting good marks in
his BA. Shortly before he left, he met the Baxter family through the
local church, and, he told Williams, fell briefly in love with their pretty
daughter Viola. He took her out driving a few times, and was invited
to supper by her family, but that was about as far as that romance developed, though, as so often, he kept in touch with her all his life. (Williams,
whom Pound later introduced to Viola, was to have a complicated love
affair with her, and later she and H.D. were to become friends. Many
years later, when Pound was in St Elizabeths mental hospital, Viola sent
him regular supplies of her home-cooked fudge brownies; he complained
when she forgot that he liked walnuts in them.) This friendship with
Viola seems to have been his first real move towards a heterosexual relation with someone from his own age group. The previous summer he
had had a holiday with a Philadelphian family, the Skidmores, and spent
some time playing tennis and sailing with, among others, one of their
daughters, Louise. Louise Skidmore was later to be named as one of
Pound's other girlfriends to H.D., but she does not appear to have had
at this early stage the impact, even if short lived, of Viola.

Pound had arranged to return to the University of Pennsylvania to
take an MA in Romance Languages. During his final year at Hamilton,
when there was tension, as there frequently was, about money, Pound

would make soothing noises to his parents about taking a teaching job instead. Nothing came of it. He had kept in touch with William Carlos Williams, still in Philadelphia on his lengthy medical course, and their friendship resumed. He had also remained in touch with H.D. It was during this coming year that their love affair was to develop.

H.D. was now in her first year at Bryn Mawr College, and no happier than Pound had been in his freshman year, though for rather different reasons. Like Pound, H.D. had found Philadelphian education blighting to the spirit, but had come to it later than Pound, and through a very different route. If for Pound starting school was when the serpent entered, for H.D. her family's move to Philadelphia was the crucial break in her childhood years. Bethlehem was only about fifty miles from Philadelphia, and in the same state, but for the young H.D. the two places were in different universes. They were certainly in different time frames; Bethlehem might have massive steel works in the new town to the east, on the other side of the Lehigh River, but the old town, built on a bluff high above the new development, remained part of an earlier world. Life for H.D. in Bethlehem was enmeshed in family – aunts, uncles, cousins, her much-loved grandparents, known as 'Papalie' and 'Mamalie' – and in the charm and beauty of Moravian ritual. The parents and grandparents lived in the same street, two houses, but one garden; the children at one stage even believed they had 'two fathers and two mothers, for we thought that Papalie and Mamalie (our mother's parents) were our own "other" father and mother, which, in fact, they were'.[75] The world that H.D. described in her memoir of her early years, *The Gift*, is not one entirely free of anxiety and unhappiness. There was her sadness that her brother meant more to her mother than she did, and she was always conscious, she says, of the dead children in the cemetery, and that for some reason it was 'always a girl who had died'.[76] There was Fanny, who was her mother's elder sister, Alice, the child of her father's first wife, 'the Lady', also dead, and Edith, her own elder sister. There was a little girl who had been at school with her mother whose crinoline had caught fire from a Christmas tree and who was burnt to death at the Young Ladies' Seminary in Bethlehem, where H.D.'s grandfather, a minister and a writer of botanical treatises, had been headmaster.

Yet for an imaginative child Bethlehem was a world of great richness, one of the sources, H.D. came to feel, of her creativity as a poet. In *The Gift*, which she wrote during the London Blitz in 1941, recalling the childhood that she had buried until her sessions with Freud, she evokes that Bethlehem world as the child experienced it, letting 'the story tell itself or the child tell it'.[77] There was Papalie, who knew everything about tarantulas, algae and other exotica, and had a microscope and an alligator which was the survivor of twins called Castor and Pollux, no one knew which. There were the Grimm fairy tales, read again and again by the indulgent family servant Ida; there were nursery rhymes; there were the *Arabian Nights*. There was the schoolteacher Miss Helen, with her brown paper map of Africa which the children covered with pictures of camels and palm trees cut out from magazine advertisements, and who, on Friday afternoons, would read them *Tanglewood Tales* (Hawthorne's retelling of Greek myths for children), 'if [they] were good, instead of lessons'.[78] 'Those stories,' she told Freud in 1933, 'are my foundation or background, Pandora, Midas, the Gorgon-head . . . Perseus and the guardian, Athené.'[79] The Greek settings and images of her later poetry had their roots in the young child's entrancement by these stories. There was the Moravian Christmas, with its Christmas trees and glass balls and gilt pine cones and its crib and its music, and Papalie, as the minister, saying.

I am the light of the world, when the doors opened at the far end of the Church and the trays of lighted beeswax candles were brought into the church by the Sisters in their caps and aprons, while Uncle Fred in the gallery at the organ, was playing very softly, *Holy Night*.[80]

Christmas, that celebration of a birth 'in a town that had the same name as ours', had especial significance in the children's year, not only for its magic and colour but because they all helped to 'make' Christmas. It was H.D.'s first introduction to the delight of creation:

We were 'making' a field under the tree, for the sheep. We were 'making' a forest for the elk, out of small sprays of a broken pine-branch. We ourselves were 'making' the Christmas-cakes. As we pressed the tin mould of the lion or the lady into the soft dough, we were like God in the first picture in the Doré Bible who, out of chaos, created Leo or Virgo to shine forever in the heavens. 'We' were like that, though we did not know it. Our perception recognised it, though our minds did not define it.[81]

Then there were visiting players, like those who came in a procession to perform *Uncle Tom's Cabin*, 'shoddy strolling players' through whom the children discovered 'art, or many of the arts':

O well, I know it was only Little Eva in a jerry-built, gold chariot, and yet it was the very dawn of art, it was the sun, the drama, the theatre, it was poetry, why, it was music, it was folklore and folk-song, it was history . . . [and] the three children . . . who stood watching were all the children of all the world; in Rome, in Athens, in Palestine, in Egypt, they had watched the golden-chariots, they had seen black-men chained together and cruel overseers brandishing whips. It was Alexandria, it was a Roman Triumph, it was a Medieval miracle-play procession with a Devil who was Simon Legree, and the poor dark shades of Purgatory, who were negroes chained together, and it was Pallas Athené in her chariot with the winged Victory poised with the olive-crown, who was coming to save us all.[82]

This sense of a unity of meaning beneath diversity, the belief that the Greek, the Christian and all the other myths were one, was to be central to the adult H.D.'s philosophy, a belief which she would share with Pound and Yeats and other modernists, though the mythic pattern they discerned might vary. As a child she accepted, as children do, all the different systems she met, Christian and pagan, science and fantasy, as equally true. Moravian tolerance perhaps made it easy to hold on to this catholicism of belief. She did not have to struggle with the less flexible world of mainstream Protestantism, as Pound did. One story H.D. was told when she was very small was of the Indians who said that the Christmas Eve music from the Moravian church was the voice of the Great Spirit: 'so,' the small H.D. concluded, 'the Great Spirit who was the Indian's God, was part of our God too'.[83] In the chapter in *The Gift* entitled 'The Secret' she tells a story, evidently her invention, but characteristic of what she felt about the Moravians, of an early eighteenth-century pact between a breakaway group of Moravians and the chief medicine men of the friendly tribes, who jointly pledged to share their secrets, making a new and deeper truth. H.D. here goes rather further than the Moravians; although it was true they preferred converting Indians to killing them, and although they respected the Indians' religious spirit and their freedom from acquisitiveness, it was no part of their plan that the Indians should, even partially, convert *them*.

When H.D. was nine, her father moved from Lehigh University in south Bethlehem to a much more prestigious position at the University of Pennsylvania, and life changed. The note was struck for the young H.D. when, after reaching the new house, she found her mother had not brought her Grimm, but given it away to some needy child. H.D. was broken-hearted.

I could see the first picture, the bright princess with the ball and the frog in the corner to the left and then the large dancing-bear and the girl going up the glass-mountain with spikes she stuck in the ice-sides of the mountain.

I was part of the ice of the mountain.[84]

Grimm remained the symbol of the childhood she had lost. The family moved just after Christmas, a strange last Christmas in Bethlehem because 'Papalie was dead, there was a new baby'. Papalie was 'the first "dead person" [she] had ever known', and his death deepened her sense of the irrevocable fissure between the old world and the new.[85] The new baby, also a boy, brought yet a further loss of her mother's attention. H.D. missed the fluid extended family of Bethlehem, where nearly everyone was 'a relative or friend', where 'in a sense every one is related for there is the church and we all belong together in some very special way, because of our candle service on Christmas Eve'.[86] No longer were all her mother's women friends known as 'Sister' in Moravian fashion: they were now the 'University ladies' or 'faculty ladies' who whispered and gossiped and were later to do such damage to the young Pound's Philadelphian reputation. The children went to a new and 'horrible' school, which H.D. and her younger brother Harold did not like, although the older Gilbert was happy there. It was too far to come home to lunch, and the school day felt very long. Of course, had H.D. stayed in Bethlehem her feelings might have been different. For a teenager Bethlehem might have felt narrow and cloying. But for H.D., leaving when she did, in her memories Bethlehem, though such a tight community, was never oppressive and suffocating as she felt the provincial, genteel society of the Philadelphian bourgeoisie to be.

During the nineteenth century, thousands, probably millions, in America and Europe had experienced a move from a rural childhood to an urban adulthood, from a small, intimate community to the anonymity and often anomie of city life, from a pre-industrial world to the stresses of modernity. In the nineteenth century anthropologists claimed that the crucial step into civilisation was the evolution from societies based on blood-relations to those organised instead on property and status, an assertion which perhaps had as much to do with their own changing society as it did with any putative history of the race. H.D.'s move was one variant of this sudden change in lifestyle, though an unusual one, for it was a move from a town to a house two miles from the city edge, surrounded by farms. Yet Bethlehem had, more than most places, preserved a culture in which, as in the pre-modern world, relations were based on kinship, including the kinship of the extended religious family: they were the Moravian Brethren, the *Unitas Fratrum.* Although they no longer held their possessions in common as they had done in the eighteenth century, the ethos of sharing and exchange remained. In Upper Darby and West Philadelphia H.D. found a modern society of individual property owners, who associated with those of their own class and status: her family met and exchanged visits only with the university families and a few other professional and comfortably placed families in the neighbourhood. H.D. had to endure something worse perhaps for a teenager than the anonymity of the city. She met, not an urban life of nameless strangers, but a suburban life of acquaintances, who might not fully understand their neighbours but who would not hesitate to judge them. At the turn of the century, the respectable East Coast bourgeoisie felt itself under threat, from a newly rich and, they claimed, vulgar Middle West, from a tide of working-class, ethnically suspect immigrants, from the New Woman, from labour unrest. Conformity was the price of acceptance in the suburbs, particularly for women.

As a small child, H.D. had pondered what it meant to be a girl, and life in Upper Darby highlighted even more how strangely different were the worlds in which her mother and father lived. The Moravian religion in principle gave women a more equal role than other sects; when H.D. told Freud about the Christmas services with the beeswax candles, he commented:

There is no more significant symbol than a lighted candle. You say you remember your grandfather's Christmas Eve service? The girls as well as the boys had candles? . . . If every child had a lighted candle given, as you say they were given at your grandfather's Christmas Eve service, by the grace of God, we would have no more problems . . . That is the true heart of all religion.[87]

But Freud was too sanguine. H.D. was still left with problems. The Bethlehem Moravians of her youth, like the majority of their contemporaries, believed that a woman's role was to care for a man, and indeed their ideals of loving service made that all the more an obligation. H.D.'s mother was always harassed, shopping, organising meals, the household, everyone's clothes, caring for the children but above all making sure they did not disturb their father or his academic visitors. Life in the Doolittle household revolved around the Professor, even though for so much of the time he was absent from it, in the 'transit house', watching the stars. In Upper Darby the young H.D. tried to think it out:

What it was, was, Mama had Uncle Fred and Uncle Hartley and Aunt Laura and Aunt Aggie and Mamalie and the old school and Cousin Edd and everybody in the old-town really. She had Gilbert and the new baby upstairs. She had Harold.

Ida and Annie [they now had a second maid] belonged to the house and the kitchen and the baby.

What Papa had was the Transit House now and his classes at the University and people who came to see him about the new instruments and reporters from the papers. What Papa had was outside, the old Observatory on the hill, the walk across the bridge at night, 'like a thief or an astronomer' as he would say. What he had was the high walled-in book-shelves here and in the old study . . . What he was, was a pathfinder, an explorer . . . What it was, was that he was separate, he was not really part of this table with the glass-balls, with the tinsel paper, with the work-basket, with the paste-pot, with the old gilt fir-cones that Mama said we could paint over with some new gilt that she would get when she went in to shop in Philadelphia.[88]

Her father's life seemed heroic, but always lonely. As a non-believer, he was not part of the Moravian church family: he was left out of the Moravian love feasts, their central and unique ritual. Everything she knew about his early life was bleaker than her mother's. As a boy, he had had no Christmas tree and was miserable on Sundays; when he came back from the Civil War, his mother cried because he and not his brother Alvin had survived.

Freud said to H.D. that her father sounded a cold man, and whilst she could not accept that, it was true that to the young H.D. he was remote and awe-inspiring, and his gestures of affection, when he took her hand and called her '*Töchterlein*', frightened rather than reassured her. Yet it is surely significant that while she mentions the other children, Hilda herself does not figure in either her mother's or her father's world. H.D. never felt as close to her mother as she wanted:

It is *she* who matters for she is laughing, not so much at us as with or over us and around us . . . About *her* there is no question. The trouble is, she knows so many people and they come and interrupt. And besides that, she likes my brother better. If I stay with my brother, become part almost of my brother, perhaps I can get nearer to *her*.

But one can never get near enough.

Later H.D. came to feel that it was from her 'musician-artist mother, through her part-Celtic mother, through the grandfather of English and middle-European extraction', that she had inherited her 'imaginative faculties', though she was also to be a 'pathfinder, an explorer' like her father, and like him, dedicated, indeed devoted, to her work.[89] By the time she came to write *The Gift*, or perhaps indeed *by* writing *The Gift*, H.D. was able to accept her inheritance from both her parents, much as Virginia Woolf, writing of her not dissimilar parents, came to do through writing *To the Lighthouse*. But that was not for many decades after the move from Bethlehem. In her Philadelphian years, she was torn apart by conflicting models, expectations and desires. Her parents represented two worlds, each essential yet impossible for her.

VI

FOR H.D., however, in spite of her sadness at leaving Bethlehem, the first few years in Philadelphia brought compensations. She had, perhaps for the first time, girl friends. Like her mother, she had a gift for friendship. What she inherited or learnt from her mother's blend of good manners and Moravian loving-kindness was considerable charm and sensitivity in her relationships. Soon after her arrival in Upper Darby, she made friends with two girls her own age, Margaret Snively, whose family were their closest neighbours, and Martha Wells, who lived only a little further away. Dr Snively was the Episcopalian minister of their nearest church, and warden of an orphanage for clergy daughters. The family lived in a wing of the orphanage building, and it was there that H.D. first met Pound at the Hallowe'en party, one of many parties and dances held there. It was Margaret's brother DeForrest who originally introduced her to Pound; later some of H.D.'s illicit meetings with Pound took place at the orphanage with Margaret's connivance. But that was in the future. As adolescents H.D., Margaret and Martha would explore what William Carlos Williams later nostalgically described as 'the really lyrical Upper Darby country of those days', rich in wild flowers.[90] Together they would escape some of the humid sultry heaviness and constraints of the Philadelphian summer, when the three girls would go with Margaret's family on holiday to the New Jersey coast, or with Martha's to the Casco Bay islands off the coast of Maine. The sea coasts so often evoked in H.D.'s poetry owed much, she said, to those early holidays.

Talking of her girlhood friends, H.D. told Freud that early adolescence was a return to happy childhood. But that seems to have been out of school, or at any rate out of the classroom. The change from happy to most unhappy schooldays came, she said, with the advent of long division, which probably coincided with the move to Upper Darby. School now became a diminishment, no longer the opening of enchanting vistas. In her first autobiographical novel, *Paint it Today*, the narrator describes the character representing H.D. changing from the eager child 'on the trail of the Pennsylvania foothills breaking her first bunches of the wax-pink mountain laurel', to one 'blurred in the process of civilizing, of schooling, of devitalizing'.[91] H.D. never said much about her school years, but she did recall being

publicly reproved at Miss Gordon's school in West Philadelphia, when I was fifteen, because I firmly stated that Edgar Allan Poe was my favourite among American writers. I was told by Miss Pitcher who had otherwise encouraged me, even at that age, in my literary aspirations, that Poe was not a good influence, he was 'unwhole-some, morbid.'[92]

Poe, the aesthetician, the explorer of the dark places of the psyche, had been rejected by the respectable American middle classes, as well as by the Bostonian men of letters who decreed what constituted critical and moral correctness in nineteenth-century America. Britain was equally unreceptive. Where his work had been enthusiastically received, of course, was in France, especially by Baudelaire, whose *Fleurs du Mal* could be said to be the finest tribute to Poe's perturbing art. Poe's heritage, by and large, only re-entered the English language tradition through the impact of Baudelaire and the French *symbolistes*, first on the nineties poets, and then on the modernists. But on H.D. the influence was direct; she defiantly continued to love Poe's poetry all her life, especially his poem about Helen of Troy:

> Helen, thy beauty is to me
> Like those Nicean barks of yore,
> That gently, o'er a perfumed sea,
> The weary, way-worn wanderer bore
> To his own native shore.
>
> On desperate seas long wont to roam,
> Thy hyacinth hair, thy classic face
> Thy Naiad airs have brought me home
> To the glory that was Greece
> And the grandeur that was Rome.

Helen was her mother's name. *The Gift* is dedicated 'to Helen, who has brought me home'; she quotes the poem many times in her prose writings, including *Tribute to Freud*, in which she records that Freud suggests that her fascination with Greece (Hellas) was linked with her search for her mother (Helen). But this admiration for Poe is also a sign that H.D. was one of a generation, to whom Pound also belonged, who were beginning to question the definitions of morality and 'wholesomeness', duty and earnestness that had dominated American culture, perhaps even more powerfully than in Britain, since its inception. To love Poe's poetry was to opt for pleasure rather than duty, beauty rather than moral endeavour. This shift in literary sensibility was just one aspect of a wider cultural change through which H.D. was living, a change particularly significant for young women, who, like the generation Virginia Woolf described on the other side of the Atlantic, 'could sport with infidel ideas . . . of a life different from [their mother's]; in Paris, perhaps; a wilder life; not always taking care of some man or other'.[93]

At the time, however, the accusation of having 'unwholesome, morbid' tastes went deep. She asked to change schools because she was unhappy – exactly why isn't clear, but Miss Pitcher's comments cannot have helped. The Quaker Friends' Central School to which she moved was not a great improvement. The atmosphere, she suggests in one of her novels, was 'tepid' and the girls snobbish.[94] It was in fact a co-educational school – her brother Gilbert was there – but strictly segregated, points being deducted from the end of term grades if boys or girls were seen speaking to each other in school time. Yet although she was not particularly happy at school, she was much liked. She was praised in the 1905 yearbook for her 'charming affability', and voted the class member 'with the best disposition'.[95] One of her classmates described her memories of H.D. shortly after her death, 'the tall, loveable girl who became the famous H.D. of poetry . . . so friendly to all, so ready to help . . . So modest . . . She had no desire for the leadership she could have had and lived in a beautiful world. I sat near her during our senior year and remember her gazing out of the high windows watching the horse-chestnut leaves unfurl in the spring. Yet she never kept herself aloof and was always one of us in our group activities.'[96] The young H.D. loved social get-togethers, but faced with academic pressure she would withdraw from competition and the classroom into her inner world. Her problem was that the other world, of achievement and grades, kept dragging her back. And whilst she was liked, there were also jokes in the yearbook about her height and her name, subjects about which she was deeply sensitive. She never suffered anything like Pound's ostracism; quite the reverse. All the same, she found searing enough her share of the common, casual callousness of schoolchildren.

The Friends' Central School had a high academic reputation, and its pupils, including the girls, were expected to gain entrance to the best colleges and universities. Most of them did, the girls going on to famous women's colleges in New England and Pennsylvania, such as Smith, Vassar, Wellesley and Bryn Mawr. By this date, most of the more recently opened colleges and universities in the American West were co-educational, but in the older established colleges of the East single sex education remained the norm. A higher percentage of women went into higher education in the States than in Britain – indeed those western colleges were co-educational largely because they could not have made up their numbers without women students. The relationship between education and gender had complexities in the States not experienced in England. On the one hand, as in England, there were colleagues of Dr Mitchell who took an even more extreme view than he did of the harmfulness to women of intellectual activity, prophesying neurasthenia, infertility, hysteria and general debility in the wake of too much mental activity in adolescence. Yet traditionally, for many sections of American society, education and bookishness in general were regarded as a womanly indulgence; real men went into business or politics or some kind of active life. The zealous reforms in the university system that Pound disliked so much, the emphasis on the scientific and the vocational, the fact-crunching, philological bent of the humanities, was in part a response to this perception of the feminine taint of education. But whilst many middle-class women might go to college, there were still few whose families considered any profession apart from teaching acceptable for them. H.D.'s mother had pursued a very common pattern: a good education, teaching until married, dedication after that to husband and family. William Carlos Williams' mother was very similar; in his autobiography Williams describes how, as a small boy, he had found his mother's discarded oil-paints, and was amazed to learn of this earlier life of which he had known and suspected nothing; she was simply his mother, and his father's wife. Pound's mother had not been to college, though she too was well educated and reasonably well read, even if Pound were to be exasperated in later life when he could not persuade her to prefer Stendhal to Marie Corelli. But there was no question of her taking paid employment. Isabel Pound would walk to meet her husband at the station every evening; when she was older and could not manage the steep hill, she would stand on her front porch to await Homer's return home up the hill. That was her place. Of course, this state of affairs did not apply to the working classes; as in England, working-class women worked out of necessity. H.D. later wondered why, in the Philadelphian years after she left college under a cloud and felt chained to the house, she had never thought of working as a shop girl, or becoming a hat- or dress-maker, just to gain independence. But at the time it was inconceivable.

H.D.'s father, unusually, had ambitions for her, but not ambitions that made her happy. It was he who wanted her to go to Bryn Mawr, the women's college with the highest entrance requirements in the States, the equivalent of Harvard for young men, and rare among women's colleges in offering postgraduate and doctoral work. 'He wanted,' she wrote, 'eventually (he even said so) to make a mathematician of me, a research worker or scientist like (he even said so) Madame Curie. He did make a research worker of me but in another dimension.'[97] It was he who insisted on her 'preparing for college', which meant not just the usual high school curriculum and leaving certificate, but intensive coaching and extra study for the very demanding Bryn Mawr entrance examination. H.D. took the examinations twice, firstly in June 1904. Her September birthday meant that she would either be one of the youngest or one of the oldest in her academic year. If she had been successful, she would have been not quite eighteen when she enrolled. She failed, discouragingly, but in 1905, on the second attempt, she passed.[98] She entered the same year as Marianne Moore, who was four-teen months younger. Intriguingly, on H.D.'s Bryn Mawr record, her date of birth is wrongly given as 1887 – presumably a clerical error that may have owed its origin to the fact that most of her year were younger than she was. Another reason, perhaps, for feeling ill at ease.

In spite of her eventual success in the entrance examination, H.D. at this period felt increasingly out of place in the Philadelphian world. She chafed under her parents' requirements. She was turning out neither sufficiently feminine for her mother, nor sufficiently scholastic for her father. She was totally undomesticated; she liked to rush round the countryside, her clothes thrown on anyhow, her hair wild. She never fitted in with the ideals of Moravian womanhood, which in the environs of Pennsylvania mapped seamlessly on to conventional middle-class morality. Everyone who met her commented on her beauty, but she felt ugly. She was awkward, ashamed of her height and unsure of herself. (In *Paint it Today*, the character representing H.D., ironically named Midget, has 'stiff legs and arms and short hair and no grace and beauty of girlhood', and 'seems of an inferior race' compared to her girl friends.)[99] At school and college she felt equally inferior. Her father wanted all his children to be academically successful; they all were, except H.D. Describing herself at that time, H.D wrote: 'I was clothed with confusion. I had been forced into the wrong groove. Is every groove wrong? I resented the years preparing for college that might have been spent with music, drawing.'[100] H.D., as a schoolgirl, had had, she said, 'a craving, a hunger for music', which sometimes she was able to assuage by visits to concerts at the Philadelphia Academy of Music, but she never had enough.[101] Years later Freud said to her that her unconscious childhood wish had been for a house with a piano and no boys. Her mother had given up her own music, and though H.D. learnt to play, she never had much confidence in her talent. In *Asphodel* Hermione, or Her as she is generally called, asks herself 'why didn't they really let me sing' and thinks of a singer she had heard as a girl with 'a voice that would make you crouch in your chair and wish you were dead'. The singer, much sought after by Philadelphian parents who 'begged her, prayed and implored but she wouldn't take their daughters', says to Her: 'You have a quality in your voice. I would make you a good singer but only of chamber music, you understand. I will take you for nothing. Who are you?' And she replies nervously: 'My – father – is a – a – professor of – of theorems and things. I don't think I care for . . . music.'[102] This story may not be literally true, but the sense of loss and inhibition was. In an equivalent English school at the time, as a young lady she would have learnt music and drawing, for which she also had quite a talent, though she would certainly not have been expected to make a career out of either of them – yet when she reached London, she would meet young women who had defiantly done just that. But at the Friends' Central School and Bryn Mawr, such frivolities had no part. Only scholastic subjects were studied, and those with an eye on examination success. Professor Doolittle, during H.D.'s time at Bryn Mawr, rather generously offered to give the students some lectures on astronomy. The president turned his offer down, on the grounds that astronomy was not part of their academic programme, and therefore there was no point in the students knowing about it.

H.D. started her first year at Bryn Mawr, apprehensive and uneasy. Bryn Mawr College was only a few miles from her home, built in one of the fashionable suburbs along the 'Main Line', the railway that ran from the centre to the most prestigious suburban areas west of the city. Most students were resident, but H.D., living locally, travelled daily.

The reason was undoubtedly her parents' desire to keep her under their protective eye at home. They were well off, and could easily have afforded to pay the residential fees. H.D. might have been happier if she had had the chance to take more part in college social life. She did not, for example, get to know Marianne Moore, although they took two courses together, and they remembered each other by sight. At the Friends' Central School, H.D. had been in the Classical Section, the 'academically elite' stream, where she learnt Latin, French, German, English Literature and Ancient History, as well as Mathematics, Physics and some Botany. She was one of four students chosen to read an essay at the graduation ceremony, hers being on 'The Poet's Influence', a title which suggests that the 'literary aspirations' that Miss Pitcher had encouraged, at any rate until her unfortunate comment on Poe, were undiminished. At Bryn Mawr she took three courses, Latin, English and Chemistry, a science component being compulsory. Although she had far fewer courses than Pound, each had very demanding requirements. She coped, but that seems about all. In English the students were given an enormously strenuous programme of private reading, which included, during the first year, five histories of England, Carlyle's *Heroes and Hero-Worship*, Andrew Lang's *Myth, Ritual and Religion*, E.B. Tylor's *Anthropology*, the Icelandic Eddas, all the main Anglo-Saxon works, Matthew Arnold's poems and criticism, the *Chanson de Roland*, *Aucassin and Nicolette*, *Le Morte d'Arthur*, Dante's *La vita nuova* and his poems in Dante Gabriel Rossetti's translations, Chaucer, Sidney, Spenser, ballads and other early poetry. And that was only part of the course. H.D. certainly enjoyed the literature; what she felt about the history and anthropology she doesn't say, but later she was to take a keen interest in anthropologists like Sir James Frazer and Jane Harrison, so perhaps that earlier introduction bore fruit. Bryn Mawr turned its students out well-read – at least in the literature of the past. Even if H.D. had not left early she would not have been asked to read a literary text more recent than Keats – apart, that is, from Matthew Arnold (Rossetti was only there as a translator). The inclusion of Arnold's criticism in that first year course might suggest that some in the Bryn Mawr English department believed the study of literature should bring sweetness and light rather than philological competence, but H.D., much as she loved literature, found the teaching dry.

H.D. was also pursuing her own interests, perhaps to the neglect of her prescribed work. She did some translations from the lyric Latin poets that year, but not from the writers on her course, Horace, Livy and Cicero, none of which she ever seems to have liked. Even before she began Bryn Mawr, H.D. had started to teach herself Greek – not a subject generally offered to schoolgirls.[103] Her childhood fascination with Greek myth had been rekindled when at sixteen she went to a performance of Euripides' *Iphigenia in Aulis*. It was a student production, put on by the University of Pennsylvania. Pound had been in the chorus, dressed, according to Williams, in 'a togalike ensemble topped by a great blond wig at which he tore as he waved his arms about and heaved his massive breasts in ecstasies of emotion'.[104] But the Messenger, whom even the cynical Williams agreed was 'superb', 'awakened' H.D. to the riches of Greek drama: she felt, she recalled fifty years later, that she 'had heard Greek at last'.[105] And among the Greek dramatists, Euripides, anti-war, a defender of women, was to remain the most central for her. She drew on his work all her life, working in her London years on translations from *Iphigenia in Tauris*, *Hippolytus* and *Ion*, producing poems based on his plays throughout the 1920s and 1930s, and in her late poem *Helen in Egypt*, published the year before her death, drawing on his play about Helen. Ironically, although Pound was in the production that inspired her so much, Greek was the shakiest of his languages (none of them were very steady) and one is tempted to think that one motive, perhaps an unconscious one, for H.D.'s ongoing pursuit of Greek was that it was not under Pound's mastery. H.D. herself always read Greek with some difficulty, liable to condescension from male scholars. Greek was still a club that only gentlemen were expected to join. Yet she persevered. Williams, to whom Pound had introduced her, had learnt no Greek as a medical student in the USA and only rudimentary Latin. He was envious of those who had, and was impressed by H.D.'s study of Greek, but his own timetable was too pressured to emulate her. H.D., who always felt in danger of having her efforts shattered by the explosive egos of the male poets around her, had already by the age of nineteen identified the poetic field that she would make her own.

VII

WILLIAM Carlos Williams and H.D. had first met in 1905. Writing to his brother that April, he mentioned that Pound, 'a fellow who used to be at Penn but now goes to a little college way up in New York State', was back visiting, presumably for Easter, as he didn't leave Hamilton until later in the summer: 'We were good friends,' Williams wrote, 'and he certainly treats me great whenever he is at home'. On this occasion Pound had organised a supper party, 'five fellows' and 'five girls', presumably hosted if not actually cooked by the long-suffering Isabel. Williams was very taken with the

ladies . . . a deuced of an intellectual bunch, daughters of professors, doctors, etc. but they are fine. Not one is good looking, I mean pretty, but they are all pleasant to look upon because they are so nice. One in particular struck me. She is tall, about as tall as I am, about eighteen and, well, not round and willowy, but rather bony, no, that doesn't express it, just a little clumsy but all to the mustard. She is a girl that is full of fun, bright, but never telling you all she knows, doesn't care if her hair is a little mussed, and wears good solid shoes. She is frank and loves music and flowers and I got along with her pretty well.

She was, he goes on, the daughter of the Professor of Astronomy, and she invited Williams and Pound to her house the following Saturday. There was another party, this time of 'eight girls and eight fellows all in their old clothes; these fellows never dress up, which is slick'. They set off for a walk: 'Away we went, despising road and paths, right across fields on the run just like a game of hare & hounds. It was great. We went over fields, through woods, climbed fences, jumped streams, and laughed and talked till everyone simply had to get into the game.' During the course of the afternoon, Williams and H.D. managed to fall behind

the others and 'had a great two hours walk by [them] selves', during
which time they had 'gotten pretty well acquainted'. 'We talked of the
finest things,' Williams told his brother, 'of Shakespeare, of flowers, trees,
books & pictures. . . . She said I was Rosalind in *As You Like It* and she
was Celia, so I called her that, although her real name was Hilda'.[106]

Bearing in mind what a macho image Williams later wanted to present,
it is intriguing that at this stage he didn't mind this gender-bending
nomenclature: Williams' good looks were thought to be somewhat feminine by the Penn students – he was described in one student publication
as 'a dark Spanish beauty'.[107] H.D. was always attracted by androgynous
looks, but if that were the implication Williams did not take offence. Of
course both Celia and Rosalind would originally have been played by male
actors, so the gender bending could go either way. It is clear from this
letter that on this occasion Williams was much more interested in H.D.
than Pound was. Who was Pound talking to on that walk? Perhaps Williams'
unmistakable attraction to H.D. aroused the ever competitive Pound's
attention, though between this April and his return to Penn, Pound's brief
falling 'in love' with Viola Baxter was to occur. Williams himself would
always downplay H.D.'s striking looks, later asserting that Pound 'exaggerated her beauty ridiculously'.[108] Even in that first letter, it is clear that
it is not her beauty that first attracted him. His statement, 'not one is
good looking', seems surprising, given the evidence of most contemporary photographs of H.D., though she could look awkward and gauche,
but generally when she is clearly having to wear clothes she dislikes. But
in any case her looks – being so tall and 'bony' – were possibly too unlike
the norm for Williams to appreciate straight away. 'She fascinated me,'
he said, 'not for her beauty, which was unquestioned if bizarre to my
sense, but for a provocative indifference to rule and order which I liked.'[109]
But as Emily Wallace has shrewdly pointed out, although Williams always
claims to be uncertain about H.D's beauty, he always mentions it.[110] Once,
when again dismissing her as 'not beautiful enough', he would admit that
'her smile could be maddening when she allowed herself to play with
it'.[111] H.D., for her part, was certainly fond of him: he would be her confidant when her relationship with Pound was in crisis, and she admired
him for the 'interest and love for humanity' that led to his dedication as
a doctor.[112] She and Williams continued to be good friends, though no
more, in those Philadelphia years, and to talk about poetry.

Williams' account in his autobiography suggests that by the time they
met again, H.D. had become 'Pound's girl'. 'Ezra was in love with the
girl – or thought he was,' he wrote later.[113] Williams' letters make clear

that Pound had kept in touch with H.D. after that first meeting at the Hallowe'en party, but it was not until Pound met up with her again on his return to Penn in the autumn of 1905 that their relationship began. They were drawn together, among other things, by their shared sense of discomfort in Philadelphia and their passion for poetry, and Pound brought H.D. all his enthusiasms:

He read me William Morris in an orchard under blossoming – yes, they must have been blossoming – apple trees . . . It was Ezra who really introduced me to William Morris. He literally shouted 'The Gilliflower of Gold' in the orchard. How did it go? *Hah! hah! La belle jaune giroflée*. And there was 'Two Red Roses across the Moon' and 'The Defence of Guenevere'. It was at this time that he brought me the *Séraphita* and a volume of Swedenborg – *Heaven and Hell*? Or is that Blake? He brought me volumes of Ibsen and of Bernard Shaw . . . He read me 'The Haystack in the Flood' [also by William Morris] with passionate emotion . . . There were a series of Yogi books, too.[114]

This selection owes, one can see, some elements to Brooke Smith's influence – the Pre-Raphaelites (Morris, and H.D. elsewhere mentions that Pound brought Rossetti and Swinburne), as well as the infamous playwrights (Ibsen and Shaw) so disturbing to Philadelphian calm. The rest, H.D. surmised later, Pound had met through Kitty Heyman's penchant for the mystical and the occult – Swedenborg and the Swedenborgian mystical novella, *Séraphita*, by Balzac, and the 'Yogi' books. Pound came to see her, she recalled, with '(literally) armfuls of books,' passing on a different set of values and desires from those approved by Philadelphia.[115] Pound and H.D. were only two of the many young people – and the not so young – of the late nineteenth and early twentieth century who found entry into a new and more satisfying world through 'advanced' books; books which often aroused horror, and even panic, among those anxious to preserve the status quo. A pile of books – sometimes just a single book – becomes in many texts of the period, both fictional and autobiographical, the symbol of emancipation. Mrs Alving, in Ibsen's *Ghosts*, scandalises Pastor Manders when he catches sight of certain books on her table, but she defends them stoutly – to paraphrase Jane Austen, a welcome case of the heroine of one scandalous text patronising those of others. In *Stephen Hero*, the early version of *Portrait of the Artist as a Young Man*, Stephen Dedalus is similarly inspired by his reading of Ibsen, and equally condemned by his college president, who, in a neat intertextual twist, has not actually read Ibsen any more than

Pastor Manders in *Ghosts* has read the books that he is so outraged to see in Mrs Alving's house. What Ibsen has Mrs Alving say of her books (we are never given any specific title) is revealing. They only say, she tells Pastor Manders, what many people really think, even if they don't talk about it. They only tell her, in fact, what she has come to feel for herself: their importance is that they make her more confident of her own judgement. The same is, I think, true of Pound and H.D's generation. There was already an undercurrent of dissent that these radical, questioning writers met as much as they created. Such books gave a language to what those like Pound and H.D., perhaps in a muddled and incoherent way, already felt, or were coming to feel. Pound and H.D. both fretted under the restrictions of respectable bourgeois life. Progress, so called, only seemed to produce an uglier and crueller world. Modern education, they complained, filled them with facts from which the life was drained away. Now, however, from the Pre-Raphaelites and the aesthetes they had support for their sense that the beautiful was more important than the commercial, and art than examination success. After Ibsen and Shaw, they had a language with which to argue against Philadelphia's combination of complacency and corruption. As for the occult and mystical texts they read, these confirmed their sense that the world of visions and the imagination was more significant than the practical demands that middle-class life made on them, that there were alternatives to the Philadelphian view of things, that truth might reside elsewhere than in the American way of life. Of course, many of the really advanced, much more explosively scandalous texts read by young intellectuals in Europe (and even in Boston), they had yet to hear of – in Pound's armfuls of books there were no French realists, no Yellow Books, no Baudelaire, no Nietzsche, no Marx, not even William Morris' political writings. Yet even with this limited access to new ideas, they were moving away from the assumptions of their upbringing towards new hopes and the scent of new possibilities.

One other work that Pound had urged on H.D. was Whistler's 'Ten O'Clock Lecture', an artistic manifesto, as it would later have been called, that Whistler had delivered in 1885, and which became one of the most famous statements of the doctrine of Art for Art's Sake. Of the aesthetes, the flamboyant and outrageous Whistler – after all, a fellow American – was the one on whom Pound would most directly and ostentatiously model himself. When Pound sent H.D. poems, he signed them with a gadfly, in imitation of Whistler, who famously signed with a butterfly. Many of Whistler's provocative statements were foundational truths for the young Pound. Whistler believed in the artist as solitary genius, whom neither the vulgar public nor the scarcely less vulgar critic can appreciate, and who scorns the amateurs and dilettantes who merely mimic him. (Whistler had Wilde in mind, or so Wilde thought.) Art, Whistler wrote, is 'selfishly occupied with her own perfection only – having no desire to teach – seeking and finding the beautiful in all conditions and in all times'.[116] For H.D., however, enthralled though she was with the quest for beauty, Whistler's version of the artist – public, pugnacious and assertive – could not provide any kind of role model. In her London years, what she loved was being part of a close-knit group of poets; flashy individualism in the Whistler/Pound mode was not for her.

Pound also brought H.D. exquisite reprints from a firm in Portland, Maine, owned by Thomas Bird Mosher, who published what were essentially pirated copies of books that had legitimately appeared in London, brought out by the aesthetically inclined presses such as the Bodley Head. Mosher's books were cheap enough to tempt students, yet beautifully produced with elegant art nouveau designs. In 1915 Pound would recall that back in America in those years 'one was guided by Mr Thomas Mosher'.[117] H.D. mentions in particular the Mosher *Romance of Tristram and Iseult* that Pound gave her, and which provided one of the models for his courtship: 'He called me Is-hilda and wrote a sonnet a day; he bound them in a parchment folder.'[118] This was *Hilda's Book*, lost for many years, but now rediscovered, a collection of Pound's love poems to her. The poems are derivative, as one might expect (William Morris, Rossetti, Swinburne, Chaucer, Yeats, Fiona Macleod are all there), but never merely so. (Few of them incidentally were sonnets – poetic licence on H.D.'s part.) One is a reply to Rossetti's 'Blessed Damozel', who looks out from the bar of Heaven longingly to her earthly lover. Pound (his passion for foreign titles already established – his books would later include *A Lume Spento, Personae, Lustra, Des Imagistes, Quia Pauper Amavi* and *Canzoni*) called his version, 'La Donzella Beata'

> Soul
> Caught in the rose hued mesh
> Of o'er fair earthly flesh
> Stooped you again to bear
> This thing for me
> And be rare light
> For me, gold white
> In the shadowy path I tread?

> Surely a bolder maid art thou
> Than one in tearful fearful longing
> That would wait Lily-cinctured
> Star-diademed at the gate
> Of high heaven crying that I should come
> To thee.[119]

One of the intriguing things about this poem is that it looks as it stands on the page as if it is a piece of free verse, although Pound did not consciously attempt to write free verse for some time. Pound's poem is much briefer than Rossetti's, though it picks up many of its images and words (white, light, gold, lilies, stars). The relation between the two has something in common with Pound's later cuttings and slashings at his own and his friends' poems. The 1890s had already seen a move away from the long poem to the lyric: fragmented form, so central to early modernism, was something poets were feeling their way towards even before they developed a conscious sense of its aptness for their time. Of course, such archaic, poeticised diction would be denounced (though often still used) by the later Pound, but all the same Pound's mocking reversal of Rossetti's story is indicative of his later development. Whilst Rossetti's Blessed Damozel longs for her beloved to join her in Heaven, Pound's *donzella beata* comes down to meet her living lover, 'declar[ing]' as Pound would later advocate, 'for life'.[120] When Pound published a version of this poem in *A Lume Spento*, he separated it into stanzas and evened up the lines, and it looks a much more conventional poem. Perhaps he was worried about his readers, or possibly he himself wasn't yet ready for his own experiments

As with Paolo and Francesca, Dante's doomed reader-lovers, a pair often evoked by Pound, it had not taken long, as these poems show, before the shared pleasure in reading had developed into shared pleasure in each other. As with Paolo and Francesca, the move brought both joy and devastation, at any rate to H.D. Their love affair began, according to H.D., in winter, which must have been that of 1905–6, in the woods that surrounded the Upper Darby house. In *Winter Love*, the poem she wrote for Pound in 1959, the wintry trees appear again:

> . . . a drift of snow
> slides from a branch
> then, silence more intense.[121]

Besides Is-hilda, Pound would call her Dryad – the name he continued to use for her till the end of her life – associating her with the trees that screened their meetings. *End to Torment*, the late memoir of H.D.'s relationship with Pound, gives, in its elusive, fragmentary elision of past and present, a sense both of the passion and the pain the relationship brought. 'First kisses? In the woods, in the winter – what did one expect? Not this. Electric, magnetic, they do not so much warm, they magnetize, vitalize.'[122] It was intoxicating, overwhelming. They would spend hours in a 'crow's nest', a tree house that her younger brother had built, 'hidden [from the house] by the great branches . . . He must not miss the last "car" . . . "There is another trolley in a half hour," I say, preparing to slide out of the crow's nest. "No, Dryad," he says. He snatches me back. We sway with the wind. There is no wind. We sway with the stars. They are not far.'[123]

H.D.'s parents were never happy about the relationship. H.D. dreaded their disapproval.

'He was late again.' My father was winding the clock. My mother said, 'Where were you? I was calling. Didn't you hear me? Where is Ezra Pound?' I said 'O – he's gone.' 'Books? Hat?' 'He'll get them next time.' Why had I ever come down out of that tree?[124]

Pound had not lost his dubious reputation in the University of Pennsylvania, even though in that first year back he was working well. He had returned to Penn full of enthusiasm about his forays into medieval Romance literature, signing up for an MA in the Department of Romance Languages, and taking every course offered bar one: Old Spanish, Spanish drama, Spanish literature, Old French, Provençal, Italian and more. He was writing poetry apace, but was not inclined to take H.D.'s own efforts seriously. '"You are a poem, though your poem's naught," quoted Ezra. From what? I did not ask him.'[125] At the time H.D. appears to have accepted his judgement. But she went on writing poetry.

Meanwhile the three-way friendship between Pound, H.D. and Williams continued. Whether or not Williams and H.D. were comforted by the fact that Pound was equally dismissive of both their poetic efforts, neither of them say, though possibly one of the important things they gave each other was the realisation that one could be a poet in a different mould from Pound: posturing and histrionics were not necessary adjuncts. H.D. and Williams were, of course, to be in two very different modernist traditions: she, like Pound, belonged to the internationalist, he to a specifically and committedly American modernism. In the wrong mood, Williams could later be damning about H.D.'s Hellenism, which he once described as 'too staid, too chilly, too little fecundative to impregnate my world'.[126] Did this charge of metaphorical sexual inadequacy betray a buried rancour, some resentment that sexually she had responded to Pound and not to him? Williams later wrote of those Philadelphia years: 'before she began to write poetry or at least to show it to anyone [H.D] would say, "You're not satisfied with me, are you Billy? There's something lacking, isn't there?" When I was with her my feet always seemed to be sticking to the ground while she would be walking on the tips of the grass stems.'[127] In the practical organisation of her life, H.D.'s head certainly remained in the clouds, but in some ways she was as aware of the ground beneath her feet as he was. As Williams acknowledged, one thing he and H.D. shared was a passionate love of the Pennsylvanian countryside, especially its wild flowers. While Pound's roses and lilies grew in poetry books, Williams and H.D. saw the dark blue grape hyacinths and violets that they found in the Upper Darby fields, and what they saw found its way into their poetry. Both wrote poetry 'close to the thing', as Pound would one day put it.[128] They were both to develop a direct, stripped poetic mode, though H.D. would achieve it, or at any rate use it publicly, before Williams: it is possible he learnt from her early poetry, for which he was eventually to admit deep admiration. Even in those student days, however, Williams later claimed, he was secretly composing Whitmanesque free verse, which he certainly never showed to Pound, nor, as far as one knows, to H.D. His earliest poem was in free verse, he says, and 'came out of the blue, with no past:

> A black, black cloud
> Flew over the sun
> Driven by fierce flying rain.

The thrill, the discovery. At once, at the same instant, I said to myself, 'Ridiculous, the rain can't drive the clouds'. So the critical thing was born at the same instant.[129]

That prosaic, though entirely logical, afterthought marks his sensibility as very different from H.D.'s, who, though also a great invoker of weather in her poetry, would more likely be pondering the psychic charge of the black, black cloud rather than worrying about meteorological precision. Perhaps that difference in sensibility was one reason why they remained friends rather than lovers.

In his account of his poetic life, Williams writes that 'Together with Hilda Doolittle ("H.D.") I discovered in those days, the wonders of *Aucassin and Nicolette*, the prose and the verse alternating'.[130] *Aucassin and Nicolette*, a thirteenth-century love story, had become in Andrew Lang's translation something of a cult book of the period, having been popularised by Pater's enthusiastic endorsement in *The Renaissance*, where he praised the story as a folk version of Provençal love poetry, 'reaching, by lightness of form and comparative homeliness of interest, an audience which the concentrated passion of those higher lyrics left untouched'.[131] In a footnote to the 1893 edition, he recommended Lang's 'poet's translation', which soon became a bestseller: in the USA, Andrew Lang's *Aucassin and Nicolette* had been duly pirated by Thomas Mosher, and in turn duly bought by Pound, who wrote in *The Spirit of Romance* in 1910 that the story 'owes its immortal youth purely to the grace of its telling . . . Andrew Lang was born in order that he might translate it perfectly, and he has fulfilled his destiny, bringing into his English all the gay, sunlit charm of the original.'[132] What, however, had seized Williams' interest, significantly enough, was not the story's romance but its experimental form, the way it blurred the categories of poetry and prose as he was to do so much himself. Williams may not have known what Pater said about its form, though H.D. and Pound undoubtedly did, but intriguingly in Pater's interpretation *Aucassin and Nicolette* uncannily echoes the tentative moves towards new possibilities in poetry that the three young poets were making. *Aucassin and Nicolette*, Pater points out, is a *cantefable*, a prose tale, with songs inserted here and there. The prose, he suggests, was only added to give a framework for 'so moving and attractive' a series of songs. 'Yet,' he continues,

here, as elsewhere in that early poetry, much of the interest lies in the spectacle of the formation of a new artistic sense. A novel art is arising, the music of rhymed poetry, and in the songs of Aucassin and Nicolette, which seem always on the point of passing into true rhyme, but which halt somehow, and can never take flight, you see people just growing aware of a new music in their possession, and anticipating how pleasant such music might become.[133]

Pound, H.D. and Williams were to spend the next few years discovering how to capture their new music, in their case, however, moving away from the rhymed poetry that the folk poets behind *Aucassin and Nicolette* were feeling their way towards, but like them engaged in the 'formation of a new artistic sense'.

VIII

AT the end of the academic year, in the summer of 1906, Pound was given his MA, and a scholarship so that he could continue at Penn to do a doctorate. (The scholarship, worth $500 a year, was a 'Harrison fellowship' funded by W. W. Harrison, known as the 'Sugar King', whose vast house, Grey Towers, was not far from Pound's own more modest home in Jenkintown.) His parents must have been relieved. H.D. had not done so well. She had failed English, which 'somewhat shocked [her]'. Commenting on this later, she wrote: 'I don't know how or why this shocked me. I really *did* love the things even when they were rather depleted of their beauty, *Beowulf* and such like.'[134] The worst of it was that it meant she would not be able to take English in her second year. She had to take Mathematics instead. However, no more than Pound's criticism did it deter her from her 'literary aspirations'. Quite the reverse: 'I suppose that was one of the spurs towards a determination to self-expression,' she said.[135] Pound, meanwhile, went off to Europe for the summer, paid for by the scholarship funds, supposedly researching the buffoon in the plays of Shakespeare's Spanish contemporary, Lope de Vega, the speciality of his professor, Hugo Rennert. It was an unfortunate assignment. Spanish was the Romance language he liked least. He had written to his mother from Hamilton with the odd puritan squeamishness that he never lost: 'I don't like the beastly language any better than I liked the people. It seems to have been made for the sole purpose of saying vile things easily. Sort of loose lipped filthiness inseparable from it. And fools compare it to Italian.'[136] Pound does not explain what prompted this outburst, but it was perhaps an early forewarning of the frenzied xenophobic disgust, later largely directed against the Jews, that would become so much part of his psychic life in his Fascist years. Pound later was to have more time for the Spanish, but it is hard to think that in 1906 the Spanish playwright would have been his own choice; he was much more likely that of his supervisor. When Pound left Hamilton, he had hoped to do research on the Provençal trouba-dour, Peire Cardinal, whose satires had particularly attracted him. 'Peire Cardinal,' he wrote 'is extremely lucid on the imbecility of the belliger-ents and the makers of war . . . [His] violent invectives against the corruption of the church temporal should be read by anyone interested in the . . . period.'[137] The angry prophet was one of the roles Pound already knew would be important for him. The buffoon was a sideline.

Whatever the reason, his temporary enthusiasm for the academic life was fading. In Europe he spent more time sightseeing than researching, visiting Madrid, Paris and London, though in London he made his first acquaintance with the British Museum Reading Room. The *Jenkintown Times-Chronicle*, with all the naïve pride of a local newspaper, reported shortly after Pound left that 'Wyncote has been represented at Madrid, Spain, during the wedding of the young King, by Ezra, son of Homer L. Pound, who expects to be there several weeks.'[138] This was the wedding of Princess Victoria Eugénie, to King Alfonso: Pound in fact witnessed not the wedding but an attempted assassination of the couple, and used it as an excuse for cutting short his studies there, claiming the police failed dangerously to distinguish between 'anarchist suspects and uncatalogued foreigners'.[139] When he returned, he wrote an article attacking philological erudition in the *Book News Monthly*, which was published by the John Wanamaker Store in Philadelphia. This piece, his first published prose work, denounced what he called the 'Germanic ideal of scholarship'. Such scholars

are no longer able as of old to fill themselves with the beauty of the classics, and by the very force of that beauty inspire their students to read Latin widely and for pleasure . . . The scholar is compelled to spend most of his time learning what his author wore and ate, and in endless pondering over some utterly unanswerable question of textual criticism.[140]

Pound advocated an engaged, vital and discriminating criticism, denouncing university professors as desiccated accumulators of know-ledge. Once again he was probably following Pater, who called in *The Renaissance* for 'aesthetic critic[s]' who possess 'the power of being deeply moved by the presence of beautiful objects', and whose 'function . . . is to distinguish, to analyse, and separate from its adjuncts, the virtue . . . which . . . produces this special impression of beauty or pleasure'.[141]

Pound's article gives a foretaste of his later critical theories, but it cannot have made for good relations with his professors.

On his return, in the autumn of 1906, Pound signed up for a large number of courses besides his research work, perhaps a sign of his restlessness. He apparently did little work at any of them, even though he took 'an odd sort of post-graduate course' on contemporary poetry with Cornelius Weygandt, who perhaps did more for his poetic education than Pound later liked to admit.[142] Weygandt was neither a pedant nor a philologist, but was an avid admirer of the nineties poets, of the Celtic Renaissance and above all of Yeats, whom he met on a holiday in Ireland in 1902, a meeting he described to succeeding generations of students many times. He met Yeats again in November 1904, when the latter came to both Bryn Mawr and Penn on his highly successful lecture tour of the USA. (Pound missed this visit, having left for Hamilton; so did Williams, because of work; H.D. had not yet started at Bryn Mawr. They all three had to wait till they reached London to see Yeats in the flesh.) It could well have been Weygandt who introduced Pound to Yeats' poetry, which he seems to have discovered only after his return to Penn, as well as extending his knowledge of the other members of the Rhymers' Club, which had been founded in 1890 by Yeats and Ernest Rhys, a group of young, mainly Celtic poets who met at the Ye Olde Cheshire Cheese pub in London's Fleet Street, and whose survivors Pound would eagerly seek out when he reached London. Weygandt's books give a vivid picture of his passion as a young man for this poetry, detailing his first delighted discovery of Lionel Johnson, his admiration for John Davidson's tempestuous, acerbic verse, and his even greater veneration for Ernest Dowson.[143] Yet Pound's only positive mention of Weygandt was in 1915, when he wrote that it was from him that he first learnt of the poetry of Lionel Johnson. Pound could in fact have learnt more than he did from Weygandt. He read none of Symons' criticism, which Weygandt admired greatly, and so missed *The Symbolist Movement in Literature*, the book that had such an influence on Eliot's development.

That same autumn of 1906, H.D. was having an unhappy time at Bryn Mawr. She was miserable studying Mathematics, and was not doing well. How much this was due to resistance, conscious or unconscious, to her father's plans, one can only guess. To the young H.D., her father's mathematical and astronomical measurement drained life from the universe: the Greek myths that had nourished her young imagination for him simply provided names for the points on a diagram. 'My love of the gods, as fairies and beings was alive in me, before I struck the bare cold reality of "facts" or the numeral star-symbol,' she wrote later.[144] During her analysis with Freud in 1933, H.D. had a dream about a scorpion, which she identified with her father, a Scorpio. Describing it to Bryher, she wrote:

The clue is the fear and dread of the Scorpio, my father, a cold, distant, upright, devoted father and husband but for whose profession I had only terror, a blind fear of space and the distances of the planets and the fixed stars. But no. Scorpio grew wings in my dream. I ran across a . . . floor to open a door so that this deadly insect might run out. But as I open the door, he spreads bright translucent needle-like wings and with a sword like directness, flies into the branches of a small tree, in the dark hall-way. We have not interpreted this finally, but it is obvious that the fear is removed, the mystery, the glamour remains, and is now recognizable in my reading and romantic interpretation of star-values which my father measured with . . . cruel (to me) accuracy, with a cold hermit logic and detachment.[145]

That imaginative transformation was in the future, though in her rejection of positivist nineteenth-century science H.D. was typical of many artists of her generation. Taking Latin, Mathematics and Chemistry, when what she wanted was English and Greek, felt like the road to an alien existence. She left college half-way through her second year. In *Her*, Hermione has failed in 'Conic sections [which] would whirl for ever round her', but although H.D. left with a sense of failure, it was not apparently literal examination failure that prevented her going on.[146] H.D. told Norman Holmes Pearson: 'I must choose, because my life depends upon it, between the artist and the scientist. I manage in the second year of college to have a slight breakdown and I manage to get engaged to Ezra Pound.'[147]

Marriage was still a career for a woman. An engagement could be claimed to be an alternative to college. In the years 1905 to 1907, while Williams was still at Penn, it was already clear to him that Pound and H.D. were a couple, but after H.D. left Bryn Mawr some more definite sort of informal engagement or understanding existed between them, although there would, it seems, be no formal engagement until 1908. H.D. records her physician and friend Erich Heydt, who played an important role in encouraging her to write *End to Torment*, trying to make sense of the events:

'But you did not say you were actually engaged.' 'It's implied . . . Anyway, would she, this – the period Miss of our narrative, have gone on with the fiery kisses that I speak of, in the beginning, unless there had been – had been – at least, an understanding?"[148]

H.D. regarded it as an engagement, but for Pound it may have been very different. She clearly did have a 'slight breakdown', though her mother described it later to Amy Lowell as simply a physical one. One might expect a mother at that time to do so outside the family, whatever she privately thought, but H.D. was lucky in that her family did apparently take her ill health to be purely physical and did not subject her to the attentions of a Dr Silas Weir Mitchell. The East Coast bourgeoisie were in general perturbed by those who did not follow the strenuous success ethic fundamental to their still Puritan culture, and deviance from it was rapidly diagnosed as mental disease. In 1900, parents were warned that if 'a son or daughter at home loses interest in study, drops out of school or neglects work, formerly well done, and lounges about the house', or shows other forms of 'silliness' or 'contrary disposition' – in other words, behaves just as H.D. did – 'dementia praecox', i.e. what we now call schizophrenia, might be beginning.[149] Luckily H.D.'s parents did not see it that way. In any case, her breakdown, though the product of psychic turmoil, must have had physical symptoms, for reports reached Williams of how weakened she was. Many people commented on how thin she was for her height, and whilst this was partly genetic – her father was also tall and thin – she appears to have been intermittently anorexic for much of her life, and her fragility may have been partially at least a product of the nervous and physical exhaustion that accompanies anorexia. In her fiction she recounts her mother's efforts to make her eat in the post-Bryn Mawr period. After the Second World War, during which H.D. lived in London, the severe mental breakdown that she had then was ascribed partly to malnutrition. Food had of course been rationed, but it provided a very healthy diet, and Britain as a whole was much better nourished by the end of the war than before. The malnutrition might not have been helped by the fact that the Second World War was the only period in H.D.'s life when she had to cook, but by and large it was stress of war that stopped her eating. Like Virginia Woolf, H.D. would have recurrent breakdowns all her life, though they were not generally described as periods of madness, as Woolf's were. The difference was, however, perhaps in degree rather than in kind of mental turmoil.

One guesses it was no coincidence that Pound's attendance at Penn was poor in the months after H.D. had left Bryn Mawr. He even failed one examination, in literary criticism, but, unlike H.D, claimed in later years to have been outraged rather than humiliated, insisting that he had been 'so far as I know . . . the only student who was making any attempt to understand the subject of literary criticism and the only student with any interest in the subject'.[150] However, he appears to have hidden this failure from H.D., which suggests his *amour propre* was more damaged than he liked to admit. But if H.D. had freed herself from one conflict she had intensified another. Her parents might now have to accept that she would never be a scientist, but they remained uneasy about her relationship with Pound. More important, she herself was uncertain. It was not that her feelings were not intense. She had, she said, a 'deep love' for Pound: 'no "act" afterwards, though bio-logically fulfilled, had had the significance of the first *demi-vierge* embraces. The significance of "first love" can not be overestimated.'[151] But, as Williams put it, 'there were others, and she . . . knew it'.[152] Pound stirred her depths, and then betrayed her. 'What had you done/had you been true,/I can not think,/I may not know,' she wrote later.[153] Then there was the guilt that their lovemaking inevitably engendered in 'this period Miss', and indeed, in this period Philadelphian youth. Young Americans of their class were given much more freedom and privacy than their British and European counterparts, but chastity was no less sacred, for men as well as women. On one devastating occasion, her father caught them kissing. 'We were curled up together in an armchair when my father found us. I was "gone". I wasn't there. I disentangled myself. I stood up; Ezra stood by me. It seems we must have swayed, trembling. But I don't think we did.' Her father had said, 'Mr Pound, I don't say there was anything wrong . . .'[154]

Looking back, H.D.'s comment was: 'Mr Pound, it was all wrong. You turn into a Satyr, a Lynx, and the girl in your arms (Dryad, you called her), for all her fragile, not yet lost virginity, is *Maenad, bassarid* . . . Mr Pound, with your magic, your 'strange spells of old deity', why didn't you complete the metamorphosis? Pad, pad, pad, . . .'[155] She is referring here to Canto 79, one of the *Pisan Cantos*, which she was reading as she wrote her memoir, where the Lynx appears as the animal associated with Dionysus. Most commentators assume that the Lynx represents a woman in Pound's life, but H.D. takes the Lynx to be Pound/Dionysus himself, while she is 'maenad' or 'bassarid', one of the hysterical women worshippers whom Dionysus drives mad. In the canto, only the word bassarid is used, not maenad, though there are references to 'maelid', another name, like dryad, for a tree-nymph. So she is dryad turned bassarid, maelid turned maenad, in Pound's arms. What drove her mad? What was all wrong? Those others? That Pound insisted on labelling her an ethereal spirit instead of recognising she was a passionate woman? That it was impossible, in 1907 Philadelphia, for them to contemplate consummation? That Pound really wasn't interested in consummation? There are similar moments of mixed emotions in *Her*, when George Lowndes makes love to Her:

George was like a great tawny beast, a sort of sub-lion pawing at her, pawing with great hand at her tousled garments . . . but if he had simply bared teeth fangs, torn away garments with bared fangs, she would have understood, would have put narrow arms about great shoulders, would have yielded to him . . . 'Why did you come so near' was the sound her heart made, was her accusation, or 'Having come so near' was her accusation, 'why didn't you come nearer?'[156]

Yet elsewhere she suggests another reason why this relationship was so disturbingly dangerous to her:

It was not chastity that made me wild, but fear
that my weapon, tempered in a different heat,
was over-matched by yours, and your hand
skilled to yield death-blows, might break

With the slightest turn – no ill will meant –
my own lesser, yet still somewhat fine-wrought,
fiery-tempered, delicate, over-passionate steel.[157]

The scornful dismissal of her poetry rankled. In retrospect H.D. felt she had dreaded, at some level, that her own talents would be crushed or prematurely stifled by Pound's demanding, coercive creative drive. H.D. was, in her own way, as driven as Pound, but it was a struggle to achieve poetic independence. She was to spend most of her imagist years resisting obliteration by one or other of the powerful poetic egos she met. Her relationship with Pound was the first of several in which she struggled for artistic survival. In *Her* she writes: 'He wanted Her, but he wanted a Her that he called decorative. George wanted a Her out of the volumes on the floor . . . There was something stripped of decoration, something of somewhat-painful angles that he would not recognise . . . George never understood me.'[158] *End to Torment* makes clear that part of her was bewitched by the way Pound identified her with Isolde, Nicolette, Rossetti's Lady, Greek nymphs and the rest, enchanted by the torrent of poems in which she appeared recast as one of these literary loves. But she needed to be a poet herself, not just a poem, and Pound could not, or would not, understand that.

IX

MEANWHILE, Pound's second year of graduate work at Penn continued to go badly. His fellowship was not renewed, and he left at the end of the summer term in 1907. His parents must have been mortified, as no doubt was Pound himself, but there is no sign he was prepared to admit it. He found a summer job as a private tutor in New Jersey, in the town of Trenton, north-east of Philadelphia, and an easy train journey from Jenkintown station, though in quite the opposite direction from Upper Darby. It was here he met the most significant of those 'others' of whom Williams spoke. As far as H.D. knew, there was no change in their 'understanding', but in Trenton Pound began another relationship. Perhaps Pound found his love affair with H.D. in some ways as overwhelming as she did, and needed some space; in addition, at this particular time, visits to Upper Darby must have been associated with the humiliating end to his Penn career. Here he could cut a fresh dash as a brilliant private teacher. Whether or not Pound was trying to loosen his ties with H.D., he needed admiration and he needed an audience, and he found women much more ready to satisfy such needs than men. He was mocked by most of his male confrères, but with his fine features and fiery curls, he had more success with women.

The young woman who provided the welcome audience in Trenton was Mary Moore, daughter of the well-to-do vice-president of the Trenton Street Railway, a lively, attractive woman, a year or two older than Pound, intelligent but without intellectual pretensions. She was very taken with Pound, but she laughed at him a great deal, which he seemed to enjoy for a change. He did not tell her about his 'understanding' with H.D., nor, it appears, H.D. of his new attachment to Mary. According to Mary Moore, things never went further than a peck on her forehead; they were, she said later, just 'warm, loving friends'.[159]

Even if this may have been a little economical with the truth, this love affair appears to have had little of the physical or the poetic intensity of the relationship with H.D., which was surely not all on H.D.'s side. Pound may well himself have felt a certain guilt over that passionate, if unconsummated, relationship. Nicely brought up American young men of his day were often almost as sexually inhibited as the young women – T.S. Eliot and John Gould Fletcher are cases in point. His relationship with Mary Moore was good-natured fun, which he seems to have found quite a relief.

At the end of the summer of 1907 Pound found a job at Wabash College, in Crawfordsville, Indiana, in the Midwest. The principal, Dr George Mackintosh, had journeyed to Wyncote to interview him, and promptly offered him a post. Things had clearly been sticky at home since he failed to have the scholarship renewed, and Pound wrote triumphantly to his mother, on holiday in New York: '& blessed of most blessed jokes on you dear I did it all without those essentials of all life, a coat, a collar, or a necktie, also my shoes were not shined'. He was to be chairman and entire staff of the new Department of Romance Languages, so would have the 'whole d——d dept [of] French Spanish & Italian to run as I hang please'.[160] He had been imported to help modernise the curriculum, which up till then had taught no modern languages. Competition for students was fierce, and Wabash had to catch up with what the more established East Coast colleges were offering. Wabash College was Pound's first experience of the Midwest. If he thought Philadelphia provincial, he now discovered he had hardly realised what the concept meant. He would have shocked Crawfordsville without trying, but his reaction to its almost uniform sobriety was to become more flamboyant than ever. He taught with his feet on the desk; he ostentatiously poured rum into his tea; he smoked because it was forbidden and he strenuously avoided chapel, though not only because it was compulsory. Student opinion was divided: some idolised him; many were disapproving. The faculty was nervous.

Pound tried to make friends, and even had one or two flirtations, but there is no doubt that for the most part he felt intensely lonely. In one of the poems he wrote there, 'In Durance', he says,

> I am homesick after mine own kind,
> Oh I know there are folk about me, friendly faces,
> But I am homesick after mine own kind

... that know, and feel

And have some breath for beauty and the arts.[161]

If congenial friends were not there, Pound at any rate could write to them. Letters poured out from Crawfordsville to Mary Moore, as well as to H.D, and to Viola Baxter, with whom he had corresponded since 1905, and no doubt as well to William Brooke Smith, who was spending the summer with his friends Sheeler and Schamberg, painting in the fishing port of Gloucester, Massachusetts, debating whether after all, in the face of family opposition, to continue to study painting. In his exile Pound was writing a good deal of poetry, and beginning to formulate his own poetic theories, still largely in the Paterian mode, but with hints of a new direction. His letters to H.D. and Will are not extant, but the ones to Mary Moore and Viola Baxter include speculations on art – and copies of his poems – and no doubt H.D.'s and Smith's did too. By now he was emphasising different literary masters from those in the 'armfuls of books' he carried to H.D. Yeats' poetry and essays (themselves much influenced by Pater) had by now become important to him, and Pound's nascent theories of art were heavily dependent on his *Ideas of Good and Evil*, published in 1903, particularly the essays on William Blake, in which Yeats presents Blake as the poet-artist who 'announced the religion of art', and for whom 'the world of the imagination' was the same as 'the world of eternity'.[162] Following Yeats, even using the same Blake quotations, though often misquoting them, Pound draws on Blake to put forward a view of artistic creation as a mystic path to the divine: 'Wm Blake,' he tells Viola Baxter, 'has given us this dictum: "Noah's rainbow, the triple bow of music, poetry, painting," by which we ascend "to meet God in the air".' Pound had by 1907 rejected conventional religion as 'Another of those numerous failures resulting from an attempt to popularize art'. Now his imaginative engagement with the visionary was, like Yeats', translated into aesthetic terms. Swedenborg's 'angelic language', he tells Viola Baxter, 'I choose to interpret into "artistic utterance"'. 'I am interested in art and ecstasy,' he explained, 'ecstasy which I would define as the action of the soul in ascent, art as the expression and means of transmuting, passing on that ecstasy to others.'[163]

All the poems in *Hilda's Book* had been 'ecstatic' in one way or another. For the most part they were visionary love poems, singularly, almost innocently free of the pains of disappointed desire and the cruel *femmes fatales* that mark Rossetti and Swinburne's poetry. Some recorded a kind of pantheistic mysticism, where the poet 'draw[s] back into the soul of things', in a mode which was perhaps influenced again by Yeats. Several critics have pointed out that the poem 'The Tree' ('I stood still and was a tree amid the wood/Knowing the truth of things unseen before'), which Pound was to reprint many times, is indebted to Yeats' 'He Thinks of his Past Greatness': 'I have drunk ale from the Country of the Young/And weep because I know all things now:/ I have been a hazel-tree . . .'[164] Others, however, such as Louis Martz, have suggested that on another level Pound is recording or emulating here the very passionate response of H.D., his 'Dryad', to the Upper Darby woods. Pound writes elsewhere in *Hilda's Book*, that 'She hath some tree-born spirit of the wood/About her', and 'She swayeth as the poplar tree/When the wind bloweth merrily.'[165] Did Pound learn from H.D.? In *Her*, which is threaded with allusions to this particular poem, there is very much the suggestion that the George Lowndes figure wants to enter Hermione's feelings about trees but never quite does: 'he hadn't known it was a live oak till she told him . . . he would never love a tree . . . George smells of morocco bindings . . .'[166] Perhaps H.D extended Pound's response to the natural world, or at any rate his sense of the need to respond; he would later write of the importance for the poetic mind of being close to 'the germinal universe of wood alive, of stone alive'.[167] For now, however, it remained for him a universe very much mediated through books, and at this stage, at any rate, Pound seems to have valued what precipitated the visionary state, be it girl or tree, more for the ecstasy induced rather than as a being in her or itself. All the same, when Pound's collected shorter poems appeared in 1926, incidentally when H.D. was beginning work on *Her*, 'The Tree', the only poem preserved from *Hilda's Book*, appears first, as what has been described as a programme leader for the entire volume.[168]

Pound was later to say dismissively that he spent all those early years in a haze of mysticism, but he was never to lose his belief that one role of art was to keep alive a sense of vision and transcendent beauty. But much of Pound's poetry, then and later, dealt with states of mind besides ecstasy; he needed other theories as well. Besides Yeats, Pound was attracted by the more terrestrial poetry of Robert Browning, who led him to rather different ways of thinking about the writing of poetry.[169] From 1906 onwards he had begun to draw on Browning's dramatic monologues, set for the most part in Renaissance Italy, passionate, vivid, psychologically subtle, as a model for his treatment of Provençal figures. He wrote to Viola that 'Ovid began that particular sort of subjective personality analysis in his "Heroides" & Browning is after 2000 years about the first person to do anything more with it. I follow – humbly of course? doing by far the best job of any of them? not quite."[170] Like Browning, Pound takes a figure, often historical, often indeed, in Pound's case, a poet, presenting him (or very, very exceptionally, her) in his or her own words. Pound gives much less circumstantial detail than Browning. As he explained to Williams the next year:

> To me the short so called dramatic lyric – at any rate the sort of thing I do, is the poetic part of a drama the rest of which – to me the prose part – is left to the readers immagination or implied or set in a short note – I catch the character I happen to be interested in at the moment he interests me – usualy a moment of song, self-analysis, or sudden understanding, or revelation. & the rest of the play would bore me and presumably the reader. I paint my man as I *conceive* him.[171]

Browning's often lengthy explorations became Paterian moments. For Pater himself, who like the Pre-Raphaelites greatly admired Browning, it was indeed the moment of epiphany at the heart of the Browning poem that was its core. Browning, Pater says, 'apprehends' a character in 'some delicate pause of life' . . . 'we have a single moment of passion thrown into relief after this exquisite fashion'. But to do this, he has to employ 'the most cunning detail, to complicate and refine thought and passion a thousandfold'. Pound's aim was to go straight to the heart of the matter.[172] Yet Pound's glancing, oblique use of personae might be seen, not only as the continuation of Paterian aesthetics, but also as one of the significant proto-modernist aspects of his early poetry in its emphasis on subjectivity. Browning's personae, embedded as they are in a very specific historical world, have a particularised context like a character in a realist novel. Pound, as he explains to Williams, is interested in a psychological moment. Any historical context for his personae is at most implied, or sometimes provided by a note or the title; what Pound presents is a fleeting insight. His concern is with what Virginia Woolf – and the Bloomsbury group were also very much the heirs of Pater – would describe as 'moments of being'.

Each of the figures that Pound dramatised, he told Viola, was a persona, or a mask, through which to 'give you that part of me which is most real, most removed from the transient personality'.[173] In this he may be thinking to some extent of Blake's distinction, described by Yeats, between the immortal and the mortal man, but he is also in tune with a very contemporary change in the understanding of the psyche.

With his distinction between the real and the transient personality, the underlying and the apparent, he sounds akin to Lawrence in his later desire to get away from the novelistic convention of 'the old stable ego of character', which for Lawrence is a psychologically false ascription of essential identity to surface qualities: as Lawrence was to write to Edward Garnett in 1914:

There is another ego, according to whose action the individual is unrecognizable, and passes through, as it were, allotropic states which it needs a deeper sense than any we've been used to exercise, to discover are states of the same single radically-unchanged element. (Like as diamond and coal are the same pure single element of carbon. The ordinary novel would trace the history of the diamond – but I say 'diamond, what! This is carbon.' And my diamond might be coal or soot, and my theme is carbon.')[174]

Both Lawrence and Pound's formulations can be seen as variants on Freud's ego and the unconscious (in Lawrence's case probably a conscious variation). The public face, ready, as Eliot puts it, 'to meet the faces that you meet', the prepared manner, would be for the modernists necessarily a surface only.'[175] Pound, as a shameless self-fashioner, was always aware of that. In addition, in the twentieth-century world of movement and change, the possibility of even apparently stable identities was disappearing. Pound already knew he had no secure identity as a Philadelphian, nor as a Presbyterian, nor, with his parents' uncertain social standing, as a member of a definite social class. In the metropolitan world of London, most of his fellow-poets of the imagist years were drifters and hybrids like himself, *déclassé*, expatriates, outsiders anywhere. The use of the persona, he wrote later, was part of an endless search:

In the 'search for oneself', in the search for 'sincere self-expression', one gropes, one finds some seeming verity. One says 'I am' this, that, or the other, and with the words scarcely uttered one ceases to be that thing.

I begin this search for the real in a book called *Personae*, casting off, as it were, complete masks of the self in each poem.[176]

As these letters to Viola show, Pound had begun the search even before the 1909 *Personae*. The self has become something momentary, provisional, changing. Like Yeats and Eliot, he uses these masks as a way of exploring this; for them all the self was elusive, divided, contradictory, only to be understood indirectly and through metaphor. In Crawfordsville he had already discovered what was to be one of his most necessary poetic forms. In the early years these personae were generally Provençal or other medieval figures – Cino, Peire Vidal, Bertrans de Born: in his *Cantos*, Pound takes on the persona of Odysseus. His 1926 collection of shorter poems he again called *Personae*, to stress his central poetic method; even his translations, he admitted, were in their way just more elaborate forms of these masks.

The influence of Browning on Pound was not necessarily in opposition to that of Yeats, who himself in *The Wind Among the Reeds* speaks through a variety of different figures, also identifiable as personae. Yeats was himself developing a theory of the mask, but Pound could not have been aware of that, though he may well have known Wilde's dictum that 'man is least himself when he talks in his own person . . . give him a mask and he will tell you the truth'; one of Wilde's essays was, after all, called 'The Truth of Masks'.[177] The majority of Pound's personae are exiles, itinerant, out of favour with the world, defiant, like, for example, Cino Polnesi, a wandering, unsuccessful poet, in another poem he wrote in Crawfordsville:

> Bah! I have sung women in three cities,
> But it is all the same;
> And I will sing of the sun.[178]

This persona has clear links with Pound's own predicament, the unacknowledged poet in a hostile environment; even the small detail about the women, 'they mostly had grey eyes', could well owe something to Mary Moore and H.D.'s grey eyes. Pound wrote to Viola Baxter of his poetry, 'Some is literature, some mere autobiography'; it was perhaps, at some level, both, but it is not autobiographical in any straightforward sense.[179] The careless insouciant Cino is as much what Pound desires to be as what he is.

Yet if Pound was constructing personae who had no truck with domestic and bourgeois life, his letters to Mary Moore, when not about poetry, were much concerned with plans for creating an agreeable home. He wrote to her almost daily, warmly and affectionately, discussing at length his choice of living accommodation, and apparently taking it for granted that she would join him out there as his wife. Not having her replies one can only guess her response. Whatever she felt about Pound, her upbringing in an elegant and rich home on the East Coast could not have made her eager to join him in a place that he later described as the 'most God-forsakenest area of the middle west' and where he eventually admitted the plumbing was beneath one of her upbringing.[180] The Moore family house was on a grand scale, used as alternative accommodation for the New Jersey Legislature when the State House was being repaired. Pound talks enthusiastically about his efforts to make Hell into a home on $3 a week, how he intends to follow William Morris' advice to have one big room in which one might cook and sleep in different corners, his anxiety that even if they can lead the simple life they will scarcely find enough to eat'.[181] In London Brigit Patmore, who was to become a close friend of himself and H.D., was to comment on Pound's skill in making a place home-like on a shoestring, but at this stage these plans were in vain. The letters read in fact as if he is constructing a fantasy of togetherness to protect himself against his lonely actuality, and he may not have paid much attention to Mary's prevarications. He even sent her Kitty Heyman's ring, there being nowhere to buy a ring in the neighbourhood, and told her they were engaged. A few weeks later she wrote to say she was engaged to someone else, one Oscar Macpherson. Mary Moore did not marry Oscar Macpherson; one might wonder if he was invented solely for the purpose of quieting Pound down, but a further letter from Pound indicates that Oscar was an earlier admirer whom Pound had only temporarily succeeded in displacing. Pound blamed himself for writing to her about poetry – it was his 'Mat Arnoldesque high seriousness' that he was sure had put her off: 'You don't like geniuses'.[182] He went on writing to her, in as affectionate a manner as ever. She must have returned the ring, because by Christmas Pound was formally engaged to H.D. and the ring passed on to her. H.D.'s version of this emerges in another exchange she records with her physician/confidant Erich Heydt:

'You didn't say he gave you a ring. Did he give you a ring?' 'Of course . . .' 'It was announced, everyone knew it?' 'O, how you get hold of the unimportant details. Yes, no. I mean, it was understood but my parents were unhappy about it and I was shy and frightened. I didn't have the usual conventional party – lunch, dinner or announcement dance, if that is what you mean. But *what* does it matter?'
    'His parents came to see you?' 'Of course.' 'They were pleased?' 'Very – mine weren't, as I say. Mrs Pound brought me an exquisite pearl pendant.'[183]

Pound's parents were indeed delighted. They were very fond of H.D., and she of them, but her own parents remained anxious. Their fears were justified. On 17 February 1908 Pound wrote to his father: 'Dear Dad, Have had a bust up but came out with enough to take me to Europe. Home Saturday or Sunday. Don't let mother get excited.' And he added as a not entirely coherent afterthought, 'I guess something that one does not see but something very big & white book of the destinies has the turning & the leading of things & this thing & I breathe again . . . In fact you need say nothing to mother till I come.'[184]

What exactly had happened has never been entirely clear. It appears to have been the last in a series of unfortunate events involving Pound that had made the college authorities increasingly twitchy about him. The story he told H.D. is probably as reliable as any of them about the final incident, which involved an actress: 'I found her in the snow, when I went to post a letter. She was stranded from a travelling variety company. She had nowhere to go. I asked her to my room. She slept in my bed. I slept on the floor.'[185] He was dismissed forthwith, but when he challenged the college to prove immorality they realised they could not and offered payment for the rest of the year if he went quietly; they then rethought and offered him his job back, but he refused it, apparently to the satisfaction of all concerned. Pound was, it was said, 'a Latin Quarter type', not suitable for the puritan Midwest.[186] Crawfordsville remained for Pound the epitome of an environment that destroyed artists. In the first version of the second of his *Cantos*, published in 1917, he tells the story of a painter who had returned there after ten years in Paris, and was now utterly unable to practise his art:

> And when I knew him,
> Back once again, in middle Indiana,
> Acting as usher in the theatre,
> Painting the local drug-shop and soda bars.[187]

Pound felt that he had had a lucky escape.

When he returned home, Philadelphia was aflame with rumours. 'There is more to it than that . . .' was the general verdict on Pound's tale. Pound was delighted to escape Wabash and excited by the possibility of an escape to Europe on his Wabash earnings, but whilst he enjoyed shocking pink-and-drab Philadelphia he was simultaneously and contradictorily hurt by the hostility. This was to be a repeated pattern in his life: he relished shock tactics, but was dismayed by the enmity they aroused. H.D. wrote that 'almost everyone I knew in Philadelphia was against him, after that Wabash college *debâcle*'.[188] To Williams she said that Pound was 'torn and lonely'.[189] Professor and Mrs Doolittle felt the engagement was now impossible; 'it terribly upset [Pound's] parents,' H.D. recalled, 'and at the time, Mr Pound more or less formally asked me not to "drop" Ezra.'[190] She might possibly have stood out against her parents had it not been for a revelation from a friend. '"Anyway," an old school friend confided, as if to cheer me up, "they say he was engaged to Mary Moore, anyhow. Bessie Elliot could have had him for the asking. There was Louise Skidmore, before that" . . . The engagement, such as it was, was shattered.'[191]

At the time, H.D. was devastated, but in retrospect she came to realise, not just that 'Ezra would have destroyed me and the center they call "Air and Crystal"', but that, in spite of the cataclysmic end, she had gained immeasurably from that relationship:

> You would have broken my wings,
> but the very fact that you knew
> I had wings, set some seal
> on my bitter heart, my heart
> broke and fluttered and sang.[192]

Pound, she thought, 'broke [the engagement] by subconscious or even conscious intention'.[193] He feared control, perhaps especially by women. At this point, in his isolation, he probably longed at one level for companionship, but he was also making it impossible. He was seeing Mary Moore as well as begging H.D. to go to Europe with him. It was bound to come out. Who was more important to him, H.D. or Mary Moore? Biographers are divided. He was clearly attached to both, in very different ways. Pound loved flirtations. He loved acting the part of the lover. But whether he ever cathected, as Freud would put it, to an object of desire, whether he ever felt a particular woman was essential to his happiness, as opposed to helpful to his art, is hard to estimate. The women in his love poems were, as H.D. complained, out of books. The erotic charge in his poetry comes from the masculine energy of his poetic lovers. Pound was well aware of each of his women as an individual human being, and he always wanted to remain, and mainly succeeded in remaining, good friends, years after any dalliance might have passed. To his women, he was faithless as a lover, but loyal as a friend. It made some of them, like H.D., deeply unhappy.

Pound remained immensely fond of Mary Moore, but he appears to have been content for their relationship to be that of 'warm, loving friends', as she put it. He found it harder to make the break with H.D., who had a more problematic hold over him, as we shall see. Norman Holmes Pearson was to write to H.D. fifty years later: 'if there is a single person to whom Ezra has been constant (don't laugh, my dear) it is you'.[194]

Pound left for Europe, by himself, on 17 March 1908.

PART II

ENTRY INTO EUROPE

I

POUND reached Gibraltar on 23 March 1908. He had been there in 1902 with his parents and Aunt Frank, and two years before as the promising Harrison Fellow; this time he was by himself, and in disgrace. A pariah at home, he was now an alien abroad. It was a low moment. As he put it many years later, 'my k-rear as a prof in the corn belt ended in smoak/ and DEEEspair of the future etc.'[1] At least he was on dry land after the tribulations of an equinoctial crossing, and was able to tell his mother, in chilly pre-spring Philadelphia, that 'Gibraltar is a delight of roses and wisteria'.[2] Happily he was recognised (by that hair?) from his earlier visit by a Jewish guide, Yusuf Benamore, who took him under his wing. He later commented, 'Life saved by Yusuf Benamore.'[3] They visited a synagogue together; in 1910, in one of his periodic disputes with his mother over his church attendance, he would write that the only worship that had ever interested him 'was a little syna-gogue in Gibraltar & San Pietro at Verona', adding that 'Most of the so-called Christian sects ought to be sued for breach of copyright'.[4] At this stage, Pound appears to have been fairly free of anti-Semitism – more so than might be expected, not just in the light of his own later views, but because anti-Semitism was then so pervasive among East Coast Americans. There is nothing in his personal correspondence at that period to compare with the throwaway anti-Semitism of some of those who will appear later in this story, such as T. S. Eliot, John Quinn, Amy Lowell or John Gould Fletcher. Doubly ironically, in terms of Pound's later fulminations against usury, Yusuf helped Pound to an extension of his funds by finding him someone who would give him interest on the $80 he had brought with him.

Pound did not stay long in Gibraltar. He had planned to earn money as a guide for visiting Americans, but that turned out not to be the easy

option he had hoped: on his first – and last – attempt he found himself
expected to look after four children. Never again. He moved on to
Venice, where he also made desultory attempts to earn money. He was
getting through his $80, and although he was still receiving payment
from Wabash – sometimes rather delayed – he needed more. Some kind
Americans bought him meals; others paid him to teach them Italian.
But his main strategy was the most congenial: to make money by writing.
He had been writing furiously since he arrived, and not only poetry.
He sent home an article on Tangiers, which he had briefly visited again
with Yusuf, asking his father to place it in a suitable magazine. He sent
stories for his mother to type and sell. 'In typing leave good triple space
between the lines,' he told her, 'it is much easier on the editorial eye and
consequently on the temper.'[5] In his letters home, the imperative mood
– and tone – was Pound's favourite. Someone once said of Pound, 'Ezra
must have found very early in life that being a belligerent baby paid'.[6]
As far as his parents were concerned, it continued to pay. He had ideas
for articles on figures on the Venetian scene for which his father was
deputed to find a publisher: 'Send Dad to Book News to talk up that
"personalities" stunt . . . he can bluff better in person than I can on
paper'.[7] But he did not have much luck with his prose, and in addition,
his stories bothered his parents – even the kindly Homer went so far
as to say some of them seemed a bit 'off'. Pound was cross. Like most
of his poems, they were in the first person, but he told Homer with
some irritation they were only characters, nothing to do with him, and
he had no patience with his mother's uneasiness about his language.
'My dear mama . . . diction etc may not be exactly what you would have
used, but most of it is carefully considered and used for purposes perhaps
more clearly seen on the third reading than on the first . . . So even
where you object I ask a fairly exact copy.'[8] In any case, he insisted, 'I
am not a short story writer & do them as a matter of necessity'.[9]

His main project, and the only one which appears to have met with
any success at all, was the decision to publish his first book of poems,
compiled from poems written in the States, including some from *Hilda's
Book*, along with a few new ones. He had sent the manuscript to Thomas
Mosher shortly before he left America, but Mosher wasn't interested.
So although in the long term he hoped to make money from his poetry,
for now he decided to pay for the printing, though a return on his
money was urgent. He put his mind to the problem: Venice marked not
just the appearance of Pound's first published book, but the start of his
parallel life as literary impresario. For now, however, the latter role was

an undercover job. Instructions poured home to his parents on advertising, cajoling, eulogising:

It pays to advertise, ergo spread this precious seed . . . It is poetry & of course not a popular work, but you neednt mention that fact . . . As you don't know whats in the book you are expected for the present to say anything that will stir up advance orders. The Inquirer or Bulletin may note 'Another University man in the Literary Field. Mr E.P. Sometime Fellow in U. Penn . . . a promising magazine writer, etc' . . . You understand that what we want is *one* big hoorah of fore announcements & *one more* big hoorah of reviews. I give you & mother carte blanche to incite all our numerous family . . . You understand that what people think after they get the book is a secondary matter. What I want *now* is advance orders culled from general curiosity. The sale on pure & exalted literary merit will begin later . . .

Wham – Boom – Boom – cast delicacy to the wind for I must eat.

Of course I figure as the modest retiring man in all this.[10]

The role of modest violet, as he put it in another letter, was one that he was rarely to play again, but that parallel conviction of the need for self-promotion and the 'pure and exalted literary merit' of his work would endure. Homer as a young man had known the sentimental poet Ella Wheeler Wilcox – she had been quite sweet on him – and was urged to contact her: 'a review from her would about keep me in "orzo" id est barley soup for a month'.[11] 'No vulgarity of publicity,' he assured his parents, 'need be shunned.'[12] As Amy Lowell was later to comment: 'Ezra is thoroughly American in his understanding of the value of advertisement'.[13]

Only 150 copies were to be printed in the hope that the book would sell out, and then be republished, this time at a publisher's expense. The collection was originally to have been called *La Fraisne*, the title of the first full poem, spoken through a persona, though one more reminiscent of Yeats than Browning, a man driven mad by disappointment in love; it draws on a Provençal story, though with a note that suggests parallels with Yeats' *The Celtic Twilight*. Though the pain of unrequited love is the principal theme of the Provençal poets, for all Pound's indebtedness to them it is not one that often attracted him. His personae are generally in trouble for one reason or another, but only rarely because their love has been rejected. Even in this poem the crazed protagonist (we are told in the note he is the troubadour Miraut de Garzelas) finds happiness in mystical communion with nature: his bride is now 'a pool of the wood', who has for him 'a great love/That is sweeter than the love of women/That plague and burn and drive one away'. The vocabulary and imagery is close to Yeats, but the flexibility of line-length and movement, the gradual breakdown of regular rhyme as Miraut begins to remember what drove him mad, all create a very different voice. It moves towards a free verse form, increasingly fragmented and disjointed: '. . . I do not remember . . . /I think she hurt me once but . . . /That was very long ago.'[14] Pound's note implies that Miraut has found 'a peace great and of the woodland', which comes when 'the soul is exhausted of fire', suggesting that he wanted the poem to be read as a tribute to the power of the artist's imagination in the face of the world's rejection, perhaps why he chose its title for the original name of the collection, but in the poem itself the resolution of Miraut's pain is more ambiguous.[15]

Shortly before the book went to print, however, Pound heard that only a month after he had left America William Brooke Smith had died. He too had been planning to visit Europe that year, along with Sheeler and Schamberg; they went without him, discovering on that visit the Cubists and Fauvists, and seeing paintings by Cézanne, Picasso and Matisse, an experience that transformed their work. Had Smith lived, he too could have made the same discoveries, and Pound might have felt the impact of the modernist movement rather earlier than he did. Pound was profoundly saddened by Smith's death. He decided to dedicate this first book of poems to him, changing its name to *A Lume Spento*. The full title-page read, in the polyglot web of allusions that would be Pound's hallmark:

This Book was LA FRAISNE (THE ASH TREE) dedicated *to such as love this same beauty that I love, somewhat after mine own fashion.* But sith one of them has gone out very quickly from amongst us it [is] given A LUME SPENTO (WITH TAPERS QUENCHED) in memoriam eius mihi caritate primus William Brooke Smith Painter, Dreamer of dreams.[16]

That last phrase comes from near the beginning of William Morris' long poem, *The Earthly Paradise*, one of the poems Pound read with H.D., and may well have first met through Smith:

> Dreamer of dreams, born out of my due time,
> Why should I strive to set the crooked straight?

That sense of being out of sympathy with the times is echoed by the title, *A Lume Spento*, this time a phrase from Dante's *Purgatorio*, where it refers to the funeral of the thirteenth-century Ghibelline leader, Manfred, who died excommunicate, hence buried 'with tapers quenched'. Pound is suggesting a parallel between that excommunication and the 'heretical' religion of beauty, which he and Brooke Smith shared with those few 'who love this same beauty that I love'. Pound associated the Albigensian heresy with the Provençal cult of love, as Pater and Swinburne did; like them he saw Simon de Montfort's twelfth-century campaign to stamp out the Albigensians, a campaign which did indeed destroy the courts and castles where the Provençal poets had flourished, as one of history's most horrendous examples of the persecution of the artist. The reference to that excommunicate burial, made at a particularly lonely moment in Pound's life, is a way of construing those lovers of beauty as a tiny group of heretical exiles in a philistine society, as Pound was so often to see himself and his chosen few, 'mine own kind that know, and feel/And have some breath for beauty and the arts', as he had put it in 'In Durance'.

By July 1908 *A Lume Spento* was published. In spite of Homer's efforts it did not attract much comment, even though his erstwhile acquaintance Ella Wheeler Wilcox wrote a few gushing words. A complimentary review appeared in the London *Evening Standard and St James's Gazette* written by a 'Venetian critic'. Humphrey Carpenter suggests this was Pound himself.[17] It seems all too likely; one wonders if Pound knew that Whitman had done the same thing for *Leaves of Grass*. *A Lume Spento* was in its way an impressive collection for such a young poet, still only twenty-two. Pound would reprint fourteen of the forty-five poems, including 'La Fraisne', in his collected shorter poems in 1926. Already he had another notebook of poems for which he hoped to find a publisher, again some written in America and some in Europe. This set of poems was to have been called 'San Trovaso', after the quarter of Venice in which Pound lived for his last month or so there, but it was never published in its entirety, though a few of the individual poems appeared in later collections. On the whole these poems were a weaker group, identified by Pound even then as second division, though he was still to be put out by his failure to get them published. None appeared in the 1926 collection. The notebook, however, contains a curious and intriguing 'essay', as the index calls it, only about 300 words long. In it he writes:

All art begins in the physical discontent (or torture) of loneliness and partiality. It is to fill this lack that man first spun shapes out of the void. And with the intensity of this longing gradually came unto him power, power over the essences of the dawn, over the filaments of light and the warp of melody.[18]

Pound still held to his Blakean belief that art ought to be about ecstasy, yet in this little essay he is perhaps at times more open than he would usually be about the relationship of pain and art. Pound goes on to say that 'Of such perceptions rise the ancient myths of the origin of demi-gods', and explains that his poem 'The Tree' had been 'an attempt to express a sensation or perception which revealed to me the inner matter of the Daphne story': the transformation of pain, his torturous 'lone-liness and partiality' into ecstatic 'cosmic consciousness'. The word 'partiality' in the context appears to mean 'desire' or 'love': and Pound would insist that there was a close connection between poetic compos-ition and desire, though for now he believed unfulfilled desire was probably best, at any rate for the production of art. Williams reported the problem back in Philadelphia in much less elevated terms: 'We talked frankly about sex and the desire for women which we were both agonizing over. We were both too refined to enjoy a woman if we could get her. Which was impossible. We were too timid to dare. We were in agony most of the time.'[19] In Venice, Pound was definitely aiming for sublim-ation: 'Art and marriage,' he ends, 'are not incompatible but marriage means art death often because there are so few sufficiently great to avoid the semi-stupor of satisfied passion.'[20] This was not going to be the problem with Pound's own marriage, but he did not as yet have much insight into the complexities of marital relationships. The phrase 'semi-stupor' suggests he was not as yet free from Philadelphian suspicions of sexuality; perhaps his belief that unsatisfied desire was best for poets was a way of reworking sexual fears into aesthetic doctrine. Herbert Sussman suggests that Pater's celebration of aesthetic pleasure is put in terms of intense but unfulfilled desire, as in his famous call 'to burn always with this hard gem-like flame, to maintain this ecstasy'. For Pater, male sexual potency was not, as Carlyle for one believed, to be subli-mated into work and achievement, but passion to be cultivated for its own sake, though always contained; this he insists is what should be regarded as 'success in life'. Pound may at this stage have gone along with this to some extent, though even then success for him necessitated the acquisition of fame as well as 'the highest quality to your moments as they pass'.[21]

One of the poems in the San Trovaso notebook not published until after Pound's death was a short poem called 'Shalott', alluding to

Tennyson's Lady, who is cursed to see the world only in her chamber's mirror, weaving 'the shadows' into her web. Pound's poem goes:

> I am the prince of dreams,
>   Lord of Shalott,
> And many other things long since forgot.
> Oer land & sea
> I roam where it pleaseth me
> And whither no man knoweth
> Save the wind that bloweth   free.[22]

That gap in the last line is there in the original, and is perhaps Pound's first experiment with using the visual appearance of a poem to add to the meaning. 'Free' becomes the key word. If Tennyson's poem is about an imprisoned and doomed artist, Pound's free spirit is a much more cheerful view of the poet, though, it is worth noting, just as solitary a one. However, in 'Shalott' he was now able once again to construct a defiantly carefree persona, who trusts his poetic drive, 'the wind that bloweth', to take him where he needs to be. He was shortly to decide that was London. Yet this brief poem appears immediately before the essay with its emphasis on the misery of isolation. Pound was in an emotionally tumultuous state. At one moment he felt so depressed he thought of dropping the proofs of *A Lume Spento* in the canal and giving up poetry altogether. He also copied out in the notebook the text of II Chronicles 14:11:

And Asa cried unto the Lord his God, and said, Lord, it is nothing with thee to help, whether with many, or with them that have no power: help us, O Lord our God; for we rest on thee, and in thy name we go against this multitude. O Lord, thou art our God; let not man prevail against thee.[23]

One could read this as an expression either of Pound's confidence in his mission, or of his feeling that he was beleaguered and alone. He probably felt both.

While Pound was waiting for the printers to produce his book, he met up again with Kitty Heyman, who had come to Venice to perform, and set himself up as her agent, an arrangement which did not last long, probably because Pound was too busy promoting himself to have time efficiently to promote anyone else. Yet he could not afford just to sit in the Venetian sun; higgledy-piggledy Venice, no right angle in sight, a

glorious maze rather than the oppressively orderly criss-cross of rectan-
gles of Philadelphia, may have soothed his spirit, but he had brought
his Presbyterian compulsions with him. Something had to be done about
money. Pound's letters to his parents are always largely concerned with
what is of interest to him at that particular moment – what he is reading,
writing, whom he has met – but a repeated refrain, or leitmotif, that
appears regularly in his letters from Hamilton onwards, at any rate until
1910, was the request for funds, which would be balanced (strophe and
antistrophe) by his latest tentative and unwilling plan to get an academic
job. The letters from Venice are no exception. As well as asking for
money, he told his parents of his applications, clearly dutiful but un-
enthusiastic, for university jobs back in the USA. Luckily he didn't get
them. But the prospect of a part-time position came up in London. 'It
was only a question of a year or so,' he wrote home, 'before I should
have attempted to establish myself in London. And as events have always
shaped themselves to hurry me along a bit faster than I should have
moved myself, it may be that I am not to wait.'[24] Above all, as he told
them, he wanted to meet 'Bill Yeats'.[25] When he reached England he
would learn that no one called Yeats Bill; he was Willie to his friends.
But that was the least of what he had to learn. At the beginning of
August 1908 he left for London.

II

POUND'S first few months in London were largely lonely and impecunious, even though he wrote to his father in his usual upbeat way, 'I've a fool idea that I am going to make it good in this blooming village', and three weeks later was saying, 'Have a vague idea I am going to be a success. I continue to meet people who seem alive'.[26] It was only six months after his arrival, when things were looking up, that he was prepared to admit to Mary Moore, albeit still rather indirectly, that it hadn't all been 'fun' to start with.[27] One letter to his mother suggests that being far away and friendless made him reconsider – temporarily – his attitude to her. She had just sent him a photograph of herself – 'more like a proud presbyterian peacock than ever' was his filial comment – but the photo seems to have awoken or increased his homesickness and his guilt towards her. The letter goes on to offer what he describes as 'some sort of apology':

It dawns for me gently that perhaps the holding of a contrary opinion on your part is not a sin against the eternal order of things, and that however diversely we may regard life, society, etc. we may at least commence a polite acquaintance, or even broach some unexplosive intercourse . . . The necessity of reforming you does not any longer seem imperative.[28]

Nothing in his later letters suggests that this moment of open-mindedness lasted. As his spirits recovered, he was soon back to scolding her for not following his judgements.

If Pound's chief aim in coming to London had been to meet Yeats, or, failing him, his fellow Rhymers of Ye Olde Cheshire Cheese days of the 1890s, he first needed to find some way of supporting himself. He had arrived with £3 and as many of the unsold copies of *A Lume Spento* as he could carry, and while Noel Stock in his *Life of Ezra Pound* suggests he might have sold a few to bookshops, he was in urgent need of funds. He had two main strategies for earning money – publication and lecturing – but he had only been in London a few days when he wrote back to his father that nothing was doing immediately on either front ('You'll have to stand the guns for a month or so').[29] But Pound's efforts slowly paid off. The Regent Street Polytechnic, which he had approached in the hope of lecturing on medieval poetry, had a lecturer 'obliging enough to die', as Pound put it, and at the end of September he was offered teaching for the new year.[30] The two publishers whom he contacted, Elkin Mathews and John Lane, were slower to respond, but Mathews, even if he did not, as Pound had hoped, immediately offer to republish *A Lume Spento*, made kindly noises about possibly publishing 'San Trovaso' later in the year. Mathews, doubtless chosen by Pound because he was the publisher of Yeats and many of the other Rhymers, was later to give Pound some useful introductions, but few of these appear to have come before the new year, and most of the autumn must have been bleak. In early October Pound was still telling his father that he would need his continued support for a while, and when the next subsidy took some time to arrive he was put out of his first lodgings along with his bags for non-payment of rent. Yet once funds came, and he was settled in lodgings he could just about afford, Pound renewed his card for the British Museum (sponsored by a friend of Katherine Heyman, a contralto, who also lent him ten shillings in his financial crisis), prepared his lecture course, and wrote a few poems, all preoccupied with his desire to be a poet.

Pound's parents were obviously edgy – understandably – about his lack of clear prospects, and Pound, always believing attack was the best form of defence, tried to ward off their criticisms by blaming Homer for failing to find an American publisher for *A Lume Spento*. And he had one small success. In October he had the satisfaction of having a poem appear in the *Evening Standard and St James's Gazette*, which, he told his father, had a circulation twice that of any other two London evening papers put together. This poem was a curious piece called 'Histrion', another attempt perhaps to explain his use of personae. Here he suggests that the poet gets taken over, or even possessed, by the great poets of the past, by Dante, or 'one François Villon' or 'such holy ones I may not write'. The poet is, as it were, a medium through whom the spirits of the dead speak. At one level this poem is another stage in his exploration of the fluid, ever-changing psyche:

> 'Tis as in midmost us there glows a sphere
> Translucent, molten gold, that is the 'I'
> And into this some form projects itself.[31]

As almost the only contacts Pound had in London were through the occultist Kitty Heyman, one might wonder if he had been to a seance and taken the metaphor from that, though it has to be said there seems little evidence that Pound, unlike H.D., ever had a practising as opposed to a poetic interest in spiritualism. But it is more likely in any case to be again a metaphor from books rather than life. As Thomas Jackson has pointed out, the idea is taken very directly from a Yeats story, 'Rosa Alchemica,' where the 'divinities' under whose power the imagination may fall include such figures as Hamlet, Faust, Lear and Beatrice, created rather than creative figures.[32] As Pound has expressed it here, the idea is in fact curiously inappropriate to his own poetic practice. Pound's personae are not those of the established famous writers like Dante, certainly not prophets or angels or whatever kind of holiness he hints at, but less well known and more maverick figures. For example, one of the other poems Pound wrote at about the same time as 'Histrion', 'Marvoil', is spoken by a typical Pound persona, a little-known Provençal troubadour, 'Arnaut the Less', who is on the road, disconsolately but defiantly tucking his verses away in holes in the wall. 'Marvoil' is a much more successful poem than 'Histrion', but the latter's uplifting tone and Browningesque blank verse were less challenging for the *Gazette*. But 'Histrion' ('Histrion', Pound explained to his father, was, like 'histrionic', describing an actor) indicates all the same how powerful was Pound's sense of his poems as performances, vivid and alive. F.S. Flint, whom Pound had still to meet, was to comment rather sardonically on this poem that 'though [Pound] would have it that "the masters of the Soul" speak through him, it seems truer to say that he himself speaks through the glamour which their names cast over him'.[33] Pound was still entranced by his past masters; to him indeed they were not the past, but his own present.

Pound's poetic personae, such as the resilient Arnaut or the irrepressible Cino, though drawn from the past, exemplify for him what the spirit of the modern poet should be. Like other male writers at the period, he was anxious to banish the still widely circulating image of the effeminate poet. Many of the male modernist artists and writers with whom he would work would be much concerned with the creation of a masculine, not to say macho, persona for the artist, though they were to set about it in different ways; Pound, I suggest, found a very American answer. During the nineteenth century, poets or artists, as people who failed to contribute to the thrusting development of a dynamic capitalist economy or to the acquisition of territory, whether in the American West, or in the case of the British, in the Empire, were always suspiciously unmanly. In the latter part of the century, the aesthetes had, to some extent, simply mocked conventional views of masculinity, with their velvet jackets, soft ties, flowing hair and languid movements, but the trials and disgrace of Oscar Wilde had dealt a blow to that form of defiance of gender norms: 'effeminacy' and unspeakable vices had become identified in the public mind. In America, whilst the impact of the Wilde scandal was less, the world of the arts and culture had always been considered even more shamefully effeminate than in Britain. Pound needed to create a persona that escaped this ignominy. In America, as in Britain, there were several competing models of masculinity; David Leverenz has argued that by the mid-nineteenth century the entrepreneur, the self-made man, who suffers knocks, picks himself up and goes on to success, was firmly established and remained as the dominant type of American manhood, taking the place of earlier models of masculinity such as the patrician or the artisan.[34] American writing in the late nineteenth and early twentieth century is full of examples of the now emasculated patrician, well-bred but timid men, who lack the courage to act in crucial testing situations; among them Winterbourne in James' *Daisy Miller*, Leonard Strethers in Wharton's *The House of Mirth*, her Newland Archer in *The Age of Innocence*, and Eliot's Prufrock. One might contrast them with the entrepreneurial Caspar Goodwood, in *The Portrait of a Lady*, manufacturer of the small domestic article, who at the end of the novel is still refusing to take no for an answer. Pound's Provençal poets can also be seen as versions of the entrepreneur, down on their luck, but never giving up. You could link them too with another version of American masculinity, on which Leverenz does not touch, the outlaw; the roads of southern France on which Pound imagines his poets wandering may be very different from the Wild West, but they have equally escaped the feminising domestic space. One last model of artistic manhood Pound might have associated with his troubadours and their anarchic extra-marital passions is what Herbert Sussman describes, in his book *Victorian Masculinities*, as Dante Gabriel Rossetti's 'Bohemian' masculinity, the rejection of bourgeois monogamy and the celebration of desire and artistic freedom.[35] At the time Rossetti was still seen as far too feminised – far too much feeling, dreaming, myth-making – but 'Bohemian' masculinity would be an important model for many of the modernists, though they freed it further from those feminised associations.

But as far as his career was concerned, Pound, like his troubadours, was still hopeful his luck would turn. Though his original optimism in August that he was 'going to make it good in this blooming village' was not likely to have been based on any knowledge of the London scene, in fact he was right to be sanguine. Literary London was indeed in some ways a village, in which it was not as difficult as might be thought to make one's way. In 1908 London's intellectual and creative life was based on a series of interconnecting, loosely constituted groups (Pound would describe them as 'gangs') which gathered around certain publishers, editors, writers, literary hostesses and actresses, as well as in societies and informal discussion groups. Once a hopeful writer came to meet one circle, other contacts would surely follow, and most circles – though not all – were ready to include a colourful new arrival. Fresh ideas and personalities were welcomed, often indeed eagerly sought. Human nature may, as Virginia Woolf said, have changed around December 1910 (incidentally while Pound was out of the country) but it did not change overnight. The theatre had been a centre of radical questioning since the 1890s. The novel was in vigorous form: Conrad, James, Bennett and Wells were all publishing, and whilst conventionally the latter two are labelled as Edwardian and the first two proto-modernist, they all in different ways were producing deeply etched critiques of their society. There were several flourishing radical, intellectual journals, perhaps most notably in this context, the *New Age*, where all manner of new movements could be discussed, and where all manner of newcomers, Pound would thankfully discover, could earn some useful cash. The six years between Pound's arrival and the First World War were politically tense and volatile; the suffragette movement was under its tempestuous way; social unrest and the fear of revolution loomed; the Irish question grew more urgent. The purely literary magazine only came into existence at the end of these years: most of the journals which were to publish Pound's poetry were also those that debated Home Rule, votes for women, anarchism, socialism, Fabianism, syndicalism, Nietzsche, Bergson and the fourth dimension; the more advanced added prostitution, birth control and free love. There had of course been a Victorian tradition of highly respectable Men of Letters, of whom Virginia Woolf's father Sir Leslie Stephen was a celebrated example – though it should be noted his letters never included fiction or poetry.

There were writers in Edwardian London who achieved positions within the establishment: Sir Edmund Gosse, for example (also better known for his prose than fiction or poetry, though he had published quite an amount of the latter), had been made librarian of the House of Lords in 1904. But even Gosse was a tireless supporter of the still dubious Ibsen, and a loyal friend to the questionable Swinburne. His masterpiece, his autobiography *Father and Son*, published in 1907, was a delicate pricking of the bubble of Victorian high-mindedness, and much admired by Pound. In later years Pound was to rewrite history with himself as the bearer of light to Edwardian London's Stygian gloom, insisting that 'Gosse's generation . . . was contemptible, mingy, they were carrots, not animals. Born under the Victorian fugg, insularity, a meagreness, a dwindling.'[36] This was a travesty, and certainly not the way that Pound saw the literary world in 1908. In the pre-war years London cultural life combined Edwardian hospitality with a relish for the new and the young. It was a good period for aspiring writers.

Much of Edwardian society, of course, remained hierarchical, hidebound and oppressive – hence the attacks of socialists, suffragists and reformers of every hue. John Gould Fletcher, in his autobiography *Life Is My Song*, comments that when he first came to London, he met only the radical side of London life, and it was several years before he realised that what he saw as the norm was in fact exceptional. Pound himself had a not dissimilar experience, although he never analysed it so clearly. In addition, he would find that some of those who were open minded in their approach to literature could turn out to be alarmingly rigid when it came to observing social conventions, as Pound was to find to his cost. But the metropolis in modern times has always been the place where class barriers are most permeable, and the first years of the century were seeing a shift – a slow shift – towards at any rate elements of a meritocracy, though there were many, both snobs and socialists, who complained that it was becoming more of a plutocracy. There was some truth in the latter accusation, though even that had the merit of weakening the old class structure. Douglas Goldring, an aspiring writer whom Pound would shortly meet, and whose sparkling memoir, *South Lodge*, gives a vivid picture of contemporary cultural life, argues that there was, before the First World War, a community in London which could be called the 'literary world', his main home, distinct and very different from 'Society', in which he also had a walk-on part, being an impecunious but well-bred ex-public schoolboy, as a partner at débutantes' balls. To a Society woman, Goldring writes, 'Every man belonging

to any of the Services, [he means, naturally, as an officer] was . . . automatically "pukka", while writers and artists – unless, of course they
were rich, famous or titled – were . . . automatically "awful".'[37] This was
a situation that distressed some, like Ford Madox Hueffer, who wanted
to be thought a gentleman, and who complained that the English
regarded writers as socially somewhere between a governess and a butler.
Compared with Paris, there were few bohemian enclaves in London, at
any rate when Pound arrived, and certainly no absence of class-
consciousness among London writers and artists, but class worked more
flexibly with them than in many other sections of society. Pound would
meet a range of gifted individuals who came from working- or lower
middle-class backgrounds, including D. H. Lawrence, F.S. Flint and
Desmond FitzGerald, who made their way none the less. The upper
and upper middle classes were not in any case as uniformly philistine
as Goldring suggests. One perhaps should bear in mind Shaw's
distinction between Heartbreak House and Headlong Hall, between
what one would now call the chattering classes and the huntin' and
shootin' brigade. There were a number of well-to-do hostesses who were
delighted to entertain intellectuals and artists regardless of class or
nationality – the most famous, of course, being Lady Ottoline Morrell,
satirised so cruelly for her pains as Hermione Roddice in *Women in
Love*. Pound himself does not appear to have met Lady Ottoline until
the post-war years, but there were others ready to tolerate or indeed
welcome a noisy and boisterous American poet. In his early days in
London, he helped to keep them entertained, while they helped to keep
him adequately fed. During the autumn of 1908, however, Pound had
not yet come across such hostesses, nor seen much sign of literary circles.
All the same, when not in the British Museum, he hovered hopefully
round Elkin Mathews' premises, surmising, with sound instinct, that
something would turn up.

III

ELKIN Mathews published from what Ernest Rhys described as 'the smallest shop in the world' in Vigo Street, just off Regent Street, on the corner of Savile Row, whose tailors must have been well beyond the pockets of most of Mathews' customers.[38] The tiny bookshop – tiny in size that is, but stuffed with books from floor to ceiling on shelves and in piles – doubled, Pound was to discover, as an unofficial club for aspiring writers. In the late 1880s Mathews had joined forces with John Lane, the other publisher whom Pound had approached, in a publishing firm that brought out all the leading nineties poets under the imprint of the Bodley Head. They specialised in printing beautifully designed, limited editions of poetry, although they had some prose on their list too. Poetry was not selling as well as earlier in the century, and the fine limited editions were, paradoxically, a way of making poetry pay. Generous margins and large type were used to keep the typesetting costs down. The high-quality paper they were able to buy as cheap ends of rolls. They didn't pay authors much in royalties, but the copies were not expensive, so their limited runs, calculated to meet the small market that still existed, sold well. Their literary adviser was the flamboyant Richard Le Gallienne, one of the Rhymers' Club, known as 'Narcissus' in literary circles – according to Mathews, 'neither Byron nor Shelley looked more the poet than he did' – and on his recommendation, the Bodley Head published such writers as Le Gallienne himself, Lionel Johnson, Ernest Radford, Walter Crane, Arthur Symons, John Addington Symonds, Francis Thompson, John Todhunter, John Davidson, Oscar Wilde – including the edition of *Salomé* illustrated by Beardsley which had shocked Pound so much – as well as the *Book of the Rhymers' Club* in which Yeats appeared.[39] For a while all went well, and the shop acquired the nickname of Parnassus because there were so many poets to be found

clustered around it. In the public perception the Bodley Head was associated with all that was decadent, as Owen Seaman's parody, 'Ballad of
a Bun', vividly illustrated. This parody mocked – or perhaps castigated
– Davidson's 'Ballad of a Nun', a highly disturbing, though compelling,
poem about a self-flagellating nun tormented by sexual fantasies. The
nun eventually manages to lose her virginity and her 'passion's hoard',
but is saved from punishment by the Virgin Mary, who kisses her and
calls her 'sister'. Seaman's poem went:

> A Decadent was dribbling by;
> > 'Lady,' he said, 'you seem undone;
> You need a panacea; try
> > This sample of the Bodley bun.

> 'It is fulfilled of precious spice,
> > Whereof I give the recipe; –
> Take common dripping, stew in vice,
> > And serve with vertu; taste and see!

> 'And lo! I brand thee on the brow
> > As kin to Nature's lowest germ;
> You are sister to the microbe now,
> > And second-cousin to the worm.'[40]

Mathews, 'a gentle Lamb-like figure', as Le Gallienne describes him,
was on the whole remarkably tolerant of 'decadence' in poetry, but there
were times when he felt it went too far.[41] The partnership between
Mathews and Lane had begun to crack by 1893. Mathews became,
according to James Nelson's history of his career, alarmed by Oscar
Wilde's increasing lack of discretion, both in the publication of 'The
Portrait of Mr W.H.', which overtly treated 'Uranian' love, and by the fact
that Wilde had seduced one of their clerks. But, paradoxically, the *coup
de grâce* came the next year when Lane failed to tell him there was to
be a dinner to celebrate the first issue of the *Yellow Book*, the notorious
quarterly he would continue to publish until 1897. Lane suavely
presented the unknowing Mathews' apologies, and took all the credit
for bringing out the controversial volume for himself. They separated
in late 1894. Parnassus, the *Athenaeum* reminded its readers, had, after
all, two peaks, a joke that must still have been circulating in London
when Pound arrived, for he was to repeat it almost fifty years later, when

he described his arrival in London from Venice with *A Lume Spento*, 'copies of which DEEPosited with Elkin Mathews and "Indigo" Lane, the two peaks of Parnassus'.[42] Mathews kept the Vigo Street shop, Lane the sign and imprint of the Bodley Head. Wilde for a while was thoroughly fed up with both of them, and planned to call the two menservants in *The Importance of Being Earnest* Lane and Mathews, though in the end he took pity on the gentle Mathews and named them Lane and Merriman.[43]

Mathews continued to publish elegant 'belles-lettres', which he defined as 'essays, poetry, drama, and that higher fiction in which the educated classes may be supposed to take an interest'.[44] He went on publishing the Rhymers and their associates – Dowson, Johnson, Selwyn Image, Michael Field (pseudonym of Katherine Bradley and Edith Cooper), Fiona Macleod and Yeats, including *The Wind Among the Reeds*, the collection Pound admired so much. Mathews had, in fact, himself attended the Rhymers' Club meetings. He was deeply sympathetic to the Celtic Revival, and had been for some years a neighbour of the Yeats family in Bedford Park, the aesthetic hotbed of west London, so he had many personal links with these writers. But sales of poetry, after the Wilde trials in 1895 and the public turn against the decadents, had declined still further; the counter-decadent, pro-British *National Observer*, edited by W.E. Henley, whose journalists were nicknamed by Max Beerbohm 'the Henley Regatta', thundered:

There must be another trial at the Old Bailey, or a coroner's inquest – the latter for choice; and of the Decadents, of their hideous conceptions of the meaning of Art, of their worse than Eleusinian mysteries, there must be an absolute end.[45]

The only kind of poetry to flourish was the stirring imperialist strain that emerged from the ashes of decadence, like that by Rudyard Kipling, William Watson and Henry Newbolt, the last of whom luckily published several hugely popular volumes with Mathews. (Mathews never published any Rudyard Kipling, but in the highly successful run of exquisite children's books that Mathews began to bring out in the late 1890s, after he had become a father himself, he brought out verses by Kipling's mother and sister.) Mathews, however, was still dedicated to the cause of aesthetic poetry, and he conceived the idea of a series of slim, paper-wrapped volumes, still beautifully designed but cheaper yet again. The first was a Shilling Garland series, followed by several more, of which the most extensive was the Vigo Cabinet series, in which over

150 volumes appeared, generally at one shilling or 1s. 6d. In America
Pound had of course known some of the Bodley Head's and Mathews'
authors through the books pirated by Thomas Mosher, though the
edition of *Salomé* that shocked him so much was probably the one
brought out by the authorised American firm, Day and Copeland.

Though Mathews' heart was in the nineties, by the time of his death
in 1921 he had published a remarkable number of works by early
modernists, or, as in most cases one should say, early works by modernist
writers, in 1905 and 1907 publishing plays and prose by Synge, and in
1907 James Joyce's book of poems, *Chamber Music*. He was to publish
most of Pound's books up to 1920, as well as Ford Madox Ford (then
Hueffer), F.S. Flint, William Carlos Williams, Richard Aldington, Nancy
Cunard, and the *Cubist Poems* by the avant-garde American artist and
poet Max Weber. He did, it must be admitted, also turn down some
famous volumes – *Dubliners* and *Prufrock and Other Observations* among
them – and some of the later Pound he found hard to stomach. In spite
of his initial caution, however, he was enthusiastic about the early Pound.
Even during that first autumn, he occasionally asked Pound home for
a meal and the night: Mathews had now moved from Bedford Park to
the then village of Chorleywood, in Hertfordshire. His eleven-year-old
daughter Nest was shocked by how thin Pound was, how 'pallid' and
'spotty', and noted in her diary: 'I think Mr Pound is a very sickly
young man'.[46] Perhaps the kindly Mathews thought the same.

Whatever the state of his health, Pound's spirits may have dipped.
Apart from the publication of 'Histrion', he was receiving little encouragement. Mathews was still making no commitment to the 'San Trovaso'
manuscript that Pound had put together in Venice, and it had been
rejected outright by Dent. Pound's parents were criticising his poems
as they had criticised his prose, his mother in particular complaining
they were all far too self-absorbed, and suggesting that Kipling would
be a good alternative model; both H.D. and Williams had been discouraging about *A Lume Spento*. Pound set about defending himself.
To his mother he insisted that he wanted to write dramatic, not descriptive verse; after all, he pointed out, Shakespeare nearly always wrote in
the first person. What he said to H.D. is lost, but to Williams, though
touchingly grateful to him for reacting at all ('I am dam glad to get
some sincere criticism any how'), he wrote 19 pages refuting his objections.[47] Williams had complained – much to Pound's indignation – that
many of the poems had 'bitter personal notes', and were full of 'poetic
anarchy', which laid them open to condemnation in the 'eyes of too

ruthless public'[*sic*]. Pound admitted to the collection's being rather
sombre, though he assured Williams it could have been worse – he had
'[k]ept out of it one tremendously gloomy series of ten sonnets à la
Thompson of the "City of Dreadful night".' Williams had also accused
him of 'unconstrained vagabondism', to which Pound responded: 'If
any body ever shuts *you* up in Indianna for four months & you don't
at least *write* some unconstrained something or other, I give up hope
for your salvation.' He pointed yet again to his use of a persona to deflect
the charge of writing 'personal' poetry, and says he does not care about
the public ('damn their eyes'). In Williams' condemnation of his poetic
anarchy Pound came up against the charge constantly levelled at him
in the early reviews: Pound, who thought of himself, with some justification, as a tireless experimenter with complex and subtle forms, was
repeatedly charged with formlessness.[48] (The reception of the *Cantos*
would repeat this pattern.) 'Sometimes,' he told Williams stiffly, 'I use
rules of Spanish, Anglo-Saxon, & Greek metric that are not common
in the english of Milton's or Miss Austin's day.'

Williams had also attacked the collection for lacking the 'ultimate
attainments of poesy'. Pound responded indignantly, 'I wish no fooling
that you would define your ultimate attainments of poesy', and then
went swiftly on to give his own:

1. To paint the thing as I see it.
2. Beauty.
3. Freedom from didactisism
4. It is only good manners if you repeat a few other men to at least do it better
   or more briefly. – utter originality is of course out of the question.

The first three of these still closely follow Pater, who, besides advocating the pursuit of beauty for its own sake, had emphasised the
capturing of a subjective impression in art, arguing that 'in aesthetic
criticism the first step towards seeing one's object as it really is, is to
know one's own impression as it really is'.[49] But in Pound's fourth point,
one might note, he is going beyond Pater; in asserting that 'utter originality' is out of the question, he is making not just a modernist, but
almost a postmodernist admission.

As a *coup de grâce*, Pound had said dismissively to Williams: 'I doubt
however if you are sufficiently au courant to know just what the poets &
musicians & painters are doing with a great deal of convention that has
masqueraded as law'. Quite which artists Pound has in mind here would

be interesting to know, because at this stage he was not yet so *au courant* himself with contemporary experimentation. Music he might have known a little about from Kitty – she took a keen interest in avant-garde composers – and although he had apparently read little Whitman, he did know at least one *vers libre* poet, W. E. Henley, a gritty poet of contemporary life, as well as the anti-decadent editor of the *National Observer*. Henley's work had made an impact on him while still in America, though he never appears to have mentioned him in any positive way after he reached England: perhaps he discovered Henley was too much associated with Kipling and imperialism to be altogether someone he wanted to acknowledge as an influence. That vigorous, masculinist writing, however, probably had more impact on Pound than he liked to think. While he had been at Hamilton, Pound had mentioned to his mother he had borrowed from the library two of Henley's most innovative and powerful collections of poetry, *London Voluntaries* and *In Hospital*, which like so much contemporary French writing made the modern city its subject matter, and both of which included poems that experimented with a form of free verse, generally one that still used some rhyme, but in an irregular and free way, with no fixed metre. Pound was not yet to acknowledge any concern with free verse, but he did send a poem based on Henley to Mary Moore. In 1908, Pound preferred complex, esoteric verse schemes, but the *Zeitgeist* was against his conscious preferences: although always musical and rhythmic, Pound's pre-imagist verse often moves further in the direction of free verse than he was prepared to admit at the time. Henley was also to influence T.E. Hulme and Richard Aldington, though in each case they admitted it only to dismiss him. Henley has been unjustly neglected in the history of modern verse; he deserves his place in the story of the emergence of imagism.

In spite of these attacks and rejections from friends and the world at large, Pound did not lose heart. If no one would pay to publish his poems, once again he would do it himself. He arranged to pay a printer to bring out a booklet of fifteen poems, selected from his 'San Trovaso' manuscript. He called this selection, with his instinct for marketing, *A Quinzaine for this Yule*, in the expectation of catching the eye of Christmas shoppers. It was a classic Pound title – French and Ye Olde English mixed – and it worked. The 100 copies he could afford to have printed soon went, and he was able to persuade Mathews to pay for another 100 copies to appear under the Elkin Mathews imprint in late December, and at Mathews' expense. He was launched.

IV

In January 1909 Pound began his lectures at the Regent Street
Polytechnic, with a fluctuating audience whose vagaries he put down,
perhaps rightly, to weather and transport; if he didn't always have the
55 with which he began (he observed gleefully to his father that
Shakespeare's Comedies only had 19) he still had a good turnout. Pound
was not just concerned about his popularity; payment depended on the
numbers who attended. Then, to his delight, Mathews agreed to publish
a collection, in his 'best series', that would bring together some of *A
Lume Spento* poems, some of *A Quinzaine*, as well as some other earlier
and more recent poems. Mathews even said that he would again pay for
the publication, a fact of which Pound made a great deal, since unknowns
generally had to pay their way as he had done in Venice and with the
first edition of *A Quinzaine*. Pound put this largesse down to his own
exceptional talent, but in fact the generous-hearted Mathews appears
to have done this quite often.

Things were looking up in other ways as well. Pound was at last
beginning to make friends. Mathews introduced him to a young poet
his own age, James Griffyth Fairfax, of Australian origins, though he
came from the class that governed Australia, and had been given a thoroughly British upper-class education, which the higher echelons of
British colonials always insisted on for their sons. Jim Fairfax, as he was
generally known, had been to Winchester College and New College,
Oxford, as had the late Lionel Johnson, one of several of the Rhymers
to die young. Fairfax's first book of poems, *The Gates of Sleep*, which
Mathews had published in 1906, when Fairfax was still an undergraduate, is clearly the work of an avid disciple of Johnson's work and is
dedicated 'To Lionel Johnson. From one who stands at the foot of the
heights to one who has ascended them, from a Wykehamist to a

Wykehamist, greeting.'[50] (With a dedication like that, it is not surprising that he eventually gave up poetry and became a Conservative MP.) Fairfax, who was only Pound's age, had brought out a much-admired second book of poems in 1908, and Pound told his father that Fairfax was quite possibly to be the Tennyson or Swinburne of the next generation; his letters to his parents for the next few months are full of such extravagant comparisons. He needed to impress them with the high potential, if not actual achievements, of those he met.

Taken under the wing of the well-connected Fairfax, whose parents had now returned permanently to England, Pound began to make contacts. At the home of Mrs Eva Fowler, an American married to a Leeds businessman, who hosted a salon as well as organising seances, he met Yeats' friend and, though Pound would not then have known this, former lover, Olivia Shakespear. Pound wrote back excitedly to his parents that she was 'undoubtedly the most charming woman in London'.[51] Many would probably have concurred, though as Pound up to that time appears to have met very few women in London, apart from several landladies, one of whom had thrown him out, he had scarcely the authority to make such a pronouncement. But Pound never regarded factual evidence as necessary for authoritative dicta. Olivia, then in her forties, was still a remarkably beautiful woman, highly intelligent and well read, a novelist and playwright, and, like most of Yeats' friends, interested in the occult. Lionel Johnson had been her cousin, and it was through him that she had originally met Yeats. Yeats, though spending much of his time in Ireland, still kept the flat in Woburn Walk where Olivia had helped him lose his virginity, and she assured Pound that she would soon effect an introduction. In the meantime, her drawing-room was a constant meeting place for writers and artists. Olivia had a twenty-two-year-old daughter, Dorothy, also very beautiful, though in a somewhat reserved and proper way; Yeats described her as looking like porcelain. Olivia had brought up her daughter with very English care. Both Olivia and her husband Hope came from Anglo-Indian families, often, as E. M. Forster was to point out, more fiercely English than their compatriots at home, and she took no chances. (Olivia Shakespear's father had been in the Indian Army; Hope's grandfather, Sir Hope Shakespear, had taken part in the relief of Lucknow during the Indian Mutiny, while his father had been in the Indian Civil Service.) Dorothy was sent to a select girls' boarding-school, spent a year in Geneva perfecting her French, and then remained at home, an unusual home in so far as it was frequented by literary and artistic figures, many

of whom led far from conventional lives, but Dorothy herself was
watched over with utmost propriety. She read, painted, sewed, went out
to concerts and lectures, but always with her mother. Dorothy was a
gifted artist, but she never seems to have felt she deserved a career as
an artist in her own right. Until this time, she appears to have accepted
this life, content to remain a cool observer rather than a participant.
There is nothing to indicate that Pound particularly noticed Dorothy
at first, but she was very taken with him, and found him deeply romantic.
She wrote in her diary, after his second visit: 'He has a wonderful, beautiful face . . . Some people have complained of untidy boots . . . how
could they look at his boots, when there is his moving, beautiful face
to watch? . . . Oh Ezra! how beautiful you are! With your pale face and
fair hair! I wonder – are you a genius? or are you only an artist in
Life? . . . I think he has passed most of his life in tracts of barren waste
– and suffered that which is untellable.'[52]

Pound had been invited to tea at Olivia Shakespear's along with
another of Fairfax' friends, Frederic Manning, four years older than
Fairfax and also from the Australian governing class. As a child and
youth Manning had suffered from asthma, and though academically
gifted, had been educated almost entirely at home. In his teenage years
his tutor had been an Englishman, Arthur Galton, an accomplished
classical scholar, who had gone to Australia as a private secretary to the
Governor. When Galton, a close friend of Lionel Johnson, decided to
come back to England in the later 1890s, he brought Frederic with him
to complete his education, introducing him to his many aesthete friends
and taking him on European visits. In the wake of the Wilde scandal,
however, Galton became increasingly conservative; he had converted to
Catholicism in his twenties, but now became an Anglican vicar, writing
anti-Catholic theological tomes rather than the literary criticism that he
had earlier published. By 1909 he had been settled for some years in a
parish in Lincolnshire, and his vicarage in Edenham remained Manning's
main home, though he regularly visited London. To aficionados of *Bleak
House*, Lincolnshire scarcely seems a good choice for an asthmatic, but
Dickens was perhaps guilty of meteorological slander, and Manning in
any case needed the quiet. Under Galton's tuition, he had become formi-
dably erudite, and hoped for a literary career himself, but although he
enjoyed meeting Galton's cultured London acquaintances, his physical
strength was never great, and the long periods back in Edenham were
essential to him.

Galton was a friend of Olivia Shakespear, whom, like Yeats, he had met through her cousin Lionel Johnson, whose somewhat inefficient literary executor he now was. Pound was impressed to discover that Manning, as an adolescent, had met Johnson himself. Manning is now best known for his powerful novel about the First World War, *The Middle Parts of Fortune*, brought out anonymously in 1929, and not generally available unexpurgated until 1943, but at the time Pound met him, Manning had just published a long and melodramatic, though racily told verse narrative, *The Vigil of Brunhild*, about the passionate life and hideous death of a seventh-century Merovingian queen. Pound reviewed it enthusiastically that April for the Philadelphian *Book News Monthly*. (Other reviews were not so positive; significantly *The Vigil*'s only other admiring reviewer was Sir Henry Newbolt.) Manning's poetry at this stage was derivative (shades of Morris sagas, with a touch of nineties decadence) and most of it was rather more static than the vigorous *Vigil*, but it had its own individual stamp. It is not surprising that during the next few years Pound was to be a great deal more friendly with Manning, even though they had intermittent rows, than with the more conventional Fairfax. Like Pound, Manning loved the past: later that year, he published a prose work entitled *Scenes and Portraits*, imaginary conversations between figures, some historical and some fictional, a form Pound would later imitate. The conversations were witty, subtle and ironic yet also melancholy, a Pater-inflected probing into some kind of spirituality on the other side of organised religion, a theme that deeply appealed to Pound, and clearly to others of the day, for the book was a critical success. In addition, Manning, like Fairfax, had excellent contacts, and he was ready to put them at Pound's disposal.

Manning promised to send a copy of Pound's poems to Sir Henry Newbolt and to introduce Pound to Laurence Binyon, the 'Wordsworth-Matthew Arnold of today' as Pound described him in his letter home.[53] Binyon had not been a member of the Rhymers' Club – he was still an undergraduate at Oxford when that was formed – but he had published several volumes of poetry with Mathews, as well as editing the Shilling Garland series for him. As far as subject-matter was concerned, the poems of his first and second book of *London Visions* (1897 and 1898) were considerably more modern than anything Pound had written so far, focusing on the urban everyday scene: those who have 'visions' are the poor and the ordinary, not the rich or the cultivated. The poems, compassionate and moving, have titles such as 'The Convict', 'Whitechapel Road', 'The Road Menders, 'To a Derelict' and 'The Rag-Picker'. Their language is a curious mixture of the direct and the contrived, natural speech rhythms cut across by poetic inversions, but if Binyon was an uneven poet, he was a man of deep sympathy, which gives his work a most attractive humanity and serves as a reminder that many of the nineties poets, contrary to their image as dreamy aesthetes, had socialist sympathies of one sort or another. Yeats and Ernest Rhys, the founders of the Rhymers, originally met at a socialist gathering at William Morris' house, though that was, on Yeats' part at any rate, a short-lived enthusiasm.

Binyon, like Pound in these years, and so many of the poets of the 1890s, loved experimenting in old and new metrical forms, but with the turn of the century he came, like others at the time, increasingly to value the rhythms of speech. In 1901 he joined another group of writers and artists associated with Yeats, mainly based in Bedford Park, who were later known as 'the Masquers', aiming to promote Yeats' ideas about a 'Theatre of Beauty', in particular his emphasis on musical speech in drama. Perhaps it is no coincidence that Binyon's best-known lines, from his war poem 'For the Fallen', are more 'musical speech' than conventional poetry:

> They shall not grow old, as we that are left grow old:
> Age shall not weary them, nor the years condemn.
> At the going down of the sun and in the morning
> We will remember them.[54]

Binyon's own poetry always remained to some extent wedded to metre and rhyme (and indeed inversions – when Pound reviewed Binyon's translation of the *Inferno* in 1934, which in general he admired, he thought the inversions its chief blemish), but he is an example of the zeal for new directions in poetry, particularly for speech rhythms, already present in London when Pound arrived. Binyon was another possible route to Yeats, though Pound liked him very much for his own sake, finding time spent with him 'delightful', and writing to his father: '[Binyon] seems to be one of the best loved men in London, a sort of pervading slow charm in him & his work'.[55] Binyon's 'slow charm' was obviously memorable; much later Pound was to write of him in Canto 87, 'BinBin "is beauty"./"Slowness is beauty"'.[56]

Binyon's most important influence on Pound was, however, in alerting him to the wealth of Far Eastern art. Binyon earned his living as an Assistant Keeper in the Prints and Drawings Department of the British Museum. He spent most of his working day researching and writing as he pleased – Pound was envious of the lightness of his duties, writing to his father that 'Binyon gets paid for doing pretty much what I do in the museum'.[57] Binyon was already an authority on Chinese and Japanese art, of which the British Museum had some wonderful examples, not all of them obtained by the most ethical of means. Binyon's first book about this art, *Painting in the Far East*, had been published in 1908, and in March 1909 Pound went to some lectures that Binyon gave on Oriental and European art, which he found of great interest. Though it was some time before that interest would bear fruit, Binyon played a significant role in leading Pound to appreciate the Far Eastern aesthetic. Binyon was another friend of Olivia Shakespear, and later helped to arrange for Dorothy to make copies of Japanese woodcuts and other Chinese and Japanese painting in the British Museum, something she began to do as a way of training herself as an artist well before Pound had come to feel that the Chinese ideogram was vital for his conception of poetry. Two of the delicate line-drawings she copied from Chinese prints in the British Museum have been reproduced, with her son Omar's permission, in Zhaoming Qian's *Orientalism and Modernism*.[58] Half a century after she first discovered this art, in her rather sad old age, Dorothy wrote to Patricia Hutchins that at least the mountains around her in Italy were a continual delight; they reminded her of Japanese and Chinese drawings.

Pound, to his great joy, also began to meet some of the original members of the Rhymers' Club. He was introduced to Ernest Rhys, now more preoccupied with setting up the Everyman's Library for Dent than with poetry, but kindly and hospitable. He invited Pound to his home in Hampstead, as he had started up there a weekly gathering of literary people, to which later in the year he would invite D. H. Lawrence, 'resuming', as he puts it in his autobiography, 'the evenings at the Olde Cheshire Cheese', though instead of 'old ale and other time-honoured liquors', after supper they had a 'claret-cup with a little tarragon and pomegranate juice interfused'.[59] These meetings worried Pound's parents, who knew enough to connect Rhymers with decadence; quite unfairly so as far as the domestically inclined, uxorious Rhys was concerned. Pound wrote back emphatically that 'Rhys's crowd has the wholesomest to perhaps most delightful atmosphere I have found in London'.[60] He also met Selwyn Image, who had written some poetry but was principally a designer and stained-glass maker, one of the founders in 1882 of the Century Guild, an arts and crafts guild whose exquisitely produced journal, the *Hobby Horse*, had been published by the Bodley Head. Image had designed many of Mathews' books, including the Shilling Garland series, and although ten years older, was a close friend of Binyon's and the Shakespears. Not long after Pound met him, he was appointed the Slade Professor of Fine Art at Oxford. Pound was greatly taken by his charm (Rhys described him as 'the most naturally urbane man you could meet'), and Pound was most excited by his stories of meeting Verlaine and others.[61] When he met another of the Rhymers, John Todhunter, he reported home, clearly impressed, that he had known Browning and Morris.

Pound was now in the best of spirits: 'Everyone seems to treat me rather decently and I don't mind at all,' he told his parents. He had a good word for everyone, especially the Shakespears, 'the nicest people in London'.[62] Not only was London welcoming, but it liked his poetry. Sir Henry Newbolt himself had sent a note praising *A Quinzaine*. The Shakespears asked him to read his unpublished work in their drawing-room. Fairfax saw to it that his poems were praised in the Oxford magazines. Maurice Hewlett, the well-known novelist, had agreed to write a preface for the new collection, now entitled *Personae*, though in the event he was ill and couldn't do so. Particularly kind was another new acquaintance, who was to remain a staunch supporter and loyal friend, the novelist May Sinclair, whom he met at Ernest Rhys' house. She sent a warm letter of congratulations on reading *A Quinzaine*, saying some of the poems were perfect, that his voice was excitingly new and that he had things to say. All of this Pound relayed to his parents, who were getting bothered again at his lack of settled income. In a low moment in the autumn he had agreed to return to America after his lectures finished in late February 1909. Now he was insisting it was far too soon. Quite apart from anything else, Yeats was arriving in the near future: 'I don't think such chances of acquaintance should be lost . . . This being in the gang & being known by the right people ought to mean a lot better introduction of "Personae", reviewing etc.'[63] Pound's instincts as self-promoter were at work again. There can be no doubt he wanted to meet Yeats because of his immense admiration for him, but he was also very clear-eyed about the advantages that might be drawn from that contact.

If Londoners were ready to praise Pound's poetry, he was ready to return the compliment. He wrote to his father that Mathews had given him a free run of his shelves, and that he had found that 'the contemporary people seem to be making as good stuff as the theoretical giants of the past'.[64] He repeated his praises to Williams; already by early 1909 he was writing that 'London, deah old lundon, is the place for poesy'.[65] For now Pound was not to dispute the judgements of London. His usual opposition to all received opinions was in abeyance. He was so relieved to have escaped from the soulless bigotry of Crawfordsville that he accepted literary London without quibble as the antidote to American provincialism. In May he was still full of admiration. Williams had sent him a copy of his first book of poems (printed at his own, or rather his father's expense for $50; four copies sold at 25 cents each). Pound was not complimentary, but then, Williams had been pretty lukewarm about *A Lume Spento*. The poems were on the whole derivative, but even so Williams at times makes subtle moves with unusual enjambment from one stanza to the next, presaging his later experiments. There is one poem on a street market in New York that suggests the route he would eventually take, in which, significantly, he writes about noticing this urban world for the first time: 'For many a year gone by/I've looked and nothing seen/But ever been/Blind to a patent wide reality.'[66] Pound, although conceding Williams had 'poetic instincts', was fairly damning. Williams' trouble, he said condescendingly, was that he was 'out of touch':

if you were in London & saw the stream of current poetry, I wonder how much of it you would have printed . . . If you'll read Yeats, & Browning, & Francis Thompson, & Swinburne & Rosetti you'll learn something about the progress of Eng. poetry in the last century.

And if you'll read Margaret Sackville, Rosamund Watson, Ernest Rhys, Jim G. Fairfax, you'll learn what people of second rank can do & what dam good work it is.[67]

For those who think of Pound as an apostle of the avant-garde, those last four are an odd choice. Fairfax was a competent versifier, though scarcely more; perhaps in his case Pound's judgement was influenced by his new friend's kindness to him. Rhys was a cheery and charming lyricist, as well as a generous host, but now remembered for the Everyman Library rather than his poetry. Rosamund Marriott Watson, who lived an excitingly scandalous life, has recently, having been forgotten for many years, received some notice from feminist critics for her powerful and arresting use of myth. No one has yet attempted to rescue Lady Margaret Sackville's reputation. This may just be because of the vagaries of critical fashion, for she could also write arrestingly, but whilst feminist literary critics have applied themselves to rediscovering, on the one hand, Victorian and, on the other, modernist women writers, they have so far shown little interest in Edwardians (Lady Margaret's first collection was 1901) who continued to write in traditional forms. Margaret Sackville was regarded as a much more respectable figure than Watson, though in fact she had affairs with no fewer than two figures who might be thought unlikely lovers for the daughter of an earl, the anti-imperialist Wilfried Scawen Blunt and the first Labour Prime Minister, Ramsay MacDonald. She wrote fluent, musical verse-tales and lyrics, evocative and full of energy, much influenced by the early Yeats, whom she greatly admired.[68] Pound still recalled some of her poetry with affection in the 1950s. What these four had in common was that they were all writing melodious and technically accomplished verse in the mode of the nineties. Pound still had lessons to learn from the nineties, particularly in terms of the Rhymers' opposition to rhetoric and embellishment, but it is striking that there is no sign at all at this stage that he felt the need for any kind of change in poetic language. One of the most recalcitrant myths recycled in accounts of the period is that Pound set about modernising English writing as soon as he arrived; quite the reverse, for four years after he arrived, as will become apparent, various writers tried earnestly but ineffectively to modernise *him*. In 1909 Pound the moderniser was still in the future.

V

BUT change was in the air. By April 1909 Pound was to come across two separate 'gangs', as he called them, who wanted to bring new vitality into English writing, and who were beginning to discuss the ideas that would come to be known as modernist, ideas which in three years' time would be invaluable to Pound in the formation of imagism. Although Pound at this stage was not particularly keen to listen to anything new, he was delighted to meet any likeable literary company. One of these 'gangs' was the circle around Ford Madox Hueffer and Violet Hunt, who met at the *English Review* offices and at South Lodge, Hunt's large house in Kensington; the other was the famous 'school of images', as Pound would later call them, who met in the Tour Eiffel restaurant in Soho.

Hueffer had been christened Ford Hermann Hueffer, though from 1900 he had written under the name of Ford Madox Hueffer, and changed his legal name to the latter by deed poll in 1915. He would change his name again in 1919 to Ford Madox Ford, as we now know him. Ford – as I shall call him for simplicity – had launched the *English Review* at the end of 1908, in order, he claimed, to publish a poem by Thomas Hardy that more conventional journals 'found too – let us say – outspoken for them to print'.[69] This was a poignant ballad, 'A Sunday Morning Tragedy', about a young girl, pregnant, deserted, whose mother gives her a herb, begged from a knowledgeable shepherd, reputed to 'balk ill-motherings'.[70] The daughter dies from the abortion as the repentant lover turns up to make her his wife. Hardy had given up writing novels after the moralistic censure he had suffered because *Tess of the d'Urbervilles* and *Jude the Obscure* had offended late nineteenth-century English prudery. It was impossible, he complained, to write novels for grown-up people in English. Ford, a great admirer and defender of French fiction, particularly Flaubert, was eager to enter the fight against what Hardy called the 'hypocrisy of the age'.[71] Publishing 'A Sunday Morning Tragedy' could be seen in itself as a significant landmark in the opening of Anglophone modernism, the refusal any longer to hide behind the euphemisms of British (or even worse, genteel American) propriety, where hints and circumlocutions only were permitted. The championing of greater sexual openness was to be a central cause for the Anglo–American modernists, though they were often loath to admit it in those terms, a reluctance that was in itself perhaps a sign of the problem. On the whole (Lawrence of course was an exception), they would only say they were defending the cause of art.

Yet if Ford's original impetus had been his desire to publish Hardy's poem, he succeeded in creating in the *English Review* an outstanding journal that would bring together the best of the established writers and some, at least, of the best of the new. In that first issue (186 pages for 2s. 6d.) were pieces by Conrad, James, Wells, W.H. Hudson, Galsworthy and a Constance Garnett translation from Tolstoy. Soon Ford would also include those he called 'les jeunes', Lawrence, Wyndham Lewis, Pound, F.S. Flint and Norman Douglas, several of whom, such as Lawrence and Wyndham Lewis, were given their first publication there. Lawrence, then a young schoolteacher in Croydon, had read the *Review* from the first issue, and recommended it to Jessie Chambers and her family, who were, she said, 'delighted with it. The very look of [it] with its fine blue cover and hand-some black type, was satisfying ... The coming of the *English Review* into our lives was an event, one of the few really first-rate things that happen now and again in a lifetime.'[72] Many felt the same, not enough, it is true, to prevent the journal, whose contributors were generously paid, from losing money from the first issue; but it was undoubtedly a *succès d'estime*.

The *Review* was published from 84 Holland Park Avenue, which housed the editorial office, Ford's living quarters and, on the ground floor, a combined poulterer's and fishmonger's. Violet Hunt, who would shortly become his companion and supposed wife, recalls in *The Flurried Years* that

There was a chaste brown door – the side door of the shop originally – with a gilt plaque, ENGLISH REVIEW, LTD., just over the bell. There was no need of a bell, for, from the date of the installation of the Review, this, the editor's house and home, was left permanently open to all and sundry, contributors, burglars, and political refugees. Vera F——, the woman who shot at Stolypin, found an asylum here in 1908. An English burglar contrived, one summer afternoon, to steal all the editor's spare tall hats, while Azef, the Russian spy, so he informed me, was in the habit of coming in and ransacking the editor's desk. Altogether, 84 Holland Park Avenue seemed to

be a mark for all sorts of Communist, Bolshevik attempts, a regular danger-spot. On
the pavement outside a man had been sandbagged and left for dead; and Mr Chandler,
the poulterer, his landlord, and a big, hefty man carried his takings to the bank each
day, but went continually in fear of a knife in his back. The editor rather liked it.

Luckily, as she entered, 'nothing more terrible than the sickly, depraved
smell of chickens assailed [her]'.[73] The open door and the smell have
been amply testified to elsewhere, but while Ford was certainly in touch
with the world of Russian émigrés – his sister was married to one –
whether his office was quite such a centre of Bolshevik intrigue is another
matter. He no doubt liked to give that impression.

Pound was introduced to Ford by May Sinclair. She was a friend of
Hunt's, both of them being ardent supporters of women's suffrage and
in 1909 considered by many the two best living women novelists. In
other ways they were very different. Hunt's life was a succession of
badly managed indiscretions, while May Sinclair combined advanced
views with an air – and probably a life – of invincible propriety. She
was beautifully mannered and immensely kind. H.D. recalled Pound
rounding Richard Aldington and herself up in Kensington one morning
to 'look in on May'.

Miss Sinclair opened the studio apartment door. Her somewhat Queen Mary bang
or fringe was done up in curl papers. I tugged at Richard's sleeve to suggest that
we go home, but Ezra had already swung on into the studio. May Sinclair made
no reference to her early morning appearance. She was as Norman Douglas once
said, 'a rare thing nowadays, my dear, a gentlewoman'.

Pound meanwhile had found a pile of books on her table, which he
threw on to an inaccessibly high shelf:

'People *impose* on you,' he said, 'you can't get those books down. You can't write
letters to all those people' . . . This was a swarm of minnows, according to Ezra,
poets in the manner of the underprivileged hero of *The Divine Fire* [May Sinclair's
1904 novel] . . . I still think of those books, slim volumes of verse, first books I
should imagine for the most part. No doubt Miss Sinclair summoned a janitor, a
window-cleaner or a fireman with an imposing ladder. She wouldn't, with her
amazing Edwardian courtesy, neglect her minnows.[74]

For now Pound was her minnow, and she was not going to neglect him.
'Ezra,' Ford recalled, 'was brought to my office by Miss May Sinclair

who said she wanted to introduce the greatest poet to the greatest editor in the world. She could invent these courtesies when she wanted to.'[75] The invention was more likely Ford's. Sinclair was impressed by Pound's poetry but surely not that impressed.

At the time of this introduction, Ford was thirty-five, and had already published over twenty books, no fewer than six in 1907 alone, one of which was *The Pre-Raphaelite Brotherhood*, a title which might have excited Pound's interest, though there is no indication that he read anything by Ford on this first visit to London.[76] Ford himself had strong connections with the Pre-Raphaelite era, his mother being the daughter of the painter Ford Madox Brown, not actually one of the Brotherhood, but associated with them. Her sister had married William Michael Rossetti (brother of Dante Gabriel and Christina). Ford was partial to talking of his 'Aunt Christina', whom he once described as 'the greatest master of words and moods that any art has produced', and he was immensely proud of his association with them all.[77] He had a Chippendale bureau in his office at which he claimed Christina wrote her poems, and he had inherited Dante Gabriel's velvet jacket, which he always wore. It was from Ford Madox Brown, Ford's biographer suggests, that Ford inherited his gift for 'lavish and picturesque' anecdote, though according to Ford himself all the Pre-Raphaelite circle had engaged in 'the habit of anecdote, incisive, however wanting in veracity'.[78] That was certainly the tradition he emulated. Ford's father was a musician, a German émigré, who Hunt says first came to England 'merely to edit the Tauchnitz edition of Rossetti's poems and play backgammon with him', but then never left.[79] Franz Hüffer or Francis Hueffer, as, after some variations on the way, he became, wrote a book about the Provençal poets, much read by the nineties poets. Pound, one would think, must have known about this book, but again there is no evidence that he ever read it. But Ford's Pre-Raphaelite backdrop delighted him.

Ford was a man of many talents. Douglas Goldring, who worked as Ford's secretary at the *English Review*, has a story of one day arriving at 84 Holland Park Avenue and finding Ford seated at the grand piano, whose presence in the office often surprised his visitors, 'humming a song and playing over the accompaniment ... "One of my few popular successes, my dear Goldring" Ford remarked as he got up from the stool and shut the piano. "I didn't put my name to it, out of respect for my father's reputation, but it was sung everywhere for a couple of seasons".'[80] Even at the time Goldring thought this story might well have been true ('I doubt if "l'honneur" would have allowed him to claim the authorship of something which was not his,' he commented). More recently it has been discovered that as a young man Ford composed extensively, pieces for voice and piano, following his father's admiration for the Provençal fusing of verse and music.[81] He was also talented as a painter, not perhaps surprisingly given the other side of his genetic inheritance. As a writer, his fiction brought him most fame, though in 1909 his best-known works, *The Good Soldier* (1915) and the four novels that make up *Parade's End* (1924–28) were in the future. He also wrote poetry of which Pound was to say in 1913, 'Hueffer has . . . the gift for making lyrics that will sing . . . Hang it all, if "a lyric" means a song calculated to be sung . . . we would not be far wrong in calling Mr Hueffer the best lyricist in England';[82] few would agree today. Pound, in fact, was to admire him most as a critic, though he paid scant attention to Ford's ideas until 1912.

Ford's father had been an intense Anglophile, who insisted his children learnt to behave in accord with English upper middle-class mores, yet his upbringing was very un-British. For one thing he lived in a milieu of artists, writers and – through the Rossetti connections – revolutionaries. He had German relations; his Rossetti cousins had Italian ones. He didn't go through the preparatory and public school, Oxbridge route of his class. He was sent to a co-educational Froebel school, run by a German couple, where the children spoke English, French and German on different days in rotation. By the time he was twenty, he had, he said, spent three winters in Paris and two summers in Germany. ('Fordie,' Brigit Patmore once heard a relative say to him, 'don't speak French so well. Englishmen consider it affected and therefore it is not *done*.')[83] After his father's unexpected death when he was fifteen, he went to live with his grandfather, Ford Madox Brown, two doors away from William Rossetti and his family, and spent a couple of years at University College School as a day boy. He left at seventeen, not to go to university, nor get a job, but to discover in what artistic field he would best shine. As the very English Goldring commented with some amazement: 'Ford is the only man I have ever heard of who was actually commanded by a relative – his Madox Brown grandfather – to follow an artistic career.'[84]

Direction was Ford's problem. He wondered about music, but decided that there he would not be a bright enough star. His first book was published in 1891, when he was eighteen, and two more in 1892. At twenty he converted to Catholicism, the religion of his father's southern German family; he liked the ritual and tradition of Catholicism, though it doesn't appear to have had much influence on the way he lived his life. At twenty-one he eloped with and married a former school friend, a romantic escapade that, like most of his later ones, was to end in misery. He was hard up, but not impecunious, and he went on writing – art criticism, some poetry, and a biography of his grandfather, who died in 1894. What changed everything, his biographers and critics agree, was his meeting in 1898, when he was aged twenty-five, with Joseph Conrad, to whom Edward Garnett introduced him. Conrad, already a much-praised writer, suggested they collaborated. Ford was writing unsuccessful fiction, both in his own estimation and that of his publishers; Conrad was, he told Ford, still struggling with English, his third language, laboriously translating from French. The result of this collaboration, as one critic puts it, was that 'Ford was converted whole-heartedly to the Novel; not however, to the English tradition of Fielding and Thackeray, but to the art of Henry James and the French and Russian masters, particularly Maupassant, whose preface to *Pierre et Jean* (1888) had set out new aims for practitioners of the craft of fiction.'[85]

Maupassant's preface, already translated into English by 1890, was both the summation of Flaubertian principles and an indication of the way in which the modernist novel, and indeed poetry, would develop. According to Maupassant, the novelist who cares for his art should not simply 'show us a commonplace photograph of life, but . . . give a presentment of it . . . more complete, more striking, more cogent than reality itself. To tell everything is out of the question . . . a choice must be made.' Above all, the artist-novelist 'knows what to eliminate'.[86] Ford described the technique that he and Conrad had evolved following Maupassant's precepts as 'Impressionism', for the Impressionist painters too had abandoned photographic realism, wanting to paint not the scene itself but something 'more cogent than reality', the sensations that the scene evoked in them. Conrad and Ford were concerned to *show* or *present*, rather than *explain* or *describe*, the essence of Impressionist technique being selection, not the piling up of information but the choice of the illuminating detail that conveyed what Ford described in Henry James' work as 'vibrating reality'.[87] Like Maupassant and the Impressionist painters, Ford believed the subject-matter to be treated in this way was the modern world: 'Facts,' he wrote in 1909,

so innumerably beset us, that the gatherer of facts is relatively of very little value. And when, each man by himself, we are seeking to make out the pattern of the bewildering carpet that modern life is, it matters very little whether the facts are those collected by the scientific historian, by the socio-political economist or by the collector of railroad statistics. But to be brought really into contact with our fellow men, to become intimately acquainted with the lives of those around us, this is a thing which grows daily more difficult in the complexities of modern life. This, vicariously, the artist is more and more needed to supply.[88]

Ford would pass these precepts on to Pound to apply to poetry, most successfully the exhortation to eliminate: indeed Pound's expertise at elimination, slashing out unnecessary or redundant words, was to become legendary, and 'showing' or 'presenting', rather than 'describing', would be central to imagism. For Ford himself, in practice 'Impressionism' meant less eliminating than embroidering facts. Even in memoirs like *Return to Yesterday* and *Thus to Revisit* he quite blatantly embellished his stories, but he insisted that by so doing he gave a better impression of how things actually felt. In the past, it has to be said, some of Ford's more baroque flourishes have been taken by earnest literary historians as sober documentary. Even the compiler of the history of the Pound–Ford literary friendship solemnly repeats Ford's assertion that Pound crossed to Europe on a cattle boat: it was actually RMS *Slavonia*. Fortunately she draws the line at endorsing Ford's version of Pound's birth: 'Born in the blizzard, his first meal consisted of kerosene. That was why he ate such enormous quantities of my tarts, the flavour of kerosene being very enduring. It also accounted for the glory of his hair.'[89]

Ford had been acquainted with these French and Russian writers before meeting Conrad, even if he had not yet been influenced by them. He had known the Garnett family, tireless promoters of the Russian novel, since boyhood, for Edward, whose father Richard was Keeper of Books at the British Museum library, and its first cataloguer, had lived next door to William Rossetti. (According to David, Edward's son, his grandfather had only reached the letter S when he retired; perhaps that gave Virginia Woolf, whom David Garnett knew well, the idea that Mr Ramsay should stall at R.) By 1898 Edward's wife Constance had already translated much of Turgenev's work. Constance, whose output was prodigious – she translated seventy books in thirty-five years – later moved on to Tolstoy, Chekhov and Dostoevsky, but Turgenev was to remain the important Russian influence on Ford, as he had been on Henry James. Ford's own wife, Elsie, was translating Maupassant, a factor which has perhaps not been given its due weight, and his sister Judith, who married a political exile from Russia, was later to collaborate with Constance, and to produce acclaimed translations of Russian poetry.[90] The Garnetts were sympathetic to the opponents of the Tsar, and the neighbourhood of the Cearne, the Garnett cottage that Lawrence would later visit, became known as 'Dostoevsky Corner' on account of the number of Russian exiles and émigrés around. At the International Social Democratic Conference in London in 1907, Constance met Lenin and Trotsky, whom she admired, and Stalin, whom she thought a 'bank robber'.[91] Perhaps Azef the Russian spy really did keep an eye on Ford after all. Yet if Conrad by no means introduced Ford to the European novel, it appears to have been working with him that revealed to Ford how he could use the example of these writers to shape his own fiction.

Ford's first book to excite real praise was published in 1905, not as it happened fiction, but an extraordinarily evocative account of the modern metropolis, called *The Soul of London*. His marriage, however, was rapidly falling apart, not helped by an affair with his wife's sister. By now Ford and Elsie had two daughters, to whom he was devoted, but possibly the extra burden of family expenses on a slender income was an added stress. Ford had had a nervous breakdown in 1904, and the doctor insisted he went abroad by himself. The couple never again lived together for any length of time. By 1909, when the *English Review* was already in financial trouble, Elsie was asking for a divorce, which Ford resisted, though in great distress about the relationship and his life in general. He was profoundly depressed, even, according to Violet Hunt, on the verge of suicide. In *The Flurried Years* Violet relates how she was round at 84 having dinner one night, when Ford began to talk, in deep dejection, about his plans to kill himself. He would take poison and then immediately throw himself under one of the many buses that trundled past from Notting Hill, so it would look like an accident, and Elsie would get the life insurance:

What can a woman do? There is the old, traditional way of comfort . . . something of the sort . . . I put one hand on the lapel of his coat, using, I think it was, the simple outsider's phrase:

'Don't look so unhappy!'

The other hand, by the will of Providence, stole to the loose, open pocket of the brown velvet jacket that Rossetti had once worn. It fished out a dark, fluted bottle, inscribed in the Futurist colours of danger, POISON. The blunt letters were like the head of a cobra suddenly reared. I took it to the light, and he waited like a condemned criminal.

'Were you?' I said; and he answered, 'I was.'

'Donkey', I said.[92]

She then, as Douglas Goldring puts it, 'proceeded to take Ford in hand and put the all-but-shipwrecked genius under entirely new management'.[93]

Violet Hunt was seven years older than Ford. They had known each other as children. Hunt's father, Arthur Hunt – no relation, as it happened, of Holman – was another Pre-Raphaelite painter, a friend of Ford Madox Brown and the Rossettis, but she and Ford only met up again in 1907, at dinner with the Galsworthys. She had approached Ford in 1908 to see if he would publish one of her short stories in the *English Review*, which he did, the occasion on which she first attempted the dangerous environs of his office. Violet, a woman of enormous charm and wicked tongue, had a wide acquaintance in the London literary and artistic world, and her 'At Homes' were famous. She lived with her mother, also a novelist, in Campden Hill Road, only a few minutes from Ford. According to Goldring, her novels had an alluring reputation for 'Nastiness', and a haze of scandal always hung around her. 'She was regarded,' he wrote,

as an English Colette with whom, indeed, she had much in common, besides a passion for cats . . . Popular rumour credited her with being very French and fast, a fashionable and faintly vicious blue-stocking. People I met discussed in a knowing way the tragic 'grande passion' of which *Sooner or Later* [her 1904 novel] was supposed to be a projection. Violet was never notable for emotional reticence and had already wept copiously on several famous shoulders, so she had herself to blame for being talked about. Even in her girlhood her friends had nicknamed her 'the immodest Violet'.[94]

The 'grande passion' had been for Oswald Crawfurd, her second lover, roué, diplomat and married man, who, when his invalid wife died, married someone else, leaving Violet with a broken heart and syphilis. She had had affairs since with Somerset Maugham and H.G. Wells. (The only person ever to propose to her, or perhaps the only suitor she felt worth recording, was Oscar Wilde, when she was about seventeen; how it would have worked out emotionally one can't tell, but dinner conversation between them would have been of a high order.) She attempted, possibly out of habit, to seduce the untemptable Henry James, who remained (for now) an excellent friend. Ford was her second 'grande passion'. She was never to recover after he left her.

Violet Hunt had captivating looks, although those who disapproved of her morals said she just missed beauty through her frivolity of expression. Even Brigit Patmore, who knew what it was like to be condemned as frivolous, and who has left one of the most sympathetic accounts of 'the startling beauty of [Hunt's] eyes . . . their clear curious green colour and the perfect leaf-shape of the lids round them', wrote that:

In conversation she was inconsequent, a verbal dragon-fly. When she was young, had it not been a crime for a girl to be clever? Blue stockings were more shameful than bloomers, therefore be amusing and again amusing . . . Truthfully, a friend of hers said 'Violet prefers her worst epigram to her best friends.'[95]

Violet Hunt thought of herself as a New Woman, but she was still bound by some of the old chains. She certainly had sexual charisma (even one of her enemies described her as 'a thin viperish beauty') and continued to use it.[96] Goldring describes her, some fifteen years later, over sixty, surrounded by young men laughing at her witticisms, 'the centre of attraction, a regular "honey-pot", sparkling, flirtatious and lavishly endowed with sex-appeal. "The brave old dear!" murmured a man who had known her as long as I had, as we watched her flash her still lovely eyes at the youth who was handing her a cocktail. "She *does* keep her end up!"'[97] Ford, plump, pasty and adenoidal, appeared a much less likely recipient of a 'grande passion'. Wyndham Lewis described him as a 'flabby lemon and pink giant, who hung his mouth open as though he were an animal at the Zoo inviting buns', and some women are on record as finding him simply repulsive: Rebecca West, a few years later, memorably commented that being kissed by him was 'like being the toast under a poached egg'.[98] Yet a series of women fell hopelessly in love with him (including, for a while, Jean Rhys, though unlike Hunt she recovered with a vengeance), but perhaps it was more for his golden tongue than his straw-coloured hair.

Part of Ford's charm for his women may well have been his warm encouragement and promotion of their own talents, for he was always generous in his support and help. This was certainly the case with Hunt, though as an established writer she was in a very different position from Rhys, who was first published by Ford. But in addition Hunt was grateful to Ford for his support in other ways. They were drawn together not only by literature but by what Hunt describes as the 'lien' of 'our mutual passion for women's suffrage'.[99] Ford, a natural libertarian, had been converted to 'the Cause' by his mother and sister, and was delighted to support Hunt's efforts. Ford's politics were, like much about him, very contradictory. He insisted he was a Tory, but the two political causes he cared deeply about, suffrage and Irish Home Rule, were denounced by the Conservative Party of the period. His account of the London poor in *The Soul of London* has a profound humanity that seems miles away from a Tory party engaged, as it was in those years, in bitterly resisting attempts to introduce the first rudiments of a welfare state. Ford attributed these contradictions to his upbringing: 'To irritate my relatives, who advocated advanced thought, I dimly remember that I professed myself a Tory. Amongst the bourgeoisie whom it was my inherited duty to *épater* I passed for a dangerous anarchist. In general speech, manner and appearance, I must have resembled a socialist of the Morris group. I don't know what I was: I don't know what I am.'[100]

The Rossetti family must have been the ones that Ford had most wanted to provoke by his 'Toryism'. His sister Judith had gone to live with them when he and his brother went to their grandfather's, and recalled their political zeal: 'I had four cousins, who, though they were young, were social reformers. Mary was seven; Helen was nine; Arthur was about fourteen; and Olive was fifteen at least. I was eight, and I became a social reformer too. We were anarchists. We believed that all people should be equal, and nobody should possess more than anybody else; and we hoped for the social revolution.' On 'an anarchist printing press' in the basement they printed an anarchist paper called the *Torch*, written mainly by Olive and Arthur but with occasional contributions from 'real outside social reformer[s]', selling it at railway stations and in Hyde Park. 'I think,' she recalled, 'it must have been interesting and uncommon, because whenever anybody bought a copy they would first stand some time staring at the cover, and as soon as they got to the title of the first article they would to an absolute certainty (we knew because we used to watch) turn round suddenly and stare after us.' (The *Torch*, as Max Saunders points out, is one of the magazines sold by Mr Verloc in Conrad's *The Secret Agent*, a book for which Ford supplied the plot and many details.) Judith, Mary and Helen had 'a special mission' of their own. 'It was the reformation of policemen . . . What we had to explain to the police was that it was very unfair to put a man in prison merely for taking what he needed from another man who had more than the first man had.'[101] Judith's own son was later to become Attorney-General in the Attlee government, clearly inheriting her left-wing views and powers of persuasion, if not perhaps her view of policemen.

Ford, in fact, could be as critical of present ills as any anarchist social reformer, but he felt acutely the need to understand, or to attempt to understand, the nature of the modern, which he feared was spreading a lamentable uniformity. This was the central concern of *The Soul of London*, for in London, the sprawling, cosmopolitan metropolis, is to be found, Ford says, 'the highwater mark achievement of the Modern spirit,' about which Ford was deeply ambivalent. He writes of London that 'it is one gigantic pantheon of the dead level of democracy':

If in its tolerance it finds a place for all eccentricities of physiognomy, of costume, of cult, it does so because it crushes out and floods over the significance of those eccentricities . . . In its innumerable passages and crannies it swallows up Mormon and Mussulman, Benedictine and Agapemonite, Jew and Malay, Russian and Neapolitan. It assimilates and slowly digests them, converting them, with the most potent of all juices, into the singular and inevitable product that is the Londoner – that is, in fact, the Modern. Its spirit, extraordinary and unfathomable . . . spreads, like sepia in water, a tinge of its own over all the world. Its extraordinary and miasmic dialect – the dialect of South Essex – is tinging all the local speeches of England. Deep in the New Forest you will find red brick houses trying to look like London villas; deep in the swamps of coastal Africa you will find lay white men trying to remain Londoners, and religious white men trying to turn negroes into suburban chapel worshippers.

Apart from his remarkable prophecy of the emergence of estuary English, Ford's insight into coming globalisation is striking. He goes on: 'London is the world town, not because of its vastness; it is vast because of its assimilative powers.'[102] Yet if for him that process of assimilation was of dubious value, it is worth noting that assimilative powers were also a characteristic of modernist art and poetry. Douglas Goldring once referred caustically to Ezra Pound's poetry as 'stuffed with cultural bric-à-brac, classical allusions and rather pretentious souvenirs of the European Grand Tour'.[103] But it was to become more of a World Grand Tour, albeit a highly eclectic one. Whether it was pretentious or not is another matter, but Pound, like other modernists, came to realise, as Ford put it, that the modern 'owes its being to no one race, to no two, to no three'.[104] Like metropolitan culture, modernist poetry was formed by an increasingly multicultural world.

It would be some years before Pound could be won over to Ford's view that the modern world necessitated new endeavours for the artist. For now, if Ford published his poetry, invited him to tea, introduced him to interesting people and gave him a good deal of amusement, that was quite enough. By the following March, when Pound left England again, he had had nine poems appear in the *English Review*, with considerable benefit to his finances. And if he enjoyed Ford's company, Ford found Pound irresistibly comic.

Ezra . . . would approach with the step of a dancer, making passes with a cane at an imaginary opponent. He would wear trousers made of green billiard cloth, a pink coat, a blue shirt, a tie hand-painted by a Japanese friend, an immense sombrero, a flaming beard cut to a point, and a single, large, blue earring . . . he was astonishingly meagre and agile. He threw himself alarmingly into frail chairs, devoured enormous quantities of your pastry, fixed his pince-nez firmly on his nose, drew out a manuscript from his pocket, threw his head back, closed his eyes to the point of invisibility and looking down his nose would chuckle like Mephistopheles and read you a translation from Arnaut Daniel. The only part of that *aubade* that you would understand would be the refrain:

'Ah me, the darn, the darn it comes toe sune!"[105]

Pound and Ford met some time in March or April; they certainly knew each other by the end of April, when Pound wrote home that Ford had advised him to stay in London rather than go to Italy, his latest plan for saving money.[106] By then he had also met the other 'gang' who were to attempt to modernise him.

PART III

THE SCHOOL OF IMAGES AT THE TOUR EIFFEL

I

THIS other 'gang' with whom Pound became acquainted in the spring
of 1909 was a small group of poets, mainly young, who met on Thursday
evenings at the Tour Eiffel restaurant, and whose discussions formed
the first phase of imagism, or perhaps one should say, proto-imagism.
Unlike the Ford/Hunt circle, who carried on the tradition of lavish
Edwardian hospitality, the Tour Eiffel poets' meetings emulated Parisian
café life, importing a new style of literary culture. This group was the
rebellious offshoot of the Poets' Club, itself established only a year earlier
by a Scottish banker and amateur poet, Henry Simpson, who was joint
president along with Henry Newbolt. The Poets' Club met for dinner
in Mayfair once a month at the United Arts Club, which shared No.
10 St James's with the Junior Army and Navy Club. After dinner there
would be one or two speeches or readings from both well-known and
aspiring writers. Quite a number of successful writers joined: Edwardian
cooking was very good, and taken seriously, and a literary dinner served
at a reputable club was guaranteed to get a good attendance from
the well-to-do literati. Mathews had offered to take Pound along to the
Poets' Club in February, and Pound wrote home excitedly about the
prospect, telling his father that one of the 'attractions', as he put it, was
to be Hilaire Belloc. Belloc is now better known for his comic than his
serious verse, but Pound was probably most interested in him as the
translator of the version of the Tristram and Iseult story that he had
given to H.D. in Philadelphia.[1] The other 'attraction' was the writer,
wood-engraver, designer and friend of Yeats, Thomas Sturge Moore,
whom Pound must have noted as yet another Yeatsian contact, but in
the event Sturge Moore didn't turn up. Shaw spoke instead, a fact that
impressed Pound, but overall he found the evening dull, and was not
to return for some time. It was his first minor disappointment with

..erary London. When the breakaway group set up in March, it is not surprising that Pound soon found his way there, and stayed longer.

The Tour Eiffel restaurant at which the rebel group met was in Percy Street, off the Tottenham Court Road, an area then regarded as part of dubious Soho, very different from gentlemanly Mayfair. The Tour Eiffel was near the British Museum, at which Pound was now spending much of his time, and at that time still inexpensive – Douglas Goldring recalled that in 1912 it did 'an admirable table d'hôte lunch for 1s 6d' – the Poets' Club's dinners were 3s. 6d. in 1908 – and was to be much frequented by artists and writers. In 1915 Wyndham Lewis decorated a room for the owner, Rudolf Stulich, who features, bringing cake, in William Roberts' picture of the Vorticists at the Tour Eiffel. Goldring said he knew 'no restaurant in London, or anywhere else, which has quite the same intimate atmosphere as the Eiffel Tower. Many of the most amusing evenings of my life have been spent chez Rudolf. I should like to read his "Reminiscences," if he ever bestirs himself to write them, for no *restaurateur* ever has had a more interesting clientèle.'[2] Rudolf Stulich (or Stulik, as his name is also given) was from Vienna, and claimed to be a former chef of the Emperor Franz Joseph and the product of a romantic attachment between an aristocrat and a ballerina. However that may have been, Stulich liked writers and artists to come to his restaurant, and was no doubt as generous and kind to these poets as a few years later he was to the Vorticists.[3]

The Tour Eiffel meetings originally came about as the result of an argument between two young men from very different backgrounds: T.E. Hulme, then twenty-six, son of a well-to-do Staffordshire businessman and landowner, a Cambridge man sent down for a series of what his tutor described as 'foolish scrapes', ex-mathematician, self-taught philosopher and, at this time, poet; and F. S. Flint, aged twenty-three, from the London working class, educated at night school, a Post Office clerk, aspiring poet and critic, a gifted linguist, and eventually to be a central member of the imagist group.[4] They had first come across each other only two months before, in February 1909. Flint had published an attack in the *New Age* on the bourgeois stuffiness of the Poets' Club, of which Hulme was then honorary secretary, deploring an anthology of poems that the club members had recently produced, entitled, somewhat portentously, *For Christmas MDCCCCVIII*, apparently aimed, like Pound's *Quinzaine*, at the Christmas market. The anthology contained Hulme's 'A City Sunset' and 'Autumn', the latter probably now his best-known poem, and one of the few poems which Flint singled out in the review for tepid approval. Like Pound, he was impressed with Margaret Sackville, whose 'Ode to Aphrodite', also included in the collection, he praised rather more warmly than he did the Hulme poem. As far as the rest were concerned he simply lamented the anthology's trite conventionality compared to the collection of recent French poetry he reviewed along with it.[5] Flint insisted, with youthful doctrinaire conviction, that poetry could only be revolutionised in the kind of bohemian French cafés frequented by Verlaine.[6] Whilst Hulme mocked this notion in a letter he wrote to the *New Age* in response, calling Flint 'a belated romantic' – possibly true – with 'all the sentimentality of an orthodox suburban' – quite wrong – and citing Mallarmé's appearances in evening dress, he was clearly attracted by this suggestion of a counter-culture.[7] In this letter he invited Flint to come to the next Poets' Club dinner, on 23 February, the dinner attended by Pound. It seems unlikely that either Hulme or Flint was there, as Pound saw them for the first time at the Tour Eiffel, but Flint and Hulme certainly met up. Hulme would have realised from Flint's reviews in the *New Age* that they both wanted to introduce into English poetry something akin to French *vers libre*, and that they ought to be collaborators rather than opponents. According to Flint's later 'History of Imagism', published in the *Egoist* in 1915, Hulme had had a 'violent' disagreement with the Poets' Club (Simpson later said he had always been an 'extremely trying' secretary) and left, after which he proposed to Flint the weekly meetings 'with a few congenial spirits' at the comparatively bohemian Tour Eiffel.[8]

Hulme and Flint had come to this shared interest in new poetic forms through very different life experiences. Hulme's upbringing, though much more affluent than Flint's, was harsh enough in its own way. His father was an irascible, authoritarian man, provincial and narrow in his outlook and concerns. Hulme's mother was strong-minded, an enthusiastic cyclist and a wit, but not a warm woman; like her husband she believed in discipline, and it was she who would beat both her two sons and her daughter. Neither of Hulme's parents appears to have had any intellectual or cultural interests. His mother would play draughts with him – perhaps the origin of Hulme's later passion for Go, a Chinese game perhaps best described as a more sophisticated form of draughts – but she was much more interested in her cycling, and Hulme's father's only pastimes were fishing and shooting. He had at one stage been a farmer, and Hulme grew up in the country, having been born at Gratton Hall, near Leek. His father in some ways lived the life of a local squire, but he was not in class terms gentry, perhaps more a successful, abrasive

Mr Tulliver, the family fortune having been established by Hulme's pawnbroker grandfather.

Hulme went to an excellent school, Newcastle under Lyme High School, which he attended as a day boy. He was lazy, but very clever, and a natural leader. The staff found him difficult – he once reduced his housemaster to tears – but he was popular with the other boys. His mathematical talents were striking, as was his ability (and desire) to argue. In spite of his lack of application, Hulme won an Exhibition for Mathematics at St John's College, Cambridge. According to one of his contemporaries, Hulme 'didn't seem to work much at College but he did talk', and he was 'the first and the chief of the debunkers. He was far too original and radical to be content to be merely unconventional'.[9] Hulme never made any attempt to disguise his Midland accent, and prided himself on his country directness – when lecturing to a select London audience he told them, 'I want to speak of verse in a plain way as I would of pigs: that is the only honest way'.[10] To have a regional accent, and to come from a trade background, would generally be thought insuperable obstacles to social success in the gentlemanly culture of Oxbridge, but Hulme regarded the refined world of Cambridge as decidedly effete, and his dazed admirers accepted his judgement. Hulme all his life retained the bluff uncompromising truculence of a North Country farmer or unpolished manufacturer: like the other modernist artists associated with Pound, he firmly rejected the model of the cultured, well-bred gentleman. Hulme founded and became first president of a student group appropriately named 'The Discord Club'; he was always in debate with someone over something, and he was as interested in philosophy and art as in mathematics, though as mathematics was at that time wrestling with deeply philosophic problems, they were not areas as different as might be thought. J. C. Squire, another contemporary, later Sir John Squire and a leading conservative literary critic and editor, who would denounce the imagists, and, later and even more vehemently, *The Waste Land*, described him as 'a huge, ham-faced, idle man, but one of great wit and lightning intellect'.[11] The phrase, 'ham-faced' puts one in mind of 'the ruddy moon . . . Like a red-faced farmer' in Hulme's poem 'Autumn'.[12] But Hulme was not yet writing poetry at Cambridge, nor indeed anything much at all, it appears, and when not talking was behaving badly. There are a number of different legends about the offence for which he was sent down, from hitting a policeman to continual rowdy parties, but his latest biographer suggests that it was the accumulation of incidents rather than any single one that drove the authorities first to rusticate him and then to send him down.[13] Hulme left Cambridge in style, seen off by a long procession of his fellow-students in a mock funeral to mark the death of his academic career. His biographer Robert Ferguson comments that it is a measure of 'Hulme's extraordinary ability to arouse interest in his person . . . that the *Cambridge Daily News* saw fit to cover it in detail'.[14]

His family was furious at this failure – especially when Hulme refused to enter his father's ceramic transfer business, which as elder son he was expected to do – and at first threatened to cut him off. However, through the good offices of a sympathetic 'aunt', his mother's cousin, Alice Pattinson, his father agreed to give him another chance at University College London: not to read Philosophy as he would have liked, but, at his father's insistence, Biology and Physics. He spent most of the next two years back in Cambridge, unofficially attending philosophy lectures, and never took a degree at UCL, though, according to J.B. Harmer, he entered the examinations for the Indian Civil Service and failed.[15] He sailed for Montreal, probably working his passage as a ship's steward, having told Alice Pattinson he 'would rather live on bread and cheese than go on with studies he disliked; and he hated the thought of entering the civil service'.[16]

Once in Canada, he worked his way across the continent and was profoundly moved by the vastness of its spaces. It is from this period that his first surviving account of his intellectual and psychological odyssey dates, a collection of fragmented notes that he entitled 'Cinders', recording his experience on the prairies of a personal and searing sense of the limitations and frailty of human knowledge, limitations that he had earlier recognised intellectually, the notes reveal, but now felt existentially. 'Travel,' he writes, 'helps one to discover the undiscovered portions of one's own mind'.[17] 'Cinders', mostly it seems drafted during his eight months in Canada, was never published in his lifetime. It is influenced both in form and thought by his reading of Nietzsche, whose radical critique of traditional Western assumptions troubled but compelled him.[18] At the time, Nietzsche, at any rate in English-speaking cultures, was generally seen more as a prophet than a philosopher, known primarily for his denunciation of Christianity and its 'slave morality'. Hulme, who would later point out that the 'metaphysical part of Nietzsche, generally neglected, is really the root of all his views', interpreted Nietzsche very much as he is more often read today, when he has come to be seen as the father of modern deconstruction.[19] For Hulme, as for present-day deconstructionists, what was central was

Nietzsche's recognition that neither language nor logic can ever represent reality. The order language imposes on the world is illusory: Hulme quotes with approval Nietzsche's dictum: 'What can be conceived is necessarily a fiction.'[20]

In 'Cinders' Hulme, following Nietzsche, builds up his ideas through metaphor rather than logic. It reads, curiously enough, more like a modernist prose poem than anything else, discontinuous, threading together images rather than argument, full of sudden and striking juxtapositions. Its style was perhaps a response to his surroundings and the inner turmoil they caused: 'the first time I ever felt the necessity or inevitableness of verse,' he wrote a couple of years later, 'was in the desire to reproduce the peculiar quality of feeling which is induced by the flat spaces and wide horizons of the virgin prairie of western Canada.'[21] 'Cinders' may have been his first move towards poetry. In contrast with the neat hedges, fences and stone walls that parcelled out the Midlands countryside into bite-size pieces, the undifferentiated, seemingly boundless prairie mirrored for Hulme the dissolution of definite meaning insisted on by Nietzsche and others of the period, who argued that philosophical systems, scientific theories and language itself were simply a misleading and falsifying set of abstractions. 'The flats of Canada,' Hulme writes, 'are incomprehensible on any single theory . . . The plurality consists in the nature of an ash-heap. In this ash-pit of cinders, certain ordered routes have been made, thus constituting whatever unity there may be – a kind of manufactured chess-board laid on a cinder-heap. Not a real chess-board . . . but the gossamer world of symbolic communication . . . The aim of all science and of all thought is to reduce the complex and inevitably disconnected world of grit and cinders to a few ideal counters.'[22]

These abstractions are simply conventions, though necessary to enable some sort of communication: Hulme suggests that we have evolved what Wittgenstein would later call language games, but that our danger is that we take the conventions of the game, 'the gossamer world of symbolic communication', for truth itself. Then, Hulme argues, 'we get the curious phenomena of men explaining themselves by means of the gossamer web that connects them. Language becomes a disease in the hands of the counter-word mongers. It must be constantly remembered that it is an invention for the convenience of men.'[23]

What is the cure for diseased language? Is it possible to find a way of using language without the distortions of convention? Hulme's intuitive answer was that poetic language could achieve this, but what sort of poetry and why? Certainly not conventional poetic language. That too had to go. Being really more a philosopher than a poet Hulme needed a theory, and over the next two years he was to think out his philosophical justification for his position, yet his starting-point remained his need to express the overwhelming experience he had had on the prairies. As he wrote later: 'I came to the subject of verse from the inside rather than the outside. There were certain impressions which I wanted to fix.'[24] Alun Jones sees Hulme's vision on the prairies as essentially a religious one, but it certainly was not so in any orthodox way: Hulme denounces the word 'God' as a counter along with the rest. One critic has compared 'Cinders' to Pascal's *Pensées*, a work that Hulme greatly admired; what Pascal says there about his response to the open skies is echoed by Hulme: 'The eternal silence of those infinite spaces terrifies me.' One could perhaps read 'Cinders' as *The Waste Land* has been read, as the work of someone agonisingly convinced that the death of God has drained meaning from modern existence. Hulme's quest from now on would be to find some kind of certitude to which he could hold in defiance of the shifting sands of nihilism. Hulme might, like the postmodernists, recognise Nietzsche's radical scepticism, but, at the same time, like so many modernists, particularly the male modernists, when faced with the breakdown of his world's traditional certainties, he wanted to find a new certainty of his own.

There is another story about how Hulme came to poetry, which might be thought to contradict the version he gave himself, but which may throw a different light on his quasi-religious search. Desmond FitzGerald, another of the Tour Eiffel group, in an unpublished note, wrote in 1930 that Hulme was an 'erotic':

The first poetic work that appealed to him was the Song of Songs. He had no illusions about himself and quite realised what side of his nature responded to that poetry. But he also realised that it was great poetry, and that to be great poetry was very great. But he did not exalt his eroticism to the sphere of greatness – it was rather a flaw – an element of disorder in himself. If the whole significance of poetry was the appeal it made to that disorderly element in him – then it was less than nothing. But the other side of his nature also affirmed the greatness of great poetry.[25]

One imagines that Flint had also heard something of the sort, as in his 'History of Imagism' he writes that

Somewhere in the gloom of the year 1908, Mr T. E. Hulme . . . excited then by
the propinquity, at a half-crown dance, of the other sex . . . proposed to a companion
that they found a Poets' Club.[26]

Of course, in FitzGerald's account he is speaking of Hulme's first
response to reading poetry, while Hulme's story of his prairies experience is about first wanting to write poetry for himself, so they could
both be true. Hulme was certainly known as an 'erotic': there are many
accounts of his preoccupation with sexuality. Wyndham Lewis, for
example, wrote that Hulme 'was very fond of the girls. His conversation
mostly bore on that subject.'[27] Richard Aldington, who was also 'very
fond of the girls', but, unlike Lewis, a romantic, said that 'Hulme had
a coarse and cynical way of talking about women which repelled me'.[28]
It is probably an indication of Pound's own sexual inhibitions that, when
asked about Hulme's preoccupation with women, he would only say,
'Can't recall T.E.H. divagating from ideas to personal tosh.'[29]

Hulme's writings are sprinkled with references to 'pretty girls' and
his reactions to them, often used as analogies to make philosophical or
poetical points; in his unpublished notes 'tarts' are employed in a similar
way. In conversation, Hulme was happy to leave the impression of well-
exercised sexual prowess, but how much of that was talk one cannot
know. David Garnett relates an often repeated tale of Hulme leaving
the Café Royal for an appointment, and returning twenty minutes later,
complaining that 'the steel staircase of the emergency exit at Piccadilly
Circus Tube Station was the most uncomfortable place in which he had
ever copulated'.[30] Piccadilly Circus station is, it is true, very close to
the Café Royal, but it still sounds a tall story, though whether the tall
story was Garnett's or Hulme's is harder to say. FitzGerald's note,
however, is illuminating about Hulme's attitude to sexuality; unlike the
others, he stresses Hulme's sense of guilt: his eroticism was 'a flaw –
an element of disorder within himself'. By 1930 FitzGerald had returned
to the fold as a devout Catholic, and in any case he had become very
critical of Hulme's later theories well before Hulme's death, so some of
the disapproval may have been projected; but in general his interpretation fits, if not with Hulme's public persona, at least with some of the
hints in his writings. Hulme was a puritan at heart, who by 1912 would
return emphatically to the idea of Original Sin. Already in 'Cinders',
for example, he writes of 'the pathetic search for the *different* . . . Where
shall they find it? Never found in sex. All explored sex is the
same.' There are two moods in life, he says. One is the personal,

'withdraw–into–oneself mood . . . ennui and disgust . . . the sick disgusting moments'. The other is 'Flying along in the wind (wind in the hair, on a motor bus) . . . impersonal'.[31] The modernist quest for impersonality, which became increasingly important to him, and which he shared with Eliot (and, Maud Ellmann argues, Pound too), had, perhaps, much to do with sexual anxiety, and with the desire to escape all that was associated with the messy emotionality of the feminine; through the idea of impersonality it was possible to construct a hyper-masculine persona for the poet or artist, uncontaminated by contingency of personal feelings.[32] Hulme was a radical in many ways, but in his sexuality he reproduced the contradictions of his time: sexual prowess was something a man should boast of; sexual feelings were disgusting and a sign of effeminate weakness. David Trotter has coined the term 'anti-pathos' to describe Wyndham Lewis, and it is equally applicable to Hulme.[33] This conflicted approach to sexuality can be seen in the theory of poetry that he later developed – along with much else, of course. As he quoted approvingly from Nietzsche, 'Philosophy is autobiography.'[34]

After his return from Canada, Hulme went to Brussels, partly to earn money by teaching English in a Berlitz school there, but also to improve his own languages. He was reading widely, probably some French symbolist and post-symbolist poetry, but very definitely French poetic theory, psychology and philosophy. Most importantly, he discovered the work of the French philosopher, Henri Bergson. Bergson's ideas would dominate Hulme's thought, including his approach to poetry, for the next four or five years.[35] Hulme has been chastised for being derivative, though as Pound had already realised, 'complete originality is out of the question'. Many of the ideas Hulme puts forward can be found elsewhere, and indeed Hulme, as his detractors again point out, sometimes appears reductive in his adaptations; certainly his versions of Bergson's poetically expressed ideas sometimes become profoundly more prosaic. The poetic style of 'Cinders' is not a feature of his later prose, which is very workaday, pigs is pigs, as Hulme might have himself put it. But Hulme selected – spotted – the ideas that were to be at the core of modernist thinking. In the 1950s, Pound was to say that Hulme's greatest achievement was that he gave the sculptor Jacob Epstein a language through which to talk about his art; but he also played his part in giving Pound and the other imagists a language in which to talk about poetry.

II

THE route by which Frank Stock Flint reached the Tour Eiffel on
Thursday evenings was very different from that of either Hulme or
Pound, although he had discovered some of the same writers and thinkers
on the way. Already by 1909, at the age of twenty-three, Flint, who had
left school at thirteen and was working full-time in the Post Office, was
the regular poetry reviewer for the left-wing intellectual weekly, the
New Age, a remarkable achievement in itself. A photograph of him in
1914, the earliest I know of extant, shows him as a tall, slim, good-
looking young man, with a sensitive and vulnerable face. Flint, like
Pound, was born in 1885, but unlike him, in poverty that was to become
destitution by the time he reached the age of three. In the London of
the late nineteenth century, poverty, as in Philadelphia, could be absolute.
Flint's childhood had more in common with that of the children in the
missions visited by Pound's parents than with Pound's own; even Flint's
adult face suggests 'the wistful stars/With white faces like town children' that Hulme recalls in his poem 'Autumn'.[36] He had been the kind
of child Hulme and Pound had known about rather than understood,
and neither of them could empathise with the legacy of that childhood.
The robust, self-confident Hulme would at times simply bully Flint,
whose diffidence he saw as weakness. Pound was kind, but often patronising. He would particularly bemoan Flint's lack of energy compared
with his own, without apparently pausing to consider the fact that Flint
had done half a day's work by the time he had got out of bed – Pound
believed in lying in – but in fact Flint's energy was prodigious: he
worked at his demanding and dispiriting job all day, and read, wrote or
translated all evening. Dominic Hibberd writes that 'he reminded people
of a volcano, with his restless green eyes, fiery red hair on end as though
overcharged with electricity, tall frame always in movement, and sudden

bursts of emotion'.[37] Pound and Hulme were ready enough, they thought, to accept Flint as one of themselves, but they could not understand that he was deeply wounded by the experiences of his early life. He never recovered from the sense of deep betrayal that had seared him then. Like Dickens, though his experience was more extreme in some ways, he could never forget, as he put it, 'the child for whose wounds I bear the scars'.[38]

Flint was born in Wood Green, not then part of London, though he grew up largely within London itself. Of all the imagists his poetry was most often concerned with urban life, and was the most directly personal. No one has verified the facts of his life with the painstaking zeal that has been applied to Pound's, and so far the best source of information about his youth is the unpublished manuscript of an unfinished autobiographical novel, or perhaps, as it reads, an autobiography under an assumed name. Some of the events appear again in poems, and some of the information was repeated in an interview with Glenn Hughes in 1929. One can't guarantee the literal truth of all the details; in fact he warns the reader that 'truth and lie are to jostle each other; for no man tells the truth about himself, and autobiography is metaphysics' – possibly an intended reversal of Nietzsche's 'philosophy is autobiography', for he was a keen Nietzschean too. Yet the narrative undoubtedly represents how Flint felt about his youth. It is told very differently from H.D.'s fragmentary, elusive accounts, or from the leisurely and polished memoirs of upper-class Edwardian life. It perhaps has more in common with late nineteenth-century French realism, detailed and thoughtful, often understated and frequently painful. It is entitled, poignantly, *Failure*, and begins: 'My name is John Graham Giltrow, and I am a failure.' His father was a commercial traveller, of peasant stock, he says, 'clever, much too clever'. His mother, who had 'a strong strain of illegitimate gentility', had been brought up in a flat in 'a West London house that had seen better days', one of those 'dismal habitations still haunted with the broken spirit of bygone slaveys'. In Wood Green, though their house was only 'one of a row of similar small and ill-conceived sublimated rabbit-huts' which spread over much of the district, 'you might at any moment come upon a lane leading into unspoiled meadows, where daisies and great stretches of golden buttercups and huge and gorgeous dandelions grew'. For his first three years, all was happiness; then, as with Pound, though for very different reasons, the serpent entered the garden early. 'My father's incurable cleverness involved us in financial disaster which was to drag us out of our maisonette into the byways and purlieus of London's poverty'.

For two years they lived in terrible hardship, sometimes without food in the house or the prospect of money to buy it: 'London ground our faces.' When he was about five and a half, everything changed again: 'I was taken away from my sister and a newly arrived brother to live with my grandfather. My mother's spirit was broken'. He moved to Islington, then a very poor part of London (as Pound discovered in a brief sojourn there in the autumn of 1908), to his father's parents, 'thoughtful working people. Their philosophy of life was formed from their battling with it; their wisdom was the wisdom of working folk, gained with hard knocks and mental and moral abrasions'. The grandparents were, unlike their son, the respectable, industrious, cautious and deserving poor. The grandmother's parlour, used once a week when 'the awfulness of Sunday held sway with impregnable rigour', contained a piano, and books – a large bible, a history of England, a life of Dickens, a book entitled *Old and New London*, an encyclopaedia in three volumes, one-volume editions of Longfellow, Byron and Shakespeare, and 'volumes of pious stories, Sunday school prizes these', devotional books, and even one or two of Scott's novels. The young Giltrow/ Flint was taught to read by his aunt, who was a schoolteacher. He began 'to develop a taste for words – words that have since intoxicated, and thrilled me, when strung in the "right order" as Coleridge says, and that I now use as a burial ground for my fallen self'. But, one day, his father came to retrieve him, and he was taken off, both fearful of leaving the calm if stolid safety of his grandparents' home, and overjoyed to be reunited with his mother. But his happiness was short lived. His parents were no longer destitute but they lived on the edge. His father worked a twelve-hour day of 'heavy drudgery' in a mineral water factory. The house was always untidy, and rows were constant. According to the story he tells here, two incidents in particular, tiny in themselves, shattered the small boy's faith in his parents, the world and his own worth. He had brought back from his grandparents a money box, probably not with much in it to start with, but one morning he found it empty. He was told the money must have been stolen, but later he overheard his parents talking, and realised it had been taken by his father. He had also brought back from his grandparents a much-prized sailor suit, which also soon vanished – he learnt, eventually, to the pawnbrokers. 'I had been wounded and the depth of the wound was not then, nor is it even now, calculable.'

His parents were now living in Camberwell, in a house with two other families, and he was sent to a 'school complying with the English demand that everything free shall be unattractive, for an Englishman would rather lose his soul, or the souls of his children, which is the same thing – than spend money on comeliness'. It was strict, punitive and narrow.

All our attitudes were regulated according to some pre-arranged plan and the restless young animal in us curbed and restricted by the cruel inventions of the pedantic pedagogue . . . [W]e might have had our eyes opened to beauty, and rhythm and colour, and in our squalor carried with us dreams of better things; but in place of all this, we went through a dreary drill which was called our curriculum, invented for us by men without imagination or sympathy, who dealt with us in the forbidding spirit that men assume when they have to control the conduct and lives of other people.

Outside school, he loved reading, and escaped from the harshness of his surroundings into a different world, generally in adventure stories, which he would get from the public library: 'The world of today is not so real to me as the world that was conjured up in my perfervid boyish imagination by those books'. At this stage he had been put off poetry – the example he gives of what they were offered is Felicia Hemans' 'Casabianca' ('The boy stood on the burning deck/Whence all but he had fled'). He says indignantly that such stuff is not poetry, but he does not mention his feelings about the subject-matter, which he must surely have found disturbing – the blindly conventional child commended for choosing death rather than disobedience, or, no doubt in the young Flint's opinion, death rather than independent thought. All the children he knew, including himself, were similarly trained to be blindly obedient martyrs, to accept their half-lives and their meagre existences while being instructed in the belief that the sacrifice of their happiness for the good of the country was just and right and not to be challenged.

His mother, he says, did her best for them, trying to keep them 'respectable', mainly by keeping them indoors. As for his father, 'all the impulses of his better nature were stifled by poverty'. It was not that he was without feelings, but they were 'buried beneath an ever-increasing thickness of the scoriae of a poor man's life, which hardened and hardened as he grew older, and welded into a solid mass. Beneath that mass it still lurks, and awaits the emotional upheaval, which, if it ever come, will make my father articulate'. Ultimately, he says, he does not blame his parents. Whatever their weaknesses or shortcomings, they were themselves the victims of circumstances: 'society can, and does not, see to it that children shall not suffer . . . and children do suffer, and the crime lies against society'.

Even while at school, Flint had to work in the evenings and week-ends as a barber's lather-boy.[39] At thirteen and a half he left school: it should have been fourteen, but he had passed all the examinations and they let him go. He did various odd jobs, including working in a ware-house. Then at seventeen, he told Glenn Hughes, his life changed. He bought a copy of Keats from a street stall, fell in love with poetry, and began to write. He enrolled at night school, learning among other things Latin and French and discovering that he was a gifted linguist. At nine-teen, in about 1904, he managed to get a civil service job as a typist. By 1906 he was living in Islington once more, apparently in lodgings, not with his family, and beginning his first literary venture, a home-produced magazine.

Two issues of this magazine (possibly the only two produced), dated that year and edited by Flint, are among his papers. Called the *Agora* ('Agora' is Greek for marketplace, perhaps a reference to the market-place at the beginning of *Thus Spake Zarathustra*), it is subtitled *A Journal for All and None*, price twopence. Pieces are generally signed by initials – including, of course, F.S.F – and occasionally by names. Some of these may simply be the editor writing under other names; the only one that can be recognised as one of Flint's later acquaintances is T.D.F-G., his fellow Tour Eiffel poet, Desmond FitzGerald, whose comments on Hulme I quoted earlier. Possibly Flint put the magazine together with some other young people, like him interested both in socialist politics and in literature, the twin themes of the publication. The magazine makes clear that by 1906 Flint had given himself a thor-ough education in modernity; he is much more immersed in current philosophical and intellectual debates than Pound at the same date. The *Agora* is iconoclastic, irreverent, anti-capitalist and outspoken. The prin-cipal influences appear to be Nietzsche, Wilde and Shaw, though the last is at one point taken to task for his approbation in *The Quintessence of Ibsenism* of the 'higher love': the magazine advocates 'the love in which both mind and body participate'. Both issues contain poems (mainly rather bad, it has to be said), reviews (including one of a Manet exhib-ition, criticised for only including his earlier, more realist works), dialogues, brief articles and epigrams. The editorials are trenchantly polemic, the first attacking a new department store as a 'monument . . . to plutocratic vulgarity'. In the second issue there is a series of 'Open

Questions', which are clearly Flint's own. These include a Blakean piece
– perhaps in this case Blake read through Wilde and Nietzsche – on
Milton:

Paradise Lost is great art, and in so far, un-Christian; for Christianity . . . means
the denial of life in favour of the Beyond; whereas art affirms life, and by the fact
of its existence, tacitly denies the Beyond. It is a commonplace of criticism to point
out that Milton's Devil is intellectually superior to his God; and here we have
evidence of the superiority of [Milton's] art over his theology.

Several of the other 'open questions' are pure Nietzsche. There is full-
frontal attack on Christianity, under whose mask, Flint writes, 'has been
rampant man's true, cruel nature, made worse by its enforced subjec-
tion . . . [to] an emasculating creed'. He describes the present as a 'period
of disintegration', not just, as for Hulme, the loss of all certainty, but
moral and social breakdown, a corrupt and decaying society. Elsewhere
in his unpublished papers is a copy of a letter to the editor of the *Daily
Express* opposing their campaign against socialism, in which he argues
fiercely that

Socialism is a scheme for the welfare of the human race . . . the Capitalist can only
live one life; but he can and does spoil thousands . . . As money hogs the capitalists stand for themselves, and leave labour rotting in the gutter, where he is fool
enough to lie, while men like you squirt mud at him. That is the position as it
stands today: money hogs on the one hand showing all the evil effects of gluttony,
fat, unwieldy, apoplectic, on the point of bursting; and on the other, the starving
proletarian rotting in the gutter: both rotting.

Like many at this period, Flint found socialism entirely compatible
with admiration for Nietzsche. That Nietzsche's work should come to
be used as support for a totalitarian Fascism would have seemed inconceivable. Both socialists and Nietzscheans were appalled that the mass
of humankind lived degraded, impoverished and hopeless lives. Both
insisted that humankind must be aroused and realise its true strength.
Nietzsche was mistaken in one way, Flint suggests, in that his broad
attack on Christian meekness ignores the fact that it was preached from
the pulpits to dupe and control the people: those in power never espoused
the humble subservience they advocated. Pieties about Christian self-
sacrifice were 'but a mask for the fierce hell of jungle anarchy' by which
power is maintained. Although some left-wing critics of Nietzsche

complained that he was only for individual rather than collective change, in a society where there seemed little hope of collective reform, the promise that the individual could change him or herself was liberating, as the spectacular success of Samuel Smiles' *Self-Help* had earlier shown. Flint in his early twenties still knew the enervating and corrosive effects of poverty at first hand; he wrote in a despairing note dated 12 June 1906 that his desire to write anything original was defeated by the sordidness of his circumstances: 'this room, this hideous room, with its horrible surroundings, its poverty of suggestion, its proximity to the wailing and screaming of dirty children, and the raucous voices of coarse men and women, stifles and suffocates me. Life is a universal dungheap on which a few cocks crow.' Only revolution will change this, he continues, for 'such tinkering as is the work of Parliament is useless, a mere ineffectual screen drawn over the filth'. Yet he has little hope of a better world: 'The dungheap is content. It seeks only to be left alone for the sun to shine upon it; or that it may revel in its own reekings. It recks not of the few, like me, who shrink from its malodourousness, like me, who am deafened by its clamour, crushed by its idiocy, and forced to level myself to its filth.' Flint ends by declaiming, 'All hail to thee, O Nietzsche, thou one bright fervid critical star!'

Flint was in fact achieving remarkable things in spite of his dire circumstances. In his notebooks and jottings of this period are references to a wide range of writers such as Ibsen, Mallarmé, Verlaine, Flaubert, Balzac, Zola, Pierre Loüys, Thackeray, Shelley, Dowson, Symons and Yeats.[40] If like Hulme he read Nietzsche, like Pound he read Pater, and he had worked out for himself a synthesis of the two. As he points out in his notes there are important shared ideas. They were, he comments, contemporaries, often writing the same thing at almost the same time. Both of them are writing after what Nietzsche called the death of God, and both are asking what is the significance of life in the wake of that; for both the answer is to live with intensity. Flint copied out into a notebook nearly the whole of the conclusion to *The Renaissance*, transcribing the version that uses the contentious phrase 'art for art's sake', which Pater later modified as it was thought so scandalous.[41] He puts one further quotation at the end: 'the aim of our culture should be to attain not only as intense but as complete a life as possible', adding in brackets, 'this might have been written by Nietzsche'.[42]

Flint's first significant contact with those who could help him towards publication and contact with the literary world came in 1907. Among his papers is a copy of a letter, dated 30 July that year to Mrs Eder, whose husband, David Eder, was closely connected with the *New Age*. Flint had met her at a political meeting the previous night, and she had invited him to call. He is replying to say he will be delighted, though he also explains that this will be the first time he has ever been asked 'to call' at anyone's house. 'I am not in the least a calling person. My private life so far has been Bohemian of a kind, that mean, poverty stricken, envious Bohemianism.' He is delighted to know 'there is a house where [he] may find educated people to talk to for half an hour or so'. But this comes only at the end of a long letter, which up till then has been carrying on the arguments of the previous evening with a passion which suggests why she had been so taken with this penniless twenty-two-year-old. They had clashed over the Fabians, whom he had described as 'shilly shally' in contrast to the new and fiery Socialist Independent MP Victor Grayson, who had just had an unexpected by-election victory in the Colne Valley, in Lancashire. The Labour Party had in 1906 increased its parliamentary representation from two in 1900 to fifty-three, thanks to an electoral pact with the Liberals not to split the anti-Conservative vote, but it was generally still regarded as politically insignificant; Grayson clearly gave Flint fresh hope. In the letter he slightly withdraws his comment on the Fabians, but still insists there is something 'stodgy and unlifelike' about them. He recounts a story told him by an architect friend, about a woman he has seen that day, dying in utter poverty in an East End tenement, with sewer fumes seeping into her room, and a landlord attempting to evade spending any money on repairs. Flint adds:

And the yellow press talks of the responsibility of the parent and state interference with the individual, all damnable lies and hollow cant . . . A few more Graysons, say I, with passion and argument and ridicule and fun to stir up and dispel the dead mass of inertia which weighs like an incubus of poisoned air on the people of London. I look at these people, at their dull eyes and ask myself whether the poets and artists are not wasting their time while these exist, whether it is not a crime against humanity for a man to write anything except warsongs, or for an artist to paint anything except cartoons. And the utter despair of the whole thing makes us wish for some star 'beyond Sirius' to leave its course and smash the world into blinding, beautiful, pure incandescence, washing it pure of its putrescence in the white stream of fire.

Mrs Eder must have been impressed, not surprisingly, because soon her husband was helping Flint (who, in spite of his doubts, wrote poems other than war songs) to get published.

David Eder was a remarkable man, then forty-one, a little later to become the first British psychoanalyst: as Freud himself put it, he was 'the first, and for a while the only doctor to practise the new therapy in England'.[43] He had trained as a medical doctor, and practised in South Africa and Latin America, before returning to work in the East End. He was a member of the Fabian Society, though rather to the left of many there. One of the political issues for which he campaigned, and wrote about in the *New Age*, was a family allowance to be paid to mothers, a benefit which he rightly believed could have a profound impact on the health of the London poor. In 1911 he read a paper to the British Medical Association on a case of hysteria and obsession; the chairman and entire audience walked out. Eder wrote about Freud in the *New Age*, and produced the first authorised, public translation of *The Interpretation of Dreams* in 1914. (The 1913 translation had been available only to 'Members of the Medical, Scholastic, Legal and Clerical Professions'.)[44] During the war he became a Zionist, though apparently without giving up his belief in international socialism. He died in 1936, three years before Freud, who wrote a moving foreword to a book of memoirs about him, in which Freud shows both affection and respect. When he heard of his death, Freud wrote sadly to Eder's sister-in-law, identifying with him as a fellow-Jew in the dark days of the late thirties: 'The world,' he said, 'has become so sad that it is destined to speedy destruction – this is the only palliative for me. I can easily imagine how he, too, must have suffered under the bitterness of these times. We were both Jews and knew of each other that we carried in us that miraculous thing in common which – inaccessible to any analysis so far – makes the Jew.'[45]

Perhaps it was Eder's own experience as a Jew that made him particularly sympathetic to outsiders of all sorts. He had always had a keen interest in literary matters; as a young man his closest friend and flatmate was his cousin, the novelist and playwright Israel Zangwill. Flint was not the only working-class writer helped by Eder; he was also a good friend to Isaac Rosenberg and D.H. Lawrence. Flint's first publication was a poem that appeared in the *New Age* towards the end of the year, quite traditional, but straight from his experience. Flint has been described as a confessional poet, and certainly many of his poems directly deal with his own life. Here he is in his cheap rented London room, dreaming of the country:

> I was thinking this evening, surrounded by my books
> In a dull, drab room, in a drab, noisy street,

> That the woods are still there, with their intimate nooks,
>> And the bloom on the bramble and wild rose is sweet:
> Epping and Hainault, Saint Cloud on the hill,
>> And all their green silence, unreal though it seem,
> Are there in the darkness – indefinite – still;
>> But to me in my drab room they seem but a dream.[46]

'Drab', of course, was the word Henry James chose to characterise Philadelphia, though for very different reasons from those that led to Flint's use of it for the mean backstreets of working-class London. Yet Pound and he were both to be in revolt against their backgrounds, different though they were, for more similar reasons than one might have thought, not least their indifference to aesthetic pleasure.

Three more of Flint's poems appeared in the *New Age* in the first half of 1908, and when in July the weekly needed a new poetry reviewer, Eder recommended Flint. His literary career had begun.

III

THE *New Age*, for which Flint was now writing, was, in the years before the First World War, perhaps the quintessence of Edwardian radical culture – heterogeneous, eclectic, contradictory, sometimes brilliant, often cranky; above all, always open to anything new. It had existed as a left-wing magazine since the 1890s, but the present incarnation dated from 1907, when it had been given new backing by Bernard Shaw and a theosophical banker, Lewis Wallace. Its editor was A.R. Orage, for the first year jointly with his friend Holbrook Jackson, and after that by himself. Jackson had supplied the poetry criticism, and it was his departure that gave Flint his break. Jackson and Orage both came from Leeds, where Jackson had been a lace merchant and Orage a school-teacher, and they had jointly set up the Leeds Art Club. Like Flint, Orage was a Nietzschean and a socialist, and, again like Flint, a socialist in the William Morris tradition. (Orage had also had a phase as a theosophist, hence the connection with the theosophical banker.) For Orage, social change required cultural change. He and Jackson, as his biographer put it, wanted 'a reform of *taste* in art, manners, thought and discussion. This aesthetic revolution was gradually to engender a social force capable of overthrowing the supreme evil of the age, Plutocracy.'[47]

By 1906 Orage and Jackson were both in London, trying to persuade the Fabian Society – then dominated by figures like Sidney and Beatrice Webb, with their passion for compiling factual information and statistics – that economic reform would never come on its own, nor simply through collectivist activity. Changing individuals was important. The Fabians' mistake, Orage told H.G. Wells, was that they were too materialistic. Their 'collectivist proposals have been designed solely to make economic poverty impossible; it is necessary to design them not only

to make economic but also aesthetic poverty impossible'.[48] Jackson and
he set up the Fabian Arts Group, which was to be 'a platform for the
discussion of the more subtle relationships of man to society . . . in the
works of such modern philospher-artists as Nietzsche, Ibsen, Tolstoy,
and Bernard Shaw.'[49] The *New Age* was in some ways an extension of
the Fabian Art Group's activities, a periodical in which political, philosophical and cultural issues were all debated. Orage and Jackson first
published it under the title of *The New Age: An Independent Socialist
Review of Politics, Literature and the Arts*, but by the time Flint joined
it its subtitle had become simply *A Weekly Review of Politics, Literature
and the Arts*, indicating the degree to which Orage wanted free and
untrammelled debate. By 1909, Orage would write, 'We are sometimes
told by the old Socialist buccaneers that *The New Age* is too damned
literary, or too damned aesthetic, or too damned something or other.
But the fact is that Socialism in *The New Age* is losing its statistical
aspect and putting on the colours of vivid life.'[50]

Part of the charm of the *New Age* was that Orage rarely insisted that
his contributors agreed with his views in any field. For most of the pre-
war years, there was no *New Age* line on any question. As Samuel Hynes
put it, 'If it had an editorial policy, it was simply an open-door policy.'[51]
Certainly it was generally leftish, though as the far from leftish G. K.
Chesterton later wrote, Orage 'very generously allowed that monster,
the Chester-Belloc, to roll and wrestle all over his paper, in warfare with
two such giants as Bernard Shaw and H.G. Wells'.[52] But left-wing politics in any case came in many forms, most of which found their way
into the *New Age*. Socialism then, says Samuel Hynes, was 'a slumgullion
of fads and dissensions that could accommodate any view, so long as it
was unconventional'.[53] Orage himself described early socialism as

a cult, with affiliations in directions now quite disowned – with theosophy, arts and
crafts, vegetarianism, the 'simple life', and almost, one might say, with musical
glasses. Morris had shed a medieval glamour over it with his stained-glass *News
from Nowhere*, Edward Carpenter had put it in sandals, Cunninghame Graham had
mounted it on an Arab steed to which he was always saying a romantic farewell.
Keir Hardy had clothed it in a cloth cap and a red tie. And Bernard Shaw, on
behalf of the Fabian Society, had hung it with innumerable jingling epigrammatic
bells – and cap.[54]

Orage himself came to favour Guild Socialism, a Morrisite return to
craft-guilds though in support of direct action by the trade unions, a

kind of modified syndicalism, but that was never more than one of the varieties of left-wing thought debated in its pages.

The treatment of the controversial issues of the day was equally unpredictable. Orage was personally against women's suffrage, but there were articles both passionately for and steadfastly against in the magazine's pages. The Irish question was asked and answered from all conceivable angles: the balance of opinion during the pre-war years perhaps moved slowly to the side of Home Rule, though earlier the favourite argument was that the common enemy of the English and Irish peoples was the capitalist class, which they should jointly resist. There was general agreement that the British were behaving disgracefully in many parts of their empire, but less unanimity about whether imperialism in itself was a good or bad thing. On the whole, the verdict was that British colonialism was a good idea badly executed. One writer argued, in protest against what he called the 'oxonisation of the Empire', by which was meant the pressure for all colonial universities to be modelled on Oxford and Cambridge, that what one should ideally have is 'a commonwealth of nations, each with its own individual spirit exemplified in education and in life', a surprisingly early recognition of the value of cultural diversity.[55] The rights and wrongs of contemporary marriage, the existence of the white slave trade, the laws against homosexuality, all were chewed over and pronounced upon emphatically from a whole range of positions.

As far as the arts were concerned, some of the coverage was deeply resistant to change – Pound would be parodied more than once, and attacked on numerous occasions – but in the years before the war the *New Age* also carried some of the most avant-garde literary and arts criticism in London. It gave the first Post-Impressionist Exhibition of 1910 one of its most favourable reviews, and published in 1911 the first reproduction of a Picasso painting in London, admittedly to the horror of some of its readers. Pound, Hulme, Wyndham Lewis, Katherine Mansfield, Middleton Murry, Desmond FitzGerald and Richard Aldington were all to write for the *New Age*. It was notably internationalist in its coverage of the arts, publishing fiction by Dostoevsky, Chekhov, Gorky and Anatole France, and discussing many other European novelists, such as the de Goncourts, Gide, Rémy de Gourmont and Turgenev, particularly in the columns written by Arnold Bennett from 1908 to 1911 under the pseudonym Jacob Tonson.[56] It introduced its readers to modern French poetry, aided by Flint, Bennett again, and later Pound. Modernist literature, art and sculpture were all championed – and denounced – in its pages.

Orage himself had little admiration for the avant-garde art and poetry that he published, and it speaks volumes for his tolerance, belief in artistic freedom and editorial shrewdness that he gave so much space to its noisy perpetrators. He would frequently enter the debates himself. He allowed Marinetti to publish his Futurist Manifesto one week, and the next wrote, 'My view is that Mr Marinetti is reviving an old quarrel that ought to have been drowned and damned by the flood . . . and that he is on the wrong side of the controversy.' He published Pound regularly from late 1911 until after the war; indeed, Pound was to say that Orage 'did more to feed me than anyone else in England'.[57] Yet he thoroughly disliked Pound's poetry, with the exception of *Cathay* (Pound's 1915 translations from the Chinese), which he would describe as Pound's 'best and even . . . only good work so far', adding to this barbed praise the comment that he would have enjoyed the poems even more if they had had rhyme and regular metre. Wyndham Lewis appeared in his pages, yet Orage wrote of *Blast*, Wyndham Lewis' short-lived Vorticist magazine: 'It is, I find, not unintelligible – as most of the reviewers will doubtless say – but not worth the understanding.'[58] He does appear to have liked the work of Jacob Epstein, as he had a bust of Hulme carved by Epstein in his house, but on the whole he had no time for modernist innovation. He was a radical himself, but of an earlier generation. As has been pointed out, the *New Age* cannot be called a modernist magazine, and indeed it grew more reactionary in aesthetic terms as the arts became more radical.[59] Yet Orage's importance for those writers was not simply that he gave them a chance to publish and to eat. In one way his approach to the arts had a profound influence on the London modernists. The fundamental belief on which he had founded his arts groups and his magazine, that there is an intimate connection between the appreciation and state of the arts and the social health of a culture, was later to be central to many of them, particularly Pound, who perhaps had already imbibed some of this Ruskinian notion of culture from Brooke Smith.

At the time Flint started writing for it, the *New Age* had 22,000 readers. It was read by well-to-do intellectuals in London and elsewhere, but at threepence a week in 1911 (compare the *English Review* at 2s. 6d.) it was easily affordable to the new audience of educated working and lower middle class that emerged in the wake of the nineteenth-century Education Acts. D.H. Lawrence was a subscriber when he was in Croydon (in *A Collier's Friday Night* Mrs Lambert reads her son's copy of the *New Age*) and the *New Age* may well have been where Lawrence first learnt about Nietzsche, who was much discussed in its pages, as, later, were the philosophy of Bergson and Freudian psychoanalysis. The *New Age* was a higher education in itself. Ford Madox Ford in impressionistic vein wrote of its audience:

The readers of *The New Age* are very numerous and come from widely different classes. I have known several army officers who regularly studied its pages, together with at least two colonial governors, quite a number of higher Civil Service officials, solicitors, and members of the Bar. On the other hand, I have known it read regularly by board-school teachers, shop assistants, servants, artisans and members of the poor generally.[60]

It was a natural home for the aspiring young Flint. Perhaps indeed Flint's association with those connected with the Fabian Arts Group, like David Eder, and his early reading of the *New Age* had been what encouraged him to believe there was still a place for poetry other than socialist battle songs, and helped him to reconcile his aestheticism and his politics. Orage interviewed him before he started work, and clearly liked him. Perhaps they talked about Nietzsche. Flint left, he told Wallace Martin, with a pile of books under his arm.

  Flint's reviews were full of vigour and conviction: with scant respect for established reputations, he was ready to point out the weaknesses he saw in those he admired, like Yeats, and was scathing towards work he disliked. Even before he joined the Tour Eiffel group, these reviews show that he was beginning to question conventional poetic forms, though without any certainty of what he wanted to substitute. As he wrote on 26 November 1908: 'Amid much that may be contradictory, one thing has been insisted upon in what I have written here about modern English poetry: the need for a revaluation of all poetical values.' The second poem he had published in the *New Age*, 'Palinode', which had appeared the previous January, had begun:

  I have grown tired of the old measures in which I beat my song,
  And as the sounds on the hill-top where the winds and sea-birds throng,
  And the broad and mournful monody of the singing sea,
  In heart-harped rhythms my song henceforth must well from the soul of me.[61]

Though he is still using a rhymed, stanzaic form, the poem bears the seed of the later imagist belief that each poem should find its own form and rhythm, a continuation of the poetic doctrine, advocated by Coleridge, a poet often mentioned by Flint, of 'organic form'.

Flint's very first review was in itself a striking foretaste of later imagist ideas and practice. He was reviewing no fewer than six books, no doubt the pile he carried off from Orage's office, and was not impressed by any except the first he mentions, translations from the Japanese. Even these he suggests have been spoilt by being turned into 'heavy English rhymed quatrains', typical of the florid versifications that English translations of Japanese and Chinese poems employed at the time. 'I could wish,' he wrote, 'that the poems in this book had been translated into little dropping rhythms, unrhymed.' He quotes a couple of examples of such translations of 'haikai', as he calls them, which he in turn had translated from the French:

> Alone in a room
> Deserted –
> A peony

and

> A fallen petal
> Flies back to its branch:
> Ah! a butterfly!

The haiku was to be more influential on the imagist movement overall than any other form, and this pair could lay claim, with their brevity and fleeting images, to be the first published imagist poems. Many imagist poems were to be translations, or quasi-translations, so that these haiku were translations of translations is entirely fitting. As J.B. Harmer first pointed out, Flint had found them in a series of articles in a French journal – his reviews indicate he was reading several of the leading cultural French journals even at this stage, as well as French poets such as Mallarmé and Verlaine. These articles had been sent home from Japan, shortly after the end of the Russo-Japanese war, by a remarkable young French doctor, poet and philosopher, Paul-Louis Couchoud, who had seen the delicate minimalism of Japanese poetry as the fulfilment of the ideals of *l'orphisme mallarméen*, the evocative, suggestive lyric style that Mallarmé thought had been lost to the West since Homer, and that he sought to recreate.[62] Flint repeats the comparison:

'to them in poetry as in painting, the half-said thing is dearest' – the suggestion not the complete picture (one thinks of Stéphane Mallarmé) . . . To the poet who can catch and render, like these Japanese, the brief fragments of his soul's music, the future lies open . . . The day of the lengthy poem is over – at least for this troubled age.[63]

Couchoud's account of the Japanese undoubtedly appealed to Flint, as he stresses that they are lovers of nature and of beauty, less materialistic than the West, simpler in lifestyle but richer in aesthetic response. The militarist West is at last beginning to treat them with respect, Couchoud says, solely because they have defeated Russia and Germany, whilst the respect should have been given sooner for their artistic and cultural life, in which all participate, not just an aristocratic few. Japanese art is perhaps less developed than the art of the West, Couchoud comments (though that is not a sentiment Flint ever echoes), but he insists it has a more valuable social function than European art. These points are just the ones the American supporters of imagism were to make about Native American life and poetry a few years later and, like them, Flint fears this utopian way of life is endangered by the West: 'The Japanese, we are told, are quick to take an artistic hint; in fact even the most lowly are all poets (or should we say, *were* poets?)'.

Flint ended the review by suggesting poetry of the future would be written with 'more subtle rhythms and broken cadences', and in November he found a poet who believed the same, and who like himself had 'drawn inspiration from France'. This was Edward Storer, who would become one of the Tour Eiffel poets, and whose book of poems, *Mirrors of Illusion*, ended with an essay advocating free verse. Like Hulme, Storer began from the premise that 'everything in this world is a convention'. Nothing is sacrosanct. 'One does not despise one's ancestors for having ridden in stage coaches,' he writes, 'but one can use a railway train oneself without disrespect to the dead.'[64] Storer, Flint told his readers, has rejected 'mere wordiness and mechanical rhythm' and 'fought his way out of convention, and formed for himself a poétique'. This *poétique* or poetics – Flint signified his approval through use of the French – was radical:

Mr Storer makes war on all poetic conventions; sonnet, ballade, villanelle, stanza, poetic drama, narrative, didactic and descriptive poem, heroic blank verse – all are wrong; even rhyme is only admitted on sufferance, as an occasional embellishment; and the sole poetry is the *vers libre* – heroic blank verse cut up and phrased according to the flow of emotion and the exercise of the sixth sense.[65]

Free verse in English was to be rather more than 'blank [i.e. unrhymed iambic pentameter] verse cut up', though perhaps a first step; as Pound would write, 'To break the pentameter, that was the first heave'.[66] But as Storer's essay shows, in the England of 1908, conventional rhyme and metre were – at any rate to a few – beginning to look like chains.

Although Flint praised Storer's theories, he does not appear to have thought Storer's poetry altogether successful. Storer drew on much the same poets as Eliot was to do shortly after, and some of his urban poems, which are often set in Paris, read like a cross between Jules Laforgue – the self-mocking *flâneur*-poet so admired by Eliot – and Edward FitzGerald's *Omar Khayyám*: 'Let us two go./Dances and song and purple laugh of wine,/And kisses if we pay for them'. Storer's imagery and language has the feel of late nineteenth-century decadence, a very different tone from much of the modernist experiments to come, even though in form he sometimes anticipated them. His poetry is dream-like, sensuous, exoticising, using assonance rather than regular rhyme, like much French *vers libre* ('I heard the music of a violin/Pierce the pale night with silver sword of song').[67] But in November 1908 Flint was not yet a total convert to free verse. He felt a little cheated, he said, that Storer often deprived the reader of the 'sweet chime of rhyme'. The poem that he liked best, 'The young Bride' – as it happened, also the poem picked out by the *Daily Chronicle* and the *Mercure de France* – was in fact rhymed. Flint was not yet sure, as his own poems showed, quite how far the new forms should move from the old.

Yet if Flint was hesitating in late 1908, Hulme was not. Hulme had returned to England from Belgium in the spring, full of enthusiasm for poetic reform. A couple of weeks before Flint's review of Storer appeared, Hulme delivered a lecture on 'modern poetry', as he firmly called it, to the Poets' Club, in which he insisted on the need for *vers libre*. Like Ford he believed modern writing must be appropriate to the modern spirit, and, like Ford, he associated this modern form with Impressionism. 'We can't escape from the spirit of our times,' he told the Poets' Club. 'What has found expression in painting as Impressionism will soon find expression in poetry in free verse.' Old forms must go. 'Those arts, like poetry,' he argued, 'whose matter is immortal, must find a new technique each generation. Each age must have its own special form of expression, and any period that deliberately goes out of it is an age of insincerity.' In a declaration clearly designed to make the Poets' Club bristle, he added, 'Personally I am of course in favour of the complete destruction of all verse more than twenty years old.'[68]

This faith in the importance of a new poetry is very different from Hulme's despair at the moribund conventions of human communication two years earlier in Canada, when for the first time he felt the need for poetry just at the moment when his faith in language crumbled away. What had happened to change him? It has been claimed that his lecture is simply a patchwork of translated quotations – the same, of course, could be said for much modernist poetry; later indeed, with Eliot and Pound, the quotations were not always even translated. Yet like the later modernists, Hulme has made something new from the pieces. His lecture was the fruit of his search to find how he could 'fix' the kind of 'impressions' that he had had on the vast prairies. While he was in Belgium, Hulme had put down his thoughts in a second collection of aphorisms and comments, apparently a continuation of 'Cinders', but now concentrating more on the possibilities of poetry than on the disease of language.[68] His mood is more positive here, with only occasional references to grit and cinders; he spends more time devising the startling analogies that he loves to make. Analogy and metaphor – or images, as he would come to call them – are in fact his chief concern. In 'Cinders' he had written, while wrestling with his sense of the inadequacy of language and systems: 'The truth is that there are no ultimate principles, upon which the whole of knowledge can be built once and for ever as upon a rock. But there are an infinity of analogues, which help us along, and give us a feeling of power over the chaos when we perceive them.'[69] Poetry, depending as it does on metaphor and analogy, could therefore, at the least, 'help along'. But he wanted it to do more.

While he was in Belgium, Hulme had read all he could on language, poetry and perception. Like Ford and Flint, he had come to believe in the value of selection; like Pound, Pater and Flint again, he believed in the heightened moment. He wrote in his notes: 'Life as a rule tedious, but certain things give us sudden lifts. Poetry comes with the jumps, cf. love, fighting, dancing. The moments of ecstasy. Literature, like memory, selects only the vivid patches of life . . . Life composed of exquisite moments and the rest shadows of them.'[70] Yet there were other elements in his approach to poetry that go further, and which would have an important and different influence on the development of modernist poetry. Among the thinkers that Hulme discovered, he came across the work of the Nietzschean French writer, Rémy de Gourmont, poet, novelist and critic, a figure forgotten today by all but the most assiduous modernist critics, but deeply influential on the Anglo-American modernists, including Pound and Eliot.[71] De Gourmont was a libertarian who championed sexual openness and individualism. Richard Aldington described him as 'the defender of liberty of expression, liberty of morals, liberty of action . . . All Gourmont's work is a magnificent protest against the over-organization of society for the benefit of human mediocrity'.[72] 'Truth tyrannises; doubt liberates', was how de Gourmont summarised his philosophy.[73] Hulme, was very taken by de Gourmont's argument (a development of Nietzsche's view of language) that poetry introduced fresh and vital metaphors into the language, which would eventually pass as dead metaphors, or in Hulme's terms, 'counters', into prose. Hulme was now convinced, as he phrased it, in typically aggressive terms – he would later take to wearing knuckle-dusters – that 'Poetry [is] always the advance guard of language'. 'Prose,' on the other hand, 'is a museum where the old weapons of poetry are kept.' 'The Prose writer drags meaning along with the rope. The Poet makes it stand on end and hit you.' As he put it in his lecture to the Poets' Club: 'The direct language is poetry . . . because it deals in images. The indirect language is prose, because it uses images that have died and become figures of speech . . . One might say that images are born in poetry. They are used in prose, and finally die a long lingering death in journalists' English.'[74]

This might now seem a very arbitrary division between poetry and prose, and many of the later imagists would not have made such a distinction, for all that they embraced Hulme's emphasis on the image. In this respect Flint's views prevailed. Flint had already quoted that August, as an epigraph to a review in the *New Age*, Stéphane Mallarmé's words: 'In truth there is no prose; there is the alphabet, and there are verses more or less compact, more or less diffuse. Each time there is effort after style there is versification.' This argument, that it was simply intensity of language, not a special form, that produced poetry, was one that Flint maintained, and that was essential to the later imagist programme. But Hulme is really talking about two different kinds of language use, and indeed two different kinds of knowledge, which he had found defined in Bergson's philosophy.

Henri Bergson was then almost fifty, and at the height of his influence over French art and culture. His lectures at the Collège de France had become famous, and drew a wide range of students, intellectuals, artists, writers and the cultured *haute bourgeoisie*, much as did Alexandre Kojève's lectures on Hegel in the 1930s, and Lacan's seminars in the 1950s and 1960s. The intellectual star is of course a strictly Parisian phenomenon, for which there is no trace of a parallel in London. Hulme, however, was not to hear Bergson lecture until 1911. At this stage he knew him only through his writing. Bergson's theory of language, like Nietzsche's, was an attack on the artificiality of conventional systems, but it gave Hulme hope in a way that Nietzsche had not. Language, Bergson says, breaks up into crude segments the fluidity of experience, the stream of time: it is a pragmatic tool that makes human action possible, yet the intellectual knowledge it yields is always a distortion and simplification. Language and the intellect prevent one from making contact with the ceaseless flux of being, which we can only know through intuition. As Hulme paraphrased it, 'one must dive back into the flux . . . if one wishes to know reality'.[75] Hence for Bergson the importance of art, which works through intuition and the imagination and leads one back into contact with the complex, shifting mutability of experience. Philosophers, artists and writers of the period were coming to understand the world in similar terms: the dead cloak of convention, rationality, factuality, measurement, hid the vital, dynamic, pulsing nature of human life; the rational, conscious ego was unaware of its unconscious passions and desires; the unruffled surface hid its tumultuous depths.

Hulme was particularly interested in the relevance of Bergson's thought to poetry. He seized on the suggestion that Bergson makes in *Introduction to Metaphysics*, an essay written in 1903 that Hulme and Flint were later to translate, that the juxtaposition of disparate images sparks intuition. 'Now the image,' Bergson writes, 'has at least this advantage, that it keeps us in the concrete. No image can replace the intuition of duration, but many diverse images, borrowed from very different orders of things, may, by the convergence of their action, direct consciousness to the precise point where there is a certain intuition to be seized.'[76] Bergson, who recommends using images 'as dissimilar as possible', is here describing the practice of the French *symboliste* and post-*symboliste* poets, whose strange and unexpected images were created to convey, as Mallarmé puts it, like the Impressionists, not the object seen but the emotion it evoked. In his lecture Hulme gives his own version of this poetic programme: 'Say the poet is moved by a certain landscape, he selects from that certain images which put into juxtaposition in separate lines . . . suggest and . . . evoke the state he feels. To this piling-up and juxtaposition of distinct images in different lines, one can find a fanciful analogy in music . . . Two visual images form what one may call a visual chord. They unite to suggest an image which is different to both.'[77] This selectivity, brevity and duality of images is evident in his poem 'Autumn':

> A touch of cold in the Autumn night –
> I walked abroad,
> And saw the ruddy moon lean over a hedge
> Like a red-faced farmer.
> I did not stop to speak, but nodded,
> And round about were the wistful stars
> With white faces like town children[78]

The vivid association of the 'ruddy moon lean[ing] over a hedge' with the 'red-faced farmer', and the 'wistful stars' with the 'white faces' of 'town children' employs the very traditional device of personification in a new way. Given that Hulme had come to poetry to fix the terrifying spaces of the vast prairie skies, one might guess this homely evocation of the English night sky is his effort on his return to tame and re-domesticate those cosmic depths, a constant preoccupation of his verse.

Yet there is another element in Hulme's writing, less attractive, though also significant in the formation of a certain strand of modernism. Hulme is always more confidently brash in his presentation of ideas than Bergson, for whom art is an approximation, a hint, the closest one might get, but never an entire escape from the limitations of the intellect. For Hulme, visual images are responded to physically and directly, and are intimately connected with a test of male virility. 'All poetry,' he had written in 'Cinders', 'is an affair of the body – that is, to be real it must affect body . . . Teachers, university lecturers on science, emancipated women, and other spectacled anaemics attending the plays at the Court Theatre, remind me of disembodied spirits, having no bodies to rest in.'[79] In his lecture on modern poetry, he identified the poetry that he wanted to sweep away with these effeminate wraiths: 'The latter stages in the decay of an art form are very interesting and worth study because they are peculiarly applicable to the state of poetry at the present day. They resemble the latter stages in the decay of religion when the spirit has gone and there is a meaningless reverence for formalities and ritual. The carcass is dead and all the flies are upon it. Imitative poetry springs up like weeds, and women whimper and whine of you and I, alas, and roses, roses all the way. It becomes the expression of sentimentality rather than of virile thought.'[80] This association of the whimpering women with the decomposing, fly-ridden carcass indicates a deep revulsion from the feminine, and suggests that his fear of open spaces and his fear of uncontrolled emotionality are closely connected. What the Poets' Club made of this one can only guess. Hulme would have more luck in expounding his theories to those at the Tour Eiffel, though they had their theories too. Although Pound, in his visits to the Tour Eiffel, was to take little notice of what Hulme had to say on many matters at this stage, two years later these ideas would take on a fresh importance for him; but Hulme's desire to prove that poetry was virile was already close to his heart.

IV

THE first of the Tour Eiffel meetings took place on 25 March 1909, less than six weeks after Flint's attack in the *New Age*: Hulme and Flint had already become allies. Hulme initiated that first meeting, writing to Flint: 'Can you come to the Tour Eiffel Thursday at 7.30pm. Only poets this time, Ernest Radford, Rhys, Seosamh MacCathmoil [the Gaelic name of the Irish poet Joseph Campbell, as it happens misspelt], the man Storer, whose poems you reviewed in the new Age and 4 or 5 other "versers".'[81] The latter would include Flint's friend, T.D. FitzGerald, the actress and close friend of Yeats, Florence Farr, and a poet called Francis Willoughby Tancred, forgotten today, but already with two published volumes of poetry to his credit. Ernest Radford had been a member of the Rhymers' Club, and he and his wife Dolly, a short-story writer, were later to be good friends to D.H. Lawrence and Frieda, but if he and Ernest Rhys turned up that Thursday, it was probably the only time, because they are never mentioned again: this was a new generation.

The Tour Eiffel poets were a curiously disparate group, English, Irish, American, from very different class and social backgrounds, the sort of group unlikely to be found dining together anywhere else in the early twentieth century than in a great metropolis like London. Pound had spent six years at university; Storer had trained as a solicitor; Tancred was a stockbroker, then as now a lucrative occupation, though looked down on for its association with trade by the best society; Farr was the daughter of a distinguished doctor, a friend of Florence Nightingale, whose namesake she was. Flint and FitzGerald were Civil Service clerks; Campbell did some teaching; all the last three were hard-up, and none of them had any higher education. They had largely educated themselves, though in the case of Flint and Campbell – and

FitzGerald perhaps to a lesser extent – the role of night school was crucial. So many lives at that period were transformed by night school education (the Workers' Educational Association was founded in 1904), which made it possible for the able children of poor parents to learn skills and knowledge that could change their future. Perhaps equally important, though in less quantifiable ways, were the new ideologies – whether Nietzscheanism, socialism, Irish nationalism, feminism, or frequently a fusion of two or more of these – that gave a new sense of self-worth to those low in the pecking order of a highly hierachical society. Social mobility of course at that period often ended in grateful conformity to the newly acquired station, but some emergent figures, *déclassé* and marginal, like those at the Tour Eiffel, used their new-found knowledge and growing confidence to challenge the assumptions of the system that had earlier consigned them to a lowly role.

Hulme was clearly impressed by Storer, whose radical ideas about poetry had much in common with his own. *Mirrors of Illusion* was Storer's second book of verse; his first, entitled *Inclinations*, had been published in 1907, also largely in free verse and at times strikingly experimental, in some poems language and syntax breaking down completely, in a way that foreshadows Eliot's technique at the end of *The Waste Land*. Storer had given up work as a solicitor the year before; he clearly had independent means, as even when he had no steady job, a year or so later, Desmond FitzGerald would describe him as, after an abortive romance, 'being bored in a large and expensive way'.[82] When he told FitzGerald in the early 1920s that he was now earning his living, FitzGerald was amazed and half incredulous, which suggests that the persona of urbane *flâneur* in *Mirrors of Illusion* was one he cultivated in his life as well as in his poetry. Yet he must in his own way have been hard-working, because he was to produce books steadily for most of his life. He wrote, in addition to several volumes of poetry, a biography, literary criticism and numerous translations, many, after he settled in Italy at the end of the First World War, from Italian, including works by Pirandello. He also edited at least one literary magazine in Italy, soliciting contributions from his earlier poetic companions. The poems in *Mirrors of Illusion* suggest he had spent much of the year before the Tour Eiffel meetings in Paris, which might explain why he had never joined the Poets' Club. Perhaps, of course, he already shared Flint's low opinion of it.

Joseph Campbell, who, like many Irish nationalists at the period, preferred to use the Gaelic form of his name (actually Seosamh

MacCathmhaoil), was the most established poet of the group, just about to bring out his fifth book of poems. His life was ultimately to be a tragic one, but he was a fine poet, whose work deserves to be better known than it is. Of the poets in the Tour Eiffel, it was his poetry to which Pound first responded, and he would continue to promote it for a number of years. At this time Campbell was the honorary secretary of the Irish Literary Society, supporting himself by teaching in a London County Council school. Campbell's background was very different from any of the other members of the group. He had been born in Belfast in 1879 into an artisan Catholic Nationalist family, in which he was the seventh of ten children; his grandfather was a farmer and stonemason in County Armagh, but his father had moved to the city to become a road contractor. Campbell's early years were coloured by Irish nationalism, both political and cultural. In a broadcast about his early years, he tellingly points out that he was born in the year when Parnell took over leadership in the struggle for Home Rule, and that the first public event he remembered was the assassination of the newly appointed Chief Secretary of Ireland and his deputy in 1882 in Dublin's Phoenix Park: 'I was less than three years old at the time,' he said, 'but what had occurred burned itself into my precocious mind, and gave a trend to it which has remained ever since.'[83] His father's father, to whom young Joseph was deeply attached, described to him how he had been beaten at school for speaking Irish, and made to wear a wooden mouth-gag. His mother, the child of a mixed marriage, Catholic mother and Presbyterian father, was, Campbell said, the first to arouse his interest in Irish folklore, as well as in the richness of the Antrim dialect, the county from which her mother came. Gaelic he began to learn on his paternal grandfather's farm, where he would often spend his holidays, it still being spoken in that part of Armagh.

As well as a precocious observer of the political scene, Joseph was a precocious reader, and at the age of seven, when he had read all the books available in the house, his father bought a four-volume *Cabinet of Irish Literature*, which gave him an early introduction to the idea of an Irish literary tradition. He was learning about other Irish traditions as well: that same year, there were stormy troubles in Belfast over the Nationalists' support for Parnell's campaign for Home Rule. Earlier in the century, Belfast had been a predominantly Protestant town, but after the famine of the 1840s, and with the growth of the city's industrial wealth, Catholics had poured into Belfast in the hope of work. In Joseph's youth, they still made up only 25 per cent of the population, excluded from many jobs, and they were regarded with deep suspicion by the Protestants; violence flared frequently. Joseph's father was an ardent believer in Home Rule and a staunch supporter of Parnell. He and his family remained loyal to Parnell, as James Joyce's father did, even after the scandal of Kitty O'Shea's divorce ended Parnell's career when Joseph was eleven years old. One cousin, family tradition proudly related, actually walked out of mass when the priest began to denounce Parnell. When the news of Parnell's death came a year later, they felt, Campbell recalled, that 'the Uncrowned King [had been] thrown to the wolves by his own people'.[84]

Yet in spite of the setback to hopes of Home Rule – and hope by no means died – a vigorous cultural and literary nationalist movement was growing up, though Campbell learnt little about this until he left school. Not, as it happens, that this was so long ahead. He was doing well at school, winning an Exhibition in 1892, and a composition prize in 1893, but his father decided that Joseph must abandon his schooling at the age of sixteen, as he wanted to apprentice him as a road-maker. Joseph's only older brother had already become a priest; Joseph was expected to help his father in his work. In actual fact, he was to do little formal work of any sort for the next three years. The year that he left school, while he was staying on the Armagh farm, his grandfather was suddenly taken ill and died, leaving Campbell traumatised: 'The experience unnerved me,' he said in his broadcast, 'and I was ill for quite a long time after; afraid of day, afraid of night, distrustful of my own shadow.'[85] Campbell was to remain prey to melancholy all his life, but one wonders how much the depression and inability to work may have owed to his being forced into an uncongenial career. For the next three years he stayed at home, reading everything he could lay his hands on, and he began to write. He made friends with Francis Joseph Bigger, whose house was the centre for the Celtic revival that was taking root in the Belfast region. One of Campbell's cousins, Anne MacManus, who published as Ethna Carbery, with another young woman, Alice Milligan, started a magazine, *Shan Van Vocht* ('The Poor Old Woman', i.e. Ireland), dedicated to publishing writing that drew on Irish cultural traditions. In 1899, Campbell had his own first poem published in the *Belfast News-Letter*, but he was still, he later said, living in a 'penumbra':

I was vaguely aware of the celebration of the centenary of 1798 [the Irish rebellion led by Wolfe Tone] . . . and there were rumours of green branches and black-helmeted police clashing on the Hannahstown Road. Kruger and Cronje and De

Wet were names, too, that floated across sea from the South African veldt. And somebody called Victoria died . . . and Oscar Wilde was being waked with guttering candles and the prayers of nuns in a shabby room in Montmartre . . . and then my father, William Henry Campbell, caught cold, and despite my mother's assiduous nursing, did not rally out of it.

It was the end of an epoch. Too dazed by my introspections, I could not realise it was the beginning of another.[86]

For the next two years Joseph and his brother John had to run the family road-making business. His father had had a two-year contract for a drainage scheme they could not break. He and his brother got up at dawn, and worked all day in the open with navvies recruited from the nationalist Falls Road. In a strange way it brought him back to life. He never forgot those labourers. 'I gained, from intimate daily contact with them,' he said in his broadcast, 'experience that proved of more value to me than if I had spent this preclusive time in libraries, or in aimless mooning about.'[87] Like the majority of the Catholics in Belfast, they were only first- or second-generation town-dwellers, not far from their peasant roots, and Campbell felt that through them he was meeting the real people of Ireland. From then can be dated what one of his sisters described as his 'socialist tendencies'.

Along with his brother John and the navvies, he succeeded in fulfilling the contract, and the family benefited from a handsome profit of £700. But it had to last them some time; there was no more work. Recession hit Belfast after the end of the Boer War, and in times of recession it was even harder for a Catholic to find employment. At least, however, there was a chance for Joseph's literary interests to develop. In 1904 he helped to organise the first big *Feis na nGleann* – Festival of the Glens of Antrim – and there he made two significant new acquaintances. One was the consul Roger Casement, the humanitarian and nationalist, just back from a harrowing time in the Congo and fighting to get his report of the scandalous abuse of African workers there accepted by the international community. The other new contact was the poet Padraic Colum, then working as a railway clerk in Dublin, and like Campbell a Catholic. Colum, only twenty-one, two years younger than Campbell, had already published stories and poems in the *United Irishman*, edited by Arthur Griffith, founder of Sinn Fein and later the first President of the Irish Free State; one of these poems, 'The Drover', was to remain among his best-known and was later a favourite of Pound's. Campbell had read and admired Colum's work, and he and Colum became immediate friends.

Soon, like Colum, Campbell was having his work published in the Dublin-based *United Irishman*, as well as in places like the *All Ireland Review* and the *Gael*, journals whose titles make their sympathies clear. The aim of the Irish literary revival can be summed up in the title of a famous address given by Douglas Hyde in 1892, the year after Parnell's death: 'The Necessity for Deanglicizing Ireland'. If liberating Ireland politically was proving slow work, she could find cultural liberation through reviving and celebrating her language and traditions. Douglas Hyde founded the Gaelic League – which Campbell had joined – a year later in 1893, to promote the Gaelic language and its literature. But he did more than revive Gaelic; he Irished English. That same year he published a collection of traditional Gaelic lyrics, *The Love Songs of Connacht*, both in the original Gaelic, and in translation. Earlier in the century translations of Irish ballads had been into standard Victorian English verse, but this was different. On the left-hand page was the Gaelic, on the right Hyde's translation into what became known as Hiberno-English, a language which aims to capture the rhythms and idioms of English as spoken by the Irish peasantry, incorporating Gaelic place-names and Gaelic idioms and usages. Hyde's Hiberno-English was an early and tentative version, still more English than Hiberno, though he had already taken the significant step of attempting to reproduce Gaelic poetic forms and characteristic devices like assonance and the use of internal rhyme. One can see the adoption of Hiberno-English as very much the equivalent of the move that came about in Caribbean writing much more recently, as it shed its allegiance to standard English and began to use what Edward Braithwaite (who, in a gesture similar to the Irish adoption of Gaelic names, now prefers to be known as Kamau Braithwaite) named significantly 'nation-language'. As in the Caribbean, this 'vernacular' Irish was rarely the vernacular of the writer, certainly not as an adult, though for Colum and Campbell it was not as distant as it was for others. The apotheosis of this movement was perhaps Synge's wonderfully evocative creation of the speech of western Ireland, though once again for all Yeats' celebration of him as a peasant-poet, it was not his own speech; but he had listened well.

Campbell's first book-length publication was, not surprisingly, a book of folk songs. His brother John – probably not long before the *Feis na Gleann*, although the precise date is uncertain – travelled with the composer Herbert Hughes to Donegal, a county that was then part, as it had always historically been, of Ulster. (It was only when partition came that it was to be split away from the rest, on account of its predominantly Catholic population.) There they took photographs, and collected traditional airs; John was a gifted artist, so presumably the former task was allocated to him, and the latter to Hughes. On their return, Hughes asked Joseph Campbell to supply words. The original Gaelic verses had been lost, but Campbell was already by then knowledgeable in Gaelic culture, and he wrote lyrics as close as possible to the spirit of Gaelic folk verse. He first learnt through this exercise, according to the poet Austin Clarke, who edited Campbell's collected works in 1963, the 'directness' and 'concentrated simplicity' later characteristic of his own poetry.[88] Hughes would come to his house; 'seated at the piano,' Campbell recalled, 'he would play over the airs, improvising an accompaniment as he proceeded – first in their natural tempo, and then more slowly, so that I could catch and absorb the peculiar quality in each.'[89] The words and music were published in 1904 as *Songs of Uladh* (i.e. Ulster), and illustrated by his brother John, under the name Seaghan MacCathmhaoil. Many of these songs have passed into general circulation and are regarded as anonymous and authentic folk songs, some of them, like 'The Blue Hills of Antrim', being made famous worldwide by James Joyce's tenor friend, John McCormack. It is a curious fact that some of Campbell's poems are so much better known than his name; it is certainly a story that illustrates the very fine line between the discovery and invention of folklore at this period.

The year 1904 was an important one for the Ulster literary movement. Campbell and others started a periodical in Belfast, called simply *Uladh*, to which Casement among others contributed, and the Ulster Literary Theatre was founded, also in Belfast. Campbell published in the journal, acted in the theatre, and the next year put on a none too successful play. He also brought out a book of poems, *The Garden of the Bees*, also far from successful; even his friend Padraic Colum said it showed 'little reverence for form'.[90] Campbell at that point was trying to incorporate several different influences, most notably Whitman and Blake in addition to Gaelic literature, and at this stage they pulled against each other. Colum on their first meeting had lent him *Leaves of Grass*, which he had read with passion, finishing it by the next morning. Whitman, as a poet who celebrated the nationhood of a country trying like Ireland to escape from the yoke of traditional English culture, was an important influence on the Irish literary revival, though Campbell was unusual among Irish poets in being attracted by Whitman's use of free verse, which drew both on biblical language and Blake's Prophetic

Books. For Campbell, Whitman had a further significance: he was not only a national poet, he was the poet of democracy, the poet of the people, the poet of liberty. Whitman's bid for freedom from traditional verse forms clearly struck him as an essential part of this. Unlike Flint, Storer and Hulme, Campbell first learnt free verse not from the French post-*symbolistes* but from the American poet – a more direct route, one might say, as Whitman had been a key influence on the development of *vers libre* in France. Campbell was, according to Austin Clarke, the first poet in Ireland to use free verse.

Trying to yoke together Whitman's long, loose paratactic lines and Gaelic folk poetry, whose simplicity, restraint and brevity Campbell so admired, was not easy, and his first collection showed it. The lukewarm reception that the uneven poems of *The Garden of the Bees* received was a blow. He was also still unemployed, and decided to try to find work in Dublin, where the well-connected Roger Casement, now a famous figure since the painful truth of his report had been established, could give him help. With Casement's support, Campbell was admitted on a probationary training course as a civil servant, and did some acting for the Abbey Theatre, which had just been opened the previous December as the home of the Irish National Theatre Society, in which Yeats and Lady Gregory were prime movers. Ronald Schuchard reports that Campbell trained as a chanter there, and as Campbell had a remarkable speaking voice, deep and musical (Austin Clarke described it as 'strong, vibrant . . . rich and warm'), he would certainly have been an asset to the theatre.[91] At the Abbey, 1905 was a stormy year. Synge's *The Well of the Saints* did not do well, while Padraic Colum's play, *The Land*, was a great success. Yeats' response to what he regarded as poor judgement on the part of the public caused friction, and by early 1906 Colum and others had split away. Campbell would have discovered by then, if he did not already know, that Irish nationalism was increasingly factional. The name of the *United Irishman* bore little relation to the disunited Irish and their feuds.

When Campbell finished his Civil Service training course, he was still unable to find work. In Belfast he might be ostracised as a Catholic; in Dublin he was ostracised as an Ulsterman. He decided to move to London. Before he did so, his third book of poetry, *The Rushlight*, was published, and this time he was highly praised. The majority of the poems there were written in traditional ballad forms, drawing on Irish folk traditions. Campbell had a quasi-mystical sense of the relation of the poet, the people and the land in Ireland. In *The Rushlight* he identified himself as 'the

Mountainy Singer', later using that as the title of his 1909 book: a poet who speaks for the peasant and the living spirit of the Irish countryside:

> I am the mountainy singer –
> The voice of the peasant's dream,
> The cry of the wind on the wooded hill,
> The leap of the trout in the stream . . .
>
> Beauty and peace I sing –
> The fire on the open hearth,
> The cailleach spinning at her wheel,
> The plough in the broken earth.
>
> Travail and pain I sing –
> The bride on the childing-bed,
> The dark man labouring at his rhymes,
> The ewe in the lambing shed.[92]

'The dark man labouring at his rhymes' is of course Campbell himself – 'the darrk man frum th' narth', as Pound learnt to call him, doubtless a description Campbell acquired in Dublin.[93] For Campbell, the poet is an integral part of Ireland and its travail, a bringer to birth, he hoped, of freedom as well as beauty. Whitman is less in evidence in *The Rushlight*, Blake perhaps more so at this stage, and the simplicity and apparent childlike directness of Campbell's lyrics is often reminiscent of the *Songs of Innocence and Experience*.

In London Campbell made contact with the Irish Literary Society, which had been set up in 1892, with Yeats as one of the moving spirits in its creation. The Society, based at 20 Hanover Square, was the leading centre for Irish writing in London, as well as being closely involved in debates about Home Rule and Irish independence. Significantly, in terms of the importance of expatriate Irish to the Irish literary revival, it was founded even before the National Literary Society in Dublin, for whose first presidential address Hyde had delivered the lecture on deanglicisation, and had been in existence for some five or six years before the Irish literary revival reached Ulster. The Irish Literary Society was one of the most lively arts venues in London, and both expatriate Irish and sympathetic non-Irish had always flocked to its events. Campbell was quickly asked to become secretary, and appears to have been a great success. He was a distinguished and romantic figure, tall, powerfully built, with dark handsome features, a man, according to Austin Clarke, who 'looked like a maker of sagas rather than a lyric poet with a singularly delicate touch'.[94] He took to wearing a kilt, seen then as a badge of Celtic identity, apparently with no historical justification but considered very dashing by English sympathisers. At the Society he gave lectures, directed musical evenings, acted and gave poetry recitals, which were enthusiastically received.

In 1907, Campbell published two more small collections. *The Gilly of Christ*, the title poem of which had also appeared in *The Rushlight*, was a series of poems drawn from folk religious beliefs: delicate and evocative pastiche folk poetry, it consisted mainly of lyrics, but with some free verse. *The Man Child* was more experimental, but less successful. Meanwhile, Campbell was reading widely in European literature, learning Russian, French and German at night school. Yeats had argued back in 1893, in a lecture entitled 'Nationality and Literature', that Irish writers should not rely solely on Irish traditions, but search throughout the world for the best models available. Although he stressed 'we must not imitate the writers of any other country', he was convinced that 'we must study them constantly and learn from them the secret of their greatness. Only by study of great models can we acquire style.'[95] The Irish, Yeats said, too often believed they could rely on inspiration but that 'comes only to him who labours at rhythm and cadence, at form and style, until they have no secret hidden from him. This art we must learn from the old literatures of the world. We have hitherto been slovens.'[96] Like Yeats, Campbell believed that Irish poets should be citizens of the world, and should labour at their art. Indeed, had he not, he would not have come to the Tour Eiffel. *The Mountainy Singer*, published a few months after the Tour Eiffel meetings began, shows Campbell experimenting with a variety of verse forms. Austin Clarke, who first met Campbell in 1917, commented that, for all his deep knowledge of Gaelic traditions, he 'was not merely a traditionalist. Paradoxically enough, he was immensely interested in every phase of modern poetry in England and elsewhere.'[97]

Pound had already visited the Irish Literary Society before he joined the Tour Eiffel. He may have first gone primarily in search of Yeatsian contacts once again, but he had not yet lost the general enthusiasm for the Celtic imagination that Fiona Macleod had inspired in him. Dorothy Shakespear had noticed with surprise that Pound affected an Irish accent when declaiming Yeats' poetry, and indeed much of the time. It was not surprising that Pound had moved on in 1906 seamlessly from the Pre-Raphaelites to the Celts. That was entirely what the Irish literary revival itself had quite consciously done, carrying on Morris' and Ruskin's campaign against utilitarianism and greed and their search for creativity and beauty but moving these categories into national terms. When Yeats visited the United States in his tour of 1903–4, he had presented the American public with, in R.F. Foster's words, 'high claims for Irish culture over English materialism'.[98] That there was a nationalist as well as a literary dimension to such claims did not matter to Pound: for him, Celticism, like Pre-Raphaelitism, celebrated the imagination and art, unlike American business, which celebrated profits and possessions.

The part the Irish played in the Tour Eiffel group was a significant one. Hulme, like Pound, was attracted to the creative energy of the Celtic movement, though he was actually against Home Rule, yet his use of Campbell's Irish name in his letter to Flint indicates that he liked its defiant signal, and that he saw Campbell as a fellow opponent of the status quo. He recognised that Campbell and he shared a common cause in trying to find new forms that escaped the received traditions of Victorian English poetry. Celticism served as a model of how to break the dominant mode. Anglo–American modernist poetry, and especially imagism, owed a bigger debt to the Celtic revival than is often realised.

V

IN his 'History of Imagism', Flint says that Pound joined the Tour Eiffel group on 22 April 1908, 'introduced, I believe, by Miss Farr and my friend T. D. FitzGerald'. It is possible that Pound had met Florence Farr at the Poets' Club, to which she belonged, and which she had entertained earlier the previous year to her own arrangement of dramatised readings from *Thus Spake Zarathustra*. Alternatively, he might have met her at Olivia Shakespear's, for the two women were good friends. It is most likely, however, since he was introduced by Farr and FitzGerald in tandem, that he first met them together at the Irish Literary Society, which they both frequented. While Farr and FitzGerald would both already have known Joseph Campbell, it was probably Flint who had invited FitzGerald, whom he had known for a couple of years. Florence Farr, a letter to Flint confirms, was first invited to the Tour Eiffel by Hulme, who had met her soon after he first came to London.

Pound was delighted to meet Florence Farr: as he reminded his father, Yeats had written with ecstatic admiration about her method of reciting poems to a musical accompaniment in 'Speaking to the Psaltery', one of the essays included in *Ideas of Good and Evil*. (The psaltery was a kind of harp, made specially for her by Arnold Dolmetsch, on which she would pluck notes while speaking the lines.) He was impressed by her part in the radical theatre productions of which he had heard from Brooke Smith; she had played Rebecca West in the first English production of Ibsen's *Rosmersholm*, and had been the lead in Shaw's first play, *Widowers' Houses*. Shaw had written *Arms and the Man* especially for her, which was produced as a double act with *Land of Heart's Desire*, written for her by Yeats. More recently, in 1905, Farr had produced the first London performance of Wilde's *Salomé*, and acted herself in many of Yeats' plays in London and Dublin. She was older than the other

Tour Eiffel poets, though she was still a very attractive woman; in 1912, when she left England for Ceylon at the age of fifty-two, the young Clifford Bax, then nineteen, recalled that 'she was still beautiful, and no one who saw her could forget her starry eyes'.[99] Pictures of her in the 1890s show her as slenderer than was generally fashionable at the time, with a piquant, Burne-Jones face and finely but firmly chiselled features that suggest a certain underlying toughness and determination. Perhaps significantly enough, in his poster for her appearance in a John Todhunter play in 1894, Aubrey Beardsley depicts her as a powerful and sultry *femme fatale*. Shaw, who had an affair with her for a while in the early 1890s, described Farr as 'in violent reaction against Victorian morals, especially sexual and domestic morals; and when the impact of Ibsen was felt in this country, and I wrote somewhere that "home is the girl's prison and the woman's workhouse" I became *persona grata* with her'.[100]

Farr was the New Woman *par excellence*, turning her back on her highly respectable education at Cheltenham Ladies' College and later Queen's College, the first college for women in London, and going on the stage in her early twenties. Her father died when she was twenty-three, leaving her a small income (£50 a year), which she always successfully supplemented. She was briefly married to an unsatisfactory actor, Edward Emery; she insisted on his emigration to the United States after three disagreeable years, eventually divorced him and never married again, though she had many lovers. There are numerous reports of her beautiful voice, and much criticism of her acting. She thought spontaneity mattered much more than training, and would only put as much effort into a play as the whim took her. Although she had some successes she was unwilling to take direction or advice, and could drive playwrights, even when they were admirers, to distraction.

Yeats met Farr in 1890, when he first began to think about the possibilities of a non-realist theatre, and decided that she was 'an almost perfect poetic actress'.[101] From the beginning he consulted her regularly about his writing, that first year reading her *The Countess Cathleen*, on which he was then working: he introduced her to the Hermetic Order of the Golden Dawn, delighted that her fascination with the occult matched his own. (The Order of the Golden Dawn was an esoteric Rosicrucian society, founded in 1888; Yeats had joined in early 1890, after becoming exasperated by Madame Blavatsky's autocratic rule in the Theosophical Society.) Yeats was fascinated by Farr from the start, and very jealous of Shaw. Farr to a certain extent played the two of them off against each other, but her interests in the occult and in the chanting of verse coincided much more with Yeats' than with those of the more down to earth Shaw. Farr firmly believed one should not form exclusive attachments, and, unlike some who espoused that view, she never appears to have found her heart acting against her head. She never lost her regard for Shaw, and they remained excellent friends. With Yeats too she remained close, before and after a brief affair in 1903. Farr was not of course in any way a rival to Yeats' devotion to Maud Gonne, but she was of great importance to him. He wrote to her in 1906: 'You cannot think what a pleasure it is to be fond of somebody to whom I can talk – as a rule any sort of affection annihilates conversation, strikes one with a silence like that of Adam before he had named the beasts. To be . . . one's own self . . . because one has found an equal, this is the best of life.'[102] Yeats said of her to his wife, whom he married in the year of Farr's death, 'She was the only person to whom I could tell *everything*'.[103] Shaw had said, in a rather similar vein, that with Farr he had discovered the 'full intellectual and emotional companionship of love'.[104] She was clearly a remarkable woman. Yet Shaw's letters to her are often full of incandescent outrage at her refusal to follow his bidding as an actress. 'Miserable wretch!' he would address her, 'You want someone with a whip to keep you up to the collar . . . Murray asks whether you have not a mother with a large stick to keep you awake' – not, one would think, the best way to gain co-operation from Florence Farr.[105] So much for full companionship. Yeats was also to say that he 'formed with her an enduring friendship that was an enduring exasperation', and later told Sturge Moore that she had been a 'china egg' that he 'had been sitting on for years'.[106] One wonders what he had hoped she would hatch into.

Farr was also a writer, and it was presumably in that capacity she had been asked along. Hulme obviously took her presence seriously, because he wrote to Flint delaying the second meeting of the group until she could make it and telling him reassuringly that Farr had much admired a poem of his. The poem in question was 'The Mask of Gold', not yet published, as far as I can ascertain, so it suggests that Hulme and Flint were already swapping manuscripts. Farr would have known of Flint even if they hadn't met, for she too had been a regular contributor to the *New Age*, having recently written a series of articles on Ibsen's women. She had had a brief and racily written 'New Woman novel', *The Dancing Faun*, published by Mathews and Lane in 1894, whose heroine, Lady Geraldine, has no truck with conventional mores, apart, that is, from having made what Farr regarded as the common and foolish mistake of falling in love. Lady Geraldine is ready to forgive the cad she adores for having cheated at cards, even for having a wife already, but when he refuses to run away with her because her yearly income is only £800, she shoots him dead – and gets away with it.

Since then Farr had published a book on ancient Egyptian beliefs, which Pound mentioned admiringly to his parents; incidentally, it had infuriated Shaw, who thought her occult interests a waste of time. No doubt Shaw was equally outraged when she wrote two plays with Olivia Shakespear on occult Egyptian themes. And the very month that the Tour Eiffel meetings began, Elkin Mathews published a book by her entitled *The Music of Speech*, a book that Yeats had been urging her to bring out for years, and which she dedicated to Yeats and Dolmetsch. The greater part of *The Music of Speech* consisted of the re-publication of admiring reviews of Farr's performances with the psaltery, followed by a rather briefer section explaining the technique and principles of what she called 'cantilating', and giving examples of musical accompaniments for poetry. Pound's eye must have been caught by a review which said: 'A new Troubadour has come chanting through Provence . . . Florence Farr has re-found the Troubadour's secret and some other, older and more precious secrets as well.'[107] Farr's insistence on the link between music and poetry undoubtedly made a considerable impact on Pound, for it was only after meeting her that he began to research seriously the musical accompaniment to Provençal poetry, and to emphasise the musicality of verse. Flint too, who once said that he had never heard poetry spoken as beautifully as by Farr, was always to stress the role of cadence. Farr's views must, however, have led to arguments with Hulme, who had asserted in his lecture of the previous November that in future poetry would be silently read, and its typographical appearance on the page would come to matter more than its sound. As far as the increasing importance of typography in modernist poetry goes, Hulme was quite right – one thinks of e. e. cummings, or Apollinaire's *Calligrammes*, his poem/drawings that look like their subject-matter – falling rain, carnations or lutes. But those developments were not necessarily at the expense of the musicality, as the imagists would insist. One of the characteristics of modernist poetry was that it paid close attention to the materiality of words, whether as auditory sound or visual shape. Farr and Hulme had as it happened other differences as well to argue over: Hulme believed strongly in women's domestic role, and had in theory no truck with

New Women. Yet he clearly thought highly of the strong-minded and spirited Farr.

Desmond FitzGerald, the second Irish member of the group, and along with Farr responsible for introducing Pound to the group, has always been a shadowy figure in accounts of the imagist movement, though far from shadowy elsewhere. He later became something of an Irish nationalist hero, taking part in the Easter Rising, being imprisoned, and then elected as a Sinn Fein MP while still in jail. When the Irish Free State government came into being, he became Minister for External Affairs, and was eventually, like Yeats, to be a Senator, though, unlike his son Garret, never Taoiseach. FitzGerald was to be something of an icon to Pound – he fulfilled his idea of the poet/man of action – the more so as the two of them moved steadily to the right. FitzGerald never became a vociferous supporter of Fascism like Pound, though Pound was keen to remonstrate with him (fruitlessly) in the area where he felt FitzGerald went too far, his support of Irish censorship. Pound was to say later that he preferred FitzGerald's poetry to that of either Flint or Storer 'for its insides, but they didn't get a bullet-proof cover on it any of 'em', and he remained proud of his association with him, always striving hard to have his presence acknowledged in accounts of the Tour Eiffel group, such as those he gave to René Taupin in 1928, and to Patricia Hutchins in the 1950s.[108] He would have been very disgruntled by FitzGerald's invisibility in more recent accounts. In an unpublished memoir, written in middle age, FitzGerald recalled rather regretfully how as a young man 'my two interests were philosophy and poetry, and so I should have thought that at my present age I should be talking about philosophers I had known, and the writers I had known, and the works they had written'.[109] Historical events changed all that. In 1909 he was involved in the cause of the Irish cultural revival, but for him, as for many of his nationalist compatriots, this cause would be transformed a few years later into a violent and bloody political struggle.

FitzGerald was only twenty-one in 1909, the youngest of the group. Born in England of Irish emigrant parents, he came to identify strongly with the Irish cause. His father Patrick had earlier been a stonemason but became a builder, and the family lived in West Ham. He was the youngest of six children, though there was a considerable gap between the first two and the last four, his mother having left his father at one stage and returned to Ireland for almost six years. He had been christened Thomas Joseph, but adopted the name of Desmond. As his son Garret explains, 'Desmond, from the Irish for "South Munster", was one of the two earldoms that the FitzGeralds had held in Ireland in the Middle Ages', and the young FitzGerald clearly felt it was more romantic and more celebratory of his Irish ancestry than the workaday Thomas.[110] His mother continued to call him Tommy, so he could not repudiate it altogether, and during the Tour Eiffel days he was always known as T.D. FitzGerald. Desmond had loved poetry since he was very young. His son reports a family story 'presumably exaggerated, at least in relation to his age! – that when he was seven he walked from his home in West Ham six or seven miles into the West End in the hope of seeing W.B. Yeats going into the Café Royal'.[111] When he left school, one of his brothers, William, who was fifteen years older than Desmond and a successful magazine editor, offered to fund him through university, but he turned the offer down and became a civil service clerk, an unhappy choice. How long he was in the civil service is not clear: by the time he was married in the summer of 1911, he was, according to his marriage certificate, a 'commercial clerk', though just about to escape to a freer existence abroad. Why he refused to go to university is unknown. It certainly was not lack of ability. Desmond became a fine linguist, knowing several languages, if not quite so many as the prodigious Flint – though FitzGerald was delighted, in 1914, to be able to point out to Flint that he knew and could speak one language of which Flint was entirely ignorant: Irish.[112]

What family history does relate is that as a young man Desmond was determined to be a poet; perhaps he turned down university because his brother was offering to fund him through an uncongenially practical degree. His mother and some at least of his siblings appear to have taken his ambitions seriously, for one of his nieces records – rather disapprovingly – visiting the family home, then in Upton Avenue, Forest Gate, and seeing Desmond with his long artistic curls languidly lying on the settee, his mother and a brother and sister waiting on his every need.[113] No wonder he found the life of a civil service clerk dismaying. Where he met Flint, another would-be poet imprisoned in the role of civil service clerk, is not known. As the only other friend of his own age of whom there is any record before 1909 was a left-wing journalist, Langton Everard, also a friend of Flint's, it seems most likely that FitzGerald had socialist as well as poetic sympathies himself at that stage and that they met at a gathering akin to the Fabian Art Group, or some sort of left-wing literary group. (I have to say that when I suggested this to his son he was deeply sceptical, because of his father's later right-wing political views, but there are many examples of such a switch, and certainly a letter from Everard to him is on the writing paper of the *Labour Leader*.) FitzGerald certainly admired William Morris' literary works, but he may have had only a vague interest in his politics; yet the left was where a bohemian, as he thought of himself, would head for congenial culture in Edwardian London. In 1911, Hulme was still lamenting 'the landslides amongst the intellectuals to the Socialist side'.[114]

Desmond's interest in Gaelic culture had begun early. He had been taken to Ireland by his father; though probably only once or twice, but he was deeply attached to it. When he left school, he began to write for publications devoted to encouraging the Irish Literary Revival, as early as 1907 publishing a short play in the magazine, the *Shanachie* ('The Storyteller').[115] In 1919 he was eventually to have a play put on at the Abbey Theatre in Dublin, but it is hard to imagine that the earlier effort, which was entitled *The Passing*, would have tempted a director. It is set in Ireland, and the Irish language – that is, the Hiberno-English – is quite melodiously done: shades of Synge perhaps, whose work appeared regularly in the *Shanachie*. But *The Passing* is deeply gloomy. There are only four characters, two of whom are ghosts of the just departed; the other two – an old woman and a widow – are dead by the end of the play. Perhaps the story symbolised for FitzGerald the feared death of Irish culture. Looking back at his youth, FitzGerald wrote: 'When my generation woke to consciousness we found that our country did not exist as a nation . . . Some at least of us, felt wounded and bruised by the condition we inherited.'[116] The play comes, perhaps, from the pain of that wound. The Irish had been one of the groups most despised by the English in the nineteenth century; as the flood of Irish emigration took place into England's industrial cities at the time of the famine, the Irish became characterised as 'white negroes' or subhuman apes: the 'Irish Yahoo' was in some quarters the obvious candidate for the Missing Link.[117] Deanglicising Ireland included a refusal to accept the English definition of Irishness, fighting back against such racist valuations as well as challenging English aesthetic and cultural norms. The Irish Literary Revival gave the younger generation at the turn of the century – people like FitzGerald, Campbell and Colum – a much more positive sense of their inheritance; it aimed to bring Irish culture and the nation back to life. By 1908, FitzGerald was taking part in that endeavour, studying Gaelic at a class run by the Central Gaelic League.

The year 1908 was also the year that FitzGerald's father died, aged about seventy; his loss may have intensified young Desmond's desire to know more of his roots. His sister described their father as 'very Irish, but quiet' whilst their mother, on the other hand, was 'not very Irish'; his mother was reported by the family to have had nineteen very happy years after her husband's death, which suggests her married life had not been particularly felicitous.[118] There was a family rumour that the father drank – which by some certainly might have been considered 'very Irish', but often not 'quiet' – but whatever criticisms his family had of Patrick FitzGerald, his death, it appears, hit his youngest son hard. His father died on 1 August and on the blank half-page at the end of a letter sent to him by Everard on 11 August Desmond wrote some intriguing fragmentary sentences. They are in the third person, and read like the first attempt at a story, for FitzGerald would also try his hand at fiction, but the emotions the passage attempts to deal with are, one suspects, in many ways his own. 'It was the most bitter hour of his life,' he begins, and then goes on: 'How he had longed for success & before success came his father died his father whom he had loved and wronged . . . All the time he had been living with Phoebe [his religious faith] had added gall to his every joy and now it whispered to him that he tasted the sorrow of sin. Ah what an epiphany of despair to know that he was weary of her year in and year out, he must go on living with her for he knew he had not strength enough to send her . . .'[119] The fragment ends there. Though by his thirties FitzGerald was a deeply devout Catholic, the faith in which he had been reared, there is little indication that he was much concerned with religious practice in the Tour Eiffel days; nevertheless, this passage suggests how strong the underlying pull of his belief was, as if his father's death had precipitated a wave of guilty horror at his apostasy, or at any rate slackness, followed by a short-lived – for now – return of religious fervour. Desmond lived at home until he married in 1911 – he certainly had no literal live-in lover named Phoebe – but he may well have felt he was sowing his wild oats in some form or other. The few poems that date from his Upton Avenue days are preoccupied for the most part with very Catholic sexual guilt and with the need for renunciation of the beloved in favour of heavenly reward, and though conventional in form are quite Donne-like in the complexity of their imagery, an indication perhaps of his philosophical bent. Whether FitzGerald practised the renunciation his early poems advocate is another matter. His letters from 1910 and 1911, written to his future wife, Mabel McConnell, suggest that he was a great deal more occupied with her and social life generally than with either religious observance or self-denial. Yet what is also striking in the fragment on his father's death is his ambition, which at this stage was firmly set on literary fame; had his father lived, he would have seen his son achieve success, but not in that way.

Although FitzGerald and Flint both worked as civil service clerks, FitzGerald was apparently the better off of the two, as in a letter he refers to his pleasure in finding someone who may be able to be of use to the impecunious Flint.[120] FitzGerald came, of course, from a more comfortable if not actually affluent background, and it may well have been that one or other of his older brothers gave him some sort of an allowance, because in another letter he talks of a row with a brother which will leave him financially poorer, though spiritually healthier – not that there appears to have been any great change in his circumstances, so presumably reconciliation took place quite quickly. Pound suggests in a parody he wrote of Burns' 'A man's a man for a' that' that both Hulme and FitzGerald were considerably better off than himself. He compares his own penniless position with their apparent comfort:

> Is there for feckless poverty
> That grins at ye for a' that!
> A hired slave to none am I,
> But underfed for a' that . . .
> The tails I shun and a' that,
> My name but mocks the guinea stamp
> And Pound's dead broke for a' that . . .[121]

This was probably written in 1910, though not published until the first imagist anthology came out, where it was entitled 'To Hulme (T.E.) and FitzGerald', with a note explaining that it was 'written for the cénacle of 1909'. But Pound's justification of what he describes here as his 'time to loaf and will to write' sounds as if the real spur for this poem may well have been one of his recurrent fits of guilt at his own lack of a steady job, rather than his friends' affluence. Hulme was certainly no more a 'hired slave' than Pound was, and neither Hulme nor FitzGerald would have felt that any subsidies they had from relatives promoted them into the category of what another verse describes as 'the man of independent means'.

According to Ronald Schuchard, FitzGerald was assistant secretary to the Irish Texts Society at this period, an organisation that undertook the publication of Gaelic texts and was closely linked to the Irish Literary Society. Like Campbell's position, this would have been purely honorary.

FitzGerald's Gaelic interests were, one would guess, cultural rather than strongly political at this stage. When he began courting his future wife Mabel in 1910 – a determined nationalist in reaction against her Ulster Unionist background – it is clear from his letters that she thinks he spends far too much time in literary circles with those who do not, as he puts it, 'shout' for the cause. When Pound spoke of FitzGerald to his father, he described him as 'journalising and poetizing somewhat'. If one could discover where he 'journalised', one might have a more precise understanding of his attitudes at that stage; given his friendship with Flint and with Everard, who had left London in 1908 to work on the Manchester-based *Labour Leader*, it might have been in the radical press, possibly on the question of Irish Home Rule. (Incidentally, 'English journalist' was the cover that FitzGerald – with his English accent – was to use with some success when evading capture by the British Army in Ireland a few years later.)

FitzGerald's poetry is not much easier to locate than his journalism, one reason why he has figured as no more than a name in most accounts of the Tour Eiffel. Though their imagery can be striking, the poems surviving from his days at Upton Avenue do not attempt *vers libre*; FitzGerald appears to have had a more cautious approach to experimentation than someone like Campbell. Even in 1914, when he was living in Ireland, he was to write to Flint, having read some of his imagist poetry in the *Egoist*: 'I liked your poems . . . Mind you, I don't commit myself to acknowledging that as the highest poetical form. I don't even say that it isn't prose. But what I liked was that you had something to say and said it gracefully and straightforwardly. The matter of where one line ends and another begins did not bother me. You arranged your lines in a way consonant with the rhythm of the words which made the reading very pleasant.'[122] Yet the early discussions perhaps took root, and bore fruit in his later poems, though none were, as far as I can find, published before 1917.

Even though Hulme spent so much time at the Irish Literary Society, given his opposition to Home Rule for Ireland, he would have been no more in tune politically with FitzGerald and Campbell than he was with Farr. Yet two other Irishmen appear to have come along intermittently, Campbell's friend, Padraic Colum, and Dermot Fryer, with whom Hulme had become friendly at Cambridge, but whose writing, as far as I have found, never featured in the magazines in which the later imagists published, although he eventually published a volume of short stories. Of the '4 or 5 versers' mentioned by Hulme, the only other one that can be identified is the stockbroker Tancred; according to J.B. Harmer he was somewhat older than the others, apart from Florence Farr, probably in his mid-thirties, and a great admirer of Hulme. Tancred had also been a member of the Poets' Club, and had brought out a small book of poems in 1907, and another in 1908 under the aegis of the club. (Flint reviewed the latter unenthusiastically in the *New Age*.) Tancred's pre-Tour Eiffel poetry is unusual for the period, but certainly not because he is experimenting with free verse. He somewhat defiantly wrote poetry in imitation of Herrick and his contemporaries, whom he described as 'the conspicuous poets who have jewelled the auspices of the House of Stuart'.[123] Herrick was, incidentally, a poet whom Campbell also admired, but was not generally in high esteem at the time. Yet if one looks a few years on to Eliot's celebration of Herrick's contemporaries, one might think of Tancred as being slightly ahead of the game. One poem in the 1907 collection is written to Selwyn Image (the poet, designer and stained-glass maker whom Pound had met earlier in 1909), rebuking him for not having returned some of Tancred's poems, and is more ironic pastiche than imitation ('Doubtless, my Selwyn, they are used/As shaving papers, or diffused/As pipe-lights, or they tautly curl/The neat fringe of your servant girl').[124]

Like Flint, Tancred had become interested in Far Eastern poetry before he joined the Tour Eiffel group; Robert Ferguson points out that in the first Poets' Club collection, the title of his poem, 'On finding Selwyn Image not at home when calling upon him at lunch' (Image was obviously an important person in his life), is a reference to a poem by Li Po, whom Pound would later translate, 'On visiting a Taoist master in Tai-T'ien and not finding him at home'. According to Alun Jones, Tancred was a descendant of the bestselling nineteenth-century poet, Felicia Hemans, whose poem 'Casabianca' – 'The boy stood on the burning deck' – Flint recalled with such distaste in his unfinished novel. The British Library copy of Tancred's poems has a letter attached to one of the opening pages, explaining that the poems are 'published to endow a cot in the memory of Felicia Hemans'; one hopes they sold well enough to do so. Neither Pound nor Flint ever mentions Tancred's connection with Hemans, so perhaps Tancred felt in these circles it was best not to acknowledge such ancestry. Harmer points out that Hulme took Tancred's critical judgements quite seriously, so he was apparently not regarded as a negligible member of the group at the time. Pound was rather irritated by him, as he tended to be by other people's disciples, though he forgave Tancred when he praised his own poems.

Tancred published very little, so how his poetry developed after he joined the group is hard to discover. After the war, he developed a mental illness, and died in an institution. Flint described him as 'a poet too little known, perhaps because his production is precious and small, [who] used to spend hours each day in the search for the right phrase'.[125] One wonders how his stocks and shares fared as he searched.

VI

WHAT happened at those Tour Eiffel meetings? There were certainly no formal after-dinner speeches in the manner of the Poets' Club. In fact, Flint never mentions whether they actually ate or not, though Pound says they did, and many years later would recall them as 'Hulme's dinners', so they presumably did.[126] Even the kindly Stulich would surely have taken it ill if they had not at least had drinks. They certainly couldn't afford a private room – Flint recounts how a waiter resorted to putting a screen round them on one occasion, when Pound was bellowing a poem at full force. The rest of the clientèle must have wondered what was going on. The Tour Eiffel gatherings appear to have operated much more as contemporary poetry workshops do; the members read each other their poems, praised, objected, criticised and dissected them, talked over their ideas about poetry, argued and encouraged each other to experiment with different forms. Although Pound later described the Tour Eiffel poets as a 'school', by analogy with the avant-garde coteries in Paris, that was a misnomer, a rhetorical gesture for his own ends. There was no shared programme, though there were shared questions, the most central of which was what form modern poetry should take. In Flint's somewhat self-mocking 'History of Imagism' written in 1915, he gives an indication of their discussions:

I think that what brought the real nucleus of this [Tour Eiffel] group together was a dissatisfaction with English poetry as it was then (and still is, alas!) being written. We proposed at various times to replace it by pure *vers libre*; by the Japanese *tanka* and *haikai*; we all wrote dozens of the latter as an amusement; by poems in a sacred Hebrew form, of which 'The House that Jack Built' is a perfect model; Joseph Campbell produced two good specimens of this, one of which, 'The Dark,' is printed in

'The Mountainy Singer'; by rhymeless poems like Hulme's 'Autumn' and so on. In all this Hulme was ringleader.[127]

In Flint's list of poetic forms with which the Tour Eiffel poets experimented, he characteristically first mentions *vers libre* and Japanese poetry. For Flint they remained the two essential models for change. As he had stressed in his *New Age* reviews, he was convinced that they were akin, both evocative, imagistic, impressionistic, visionary. Arthur Symons had said of symbolist poetry – in his book, *The Symbolist Movement*, that was to influence Eliot so much – that it was an attempt

to evade the bondage of rhetoric, the old bondage of exteriority. Description is banished that beautiful things may be evoked, magically; the regular beat of verse is broken in order that words may fly, upon subtler wings.[128]

This was Flint's view of both French *vers libre* and of the Japanese haiku. In a review Flint had described Storer's proto-imagist poetry as 'aiming at a form of expression, like the Japanese; in which an image is a resonant heart of an exquisite moment'; this was the form in which imagist poetry would first emerge, as the brief, intense epiphany.[129]

Although he modestly does not make the claim, Flint himself, rather than the 'ringleader' Hulme, was probably the one who introduced the tanka and haiku to the group.[130] As he says, the haiku was quickly taken up by the others, including Hulme, though not yet by Pound. By 1909, when the Tour Eiffel poets met, Japanese art had already had a profound impact on European, especially French, painting. Since it first became known after the opening up of Japan in the 1850s, painters such as Manet, Degas, Monet, Mary Cassatt, Van Gogh, Gauguin, Seurat, Toulouse-Lautrec, Bonnard and many others had been deeply influenced by its minimalism, its simplicity and its use of line and block. Impressionism as a movement owed much to the discovery of Japanese art, and Japanese influence played no small part in bringing about the late nineteenth-century / early twentieth-century move away from representational towards more abstract art. In England and America, the arts and craft movement had spread the fashion for Far Eastern design in furniture and ceramics, but while *chinoiserie* had been in vogue since Horace Walpole and Strawberry Hill, from the 1860s onwards the new interest was in Japan. (Gilbert and Sullivan's *Mikado* [1885] was among other things a satire on the public fascination with all things Japanese.)

Significantly for later interest in England, Whistler's work was profoundly influenced by Japanese art, as was the whole development of art nouveau. At the end of the work Pound admired so much, the 'Ten O'Clock Lecture' (also 1885), Whistler names as the two supreme touchstones of beauty, 'the marbles of the Parthenon' and a fan painted by Hokusai. For many in the mid-1880s, such a coupling was still an outrage; Far Eastern painting might be interestingly exotic, but not comparable to the Graeco-European tradition: it could be a source of delightful knick-knacks, but not High Art. Even Swinburne, regarded as so radical and deviant by the respectable, was shocked by what he regarded as this blasphemous promotion of non-European art to a level of equality with the European, and wrote an outraged response in the *Fortnightly Review*, deploring Whistler's suggestion that 'the highest expression of his art is to be realized in the reproduction of the grin and glare, the smirk and leer, of Japanese womanhood'.[131] The two pieces were sometimes published together, as if Swinburne, for once, could be antidote rather than poison. As Swinburne's piece hints, to many Japan meant decadence and immorality, its courtesans all the more shocking because highly cultured. The influence of Japanese art on the dubious aesthetic movement, of course, told its own tale. It was Arthur Symons, the pointer in so many ways to the future development of modernism, who in *Dramatis Personae* quoted approvingly Goncourt's commendation of the 'search after *reality* in literature' and the 'triumph of *japonisme*' as two of the 'great literary and artistic movements' of the later nineteenth century.[132]

Writers took longer to see a potential model in the Japanese forms than the visual artists, though one can argue, as Earl Miner does, that some were influenced at second hand through the Impressionists; there is a clear link, for example, between the version of Impressionism Ford Madox Ford absorbed from Maupassant – the selection of the telling detail, the hint, not the detailed account – and Japanese art forms. Until the late nineteenth century, little Japanese, or for that matter Chinese, poetry had been translated into English, at any rate outside the academy. Poets in Britain and America had continued to look to the European past for their models.[133] Yet that was now changing. Herbert Allen Giles, a British diplomat based in China for many years, later Professor of Chinese at Cambridge, brought out a two-volume *Gems of Chinese Literature* in 1884 and *A History of Chinese Literature* in eight volumes in 1901, a book Pound was later to read to great effect. In 1880, Basil Hall Chamberlain, an Englishman living in Japan, who rather remarkably became Professor of Japanese and Philology at the Imperial University of Tokyo, published a book of English translations aimed at the general reader, entitled *The Classical Poetry of the Japanese*. His translations still used conventionally rhymed stanzas of the kind denounced by Flint, always, for example, translating a tanka, the 31-syllable poem, as a four-line stanza, such as this one, entitled simply 'Spring':

> Spring, spring, has come, while yet the landscape bears
> Its fleecy burden of unmelted snow!
> Now may the zephyr gently 'gin to blow,
> To melt the nightingale's sweet frozen tears.[134]

Surprisingly for us today, Chamberlain never mentions the existence of haiku in this work; chronologically the haiku emerged later than the poetry he includes here, but considering that thirty years later Japanese poetry and the haiku would have become synonymous in Europe, the absence of a reference is striking. In 1899 W. G. Aston published the first history of Japanese literature, which has a brief mention of the haiku form, and gives translations which interestingly are not forced into rhyme, though still Victorian in diction.

When Chamberlain reissued his collection with the title *Japanese Poetry* in 1911, he included an essay on the haiku, entitled 'Bashō [*sic*] and the Japanese Poetical Epigram', which he had originally published in a scholarly journal in 1902, and in addition a new introduction, strikingly different from the previous one. In 1880, Chamberlain had been deeply patronising about Japanese poetry. The Japanese, he said, were imitators rather than creators; their poetic metre, which depended solely on the counting of syllables, without 'rhyme, tone, accent, quantity, nor alliteration', was 'primitive'; the chief characteristic of their poetry was its 'prettiness'; and 'there are no soundings of the depth of the human heart'.[135] The one quality he ascribes to them that might have caught the aesthetes' attention is that 'the Japanese muse . . . does not consider it her mission to *teach* at all', precisely the point about art that Whistler was making in his lecture. 'What we find,' Chamberlain wrote, 'is the expression, in natural language, of the simple feelings common to all mankind, – love, regret, loyalty, attachment to the old traditions, and in the place of religion and of moralising, nothing but that hopeless sense of the transitoriness of life, which precedes, as it survives, all culture and all philosophy.' The 1911 introduction contains a much more detailed account of the development of Japanese poetry;

Chamberlain evidently by then knew a great deal more about it. Comments on its prettiness or primitive state have entirely vanished. In a preface before the introduction, he explains that while he has republished the original translations at the 'urgent request of friends', they 'no longer satisf[y] him, because he allowed himself too much freedom'. He has now 'gone over into the camp of the literalists', as he shows in the much sparer translations included in his essay on the haiku. There he emphasises the qualities which would make this poetry so important for modernist poetry – its fragmentary, elliptical nature, its intense condensation of meaning. He describes it in terms of painting: 'It is the tiniest of vignettes, a sketch in barest outline, the suggestion, not the description, of a scene or a circumstance. It is a little dab of colour thrown upon a canvas one inch square, where the spectator is left to guess at the picture as best he may.' He goes on to comment that 'the spirit of the seventeenth century Japanese poet is identical with that which informs the work of the Western water-colourist of to-day. It is intensely modern, or at least imbued to the full with that love and knowledge of nature that we are accustomed to consider characteristic of modern times'.[136]

This was very much Flint's view, though the writer whose accounts of the Far East captured the widest audience in the 1890s and early years of the twentieth century, including several of the future imagists, was the Greek-Irish-American Lafcadio Hearn, who published several books on Japan, many of them with titles, as Earl Miner notes, that suggest a romantic vision of an exotically mysterious land: *Glimpses of Unfamiliar Japan*, *Gleanings in Buddha-Fields*, *Exotics and Retrospectives*, *In Ghostly Japan*, *Shadowings*. Hearn was one of the many intellectuals increasingly pessimistic about Western modernity, and he had been entranced by Japan. His books created a picture of a Japan that was wise, calm, beauty-loving and mysterious, a 'fictive nation' that became Japan for a generation in the West, though Hearn himself, having settled there, soon began to despair of the Japanese desire to modernise.[137] Although Hearn failed to learn Japanese, his books occasionally included translations by others, but the only volume of Japanese poetry in translation published in his name did not appear until after his death, in 1915, when the vogue for the haiku was already flourishing. All the same, his evocative descriptions of the role of poetry in Japanese life and his aestheticising vision of Japanese culture helped to raise the interest of poets in forms such as the haiku, as significant in the evolution of modernist poetry as the discovery of Japanese art had been earlier for Impressionist and post-Impressionist artists.[138]

By 1909 the leading modernist painters had moved on to new areas. Since about 1890, inspiration began to be sought in so-called 'primitive art' – whether of the past or from exotic cultures, or peasant or even child art – anything that did not employ the careful mimesis of the Western tradition, anything that could put artists in touch with a spontaneity and freshness they felt was lost in modern civilisation. It was to these areas that artists such as Picasso, Vlaminck and Matisse were now turning, having come to feel, as the French artist and critic Maurice Denis put it, that Japanese art was still too sophisticated and self-conscious. As the art historian Colin Rhodes points out, these artists argued of their new eclectic range of influences that 'the strand that . . . drew these disparate elements together was the search for clarity and simplicity', and the appeal of the direct and spare haiku form for early modernists like Flint had much in common with this; it was also similar to the attraction that Gaelic forms had for a poet like Campbell.[139] For their generation, the modern, so-called civilised world of convention was a world of surfaces, obscuring the depths below; this apparently simple, pure, direct poetry gave, they felt, access to a more authentic kind of experience.

Hulme must quickly have realised that the haiku could be interpreted to fit in perfectly with his Bergsonian conception of art as the intuitive dive into the flux, as Paul-Louis Couchoud, the French doctor whose articles were Flint's source of information, had already realised. If Flint had not recognised Couchoud's Bergsonian language when he first read him, after meeting Hulme he undoubtedly would. In Couchoud's account, Japanese poetry's supreme gift is that it offers an image which captures an instantaneous response before its freshness is destroyed by ratiocination; its brevity and directness make it possible to evade the loss of authenticity suffered once syntax interposes its conventions:

Du poème japonais surtout le discursif, l'explicatif sont extirpés. La bizarre fleur se détache unique sur la neige. Le bouquet est interdit. La poème prend à sa source la sensation lyrique jaillissante, instantanée, avant que le mouvement de la pensée ou de la passion l'ait orientée et utilisée . . . Les mots sont l'obstacle. La chaîne des mots introduit un ordre élémentaire qui est déjà un artifice.

('Above all, Japanese poetry avoids wordiness and explanation. A single flower lies by itself on the snow. Bouquets are forbidden. The poem springs from an instantaneous lyric impulse, that wells up before thinking or passion have directed or made use of it . . . Words are the obstacle. The chain of words introduces an elementary order that is already artifical.')[140]

Couchoud here follows Bergson in his contrast, so important to Hulme, between the *immédiatement donnée* of direct intuition and the deadening language of intellectualised knowledge. The brief, momentary haiku, he suggests, gives direct access to experiences which words by their very nature obscure. Its sudden juxtaposition of two sparsely presented, very different images that fuse to give a new perception precisely illustrates the Bergsonian poetic theory that Hulme had expounded to the Poets' Club, the philosophy which lay behind his theory of 'the image', or rather of 'images'. Hulme had the theory; Flint had found the form. The haiku's qualities of simplicity, brevity, fusion and instantaneous impact were all to be central to later imagism. In addition, the haiku's use of juxtaposition, also apparent in the fragmented forms of modernist art and soon particularly in the technique of collage, was to be perhaps the most important innovation in modernist verbal and visual art. Though in one sense these poets turned to the haiku to find an alternative to what they saw as the tired, stale, deadening present, they were also seeing in it a poetry appropriate to the modern world: juxtaposition and collage were to be the art forms of the modern metropolis, a world of heterogeneity, rupture and shock.

VII

FLINT would later comment that the Tour Eiffel meetings had been started for 'solace and amusement' by Hulme, and the participants appear to have found them lively entertainment; even Pound would eventually admit that they had been 'fun'.[141] But they were also serious discussions about poetic form. One intriguing feature of Flint's list of forms with which the Tour Eiffel poets experimented is the distinction he makes between 'pure *vers libre*' and Hulme's 'rhymeless poems'. As Flint knew well, French *vers libre* does not mean 'free verse'. *Un vers* is a line, not a verse, and *vers libre* meant in the first instance getting away from fixed line length, as Storer had advocated for the English pentameter. *Vers libre* still had form: not a prescribed one, but the form that the poet felt best suited to the poem. Much French *vers libre* continued to use some rhyme, generally irregularly, with mid-line rhymes, half-rhymes, assonance, etc., and what Flint later translated as 'rhythmic constants', echoing or repeating cadences. (Much of T.S. Eliot's poetry follows this form.) Of the five poems that are preserved in 'The Complete Poetical Works of T.E. Hulme', only 'Autumn' is completely rhymeless. The other four, although they have no fixed form, use irregular rhyme and rhythmic cadences; for example, 'The Embankment', which Hulme subtitled: 'The fantasia of a fallen gentleman on a cold, bitter night':

> Once, in finesse of fiddles found I ecstasy,
> In a flash of gold heels on the hard pavement.
> Now see I
> That warmth's the very stuff of poesy.
> Oh, God, make small

> The old star-eaten blanket of the sky,
> That I may fold it round me and in comfort lie.[142]

Lines 1 and 4 rhyme, lines 3, 6 and 7 rhyme, and 'me' in line 7 gives an internal rhyme back to lines 1 and 4; the poem uses plentiful alliteration (all those 'f's, for example). Yet for all the variable length of its lines, the poem is as close to the iambic pentameter as many passages of late Shakespeare. Incidentally, yet again, like 'Autumn', it is a poem that strives to domesticate and soften a cold and indifferent universe, the final couplet enwrapping the 'I' of the poem in the homely, star-eaten blanket. Of the eight poems published in the most recent edition of Hulme's writing, all but one mention the sky; Hulme was still reworking the Canadian sky's vast emptiness. Yet 'The Embankment' perhaps also marks the move from the nineties decadence of the flashy beginning to the plain, unadorned writing Hulme thought appropriate to modern poetry at the end.

In the rather wider selection of Hulme's poems that Alun Jones published, the majority of those previously unpublished were rhymeless, and whilst they are less successful on the whole, clearly Hulme's boldness in completely abandoning rhyme impressed the Tour Eiffel group. Free verse as it has developed in English has been most typically rhymeless, rather than 'pure *vers libre*'. Campbell included some rhymeless poems in *The Mountainy Singer*. Take the following poem, for example, one of a number drawn from his 'tramps' in the Ulster countryside.

> Night, and I travelling
> An open door by the wayside,
> Throwing out a shaft of warm yellow light.
> A whiff of peat-smoke;
> A gleam of delf on the dresser within;
> A woman's voice crooning, as if to a child.
> I pass on into the darkness.[143]

This poem – by design or not – illustrates Hulme's Bergsonian poetic technique of 'piling up of distinct images in different lines', evoking in their combination a sudden moment of light, warmth and humanity surrounded by the darkness of the first and last lines. His poem, 'The Dark', in the 'sacred Hebrew form' that Flint mentioned in his 'History of Imagism', is a powerful poem in its own right, and although that kind of long cumulative repetition did not feature in later imagist poetry, simpler forms of such biblical or liturgical repetition of words and cadences (such as the pattern, 'The Lord bless you, the Lord be with you, the Lord keep you and shield you') certainly do, particularly in H.D.'s work ('Whirl up, sea –/whirl up your pointed pines,/splash your great pines'). But Campbell also experimented with very brief imagistic poems:

> Darkness.
> I stop to watch a star shine in a boghole –
> A star no longer, but a silver ribbon of light.
> I look at it, and pass on.[144]

As always, Campbell's subject-matter was Ireland, but he presented it in both experimental and traditional forms. Although neither of these brief, rhymeless poems is a haiku as such, one could hazard the guess that their simplicity and brevity shows the Japanese influence, fused perhaps with that of Gaelic poetry. Campbell's sense of the Irish poetic tradition had much in common with the view of the Japanese that Flint would have gained from Couchoud; both believed they had uncovered the art of an innately poetic people, immediate and direct, capturing the ever-mobile fluidity of the natural world.

Flint too still wavered between traditional and freer forms. He wrote in spring 1909, in the preface to his book of poems, *In the Net of the Stars*, that 'I have, as the mood dictated, filled a form or created one. I have used assonance for the charm of it, and not rhymed when there was no need to. In all, I have followed my ear and my heart, which may be false. I hope not.'[145] Even if in practice few of his poems of this time are as innovative as Campbell's or Hulme's, one can see the direction in which he would develop, and indeed most of the poems in that collection must have predated the Tour Eiffel meetings. But form was not all they discussed. Hulme insisted, Flint says, on 'accurate presentation and no verbiage' and 'there was also a lot of talk and practice among us . . . of what we called the Image'.[146] Not, of course, that they called themselves imagists. Pound was not to invent the word for another three years, but it would be out of these debates that imagism would emerge. If they had felt themselves unified enough – which they did not – to give themselves a name it would be more likely at that stage to have been impressionist, since Storer, like Hulme, had insisted that was what modern poetry should be: 'To argue for or against impressionism at this time of the day would be as foolish as to write a treatise proving the

circulation of the blood,' he had said in his essay in *Mirrors of Illusion*.[147]
In the England of 1909, the year before Roger Fry's first Post-
Impressionist Exhibition, Impressionism still represented all that was
most modern in art.

Pound himself, it is generally agreed, took little part in their discussions. Humphrey Carpenter suggests the trouble was that Pound
was not a good listener, which he was not, but it was also the case that
he was not ready for these ideas. He had no interest as yet in *vers libre*.
As Flint wrote, Pound 'could not be made to believe there was any
French poetry after Ronsard'; his heart was still with his troubadours.[148]
Pound's only response to the modern world was still rejection. Yet even
if these avant-garde poetics meant little to him at the time, Pound liked
to have literary friends; in addition, the Tour Eiffel meetings gave him
a captive and appreciative audience for his poems. Although Pound may
not have been much concerned with their quest for modern poetry,
some of the group at any rate appear to have realised that Pound's poetry
had a distinctive voice, and that he, like them, cared deeply about technical experiment, even though for different reasons. On his first visit
to the Tour Eiffel, Pound read – indeed shouted – his latest Bertrans
de Born poem to the assembled poets, presenting it with some confidence, for it had already been accepted by the prestigious *English Review*.
Entitled 'Sestina: Altaforte', it began: 'Damn it all! All this our South
stinks peace./You whoreson dog, Papiols, come! Let's to music!/I have
no life save when the swords clash.' ('Altaforte' refers to Born's castle,
Altafort, nowadays Hautefort; not, as I imagined for many years, being
an obscure musical term meaning 'high-pitched and loud'.) Whatever
else Hulme thought of it, he must have conceded that here was a poet
who like himself wanted to forge a masculine poetry. Flint was later,
with some justification, to describe this poem as a rant. The waiter at
the Tour Eiffel apparently thought the same, as this was the occasion
when he hastily screened them off from the other guests. Like so many
of Pound's poems, then and later, it is a curious mixture of the colloquial and the archaic, as well as a disturbing mélange of violence and
glamour: 'No cry like the battle's rejoicing/When our elbows and swords
drip the crimson . . . May God damn for ever all who cry "Peace!"'[149] It
feels unpleasantly in tune with the growing militarism of the pre-First
World War political world; perhaps by 1913 Pound – though still proud
of its technique – had become uneasily aware of this, as he was to
comment then that a poem with such a theme could not be an important one. At the time, however, he triumphantly described it to his parents

as 'the most blood-curdling thing the good city has seen since dear Kit Marlowe's day – unadulterated lust for battle & incidentally B de B in a peevish humour – accurate reading would require 54 inch chest.'[150] The Tour Eiffel must have been thankful that Pound's chest was luckily so inadequate, but the group could not have failed to realise that 'Sestina Altaforte' used a form that had very little in common with conventional English rhymed stanzas. While Pound prided himself on his antiquarian mastery of this intricate twelfth-century form, to the other members of the group he was an experimenter like themselves, using unusual models to write new poetry.

Flint does not mention what other poems were read on Pound's first night at the Tour Eiffel, but one can deduce that Campbell either read from his 1907 collection, *The Gilly of Christ*, or lent it to Pound, because Pound was back a week later with his own version of the title poem. If he was not concerned with their theories, he took more interest in the poetry itself. Although Pound and Campbell's subject-matter – medieval Provence and peasant Ireland – might appear very different, their poetry shared common traits. Like Pound's, Campbell's poems were characteristically first person, spoken through a persona, colloquial, taken from an earlier, fresher tradition, often drawing on myth or the past, and, often, as even in Campbell's free verse poems quoted above, about a wanderer, someone on the move. Ireland, like Provence, had a tradition of the wandering minstrel, a figure centrally important to both Pound and Campbell. Both of them frequently produced poems that hover between translation and pastiche, imitation or re-creation. In addition Campbell's approach to poetry was, like Pound's at that stage, much more quasi-mystical than the highly theoretical Hulme. Like Yeats, Campbell was fascinated by the Irish peasants' fusion of Christianity and pre-Christian myth, and it was, after all, less than a year since Pound had, in *A Lume Spento*, compared the Provençal mingling of pagan and Christian beliefs with those recorded in *The Celtic Twilight*. Campbell's *The Gilly of Christ* is another version of this.

The Gilly of Christ poems are based on legends about Christ's appearance in the West of Ireland that Campbell had found in Hyde's translations of the religious songs of Connaught, and the poem after which the collection is named is spoken by one of Christ's disciples, though called in this context, with Christ roaming round the Irish countryside, his 'gilly', from the Gaelic *giolla*, a servant. The poem has a very simple ballad form, and is possibly influenced, at any rate in conception, by Blake's 'Jerusalem' ('And did those feet, in ancient time,/Walk

upon England's mountains green') as well as by the Gaelic folk legend.
It begins:

> I am the gilly of Christ,
> The mate of Mary's Son;
> I run the roads at seeding-time,
> And when the harvest's done . . .
>
> No eye has ever seen me
> But shepherds hear me pass,
> Singing at fall of even
> Along the shadowed grass . . .
>
> All know me only the Stranger,
> Who sits on the Saxons' Height
> He burnt the bacach's little house
> On last St Brigid's night.
>
> He sups off silver dishes,
> And drinks in a golden horn,
> But he will wake a wiser man
> Upon the Judgment morn . . .[151]

This fusion, in a swiftly moving verse form, of folk traditions,
Christian judgement and anti-British feeling (in the reference to 'the
Stranger' who burns the peasant's cottage) is Campbell's reinvention
of Celtic forms as a means of resistance. The next week, Pound
produced his own version of disciplehood, in his case spoken by a
different 'mate of Mary's son' and an attack on contemporary
Christianity rather than on the British in Ireland. Pound's poem was
entitled the 'Ballad of the Goodly Fere', with an introductory note
telling the reader that 'Simon Zealotes speaketh it somewhile after
the Crucifixion', and another note explaining that 'Fere = Mate,
Companion'. The language, as in the 'Sestina', is both vigorously
colloquial and archaised, and if the Christ who emerges is not as
bloodthirsty as Bertrans de Born, he is still a great deal more phallic
than most pious versions of Christ:

> Ha' we lost the goodliest fere o' all
> For the priests and the gallows tree?

Aye lover he was of brawny men,
O' ships and the open sea.

When they came wi' a host to take Our Man
His smile was good to see,
'First let these go!' quo' our Goodly Fere,
'Or I'll see ye damned,' said he . . .

Oh we drunk his 'Hale' in the good red wine
When we last made company,
No capon priest was the Goodly Fere
But a man o' men was he.[152]

And so on for another ten verses. Pound was immensely pleased with
it. He wrote to his father that it was 'probably the strongest thing in
English since "Reading Gaol" and a thing which anyone can under-
stand'.[153] This desire to be comprehensible was something new for
Pound, who had written in 1907 to Viola Baxter full of scorn for Thomas
Mosher's suggestion that he should make his poetry easier for his readers
to comprehend; perhaps Campbell's simplicity had impressed him,
though again it was not something he would always aim for in the future.
'The Ballad of the Goodly Fere' was to be accepted by the *English
Review*, although Ford must have guessed the trouble it would cause.
To Pound's delight, 150 readers cancelled their subscriptions in outrage
at the poem's apparent blasphemy. A sexualised Christ ('no capon priest'),
and possibly (as a 'lover o' brawny men') one of dubious sexual preference, was too much. For Pound, the ballad simply restored what centuries
of hypocrisy had obscured. Four years later Pound was solemnly to
affirm that he had written the poem because *he* had been shocked by
listening to blasphemous talk, but this was surely a coat-trailing exercise
to perplex the easily scandalised.[154] When Pound was next invited to
the Poets' Club, not in fact till December, he asked Campbell – who
obviously knew its origin – to read the poem for him, telling his father
that 'Campbell, "the dark man from the narth" read the "Goodly Fere"
splendidly. I wish I had his voice.'[155]

With those not outraged, this ballad became one of Pound's most
popular poems, and perhaps not only because anyone could understand
it. It caught the mood of the moment. His rejection of the image of the
'pale Galilean' whom Swinburne had condemned because the 'world
had turned grey with [his] breath' appealed deeply to those impatient

with the subservience, or in Nietzsche's term, the 'slave morality', that they felt Christianity and a so-called Christian, in fact hierarchical and unjust, society imposed. Yeats, for example, an ardent Nietzschean, although often ambivalent about Pound's work, greatly admired the poem. Eliot, on the other hand, having praised it in 1917 for its metrical skill, which is considerable, had come, once a Christian, to disapprove of it strongly, and excluded it from his 1928 Faber edition of Pound's *Selected Poems*. Pound, who believed with increasing conviction that Christ like the pagan Greeks had celebrated sexuality rather than condemning it, would say in a poem the next year that he suspected Nietzsche of being 'the one modern Christian'. 'I am sick,' he wrote there, 'of the toothless decay/of God's word as they usually preach it;/I am sick of bad blasphemous verse/that they sell with their carols and hymn tunes.'[156] If anything that he thought 'blasphemous' had contributed to this poem, it would have been what was more conventionally known as pious. When Pound himself refused to let Edward Marsh have it for *Georgian Poetry* in 1912 on the grounds that it illustrated no '*modern* tendency', as far as the theme went he was not entirely correct.[157]

When, some time later, Ford Madox Ford paid Pound £5 for the 'Ballad' and two other poems, Pound promptly spent the money on an outrageously dandified velvet jacket. Concern about decent clothes had been a repeated theme of his letters home. In 1909 clothes were the badge of class; one could skimp on one's lodging or food, but social exclusion threatened those who did not pass muster with their outfits – a situation which on various occasions was to rack both Flint and Lawrence. Robert Louis Stevenson had recounted ruefully, a little earlier, how, when a row with his father left him impoverished for some months and he was forced to don working-class clothes while travelling steerage to the States, he found himself to his mortification suddenly invisible to the better-off young ladies on board. Pound, of course, was never in danger of being invisible. His flaming hair saw to that. And he had no intention of dressing simply to conform. He was bent on continuing the habits of his student days, dressing the part of the aesthetic genius. There was, perhaps, a closer link between his dress style and his choice to remain on the margins of the Tour Eiffel group than might at first appear. Pound continued to model himself partially on Yeats, but even more on Whistler, the towering individualist artist, contemptuous of the common herd, and in a year or two would actually begin to sport a version of Whistler's grey waisted jacket, and invest in a similar ebony cane. The kind of artistic life that was soon to be imported into the English scene from the continent, the avant-garde school or movement rather than the solitary genius, was still beyond his imagination. If he had offered to be Kitty Heyman's impresario in Venice, for now the only artist he was anxious to promote was himself. It would be some time before the potential excitement of the position of a leader of an artistic guerrilla force would tempt him into other paths, and his extraordinary skills – and blind spots – as an impresario of the literary world would change his direction for ever.

PART IV

SUDDENLY SOMEWHAT OF
A SUCCESS

I

On 15 April 1909, the day before *Personae* was published, and a week before he joined the Tour Eiffel group, Pound had written home in what was clearly a fit of uncertainty and depression. He was getting nowhere, he complained. He was stagnating. He needed to go to Italy for sun, a cheaper life and better food. His irritable spirits may have been exacerbated by pre-publication nerves. *Personae* would, after all, be his first full collection to be brought out at the publisher's expense; he could now claim to be a professional, not just an amateur writer; he was getting known in London literary circles. But he was still a young man, not yet twenty-four, on the edge of things; would he be acknowledged as a serious poet? would he be given the kind of praise he craved? Pound was desperate to be acclaimed. Italy would perhaps have been a bolt-hole if failure were his fate.

In the event, a bolt-hole wasn't needed. By the end of the month Pound was back in ebullient form. Success was on its way. During that month he had effortlessly entered the Ford Madox Ford circle; he had been welcomed by the Tour Eiffel group; he had had his first poem accepted by the *English Review*; and, most cheering of all, he had seen the publication of *Personae* to remarkably kind reviews. Acceptance and acclaim appeared assured. On 30 April he was telling his father that the 'London game seems to have too many chances in it to risk missing them by absence'.[1] No less an authority than Ford advised staying in England. Two more books, Pound reported, should be out by autumn.

Pound had yet another reason for his revived spirits. It looked as if he would finally meet Yeats, the lodestar that had originally drawn him to London. During the eight months Pound had been in London, Yeats had scarcely visited the capital, having been in Ireland or France for most of the time, but Pound had told his father in early March that, though Yeats had been delayed, 'Mrs Shakespear has him nailed to meet me when he does come.'[2] In May, Yeats was finally 'nailed'. Olivia took Pound round to Woburn Place to one of Yeats' Monday evenings, which Pound would soon attend regularly during Yeats' time in London. By the end of May Pound was describing his usual week as if its pattern had been established for years: 'Victor Plarr of the old Rhymers Club . . . is in on Sunday supper-&-evenings, Yeats, Monday evenings, a set from the Irish Lit. Soc eats together on Wednesdays – & a sort of new Rhymers gang on Thursdays.'[3] He was not to give any further details of the 'new Rhymers gang', as he significantly entitled his Tour Eiffel poets, until August: they had not on the whole impressive enough connections. When he eventually produced information, under questioning, it was carefully edited. Florence Farr was given star billing, as friend of Yeats and a famous actress; he had, he told his father, been working with her on psaltery settings. But he was more careful in his descriptions of the rest. He forbore to say that Flint and FitzGerald worked as office clerks, only mentioning their writing. Hulme, Pound said, 'writes articles on Philosophy', although Hulme had only just had his very first article on Bergson published in the *New Age*.[4] Pound promised to send a copy of Storer's poems in lieu of other credentials – incidentally an indication that Pound thought more of him then than he would later admit. That Tancred was a stockbroker he did acknowledge, the only one apart from Farr whose occupation he felt he could mention. With Yeats, however, the situation was different. Pound's letters home from the start made the most of his eminent new connection.

Pound, indeed, succeeded in making a remarkably rapid impact on Yeats. A week after the first Monday evening he was delighted to get a note from Yeats inviting him again, along with an Italian poet, Florence Farr and her psaltery. Farr had perhaps put in a good word for Pound, but Yeats was in any case very taken with this 'queer creature', as he was to describe Pound to Lady Gregory.[5] As R.F. Foster suggests, Pound arrived in Yeats' life at a moment when the admiration of an ardent young poet was particularly welcome. The reason Yeats had not turned up in March was that his friend and fellow playwright Synge was dying at the age of only thirty-eight, and his death on 24 March was a bereavement that Yeats felt acutely on several levels. It was a bitter personal blow, but in addition, as Foster puts it, 'since Synge had . . . stood for the freedom of the artistic imagination against the middle class of (largely Catholic) nationalist Ireland, his loss was enormous. It was easy, in retrospect, to see Synge as the victim of Dublin philistinism rather than of

Hodgkin's disease.'[6] For the last few years Yeats had been pouring all his efforts into the theatre, and was beginning to feel it fruitless expense of spirit. The attacks on Synge and himself by the Irish nationalist press, especially those that followed the opening of Synge's *Playboy of the Western World*, disheartened and depressed him. The Theatre of Ireland, to which Padraic Colum and others had transferred their allegiance, was flourishing at the Abbey's expense, and Yeats felt himself increasingly isolated in Dublin. London, where he could enjoy the relaxing friendship of Olivia Shakespear and Florence Farr, was more and more congenial. Other chapters of his youth appeared to be closing. He was seeing Maud Gonne again; it was she who drew him to France, where she was now living. Gonne had admitted to him the disaster that her marriage to John MacBride had been; it is likely, as Florence Farr drily put it, that Yeats's 'long years of fidelity ha[d] been rewarded at last'.[7] But Gonne had also made it clear her Catholicism made a second marriage impossible, and the continuation of an illegal union unacceptable. That relationship offered no future. Arthur Symons, Yeats' closest friend among the Rhymers, had collapsed into psychosis, and his illness brought back to Yeats the deaths of his other Rhymer friends, Lionel Johnson and Ernest Dowson. Though the majority of the ex-Rhymers were in fact still in robust health, to Yeats it felt as if he were the last remnant of that 'Tragic Generation', as he was memorably to name them. As well as these emotional blows, Yeats was growing impatient to have space to work once more on his poetry. His work in the theatre had, he complained, 'dried the sap out of my veins, and rent/Spontaneous joy and natural content/Out of my heart . . . My curse on plays.'[8] To meet with an energetic young poet, whose veins fairly pounded with sap, who thought Yeats the greatest living poet, who, moreover, neither knew nor cared about the politics of Irish nationalism, and who would have been incredulous at the steady criticism Yeats received in Dublin, a young man who had no interest in anything except poetry, nor any wish to broach any other subject – all this was balm and refreshment to the grieving, beleaguered Yeats.

Pound's close association with Yeats was not to develop fully until his next visit to Europe. But he was able to write proudly to Williams: 'I have been praised by the greatest living poet. I am after eight years hammering against impenetrable adamant become suddenly somewhat of a success . . .'[9] Douglas Goldring, who had recently met Pound through Ford, describes as 'one of his greatest triumphs in London . . . the way in which he stormed 18 Woburn Buildings, the Celtic stronghold of W.B. Yeats, took charge of his famous Mondays . . . I shall never forget my surprise, when Ezra took me for the first time . . . at the way in which he dominated the room, distributed Yeats's cigarettes and Chianti, and laid down the law about poetry.' Goldring, however, may be referring to the next year; even 'Ezra's transatlantic *brio*', as Goldring called it, may not have accomplished domination quite immediately.[10]

Yet Pound had indeed become, as he told Williams, 'somewhat of a success'. It was clearly a sweet moment. Yeats was not the only one to praise him. *Personae* was Pound's most well received volume, with the sole exception of *Cathay*, his translations from the Chinese, which he would publish in 1915. There were negative notes, but overall, as the *Bookman* commented in 'New Notes' that July, it 'met with an unusually appreciative reception', accompanying this note with a photograph of Pound in profile and the carefully honed information, doubtless supplied by Pound himself, that he was

a young American of English descent, his forbears having been among those early settlers who went to the New World in the seventeenth century. On his mother's side he is distantly related to Longfellow, whose poetry he does not admire; he is a Fellow of the University of Pennsylvania; has travelled much in Spain; lived for some while in Venice; and is now making his home in England with no particular desire to depart from us, though he has a very much greater liking for the English people than for their climate.

Whether it was entirely true, as the piece also asserts, that 'he had written and burned two novels and three hundred sonnets' is a matter for conjecture, but it gave the right impression: Pound was an excellent spin-doctor long before the term had been invented.[11] He had sent home the first review that appeared – quite an important one, as it happened, by W.L. Courtney, editor of the influential *Fortnightly Review*, which would later print some of Pound's most significant articles – with orders for his father to take it to the *Philadelphia Inquirer* and to his old support, the *Book News Monthly*, for re-publication.[12] His father does not appear to have had any luck with this venture, though the *Book News Monthly* published one of the poems from *Personae*, 'Piccadilly', and in November the American *Literary Digest* – the first of several American papers to boast of Pound's success in England – ran a feature on him under the title of 'An American Poet Discovered in London', quoting liberally from English reviews, including a piece from *Punch* – real fame, Pound claimed – in which he was presented as 'Mr Ezekiel

Ton . . . the most remarkable thing in poetry since Robert Browning . . . by far the newest poet going'.[13]

Pound had told his father at the end of April that the *New Age* was 'howling' for a review copy of *Personae*, which must mean that Flint had offered to review it, Pound having no other contact with the *New Age* at that time, and, indeed, a review by Flint duly appeared.[14] This review was one of the most perceptive, and of considerable interest as confirmation that, notwithstanding Pound's devotion to the Middle Ages, the Tour Eiffel group had welcomed him as a fellow-revolutionary and a fellow-craftsman. 'Mr Pound,' Flint wrote, 'is a poet with a distinct personality. Essentially, he is a rebel against all conventions except sanity; there is something robustly impish and elfish about him. He writes with fresh beauty and vigour . . . Let us once and for all acknowledge what Mr Pound owes to Browning, his mediaeval poets, mystics and thinkers, and, perhaps, a little to Mr Yeats and Thompson; and take his poems as poetry, without references to sources of raw material. I think there is sufficient craft and artistry, originality and imagination in *Personae* to warrant one giving them high praise . . . Mr Pound . . . is working towards a form that other English poets might study.'[15]

Flint was the reviewer to see most clearly that Pound was the forerunner of an innovative movement in poetry, though others agreed that, for all his medieval subject-matter, he was doing something original and new. The first of Edward Thomas' reviews – he wrote several – was entitled 'A New Note in Poetry', and Rupert Brooke, in a review later that year, which acknowledged Pound's 'great talents', actually criticised him for writing *vers libre*, scarcely Pound's intention at this stage.[16] Yet, as Humphrey Carpenter perceptively comments on Pound's opera, *Le Testament de Villon*, which he wrote in 1921, 'He achieved strikingly modern effects chiefly by straining after revivalism'; something similar was happening here.[17] For example, in 'Praise of Ysolt', one of the poems that appeared for the first time in *Personae*, the persona is an unnamed troubadour, worn out by 'the wandering of many roads', desolate because he has lost the woman he loved and for whom he composed his songs. Pound uses a refrain, an envoi and the traditional imagery of a Provençal poem, but his shifting rhythms, irregular line lengths and paucity of rhyme convinced Brooke that this was modern experimentalism:

> In vain have I striven
>
> to teach my heart to bow;

> In vain have I said to him
> 'There be many singers greater than thou.'
>
> But his answer cometh, as winds and as litany,
> As a vague crying upon the night
> That leaveth me no rest, saying ever,
>   'Song, a song.'[18]

Other poems used no rhyme at all, but Pound was well aware that many earlier forms of verse – Latin, Greek and Anglo-Saxon for example – had not; he would not yet accept that he was using anything so newfangled as *vers libre*. One of the few strongly negative reviews – and even it admitted that 'Pound makes a lively din' – appeared anonymously in the *Nation*, protesting indignantly that Pound was trying to change poetry the way such modern composers as Debussy and Strauss were changing music.[19] (Debussy's *Pelléas et Mélisande* had just had a controversial production at Covent Garden, and reports of Strauss' latest scandalous opera, *Elektra*, had reached London, though it had not yet been performed there.) The reviewer spoke truer than he or the Pound of 1909 realised.

More than half of the poems in *Personae* had appeared in *A Lume Spento*; some, like 'In Durance' ('I am homesick after mine own kind'), had been written in America and a few, like 'Marvoil', since he arrived in London. The collection contained some of the best of the poems that Pound was to produce before 1912. Many were, as the collection's title implies, 'persona' poems, the form he had evolved for himself in Crawfordsville, full of life and drama, in one way or another exploring themes of loneliness, rejection, exile and defiance. The speakers in the poems are, as usual, poets and lovers, generally, of course, troubadours, outsiders, ne'er-do-wells, who have failed in worldly matters but not (with rare exceptions) in vigour, vitality or hope. Over the two years or so during which these poems had been written, Pound had known rejection, from fellow-students, from Crawfordsville, from Mary Moore, from H.D., from a series of publishers. Like the personae he created, he refused to give up; perhaps creating these personae enabled him to keep going.

Several reviewers besides Flint recognised the debt Pound owed to Browning for his dramatic monologues; as one poem directly mentioned and another quoted him, it was not a hard task. Another poet mentioned in several of the reviews was Whitman, whose 'dangerous influence' was, according to Rupert Brooke, apparent in Pound's 'many poems in unmetrical sprawling lengths'.[20] Brooke's strong disapproval of Whitman was not echoed by the other reviewers: Whitman was on the whole more admired on the European side of the Atlantic than in his home country, being regarded by the bourgeoisie in the States as a vulgar, sensual poet. Pound had, he says, never really read Whitman before he came to Europe, let alone imitated him. Yet once in England, as soon as Pound introduced himself as an American poet, Whitman would be immediately evoked by his British literary contacts, and he was finally forced to pay attention to his fellow-countryman. He had written a short piece that February, in which he comments that 'From this side of the Atlantic, I am for the first time able to read Whitman', but his response remained deeply ambivalent. Whitman '*is* America', he wrote. 'His crudity is an exceeding great stench, but it *is* America.' Pound, having spent his youth inventing himself as a child of Europe, had needed to come to Europe to discover he was American. He now admits that 'Mentally I am a Walt Whitman who has learnt to wear a collar and a dress shirt (though at times inimical to both).' Whitman's poetry, he complained, was at times painfully bad, but Pound acknowledges that he himself sometimes – when writing of 'certain things' – found himself using similar rhythms. Moreover, the 'vital part of [their] message, taken from the sap and fibre of America, is the same', and he adds with no undue modesty, 'I am immortal even as he is, yet with a lesser vitality as I am the more in love with beauty'.[21] Though Pound would some four years later write a poem making a 'pact' with Whitman, he remains a very different poet from 'his spiritual father'. Wyndham Lewis was to comment shrewdly much later: 'Pound's nearest American analogue in the past is not Whitman . . . or Mark Twain, but a painter, James McNeill Whistler.'[22]

Shortly after *Personae* appeared, Pound briefly moved to Hammersmith, in the hope of finding cheaper accommodation. To his dismay the bus fares, as he told Patricia Hutchins many years later, cancelled out the saving in rent. With his increasingly frequent visits to the Shakespears and the Ford/Hunt circle – shortly to become a ménage when Ford moved as a 'paying guest' into South Lodge, with Violet's near-senile mother as supposed chaperone – Pound decided Kensington was the place to be. It was full of associations with the Pre-Raphaelites, but luckily not anything like as affluent as today. He moved in August, having found a room in a working-class street, 10 Church Walk, by the graveyard behind St Mary Abbots. Pound had no objection to graves, but he found the constant ringing of St Mary's bells

deeply irritating, and complained about them well into his old age. It
was another wedge between himself and organised religion. The house
was owned by a grocer, Sam Langley, whose wife let out the rooms, and
who would cook for Ezra if he were in. The Langleys, Pound said, were
'positively the best that England can produce at ANY level'.[23] Pound
was still there in 1914, when he married and moved to a flat. But the
flat was only just round the corner, and Mrs Langley would still sometimes come and cook.

Praise continued to come ('even from Paris I am felicitated,' he
reported home) but by the autumn he was forced to face the fact that
praise had failed to turn into adequate funds.[24] Mathews had not recovered his money on *Personae*, although he was not reneging on his
promise to bring out a fourth collection for Pound, *Exultations*, whose
organisation was causing Pound headaches. But if Pound was not earning
much, he was not spending much either. He walked to the British
Museum or the Tour Eiffel, and could rely on the hospitality of literary
London for much of his diet. Kathleen Cannell, the wife of the poet
Skipwell Cannell, who would later contribute to the first imagist
anthology, remarked in her memoirs on the penniless writers at Ford's
teas devouring food as if it was their only meal of the day; Pound was
one of those. He was becoming a regular at South Lodge parties, and
even introduced a new form of entertainment to the Ford/Hunt circle.
Opposite South Lodge was a communal garden with tennis courts, and
Pound decided they should be used by Ford and his friends. He sent
home for his tennis racquet, and, as Douglas Goldring put it, 'The
garden was taken over and every afternoon a motley collection of people,
in the oddest costumes, invaded it at Ezra's instigation, and afterwards
repaired to South Lodge – or to 84 Holland Park Avenue, – to discuss
vers libre, the prosody of Arnaut Daniel, and, as Ford records, "the
villainy of contributors to the front page of *The Times Literary
Supplement*" '.[25]

Violet Hunt recalled Pound's 'demon' play, as he sprang round the
court, 'the flaps of his polychrome shirt flying out like the petals of
some flower and his red hair like a flaming pistil in the middle of it'.[26]
Ford was unfailingly mocking of Pound's tennis, describing him as
playing like 'an inebriated kangaroo', but the games gave Ford a welcome
and amusing diversion from the mounting debts at the *English Review*
and from the conflicts of his emotional life.[27] In 1909 he and Pound had
not yet developed their later 'intimate friendship', as Goldring put it,
though that was never to be intimate in the sense that they would share

personal troubles, but then, as later, Pound's 'transatlantic *brio*' could certainly cheer Ford up.[28] In addition, Hunt said, 'Ezra, a dear . . . was very kind to the editor, and would do any sort of job for him or me'.[29] Pound, in fact, in spite of his eccentricities and lack of polished manners, was becoming something of a social as well as a poetic success in London literary circles. It was a far cry from the disapproval and loneliness he had experienced in his university days in the States. No wonder he was reluctant to return home.

WHEN Pound had written home for his tennis racquet, he had also asked for his copy of Dante, because, much to his relief, the London Polytechnic had agreed to employ him again, this time for a series of twenty-one lectures, beginning in October 1909, on 'The Development of Literature in Southern Europe'. In addition, the kindly Rhys persuaded Dent that they should publish the lectures as a book, which Pound decided to call *The Spirit of Romance*. He had found the phrase in a lecture by Oscar Wilde, 'The English Renaissance of Art', first delivered in 1882, appropriately enough on an American lecture tour funded by the D'Oyly Carte Opera Company. 'The English Renaissance in Art' was Wilde's name for the Pre-Raphaelites and the aesthetic movement, and at the time the lecture, described as Wilde's 'full-length manifesto of aestheticism', caused considerable stir; though much reported and misreported, it had its first full publication only in 1908, in a collection of Wilde's *Essays and Lectures* edited by his friend Robert Ross. That Pound was quoting it in 1910 is another reminder that he was a committed aesthete still; the essay's central message chimed with his own creed: 'Love art for its own sake, and then all things that you need will be added to you.'[30] But the distinction Pound was to seize on for the title of this book was that made by Wilde between what he calls 'the Hellenic spirit' and 'the spirit of romance', romance here referring to the cult of medievalism. These two Wilde describes as the twin sources of that English Renaissance of Art, insisting that 'It is really from the union of Hellenism, in its breadth, its sanity of purpose, its calm possession of beauty, with the adventive, the intensified individualism, the passionate colour of the romantic spirit, that springs the art of the nineteenth century in England.'[31] At this stage, Pound's interest in Hellenism was fairly minimal, even though he thought his

Provençal poets had rediscovered the pagan gods. 'The Spirit of Romance' had him in thrall.

When Pound came to write the book, he found it a great deal more of a trial than he had expected. For all his enthusiasm for his chosen medieval writers, his knowledge of conventional literary history was shaky. Questioned a year earlier by his father, he was extremely vague about where in western Britain Tintagel was to be found, and when asked at what period Villon wrote, replied that he was a poet of 'the XIII century or XII or XIV. I am no good at dates'.[32] Villon was in fact a fifteenth-century poet. Pound sent home for his college textbooks, and was forced to apply himself to them. His lecture course itself, he was to admit more than half a century later, had only been 'a very raw summary of things in Rennert's Seminar at the University of Pennsylvania'.[33] He had begun hopefully enough, cribbing some of the first chapter, he acknowledged later, from J.W. Mackail's *Latin Literature*, one of the textbooks his father obligingly posted across the Atlantic, and writing the next two chapters on his beloved Provençal troubadours. But boredom soon set in. Already by October, when his lectures began, he was grumbling that he was 'sweating on this fool book for Dent – the prospect is very horrible. I think breaking stone would be preferable to compiling a literary history'. For one thing he had no typewriter, which made the physical task more onerous, but he could not afford to buy one, nor apparently could his parents, though he repeatedly begged them to send one. Thankfully Olivia Shakespear, he told his father, had 'angelically offered to do emanuensis work' for him, which would have the added bonus that she would 'insist more or less on my getting it done.'[34] Letters from Pound to Dorothy early the following year indicate that she had been helping too, although that had not been mentioned to Homer.

Perhaps worst of all, however, Pound found the writing of a continuous narrative deeply uncongenial. *The Spirit of Romance* contains some brilliant *aperçus*, but the description of texts is at times plodding, and he filled the pages with translations, often his own, which he found easier than commentary. Pound was to produce many essays during his life, but the majority are a series of staccato points, aphoristic, forceful and jerky, assemblages of statements and opinions rather than reasoned arguments. Much the same could be said of his poetry; even the *Cantos* are a collage, an assemblage of shards and fragments. He wrote to his mother in February with striking self-awareness: 'My mind, such as I have, works by a sort of fusion, and sudden crystallization, and the effort to tie that kind of action to the dry work of prose is very exhausting. One should have a vegetable sort of mind for prose. I mean the thought formation should go on consecutively and gradually with order rather than epigrams.'[35] Consecutive thought, as opposed to the striking image or phrase, was never to be his forte. Pound, seizing on Hulme's notion of the inferiority of prose to poetry when it suited his purposes, described his problem as that of the artist-poet condemned to the slavish labour of prose. 'Of course your ideas on prose are quite erroneous,' he told his mother. 'I should never think of prose as anything but a stop-gap, a means of procuring food exactly on the same plane with market-gardening. If anything is not sufficiently interesting to be put in poetry, and sufficiently important to make the poetical worth while it is hardly worth saying at all.'[36]

Olivia and Dorothy both attended Pound's lectures, which were, Dorothy confessed many years later to Noel Stock, 'dismal' – though she loyally explained that this was because 'Ezra did not manage to get through to his very small audience because (she said) of his habit of over-estimating their intelligence.'[37] The thin attendance was a disappointment to Pound, compounded by the lukewarm reviews of *Exultations*, which Mathews duly published in October, 1909. (*Exultations* was, incidentally, one of the few volumes of poetry published by Pound with an English – if unusual English – title.) Edward Thomas reviewed it much less enthusiastically than he had *Personae*, entitling his piece this time 'The Newest Poet', the phrase *Punch* had used to describe Mr Ezekiel Ton, so now Pound's newness became something of a put-down rather than the welcome given the previous spring to 'A New Note in Poetry'. Thomas complained about the poetry's 'turbulent opacity', and was dismayed by the way that Pound's verse was 'dappled with French, Provençal, Spanish, Italian, Latin and Old English, with proper names that we shirk pronouncing, with crudity, violence and obscurity, with stiff rhythms and no rhythms at all'.[38] Even the *English Review*, during that first visit to England probably Pound's main source of income – after his father and the Polytechnic – gave him a somewhat mixed reception. 'Richard Coeur de Lion, as we imagine him, violent and unbridled, was also the friend of the Troubadours and Mr Pound handles his verses very much as Richard I handled the events of his day.' The anonymous reviewer (I suspect Ford himself) did, however, admire his energy: 'he is the most alive as he is the most rugged, the most harsh and the most wrong-headed ... his very thoughts ... are apt to be obscured by the derivative nature of his language. But he uses his language with such force, hammering as it were word into word, that we can have no doubt as to his vitality and as to his determination to burst his way into Parnassus.'[39] In the *New Age*, Flint, though he had reservations, was more upbeat; he was – and would continue to be – sharply critical of Pound's use of archaisms and snatches of foreign languages, but he was emphatic that Pound was breaking new ground:

> One thing is proved by these two little books of his 'Personae' and 'Exultations', and that is that the old devices of regular metrical beat and regular rhyming are worn out; the sonnet and the three-quatrain poem will probably always live; but for the larger music verse must be free from all the restraints of a regular return and a squared-up frame; the poet must forge his rhythm according to the impulse of the creative emotion working in him.[40]

Flint realised that modernism was on its way.

The poem in the collection that was most admired, was, perhaps predictably, the 'Ballad of the Goodly Fere' – both comprehensible *and* rhyming. Pound himself had been uneasy about *Exultations*, though he was not to take notice for some time of the criticisms of his fondness for the derivative, the archaic and the obscure – indeed they are qualities that at times remain defiantly and sometimes productively present in the *Cantos*. Noel Stock suggests that the poem which gives most clue to the way Pound would develop in the imagist years is a very simple poem entitled 'Francesca', an unrhymed poem free of archaisms and rhetoric, beginning 'You came in out of the night/And there were flowers in your hands'.[41] Later Eliot was to say he had read *Personae* and *Exultations* shortly after they came out but hadn't thought much of them, but one wonders if these lines or this image had lingered in his mind, to re-emerge in *The Waste Land* as the hyacinth girl returning from the garden, also with her arms full. Pound's poem is very much the evocation of an epiphanic moment, and in that way too looks forward to imagism: 'I who have seen you amid the primal things/Was angry when they spoke your name/In ordinary places.' But it would be some time before he would attempt such poetic minimalism again.

Flint's first book of poetry, *In the Net of the Stars*, and Campbell's fifth, *The Mountainy Singer*, appeared at much the same time as *Exultations* – the Tour Eiffel group was making its mark – and some reviews linked Pound with one or the other. The *Nation*, which, exceptionally, thought *Exultations* a slight improvement on *Personae*, welcomed Campbell's book with relief as an alternative to Pound's 'somewhat feverish eccentricities'.[42] Pound and Flint, on the other hand, were largely condemned for the same faults. The *Birmingham Daily Post* lamented: 'Mr Ezra Pound is a poet, we fear, in danger of being misled by the unwise. His technique in *Exultations* finds a parallel in the work of Mr Flint recently reviewed in these columns. Again we have the spectacle of a really sincere and vigorous artist driven by his revolt against the abuse of law and convention into mere chaos.'[43] One wonders if Pound were thinking of reviews like that when he later added a footnote to the chapter in *The Spirit of Romance* that discusses the *Poema del Cid*:

As to its 'irregular' metre, I can still see Dr Rennert [his supervisor at Penn] manicuring his finger nails in seminar, pausing in that operation, looking over his spectacles and in his plaintive falsetto, apropos someone who had attempted to reprint the *Cid* with ten syllables in *every* line: 'Naow effa man had sense enough to write a beautiful poem like this, wudn't yeow think he wudda had sense enough to be able to keount ep to ten on his fingers *ef he'da wanted tew?*[44]

The Net of the Stars, like *Exultations*, was reviewed in the *English Review*, but the only comparison made between them was to note they had both had poems published in the journal. Three of Flint's poems had appeared there that July; Pound may have sent them in for him – he was to do so for others – or made the suggestion that Flint should approach Ford. Flint like himself became a regular visitor at South Lodge – another example of the class fluidity of that circle – and was to remain a good friend of Ford's for many years. Ford and Douglas Goldring both admired Flint's poetry, rather more than Pound came to feel they should. The poems that had been published in July had moved further away from regular stanzas than those he had published in the *New Age*. They were clearly very much the product of the discussions in the Tour Eiffel, strongly influenced by French *vers libre*, with irregular rhyme schemes, alliteration and assonance, and what Flint called the 'Hebrew' form of anaphora, also cultivated by the French *vers libristes*: the *Birmingham Daily Post* would undoubtedly have found them alarmingly chaotic. They were love poems, the titles and imagery reminiscent of Yeats, but they are less successful and individual than his poems that rail against urban drabness, and the anonymous reviewer (again probably Ford) in the *English Review* agreed, commenting that 'Mr Flint occasionally attempts to render some aspect of modern life. And it is from such rendering that – if ever it will – poetry will once more regain its hold on the attentions of the English-speaking world.'[45]

That poetry should be concerned with the modern world was the message Ford would hammer home to contemporary poets in general, and later the imagist poets in particular. The poem that the reviewer picked out to quote begins, at any rate, in the urban present:

> As I paced the streets, there came to me,
> Although the air with smoke was dim,
> And bleak, black walls were frowning grim,
> The vision of a sunlit sea,
>
> A crumbling cliff all hacked and torn,
> A waste of sand dunes, grey and wide,
> And wheeling gulls that dipped and cried,
> And scarlet poppies in the corn.
>
> The traffic's jangle and its roar
> And human clamour could not quell
> The low murmur and the spell
> Of languid waves that laced the shore.[46]

In the Net of the Stars was dedicated to 'Violet'. Flint had married during the course of the year, his new wife being the daughter of his landlady. He was devoted to her, though on his meagre salary it was scarcely objectively a sensible act, and over the next few years he was to feel increasingly ground down by what Maupassant had called, as Flint would know, the '*petites misères*' of life. They both came from large families – Flint had ten younger brothers and sisters by then, Violet's family was the same size – and there was no family assistance with finance. It was not at this stage to stop him writing poetry, but it would heighten his sense of social injustice. His better-off acquaintances were apt to regard the marriage as a grave mistake, and at times Flint was in despair under the pressures of penury and family obligations. Their first child, Ianthe, who would become a great favourite with H.D., was born the next year. Flint's new domestic commitments may be one reason why the Tour Eiffel group appears to have disintegrated by early 1910. In addition, Hulme was beginning to lose interest in poetry. Storer, whose next book, *Ballad of the Mad Bird*, was also reviewed, somewhat harshly, in the *English Review*, had lost his enthusiasm for *vers libre*. Campbell and FitzGerald were both embarking on relationships that would end in marriage and take them away from

England. One phase in the development of imagism would soon be over.

Pound did not mention Flint's marriage in any of his extant letters during this London visit, though his mother in September began to raise the issue of marriage with Pound himself. Perhaps she was afraid his reluctance to return home was due to an affair of the heart – which in a sense it was, but the affair, it seems, was more with literary London rather than with a woman. Pound had dedicated *Personae* to 'Mary Moore of Trenton – if she wants it'. He had dedicated *Exultations* to his former minister and co-editor of the Philadelphian *Book News Monthly*, Carlos Tracey Chester. No suggestion of a London attachment in either. Yet given Pound's dependence on female attention in the States, it might seem rather surprising if, in that first year and a half in England, Pound had not found any substitute or substitutes for his H.D.s and Mary Moores and Louise Skidmores. Pound of course would not mention any such relationship in his letters home, merely telling his mother that it should be illegal for artists to marry, but in any case the evidence suggests that on this visit Pound's desires were overwhelmingly directed towards poetic success. In London he could attract the admiring gaze of whole drawing-rooms; he did not have to be content with one young woman at a time. Dorothy Shakespear was certainly in love with him, but his attitude to her is harder to gauge. Their relationship would blossom in Italy the following spring, but in 1909 it seems unlikely that there was more on his side than a little gallantry, which he appeared to show to Olivia and Dorothy equally. In July Dorothy had copied a poem by Pound into her journal with a note that it was written for her that month.[47] This poem, 'Planh', whose title meant, he explained to his father, a lament, and which appeared in *Exultations*, gives an uncertain message. It is in no way a straightforward love poem, but addresses a 'White Poppy, who art wiser than love':

> White Poppy, heavy with dreams,
>   Though I am hungry for their lips
>   When I see them a-hiding . . .
> But if one should look at me with the old hunger in her eyes,
> How will I be answering her eyes?[48]

It reads like a moment of insight into his ambivalent attitude to women, on the one hand the 'fiery' kisses that H.D. records, on the other the refusal to commit himself.[49] 'Planh' contains the lines: 'O White Poppy,

I come for peace, yea from the hunting', which suggests that for now he is coming to Dorothy for companionship rather than love. Dorothy feared just that: she confessed to Pound two years later that she had been afraid that the poem meant only a 'friendship – rather cold & blue'. The hunting with which Pound was concerned in 1909 he summed up in a short poem in *Personae*, 'The White Stag', which describes the chase: 'Lo! they pause not for love nor for sorrow . . . *'Tis the white stag, Fame, we're a-hunting, / Bid the world's hounds come to horn!*'[50]

Yet there are some less indecisive love poems than 'Planh' in *Exultations*, notably the poem 'Francesca', and since Pound's other love poems were at any rate loosely associated with a real woman – H.D. or Kitty Heyman, for example, however reworked into a literary device – it may be there was someone for whom they were specifically written, though Pound, according to H.D., was apt to make any love poem serve a variety of recipients: a sequence in *Asphodel* goes: ' "O George I thought you'd written them to *me*." "What made you think that Lointaine?" "I thought you'd told me you had." "O but I tell that to everyone." '[51] When William Carlos Williams came to see Pound in February 1910, he discovered that Pound had, in a typically theatrical gesture, constructed a little shrine in his room with a woman's photograph before which a candle always burnt. Williams never discovered who she was, so it cannot have been Dorothy, whom he met on that visit, and would surely have recognised. Noel Stock suggests the photograph was that of Bride Scratton, a strikingly beautiful married woman, for whom he thinks Pound developed a romantic admiration during that first year in London. If that is so, it is possible that the poem 'Francesca' was also written to her. Pound knew no Frances or Francesca in London, as far as is known, but, given his devotion to the Paolo and Francesca story, 'Francesca' could well signify a lover's name for a married woman. Pound had met Bride Scratton at one of Yeats' Mondays; according to Stock she was unhappily married, dissatisfied with upper middle-class drawing-room life, and anxious to meet poets and artists. Yet there is no evidence that there was much more at that time than courtly worship of her beauty and charm in Pound's attitude to her, conducive to the writing of poetry. Later, in the early 1920s, when Pound was living in Paris, he became closer to her, helped her to publish some prose, and was cited as co-respondent when she eventually divorced her husband – but even that, Stock loyally maintains, was only Ezra 'being gallant and getting Bride out of a ghastly marriage'.[52] Possibly there was more to it; Bride is remembered in the *Cantos* under the name 'Thiy', after an early Egyptian queen, so she was not unimportant to Pound. All the same, in 1909–10 she was probably no more than a muse.

One young woman with whom Pound may have had some kind of Philadelphian flirtation was the twenty-year-old Grace Crawford, whom he met at the end of July 1909. Grace was attractive, cultured and cosmopolitan. She had American nationality and parents, but had been born in Paris, growing up for the most part in London. Grace's father, then a political journalist, had been posted to London some years before Grace was born, to supply news on English affairs. When he went to report on the London visit of Buffalo Bill's highly successful travelling Wild West Show, he was so taken with it that he set up a syndicate to fund a continental tour, and, dispatching his notice to the States, installed himself as Buffalo Bill's (alias William Cody's) financial manager. Grace was born while the show was in Paris. After the tour was over – it lasted a couple of years, one of the highlights being a performance in the spectacular Roman Arena in Verona – her father supported them in remarkably fine style through a series of risky but largely rewarding business speculations. Although Grace later wrote that 'like all gamblers he had his ups and downs', the family, she notes, never had to reduce its expensive way of life; successful ventures quickly made up for any disasters.[53]

Grace's mother came from a respectable New England family, her own father being in the House of Representatives. Her passion was music, and she had longed to become a professional pianist, but her father had refused to countenance this. Grace had inherited her mother's gift for music, and her mother hoped that Grace would become the professional musician she had never been allowed to be. Grace was taught the piano by none other than Pound's friend Kitty Heyman, but although she, like her mother, loved music, and practised the piano two hours a day, her real wish was to go on the stage, a profession which was in turn too shocking for her mother to contemplate. Training as a singer was the compromise they agreed on. Grace had never been sent to school, and was taught by governesses and tutors, being brought up to speak French and Italian as well as she did English. She also knew German, and was well read and knowledgeable about the arts. Although she lived at home, and both her parents doted on her, she had established a degree of independence unthinkable for most respectable English daughters of the time, having her own sitting-room to which she could invite her friends, and going out unchaperoned to theatres and concerts.

Pound was brought to tea by Kitty Heyman, who had told the Crawfords (mother and daughter that is, Grace's father being away on business) that he was a lonely young American poet who would love to meet an American family. As this was in late July 1909 Pound was already a good deal less lonely than he had been.[54] Kitty was clearly very fond of Grace, and it is possible that she was attempting a little matchmaking. Grace was by no means as struck by Pound's beauty as Dorothy had been, describing him as 'thin, loose-limbed and gawky, pallid and with a mop of long, tangled pale gold hair'. She was, however, intrigued by his outfit. Pound arrived, Grace wrote,

dressed in a loose fitting grey suit – without a waistcoat – a sky-blue shirt and an apricot-coloured tie held in place by a gold finger ring. All of this was most negligently worn but obviously far from negligently chosen. Around his neck was a narrow black riband to which was attached a pair of rimless pince-nez. The position of these was constantly varied as he talked, sometimes worn normally, sometimes far down his nose to be frowningly peered over, sometimes wildly waved in the air to emphasize a point or dropped and completely forgotten.[55]

Yet even if, as this suggests, she was amused by his posturing, they rapidly became friends. After tea, they spent a couple of hours alone in her sitting-room, Pound being delighted to discover copies of Villon and the early Italian poets on her shelves and Grace to find that 'he really liked and understood music'. He stayed for dinner and lingered on talking until 'Mama proclaimed a curfew'.

After that he would frequently spend the afternoon with Grace in her sitting-room, arriving unannounced and often staying to dinner afterwards, for Mrs Crawford liked him and encouraged his visits. Grace had her own piano, and Pound persuaded her to collaborate on a project on which he was working, trying to bring spoken poetry and music closer together by finding a 'vocal line, neither quite speech nor quite song, but a fusion of both which would completely fit the rhythm of the verse'. Grace was 'to pick up on the piano the rhythms and musical intervals as he chanted the words and transfer these to music paper so that they could be repeated for him to polish and amend'.[56] Since meeting Farr Pound had become very attentive to the links between music and poetry, and she may well have told him, if Yeats himself had not, of Yeats' own collaboration with Arnold Dolmetsch, who, Ronald Schuchard tells us, 'sat up many hours writing the musical notation of Yeats chanting his poems in trancelike states'.[57] Pound and Grace started work with Provençal and the early Italian *dolce stil nuovo* poems, and then tried some of Pound's own. 'Our work sessions were never plain sailing,' Grace wrote, 'and we occasionally fought over some disputed point, but these hours of a close working association were among some of the most stimulating which I have ever spent.'[58] They didn't only work; they talked, read books to each other, went for walks around London together and went to see plays. Pound introduced her to Ford and Violet Hunt, with whom she became good friends, and he took her once to a Yeats Monday, which she found quite terrifying. She played tennis in a foursome with Pound, Ford and Mary Martindale, Ford's sister-in-law with whom he had earlier had an affair and who had for no very clear reason also moved into South Lodge. All the tennis equipment was kept at South Lodge, not an entirely satisfactory arrangement, as, Grace reported, old Mrs Hunt loathed both Ford and Pound and would hide away their tennis racquets every week, always in a different place, so the game had regularly to be preceded by a house search.

Grace only goes so far as to assert friendship with Pound, but since for a while she was seeing him almost daily, often unchaperoned, that could perhaps be taken for code that their intimacy included at least the unconsummated embraces that were acceptable between the American middle-class young, though not yet the English. Yet there is certainly no hint of romantic intensity in her account; more good-natured companionability. Their relationship appears to have more in common with Pound's warm, friendly relationship with Mary Moore than his intense love affair with H.D. Grace said that Pound never wrote to her, perhaps understandably while they were both in London, but that he did not continue to correspond with her, as he did with H.D., Mary Moore and his early lust, Viola Baxter, is quite surprising. Their friendship had already faltered before Pound left England in March, for reasons that will emerge. It is not impossible, though it is unlikely, that it was her picture that Williams saw. It may be significant that Pound never took her to the Shakespears', though they once bumped into Olivia at the theatre. He certainly never introduced Grace to Dorothy; his old habit of compartmentalising again, perhaps. He may not have been ready to develop a relationship with Dorothy, but he must have been aware that she would not like to feel she had a rival. Perhaps he did not want to spoil his chances there. Yet for his 1908–10 visit, his principal object of desire remained 'the white stag, Fame'.

III

WHILE Pound was busy pursuing fame and fortune, and, if not yet achieving either, gaining a name as a promising newcomer and gathering advantageous literary contacts, another young American poet in London was having a much bleaker and lonelier time. This was John Gould Fletcher, just a few months younger than Pound, a melancholy, withdrawn poet from Arkansas, and as introverted as Pound was extrovert. Unlike Pound, he lived a largely solitary life, making little attempt to meet other writers. Although Fletcher arrived in London in May 1909 and had his main base there for the next four years, it would be only a chance meeting in Paris in 1913 that introduced him to Pound and eventually drew him uneasily into the imagist camp. In 1909 he had met Hulme, who invited him to join the Tour Eiffel group, but he was too painfully shy to risk it. Although Pound's fellow-countryman, Fletcher came from a very different part of the States. He had been born in Little Rock, son of a prosperous businessman who had earlier been a colonel of Confederate troops in the Civil War. His mother, Adolphine Krause, came from a cultivated German family, her parents being immigrants who had very much maintained their European way of life. According to Fletcher's biographer, Ben Johnson, the Krause family were well-read and musical: they subscribed to journals 'unknown in most Arkansas homes' and lived a life of 'cultured gentility which must have been hard-won in a community still largely a frontier outpost'.[59] Arkansas remained a frontier state until Fletcher was sixteen, for it was not until 1902 that the region on Arkansas' western border became Oklahoma. At the time of Fletcher's birth in 1886, it was still Indian territory, in name and in fact. When Adolphine was born in 1854, the railway had not reached Little Rock; communications were by the slow river networks. Sewers, clean water, pavements and lighting were just appearing around the time young John was born. Before the Civil War the cotton-growing slave plantations in the south of the state had brought wealth to their owners, 'fine Arkansas gentlemen who . . . walked in pomp', as Fletcher put it.[60] While he grew up, however, Arkansas was experiencing the widespread poverty and depression suffered by all the former Confederate States in the post-Civil-War years. Only a few opportunistic entrepreneurs, like his father, were doing well.

Adolphine Krause had hoped to have a career as an opera singer, but had had to leave school early to care for a sick widowed mother. After her mother's death, like so many women of her generation, she settled for the safety of marriage. She was twenty-three, her husband forty-six. John was her second surviving child, with an elder and a younger sister. When he was three, the family moved into a large, dilapidated but still elegant colonial-style house, one of the most impressive in Little Rock (today the Arkansas Decorative Arts Museum), dating from 1840 when the frontier line ran through the spot on which the house stood. The house had a dark, Faulkneresque history; it had been built by one Alfred Pike, poet, journalist and political schemer, with 'flowing locks and Jove-like appearance'. Pike acquired a fortune through marriage, fought in the Mexican war, abandoned his family, and infamously instructed his soldiers in the Civil War to scalp Federal troops. Back in the house, his deserted wife went mad. When Union troops were quartered there during the war, she would wander, it was reported, 'vacantly around the dreary wreck, seeming to scarcely notice anything that pass[ed] around her'. There were other strange, disturbing stories about the house that Fletcher was told as a boy:

It was said that one of the Pike children had either jumped or fallen into a heap of burning leaves on the lawn and been burned to death; it was said that silver, buried since the Civil War, might be found there by digging; it was said that Mrs Pike, in her last years, had once become so angry with a Negro servant who was brushing out her hair, as to drive the girl to leap out of the central window upstairs and break her leg on the downstairs veranda floor; it was said that the old lady's ghost had been frequently seen in the library downstairs, rocking herself in a certain rocking chair. All this, no doubt, served to color my youthful imagination.[61]

Fletcher always felt the house was haunted, though as much by the ghosts of his own childhood traumas as by the crazed Mrs Pike. One of his most moving and successful poems would be called 'The Ghosts of an Old House', evocative and painful recollections of his youth. Fletcher's own childhood had some of the aspects of a Faulkner tale. His father was silent and severe at home, and imposed a dead, grim Sabbath on his household, even though he was not a church-goer himself. On the other hand, he was ready to go along with his wife's desire to furnish the house sumptuously from expensive New York suppliers, thus demonstrating her superiority to what she considered the uncouth bumpkins of Arkansas. They had vast chandeliers, and a dining table that seated twenty-seven. Ironically, as the years went by, Adolphine refused to entertain even her husband's relatives. Fletcher's father, out of the house, was an aspiring politician, who campaigned unsuccessfully as State Governor, but the family at home lived, apart from the servants, largely in isolation.

According to Fletcher's account of his childhood, Adolphine wanted to keep her children apart from the vulgar *canaille* for as long as possible. She hoped to form them, particularly John, as artistic cultivated spirits, untouched by the ignorance and coarseness of their Arkansas neighbours. In an unpublished autobiographical novel, Fletcher wrote of his birth: 'So John came into the world and in him his mother reembodied all her vanished ambitions.'[62] He was to be the musician fate had not allowed her to be. Until he was ten, Fletcher never went beyond the grounds of their estate unless taken by his parents, generally in the carriage. His mother taught the children to read, and encouraged her son's love of poetry, although she proscribed certain 'dangerously exciting' adventure stories, such as *The Count of Monte Cristo* and *Tom Sawyer*.[63] At the age of six he had a tutor who taught him German and Latin, and gave some lessons to his elder sister (also called Adolphine), although she, four years older than he was, had been allowed to start school at seven. Fletcher showed limited aptitude for languages, something that distressed him greatly in later years. But worse, he showed no promise as a musician. When he was small his mother played the piano and sang to herself for hours. He loved to listen, but when she attempted to teach him she found that he was too physically clumsy to make his fingers move as they should. She abandoned the experiment in disgust. He had failed to make good her frustrated hopes. Eventually she ceased even to play the piano herself, and as the years went on grew increasingly bitter. (This experience was too painful to be included in Fletcher's published autobiography, in which he claims simply that music 'was thought effeminate in those days for a boy to learn'. True enough in many instances, and his father had forbidden a violin on those grounds – 'I won't have my son a damned fiddler' – but not the piano.)[64]

By the time Fletcher was twenty his mother had become chronically, angrily depressed: Fletcher remembered in 'The Ghosts of an Old House', that

> She would sit all day and listlessly
> Look on the world that had destroyed her,
> She would go down in the evening
> To the room where she would sleep,
> Or rather, not sleep, but all night
> Lie staring fiercely at the ceiling.[65]

By twenty Fletcher himself had already begun to experience the pattern of extreme mood changes that would dog him all his life until his suicide in 1950. The rollercoaster leaps and dives of his journals suggest this may have been a form of manic depression, or, since depression certainly predominated over mania, a form of melancholia like his mother's. Whether one should ascribe Fletcher's psychological suffering to his genes or his strange upbringing or both must be a matter of conjecture. It was undoubtedly very real.

Fletcher was four when his second sister, Mary, was born, and it was she who was his main companion until he went to school at ten. They played together, games that fed his imagination more than anything else in his odd childhood. Mary, however, suffered several life-threatening illnesses as a child, and though she survived, the recurrent periods of fear and loneliness added to the bleakness of John's childhood. Another of the sections in 'The Ghosts of an Old House' is about one of these:

> In the tired face of the mirror
> There is a blue curtain reflected.
> If I could lift the reflection,
> Peer a little beyond, I would see
> A boy crying
> Because his sister is ill in another room
> And he has no-one to play with:
> A boy listlessly scattering building blocks,
> And crying,
> Because no one will build for him the palace of Fairy Morgana.
> I cannot lift the curtain:
> It is stiff and frozen.[66]

It is a moving evocation of the solitariness of the desolate child, hungry
for play, companionship, imaginative life. Yet one has to note that what
is uppermost in his recollection is not anxiety for his sister, but pity for
himself. Is this an example of the self-absorption so typical of Fletcher's
later life? Or is it commendably honest about the self-centredness of
childhood? Perhaps both.

Ben Johnson suggests that in Fletcher's relationship with his younger
sister began the pattern that so many of his later friendships and love
affairs followed: fierce possessiveness that soon turned to distrust, and
thereafter oscillated between the two. Both his sisters had much more
affectionate relationships with his father than he had, but John wanted
all Mary's affection and attention for himself. He depended on her
companionship and indeed her building bricks and dolls. His own expensive German toy cars remained locked away, too valuable for everyday.
Circuses and any kind of travelling entertainments were off limits to
the young Fletchers. Fletcher recalled later hearing the distant sounds
of Buffalo Bill's Wild West Show, only able to fantasise about its exotic
vitality and colour. It is not surprising that Buffalo Bill was the entertainment he minded missing most. Like many American intellectuals of
his generation, particularly those like himself who grew up not far from
Reservation lands, he was never to lose the image of Native American
culture as a romantic alternative to the greyness of modern life, but in
childhood he knew them only in books and his imagination.

At ten he started school at a private academy. His mother had cut
off the long hair he had worn till then, but he was still an outsider,
teased and bullied as Pound had been. He did not do well. His one
solace was that he was now allowed more freedom in his reading, and
he devoured novels, especially those of Walter Scott. There was a vogue
for Scott among Southerners, who identified with his defeated but
romantic Highlanders, but whether Fletcher, who had been taught by
his mother to despise the South, saw them that way is dubious. At thirteen he moved to public school (in the American sense) which he enjoyed
no more than the private. There are some pictures of Fletcher at this
age held by the Beinecke Library, studio pictures taken by a Little Rock
photographer. He has an extraordinarily vulnerable, sensitive face, and
is holding himself apparently motionless, his face completely contained,
every hair in place, as if he were making a desperate attempt to conform,
to please, to be what he was wanted to be. He was not to succeed.

His mother believed her children's education needed to be completed
in the North. Adolphine was sent to Vassar, and it was planned that

John should go to Harvard. Although his parents had engaged a tutor to coach him out of school hours, at his first attempt, at sixteen, he failed, as H.D. had done at Bryn Mawr. Harvard told his father he should be sent to a New England preparatory school to be trained up to the standard required by the entrance examination, and he was duly dispatched. Life if anything took a turn for the worse. New Englanders despised 'filthy Southerners', in a complex double bind both for their moral inferiority as erstwhile slave-owners, and simultaneously for their cultural affinities, real or supposed, with the Southern blacks. T.S Eliot suffered much the same, being mocked when he went from St Louis to Massachusetts for his 'nigger drawl'. Like Fletcher, Eliot came from the defeated Confederacy area, but not from the true Old South, with the possible consolatory identity that offered. In addition, Eliot's family were New Englanders, foreigners in St Louis, 'northerners in a border state [who] looked down on all southerners', as Eliot described them.[67] Fletcher too had been brought up to consider himself an alien in Little Rock, and to scorn its culture. Later in life Fletcher was to reinvent himself as a Southerner; Eliot, of course, famously turned himself into an Englishman. But for both of them their student days in New England left them without a sense of identity or roots.

Fletcher passed his entrance examinations at the second attempt, and entered Harvard. Although he found the first year's work disappointingly routine, he was reading eye-opening books he had never found in Arkansas, nineteenth-century realist novels, for example, which did not yet lead him to any great questioning of his society's sexual mores, at least in personal terms, but at any rate gave him his first encounter with writers who dealt with the modern urban world, with which so much of his own poetry would be concerned. In his first year, he appears to have got to know few of his fellow-students except for those with whom he played poker, and to whom he frequently lost money. In his second year, however, he found a friend, or perhaps one should say a guru. Fletcher at various points in his life would develop intense hero-worship for another man, on whom he would become fixated and dependent, until disillusionment and the conviction of betrayal set in. Lyman Willets Rogers was the first, a handsome aesthete who wrote poetry and introduced Fletcher to the work of Wilde and Nietzsche. Unlike Pound, Aldington and H.D., Fletcher never had more than a passing interest in the Pre-Raphaelite poets, though he recorded the more exotic *Omar Khayyám* as his favourite book in 1903. It was not till he went to Europe that he became attracted by Ruskin's idealisation of medieval times, and then not for long. For now what was important to him was that Rogers taught him, as Ben Johnson puts it, that 'his own alienation and general dissatisfaction indicated an artistic temperament'. Loneliness was a sign of a superior nature. Rogers expounded his Nietzschean conviction that Christianity aimed to 'shackle men of genius', freeing Fletcher at a stroke from his Southern Calvinist practices; its sense of doom he would never escape. He wrote in his diary: 'Determined to follow Rogers' plan and eliminate the Sabbath from my calendar.'[68] Like Hulme and Flint, in their different ways, Fletcher found Nietzsche a revelation, and would read him enthusiastically over the next few years, liberated from Christianity into new possibilities. He wrote in his autobiography: 'my becoming a Nietzschean, and my break with the religion of my boyhood, made it certain that I would go on writing poetry. Men must believe in something; if they cannot believe in the accepted religion they will believe in art, or in fate, or in machinery, or in progress, or in communism. For my part, I believed, since severing my alliance with Christianity, all the more completely in art.'[69]

Oscar Wilde, he noted, was the most important writer in his life in 1903, and to a lesser extent Pater. Fletcher became an aesthete. He began visiting art galleries instead of lectures, listening to concerts rather than writing essays, wearing the obligatory flowing tie. He wrote in his journal, in terms with which Pound would have concurred: 'There is but one true religion in this world – the religion of beauty. But the tables of the Law are broken, and the people are now all worshipping the Golden Calf of Commercialism.'[70] Fletcher had already become, as well as an aesthete, an anti-capitalist, a position he was to maintain all his life, from a variety of stances, both left and right.

It was during this academic year that Fletcher discovered the work of James Thomson, the most Dostoevskian of English poets, whose best-known poem, *The City of Dreadful Night*, had appeared in 1874. Thomson's mapping of psychic turmoil and despair on to the dark streets and garish lights of the crowded city was later to provide Fletcher with a powerful trope, but Thomson did not immediately help him find a poetic mode. Fletcher had also, however, perhaps under Rogers' guidance, read Symons' *The Symbolist Movement in Literature*, from which he first learnt of Baudelaire and French symbolism. He had as it happened reread the works of Baudelaire's mentor, Edgar Allan Poe, the previous summer vacation, which must have served as a useful preface. He began to read French literature in translation – his French was not yet up to reading in the original – Baudelaire's 'incomparable'

Fleurs du mal, Gautier's *Emaux et camées*, Flaubert's *Trois contes*, works which he read for 'their perfect craftsmanship . . . their supreme aesthetic delight'.[71] Gautier's jewelled precision, later so much admired by Pound, but admittedly less obvious in translation, had little specific influence on Fletcher's poetic work, though undoubtedly in general terms led him to his later concern with poetic technique. Many of his early poems, however, are Baudelairean evocations of the modern city and modern angst. He visited California that summer with his older sister Adolphine; as with T. E. Hulme, his own first impulse to write poetry came from his journey across the empty spaces of the continent – 'the Arizona desert, intensely hot and scorched by relentless sun'.[72] All the same, his first poem was not about the desert but about a Los Angeles actress, and was, he said, 'a palpable imitation of a Baudelaire translation'.[73] It is curious that although the impulse to write arose from travelling through rocky wastes, the poem when it came was about the experience of the city; the Baudelairean model was dominant, though on the return journey through the Yosemite park, Fletcher recalled that poems poured out. It was the first time he knew what it felt to be intoxicated by poetry. Fletcher later was to write a number of poems about solitary places, particularly the American South-west (including a sequence of poems, 'Arizona', which he first published in 1916). In fact, the landscape of his poems is generally either intensely urban or remote – he had no affinity with the gentle settled countryside that made up so much of the English Georgian poets' subject-matter.

Baudelaire was significant to Fletcher on many levels. Though in his autobiography he claims he admired him simply for his craft, perhaps Baudelaire's depiction of modern consciousness torn between *spleen* and *idéal* – on the one hand self-loathing, boredom, disgust, on the other tortured, unfulfilled desire for love and beauty – gave Fletcher a way of understanding his own tormented psyche. Fletcher's French was to improve, and although he always struggled, he later made translations himself, several of which appeared in his first books of poetry in 1913. Although awkward and uneven, they convey something of the un-expectedness and black vitality of the original, qualities lost in translations that search for the idiomatic and tamer English version. What Fletcher lacked, then and later, is Baudelaire's elegance and technical skill; his work so often has the maladroitness of his social being. He was aware of his awkwardness, but argued from early on that 'posterity will the more willingly accept the unfinished genius than the polished artisan', a view that links him back to Whitman and on to more recent traditions of experimental American writing.[74] That is the argument by which some of Pound's admirers would now defend the *Cantos*, though it was not Pound's own view during the Imagist years, and he could be cutting about what he saw as Fletcher's sloppy technique. Yet some of Fletcher's poetry has striking originality and power, even if at the moment most literary critics pass him by.

The next academic year, 1905–6, Fletcher saw less of Rogers, who was absorbed in poetry, Nietzsche and opium-taking. Dejected, Fletcher returned to the poker tables, though not to his lectures, and managed to lose $1,000 as well as failing several examinations. He was sure he wanted to be an artist of some sort, but knew his father was determined he should enter law or business. In mid-November he wrote in his diary:

Tomorrow is the hour-examination in French, which I know I will fail, as I have not studied at all for it. What will happen to me then, as I have already failed in German, I don't know, and only wish that I didn't care, I know in my innermost heart, that I cannot, cannot study. I have tried to do so. The result was that I was plunged into the depths, and while in this state drew a 'Melancholia', the finest thing I have ever yet made, and one which almost makes me wonder if I couldn't have done something in the way of art, and also makes me curse the day I ever heard the word 'art'. If I could only be practical! I am almost sure I could be if I could only stop this foolishness, which will ruin me if I stay up here much longer. However, it looks now as if my stay will be brief indeed. I don't want to cause a tornado at home, but I can't help it! I can't! I can't![75]

But he did not cause a tornado at home. A different kind of disaster struck the Little Rock mansion. At the end of January 1906 his father unexpectedly died. His mother closed the shutters for a year; even deeper gloom descended on the house than had surrounded it in his childhood.

IV

FLETCHER went home for the funeral, uncertain of what the future would hold, as apprehensive now that he would be made to leave Harvard as he had been a short while ago that he would be forced to stay. His father had always been a distant figure, already fifty when John was born, with little understanding of his uneasy, awkward son's artistic bent. In his autobiography, however, Fletcher says, ironically perhaps, that he had come to feel more warmly towards his father since the time he lost the race for the Arkansas governorship; in defeat, the apparently all-powerful father could seem human, even lovable, now his son discovered his power was, after all, limited. In retrospect Fletcher came to see his father, like himself, as a tragic failure, a martyr to his idealism in a mercenary, unscrupulous world. Like so many of his generation, including Pound and H.D., Fletcher became deeply disillusioned with American political life. His teenage years had seen first the revelations after the 1898 Spanish war, which made apparent, as he put it, 'greed, official incompetence, imperialistic ambition masquerading as humanitarian motive', and later the muckrakers' devastating exposures of civil corruption.[76] Fletcher's experience of what he judged his father's unjust humiliation sharpened his disgust.

At the funeral Fletcher's mother and sisters were distraught. Fletcher was repelled by their 'loud sobs', maintaining what he described as a 'manlier' self-control.[77] With his father's death Fletcher appears to have felt for the first time able to assert his masculinity. Until then what he described as his 'puny appearance' as a boy compared to his patriarchal father's six foot, powerfully built imposing presence, as well as his awareness that he had more in common temperamentally with his mother than his father, had made him uncomfortably part of the women's household group.[78] Now he began to contrast himself with them, but it is a mark of his insecurity that for him 'manliness' generally took the form of misogynistic denigration of the women in his life. In some ways he felt more relief than grief over the death of his father, and his sense of loss was tempered by his discovery that his father was far wealthier than he had realised. He returned to Harvard, but this time with the knowledge that when he came of age in a year's time, he would be financially independent. He need neither return to Little Rock, nor become a lawyer or businessman. He would be able to pay his debts, and he need not worry if he failed examinations. However, the solution of all his immediate problems was never to prevent Fletcher from finding cause for misery. He discovered his friend Rogers had taken desertion one stage further by falling in love with a music student, Louise Howard, who was training as a professional singer. Fletcher promptly fell in love with her himself, and wrote her passionate poems, but to no avail. She and Rogers eloped in May – Harvard undergraduates were not allowed to marry – and he was left without either of them.

In the summer of 1906, Fletcher had a bitter quarrel with his mother. In six months he would be of age, and he asked his mother to let him have his share of his inheritance immediately so he could embark on life as a poet. She refused in outrage, insisting he had to continue to prepare prudently for a career in law or business. Fletcher felt betrayed; he had expected her to sympathise in a way his father could not. 'It is from [my mother],' he wrote in his autobiography, 'I trace all those aesthetic hankerings which have made me into a poet – all that love for pictures, architecture, music, that has sustained me through life, and has even led me to the extravagances and excesses that the artist usually has to commit in this world . . . my father . . . showed ability on the practical, but was deficient on the aesthetic side. My mother's aesthetic side, on the contrary, was overdeveloped.'[79] Yet she was now rejecting him for a second time, refusing to recognise the aesthetic needs she had implanted herself. Not only was she the cause of all that was weak in his nature, she was blindly refusing to recognise the gifts she had passed on. Fletcher returned disconsolately to Harvard. 'Feeling like an outlaw, without a soul who cared either to listen to me or to understand me, I crept back to college.'[80]

The excesses and extravagances he blamed on his mother were his only consolations. He was experimenting with opium. He drowned his sorrows in wine – generally rather good wine, Rogers having introduced him to the sophisticated pleasure of wine-drinking while most Harvard students stuck to whiskey. He was gambling, for increasingly high stakes.

After Rogers' departure, apart from his poker companions he had few friends among his fellow-undergraduates, confining himself to pouring out his thoughts and emotions into his journal. He was now reading Nietzsche extensively, and justified his crippling shyness as scorn for inferior souls; a pity, perhaps, because he could have found congenial companions, not necessarily inferior at all. Conrad Aiken, later one of his most loyal friends, was at Harvard, but they did not meet at this stage. Van Wyck Brooks, for whose journal, the *Freeman*, Fletcher would write in the twenties, only remembered Fletcher's 'queer, white, skull-like face peering out through the crimson curtains of the Harvard Union'.[81] T.S. Eliot arrived at Harvard in the fall of 1906, but Fletcher would not get to know him until they were introduced in London in 1916. After the war, although never intimate – neither of them was ever easily intimate – they had what for Fletcher was an unusually untroubled and pleasant friendship. He and Eliot had more in common than their shared sense of placelessness, of belonging nowhere, so much part of the modern rootless urban existence. Brought up away from the culturally superior New England with its historic traditions and its European links, they were both acutely conscious of the new America's rapid and unlovely urban growth, steadily sprawling over the continent without the romance of past associations. For both, beginning their poetic careers, urban existence was the modern condition and inevitably the subject-matter of modern poetry. Eliot was already, as Pound would later put it, 'modernis[ing] himself' on not dissimilar lines to Fletcher. He too was deeply influenced early on by the poetry of the city, first that of James Thomson and then Baudelaire. Both were to be great admirers of Rimbaud, though the gauche, over-intense Fletcher never seems to have been particularly attracted to Jules Laforgue's wry self-ironising poems, which were to influence Eliot so much. Nor does Fletcher appear to have come across the poetry of John Davidson, another early passion of Eliot's, and a poet whom Fletcher would probably have admired. Davidson (author of the torrid 'Ballad of a Nun' lampooned by Owen Seaman) was another impassioned poet of city life, uneven and unbalanced like Fletcher himself. Indeed, Lionel Johnson's notes on Davidson's work are curiously applicable to Fletcher: '[His] work often requires a last refining touch to transfigure it into a very wonderful thing . . . [He] has tried so many ways and done so much. Has put genuine passion into his poetry, not an "artistic" pose . . . Has not quite "found himself" in literature or life.'[82]

In early 1907, shortly after his twenty-first birthday on 6 January,

Fletcher made his first attempt to find himself. He withdrew from Harvard, which at twenty-one his mother could no longer force him to attend, but did not return home. He continued his solitary life in Cambridge, writing poems, continuing his journal jottings, which are often in the form of a series of brief, gnomic comments – to some extent imitating Nietzschean aphorisms, though he refers to them dismissively at one stage as 'paltry fragments'.[83] In the summer he visited the desert once more, going this time on an archaeological expedition to Colorado. One friend whom he had made during his latter days at Harvard was Silvanus Griswold Morley, later a famous authority on the Maya, then a student of American archaeology. That, Fletcher thought, was what he should have taken up. 'Why,' he asked himself, 'had I not been allowed to study American archaeology? Here was a field that offered more, it seemed, to a man of my type than any other; it required imagination, courage, linguistic, cultural and aesthetic knowledge to pursue; its rewards were the remote, the romantic past of the Indian.'[84] He read avidly in the subject. His fascination with the primitive was very much of the moment, and, as he would discover, widespread among artists and writers at the time. This was the year of Les Demoiselles d'Avignon, Picasso's famous work, often seen as the first truly modernist painting, in which he incorporates the form of African masks into his depiction of Paris prostitutes. In America itself, a whole new preoccupation with Native Americans and their art forms was just beginning among the intelligentsia, and 1907 saw the publication of the widely admired Indians' Book, compiled by Natalie Curtis, a collection of Native American music and poetry. Natalie's namesake Edward Curtis was already beginning his great anthropological study of the North American Indian, illustrated with his elegiac sepia photogravures, soon to be some of the most famous images of Native Americans. American modernist painters, like Marsden Hartley and Max Weber, would in a few years be using Native American motifs, and there would be considerable interest in Native American poetry among supporters of imagism in the States. The stereotype of the bloodthirsty warrior was giving way to a cult of the Native Americans as beauty-loving, gentle artists. For American intellectuals like Fletcher, disillusioned with present-day commercialism, the one element of history and romance America had was Native American culture. So Fletcher set off to discover what the ancient rock houses of the South-west could reveal of this exotic past.

To start with all went well: they felt like explorers, he said, rather than archaeologists: 'In that vast upland of twisted piñon and juniper and sagebrush, with the long, absolutely soundless yellow canyons running off to the south, where blue-grey Ship-Rock hung and quivered like a mirage in the glare above the Navajo desert, we were seeing a country which, except for a few archaeologists and cattle rustlers and horse thieves, no white man had ever seen.'[85] He was entranced by the sight of the great cliff dwellings of the Mesa Verde, whose origins then were still mysterious. But when they got down to work, it was different: the heat, the discomfort, the primitive conditions were bad enough, but what was worse still was the boredom. Fletcher had not been prepared for the fact that the archaeology, at any rate for the assistants, was largely a matter of scrabbling in the dust. Remarkably, though with increasing misery, irritation and frustration, he stuck it for almost two months, and then abruptly returned home. Archaeology was not for him; primitive life was all very well as a romantic myth about other people, but actually to experience it was dismaying. Some poems came out of this experience, however, although not till later, when they would appear in one of Fletcher's most warmly reviewed collections, *Breakers and Granite*, in 1921. The allure of the primitive would remain powerful for Fletcher, something else he shared with Eliot, who was intrigued not by archaeology so much as by anthropology, but it was another way in which they were ready to meet European modernism earlier in their development than Pound.

By now Fletcher was certain that he wanted to be a poet, and was convinced that he would need to go to Europe to become one. He had one problem. Most of his wealth was tied up in the estate, and his mother refused to release any of it to him. He was still living on an allowance. In May of 1908, however, his mother was diagnosed with breast cancer, and his sister Adolphine took control of family affairs and agreed to make a settlement. In return for his ceding to his two sisters two-thirds of his share of his father's estate, they each paid him $25,000, half of it immediately, and the rest a promissory note. In August 1908, just as Pound was arriving in England, Fletcher sailed to Europe. Like Pound, he first spent time in Italy, in his case ten months, reading Ruskin, lamenting the modern industrial world and writing dark poems. In May 1909 he went to London, where he would live off and on for the next five years, with frequent visits back to mainland Europe.

Fletcher says little about his meeting with Hulme, nor how it came about that Hulme invited him along to the Tour Eiffel. They had met through the *New Age*, where the first, and for some time only, friend Fletcher made, S.J. Hobson, was a regular contributor on political events.

Fletcher had been deeply shocked by the poverty of the London slums, and was briefly attracted by socialism. His biographer, Ben Johnson, argues that his anti-capitalism sprang more from his hatred of commercialisation and degradation of culture than from sympathy with the poor, but at least he noticed their suffering. Yet after accompanying Hobson to a Labour Party rally in Lancashire, he decided in a Nietzschean way that the workers connived in their own exploitation, and became a nihilist In London he was meeting few people with any interest in the arts: he continued writing poetry, but did not attempt to publish. In general he was still using traditional forms, though he did experiment with some free verse, which he had discovered through Whitman shortly after he had turned down Hulme's invitation to join the Tour Eiffel group. With his customary extremism, he wrote in his diary for 2 June 1909: 'Sat down at five pm to read Walt Whitman . . . amazing in every way. I think Whitman will be my next demigod'.[86] He was soon on to other enthusiasms, however, reading avidly, and by the next year would put down his responses on a whole range of topics in a new series of Nietzschean aphorisms: what he admired in Nietzsche, where he differed from him, his now limited support for socialism but total loathing of capitalism, his impatience with traditional Christianity, his interest in early Greek philosophy, his recent fascination with William Blake, his irritation with Shaw, and, centrally, his hopes and despairs about his own writing: 'With conditions more favourable,' he wrote, 'I could certainly have produced another Zarathustra. Primarily, I am a poet, drunken with the highest flights of the imagination, but not strong enough to get them on paper . . . I am accursed. I am also a madman.'[87]

He was certainly lonely; the friendship with Hobson did not last long. If Fletcher had joined the Tour Eiffel group his life just might have been happier, and it is certainly possible that his poetry would have developed differently. Later he was to be deeply impressed by Japanese culture, publishing a volume entitled *Japanese Prints*: had he learnt then about the haiku form and of Hulme's insistence on sharp, direct presentation, it might have counteracted the looseness and sprawl of some of his early poetry. Given, however, his capacity for falling out with people, he might easily have irrevocably quarrelled with Pound well before the imagist movement was born in 1912, and never have been associated with the imagists at all. As it was, he remained for now working by himself.

V

POUND, meanwhile, unlike the solitary Fletcher, continued to make new literary acquaintances. In September 1909 he had been delighted finally to meet Arthur Symons, the most famous of the living Rhymers after Yeats, now much recovered from the mental breakdown by which Yeats had been so distressed. Their second meeting was at tea at the Shakespears', to which Symons came with an American friend, Alice Tobin, and when Symons presented Olivia with a single red rose, Alice, not to be outdone, promptly presented Pound with a turquoise ear-ring, which he would delight in wearing *pour épater la bourgeoisie*. (If Pound had read *The Symbolist Movement in Literature*, he would have come across – but would probably have ignored – Symons' observation that 'Nothing, not even conventional virtue, is so provincial as conventional vice; and the desire "to bewilder the middle-classes" is itself middle-class.')[88] There are numerous accounts of Pound with his ear-ring. As an attention-seeking device it certainly worked.

Arthur Symons was another figure from the glorious past to add to Pound's tally, but he was also meeting some of the young artists who like himself would emerge shortly as central figures in the revolution in literature that broke out before the First World War. In November he was introduced to D. H. Lawrence. Pound's relationship with Lawrence was not to be an untroubled one; they would become increasingly cool towards each other, though they began on the friendliest of terms. There was no particular point at which they fell out, but as Pound was apt to patronise, and Lawrence bitterly to resent patronage, the early warmth of their relationship turned to mutual irritation. Pound later helped to publish and publicise Lawrence's poetry and stories; he recognised that Lawrence's writing was important, but had no real liking for it. Even in the years when he claimed to champion artistic freedom, he remained disturbed by its erotic charge. Lawrence was to become much more friendly with Richard Aldington and H.D. than he ever was with Pound – though Lawrence's friendships in general were rarely straightforward or easy, and those friendships were no exception.

In 1909, however, Pound's similarity in age, his relative poverty and the fact that he was also an outsider in London society, even if culturally rather than in class terms, may have made him appear potentially an ally in the new world Lawrence met that autumn. D.H. Lawrence, though a collier's son and in 1909 still a teacher in a Croydon elementary school, was, like Pound, meeting many of the figures who were to launch him on his career through a series of expansive invitations. When his ex-girlfriend and still loyal friend, Jessie Chambers, sent the *English Review* some of his poems, Ford not only accepted them for publication in that November, but asked Lawrence to visit. Lawrence described the visit to an old college friend, later for a while, his fiancée, Louie Burrows: 'Last Sunday I went up to lunch with Ford Madox Hueffer, and with Violet Hunt, who is rich, and a fairly well-known novelist. They were both delightful'. Ford took him on to tea at Ernest Rhys' ('very nice indeed'), and then to call on H.G. Wells, ('a funny little chap').[89] Two days later, Violet Hunt invited Lawrence to an 'At Home' at the Reform Club at which Pound was also a guest. Lawrence told Louie that Pound was 'a well-known American poet – a good one' and 'jolly nice'. Pound took him out to supper and back to his room – 'He lives in an attic, like a traditional poet – but the attic is a comfortable well furnished one'. He was impressed by Pound's MA and the fact he was lecturing at the Polytechnic, and commented that 'He is rather remarkable – a good bit of a genius, and with not the least self consciousness.'[90]

Pound asked Lawrence back to London the next weekend, taking him out to meet friends who did not demand evening dress – an important issue for them both. The friends in question were probably the Crawfords, Pound having conveyed the impression to Grace – who had heard about Lawrence at a visit to South Lodge, and was intrigued to meet this miner's son become poet – that he knew Lawrence rather better than he did. At the same time, Pound wasted no time in letting Lawrence know how extensive his acquaintanceship was in the literary world. 'He knows W.B. Yeats and all the Swells,' Lawrence told Louie: at this stage, Lawrence was as delighted with his London reception as Pound had been. 'Aren't the folks kind to me,' he wrote, 'it is really wonderful. Hueffer is splendid: I have met a gentleman indeed in him, and an artist.'[91] By 1913, although still ready to accept Ford and Pound's well-meaning if somewhat *de haut en bas* help in placing his stories and poems, he had become much more cynical, telling Edward Garnett: 'the Hueffer–Pound faction seems inclined to lead me round a little as one of their show dogs'.[92] In his late autobiographical sketches, however, Lawrence reiterates his sense of Ford's early kindness. He recounts the story of Ford's reading the manuscript of his first novel, which Ford declared had 'every fault that the English novel can have', and, as Lawrence knew well, Ford considered the number of faults the English novel – as opposed to the French or Russian – could contain to be legion:

'But' shouted Hueffer in the bus, 'you've got GENIUS.'

That made me want to laugh, it sounded so comical. In the early days they were always telling me I had got genius, as if to console me for not having their own incomparable advantages.

But Hueffer didn't mean that. I always thought he had a bit of genius himself.[93]

Towards Pound he was less respectful in his recollections. He told Glenn Hughes in 1929 that 'in the old London days Pound wasn't so literary as he is now. He was more of a mountebank then.' But, he added, Pound 'was always amusing'.[94]

Pound asked Lawrence to visit him again three weeks after that first invitation, having promised to introduce him to a 'crowd of other literary folk', perhaps the Tour Eiffel poets. Jessie Chambers, however, reports an incident that might have had something to do with the souring of this early friendship. Lawrence had asked her down to London soon after he had first visited South Lodge, and insisted that she went with him for lunch there. Jessie had been reluctant, for, as she said, she 'dreaded meeting strangers', particularly no doubt rich strangers, but she was immensely taken with Ford's 'genial warmth'. 'I suppose,' she wrote, 'never before or since has anyone talked to me with quite such charm, making me feel in the most delicate way that what I said was of interest'. His pleasantness to the maid 'confirmed [her] impression of genuine kindliness'. She liked Violet Hunt, but Ezra Pound, to whom she refers simply as 'an American poet', was another matter. He startled her 'by springing to his feet and bowing from the waist with the stiff precision of a mechanical toy', and by constantly flinging out 'observations in an abrupt way', which, she noted perceptively, was oddly reminiscent of the form his poetry took. What really disturbed her, however, was when Ezra Pound, who, as Ford said *à propos* this very incident, 'had a genius for inappropriate interpolations', asked Ford: 'How would *you* speak to a working man? . . . Would you speak to him just the same as to any other man, or would you make a difference?' Ford, a natural diplomat himself, unless he chose not to be, was taken aback, but answered after a moment's hesitation that he 'should speak to a working man in exactly the same way that I should speak to any other man, because I don't think there is any difference', thus retrieving the situation.[95] Of course, even by the standards of those more snobbish than Ford, Lawrence was not strictly a working man. His post at an elementary school put him on the middle-class ladder, albeit near the foot. But he was the son of a working man, and the working class was too near to both Jessie and himself for it to be anything other than a horribly embarrassing moment. Lawrence himself never appears to have mentioned it, but it must have entered his super-sensitive soul.

The tension between Lawrence and Pound, however, was not entirely Pound's fault; it was partly the product of Lawrence's situation and temperament. As Helen Corke observed (she was the schoolteacher friend from Croydon whose experiences, and own novel, *Neutral Ground*, provided the plot for Lawrence's second novel, *The Trespasser*): 'The patronage of the London *literati* hurt Lawrence's pride, and he became conscious of the gulf between the artist who is a working schoolmaster, and the young artists who, often penniless themselves, lived within a charmed circle of influence and wealth. After a London literary party he would savagely satirise to me its personnel.'[96] She goes on to mention specifically Ezra Pound, one of the chief victims, though the most famous of Lawrence's cruel imitations was that of Florence Farr at her 'ping-wanging', as he called her performances to the psaltery.[97] Pound and Lawrence saw each other again at South Lodge and at the gatherings at Ernest Rhys' house several times before Pound left for Italy the following March, but the invitations appear to have ceased.

Before his appearance in the *English Review*, Lawrence's only publication had been a short story submitted under Jessie Chambers' name to a *Nottingham Guardian* Christmas competition, when he was still at Nottingham University College. He had since written many poems, short stories, at least one play and the novel that was to become *The White Peacock*, but unlike Pound, with his relentless drive to achieve publication, sales and fame, Lawrence had been reluctant to expose himself to failure. As his biographer John Worthen suggests, perhaps the very unimaginability of an Eastwood miner's son becoming a writer blocked him. His poems had, after all, only appeared in the *English Review* because Jessie Chambers sent them. She recalls in her memoirs an incident when Lawrence finally announced to her that he was going to be a poet. She only had time to express her delighted support when he immediately took it back, saying incredulously, 'A collier's son a poet!'[98]

The warmth of response that Lawrence had from Ford changed all that. By late November, he had given Ford his novel (the one with every fault the English novel could have) to read and appraise. On 15 December Ford wrote to Lawrence that he should approach a publisher with the novel, telling him, both encouragingly and shrewdly, 'I certainly think you have in you the makings of a very considerable novelist, and I should not have the least hesitation in prophesying for you a great future, did I not know how much a matter of sheer luck one's career is.'[99] Lawrence sent off a copy of the letter that very day to Heinemann, the firm Ford had recommended. Lawrence never forgot Ford's support at that time, though John Worthen suggests that Ford, who was thrilled to have discovered a writer of genuinely working-class origins, had been rather disappointed that the examples of Lawrence's writing he first met portrayed so little of his origins. The poems in the *English Review* were based on his life in Croydon; there were references to his teaching and his landlord's baby, so at least Ford could feel that he was dealing with modern life, but nothing overtly tied him down to the working class. His first novel, 'Nethermere', as the draft of *The White Peacock* was then called, did not deal in any way with his mining-village background, and although the stance of the narrator/observer Cyril is to some extent autobiographical, he is given no occupation or class position. It was Ford, it appears, who encouraged Lawrence to write about the world in which he had grown up. In doing so, he could be accused of trying to make Lawrence fit his own stereotypes, but whatever caveats one might have about the reasons for Ford's advice, it was good for Lawrence's writing. By the time of Jessie's visit to Croydon, Lawrence had already written the short story 'Odour of Chrysanthemums' and the play, *A Collier's Friday Night*, two powerful pieces that drew directly on his own family life. Significantly, when Ford recounted the story of his discovery of Lawrence, he claimed that 'Odour of Chrysanthemums' was the first thing he read: it was clearly what he wanted to remember. And Ford was not alone. When Ernest Rhys described a visit by Lawrence to one of his poetry evenings – an account whose accuracy is questionable on a number of grounds – he recalls Lawrence reading a large number of dialect poems, though at that date Lawrence had only written one, and published none. Lawrence also recalls Edward Garnett, to whom Ford introduced him in 1911, and who did much to place his work, encouraging his writing of dialect poems. This was the working-class author they wanted. All Lawrence's major works were to be autobiographical to a greater or lesser extent, and if Ford were responsible for casting him back on an examination of his own experience of the world, he owed him thanks. On the other hand, his life was not to remain within the purlieus of Eastwood and he was to range widely in life and art. Few now would insist his dialect poems are his best.

Pound, Philadelphian bourgeois, and Lawrence, collier's son, came from very different worlds, but although their backgrounds and style were in stark contrast, it was their likenesses that drove them apart as much as their differences. They were both sensitive but tactless, insecure but at the same time certain they were right. Both were driven, ardent, passionate in their beliefs, and would develop into angry prophets as much as artists. Whilst their missions were very different, their crusading zeal was surely not unconnected with the fact they both grew up immersed in Nonconformist Christianity. Both of them had striking looks, with flaming red hair: in any group of which either formed part, they would be the centre of energy, the magnetic force. No wonder they soon stopped inhabiting the same groups: like poles repel.

What they also had in common was the experience of finding themselves fêted in London literary circles, when for much of their previous lives they had felt looked down on and rebuffed. Lawrence had been mocked by the other boys at his elementary school, being too delicate and sickly to play games; in addition, his mother, it was felt, had taught the family to think themselves better than their neighbours, and that did not go down well. When Lawrence went to Nottingham High School as a scholarship boy, an exceptional achievement for a miner's son (only three attended the school in the eighteen years from 1882 to 1899), he was a working-class outsider. He passed the entrance examination to college to study for a teaching certificate, but although he made some friends there, including Louie Burrows, he was bitterly disappointed by the lecturers, who were much less intellectually questioning than he was; he felt alienated once more. Coming to Croydon to teach was a bold move for a Midlander. He came, not because he wanted to move south, but because his pride would not let him teach for less than the £90 a year that his father had earned when he started at the pit, as he would have done at a Nottinghamshire school. Davidson Road School was much rougher than anything he had been used to, and teaching was a struggle, not the pleasure it had largely been at home. His first months there had been full of intense loneliness and despair, though by late 1909 he had made some friends, mainly, as so often with Lawrence, women, but without any clear view of his future; teaching these slovenly, dispirited proletarian children, writing constantly in his free time, he was lost and uncertain. Suddenly to become the darling of London literary circles was briefly immensely pleasurable. Lawrence, however, became disillusioned more rapidly than Pound was to do. He was irritated by the way Pound threw himself into playing the extravagant poetic role that his audience so much appreciated, and was much shrewder than Pound in realising how much of his welcome was a fashionable fad that might not last, though no less bitter than Pound would be when he was rejected once more.

Both Pound and Lawrence had devoured books in their youth, but what they read had been very different. Pound's knowledge of languages, particularly classical and medieval languages, outstripped Lawrence's – not that Pound's knowledge was as good as he thought, and he caused many raised eyebrows in London circles with his confident claims, so often let down by errors – or conscious and often creative liberties – in translation. 'Those were the days,' Wyndham Lewis later pointed out, 'when a man going on a long train journey would be apt to slip in his pocket a copy of the Iliad in the Greek text: and there was after all Lionel Johnson's definition of a gentleman – a man who knows Greek and Latin.'[100] But if Pound's Latin and Greek were suspect, Lawrence's were non-existent. Lawrence had been unable to take a degree as he had not studied Latin, having to content himself with a two-year teacher's certificate. He had, however, learnt modern French and German at school, and did well at them. Yet as far as anything later than medieval or early Renaissance literature was concerned, Pound's reading up till 1909 seems to have largely centered on English poetry, or writings about poetry, Wilde, Pater and the handful of mystical texts that he had met through Kitty Heyman. He had officially taken a course on the nineteenth-century novel at the University of Pennsylvania, but it appears to have been one of those for which he did very little work. He had, of course, been introduced to Ibsen and Shaw, though once they were no longer useful as weapons against his professors, his interest in them waned. Lawrence's nineteenth- and early twentieth-century reading, as well as his knowledge of the philosophical concerns of the day, was much wider.

Significantly enough, however, much of Lawrence's important intellectual growth and literary knowledge, like Pound's, had been gained outside his educational establishments. Lawrence's equivalent to Pound's visit to Upper Darby with 'literally armfuls of books' had been his visits to Jessie Chambers' home at Haggs Farm, about three miles across the fields from Eastwood. Jessie was two years younger than Lawrence, in rebellion against domesticity and passionate about reading. Haggs Farm was in Lawrence's memory an idyllic spot, frequently depicted in his later fiction, a haven where his passionate love of the natural world could be satisfied as well as his intellectual hunger. Even the father, Edmund, who did a milk round as well as work on the farm, cared for literature. Jessie remembered that as a little girl she had heard him reading *Tess of the d'Urbervilles* (daringly serialised in the *Nottingham Guardian*) to her mother. All the children – there were seven of them – grew up loving books. The family adored Lawrence, who was with them the life and soul of every occasion, very unlike the inhibited scholarship boy he was at Nottingham High School, where he was still a pupil when he first met the Chambers family. By the time his friendship with Jessie really began to flourish, they had both become pupil-teachers. Jessie's family were unable to give her the chance that Lawrence had of going to college, but both of them probably learnt more together than Lawrence did from his teachers there. In the years between 1901 and 1908, when he moved to Croydon, his happiest hours were spent at Haggs Farm. Jessie and he would borrow books together from the Mechanics' Institute library in Eastwood, and carry them back to the farm. They read the nineteenth-century novelists, Scott, Fenimore Cooper, Charlotte Brontë, George Eliot (a particular favourite with Lawrence), Thackeray, Charles Reade and Stevenson, poets like Blake and Swinburne, daring European writers such as Maupassant, Ibsen, Tolstoy, Verlaine (Violet Hunt said Lawrence knew more decadent poetry than she did), the disreputable Whitman, as well as the sages and prophets, Emerson, Thoreau, Ruskin and Carlyle, whose denunciations of Victorian capitalism and belief in great men made a lasting impression on Lawrence. During his years at college, Lawrence discussed with Jessie the philosophers and scientific thinkers that he learnt of there, Schopenhauer, Darwin, Haeckel and William James. Like H.D., Jessie found meeting this cornucopia of books an experience of heady excitement and imaginative expansion, an entry into a more spacious universe. 'To say we *read* the books gives no adequate idea of what really happened,' she wrote later. 'It was the entering into possession of a new world, a widening and enlargement of life.'[101]

Jessie's mother, like Lawrence's, regularly attended the Congregational chapel; indeed that was how the families knew each other, but her religious scruples rarely led to any censorship of their reading. The Congregationalists put great emphasis on self-improvement and education, and she was happy to encourage their explorations. The Congregational Chapel in Eastwood ran its own Literary Society, and the Sunday evening sermons were more like lengthy lectures, followed by discussion. While entirely orthodox, they promoted a habit of intellectual curiosity and rigour that could lead the young to very different conclusions from those of the minister; it has always been the bane of Nonconformity that it breeds yet further nonconformity in its children. Ford has a wonderful, fantastical account in *Return to Yesterday* of a visit to Nottingham to see Lawrence and his friends, a visit that almost certainly never took place, and definitely not like this:

I have never anywhere found so educated a society. Those young people *knew* the things that my generation in the great English schools hardly even chattered about. Lawrence, the father, came in from the mine of a Saturday evening. He threw a great number of coins on the kitchen table and counted them out to his visiting mates. All the while the young people were talking about Nietzsche and Wagner and Leopardi and Flaubert and Karl Marx and Darwin and occasionally the father would stop his counting to contradict them. And they would discuss the French Impressionists and the primitive Italians and play Chopin or Debussy on the piano. I went with them on the Sunday to a Nonconformist place of worship . . . The sermon renewed my astonishment. It was almost entirely about – Nietzsche, Wagner, Leopardi, Flaubert, Karl Marx, Darwin, the French Impressionists and the primitive Italians. I asked one of Lawrence's friends if that was not an unusual sort of sermon. He looked at me with a sort of grim incredulity.

'What do you suppose?' he said. 'Do you think we would sit under that fellow if he could not preach like that for fifty-two Sundays a year. He would lose his job.'[102]

Eastwood Congregational sermons might tackle heavy subjects like 'Religion and Science', but they were not like this. Yet, as John Worthen says, 'even allowing for [Ford's] exaggeration and invention, the account is not simply ridiculous'.[103] By the time Ford met Lawrence, Lawrence was certainly acquainted with this cultural world, and although some of the figures mentioned here – Nietzsche and Wagner, for example – he only discovered when he reached Croydon, that he led an intellectually rich life in Nottingham was absolutely true. Ford is simply dramatising the amazement he felt at Lawrence's account of his home culture, and the depth of his early engagement with ideas and the arts. Ford constructs himself as the southern English gentleman, astonished to discover this thriving northern intellectual milieu, which had a vitality and urgency that cultural life often lacked among his more genteel companions in the south. For the young intellectuals around Nottingham 'advanced thinking', as it was called, was their life-blood. It gave them weapons with which to fight the sense of inferiority to Ford's class that their official education strove to inculcate in them.

Yet something that Pound shared with Lawrence was the experience of growing up labelled effeminate, almost inevitable then for slightly built, bookish boys. In fact, one of the factors in common between Lawrence and Pound was that, while an English middle- or upper-class boy might just get away with an interest in the arts or poetry without being branded girlish (many of course did not), that was impossible in the English working class or in any class in the United States. Both grew up identifying more with their socially superior and cultured mothers than with their fathers, though that early identification with the mother was to become increasingly problematic, both personally and artistically. Both had in different ways to battle for personal emotional independence, developing ideas of masculine superiority that they would defend with hysterical vehemence. Pound had of course already begun his self-reinvention in the series of dashing devil-may-care male personae in his poetry. Lawrence was not to make the break from his mother's influence until her death in 1911 and his meeting with Frieda in 1912. Not that the masculinity either of them espoused was an entirely conventional one. Lawrence, who had happily helped with cooking as a boy, continued to do so, and had none of the traditional miner's insistence that he be waited on by the women in his life. Douglas Goldring remarked after the First World War on what an agreeable visitor Lawrence was to a servantless household, as he would always help set the table and wash up. There are no reports of Pound's feats in the kitchen as a boy, but certainly in London he would cook for friends, and do so rather well. Neither Frieda Lawrence nor Dorothy Shakespear was willing to cook, so perhaps Lawrence and Pound's culinary skills were a fortunate accomplishment.

Pound does not appear to have been particularly struck by Lawrence's poems when they were first published, though Grace Crawford maintained that Lawrence and Pound when she knew them 'liked and respected each other's work'. The three poems that Ford had accepted for the *English Review* are uneven, but there are fresh, directly observed lines which do hint at a new kind of voice in English poetry. By January

1910, *The White Peacock*, Lawrence's first novel, recommended by Ford to Heinemann's, had been accepted for publication, and would be published in early 1911. Lawrence was launched. The *Observer* had noted of Pound the previous December that 'few poets have so quickly become known to literary London', but Lawrence's acceptance was perhaps equally rapid.[104]

Lawrence appears to have unwittingly precipitated the end of Grace Crawford's friendship with Pound. Pound had told Grace that Lawrence would dislike her because of her privileged background, but perhaps he really feared that she would like Lawrence too much. It was not that Grace and Lawrence ever developed anything similar to the easygoing close friendship that she and Pound had. They always remained Miss Crawford and Mr Lawrence, but they very much took to each other, and Pound felt cut out. When Lawrence asked Grace to give him some Italian lessons, Pound turned up at the first one, trying to interrupt and distract Grace's attention, behaving like a child angry at his displacement by a sibling rival. Grace soon decided it was better to see them on separate occasions. Pound and Lawrence's friendship was, she thought, an 'odd and uneasy' one. 'Ezra,' she noted, 'was sometimes inclined to be patronising to Lawrence but this was always a failure for Lawrence would seem quite unaware until the moment came when he would insert a neat and unexpected barb into Ezra's ego.' Pound continued to resent the interest Grace took in Lawrence, and became increasingly obstreperous and badly behaved. When Grace's father, who 'where young men were concerned . . . was inclined to be more conventional than Mama', returned from America in December, Grace alleges that Pound took 'a wounding delight in trying to bait and annoy Papa out of sheer wanton mischievousness'. Grace's father at first put up with Pound's 'deliberate flamboyance of manner and apparel' and 'provocative flippancy of . . . conversation', but when Pound appeared with the addition of his turquoise ear-ring, her father was incandescent, telling her later that she really ought to see Pound less and that 'if the ear-ring was to be a permanent feature of his dress I had better drop him entirely. I was angry with Ezra but did my best to soothe Papa; but on the whole [Pound's] departure for America came as a relief.'[105] Grace does not suggest Pound's behaviour was due to jealousy of Lawrence; indeed, his constant, noisy needling of Mr Crawford and hence of Grace does not suggest adult sexual jealousy so much as once more the naughtiness of a petted child no longer the centre of his mother's attention, but perhaps there is always something of that in adult jealousy. Phyllis

Bottome, who met Pound a couple of years later, commented that 'Ezra had, as a human being, all the failings of a beloved, an only, and a spoilt child.'[106]

Pound did not of course assume the ear-ring solely to annoy Mr Crawford. He wished to provoke generally, and succeeded. He had written to Dorothy on 8 January that 'Mrs Fowler is in an azure rage on the subject of azure ear-rings'.[107] Eva Fowler was the American hostess at whose house he had first met Olivia Shakespear, and it may be significant that the two people recorded as being outraged rather than amused by the ear-ring were both Americans. The English could tolerate such eccentricities in an outsider; to the Americans he was unforgivably one of their own. Though Mr Crawford was in many ways indulgent to his daughter's artistic leanings, he was not ready to go so far as to let her marry an unsuitable artist. A little later he was to put a damper on Grace's friendship with Lawrence, whom he liked much better than Pound but still did not wish to have as a son-in-law. Lawrence's clothes also gave the wrong signals, though for very different reasons. When Grace first met Lawrence, the first thing she noticed was his 'heavy, clumpy boots'; his inability to afford better at that time caused Lawrence agonies of self-consciousness, and he knew they marked him as of an inferior class.[108] Grace did, a little later, marry an artist who passed muster, Lovat Fraser, a stage designer and an Englishman of the right background, with whom she was very happy, she says, until his tragic early death. Her last contact with Lawrence was in late 1911.

VI

AT some time during this London visit, probably in 1909, Pound was introduced to Percy Wyndham Lewis, the third of Ford's most famous discoveries among '*les jeunes*' at the *English Review* and later Pound's fellow-Vorticist.[109] Wyndham Lewis was both an artist and a writer, whose first short story 'The Pole' had appeared along with Pound's 'Sestina Altaforte' in the *English Review* of June 1909. Ford offered more than one highly coloured account of his own first meeting with Lewis and his work. Douglas Goldring gives a version of the event that he claims Ford gave him the very night the meeting had taken place: Wyndham Lewis, 'tall, swarthy and with romantically disordered hair, wearing a long black coat buttoned up to his chin', fought his way through the fishmonger's up to the *English Review* office; finding it empty, he went up to the next floor. Through the open bathroom door, he could see 'reclining on his back in the bath, in two feet of hot water, with a large sponge in one hand and a cake of soap in the other . . . the missing editor'. Lewis, 'announcing in the most matter-of-fact way that he was a man of genius', asked if he could read the manuscript that he had brought with him. '"Go ahead", Ford murmured, continuing to use his sponge.' When Lewis had finished, 'Ford observed "Well, that's all right. If you'll leave it behind, we'll certainly print it"'. 'If it didn't happen,' Goldring concludes, 'it should have done.'[110]

Ford, at a later date, gave another version of this encounter, in which there is no bath and the meeting takes place in the office itself. In this scenario, he takes Lewis to be a Russian exile, selling documents about the Tsar or the secret police. Given Ford's connections with the Garnetts and 'Dostoevsky Corner', this was not as far fetched a thought as it might appear. In retrospect, however, Ford's recollections may have been coloured by the fact that Lewis developed a reputation for being a very

Russian, 'Dostoevskian' writer. Lewis, according to Ford, certainly acted the part of a mysterious foreigner: 'Slowly and with an air of doom the stranger began to draw out manuscripts from his coat-pockets, from his trouser-pockets, from his breast-pockets, from the lining of his conspirator's hat . . . I have never known anyone else whose silence was a positive rather than a negative quality'.[111] At the time, as it happens, he referred to Lewis in a letter to his wife as 'the new Polish genius', which suggests he took him then to be something Eastern European; ironically, one of the points of Lewis' piece 'The Pole' is that all expatriate Eastern Europeans and Russians were assumed to be Poles.[112] Lewis was very dark, handsome in a slightly sinister way, and certainly did not look English, and he had clearly impressed himself on Ford as an exotic outsider. Lewis himself recounts a more mundane story – he found the office empty, and just left his manuscript behind. When he returned a few weeks later to find out what Ford thought, he was delighted to find his story in proof. He had failed to leave an address, so Ford had been unable to contact him. Lewis' version may be more accurate, but Ford's fantastical embroideries, as so often, capture much of the man's personality – his egoism, his paranoia, his brilliance, his disturbing, imperious, unsettling presence.

Ford's publication of 'The Pole' was Lewis' first appearance in print, but he was already becoming the quintessential modernist cosmopolitan. He once wrote that 'At around the age of 6 I arrived in England, a small American, and left it for France about 11 years later a young Englishman. I returned to England a European.'[113] Lewis was born in 1882 (a great year for infant modernists – Joyce and Virginia Woolf were also born then). His parents (American father, English mother) had separated when he was ten, his father, always a womaniser, causing scandal in the family by running away with his sister's housemaid. Lewis and his mother were left with little to live on. Somehow the money was found to send him to Rugby, though being a poor boy at a major public school was not an enviable position. Lewis learnt little there and was beaten a good deal, something he would recount in later life with sado-masochistic relish; these beatings played no small part, one might guess, in his lifelong conviction of (and perhaps desire for) persecution.

While at Rugby he spent most of his time painting – not part of the curriculum – but one master spotted his talent and suggested that he went on in 1898 to the Slade, an art school seeming more appropriate than university. Lewis claimed later that he was bored by the academic conventions taught at the Slade. He was sent off to the Print Room at the

British Museum to copy Michelangelo and Raphael drawings, but says he was much more interested in the Easter Island and African carvings that he passed on the way there. At that period the so-called 'ethnographic' galleries had not yet been hived off to a separate venue at the Museum of Mankind, from which they have only recently been recalled. The scramble for Africa had greatly increased the Museum holdings of African art, as it was beginning to be controversially described; if Swinburne had been uneasy about equating the value of Japanese and European artistic work, it was nothing to the anxiety caused by the linking of art and Africa. Lewis himself must have missed the great exhibition of Benin bronzes and ivories in September 1897 that followed the sacking of Benin City, but some of these remained at the Museum. Interest in their striking workmanship remained high, in spite of the fact that the Benin themselves were described in the press as bloodthirsty savages. The paradox was solved at the time by the supposition either that these works had been influenced by European art, or that the present-day Benin were the degenerate descendants of superior ancestors. If Lewis was really attracted by such works in his days at the Slade, it was earlier than Picasso by eight or nine years; whether he was rewriting the past or not, these non-European works would later suggest a new direction for his art. And even if Lewis felt such scorn for the Slade's teaching and values, he did very well at the kind of drawing they demanded. He was given a scholarship for two years, though he only remained for one, becoming a legend at the Slade both for the skill of his draughtsmanship and for clashes with authority.

Lewis was dismissed from the Slade in 1901, in the event for smoking in the building, though, as with Hulme's expulsion from Cambridge, that appears very much to have been the final straw. His father offered to support him while he took a university degree in America, but Lewis had no intention of giving up the artistic life, though he was hesitating between writing and painting. He remained in London for a couple of years, meeting Yeats' friend Sturge Moore, and the painter Augustus John, whom he had seen in the distance as a celebrity former scholar at the Slade. In 1903 he headed for Europe, where he spent much of the next four years leading an impecunious bohemian existence, made possible by regular handouts from his mother and spasmodic ones from his father, plus what loans he could cadge from those he met. He spent a good deal of time in Paris, in various garrets in Montparnasse, and visited Munich, Haarlem, and Spain, where he went first, spending several months of the late summer and autumn of 1903 in Madrid with Spencer Gore, a former fellow student at the Slade, four years older than Lewis. They had come to copy the Old Spanish Masters, and though in the end they did little painting, the work of Velázquez and especially Goya, out of fashion in England then, had a profound impact on Lewis. Those two painters' bitter vision of the savage workings of power was to be a potent influence. In Paris, he saw a good deal of Augustus John, like Gore four years his elder, someone he regarded with deeply ambivalent admiration and with whom he had a stormy friendship. He imitated John's imposing broad-brimmed black hat (there are few extant photographs of Lewis without it), his cultivation of the figure of artist-genius and his womanising, but not his style of painting.

Lewis was more attracted by the avant-garde. He was in Paris during the time of the Fauves and the early years of Cubism. He was in Munich in the early days of German Expressionism. In Paris he heard Bergson lecture; he read, like so many artists and writers in Paris, Nietzsche and Dostoevsky. He visited Brittany, still as much of a cult with artists as it had been when Gauguin was there in the late 1880s. Brittany, to the artists' colony there, was not just a remote and unspoilt home to simple and picturesque peasants, but in Gauguin's words, a 'savage, primitive' other world, a geographical and spiritual escape from modernity. Gauguin had written that 'When my clogs echo on this granite earth, I hear the dull, muffled, powerful note that I am seeking in my paintings'.[114] Lewis was to look for granite-like power in his paintings too, ultimately in a much harsher note than Gauguin's; he admired the violence of the Breton fishermen, who 'brawled about money over their fiery apple-juice', as well as the stoical courage with which they set off to Iceland in their tiny boats 'much at home in the huge and heaving Atlantic'.[115] Lewis had written poetry in his Slade days, but in Brittany he began to write short stories. Although, as Paul Edwards suggests, he had probably been attracted by Gauguinesque Romantic primitivism, the stories suggest that he quickly developed a more cynical view of the Bretons than Gauguin's. These allegedly 'savage, primitive' peasants, it has been pointed out, were already taking shrewd advantage of the tourist trade that their perceived pre-modern simplicity was attracting, and Lewis' stories – half-way between travelogue and fiction, between racist stereo-type and satire on racism – register this social fact. The Bretons in his stories are greedy, narrow and deeply limited innkeepers and hoteliers, though they make good money, on occasion, by selling the left-behind sketches of their artist clients; there is no touch of savage grandeur in sight. The pieces are written with great panache, and remain highly entertaining if politically questionable, full of inbred scorn for foreigners and the lower classes. Lewis would continue to exoticise the qualities of savagery and aggression, but he was a generation too late to find an unproblematic primitive in the Breton. Gauguin himself, after all, had moved on to Tahiti some fifteen years earlier. Yet Edwards argues this was a crucial period for Lewis, when he was developing a form of modernism that owed much to but radically transformed this Romantic cult of the savage other; in the 1920s he would rework his writings about the Bretons in a book significantly entitled *The Wild Body*.[116]

Lewis had returned for short periods to England during this period, but in late 1908 he settled back in London. He might have wondered how good a move that would be for his art, as London was artistically still well behind Paris. Augustus John, back in London earlier in the year, had been shocked to discover that '"Impressionism" [was] still lectured on as the new gospel by certain persons of importance'.[117] Lewis, however, met more innovative figures such as Roger Fry, and knew the sculptor Jacob Epstein, with both of whom he would later work for a while. Lewis may have returned to escape from the demands of his German mistress, Ida, whom – as Tarr finds with Bertha in the novel that Lewis was to write about these Parisian experiences – he could neither love nor leave. She was heavily pregnant, probably though not necessarily with his child, and the urge to escape paternal responsibilities might finally have given him the resolution to make the break. His life, as his biographers point out, was beginning to follow the pattern of his father's irresponsible womanising. He was eventually to abandon several more children and many more women. Lewis was devoted to his mother, but her miserable experience of desertion did not deter him from becoming a multiple deserter. He treated women badly, and despised them for allowing it; at some unconscious level perhaps he despised his mother for her misfortunes. His mother had, ironically, advised him to leave Ida and her child. So did his London mentor, Thomas Sturge Moore, whom he had met on a visit back in 1902, and who took a keen interest in his career.

Sturge Moore was, like Lewis, both a writer and an artist, in his case poet and illustrator; a brother of the philosopher G.E. Moore, he was thought of by all as a gentle, sensitive man, yet he wrote to Lewis saying that Ida was the kind of woman who used the 'slop of sex' to catch a man. With such a woman, he assured him, 'if [a man] puts his genius between her legs she will cover it with any petticoat that takes her fancy, and no one will see it again'.[118] So much for Edwardian gallantry. The 'slop of sex' is a phrase that recurs in *Tarr*, where it represents all that the artist must avoid; not sexual activity as such, but emotional involvement.

'In this department of my life,' Tarr insists, '*I have not a vestige of passion.*' Like Hulme, Lewis distrusted emotional ties; for him, the artist had better things to be passionate about than a sexual partner. 'With most people,' Tarr claims, 'not describable as artists, all the finer part of their vitality goes into sex. They become third-rate poets during their courtship . . . The artist is he in whom this emotionality normally absorbed by sex is so strong that it claims a newer and more exclusive field of deployment. Its first creation is *the Artist* himself, a new sort of person; the creative man.' Tarr is not wholly successful in his efforts to separate the realms of Art and Life, but womanly feelings certainly disgust him: 'Women's stormy weakness, psychic discharges, always affected him like the sight of a person being sea-sick.'[119] Such a reaction suggests fear and revulsion as much as callousness, possibly true of Lewis himself, even though he regularly responded with an apparent stony indifference to the unhappiness of women in his life; he was, like Hulme, in David Trotter's phrase that I quoted earlier, 'anti-pathos'. He wanted to construct a hyper-masculinity for the artist which attempts to eschew personal feelings. All the artist's libido is directed towards his art.

It was probably Sturge Moore who had headed Lewis in Ford's direction. Pound and Lewis' first meeting was at the Vienna Café, five minutes from the British Museum near Bloomsbury Square, which was, according to Lewis, apart from the Café Royal, 'the only continental café' in London.[120] It occupied the 'wedge formed by Hart Street and Holborn', and its first-floor room was triangular with a wonderful 'ceiling of glass, which reflected all your actions as if in a lake suspended above your head, surface downwards'.[121] Pound spent a considerable amount of time in the Vienna Café over the years, and was deeply disgusted when during the First World War it was closed down, and eventually became a bank. On this occasion, however, Pound was with Binyon, a steady *habitué* of the Vienna, and Lewis with Sturge Moore. Pound gave his own myth-making version of the meeting in the *Cantos*:

> So it is to Mr Binyon that I owe, initially,
> Mr Lewis, Mr P. Wyndham Lewis. His bull-dog, me,
>   as it were against old Sturge M's bull-dog, Mr T. Sturge Moore's
>   bull-dog.[122]

Oh boastful Pound! In those days he perhaps could be compared to a noisy fox terrier, but he was certainly no bulldog. The two of them had nothing to say to each other at the time. They both, as Douglas Goldring put it, made 'no secret of their calling', playing the part of the bohemian artist to the full.[123] But their life experiences had been extraordinarily different. As Lewis said of himself, he was now a European; Pound was still in many ways an American provincial. Lewis was sexually experienced – in fact he had already had his first bout of venereal disease. Pound was very possibly still a virgin. While they were both short of money, even in Italy Pound had mixed mainly with the many well-to-do American expatriates; in London he was circulating through polite drawing-rooms. Lewis' time in Parisian poverty, though admittedly also mainly with expatriates, including Augustus John's irregular and explosive household, was another world. Pound could only rely on, in Goldring's phrase, his 'transatlantic *brio*', whilst Lewis, as he said of himself, had 'the tarnished polish of the English Public School, of the most gilded cafés of five or six continental cities'.[124] Pound was obsessed with the Middle Ages. Lewis was aware and already part of the beginnings of the modernist revolution. It is perhaps significant that in his wanderings through Europe Lewis never went to Italy, the mecca for Victorian and Edwardian English and American tourists. Italy represented a traditional ideal of civilisation he already wanted to repudiate. When they first met, Lewis claims, he felt no interest in this 'cowboy songster'.[125] He found Pound 'an uncomfortably tensed, nervously straining, jerky, reddish-brown American . . . The impression he made, socially, was not a good one. He was a drop of oil in a glass of water. The trouble was, I believe, that he had no wish to *mix*: he just wanted to *impress*.'[126] Lewis, of course, wanted to impress too, and neither of them had any interest in being impressed by the other. Their friendship and collaboration was still in the future.

VII

THE writer with whom Pound became most friendly during the autumn of 1909 was, in fact, a member neither of the Tour Eiffel group, nor of the Ford/Hunt circle. He was Frederic Manning, whom he had met back in January at Olivia Shakespear's, and who, like himself, was still very much under the spell of the aesthetic tradition: Pound clearly felt more in tune with Manning's backward gaze than with critics of the Edwardian status quo like Hulme, Flint, Lewis and Ford. Eliot would say of Manning, after his death, that he 'had a style of writing, and a frame of mind, suited to a more cultured and better educated age than our own', and his erudite elegance much appealed to Pound.[127] By the time Pound left London in March 1910, he told his parents that he and Manning were in agreement that they two were the only significant writers under thirty. Many years later Pound was to write that his relationship with Manning was 'the first licherary ComPanionship in Eng/of Ez'.[128]

Like Manning, Pound was now securely part of the Shakespear circle, and they saw each other frequently there. In October 1909, Manning invited Pound up to Edenham in Lincolnshire to spend a weekend with his guardian, Arthur Galton; although Galton was later to disapprove of Pound greatly, and Pound to scorn Galton for what he saw as his conservatism and stuffiness, all went well on this visit. Manning and Galton, he told his mother with unusual modesty, 'probably know their latin literature much better than I do', and were able to help him with advice for the early part of *The Spirit of Romance*.[129] Manning would never marry, and it has been suggested that he was gay: one biography of Manning is actually entitled *The Last Exquisite*, a phrase coined by T. E. Lawrence, with whom Pound also became friendly, who later commented, 'Manning is a very exquisite person; so queer'.[130] Quite what he meant by that second adjective is uncertain; the modern meaning of queer was then only just coming into use. No one ever described Pound as exquisite, but at this stage he certainly admired Manning's aestheticism, and enjoyed the retreat into the homosocial learned world of Edenham. Pound even copied out one of Manning's poems that he particularly admired in a letter home, a quite unprecedented event, shortly afterwards sending the same poem to Ford to print in the *English Review*, with a note saying 'Manning has . . . written this quite beautiful "Persephone" which I can praise without reservation'.[131] Ford took the poem, which appeared in the December issue, and then printed in January a poem by Pound, accompanied by a note saying it was 'written in reply to Manning's "Korè"' (another name for Persephone).[132] Manning's poem describes Persephone passing sadly through a beautiful, melancholy autumn countryside on her way to the underworld; it has a certain charm, very much in the nineties tradition, but what is most striking about it is that Manning describes Persephone as the 'yearly slain', a phrase Pound seized on for the title of his reply, 'Canzon; the Yearly Slain'. Such a phrase strongly suggests that Manning must have been thinking of *The Golden Bough*, in which Sir James Frazer associates Persephone with the fertility rituals and myths that centred on the figure of the dying god, 'who', in Frazer's words, 'dies in winter to revive in spring'.[133] In 1909 only one volume (and it was to be revised) of the famous 12-volume third edition had been published; Manning had probably come across the second edition, which came out in 1900, and which, though not the bestseller that the third edition was to be, had been widely reviewed and read. Manning was deeply sceptical of the Catholicism in which he had been reared, and had no intention of embracing Galton's Anglicanism, but he was widely read in anything to do with theology or philosophy, so it is not surprising that he knew Frazer's ideas.

Pound might have already come across Frazer's name through his reading of Yeats, who had quoted from the first edition of *The Golden Bough*, published in 1890, in the notes to *The Wind among the Reeds*, but Manning probably gave Pound his first real introduction to the work. Pound's later poetry – like so much modernist writing – owed much to a set of ideas derived, albeit transformed, from Frazer. Frazer's work appealed to the widespread fascination with the 'primitive' among artists and intellectuals at the period. If on the continent, Picasso, Matisse, Vlaminck and Kandinsky, among others, were already drawing on African and other kinds of non-Western art, in Britain Assyrian,

Egyptian and African art would be vitally important in modernist visual art of the period just preceding the war, influential, for example, not just for Lewis, but also Jacob Epstein and Gaudier-Brzeska; the Tour Eiffel poets were, of course, already looking to other cultures for fresh poetic forms, but Frazer did more than provide just one more source of exotic material. Frazer led writers such as Pound, and perhaps even more H.D., to a particular engagement with the world of myth that shaped much of their work, giving them new metaphors by which to frame their art, and from which to form a very specifically modernist aesthetics.

That Frazer's work was significant for modernist writers has long been established (as well as Yeats, Pound and H.D., he was also important to Eliot, Lewis and Lawrence), but paradoxically all these modernists read 'Frazer *contra* Frazer', as Warwick Gould has put it.[134] They made of what they found in the capacious pages of *The Golden Bough* something very different from Frazer's own convictions. What Pound believed was 'essential to contemporary clear thinking', as he would later describe Frazer's work, was undoubtedly this creative misreading of his arguments.[135] Frazer himself approached his subject, as his subtitle put it, 'a study of magic and religion', from the viewpoint of a Victorian scientific rationalist. Like other anthropologists in the latter half of the nineteenth century, he was searching for a pattern of cultural evolution that would parallel the Darwinian biological one, using as evidence both investigations into the past and contemporary examples of 'savage' societies, seen as 'survivals' from an earlier stage of human development. Museum-based anthropologists were busy working out this evolutionary story in a material progression that they constructed from 'savage' through 'barbarian' to 'civilised' artefacts. For Frazer what mattered was what he called 'mental anthropology', a history of thought; he was an 'armchair anthropologist', as a younger generation, who placed fieldwork at the centre of the discipline, would scornfully put it: he used evidence from the classics, from histories, from travellers, from missionaries, from folklore, from the Bible, even on occasion from the newspapers. Armed with this plethora of miscellaneous facts, Frazer mapped out the sequence of human mental development as a movement from belief in magic, to religion, to a scientific view of the world. Central to both magic and religion, Frazer asserts, are fertility rituals designed to ensure the continuity of life. In *The Golden Bough* he charts particular motifs, in which the dying god is central, across Greek, Phoenician, Egyptian, Christian, Native American, Roman, Cambodian, Jewish, West African, Zulu and many more sets of myths and rituals. In fact, for all his flowing, golden prose – and Frazer was masterly in his evocations of the beauties or terrors of places to which he had never been – he is proto-modernist himself in his profusion of heterogeneous juxtapositions. The evolutionary narrative vanishes as he excitedly piles up comparisons from round the world and from all ages. When Eliot acknowledged the indebtedness of *The Waste Land* to Frazer, critics have assumed he was drawing attention to his use of Frazerian symbols, but equally, consciously or unconsciously, he uses this Frazerian technique of collage. Eliot's text is fragmentary, fissured and jaggedly abrupt rather than woven together as Frazer's is by his magisterial periods, but juxtaposition of the heterogeneous is the structural principle for them both, as it had earlier been for the imagists. It is not for nothing that *The Waste Land* has been described as a long imagist poem.

The subtext – not always so concealed – of this project was Frazer's critique of Christianity. He wrote to his publisher before he brought out the first edition: 'The resemblance of the savage customs and ideas to the fundamental doctrines of Christianity is striking. But I make no reference to this parallelism, leaving my readers to draw their conclusions, one way or another.'[136] Frazer, however, does a fine line in irony, and any alert reader would see exactly what he was getting at. When his wife Lilly constructed the 1922 abridgment of *The Golden Bough*, which she did as a scissor and paste exercise, she literally cut out any controversial references to Christianity. These she felt, no doubt correctly, were not good for her husband's career, but she thereby deprived his work of much of its edge. In Frazer's original account, Christianity becomes just one of many mythic systems, but if to him that suggested the dubiousness of Christianity, to the modernists it proved the importance of the non-Christian myths. If to Frazer these myths, Christian and non-Christian alike, were based on pre-scientific and mistaken beliefs about the nature of fertility that the sound study of natural science rendered redundant, to them they embodied truths about the nature of existence, truths which had become lost by and large to modern civilisation, and which remained obscured in modern Christianity. Something similar was of course already being argued by the theosophists, who believed there was a deeper, older alternative truth about existence lost to modern rationalism, which could be discovered particularly in Eastern religion and philosophy. Some theosophists and occultists, such as Yeats himself, immediately recognised the relationship. According to Warwick Gould, the occult society in which Yeats was deeply involved, the Order of the Golden Dawn, increasingly absorbed and adapted Frazerian motifs.

Like many of their generation of artists and intellectuals, Pound, H.D., Hulme and Lawrence no longer accepted the rational, determined world of Victorian science, which came to them inseparably entwined with the belief in progress and the superiority of the modern world. The developmental metaphor that had been behind and structured so much nineteenth-century thought had ceased to make sense to them. Even Frazer himself, for all his claimed adherence to a progressive trajectory, shows considerable anxiety about the future of civilised society. Civilisation depended, he believed, on a small elite. It is, he lamented, 'the dull, the weak, the ignorant, and the superstitious, who constitute, unfortunately, the vast majority of mankind'. There exists 'a solid layer of savagery beneath the surface of society . . . unaffected by the superficial changes of religion and culture', something that can only be considered as 'a standing menace to civilisation. We seem to move,' he writes,

on a thin crust which may at any moment be rent by the subterranean forces slumbering below . . . Now and then the polite world is startled by a paragraph in a newspaper that tells how in Scotland an image has been found stuck full of pins for the purpose of killing an obnoxious laird or minister, how a woman has been slowly roasted to death as a witch in Ireland, or how a girl has been murdered and chopped up in Russia to make those candles of human tallow by whose light thieves hope to pursue their midnight trade unseen.[37]

Whether progress would continue or be undermined by this underlying savagery, he is unsure.

Though many of the modernists were quite as elitist in their way as Frazer, his view of the peasantry is a very different one from, for example, that of Yeats or Campbell, who went to the Irish peasants to learn what the modern world could no longer tell them, or from E. M. Forster's, whose fiction at that very period depicted Italian peasants as full of the vitality and passion drained from contemporary society. (Their romanticised view is not of course necessarily any more to be relied upon than Frazer's apprehensive disgust, though it was not primarily the peasantry who caused the volcanic eruption of carnage that was shortly to come.) That there was a 'solid layer of savagery beneath the surface' was accepted but not necessarily seen as alarming by the modernists, though for many of them modern civilisation was as fragile a crust as it was for Frazer. Yet Frazer's fear of degeneration was widespread in the 1890s and the early twentieth century. What can progress can also decline. The linear metaphor itself had become a trap. Paradoxically, what the modernist writers took from Frazer, in spite of his intentions, was a way of escaping that linearity, through what Eliot, in an essay on *Ulysses*, was to call the 'mythical method'.[138] The old myths could be read as maps of experience, which could explain the present in as illuminationg terms as they had originally explained the past. Repetition not development was the key. Joyce could use the mythic adventures of Ulysses to model a day in the life of Leopold Bloom. Eliot could use Greek myths, *The Tempest*, medieval quest literature, tarot cards, the Christ story and much more, all to give the same message of sterility and of diseased, violent sexuality in *The Waste Land*. H.D. could argue that Greek and Egyptian myth, Native American beliefs, Moravian religion, psychoanalytic theory all reveal a universal key which could unlock the mysteries of the psyche and explain the vicissitudes of twentieth-century history. Pound could bring together his early poets, the Eleusinian mysteries, the Homeric stories, his own version of Christianity, medieval theology, and Confucian wisdom in his voyage through the *Cantos*.

In short, Frazer – duly reinvented – helped Pound's generation of writers to find an alternative to the narrative of Western progress, or indeed, decline; 'the mythical method' changed the relationship between past and present. In addition, for these young early twentieth-century writers, what Frazer added to the theosophists' synthesis was his conviction that the central meaning behind these myths is anxiety over fertility, or, in human terms, sexuality. (One of Frazer's more risqué passages is an extended comparison between Catholic celibate nuns and pagan sacred prostitutes; alternative versions of same thing, he argues, both illustrating that sexual practices are at the heart of religion.) Frazer's third edition was to appear at the same time as the first translations of Freud into English were published. Like Freud (of whom, as it happened, Frazer strongly disapproved, although Freud was also a nineteenth-century scientific rationalist), Frazer argues that the truth of the human condition is hidden under a shallow layer of civilised conventions, and that this hidden truth centres on sexuality. That sexual desire is the most important constitutive element in human nature, the deep truth of our being, has been one of the most potent beliefs of the twentieth century, and still has power today, though the horrors of the Second World War were to make aggression or the will to power seem to some more meaningful alternatives, and post-structuralism in its various forms has steadily deconstructed those metaphors of surface and depth on which such beliefs rely. In the early part of the twentieth century, however, the power of the libido was the explosive revelation that exposed the hypocrisies of Victorian society.

Frazer was not equally influential for all these writers; Joyce, for example, although Eliot's prime example of the mythical method, owed more to Vico's theory of the cyclical nature of history than to Frazer, and Eliot himself was to revert to Christianity, though of these writers he was the one who most closely shared Frazer's distaste for the 'solid layer of savagery beneath'. H.D. was certainly influenced, though probably also owed much to the classicist/anthropologist, Jane Harrison ('the great J.H.' much admired by Virginia Woolf, whose ghost flits across the college grass in *A Room of One's Own*). For Pound, Frazer confirmed his earlier fusion of the pagan gods and the troubadours' Religion of Love. In his 'Canzon: the Yearly Slain', the 'Yearly Slain' is no longer Persephone but the God of Love, the figure who is so central for the Provençal and even more so for the early Italian poets, who were to become increasingly important to Pound over the next eighteen months. It is with the *Cantos* that the significance of the mythical method for Pound became most apparent, but Pound's 'Canzon', which makes the troubadours' God of Love a Frazerian dying god, although very different in form from his later work, was an indication of those further fusions to come.

Pound's 'Canzon: the Yearly Slain', in fact, marked a turn in his development, though not only because of the Frazerian influence, and not in the short run for the better. The next two years were to see Pound move away from his earlier persona poems, with their vigour, their directness, their defiance, their evocation of speech. He would concentrate on producing in English the formal complexities first of Provençal poetry and then of Guido Cavalcanti's sonnets. The form of 'The Yearly Slain' was derived from Arnaut Daniel: a seven-line stanza which has no rhyming lines, but each successive stanza has to rhyme line for line with the first, a form which places considerable demands on the ingenuity of the poet, but without offering the auditory rewards that rhyming within a stanza gives; the reader can only appreciate the scheme intellectually. Other *canzoni* use different if equally complex forms, but in them all the language that Pound uses is archaic, the conceits elaborate, and many of the symbols derivative. Individual images can be striking, some passages characteristically musical, but the overall effect is stilted and inert. Was Pound reacting against the whole tenor of the Tour Eiffel discussions, certainly against Hulme's campaign for directness? One might almost hazard a guess that Pound was picking up on something he had found in 'The English Renaissance of Art', where Wilde praises Pre-Raphaelite poetic practice: 'all this love of curious French metres like the Ballade, the Villanelle, the Rondel; all this increased value laid on elaborate allit-erations, and on curious words and refrains, such as you find in Dante Gabriel Rossetti and Swinburne, is merely the attempt to perfect flute and viol and trumpet through which the spirit of the age and the lips of the poet may blow the music of their many messages.'[139] Perhaps having read this, Pound had decided to redouble his efforts to hone his art through a return to the complexities of Provençal and early Italian verse. Manning was writing similarly archaicisng poems, and his influence was no doubt significant. Yet perhaps, like Hulme and Flint and Campbell, even here Pound was trying to renew English poetry by the use of exotic, in this case exotically archaic, forms, as Flint had earlier implied. The Provençal and the other early Italian poets were after all the avant-garde of their day; the latter the *dolce stil nuovo* poets, writing in 'the sweet new style'. Later Pound conceded that his use of the *canzone* form had been something of a mistake. 'I have proved,' he later wrote, 'that the Provençal rhyme schemes are not *impos*sible in English. They are prob-ably *inadvis*able.'[140] He was to admit that no one can ever 'learn English, one can only learn a series of Englishes. Rossetti made his own language. I hadn't in 1910 made a language, I don't mean a language to use, but even a language to think in.'[141] Much of this period of intense anti-quarianism coincided with his period out of England. It was not until after his return that a new phase in his development would begin.

PART V

AMERICAN INTERLUDE

I

DURING the time Pound was in England from 1908 to 1910, he had ignored both British politics and English social problems, though he must have heard them discussed at South Lodge, since one of Ford's good friends was the Liberal MP Charles Masterman, determined, his wife Lucy was to say, to banish 'at any rate the blackest pits of poverty' so prevalent then in Britain. Since Ford and Hunt and many of their friends were staunch supporters of Irish Home Rule and the suffragettes, Pound must have known about those too.[1] Did Flint ever attempt to discuss socialism with him? If he did, Pound appears to have taken no notice. When Jessie Chambers visited London, she was appalled at the homeless poor sleeping under Waterloo Bridge, pointed out to her by Lawrence, but Pound made no comment on anyone's poverty except his own. Just one poem, 'Piccadilly', deals with the urban destitute, and even there Pound says that while he could feel pity for those with 'beautiful, tragical faces', when it comes to 'The gross, the coarse, the brazen,/God knows I cannot pity them, perhaps, as I should do,/But, oh, ye delicate, wistful faces,/Who hath forgotten you?' This is honest enough, but if only the aesthetic needy are to stir compassion, it would be a bleak world.[2]

At this stage Pound's only interest in British politics was in its impact on his literary production. On 5 February 1910, he had written home in some irritation that 'the election has held up everything for a month' and at the beginning of March, even more crossly, 'if they have another be damned "General Election" it will interfere with my next set of reviews. I trust Lloyd George will suffer torments hereafter'.[3] The political scene was a troubled one at the time, causing problems beyond Pound's publishing plans, and many were anxious about the future. When Frazer expressed his fears about the future of civilisation, his sense that 'the ground beneath our feet is . . . honeycombed by unseen forces', he was responding to a widespread sense of menace, from the discontented proletariat, from disruptive women, from the resentful Irish.[4] The elections that Pound mentions were the consequence of a battle between the Commons and the Lords: Lloyd George had been endeavouring since the previous July to pass what became known as the 'People's Budget', which he described to the public as 'a war budget . . . for raising money to wage implacable war against poverty and squalidness'.[5] The Liberals had recently introduced for the first time a National Insurance scheme and wanted to give more help to the unemployed, measures that they believed were vital to alleviate the extremes of poverty in the country, and to calm the discontent that many feared might lead to violence or even revolution. Money was needed to pay for these rudimentary social services, and Lloyd George wanted income tax increases, including a supertax of sixpence ($2\frac{1}{2}$p) in the pound for those with more than £5,000 a year, increases in death duties and in taxes on alcohol and tobacco, and new taxes on the latest toy of the aristocracy, the motor car. Most peers were appalled, and adamant that they would not tolerate such socialist outrages, which they believed were 'the beginning of the end of the rights of property'.[6] Asquith, the Prime Minister, was threatening to create 500 new peers to get the budget passed (he had in mind, among others, Thomas Hardy, J.M. Barrie and Bertrand Russell), but the Lords in the end conceded, and Pound was saved from further electoral disturbance to his reviews.

On Pound's return to England he would gradually become more aware of British politics, but at least in 1910 he was also still free of his later dark obsessions. When Ford was forced to sell the ailing *English Review* at the beginning of 1910 to the financier Alfred Mond, Pound's only comment to his parents was a cheery note to the effect that the new proprietors had said they would still welcome his work. In retrospect, he was to see this takeover as an evil Jewish conspiracy. As it happens, John Gould Fletcher, who had spent the summer of 1909 taking his sister Mary, about to start at Vassar, on a grand European tour, was now back in England, and wondering about purchasing the *English Review* himself. Indecisive as always, he did nothing about it.

Pound was out of England from March 1910 until the end of August 1911 for all but a few days. He had realised for some months that he was not going to make enough money to convince his parents that it was worthwhile for him to stay. He had continued to have regular handouts from Homer; he felt guilty about this, but not guilty enough to take up uncongenial work: 'no literature,' he had told his long-suffering father the previous year, 'is made by people in other professions'.[7] (Williams, for one, would prove him wrong.) But he could not expect the subsidy to continue for ever. He was still – under a certain amount of parental pressure – toying reluctantly with the idea of an academic post, and making desultory enquiries. Had *Exultations* been more of a success he might have felt differently, but in spite of being able to report to his parents that he had been praised in the Parisian *Mercure de France*, he had also to admit that the reviews in London had included some 'violent' attacks. Although Ford and Violet Hunt had found him some well-paid private teaching of affluent society ladies, including Olivia Shakespear's friend, Eva Fowler, his lectures had not picked up. It seemed that returning home was inevitable. All Pound could do was delay the evil hour. It would be much more sensible, he argued, to arrive in the States in June when *The Spirit of Romance* came out, he hoped to glowing reviews, and jobs would therefore be more readily forthcoming. In the meantime, with the book completed, and payment from the *English Review* for three more poems, he had enough to get to Italy, always cheaper than England; he asked his father to send his next remittance there, and to continue with a little more modest support for the next few months. On 22 March he had a final day of London hospitality, lunch with Violet Hunt (he had been out with Ford the day before) and tea with the Shakespears, before taking the night boat train to Paris. There he had arranged to visit a musician, Walter Morse Rummel, later one of the foremost exponents of Debussy's music, and, like Pound, interested in Provençal song settings. They had met briefly in 1908, probably introduced by Kitty Heyman. Rummel, handsome and charming as well as musically gifted, had been born in Berlin of a German father and American mother, and was now settled in Paris. Pound had intended to have breakfast only, but they got on so well he stayed two days. 'He means to music about what I do to poetry,' he commented a little later.[8]

Pound went on to Italy, where he first stayed in Verona, which he had visited during his time in Venice; it was always one of his favourite cities, partly for its associations, as the city to which Dante had fled, and where under the protection of Can Grande della Scala, Lord of Verona, he had written much of *The Divine Comedy*, dedicating the *Paradiso* to Can Grande himself. Pound admired Verona's architecture, particularly the tall, elegant and imposing San Zeno, described by the 1906 Baedeker as 'one of the finest Romanesque churches in North

Italy', with 'most noble proportions'. Pound, who like most Americans of the period took his Baedeker seriously, did not dissent. He pronounced it 'ultimate perfection', and said it had 'the abiding spirit in it as no other church in Europe'.[9] Although there had been a church on the site since the fourth century, the present basilica and campanile date from the twelfth century, Pound's favourite period. In *The Spirit of Romance* he had written, 'The twelfth century, or, more exactly, that century whose centre is the year 1200, has left us two perfect gifts: the church of San Zeno at Verona, and the canzoni of Arnaut Daniel; by which I would imply all that is most excellent in the Italian-Romanesque architecture and in Provençal minstrelsy.'[10]

Pound could find nowhere to stay cheaply in Verona, so he moved on, very much by chance, to nearby Sirmione, 'a village that you could hide under a thimble', as he described it in one letter, on a finger of land that ran out into the lake in a narrow peninsula at the southern end of Lake Garda. It is now a popular day out from the northern Italian cities, and packed on sunny weekends; even then it had half a dozen hotels, which catered mainly in the spring and autumn for German tourists, for many Germans of the period, like Aschenbach in Mann's 1912 *Death in Venice*, had a passionate love for Italy and the romantic south. In the summer, the Italians would come to take sulphur baths, but there were, to Pound's relief, very few Americans. He was able to live at the aptly named Hotel Eden for seven lire a day, even then admirably cheap; his one quarrel was with its writing-paper, on which he would regularly and disapprovingly cross out the address of 'Gardasee' and substitute 'Lago di Garda'. The entrance to the village itself was guarded by a small and picturesque castle built by one of the della Scala family and surmounted by the same swallow-tailed crenellations as the great Castelvecchio built by Dante's patron in Verona itself. The wild headland north of the village was covered with olive trees and ruins, and across the lake could be seen the beginnings of the Alps, with Mount Riva towards the northern end.

Pound spent a couple of rather lazy months in Sirmione, correcting proofs and sitting in the sun. He had, after all, in the two years since he arrived in Europe, published four books of poetry, and written one book of literary criticism, as well as doing a fair amount of lecturing, reviewing and other journalism. In addition he had had the highly demanding task of performing the role of intense and aesthetic poet for literary London. Even if financially he had not been a success, it would not have been surprising if he felt he were due some relaxation. But there was more to his holiday mood than that. Soon after arriving he wrote to his father: 'No I dont think you have to pay for my passage & I dont think you have to send me anymore remittances'. He added enigmatically, 'the financial condition is decidedly comforting'.[11] When his parents asked in some bewilderment how he had suddenly at last become – even briefly – self-supporting, he wrote indignantly back:

'sudden occasion of wealth' . . . I've jawed all winter at the Polytec. I've been writing a book for six months, I've given lessons in advanced kindergarten aesthetics. My poesia begins to go in the magazines at about £5. a dip. Jan. Eng. Rev. paid in March. April Eng. Rev. just paid. Fortnightly proofs returned. Eng. Rev. 3 new poems received & presumably to appear. Sudden! – hm – well, we hope we're on the way.[12]

Pound was not being entirely frank. He had not told his parents that while he was in Paris, Walter Rummel had introduced him to a young American woman, called Margaret Cravens, who had offered – and already begun to supply – financial support. Perhaps it was not only Pound's admiration for Rummel that had delayed him on that occasion. Margaret Cravens, like other young Americans of the period, had come to Paris to pursue an artistic life, in her case as a musician, a life that would have been impossible in the States for a woman of her class. She came from a wealthy family, having grown up in Madison, the second biggest city in Indiana, where she had been cared for by a formidable maiden aunt, and she had a comfortable, if by no means large, allowance. After Pound's own tribulations in Indiana he would undoubtedly have sympathised with her flight to Europe. Pound was later to realise Margaret was full of inner anguish, but he probably only learnt of her tragic early life after her death. In the *Cantos* he refers to her as 'Margaret of the seven griefs', referring perhaps to the seven deaths in Margaret's immediate family, her mother having died when she was four, and Margaret herself being the only one of five children to have survived.[13] She saw little of her father, and was brought up by grandparents. Her grandfather died when she was eight, and her grandmother when she was thirteen, at which point she was handed over to the intimidating aunt. That childhood surrounded by death had left her with a deep inner melancholy, and also perhaps a need to find a passionate cause to give sense and human connection to her bereft existence.

Pound must have made an intense impact on Margaret; he convinced her of his genius, and she offered to give him a substantial proportion of her income to free him to write. Since his arrival in Sirmione, she had already sent him $100, enough to support him for six weeks, and was putting more in a Paris bank for him to drawn on as he needed it. From his letters to her it appears that she had wanted to settle on him a lump sum, but Pound, rather honourably, dissuaded her from that, suggesting that she 'send [his] salvation in smaller amounts'.[14] As with his parents, he had some qualms about accepting her generosity, but not so many as to refuse it. It was for his art, he argued, not for him, and he was deeply grateful, not only for the money, but also for her belief in the value of his talent. In his first letter of thanks, which he wrote before he left Paris, he appears almost overwhelmed. 'Of course it is all out of the Arabian Nights or some book of magic . . . I haven't quite realised things yet. I mean you've brought me back to a number of things.' One of those 'things' she brought him back to was self-belief. He wrote again a couple of days later after his arrival in Italy: 'You have given me so much – I dont mean the apparent gift – but restorations of faith. Your "largesse" in all that a forgotten word should mean! – and then the apparent gift comes, as a sort of sign from beyond that my work is accepted. It couldn't have come unless there was some real reason, behind us all, for the work to go on unfettered.' His future mission and greatness as a poet was confirmed. Curiously enough, in his letters to her from Italy he mentions Hamilton several times, somewhat to her confusion, as she had no idea what or where Hamilton was. It suggests he was vividly comparing her faith in him with his pariah status there – 'Life is bitter in an American College,' he told her. Life was very sweet now for a newly confident poet, without financial worries, living in the warmth by a 'lavender lake'.[15]

Pound soon had some more good news. He heard shortly after his arrival that he was to have a book of his poems published in the United States for the first time. Smith, Maynard & Co. had agreed to bring out later that year a selection of poems from *Personae* and *Exultations*, with a few new poems included. Pound settled down to enjoy Italy. He loved Sirmione, unusually so; he was in general much more interested in people than places, and in conversation, or at least an audience, than in scenery. He was fascinated by the town's literary associations; past the village, in the wilder northern end of the peninsula, the Roman poet Catullus had lived; one of the ruins was thought to have been his house. Sirmione had also been the home of one of Pound's favourite Renaissance Latinists, Marcus Antonius Flaminius, about whom he had written in *The Spirit of Romance*. Pound had included one of Flaminius' poems in *Exultations*, something of a direct act of plagiarism, or to put it more kindly, *l'art trouvé*, for it was in essence an only slightly adapted version of a seventeenth-century prose translation that he also quoted in *The Spirit of Romance*, commending Flaminius for his 'sensitiveness to nature' and to the 'spiritual presences therein'.[16]

In addition to his sense of this poetic heritage, the sheer beauty of Sirmione moved him, though perhaps the golden light shed by Margaret Cravens' 'largesse' helped him to appreciate it. He wrote to H.D. (the only early letter to her that survived), 'I've been watching the "Garda" for a month trying to see it in paint . . . No paint can ever get the intensity, the brilliancy, the transparency, the depth . . . Sirmione is the peace of God. I've been about a little & I know paradise when I see it'.[17] He told Margaret Cravens, 'I am quite convinced . . . that the gods have returned to [Mount] Riva or to be more exact they have never left it'.[18] In Sirmione, he could experience for himself the return of the old pagan gods of whom Pater spoke, who had liberated his Provençal poets from the dead hand of the medieval Church. Sirmione, he would continue to maintain, was the original world of the gods.[19]

Italy, with so many reminders of the pagan past, must have made it easy for him to imagine himself back into that world, though it may also have been his recent introduction to Frazer that made his mind run so much on the pre-Christian gods. He was working on a series of poems, much concerned with a quasi-pagan, visionary religion of love, most of which would be published the following year in the collection entitled *Canzoni*, though he would include a few in the *Provença*, the American selection of his poems that would come out later in the year. His chief focus of interest was moving on from the Provençal poets to the early Italians, as *The Spirit of Romance* had already signalled, particularly Guido Cavalcanti, the most famous of the thirteenth-century Tuscan *dolce stil nuovo* poets. Pound had given him only two pages in *The Spirit of Romance*, though he had praised him warmly: 'Dante himself,' he said there, 'never wrote lines more poignant, or more intensely poetic than did Cavalcanti.'[20] In Sirmione, Cavalcanti appears to have taken on a new significance, and he began work on what would be a book of translations, *The Sonnets and Ballate of Guido Cavalcanti*, which eventually appeared in 1912. Cavalcanti's work does not have the bravado and panache of the Provençal troubadours, though influenced by them, but his beautifully wrought poetry incorporates a mystical philosophy that fascinated Pound. When the Provençal poets fled after the brutal crushing of the Albigensian heresy by Simon de Montfort, spreading their love poetry to other parts of Europe, Tuscany was particularly receptive. The Tuscan poets took over much of the Provençal imagery and forms, their conception of love becoming fused with Neoplatonic doctrines of light, possibly Arab in origin. The light that shines in the eyes of the lady is a light that is also the mystical heart of being. Those of 'cor gentil' (noble heart), with the sensitivity to respond to this radiance and beauty, are a small, elect group. Both this elitism and the fusion of earthly love and mysticism, brought to consummation in Dante, appealed powerfully to Pound, as it had to the Pre-Raphaelites, especially to Rossetti, on whose *Early Italian Poets* Pound had relied heavily in his chapter on the Tuscan poets. This fusion of the love of beauty and the love of God could be justified in Christian theology too, at any rate in the writings of Pound's favourite theologian, Richard of St Victor, who held that in loving any mortal beauty one was in essence loving God. This idea was already present in the Provençal poets but it was developed into a more systematic mysticism in Tuscany.

Pound came to see Cavalcanti as one of the most subtle expositors of the psychology of the lover/mystic, but he found it hard to convey this, and his translations when they appeared in 1912 were not a success. They were castigated for their errors, but beyond that they fail to come to life as poems. They have the awkward leaden stasis of many of the poems in *Canzoni*, Pound remaining too trapped within their literary conventions to make them living things of his own. By 1915 he would admit to James Joyce that they were not a good translation.[21] His search, however, to find a mode of expression for this mystic, yet erotic, 'radiant beauty' would go on, and for him imagism was in some ways just that. Yet with concerns like these, it is no wonder Pound in 1910 had been unable to find any common ground with the antipathetic Lewis.

Pound was not writing love poetry in Sirmione simply as an exercise. In *The Spirit of Romance* he had quoted a dismissive attack on a worthless troubadour: 'And he made canzoni because he had a will to make canzoni and not because love moved him to it; and nobody thought much of him or of his songs either.'[22] Love moved Pound. In late April Olivia and Dorothy Shakespear came to stay. Both of them had been researching on Pound's behalf in his absence; having lectured them at his classes at the polytechnic, Pound considered them trained assistants, and they were sent to check information for queries in the proofs of *The Spirit of Romance* or to copy Provençal or Italian originals for Pound's new translations. Dorothy felt ill at ease in the British Museum Reading Room; her upbringing had not prepared her to go alone to public places, but her writing was more legible than Olivia's, and, Pound thought, she produced a more decipherable and therefore reliable copy. The tasks associated with the proofs were light, but the transcription of a considerable number of Arnaut Daniel and Cavalcanti sonnets demanded more intensive labour. Pound was aware that they might rebel: 'I write with no confidence that the Griselda type has survived the Ibsen revolt and the last election,' he said apprehensively when sending yet another request to Olivia.[23] In spite of his indifference to British politics in general, even Pound had noticed the suffragette agitation.

During the past fifteen months in London, although Pound and Dorothy saw each other frequently, there is no indication that they ever met without Olivia's chaperoning presence, certainly not for more than a few minutes. While at Sirmione, the careful watch Olivia kept over her daughter in London appears to have slipped. Pound and Dorothy managed to escape together a few afternoons to the olive groves, ruins and cliffs of the northern end of the Sirmione peninsula, perhaps leaving Olivia having a siesta in the Hotel Eden. Dorothy wrote in her diary that it was the first time she had been really happy, and the following summer (not having seen Pound since) she was to write: 'Last night I remembered all S[irmione] so well. I lived those exquisite days again: more clearly than I have for months been able to see anything. The Tower, & the two other afternoons. Truly my life was lived then.'[24] She told Noel Stock many years later that it was 'the first time [she] ever saw colour'.[25] Now Pound wrote her a poem that was a much less ambiguous statement of his feelings towards her than 'The White Poppy', suggesting the only heaven worth having was being together in the earthly paradise of Sirmione 'wherein the sun/Lets drift in on us through the olive leaves/ A liquid glory . . .'[26] The couple of weeks they spent there had been decisive.

The ecstatic visionariness revealed in that poem was what Dorothy admired most deeply about Pound, apart, perhaps, from his beauty, the two qualities she comments on most frequently in the extracts from her journal. Pound's search for visionary states of mind was not something that most of his London acquaintances had noticed. To them, his extraordinary garb and eccentric behaviour implied someone far too noisy and obstreperous for mystical experience. Already, however, Dorothy's notebook had suggested a very different view of Pound from the general. She wrote of him very shortly after their first meeting: 'He has conquered the needs of the flesh – He can starve; nay, is willing, to starve that his

spirit may bring forth the "highest of arts" – poetry . . . He has attained
to peace in this world, it seems to me. To be working for the great art,
to be living in, and for, Truth in her Greatness – He has found the
Centre – TRUTH."[27] Dorothy saw Pound with the eye of love, but her
insight was not entirely flawed. It is true that Pound wanted fame; he
wanted to be recognised; he liked to act the artist-dandy; he was not
quite so ready to starve as she thought – he had written indignantly to
his father the previous May when his parents had sent him less than
he demanded: 'what am I to eat if you send me $10 instead of $20?'[28]
Yet visionary, mystical experience remained immensely important to
him, seemingly still as central as it had been back in Wabash when he
wrote to Viola Baxter about art and ecstasy, or as it had been in Venice,
when he wrote of 'the essences of beauty' and 'flashes of cosmic
consciousness' that he associated with art.[29] Dorothy's recognition of
this strain in him must have been an important part of her attraction
for him. It may also have encouraged him to indulge it, for a while at
any rate, not necessarily to the benefit of his poetry.

At some point during this visit Olivia began to realise Pound and
Dorothy were attracted to each other. She may earlier have thought that
Pound was already tied up with Grace Crawford, as she had met them
together at the theatre, and in English decorum – as she would later
point out to him – appearing as a couple together in public implied an
understanding at the least. She had evidently come with no expectations – or perhaps one should say fears – of an entanglement between
Pound and Dorothy. Olivia was not pleased: the Shakespears returned
home, and Pound was forbidden to visit or write to Dorothy, although
he would continue to write to Olivia at regular intervals while he was
in the States. Humphrey Carpenter regards Olivia's behaviour as
distinctly odd, and suggests that what was most galling to Olivia was
that she had believed Pound had a *tendresse* for herself, indeed hoped
to become his mistress as she had been Yeats', but that seems unlikely.
Pound certainly admired Olivia, and had made his admiration clear, but
only as a younger man to a charming and respected older woman. In
his letters he always addresses her as 'your highness', which, though a
little mocking, suggests he was always aware of the gap between them.
According to Grace Crawford, Pound was quite in awe of Olivia. Olivia
was a serious and sensitive woman; her marriage was unhappy, but her
feelings for Yeats had, and still did, run deep. She had broken off their
relationship in the 1890s, when she was traumatised by the discovery
that Yeats was still in love with Maud Gonne. Their friendship had gone

into abeyance for some time, but it had resumed as an important part
of both their lives some time before Pound arrived in London. They
may never again have been lovers – though it is possible they were at
this very period, and some of Yeats' biographers state this as a fact –
but, whatever the sexual element, it was a close and intimate friendship,
and there was a strong emotional bond between them. Olivia's liking
for the ebullient Pound was not in any way comparable.

Whatever her feelings for him, however, as a responsible, upper
middle-class mother in the England of 1910, her reaction was entirely
predictable. This was not the United States, where a certain amount of
pre-marital flirtation could be condoned. Pound may not yet have read
much Henry James, but if he had known *The Awkward Age* he might
have understood better. A married woman's liaison – as long as there
were no scandal and no marital separation – could be silently overlooked,
but the unmarried young woman's reputation had to be spotless; there
must be no possible hint of dalliance. The penniless Pound was a disastrous proposition as a husband, and there is no doubt that Olivia
would know quite how penniless he was. Pound was rather proud of his
role as poverty-stricken artist. Lucy Masterman, the wife of Charles
Masterman, recalled one lunch when '[Pound] assured me that he was
living on 10/- a week which dismayed me, as even in those days when
£s were £s it was very small'.[30] Whilst as an acquaintance Pound's
poverty might promote sympathy, as a prospective son-in-law in 1910
England it could induce only horror. Dorothy had other and more acceptable admirers – for example the well-to-do and well-connected Fairfax,
a much better proposition in accepted London terms. Pound – penniless, *outré*, scandalously short of drawing-room manners, and lacking
any economic prospects – was out of the question. Olivia might be ready
to tolerate the unconventional in art, but not in life. In June, Dorothy
wrote to Pound that she took it he had been forbidden to write to her.
'As yet, I have had no lecture – and have given no promise not to write
to you – we pray I shall not be asked for the promise anyway.'[31] Apparently
she was not, as she continued to write, but without letting Olivia know.

Pound left no evidence as to what his feelings were in the time he
remained in Sirmione. He had sounded in the best of spirits when he
reported the arrival of his *amies anglaises* in a letter to Margaret Cravens,
but made no comment on their departure. A few weeks later he returned
to Paris, spending some time with Margaret, who realised Pound was
in low spirits. For Pound to let someone else know he was unhappy was
uncharacteristic ('if he ever gets blue nobody knows it,' as Williams had

commented), but Margaret herself was depressed, and his own un-happiness may have emerged as he tried to cheer her. He gave, apparently, no explanation. After a few days he left Paris for London, where a week later, on 18 June, he would catch his boat to New York.

During Pound's brief stay in London, he saw Dorothy, but only, as she sadly noted, across 'a roomful of people'.[32] While the Shakespears were with him at Sirmione, Edward VII had died on 6 May and was much mourned, George V being generally agreed to be a dull dog in comparison, but the only reference Pound made to the royal death was to lament that it interfered with the concerts Rummel was giving in London at the time. He spent some time with Yeats, and went to spend a last evening with Ford, where among others he caught up with D.H. Lawrence, who gave an illuminating, if unkind description of the returning poet in a letter to Grace Crawford. 'He was just back from Sermione [*sic*] – which he announces as the earthly paradise,' Lawrence reported mockingly, though he was to have a similar response himself when he visited that part of Italy two years later. Pound, he told Grace, had been dressed more affectedly than ever: his 'David Copperfield curls' had been cut, and

His great grandfather's black satin stock, which would throw into relief the contour of his chin four months ago, had given place to a tie of peach-bloom tint and texture. He wore a dark blue cotton shirt, no vest, and a Panama hat. What is the guise? – sort of latest edition of jongleur? Italy had improved his health; I was glad of that. It had not improved his temper: he was irascible. He discussed, with much pursing up of lips and removing of frown-shaken eyeglasses, his projection of writing an account of the mystic cult of love – the dionysian rites, and so on – from the earliest days to the present. The great difficulty was that no damned publisher in London dare publish it. It would have to be published in Paris. Then how about sales.

Lawrence would have his own problems in persuading publishers to print his views on love, but for now he was not sympathetic. His comment is confirmation, however, that Pound in Sirmione had been ruminating on his belief, which would be increasingly important to him, that Cavalcanti *et alia* were descendants of the Eleusinian mysteries, one of the most ancient of the Greek cults, fertility rites associated with Demeter and the return of her daughter Persephone from the underworld, and with Dionysus, god of wine and ecstasy, where a sacred marriage was celebrated, for Pound the oldest and exemplary 'mystic cult of love'.

Was Pound irascible because he was unable to see Dorothy? Or because he was returning to America? Probably both. Of course, if he noticed, at that particular moment he may also have been cross because Lawrence was laughing at him. Lawrence produces one other intriguing piece of information in the same letter. Pound was going back to America, he announced to Lawrence, to make money. 'Having had all the experiences possible for a poor man, he will now proceed to conquer riches . . . He will sell boots – there is nothing in that blown egg, literature. I ventured he should run a Cinematograph: a dazzling picture palace; for which valuable suggestion he tendered me a frown.'[33] It seems unlikely that Pound was really thinking of giving up that 'blown egg, literature', just when he had found a patron; the sudden enthusiasm for making money must have been a plan to make himself a suitable suitor for Dorothy, for she wrote him a sympathetic letter shortly after saying that she realised it was difficult to find £5,000 a year in a fortnight. The figure Olivia had in mind was £500, but Pound believed in overkill.

Pound appears to have made no promises about the future, except for saying to Dorothy, as she recorded in her notebook, 'if ever you want me, I will come, at once'.[34] His parents, he knew, expected him to find a respectable and well-paid job in the States, a prospect he dreaded. *The Spirit of Romance* would be out shortly, and *Provença* by the end of the year. Much might depend on their success. And then there were those ex-fiancées. He would undoubtedly see H.D. as soon as he reached Philadelphia. Pound crossed the Atlantic to an uncertain future.

II

WHEN Pound left for Europe in the March of 1908, H.D. had remained at home, wretched and confused, her engagement, as she said, 'shattered like a Venetian glass goblet, flung on the floor'.[35] As she describes it in her quasi-autobiographical novel *Paint it Today*, she was 'drifting, unsatisfied, hurt and baffled out of a relationship with a hectic, adolescent, blundering, untried, mischievous, and irreverent male youth'. She was wounded by Pound's casual and callous – as it seemed to her – philandering. For her, their love had been a passion; for him, it appeared in retrospect, a pastime. She felt betrayed, as if what to her had been sacred he had desecrated, and she had 'gained nothing from him but a feeling that someone had tampered with an oracle'.[36] By the time she came to write *End to Torment* she could acknowledge what she had gained as well as suffered, but perhaps the fiction reflects something of her feeling of desolation and despoliation at the time.

H.D. wrote repeated accounts of her life up to the end of the First World War, sometimes as memoirs and sometimes as *romans à clef*. Memoirs are always in themselves only partially reliable reworkings of the past, but fictional accounts, though often illuminating, have to be drawn on with particular caution. The novels that deal most explicitly with this period are the two I have already mentioned, *Her* and *Paint it Today*, and two more, *Asphodel* and *Bid Me to Live*. *Paint it Today* is quite short, written in 1921 or 1922, after H.D.'s return visit to America with her companion Bryher. It covers, in fleeting fragments, her life from her childhood to the end of the First World War. The first draft of *Asphodel* was also written about then, but the surviving version is from a revision made in 1926 or 1927, written at much the same time as *Her*, the H.D. figure in both being Hermione or Her Gart. *Her* is specifically about the years between Bryn Mawr and her departure for

England, her Philadelphian life, her early love affairs, and her struggle to find some autonomy. *Asphodel* takes the story on from her arrival in Europe to the immediate post-war years, and her discovery of herself as a writer. All give significant insights into H.D.'s psychological and artistic journey in the early years, but her plots do not necessarily follow the precise historical sequence. Though *Her*, for example, encompasses many of the central events of H.D.'s life between 1905 and 1911, the order has been shifted, and the novel weaves them together not as a factual or exact account but as an attempt to understand, as the text puts it, Her's 'yet unformulated consciousness and her consciousness of America', her gradual growth, if not fully to self-understanding, to a sense of necessary direction.[37] All of these novels are *Künstlerroman*, that is, stories about her development as an artist, not as systematic as say Joyce's *Portrait of the Artist as a Young Man*, but equally concerned with the evolution of an aesthetic path, and her allusions to particular poems or writers always carry rich resonances. When H.D. came to write the novel *Bid Me to Live*, set in the First World War, and the only one of these four to be published in her lifetime, she records that Freud advised her to tell her story as directly as she could, and not to re-pattern events as she does in these earlier versions. Yet even in the other three, many details can be corroborated outside the text, and H.D. certainly had a wonderful ear for dialogue. The Pound character sounds unmistakably like him, and in *Asphodel*, which covers her years in England from 1911 to 1919, Aldington is mimicked, or perhaps even quoted, brilliantly. H.D. was later to refer to the four novels as her *Madrigal* cycle, recording with different rhythms and emphases these years, which included both trauma and great happiness. In each case she paints it as she sees it at the moment of writing, as the title of *Paint it Today* indicates. None of them is a definitive account, but all can help interpret H.D.'s attitudes to her work and her complex emotional life.[38]

One incontrovertible result of H.D.'s abortive love affair with Pound was that it seared for ever her relationship with her parents. She was dismayed and angry at their apparent lack of sympathy for what she cared for in Pound, his passion for poetry, for beauty, for life, irritated that they were so easily prey to what she saw as the blinkered judgements of Philadelphia. In their opposition to her feelings for Pound – perhaps all the more because they had been partly justified – they had, she felt, rejected what was most important in her. Yet though her relationship with Pound was a turning-point, one that would eventually set her on the path to her life as a poet in Europe, she was for now still the dutiful daughter at home. The H.D./Midget character in *Paint it Today* had never, she wrote, 'said to her mother, "I can't," or to her father, "I won't" . . . it was a subterranean sort of struggle. It was a question of atmosphere and pressure and tyranny of affections, but Midget had never faced a direct issue with absolute defiance.'[39] Both H.D.'s mother and father were figures of authority, as Williams noted on his visits there. Her mother ruled the house, though as he observed, not 'obtrusively', and saw to it that Professor Doolittle, with his 'flowing beard', was treated as the revered patriarch of his tribe: 'At a meal, usually supper, with every place taken by the children and others, if the alert Mrs Doolittle detected in the general din that the doctor wanted to say something, she would quickly announce: Your father is about to speak! – Silence immediately ensued. Then in a slow and deep voice, and with his eyes fixed on nothing, as Ezra Pound said . . . nearer than the moon, he said what he had to say. It was a disheartening process.'[40] But, and perhaps Williams did not quite see this, if they were authoritative they were never authoritarian, and they loved H.D. dearly and she them. Had it not been the case, her escape might have been much easier.

As it was, her attempts at finding a substitute for a Bryn Mawr education did not go well. In one of Pound's letters to his mother while still at Wabash, he had mentioned that H.D. was studying music at the *conservatoire*, but that apparently did not last long. Many years later, she told the composer Eric White, who set some of her poems to music in the 1930s, that she had been discouraged because her musical uncle Frederick Wolle, the one who had founded the Bethlehem Bach Choir, had disapproved of her liking for Beethoven, whom he considered a much inferior, and far too modern, composer. She registered for a teacher training course at the University of Pennsylvania, but didn't pursue it, though she said in *Tribute to Freud* that she would have liked to be a teacher, and that one of the things that later drew her to Lawrence was that he had been a schoolmaster. H.D.'s 'provocative indifference to rule and order', which Williams had earlier admired, appears to have been temporarily crushed, but neither had she any faith in her ability to follow any systematic path. As she put it in *Paint it Today*, 'She had not the strength nor courage to snap fresh and vivid from the surroundings of her childhood. She had no sap or vivid living power left in her. She felt instinctively that she was a failure by all the conventional and scholarly standards. She had failed in her college career, she had failed as a social asset with her family and the indiscriminate mob of relatives and relays of communal friends that surrounded it. She had burned her candle of rebellion at both ends and she was left unequipped for the simplest dealings with the world.'[41]

That could, one imagines, have been the end of the story of H.D's poetic career. A few scribbled poems, a few dreams, put away, like Williams' mother's oil-paints, in the attic of some respectable Philadelphian academic or lawyer whom she had married after a year or two of helping her mother with the household tasks and the giving and attending of tea parties. But, for all her sense of defeat, incompetence and hopelessness, her survival instincts came to her rescue. As she wrote in *End to Torment*: 'the two-edged humiliation, from the friends and family, from Ezra, was carefully camouflaged, covered with the weeds and bracken of daily duties and necessities, and a bridge finally crossed the chasm . . . a forceful effort toward artistic achievement'.[42] She went on writing; she went on reading. Pound had given her a volume of Renaissance Latin poets – easy Latin, she said – and she translated some of them.[43] She translated some German poetry, German being her grandparents' language, for which she had a special affection. She wrote charming, gently subversive, children's stories, which Homer Pound helped her to publish in the Presbyterian Press. She filed papers and articles for her father, and when schoolchildren poured in to visit the Observatory in 1910 as excitement rose over Halley's Comet, she told them (again somewhat subversively) Greek myths about the origins of the stars rather than scientific data. She began to read works by the French astronomer, Camille Flammarion, who had written a book about such myths, as well as one about mysterious psychic forces in the universe, and who was considered 'unreliable and sensational' by her father.[44] And it was also in 1910, 'the comet-year', she says in *Tribute to Freud*, that she found another rebel outsider with whom she could bond, another irritant to her family to save her from reabsorption into the blight of Philadelphian 'blandness' and 'immeasurable bourgeois blankness', to quote Henry James once more.[45] The fresh irritant, the new outsider, was Frances Gregg, who, as H.D. recalls in *End to Torment*, 'filled [her Philadephian life] like a blue flame' after Pound had gone.[46] It was her first lesbian love affair, and as significant and unforgettable as her first heterosexual affair with Pound.

H.D. met Frances through an acquaintance (according to Barbara Guest, Nan Hoyt), who appears as Mary, a 'relic of the tepid school', in *Paint it Today*, and as Nellie Thorpe, a Bryn Mawr acquaintance, in *Her*.[47] Frances, who was one or two years older than H.D., had had a scholarship to the 'tepid' school, but had had to leave early, probably before H.D. had moved there. She was later a student at the Philadelphia Academy of Art, to which William Brooke Smith had hoped to go if he had lived. Frances was poor, compared to most of H.D.'s circle, who were 'the daughters of lawyers, doctors, professors, and oversuccessful wholesale merchants'.[48] She lived with her mother, Julia, presumably widowed, certainly husbandless – Frances' father, an Englishman called Oliver Gregg, was said to have gone prospecting out West, never to return. Julia was told he had died of exposure. In H.D.'s fictional accounts of her relationship with Frances, Fayne Rabb, the Frances figure, wonders if her mother had ever been married at all. Frances and her mother shared a small flat in an unfashionable area of West Philadelphia, though when Frances was younger they had lived in a poorer district still, on the edge of a slum, where, according to her son, Frances had 'heard negro jazz, saw negro dancing, and a lynching'.[49] Frances had, like Pound, been born out West, probably at Fort Worth, but moved with her mother and grandmother back East when still very young. Mrs Gregg came from one of the old Dutch families who preceded the British in the New York area; she liked to be known as Mrs Van Ness Gregg, and was proud of being related to the Roosevelts, but in Philadelphia status depended first and foremost on money.[50] Ancestry might count, but not in shabby surroundings.[51] The very fact that Frances was not part of Philadelphia's snobbish, tribal upper middle class appealed in itself to H.D., but H.D. was only the first of several, including most notably John Cowper Powys, to be entranced, and frequently made wretched, by Frances Gregg.

Frances Gregg was different from, as well as indifferent to, the well-bred young ladies of Philadelphia. In her own short story, 'Male and Female', based on the events of this period and only published posthumously, Frances says of her fictional self: 'There was about her . . . a touch of something both neurotic, and exotic, that made her women friends regard her with envy, suspicion and a deep-rooted, if blind, jealousy. Somehow they knew she was not "good", in their sense of being suppressed, nice women, but they also recognised something bold and clean and fierce that commanded their respect but, oddly enough, made them hate her all the more'.[52] In H.D.'s fiction the Frances figure always arouses considerable disapproval, but both in fiction and real life she is described as bewitchingly lovely, something borne out by the extant photographs. In *Paint it Today*, like Frances' other admirers, H.D. stresses her eyes, 'an unholy splendor', whose colour fluctuated mysteriously from blue to slate or 'rain gray'.[53] Richard Perceval Graves, in his memoir of the Powys brothers (whose complex relationship with Frances will emerge later in this story), describes her, more conventionally, as 'very beautiful' with 'the large appealing eyes of a star of the silent screen'.[54] The Ezra Pound figure in *Asphodel* calls her a 'Burne Jones fury', which captures better the dangerously compelling intensity of her eyes.[55] She was shy and vulnerable looking, but also clever, witty, quick and often cruel. She worked as a teacher – the usual fate of the unmarried and less than affluent middle-class American woman, but perhaps it was she who made H.D. admire the calling – following in the footsteps of her mother, who had founded a school for Italian immigrants, and, Graves claims, 'made their home a centre for outcasts of all kinds, in particular ill-treated children and animals'.[56] If this were true – and Frances' son repeats the story – Mrs Gregg was a rather nicer character than most accounts of her have credited. Frances' grandmother, who had lived with her daughter and granddaughter till her death, was a powerful and resilient woman, much admired by Frances. Her husband had died in the Civil War, leaving her with five children, four of them boys, to bring up single-handed. She worked, like her daughter after her, as a teacher, and was also, according to Frances's son, 'a formidable lecturer on temperance, venereal disease and women's rights'.[57] There was something of her zeal and resolution in Frances, though she would devote those qualities to rather different causes. Frances' mother Julia was more conventional. She was, Graves says, 'a devout Evangelical Christian' (Frances spent hours of her youth in revivalist camp meetings) but 'Frances herself had no time for the Church, though she very much admired the way in which, as she saw it, Christ had courageously launched a movement which challenged the established order of the entire universe. She thoroughly disliked the social and intellectual establishment on earth; she had a particular loathing for the police.'[58] No wonder she appealed to H.D.

H.D. wrote in *Paint it Today* that since she was about ten she had longed for a sister, a twin sister, even a baby sister. Frances filled that role, although, as H.D. was to discover, sisterly emotions come in many forms. In the satirical novel that Frances helped her husband to write some years later, *The Buffoon*, which is in many ways very cruel about H.D., and very comic about Pound, the heroine is a curious fusion of Frances and H.D., and there were likenesses between them, in their sense of isolation, in their interests and even in their looks. When Llewelyn Powys later described Frances as he first saw her, it sounds remarkably like H.D. He even calls Frances a dryad, as Pound did H.D.:

The first impression she produces is of one walking in a trance, her head full of dreams . . . The next is of an extraordinary timidity and shyness – more than shyness, a certain reluctance to step into the world at all – precisely like the look of a Hamadryad standing waiting at the entrance of her hollow tree till the steps of some passing faun have died into silence . . . She is tall and dark and very supple and slender . . . yet moulded with quite girlish and almost Tess-like contours.[59]

H.D.'s contours were never described as Tess-like, but the tall, slender shyness and the sense of unease in the world would apply equally well to her. When they later travelled together they were often taken to be sisters.[60] But in spite of their shared social diffidence they were both strong characters, though Frances' strength was a more active force. She was a much more overt rebel than H.D. ever was. H.D. was always attracted by rebels; she needed them to help, or make, her escape. Pound, Frances and Aldington were all stirrers, out to disturb the bourgeois peace of mind. H.D., frustrated as she might be by conventional expectations, was much more inclined to remember that the bourgeois were after all human beings. She was polite; she was tactful; she hated hurting people's feelings. She was consumed by guilt when she realised that she had done so. H.D.'s own strength lay in her largely silent, sometimes stoic powers of endurance. Many of her early poems are about endurance – 'Sea Rose', for example, where the traditional feminine emblem of the rose loses its beauty and sensuousness, but equally it becomes, instead of an image of fragile mortality, a survivor:

Rose, harsh rose,
marred and with stint of petals,
meagre flower, thin,
sparse of leaf . . .

Stunted, with small leaf,
you are flung on the sand,
you are lifted in the crisp sand
that drives in the wind.

Can the spice-rose
drip such acrid fragrance
hardened in a leaf?[61]

H.D. wrote that poem in England during the First World War, but already she often felt marred, meagre, sparse and stunted. Frances, like Pound, brought her fierce joy and great pain.

Frances had an intense, almost suffocating relationship with her mother, who was deeply possessive of her, something Frances both depended on and hated. Julia, Frances' son says, was 'the bane and spur of her life'. She and her mother had constant, bickering rows, though 'when the battles were over . . . [they] would . . . begin to laugh'.[62] That seems to have been the model for most of her relationships; she would bind people to her, alternatively slashing them pitilessly and enchanting them with her vitality and spirit. John Cowper Powys said later of her cruelty to him: 'She is really wicked – beyond anything it is possible to imagine'.[63] In *Her* and *Paint it Today* she is compared to the beautiful, sadistic Roman Empress Faustine in Swinburne's poem of that name, to whom the slaughter of the gladiatorial contests was an addiction; she 'loved the games men played with death,/Where death must win;/As though the slain man's blood and breath/Revived Faustine'. Frances Gregg wrote later in another short story. 'I could never let anything alone. My instinct was to draw a thing to me, then strip it of every defence, every self-illusion, every self-deception . . . Certainly there was a fury in me, a bitter hatred of people, and a vindictive malice toward life, – but there was too, a love, and a pity that broke my heart. I am queer. I am solitary.'[64] Yet just as H.D. recognised that Pound was 'torn and lonely' under the bravado and gaucherie, so too perhaps she recognised Frances' love beneath her destruction of it, the pity beneath her cruelty. And Frances cared about books, cared about poetry, cared about ideas. She too wanted to write. She was intellectually and artistically H.D.'s salvation.

Frances's extra two years, the toughness of her life, and her time at the Academy of Art had all combined to make her a more sophisticated and knowing young woman than H.D. In retrospect, it has been easy for commentators (like, for example, Barbara Guest) to think of H.D., the famous poet, in this friendship/love affair with someone who never made a name, as being the more dominant of the two. But Frances believed passionately in her superiority to the world at large and in the moral rightness of her own unorthodox convictions; perhaps, in the face of Philadelphian condescension, such passionate self-belief was necessary. She would castigate H.D. for her bourgeois softness and compromises well into the 1920s and 1930s, and H.D. both admired and feared her fierceness of principle. Frances was, according to her son, appalled by the suffering of the world; if there were 'fury' and 'bitter hatred of people' in her, it came out of her terrifyingly bleak view of the human condition and her conviction of the constant inhumanity of man to man. Unlike H.D. and Pound, she had lived close to the most exploited groups in American society, the blacks and the immigrant poor, and she knew the brutality of the law-keepers and the respectable. She was heir to the New England tradition of hell-fire preaching – she had heard plenty of it in her youth – and, like the famous Jonathan Edwards, she was ready to terrorise people for what she thought was their good. Her letters to Powys could be savage: she saw them as necessary tools of reformation. In *Her*, when Fayne Rabb talks about George Lowndes, she describes a similar technique: 'George is lie upon lie upon lie. George interests me because I try out on George the thing that is in me . . . Truth, pure truth, that atomic center of me, draws George to me, separates George from George like some deep distilling acid. The thing in me, pure upon pure truth, disintegrates George and I watch the disintegration, matching element to element, saying this *is* George, this *was* George. The George that is to be.'[65] It has to be said, if this is based on Frances' treatment of Pound, the reformation did not succeed.

Cassandra Laity points out that the Fayne Rabb figure is depicted by H.D. as a *femme fatale*, which is certainly the case, but one wonders whether it was not Frances who first modelled herself on the beautiful, forceful and exciting *femmes fatales* of the late nineteenth century. Her sinister stories rather suggest that she did. Her writing has a dark, disturbing Gothic quality – she published some stories appropriately entitled 'Contes Macabres' in the *New Freewoman* – and her imagination was powerful and perturbing. Like other rebellious women at the time, as Rita Felski has suggested, she may well have found the *femme fatale* a much more attractive role model than the 'nice', 'good' woman. In addition, Frances had a strong interest in the occult, and was, she claimed, a medium, another role through which late nineteenth- and early twentieth-century women could claim a position of psychic power generally socially unavailable to them.[66] H.D. depicts Frances on occasion as a kind of vampire, like Swinburne's Faustine, feeding on others' souls; 'she is psychic klepto-maniac', she told Bryher in 1930: 'She must get and break'.[67] In the autobiographical novels Fayne Rabb is never depicted saying a kind or tender thing. One can understand why Bryher later described Frances as 'very dangerous', but she gave H.D. an alternative and fascinating model of what a woman could be.[68]

III

UNTIL 1912, perhaps beyond, it was always assumed (by Pound as well as others) that, of the two young women, Frances was to be the writer; in the event, she would publish, if not a great deal, enough to make clear that she had great promise. No one yet believed in H.D., except, very uncertainly, H.D. herself. Yet H.D. was writing poetry, still apparently largely translations. Now she wrote poetry for Frances, or about Frances. In *Paint it Today* she includes a translation from the German poet Heine, whom Pound, in spite of his inadequate German, would also attempt to translate, perhaps following H.D.'s example, in the *Canzoni* which were published a year after his return home. Heine, who has been rather neglected by Anglophone audiences in recent years, was widely read in the late nineteenth/early twentieth century; an outsider, first as a Jew in Germany, and later, when he moved to Paris, as a German in France, for the incipient modernist, and perhaps especially H.D., he was an important early emblem of the poet as exile. Some of his poems, significantly enough, were in a form of *vers libre*, but H.D. was here apparently translating from his rhymed lyric love poetry:

> I have come again away from the dead,
> Drawn by strange powers to thee,
> Quicken me now nor fear to give,
> Too much of yourself to me.

'She had translated it painstakingly from Heine,' she explains, 'and she knew that she had brought over a little the fragrance of the German. She worried about the "thee" and the "yourself" but "thyself" sounded stilted, unnatural.'[69] This is not yet the *vers libre* that she is known for, but it has a simplicity and reticence that continue to be qualities of her verse. She writes in *Paint it Today* about trying to find the right sort of poetry for her. 'Poetry and the beat and the swallow wings. Large, epic pictures bored her, though she struggled through them. She wanted the songs that cut like a swallow wing the high, untainted ether, not the tragic legions of set lines that fell like black armies with terrific force and mechanical set action, paralyzing, or broke like a black sea to baffle and crush.'[70] Like the young poets that Pound was meeting in London at the Tour Eiffel, she knew that traditional verse forms no longer worked for her, and like them she had found it hard to discover forms in English on which she could model her poetry. Again like them, she looked elsewhere for her models.

One of the first models that H.D. drew on for verse 'that cut like a swallow wing the high, untainted ether' was the Greek poet Theocritus, the founder of the pastoral tradition. Pound had introduced her to Andrew Lang's translations, which were published in a single volume along with his followers Moschus and Bion. Pound himself always admired Theocritus, referring to him repeatedly as one of the touch-stones of poetry, but, unlike H.D., in practice he rarely drew on him. That collection appears to have been the one that first led H.D. to her love of the Greek lyric poets, with their combination of passion and economy, the defining qualities of her own poetry. In *End to Torment* she gives an example of the sort of Greek pastoral poem she wrote to Frances – in this case she says in 'Bion and Moschus mood', rather more melancholy, at any rate in Lang's selection, than Theocritus himself – though this particular poem sounds more a parody of the sort of thing she would have written than a carefully preserved morsel of her early writing, as some critics take it to be. H.D. was a very witty writer, but her more earnest admirers sometimes miss her jokes:

> O hyacinth of the swamp-lands,
>   Blue lily of the marshes,
> How could I know,
>   Being but a foolish shepherd
>   That you would laugh at me?[71]

In *Her*, Fayne Rabb dismisses Hermione's poetry out of hand, much as Pound had done H.D.'s: "'Your writing is nothing really. It is the pulsing of a willow, the faint note of some Sicillian shepherd. Your writing is the thin flute holding you to eternity. Take away your flute and you remain, lost in a world of unreality". "It's not – I mean – *all*."

"It is all – *all* unreal. You accept false, superimposed standards" . . .
"But I'm trying to escape them.'"[72] If that poem of the swamps and
marshes is anything to go by, H.D.'s writing had some way to go, and
perhaps she records this attack because she knew it had some truth.
Fayne repeatedly berates Hermione for her conventionality: 'You aren't
firm enough. You are transient like water seen through birch trees. You
are like the sparkle of water over white stones. Something in you makes
me hate you . . . You are yet repressed, unseeing, unseen . . . Really at
the end you are just like other people.'[73] Did Frances talk like this to
H.D.? Or is H.D. putting her own self-criticisms in Fayne's mouth?
One way or another, Frances was needling her out of her safe conformity.

As in her love affair with Pound, books were a central focus of H.D.'s
relationship with Gregg. In *Her*, she describes Fayne as 'the girl with
the wild eyes that were the only sane eyes (possibly except Bertrand's)
that Hermione had yet seen'; Bertrand (based on H.D.'s much-loved
and brilliant elder stepbrother Eric) is significantly the first person in
this novel to introduce her to books, including the story of that other
solitary rebel, *Jane Eyre*.[74] H.D. introduced Frances to the writers that
she had met through Pound, while Frances told H.D. of other writers
of whom she had never heard. In *End to Torment*, H.D. writes, 'I read
her some of the poems Ezra and I had loved together, chiefly Swinburne.
"You read so beautifully," said Frances'.[75] In the version of their meeting
that H.D. gives in *Her*, books are their first topic of conversation; this
is of course a fictionalised account, but the books selected are probably
representative. At the polite young ladies' tea party at which they first
encounter each other, Hermione finds it hard to express a view of her
own. Everything is referred to the Pound character, George Lowndes.
When Fayne asks about Meredith, she says 'a friend of mine – a man
I know – George (he is George too) Lowndes, have you heard of him?
he writes; George Lowndes says Meredith shows in every other syllable
that his father was a tailor.' When asked what he means by this, she is
unable to explain in any articulate way. Fayne says to her, '"Who is
George?" . . . "Oh, he knows people who write. He writes." . . . "What
then is George like?" "Oh, I don't know – rather like Aucassin and
Nicolette [the anonymous medieval work translated by Andrew Lang,
that H.D., Pound and Williams had all read]. I mean, he once said I
was." "Like –" "One or the other. Aucassin, you know, and Nicolette,
you know." "I don't know."'[76] They discover they have Dante, Ibsen,
Shaw and Maeterlinck in common, but when Fayne asks her if she likes
Maeterlinck, all she can say is '*The Bee* – yes, George said it was nature

faking.' Fayne, in the midst of the conversation about George Meredith, had dropped the unexpected and unwelcome question: 'What about Dostoevski?' 'Dostoevski rang no bell,' the text goes on. 'Dostoevski was a shaggy word, it did not suit them'; the conversation returned to Meredith.[77]

The 'Dionysian' Dostoevsky, as he is described here, perhaps stands for a dimension of psychological complexity and darkness that Pound's version of the aesthetic programme, let alone polite Philadelphia's cultural map, did not include. Frances' short stories often have a tormented Dostoevskian feel. Dostoevsky, before Freud, had traced the divisions and contradictions of the mind, and perhaps helped H.D., who, unlike Pound, was an avid reader of fiction, to understand some of the battles that her unconscious waged with her conscious mind. His influence can certainly be seen in H.D.'s fiction, but even before she turned to novel-writing, reading Dostoevsky may have helped her comprehend the psychic conflicts that she was to suffer during the war years, recorded in her imagist poetry. In fact, that poetry, one might guess, though so often spoken through mythic Greek personae, owes much of its psychological intensity to her reading of fiction. According to *Asphodel*, by the time Hermione reached Europe in 1911 she had also read Flaubert, Maupassant and Pierre Loti, which if true of the real-life H.D., would have put her well ahead of Pound. She and Frances went together to what Frances described as 'those maddening, exalting, incredible' University Extension lectures on literature in Philadelphia (it was at one of these that Frances was to meet John Cowper Powys), and these no doubt extended the range of reading she had met up till then.[78] H.D., like Pound, had her fundamental approach to writing formed by her first meeting with the Pre-Raphaelites and the aesthetes, especially Swinburne and Pater, and that influence would remain, but her art would in addition be fed from many other sources.

It was undoubtedly significant that in *Her*, H.D. describes Hermione talking to Fayne about George long before she gets on to herself. In 1910 H.D. was still obsessed by Pound, and her stories of Pound, the evidence suggests, played a central part in her relationship with Frances, intriguing and irritating the latter, well before his return. By now Pound had made his name. Philadelphia was proud of its young poet who was able so to impress the English public. As Pound was caustically to point out, that was the only way to get oneself taken seriously in America in 1910, though even so, when he actually arrived, the praise became more tempered. Yet undoubtedly H.D. could not help but be proud of the reports of his success, which were to some extent a vindication of her fight with her parents. An exchange between Her and her mother goes: (her mother) 'I thought you said he was getting on famously, that all London, Munich, Paris and Berlin were at his feet, that he was chanting his verses to crowded houses, at tea parties –'; (Hermione) 'I didn't say anything of the sort. I said that Yeats had praised him in a review, that Madox Ford wanted him to help in a new book he's doing, that – . . .'[79] All in fact wildly inaccurate, apart from chanting his verse to crowded houses and at tea parties, in the limited purlieus of London, but indicative of the vibrations of Pound's small successes as they reached Upper Darby.

Yet if H.D. poured out to Frances the story of 'her infatuation' with Pound (as Fayne Rabb describes it in *Her*) she was also 'infatuated' (as H.D. put it to Freud many years later) with Frances herself. How H.D., in the bland Philadelphia of 1910, defined or understood her passion for Frances is hard to say. Writing about this period in the 1920s, H.D. avoids labels or categories. In *Her* she mocks the fashionable sub-Freudian jargon of the post-war years that would have defined and pigeonholed her feelings, her failures, her struggles to find herself. 'Her Gart had no word for her dementia . . . She could not predict later common usage of uncommon syllogisms; "failure complex," "compensation reflex," and that conniving phrase "arrested development" had opened no door to her . . . Words that had not (in Philadelphia) been invented, beat about them: Oedipus complex, inferiority complex, claustrophobia.'[80] Not that the text suggests doors would have been opened to her even if she had known such words, but perhaps she would have known that her confusion, her sense of failure, was not uncommon. But how she explained or understood her feelings for Fayne/Frances, 'her sister love', is never resolved, and no more precise formulation is ever offered in the novel. *Her* was not written to be published, so it was not fear of censorship. As with *The Gift*, which is written 'as the child saw it', H.D. is telling the story of *Her* as the young woman in 1910 would have understood things, so she would not put it in language only available to her a decade and a half later. But there are perhaps other reasons that H.D. does not introduce the vocabulary of the 1920s here. Though by then H.D. knew a great deal more about sexology than she could have done at twenty-three, for her the theories that were current were not very helpful. She did not feel, as her then companion Bryher did, that she was a boy trapped within a woman's body. Gender inversion was the most common explanation of homosexuality at the period, and

Bryher had the comfort of being assured by Havelock Ellis himself that in deciding she was inwardly a boy she had diagnosed her problem correctly. H.D. admired Havelock Ellis in many ways – he was a good friend, and possibly at one stage a lover, and it was she who had put Bryher in touch with him – but his theories were alien to her experience. In Radclyffe Hall's *Well of Loneliness*, which appeared in 1928, shortly after H.D. had finished *Her*, gender inversion is also the theory embodied by Stephen Gordon, who again sees herself as a boy unhappily trapped in a female body. Such a concept was not much use to a bisexual like H.D., who felt uncomfortable with contemporary definitions of both masculinity and femininity. As Her says to Fayne in *Asphodel*, 'I don't want to be (as they say crudely) a boy. Nor do I want you to so be. I don't feel a girl. What is all this trash of Sappho? None of that seems real, to (in any way) matter. I see you. I feel you . . . My brain reaches some height of delirium. Do people say it's indecent? Maybe it is. I can't hear now, see any more, people. Some are kind, some aren't. That's all the division I can ever have between them.'[81] By the time H.D. came to write *Her* and the extant version of *Asphodel*, she was in love with Kenneth Macpherson, though with no desire to break away from Bryher. Her complicated emotional life still refused easy definition.

Freud's theories would later be more helpful to H.D., but when she was writing *Her* she was warily taking an interest in them for the first time. There are brief allusions to Freud in the novel, but Hermione is mistrustful of his theorising: 'I mean abstractions are so frightening,' she comments.[82] That mention of the 'conniving phrase "arrested development"' suggests his theory that the homosexual has for some reason remained trapped in an immature stage, an idea H.D. was never to accept. Fayne is said to have an uncle doctor, 'very advanced', in North Philadelphia, who is translating some psychoanalysis: 'it was mother and father and Oedipus complex'. Fayne, Her says, 'read a lot of books, wanted to lend me some books, psychoanalysis, German books . . . German that ran on and on, and the translations read odd, didn't mean the same thing.' What she does discover from them is that 'there were people who loved . . . differently'.[83] This simple statement, not wrapped in scientific terminology or medical jargon, is all she wants to accept here.

H.D. insists several times in her letters that Pound was the first person to mention psychoanalysis to her, and that he did so in 1912; Frances also said she first learnt of Freud from Pound, presumably at the same

period: Fayne's uncle must be a fictional device so that she can introduce the references to her awakening interest in Freud. It is, as it
happens, quite likely that some 'advanced' doctors in Philadelphia were
reading Freud at the time; the lectures he gave on his famous tour to
the States in 1909 were not only, as I mentioned earlier, reported in the
press, but were published in the *American Journal of Psychology* in 1910,
and any doctor with a serious interest in mental health could well have
known about him and decided to find out more. The very considerable
influence of Freud in America was certainly beginning. According to
Gregg's son, Oliver Wilkinson, Frances did not know before her marriage
the sexual meaning of 'lesbian', nor did she realise that heterosexual
relations involved penetration; if true, something hard to believe of a
student of Freud.[84] Even if psychoanalysis were already infiltrating
corners of Philadelphia, the reference indicates not literal knowledge
then, but simply how important culturally Freud had become by the
time the fictions were written. Freud differed from sexologists such as
Krafft-Ebing and Havelock Ellis, who saw homosexuality as innate; for
Freud both homosexuality and heterosexuality are acquired. To understand your sexuality, you had with your analyst's help to revisit and
retell the story of your life. When H.D. went to see Freud in 1933 she
had already spent over a decade attempting to find a way to retell the
story of her life in her fiction, though without the help of an analyst.
So, although, as Diane Chisholm argues, H.D. very much 'translated'
Freud's scientific categories into her own poetic language, Freud's
method was ideal for her.[85]

At the time H.D. met Frances in 1909 or 1910, it is much more likely
that her understanding of sexual desire and her knowledge of how people
'loved . . . differently' came, not from sexology or psychoanalysis, but
from literature, and in particular Swinburne, whom Pound had read to
her, and whom she read to Frances. As critics have pointed out, it is
often through quotations from him that she expresses her complex
passions in these autobiographical novels. Swinburne was at his best a
superb lyricist as well as a shockingly iconoclastic writer, a combination
of qualities which endeared him to poetic young rebels, and many of
the modernist generation admired him fervently in their youth. Pound
in these years saw Swinburne as an apostle of life dispelling pious
Victorian gloom, 'the lifter of the hearts of men'.[86] Unlike H.D., he
never refers either to Swinburne's exploration of deviant sexuality nor
to the dark melancholic strain in his poetry. Swinburne published his
Poems and Ballads, First Series, the collection from which Pound and

H.D. both quote, in 1866, just as the first works of sexology were beginning to appear in Germany, at the very start of the period when, Michel
Foucault has argued, the idea of a homosexual was born; that is, the
homosexual as a distinct type of human being who only desires those
of his or her own gender, as opposed to human beings who might from
time to time, or indeed frequently, commit homosexual acts. Swinburne's
poems in this collection are psychological studies of states of desire,
deeply influenced by Baudelaire, exploring the complexity and diversity
of human sexual passion. Jonathan Culler says Baudelaire saw 'passion
as a sought-for hell', and the same could be said of Swinburne: he writes
of lesbian, male homosexual, bisexual, heterosexual, incestuous and
masochistic desires, in all of which pain and pleasure, ecstasy and
suffering, are inextricably mixed.[87] Swinburne is a master of lyric beauty,
even when his subject-matter is at its most disturbing. What he says of
Baudelaire could apply equally to his own *Poems and Ballads*: 'he has
chosen to dwell mainly upon sad and strange things – the weariness of
pain and the bitterness of pleasure – the perverse happiness and wayward
sorrows of exceptional people. It has the languid, lurid beauty of close
and threatening weather – a heavy, heated temperature, with dangerous
hothouse scents in it; thick shadow of cloud about it, and fire of molten
light . . . The style is sensuous and weighty; the sights seen are steeped
most often in sad light and sullen colour.'[88]

Unlike Baudelaire's, the settings of Swinburne's love poems are generally mythic, or at least they are set in classical Greece or Renaissance
Italy, not in his own day. That would have been too much for an English
audience, though even so his publishers, the respectable firm of Moxon,
withdrew the collection as soon as they had released it. Swinburne had
to have it reissued by a firm of dubious reputation whose owner had a
taste for erotica. The collection sold well, going into numerous editions,
in spite, or possibly because, of the frequent attacks on it. The poem
that caused most affront and was deemed 'especially horrible', according
to the reply Swinburne published to his critics, was 'Anactoria', a version
of a Sappho poem in which she expresses passionate love for a young
woman of that name. During much of the nineteenth century, translations of Sappho quietly changed the gender of pronouns, or substituted
'youth' for 'girl', so her poetry became heterosexual.[89] As Swinburne
(who had been to Eton) pointed out, this was in spite of the fact that
every schoolboy – every schoolboy, that is, who belonged to the classes
who were taught Greek – was 'compelled under penalties to learn, to
construe, and to repeat . . . the imperishable and incomparable verses

of that supreme poet'.[90] It was women and the working class who were being 'protected' by these bowdlerised translations. The first English edition to break with that tradition was brought out by H.T. Wharton in 1885, the edition from which H.D. would later work. Swinburne in 1866 was in the vanguard. 'Anactoria' is still startling for the violent intensity of passion that Sappho pours out, the scandal of this poem being compounded by its blasphemous denunciation of God. Swinburne subverted every Victorian idol: patriarchy, family, religion, even the monarchy, for he was a republican into the bargain. To the questioning young, impatient with the status quo, he gave new breath.

H.D.'s writings echo the sense of the ambiguities and ambivalences of all forms of desire in Swinburne, whose gallery of passion is much closer to Freud than to the early scientific work of the marshalling and cataloguing sexologists. To Swinburne, as to Freud, all desire is more or less perverse; in some forms the inevitability of its pain, its frustration, its disruptive force are clearer than in others, but they are not essentially different in kind from the form society decrees 'normal'. Like Freud, Swinburne sees human desire as insatiable, never to be totally fulfilled, always threatening to tear apart the fragile veil of social order; family relationships are often erotically charged, and frequently destructive. In the sexologists' work, genders may become inverted, but most sexologists had a strong and generally conventional late nineteenth-century sense of what masculinity and femininity ought to be. In Swinburne's poems, as to some extent in Freud, those certainties vanish. Like other Pre-Raphaelite and aesthetic poets and artists, his work is full of disturbing *femmes fatales*, androgynous bodies, and suffering, vulnerable men. It was perhaps this move away from conventional gender binaries that H.D. particularly valued in his writing.

The Swinburne poem H.D. quotes most often to describe the intensity of love and pain in Her's response to Fayne is one of Swinburne's most poignant and delicate poems, 'Itylus', not explicitly concerned with sexual love at all, though the emotions as always in Swinburne are tinged with eroticism, and the backdrop to the poem, as contemporary readers would have recognised, is rape, mutilation and child murder. Its mixture of bitterness and sweetness, allure and rejection, violence and pity is, perhaps, what makes it so meaningful for her. Frances was never an easy person. In her 'Autobiographical Notes' for 1910 H.D. comments, 'Frances is un-even as always'.[91] Their relationship was, as Frances' son later said, 'deep' but 'bitter-sweet'.[92] Yet, if her relationship with Frances was always difficult, H.D. does suggest in *Her* that

the experience of falling in love with a woman was in itself an important step in accepting herself. All through her life and work, she was
struggling against an upbringing and a culture that devalued her as a
woman and that gave young men – at least middle-class young men –
a sense of effortless superiority over her or any woman. The modernist
avant-garde would create its own problems for the woman artist, as she
would find. But, with Frances, a fellow-woman whom she loved and
whose worth and power she felt, she could believe that she too, although
a woman, could have value, and could create. Her love for Frances made
possible her first blossoming as an artist, whereas, although she learnt
so much from the young Pound, he had in many ways, in that first love
affair between them, silenced her, with his chant of 'You are a poem,
though your poem's naught', or, as George puts it in *Her*, 'your pomes
were rotten'.[93] Both Pound and Frances, she concluded later, were necessary to her development as a poet, but after Pound's awakening, Frances,
as she says in *End to Torment*, 'completed or "complemented" the Dryad
or Druid that Ezra had evoked so poignantly'.[94] After Pound had left
the first time, she writes,

A sort of *rigor mortis* drove me onward. No, my poetry was not dead but it was
built on or around the crater of an extinct volcano. Not *rigor mortis*. No, No! The
vines grow more abundantly on those volcanic slopes . . . I was separated from my
friends, my family, even from America, by Ezra. I did not analyse this. When
Frances came into my life, I could talk about it – but even so, only superficially.
But I read her some of the poems that Ezra and I had loved.[95]

It was at that point, she says, that she could begin to write again. As
she puts it in *Her*, 'Love is writing'.[96] Writing is in H.D.'s eyes in itself
an erotic – a bisexually erotic – activity.

H.D. never lost her affection for Swinburne's poetry, but he cannot
have been an entirely encouraging guide for youthful ardour. In
Swinburne's late nineteenth-century view of sexuality, all desire is ultimately doomed to pain and self-defeat; for all his atheism and claimed
paganism, the pallor of evil still colours eroticism in his poems; his
depiction of lesbianism depends on his readers' knowledge that this is
forbidden, shocking desire. In these poems, sexuality is central, as it
was to be for the modernists, but for Swinburne it is an inevitable curse,
not a hope. Like Baudelaire he believes that 'the unique and supreme
pleasure of making love lies in the certitude of doing evil'.[97] H.D.
continued in her poetry to show desire as intense and violent, painful

and ecstatic, just as Swinburne does, but, as she says in *Asphodel*, she wants to resist the labelling of her desires as 'indecent'; the decadent delight in sin was not for her generation, or at any rate not for most of them: Eliot, who was perhaps an exception, at any rate in hanging on to the sense of sin, if not delighting in it, wrote, in 1927, the year in which he became an Anglican, that Baudelaire 'was at least able to understand that the sexual act as evil is more dignified, less boring, than as the natural, "life-giving", cheery automatism of the modern world'.[98] H.D. had no liking for 'cheery automatism' either, but neither did she desire the stigma of evil.

One thing that is striking about H.D. is the intensity of response she gave to her relationships. Pound, Frances, Aldington, Lawrence, Bryher, Kenneth Macpherson and others she felt about with a strength of passion, though of very different kinds, that absorbed her whole being for the time, and that she never forgot, revisiting and exploring each encounter in her poetry and fiction again and again, weaving them together in mythic patterns. Where others might be emotionally wary, H.D. gave herself unguardedly, frequently to be painfully hurt. And yet, that said, as with Pound, there was always one passion that was stronger: her need to write. Those with Pound and Frances were perhaps the two most intense relationships she had, but she would not have sacrificed her poetry to either of them. Already in 1910 she knew she wanted to be a poet; but she also knew she loved Frances; and she was soon to discover that she still loved Pound. Pound had shocked Philadelphia, but a woman loving a woman was more shocking still. She might feel her desires ought not to be labelled 'indecent', but she knew that, if uncovered, they would be. H.D. always went in fear of social ostracism. She was rebellious, but largely covertly; she knew that a woman who overstepped the mark could be psychically destroyed. When Pound returned to Philadelphia their relationship would begin again, but this time there was also Frances. How would that be resolved?

IV

POUND arrived in New York in late June 1910, after a terrible crossing. He was always a bad sailor, and on this occasion, he said, 'the Lusitania had delirium Tremens in the end of it I used'.[99] Once safely back on dry land, he spent a couple of nights in New York, then headed home. In August he would return to further his fortune-making plans, but for now he took things easy. His parents were not in Wyncote at that point, but were living temporarily in the suburb of Swarthmore, having rented out the Wyncote house, something they did regularly. H.D. later surmised this was in order to finance Pound's London life, but Pound never commented. The Swarthmore house, which was large and spacious, belonged to a journalist, at whose 'huge desk' Pound was able to work. Although he complained about the 'absurdly' hygienic quality of American suburban life, after the friendly squalor of London, he was happier to be home than he had thought he would be.[100] As he later put it, 'To return to America is like going through some very invigorating, very cleansing sort of bath.'[101] He wrote to Margaret Cravens from Swarthmore on 30 June, a few days after his arrival, 'The country seems strange to my eyes that have grown more European than I knew – strange but not so unpleasant as I expected.'[102]

In spite of being separated from Dorothy, Pound had cheered up. He told Margaret that she would be 'relieved' to know that he was feeling much more optimistic, and was sorry for worrying her in Paris. Now, he told her, he had a new sense of purpose:

with the new fight before me (mad enough tho' it seems), there has come a curious renewal of that kind of energy that I had before the first *battaglia* . . . I have come to another starting point, and I am neither weary – nor am I any longer filled with that virus that makes one ask 'to what end the attempting?'

What does he mean by the 'new fight'? The first *battaglia*, he explains, was his attempt, on arrival from Gibraltar, to take London – to echo his military metaphor – by storm. Now once more he has 'the same absolutely unfettered puerile sort of feeling for the attack as I had when I first went up against London with a sheaf of verse'.[103] When in March he had first met Margaret in Paris, he had begun seriously to doubt that he would ever make his way as a poet, just as after his expulsion from Wabash he had been through a period of similar near-despair. He was generally loath to admit to despondency; in his 1912 lecture 'Psychology and the Troubadours', one of the things for which he praises his troubadours is that in their love religion, 'though the servants of Amor went pale and wept and suffered heat and cold, they came on nothing so apparently morbid as the "dark night".'[104] But Pound himself clearly did have 'dark nights of the soul', and though remarkable in the way that he would pick himself up again after a setback, perhaps his best poetry came, as in the *Pisan Cantos*, when he allowed himself to acknowledge them.

For now, however, Pound was full of hope once more. For one thing, as he told Margaret, his brief reunion with Yeats in London had cheered him:

> Yeats has been doing some new lyrics – he has come out of the shadows & declared for life. Of course there is in that a tremendous uplift for me – for he and I are now as it were in one movement, with aims very nearly identical. That is to say that the movement of the 90'ies for drugs and shadows has worn itself out. There has been no 'influence'. Yeats has found within himself spirit of the new air which I by accident had touched before him.[105]

These 'new lyrics' were the poems that Yeats was to publish later in the year in *The Green Helmet and Other Poems*. Pound does not in any way yet identify this 'spirit of the new air' as a modernising project in terms of style, in the way Hulme or Flint would have advocated; that was to come. It is true that Yeats' poetry in that volume has, as R. F. Foster puts it, a 'sharp new edge', and the change in Yeats' writing, even more pronounced in later volumes, has sometimes been retrospectively attributed to Pound's influence. But Pound had as yet no interest in sharp edges, and Yeats, Foster points out, had been 'hon[ing]' his writing for some time.[106] What had delighted Pound in these poems was more a question of mood than style, the fact that Yeats was moving away from nineties melancholy. Pound's 'revolt against the crepuscular spirit in modern poetry', as he had phrased it in the title of one of his *Personae* poems, was the one criticism he had so far made of that earlier generation, writing in his introduction to *The Spirit of Romance* that 'Art is a joyous thing'.[107]

Pound was right that the 'spirit of the new age' refused defeat and resignation. Pre-war modernism would be combative and often aggressive, but it had energy and drive. Hulme, Flint and Lawrence would all have agreed that art should be vital and vigorous. All three, like Yeats, had been deeply influenced by Nietzsche's insistence on the affirmation of life, and his belief that 'Art is the great stimulus to life'.[108] Pound had perhaps got there through Swinburne, though when he met Nietzsche he recognised their points of agreement. The First World War and its physical and spiritual death-dealing would bring this vitalist view of art to a crisis, but that was in the future. Yet, at this moment, for all his talk of 'the spirit of the new age', Pound was really only interested in himself and Yeats. He had written to his mother at the beginning of the year, when Yeats went back to Dublin, 'He is the only living man whose work has anything more than a most temporary interest.' And from Sirmione he had reported with some excitement to his father that 'News comes from London that Yeats has been saying nice things about me – not so valuable in private as they would have been on the platform but as gratifying personally to the effect that "there is no younger generation (of poets). E.P. is a solitary volcano".'[109] Pound had no intention at this stage of having a poetic pantheon of more than two.

Pound arrived home with hopes of a new beginning in America. He expected to be treated very differently now he had achieved a *succès d'estime* in Europe. Yet perhaps the fact that there exists no adequate Anglo-Saxon version of that phrase hints at why he was to be disappointed. He had acquired status in Philadelphia, particularly within his own circle, but for all the press coverage during the previous year of his London success, Pound was to find America, by and large, as unappreciative of him and his work as ever. *The Spirit of Romance* was published in June in England and in July in America, his first book to be published there. Though in *Her* we are told, 'everyone was taking George so to speak "up" because of that volume on Dante', the truth was more mixed.[110] Locally it did perhaps give him a certain cachet, but nation-wide the verdict was less kind. In 1968 Pound was to write of this book, 'As far as I remember it elicited no comment from the press'.[111] Repression perhaps was at work; though it certainly was not widely reviewed, he might have preferred to forget what comments there were. *The Spirit of Romance*, the book that Pound had suggested to his parents would guarantee his academic employment in the States, originally sprang out of his loathing for American university literature teaching, so its lack of success within the academic world there was not entirely surprising, particularly as Pound's introduction had started with an attack on the 'slough of philology', in itself likely to inflame many.[112] There are good moments and some memorable turns of phrase in *The Spirit of Romance*; the introduction especially has an engaging youthful exuberance and is an intriguing early manifesto of his poetic beliefs. Yet Pound's haste and boredom in its writing at times show through. The first review, which appeared in the American *Nation*, said unkindly that 'the few bits of really good comment are too rare to be worth hunting for'.[113] Another American review praised Pound for his insight but condemned his hunger for publicity, which was perhaps, in this instance, for once unfair; Pound's views on literature were deeply felt and not simply meant to shock. Presumably the reviewer has in mind, besides the attack on the philological method, comments like, 'Milton's god is a fussy old man with a hobby'; or '[Arnold's] definition of literature as "criticism of life" is the one notable blasphemy that was born of his mind's frigidity . . . Poetry is about as much a "criticism of life" as red-hot iron is a criticism of fire.'[114] In Pound's view, this was simply fair comment.

H.D. herself admired *The Spirit of Romance*, perhaps partly as a record of the eclectic enthusiasms that Pound had brought to her during their relationship.[115] In *Paint it Today*, she uses as a repeated motif the refrain of the anonymous hymn to Venus, from about the second century AD, the *Pervigilium Veneris*, which Pound praises and translates in his first chapter, to which he had undoubtedly earlier introduced her. This hymn was to be sung on the eve of the feast that, Pound says, has survived as May Day, and the refrain goes, '*Cras amet qui numquam amavit/Quique amavit cras amet*' ('Let whoever never loved, love tomorrow/Let whoever has loved, love tomorrow').[116] Pound sees this hymn as an early anticipation of the Provençal love lyric, pointing out that its metre uses stress, rather than quantity like traditional Latin verse, a shift which, he says, 'probably indicated as great a change of sensibility in its day as the change from Viennese waltzes to jazz may indicate in our own'.[117] In H.D.'s novel the refrain becomes the centre of her reflections on the nature of her different love affairs, and on the nature of love itself. H.D was to read *The Spirit of Romance* again in 1948, and found it returned her to the early Pound, at a period when she was appalled by the raving anti-Semite so prominent in the newspapers.

Pound's chapter on Villon, one of the most successful, perhaps indicated what was going wrong with his own poetry at the time. Villon was, he says, 'poet and gaol-bird, with no care whatever for the flowery traditions of medieval art, and no anxiety to revive the massive rhetoric of the Romans'. In his work were the 'seeds and signs of a far more modern outbreak' even than Dante's. 'From Provence,' he argues, 'the Tuscans have learned pattern; the Elizabethans a certain lyric quality; Villon carries on another Provençal tradition, that of unvarnished, intimate speech'.[118] In Pound's early poetry, much of what was most successful was the poetry that like Villon's took from troubadours the direct, speaking voice, and the defiant, iconoclastic personae. Now in his elaborate *canzoni*, in his painstaking translations of Cavalcanti's exquisitely fashioned sonnets and ballads, he was imprisoning himself in an alien formal pattern. No longer uttering defiance at a world in which he did not fit, he was weaving an elegantly wrought barrier behind which to hide, locking himself in more effectively than keeping the world out.

Pound may never have seen that first dismissive review of the book that he had produced with such pain, and for the first couple of months back home his letters to Margaret remain cheerful. She wrote that she liked the 'S. of R.', as he put it, and was able to tell him of an encouraging review of the book in the *Mercure de France*.[119] Pound's letters to Margaret are very different in tone from the lectures he delivered to Viola Baxter, or even the condescension that is often present in his letters to Williams. Pound treats her much more as an equal. Perhaps her generosity and belief in his gifts made it possible for him to find a saner way of relating to the world than hitherto. It was not to last, but perhaps it might have done if events had turned out differently.

Pound had said nothing to Margaret about Dorothy, who had figured in the letters from Sirmione simply as one of *les amies anglaises*: Margaret and Dorothy were in separate compartments of his life. This is not to suggest that they were rivals; there is no hint in Pound's letters to Margaret of any romantic involvement, though that is not to say her feelings for him were not already more than disinterested admiration for his art. But back in Philadelphia there was a rival. Although Pound said nothing to Margaret about H.D., in his first letter from Swarthmore he tells her he is reading Swinburne for the first time in three years, possibly an indication he was in touch again with H.D. They had been corresponding regularly, and he had written to her from Italy (at any rate according to her fictionalised account) that he was coming back to 'Gawd's own god-damn country'.[120] H.D. had kept in touch with Pound's parents, to whom of course Pound had said nothing about his involvement with Dorothy, and who clearly still hoped for a marriage between her and their son. But Pound could resist his parents. It was perhaps his own feelings for H.D. that he trusted less. While in the States, he would also see Mary Moore and Viola Baxter, but they had both settled – it appears, though one cannot be quite certain – into the role of good friend.

As with Pound's first courtship of H.D., the evidence for their relationship over the next few months is patchy. William Carlos Williams recalled being visited by the two of them later in the year, but whether their engagement had been renewed isn't clear. It appears to have been back to the status of an 'understanding'. Perhaps, like Olivia, H.D.'s parents felt nothing more formal could be finalised until Pound had a visible income. After all, at the time of the original engagement, when Pound gave H.D. Kitty Heyman's ring and his mother gave her the pearl pendant, he was still employed by Wabash College. As Eugenia, Hermione's mother, says in *Her*: 'You can't live on nothing. Your father won't permit it. Do you think your father and I would have such inhumanity as to let you – to *let* you marry a man of George Lowndes' reputation and marry a man of George Lowndes' reputation on simply nothing?'[121]

Her's fictional account of the ambivalence with which Hermione hears of George's return from Italy, and of how she eventually succumbs to his renewed lovemaking, may be close to what in fact occurred. Certainly the way in which, in the novel, in spite of Pound/George's new-found fame, Philadelphia still murmured about the scandal which had sent him to Europe, rings very true. In *Her*, George and Fayne, to Hermione's intense distress, have some kind of affair, and Gregg's memoirs confirm that this was true of Pound and Frances. When H.D. discovered, she was distraught. If Pound had become so instantly jealous when Grace Crawford, who was far less important to him than H.D., offered Lawrence Italian lessons, one can imagine that he was outraged on his return to find H.D passionately involved with another woman, though he may have taken some time to appreciate the situation. Once he did, he was very ready to take a moral high line on the scandalous bond between them. In the fictional account, George says that they are witches and should have been burnt at the stake, an extreme response for an aficionado of Swinburne, who might have been expected to show greater tolerance. In *Her*, Hermione is under the impression that he disapproves of Fayne as much as her mother does, one reason why the betrayal is so unexpected. But Pound appears to have been more shocked by finding a rival than anything else. One element in his advances to Frances may have been the desire to revenge himself on H.D. for daring to have another love, as well as his childish hatred of being left out. When Pound first met Bryher, she says in her autobiography, he tried to make a pass at her, doubtless for the same complex reasons, but she froze him out very effectively. Yet Pound in his relationship with H.D. would repeatedly make advances to her, and then retreat in one way or another, and this betrayal, like the earlier ones, may have also been a means of escape. In Frances Gregg's short story, 'Male and Female', she has a perceptive analysis of what was going on. She sets up the triangle of 'Kiah' (based on Pound, short for Hezekiah), in her version an acclaimed young painter who intended, he said, to 'become the greatest artist since Leonardo', 'Sheila' (based on H.D.), his fiancée, and 'Jennie' (based on herself). Kiah has already made a name for himself: 'It was before the days of "publicity", but Kiah had invented a technique of personal publicity that was working like a dream.' Having acquired fame since his engagement to Sheila, he is now 'launched with a number of new loves. His only anxiety was just how to be off with the old. Sheila had a strong will, but more tricky to handle was the tie of his own affection and an old fealty to Sheila. That was where Jennie came in.'[122] Once again, as in the weeks immediately before he left for Europe in 1908, Pound may have attempted to resolve his ambivalent attitude to H.D. by driving her away through his infidelity.

When precisely this happened isn't certain, but it was probably in September, when Walter Rummel came to stay in Swarthmore. A tentative reconstruction of the timetable might be this: on his return Pound laid siege to H.D.'s affections once more. She was still in love with him, though angry as well, and in spite of her feelings for Frances, found him hard to resist. But Pound had his own divided loyalties. He was still busy translating Guido Cavalcanti, and in the introduction, which he wrote later in the year, he raises the question of whether Guido's lady was 'one' or 'several'. Pound's ladies were definitely in the plural. In August he returned to New York, clearly guilty about Dorothy, whose tender, admiring letters he was receiving, even if he was not allowed to write to her. He threw himself into attempts to make money, as he had promised her he would. Pound's idea, according to Williams, was to

H.D. at fourteen, just before she met Ezra Pound

H.D.'s mother, Helen Doolittle, née Wolle, as a young woman,
with her paintbrushes

H.D.'s home in Upper Darby, near the Flowers Observatory

Ezra Pound at Cheltenham Military Academy in 1898. Pound is in the upper middle of the picture, the only boy with glasses

Pound, second from left, as a maiden in the 1903 University of Pennsylvania production of Euripides' *Iphigenia in Tauris*, seen by both Williams and H.D.

H.D. (front row on the right) at Bryn Mawr, c.1906

Elkin Mathews'
bookshop at
6b Vigo Street,
'the smallest shop
in the world',
Ernest Rhys said,
as it appeared in
an ink drawing,
c.1891

Ford Madox Ford, then Hueffer,
c.1915. When Pound met him
in 1909, Ford was editor of the
English Review, 'the greatest
editor in the world', as he claimed
May Sinclair described him

Dorothy Shakespear, c.1910,
about the time when she met Pound;
she looked, Yeats said, 'as if her face
was made out of Dresden china'

Olivia Shakespear, c.1910,
'undoubtedly the most charming woman
in London', according to Pound

T.E. Hulme, probably in his late twenties, in a pencil sketch by Dolly Kibblewhite

F.S. Flint, poet, linguist and socialist. He never forgot his painful childhood, or as he put it, 'the child for whose wounds I bear the scars'

Aubrey Beardsley's title page for Florence Farr's 1894 New Woman novel, *The Dancing Faun*. (The faun here is probably a caricature of Shaw, one of Farr's lovers and satirised in the book)

Songs published for the 1904 Festival of the Glens, which Joseph Campbell helped organise, a central event in the Ulster Celtic Revival

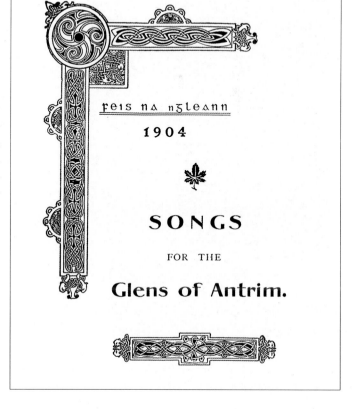

Feis na nGleann

1904

SONGS

FOR THE

Glens of Antrim.

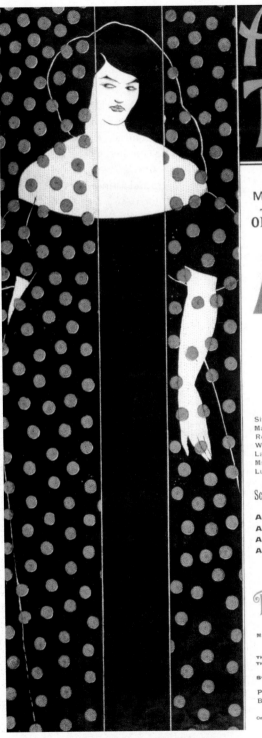

Aubrey Beardsley's poster, regarded as very shocking at the time, but widely exhibited none the less, for Florence Farr's 1894 season at the Avenue Theatre, on the London Embankment, in which she appeared in Yeats' *The Land of Heart's Desire* and Shaw's *Arms and the Man*

W.B. Yeats in about 1910, when Pound first met him, introduced by Olivia Shakespear

John Gould Fletcher in 1914, a moody and reluctant imagist, who thought of himself as a 'grey ghost' and 'one of the never born'

Frances Gregg, c.1912. H.D. wrote of her that, after Ezra left for Europe,
Frances filled the gap in her life 'like a blue flame'

A DECADE'S PROGRESS.

I.—MRS. BROWNE, MRS. BROWNE JUNIOR, AND MRS. BROWNE JUNIOR'S LITTLE GIRL AS THEY WERE IN 1901 AND—
II.—AS THEY ARE TO-DAY.

'A Decade's Progress': *Punch*'s version of the changes in women's fashion from 1901 to 1911, the last year of Victoria's reign to the year after the death of Edward VII

Brigit Patmore, whom Pound described as one of the 'charming people on the planet'; from 1911 until his marriage in 1914, much of his time was spent with Brigit, H.D. and Aldington

Rabindranath Tagore, the gifted Bengali writer, musician and painter, in a drawing in sanguine and black and white chalk by William Rothenstein, 1930. Pound watched Rothenstein paint Tagore's portrait in 1912, shortly before the publication of his poems, *Gitanjali*, Pound's first great enthusiasm in non-Western literature make a great deal of money very fast, so he could quickly settle back into the literary life Nothing came of this excursion into the business world, not even of Pound's suggestion that he and William Carlos Williams should go into partnership selling a recently developed anti-syphilis drug to North African 'nabobs', which Pound was convinced would make their fortune in a year. He had no luck. Most projects he attempted demanded capital, to which Pound had no access. Finding himself an income to placate Olivia was going to be harder than he thought. What is surprising is that Pound thought he had a chance of making a fortune in business, but he found it hard to accept that there were skills that he did not possess. Margaret probably had quite good business contacts, and had he asked her for them he might have done better.

While in New York, Pound went to call on Yeats' father, the painter John Butler Yeats, now living in the city. They took to each other greatly; Yeats *père* (as Pound described him) appreciated Pound's enthusiasm for his son's work, and Pound, ready in any case to admire any relation of Yeats, appears genuinely to have liked John Butler. Yeats' father introduced him to John Quinn, an Irish-American lawyer with strong artistic interests, particularly at this stage in the Celtic Revival. Quinn had bought paintings by John Butler Yeats and his son Jack, and had organised Yeats' lecture tour in the States, and also one by Florence Farr. (He was one of her many lovers.) Quinn, Yeats *père* and Pound all went together to the amusement fair on Coney Island, which greatly diverted Pound. He claimed later to scorn 'its sham fairy-land', but at the time he enjoyed it immensely, and was especially delighted by the sight of the father of the man he thought the greatest living poet riding an elephant.[123] It was the highlight of the August visit. John Quinn later became a generous patron of modernist art, supporting Pound's friends on Pound's advice, so that August visit was not in the end without its financial benefits, even if Pound would not realise that until 1915.

When Rummel joined him at the beginning of September, after a concert tour in the States, in the course of which he had given the American première of Debussy's *Preludes*, Pound took him back to Swarthmore. There, Pound was to tell Dorothy later, he and Walter Rummel had a fornight 'that mattered': Pound gave her no explanation of why.[124] It was, undoubtedly, partly to do with the Provençal settings in which Pound was so keenly interested, and on which he would work with Rummel the following year in Paris. Yet more important, perhaps, was the musical philosophy that Rummel had absorbed from Debussy, which was to be crucial to the next stage in the development of Pound's poetic theories. Many of the ideas that Pound absorbed from Rummel, or worked out together with him, were to remain fundamental to his poetic practice. It may well be that Rummel was the person referred to in a letter Pound wrote the following January, in which he said that in his seven months in the States, he had only found one man to whom he could talk, or, he added with some self-knowledge, at whom he could talk. Pound always took his male friends more seriously than his female, and during his time in America, although he made a few brief visits to see Williams, he appears to have lacked any close male literary or artistic companionship, so perhaps that fortnight stood out. Pound believed, as Brigit Patmore recalled, that women expected to be instructed, amused or made love to. He didn't expect them to be intellectual or artistic equals. He had said to his mother earlier that year that he had no objection to intelligence in a woman, and the women to whom he made love were certainly all intelligent and gifted. But when it came to 'licherary' or any kind of artistic 'ComPanionship' he turned to men. This was precisely the bone of contention between himself and H.D., though neither may have been able to put it into words at this stage. She wanted to be a literary as well as erotic companion; he wanted a woman who would be muse and acolyte simultaneously.

In Swarthmore, Walter Rummel gave at least one informal concert in the Pounds' rented house, to which H.D. and Frances came. For H.D., with her intense love of music, it was, she recalled many years later, 'sheer bliss'.[125] She was very taken with this charming, handsome musician, and was intrigued by the fact that his grandfather had been Samuel Morse, who invented the Morse code, so that like her he was an artist who sprang from scientific stock. (As she puts it in *Asphodel*, 'It's the Gart formula and the Morse Code between us.')[126] In Frances' fictional account of events, Kiah begins to flirt with Jennie while Sheila is engrossed in talking to his aesthetic friend, not at all an unlikely scenario. Frances had, it appears, been immediately attracted to Pound; she had heard enough about this scandalous poet to make her in love with him before he arrived. Although she was bisexual – later apparently predominantly heterosexual – she had had no kind of a relationship with a man up till then, in spite of her age – she was twenty-six that September – notwithstanding her striking looks. In her story 'Male and Female', she says of her persona Jennie, 'Believing that no one would ever choose her as a wife, a belief which her mother had nurtured in her, she loudly acclaimed that she disliked all men and never intended to marry.'[127] H.D. in *Paint it Today* also says of Fayne Rabb, 'she had always repudiated all talk or thought of marriage'.[128] It is not unlikely that Frances' mother wanted to hold on to her only daughter, but she may also have felt Frances' comparative poverty meant that she would not land a husband of the social standing she deserved. Better not to marry than to marry beneath her. Pound was the first man to kiss Frances, and, she said, in the dramatic terms of the day, it awoke her as a woman.[129]

'Male and Female' is very entertaining, though like all Gregg's fiction astringent and disturbing; it is bitter in its depiction of all the figures involved, including Jennie herself, who outwits the others ruthlessly and cynically, including the aesthetic friend, Aloysius, who evolves into a caricature of Gregg's husband Louis Wilkinson, whom she was to marry two years later. When Kiah kisses her, it is 'suddenly, roughly, with hard, vehement greed', followed by an outburst of rage and hatred for women.[130] In this fictional account, Jennie is aware that she is hopelessly in love with Kiah and simultaneously that he is quite unworthy of such passion. His words, she records, were a 'blather of vanity and nonsense'. He describes to her 'the wonders of his personality, genius and beauty, as ascribed to by his friends, family, the public, and, of course, himself', and tells her that 'Nothing would induce me to boast, or blow my own horn – trust pater for doing that – but I should just like you to know that I am the greatest painter of my generation.'[131] In real life, Frances certainly was very much in love with Pound, and remained so for some time, but whether she so clear-sightedly saw his faults from the start is another matter. In 1914, she was still saying he was one of the two fixed points of her affections, and recalled her passionate response to him in her late memoir. (The other, incidentally, also mentioned in the memoir, was a woman called Amy Hoyt, presumably related to, or possibly even identical to, the maligned Nan Hoyt.) Even though Pound was much mocked in the 1916 novel that Frances co-wrote with her husband, *The Buffoon*, in the end the heroine, the ambiguous H.D./Frances figure, marries him, perhaps a piece of fictional wish-fulfilment.

Sheila disappears from Jennie's life in the fictional version, but Frances' feelings for Pound don't appear to have changed hers for H.D., at any rate in the short run. She wrote in her diary: 'Two girls in love with each other, and each in love with the same man. Hilda, Ezra, Frances'.[132] Her son, in the introduction to a collection of John Cowper Powys and Frances' letters to each other, says that Pound and H.D. were the loves of her life. Perhaps that is true, and there were surely many complex emotions at work on her side too, including jealousy and competitiveness, behind her liaison with her lover's lover, something that 'Male and Female' makes very clear. Frances and H.D.'s relationship was never simple. When H.D. was writing *Her*, she had recently met up with Frances Gregg again, and on this occasion, Gregg's then lover, the twenty-four-year-old Kenneth Macpherson, fell in love with H.D. and deserted Frances. In her 'Autobiographical Notes', H.D. suggests Frances sent him to her, as if he were a gift. But Frances was bitterly hurt; perhaps there was an element of unadmitted revenge there on H.D.'s part for Frances' earlier betrayal.

V

POUND remained friendly with Frances Gregg for some years, possibly more than friendly: John Cowper Powys would suffer torments of jealousy when he knew she was seeing Pound. Pound always referred to her as the 'Egg' (egg-head? egoist? – it could be either), and later would help her get her work published. Yet the strength of feeling that Frances had for him may be related to his somewhat casual attitude to her. H.D.'s and Powys' infatuation with her she appears to have responded to with some ambivalence. How soon H.D. discovered what was happening between Frances and Pound one can only guess, because she only mentions that particular wound in her fiction. She may have found it too painful to speak of in *End to Torment*, where she records those earlier betrayals, and marks out betrayal as the canker which destroyed her relation with Pound from within more disastrously than the outside forces. That discovery may be what precipitated her move away from Philadelphia and Frances to New York in October, to share a flat with a Philadelphian acquaintance, Julia Wells, in the hope of finding work as a writer. What she clung on to was her resolute need to write. But she must have known that Pound would be in New York too, and that she would inevitably see him there. Once there, reconciliation – for now – appears to have been swift. In Noel Stock's account she arrived in New York in late October, and almost immediately went with Pound on the visit to Williams, where she met Williams' future wife Flossie; Williams, in his curmudgeonly way, asserts that Flossie didn't much care for either Pound or H.D.

H.D. remained for probably a couple of months that autumn in New York, living on the edge of Greenwich Village, whose bohemian life was just beginning. She stayed in Patchin Place, later one of the famous Greenwich Village addresses, home to Djuna Barnes and e.e. cummings, among others.[133] It has been suggested that Pound cold-shouldered H.D. while in New York, but there really is not much evidence one way or the other, and they did see a certain amount of each other. Julia Wells in later life referred to this period more than once as if both H.D. and Pound had stayed with her. Pound in fact lived elsewhere in New York, but the implication is surely that he spent quite some time at her flat. Julia Wells recalled that he wrote the Heine translations that appeared in *Canzoni* in Patchin Place, perhaps drawing on H.D.'s knowledge of German.

H.D. was unhappy in New York. She must still have been bruised by the Pound/Frances affair, but if she had been hoping to make a new life for herself, she was disappointed. In her 'Autobiographical Notes' she says enigmatically of that visit, 'it does not synchronize'. Perhaps she means it was not the right place for that time in her life. She found Julia 'discouraging', and the conditions in Patchin Place 'sordid'.[134] John Cowper Powys, who met Julia Wells in the 1920s, still in Patchin Place, described her as 'a quaint little old-fashioned Dickens character', which hardly sounds like a soul-mate for H.D. He comments that she lived 'in extreme poverty', which is perhaps what H.D. means by 'sordid'.[135] Presumably Julia had no servants, and H.D. was completely undomesticated. In 1910, though America was ahead in labour-saving gadgets, keeping one's living space civilised required constant manual effort. In London, until she married Richard Aldington, H.D. always lived with landladies, professionals in keeping sordidity at bay. She had none of Pound's skill at surviving in garrets, metaphorical or literal. Yet in 1911 Pound himself told Margaret Cravens that Julia Wells' life for the last ten or fifteen years had been 'rather sordid', so even he had been shocked by the degree of poverty in which she lived.[136] Julia Wells came from a well-to-do Philadelphian family, who, Powys surmised, had cut her off, presumably on account of her bohemian lifestyle. H.D. must have felt that Julia was a warning against women who rejected family life. And in New York she also suffered from the snow and cold, undoubtedly unalleviated by adequate heating, and, worst of all, could get no work published. One bright spot was that she met Viola Baxter, presumably through Pound, with whom she became good friends. Viola took H.D. to see her office. A woman working in an office: it was becoming increasingly common, but H.D. was impressed.

One letter survives that H.D. wrote to Isabel Pound from New York. She puts a brave face on things, and though she doesn't mention Ezra, she does say that Homer has been to see her, possibly when in New York on Presbyterian affairs, which seem to have been his main leisure activity. She fears that Homer's report on the place 'hasn't made things attract-ive', but insists all is really fine: 'There are stories to write and shredded wheat biscuits to buy, and stoves to build fires in – and people – numerous ones – to talk to!' The atmosphere was entirely European – everyone came from the 'old country' – and she was flattered that she and Julia were mistaken for 'English ladies'.[137] All this suggests H.D. was, like Pound, feeling deeply alienated from America, and longing to be in Europe. New York had appeared the next-best thing, but on closer acquaintance H.D. found it an inimical place. For someone who had spent her first years in Bethlehem and later youth in the countryside of Upper Darby it was too violent a shock. She wrote in *Paint it Today* of the sounds of New York, 'Have you heard New York shriek real terror, real emotion, reality, Europe and Asia in one voice, swift, penetrating, intimate and unrepentant?'[138] H.D. was not exaggerating: the sounds that one heard in Patchin Place were in truth often those of 'real terror'. Alyse Gregory, later managing editor of the *Dial* and later still wife of Llewelyn Powys, moved to Patchin Place shortly after H.D.'s time there, and found its sounds heart-rending. 'Patchin Place,' she points out, 'lies under the shadow of the old Jefferson Court, with its sham Gothic tower, where a great clock points out the hours to damned and saved at once.' On the upper floors of this grim prison were cells where pris-oners would be detained, and Gregory heard desperate women calling and crying through the night: 'On one occasion a woman howled half through the night. I could hear her as I lay stiff in my bed, this howl of a trapped animal, rising to a shriek of frenzy and subsiding to a low wail of unutterable terror and despair.'[139] This was where rebellious women ended, H.D. might have noted. She gave up her first attempt at independence, and returned home to Philadelphia.

Whether or not Pound neglected H.D. in New York, it is true, of course, that his eye was chiefly on his career. During these months he was engaged in discovering New York's literary life and trying to estab-lish himself in it. He began with a certain amount of enthusiasm. Pound had a warmth of feeling for New York that he had never had for Philadelphia, which may have been born of his earlier visits to Aunt Frank. He was, perhaps surprisingly, very taken with the New York skyscrapers, as he told Margaret Cravens, repeating his praise in a series of articles about his homeland that he would publish two years later, with the typically Poundian title of 'Patria Mia'. American architecture, he suggests there, 'is our first sign of the "alba"' of America, that is,

its artistic dawn.[140] In New York, 'electricity has for [the new metro-
politan] made the seeing of visions superfluous'; it is, he claims, not far
from being the most beautiful city in the world, at any rate by night:
'Squares after squares of flame, set and cut into the aether. Here is our
poetry, for we have pulled down the stars to our will.'[141] Pound's excitement at the skyline of New York would be echoed by a range of modernist
artists, including Francis Picabia, John Marin and Max Weber, in the
coming decade.[142]

Pound wrote a first draft of these articles that winter of 1910–11,
and the resulting 'Patria Mia' reveals a good deal about why he decided
to return to Europe in early 1911. In spite of his praise of those New
York buildings, architecture, he concluded, was the only flicker of
American artistic life there was. In all other ways America was still a
cultural desert: 'I have declared my belief in the imminence of an
American Risorgimento. I have no desire to flatter the country by
pretending that we are at present enduring anything except the Dark
Ages.'[143] There is, he says sweepingly, 'no man living now in America
whose work is of the slightest interest to any serious artist'.[144] America
produces artists, certainly, but they all leave for Europe: his two great
examples are Whistler and Henry James, but doubtless he was also
thinking of himself. In America, he claims, literature is destroyed by
'dry rot, magazitis', conventionality and provincialism.[145]

Pound told Margaret in late November that, while in New York, he
devoted all his time when not writing 'to a wild & desperate search for
people', but so far he had only met one who qualified for that status, an
'intelligent editor' named William Shepard Walsh.[146] He met several
aspiring poets, including Orrick Johns, whom he would later publish in
his *Catholic Anthology* of 1915, but appears to have developed no friendships. Why was Pound so unlucky in his time in New York, which shortly
would be alive with experimental and innovative poets? He was possibly
just a little early. The poetry revival in the States is generally dated to
1912; Julia Wells, writing to the *New York Times* in 1928, saw the visits
of H.D. and Ezra Pound as marking the very beginning of that period
of artistic flowering.[147] David Frail suggests that although writers and
artists had lived in Greenwich Village since Edgar Allan Poe's day, and
the number had grown in the first decade of the century, it was only
'in late 1912 or 1913, most participants' accounts agree, some critical
mass was reached that made it a "self-conscious" community aware of
its own distinctive values and style'.[148] Pound certainly was not aware
of an artistic community there. His friend Williams would later be deeply

involved with the New York scene, but at this stage, in spite of his years as what we would call a house-doctor in the French hospital in New York, he knew no Greenwich Village artists or intellectuals. He had not had the time available to make such contacts, and had no introductions to offer. But Pound was perhaps looking for the wrong things in New York. There were no established figures to whom he could look up, no sense of a tradition in the way he experienced it in London. As Edith Wharton shows in her novels and memoir, the upper classes of New York shrank from writers and artists; there was no hospitable network of the literary and cultured well-to-do. Mabel Dodge Luhan's famous salon, where everyone of any consequence in the artistic or intellectual world met, was not established until 1913, when she returned to America from Italy. There was a younger generation that was soon to make its mark, but as with the younger generation in England, Pound at the moment took little notice.

Pound too was predominantly looking for literary contacts, while the centre of artistic life in New York at the time, which he appears to have missed, was Alfred Stieglitz' 291 Gallery in Fifth Avenue, which had opened in 1905. Although the moment when modernist art erupted in New York's general cultural consciousness was the Armory Show in 1913, with its 1,300 paintings, Stieglitz had already introduced many modernist artists in his own smaller exhibitions. His beautifully produced magazine, *Camera Work*, which first came out in 1903, gave coverage to the latest movements in continental art, as well as promoting photography as an art form; if Brooke Smith had lived, Pound would have known of it by 1910. Stieglitz had already initiated what was to be the favourite New York form of social gatherings of artists, a meal at a large hotel table, the most famous of which was to be at the Algonquin Hotel in the 1920s. He had set up what became known as his Round Tables: the participants – artists, writers, poets – would gather at noon, at a round table in the dining-room of the Prince George Hotel, and put the world to rights; Pound, however, never found his way there. He mentioned in 1920, in a letter to Williams, the memory of visits to Mouquin, a French restaurant later used by the group who planned the Armory Show, but he did not appear to meet any of the avant-garde there in 1910.[149]

There is perhaps one other reason why Pound failed to make links with the young intellectuals who were in New York in 1910. By and large they were politically both more radical and activist than he was; they would have been impatient with his aestheticism, and he with their politics. Pound himself was already increasingly in favour of elites, order and hierarchy. In the first instalment of 'Patria Mia' in the *New Age*, he was to write: 'America, my country, is almost a continent and hardly yet a nation, for no nation can be considered historically as such until it has achieved within itself a city to which all roads lead, and from which there goes out an authority.'[150] This notion of centralised power, even though for now Pound is really only concerned with its cultural rather than its political impact, could not have been more different from the position of the young New York intellectuals, who supported not the official American Socialist Party but the more romantic syndicalists who formed the International Workers of the World (generally known as the IWW or the Wobblies). Max Eastman wrote in his autobiography that the journal *The Masses*, which he edited from 1912 to 1918, 'provided for the first time in America, a meeting ground for revolutionary labor and the radical intelligentsia', a forerunner of the hopes of 1968.[151] Eastman, later a poet and critic, as well as editor of Marx and the author of a widely read book, *The Enjoyment of Poetry*, published by Elkin Mathews in 1913, was in 1910 a lecturer in philosophy at Columbia, in Washington Heights, considerably north of where Pound lived, perhaps one reason why their paths did not cross. That November Eastman had launched the Men's League for Women's Suffrage in the City Club, not an event that appears to have attracted Pound. Women's suffrage was another cause warmly supported by the 'radical intelligentsia' of Greenwich Village, but though Pound did not oppose it, he never thought it important. Like a certain brand of Marxist to this day, he saw women's rights as a distraction.

Yeats' father made an intriguing comment on Pound's relationship with other writers in New York. He wrote to his son that he himself liked Pound very much, though surprisingly thought him rather quiet, but that 'the Americans, young literary men whom I know found him surly, supercilious and grumpy'.[152] The English literati had thought Pound could be bumptious, and certainly his scorn for American culture may have come across as superciliousness. But in London no one suggested that Pound was either 'surly' or 'grumpy'. Perhaps the final reason for Pound's failure to find '*people*' in New York was that while he could admire its skyscrapers, his early years in the States had been too bruising for him to be other than on the defensive with the young Americans he met. He may never have given them a chance. Yet by the time he published 'Patria Mia' two years later, the American *Risorgimento* that he believed was still distant had already begun.

For the meantime, Pound occupied himself with his translations, though he only succeeded in getting a few publications on this visit: the *Forum* published one of his *canzoni* in October, and accepted what he described as a 'vitriolic' article a little later, though they were not to get round to publishing it for over a year; eventually it appeared as 'The Wisdom of Poetry' in April 1912, though by then revised, moderated and embodying some of the ideas he began to evolve when he returned to London in 1911.[153] For now Pound had to be content with placing a version of it in his Philadelphian standby, the *Book News Monthly*.

If Pound was to make few new friends in New York, he was at least able to see some old ones. His Aunt Frank no longer lived in New York, though he did see her on that visit to the States, but Kitty Heyman was back visiting, and not apparently holding his break with her protégée Grace Crawford against him. He also saw Viola Baxter, and made occasional visits to New Jersey to see William Carlos Williams and his family. Williams had returned to the States at much the same time as Pound, having completed a course of postgraduate medical study in Leipzig, and had already started work as a doctor back in Rutherford, New Jersey. Williams felt as ambivalent as ever towards Pound, an ambivalence that in recollection could verge on hostility. Pound had obviously much enjoyed Williams' visit to London earlier in the year, reporting home that, by the time he left, 'Bill seemed to feel educated'.[154] Williams' version of events was rather different; he had felt not so much educated as patronised, and had been much irritated by Pound's pretentiousness. Williams had little patience with Pound's exaltation of art to a visionary plane. Although Williams was not to develop his modernist style for another three years, he had already come to believe that art should deal with the quotidian world. He had written to his brother Edgar in 1909 that 'Art . . . is an everyday affair and does not need a museum for its exposition,' adding, 'it should breathe in the common places'.[155]

These occasional meetings with friends were scarcely enough for the generally convivial Pound. By January he was back in Philadelphia with his parents, then living in another rented house near the Mint. He confessed to Margaret Cravens that he had had a miserable December. 'I had given up the fight more or less & was deciding that the country wasn't worth saving.'[156] Some of the misery may have been increased by the early stages of jaundice, to say nothing of the cold, of which he complained to Olivia, but what must have especially blighted his spirits were the generally hostile reviews of *Provença*, which had been published in late November. *Provença*, a selection of previously published poems plus a small final section with some of the new *canzoni*, contained many of the best of his early poems, highly praised in England, and Pound was stung to the quick by his home country's indifference. William Stanley Braithwaite (an unusual figure in that he had made his way into the cultural mainstream in spite of being African-American, but conservative in his tastes none the less dismissed the collection in the *Boston Evening Transcript* on 7 December: 'We began ... this book of poems with great expectations and we lay it down with considerable contempt for the bulk of English criticism that has pretended to discover in these erratic utterances the voice of a poet.'[157] This snub may have been partly inspired by a Bostonian distaste for being told by England what to think, but it was hurtful none the less. Pound, who had returned home with high hopes of poetic triumph, was, at any rate briefly, crushed.

In January one enthusiastic review finally appeared, written by Floyd Dell, at that time though only twenty-two already an associate editor of the *Friday Literary Review* of the *Chicago Evening Post*, and soon to be editor of *The Masses*, a poet and later a significant figure in New York intellectual life. It was a remarkable review: Floyd Dell realised the joint problem of unfamiliarity and difficulty that modernist art and writing gave its audience. Though Pound had been admired in England, Dell noted, his work had also caused some 'bewilderment', an emotion with which he believed many readers in America would have some sympathy. 'For Mr Pound,' he continues, 'is a very new kind of poet. Thinking of the art exhibition just held in London, one might, for want of a better figure, call him a Neo-Impressionist poet'. (He is referring, of course, to the 1910 Post-Impressionist Exhibition recently organised by Roger Fry.) Like these painters, and like the Impressionists earlier, 'Mr Pound is open to misunderstanding', but, he goes on, 'though these poems have often an unconventional form, bizarre phraseology, catalectic or involved sentence structure and recondite meanings, yet it is always apparent that the poet knows what he is doing. This sense – the sense that effects which are beyond one's immediate power of comprehension have been exquisitely designed and exactly carried out – is at the base of the pleasure afforded by all art of a high order.' Ezra Pound, he concludes, is a 'true poet'.[158] This was the warmest review that Pound had so far received and he wrote to Floyd Dell expressing his happy appreciation. Looking back, Floyd Dell's comparison between Pound's poetry and Post-Impressionist painting may not appear surprising, but at the time it had not even occurred to Pound himself. Pound told Floyd Dell in his letter that he was glad he 'felt the contemporaryness of the work', and agreed that poets should be engaged in making 'emotional

translations of their time'. This was a new idea for Pound and possibly
the product of his discussions with Williams. Pound told Dell that he
did not expect to be liked in America, 'for I dont think many people
have had "the ninetys"', adding by way of explanation in his next letter:
'The whole set of "The Rhymers" did valuable work in knocking
bombast, & rhetoric & victorian syrup out of our verse.' American
readers, he implies, still expected Victorian syrup. Yet he is not advocating
simple imitation of the Rhymers. 'They are not *us*. They are not america,
but they ring true.'[59]

Pound was to receive one other sympathetic American review, though
it did not appear until April, after he had left the States, and he apparently never saw it, though its praise for his poetry's virile qualities would
have delighted him. It was by H.L. Mencken, who became a well-known
and influential critic, and later editor of the *Smart Set*, in which this
review appeared, and for which Pound would become an English agent.
Mencken was an enthusiastic admirer of Nietzsche, and his review echoes
Nietzsche's railings against an effeminate culture. Pound, he says, is in
revolt against 'the puerile kittenishness' of contemporary poetry.
'Nine-tenths of our living makers and singers it would seem are women,
and fully two-thirds of these women are ladies. The result is a boudoir
tinkle in the tumult of the lyre.' Pound's poems on the other hand have
often 'an arresting and amazing vigor. The pale thing we commonly call
beauty is seldom in them. They are rough, uncouth, hairy, barbarous,
wild. But once the galloping swing of them is mastered, a sort of stark,
heathenish music emerges from the noise. One hears the thumping of
a tom-tom. Dionysos and his rogues are at their profane prancing. It is
once more the springtime of the world.'[160] It sounds as if written in
anticipation of Stravinsky's *Rite of Spring*.

Meanwhile, back in January, Pound had no strength for profane
prancing, and was reproaching himself for his wild hopes. 'I'm always
so ludicrous with my toys, my ambitions, imagine anything thinking it
could turn America into a paradise of the arts,' he wrote to Margaret.
His illness appears to have been quite severe, and worried his mother
considerably. Pound was thin enough at the best of times. A month later,
on 4 February, he was having his first full day up, feeling 'a bit too light
for a weather vane', still in a state of indecision and ambivalence. He
had hoped to leave the States the next day, he told Margaret Cravens,
heading for Paris to recuperate, but the doctors insisted that he wouldn't
be fit to travel for some time. He had resigned himself to this as a 'sign
from heaven' that he should 'continue the battle' in America after all.

He had been talking over the possibility of a fellowship in the Romance Department at the University of Pennsylvania with his old professor, Hugo Rennert. Having finished the Cavalcanti, he mentioned that he was now working on translations of Arnaut Daniel, 'a quite impossible job, but . . . I must have some occupation which will prevent me from becoming contaminated with american methods of thought.' Later in the same day he added a note to the effect that he had discovered the fellowship could not be taken up until the autumn, so he might be 'blown anywhere in the interim', implying Paris was back on the cards.[161] His sign from Heaven to continue his American mission seems forgotten.

Pound returned briefly to New York, paying a visit to the Poetry Society of America, where Amy Lowell would later have one of her greatest triumphs. The Poetry Society had been formed the previous year, and had had its first meeting in October in the National Arts Club. At least one person noticed his presence, perhaps significantly a woman. This was Jessie Rittenhouse, secretary to the Society, who wrote in her memoirs, 'Surely no-one could have been more charming, more boyish, more provocative than Ezra that night. Young and handsome, with his mass of golden-brown hair, his keen merry eyes, his careless ease of dress.'[162] Yet, though he joined in the discussion, no one else seems to have been impressed. He had already written to his mother urging her to read an article in the February issue of the *Forum* on 'The New Art in Paris', in which she would find 'an answer to a number of things that ought to prove my instinct for where I can breathe. It's mostly news to me but the right sort.'[163] The article discusses what it describes as *libre-versistes* as well as painters, and stresses the way they both return to a primitive past, but Pound was probably most attracted by its celebration of Paris as a place where the 'thinking genius' has full freedom of expression, and the arts are taken seriously by 'the intellectual, contemplative Parisian people . . . This is not a town, but a soul. This is not a people but an intelligence.'[164] That was where he should head. The day after he visited the Poetry Society, 22 February 1911, he left the States, sooner than his doctors advised, but he had had enough. He would not return until 1939.

What had happened with H.D.? Pound has one ambiguous comment in his February letter to Margaret which might explain a little: 'I feel better than I did before my illness, and by it & by the determination to go abroad I've managed to cut loose from all the threads that seemed to be winding themselves around me so that I feel freer, free almost as if I were in Paris'.[165] Some of those winding threads must have come from his parents, who were loath to part with him again. But some were probably from H.D. Was Pound trying to detach himself in preparation for a return to Dorothy? Yet Pound's attitude to H.D. appears never really to change, though how conscious he was of his feelings at any given time is hard to tell: he was strongly attracted to her, deeply fond of her, but he did not want to settle down and marry her. H.D.'s attitude was much the same towards him, though that didn't prevent her from being hurt when she felt he was rejecting her. He required a selfless disciple; she had no intention of being one. But at this stage it was not a clean break by any means. H.D.'s 'Autobiographical Notes' suggest their relationship went better when Pound returned to Philadelphia, as 'I am more "myself" in nice house and surroundings'.[166] When Pound left, his parents expected him to return, and presumably so did H.D. When she later followed him to Europe, she was unsure of whether or not their engagement still stood. Things had been left vague. Yet, she always maintained, if it had not been for Pound she would never have gone to Europe. He may or may not have persuaded her to follow on, but he certainly made her want to be there.

ON his return to Europe, Pound had just three days back in London before moving on to Paris, during which time he saw Yeats, Victor Plarr, May Sinclair and Ford, but not, apparently, the Shakespears. He explained to his mother that his rapid passage through the city was on grounds of health, as he was not yet up to 'the eight hour conversation day'.[167] The Shakespears might have been out of London at the time, but Pound gave no sign of being anxious to see Dorothy, not even, as in the previous June, across a crowded room. He had sent the Shakespears a copy of *Provença*, in which the final group of *canzoni* was dedicated to Olivia and Dorothy, but perhaps he felt, honourably enough, that while he was uncertain about H.D., and unsure how long he would stay in Europe, it was better to keep away. In Paris, he stayed first in a *pension* in the rue de l'Odéon, which runs south from the Boulevard Saint-Germain on the Left Bank, but in less than three weeks he had moved into Rummel's flat on the more affluent Right Bank, near the Trocadéro, attending concerts with him, and working with him on his study of troubadour music. Rummel, unlike Pound, appears to have been quite comfortably placed financially; he came from a well-to-do family and must have earned well as a concert performer and piano teacher. Presumably paying no rent, and with money from his patron, Pound could convalesce without financial worries. He was regularly in touch with Margaret, as she lived not far from Rummel off the Champs-Elysées, and he took advantage of her knowledge of literary Italian as he continued to polish his Cavalcanti translations for publication. The introduction to the translations, though dated 15 November 1910, was, he said later, finished in her apartment some time that spring.[168]

This introduction, in which Pound always refers to Cavalcanti as Guido, as if he were a personal friend, appeared with the translations in 1912, and is much concerned with the links between poetry and music. While this was a continuation of the preoccupations he shared with Yeats and Florence Farr, by now it drew too on his conversations with Rummel, first back in Swarthmore and then on this Paris visit. Pound and Rummel were co-operating closely now, working more in partnership than Pound had done with Grace Crawford, but on a similar quest to find the musical equivalent of his verse. By the age of twenty-four, Rummel had achieved a remarkable reputation. He was acclaimed as a pianist, and his compositions, mainly settings or arrangements of songs, were greatly admired in America, Paris and London.[169] The great Paderewski had heard Rummel play when he was only twenty-one, and was so impressed by his talent he had offered to tutor him himself for a year. Rummel had refused: Paderewski saw his future as a performer, he wanted to be a composer. He went to Paris to work by himself on his ideas about the nature of music, particularly the relation between text and music, for like Pound, Rummel had been concerned with the translation from word to music for some time. He studied medieval French music, including Provençal songs and their settings, though he was also interested in baroque music, and loved chamber music, quite unfashionable in the days of ever-expanding orchestras. Like Pound he turned to these early sources not as a historian but to learn techniques for his own compositions. In this, he was following Debussy, whom he had come to know well in Paris and who was described, in the context of his influence on Rummel, as 'the most pronounced exponent of the old French beauty reclothed in modern garments'.[170]

Debussy was fascinated by the relation of poetry and music. He had been close to the *symboliste* poets, a regular attender at Mallarmé's Tuesdays, and had set many of their poems to music, perhaps most famously Mallarmé's *L'Après-midi d'un faune*; his opera *Pelléas et Mélisande* had used Maeterlinck's symbolist drama as its libretto. The symbolists believed, like Pater, that all art, in their case poetry, should aspire to the condition of music, and Debussy took on the task, as Rummel did, of transforming that music-like poetry into poetic music. Debussy's approach to music was close to the *symbolistes*' view of poetry. They believed poetry should evoke rather than describe; it should not represent external reality, but the world of dreams, of the interior, the subconscious. Many *symbolistes* were, like both Debussy and Rummel, attracted by the occult and saw their poetry as a bridge to a higher world, though the desire to record this shadowy world can also be seen as part of the pre-Freudian fascination with the unconscious mind, which was how Flint would interpret symbolism to the London public in 1912.

For Debussy – and Rummel followed him – music was to be discovered rather than written. For Debussy it came predominantly through the natural world, but Rummel was trying to hear not so much the music of nature as of the past. He said of some Fiona Macleod settings he had made that they were 'the transmission of a very old beauty lying latent in the great memory-book of Celtic Beauty of old forgotten days'.[171] During that spring, Rummel set three of Pound's poems to music, 'Au Bal Masqué', 'Aria' and 'Madrigale', the last two of which Pound had dedicated to Margaret Cravens, writing, in terms which suggest he shared Rummel's view that the aim of art was to recapture a lost beauty, 'To the Weaver of Beauty, the comfort of these forgotten strains redreamt'.[172] An interview with Rummel said that his aim was 'to expose the relationship between the inner rhythm of words to that of music . . . It is this inner rhythm (distinct from the outer, scholastic scanning) that seems to be the characteristic of modern poetry – as, in fact, of all modern art'.[173] Pound, shortly after that significant fortnight spent in Swarthmore with Rummel, had spoken of something similar to 'inner rhythm' to Floyd Dell, whom he had told of his belief in 'absolute rhythm, – an exact correspondence between the cadence-form of the line & some highly specialized or particular emotion . . . There is in every line a real form or inner form & an apparent.' Since he was fifteen, he told Dell, he had believed 'unconsciously' in this idea of 'sincere rhythm. – I mean the thing that isn't the beat of the metronome.'[174]

Omar Pound and Robert Spoo, who edited Pound's letters to Margaret Cravens, say that, during the spring of 1911, 'Ezra's friendship with Margaret grew, and he visited her often now at her new apartment.'[175] Quite what that 'friendship' consisted in has been a matter of speculation. H.D., like quite a few others, thought there had been 'kissing'. But there is no evidence, though the two poems Pound dedicated to Margaret were both love poems, and she must have wondered how to read them. It is hard not to believe that she was in love with Pound. As well as her generosity in both economic and emotional support, that spring she commissioned an American artist living in Paris, Eugene Paul Ullman, to paint portraits of each of them. Yet by that August, when Pound had returned to England, it is clear he had taken Margaret into his confidence about Dorothy, so he was not at any rate deceiving her about his intentions. In late April, a tragedy struck Margaret, to add to the many tragedies of her early life. She heard that her father had shot himself. She had never, it seems, spent much time with him, so they had no intimate relationship, but the fact that she was now the only living member of her family, her parents and all four siblings dead, must have affected someone so prey to depression and melancholy. She may have returned to America for a while, for Pound does not mention seeing her in the next few weeks. Possibly she went out of Paris to somewhere quieter in France; later in the summer she certainly spent some time in a resort on the south-west coast, Saint-Jean-de-Luz.

In May, to Pound's delight, Yeats and Lady Gregory arrived in Paris. They were working, as Yeats told his father, on 'the big book on Fairy Belief that we have been doing for years. My part is to show that what we call Fairy Belief is exactly the same thing as English and American spiritism except that fairy belief is very much more charming'.[176] While Yeats was there, Pound saw him daily. Yeats read portions of 'the big book' to Pound, who was much flattered by his role as critical adviser, though there were still many more years to go before it eventually appeared, in 1920, when it was published as *Visions and Beliefs in the West of Ireland*. Yeats was becoming deeply interested in the Society for Psychical Research, which aimed to investigate spiritualism and psychic phenomena through scientific means, and Pound was immediately intrigued. The article he had published in *Book News Monthly* the previous December was a withering review of a book by Hudson Maxim on *The Science of Poetry and the Philosophy of Language*. Maxim's day job was as a manufacturer of gunpowder, and his brother, with whom Pound would later confuse him, was the inventor of the notorious Maxim gun, one of the great tools of colonialism in the late nineteenth century. Whilst Pound undoubtedly felt that Maxim would have done better to stick to gunpowder, he concluded that his book was right in asserting that poetry 'admits new and profounder explanations in the light of modern science', but scientific truth was not for Pound, any more than for Yeats, separable from his mystical beliefs.[177] It is probably his conversations with Yeats about psychic research that lay behind some of the ideas he puts forward in his introduction to the Cavalcanti, where he speaks of radium, with its 'noble virtue of energy', as akin to the 'magnetism' of Cavalcanti's Lady, and he describes Cavalcanti's concept of *virtù*, the 'potency, the efficient property of a substance or person', as a 'spiritual chemistry', something that 'modern science and modern mysticism are both set to confirm'.[178] Nowadays science and mysticism may appear to have very different grounds for their truth claims, but there were many intellectuals in 1911 ready to believe that there could be a scientific basis for the occult, the paranormal or the mystic. Pound would later develop a series of scientific analogies for the power of poetry, such as light, electricity, radioactivity or magnetism, which has been interpreted as a sign of his 'modernity', but he is not 'modern' in the sense of 'secular'. Pound does not use science like the nineteenth-century positivist thinkers, for many of whom it was a liberation from religious authority, though for others a painful emptying from the universe of the presence of God. Pound belonged to a later generation who, in one way or another, found scientific materialism as wanting as orthodox religion; unorthodox religion and a spiritualised science were quite another thing.

Yeats, R.F. Foster notes, was at this time moving towards the decision to end his involvement with the Abbey Theatre, and he suggests that his revived acquaintanceship with Pound reinforced his desire to return more fully to his poetry. Pound, for his part, was enjoying Yeats' visit immensely, and told his father he had decided that Yeats was a 'very great man and improves on acquaintance'.[179] During his first few months in Paris, Pound saw little of Paris apart from Margaret and Walter's apartments. He had made scarcely any attempt, possibly due to his state of health, to find out more about the 'New Art in Paris' of which he had spoken so eagerly to his mother; when Yeats appeared, however, Pound began to venture further afield. He saw some Cézannes, and went to the Salon Indépendant, where he saw some Matisse paintings, of which he only liked one. Floyd Dell's comparison of his own poetry with post-Impressionist art may have piqued his interest, but he did not immediately respond with any enthusiasm.[180] Yeats introduced Pound to some figures in the Paris literary world, including Henri Davray, editor of the leading French literary journal, the *Mercure de France* and author of the warm review of *The Spirit of Romance* that had appeared there. But the admiration that Pound was to develop for French poetry a year later had not yet been born. He wrote home that the French poets he met were 'a rather gutless bunch, given over to description'.[181] As Noel Stock points out, Pound had earlier missed another opportunity to find out about French literature, when, about a fortnight after he arrived in Paris, he dined with Arnold Bennett, who was then living there and engaged in writing a series of well-informed pieces for the *New Age* on French writers, including several who would later become important to Pound, such as Stendhal, Rémy de Gourmont and Tristan Corbière. No friendship developed between Bennett and Pound, though

Pound acknowledged that he might have enjoyed the workaholic Bennett's company more if he had been feeling more 'vigorous'. Pound's main interest in Paris continued to be music, and he raved in a letter home about a performance he attended of Debussy's *St Sébastien*. For the next couple of years Pound would use Debussy as the touchstone for what was finest in music, although he would later turn entirely against his music, in 1921 condemning *Pélleas et Mélisande* as a 'mush of hysteria'.[182]

In mid-May, the proofs of *Canzoni* arrived, and Pound applied himself to them, though with some anxiety. He wrote in July to Dorothy, when the book was out (addressing her ambiguously as 'Dearest Coz'), explaining to her that 'Artistically speaking its supposed to be a sort of chronological table of emotions: Provence; Tuscany, the Renaissance, the XVIII, the XIX, centuries, external modernity . . . subjective modernity, finis'; in the term he had used to Floyd Dell, 'emotional translations' of a range of periods.[183] At the last minute he had cut out the three poems that formed the 'external modernity' group, because he felt they were too 'rough' and unfinished, but now he feared that no one would recognise his trajectory. The pages cut included the Robert Burns parody addressed to FitzGerald and Hulme, and a poem called 'Redondillas', very directly concerned with contemporary life ('I sing the gaudy today and cosmopolite civilization'), a lively and entertaining piece but worlds away from the more rarefied love poetry of the opening pages.[184] Had Pound included this section, all rather comic poems, his readers might have realised that here was a poet who, although he had not yet found a voice, or, as he would later put it, a language, might develop in any direction; as it was, many rather assumed that his work was now an unremitting retreat into archaisms and the past. Perhaps part of his problem was that both Margaret and Dorothy saw him as an elevated and visionary poet, and might have been taken aback by this lighter vein. He did retain a long and uneven poem in eleven parts, called 'Und Drang' (after the German Romantic *Sturm und Drang* or 'Storm and Stress' movement), presumably filling the role of 'subjective modernity', and containing much mention of 'modernity/Nerve-wrecked, and broken', 'confusion, clamour', and 'the flurry of Fifth Avenue'.[185] It is hard to tell if this is a parody of modern angst, or an attempt to convey it. But the balance of the collection remained with the elaborately wrought poems of the earlier period.

One other pointer to Pound's uncertainty about this collection was that he added at proof stage a defensive note: 'The canzoni have already been assailed and on this account [I] feel I may be permitted to venture toward that dangerous thing, an explanation.' The *canzone* form, he said, celebrated a 'love of Beauty' which belonged to 'the permanent part of oneself', not to a 'sudden emotion or perception': 'the canzone is to me rather a ritual, the high mass, if you will, of poetry, than its prayer in secret', quite the opposite of the dramatic and psychological moment he tried to capture in his persona poems.[186] Yet he must have decided this defence would not help, because he then cancelled this note as well. Both Margaret and Dorothy had been shown several of the poems before, including of course those published in *Provença*, and they admired them deeply, though Dorothy was to admit she could not judge them impartially; they were, she said, too close to her. For now, however, Pound allowed their admiration to reassure him.

By the beginning of June 1911 Yeats had returned home. Walter had gone to London, presumably on another concert tour; Olivia and Dorothy met him and heard him play, and both took to him very much. He gave Dorothy news of Pound, to whom she wrote saying that she thought Walter must have helped him a good deal. Pound continued work on the Arnaut Daniel translations, making use of the Bibliothèque Nationale, and, remarkably, given his struggles with *The Spirit of Romance*, toying with the idea of writing another prose book, covering the same period but dealing with philosophy, beginning, he told his parents, with Richard of St Victor and ending with the Renaissance Neoplatonist, Pico della Mirandola. This, unsurprisingly, never materialised. His future was still in complete doubt. Would he go home or would he stay? What would he do about H.D.? By now he must have heard that she would be leaving for France in July. What about Dorothy? He was still avoiding London, and when Dorothy wrote to him in July, she sounded very uncertain of his intentions, saying anxiously that if he came to London, she hoped he would come to see her. *Canzoni* had been dedicated to her and Olivia jointly, and Pound had told her that she had inspired many of the poems, but she apparently had little hope for the future, sadly saying she would probably never see Sirmione again, because 'being a woman one cannot wander alone'.[187] Evidently she had no thought of seeing it with him. They would in time visit it again together, but not until after the war.

In May, Isabel's letters had been so mournful that Pound even suggested briefly that he would return home in June. Then he heard – somewhat, one suspects, to his relief – that he had been turned down for a fellowship at the University of Pennsylvania. He would not return for now, he decided, but promised to look for a job in Europe. There was something, he said mysteriously, that he would know about in September. By mid-July he appeared to have decided that, whatever the outcome of the September mystery, he would stay in Europe until the next spring at least, but would let his parents know in September whether he would return in 1912 or not. Pound's primary motivation for remaining in Europe was almost certainly his desire to re-enter the congenial world of the London literati rather than go back to what he saw as the barren and philistine wastes of America. But if affairs of the heart, now that both H.D. and Dorothy would be in Europe, played any part in his decision, he may have been influenced by the fact that Olivia seemed to be relenting slightly: Dorothy was told she might write to Pound to thank him for her copy of *Canzoni* – she forbore to mention to Olivia that she had already done so – and Pound was allowed to reply. In his letter he assured her he would soon bring her the Cavalcanti proofs to read; he had at last, it seemed, decided to return to England.

But not yet; for now, he retreated once more to Sirmione. Williams' brother Edgar, the architect, came to stay with him, and they travelled together round some of the cities of northern Italy, including Verona. They went together to Pound's beloved San Zeno, and Edgar pointed out to Pound the signature of the mason on one of the columns, saying, 'how the hell do you expect us to get any buildings when we have to order our columns by the gross', a comment quoted twice by Pound in the *Cantos* to illustrate the falling away of the modern world from the artistic integrity of the past.[188] Architecture was still the only one of the visual arts in which Pound was as yet seriously interested, and he thoroughly enjoyed Edgar's company. He went on to Milan, apparently now by himself, to look up an Arnaut Daniel manuscript that had music included. He wrote excitedly to his father that he had 'had a delightful morning in the Ambrosiana, found a mss of Arnaut with musical notation that accords exactly with my theories of how his music should be written, which same very comforting'. In a letter a few days earlier, Pound had responded rather stiffly to an enquiry from his parents about H.D.: 'Hilda is I believe spending the summer some where in Tourraine'.[189] His parents, and possibly H.D. herself, had apparently thought that Pound would be anxious to see her once she arrived. Pound makes no comment. He was now planning to leave Italy, but still not in the first instance for London, where he could see Dorothy, or for Paris, where he could have seen H.D. He was off, somewhat reluctantly, to Giessen, a small town a little north of Frankfurt, on a tributary of the

Rhine, to join Ford as his secretary. Whether he went out of friendship for Ford, perhaps flattered by his insistent desire for his company, or because he was prevaricating one last month, one can only guess. A few days after Pound had left Sirmione, H.D. arrived in France.

PART VI

H.D. COMES TO EUROPE

I

H.D. reached the French port of Le Havre in early August 1911. When Pound left New York in February, the Doolittles had no plans for H.D. to go to Europe that summer, and she only gained their agreement shortly before she left. In her fictional version of events, H.D. reproaches herself for the sadness her departure brought her mother, yet it may not have been as distressing as it might have been earlier. Shortly after her return from New York, H.D.'s niece Helen was born, the first child of her brother Gilbert, her mother's favourite. The baby was the cause of great family excitement, and whilst H.D. was herself very taken with little Helen, she was also, no doubt, grateful to her for giving her mother a new interest that softened the pain of letting her only daughter leave the country. On 23 July, five months after Pound had left the States, H.D. sailed from New York along with Frances Gregg and her mother, her parents having agreed to let her join them for a four-month sight-seeing visit to Europe.

William Carlos Williams came to the quayside to see her off. Her father was there, but not her mother. 'The picture of Professor Doolittle at the pier on the departure of his daughter for England!' Williams recalled later, 'to meet Ezra Pound (as he well knew) impressed me deeply. He was alone with her, aside from myself. He was sitting on a trunk, completely silent. No word to me or to anyone.' Perhaps Williams is right, and Professor Doolittle was worried about the equivocal engage-ment, even though officially the visit was only temporary. Perhaps he had a premonition that his favourite child would not return to America in his lifetime. He and H.D. were very alike, and he may well have realised that H.D. was following a quest to which she would be as dedi-cated as he to his stars. Whatever its cause, her father's silent, reproachful misery must have been acutely painful for the affectionate and easily guilt-ridden H.D. But if she was going to meet Ezra Pound, she was still entranced by the mercurial Frances, and if she was conscience-stricken by her parents' distress, she was enormously excited about her visit to Europe. Many years later, answering a questionnaire in the *Little Review*, she said that the happiest moment of her life had been when she had first left for Europe along with someone she loved. But what about Frances? She said later of that moment, 'If, out of the long dead years, I could choose one episode to relive, it would be, I think, that embarkation'.[2] But what did she hope for? Her feelings may have been equally divided. She had after all originally planned to go without H.D. Perhaps she too was going in search of Pound.

Given their poverty, it may seem surprising that the Greggs managed to afford a European trip, but Americans could visit Europe very cheaply in those days. H.D. was paying her own way, that is to say, her parents were paying, and as she was given rather more spending money than the Greggs were likely to have, in the event she may have partially subsidised their visit. According to Barbara Guest, she and Frances spent the early days of the voyage hiding from Mrs Gregg, kissing in a lifeboat under the tarpaulin.[3] Then the weather worsened and the rest of the voyage was grim; they finally reached Le Havre a week late. But, having put the miseries of the crossing behind her – it makes one feel, hearing these accounts, that jet-lag is a small price to pay – H.D. was delighted with France. She sent a series of excited postcards to her mother – she was writing letters too, but those her parents did not save. 'Dearest,' she wrote on one card, 'Often think of you here – the crowds of real French – and the green hills would so delight you . . . My life is so exuberantly full, I know you rejoice with me.' They stopped in Rouen on their way to Paris, the route recommended by Baedeker. H.D. sent her mother a postcard of the famous cathedral door, 'Where I sat and wrote your last – overhead the open sky – and red geraniums in the stone niches at the gate entrance. We are so happy here that even Paris seems anti-climactic – markets with plums, pears, etc. in the open – Attended pageant service in the Cathedral to-day – Tuesday – annunciation of the Virgin – I am still intoxicated with it all.' But when they reached Paris it was far from an anticlimax. 'Am enjoying all things,' she told her mother. 'I grow happier and freer and more exuberant every day'.[4]

Once in Paris ('very hot,' H.D recalled), they threw themselves into sightseeing. H.D. loved the art galleries.[5] To their disappointment the Louvre was shut when they first arrived; the *Mona Lisa* had been stolen, an event that H.D. would recount later as if it had symbolic import for her. Although she was at one level ecstatic in her liberation, she was also apprehensive about where this bold step out from the family home would lead; the capture of the *Mona Lisa* is one of several images in her writing about this period that suggest the violation that women risk when they venture into the public sphere. (H.D. was not alone in seeing her as an archetypal woman: in *Blast* Lewis would comment that Leonardo's 'Mona Lisa eloped from the Louvre like any woman. She is back again now, smiling with complacent reticence, as before her escapade; no one can say when she will be off once more, she possesses so much vitality.')[6] When the Louvre reopened, H.D. spent many hours there, writing to her mother that 'I am still just beginning to get into the Louvre. A life-time would be short in which to really study it – We are so very happy!' Aldington was later to write of H.D. that 'To look at beautiful things with H.D. is a remarkable experience . . . She responds so swiftly, understands so perfectly, re-lives the artist's mood so intensely, that the work of art seems transformed.'[7] The art that H.D. sought out on this visit were the established greats: Greek statues and Renaissance paintings, works whose praise she would have read in Pater. There are no references to her seeing any avant-garde or recent painting or sculpture on this first visit. She would never, in any case, lose her passion for Greek statuary.

H.D. was also carrying on a busy social life. Pound had written to his mother the previous May, 'I'm not sure but Paris is the easiest place to see "London"': H. D. might well have said the same about seeing 'Philadelphia'.[8] Paris was full of Americans. Margaret Snively and her father were there for some of the time; so was H.D.'s cousin Francis Wolle, who took her to Versailles and to Gounod's *Faust*. She met up again with Walter Rummel, now back from London, who invited her and the Greggs out to his studio in the rue Raynouard, in Passy, 'a lovely suburb where Maeterlinck lived'. They went several times to see him: 'Such music!' she told her mother. In *Asphodel*, where Rummel appears as Walter Dowel, it is said that people collected underneath his window while he played.

H.D. was as enchanted as she had been in Swarthmore; she was always acutely responsive to music. In *End to Torment* she tells a story of going by herself to the Philadelphia Academy to hear Paderewski. At the end 'too shattered to move', she 'found [herself] alone in the vast empty circles of balcony benches'. Below her, she saw 'a furtive handful of dark figures'. They were not part of 'the fastidious, fashionable

audience that had just surged out . . . We [were] of a secret order.'
Paderewski returned, and played for them for another hour.[9] She sat
entranced. She appears to have been equally moved by Walter's playing,
which had been admired, of course, by Paderewski himself. Over forty
years later, when she heard of Rummel's death, she still remembered
how magical she had found that music. In her fictional account in
Asphodel (in which Hermione is for a while dazzled by the combination
of his music, 'Byronic face', courtesy and sophistication)[10] she writes:

It was winter when Walter played. Cold and chill and the sound of the notes was
the last drop of an icicle that started to melt in the spring, melting, it must melt
but it decided not to melt and broke off a little crystal bead and fell down, down,
down and broke, with an infinitude of sound, the lightest sharp cold ice note at
the top of the piano, making the whole world vibrate.[11]

'That is Walter,' she says a little later: 'Fire frozen.'[12] This imagery
recalls the fiery kisses given by Ezra, that 'do not so much warm, they
magnetize' – '*rigor mortis*. I am frozen in this moment,' as she puts it.[13]
H.D. often describes ecstasy as others might describe agony, the singer
with 'a voice that made you crouch low in your chair and pray to be
dead', the moment of epiphany as a moment of death.[14] Yet in the case
of both Pound and Rummel the fiery coldness is also perhaps a comment
on their ultimately ruthless dedication to their art. Walter in her account
emerges as in the end somewhat detached from humanity, as if, for all
his charm, his immersion in his music and occult pursuits held him
apart from the warmth of human interaction.

In spite of this, H.D. was attracted and intrigued by Walter. In the
fictional account, Walter spends time with Hermione, discussing music
and telling her of his efforts to reinvoke the ancient music that the
Egyptians had played: 'He believes he can *hear* things . . . He thinks
it's all written if one could only get it.' He tells her she is 'all wrong'
to prefer the Greeks to the Egyptians, and because of that 'she couldn't
be expected to understand – the *real* things'.[15] Egyptian art was to
become a source of inspiration to many modernist visual artists,
including the London Vorticists, and, by the time she wrote *Asphodel*,
to H.D. herself. Rummel may well, in 1911, have felt H.D. was rather
old-fashioned in clinging to nineteenth-century Hellenism. Rummel
himself did not venture as far as Debussy, whose work was profoundly
influenced by Javanese and Cambodian music, which he had discovered
through the Paris *Exposition Universelle* of 1889. These great international

exhibitions of the turn of the century years were celebrations of colonialism, structured to exhibit the superiority of the coloniser to the exotic but backward colonised, but what Debussy took from this music was symptomatic of the new readiness among artists to value non-Western art: if we forget our European prejudices, he wrote, we can see that 'Javanese music is characterized by an art of counterpoint compared to which that of a Palestrina is mere child's play.'[16] Rummel felt that the Egyptian past took him in a very similar way beyond the limitations of European prejudices. Through him, H.D. was meeting for the first time the modernist critique of traditional European forms, the search for alternatives already intuitively part of her own artistic practice. Even if she had not yet met Parisian avant-garde painting, through Rummel she was introduced to what was then the avant-garde in music.

Meanwhile, H.D.'s relationship with the Greggs continued to be volatile. Frances was, as H.D. put it, 'uneven as always'; Mrs Gregg saw H.D. as a rival for Frances' affections, and resented her. In addition, judging from H.D.'s own postcard-recorded schedule, Frances and her mother could well have felt indignant about how much time she spent away from them, and it may have been H.D.'s passion for Paris that prevented the visit to the Loire region that Pound had thought they would make. In *Asphodel* Hermione's earlier desire to see Chartres vanishes when she discovers Paris; if the Greggs' plans were altered to suit her, they may well have been irritated by her change of mind. They stayed a while, H.D. recalled in her 'Autobiographical Notes', 'in a dreadful little place, on the outskirts of Paris'. ('Siamese cats,' she adds darkly.)[17] Yet none of this appears to have stopped her enjoyment. Towards the end of September they left Paris for a few days on the Pas de Calais coast at Paris Plage, near Etaples, south of Boulogne, before moving on to England. H.D. wrote to her mother: 'We enjoy the people here so very much & the living in more or less aristocratic surroundings. The sea is, as always, wine in my veins.'[18] According to *Paint it Today*, Hermione and Fayne tried to take photographs of each other in the nude in an old boat on the shore, but 'Julia [Fayne's mother] shouted there was a man (and a *French* man) coming and we must get dressed at once . . . even our shoes must go on.'[19] H.D. in England would discover the delights of swimming naked, much advocated by the younger generation of writers and artists. Rupert Brooke and his friends, christened by Virginia Woolf the Neo-Pagans, were particular devotees of this, and his young girlfriend, Noel Oliver, had already caused a scandal at her supposedly progressive co-educational boarding-school, Bedales, by diving nude into the school swimming pool.[20] What would a Philadelphian evangelical like Mrs Gregg say to that? H.D. and Frances undoubtedly, like Hermione and Fayne in *Paint it Today*, for now 'bathed in clothes'.

In *Paint it Today*, H.D. also recalls that French shoreline – and shorelines were to remain a central locus for her poems – as the place where she became conscious of the intense difference of Europe from America: 'The wind against an old hulk on the sands below Etaples, was not yet wind, not wind that is when contrasted with that rush of swords that cut the sand stretches into snow and ice patterns and blared through the Maine pines and tore in midsummer, tornadowise, walnut and tough oak branches from the walnut and great oak trees . . . Yet what they had lost in the sting and dash of spray, in the rains and wind, they gained elsewhere.' What on the shore 'inflamed their imaginations' were the half-obliterated letters on the bow of 'the old hulk, blown windward, half filled with heavy, earthlike sand . . . The letters, cut with a slightly Gothic twist, might have stood for an Andros, or Arcadia or Helenis stranded there from southern waters'.[21] The twisted letters evoke both a medieval and a classical past. Europe was the continent of history, of myth, of a past whose fragmentary remains surrounded the living, offering depth, entrancement, poetry, secrets to be teased out. But it was a peopled continent. Even though 'the sun was not a sun . . . these people trailing up from the sand were people, authentic people . . . Here in France, at Etaples, the people were a reality. In America, it was the white sand that lived, the wind, the stainless rout of stars.'[22] This might seem a strange view of America coming from someone who grew up on the edge of a great city of the East in the early twentieth century, even for someone with a father whose life was largely spent with 'the stainless rout of stars'. But that sense of the dwarfing of humanity by the immensity, in size, in power, in danger, of the natural world of the American continent (something akin to what Hulme had felt on the Canadian prairies, or Fletcher in the Arizona desert) never left H.D. Weather in her poems is always that American weather of extremes ('you are unsheltered,/ cut with the weight of wind – you shudder when it strikes'; 'O wind, rend open the heat,/ cut apart the heat/ rend it to tatters.')[23] It would be her discovery of Sappho, when she reached London and started to use the British Museum Reading Room, that showed her how to use that imagery as a way of understanding her life. Images of wind and heat, along with the lashing of the waves, are central to her poetry of those early years; their physical lacerations give a language to her psychic turmoil.

H.D. retained all her life this intensity of response to the natural world, but she is not a poet who 'describes' the natural world. Rather, and this is perhaps what is distinctively modernist about her, she wants to capture the subjective response to 'the sting and the spray', or to the scent of a flower. 'She, Midget,' she writes in *Paint it Today*,

did not wish to be an eastern flower painter. She did not wish to be an exact and over-*précieuse* western, a scientific describer of detail of vein and leaf of flowers, dead or living, nor did she wish to press flowers and fern fronds and threads of pink and purple seaweed between the pages of her book. Yet she wanted to combine all those qualities in writing and to add still another quality to these three. She wished to embody, as this other quality, the fragrance of the flowers.

You cannot paint a fragrance, you cannot be a sculptor of fragrance, you cannot play fragrance on a violin. Yet you can, with a pencil, at least attempt to express something in definite terms, before which the violin, the chisel, and the brush are powerless.[24]

In *Asphodel* H.D. tells the story of her first response to France rather differently; there her coming to Europe makes her grasp for the first time that she could and should be a writer. The H.D. character, Hermione, arrives with a plethora of fictional images of French life derived from her reading, images that in America had seemed dream-like and fairy tale but which in Europe tumble into actuality. She is taken aback by how like Maupassant and Pierre Loti the French appear to be; what had seemed totally fictional is suddenly there in front of her: '*that* was France, de Maupassant was true. Literature was true. If de Maupassant was true then life and letters met, were not sub-divided, hermetically shut apart. *Helen thy beauty is to me* was still hermetically sealed and a star, but de Maupassant in one terrible instant became real, a reality. Terrible and strong . . . Writing. How marvellous. Writing. She must write.'[25] In America she had only understood writing as a dream world, a visionary alternative to a society in which she felt ill at ease. Now she saw that writing would be her way forward in understanding the confused reality of her life. H.D. was to say many times that she could not have become a writer if she had not come to Europe. Whether she literally had one such moment of revelation as here, or whether it was a more gradual realisation, by the time she had reached England she knew she 'must write'. By the end of the next year she would have achieved her first recognition as a poet.

H.D. and the Greggs crossed the Channel on 29 September 1911, either with or at much the same time as Rummel.[26] By early October they had all arrived in London.

II

IN London, Pound was expecting them. Much had happened to him during the two months they had spent sightseeing. If H.D. was resolving to pursue a writing career, Pound was reappraising his. If H.D. was still pulled emotionally in different directions, mesmerised by Frances, fascinated by Pound, attracted to Walter, Pound's relationship with Dorothy had moved into a new phase. His visit to Giessen had proved memorable, even if it was not at the time a pleasure. He had arrived in Giessen in early August, after a gruelling train journey, only to find that the cheery friendship he had enjoyed with Ford in 1909–10 had, at any rate for the time being, degenerated into mutual impatience. Ford's private life was growing increasingly messy, and his spirits were low. Since Pound had left London in March 1910, the complications surrounding Ford's relationship with Violet Hunt had taken a heavy emotional toll. In 1908, at the time when Hunt had snatched the poison from his Rosssetti jacket pocket, Ford had been unwilling to give his wife the divorce for which she was asking; within a few months he was, with Violet's encouragement, anxious to do so. As soon as he changed his mind, Elsie changed hers, and announced that divorce was anathema to her. In 1910 a case was brought against him for restitution of conjugal rights, which was not enforced, but Ford was put in prison for a fortnight. Pound, according to Hunt, had written with much merriment to Ford at the time (it was during his first visit to Sirmione), calling Ford an 'Apostle in Bonds' and 'perpetrat[ing] shocking parodies on the comic event in the style of "The Ballad of Reading Gaol"'.[27] Ford's continued residence as a lodger in Hunt's house provoked much gossip among their acquaintances, even though they now had several chaperones in place to keep up a façade of respectability; as well as Violet's near-senile mother and his sister-in-law, Mary Martindale, who had joined in the tennis foursomes with Grace Crawford in 1909, they had added Ford's mother. In the autumn of 1910, when Pound was in New York, Ford and Violet had visited Ford's relatives in Germany, on that occasion rather oddly taking with them as chaperone the widow of Violet's first *grande passion*, Oswald Crawfurd. While they were there, someone made the suggestion that if Ford were to take up German nationality again, he could divorce Elsie under German law without her consent, and marry Violet in Germany. Such a marriage would not be valid in England, but Ford and Violet don't seem to have let that concern them. Although Violet had to go home, partly because of ill health, for the complications from her syphilis were causing her great pain, Ford remained in lodgings in Giessen, in his view a town of stultifying boredom, but one where there was a good lawyer, recommended warmly to them by Ford's German relatives. Ford and Hunt believed they could rely on him to solve their problems.

Ford had nothing to do but write. He described himself in a letter as

well, prosperous and occupied. With my right hand I am writing a history of cholera in Ireland; with my left an historical novel dealing with the divorce of Anne Boleyn, using it as a peg on which to hang many disquisitions on Divorce in general. My feet are dealing with the treadles of a type-writing machine that pours out the history of literature in England during the last two years, whilst my eyes are engaged in perusing the material for my gigantic life of Sejanus.[28]

But in spite of his frenetic activity, Ford missed his friends. He was, after all, a great talker, and needed an audience. In late May or early June Ford wrote to Pound, whom he had last seen in early March on a brief visit home, begging him to come and join him in Hunt's absence. At first Pound was reluctant to undertake the 24-hour rail trip north from his beloved Sirmione, so Ford returned to England again for six weeks, in the first instance to see George V's coronation. The candidate for German nationality briefly turned back into a loyal British Tory and wrote a piece for the *Sheffield Daily Telegraph*, full of emotional yet sonorous reverence. By August he was back in Giessen, with Pound as secretary.

According to Brita Lindberg-Seyersted, who edited the Pound/Ford letters, the role of secretary cannot have been entirely notional, for Pound wrote at least one letter for Ford (in which he managed to misspell Ford's name), but one suspects Ford really wanted his companionship, even if in the event he was too full of anxiety to enjoy it as he had expected. He and Hunt had been having terrible rows, particularly about money; she was finding the strain of widespread social disapproval painful, and he was growing ever more unsure of his feelings for her, though believing miserably that it was impossible to withdraw at this stage. It is unlikely that any of this was told to Pound; Ford and Pound did not discuss personal pain, and Pound was probably only given a wittily edited version of Ford's recent life. All the same, the mood of unease communicated itself. It was, moreover, according to Douglas Goldring, the hottest summer in Germany since 1453, and the heat may have increased the friction. Pound did not write to his parents at all while in Germany, perhaps too disgruntled to do so, but, when he finally reached England at the end of August, he sent a letter oozing with ill humour: 'I had very little time to myself while with Hueffer, not that there was much work done, but we disagree diametrically on art, religion, politics and all therein implied . . . I was dragged about to a number of castles, etc, which were interesting and about which I persistently refused to enthuse.'[29]

The climax came when Ford poured scorn on Pound's poetry. Pound had brought with him a copy of *Canzoni*, which, since Ford had published the first few poems in the *English Review*, he must have hoped would earn him some praise. He would soon realise his mistake. Ford already had reservations about Pound's poetry, which he felt was vigorous but weighed down by its archaisms and affectations, and *Canzoni* certainly paraded all the qualities in Pound's verse that he disliked most. Ford's general lowness of spirits may, however, have been responsible for the sharpness of his criticism, which was clearly the main irritant behind Pound's jaundiced complaints home. Yet, although at the time Pound insisted he and Ford 'disagree[d] diametrically on art', he was later to turn this visit into a legendary moment in his life, a road to Damascus experience. In the obituary that Pound wrote for Ford in 1939, he recalled Ford's reaction to the book:

he felt the errors of contemporary style to the point of rolling . . . on the floor of his temporary quarters in Giessen when my third volume [it was actually his sixth] displayed me trapped, fly-papered, gummed and strapped down in a jejune provincial effort to learn, *mehercule*, the stilted language that then passed for 'good English' in the arthritic milieu that held control of the respected British critical circles . . . And that roll saved me at least two years, perhaps more. It sent me back to my own proper effort, namely towards using the living tongue.[30]

In the immediate aftermath of the roll, Pound was not at all grateful. His defensive note on the *Canzoni* proofs had shown that he was already feeling uneasy about the direction his work was taking, and criticisms that strike home are always the most painful. His 1939 account of that Giessen event is strikingly misleading in several ways. Firstly, it suggests Ford made him change direction from that point, while actually he was to resist and argue with Ford's views well into the next year. Secondly, it was wholly unfair to suggest *Canzoni* was a typical example of 1911 style, and to blame its archaic and artificial language on the literary establishment's idea of good English. If Pound had expected it to be taken as such, he must have been swiftly disillusioned when he saw the generally unfavourable reviews, which were beginning to appear while he was still in Giessen. Such rewriting of history to shift the blame from himself to the establishment is typical of Pound. And finally, the 'milieu' of London literary and intellectual life, as Pound put it, was very far from 'arthritic', although for decades many literary historians meekly accepted Pound's judgement on the case. Yet it is true, as he said in 1939, that Ford was influential not so much in making him do something new as in sending him back to the 'living tongue' of his persona poems. Reviewers had again and again criticised him for his affectations, but he had ignored them. Ford's roll stung him to the quick, and certainly played its part in the changes he would come to make during the next year.

Yet Pound's poetry was already changing, at any rate in his own terms, if not yet in Ford's. Another indication that Pound at one level knew he was on the wrong track in his elaborately wrought visions in the *Canzoni*, was that in Sirmione, even before Ford's attack, he had already returned to his persona poetry and had written one of his most successful poems to date, and indeed of his career.[31] This was 'The Seafarer,' a translation from an early Anglo-Saxon text, and an evocation of lonely, stoical endurance. Pound himself argued, and he may well have been right, that the verbal inventiveness and technical mastery that he learnt through the *Canzoni* experiment, even though at the time it failed to produce living poems, was an invaluable discipline that strengthened his later work. Certainly Pound's imaginative and verbal skill in creating an English that echoes the sound and movement of the Anglo-Saxon might owe something to those labours. Pound's method of translation in 'The Seafarer', as always in his best translations, can perhaps be compared (though he might have thought the comparison *lèse-majesté*) to that of British films *circa* 1950 about the Second World War, in which, on German battleships and in officers' messes, the German-speaking Germans are represented by actors speaking English with a German accent. Pound translates into the appropriate accent, brilliantly so. He had perhaps learnt from Campbell's Hiberno-English, even more than from working with Shepard on the Provençal, to shape a translation that conveyed the forms and movement of the original. Here he takes the basic form of Anglo-Saxon verse, which uses not rhyme and metre but alliteration and stress, each Anglo-Saxon line having a caesura in the middle, with two heavy stresses before the caesura, and one after, each stressed syllable beginning with the same letter. Pound does not use this pattern for every line, but overall that is the effect, and he also imitates the highly conventionalised compound words that Anglo-Saxon poetry uses with great frequency. So for example:

> Coldly afflicted,
> My feet were by frost benumbed.
> Chill its chains are; chafing sighs
> Hew my heart round and hunger begot
> Mere-weary mood. Lest man know not
> That he on dry land loveliest liveth,
> List how I, care-wretched, on ice-cold sea,
> Weathered the winter, wretched outcast
> Deprived of my kinsmen;
> Hung with hard ice-flakes, where hail-scur flew,
> There I heard naught save the harsh sea.[32]

Pound had two methods of translation, he had told Floyd Dell, one of which was translating the words fairly literally, as in the translations in *The Spirit of Romance* (and, it appears, in the Cavalcanti poems), and another which was a 'freer mode for translation of spirit plus expression of oneself', as for example, he says, in 'Sestina Altaforte'.[33] 'The Seafarer' is one of the latter, Pound taking on the persona once more of the *isolato*, the exile, the outcast, a figure like those who appeared earlier as Cino, Marvoil or Piere Vidal. For all the deliberate archaising, he has gone back already to something much closer to the 'living tongue'. Rhythm and sound are all important, and by freeing himself from the constraints of rhyme he is able to explore a different kind of verse movement. Pound never bothered overmuch about the accuracy of his translations, and this poem was no exception, as scholars have been pointing out ever since, though Anglo-Saxon scholars took a rather more tolerant line than the Latinists when he came to produce *Homage to Sextus Propertius* some years later. (In September, when he was back in England, Pound asked his mother to send over his Anglo-Saxon Grammar, so he presumably made some attempt at checking it before publication.) In his interpretation of the poem, Pound decided to go with a particular scholarly argument about the extant Anglo-Saxon text, which suggested that the body of the poem was pre-Christian, but that a monk had later inserted Christian references and added a Christian coda, to make it acceptable in Christian times. Pound ignored the coda, and removed any Christian references in the body of the poem, so it becomes totally pagan. Death is the end, and all that can be claimed is that 'Tomb hideth trouble'.[34] Pound's dislike of institutional Christianity had continued to grow.

The nub of the poem, however, and the reason perhaps why it appealed to Pound, is the seafarer's passionate dedication to his sea-voyaging; the journey may be painful and hazardous, but it is his life. The harsh quest is ultimately self-chosen. The seafarer has no wish to linger among the 'wealthy and wine-flushed' 'burghers'. (Peter Brooker suggests that Pound uses the anachronistic word 'burghers' precisely to turn it into an anti-bourgeois poem.) If he is at home, the seafarer says, 'Moaneth alway my mind's lust/That I fare forth, that I afar hence/Seek out a foreign fastness'. Any 'mood-lofty man' will find 'longing comes upon him to fare forth on the water . . . Burgher knows not – /He the pros-perous man – what some perform/When wandering them widest draweth'.[35] The seafarer had become for Pound a symbol of the artist devoted to his mission to perfect his art. Earlier in the year, when he was making his painful farewells to his family, he had written to his father, 'I am sorry for the desolation in my wake, it has not been particu-larly easy for me to go', for there is 'more than comfort left behind'. He told him that 'Whatever I may seem to have done or left undone, my time is still a time of preparation not a time of accomplishment'. He had to leave America on his travels again because 'here there is nothing so new or so different to build into the work'.[36] So many of Pound's earlier poet/wanderers had been on the road. Now he used the image of the sea voyage, an image that would become central to the *Cantos*, which begin with Odysseus and his men setting sail: 'And then went down to the ship,/Set keel to breakers, forth on the godly sea'.[37] At Sirmione, making his decision to stay in Europe, aware of his parents' disappointment, unsure about his future, 'The Seafarer' becomes his latest 'mask of the self' through which to find a voice.

'The Seafarer' would be published in November 1911, in the *New Age*, and even if Pound was still not using the contemporary language and contemporary subject-matter that Ford called for, the translation was much praised. *Canzoni*, however, was not; Ford was not the only one of Pound's earlier advocates who felt his latest collection was, if not a failure, at any rate a mistake. In an article she wrote in 1920, May Sinclair, who had been such an enthusiastic admirer of Pound's early work, recorded the disappointment felt by those who had been impressed by his earlier poems' 'strange, foreign beauty'. *Canzoni* was 'a set-back to extravagant expectations. The elaborate form, the artificial sweetness, the dextrous technique, the sheer convention of the thing, were felt to be incompatible with unfettered, unpremeditative genius'.[38] In most reviews of *Canzoni*, the volume was much criticised, denounced as a 'lamentable failure' and 'a medley of pretension' which exhibited 'affectation combined with pedantry'. Some months after Pound's return to England, J.C. Squire wrote in the *New Age*, where he had taken over as poetry reviewer from Flint, that 'the plupart of the poemata in this opus (one falls insensibly into polyglottery after reading Mr Pound) are essays in Early Italian and kindred forms . . . [whose] rigid elaborateness . . . induces, or at any rate favours, at worst a frigidity, and at best a trivially and sentimentally titillating content'. Yet Squire, like most of the reviewers, was in the end quite kind to Pound, pointing out 'how excellent is Pound's artistry within the limits he has imposed on himself'.[39] One has the impression that London literati were really quite pleased to have their favourite bohemian back with them. Even before Pound's return, an affectionate burlesque had appeared in *Punch* announcing a new publication from 'Boaz Bobb, a son of the Arkansas soil, who has long been resident in London studying Icelandic literature for the purposes of a new saga of the Wild West'.[40] Pound was delighted with the attention, and wrote home to his father to give him the news with deep satisfaction. He said nothing about the adverse reviews.

Immensely relieved to have escaped from Giessen, Pound returned to England near the end of August, to a London even emptier of its better-off inhabitants than it usually was during the summer months. As in Germany, it had been immensely hot, a factor, it was widely believed, behind a crippling strike that month of London transport workers, which had paralysed the docks and had left tons of food rotting on the docksides. Those who had fled did not, however, include the Shakespears, who were still in town. Pound, in contrast to his wariness on the March visit, now lost no time in making contact with Dorothy. He wrote to Margaret two days after his arrival with cheerful lover-like concern over his discovery that Dorothy had a bad cough, and adding, 'you two *are* going to love each other which is something to be thankful for'.[41] In the same letter he mentioned H.D., suggesting there was no point in Margaret meeting her, as they would, he implied, have nothing in common. When H.D. and Margaret eventually met next year, they took to each other very much indeed, as Pound must surely have known they would. He clearly did not want his story of devotion to Dorothy to be compromised by revelations of possible other engagements.

A few days later Dorothy was in Dorset, on the first of a series of visits to friends, for the most part with her parents, and would be out of London until early October. Visits to friends with country houses were a regular feature of the Shakespear lifestyle, and there is no reason to think she was sent off because of Pound's arrival. Dorothy wrote on 26 August to say she was reading the Cavalcanti translations, delivered as promised in July, and she comments that Ezra is probably at that moment interviewing 'Madame ma mère'. It may have been in connection with this interview that Olivia wrote to Pound about Dorothy just about that time; only the latter half of the letter has survived, so one can merely speculate on whether the beginning may have queried Pound's suitability as a husband. The extant section is, however, concerned with Dorothy's failings:

What distresses me is that I see her becoming always more fundamentally selfish and self-absorbed. Of course this does not show on the surface, as her manners are too good – but I don't really believe she would stir a finger to help her dearest friend if it cost her a moment's trouble or inconvenience – she seems to have a perfect horror of being of any use to anybody.[42]

How fair this was to Dorothy is hard to say, but it failed to convince Pound. To Pound Dorothy was undoubtedly of use, in her unwavering admiration and constant engagement with his work. One of the things that Olivia complains about is that Dorothy does not go to the studio, presumably to practise her painting more professionally. Yet had she been someone dedicated to her own art rather than to his, Pound would probably have lost interest. Olivia also complains that Dorothy 'has modelled her social life quietly[?] on mine – but she has not the sense to see that what is suitable for a worn out woman of my age, & a girl of hers, is very different'.[43] Olivia was here, though she did not recognise it, fighting a battle against history that she would surely lose. Dorothy's generation no longer accepted the circumscribed and restricted lives with which well-bred young women were still expected to be content. Dorothy must have resented the fact that Olivia had freedoms she was expected to eschew. She and Olivia carried on a perfectly civilised relationship outwardly, but she told her mother nothing about her feelings. In this way, she acquired a certain limited independence, which she pragmatically accepted as the most she could have, at any rate for the present.

While separated again for these five or six weeks, Pound and Dorothy now kept in touch regularly by letter. There had been a declaration, received with much happiness, and Pound had been given permission to write. In the meantime, he was welcomed back by his London acquaintances, or as many as were around. It was still early for the well-to-do to return to London, but he immediately received invitations to visit Manning in Lincolnshire, to spend weekends at Eva Fowler's cottage in Kent and to visit Olivia's friend, Lady Low, another of those whose hospitality had been so important in keeping Pound alive during his first London visit, and who was one of the small group of wealthy ladies who had attended his private classes in the winter of 1909–10. Lady Low's place was also in Dorset, though not the part that Dorothy had visited. Pound was deeply and unusually moved by the wild Dorset coast he saw, perhaps sensitised to its beauty by the power of his reawoken feelings for Dorothy. Dorothy's own letters to him were full of her delight in landscape, and she had already told him that he would see 'some queer Dorset country – very, very beautiful'.[44] He wrote to her on 10 September:

Yesterday 'we' went down to the 'edge' (front? – whatever it properly is – at least in 'Darset') it was proper bleak & gray – & 'very odd' = very unpleasant, very poetic, & strong beyond anything. There is no place for senses in this scheme of things – only for feelings that last life out – deeper, more intense than all Italy, and silent. There are several of my family names about here – but that apart it is like getting back to the roots of things.

It is a place that would be very strong on one.[45]

The harsh poetry of this countryside, captured so powerfully by Thomas Hardy (as Dorothy knew, though Pound apparently did not), offered a new image for his feelings for Dorothy, deeper than the visionary paradisal depiction of Mount Riva in his poetry of the Sirmione visit.

This Dorset scene appears in a poem that Pound would publish the next February, and which would remain one of his most admired. Entitled 'Δώρια' (Doria), probably a reference to both Dorothy and Dorset, it goes:

> Be in me as the eternal moods
>   of the bleak wind, and not
> As transient things are –
>   gaiety of flowers.
> Have me in the strong loneliness
>   of sunless cliffs
> And of grey waters.
>   Let the gods speak softly of us
> In days hereafter,
>   The shadowy flowers of Orcus
> Remember thee.[46]

It is very different from his earlier love poetry. From ethereal, the imagery has become chthonic; from visionary, it has become elemental. There is still a sense of the sacred there, of something that gives pause, a moment of stillness and recognition, but it is simpler, more direct, not reliant on conventions of love from a very different period. There is still the hint of a reference to the Demeter and Kore myth in 'the shadowy flowers of Orcus', for Orcus was another name for the god of the underworld. Yet this strong, spare poem is a new step. In retrospect, it has been identified as free verse, but that is not how Pound saw it at that stage. At the time he claimed to be experimenting in 'sapphics' and was developing a new interest in trying to use 'quantity', the Latin and Greek metres that depend on short and long syllables, rather than stress, which modern European poetry uses. There was a revived interest at the time in quantitative verse, pursued by among others, Robert Bridges, whom Pound would soon meet; in addition there was, great excitement in literary circles about the newly discovered Sappho manuscripts, found in excavations in Egypt, some of which were first published in England in 1909, and more in the next few years. Pound was moving away from rhyme – not present in quantitative verse – but he was still intently aware, as he would remain, of form and technique. In spite of his insistence to Margaret Cravens that 'I *must* make a perfect Sapphic ode before I pass on', in general Pound appears to use 'sapphics' as an imprecise term, not, as it should strictly be used, for just one of the forms of verse employed by Sappho, a form incidentally very difficult to use well in English.[47] Though Pound did send one strained stanza to Dorothy in this form in September, his somewhat stilted poem '*Apparuit*' was the only true sapphic verse that he published. He was criticised at the time for his loose application of the term, but for Pound the term refers more broadly to Sappho's melic poetry, written to be sung. He wrote to Dorothy: 'My one comfort is this sapphic affair. Surely all systems of metric since have been a vulgarity & a barbarism, and their beautiful results have been due to genius & accident & not to any virtue inherent in the "system".' Plato, he reminded her, had written that 'melos . . . "is compounded out of 3 things, speech, music & rhythm" . . . And unless you write in quantity (by intent or accident) those three things mean mess.'[48] Pound is using quantity, not as an alternative regular metric, but as a way of achieving a rhythm free, as he would put it, 'of a metronome', another way of drawing poetry and music together.[49] 'Δώρια' is a poem that emphasises long, strong syllables, though not in any formal pattern. Sappho was a new and important influence at this stage, as her fragmented, passionate yet spare poetry gave him a model that allowed him to escape from the over-intricate and often wordy poems he had produced for *Canzoni*. Her influence was making his poetry sound more modern, even if he would not have acknowledged that; at the time he saw himself as returning once more to the past to learn from the masters of earlier years. The language of 'Δώρια' after all may be direct, and its imagery may spring from Pound's contemporary experience, yet he still calls the poem after a region of Greece, 'Doria' (the region around Sparta, appropriately austere), and gives the name in the Greek alphabet.

Pound's thoughts on poetry found an appreciative and unfailingly supportive listener in Dorothy. All the same, their renewed relationship had clearly made him wonder, yet again, if really he should be thinking about a proper job. When asked about 'economy' Dorothy replied: 'I have always designed (not the same thing as making) my own clothes, & often trimmed hats. And I should like £1,000 a year for my clothes, & I shall never have it – oh! dear.'[50] Yet she assured him, no doubt to his relief, that she wanted him to be a poet, and would only accept the £1,000 if earned by verse alone; so, as Pound reported to Margaret, 'there wont be much need of an extension for purposes of wardrobe, or staff to keep it in order – at least not for some time'.[51] Dorothy considerably underestimated the horror with which her father would respond to the prospect of so insufficiently financed a son-in-law, though, to do her justice, even when she discovered, she never suggested that Pound should do other than follow his vocation. So far, however, her father remained oblivious to the growing entanglement. That was something to await her return to London. In the event, Dorothy came back to London almost the same day as H.D arrived for the first time. Pound had told Dorothy something about H.D., quite how much one cannot be sure, though Dorothy did ask some uneasy questions about a poem Pound had written about H.D. when back in Philadelphia, in which he describes how 'she danced like a pink moth in the shrubbery'.[52] As far as H.D. was concerned, it is possible that Walter had mentioned Dorothy to her, but she certainly had no idea of the part she played in Pound's life, and it would be some weeks, possibly some months before she did so.

III

THE England in which H.D. arrived in 1911 had changed from the England that greeted Pound in 1908, not greatly, but significantly. Edward VII's death in May 1910, hastened, many thought, by political anxieties, was not precisely the end of an era, as is indicated by the very fact that 'Edwardian' is often used to denote the whole period from 1901 to 1914. Yet the Britain George V reigned over was already altering, and Virginia Woolf, for one, thought 1910 marked the end of the Victorian period and the beginning of a different world. The years from 1910 to 1914 were increasingly unsettled, and the disturbances in the country that even Pound had found hard to ignore by the end of his first visit would cause growing tension and anxiety. If the devastation ahead was still unimaginable, in retrospect the fragility of the social and political order is clear. The political battle, under way when Pound left the previous spring, between the Liberal Government in the House of Commons and the Conservative majority in the House of Lords, or, as the Liberals preferred to put it, between the People and the Peers, had finally been resolved in August 1911 with the passing of the Parliament Act. Now the House of Lords could no longer veto, but only delay, House of Commons legislation. But the resolution of social conflict that the Liberals hoped would follow in the wake of their victory, now they had the freedom to implement more generous and progressive measures, would continue to elude them.

Lloyd George's People's Budget had been passed in April 1910, while Pound basked in Sirmione. Whilst its aims – to raise more money from the rich to fund the beginnings of a welfare state, with pensions, health insurance and unemployment benefit – were laudable, progress was slow and workers' discontent grew. Poverty was widespread in Britain. A survey by Seebohm Rowntree indicated that over 30 per cent of the

urban population lived in poverty. Real wages were falling. The deference the workers had by and large felt in the nineteenth century towards
those who thought themselves their 'betters' was fading. As G.K.
Chesterton wittily pointed out in 1905, upper-class privilege was not
the result of merit: 'it rests on the perennial and unfailing kindness of
the poor'.[53] The poor were – through a combination of the effects of
universal education, working men's institutes and the growth of socialism
– no longer inclined to be so kind to the rich. Flint's Nietzschean rage
against an exploitative society was in the spirit of the time. The great
dock strike that Pound just missed on his return was one of many
portents of labour unrest. There was, as George Dangerfield commented
in his famous study of the decline of Liberal England, less of what one
might call organised anarchism or theoretical syndicalism in Britain
than on the continent, but the trade unions were very ready to take
direct action; they in practice behaved in the best anarcho-syndicalist
fashion. 'Between 1910 and 1914,' he notes, 'and against the wishes of
their leaders, [the workers] plunged into a series of furious strikes which,
but for the declaration of War, would have culminated in September
1914, in a General Strike of extraordinary violence. The exact prescrip-
tion for a syndicalist revolution.'[54]

Then there was the suffrage movement, which reached a militant
phase in late 1910. If the male workers were losing their deference, so
were women. Not all those supporting votes for women agreed with
militancy, but to the country at large it looked as if womanhood would
never be the same again. The suffragettes stormed Parliament; they
chained themselves to railings; they broke innumerable panes of glass;
they committed arson; they poured dye into pillar-boxes; they burnt
the suffragette message in acid on golf courses; Emily Davison eventually, in 1913, flung herself under the King's horse at the Derby. The
authorities took a far from gallant, and indeed ever more brutal attitude to the women; the police moved against them aggressively; most
infamously, in prison, the suffragettes who went on hunger strike were
violently force-fed. But they did not give up, even when the Cat and
Mouse legislation was passed, by which women being force-fed would
be let out when their health was failing, to be re-arrested a fortnight
later and taken back for another session, so that the maximum cruelty
was exerted without producing an undesirable martyr. If the New Woman
had appeared a dangerous and unnatural creature, the suffragette was
her apotheosis. Virginia Woolf's remark about human nature changing
in December 1910 has not generally been thought of in connection with

the workers and the women suffragettes, but to contemporaries it would have made sense. Indeed, the example Woolf gives is of a worker *and* a woman, the cook:

The Victorian cook lived like a leviathan in the lower depths, formidable, silent, obscure, inscrutable; the Georgian cook is a creature of sunshine and fresh air; in and out of the drawing-room, now to borrow the *Daily Herald*, now to ask advice about a hat. Do you ask for more solemn instances of the power of the human race to change?[55]

The old hierarchies were breaking down; only slowly, perhaps, and the liberal yet upper middle-class Woolf was possibly ambivalent about it, but change was on the way.

The other fraught area for the government was Ireland. Many, including Yeats, thought that the passing of the Parliament Act meant that Home Rule, to which the Liberals were sympathetic, was assured. They reckoned without the Ulster Unionists, who were not to allow any such devolution to go ahead. But in any case that hope of demo-cratic concession came too late. In 1910 the Irish Republican Brotherhood was reborn. Paramilitary organisations began to form in Ulster and the West. By 1914, all the elements that shaped Ireland's bloody twentieth-century history were in place, and the slow and painful dissolution of British Imperial rule in that island would begin.

It was in this unsettled Britain that H.D. arrived. Of course, on the surface much seemed as usual. The drawing-rooms to which Pound had been invited were as hospitable and well provided as ever, as she would gratefully discover. For the very rich, whom H.D. was rarely to meet at this stage, it was even a time of increasing opulence. Douglas Goldring asserts in *Odd Man Out* that it was in the ten years before the war that money began to be accepted as a passport into Society and 'the aris-tocracy of birth was beginning to wilt under repeated shocks'.[56] He may not be right about the newness of this trend, for the English aristocracy was always pragmatic about accepting trade-money into its ranks, but perhaps the process was accelerating. It was undeniably a good period for the wealthy, and his memories of the champagne that flowed at Society balls hosted by new money were undoubtedly correct.

Pound himself gives no hint of registering any particular change in atmosphere when he first arrived back. If he made comparisons, indeed, it is much more likely that he would have been struck by how different on a personal level this arrival was from that in 1908. Then he was

almost penniless, unknown and friendless. Now if not rich he was a
great deal more comfortably off; his name appeared everywhere; he had
published seven books and had many friends. During his first couple
of months back, Pound spent most of his time with the conservative
well-to-do, protected from social unrest. None of Pound's more political or radical friends were around. The Shakespears themselves had
firm views about social hierarchy. Apart from occasional wry comments
on 'the woman question', one of the only political events that Dorothy
mentioned in her letters to Pound before their marriage was the revolution in China: she was shocked that they would now be ruled by a
president rather than an emperor. The admiration for Chinese art that
Laurence Binyon had encouraged in her remained strong, but for her
China was an ancient aristocratic civilisation, and should not be sullied
by attempts at modern democracy. Yet in many parts of the world beyond
Europe old orders were crumbling. The Ottoman Empire had collapsed
in 1908, there had been a revolution in Mexico in 1910, and revolutions would also take place in Persia and Morocco. Eric Hobsbawm has
argued that the destabilisation of these societies was in many ways due
to the impact of Western expansion and trade development on the non-
European world.[57] In turn, the competition between the Western powers
for new spheres of influence in the wake of these revolutions was one
of the precipitating causes of the First World War. A time bomb was
ticking.

H.D., coming to London without her family, seeing it all in a haze
of excitement and with a sense of escape, noticed the mood of rebellion from the beginning. She was taken to a suffragette meeting soon
after her arrival; 'most thrilling,' she told her mother. H.D., impatient
as she was with the rules laid down for women in bourgeois Philadelphia,
savoured the suffragettes' defiance; perhaps it gave her hope for her
new life in Europe. Women's fashions were changing strikingly at this
time, in line with the new lives young women were seeking. Voluminous
skirts and corsets were beginning to disappear. Dresses became slim
and flowing, and hems were just beginning to rise. The Paris designer
Paul Poiret was widely credited with bringing in the new look in 1908,
with his high-waisted, slim-fitting Empire gowns, but his designs were
part of a general trend. Isadora Duncan had created a fashion for fluid
Grecian lines, and the couturier Mario Fortuny brought out Greek-
inspired fashions. H.D., who had hated the many layers of stiff material
required for respectable attire earlier in the century – particularly unsuitable for hot humid summers like those of Philadelphia – loved the

new and infinitely more comfortable styles. After her earlier irritation
with conventional dress, she now began to enjoy clothes, and later
observers commented on how gracefully and elegantly she dressed. The
fashion had changed not just in design but in women's figures. Statuesque
Edwardian battleship bosoms were out. To be tall and slender like H.D.
was suddenly absolutely right. As *Vogue*'s Paris correspondent in May
1908 had commented, 'The fashionable figure is growing straighter and
straighter, less bust, less hips, more waist, and a wonderfully long, slender
suppleness about the limbs . . . The long skirt . . . reveals plainly every
line and curve of the leg from hip to ankle. The petticoat is obsolete,
pre-historic. How slim, how graceful, how elegant women look! The leg
has suddenly become fashionable.' The colours women wore were
changing too, becoming brighter and more varied, though H.D., at any
rate in the version of herself in *Asphodel*, continued for some time to
wear the silvery greys and pastels that she had been used to in
Philadelphia, and was rebuked by George Lowndes for being 'too nun-ish'.[58]
Yet those she felt happier in. In her clothes as in life more generally,
she was finding a style that suited her.

The sphere of rebellion with which H.D. and Pound would of course
be most associated was that of the arts, though it would be the best part
of a year before either of them would align themselves with the modernist
revolution that was entering British cultural life. The impact of continental art movements had belatedly registered in London during Pound's
absence. The famous threshold moment is traditionally ascribed to Roger
Fry's 1910 exhibition at the Grafton Galleries, 'Manet and the Post-
Impressionists', which coincided with the Welsh coal-miners' strike and
the first wave of suffragette violence, and was seen by the conservative
press as an equally dangerous and perturbing outbreak of disorder, 'a
wide-spread plot', as an alarmed Robert Ross put it, 'to destroy the
whole fabric of European painting'.[59] 'Like anarchism in politics,' *The
Times* complained indignantly, 'it is the rejection of all that civilization
has done.'[60] Manet was already well known, the respectable bait to lure
the public in to see the works of Cézanne, Van Gogh, Gauguin, Matisse
and others, including a few Picassos, though none of his recent Cubist
paintings. As Pound's friend Laurence Binyon put it in his largely
unsympathetic review in the *Saturday Review*:

By an admirably discreet arrangement, reminding one of a Turkish bath, the shock
of the revelation is only administered by degrees. In the first room you need scarcely
be uneasy; Manet reigns there, and Manet is already a classic; in the second room

the temperature is more exciting, you are in the face of Gauguin and Van Gogh; and only when sufficiently acclimatised need you venture yet further into the wild realms of Matisse and his compeers.[61]

Although the show was greeted, as Roger Fry predicted, with 'a huge campaign of outraged British philistinism', it was commercially a great success.[62] As in the 1999 'Sensation' show at the Royal Academy, people swarmed in to be excitingly shocked. Paul O'Keeffe has pointed out that the four painters central to the exhibition, Manet, Gauguin, Van Gogh and Cézanne, were all dead, though apart from Manet little was known of their works by the public at large, or even by many in the art world. Cézanne, for example, had been exhibited very occasionally in England, but no one – apart from Roger Fry – had thought much about him; his death in 1906 had passed virtually unnoticed by the British press.[63] To many of the exhibition's first visitors, for whom the detailed realism of Sargent's society paintings or of Alma-Tadema's Grecian nudes represented the best of modern art, the paintings appeared crude, careless failures that ignored rules of perspective. Probably not untypical of the older generation was Wilfrid Scawen Blunt, quoted by Virginia Woolf in her biography of Roger Fry, in which she recalls with some glee this moment of cultural upheaval. Blunt wrote in his diary: 'The exhibition is either an extremely bad joke or a swindle. I am inclined to think the latter . . . these are not works of art at all, unless throwing a handful of mud against a wall may be called one. They are works of idleness and impotent stupidity, a pornographic show.'[64]

The Times was right to link the paintings with the current political unrest, for the changes in art were a sign of a new desire to rethink the accepted order of things, but the outrage provoked by the pictures was perhaps in part a symptom of the fears of the conservative bourgeoisie of other insurrections. The Labour-supporting Daily Herald had an equally political reading of the paintings, though from the opposite angle, writing: 'The Post-Impressionists are in the company of the Great Rebels of the World. In politics the only movements worth considering are Women Suffrage and Socialism. They are both Post-Impressionist in their desire to scrap old decaying forms and to find for themselves a new working ideal.'[65] As Frances Spalding points out, in these paintings, 'Nothing now was allowed to come between the artist's sensibility and his mode of expression: liberties could therefore be taken which before had been only allowable in a sketch. At a time when formality in dress and behaviour sustained a man's or woman's position in life, the informality of these paintings looked shockingly subversive, their lack of finish impolite. In their expressive vigour, they hit an English audience like a rude unwelcome shock.'[66] Blunt is, politically speaking, an interesting case in point; he was a fierce anti-imperialist who had been put in prison for his support for the Irish, but he was a Tory none the less, a believer in aristocratic values, with a fierce hatred of modernity and a horror of the decay of established traditions that to him these paintings symbolised. Significantly, his visit to the Grafton Galleries was one of the few non-political – or not obviously political – entries in his published diaries.

The papers divided largely on party lines: all the Tory papers hated the exhibition and most of the Liberal ones were more tolerant. The left-wing *New Age* gave it a cautious welcome in more than one review, one being by none other than Arnold Bennett under his pseudonym 'Jacob Tonson', though, as the letter pages testified, many of its readers were outraged. Pound's old acquaintance from the Tour Eiffel, Edward Storer, sent a letter arguing, in line with his earlier comments on convention in *Mirrors of Illusion*, that these artists – he particularly admired Matisse – had naturally moved on from the now overworked Impressionist conventions to their own set of 'rules and canons', which in fact drew on very old precepts.[67] Fry, looking back in 1920, felt the reason the 'cultured public' turned against him was that they regarded traditional high art as 'one of their social assets . . . it was felt that one could only appreciate Amico di Sandro when one had acquired a certain considerable mass of erudition and given a great deal of time and attention, but to admire a Matisse required only a certain sensibility. One could feel fairly sure one's maid could not rival one in the former case, but might by a mere haphazard gift of Providence surpass one in the second.' The condemnation of these painters, he argues, came out of 'social rather than aesthetic prejudice'.[68] The vehemence of many of the attacks on the exhibition reflected the violence with which the more obviously political rebels were being repressed: Winston Churchill sent the troops in to break the miners' strike, and the police were growing ever more aggressive towards the suffragettes.

'Post-Impressionist' was a name that had been seized on by Fry as a catch-all for these very different painters, and is a term he is generally credited with inventing; although in fact it had been used a couple of times before, it was he who gave it general currency. As he tried to explain to a confused British audience, what these artists had in common was a move away from the mimetic representational art that had dominated

Western painting since the Renaissance. 'They are,' he said, 'in revolt against the photographic vision of the nineteenth century, and even against the tempered realism of the last four hundred years . . . Like the Anarchists with whom they are compared, they are not destructive and negative, but intensely constructive.'[69] In spite of its many detractors, 'Manet and the Post-Impressionists' was to be an exhibition that dramatically and rapidly changed the course of much British art. Vanessa Bell, for example, already training herself as a painter, found it a revelation. 'It is impossible,' she said later, 'that any other single exhibition can ever have had so much effect as did that on the rising generation . . . here was a sudden pointing to a possible path, a sudden liberation and encouragement to feel for oneself which were absolutely overwhelming . . . It was as if one might say things one had always felt instead of trying to say things other people had told one to feel.'[70] She was one of many for whom the new art forms or new ideas or new mores appeared to offer 'sudden liberation' from Victorian hypocrisy and oppression.

Although the 1910 exhibition seemed to London like an overnight revolution in the world of art, the changes it charted had emerged over half a century. Fry himself was well aware of this progression, pointing out that in their desire to undo post-Renaissance realism, the Post-Impressionists were 'true Pre-Raphaelites', but though he pointed to the long roots of this art, his language played with images of violence and revolt, as in his reference to the Anarchists, quite as readily as his detractors. The sense of revolution in the arts initiated by this exhibition would remain in the air for the next decade. The frequently xenophobic British press was quick to note that this artistic revolt had a continental source, and other signs of this continental menace were appearing in London. Even before the arrival of Fry's exhibition, the theatrical Futurist poet and painter Marinetti had visited, but though at that stage he caused a stir, he was regarded as too obviously foreign to be a threat to British culture. In any case, there had so far been no exhibition of Futurist painting, though Douglas Goldring had published one of Marinetti's Futurist manifestos in his magazine the *Tramp*, in which Flint and Lewis were also appearing. Diaghilev's Russian Ballet came in 1911, but whilst Edward Marsh astutely described it as a 'Post-Impressionist picture put in motion', it came in for much less attack, and indeed was greatly admired. On the other hand, when the *New Age* in November 1911 published a black and white reproduction of a Picasso Cubist painting, the storms of the previous winter blew up once more. Picasso was defended by the *New Age* art critic, Huntly Carter, and by

Middleton Murry, who caused near apoplexy by talking warmly of Picasso's Platonism. The letters flooded in to protest, the most vehement coming from Ebenezer Wake Cook, a Royal Academy painter in his late sixties, who warned darkly that 'While there are any deeper depths of degradation, inanity, or of sheer lunacy to be gone through the Continental anarchists will drag the dishevelled Goddess of Art through them.'[71]

Pound must have heard about the 1910 exhibition in the States, if only through Floyd Dell's reference to it, but although Dorothy, who rarely missed any significant cultural event, would almost certainly have been one of the visitors to the Grafton Galleries, and the aftershocks of the 'Art-Quake', as Desmond MacCarthy dubbed it, still rumbled away in the press on his return, such events were not yet of interest to him. If Pound had read the Wake Cook letter, it would scarcely, one imagines, have occurred to him that in a couple of years, through his association with the Vorticists, he would be hailed as the next dreadful step downwards. The future Pound would rejoice in provoking such diatribes, but for now he paid little attention to this modern movement, even though his 'Δώρια' poem, in its bare simplicity and elemental power, has a quality that evokes the chthonic weight and strength of Cézanne's Mont Saint-Victoire paintings. Pound's imagism, when it emerged the next year, was to have much in common with this rigorous simplification, as well as with the move beyond conventional representation. But for now mysticism remained more significant to him than the artistic avant-garde. He wrote to Margaret in early October about his meeting with the Persian 'Abdu'l-Bahà, creator of the Baha'i religion, who had come to London to preach world love and unity, a worthy if perhaps over-optimistic platform, urging her to hear him in Paris, as 'Its more important than Cézanne'.[72] Yet even his interest in the 'Bahi', as he called him, was perhaps an indication that he would soon, like so many of these painters, turn to non-Western sources as models for his art. In late August, the Japanese poet Yone Noguchi, whose work had been published in translation by Elkin Mathews, sent him two books of his poetry and asked Pound to send him some of his. Pound was very struck by the poems, and wrote to Dorothy, prophetically in light of the later impact of Far Eastern poetry on him, 'His matter is poetic & his stuff not like everything else, he is doubtless sent to save my artistic future.'[73] He wrote back to Noguchi, saying that 'if east and west are ever to understand each other that understanding must come slowly and come first through the art'.[74]

IV

IN a letter to his father in late September 1911, Pound, now back in London after his Dorset visit, had mentioned that H.D., Frances and Walter were all expected to arrive in about a week. H.D. had written to him saying she was coming to London for a rest, and was taken aback, as she told his mother, by Pound's scorn at her ill-informed assumption that a quiet life could be lived in literary London. He had also heard from Frances, who sent him some poems, which he told his father he thought rather good; he sent them on to the New York *Forum*, which published them in December. H.D. recalled many years later that on this visit 'Ezra had hurt me . . . by picking on some rather Celtic conventional poems of F and ignoring mine'.[75] Frances later wrote some striking poems, but H.D.'s judgement of these seems pretty fair. Was this a deliberate snub by Pound? They weren't poems he would have commended even a year later, and though his comments to his father suggest that his admiration, as far as it went, was genuine, Pound's promotion of Frances' verse at this period could have been an attempt to damp down H.D.'s affections, if they were in danger of revival. Yet one suspects that Pound was equally worried about the danger of his own feelings for H.D. getting the better of him. Perhaps, just as in Edith Wharton's *The Age of Innocence*, Newland Archer hurries forward his marriage to his fiancée May when he realises that he is falling in love with Ellen Olenska, Pound, now he had both Dorothy and H.D. in close proximity, took precipitate action to make his commitment to Dorothy official. On 11 October, nine days after Dorothy's return to London, he asked Dorothy's father Hope for permission to marry her.

The results of this bold step savoured more of farce than romance. Dorothy was rather naïvely sanguine about the outcome of the proposal, telling Pound her father was 'much more likely to be perfectly sensible than not; possibly he will ask us to take breath until the New Year?'[76] Unfortunately her father had quite different ideas from Dorothy about what was perfectly sensible. He was startled by Pound's request; that Pound had any interest in his daughter had evidently not occurred to him, and he was astounded that anyone in Pound's precarious financial position should have the temerity to suggest marriage at all. Olivia had apparently told him nothing of her own anxieties about the relationship, but, like her, his first thought was money. During the interview Pound mentioned his £200 a year, but gave no hint as to its source. Nothing was resolved on the spot, Hope being too much in shock to press for clarification, but he wrote to Pound the next day, asking for more information, including detailed financial accounts for the last twelve months: 'I confess,' he wrote, with a cautious man's suspicion of the artistic life, 'I am wholly ignorant of the sources from which a man in your position derives an income.' He was surprised and relieved when Pound was able to provide him with bank counterfoils which proved he at least had a balance, but what Hope was most anxious to know was if the £200 was, as he put it, 'secured'.[77] Pound's response was to write to his father, without giving him the vestige of an explanation, saying that 'if one Shakespear, H.H.' wrote to him he was to reply 'even after this wise, altering no jot nor tittle upon pain of my wrath'. The prescribed letter was to begin:

Naturally my son has not mentioned this matter to me, but if he wants anything he is very likely to get it. Any items he may have given you about his finances are presumably correct. He is no longer in bonds of necessity. My home is at his disposal and I only wish he would make more use of it than he does.

He seemed rather preoccupied when he was last with us but that might have been Guido Cavalcanti.[78]

In his letter home Pound made no mention of Dorothy, but he did add by way of explanation of the financial guarantee that he now had $1,000 a year apart from his literary earnings and might soon have another $750. (This latter sum – in the event it was £100, i.e. $500 – was to be paid to him by Swift & Co., who were offering him, if he would agree to their being sole publisher of his work, that sum for ten years as an advance against future royalties.) By the next day, Pound clearly felt he had overdone the high-handness for once, and wrote again, with more explanations: 'I am, as you may have surmised from my epistle of yesterday, attempting to marry the gentleman's daughter.

I shall do that in any case but do not want to disturb the sepulchral calm of that english household more than need be.' He reminded his parents that they had been shown a 'poor photograph' of Dorothy when he was at home, but if they wanted to know more they should consult his published works, though one cannot imagine that they could have deduced much that was definite from one of Pound's visionary love poems. Homer and Isabel, who still had had hopes that Pound and H.D. would get together, and had been told nothing about their son's patron, wrote back in astonishment, but Pound gave no further explanations, except to say about the money that 'the source is anonymous and the donation voluntary'.[79]

It was mid-November by the time the loyal and long-suffering Homer had written to Hope in his son's support, receiving a courteous if stiff reply from Hope, written in his beautiful copperplate, so different from Pound's frenetic scrawl, assuring Homer that he had never doubted his son's word in the matter of his income, but what he needed to know was where the money came from, and most importantly, if it was 'of a permanent nature'. 'Literary work,' he continued, 'of the kind for which he is, no doubt, eminently suited is not likely for some years to furnish him with the means of supporting a Wife.'[80] One might have thought such a rebuff would be galling to an ardent young lover, and certainly the kindly Homer was worried, but Pound wrote that he need remonstrate no more with Hope as 'the status quo is very pleasant and I see no reason to disturb it with argument'.[81] To Margaret he had written in late November, when she too was expressing anxiety about him: 'the Shakespears are being quite amenable and I see D. twice a week except when the minx has the bad grace to go off to the country for a week, as she is went at present'.[82] Such easy contentment with a twice-weekly meeting and no definite prospects is surprising, and suggests Pound had decided the compensating pleasures of a bachelor existence would suffice him for a bit longer. Pound's life was in general going well. He was working productively, and besides, he was after all spending a good deal of time with H.D.

H.D. was delighted with London. She and the Greggs had moved into the Duchess Street boarding-house that Pound had used when he had first arrived, and which he had doubtless recommended. They had both Pound and Rummel to show them round, as well as introductions to friends of the Doolittles. Only two postcards are extant from H.D. to her mother from London at that period, and though she mentions on one that Walter has taken her to a couple of concerts, she says nothing about Pound, possibly because she felt her mother would rather not hear. Writing to Isabel Pound in December, however, H.D. was warm in praise of Pound's kindness in introducing her to literary London. May Sinclair had had them to tea at Pound's request – he had written to ask her to invite them even before they had arrived. H.D. had read Sinclair's 1904 novel, *The Divine Fire*, which had been a bestseller in both the States and Britain, but as she recalled almost half a century later, 'I had never expected to meet any of these famous people'.[83] Frances, she told Isabel Pound, 'was properly introduced as the rising American poetess, and I as – well, just a friend of great people'.[84] Frances was not particularly grateful, being upset that May Sinclair did not express more admiration for her poems, and recording in her diary, and her memoir, that Sinclair was 'little and mean-souled and repellent, but she could write, and I envied her'.[85] Frances might well have judged her by appearances to be old-fashioned and unbearably proper, but no one was less mean-souled than the always generous Sinclair. What H.D. thought at that first meeting she does not reveal, but she certainly came to love and appreciate May Sinclair, and was to spend her first London Christmas with her. They met the poet Alice Meynell, now in her sixties, whom H.D. describes to Isabel as the 'protectress, you remember, of the once thread-bare . . . starving Francis Thompson'. Ernest Rhys and his wife entertained them, and, H.D. wrote, were 'most interested in Frances' too.[86] She particularly liked Lilian Sauter, John Galsworthy's elder sister, and it was she who led her off to the exciting suffragette meeting. Lilian was married to a Bavarian painter, Georg Sauter, according to Noel Stock earlier a friend of Whistler's.[87] Although Pound knew the couple – they also lived in Kensington, and were friends of Ford – for once H.D. met them as acquaintances of Philadelphian friends, rather than through Pound. Lilian Sauter was almost fifty at the time, a remarkably well read and independent-minded woman, who had been an important influence on her brother's development. She had led the family rebellion against their narrow-minded and deeply conformist mother, and married Sauter, who was not only a foreigner and an artist but of peasant stock, against considerable family opposition; this act of defiance in support of the arts, Sauter himself always thought, gave Galsworthy the courage to become, in spite of family disapproval, a novelist and writer.[88]

As in Paris, H.D. visited museums and galleries, and she loved exploring the city, telling Isabel that she spent her time browsing in picture gallerys, hour after hour, – 'The National' is my favourite haunt!. Exploring old churches and church-yards – odd corners in Lincoln Inn Fields, remote byways and bridges by Hammersmith; feeding the many ducks who quack gratefully in St James' park; and sea-gulls, who look on and soar disdainfully aloft; – more ambitious adventures into Hampstead Heath and Golders' Green.

Her special delight, she said, was 'climbing up the swaying stair-cases of the horse and auto-busses, and ensconsed in state on a front seat, [to] behold all the world, panorama-wise, rolling onward for my own and special delectation'. In addition, there had been 'concerts a few and more tea-parties – a dinner once in a while, and kindness everywhere'.[89]

But this was not all. If it was in France, as she suggests in *Asphodel*, that the realisation came to her that 'Hermione must write', it seems that from very early on in her time in London she began to train herself seriously as a writer. She spent her mornings in the British Museum Reading Room, as she told her mother on one of the postcards home. On 13 October, about a week after her arrival in London, and two days after Pound had solicited Dorothy's hand in marriage, he had written to the British Museum recommending H.D. for a reader's ticket, which she obtained by 17 October. There is no suggestion that this would be temporary, so it is likely that by then she had already heard the good news that her visit was to be extended. Her mother had written to say that she and H.D.'s father were planning to visit Europe, and H.D. could await their arrival. Mrs Gregg and Frances were going back at the end of the month, and though H.D. urged Frances to remain, Frances was adamant that her mother needed her. H.D. saw this as rejection, since she herself had been ready, however regretfully, to wound *her* mother by coming to Europe with Frances. Such a reaction was not entirely fair; H.D.'s mother may have been hurt and saddened, though perhaps not as much as H.D. feared – H.D. certainly appears to be the more active correspondent: 'I look forward to mail,' she wrote a little disconsolately to her mother from France, the kind of plaint more often uttered by parents. But in any case H.D.'s mother was surrounded by family and lived in comfortable affluence. Frances' mother had only her daughter, and she needed her both for companionship and extra economic support. And Frances had her pride; she had no money and felt if she stayed it would have been as H.D.'s 'satellite and protégée'.[90] H.D.'s spell over her, she says, was broken. When sufficiently tempted, only a few months later, Frances would agree to leave her mother, if only for a while; H.D. had reason to feel rebuffed.

H.D. travelled up to Liverpool to see them off, seeing Stratford-upon-Avon *en route*, and sending her mother a postcard of Anne Hathaway's cottage, which she had visited on her honeymoon. Barbara Guest in her biography suggests H.D. was quite relieved by the difficult Frances' departure, and it's likely that at any rate her feelings were mixed, as they usually were when it came to Frances. In the version of events she gives in *Asphodel*, Hermione begs Fayne to stay, to share a flat with her in Chelsea, so that they could become writers together: 'I am burning away that's all. The clear gem-like flame. I don't want you to miss it. I'm going to write, work . . . We are the children of the Rossettis, of Burne Jones, of Swinburne. We were in the thoughts of Wilde when he spoke late at night of carts rumbling past the windows, fresh with farm produce on the way to Covent Garden. He was talking to a young man called Gilbert. They talked of Greeks and flowers.'[91] H.D. here places herself firmly in the tradition of the Pre-Raphaelites, aesthetes and decadents, the writers whom she met through Pound and passed on to Frances, love and writing being as so often for her inseparable. Yet of the two, writing remained the imperative: H.D. never contemplated returning with Frances. As Hermione says to Fayne: 'I couldn't go back. Not go back. I have to stay. I *have* to stay in England'.[92]

Whatever H.D. had felt about Frances' departure, Pound certainly appeared relieved. Frances had lost none of her passion for Pound, and there are hints that he found her fierceness of feeling wearing, writing to Margaret Cravens on her departure of his relief that the worst of his 'psychological patients' was to leave for the US.[93] Shortly after the arrival of H.D. and Frances, he had described his life as 'juggling volcanos'; having three women in London who all felt a claim on him clearly imposed a strain.[94] Pound always took his role as host to visiting Americans very seriously; while entertaining H.D. and the Greggs, he had been organising at second hand a visit to Paris by Julia Wells, the impoverished inhabitant of Patchin Place, and he would soon be masterminding a visit for Mary Moore. Frances' response to his thoughtfully arranged visit to May Sinclair suggests she was not an easy guest to please, and although Pound's friends were ready to entertain her as another of his literary protégés, her presence may have been an uneasy one. According to the fictional version in *Paint it Today*, she fitted in no better in London society than in Philadelphia. Josepha, as the Frances figure is called there, regards people in general with deep suspicion and disdain; as the narrator puts it, she 'through prenatal accident and the shocks attending a precarious childhood, had learned early to distrust [other people]. She was in turn, more or less avoided by them. Her eyes discountenanced them . . . Josepha knew all about it. She said quite clearly, "So and so hates me; so and so sees that I see.""[95] H.D. always admired, indeed was fascinated by this independence of spirit, feeling herself much more meekly conformist: the H.D. figure here is described as 'outwardly standardised by early environment'.[96] H.D. felt uneasily that the politeness and social tact she had learnt from her mother and continued to practise were sadly inappropriate to a true modernist artist, but they did make her a much more agreeable and comfortable addition to the social scene. How aware of this Pound would have been, with his own minimal diplomatic skills, it is hard to say. But he seemed delighted to have H.D. left by herself to be shown round London, and happily reported to his parents that 'she seems to get on very well with a number of people'.[97]

H.D. never explained, or perhaps never could explain, quite what her own feelings were for Pound at this time; all that is clear is her emotional confusion. In retrospect she repeatedly described her early days in London as 'drifting'. As far as her emotional life was concerned, that appears to have been true. If Frances had stayed she might well have drifted into a flat with her; if Pound had wanted it, she could well have drifted back into an engagement with him, as indeed she sometimes wondered if she had. She could have drifted into a love affair with the Byronic Rummel. As it was, she would drift into marriage with Richard Aldington. Yet as far as her desire to be a writer was concerned, she did not drift at all. That was her rudder, and it was to steer her through all the turmoil and emotional disasters of the war years. Her routine of working in the British Museum Reading Room every morning had been established by the time she had been in London a fortnight; mainly, it seems, she worked on translations, very much the way Pound had trained himself as a writer. The letter of application had said that she wanted to work on the Latin poets of the Renaissance, as she had done earlier at Pound's instigation. But she was soon to move on to the Greeks. Indeed, 'Greeks and flowers', of which she says Wilde talked to Gilbert, are the main themes of her early poetry. It may well have been Pound, with his newfound enthusiasm for Sappho, who, knowing her already powerful passion for all things Greek, drew her attention to Sappho as a model, but she was also attracted by the brevity and honed clarity of the epigrams in the Greek Anthology.[98] In her afternoons she would sightsee and attend literary parties, which also occupied her evenings and to which she would often be accompanied by Pound.

Pound told H.D. nothing of his feelings about Dorothy at this stage. He started making love to her again, more kisses, though still not consummation, and hinting at another ambiguous engagement, in which she only half, or less, believed. As she wrote in *End to Torment*, 'I remember how he said to me in London . . . Let's be engaged – don't tell . . .'[99] She was wary after her previous experience, but the shock she felt when she eventually heard of his engagement to Dorothy suggests she had let down her emotional guard once more. The account of her response to this renewed lovemaking given in *Asphodel* sounds convincing enough. There we are told that Hermione feels a mixture of guilt and gratitude; kissing now without the sanction of an official engagement worries her, and she is confused about whether the engagement is on again or not. She is fearful lest people know how she's behaving and think she isn't a 'nice girl'.[100] Yet George's lovemaking leaves her with feelings of warmth, contentment and reassurance. This mixture of emotions, guilt and gratitude, certainly fits with what one knows from elsewhere. H.D.'s relationship with Pound, perhaps because it was her first sexual relationship, beginning in her parental home under sternly disapproving eyes, appears to have filled her with guilt in a way neither her affair with Frances nor her later pre-marital lovemaking with Aldington would do. The shame of the moments of exposure back in Philadelphia that she talks of in *End to Torment*, both in front of her father and when seen by the schoolgirls, are presented as deeply traumatic. But H.D. was always sensitive about keeping up appearances; perhaps Pound exposed her to disapproval and gossip in a way that neither Frances nor Aldington did. Yet in spite of that, Pound's affection and emotional protection were very welcome. For all her excitement and pleasure in London, she was at another level anxious, vulnerable, sad to be away from her family and Frances. She wrote to her mother that she was 'very gay and almost overrushed', and to Isabel Pound, that she was 'happy but a bit too gay', as if she were in some ways quite frightened by this new world of freedom.[101] In *Asphodel*, George's kisses were less fiery in London than they had been in Philadelphia, tempered, Hermione speculates, by the London mists, but they were also more comforting: 'Her mouth lifted and kisses bent and flowered upon it . . . After all, George's hibiscus red *did* make a warm coal glow somewhere in her heart.'[102]

Where this was leading she had no idea. Her visit to England, even if extended, was still officially a temporary one. She had no notion what the future held, apart from her determination to write. In London, she was intrigued to discover, Pound was a figure of some consequence, rather than, as in Philadelphia, of notoriety: as she writes of the fictional George Lowndes: 'Here people did not laugh at George. People asked his opinion a little reverently. It was funny watching people reverencing George . . . His odd clothes not so odd, his little brush of a beard and his velvet coat and his cravats like flowers in mosaic of maroon and green and gilt and odd vermilion. George didn't look odd though he looked more odd than ever.'[103] She wrote to Isabel Pound: 'It would delight you to see how many and what devoted friends he has here.'[104] Pound, this important figure in the London literary scene, was keen to introduce her everywhere. Having a ready-made community of acquaintances, some of whom would become friends, was perhaps one reason why she was happy in London whereas she had been disconsolate in New York, where both she and Pound felt largely isolated. Yet there was also the sense of freedom, at times alarming, but also exhilarating, that she felt in moving to Europe away from the constraints of her Philadelphian upbringing. She had taken a momentous step in her struggle to become a poet.

V

DURING October 1911, Pound and Walter Rummel had shared a flat, or rather, as Pound put it in a letter home, 'part of an infinitesimal house', in Addison Road, more Holland Park than Kensington, though not far away.[105] When Pound had returned in August he discovered to his chagrin that his old room with the Langleys at 10 Church Walk had been taken, and he was forced to find lodgings elsewhere. Addison Road had many literary associations: Elkin Mathews had lived there for a while before he moved out of London; John Galsworthy and his wife lived there for many years; Jules Laforgue, the French poet so influential in T.S. Eliot's development, had been married in St Barnabas' Church in that road; and coincidentally, T.S. Eliot would marry his second wife in the same church in 1957. Pound had told his parents he and Walter would share until Christmas, but in early November he was able to move back to Church Walk, happy to return, he told Margaret, to 'my own proper corner of St Mary Abbots church yard, where it is more cheap & comfortable than any place else in London – musical accompaniment not withstanding'.[106] His former room, on the warmer, south side of the house, was not available, but he was quite content for now with one at the back, though he reported with pleasure to his mother the following August that he was back in the original one.

Yet if he was restored to Church Walk, there were still gaps in his London life. He had mentioned in a letter home in mid-September that Ernest Rhys was back in town, and that he had met up again with Laurence Binyon and Victor Plarr, the half-Alsatian former Rhymer whose Sunday evenings he had attended on his first visit, and who would later appear in *Hugh Selwyn Mauberley* as Monsieur Verog.[107] Neither Yeats nor Ford, however, was to return to London until mid-November, and Yeats only briefly, though during 1912 Woburn Walk and South Lodge would figure as importantly in Pound's cultural geography as ever. One landmark missing from Pound's literary map for rather longer was the Tour Eiffel. The group that Pound had met there, already fragmenting the previous year, had dispersed, though when the restaurant became a favourite haunt of Wyndham Lewis and the Vorticists, Pound would begin to visit it again. Although Pound might not yet have consciously recognised it, his time with those poets had had a deep impact on him. His sense of the need to draw music and poetry together, on which he had worked obsessively ever since those meetings, had come, it is true, partly from Yeats, reinforced by Rummel, but it had also come from his time with the Tour Eiffel poets, particularly Campbell and Florence Farr.[108] The way he had set about making that link had been, until recently, something of a dead end, in the elaborations of the *Canzoni*. But with his new realisation that 'melos' involved moving away from the rhythmic regularity that had dominated English verse since the Renaissance, he was now more ready to appreciate the other qualities that the group had emphasised, such as simplicity and spareness, whose value he was beginning to discover. Over the next year, his verse and his poetic theories would be profoundly influenced by two other Tour Eiffel poets, Flint and Hulme – rather ironically in the case of the latter, as Hulme had given up writing poetry, but Pound belatedly came to understand what Hulme had been trying to do in his verse. Flint would persuade him eventually to look at contemporary French verse, though Pound did not, it appears, meet Flint again until almost Christmas, and it would be some months after that before Flint's arguments weighed with him.

In the winter of 1909–10, during the months before Pound's departure for Italy and the States, as the regular meetings at the Tour Eiffel became less frequent, the poets had as often met at the Irish Literary Society in Belgrave Square as in Soho. On Pound's return he found that both the Irish members of the group, Campbell and FitzGerald, had left the country. Both had married, and both to Protestants, with strenuous opposition from the families involved; in each case their move away from England was caught up with the increasingly bitter divisions that were opening up in the struggle for Home Rule. Joseph Campbell, the road-maker's son, had married Dorothy Shakespear's closest school friend Nancy Maude, much to the consternation of Nancy's parents. Nancy had met Pound at dinner at the Shakespears' in February 1909 – possibly the first time he had dinner there – and commented on him as 'a most original person'.[109] It may well have been Pound who introduced her to Campbell later that year at the Irish Literary Society, when she was very taken with hearing 'Mr Campbell reading beautifully'. In December she dined at the Poets' Club with the Shakespears and Pound, and 'sat next to Mr Campbell', and must have had the pleasure on that occasion of hearing Campbell read 'The Ballad of the Goodly Fere' in his bardic robes.[110] Like Dorothy, Nancy came from an Anglo–Indian family; her grandfather had been for thirty-five years Court Equerry to Queen Victoria, in charge of her thoroughbred horses. Yet coming from the heart of the English establishment had not trammelled her views. She was, as Campbell's biographer suggests, something of a New Woman; she supported the suffragettes, was in favour of Irish Home Rule, attended Bernard Shaw's lectures, was an avid theatre-goer, and took a keen interest in contemporary culture and politics. She wrote some poetry herself, and in 1910 published privately a booklet of verse, dedicated to 'J.C.' and illustrated by Joseph's artist brother John; its title, *The Little People*, indicates her fascination by then with all things Irish.

When Campbell went, on 4 May 1910, to ask Colonel Maude for Nancy's hand in marriage, her parents were even more horrified than Dorothy's would be at Pound's proposal the next year. 'Mr Campbell,' her mother commented stiffly, 'is not quite in our position of life, and is a Roman Catholic.'[111] Campbell himself must have had a difficult few days. Two days later, Edward VII died, and the delicate and explosive question of how the Irish Literary Society should handle this was thrust upon him. In the end, Campbell agreed with his co-honorary secretary, Mrs Malcolm Cotter Seton, a Unionist, to postpone the evening's programme as a mark of respect. As Campbell explained later: 'My argument was this: I was an Irishman living and earning my bread in the capital of a foreign country, the King of which was dead. To Edward VII, as an Irishman, I owed no allegiance . . . Although he was nothing to me, I could not be so utterly barbarous as to dance on the dead gentleman's coffin-lid.' Other nationalists, however, took a very different view, especially Barry O'Brien, the president of the Society, who was furious with Joseph. 'The incident,' Campbell recorded, 'split the society from top to bottom.'[112] There was equal trouble in Dublin, where the Abbey Theatre had failed to close for the evening, so there was probably no way Campbell could have avoided angry dissension, but it must have added to his unhappiness. He continued as secretary, but his position had become awkward, and he must for a while have felt the world was against him. In June, on a visit back home, where he found his own family equally opposed to the match with Nancy, he wrote her a long letter, full of melancholy and self-reproach, putting forward the case against himself as a husband: he had only £100 a year, and that not assured. In addition, 'he's a weak heart, and may go "pop" at any time! He has no good looks; he is not clever; is not likely to get on in the world as he has no influential friends; is a *Roman Catholic* (oh, horror of horrors!)'.[113]

Nancy, a woman of courage and resource, was not convinced by either her parents' or Joseph's arguments. Her mother, she told a friend, 'has been rubbing it in to poor Joseph, the iniquity of imagining I can do without servants and luxuries, and how frail and delicate I am!' In the end she won her way with her parents, unhappy though they continued to be, for she and Joseph were quietly married at St Patrick's, Soho, on 23 May 1911, though without, it seems, family from either side present. Joseph went off to his class at seven o'clock that night as usual, but luckily friends brought champagne and flowers. The Catholic wedding must have been a further blow to Nancy's parents, but the marriage is another striking example of how class and cultural barriers were being broken down in London's pre-war artistic and intellectual world. Earlier Nancy's mother had exclaimed with irritation that her daughter was convinced she could live on her £60 dress allowance, but in the event her parents made Nancy a reasonable settlement, and when the young couple moved to Ireland shortly after the wedding they had an income of £400, of which at least £300 was Nancy's – probably more, because the £100 of which Campbell had spoken was probably his salary for the teaching work that he had done for London County Council. Pound must have heard the story from Dorothy on his return, though the first time Dorothy saw Nancy again was in early December, when she wrote to Pound to say: 'My friend Nancy . . . came to lunch – looking so handsome & full of so many things – married life has agreed with her well.'[114] Dorothy may have felt Nancy's final success in her battle with her parents augured well for her, but it was to take much longer for Dorothy and Pound to get agreement to their marriage. Perhaps they did not try so hard.

In March, before the wedding, Campbell had brought out another book, this time in prose, entitled *The Mearing Stones*. It consisted of a series of impressionistic sketches of his 'tramps', as he called them, in Donegal, brief vignettes, little prose poems, recalling the peasant folk he met there, from whom he was collecting legends and songs. Like his poetry, it fuses folk and modernist characteristics. Pound later described *The Mearing Stones* as a 'charming' book: 'It interests me largely because

Mr Campbell has been content to present a series of brief pictures in prose. He has cast over the attempt at continuous narrative which has spoiled so many books of walking since Heine.'[115] Pound began to plan his own travel book in early 1912; using a form analogous to Campbell's account of the countryside that had nurtured Celtic poetry, he intended to write about the places where his troubadours had lived and composed their songs. In the summer of 1912 he would undertake his own extensive tramp through southern France, and although he would never finish that travel book, what there is has the episodic, fractured form of *The Mearing Stones*; he was following Campbell's lead once more. Both Nancy and Joseph returned to England regularly for the next few years. Their marriage ultimately foundered, but it was politics not poverty that wrecked it.

Desmond FitzGerald was also gone. He had married an equally courageous and determined woman, Mabel McConnell, and it is perhaps not altogether surprising that Mabel and Nancy, who first met in Ireland at the beginning of the First World War, later became lifelong friends. Mabel was the daughter of a well-to-do Ulster businessman, John McConnell, a friend of the arch-Unionist Sir Edward Carson. One of five children, she grew up in Belfast and attended what was then Queen's College, now University, and graduated with a degree from the Royal University, Dublin. She had by then, like her elder sister, developed ardent nationalist sympathies and independent views, as she became a committee member of the Gaelic Society. After graduating, she took a secretarial course, which stood her in good stead when she moved to London in 1908, at the age of twenty-four, to study for a postgraduate diploma in teaching. In London she joined the central branch of the Gaelic League, adopting the Irish form of her name, Méadhbh Ní Chonaill, and it may have been through contacts there that she found work as a secretary with such prominent Anglo-Irish figures as Bernard Shaw and George Moore. While teaching in Upminster, she got to know Desmond's sister, who was a headmistress there, and through her, Desmond. (In his autobiography Garret FitzGerald suggested that Desmond and Mabel probably met at the Gaelic League, but letters have come to light which have led him to think they met before.) When her father realised the situation, Mabel was summoned back home for family remonstrations but she ran away back to London, climbing out of a window at night and fleeing the family home. She and Desmond married in London, and the two left for Brittany. They joined an artists' colony, and FitzGerald pursued his writing, with no thought of any other career, until in 1913 they returned to Ireland, and historical events began to push him in a very different direction.[116]

If Pound did not learn immediately where FitzGerald had gone, he would have heard it from Campbell on one of his visits, or possibly from Flint, when he finally caught up with him. Desmond said in a letter to Flint in 1914 that he returned to London as often as he could, in order to see his mother, and he certainly saw Flint, if not the others. Pound would have been aware of FitzGerald's poetry when it was published in the *New Age* in 1917, and of the romantic circumstances surrounding its publication, as FitzGerald was then in prison, a hero of the Easter Rising; by then Nancy and Mabel had become close friends, so Dorothy would have had regular news. But it was when FitzGerald obtained political office that Pound's admiration was really stirred.

Of the other figures from the Tour Eiffel, Tancred and Storer were both around on the London scene, but Pound had never been particularly friendly with either of them. He saw something of Tancred, whom he refers to casually in a letter to Dorothy the next year, saying 'The inimitable Tancred aroused me to meet the beau soleil' – Pound always got up late – '& lunched with me'.[117] He doesn't mention seeing Edward Storer again, though they would have been at some of the same social events; Storer was writing prolifically, at this period in prose, making in 1912, in the introduction to a book of selections from William Cowper, much the same onslaught on Romanticism that Hulme more famously launched around the same time. J.B. Harmer says that Storer kept in touch with Hulme, as Tancred did, though this does not of course mean that Storer took his ideas from Hulme; he had, after all, developed his earlier theories on poetry quite independently. Certainly the comments he makes in his Cowper book on 'the decadent and lifeless romanticism of our own time' predate the savage criticisms that Pound himself, rather later, came to make.[118]

Pound saw Florence Farr from time to time, as she knew the Shakespears well, but Dorothy rather disapproved of her, and she does not often feature in their letters. Farr had brought out two books in his absence, *A Calendar of Philosophy*, a beautifully produced book with woodcut illustrations for each month and a quotation for each day, drawn from a wide and eclectic variety of sources, with messages more often wry than righteous, such as 'We contract marriages as we contract fevers, partly through pure misfortune, but largely through negligence.'[119] She had also published a feminist polemic, *Modern Woman: What Does She Want?*, but that was not a question Pound would ever ask or seek to answer. The only one of the Tour Eiffel group that Pound saw much of that autumn was Hulme, who returned to London in late September. Pound was delighted to renew his acquaintance; since his return to England in August, he had spent most of his time in polite Kensington drawing-rooms or country houses, and the bluff and energetic Hulme was a welcome change. Hulme was now writing regularly for the *New Age*, and continuing to promote Bergson, though his enthusiasm would soon wane. In Paris that spring, on his way to an International Philosophical Congress in Bologna, he had met Pierre Lasserre, one of the founders of Action Française, a radical right-wing movement, Catholic, royalist and reactionary. Hulme was deeply impressed by Lasserre, but discovered they differed over Bergson, whom Lasserre considered an outdated Romantic; in particular, he was appalled by the way Bergson's philosophy was deployed by socialists and anarchists to suggest change was part of the nature of the universe. Hulme was not convinced immediately, but his confidence was shaken. He was, in addition, deeply disturbed by the fact that, partly owing to his own efforts, Bergson had become immensely fashionable in England. When Bergson lectured in October 1911 at University College, London, he drew an audience of hundreds; Hulme felt distinctly uncomfortable about now being one of a crowd of admirers. He described the first of those lectures in an article in the *New Age*, writing under the name of Thomas Gratton, which he sometimes used as a pseudonym for his more right-wing political articles, possibly, since it was drawn from his childhood home, Gratton Hall, as a tribute to his parents' political views. There he argued indignantly, in yet another of his sexually charged analogies, that presenting the subtleties of Bergsonian philosophy to this uninitiated audience was like undressing a woman in public: 'The difficulty of getting into this hall,' he maintained, 'should have been comparable to the difficulty of getting into a harem, not only in appearance, but in fact.'[120] Whilst admitting it would be childish to turn against Bergson on grounds of his general popularity alone, Hulme's unease increased. All the same, that November and December, he would give some lectures on Bergson that significantly impressed Pound at the time, though in retrospect he complained about Hulme 'fussing about Bergson and Sorel', as if he had taken no interest whatsoever.[121]

In the meantime, in October, while Ford was still in Germany, there appeared a collection of his editorials from the *English Review*, *The Critical Attitude*, whose contents undoubtedly reflect the attack Ford had launched on Pound's poetry in Giessen. The final essay in the book, on 'Modern Poetry', is to a large extent an attack on Pound himself, though with a glancing blow at Yeats and the Celtic school. It reiterates Ford's conviction that a contemporary poet should be writing about modern life, which is restless, urban, cosmopolitan, experienced as a constant stream of momentary impressions: 'We know no one very well, but we come into contact with an infinite number of people: we stay nowhere very long, but we see many, many places. We have hardly ever time to think long thoughts, but an infinite number of small things are presented for our cursory gaze. And in all of it . . . there is a note of mournfulness, of resignation, of poetry.' This quality of modern life, he asserts, hardly ever makes its way into contemporary verse: young poets need 'to come out of their book closets . . . It does not much matter where the poet goes or what he does, so long as he turns inquiring, sincere and humble eyes upon the life that is around him.'[122] Pound had addressed this argument in 'Redondillas', one of the poems he cut out of *Canzoni*:

> They tell me to 'Mirror my age'
> > God pity the age if I do do it,
> Perhaps I myself would prefer
> > to sing of the dead and the buried . . .
> We ever live in the here and now
> > it is better to live in than sing of.[123]

This refusal of any direct presentation of the present goes back to the arguments that he had had, and would return to, with Hulme, Flint, Williams and Ford himself. Pound would come to take Ford's insistence on writing about the contemporary world more seriously, though never quite in the terms that Ford advocated. The *Cantos* are both deeply political and autobiographical, and in that way are always related to Pound's contemporary world, however far away he may appear to range; Pound continued to believe that one had to turn to the past to understand the present, and that all ages feed into the contemporary moment. And he never entirely left his book-closet: the future author of *An ABC of Reading*, *How to Read* and the *Guide to Kultur* would not lose his belief in the virtues of a small, very specialised group of books. Advice to aspiring writers was always on what to read, not on paying attention to life. He also continued to view sceptically Ford's recommendations in that same article on using everyday language that expressed the poet's 'real self'. Pound did not have one voice that was the 'real' Pound; he drew on many different voices, different languages indeed, though over the next few years he would use contemporary language much more often, and with considerable skill; Ford's influence might be detected there. But for now he paid more attention to Hulme.

VI

THE meetings at the Tour Eiffel may have ceased, but Hulme created another kind of cultural gathering, in a different venue and with an extended guest list, which this time included artists and intellectuals as well as poets. He had developed a relationship some time in 1911 with a Mrs Ethel Kibblewhite, who lived at 67 Frith Street in Soho, an elegant and spacious Georgian house which had once been the Venetian embassy. Her father owned the house, and ran his ecclesiastical stained-glass business from the first floor. Dolly Kibblewhite, as she was known, had escaped with her two children from a violent husband some eight years earlier, and lived with her family on the other three floors. Hulme never moved in, but now did most of his work in a large room there put at his disposal. Dolly was a painter, who had trained at the Slade, and she drew a rather fine pencil sketch of Hulme in which he looks thoughtful, even a little melancholy, rather gentler and more pensive than he does in photographs, in which he tends to stare aggressively out at the camera. In place of his Thursday dinners at the Tour Eiffel, Hulme began to hold Tuesday soirées in Frith Street, in a large salon with, it is said, 'First Empire mirrors and chandeliers'.[124] Guests mingled, drank beer and discussed ideas, while Hulme – himself a teetotaller and non-smoker – 'argued', according to J.C. Squire, a frequent guest, 'with anyone who was willing to cope with him, or soliloquised on almost any theme, ancient or modern'.[125] Dolly Kibblewhite would be one of the few women present – H.D. would sometimes be another – but on the whole Hulme thought women distracted a man from intellectual argument.

According to his biographer, Robert Ferguson, Hulme now spent most of his afternoons in Frith Street (like Pound he was a late riser) working, or playing Go obsessively with Dolly, as he had played draughts when a boy with his mother. Dolly was ten years older than he was, and

Ferguson suggests she looked rather like his mother; perhaps emotionally she played a role in his life rather like that of his aunt Alice Pattinson,
a kindly mother substitute. He certainly, according to all reports, carried
on his promiscuous sexual activity elsewhere unabated. Dolly was
devoted to Hulme, and they remained a couple, albeit an unorthodox
one, until his death. Shortly after Pound and Hulme met up again,
Hulme introduced Pound to A.R. Orage, editor of *The New Age*, possibly
at one of these soirées. Orage could not have been unaware of the reputation Pound was building, and he took to him personally, even if he
rarely liked his poetry, putting him in touch with a publisher, Swift &
Co., who offered the stipend which Pound had mentioned to his father.
More significantly, certainly in the long run, Orage invited Pound to
write for the *New Age*. Pound was delighted, telling Margaret Cravens
on 6 November that they wanted him 'to do a Troubadour Romance';
one suspects it was Pound who suggested the subject-matter.[126] This
'Troubadour Romance' was to appear weekly over twelve weeks, and
Orage agreed to pay Pound a guinea a week, although the *New Age* did
not generally pay its contributors. (He had earlier paid Flint, so perhaps
he paid those he knew were short of money.) Pound was grateful – he
was still trying to turn himself into a good matrimonial prospect, and
in addition, to do him credit, his letters to Margaret suggest a certain
anxiety about taking her money, and an effort to reassure her that he
would soon be making his own way. Pound's income was actually better
than ever before, with his £200 a year from Margaret, and the £100 a
year from Swift & Co., but his engagement depended on earning more
than that. And if Orage's money were a welcome extra in 1911, it would
be a lifeline for Pound during the dark years of the war.

When Pound's 'Troubadour Romance' appeared, it consisted of a
mixture of translations and articles, beginning on 30 November not
with a troubadour, but with Pound's latest wandering poet, 'The
Seafarer'; the later translations were from Arnaut Daniel and Guido
Cavalcanti. The series was called 'I Gather the Limbs of Osiris', which
suggests that Pound had not lost his interest in Frazer, whose fourth
volume of *The Golden Bough*, *The Dying God*, which discusses Osiris,
had come out that month.[127] Osiris, the myth goes, was the divine king
of Egypt, who with his wife and sister, the goddess Isis, brought agri-
cultural arts and wine-making to the Egyptians, before he was murdered
and his body scattered in fourteen pieces by his brother Set.
Painstakingly, Isis gathered the scattered limbs, and Osiris came back
to life. For Pound the metaphor is that of salvaging the neglected poetic

masterpieces of the past to revive the art of poetry in the present – the process he would describe more ruefully in *Hugh Selwyn Mauberley*:

> For three years, out of key with his time,
> He strove to resuscitate the dead art
> Of poetry; to maintain 'the sublime'
> In the old sense. Wrong from the start –[128]

If Ford read these articles, he would not have felt that he was having much impact on Pound, who in this series continued to celebrate the pre-Renaissance and firmly rejected the idea of using everyday language in poetry. The main source for what was new here was Hulme, whose lectures on Bergson Pound and Dorothy both attended. These were given in a private drawing-room in Kensington, in the home of a Mrs Franz Liebich. Hulme's loyal disciple Tancred helped to sell tickets – 10s. 6d for the four. These lectures made a significant impression on Pound: ideas that he had ignored in 1909 he now seized on, and in the Osiris articles Hulmean ideas and phrases are liberally scattered across his prose. There had been similarities between his thought and Hulme's even in the Tour Eiffel days, not only their desire for a virile poetry but also their shared preference for immediacy rather than abstraction, something Pound now belatedly began to recognise. Critics have tended to set up Hulme and Ford against each other as alternative and mutually exclusive influences on Pound's imagism; indeed, the dispute has been going on since 1915, and in later life Pound claimed vigorously, though misleadingly, that Ford was by far the major influence. The truth seems to be that Pound absorbed elements from each of them, without in either case agreeing with all they said. What Pound would later say admiringly of Cavalcanti applied also to his pre-war self: 'Guido is eclectic, he swallows none of his authors whole'.[129] Yet if Pound was now ready to think about Hulme's ideas, perhaps the discombobulation caused by Ford's horror at the *Canzoni*, and his disconcerting roll on the floor, played a part in making him ready to revise his poetic theories. Hulme and Ford both wanted a more modern, direct form of writing, and Pound, as 'Δώρια' had indicated, was, like the advocates of *vers libre* at the Tour Eiffel, now moving steadily away from traditional metre and rhyme, even if he described that move in terms of a return to classical quantified verse or to Anglo–Saxon stressed alliteration.

Orage must have felt, when 'I Gather the Limbs of Osiris' came into the *New Age* office, that its title would convey little to his readers, because for the first few weeks an editorial note was appended which ran: 'Under this heading Mr Pound will contribute expositions and translations in illustration of the "New Method in Scholarship".' The reference to scholarship may seem surprising, but Pound had not yet entirely ruled out an academic job – he had in fact just had an encouraging letter from a Cambridge academic saying he thought his work deserved 'academic recognition and reward' – and he would certainly never drop his campaign to combat the way literature was taught in the American university system.[130] (And he would succeed: as Gail McDonald has convincingly demonstrated, Pound and Eliot between them were to play an important role in changing the way literature was taught in universities, and the dominance of 'appreciation' in schools of English from the 1950s to the 1980s owes much to the doctrines that Pound was already preaching in these pre-war years.)[131] The 'new method' itself, however, appears to have been directly inspired by Hulme's lectures.

The first of these was on 23 November. 'Rather good,' Pound reported home, instructing his parents, as he did Margaret, to subscribe to the *New Age*, where they could read Hulme on Bergson, one reason for taking the magazine, the other being of course his own appearance there: now he was a contributor, Pound wanted the subscription list to increase so that Orage would be persuaded he was good for sales.[132] 'Its a mad sheet,' he told Margaret, 'but I ought to be worth 3d per copy'.[133] But the enthusiasm for Hulme was genuine. The following March he was still describing him to his mother as 'a braw yorkshireman' (Pound's geography was as hazy as his history) and 'very good sort'.[134] Over the next few months, he was to see a good deal of Hulme.

The two extant essays most likely to have formed the basis for Hulme's lectures are 'The Philosophy of Intensive Manifolds' and 'Bergson's Theory of Art'.[135] Pound's 'new method' draws on Hulme's exposition, in the first of these essays, of Bergson's analysis of the two modes of understanding: on the one hand, the intellect, which is 'rational or mechanical' and which always simplifies and distorts through the crude approximations of language; and on the other hand, intuition, 'vital and more instinctive', as well as more 'complex', a mode of understanding particularly familiar to 'any literary man or artist'.[136] Hulme points out that this distinction is not new, citing Edmund Burke, perhaps a tell-tale sign, it has been suggested, of the politically conservative turn his thought was soon to take; the thinker Pound would more likely associate with the two modes was Pater, who predated Bergson in his rejection of the false solidity given to the external world by language and in his emphasis on the vital pulsating moment of experience.[137] In the first of Pound's expository articles, on 7 December 1911, he sets out his own comparable intuitive method of scholarship – that of the 'Luminous Detail', as he calls it: facts that suddenly illuminate, whose transmission is 'swift and easy' and which 'govern knowledge as the switchboard governs an electric circuit'. This method is 'most vigorously hostile to the prevailing mode of today – that is the method of multitudinous detail, and to the method of yesterday, the method of sentiment and generalisation', both of which, he asserts, as Bergson says of the rationalising intellect, distort rather than extend understanding.[138]

Pound puts forward this method of 'Luminous Detail' in part as a justification of his imitations of earlier writers in *Canzoni* and his translations of Daniel and Cavalcanti, as well as those in *The Spirit of Romance*, in whose preface he had already insisted that it was important to read the 'masterwork', not 'mediocrity'.[139] His translations were not, he insists, just the work of an antiquarian, 'rather a scholar than a poet', as one reviewer of *Canzoni* had unkindly put it: he had been picking out 'luminous details' from the past, because, he says – in defiance of Ford's insistence in *The Critical Attitude* that writers must concentrate on the present – he is setting 'forth some defence of a hope . . . that this sort of work may not fail utterly to be of service to the living art. For it is certain that we have had no "greatest poet" and no "great period" save at, or after, a time when many people were busy examining the media and the traditions of the art.'[140]

Yet what is most important in Pound's theory of the 'Luminous Detail' is not its application to 'scholarship', but his extension of it to art itself: 'The artist,' he writes, 'seeks out the luminous detail and presents it. He does not comment'.[141] (Presenting without comment is something he also learnt from Ford, so there is a fusion of influences here.) The luminous detail is perhaps his first real move towards the doctrine of imagism, where the image's impact is instantaneous and powerful, a sudden illumination, bearing out another of Hulme's propositions, that 'the essentially aesthetic emotion' is 'the excitement which is generated by direct communication'.[142] Pound's 'luminous detail' is in some ways a development of his own earlier ideas – his simplification, for example, of Browning's dramatic monologue so that only a vital, illuminating moment is presented, and his emphasis, learnt from Yeats and Wilde, on the avoidance of didacticism and rhetoric. It belatedly, one might argue, acknowledges Flint's earlier campaign for poetry like the Japanese, in which the image gives the reader 'the resonant heart of an exquisite moment'. The idea of the 'luminous detail' is also, however, a rejection of the kinds of elaboration and stasis that had crept into *Canzoni*. Pound adds a note to the effect that 'As scholarship has erred in presenting all detail as if of equal import . . . in a present school of writing we see a similar tendency'.[143] Who does he have in mind? It sounds like a forerunner of Virginia Woolf's denunciation of the fact-filled Edwardian novel in 'Mr Bennett and Mrs Brown', but Pound had read few of those novels – not that that always prevented him from making his attacks. Pound was perhaps rethinking how he should write his own poetry. Like Virginia Woolf, at that period working on her first novel, he now wanted to create art through which the vital and dynamic texture of life could be conveyed, not works in which 'life escapes'.[144]

Besides this emphasis on the centrality of artistic intuition, there are other of Hulme's ideas echoed in the articles, especially his insistence that art can be defined as 'a passionate desire for accuracy'.[145] 'Accurate', 'exact', 'precise', 'direct' are words that become central to Pound's aesthetic vocabulary, and, as for Hulme, they refer at this stage to the delineation of a psychological state: imagist poetry would aim to convey, as evocatively and tellingly as possible, a particular psychic moment.[146]

Hulme emphasises that, according to Bergson, most people at most times are limited to 'stock perceptions', because 'human perception . . . has certain fixed habits, certain fixed ways of seeing things, and so is unable to see things as they are'.[147] Hence, for Hulme, the challenge for the artist lies in conveying the 'individuality of the emotion', or 'the individuality of things'.[148] Pound follows him, warning against 'sling[ing] generalities'. One must give 'the particular case for what it is worth; the truth is the individual'.[149] He stresses, as Hulme does, the import-ance of escaping from '*cliché*', those 'magnetized groups that stand between the reader of poetry and the drive of it', and he shares Hulme's conviction that the artist has to bring freedom from stock perceptions and set ideas.[150] That society in general was convention-bound was a view Pound shared with many young people of his day: he had been acutely conscious of this in Philadelphia, and it was bearing in on him, after his attempted negotiations with the Shakespear family, that the situation was not as different as he had thought in England. The role of the artist was to bring liberation from this conventionalised thought.

Pound, however, never wholly accepted Hulme's Nietzschean, Bergsonian view of language as inherently crude and inadequate, perhaps the reason why he continued writing poetry while Hulme abandoned it: before Pound's 'Osiris' series concluded, 'The Complete Poetical Works of T.E. Hulme', five poems in all, not all Hulme wrote but the ones he presumably wished to be known by, appeared in the *New Age* on 25 January 1912.[151] There is, indeed, an aporia or logical contradiction at the heart of Hulme's argument here: given his view of the distortions inevitably imposed by language, the poet can surely never achieve total 'accuracy' in his delineation of an emotion, only some kind of metaphorical approximation. Hulme acknowledges the difficulty and the rarity of achieving this 'accuracy', but it surely is the wrong word, though symptomatic of his dilemma as a convinced metaphysical relativist who temperamentally longed for certainty and boundaries. Pound would come increasingly to need similar absolutes, but he would be more concerned with the way language is frequently used loosely and dishonestly; he repeatedly denounced rhetoric in the most rhetorical terms. The artist, he implies, meets a moral duty rather than an epistemological challenge when he tries to use language 'accurately': 'technique', as he puts it here, 'is the only gauge and test of a man's lasting sincerity'.[152]

Pound, however, also acknowledges that to be a poet is to some extent a gift. Hulme talks of different kinds of minds, some more attuned to the visual, others to rhythms and Pound has a similar but more extended discussion of different ways of thinking, including as his final category those 'favoured of Apollo', who think 'in words that hover above and cling close to the things they mean'.[153] This is an intriguing and compelling metaphor, all the more effective because it allows for approximation rather than the exactitude he demands elsewhere; Pound returned to it again a few weeks later (he rather charmingly uses inverted commas when he quotes himself), saying 'it is not until poetry lives again "close to the thing" that it will be a vital part of the contemporary life'.[154] Pound believed that there are realities beyond language that the artist strives to capture, so in that sense he is aware of language's limitations, but he wants to claim that the artist can overcome them; his poetic theories are a succession of metaphors for an Adamic, unfallen language that would bring together word and thing, poetic phrase and visionary insight, and communicate instantly and totally. As early as 1907, he had told Viola Baxter that he thought 'artistic utterance' was what Swedenborg had meant by 'angelic language', the same unfallen language that Adam spoke.[155] The 'absolute rhythm' of which he had written to Floyd Dell, and in his introduction to the Cavalcanti, which conveyed a 'particular'

and 'exact' emotion, had been another version of art's instant, accurate communication; the 'luminous detail', with its 'swift and easy'
transmission, was his latest. In his successive definitions of the image,
he would offer more.[156]

In the concluding essay of 'I Gather the Limbs of Osiris,' which
appeared on 15 February and which discusses the twelfth-century Arnaut
Daniel, Pound made it very clear that he was still at odds with Ford's
belief in everyday language: 'we must have a simplicity and directness
of utterance, which is different from the simplicity and directness of
daily speech, which is more "curial" [that is, "priestly"], more dignified.
This difference, this dignity, cannot be conferred by florid adjectives
or elaborate hyperbole; it must be conveyed by art, and by the art of
the verse structure . . . Colloquial poetry is to the real art as the barber's
wax dummy is to sculpture.'[157] Pound would in one sense always hold
to this, insisting that poetry must use a heightened, intensive language;
in that way it always differs from the looseness of everyday language.
Even though he came to draw on the language of daily speech for some
of his poetry, he continued to follow the argument put forward by Hulme
that ordinary language has to be transformed by art in order to convey
'the individuality and freshness of things'. There is no indication, it
should be said, that Pound ever thought about the Bergsonian philosophy behind Hulme's propositions, even though he concurs with many
of Hulme's conclusions. Even when they share a vocabulary they present
their points very differently. For all his critique of logical thought, Hulme
in his lectures and articles embodies his theories in a worked-out
argument, while Pound simply offers a series of pronouncements; he
thought intuitively and ignored logic, but he never employed a
Bergsonian argument for doing so.

'Bergson's Theory of Art' was Hulme's last piece of writing directly
on Bergson. His own ideas were evolving rapidly at this period, and by
the spring of 1912 he was writing political pieces, though he kept straying
back to art. In a series that appeared in a political journal called the
Commentator, under the pseudonym Thomas Gratton, posthumously
published as a single essay called 'A Tory Philosophy', he tries out a
distinction which in political terms divides Tory and Radical, proponents of Order against defenders of Liberty, believers in Constancy as
against believers in Progress, and which in art divides Classicism and
Romanticism. In each case, he himself is in favour of the first term. He
developed the importance of these ideas for art in a lecture he gave in
July, published as the essay which so impressed Eliot, 'Romanticism and

Classicism'. This essay is probably Hulme's best-known piece, misleadingly so, as far as his own thought was concerned, as it was very much
a transitional work, but it came to be seen as exemplary of the position
to which the high modernism of Eliot and Pound would move in the
1920s. Hulme himself would soon be rejecting everything since the
Renaissance as well as its Greek sources, but for now he asserts, 'After
a hundred years of romanticism we are in for a classical revival'.
Romanticism, he claims, sprang from Rousseau's dangerous and mistaken
belief that human beings were innately good, simply damaged and
corrupted by bad and oppressive laws; classicism, for Hulme, insists
that 'Man is an extraordinarily fixed and limited animal whose nature
is absolutely constant. It is only by tradition and organisation that
anything decent can be can be got out of him.' This is in line with the
'sane classical dogma of original sin'. The classical view is the religious
one: 'part of the fixed nature of man is the belief in the Deity . . . It is
parallel to appetite, the instinct of sex, and all the other fixed qualities'.[158] Romanticism follows on from 'the perverted rhetoric of
Rationalism', which turns people into agnostics, so suppressing the
natural instinct to be religious:

Just as in the case of the other instincts, Nature has her revenge. The instincts
that find their right and proper outlet in religion must come out in some other
way. You don't believe in a God, so you begin to believe that man is a god. You
don't believe in Heaven, so you begin to believe in a heaven on earth. In other
words, you get romanticism. The concepts that are right and proper in their own
sphere are spread over, and so mess up, falsify and blur the clear outlines of human
experience. It is like pouring a pot of treacle over the dinner table. Romanticism
then, and this is the best definition I can give of it, is spilt religion.[159]

Hulme's comments here on the danger of suppressing instincts suggest
some acquaintance with Freudian ideas, though he is very much turning
them to his own ends. More recent psychoanalytical theorists would be
intrigued by Hulme's own horror of 'mess' and 'blur', his choice of the
viscosity and stickiness of treacle to express all he abhors in Romanticism.
As I suggested earlier, Hulme's anxieties about masculinity are fundamental to his aesthetic and political theories. Classical verse is 'dry' and
'hard', much more suitable for men. Romantics are characterised by 'the
sloppiness which doesn't consider a poem is a poem unless it is moaning
or whining about something or other'; they think that 'poetry that isn't
damp isn't poetry at all'. Romanticism is still in the ascendancy: 'if good

classical verse were to be written tomorrow very few people would be able to stand it'.[160] But, Hulme prophesies, that will change. The kind of modern verse he had been advocating since 1908 will emerge. He no longer, however, makes the analogy with Impressionism, but notes that Maurice Denis has explained that the Post-Impressionists 'consider themselves classical in the sense that they were trying to impose the same order on the mere flux of new material provided by the impressionist movement, that existed in the more limited materials of the painting before.'[161]

Pound did not hear the lecture, but he and Hulme would certainly have discussed the ideas. He was already in sympathy with much of the gendered aesthetics here, making the very Hulmean and misogynistic pronouncement in his final Osiris article: 'As long as the poet says not what he, at the very crux of a clarified conception, means, but is content to say something ornate and approximate, just so long will serious people, intently alive, consider poetry as balderdash – a sort of embroidery for dilettantes and women.'[162] Pound's two most enthusiastic readers, Margaret and Dorothy, were women, but he appears to forget this. Poetry is to be professional, exact and virile. Pound, though showing no interest in classicism, took over much of Hulme's attack on the nineteenth century, though he still admired Swinburne, whom Hulme reviled, and was by no means ready to retract his reverence for the Rhymers, particularly Yeats. He wrote in another article that February, entitled 'Prologomena' (he meant 'prolegomena', but mispelt it by analogy, one supposes, with prologue), published in the recently founded *Poetry Review*: 'As for the nineteenth century, with all respect to its achievements, I think we shall look back upon it as a rather blurry, messy sort of a period, a rather sentimentalistic, mannerish sort of period'. (Note his distaste, shared with Hulme, for 'mess' and 'blur'.) He sees, however, a definite break beginning with Swinburne: 'The conception of poetry as a "pure art" . . . revived with Swinburne. From the puritanical revolt [he refers of course to Milton] to Swinburne, poetry had been merely the vehicle . . . the ox-cart and post-chaise for transmitting thoughts poetic or otherwise . . . Mr Yeats has once and for all stripped English poetry of its perdamnable rhetoric. He has boiled away all that is not poetic – and a good deal that is. He has become a classic in his own lifetime and *nel mezzo del cammin*. He has made our poetic idiom a thing pliable, a speech without inversions.'[163] After this tribute to Yeats, however, when he turns to the future, he has much in common with Hulme's tough talking:

As to Twentieth century poetry, and the poetry which I expect to see written during the next decade or so, it will, I think, move against poppy-cock, it will be harder and saner, it will be what Mr Hewlett calls "nearer the bone". It will be as much like granite as it can be, its force will lie in its truth, its interpretative power (of course poetic force does always rest there); I mean it will not try to seem forcible by rhetorical din, and luxurious riot. We will have few painted adjectives impeding the shock and stroke of it. At least for myself, I want it so, austere, direct, free from emotional slither.

Earlier in the article, Pound had again defended his interest in the past, what he describes as his 'pawing over the ancients and semi-ancients': this is worth stressing because he also made one other comment which is very frequently misquoted, or rather selectively and therefore misleadingly quoted. In what is probably a response to both Ford's desire for modernity and Hulme's earlier belief that all poetry more than twenty years old should be destroyed (by 1912 Hulme appears to have thought that at least Shakespeare and Pope should be spared), Pound begins a sentence by saying 'No good poetry is ever written in a manner twenty years old', a statement that is quoted in numerous literary histories as if Pound were dismissing the past and his archaisms at last, and advocating a distinctly modern style. In fact he goes on to qualify the statement markedly, continuing: 'for to write in such a manner shows conclusively that the writer thinks from books, convention and *cliché*, and not from life, yet a man feeling the divorce of his life and his art may naturally try to resurrect a forgotten mode . . . if he think he see in it some element lacking in contemporary art which might unite that art again to its sustenance, life.'[164] As long as it is well over twenty years old, that's fine. He goes on, of course, to talk of the importance of Dante and Cavalcanti. This is an argument with Hulme that Pound could be said to have won. By 1913, Hulme was advocating the study of ancient art and agreeing that for modern art it was necessary, as the French would put it, to 'se reculer pour mieux sauter', which one might freely translate as 'step backwards in order to make a better jump forward', in other words, to make the leap that would be modernism.

PART VII

THE FUTURE IMAGISTS
ASSEMBLE

I

EVEN though Hulme had given up writing poetry himself, the influence of his poetics on Pound would continue during 1912. Pound republished Hulme's 'Complete Poetical Works' at the end of his next book of poetry, *Ripostes*, which he sent into the publishers that March, a collection which suggested that quite apart from the theories, the practice of Hulme's pared, sparse poetry was also having its impact. Yet Hulme's importance to on Pound in the autumn of 1911 may have owed something to the fact that until the end of the year Pound had few other people with whom to argue over poetry. At this stage, he was not yet acknowledging H.D. as a poet, so, while he may have talked to her, it seems unlikely he would have listened to her replies. Yeats did not return to London until November from another and more controversial tour of the United States, this time along with the Abbey Company, who travelled with him performing Irish drama, including *Playboy of the Western World*, which went down almost as badly with the New York Irish as it had in Dublin; Yeats meanwhile gave lectures on the need for experimental staging and Irish Home Rule. Even after his return, Yeats was soon off to Dublin again, and so Pound can have seen little of him until the new year. H.D. was not to meet Yeats until then, and even when she did was not, as she put it, 'hyper-impressed', though perhaps less critical of him than of the fawning 'bevy of admirers' who hung on his every word.[1] H.D. was ambivalent about the Celtic revival, and was not to become a real admirer of Yeats until she read the extended version of *Responsibilities*, published in 1916.[2] In November Ford finally returned from Giessen, claiming to be married to Violet Hunt. He had failed to get either his naturalisation or his German divorce, so the marriage would not have been legal even in Germany, but they may have gone through a notional ceremony, although no record has ever been found. Violet was later to tell Rebecca West that there was a mock ceremony in Rheims performed by a defrocked priest, but Ford himself told the *Daily Mirror* in October that they had been married in Germany.[3] When Elsie read the story there, she instantly took out an action for libel; the paper paid up, so there was no public scandal at this stage. That would not erupt until early in 1913.

Pound, who had recovered from his irritation with Ford, was delighted to hear that he would be around again and expressed no suspicions about the legality of the marriage. Lawrence, still a teacher in Croydon, had been corresponding with both Ford and Hunt, and had the news of the marriage direct, but was soon alerted to its problematic nature by Edward Garnett.[4] Lawrence, like Pound, was looking forward to Ford and Hunt's return, even though he had more reason than Pound to be irritated by Ford, who had mislaid two of his play manuscripts and had been extremely critical of his second novel, eventually published as *The Trespasser*, saying of it, according to Lawrence: 'The book . . . is a rotten work of genius. It has no construction or form – it is execrably bad art, being all variations on a theme. Also it is erotic – not that I personally mind that, but an erotic work *must* be good art, which this is not.'[5] Lawrence had been so cast down that he decided not to publish it, even though Heinemann was willing to do so, and he had started work on what was to become *Sons and Lovers*. Late in 1911, however, he showed *The Trespasser*, or as it was called at the time, 'The Saga of Siegmund', to Edward Garnett, who thought much more highly of it than Ford had done, made suggestions for revisions, and persuaded Lawrence to let it be published after all.

The Trespasser came out the next year, and provided Lawrence with some much-needed income, for in November 1911 he succumbed to the double pneumonia which ended his teaching career. After convalescence in Bournemouth, he returned home to Eastwood, but before doing so rapidly and rather cruelly broke off his engagement to Louie Burrows, a college friend, now a teacher, to whom he had proposed marriage, very much on impulse, shortly after his mother's death the previous year. John Worthen suggests that Louie, warm-heartened and capable, and a favourite with Lawrence's mother, had helped him cope with his grief, and that need had now passed. In the past few months he had been greatly influenced by Garnett's own unorthodox views on marriage, saying of him admiringly that he 'is most beautifully free of the world's conventions', and Garnett may well have communicated alarm at the idea of his gifted protégé being trapped in a provincial marriage.[6]

En route home, Lawrence saw Ford and Violet Hunt, and went with Ford to a matinée at the Royal Court to see plays by Yeats and Lady Gregory, a meeting he reported in a somewhat barbed letter to Garnett, in terms that showed how immensely he had grown in self-confidence since he first met Ford: 'I found Hueffer very fat – "be not puffed up" came into my mind. But he's rather nicer than he was.' Violet 'looked old, yet she was gay – she was gay, she laughed, she bent and fluttered in the wind of joy. She coquetted and played beautifully with Hueffer: she loves him distractedly – she was charming, and I loved her. But my God, she looks old.' Poor Violet – her underlying fear was showing through. But so was Ford's: 'I think,' Lawrence continues, 'Fordy liked it – but was rather scared. He feels, poor fish, the hooks are through his gills this time – and they *are*.'[7] The comments highlight dramatically the differences between Lawrence and Pound – Lawrence with such sharp if cruel insight into the relationship, Pound in all his references to Ford commenting only on his literary views and ignoring what he would call 'personal tosh'. Possibly Lawrence's own recent realisation that he didn't want 'hooks ... through his gills' made him aware of the dangers of half-hearted alliances. He was shortly to throw himself into a most wholehearted if tempestuous partnership, this time with Garnett's blessing: in May 1912 he eloped to Germany with the wife of the Professor of German at Nottingham University, Frieda Weekley, née von Richthofen, whom he had met some three weeks after his return to Eastwood. Lawrence was not to come back to England until 1914, when he would be drawn by the unstoppable Amy Lowell into the imagist project.

Lawrence didn't see Pound again that autumn, though he told Grace Crawford in December, in what was the last letter he wrote her, that he had heard from R.A. Scott-James, literary editor of the *Daily News*, whom he had recently met, that Pound 'was in London, and considerably down at the mouth'. Scott-James must have seen Pound during the period when he was 'juggling volcanos', for by late November and December he appears to have been in good spirits, writing cheerfully home about the success of his writings in the *New Age*, which he described as publishing 'advanced' and 'usually unsound' views, though he thought the weekly most enlightened in agreeing to publish his translations.[8] The *Daily News* had liked a review he did for them, though Scott-James had told him he had 'a fantastic mind which unfits [him] for journalism', which he took as a compliment.[9] He received welcome payment for translating some songs of the French folk singer Yvette Guilbert for the music publishers Augeners, and in a splash of generosity took Dorothy out to lunch, sent his father some money with which to buy his mother a Christmas present, and his mother some for a present for his father.[10]

In spite of the pleasure Pound had expressed to his mother at Ford's imminent return, he did not see much of him that autumn, as Ford was commissioned to go to Rome to cover the story of the Investiture of the American Cardinals for the American magazine *Collier's*, an odd assignment, one might have thought, for a bigamist English Catholic, but incidentally one on which Ford became, much to his delight, the first person to send a Marconi message from the Mediterranean to New York. By mid-December he was back in London, and South Lodge life, now under the auspices of Mr and Mrs Hueffer, recommenced. Violet on her return had immediately changed her name in the telephone directory and in *Who's Who* to Mrs Ford Madox Hueffer, and referred, even in print, to 'my husband'.

Yet warm though his friendship with Ford and Violet would continue to be, Pound's close circle for 1912 revolved around a friend of Violet's, Brigit Patmore; it was she who introduced him to Richard Aldington, who with H.D., and to a lesser extent Flint, would form the centre of his social as well as poetic life for the immediate future. Many years later Pound wrote in a letter to H.D. that it had been the happiest period of his life. Violet Hunt had introduced Pound to Brigit Patmore, who in 1911 was twenty-nine, three years older than Pound. She was very lovely, a delicate Pre-Raphaelite beauty with red-gold hair, enormous eyes and white skin, full of zest for life, highly intelligent and, though unhappily married, with a great sense of fun. Although at that stage her health was not good, her letters and memoir are full of spark and energy. The art critic and writer John Cournos, who will appear later in this story, described her as one of the two most attractive women in London, while Pound said she was one of the rare 'charming people on the planet.'[11] Ford, by 1913, had fallen desperately in love with her. Douglas Goldring, indeed, suggests that 'oddly enough', Violet shared Ford's 'romantic admiration' for Brigit.[12] Violet wrote of her in *The Flurried Years*, 'My friend was very beautiful, with a queer, large, tortured mouth that said the wittiest things, eyes that tore your soul out of your body for pity and yet danced . . . She had . . . as no woman would ever admit except me – charm enough to damn a regiment.'[13]

Brigit came from a family of Ulster landowners, though she hated to be reminded of this background, stressing instead that she had, as it happened, been born in Dublin; like Ford, she was a fierce supporter of Home Rule, as well as of the suffragettes, one of the causes that drew her to Violet, with whom she would sally out to sell *Votes for Women*. Violet, rather unkindly and most unfairly, later wrote that Brigit was 'no real suffragette, though she collected with me and rattled a box at stations. Nothing but her eyes protested. Delicately cynical, she accepted things as they are.'[14] 'Delicately cynical' is a masterly summing up of Patmore's wry and shrewd analysis of her contemporary society, but she was acutely aware of the injustices endured by women. (Fascinatingly, in 1956 she wrote to Pound expressing outrage at the sexism of Osborne's *Look Back in Anger*; she must have been one of the few people to notice it at the time.) Hunt was perhaps referring to Brigit's attempts to maintain the appearance of a conventional wife, but in some ways Hunt made just the same effort, even less successfully. Brigit herself said it was because she felt 'so stifled and impatient with the late Victorian code of behaviour' that she was so delighted to meet Hunt, this 'representative of the modern times'; but Violet was going to have her own trouble with those repressive codes.[15]

Brigit was born Ethel Elizabeth Morrison-Scott; her adoption of the name Brigit must have been part of her identification with the Irish cause. Her childhood, she suggests in her memoirs, was not happy. Her father, who drank, was cruel to her mother, by repute as beautiful as Brigit herself. She died 'tragically young', having, Brigit writes, 'grieved her wild heart to death'.[16] He married again, and Brigit ran away from home at one stage, for how long, she does not say. All the same, she had had a wide education, learnt to play the piano, which she studied for a while in Dresden, and spoke excellent French and German. According to Violet Hunt, she also painted. In 1907, she married a grandson of Coventry Patmore, author, as she points out somewhat ruefully in her memoirs, for already by 1911 the marriage was not going well, of the bestselling '*Angel in the House*, the famous poem . . . celebrating the joys of married love'.[17] (According to her son, 'Edwardian gallants', on being introduced to her, would say, 'I suppose *you* are the "Angel in the House"'.)[18] John Deighton Patmore, who had a well-paid post in the insurance world, had, unlike Brigit, scant interest in literature, and while he appeared to have little tenderness for Brigit, had a weakness, according to his son, for 'pretty young secretaries', and expected Brigit to put up with it.[19] Brigit tried to take an interest in the sporting world, which was where he wanted to spend his leisure when not with the pretty young secretaries, but increasingly she spent time with her friends rather

than his. They had two sons, to whom Brigit was devoted, as they were
to her. Their son Derek writes in his autobiography that he hardly ever
saw his father when he was young; he was not, he said, 'a family man'.[20]
His 'dominant memory of those early days [wa]s that of [his] mother,
a lovely young woman . . . [whose] eyes, which were a soft grey, but
sometimes tinged with green, had a melancholy expression as if loaded
with a secret sadness'. What he recalls about his father is his saying of
his sons whenever they annoyed him, 'It's their Irish blood'; this was
clearly calculated to upset Brigit, who, Derek says, 'would always flare
up in defence of Ireland if the Irish were attacked'.[21] In many ways
Brigit had much in common with Olivia Shakespear; like her, she was
a literary hostess, and later she too become a writer of novels and translations; like Olivia, she was beautiful, charming, cultured, unhappily
married and not entirely faithful to her husband. But Olivia was of a
different generation, twenty years older, politically conservative, and she
managed to retain a veneer of respectability all her life; even H.D. did
not realise she was the Diana Vernon of Yeats' memoirs until after her
death. Brigit, however, caused a good deal more scandal. She was, her
son recorded, 'impetuous, overgenerous, extravagant with money', qualities he always found charming, but possibly not so likely as Olivia's
worldly caution to keep rumour at bay.[22] Yet, according to H.D., she
organised her love affairs with great discretion.

In 1911 and 1912, although intensely interested in literature, Brigit
had not yet enough confidence to attempt to write herself, or certainly
not to attempt publication; when she began to write later, it was with
the encouragement, indeed active persuasion, of both Pound and H.D.
Most of her own friends, however, as opposed to her husband's, were
writers; in her memoir, *My Friends When Young*, virtually all the
acquaintances mentioned are in the literary world, bar the odd Irish
revolutionary. Doubtless her husband's literary name had been part
of his attraction for her, even if it proved so misleading. As it happened,
Yeats had developed a great enthusiasm for Coventry Patmore in 1909,
particularly for his 'Essay on English Metrical Law', about which he
wrote rapturously to Florence Farr, and it is likely that either Yeats or
Farr conveyed this enthusiasm to Pound. Perhaps Pound was also taken
with the Patmore name when he met Brigit, but she had charms enough
of her own not to need her grandfather-in-law's recommendation.
Humphrey Carpenter speculates on whether Ezra and she had an
affair; Pound undoubtedly, like Ford and Violet, had a 'romantic admiration' for her, and she a *tendresse* for him. Her memoir contains a

warm and admiring description of him on their first meeting in Violet
Hunt's drawing-room at South Lodge, where Pound spent many hours,
and the picture she paints there vividly suggests what attracted artistically inclined young women of the period to Pound, as well as what
might have put off the respectable, upstanding members of the male
establishment:

I saw a long slim young man leaning back in a low armchair, withdrawn as an
animal from creatures it does not know. His head was unavoidably noticeable, not
only because of the reddish spring hair, but for the Florentine delicacy of the pale
face. His eyes were a little crinkled in closure, whether in humour or observation,
I didn't know. His mouth, sensitive and undoubtedly sweet, covered small, very
white teeth, but he revealed them seldom, neither speaking nor smiling often. Not
that he was confused or shy, no, he was as self-possessed as Violet's superb grey
Persian cat sitting on the window-sill, though fortunately he did not give out the
cold feline resentment of that beautiful animal . . . Violet . . . whispered to me, 'The
young man like a Renaissance portrait is Ezra Pound. A poet, very good' . . . Ezra
never seemed conscious of the fact that his unusual looks were beautiful, not just
the handsomeness permissible to a man in England. Perhaps in the Mediterranean
countries he had grown accustomed, like Byron, to the outspoken 'Oh, *troppo
bello*'.[23]

Brigit Patmore compared Pound with the flamboyant Polish pianist,
Paderewski, who embodied the figure of the romantic artist *par excellence* for the pre-war generation. H.D. made the same comparison, but
more warily: 'a hint of a young, more robust Ignace Paderewski . . . But
this young (already) inconoclast is rougher, tougher'.[24] Pound, Brigit
writes in her memoir, gave her a troubadour name, Vail de Lencour,
which he used when he dedicated his book of 1916, *Lustra*, to her.[25] He
also gave her the page proofs of *Canzoni* (now in the University of
Texas), including the rejected poems, hence our knowledge of that defensive note appended and then rejected for the collection. According to
her memoir, after their first meeting, Pound often called in for tea,
'probably', she says, 'because I was somewhat ailing and had to rest a
good deal and, instinctively, he would think I must need distraction'.[26]
That comment is not necessarily entirely disingenuous – Pound was
very kind in that way – but doubtless he found it a pleasanter proposition to be kind to a beautiful and witty invalid, than to a plain and dull
one. All one can say with any certainty is that Brigit and Pound were
always very fond of each other. She writes about him with amused

affection, and remained a faithful correspondent during his years of incarceration in St Elizabeth's mental hospital.

Brigit places her first meeting with Pound at South Lodge in late spring, when he was living in Church Walk; Pound did not in fact spend a late spring in Church Walk until 1912, and other evidence suggests they must have met earlier. Brigit's account of her meeting with Violet Hunt is also rather misleading, as she suggests that it was just before Hunt's relationship with Ford developed, which would have been in early 1909, when Ford was editing the *English Review*. Her son, Derek, however, says firmly on more than one occasion that Brigit did not meet Ford until he, Derek, was four years old, which was in 1912, the context for this statement being Ford's later penchant for hinting that Derek was actually his son. She probably in fact met Hunt when the Patmores moved to Kensington, most likely in 1911, the year Ford spent largely in Germany. Through Hunt she acquired a rich range of new literary acquaintances, including Pound, whom she met probably soon after his arrival back in London in 1911; by early 1912 they were good friends.

Brigit knew nothing of Pound's involvement with Dorothy for some time after they first met. She makes no mention of Dorothy in her account of the pre-war years, though they must have known each other, because Pound mentions Brigit occasionally in his letters to Dorothy in terms that imply acquaintanceship, but there appears to have been little sympathy between the two women. There are few references to Dorothy even in the memoir's account of the post-war years, and those are scarcely kind. For example, Brigit describes going dancing with Ezra and Dorothy in Italy in the early 1930s. It is clear that Pound's dancing was no better than it had been back in Philadelphia: 'Ezra danced according to no rules that I understood. New steps one may invent, but surely the music sets time and rhythm. But for Ezra, no; with extremely odd steps he moved, to unearthly beats. One couldn't face it . . . Sweet faithful Dorothy said innocently: "Ezra has a *wonderful* sense of rhythm". Yes indeed.'[27] According to Noel Stock, Dorothy in later life would always refer to Brigit scathingly as 'Patmore'.[28] She presumably took the same view of her as H.D.'s mother, who in the early 1920s decided Brigit was distinctly 'fast'.[29]

Dorothy and H.D., on the other hand, although never close, always appear to have had a perfectly amicable relationship; Dorothy gives the impression that she would have liked them to become better friends, but it never happened. H.D. probably first met the Shakespears in late November or early December, but she found Brigit's company much more congenial. Pound had arranged their meeting, asking Brigit to invite H.D. to tea, another stage in his plan to extend H.D.'s social world. 'His manner,' Brigit recalled, 'always nonchalant, was now exaggerated, and I knew he felt very diplomatic and Machiavellian.'[30] He explained that H.D. was a friend and contemporary from Philadelphia, and warned her that H.D. was very sensitive about her surname. When they met, however, it was actually H.D. who commented less than tactfully on the subject of names. She asked if her hostess' name were really Brigit, as in America only cooks were called that. Brigit says that she replied, 'How very democratic of you. Here we give it to saints', and H.D. laughed.[31] Of course, H.D. was quite right: it wasn't Brigit's real name; on both sides of the Atlantic it was a name usually found among working-class Irish Catholics. In spite of this possibly awkward start they took to each other immediately. Brigit commented on H.D.'s 'extraordinarily appealing charm . . . One had a feeling that here was a delicate work of beauty which must not be destroyed, an intellect which might blaze out into a fine clarity.' When she first saw her she was struck by the 'extreme vulnerability in her face'. Brigit was, she says, 'from that time . . . under the spell of [H.D.'s] capacity for suffering and for years was tormented by a vain endeavour to keep unhappiness from her'. Yet she also comments that for all her appearance of sensitivity and fragility, H.D. had 'a magnificent line of jaw and chin [that] gave reassuring strength'.[32] Brigit was right; simultaneously fragile and tough, vulnerable and resilient, was how H.D. was throughout her life. When they met, Brigit says that H.D. immediately asked her if she would learn Greek with her, something which in principle she agreed to do, but she was, she says, 'a lazy student'.[33] The person who would work with H.D. on her Greek was Richard Aldington, to whom Brigit soon introduced her.

It appears not to have been until December that Pound caught up again with Flint, the only other poet besides himself to belong to both the Tour Eiffel group and the later imagists. Flint was no longer writing for the *New Age*; a draft of a letter to Orage among Flint's papers suggests they had a falling out when Orage failed to publish an article he had written on Verlaine. Flint may already have proved himself too avant-garde. Orage loved to publish controversial work, but on the whole he liked the weekly's regular arts reviewers to share his views; Flint's place was taken by the more conservative J.C. Squire. Yet Flint, in spite of his demanding work, his marriage and his small daughter, Ianthe, was still writing poetry and had published several poems in the

magazine that Douglas Goldring started the previous year. This was
The Tramp: an Open-Air Magazine, so called, Goldring says, because
'the intention was to combine literary merit with the cult for what is
now called hiking'.[34] The commercial success of *Country Life*, where he
had his first job, had convinced him, wrongly, that this would be a
winner.[35] The *Tramp* was launched in March 1910, the month when
Pound left England, publishing articles about travel and walking expedi-
tions, stories, poems and reviews. When Ford had lost his job as editor
of the *English Review*, Goldring simultaneously lost his position as secretary, and starting the magazine was his first independent venture. The
Tramp's contributors were an eclectic bunch, established Edwardians as
well as those who would soon become known as Georgians or modernists.
The first issue included James Ellroy Flecker, for whom Goldring had
a particular admiration, W. H. Davies (of 'no time to stand and stare'
fame), Arthur Ransome, Arnold Bennett, Violet Hunt and Lady Margaret
Sackville, and later issues published work by Flint, Wyndham Lewis
and Ford, as well as translations of Chekhov and Maupassant stories,
and Marinetti's Futurist manifesto mentioned earlier. The places
described in the travel articles were generally either within England, in
that way looking forward to the Georgian love of the English countryside, or in Brittany, the terrain of the proto-modernist painters. The
Tramp only lasted twelve issues; Goldring, like Ford at the *English
Review*, had insufficient backing, the reason that he himself gives for
the magazine's failure, but he might also have been somewhat ahead of
his time; in the inter-war years travel writing would become immensely
popular, and Goldring's own travel books – he wrote at least ten –
brought him much more success than ever his poetry did.

The first of the poems by Flint published in the *Tramp* was entitled 'March', though it rather inappropriately appeared in the
September issue of 1910. (Perhaps this was a sign of Goldring's lack
of editorial expertise; among Flint's papers is a letter from T.S. Eliot,
written from the *Criterion* in 1925 about a poem that Flint had sent
him then; in it he comments wryly that if Flint were an editor, he
would know that the readers wouldn't tolerate spring odes in autumn.)[36]
'March' has as its subject-matter one of the themes that had appeared
in *In the Net of the Stars*, the unhappy London worker thinking of
the countryside beyond. It is quite traditional in form, but very simple,
conversational in tone – Ford would undoubtedly have liked it, in spite of
its rejection of London:

Soon will the plane trees make a shade of leaves
Along the quiet streets – alas! too few –
And in the garden where the lilac weaves
Its mantle of sweet scent and purple hue.

But I would rather be among the woods
Where the heart holds a silence dumbly stirred
By the soft mournful cuckoo call, and broods
On music which the ears have never heard.[37]

This tone, thoughtful, calm, a little melancholic, very close to everyday speech, would be characteristic of Flint's imagist free verse. In some of the other poems in the *Tramp* he is more experimental, especially in a four-part poem called 'Moods', published in the November and December issues, where he is putting into practice his belief that the subject-matter of the poem should determine the form. Here the first two parts, both love poems, are in pure free verse, and the second in particular, again very simple, looks forward to the brevity of the imagist verse-form:

You were among the apple branches.
The sun shone, and it was November.

Sun and apples and laughter
And love
We gathered, you and I.

And the birds were singing.[38]

Peter Jones includes this in his Penguin anthology of *Imagist Poetry*, in a section of poetry from the period of the anthologies, 1914–17, using the republished version from Flint's 1915 collection, *Cadences*.[39]. He may not have realised how early it had been written; it must be the earliest poem by any of the poets included, suggesting Flint was well on the way to finding an imagist style before Pound himself did, although Jones' selection also includes several of Pound's poems which were written before the word imagism was even a glimmer in Pound's eye.

Whether Pound saw these poems in the *Tramp* he does not say: probably not at the time, but when they met up again it is likely Flint showed them to him, as their discussions about poetry and poetic form began again immediately. Pound makes one reference in 'Prologomena' to these conversations with Flint, when, after lamenting the conditions of the modern poet who can no longer lie in 'a green field with his head against a tree', and play 'a ha'penny whistle' but instead has to 'holloa his verses down a speaking tube to the editors of cheap magazines', he writes that one now meets 'unkempt Amyclas in a Soho restaurant and chant together of dead and forgotten things – it is a manner of speech among poets to chant of dead and forgotten things, there seems no special harm in it; it has always been done – and it's rather better to be a clerk in the Post Office than to look after a lot of stinking, verminous sheep'.[40] Flint was the only clerk in the Post Office Pound knew, and indeed referred to himself as unkempt Amyclas in a letter to Pound many years later, but if they only talked about dead, forgotten things, it must have been because Pound would not let Flint get a word in.

II

POUND spent Christmas 1911 near Salisbury with the novelist and poet, Maurice Hewlett, whom he had seen several times that autumn. He was deeply and unforgettably moved by the sense of past lives around him on Salisbury Plain, a sense perhaps enforced by the contrast with the novel twentieth-century experience of travelling in a motor-car, which took them to see Henry Newbolt, who, he recalled in The *Cantos*, looked 'twice bathed'.[41] He told Margaret that he thought Hewlett's trilogy *The Agonists* 'very fine'; these were verse plays, written in an experimental form that Hewlett called 'stress-metre'.[42] They had received some scathing attacks, though Binyon defended them, arguing that the 'whole point of the stress-metre is the effort to bring verse-writing in closer relation to the rhythms of living speech'.[43] No wonder Pound, now returning himself to the 'living tongue', was impressed. He too was trying to write a long poem, 'much more important', he told Margaret, than anything he had done so far. Presumably this was a first draft of the *Cantos*, though Pound would not publish anything from it until 1917, when three cantos appeared in consecutive issues of *Poetry*. Dorothy wrote to him in late December, after he had consulted her about it: 'I am sure I have no suggestions for your long poem. You might damn the Commonplace – and all the unemployed, (meaning myself).'[44] Such self-deprecation was a feature of her letters, though rarely a characteristic of Pound's.

Shortly after Pound returned to London in early 1912, Brigit introduced him to another aspiring writer, Richard Aldington. Although he was always known as Richard, Aldington had been christened Edward Godfree, the first name presumably after the then Prince of Wales, as is the case for the hero of one of his novels, and it may have been the youthful Aldington's fierce opposition to the monarchy that led him to reject it. In spite of his youth – in early 1912, Aldington was only nineteen – he was already almost as full of theories and as combative in his own way as Pound himself. A friend of Brigit's had asked her to befriend him, explaining he was 'a clever boy . . . alone in London because he won't go into his father's business. All he wants to do is write.' He turned out to be 'a lively humorous boy', entertaining and engaging. He was, she said, 'tall and broad-shouldered, with a fine forehead, thick longish hair of the indefinite colour blond hair turns to in adolescence, very bright blue eyes, too small a nose and a determined mouth'.[45] He was good-looking, though in a more conventional way than Pound: with regular features, and well-built, he looked like a rugby player, which indeed he had been, though he later generally tried to keep that dark. (Harriet Monroe, the editor of *Poetry*, the magazine that would be so important to all of them, said he looked like a footballer, not a comment that endeared her to him.) When Pound met him, Richard was very poor and living on a spartan diet, with no need as yet to worry about his later tendency to put on weight. In *Asphodel* H.D. described the Aldington character, there called Jerrold Darrington, as 'square-set, a little heavy (when he wasn't too hungry)' and Darrington says of himself, 'I am a bit florid at times. True British roast beef.'[46] Aldington's robust physique led many to underestimate his super-sensitivity and the ease with which he could be wounded, particularly as he had been trained to be too conventionally masculine to admit it. Nowadays he is remembered most as the embittered, ruthless and homophobic biographer of T.E. Lawrence, but in those pre-First World War days, Aldington was full of hope, high spirits, iconoclasm and fun. Even then there was, perhaps, an underlying melancholy that emerges in some of his poems, but it was not at that stage apparent to his friends. Pound, describing the pre-war London scene to Patricia Hutchins in the 1950s, recalled 'Aldington for japes and larks . . . Don't underestimate Richard's verve in those days. It was a comfort.'[47]

Aldington was born in Portsmouth, but spent most of his childhood near or in Dover. His father was an unsuccessful solicitor with a passion for Elizabethan literature; he had written a novel (also unsuccessful, not to say tedious) about Elizabethan life. His father's family was, Aldington explained in some biographical notes he sent to Amy Lowell in 1917, 'though not noble, "respectable", as the 18th century people say', and traceable back to the sixteenth century.[48] His father had, as it was put in those days, married beneath him, though Aldington did not mention that to Amy, merely saying euphemistically that his mother was of 'old Kent stock'. The version of events Darrington gives in *Asphodel* is more colourful: 'My governor you know married a country wench. Damn clever of her. She copped the old fellow down hunting. I was born six months after though they say in hushed tones poor Ned was a seven months' baby. Damn fool the governor. One's people are one's damned ruin.'[49]

Aldington was always ashamed of and deeply hostile to his mother. He thought her sentimental and vulgar: worst of all, she wrote romantic novels, the best known of which, *Love-Letters That Caused a Divorce*, made a local stir for a while during Aldington's adolescence. It was published by a Dover newspaper, which festooned its windows with copies, much to Richard's mortification. Luckily he was a big, powerful lad, so probably he did not suffer as much as he might have done from the mockery of his school-fellows. *Love-Letters That Caused a Divorce* was a racy, and indeed very gently risqué read – the adulterous affair is true love and the wronged husband a pain – and no doubt it passed the time on the London train very pleasantly, though a rapid reader would have finished half-way. His father's novel, *The Queen's Preferment*, is a great deal longer and heavier, with wearisomely pseudo-Elizabethan dialogue ('"Tush, lad," he said, "thou forgettest that within call, aye within this royal Palace, are many who do my bidding." ')[50] It may be true that, as a later lover of Aldington's was to say, Jessie May Aldington was 'a very common woman', but she was a more successful novelist than her respectable husband was either lawyer or writer, and when his business failed she made a very competent living for many years running the Mermaid Inn at Rye.[51] Yet, scornful though he was of his mother's efforts, with two novelist parents it is not surprising young Aldington had literary aspirations.

In later life, Aldington denounced English snobbery with great vehemence, if not venom, and no doubt he had suffered from it on his mother's behalf, but there is no indication that his proclaimed contempt for class prejudice made him any more sympathetic to her, or more ready to acknowledge her abilities; his attitude to her, indeed, smacked of the snobbery he condemned in others. He gave a deeply bitter caricature of her in his war novel, *Death of a Hero*, though ironically her enterprise and energy come through there much more than in his memoir. But in the novel he claims that 'She had let George [the Aldington figure] down so badly time after time when he was a boy that he was all tight inside'.[52] Perhaps it was she who first left him with the sense of betrayal he would show so acutely later. There is evidence that Jessie May had a terrible temper, which, according to Aldington's sister, she enjoyed displaying, and in later years, Aldington alleged, she became increasingly partial to drink. In *Death of a Hero*, George says to his future wife: 'I'm glad you hate your parents or at least one of them ... I remember I used to watch the young robins exterminating their fathers, and think how right it was. But it ought to be the mothers.'[53]

Like both Pound and H.D., Aldington had found much of his formal education an unrewarding experience. A collection of recollections of Aldington is prefaced with the information that he was 'educated' at Dover College. He would not have agreed, although that was certainly the school he attended. Nor would his headmaster, whom Aldington described many years later as saying to him, after congratulating him on his literary success, 'And now tell me, my dear Aldington, *where* on earth did you get your scholarly knowledge?'[54] Aldington had enjoyed his first small prep school in a Kentish fishing village, but was deeply unhappy at Dover College, a minor public school, the sort of place, he said, that inculcated all the worst aspects of British snobbery and insularity without any of the talent and flair that might have relieved them. As he writes in *Death of a Hero*, 'They set out to produce "a type of thoroughly manly fellow," a "type" which unhesitatingly accepted the prejudices, the "code" put before it, docilely conformed to a set of rules.' The other boys accepted this: 'They wanted to be approved and be healthy barbarians, cultivating a little smut on the sly, and finally dropping into some convenient post in life where the "thoroughly manly fellow" was appreciated – mostly, one must admit, minor and unpleasant and not very remunerative posts in unhealthy colonies. The Empire's backbone.'[55] Probably there were others who resisted the 'code', and doubtless there were more inspiring teachers than Aldington admits. All the same, he learnt most of what he knew from his father's library, which comprised some 2,000 volumes, his 'home university', as he later described it to Amy Lowell.

One rather odd feature of Aldington's memoir, *Life for Life's Sake*, is that his brother and sister are never mentioned, and he leaves the impression of a lonely and wistful only child. (In *Death of a Hero*, George, when asked if he has siblings, replies, 'Yes, I believe so but I never think about it. Relatives are awful.')[56] Yet as a young boy he loved to explore the chalk downs, and became an avid collector of butterflies and moths. When he later wrote a poem about his childhood in Dover, he used for the child he had been the image of a chrysalis put in a matchbox, unable to beat its wings when they emerge.

> I was like a moth –
> Like one of those grey Emperor moths
> Which flutter through the vines at Capri.
> And that damned little town was my match-box,

Against whose sides I beat and beat
Until my wings were torn and faded, and dingy
As that damned little town.[57]

The poem is a powerful evocation of small-town dullness (Dover in *Death of a Hero* actually appears as Dullborough), but it is a trace self-pitying, a trait Aldington was never to lose. There is misery, but one feels it needs more than somewhat snobbish and misogynistic complaints about 'the sordid provincial shops – The grocer's, and the shops for women' to justify it.[58]

Aldington always loved books: 'I think,' he wrote, 'it was fortunate that my schools paid no attention to "cultural interests," so that reading was pure fun.'[59] His father had taught him 'his letters' at the age of two, and would, he said, get hold of any book that his son wanted as he grew up. As a young boy, Aldington read only adventure stories, but one day, when he was about fourteen, he came by chance across the writing of Oscar Wilde, whose complete works his father had just bought. 'I had never heard of Mr Wilde until this purchase, but from one or two of the remarks in the discussion about it, I judged there was something mysterious to be learned.' He started on *Intentions*, the volume which includes some of Wilde's most famous essays ('The Decay of Lying' and 'The Critic as Artist' among them). *Intentions* sent him on to Keats, only in fact mentioned by Wilde in passing, if with admiration, but Keats' works were luckily in his father's bookcase: 'I despair of finding words to express the effect of these two books without seeming inadequate to myself or exaggerated to other people. It was like a combination of falling in love at first sight and finding Ali Baba's treasure cave. But lovers have their woes and Ali Baba has his perils; I had neither. There was simply no fly in that ointment. By the merest chance I had stumbled into a world of enchantment.'[60] In the next two years, a year of which he was off school altogether because of a hernia operation, he went through all his father's poetry books, which included all the major British poets from Chaucer to Browning and many minor ones too, and also read his complete collection of Elizabethan dramatists. He read the Pre-Raphaelites with enthusiasm; a notebook he kept at about seventeen is full of references to Morris and Swinburne, and, as with Pound, they, along with Pater and Wilde, had an impact that would never be lost. At Dover College all the boys did by way of literary appreciation was 'parse, analyse, and (heaven help us!) paraphrase Shakespeare's *King John*'.[61] In *Death of a Hero*, Aldington describes George as 'living a double life – one life for school and home, another for himself', which comprised his walks over the downs and his explorations in books.[62] Aldington confessed to Amy Lowell that the only part of school that he enjoyed was the rugby football.

The family moved to Sandwich, whose ancient walls, tranquillity and 'air of immemorial languor' he loved.[63] There, at fifteen, he began to write poetry, which at sixteen he started to show to a neighbour, Dudley Grey, a sophisticated man of the world of about fifty, who had been a poet himself in his youth. He was wealthy and cultured, and much disapproved of in the village, because he had once let slip that he had dined with Wilde. In spite of the fact that he lived respectably with a Mrs Grey, it was decided he was a 'degenerate'; perhaps they thought his friendship with a good-looking, fair-haired sixteen-year-old boy rather odd, but Aldington says nothing about that. Dudley Grey was, he said, 'a good European'.[64] He talked to Richard about London, Paris and Berlin; he said Richard must go to Italy. Grey had not just a passion for Italy but volumes of entrancing photographs of the Italian countryside, architecture and art. He introduced Richard to French and Italian literature, and made him realise that the classics were not just 'a dreary school task' but were 'as much living poetry as Keats and Shakespeare'. Looking back, Aldington commented: 'No doubt he saw these things through the eyes of Ruskin, Pater, and Addington Symonds, but that is vastly better than not seeing them at all.'[65] (When Aldington wrote some articles about Italy for the *New Age* in 1913, his intimate knowledge of the writings of Ruskin and John Addington Symonds on Italy becomes very clear.) At sixteen, Aldington claims, he had a poem published in a London periodical. In the meantime his mother had sent off a piece of his prose to George Bernard Shaw, who wrote back: '*Madam*, Your son has obviously too much literary talent to earn his living in an honest way. I enclose a guinea which he is to spend in some thoroughly selfish manner.'[66] Aldington claimed to be shocked by this cynicism towards the calling of the writer, but even such equivocal praise doubtless gave him confidence.

The first published poem by Aldington that has been traced appeared when he was eighteen, in October 1910, in what he described as a 'leftish journal', *Justice*. Interestingly enough, it was a political poem, in a Swinburnian metre, celebrating the overthrow of the Portuguese monarchy and the establishment of a republic. Aldington was dismissive of his motivations later, writing that it was based on 'an abstract and unfounded belief that monarchies are corrupt and republics perfect *per se*', and it can scarcely be described as a good poem – only its sentiments can have secured it publication:

> We are tired of the cry of the hungry, of
> the noise of the harlot's feet –
> O, grant we be deft and courageous, and
> cunning and wise and fleet![67]

It is an indication, however, of the young Aldington's idealism, something he would dismiss derisively in later life, but which was a vital part of what drove him towards poetry, and what attracted H.D.

'A sudden change in the family fortunes', as he puts it in his memoirs, meant a move to west London. Aldington was enrolled at University College London, which, conscious that its social standing would always be over-shadowed by Oxford and Cambridge, competed through fierce scholastic rigour, not dissimilar to that introduced by Felix Schelling to Penn.[68] 'In a laudable effort to set a higher standard of learning than the two old universities, London went a bit Teutonic,' Aldington wrote in 1941, two world wars against Germany having made such a comment not only accept-able but patriotic: 'I should say it was designed to turn out philologists rather than scholars, and ten thousand pedants for one poet. Somewhere about the place is a plaque recording that Robert Browning spent a year as a student there. I think I know why he only stayed one year.'[69] Aldington was only to stay for one year himself. He was taught by some distinguished scholars, including A.E. Housman, 'who was to be seen occasionally cruising gloomily about the corridors, probably depressed by the sins of German commentators on Manilius'.[70] There was also the famous medievalist, W. P. Ker, though the lecturer whose teaching he most enjoyed was called Solomon, a classical don who loved poetry and whose enthusiasm was infectious; he would deliver his lectures, 'not from the dais, but from the right-hand corner of the room, twisting himself in and out and up and down a rope which hung down from the lofty window. It was a strange spectacle to see him hanging by one arm and leg from the rope like a learned chimpanzee in blue serge, declaiming lines from Catullus or Vergil with unflagging gusto.'[71]

At University College Aldington met Alec Randall, who remained a lifelong friend. Randall recalled Aldington as a romantic figure, 'the centre of a group of admiring friends', known to write poetry, with a velvet jacket and flowing bow-tie, *de rigueur* for a budding poet in 1910.[72] According to Randall, the poems that Aldington was writing at the time were, like his tie, influenced by the younger Yeats, as well as by Rossetti and the French symbolists, though Aldington himself said he did not know the French poets until two years later. Aldington's closest friend at university was

another poet, Arthur Chapman, who drowned in the summer of 1911, at
the end of Aldington's first and only year. It was his first experience of
real bereavement and he felt it deeply. A poem by Aldington on Chapman's
death appeared in the University College *Union Magazine*; still very traditional, a little too wordy, it is a direct and moving poem, the pain of a
young agnostic who has none of the conventional religious consolations
to protect him against the shock of sudden death. His very first imagist
poems a year later are also melancholy and more concerned with death
than one would expect of a twenty-year-old; perhaps that was just a hang-
over from the sub-nineties gloom much in vogue in the early years of the
century, so disliked of Pound and Hulme, but it may be in some measure
related to Chapman's death.

Aldington's university life ended abruptly, when his father's financial
affairs went even more badly wrong than usual. Although he disparaged
the college, if not his teachers, he must have been devastated. He had real
linguistic flair and certainly would have done well, and, more importantly,
he enjoyed the work. His mother, however, had always been opposed to
his reading for a degree; she felt he should have gone straight into a safe
profession, the law or accountancy, and family and friends pressurised him
to remedy that now. Aldington resisted. He wanted to be a writer. His
father was sympathetic. Even before he started at University College, he
had tried to get his son literary work. He wrote to the editor of the *Spectator*,
one St Loe Strachey, uncle of Lytton:

I have a son between 17 & 18, of whom one of our greatest living writers has declared
that 'he has literary ability enough for anything,' [is he or his son quoting Shaw most
accurately?] & as I am therefore anxious to obtain for him an atmosphere that would
be congenial, it has occurred to me that possibly you might be able to find him a
position that would be mutually satisfying.

As an old lover of the classics I can vouch for the boy's ability in that direction.
His knowledge of French is good, of art excellent, of English Literature, for his age
quite remarkable. His productions, particularly in poetry are equally distinctive, &
withal, he is tall, muscular & can do a twenty mile walk any day of the week.[73]

Such paternal pride and concern is touching, and though evidently
this letter did not work, perhaps he was right to present this range of
skills, from classical learning to strenuous walking. Edwardian editors
wanted well-educated, well-rounded assistants. Aldington recounts a
later interview with a Fleet Street newspaper editor who asked him to
quote from both Horace and Homer; he doesn't mention questions

about his physical prowess, but one look at Aldington would have answered that. After Aldington left university, his father, in spite of his financial troubles, gave him a small allowance, something Aldington glosses over in *Life for Life's Sake*, and omits from the account he gave to Amy Lowell. He supplemented this income with some sports journalism – scarcely a respectable activity at the time, but he was not in that way proud, and he did understand rugby. In addition, he soon found he could sell the occasional poem. He was determined to make his way as a writer. He couldn't live luxuriously – he gave up smoking and drinking and ate sparsely – but he could survive. Luckily, he soon started to be invited to literary parties and, like Pound, was able to supplement his diet agreeably as well as make contact with other writers.

Writing many years later, Aldington recalled his introduction to Pound in early 1912. By now Pound had given up his *outré* costumes – perhaps because they caused such consternation to Dorothy's friends and relations – and though still a dandy, was a more restrained and elegant one. In the days when Aldington first knew him, Pound dressed in imitation of Whistler: 'the dark suit and rolled double waistcoat, the very neat-waisted grey overcoat of Regency cut, the black cane, the hat jauntily on the side of the head'.[74] Richard liked Pound immediately: 'in 1912,' he wrote, 'Ezra was great fun, a small but persistent volcano in the dim levels of London literary society.'[75] By this time, if not exactly a celebrity, Pound was at any rate a well-known personality: 'London was interested and amused by him. The evening papers interviewed him at length and published his portrait; and even *Punch* had to notice the existence of a certain Mr Ezekial Ton who had achieved a new synthesis of Wardour Street and the wild and woolly West.'[76] The nineteen-year-old Aldington showed Pound his *vers libre* poems 'over a beef-steak in Kensington'; gratifyingly, Pound's response was, 'Well, I don't think you need any help from me!' After that they became 'great friends, very great friends'.[77] Yet, as well as their devotion to poetry, Aldington and Pound had in common a brash contempt for social conventions. They both loved to shock, and would have much pleasure in jointly doing so.

In the account that Brigit gives of Aldington's meeting with H.D., she suggests that he was from the start attracted by her, and was delighted that she accepted him instantly as a poet. What Brigit doesn't mention, naturally enough for one of her generation, is that she and Richard had already had a brief affair, to which Richard referred in a letter to her many years later, when he and Brigit became lovers once more and had an eight-year relationship. He recalled that it was 'you who first held my body';

presumably it was she to whom he lost his virginity, though he leaves the impression in his memoir that he was already quite sexually experienced by that age.[78] There is no hint in her memoir that Brigit objected to the transference of his affections. Both Caroline Zilboorg, who drew attention to this earlier affair, and H.D.'s biographer, Barbara Guest, suggest that Brigit was attracted by H.D. herself, and Zilboorg suggests she encouraged Aldington's attentions as 'a way of loving H.D. vicariously through him'.[79] Brigit was very attached to H.D. and admired her greatly, but her letters to H.D. reveal her as someone desperately needing male validation, though constantly being let down by the men with whom she became involved. She clearly liked women as people better than men, but she needed to be loved by a man. Her son Derek, who was gay himself, says he is sure she was heterosexual, though he suggests H.D. was in love with his beautiful mother. In fact the only possible sexual link that has not either emerged or been suggested between two of this foursome is between Aldington and Pound. Whatever the truth of these speculations, they rapidly became close-knit friends. Richard, like Pound, recalled later 'those magical early days in London' in the pre-war years.[80] They wrote, argued, partied, made each other laugh, more like a group of graduate students than people who had entered the serious world of work – not that literary life in London in the pre-war days often resembled the serious world of work. The war would change all that.

III

SHORTLY before Aldington first met Pound, Brigit had introduced him to another poet, Harold Monro, who was to play an important part in London literary life for the next few years. Monro had just returned to England from the continent, wanting, like Ford and Hulme, to promote poetry appropriate to the modern age. He had lived abroad for some years, in escape from an unsuccessful marriage and unfulfilling work. He came from a well-to-do family, and had a Cambridge degree, but his inability to fit in with conventional English life showed early, when he was expelled from his public school, Radley, at the age of sixteen; the official reason offered was that he had been found to have a bottle of wine in his study – possibly the case, even if not the cause for expulsion, as from Cambridge onwards drink would be an intermittent problem for him – but the truth was that he was caught, as his biographer puts it, '*in flagrante* with a younger boy'.[81] At Cambridge he had an intense but unhappy friendship with a fellow aspiring poet, Maurice Browne. Monro, who according to the poet and playwright John Drinkwater looked like a 'dejected Guards Officer', was a melancholic, and by nature reclusive; he was drawn by 'advanced' ideas, and his attempts at regular work – he was a lawyer by training who became a land agent – and his marriage – to Maurice's sister, a hockey international with a taste for society life – failed abysmally.[82] Since 1910 he had lived in Florence, where he had become a close friend of Maurice Hewlett, with whom Pound spent Christmas 1911. Monro had undergone analysis with a therapist called Max Bircher-Berger – he also treated Hermann Hesse and Thomas Mann, as well as inventing muesli – and had come to accept the fact that he was a homosexual, but although he espoused a doctrine of sexual fulfilment (in Italy at the time, homosexual relations were not illegal to men over sixteen), a series of sexual adventures with young men did not dispel his misery. Monro had already published several books of verse, but he felt that in England 'the best poetry of the time is the poetry of despair, a cry of the lost'; it needed to get back to being what it was when the poet 'expressed the keen and natural emotions of life'.[83] Given Monro's own tendency to despair, he might well have sat gloomily in Florence lamenting this state of affairs, had Hewlett not intervened. According to Flint, who became a close friend and literary executor, eventually writing the preface for Monro's collected poems in 1933,

Hewlett, in that forthright way he had on occasion, exclaimed, 'If you feel like that, for God's sake go back to England and do something.' . . . It was the turning point of his life. Hitherto, Shelley, vegetarianism, romantic idealism, a vague socialism and his own fundamental incapacity to submit to discipline had rendered him ineffective both as a man and a poet. He was to learn about men by the experience of them which money dealings give, and about poetry by the lash of other poets' tongues.[84]

Monro, who was then thirty-two, brought with him a precocious long-haired eighteen-year-old youth, Arundel del Re, half Italian, half Anglo-Irish, with whom he was in love, probably unrequited. Del Re came to be his assistant in his great project for the revival of poetry, though he was extremely sociable and frequently distracted from the cause. When Aldington met Monro, he was, with del Re's assistance, in the process of setting up the *Poetry Review*, in which Pound's 'Prologomena' was to appear. The first issue came out in January 1912; Aldington would feature there in a signed piece in June, though he also contributed some anonymous and some initialled book reviews, his first ventures into literary journalism. *Poetry Review* would also give John Gould Fletcher, still unknown to his future fellow-imagists, his first experience of literary journalism.

Aldington and Flint saw a good deal of Monro in 1912, as did Hulme, who, even if he were no longer writing poetry himself, was still interested in those who did, and who gave one of the three lectures Monro organised during the summer of 1912, most likely his 'Romanticism and Classicism'. Monro was a good deal wealthier than any of them – he had £1,000 a year, considerable riches at the time, even though he was giving money for the support of his wife and son – and he was always hospitable and generous. He retained his 'vague socialism', as Flint put it, which formed a particular link between the two of them; Dominic Hibberd describes them both as 'Fabians and reformers' (if that's so, Flint's politics must have moderated since the time he denounced the Fabians to Mrs Eder, at the fortuitous meeting that led to his appointment as literary critic of the *New Age*). Hibberd comments that Flint was one of the few literary friends with whom Monro never quarrelled.

When Monro returned to England, his intentions, according to Dominic Hibberd, 'were simple: to help young writers produce the poetry of the future, and to take their work to the people, so that poets might once again become the unacknowledged legislators of the world, bringing new answers to the old question, "How to Live?"'[85] High ambitions, which to some extent he achieved; under Monro's editorship, the 1912 *Poetry Review* and later *Poetry and Drama* published a wide range of poetry and poetry criticism, and played an important part in giving a platform both for the poets who would later be known as the Georgians, and for the imagists; if his magazines were not read by the 'people', they were by most of those interested in literary affairs. Monro, who was as keen in his own way as Pound later became to make English writers more cosmopolitan, published special issues on French, German and American poetry. Pound would later castigate Monro, in what Hibberd describes as 'one of the most grudging obituaries ever written by one poet about another' for the catholicity of his taste.[86] But Monro's tolerance and encouragement of a wide variety of poetry was his strength. If Ford in the *English Review* had produced a more purely literary periodical than the traditional generalist ones that were brought out by Victorian and Edwardian presses, Monro took a further step in developing one of the earliest examples of what was to be the prototypical literary outlet of the modernist period, the little magazine. Monro never became a happy man, but in spite of his melancholic, depressive nature, in many ways he would transform the conditions of poetic production in England. Dominic Hibberd, indeed, claims that 'no-one did more for the development of twentieth-century poetry'.[87]

Pound may well have met Monro first through Hewlett, who would certainly have talked of him during Pound's Christmas visit, and he was to write regularly for him. As early as January he told his parents that he was taking Monro along to meet Yeats, who was in London only intermittently until March, as if he had taken Monro under his wing. Whether Monro appreciated this or not, one can't tell; he certainly later developed as many reservations about Pound as Pound about him. Yet Pound always loved to be able to show off his literary contacts, and at this stage he was well disposed to Monro, and possibly flattered by the fact that Monro had included a review of *Canzoni* in the very first number. This was by none other than Flint, whom Pound, if consulted, would have been keen to recommend, since he had earlier been Pound's

most enthusiastic English critic. Flint's review had in fact been somewhat mixed; gratifyingly, he claimed that 'the true note of poetry'
sounded throughout the book, but he questioned whether that note was
Pound's own, or others', seeing so many of the poems were translations,
and even when they were not, read 'as though [they] were'. 'If you run
your eye over the pages of his books,' he writes, 'you meet Latin and
Mediaeval Latin, the "langue d'oc" and the "langue d'oil," Dante's
Italian and modern Italian, Spanish, French, German, quaint (or queynt!)
forgotten English; and lastly English. Yes, *lastly* English . . . If Mr Pound
can find a foreign title to a poem, he will do so. Queer exotic hybridity!'
But he ends by saying 'those who have the grace to and can spend
money on modern poetry should buy this book', and Pound appears to
have been content.[88] The review was, at any rate, a good deal more
positive than some of the other reactions to *Canzoni*.

Pound was equally ready to act as critic to Flint. In the first communication saved among Flint's papers from Pound, dated early February
1912, Pound writes: 'My dear Flint why don't you write some more
poetry' and in the second, apparently having been sent some, comments
that 'you could with a little decent labour and a little less "Ianthe"
[Flint's young daughter] have done it rather better'. Flint appears not
to have published any poetry during 1911, with the combined pressures
of a full-time job and a baby – plenty of 'decent labour' in fact, if not
on poetry.[89] He had, however, spent time reading, particularly French
poetry. Pound appeared delighted to be back in touch with him, and
after various lunchtime meetings, largely back in the Vienna Café,
suggested Flint and his wife came to dinner with himself and H.D.
H.D. described this meeting to Isabel Pound in a letter which makes
curious reading; although she was later condemnatory of Philadelphian
– and particularly Bryn Mawr – snobbery, her account here suggests
she was still herself at this stage quite conventionally class-conscious.
H.D. records in *Asphodel* that George Lowndes mocks Hermione for
her adherence to the Philadelphian etiquette book, and for her anxiety
to behave correctly; by the 1920s she was clearly aware, and indeed
ashamed, of her earlier social preconceptions. Her first year in London
was, however, a steep learning curve. In this letter, she tells Isabel that
her son had been very good to her, introducing her to 'celebrities and
lesser oddities – he always has some underdog on hand. On Thursday
[22 February] it was a derelict poet named Flint who made the fatal
mistake of marrying his landlady's daughter, a hapless little Cockney'.
It was clearly an uneasy first meeting. Pound had thought an invitation

to dinner 'might set them up', but Flint's wife complained about the food (H.D. decided it was the first time she had ever gone out to dinner) and told H.D. she had 'a baby whose name was Ianthe!' Quite what H.D. wanted to convey by that exclamation mark isn't clear – presumably that it was a very unexpected name for a cockney mother's baby. After 'two years silence', she tells Isabel, Flint burst into song. Yet in spite of this strained and embarrassed first meeting, they soon became good friends. Flint gave her a copy of *In the Net of the Stars*, and three months later she was writing affectionately to Flint from Paris, asking him to remember her to 'Madame and Ianthe'.[90]

The next person, she told Isabel, that Pound intended to introduce her to was Harold Monro, though whether he counted as a celebrity or underdog she doesn't say: 'Ezra,' she told his mother, 'says M. is depressed. Pleasant prospect!' H.D. almost certainly did not yet know about Pound's engagement to Dorothy. Giving the dinner party jointly could well have suggested to the Flints that they were in some sense a couple, as H.D. by now had probably been in England long enough to know. Barbara Guest indeed suggests that H.D. in this letter was trying to show Isabel how much more suitable for a poet's wife she would be than Violet Flint, but H.D. knew that Isabel had thought her a wise choice, so she had no need to prove it. All the same, she would have been unlikely to have written in quite those terms – or to have behaved in quite that way – if she had been aware that Pound had now committed himself elsewhere. She mentioned the Shakespears in passing in the letter, but again there is no hint that she knows the link: 'Mrs Shakespear,' she says, 'has been most kind, and her daughter and I have had some chats together, as well.'[91] H.D. says in *End to Torment* that she did not know about the engagement until some time after she first met Richard, probably like Pound in early 1912, and that it was Walter Rummel who broke the news, so it seems likely she would not have heard until Walter returned to London in March.[92]

Now their acquaintance was renewed, Flint began again to attempt to persuade Pound to take more interest in contemporary French poetry. But English poetry was changing too, not perhaps in the way Flint advocated, but significantly all the same. In the first issue of *Poetry Review*, just before Flint's review of *Canzoni*, a review appeared of John Masefield's *The Everlasting Mercy*, first published the previous November in the *English Review* and now appearing as a book that was already causing a sensation. The reviewer, young Arundel del Re, wrote enthusiastically: 'Mr John Masefield is a revolutionary. His latest work is an assault on cherished principles and venerable conventions . . .

Its value lies not so much in sheer audacity – though this indeed has peculiar interest – as in the influence it may have on contemporary poetry.'[93] He was undoubtedly right about the influence. *The Everlasting Mercy* is a poem written in fast-moving, diverting and highly colloquial rhymed verse, about a country ne'er-do-well who makes good in the end. Saul Kane, the protagonist, recounts the sins of his twenties: 'From '61 to '67/I lived in disbelief of heaven./I drunk, I fought, I poached, I whored,/I did despite unto the Lord.' In this year, however, he gets into a fight with his friend and fellow-poacher, Billy Myers, who accuses him of breaking their agreement to carve up poaching territory. Billy is in the right, according to poachers' ethics, and there's a fierce exchange. 'If you poach here, there'll be a fight' he says, and indeed there is. Billy insists:

> 'It's mine.'
>> 'It ain't.'
>>> 'You put.'
>>>> 'You liar.'
> 'You closhy put.'
>> 'You bloody liar'
> 'This is my field.'
>> 'This is my wire.'
> 'I'm ruler here.'
>> 'You ain't'
>>> 'I am.'
> 'I'll fight you for it.'
>> 'Right, by damn.'[94]

The word 'bloody' was omitted in the *English Review*, just a space the length of the missing word appearing, so a reader with an ear for rhythm might have been able to guess. Harold Monro later wrote of this poem: 'People who thought English poetry had died with Tennyson suddenly recognized their error ... the rapid free doggerel of "The Everlasting Mercy", its modernity, its bald colloquialism, and its narrative interest awakened the curiosity of the public in 1911, and a revival of the dormant interest in poetry was at once assured.'[95] *The Everlasting Mercy*, given Saul's repentance and reformation, is in moral terms essentially entirely orthodox, and, while lively, it is scarcely great poetry, but it helped to make a new kind of everyday language and subject-matter possible in poetry. Like Hewlett, Masefield was capturing the 'living tongue', but he was also using more modern – and earthier – subject-matter. This would be the trend of much of the poetry of the next decade, both modernist and Georgian. It would be strange if Pound had not noticed the stir caused by Masefield's poem. Aldington did, and produced an instant parody.

Pound, H.D., Aldington, Patmore and Flint, in various combinations, saw a good deal of each other for the next few months, and their conversations, as they all confirm, were much about poetry; not necessarily, as yet, with any sense of leading a literary revolution, though they were all in their different ways rebelling against traditional forms. H.D. had published no poetry so far, but she found Aldington a great deal more encouraging about her efforts than Pound had been. Aldington himself was making strides in his literary career. He exaggerated a little when he told Amy Lowell in 1917 that, by the time he was eighteen, he had had 'quite a number of poems & translations published in papers like the Evening Standard, the Westminster Gazette, the Pall Mall, etc. I got half a guinea for them & was delighted.' In truth, he was not quite so precocious. According to his painstaking editor, Norman Gates, the only poem that was definitely published when Aldington was eighteen was the truly dreadful 'Song of Freedom' that had come out in *Justice*. During the early months of 1912, however, he succeeded in having at least ten poems published in the London papers, a remarkable achievement for a nineteen-year-old largely supporting himself by sports journalism. His first poem in the *Evening Standard*, 'Chanson of Winter' (with its macaronic title, it could have been named by Pound himself), appeared shortly after he first met his fellow imagists-to-be, in February 1912. These poems of early 1912 were largely translations, mostly with conventional stanzaic forms, although four of the translations from the Greek do not use rhyme. In his early notebooks, too, Aldington can be seen to be working towards his later free verse, translating from a Greek chorus, line by line in simple rhythmic, but unrhymed phrases. These early translations bear out his claim to Amy Lowell that he had been trying out forms of *vers libre* since the beginning of 1911, not as the result of any English or French influences, but 'partly because I was fatigued with rhyme and partly because of the interest I had in poetic experiment. I got the idea from the chorus in the Hippolytus of Euripides.'[96] Aldington would later argue that these choruses were really free verse in the original Greek, and that scholarly insistence that they had a prescribed form of quantitative verse was irrelevant; good imagist verse, he would insist, was no less rhythmically shaped than the Greek. Aldington's early unrhymed poems show a keen ear for harmonious tones, but because they use very regular lengths of line and stick closely to the iambic, they lack the tautness, speech rhythms and shaped cadences of his imagist poems later in the year.

At this stage, Aldington was greatly impressed by Pound and perhaps flattered by his friendship. In a letter that year to Monro, who obviously felt Aldington listened to Pound far too much, Aldington says defensively: 'If I am so feeble-minded as to remain permanently under Pound's influence, God help me, I'm not worth bothering about. If I am so dull and stertorous-minded as not to be influenced by a man of Pound's intellect – then also God help me.'[97] There were, however, other influences. He was reading Walt Whitman, and rather unwillingly coming to like him, and although that interest was not to last long, Whitman was perhaps another pointer towards the potential of free verse. Reading Whitman's *Drumtaps* converted him to pacifism, again something that was not to last, though military regimentation was something that Aldington would always loathe. More significantly, he was to be deeply influenced by H.D., and together they fostered their love of the Greeks. Since Aldington was still too young – under twenty-one – to be allowed into the British Museum Reading Room, H.D. during her mornings there would copy out Greek poetry, including some of the newly discovered Sappho texts, for Aldington to translate, or for them to work on together.

IV

IN his article 'Prologomena', Pound had begun by saying that he 'would much rather lie on what is left of Catullus' parlour floor and speculate the azure beneath it and the hills off to Salo and Riva with their forgotten gods moving unhindered beneath them, than discuss any processes and theories of art whatsoever.'[98] Pound would repeatedly insist that it was better to read the poetic work itself than any critical exposition, though in practice he could rarely resist the missionary urge to explain what he was doing. Yet the reference to the 'forgotten gods moving un-hindered' under the Italian mountains is an indication that, in spite of the new emphasis on hardness and sanity, he had not lost his sense of the mystical power of the gods. In September 1911 he had met G.R.S. Mead, a friend of Yeats who had at one time been Madame Blavatsky's private secretary, and a leading member of the Theosophical Society until 1908, when he had resigned in protest against what he saw as char-latanism. Mead founded the Quest Society the next year, to 'promote investigation and comparative study of religion, science and philosophy, on the basis of experience' and 'to encourage the expression of the ideal in beautiful forms'.[99] Mead, like the theosophists, believed firmly in re-incarnation, though in his wish to bring science and religion together he was perhaps closer to the Society for Psychical Research. Pound, though never attracted by the notion of reincarnation, found his ideas fascinating – he told his mother that 'G.R.S. Mead is as interesting – along his own line – as any one I meet.'[100]

Mead must also have been interested by Pound, because he invited him to speak to the Society about his troubadour poets, an invitation Pound accepted with unusual apprehension; Dorothy reassuringly suggested he should claim to be a reincarnated troubadour, who *knew* what they thought: 'Are you? do you?' she asked.[101] If one believed in reincarnation it would certainly have seemed a feasible idea. The lecture was given early in 1912, and published in the *Quest* journal in October as 'Psychology and the Troubadours', and in fact its fusion of mysticism and science fitted in perfectly with the other pieces in the volume. When Pound reissued *The Spirit of Romance* in 1932, he included it as the fifth chapter, in a slightly revised form. It's an intriguing piece, bringing together many of the preoccupations that would last through to the end of the *Cantos*. The chapter has a subtitle in the 1932 edition, 'A Divagation from Questions of Technique', a description that could also apply to its place in his literary criticism of 1912, which otherwise is also largely preoccupied with 'questions of technique'. Pound had called the second part of 'Prologomena' a 'Credo', but he perhaps reveals even more of his emerging creed in 'Psychology and the Troubadours', in which, through a discussion of the 'inner significance' of the 'love code', he explores his own fundamental beliefs: art is the true religion, and artists priests. As he says, '"chivalric love" was, as I understand it, an art, that is to say, a religion'.[102]

The troubadours, Pound argues here, were visionaries with their own 'unofficial mysticism', finding their visions through the religion of love rather than the ascetic privations of medieval Christianity. 'Provençal song,' he writes, 'is never wholly disjunct from pagan rites of May Day.' The cult of Amor is an evolution from the 'Hellenistic mysteries', with their erotic core, and connected with a tradition of 'various cults or religions of orgy and of ecstasy, from the simpler Bacchanalia to the more complicated rites of Isis or Dionysus'. He quotes from Peire Vidal: 'Good lady, I think I see God when I gaze on your delicate body.'[103] Dante, though Pound does not mention him here, also bases his *Divine Comedy* on the idea that human love can lead to the divine, and sees God in Beatrice's eyes. But in Dante's case the love is a sublimated, transcendent and spiritual one, reconciling the cult of Amor and Christianity, while the Vidal line suggests an actual sexual encounter. Pound himself, in his earlier discussions of ecstasy, had favoured the Dantean visionary love, but later he would come to locate the heart of mystery in coitus itself. In 1912, his discussion remains very unclear; he had told Dorothy that he was going to be 'nebulous to Nth', and on this point he certainly is.[104] Perhaps at this stage he really was not quite sure what he thought, or possibly embarrassed to say. It is likely, as Humphrey Carpenter suggests, he was still a virgin when he married: he certainly got nowhere near Dorothy's bed, and apparently made no attempt to reach H.D.'s, so his view of the centrality of sex may have been fairly theoretical. Sex can be compared, he says, with a 'fluid force', by which he means energy, which can come as heat or light, just as sex can be either 'illumination', that is, a 'religious experience', or alternatively the 'philo-progenitive instinct', but the latter does not produce the former; they are separate and different manifestations. This distinction sounds as if he is still in Dante's camp, for all his quotation from Vidal.[105] Presumably, in Pound's analogy here, the philo-progenitive instinct is heat, and illumination, naturally enough, light. Even Pound's later celebrations of sexuality remain very much about what Lawrence would call 'sex in the head', literally so when Pound suggested in 1921 that the brain is 'only a sort of great clot of genital fluid held in suspense or reserve', a theory, he says, that 'would explain the enormous content of the brain as a maker or presenter of images', because 'the power of the spermatozoid is precisely the power of exteriorizing a form'.[106] Yet this egregiously masculinist concept is again celebrating artistic creativity by claiming for it the vital power of sexual fecundity, but by no means saying they are the same thing, or that one produces the other. In the *Cantos*, the Neoplatonic illumination and vision certainly win out. Pound was very much of his generation in feeling that sexuality must be the central force in life, but he remained too much of the Philadelphian puritan to express it in any but the most gingerly terms. Yeats was to say unkindly, many years later, that Pound remained 'the sexless American professor for all his violence'.[107]

By now the idea of energy or 'fluid force' was central to Pound's understanding of the world. Poetry, indeed all art, visions, sexuality, what Lawrence would call the 'circumambient universe', Pound had come to consider as dynamic and vitalised. We all know, he says, about our kinship with the animals; what we forget is 'our kinship to the vital universe, to the tree and the living rock . . . We have about us the universe of fluid force, and below us the germinal universe of wood alive, of stone alive . . . the strength of the Greek beauty rests in this, that it is ever at the interpretation of this vital universe, by its signs of gods and godly attendants and oreads.' Since the Renaissance, however, 'Man is concerned with man and forgets the whole and the flowing . . . when we do get into contemplation of the flowing we find sex.' Pound's vision of the vital universe is quite compatible with Bergson's, and indeed he uses the Bergsonian term 'life-force' at one stage in 'Psychology and the Troubadours', though again it is unlikely that Pound thought of his beliefs as Bergsonian.[108] What constantly fascinated him was the project of bringing together poetry, science and mysticism, or, as he would sometimes describe that last, ecstatic religion. In 'Psychology and the Troubadours', he talks of electrical currents and the workings of the telegraph (Ford must have told him his Marconi story), both leaping across distances to bring, in different senses, illumination. Yeats was also developing his interests in psychical research yet further at this time, speaking during January 1912 on a theory of apparitions to both the Society for Psychical Research and the Quest Society. Like Pound, his project was a synthesising one: science, poetry and the occult (in whatever form) all in one.

Around the time he gave this lecture to the Quest Society in early 1912, Pound was, much to his delight, introduced by Ford to Henry James, now sixty-nine. Pound had referred to his exemplary prose in 'Prologomena', though he had not read much of it as yet, but he knew him as the grand old man of American letters, and a fellow literary expatriate. Pound was deeply impressed, writing six years later of his 'wonderful conversation':

The massive head, the slow uplift of the hand, *gli occhi onesti e tardi*, the long sentences piling themselves up in elaborate phrase after phrase, the lightning incision, the pauses, the slightly shaking admonitory gesture with it 'wu-a-wait a little, wait a little, something will come'; blague and benignity and the weight of so many years' careful incessant labour of minute observation always there to enrich the talk. I had heard it but seldom, yet it is all unforgettable.[109]

James was to confirm him in his view that the only place for an American artist was in exile, and he would shortly be reporting that 'the distinguished American author' had said to him, 'It is strange how all taint of art or letters seems to shun that continent'.[110] Pound started reading James in earnest the following August, and came to admire passionately James' depiction of America, and increasingly his analysis of Europe, later claiming that only an expatriate American could really appreciate his writing. James would influence some of his poetry, as he did T.S. Eliot's; the most Jamesian poem Pound wrote was perhaps his 1920 farewell to London, *Hugh Selwyn Mauberley*, which takes another of the themes that Pound found fascinating in James, his depiction of the self-deceptions and limitations of what Pound describes as the 'literary milieux'.[111] Already by 1913, when Pound decided to try his hand at satire, James was one of his models, though he also drew on the much raunchier Catullus. James surely lies behind a poem like 'The Garden':

> In her is the end of breeding.
> Her boredom is exquisite and excessive.
> She would like some one to speak to her,
> And is almost afraid that I
> > will commit that indiscretion.[112]

From now on James joined Whistler in Pound's pantheon as one of the few great American artists; both of them, of course, had worked in Europe.

In March, Pound wrote once more to Hope, pointing out that his annual income was now about £400: £200 from Margaret Cravens, though he was still refusing to reveal the source to Hope, £100 from his publishers, Stephen Swift & Co., guaranteed as long as he produced 60,000 words in book form per year – he claimed he could easily produce that number of words in two months – and £100 from his other writing. He admitted that this might not seem to the Shakespears a large sum for a married couple to live on in England, but Dorothy 'seems to think she could live abroad for a year or so' where money would go further, adding that she would 'see a number of things & places which she probably could not see if [he] were tied to an educational position'.[113] Clearly the Shakespears, like his parents, were keen for him to have the financial security of an academic appointment, and he was as reluctant as ever to take on a regular job. Nothing came of this letter, except that Olivia suggested that Pound should get the Society for the Protection of Authors to check his contract; the next year, Dorothy went for a visit to Rome with her mother and cousin and close friend Georgie Hyde-Lees, so perhaps they took the hint about more foreign travel, even if Pound was not to be allowed to go too. Dorothy told him that her mother 'evidently thinks we are a somewhat crazy couple – which is just what we aren't. Perhaps you wish we were.'[114] That sounds rather regretful, but if Dorothy's devotion to Pound cannot be questioned, her observation of family proprieties was steely. Pound gave no sign of desperation. Things went on as before, though he began to make plans to spend the summer in France. It is possible Olivia and Hope wanted Pound and Dorothy to separate for a while. H.D. recalled something of the sort many years later.

As Pound had mentioned in his letter to Hope, he was at the time giving some well-paid afternoon lectures on medieval poetry in the private gallery of Lord and Lady Glenconner, who lived in Queen Anne's Gate. They probably used much the same material as his *New Age*

'Troubadour Romance', as one was on Cavalcanti, one on Daniel and one on Anglo-Saxon verse, and the advertisement for the series said that they would 'be considered, in part, in their possible relation to the Art of to-day'.[115] The second of these, on 19 March, Dorothy missed – being at the dentist at the time – but that same evening she went to hear the leader of the Italian Futurists, Filippo Marinetti, lecture in his breakneck French on the Futurists in the Bechstein (now Wigmore) Hall. Pound apparently did not go, though he could not have missed the impact that Marinetti was making, attracting horrified and excited coverage in the press. Marinetti was a master of publicity, with his dramatic speeches, noisy accompaniments, and extremist views. Harold Monro admired him for his success in taking poetry to the people, though he did not agree with his worship of speed and machinery. *The Times* reported that 'Signor Marinetti, founder of the Futurist movement, gave a lecture in French on Futurism in literature and art. He read his lecture in French with such an impassioned torrent of words that some of his audience begged for mercy, and of his sincerity there can be no question, but his doctrines are a morbid form of destructive revolution. There is no beauty, according to the Futurists, except in violence and strife: every museum and all the great works of the past should be utterly swept away.'[116] These sentiments are not ones that Pound would ever share, but Lawrence Rainey has suggested Pound must have been struck by the contrast between his own old-fashioned reliance on patronage and Marinetti's astute playing to the marketplace, between his *passéiste* concern with literary relics, and Marinetti's denunciation of the past and zeal for the new and machine-like, between his limited audience and Marinetti's celebrity. It was this, Rainey suggests, that drove Pound to invent imagism at that moment, by analogy with Futurism.[117] There is, however, no evidence that Pound had any such thoughts, or that he was yet planning what Aldington would call his '*mouvemong*'.[118] In his 'Prologomena', he had denied that he was part of any movement, unless one started by Swinburne in the return to poetry as 'pure art', and argues that 'only after a long struggle will poetry attain such a degree of development, or if you will, modernity, that it will vitally concern people who are accustomed, in prose, to Henry James and Anatole France, in music to De Bussy. I am constantly contending that it took two centuries of Provence and one of Tuscany to develop the media of Dante's masterwork, that it took the latinists of the Renaissance, and the Pleiade, and his own age of painted speech to prepare Shakespeare his tools.'[119] It is true that by the following

August Pound would have changed, but in the meantime he was wary of modernity. Rainey's justification for suggesting this moment for the birth of imagism is that the first mention of 'les imagistes' appeared in *Ripostes*, in a note appended to 'The Complete Poetical Works of T.E. Hulme', and Pound sent *Ripostes* off to the publishers shortly after Marinetti's lecture. Pound, however, did not deal with the final set of proofs for the volume until August. By that time things had changed, and, as will appear, the evidence shows he invented imagism then.

The first Futurist exhibition in London had opened on 1 March 1912, at the Sackville Gallery, and although Pound does not appear to have gone, his interest in modern art was belatedly arising. He had been introduced to the work of Jacob Epstein, almost certainly by Hulme, and was deeply impressed.[120] He wrote home to his parents, 'I'm not sure the little Jew hasn't more real strength than Rodin'. He was struck by a 'very fine sun-god' that Epstein had carved, which he reported might have been 'exkavated from Babylon & not questioned as to authenticity'.[121] (Richard Cork, probably correctly, identifies the model as Egyptian, but Epstein was also influenced by ancient Assyrian art.) Epstein, unlike Marinetti, was Pound's kind of modern artist: rather than embracing all that Pound found objectionable in the modern world, he returned to earlier forms, the seed-time of cultures as Pound later put it, in order to capture something that gives life again to art. Pound was also making his first discoveries in modern French poetry, telling his parents that Flint had put him on to 'some very good contemporary French stuff' and mentioning the names of Henri de Régnier and Rémy de Gourmont.[122] It was skilfully planned by Flint, because they were both poets who drew on the past, so likely to appeal to Pound in a way other modern poets would not. Rémy de Gourmont was deeply interested in the Latin Middle Ages, and one of the collections Pound and his fellow-imagists came to admire particularly was *Le Livre des litanies*, in which, Pound would say in 1913, de Gourmont made the 'most valuable contribution to the development of the strophe' since Arnaut Daniel.[123] De Gourmont here uses the rhythmic form of a Christian litany for his own secular poetry; Pound quotes from 'La Litanie de la rose':

Rose couleur de cuivre, plus frauduleuse que nos joies, rose couleur de cuivre embaume-nous dans tes mensonges, fleur hypocrite, fleur du silence.

Rose au visage peint comme une fille d'amour, rose au coeur prostitué, rose au visage peint, fais semblant [*sic*] d'être pitoyable, fleur hypocrite, fleur du silence.[124]

This technique of the repetition of words and of what the French *vers libre* poets called rhythmic constants was a feature of much of their writing, and this litany-like repetition appears in much imagist verse, especially perhaps that of H.D. Her flower poems with their subversion of traditional 'flowery', feminised associations may owe something to de Gourmont's poetry in subject-matter as well as form, as in her poem 'Garden', when she writes of a 'rose, cut in rock,/hard as the descent of hail,/ If I could break you/I could break a tree.'[125] But the book by de Gourmont that first seized Pound's imagination was his anthology of medieval Latin poetry, *Le Latin mystique*, which to his delight bore out his arguments about the fusion of religious and sexual passion in 'Psychology and the Troubadours'. Whether or not he discovered this in time to mention it in his lecture to the Quest Society that spring, he certainly quoted from it in the written-up version that appeared in their journal that October.[126]

Equally influential would be the other poet recommended by Flint, Henri de Régnier. René Taupin points out that the poem Pound wrote later that month, 'The Return', is based on his 'Médailles d'argile', one of his poems known as the 'Odelettes', which Flint particularly admired. Taupin goes so far as to describe Pound's poem as a conscious imitation, though it is scarcely close enough to assert that, but the movement of the verse is strikingly similar, and the content related.[127] In 'Médailles d'argile', de Régnier suggests his poems are, as it were, spoken to him by the gods, the forces behind the vital universe, intuited by the poet. In 'The Return', Pound's gods are also the vital forces that make poetry possible, though in his case they are re-emerging after a long period of defeat. He is going back to Pater's assertion that Provençal poetry arose at the moment which saw 'the return of that ancient Venus, not dead, but only hidden for a time in the caves of the Venusberg, of those old pagan gods still going to and fro on the earth, under all sorts of disguises', an idea which had also been lurking behind his 'Psychology and the Troubadours' lecture, and his claim there that 'Provençal song is never wholly disjunct from pagan rites'.[128] Once more, Pound suggests, the gods are returning to make poetry possible. 'The Return' is a poem that has been seen as Pound's first hesitant claim to be on the brink of discovering a new and powerful way to write poetry:

> See, they return; ah, see the tentative
> Movements, and the slow feet,

> The trouble in the pace and the uncertain
> Wavering!

Pound's poem uses de Régnier's short, broken, slow moving lines and his habit of direct address. 'Alors j'ai dit: Voici des flûtes et des corbeilles,/ Mordez aux fruits . . . J'ai dit encor: Écoute.'[129] Where de Régnier tells his readers to listen ('Écoute/Écoute') Pound instructs his to 'See'. The imagery of movement, feet and pace can, it has been pointed out, refer either to the returning gods or to poetry. The uncertain, slow movements of the returning gods are embodied in the breaks and hesitancies of the form:

> See, they return, one, and by one,
> With fear, as half-awakened;
> As if the snow should hesitate
> And murmur in the wind,
>   and half turn back;
> These were the 'Wing'd-with-Awe,'
>   Inviolable.
>
> Gods of the wingèd shoe![130]

De Régnier's gods too were counted 'une à une'. The god with wingèd shoes was of course Hermes, who, as well as being the messenger of the gods, was, in his Egyptian form, Thoth, the scribe of the gods and the inventor of writing, perhaps why Pound invokes him here. Nowadays this poem is seen as a brilliant example of cadenced free verse, and Pound himself two years later would republish it in the anthology *Des Imagistes*, but at the time he described it to Dorothy as another experiment in 'sapphics'. He would later compare this poem with Epstein's Sun-God, and it is possible that Epstein's Sun-God, with its return to the simplicity and power of ancient forms, had a direct influence on the poem, which too is re-invoking ancient forms and beliefs.[131] Pound must have been delighted when Yeats, who admired 'The Return' greatly, said that it read as if Pound 'were translating at sight from an unknown Greek masterpiece'.[132] That was undoubtedly the effect for which Pound was trying, and that he had admired so much in Epstein's carving, which could have been 'exkavated from Babylon & not questioned as to authenticity', a creation of something powerful, simplified, harking back to elemental forces that felt more vital and intense than the febrile modern age. 'The Return' is a move away from his persona poems, but it keeps their direct voice. Pound described it as a poem about 'objective reality', by which he means it is a poem that centres on the description of a scene, rather than on the psychological state or consciousness of the speaker. 'Objective reality' is in some ways an odd expression for this mythic scene, but Pound would have agreed with H.D. when she later wrote, 'Mythology is actuality, as we now know.'[133]

That spring, H.D and Aldington both moved into Church Walk, having separate rooms in number 6. Pound appeared delighted by this – doubtless he had engineered it, and he would soon begin to treat them as his poetic children. Richard and H.D. were seeing each other a good deal. Aldington, as Brigit correctly surmised, had been attracted to H.D. from the start; in a letter written from the front in 1918 he recalls the first time he surreptitiously touched her little finger at one of Brigit's parties. His open admiration of not only herself but also her poetry touched H.D., whose poetic efforts were still being ignored by Pound, though by now he appears to have been discussing poetry with the two of them. Aldington loved her passion for beautiful things; they both spent a good deal of time sketching in the South Kensington Museum, as the Victoria & Albert continued to be known. They were true heirs of the Pre-Raphaelites and the aesthetes, passionate about beauty and the power of art, dismayed at the ugliness of modern industrial society. Aldington shared H.D.'s love of the natural world and flowers, and they visited the Kent countryside together with Brigit. Perhaps because Aldington was so much younger, H.D. was, at any rate to start with, less aware of any tendency towards the kind of masculinist domination that Pound took for granted as his right. Aldington neither patronised her nor put on airs. He knew that she was, as Brigit put it, the 'chosen friend' of Pound, from which she may have acquired a certain glamour in his eyes, but he does not appear to have worried about him as a rival.[134] Richard always had enormous sexual self-confidence. In *Death of a Hero*, Pound appears as Mr Upjohn, of whom the narrator says, 'While gallantly and probably necessarily discreet as to his conquests, he was always prepared to talk about love and give subtle erotic advice, which led any man who had actually lain with a woman to suspect that Mr Upjohn was at best a fumbler and probably still a virgin.'[135] While it's unlikely that Aldington was quite so dismissive of Pound in the early days of his discipleship, he appears to have been in no way inhibited by the possibility that Pound wanted a relationship with H.D. Pound, indeed, from the beginning was keen to bring Aldington and H.D.

together; a neat solution from his point of view, though he appears to have expected to retain the proprietary right to demand kisses from H.D. when he felt like it. H.D., for her part, in her strange limbo of uncertainty about what she felt about Pound, or he about her, was charmed by Aldington's warm, exuberant admiration. All the same, when Rummel broke the news that spring of Pound's engagement, she was devastated.

It is highly unlikely Pound had mentioned the engagement to Walter himself; Pound rarely spoke of his personal affairs to his male friends, certainly not if he could avoid it. Walter had been told by Olivia Shakespear, with whom, according to H.D., he had become a great favourite. As H.D. writes in *End to Torment*, 'Walter said, "I think I ought to tell you, though I promised Mrs Shakespear not to, – don't let her know or anyone. But there is an understanding. Ezra is to marry Dorothy Shakespear. He shouldn't tell other people or imply to other people that he – that you –".'[136] When in the 1950s Erich Heydt asked her how she had felt on hearing that, she replied, 'Look – it's impossible to say. I felt bleak, a chasm opened . . . I don't know what I felt.'[137] In the fictional account in *Asphodel*, she does tentatively rebuke him: 'don't you think, George, it was just a little, just a little – odd . . . I mean if you were engaged all that time – to – kiss me . . . you might have told me.' George is unrepentant: 'Well, Dryad as I never see my – ah – fiancée save when surrounded by layers of its mother, by its family portraits, by its own inhibitions, by the especial curve of the spiral of the social scale it belongs to, I think you might be – affable.'[138] The phraseology is certainly pure Pound. Yet in the fictional version, as in *End to Torment*, the rupture sets her free to be a writer. George had continued to disparage Hermione's poetry: '*You are a poem though your poem's naught*. Why should she have questioned. Striven. George would write for them both.'[139] It is Darrington, the Aldington figure, who praises and encourages her poetry, and who is the person to whom she turns.

V

IN April, H.D. had another blow, which may have hit even harder, though in the general maelstrom of her tangled emotions it is hard to weigh up the relative shocks to her system. She received a letter from Frances, telling her that she was getting married and would shortly be arriving in England on her way to her honeymoon in Venice. H.D. was shaken and confused. If, as seems likely, she had only just learnt of Pound's engagement, here was surely another desertion. According to her son, Frances had prophesied to H.D. that she would return in 1912 with a husband. As H.D. recounts the story in *End to Torment*, Frances wrote to her that 'one of the objects of her marriage . . . in fact the chief object' was to be with H.D. again.[140] Her husband was going to lecture in Belgium and they could all go there together. Yet the fictional version of the letter in *Paint it Today* is more abrupt – no hint of continued desire for H.D., only a postscript which says 'Perhaps some day Wee Witches will grow up.'[141] H.D. was always sensitive and indignant at the Freudian interpretation of lesbian desire as immature; if Frances then or later said something like this, it would have cut deep. Yet whatever the letter said, when Frances and her husband Louis Wilkinson arrived in London, they immediately asked H.D. to go to Europe with them, to accompany them, in fact, on their honeymoon.

As such an invitation might indicate, it was an unusual marriage, but not in any straightforward way a sham, as some of H.D.'s biographers suggest. Louis Wilkinson, who would later become a novelist, memoir-writer and broadcaster, was British, and had, like Harold Monro, attended Radley School, though he was a little younger and only appears to have got to know him later. Wilkinson was the son of a clergyman, though not one of orthodox views. Even as a schoolboy Louis was a rebel, and had corresponded with Oscar Wilde in prison, at the height of his infamy. He became a close though at times abrasive friend of the three Powys brothers, later famous writers.[142] The middle brother of the three, Theodore (born 1875), had also been at Radley but was six years older than Louis so not exactly a friend, though Wikinson always admired him.[143] Louis went on to Oxford, where his passions were said to be Swinburne and poker, but was sent down with a group of others for 'blasphemy', the word referring to their celebration of Black Masses, as the authorities saw them, or 'mock masses' as the agnostic Louis described them. There was also homosexuality involved, Louis at the time being a practising homosexual, according to his son, 'out of indignation at Wilde's persecution and prosecution'.[144] The university authorities, for their own sake, drew a veil over that. During the following summer (he was by then nineteen) he met the eldest Powys brother, John Cowper (born 1872), an extraordinarily handsome and striking-looking man, as well as a spellbinding speaker. Louis wrote that he was enthralled with him: 'I had never met anyone at all like him; I could, indeed, hardly believe he was real'.[145]

Louis managed with some difficulty to get himself accepted for a new start at St John's College, Cambridge, where he met the youngest Powys, Llewelyn (born 1884), with whom he became close friends. For a while it was a 'romantic friendship', as Louis describes it, but he was soon to decide he was really heterosexual, though still indignant at Wilde's treatment, and at much else. He remained an advocate for the decriminalisation of homosexuality all his life. Through Llewelyn he once more met John Cowper Powys, who since 1904 had begun to go each winter to Philadelphia to give University Extension Lectures, becoming a particular favourite of the well-to-do ladies who flocked to his courses. Lectures like these paid a good deal better than such work in England, and he suggested that Louis might like to try his hand, which he did with almost as great success. Louis, named the Archangel by the Powys brothers, was also very handsome, with masses of auburn curly hair, rather like Pound, and, like John Cowper, a fine lecturer. Their audiences loved their Britishness (John always lectured in his Cambridge gown) and saw them, according to Louis, as 'an imported luxury, like English marmalade or Worcester Sauce'.[146] Llewelyn also tried his luck, but he was a poor speaker and desperately shy. He soon gave up the attempt, after causing Louis and John agonies of embarrassment on his behalf.

These lectures were among those Frances and H.D. had attended together, and on at least one occasion Pound had gone with them to hear John Cowper Powys during his 1910–11 visit. After her return home Frances started to attend once more, going up to speak to John after one lecture, taking with her a poem that she had written. John fell immediately and besottedly in love with her, and remained so for many years. He was impressed by her poem, which was certainly a striking and curious one, called 'Perché', which she published in 1915. Gothic and eerie, it is, perhaps, about her sense of being out of place in Philadelphia, or indeed anywhere: 'I who possess and am possessed, *Am I born and dead?*'[147] John was entranced. He was, however, already married, though the marriage had not been a success, and he lived separately from his wife Margaret for most of the time. (In Wilkinson's novel *The Buffoon*, someone says to the John Cowper Powys figure, there named Jack Welsh, 'no-one could be less married by marriage than you are'.)[148] After getting married John had found himself revolted by the prospect of a sexual relationship with a woman, and although he made passionate love to Frances, it was without penetration, something for which he had no desire. He persuaded Louis that he should marry the ravishing Frances, so at least she should be kept within his sphere.

Louis appears to have fallen in with this plan with little demur. He had gone back to the States in the autumn of 1911 feeling the time had come to get married – a feeling he later blamed on having read too much Hardy in England over the summer (a surprising response to Hardy, to say the least). His sexual behaviour since he had left university gives a curious insight into the social and moral niceties observed by a well-bred Englishman of his day. He accepted without question that he must not tamper with the honour of women of his own class, so, fancying neither prostitutes nor celibacy, he had a series of sexual partners who were shop girls or office workers – not, he stresses, factory girls. If any of them hoped for a more permanent bond, Louis did not notice, though, conveniently for him, they thought it would be below *their* station to accept money. (Such easygoing young women, known as 'charity girls' because they did it for free, or at any rate only for 'treats' or presents, were well known to the social purity campaigners of their day, who shook their heads sadly over such laxity.)[149] But, Louis says, he had decided 'this unromantic, disjointed, sensually spasmodic way of life of his could not go on'.[150] If the account in *The Buffoon* can be believed on this point, it appears that John expended all his eloquence in making sure Louis was pretty enamoured even before he was introduced to Frances. They married within three weeks of their first meeting. Louis, whom John later described as having 'an irresponsible and heathen zest for adventure', perhaps felt that if he was to marry, doing it in such a whirlwind and dashing manner was the most appropriate fashion.[151] It was decided, Frances' son says, by all 'interested' parties, including Frances and her mother, that the marriage should not be consummated for some months, probably because John felt so jealous, though it might have been an insurance in case the marriage proved an immediate disaster, as annulment of an unconsummated marriage would be comparatively easy.[152] Whether such an agreement was made, and if made, adhered to, one can only guess. Frances was desperate to get away from Philadelphia, and this was an ideal opportunity. Louis was at this stage in love with Frances, as he confirmed later, even if less deliriously in love than John, and he found Frances both attractive and intriguing. It does not appear, as is sometimes assumed – for example by Raymond (the Pound figure) in *Paint it Today* – that John wanted Louis to marry Frances in name only while she became his mistress. Even when some years later Frances left Louis for a few months and went to live with John, they did not become lovers.[153] Louis perhaps did have reservations or apprehensions about the match. He claimed later he went into it looking for 'romance', 'poetic passion' and constancy, but according to Richard Graves, the biographer of the Powys brothers, he had made Frances agree to let him have his sexual freedom after marriage. Oliver says Frances was happy with this arrangement, though she told Louis she herself would be faithful and that her main aim was to have children. Yet the anger that Louis felt when the marriage failed (Frances divorced him in 1923) suggests he had no thought of that outcome. It was, he wrote, 'the most defeating experience of [his] life'.[154]

None of the complex background of this marriage was known to H.D., who met Frances, Louis, John Cowper Powys, Louis' mother and others at Victoria Station Hotel. Ezra, Richard and Brigit came too. ('I had talked much of her,' she explains in her autobiographical notes.)[155] H.D. readily agreed to go with Frances. It was now clear that her relationship with Pound was going nowhere, and although she was seeing a good deal of Aldington, she was still quite uncertain how she felt about him. Pound, however, discovered the plan. Frances had also arranged a rendezvous with him, in which he was told about the arrangement, and possibly more. As H.D. came out of her lodgings to go to Victoria to meet them, she found a furious Pound on the pavement. 'He began, "I as your nearest male relation . . ." and hailed a taxi. He pushed me in, he banged his stick, pounding (*Pounding*) . . . "You are not going with them . . . There is a vague chance the Egg . . . may be happy. You will spoil everything.'"[156] At Victoria station, to everyone's embarrassment, especially her own, H.D. explained that she would not after all accompany the newly-weds. They made their farewells. 'Glowering and savage, Ezra waited till the train pulled out.'[157] John Cowper Powys and another of Louis' friends were, she said, 'very curt with me, "a boy wouldn't have done that", that is, let F. down at the last'.[158]

What were Pound's motives? Genuine concern for Frances? Perhaps. Genuine concern for H.D.? She was after all meant to be staying with respectable acquaintances of the Doolittles in London, not wandering the continent with her 'unwholesome' friend, as she is described by her family in *Paint it Today*. In that novel, Raymond has had a whiff of the Powys connection, and decides H.D. had been invited as a '*bon bouche*' (*sic*) for the husband, and that he was entirely justified in saving her from this moral danger.[159] Perhaps that was what Pound came to believe. But there was surely an element in this of a power struggle over H.D. He wasn't after all going to marry her, but he wasn't going to surrender her to Frances either. The sense of complete humiliation with which H.D. was left suggests that was how she felt about it. Her family – in this case the self-appointed substitute family – had defeated her again.

What about Frances' motivations? Why did she marry Louis? He was charismatic and entertaining, though perhaps she had fallen in love with the distinguished, spellbinding John and just wanted to be near him. Like Louis, of course, Frances had 'an irresponsible and heathen zest for adventure'. Life at home with her mother could scarcely compete, though such was the complicated nature of their relationship that she spent much of the voyage to England in floods of tears because she missed her so acutely, and would rarely be parted from her again. It has been suggested that she was really in love with Llewelyn, who was the same age as her; John was twelve years older. She had heard Llewelyn give one of his disastrous lectures in 1909, when he had last been in the States, and, it was said, had kept a picture of him in a poetry anthology next to a poem by Shelley that he had read. Perhaps she felt sorry for him. But it hardly adds up to a reason for marrying his friend without even trying to see him again first. Llewelyn himself was, as a matter of fact, greatly flattered when he learnt about the photograph. John had written to him from the States about his own passion for Frances, and, having crossed with Frances and Louis, he visited Llewelyn in the country and rounded him up for the honeymoon trip. Llewelyn was suffering from consumption, not really well enough to travel, but John swept him off to Venice, where he had arranged to rejoin Frances and Louis. Llewelyn was equally entranced by Frances: the four of them went round Venice together, and, as John later wrote,

[their] heads were completely turned. She insisted on dressing up as a boy; and we would accompany her in her gondola in this attire to the remotest possible spots where gondolas could be propelled ... The feelings that this beautiful girl in boy's clothes excited in me rose like flames ... [T]hrilled ... with the ambiguous beauty of this boy-girl ... I was without any doubt as completely enslaved ... as far as my peculiar type of heart, the heart of a cerebral idolator, *could* be enslaved by a human woman.

His enslavement, and 'desire not to break one link of this enchanted spell', was made all the more profound by 'our white-admiral's flutterings, now in the direction of Llewelyn, now in that of Louis'.[160]

As far as Frances is concerned, all this suggests that she was a little in love with all of them, and very much in love with being the idol of these ecstatic lovers. H.D. was to have been invited, one guesses, as another adorer, part of Frances' court, not to be courted by anyone else. Llewelyn paid for the Venetian visit with a serious relapse, much to John's remorse, but neither of them regretted it; it was, John said, 'a unique experience in both our lives'.[161] Louis' tolerance of the Powys brothers' interest in his wife might be taken to indicate indifference on his part, but Louis was never indifferent to Frances. He seemed delighted that the three of them shared this bond. Frances was clearly a captivating woman, but it is hard not to infer that at one level of this *folie à trois* this boy-girl was a token of a deep if now unacknowledged homosexual attachment between the three men. In a fictional depiction of Frances, John Cowper Powys describes her 'slender equivocal figure', and her androgynous looks were obviously part of her attraction. Louis many years later mentions this Venice visit, almost excising Frances from the narrative – perhaps not surprisingly as by then he hated her – but more tellingly emphasising how totally absorbed by John's company he and Llewelyn had been there.[162]

But to return to the disconsolate H.D. After Frances had left, she decided to escape to Paris, too bruised and cast down to face anyone in London. She left England at the beginning of May. Pound, as it happened, headed for France at almost the same time. He had gone up to Cambridge to give a lecture for Hulme on 27 April, Hulme having now been readmitted to Cambridge with a glowing reference from none other than Henri Bergson himself. Pound set out for Paris as soon as he returned.

POUND and H.D.'s near simultaneous departures in early May 1912 from London to Paris were, it seems, entirely coincidental. Pound was on his way to the walking tour in troubadour country that he had planned, which he intended to write up as a travel book on the lines of Campbell's *Mearing Stones*; he would not, he told his mother, be back until October. Dorothy was sad, but the rest of her family were greatly relieved. Dorothy told Pound after he had left that 'H.H.S's [Mr Shakespear's] only comment on your early visit on Wedy. was "I thought he was going abroad". I believe he had been under the impression, for a week at least, that you were safely awa'."[163] Pound was intending to spend a few weeks in Paris, thereafter moving south to the areas of France where the Provençal poets had lived – not simply the region we know as Provence today, and in fact only touching its western borders, but a great swathe of south-western France. The written account of his travels was to be the next book for Swift & Co.; he rather perplexingly gave it the working title of 'Gironde', after the vast estuary at Bordeaux formed by the confluence of the Dordogne and the Garonne rivers, in spite of the fact that he never actually went there. Perhaps the word worked for him as a shorthand for the whole region; apart from a brief visit to the Rhône valley and the Mediterranean coast, his journey was mainly in the water basin which empties into the sea through the Gironde.

H.D. was apparently unaware that Pound was to be in Paris, though she found out soon after she arrived. Ironically, one reason for her flight was to disprove the Powyses' implied (or possibly imagined) accusation that she was rejecting Frances for Pound. After the humiliation of the showdown over Frances, she had been anxious to bury herself in the comparative anonymity of a city in which she belonged to no social network. She was shocked and directionless, cross with Pound, wounded by Frances, maligned by Frances' new friends. Both Pound and Frances had rejected her, and if perhaps she might have felt her relationship with Aldington had held the promise of a new beginning, she was for now re-engulfed by the sense of failure that she had felt so strongly back in Philadelphia. A diary survives from that visit to Paris, the only one for her pre-war years. It is written in intense, disjointed, poetic phrases. It uses trees, wind, sea imagery, weather of all sorts, to convey her psychological state – in other words, it is very much like her early poetry. The first dozen or so pages have been cut out, but it is clear from the first remaining entry, which is for 15 May, that those earlier entries were recording the unhappiness of her first few days there, when she had felt 'despair so many morning [*sic*] as I woke, and saw the gold-gold of sun and was not of it'.[164]

She was not entirely solitary of course. She saw Rummel, who, having told her of Pound's secret engagement, now turned out, she discovered, to have a secret engagement of his own. The announcement of his impending marriage to the pianist Thérèse Chaigneau was made a few weeks after her arrival. Through Rummel, she met Margaret Cravens, to whom she felt drawn; although she was only to know her for a month, Margaret's memory haunted her for the rest of her life. In her own state of confused pain, she understood something of the emotional stress that Margaret was experiencing. Unlike Pound, who, sympathetic as he might be to Margaret's depressions, never appears to have thought about Margaret as an artist, H.D. recognised immediately both Margaret's desire to succeed in her art, her reason, after all, for being in Paris, and her anxieties about her progress as a pianist. H.D. herself only saw Pound a couple of times during the first fortnight of May; he was deliberately avoiding her, she thought – quite possible, of course; Pound may have wished to show that he had not snatched her from Frances to bind her to himself. H.D. suspected that he was seeing a good deal of Margaret, and wondered whether he was dallying with Margaret's affections as he had with her own. She never discovered that Margaret had known about Dorothy since the previous year, though that in itself doesn't preclude the possibility that Pound was, as she feared, exploiting Margaret's affection for him rather cruelly, or at any rate thoughtlessly, even if not in the way H.D. thought. Margaret, as a young American woman who, like H.D. herself, had escaped to Europe in the quest for an artistic career, uncertain and unconfident of her future, came to represent poignantly to H.D. the pains and difficulties of women artists at that time, the struggle for self-belief, the damage so easily inflicted by the insensitivity, bullying or exploitation of the male artists that they met. In *Asphodel*, the Margaret character, there called Shirley Thornton, described as 'very kind' as well as 'clever', is on one occasion deeply hurt when George Lowndes dismisses her piano-playing, just as he so brutally dismisses Hermione's 'pomes'. Hermione had asked Shirley to play, and George says, 'Gawd, don't ask her.'

Shirley looked up an odd twist to her fine straight eye-brows. A white flame of pain crossed her eyes, dark eyes, wide apart staring like a crystal gazer's. Why had George said that? Was he being rude simply? But now his rudeness seemed insanity, seemed blatant cruelty. His rudeness, his casual approach to both of them, for she was sure he had kissed, had been long kissing Shirley. Don't marry him or her – just go on kissing them . . . Wide flame of pain in the almond eyes of Shirley flashed, went, and the almond eyes of Shirley were just odd almond eyes with a little glow of passion. 'O George is like that. He thinks I play so badly.'[165]

The situation is saved by Darrington, the Aldington figure, saying some-thing kind and encouraging to Shirley, as he had to Hermione about her writing.

Aldington had arrived in Paris in mid-May, and, as her diary records, everything changed for H.D. The entry quoted earlier for 15 May goes on:

As if after great turmoil – confusion – weariness . . . Richard has come! . . . last night all the city was a new thing – revisited as one falls first upon ones first old city – to me for the first time.

Aldington had never been to Paris before, his continental visits having been limited largely to day trips from Dover. He was taking a certain finan-cial risk in coming, as it meant giving up his sports reporting, which helped his income considerably. But ever since his friendship with Mr Grey he had wanted to visit this artistic mecca. And he wanted to see H.D. When H.D. had first arrived in Paris, she had stayed in lodgings which she had shared with the Greggs in the rue Jacob (where, incidentally, the flamboyant Natalie Barney lived, in whose salon Pound would in 1922 meet Olga Rudge, the future mother of his daughter). Now H.D. was staying more centrally, in the rue de la Chaumière, and, with Aldington, she visited the Louvre day after day, sketching, making notes and writing poems. Some of these were in sonnet form, but by June her diary also contains attempts to break her fragmented, stream-of-consciousness entries into very brief lines, so that they look something like her later poems. She, like Pound, had been reading French *vers libre*, in particular Henri de Régnier, and in later life recalled her pleasure at reading him there with

Aldington. When Norman Holmes Pearson, the young scholar who became such a friend and support in her later years, asked her in the 1930s how she wrote her early poetry, she told him that 'I let my pencil run riot, in those early days of my apprenticeship, in a school copy-book . . . Then I would select from many lines of automatic or pseudo-automatic writing, the few lines that satisfied me.' She talked then about doing this in 'a dark London, autumn 1912', but the diary suggests that she had already begun that 'pseudo-automatic writing' in the Parisian summer, even though she may at that stage have found no lines at all to satisfy her.[166] She mentions in the diary that she has Flint's poems with her, suggesting that she now treated him with some respect as a poet, and it seems his recommended reading as well. De Régnier's poetry may have paved the way for both her and Aldington to move further from formal metre. Although Aldington always claimed he came to imagism purely through the Greeks, the abandonment of regular line length, and the subtler use of cadence and repetition present in his poetry by the autumn of 1912, could well have come from the French poet.

One other object H.D. mentions that she had in her room in Paris, on the same table as Flint's poems, is a 'little Venus di Milo R. brought from London'. Whether this was a small replica or just a postcard isn't clear. The Venus di Milo was one of the statues H.D. most admired, and she studied its graceful form for many hours in the Louvre, how 'the curve of the white belly and short space before the breasts brought the curve to a sudden shadow', as it is put in *Paint it Today*.[167] She had seen it earlier with Frances; she had told Aldington about their love affair, which he accepted quite non-judgementally, and the present of the Venus di Milo may relate to that. Aldington's tolerance of her bisexuality must have been very comforting at the time; it wasn't something that she had from Pound, though Aldington's reasons for tolerance were perhaps rather dubious; he was deeply homophobic when it came to gay male relationships, but found the idea of lesbianism quite erotic. Aldington would continue, long after they separated, to send H.D. postcards of female nudes, classical and other-wise. But in 1912, H.D. was his Venus; he sent his father, who thought he was on a purely cultural visit, a postcard dated 23 May, which clearly carried more than one level of meaning: 'I spend many hours with the Venus.'[168]

There is no doubt that by this time he and H.D. were very much in love. Gratitude for his belief in her poetry, as well as for his supporting warmth after her emotional traumas of the spring, played an important part in her feelings for him, but there was also their shared delight on the one hand in the Greek past, on the other in the natural world, as well as a passionate commitment to their artistic goals. In her later fiction, written after the painful end of their relationship, H.D. tends to downplay the strength of their early attachment. In *Paint it Today*, in which Aldington appears as Basil, she writes: 'She knew that she did not feel as he wanted her to feel, with warmth and depth and warm intensity . . . But the comradeship was perfect . . . Basil's friendship was like the warmth of a setting sun thrown over the ruins of an ancient city . . . The heat of mature passion would have shrivelled her.'[169] Aldington was of course very young, though in terms of relationships he could be said never to have entirely grown up. He idealised the women he fell in love with, idealised the business of being in love, and behaved with reckless emotional irresponsibility; his were never exactly 'mature passions'. Yet comradeship was certainly a key element in their early relationship; it is probably true that H.D. at this stage did not feel so painfully intensely about Aldington as she had about Pound and Frances: there was a carefree cheerfulness about the early years of their relationship, but there was also a deep bond between them. Yet again, however, H.D.'s deepest passion remained her writing, as her diary bears out; on 20 May she refers to 'the mad desire always for creation', and later, in July, writes, 'From the many, many desires, let these ones win free – the wedding of word to word as silver upon gold'; she wants to draw from 'the Greek silver verse of clarity, of tense, terse music, of drifting loveliness like Gods'. 'Tense, terse music': it is an apt description of the poetry she would soon be producing.

Now Richard had arrived Pound was seeing quite a bit of them both. Some time in May he suggested to H.D. that she and Aldington should get married, though from what he wrote to his mother, he was unsure whether she would take his advice: 'Hilda's last Englishman is also very charming,' he told her. 'He has crossed the channel and taken to drawing and velvet jacket, and they seem to share a talent for leisure. But they are probably too much alike for a "life-interest".'[170] Pound enjoyed having them there, however. He had hoped that Mary Moore would turn up as well 'to add to the general festivity', as he put it to his father.[171] She had visited Paris in the spring, and met Margaret, a meeting naturally arranged by Pound, and Mary and Margaret had taken to each other very much; in April Mary had been in London, where Dorothy was instructed to entertain her – she was rather unwilling at first, but they too liked each other. In May, however, Mary returned to the States from Holland without making a further visit to Paris, and was married later that summer. Pound would not see her again for twenty years.

During these May weeks, Pound was probably not seeing as much of Margaret as H.D. thought; he spent quite a bit of time in the Bibliothèque Nationale, studying the background of his Provençal poets. Although the two texts on which he would rely chiefly on his journey were the 1907 Baedeker for southern France and Justin Smith's *The Troubadours at Home*, written in 1898, also the record of a walking tour, Pound in addition took assiduous notes from the original manuscripts of the medieval lives of the troubadours known as *vidas* or *razos*. The scholar Gaston Paris had demonstrated in 1893 that these were largely works of fiction, but Pound accepted them as historical truth.[172] He also, he told his father, spent time wandering along the Left Bank, looking for old books in the quayside bookstalls. Oddly enough this was not how Pound had intended to pass his time in Paris. At the beginning of May he had told his parents that he would be spending three weeks there inspecting 'the state of Art', by which he probably meant literary art, but by the time he left in late May he reported that he hadn't found much contemporary work of value, apart from what he knew already, such as the work of Anatole France.[173] Following on from the admiration that he had reported in February for Rémy de Gourmont and Henri de Régnier, he had been, it seems, inclined to accept Flint's advice and look at more modern French poetry, but he rapidly appears to have lost interest, for now at any rate. He mentions that he had visited the office of the *Mercure de France*, perhaps at Flint's prompting, as H.D. reported his visit on a postcard to Flint, but though he saw the editor, Henri Davray, to whom Yeats had introduced him, he shows no interest in what the journal might be publishing; all he tells his father is that the Irish writer George Moore called in while he was there. How hard, in the event, Pound had tried to find out about current French poetry one can only guess, but *vidas* in the Bibliothèque Nationale attracted him more. The only poetry he wrote himself that May was a translation of some Provençal fragments that Rummel had discovered. He was still preoccupied with the past.

Pound set out for his travels on 26 or 27 May 1912, and went to see Margaret for the last time just before he left. It must have been a difficult visit, because on the 29th she wrote to him at Poitiers, saying that she was sorry to have been so cross, but she 'could not help it'.[174] On the night of 1 June she wrote letters to Pound and Rummel, sat at her piano, played one of the songs set by Rummel that Pound had dedicated to her as 'the Weaver of Beauty', and then shot herself. Margaret had invited H.D. and Aldington to tea the next day. H.D. learnt the news from Margaret's distraught maid when she reached the door of the apartment shortly before

Richard, and her newfound sense of reassurance and safety was rudely and ominously shattered. When Richard arrived, they went together to Thérèse Chaigneau's house. While they were there a letter arrived from Margaret for Walter; H.D. remembered it as having said that Margaret had been in love with him; Walter read it the same way, and was very shaken, saying he had been sure that it was Ezra she had cared for. When he wrote to Pound breaking the news, he said that her letter had upset him and his mind was 'not quiet'. Margaret had called on him, he said, a few hours before her death, and 'seemed so quiet and kind, that I don't understand a thing'.[175] Pound heard the news of the suicide *en route* and came straight back to Paris. There was a letter for him too. In her letter to Walter, Margaret had written that she wanted 'to say what it has meant to me to have met you, to have loved you as I have – to have seen someone the true symbol of all I have believed and *held to* in spirit always'.[176] Yet to love is not necessarily the same as to be in love; the letter is not unambiguous. To Pound, Margaret makes no such declaration, in fact says much less about the time they had spent together than one might expect, but there remains the possibility that Pound knew already of her feelings for him; perhaps she did not need to tell him. Both letters suggest she is in some heightened, euphoric state, and she insists that what she is doing is an act of courage, not cowardice. In each case, she refers to their fiancées and their future happiness, and, as she puts it to Pound, their 'final attainment'.[177]

Two years earlier, on his way through Paris before returning to America, Pound had gone with Margaret to see a production of a play, *La Vierge folle*, which culminates with one of the female characters committing suicide with a revolver; in retrospect it must have seemed a grim presage of Margaret's fate. Her death was to be a painfully memorable event for both H.D. and Pound. In *Asphodel*, Hermione sees in Shirley's fate a frightening warning to herself; Shirley had been, like her, a young woman who had strayed beyond the accepted boundaries and who had attempted to be an artist in a male-dominated society. Margaret's fate had been destruction; so might hers be. Earlier in the novel, Hermione had thought of Joan of Arc, when she had come across her monument in Rouen, as a similar warning, a 'girl who was a boy' who had seen visions, and been burned to death because of them.[178] The American press certainly saw Margaret Cravens' death as the inevitable penalty for nonconformity. The *New York Sun* published the news of her suicide under the heading 'Paris Full of Peril for American Girls', piously lamenting: 'Margaret Cravens, had she remained in America, might have been a happy wife and mother. In Paris she was one of many young women who have striven for artistic success and failed'.[179] Margaret's battleaxe aunt, Drusilla Cravens, who came to Paris after the death, also saw things that way. On her return she wrote to Pound (whom at first she had suspected deeply, presumably of having tampered with her niece's honour, but soon came to trust), telling him that Margaret's fate was due to the fact that she had 'overreached' herself. Things had gone wrong, Drusilla believed, when she had rejected life in the States: she 'grew dissatisfied and felt that her own people, however devoted and indulgent – failed to grasp her – her *intellect* and aspirations: in short she came to wander "in diverse ways" – and to the end which she precipitated.'[180] Pound, not surprisingly, does not appear to have agreed that Margaret's death was the necessary consequence of the rejection of American provincial life, or of devotion to artistic matters; neither would H.D., but to H.D. the emotional perils of a life such as Margaret's, like the one on which she herself had embarked, were very clear.

No certain reason for Margaret's suicide has ever been established. She had been subject to deep depression all the time Pound had known her; one other theory put forward in the American press, in light of her father's suicide one year before, was that it was the manifestation of a 'hereditary mental affliction'.[181] In a novel that Margaret's close friend Alice Woods Ullman (wife of the painter who had painted the portraits of Margaret and Pound) wrote ten years later, a Margaret-like figure commits suicide because she realises she lacks the talent of those who surround her in Paris. Drusilla Cravens made a comment in a later letter to Pound that is relevant to this: 'I . . . know *now*,' she wrote, 'that association with people of high order of talent if not of genius, and the sometimes cruel criticisms of these, had a very harmful influence upon the child's sensitive nature – particularly when she was in declining health and meeting with one disappointment after another. As I said at first I also say and I feel now – a *human* touch might have recalled her.'[182] It's undeniably a rebuke to Pound and Rummel, and possibly one that they to some extent deserved; both of them pursued their art fairly single-mindedly, often unaware of and uninterested in the feelings of those around them. Yet Pound had wanted to help Margaret – Rummel wrote to Dorothy that '[Ezra] tried more than the rest to help her and to develop her' – though one suspects Pound never understood that she could not be content simply in her role as patron and confidante to an artist.[183] In *Asphodel*, Hermione also blames herself for her failure to offer enough of a 'human touch', in her case because when she arrived in Paris she had been too absorbed in the pain of the Fayne Rabb débâcle to help Shirley: 'If I hadn't been so immersed in myself, so shattered with the web of myself, I would have seen her. Myself had wound round myself so that I was like a white spider shut in by my own hideous selfishness . . . Intuition and fine feeling had not been fine enough to sense this. The very proximity of this other spirit. The very nearness of this authentic sister, tangled in a worse web than she was.'[184]

H.D.'s reaction to Margaret Cravens' death is well documented. Even if one were to discount the evidence of the fictional *Asphodel*, it was an event to which she frequently returned in memoirs and letters. Pound left far less explicit evidence of his feelings, though there is some. He heard the news in Limoges, probably from Margaret's friend, Louise Morgan Sill, and he was back in Paris by 10 June. Dorothy, who heard the news from Rummel, had written, saying, 'Perhaps . . . it will not be altogether a shock to you?', possibly because Walter had told her that Margaret had 'had these attacks already often, and it was but a matter of years'.[185] Yet Margaret's death was a great shock to Pound, not something he had expected at all. He wrote back to Dorothy: 'Sadness and nobility and so many things are in the web that it is hard to exercise so wooden a Thing as my profession, that is words – even to you. Someday we will talk, perhaps – if, that is, the Thing comes near you. Write to me dear, and I will answer as best I can. I won't say, "don't write to me of trivial things", but write to [me] gravely for a little.'[186]

H.D. commented in her diary on Pound's deep sadness on his return; she certainly intuited the depths of his pain, but she cannot have realised how complex and many-stranded his grief must have been. Margaret had been a close friend; there was no other woman to whom he wrote so much as an intellectual equal. Apart from his personal sense of loss, Pound may have felt even more acutely the guilt and consciousness of failure that H.D. experienced after her much shorter acquaintance. He may have had more specific cause for guilt, as others besides H.D. were to speculate. Margaret's friend Alice Woods Ullman alleged that a letter or telegram from Pound was found in Margaret's apartment after her death, which Alice suspected of being the cause of the suicide, though her husband removed it and its contents have never been revealed. But the Ullmans might have mis-interpreted a perfectly innocent communication. Yet whilst there is no doubt that Pound grieved deeply for Margaret as a friend, for him there were other horrendous implications. Two-thirds of his regular income had disappeared at a stroke, his chances of marrying Dorothy were set back, perhaps for ever, and, possibly worst of all, he had lost the sense of divine blessing on his mission that Margaret's belief in his work had given him.

The overwhelming sense of mystic acknowledgement of his gift, which he had experienced when she first offered him support, must now have seemed a hollow irony. This patron who had revived his faith in himself because of her belief in his art had, as it were, casually abandoned him, thrown him on the waste-heap. Anger, it is said, is one of the emotions felt most acutely by those bereaved by a suicide; Pound must have felt it intensely. Not, of course, that he could ever express it, but there was a new bitterness and pepperiness that crept into Pound's relationships from then on, which might be attributable to this searing experience. It has been suggested (by Omar Pound and Robert Spoo) that Margaret had asked Pound to marry her, and he had refused in the mysterious communication suppressed by the Ullmans. It seems most unlikely; Margaret had earlier in May sent an invitation to Dorothy to come and stay – an invitation Dorothy regretfully refused on the grounds that she and Pound had no formal engagement, so she could not travel to be in a foreign city where he was. Dorothy had sent Margaret a copy of Pound's Cavalcanti translations just days before she died, and Walter was able to report to Dorothy that Margaret had spoken of her 'just a few hours before the accident, saying she knew you by correspondence and cared for you'.[187] At the level of Margaret's conscious mind, she behaved impeccably towards Dorothy, whatever her real feelings for Pound. But her unconscious motivations might have been very different. There could have been a repressed desire for revenge: suicide is an aggressive act. Intriguingly, H.D. suggested in the 1940s that it was Margaret who had introduced Pound to psychoanalysis. Yet knowing about repression intellectually does not necessarily mean that one understands one's own.

Years later, H.D. recalled walking for miles with a distraught Pound through the Parisian night. 'We were standing in the dark by an old bridge . . . Ezra waved his affected stick somewhere towards it all in a vague helpless kind of manner . . . towards the river, bridge, the lights, ourselves, all of us, all that we were and wanted to be and the thing that I wanted to say and couldn't say he said it before he dismissed me: "And the morning stars sang together in glory."'[188] As far as Margaret was concerned, Pound persuaded himself that she had found peace, reincarnated, as he wrote to Dorothy, as 'a small fat brown god sitting in a huge water-lily, splashing over the edge', an image he was later to incorporate in a poem, published in that far from peaceful publication, Blast. At the time he told Dorothy, 'Said image may sound ridiculous, but it is a great comfort to one, and so unanswerably true that I don't dare mention it to anyone else. It is however the solution of the whole affair, and we rest of us who are not ready for

such damp white-petaled beatitude may as well continue with our
paradise terrestre.'[189] This comment may hint that for a while Pound had
thought about the option of not continuing in the terrestrial world. Many
years later he would write to H.D., describing Margaret Cravens' death
as one of the most terrible 'flaying[s]' of 'destino' that he had experienced;
his belief that destiny was on his side crumbled, at any rate for the time
being.[190] Whether that drove him to consider suicide, one can only speculate. Once more, however, he picked himself up. On 16 June he reported
to Dorothy: 'I've got myself in hand again and did a real days work at the
Bibliothèque [Nationale] yesterday'.[191] He completed two chapters of
'Gironde', and on 27 June left again for his travels. But he knew he had
to rethink his life. Margaret Cravens had saved him when he thought his
career as a poet might be at an end two years earlier. How could he save
himself now?

PART VIII

IMAGISME IS BORN

I

PRIOR to the shocking news of Margaret's death, Pound had found the first period of his walking tour intensely moving, as his letters and the notes that he made on his journey reveal. That walking tour would be crucial in his development, but perhaps not in ways he expected. During the period from 27 May to 7 June 1912, travelling through Poitiers and Angoulême to the Dordogne and then north-east to the Limousin, he had passed, as he put it, 'within hale of all the best Troubadours save Piere Vidal', and he had found the land 'thick with ghosts'.[1] He had gone first by train to Poitiers (Pound, incidentally, always uses the medieval spelling, 'Poictiers'), 'mother city', in his words, of the troubadours, where the first of the troubadours, Guillaume IX, had been Count.[2] There he was so overwhelmed by his sense of the palpable presence of the troubadours that he wrote an impassioned letter to Flint, justifying his love of the early Middle Ages. Possibly Pound felt somewhat guilty, or at least embarrassed, that he had got nowhere with his survey of the state of art in Paris, and needed to explain to Flint, who had urged him to read present-day French poets, why he found the troubadours so significant. He had not ignored Flint's arguments altogether, but the beginnings of the interest he had prompted had lost out to his continuing passion for Provençal poetry.[3] He is writing to Flint, he says, as the most 'diligent' of those who had criticised his obsession with the past:

Know then that I am resolved to go back. I have as far as one may escaped the limitations of place, I attack in what seems the logical order the limitations of time . . . not that I think the 12th century any better than our own but simply that I have not been penned up within the borders of one country and I am not minded to be penned into any set period of years.[4]

Whilst he prefers Montbazillac to ale, he says, he drinks both; similarly, while he is 'as much alive in [his] time' as anyone else, he cannot see why this should stop him 'living in as many other ages as [he is] able'. It is not, incidentally, surprising that Pound with his sweet tooth should like Montbazillac, which he was drinking at that moment, he tells Flint, so he was presumably writing in a Poitiers café. In this part of the world, he says, he has found his 'land of promise', even more precious to him than Sirmione:

Garda was revelation, it was the unexpected . . . but this is my land, my chosen. And my time a time when all good things were set together. This land was English, and when England lost it my people, my own people fought some fifteen miles from here under the Black Prince and took it back again . . .

    When I say 'was English' I do not flatter you or any of our friends in London. I am no anglo-phile. I give up no jot of my own nationality. With England after 1670 I have nothing to make, but England before 1670 is as much mine as it is any man's and I decline to part with it for modern plumbing or the tower of the 'Metropolitan Life' – much as I appreciate both of these monuments to man's intelligence.

Presumably he is thinking of 1670 as around the time when the Pounds left England for America, but also perhaps as the time of Milton (the first edition of *Paradise Lost* was 1667), when for Pound English poetry went into decline. His comment on the Black Prince presages the *Cantos'* romantic and eclectic reading of history, when certain moments and figures draw to themselves intense and radiant – or sometimes darkly horrific – significance. He ignores the fact that the French reclaimed Poitiers for good twelve years later, and probably never knew that some historians argue that the Black Prince wasn't intending to recapture Poitiers at all. He happened to be doing some routine sacking and pillaging in the area when he unexpectedly met the French Army; they insisted on fighting, but luckily so incompetently that to his surprise the Black Prince found himself the victor.[5] But for Pound the heroic Black Prince is, like himself, claiming his rightful heritage; he has a visionary sense of the past and its ghosts, something Americans, he claims, are more conscious of than either 'conservative or futurist' Europeans; it is, he says, a 'sense of narrative':

I have had it once on Salisbury plain: This sense of event, of continuity, of people riding on one by one on the road, a sense of series, cavalcade, procession.

This whether we know it or not is what we come back for, we Americans with past inside of us . . . the sense of men, of men in sequence, intent upon this matter or upon that, wearing smooth the receptivities of the air with their going & coming, with their being ever upon the road for this errand or that, passing, & repassing, and giving salutation, and keeping silence.

That moment on Salisbury Plain, during Pound's Christmas visit to Hewlett, when he had also felt the presence of figures from the past, appears again in Canto 80, in a passage that is helpfully clarified by this letter:

> and for that Christmas at Maurie Hewlett's
> Going out from Southampton
> they passed the car by the dozen
> who would not have shown weight on a scale
> riding, riding
> for Noel the green holly
> Noel, Noel, the green holly
> A dark night for the holly
>
> That would have been Salisbury plain.[6]

Pound defines 'going back' in one of the few remaining fragments of the manuscript of 'Gironde'; it means, in this context, 'feeling, as well as knowing about the troubadours'.[7] Pound's acute sense of the presence of these past figures has something in common with Rummel's belief that he could and must hear the Egyptians' music, still there to be listened to; he had, after all, earlier insisted in *The Spirit of Romance* that 'all ages are contemporaneous'.[8] There is little of what Pound says to Flint in this letter that actually disappears from his project for good. Pound never gave up on the past, though there were many other periods he would look to as well as this one. This walking tour, and the troubadours, appear frequently in the *Cantos*, as well as in other poems and articles; there are several references, even in this same Canto 80, to Périgueux, to Altafort, and to Excideuil, where 'the wave pattern runs in the stone/on the high parapet'.[9] Richard Sieburth, who has transcribed, ordered and edited Pound's notes of his walking tour, argues convincingly that these fragmented, imagistic jottings, full of unexpected comparisons, references to a wide variety of artists, intended to be supplemented by extracts from the *vidas* and the poems, 'unmistakably prepare the palette for the Cantos'. The very form of these medieval *vidas*, he adds, had its own influence: Pound was drawn to them by

their elliptical compaction of information – entire poetic careers epitomised by a few dramatic gists . . . Translated and summarised in Pound's 1913 'Troubadours: their Sorts and Conditions' . . . the spare, paratactic narratives of the *vidas* point unmistakably ahead to the modernist historiography and portraiture of the *Cantos*.[10]

There is, however, a striking contrast between the emphasis on continuity in this letter to Flint and the language of rupture that Pound would soon, in common with other modernists, come to employ. To some extent, one could argue, the contrast is more apparent than significant, more rhetorical than substantive; for Pound, the rupture would be construed as a break from the immediate past (though that was a dubious claim in itself), not the past as a whole. What would be perhaps more surprising is the change in his use of the word 'modern', which in the notes on his walking tour Pound still uses only in the sense of an unsatisfactory present.[11] By October that year Pound would have moved on to use 'modern' as synonymous with 'good', just like a New Labour politician. He would not, of course, be using 'modern' to mean simply 'contemporary' or 'present'; it implied something more like membership of an elite avant-garde, that perilous ever-changing frontier, the meaning which, according to Eric Hobsbawm, 'the modern' had already acquired among French writers and artists by the 1880s.[12] It is paradoxical yet significant that one of the first times Pound used 'modern' in the sense of 'commendably avant-garde' was in reference to the Hellenic poetry written by H.D., very much the product of 'going back'.

By the time Pound was recalled to Paris, after only eleven days on his journey, already he was sure that he was succeeding in his quest to 'feel' as well as 'know' the troubadours, understanding their experience of 'the discomfort of the rd. and the boredom in the castles', living a life in which 'the condition of the weather was a necessary concomitant of every action & enjoyment'.[13] Richard Sieburth suggests Pound's attitude to the recovery of his troubadours' history is a 'positivist' one, mistakenly, I would argue. Pound certainly has no post-structuralist scepticism about historical 'facts', but his certainty about his insights into the troubadours' lives is not simply an empirical position. What Pound is claiming is an intuitive and indeed mystical or visionary contact with these past figures. At times, however, for all

his impassioned and imaginative reliving of their lives, the thought
that their world had vanished saddened him; when he visited Hautefort
(which he refers to by its medieval name Altafort) where Bertrans de
Born had his castle, he writes: 'going my way amid this ruin & beauty
it is hard for me at times not to fall into the melancholy that it is
gone, & this is not the emotion that I care to cultivate for I think
other poets have done so sufficiently'.[14] Perhaps one could see Pound's
efforts at going back into the past, recreating its vitality, 'making it
new', as he would later put it, as a way of holding the melancholy of
loss at bay.

One particular section of the notes for that first stage of the walking
tour stands out from the rest. When Pound recounts his visit to Excideuil
(with its wave pattern in the stone, referred to above), home of Giraut
de Borneil, he begins for the first time to record his thoughts, not as
prose, but broken into short lines, producing, as Sieburth puts it, a form
which 'nearly reads like stream of consciousness in enjambed *vers libre*'.[15]
Interestingly enough, it is not unlike H.D.'s writing in her diary. Again
it presages the *Cantos*, though they never follow through in so straightforward a fashion, but it is perhaps a first attempt at the flow of thought
that they present. Pound writes:

> A couple of great fields
> set up along with the church
> spire, the sky pale blue
> & white after the sunset,
> with the tree on the skyline
> outlined against it,
> & the great gentle tower
>
> clear edged,
> unascendable, and
> for no known reason
> these things wrought
> out a sort of perfect mood
> in things . . .[16]

It could have been written in the late twentieth century rather than
in 1912; this is the only passage like it in the first period of the
walking tour, but there would be several in the second. After
Excideuil, Pound's 'left shin denying [him] further assistance', he

went swiftly by tram and train to Limoges, where news of Margaret's death awaited him.[17]

It is possible Pound told H.D. and Aldington about this experiment during his time in Paris. H.D. and Aldington were still discussing literary matters in spite of the shock, but whether Pound did so is harder to gauge. One entry in H.D.'s diary reads: 'tea in "Mundora" – talked of James – Ezra came in very sad.'[18] In spite of his attempts to reassure Dorothy and H.D. that he had pulled himself together, Pound seemed still in low spirits when he began the second stage of his walking tour. He appears from his letters irritable and uneasy, full of complaints about the heat and the fleas. Dorothy had already told him in June that the Cavalcanti translations were having adverse reviews, and in July he was incandescent when Monro's friend Arundel del Re wrote a scathing piece about them in the *Poetry Review*, getting, Pound snorted, 'a good deal out of six misprints. The rest is malignant buncomb'.[19] His walking tour notes mention 'false friends/ & lying reviewers', clearly a reference to Monro and del Re, whose criticism had obviously cut to the quick, perhaps as much because of his general unhappy state as the accusation of inaccuracy, a criticism to which he was well accustomed and not something which had perturbed him particularly before.[20] The loyal Aldington, he told Dorothy, had 'withdrawn his contributions in a state of pious rage'.[21] Pound would never entirely forgive Monro. Even Dorothy's news that Yeats had pronounced 'The Return', which had appeared in the June *English Review*, 'flawless' did not appear to comfort him.[22] He was, perhaps, infected once more with the 'virus that makes one ask "to what end the attempting?"', from which Margaret Cravens had rescued him.

Pound had hoped that the countryside would rekindle some of the enthusiasm he had felt when he originally set out, but the region in which he left the train on this second visit, Uzerche in the Limousin, was not saturated with troubadour memories as Poitiers had been. It took him time to feel that he had 'reached [his] proper land again', as he put it when he got as far as the Dordogne once more.[23] Yet even when he reached Toulouse, home of Peire Vidal, and with a Romanesque cathedral that Pound thought second only to San Zeno – praise indeed – he was still somewhat morose. In a letter home, he complained bitterly to his father about 'getting this damned book written, & I've got to go on writing books for the next decade if I'm to beef on drawing pay from Swift & co'.[24] He suggested he would take up playwriting when he returned to London, an activity that he thought less uncongenial than writing prose, and more likely to earn him serious money than poetry.

Yet the open air and the physical exercise – he was covering kilometres at extraordinary speed – were therapeutic, and as time goes on his notes show him becoming calmer and more able to respond to the beauty around him. The visit to the Pyrenees was not part of his original plan, as he explains rather guiltily. 'No known troubadour', as he says, would have done such a thing; 'to go for mere mts. is decadent, I presume, & modern or at least parvenu & dating from the Ossianic movement'. But he was rewarded: 'Foix,' he says, 'was very right to come to.'[25] From the Pyrenees he moved on to Carcassonne, and then down to the coast. One thing that is striking about Pound's travel notes for the second stage of his tour is that there is less about the troubadours, with the exception perhaps of his visit to Toulouse, and more about the country-side through which he is passing. Uncharacteristically, Pound writes about what he sees, not what he has read, even if what he sees he often expresses in terms of its resemblance to works of art. When he reaches Souillac on the Dordogne River, he writes: 'the land with light subdued is like a background in Leonardo, so do his rivers curve, so do his rocks vary from white grey to dark'.[26] When he goes to the Pyrenees, he makes repeated references to Far Eastern art: at Foix he says: 'We are come again to a place where the waters run swiftly & where we have always this chinese background. The faint grey of the mountains'; at Roquefixade the sky is 'jap pink & grey', at Quillan 'at once metallic & oriental', but by Axat it is 'less Ming'.[27] As these examples suggest, what he notices most often are the qualities of light and colour of the sky and hills. Pound's response to scenery and his Neoplatonist affirmation of light reinforce each other, as they still do in the *Cantos*: in his lament for his 'green time' in Canto 115, he sees himself as

> A blown husk that is finished
> > but the light sings eternal
> a pale flare over marshes
> > where the salt hay whispers to tide's change.[28]

When Pound had begun the second stage of this walking tour, after Margaret's suicide, he had, one would guess, felt much like 'a blown husk that is finished', even at the age of twenty-seven, his future suddenly perilous and uncertain once more, his confidence in himself and his calling rudely shaken. Yet the prose in his notes at this stage of the journey is intriguingly often more intense and poetic than on the first stage, and after his rewarding 'truancy', as he puts it, in the Pyrenees, he makes more use of his loose free verse.[29] Now he becomes, as Sieburth points out, unusually frank, his lines 'bespeak a mood whose uncharacteristic autobiographical explicitness has clearly been heightened by heat and exhaustion'.[30] Pound is working through a crisis in his hastily written notebook – never intended for direct publication – in a way rarely allowed elsewhere. He passes Capestang, home of Guilhem de Cabestang, whose heart was served to his lover by her husband, a story to which Pound repeatedly returns, as if being devoured by the forces against him was a deep and constant fear. Yet there he writes:

> this walk
> was like
> a coming home,
> one expected half . . . to
> meet with one's
> people.[31]

By the time he had reached the sea coast, exhausted, full of terror at his future and exultation at the beauty of the countryside he had traversed, he had, it seems, struggled through to a resolution:

> I came here
> along the canal,
> under a mediterranean
> sky, ah
> surely I know
> my métier, there
> are artists in
> other media
> but when it
> comes to living I
> know my métier.
> I have made horrible
> mistakes, I have
> lived thru horrible
> things – but horrible –
> but still I know
> métier, as perhaps no-one

> since Flaccus [i.e. Horace]
> has known it

And he continues:

> Fools, readers of books,
> go south & live
> there. It is
> all I have to
> say for this time
> to the end of it,
> that life,
> despite all
> its damnable
> tangles & circumformations
> is worth the candle.

He has in mind Horace's 'Carpe diem', 'seize the day', which he half quotes, 'Carpe/and the rest of it/raris, the day'.[32] What is the 'métier' he shares with Horace, author of the *Ars Poetica*? That of the poet certainly – back in Crawfordsville he had written to Viola Baxter of his 'métier' as a poet – but more specifically perhaps a poet living with intensity, and pouring that intensity into poetry. While he asks, 'Can a man/be bothered making/poetry of nights like/ this!' that is precisely what he is doing. The beauty of the coastal town of Agde moves him to 'break/into dithyrambs'.[33] The question that he has settled is whether he can go on as a poet or not. Common sense, both his parents and the Shakespears would have said, doubtless voices he heard in his head as he walked, dictated that now an academic job was imperative. But he was resolved; he was not giving up on life or on poetry.

Neither was he for now showing any sign of giving up on 'Gironde', though he was getting very fed up with it; he was under contract to Swift & Co., now his sole provider of regular income. There were hints, however, of changes of direction in his thinking. He was, most unusually, reading fiction, 'completing [his] education', he told Dorothy, 'on Murger, de Maupassant, Turgenieff', though he added that, apart from the preface to Murger's *Scènes de la vie de bohème* ('surprisingly strong'), he found them less entertaining than James, Anatole France, and his friend Frederic Manning.[34] Yet the very fact he was reading them at all suggests he was rethinking his dismissal of the arguments – of those like Ford or Flint – about the need for the artist to respond to modern life.

Pound returned to Paris on about 20 July, much earlier than he had originally intended; he had already let Dorothy know he would be back in London by August. He was working hard at the manuscript of 'Gironde', and doing more Provençal translations for Rummel, who had married Thérèse Chaigneau in his absence, and, Pound complained, 'seem[ed] to have lost, eaten or mislaid certain *opii* in the excitement of his nuptials'.[35] He told Dorothy that Aldington was no longer in Paris, having been 'recalled to his "domestic den"', and asked her if he should 'bring the Hamadryad [i.e H.D.] back to England' with him; he continued, apparently, to think of himself as H.D.'s controlling 'male relative'.[36] In the event he left by himself, and got back to London in very late July or early August. He had written rather oddly to Dorothy, having been so anxious to return, 'don't bother to have me in until its convenient'; perhaps he was dreading having to reveal to her his loss of income.[37]

II

IF Pound's own life was at a critical moment, the England he returned to was itself increasingly crisis-ridden. There had been more industrial unrest in his absence, about which Dorothy complained bitterly. 'London is again messed up with Strikers – It is a rotten time,' she wrote on 22 May, and a few days later, 'London apparently will be starved out – besieged – I know not what horror – soon – all begun all over again worse than ever.'[38] Before Pound had left, indeed, the country had been almost paralysed by a miners' strike over the issue of low pay, and while he was in France there had been, among others, a second strike in the Port of London, which was only resolved as he returned. There were in all 857 disputes affecting one and a quarter million workers during 1912, in terms of industrial unrest the worst of the pre-war years.[39] Throughout the country there was now a militant refusal to continue to endure the gross inequalities of the Victorian and Edwardian eras. Whilst the Liberal government's attempts to appease the anger of the working classes through modest social provision had yet made little impact, the Tories and the Tory press were furious at even the minimal rise in taxes, and were outraged by the strikes, convinced the trouble was the fault of agitators. They were, however, as alarmed as the Liberals by the workers' mood. In January, the *Sunday Times* had put forward the widely held view that the unrest flew in the face of all 'economic and natural law'; it insisted that 'the unrest and ferocity of the masses arises . . . from innate defective civic instincts when these are incited by the invective and pungent harangues of professional demagogues . . . In the long run – and the sands of our opportunity have already nearly run their measure – those inexorable laws will destroy a nation that is foolish enough to tolerate incitory and pyrocephalic demagogues any longer . . . We are within measurable distance of civil war.'[40]

The Shakespear household took the Tory view. In late June Dorothy had written that 'The British Empire appears to be in a state, an unpleasant state, of decay . . . Every one is wild about this blooming Lloyd George's Insurance Act & H.H.S. [her father Hope] is in legal despair. Mat Mat [Manning's guardian Galton] is going to live without servants as he *won't* be Ll.G's tax-gatherer.'[41] According to Noel Stock, Hope repeatedly denounced Lloyd George for the legal difficulties caused by what he alleged was the loose wording of the Insurance Act, though one suspects it was really its content rather than its style to which he objected. Pound, having taken little interest in British politics up till then, would become considerably more condemnatory of British society in the next few years, though not from either a conventionally Tory or socialist viewpoint; instead he became convinced that an analogy should be drawn between the decadence of the Roman Empire and the present state of the British. That the British Empire was already no longer to be taken for granted was vividly apparent as far as Ireland was concerned, which was thought by many – as could have been the case – to be on the brink of a civil war between the Nationalists and the Unionists, the latter mounting forceful opposition to the possibility of Home Rule. The Anglo–American modernist revolution in which Pound would soon play a leading part was in no straightforward way aligned with this defiance of class structure and imperial power, but it was part of the same structure of feeling, a refusal to accept traditional authority. Rebellion and subversion were the mood of the time.

In Pound's absence a new venue had opened in London, introducing a touch of European bohemianism to the capital, another and different sign of the times. This was the Café of the Golden Calf, as it was provocatively named, an avant-garde night-club run by the divorced second wife of the Swedish playwright, August Strindberg, Frida. It was situated in a basement, in Heddon Street, off Regent Street, not so far from the Café Royal, and decorated with two white plaster caryatids or totem-poles (opinions vary) provided by Epstein, a gilded wooden calf by Eric Gill, and murals by Wyndham Lewis and Spencer Gore, producing, Richard Cork affirms, 'surroundings brazenly expressive of the libertarian pleasure-principle the club supported'.[42] These were all commissions, but only Lewis succeeded in getting any payment; the club was very popular among the artistic young, but it never made money. The Cabaret Theatre Club, as it was also called, had been launched in late June, following the circulation of a prospectus which announced:

The Club will open at 8.30 pm daily. From 9 o'clock to 11.30 a varied programme, with the tendency of a return of art to intuition and simplicity, will be given . . . The audience will sit round small tables . . . The cellars will be stocked by connoisseurs . . . From 11.30 Suppers – artistic suppers – . . . Spanish gypsies will play, Neapolitans sing, English poets say their verses, dancers dance.[43]

The evenings offered a form of variety show, intriguingly mixing avant-garde and popular forms. Madame Strindberg, an Austrian by birth, whose father had held an office at the Viennese Court, had modelled her café on a famous artists' night-club in Vienna, the Kabarett Fledermaus. A writer and translator herself, she had a talent for persuading up and coming artists to do things for her. She mingled with her customers at the club, would sometimes feed impecunious artists for free, and loved debate. Pound told a story of her saying to a Guards officer who had strayed into the club, presumably in error, 'Yes, I vil zleep vit you. It iss nossing. But talk to you half an hour. Neffair! Vun musst traw de line SOMMEFERE!!'[44]

The Café of the Golden Calf was one more indication, following Roger Fry's exhibition and the Ballets Russes, that European modernism was reaching London. Pound himself, within a month of his return, would decide to import some more. When he had first set out on his walking tour in late May he was determined, as his letter to Flint made clear, to remain a poet who drew deeply on the past, working as an individual artist and pursuing his own bent. By the end of August he would have taken the first steps to set himself up as the leader of an avant-garde movement, on the European model, the change in tactics that Lawrence Rainey suggests occurred to him in March but which in fact came some months later. Even when he first came back to England, his plan was still to complete his 'Gironde', which he had told Dorothy was three-quarters done by the time he left Paris – she had, incidentally, much enjoyed the first two chapters, which covered the first part of his travels, though Pound said he doubted that the 'suite' would be as good.[45] He also intended to publish a further book of translations, this time from Arnaut Daniel. Neither would ever appear. On his return to London he switched course, not overnight, but within a few weeks: he reinvented himself as a leader of a cutting-edge poetic movement. If, the previous February, he had grudgingly admitted in his 'Prologomena' that modernity might be coming in poetry, though not for a long time ahead, now he was to come to the conclusion that he needed to perform a Caesarian birth. He would be the impresario of literary modernism; for the first time he was to turn his propaganda skills to promoting a movement rather than just himself, and yet, paradoxically but probably not unintentionally, through that he promoted himself much more successfully than ever before. Pound, up to that point known best for his archaisms and love of the Middle Ages, was to be credited with being the father of the modern movement in Anglo-American literature. His own poetry had already been taking on a new spare directness and intensity: now the loss of his patron impelled his reassessment of how to be a poet in the literary marketplace. The transformation was not cynical, even though the showmanship was highly calculated, but the forces that drove Pound in that direction perhaps explain some of the contradictions in his attitudes over the next few years, and indeed beyond.

Nobody, not even Dorothy, appears to have known that Margaret had been his patron; she had insisted on secrecy in her life, and perhaps the circumstances of her death, the bitterness, as he must have felt it, of her refusal to stay alive to support his poetry, that ultimate rejection and repudiation, were too painful to acknowledge. He would not confess to his parents for some months that his mysterious patron was dead. In addition to his £100 a year from Swift & Co., he had during the last year earned approximately another £100 from other literary work, as he had told Dorothy's father, and he must have hoped that would just about keep him going. He did not ask his parents for any more subsidy. He must have known, however, that he would have to tell the Shakespears of his changed circumstances, and that was not to prove pleasant. On the other hand, in spite of the trauma through which Pound was now passing, it may have been that Margaret Cravens' patronage had not been entirely beneficial. With her money, Pound had had the opportunity to indulge his antiquarian and mystical bent unchecked, perhaps why the over-precious *Canzoni* was his least exciting collection. That was the side of Pound Margaret Cravens had admired most, and, as I suggested earlier, was perhaps why the more modern and mocking poems he had first thought of including in *Canzoni* were dropped. It is almost as if her death awoke Pound from a dream world of the literary past. Just as on the second leg of his walking tour he began to look at the countryside instead of evoking the ghosts of poets long dead, so now, back in London, he began to notice the contemporary world, perhaps not instead of, but certainly as well as seeking out visionary experiences. One should not make too much of this move: Pound had always to some extent wanted to shape his past masters anew for the present, and he would continue to be a very bookish poet. The mood of the times was changing, however; something of the same sort was happening to W. B. Yeats, who was also moving beyond his preoccupation with the world of visions and dreams. Yeats wrote in a notebook in late 1912, under the heading of 'First Principles': 'Not to find ones art by the analysis of language or amid the circumstances of dreams but to live a passionate life, & to express the emotions that find one thus in simple rhythmical language . . . The words should be swift natural words that suggest the circumstances out of which they rose . . . One must be both dramatist and actor & yet be in great earnest.' As R. F. Foster says, from then on for Yeats 'reality' meant 'not only Platonic perfection but uncompromising actuality'.[46] One could say the same of Pound. Foster, in fact, puts this change in Yeats down to Pound's influence, and perhaps Pound had already passed on his new-found conviction that 'life . . . is worth the candle'.[47] Yet Pound would still model himself in many ways on Yeats. Being 'both dramatist and actor & yet . . . in great earnest' was certainly as true of Pound as of Yeats. He was a showman, but he was deeply serious at the same.

In contrast to his return in 1911, this year Pound had been lucky to find many of his friends in London. Aldington, who had preceded him back to London, had taken on some work for a while for the Garton Peace Foundation, in wake of his conversion to pacifism, but this never appears to have taken up much time, and he had plenty left for Pound. Dorothy herself was away until mid-August, but Hulme was there, and he and Pound returned to discussing their latest views on art until late into the night, and the impact of those discussions would be seen in the new movement. Yeats was in town, enthralled by his discovery of the Bengali poet, Rabindranath Tagore, and anxious to introduce Pound to him. Ford was at South Lodge, and Pound immediately recommenced his tennis matches and literary arguments. H.D. returned to London shortly after, and Pound now saw her and Aldington on a daily basis, often with Brigit Patmore, and sometimes Flint, though unlike the others, the latter was only free at evenings and weekends, and was often working even then. Florence Farr, who had just published a partly autobiographical new novel, *The Solemnization of Jacklin*, described by the publishers as 'extremely modern', was in London when Pound arrived, but only until early September. She had decided, much to the astonishment of many of her friends, to leave England to go to be headmistress of a girls' school in Ceylon. Mabel Beardsley, the artist's sister, known for her own outrageous conversation, exclaimed in amazement:

'but a girls' school. Why she used to make even me blush!'[48] Farr probably did cause some consternation among the other colonials. She wrote in irritation to Yeats in 1913: 'In this college we are having a great bother with Christians of all kinds. We have to get people trained by missionaries dissenters church or catholic. I wish I could hear of a good Pagan like Jane Harrison who was a trained teacher.'[49] (Jane Harrison, the Newnham don whose revolutionary interpretation of ancient Greek culture was deeply unsettling to the more conservative male classicists, had been a friend of hers.)[50] But Farr loved Ceylon, finding the place extraordinarily beautiful, carrying out investigations into Tamil poetry and music, and writing to Yeats with great satisfaction: 'I am [in] the thick of politics & am having a really interesting life at last'.[51] She had left her psaltery with Yeats, who was most put out by her departure, though they continued to correspond until her premature death from cancer in 1917. Pound, when told she was to go, said sanguinely, but enigmatically, 'Ceylon ought to suit her', though he was probably sorry to lose the colour she added to London life.[52] He had written a poem about her back in January, both affectionate and gently mocking, called 'Portrait d'une Femme', unusually for him in remarkably accomplished blank verse. It began:

> Your mind and you are our Sargasso Sea,
> London has swept about you this score years
> And bright ships left you this or that in fee:
> Ideas, old gossip, oddments of all things,
> Strange spars of knowledge and dimmed wares of price.

It sounds exactly like a brief for the *Cantos*, with their ramshackle assortment of Pound's eclectic passions, scattered memories and random knowledge. The poem comments sympathetically on her unorthodox sexual alliances:

> Great minds have sought you – lacking someone else.
> You have been second always. Tragical?
> No. You preferred it to the usual thing:
> One dull man, dulling and uxorious,
> One average mind – with one thought less each year.

The poem as a whole is organised around the image of the Sargasso Sea, which has led some critics to describe it as one of Pound's first imagist poems, in spite of its traditional form. Pound certainly hadn't evolved any theories about imagist poetry at the time he wrote this, though perhaps he was instinctively moving towards them, and certainly it is already a poem about the contemporary world and its mores, like the poems he would write under the imagist label that autumn. The poem ends with a comment that could be read again as a reflection on his own poetry, so full of pastiche and allusion:

> No! there is nothing! In the whole and all,
> Nothing that's quite your own.
>   Yet this is you.[53]

Feminist critics have attacked this poem for Pound's superciliousness towards a woman, but on this occasion I think that is perhaps a misreading; it is both affectionate and a very modernist understanding of the heterogeneous fluidity of identity. Pound had sent the poem to the *North American Review*, which turned it down, on the grounds, he reported, that it had three r's in the first line, but whilst Pound waxed indignant for many years on the absurdity of this judgement, it would seem much more likely that they were worried by his unconventional comments on marriage. They had earlier accepted a rather fey and safely archaicised love poem, later published in *Ripostes* as 'Echoes', an adaptation, according to Pound, of a poem from the Greek Anthology. 'Portrait d'une Femme' had to wait for its first appearance in *Ripostes*.

This 'Portrait' had marked a new move in Pound's poetry, a poem about a contemporary woman who wasn't simply transformed into a troubadour's or Dantean Lady. During the two or three months after his return, finally turning his attention to the present day, Pound made three new discoveries, admittedly all literary, but all still connected with his new, heightened awareness of the world around him. Together they suggested to him a fresh path, a new direction which would not necessarily – or even plausibly – make him rich, though Pound was always hopeful, but one that made him feel again that there was an end worth attempting. He began, belatedly following Ford's advice, to read Flaubert; through Yeats, he met Tagore; and through Flint he discovered both more contemporary French poetry and, even more importantly, the concept of the avant-garde. Of these three discoveries, Pound scholars have tended to emphasise either Flaubert or French poetry, but all three were important. Pound's interest in Tagore, pointing forward as it did to his discovery of Chinese poetry, could in some ways be seen as the most significant of them all: just as modernism in painting only emerged by turning away from the West, the same could be said to be true about poetry. Pound would not actually meet Tagore until early October. Flaubert, however, he applied himself to as soon as he was back.

Pound's discovery of Flaubert was a continuation of the explorations in modern fiction that he had begun in France. In August he wrote to his mother to say he was giving himself 'a course in modern literature' and suggesting she should do the same. 'One is,' he said, 'always hearing of Turgueneff & Flaubert and thinking they'll be dull, and Russians are so disgustingly stupid that one can't mention 'em without a shudder, etc anyhow I've taken the plunge.' Pound often regarded literature he didn't know with such philistine prejudice, but he went on to enthuse: 'I thought Turgueneff the only sane modern, after I'd read the "Niches des gentilhommes", but Flaubert can give him points on how to write.'[54] Pound was also reading more Henry James, and therefore as usual encouraging his mother to do the same; he told his father to suggest to her she read *The American*, *Washington Square* and *Portrait of a Lady*, all apparently new discoveries of his own. In the late twenties he summed up what he had learnt that autumn: 'no man can now write really good verse unless he knows Stendhal and Flaubert . . . To put it perhaps more strongly, he will learn more about the art of charging words from Flaubert than he will from the floribund sixteenth century dramatists.'[55] (That last reference must be aimed at T.S. Eliot's admiration for Elizabethan dramatists.) *Le mot juste* was to become one of the defining principles of imagism. Already that spring, under Hulme's influence, Pound had been emphasising accuracy and the escape from cliché and convention; Flaubert reinforced this direction.

Though Pound did not yet know it, Flaubert had had an equally revelatory impact on James Joyce, whose writing Pound would promote so devotedly from 1914 onwards. Yet, whilst the 'art of charging words' was central to modernist writing, what Stendhal and Flaubert represented was not simply 'formal'; they gave to the modernists the realisation that a new form is always a new way of seeing the world. For Pound and others of his generation, what was so significant in these French writers was not just a 'style', but the view of the world and of the role of a writer that such a style implied. As Pound himself would write that autumn, 'A work of art need not contain any statement of a social or of a philosophical conviction, but it nearly always implies one.'[56] The author who removes him or herself from the text, leaving the reader to judge the world that he or she presented, made possible, these modernist writers believed, a much more searing critique of their society than more overtly polemical writing. To English-speakers, brought up on the nineteenth-century English novel, what was so deeply admirable in these French writers was their fearless commitment to showing, in the historian von Ranke's famous words, 'things as they really are'. Not people as they ought to be, not conventional sentiments applauded by middle-class morality, not a world where sexuality went largely unmentioned. Hardy had, after all, given up writing novels in the 1890s because he felt it was impossible in Britain to write novels for grown-up people. The philosophy implied by Flaubert's style was that the bourgeois view of society and people was a hypocritical sham, only kept in place by the regurgitation of clichés and verbiose banalities. Humankind could no longer be understood in Enlightenment terms, as rational and self-aware, nor in Christian terms as flawed though happiest when striving for moral perfection. If one just took a look, observed, reported, the reality of human nature would be laid bare. Pound had applauded the Rhymers' rejection of didacticism in poetry, and the exposures of bourgeois hypocrisy in Shaw and Ibsen, but Flaubert added a new dimension. He could have absorbed some of this message earlier through Baudelaire and the decadents, who had also abandoned the bourgeois view of humankind and wanted to explore evil, the irrational, the dark places of the psyche. But Pound began to take an interest in Baudelaire for the first time only towards the end of his walking tour. If the Philadelphian Pound had rejected the didactic English novel, he hadn't been up to decadence – *vide* his earlier horrified response to *Salomé*; for all his Left Bank posturing in Crawfordsville, he had felt happier with the sublimations of courtly love.

By 1912, however, he was beginning to change. Art, Flaubert had shown him, need not solely be about beauty. As he wrote the next year:

As there are in medicine the art of diagnosis and the art of cure, so in the arts, so in the particular arts of poetry and of literature, there is the art of diagnosis and there is the art of cure. They call one the cult of ugliness and the other the cult of beauty.

The cult of beauty is the hygiene, it is sun, air and the sea and the rain and the lake bathing. The cult of ugliness, Villon, Baudelaire, Corbière, Beardsley are diagnosis, Flaubert is diagnosis. Satire, if we are to ride this metaphor to staggers, satire is surgery, insertions and amputations.

Flaubert became an ally in his lifelong struggle against what he saw as provincial stupidity. Pound's belief in the artist's role as cultural critic was admirable but, given his growing certainty that the artist could accurately diagnose, and prescribe for, society's ills, also perilous. Pound had said earlier that year that poetry's importance lay in its 'interpretive power', and he would increasingly have no doubt that his interpretation in all spheres was right.[57] It would ultimately be his undoing. Yet in Anglo-American culture in 1912 there were certain areas, most notably in the field of sexual relations, where the gap between respectable appearance and practice, between bourgeois morality and behaviour, yawned wide, and the difference between the 'truth' and the social veneer appeared obvious. The first poems that Pound wrote that autumn after reading Flaubert were a collection of brief satires, first published the next year, many of them deliberately shocking in their sexual allusions to the conventional poetry readers of 1913. In his biography of Ford Madox Ford, Max Saunders points out how innocently critics have accepted the protestations by modernist writers like Pound and Ford that their interest in Flaubert and Maupassant and French poetry was simply for their 'Art'. It is clear, he argues, if you look at what they wrote under that French influence, that the much more open discussion of sexual matters was a crucial factor. Some of these satires demonstrate this new determination to be frank, yet these poems, though many of them are amusing, are by no means Pound's strongest work, and although the tone is colloquial, they are, as was quickly recognised, often modelled on Catullus, the names of people mentioned in the poems are generally Latin, the titles are still often not in English ('Tenzone', 'Ortus', 'Albatre', 'Causa') and the poems frequently employ the Renaissance convention of an address to the poem itself ('Go, my songs, to the lonely and the unsatisfied, Go also to the nerve-wracked, go to the enslaved-by-convention').[58] Yet if it wasn't for the distancing through the earlier referents, Pound might not have found a satiric voice at all at that time. The satire is gentle, and the desire to shock too blatant and jejune to be telling, although Pound got something of the outraged reaction he wanted. When successful, these satires' charm in fact comes from the mixture of modern and old; it is back to 'the living voice', but as always with Pound, through a persona, that now of the Catullus-like scourge of the bourgeoisie. The subject-matter is contemporary, even if the names are not. But the forms Pound used for those verse satires he found elsewhere, in the recent French poets of whom he learnt from Flint.

III

THE essay by Flint that was to be so decisive for Pound appeared that August 1912, in a special French issue of *Poetry Review*, the first of those devoted to foreign poetry that Harold Monro had announced the previous January. In the event almost the entire issue was given over to Flint, who provided an introduction to contemporary French poetry which was to establish his name as a French critic and to have a profound effect on English poetry in general. Flint had been arguing since his first *New Age* review that the English needed to pay attention to modern French poetry, so Monro's invitation to write such an article was a welcome opportunity. He kept up with the leading French literary journals, such as the *Mercure de France* and *Vers et Prose*; he presumably could not afford to subscribe, but both were available in the British Museum Reading Room, for which he, like Pound and H.D., had a ticket.[59] Affording the latest books was more problematic, but he was now in the happy position of being able to seek review copies.

In the months when the other future imagists were in France, Flint had been working incredibly hard. He had his full-time job at the Post Office, and after that sometimes worked two and a half hours overtime; on other evenings he spent even longer working on a translation of Bergson's *Introduction to Metaphysics* for Hulme, who was later that year to publish it under his own name. (Dolly Kibblewhite did some translating as well, and J.C. Squire claims that he also helped; Hulme clearly had quite a little cottage industry going.) Hulme had said he would pay Flint, but a fraught correspondence between them suggests money was a long time coming. In addition to this, between April and June, in preparation for his article, Flint carried out an extensive correspondence with a range of French poets, asking for information and their latest works. His main informant was Alexandre Mercereau, the editor of *Vers et Prose*, to whom Flint explained that although he had quite good knowledge of 'les aînés', the older French poets, his knowledge of 'les jeunes' was much more limited, and it was about them that he needed advice. Mercereau had his views, of course, on who counted, and Flint was to realise not long after the article was published that there were omissions.[60] But the point was not so much the comprehensiveness of Flint's account as the atmosphere of French poetic life he conveyed. He told Mercereau that what he wanted to produce was not a critical work ranking and evaluating the current rich plethora of young French poets, but a survey of the different schools and tendencies in contemporary French poetry. He was particularly interested in French poetic theories, which he was convinced could transform English verse. Although he himself, he explained to Mercereau, used *vers libre* and assonance, few others did. 'English poetry does not shine at the moment;' he wrote,

we are the suburbans of the world, – no sign of life, no curiosity about technique or psychology, apart from a few scattered young people all influenced by continental art; and, in spite of that smoking club, the Poets' Club, or that society of nicely brought up girls and genteel old ladies, the Poetry Recital Society – both of them the absolute negation of poetry and a complete plague – we are in state of utter stagnation. That's why I read French poetry, which is alive.[61]

One might note, in his references to the Poetry Recital Society (in which, incidentally, Lady Margaret Sackville was a leading light), that Flint could be just as misogynist as Hulme and Pound. Indeed, one of the most constant structurings of the modernist 'agon', as Michael Levenson has called it, an agon embraced by Flint from before his Tour Eiffel days, *vide* his complaints then about the impossibility of poetry in the bourgeois Poets' Club, was that of the artist against the forces of femininity, particularly genteel femininity, the Artist against 'the Lady'.[62] But 'a few scattered young people' – whom did he have in mind? Is he thinking of the old dispersed Tour Eiffel group, or could he be referring to the future imagists here? If the latter, he must have felt his introduction of French poetry to them had already had an effect.

When the article appeared in August 1912, few even among poetry lovers in London knew anything of French poetry later than the leading *symbolistes*; the only contemporary figure who had made an impact was Marinetti, who, though Italian, wrote in French. It was as if in the visual arts they knew nothing past the Impressionists, which indeed until

recently had been the case.[63] Flint's 1912 article was the equivalent for
poetry of the first Post-Impressionist Exhibition in 1910, and caused
its own stir: this was the only issue of *Poetry Review* to sell out – though
Monro to his chagrin later found a hundred more copies put away in
a cupboard.[64] Flint begins by defining symbolism, the movement from
which all the varied schools of present-day French poetry had developed. It was, Flint says, 'an attempt to evoke the subconscious element
of life, to set vibrating the infinity within us, by the exquisite juxtaposition of images'. The philosophy that lies behind it, like Bergson's,
emphasises intuition, and he refers his readers specifically to the
Introduction to Metaphysics. Flint sees symbolism as a psychological quest;
the original symbolists might have thought more in terms of a tran-
scendental infinity, but, as the critic Cyrena Pondrom notes, Flint elects
to make it an infinity within.[65] His reference to the 'subconscious element'
suggests the influence of psychoanalysis, which he may have learnt about
from David Eder, the psychoanalyst who first introduced him to Orage.
Much of imagist thought has analogies with Freud's ideas, on which
Pound would also draw, and while the principal influence on Flint was
still Bergson, what Freud and Bergson have in common is a model in
which a conventional, rigid exterior hides a deeper truth which can only
be discovered with great difficulty. When *The Interpretation of Dreams*
was published in English the next year, it must have seemed to followers
of Bergson that Freud's dream symbols had much in common with
Bergson's intuition-sparking images; both possible passages to the inner
depths. The word 'symbol', Flint points out, is misleading if thought
of as an algebraic sign, which stands 'in place of a reality'; on the
contrary, through a series of images 'the symbolist poet attempts to
give you an intuition of the reality itself'.[66] This would be Flint's understanding of imagism, which he always maintained was really a continuation of symbolism.

The importance of the symbolists, Flint went on, was that they created
a new manner of writing poetry. The tale of French poetry Flint tells
here serves as a lesson to the English – 'In 1885, the year of the birth . . .
of the symbolist movement, French poetry had become stagnant' – just
as, in his view, English poetry still was in 1912. Parnassian poetry, which
had advocated a return to strict forms, had come to 'stultif[y] the alexandrine'. (The alexandrine is a twelve-syllable line, the French equivalent
in many ways to the iambic pentameter or blank verse line in English,
though because the classical tradition had been so much stronger in
France than in England, the alexandrine had never been used as flexibly

and malleably as the iambic pentameter has been in English since the time of Shakespeare.) 'The French poets were impelled by an interior necessity to rid their art of the grossness of the sleep that had fallen upon it – to bring it nearer to pure music.'[67] It was to this end that they had developed *vers libre*, though, as Flint points out, it is misnamed, for it is 'by no means free': though 'free from exterior law', it still 'must follow rigorously the interior law of the poet's emotion and the idea which has given it birth'.[68] Here he anticipates Eliot's 1917 comment that 'No *vers* is *libre* to the man who wants to do a good job.'[69] *Vers libre* liberated poetry from rhetoric and cliché, but not from craftsmanship. It found new ways of using rhythm and cadence; it did not reject them. In addition, though the symbolists tended to use assonance rather than rhyme, the 'effect to be produced, and no rigid rule, was the sole arbitrament'.[70]

Having established these fundamental points, Flint went on to outline the different groupings of the avant-garde French poets, discussing a few poets individually, and referring to a bewildering number of schools – *'le néo-paganisme'*, *'l'unanimisme'* (alternatively known as *'whitmanisme'*), *'l'abbaye'*, *'l'école de grâce'*, *'le paroxysme'*, *'l'impulsionnisme'*, *'le néo-Mallarmisme'* and *'le Futurisme'*. Virtually all of these schools were associated with a particular journal, of which the leader of the school was frequently editor. It was a pattern of which Pound was quick to take note. Flint does not use the word 'manifesto', but he quotes several, and emphasises that each school has its own poetic theory, based on a philosophy of life, which it propounded with a zeal and urgency that must have appealed to Pound's own missionary spirit.

Pound was deeply impressed by Flint's picture of these dynamic avant-garde poetic schools in Paris, and their engaged poetic thought and practice. Both Flint and Pound confirm more than once that it was reading Flint's article that led Pound to create the 'imagiste' label and to form his own school. The article had suggested to Pound an entirely new way of being a poet; he would be the leader of an avant-garde poetic movement, not to say poetic storm-troops, who would take up arms against bourgeois complacency, issue battle cries, alias manifestos, and, crucially, found a magazine through which to promulgate the movement's cause. In contrast to his dismissive attitude in late May, Pound now became an advocate for modern French poetry and for *vers libre*. Flint was later to say that 'before August, 1912, Ezra Pound used to say that he knew no French poetry after Villon. After August 1912, he became like a cat in heat. He told my wife in the Ristorante Italiano, Soho, that

if I didn't write the book (on modern French poetry) *he* would. He
could not hold himself.'[71] Neither of them was to write such a book,
though Flint did write several more essays, and Pound would publish
a series of articles on modern French poets in the *New Age* a year later,
and others over the next few years. Yet though he had started talking
of the importance of Paris to poetry by the end of August, the evidence
is that he did not extend his reading of French poetry for some months.
One exception was Théophile Gautier's *Emaux et camées* (1852, so
scarcely contemporary), which he discovered through Brigit Patmore,
writing to Dorothy on 23 September that he had found 'some fine
things' in it, and adding, '[I] alternatively bless & curse my education
which has kept me from so much modern continental stuff & which
has *en revanche* allowed me so much that . . . I would never have bothered
about if I'd known the modern stuff first.'[72] He would never regret the
time he had spent 'pawing over the ancients'. Gautier's tautly shaped
poems were his model when he came to write *Hugh Selwyn Mauberley*,
and later he drew on Gautier's idea of poetry as something carved or
sculpted, but Gautier could only have indirectly influenced the *vers libre*
he began to write that autumn. Pound was intrigued by Flint's extensive discussion of *vers libre* techniques in his article, especially his
emphasis on the use of rhythm and assonance rather than rhyme, to
which Pound had always been somewhat indifferent. As Pound would
write himself the next year: 'I am aware that there are resolutions of
sound less obvious than rhyme. It requires more pains and intelligence
both to make and hear them . . . I cannot believe that one can test the
musical qualities of a passage of verse merely by counting the number
of syllables, or even of stressed syllables, in each line, and by thereafter
examining the terminal sounds.'[73] It was to this subtler form of verse
that his idea of 'absolute rhythm' had been leading, and in *vers libre* he
realised he had, for now at any rate, found what he needed.

It must have been in the first half of August that Pound first decided
to form an *imagiste* school on the lines of *les paroxysmistes*, *les néo-
Mallarmistes*, *les Futuristes*, etc. As the name indicates, his late-night
discussions of 'the metaphysics of art with Hulme', as he described
them to Dorothy, had convinced him of the importance of the image.[74]
Hulme had written the previous autumn in 'Bergson's Theory of Art'
that there were two main ways, rhythm and images, through which the
poet can transform 'ordinary language', so that it conveys 'freshness of
experience' and escapes from 'conventional ways of expression'.[75]
Rhythm, he says, 'breaks up the normal flow of our conscious life',

increasing our sensitivity to the reality beneath; rhythmical arrangements of words can 'tell us, or rather suggest, things that speech is not
calculated to express'.[76] Pound, of course, with his belief in 'absolute
rhythm' that conveyed the precise nuances of a psychological state,
needed no persuasion here; indeed, since Hulme himself had not stressed
rhythm earlier, he may well here be responding to the arguments of
Farr, Flint and Pound himself. But images, the second means by which
Hulme argued the poet could create this freshness of perception, had
not been a concern of Pound's in the past. Hulme in 1909 had emphasised the 'visual concrete' nature of the image, but now he stressed that
an image wasn't simply 'handing over any visual scene, but . . . an attempt
to get an emotion as near as possible as you feel it', and such an attempt
at capturing an emotion directly had always been Pound's aim.[77] Here
was a new way of understanding how the poetry might work; the image
was another version of the instantaneous impact of the 'luminous detail'.
In 1917 he would tell Margaret Anderson that he made the name 'imagiste' 'on a Hulme basis' and on the model of 'the French groups
catalogued by Flint in the P.R.'[78]

But having found a name for his movement, could Pound start a
magazine, a daunting prospect in his penniless state, though an accou-
trement of an avant-garde movement that these French schools or
cénacles (Pound always preferred a French term) could not do without?
He had, in the event, a great stroke of luck. A magazine came his way.
While he was still digesting Flint's article, Pound received a letter from
one Harriet Monroe of Chicago. Monroe, a poet herself, a friend of
Pound's fellow-Philadelphian, the artist Mary Cassatt, and former art
critic of the Chicago Tribune, wanted to set up a new poetry magazine
there and was writing to poets she admired, or who had been recommended to her, asking them to contribute. The idea of a poetry magazine
had come to her a couple of years earlier when, on a world tour, she
had visited China, where her brother-in-law was a diplomat. Like
Couchoud in Japan, she had been deeply impressed by what she saw as
the innate poetic sensibility of the people (anyone who visited China,
she later wrote, 'begins to suspect that every Chinese writes poetry').
On her way there, Monroe had stopped in London, where, as a feminist of the most respectable kind, she stayed at the Lyceum Club, 'then
a center for more or less militant suffragettes', and was delighted to be
able to watch the 'miles-long suffragette progression', which she followed
to 'its triumphal meeting at Albert Hall'.[79] She was introduced to May
Sinclair, another very respectable feminist, who had taken her to Elkin

Mathews' bookshop. As she recalled later in her autobiography, Mathews was 'vividly enthusiastic about the work of a young American in London, Ezra Pound. "That is real poetry!" he exclaimed, as he showed me the *Personae* and *Exultations*. I bought the tiny volumes, and later beguiled the long Siberian journey with the strange and beautiful rhythms of this new poet, my self-exiled compatriot.'[80] While in Peking, she took 'a sudden and very deep plunge into Chinese art', guided by the distinguished Detroit collector, Charles L. Freer.[81] It made her feel, she said, dissatisfied with traditional Western forms. 'Something in modern art,' she began to feel, 'goes against the grain; its realism seems over-emphatic and unrefined.' Eastern works of art, made by 'our elder brothers of the mysterious past . . . bid us pause with arresting power. Something in their quiet authority allures us; already the art of the West turns to listen and observe; and her followers must note and obey the change in her mood as she goes her way.'[82] It was perhaps this vague dissatisfaction with conventional Western art that also attracted her to Pound, though to start with she oscillated – understandably – between seeing his poetry as something from an earlier age and as something very modern. On the one hand she says of him: 'Ezra Pound's early poems, after the rich orchestration of centuries of English poetry, sound to our inner ear like Palestrina after Wagner, Schubert, Beethoven . . . They recapture primitive simplicities.' On the other, she also wrote that what charmed her on that first reading were his poems' 'strange new insinuating rhythms, their half-interval cadences, their Debussy-like under-tones and over-tones'.[83]

When she eventually returned to Chicago, she managed to raise the promise of $5,000 per year towards her venture, not necessarily from rich Chicagoans, but from a hundred subscribers who pledged to contribute $50 a year for five years; another twenty promised smaller amounts. She wanted a new kind of poetry, though she herself was not very sure what it might be, and she wanted to have poetry taken seriously by Americans. She had found another poet, Alice Corbin Henderson (who was frequently to be a mediator between herself and Pound) to be her associate editor. Henderson had known Margaret Cravens, and she wrote a very tender letter about Margaret to Pound a little later that year, referring to her 'flame-like enthusiasm', as well as letting him know how much she admired his poetry.[84] Pound appears to have been touched by this, though the only comment he made at the time in response to Alice's bafflement at the unexpected suicide of one who 'seemed to get so much joy out of life' was, 'There is no use my trying to answer the first part of your letter. She went like the god in a mystery.'[85] Yet the link was, perhaps, a promising start to their correspondence; there was always a warmth and respect in Pound's attitude to her, quite unlike the fury to which Harriet Monroe frequently provoked him. Years later Pound would say Alice was the 'only means of getting an idea into dear ole 'Arriet's hickory block. In short Alice my only comfort during that struggle'.[86] But whatever Monroe's limitations – and they were greatly exaggerated by Pound – not just founding but keeping *Poetry* afloat as an avant-garde magazine was an impressive achievement. Monroe and Henderson were the first of several women to play an important background role in making the emergence of the new movement possible – others would include Dora Marsden, Harriet Shaw Weaver and Margaret Anderson.

In her letter, Harriet told Pound that the first issue was planned for October 1912, and that she hoped he would send something that she could include; she enclosed a circular giving more details. Two aspects of the circular particularly impressed Pound. Firstly, *Poetry* would print longer and more serious poems than the popular magazines, and secondly, and most importantly, it would pay the poets. Pound's reply, written on 18 August, gives an insight into how he was still smarting from his visit home. Her plan, he assured her, was 'the only possible method' of producing a magazine that 'is not an insult to the serious artist and to the dignity of his art'. However, he continues: 'But? Can you teach the American poet that poetry *is* an *art*, an art with a technique, with media, an art that must be in constant flux, a constant change of manner, if it is to live? Can you teach him that it is not a pentametric echo of the sociological dogma printed in last year's magazines? . . . I may be myopic, but during my last tortured visit to America I found no writer and but one reviewer who had any worthy conception of poetry.' Pound himself promised to publish his own poetry in America solely with her magazine, not of course counting any books of his poetry (a promise I am sorry to say he broke as soon as someone else offered him a higher fee), and to send her some poems. In fact he offered more than his own poems. 'Are you for American poetry,' he enquired, 'or for poetry? The latter is more important, but it is important that America should boost the former.' He was asking, he said, because if she were interested in publishing poetry from elsewhere than America, he could send stuff her way. He had been 'on the verge of starting a quarterly, and it's a great relief to know that your paper may manage what I had, without financial strength, been about to attempt rather forlornly'. He promised confidently that 'If I can be of any use in keeping you or the magazine in touch with whatever is most dynamic in artistic thought, either here or in Paris – as much of it comes to me, and I *do* see nearly everyone that matters – I shall be glad to do so'. This claim might have some partial truth as far as London was concerned, but certainly not Paris – he was clearly hoping to pick Flint's brains and exploit his contacts. Earlier in his letter Pound had already told Harriet, 'you must keep an eye on Paris', something that might not have occurred to him to say three weeks before.

As far as his own poetry was concerned, he had to make an admission: 'I can't send you much at the moment, for my *Arnaut Daniel* has gone to the publisher, and the proofs of *Ripostes* are on my desk, and I've been working for three months on a prose book. Even *Ripostes* is scarcely more than a notice that my translations and experiments have not entirely interrupted my compositions'. The very act of writing this apologetic explanation may have brought home to him how much he had been neglecting his own poetry. *Ripostes* was less than half the length of *Canzoni* – one of its virtues, as it happens, but perhaps not what struck Pound then. He had only two poems to offer, though *Ripostes* had gone to the publishers the previous March, five months earlier. 'I send you all I have on my desk – an over-elaborate post-Browning "Imagiste" affair and a note on the Whistler exhibit. I count him our only great artist.' This reference to the 'over-elaborate post-Browning "Imagiste" affair', a poem entitled 'Middle-Age', is his first recorded use of the term, and suggests that Richard Aldington was right when he suggested that when Pound first invented the term *imagiste* he was not entirely sure what he meant by it. Soon Pound would have thought 'over-elaborate' and '*Imagiste*' were mutually contradictory terms, and the poem, which works through an extended if ingenious simile, has none of the immediacy and directness Pound would advocate for imagism.[87] What the imagist aesthetic was to be was in fact conveyed much more by what he went on to say about the example of Whistler; Pound was, he told Monroe, on the 'threshold of what I hope is an endeavor to carry into our American poetry the same sort of life and intensity which [Whistler] infused into modern painting'.[88] Pound had been to see an exhibition of Whistler's paintings at the Tate, which gave his long-standing admiration for Whistler a new dimension. The exhibition, he wrote that autumn, 'contains not the expected array of "Nocturnes," but work in many styles, pastels of Greek motif, one pre-Raphaelite picture, and work after the Spanish, the northern and Japanese models, and some earlier things under I know not what school'. Here was an artist who like himself had been a constant experimenter in many different styles. 'The man's life struggle was set before one. He had tried all means, he had spared himself nothing . . . There were many struggles for the ultimate nocturnes . . . What Whistler has proved once and for all, is that being born an American does not eternally damn a man or prevent him from the ultimate and highest achievement in the arts.'[89] The poem that Pound sent to Harriet praises Whistler as America's 'first great', who 'tr[ied] to wrench her impulse into art', and it emphasises the 'many fashions', 'searches' and 'uncertainties' in Whistler's artistic development. When Pound writes that Whistler 'Had not one style from birth, but tried and pried/And stretched and tampered with the media', he is perhaps offering an apologia for his own uncertain and inconsistent progress.[90] He was not yet quite sure of his way forward, what his equivalent of the 'ultimate nocturnes' would be, but he would continue to search.

This letter marks a turn in Pound's life. Harriet Monroe gratefully accepted his offer of help, and in September asked him to be *Poetry*'s '"foreign correspondent" or "foreign edtr" or something of the sort', as he explained to Dorothy.[91] Pound's long career as a promoter of 'serious artists' and a leading figure in Anglo-American modernist poetry was about to begin. He reapplied himself to writing poetry, and though he continued for a while to work spasmodically at *Gironde*, his account of his walking tour, by the time two months were up he had abandoned it completely. Some critics suggest this was because Ford criticised his prose style, which indeed he did. 'He says its as bad as [R.L.] Stevenson and that is very violent for him', Pound told Dorothy a few weeks later.[92] That was on 14 September, but he had already written to her on 13 August that 'this prose book is a dam'd nuisance', and he preferred talking to Hulme or reading *Madame Bovary*.[93] Ford did not go so far as to suggest that Pound abandon *Gironde*. On the contrary, he assured him that with some revisions it was salvageable; Pound carried on for a week or two, but then left it for good. However, his memories of that walking tour, and of the troubadour ghosts that he had felt around, would never leave him.

IV

As Pound had mentioned in that first letter to Monroe in mid-August, he was still working on the proofs of *Ripostes*. The story of these proofs is not entirely clear; the previous June he had written to his mother from Paris, telling her that he had sent off the *Ripostes* proofs, and that the book would be with her in a month or so. Dorothy had with enormous care sent him two sets of proofs to Paris, plus his original manuscript, all duly registered, and Pound had poured scorn on her for such precautions. Possibly his returned proofs, presumably unregistered, had gone astray; it may be that Swift & Co., which would not last much longer, was a rather ramshackle organisation, and simply mislaid them. Whatever the explanation, he was now checking them for the second time. Presumably he had already decided in March to append 'The Complete Poetical Works of T.E. Hulme', the five poems by Hulme which had appeared in the *New Age* in January, as one would imagine that Swift & Co. would have taken it ill if Pound had added them at final proof stage, but the preface that he included, which had not appeared in the *New Age*, and which contained the first reference to the *imagistes* in print, can only have been written in August. For one thing, if Pound had invented the term *imagiste* in March, before he sent in the manuscript, or even in June, at the first proof stage, it is inconceivable that he would not have used the term again in one of the numerous extant letters and pieces of writing he had produced since. In addition, the preface bears the signs of the new knowledge he had gleaned from Flint's article. In his newly conceived role as leader of the *imagistes*, Pound could not pass up the opportunity for a manifesto, though in this first *imagiste* pronouncement there is no definite indication that Pound was yet taking avant-gardism entirely seriously. Pound referred obliquely to the Tour Eiffel meetings, saying the poems 'recall certain evenings and meetings of two years gone, dull enough at the time, though pleasant enough to look back on'. He went on:

As for the 'School of Images', which may or may not have existed, its principles were not so interesting as those of the 'inherent dynamists' [one guesses he means the Futurists] or of *Les Unanimistes* [whom Flint had discussed at length in his article], yet they were probably sounder than those of a certain French school which attempted to dispense with verbs altogether; or of the Impressionists who brought forth

'Pink pigs blossoming upon the hillside'

or of the Post-Impressionists who beseech their ladies to let down slate-blue hair over their raspberry-coloured flanks . . .

As for the future, *Les Imagistes*, the descendants of the forgotten school of 1909, have that in their keeping.[94]

Given the mocking tone, it is not surprising that Flint was to claim later that 'the name [*imagiste*] . . . was adopted as a joke rather than the challenge it finally became'.[95] There would be at least one volume of 'post-impressionist poetry' published in 1914, though it wasn't a word much applied to poetry, but Pound was perhaps anticipating the advent of the much-discussed Second Post-Impressionist Exhibition, which was to open in October, the month when *Ripostes* eventually appeared; critics were to lose no time in discovering disagreeable similarities between them. Yet it is worth noting, in the face of Pound's later prevarications, that here he explicitly and publicly acknowledges his debt to Hulme's ideas.

Pound's next step in fashioning himself into the leader of a poetic movement was to begin to host a regular literary gathering on Tuesdays; the same day that he had held his weekly gathering back at Hamilton, though by now the choice of day was probably directly in homage to Mallarmé's famous *mardis*, described so evocatively in Arthur Symons' *The Symbolist Movement in Literature*, for Mallarmé's overarching importance as the father of the *symbolistes* had been made much of in Flint's article. These Tuesdays do not appear to have been large events – the size of Pound's room would have precluded that – and from accounts in Brigit Patmore's memoirs, it appears that she, Aldington and H.D., with whom Pound was now in almost daily contact, were the regulars. Flint also came along sometimes, and there were occasional others. Frances and Louis had returned to England, and during the later summer and autumn may have occasionally come, gathering material for their satire, *The Buffoon*. They certainly met up several times with H.D., Aldington and Pound, and might well have been asked along. Pound was now exploring new areas; on one of the first Tuesdays he invited Marjorie Kennedy Fraser to sing them Hebridean folk songs, which appear to have impressed him deeply, for the next spring he advised a would-be poet to 'fill his mind with the finest cadences he can discover, preferably in a foreign language . . . e.g. Saxon charms, Hebridean Folk Songs, the verse of Dante, and the lyrics of Shakespeare'.[96] Even before that – not much more than a week before her departure – Florence Farr chanted some of Tagore's poetry, reading 'from an unpublished english *mss* translated from the Bengali'. Tagore 'was a very great person indeed', Pound explained to his father, reporting on this event.[97] Even though he had not yet met Tagore, Pound was already on message. He told his father that Yeats was doing an introduction, and he would let him know when the book was out.

Dorothy had returned to London for the second half of August, but then left again for Devon. Pound had a busy social life in her absence: he was, he told her, playing tennis with Ford in the afternoons, and dining with Aldington and H.D. in the evenings. Given his late rising, one wonders how he fitted in his writing, but he clearly did so. He was beginning to experiment with what he now acknowledged was *vers libre*, and with satirical poems, telling Dorothy, 'I have . . . writ a few modern epigrams to keep Richard from the blues.'[98] One of them was on a tea-shop, describing the way 'the glow of youth' is fading from the girl who brings them their muffins: 'The August has worn against her'.[99] It is surely a sign of his self-reinvention that he has swapped courtly love for talk of muffins: he would later, it might be noted, dismiss his earlier poetry as 'stale cream puffs'.[100] According to Aldington, tea-shops were where Pound, H.D. and he spent much of their time, presumably after Pound's tennis matches. 'Like other American expatriates,' Aldington says, H.D. and Pound had 'an almost insane relish for afternoon tea'. He, as 'an oppressed minority', had to go along. So their poetic discussions largely took place 'in the rather prissy milieu of some infernal bun-shop full of English spinsters'. In spite of these surroundings, 'an extremely good time was had by all, and we laughed until we ached'. He couldn't, he admitted, remember what they had found so entertaining: 'I suspect that the cream of the wit lay in the fact that we were young, entirely carefree, and having a glorious time just being alive'.[101] Aldington's memories of the gaiety of the years 1912–14 may be heightened by the contrast with the sombre war years that followed, but there is no doubt they had a good deal of fun together, even if they all had their darker moments, and they all – even Aldington, in spite of the flippancy of his later comments – at heart took writing poetry deeply seriously.

Pound was making other moves to further his new persona of the leader of a *cénacle*. Aldington and H.D. were no longer just his friends. They were, he told them, somewhat to their surprise, if not bewilderment, members of the imagist movement. 'Whenever Ezra has launched a new movement,' Aldington wrote, 'he has never had any difficulty about finding members. He just called on his friends.' Pound would, he relates, often 'obliterate a literary figure by the simple assertion: "*Il n'est pas dong le mouvemong*"'. (It recalls Mrs Thatcher's insistence that her satellites must be 'one of us'.) In Aldington's account of the birth of imagism, he says that

Naturally . . . the Imagist *mouvemong* was born in a tea-shop – in the Royal Borough of Kensington. For some time Ezra had been butting in on our studies and poetic productions, with alternate encouragements and the reverse, according to his mood. H.D. produced some poems which I thought were excellent, and she either handed or mailed them to Ezra. Presently each of us received a ukase to attend the Kensington bun-shop. Ezra was so much worked up by these poems of H.D.'s that he removed his pince-nez and informed us that we were Imagists.[102]

H.D. tells the story of Pound reading these poems of hers more than once. She hadn't posted them – as they were all living in Church Walk, it is surprising that Aldington suggests she might have done. She was, she says, with Pound in the British Museum tea-room when she showed him one of her poems, rather bravely one might think, considering how often he appears earlier to have dismissed them, and indeed, Pound told Harriet Monroe, he had great difficulty in persuading her to let him see any. But if Aldington *had* praised them first that might have given her courage. This time Pound's reaction was quite different from his former scorn. As she recalls in *End to Torment*, he said: '"But Dryad . . . this is poetry." He slashed with a pencil. "Cut this out, shorten this line. 'Hermes of the Ways' is a good title. I'll send this to Harriet Monroe of *Poetry*" . . . And he scrawled "H.D. Imagiste" at the bottom of the page.'[103] This was perhaps a collaborative act not unlike the more famous partnership when Pound 'slashed' T.S. Eliot's *Waste Land*; but H.D.'s story conveys all her ambivalence about Pound. She emphasises the violence of the slashing, just as elsewhere in that memoir she makes clear Pound's aggressive bullying when he 'pounds' the taxi with his stick as he insists she is not to go with

Frances on her honeymoon. Yet that slashing with Pound's 'creative pencil', as she describes it, is also productive, setting her on her course as a poet.[104] Perhaps she wants to make it analogous to what she said about Pound's earlier betrayal of their engagement, which seared her, but put her on her path away from home and towards London and poetry; Pound, she would say, 'was the scorpionic sting ... that got me away'.[105] In her unpublished memoir, 'Compassionate Friendship', she repeats the story, explaining that 'Hermes of the Ways' was 'a rough transcription of a short poem from the Greek Anthology', which Pound 'pruned ... into *vers libre*'. 'It was one of those early poems that Ezra scrutinized and with a flourish of a large lead pencil, in the British Museum tea-room, deleted and trimmed or pruned or chiselled into the then unfamiliar free-verse'.[106] Whether the original 'rough transcription' was the kind of poetic prose or prose poetry that she had written in her diary in Paris that spring, or the kind of hesitant formal metrics she also included, one can't tell. If she had been reading Henri de Régnier in Paris, it seems surprising that she found free verse still unfamiliar, but perhaps to transpose it into English had been too sudden a move. Even Flint, who after all had been studying and advocating *vers libre* for some years, had only the previous year begun to shed formal metric and rhyme. But her diary for that summer shows that H.D. was already writing with the immediacy and intensity that characterised her poetry, though without yet being able to find a form. Pound's 'Cut this out, shorten this line' showed her what she needed. Her prose in that diary had been more intense and poetic than the formal poetry she attempted; something very close to *vers libre* was in fact what she was instinctively writing. It was the perfect form for her 'tense, terse music'.

What emerged from this chiselling and pruning was perhaps, as Cyrena Pondrom has argued, the kind of poetry from which Pound would finally develop his definition of imagism.[107] In 1915 Pound was to write to Flint saying that he had invented the name 'Imagisme' to describe the work of H.D., which cannot be entirely true, for when Pound coined the word he had not yet seen the poems to which he appended the signature, 'H.D. Imagiste'. The more likely scenario is the one he described to Harriet Monroe: 'The name appears in my introduction to T.E. Hulme at the end of *Ripostes*, and the whole affair started ... chiefly to get H.D.'s five poems a hearing. It certainly began in Church Walk with HD, Richard and myself.'[108] If that's true it would confirm, as I've suggested, that Pound invented the name of the movement first, and only began to reach a programme when he saw H.D.'s spare yet freighted poems, so imagism came to be defined by the sort of poetry that she and – to some extent – he and Aldington were writing; it was not a set of principles they had followed to produce it, hence Pound's continual redefinition of the term as he strove to analyse more exactly how he thought their verse worked. But for now he wrote to Harriet Monroe with great excitement: 'I've had luck again, and am sending you some *modern* stuff by an American, I say modern, for it is in the laconic speech of the Imagistes, even if the subject is classic . . . This is the sort of American stuff that I can show here and in Paris without its being ridiculed. Objective – no slither; direct – no excessive use of adjectives, no metaphors that won't permit examination. It's straight talk, straight as the Greek!'[109] 'Direct' was one of Hulme's watchwords, but 'objective' was Ford's, derived from the Flaubertian principle of the presentation of a story without authorial comment. It doesn't imply that there is no psychological intensity, or that it is unrelated to subjective experience. In his 'Prologomena' Pound had said he wanted poetry 'free from emotional slither', in other words, not without emotion, but the emotion, as he says in his introduction to Cavalcanti, must be 'exact'. Some critics have persuasively suggested that imagist poetry is analogous to what Eliot would later call the 'objective correlative', which for him is 'the only way of expressing emotion in the form of art', that is, by finding something external, 'a set of objects, a situation, a chain of events', that will by 'the skilful accumulation of imagined sensory impressions' give the 'exact equivalence' of the emotion.[110]

Pound's reading of H.D.'s poems must have happened very shortly before his excited letter about them to Monroe in October.[111] He had already sent some of Aldington's poems to Harriet before those by H.D., '*Choricos*' (spelt in Greek letters), 'To a Greek Marble' and '*Au Vieux Jardin*'. Aldington would later mock Pound's weakness for foreign titles, which he described as 'a rather childish form of high-hatting'; but in 1912 he was high-hatting with the best.[112] Harriet Monroe much admired '*Choricos*', and it would remain her favourite of Aldington's poems, and be one of his most popular with many others as well. Its preoccupation with death, and a strangely eroticised death at that, is recognisably in the decadent tradition, and has shades of Poe or Swinburne. Its tone and imagery must have been familiar, its diction reassuringly poetic, even if its form were new:

> O death . . .
> Thou art the dusk and the fragrance;
> Thou art the lips of love mournfully smiling;
> Thou art the sad peace of one

> Satiate with old desires;
> Thou art the silence of beauty
> And we look no more for the morning;
> We yearn no more for the sun . . .[113]

Pound was pleased to have his protégé in print. His relationship with *Poetry* had started well. He was delighted to have access to a magazine adequately funded by others; the possibility that his advice would not always be taken does not appear to have occurred to him at this stage, though he would soon learn. Although it would not be a paid position, Pound would be a regular paid contributor, and Harriet Monroe had also promised to send him some extra payment for his efforts if she could. She described him in the first issue in glowing terms, as 'Mr Ezra Pound, the young Philadelphia poet whose recent distinguished success in London led to wide recognition in his own country . . . That discriminating London publisher, Mr Elkin Mathews, "discovered" this young poet from over seas.'[114] She goes on to list Pound's books. Pound must have enjoyed the praise even if he was irritated that she managed to get the title of *Canzoni* wrong, and give an erroneous publisher for *Provença*: a correction duly appeared next time. Harriet Monroe was a curious mixture as an editor; she had an eagle eye for what she thought blasphemous or indecent nuances, but in ordinary copy-editing she was very careless. Titles of books, for example, mentioned in the prose pieces of the magazine, are randomly capitalised, italicised or in inverted commas; details about her contributors are regularly slightly inaccurate. Pound would frequently write to her or Alice Corbin Henderson to correct her statements; he does not seem to have much minded her carelessness, unless it affected his projects, but he could find her respectability very irksome.

H.D. was the only one of the imagists never to publish a pre-imagist poem, unless one counts the Heine translation in *Paint it Today*.[115] Pound's 'creative pencil' might have chiselled that first poem, but it led her instantly to her own very characteristic mode. 'Hermes of the Ways' is based on a brief epigram by a Greek woman poet, Anyte of Tegea – the choice of a woman poet is surely no coincidence – which, as H.D. says, she had come across in the Greek Anthology.[116] H.D.'s poem is longer, more developed than the original, as is often the case in her translations, yet the effect sounds as spare as a faithful translation from the Greek (though since H.D. created so powerfully our present sense of what a Greek poem should be, perhaps it sounds that way because she invented Greek poetry for the modern English reader in much the same way as Eliot would later credit Pound with inventing Chinese). The original poem, consisting of two elegiac couplets, in which Hermes welcomes weary travellers home, would have been written in the form of an inscription (which is what 'epigram' originally meant) for a herm, or boundary stone, very much an ur-Hermes, associated with the early, chthonic stages of Greek religion.[117] The speaker in H.D.'s poem, however, is not Hermes but the traveller returning after a tempestuous, battering journey: it is a persona poem, like Pound's, as many of her poems would be, growing out of a similar need to find a shape for what she would describe as the 'inchoate' self. Norman Holmes Pearson, the close friend and supporter of H.D.'s later years, was to say of her:

She used art in order to find herself. That constant search for identity marks twentieth-century American literature. You remember Cummings: 'Why do you write?'. 'I write, I dare say, to become myself' . . . Or what does Pound call the hero, the protagonist of the *Cantos*? 'A man of no fortune, and with a name to come.' You could say that H.D. devoted her life to this kind of search . . . yet again, paradoxically, one is swept up into a knowledge of one's identity by the similarities in the patterns of other lives and other races . . . she used Greek myth to find her own identity . . . she writes the most intensely personal poetry using Greek myth as a metaphor. That is, she can say these things better and more frankly about herself using these other devices than she could if she simply said, 'I, I, I.' To say 'Helen' is really to free oneself.[118]

Pearson's formulation was one that many poets of the period would have understood; the 'bundle of accidents and incoherence that sits down to breakfast', as Yeats described the poet as individual person, was bound by the distorting conventional thought of the day; to get to a truer understanding of themselves and the world they had to work obliquely through another.[119] This speaking through others, often by translating others, would be central to the imagist movement.

Whilst in her later poetry H.D.'s personae would be complex and subtle reworkings of the female mythic figures of the Homeric traditions, in her early imagist period, up to the publication of *Sea Garden* in 1916, she writes mostly about the pre-Olympian nymphs, dryads, oreads, herms and so on, the often unnamed and undifferentiated gods of archaic Greek religion, a world that embodied the radical, elemental simplicity that she wanted in her verse. She may have discovered this version of the early Greeks in the work of Farr's friend, the anthropologist Jane Harrison, whose 1905 book, *The Religion of the Ancient*

Greeks, might well have attracted her in the British Museum Reading Room. Harrison says there that Hermes in his original form as an unwrought herm or boundary stone that marked the 'sanctity of a spot' was the earliest of the Greek *theoi* or chthonic gods; the next step was 'a square limbless "Hermes"' to which the Arcadians (Tegea is part of Arcadia) were 'specially partial'.[120] There is no definite proof that H.D. read Harrison's work, but so many of her ideas appear in her work that it would be surprising if she had not, though she may have come across them at second hand. Harrison, like Martin Bernal more recently in *Black Athena*, believed that early Greek pre-Homeric culture came from Africa and Asia, something H.D. also stresses, whilst the later Hellenic culture and the Olympian gods came from the north. The archaic pre-Homeric religion gave prominence to the female deities, in particular early versions of Demeter and Kore, though Dionysus is also associated with it; the later Olympians are much more patriarchal.[121] Like Jane Harrison, H.D. recreates the Greek world; it is no longer the Victorians' masculine citadel of Homeric heroes or Athenian repose but an earlier, more elemental place where the struggles of the female psyche can be played out. H.D.'s Greeks belong to the archaic world that was also being evoked by Epstein in his statues. They are no longer the originators of Western rationalism, but represent what she sees as a non-Western intensity and passion through which she can present her own psychic turmoil.

'Hermes of the Ways' was a fitting opening poem to H.D.'s *oeuvre*. It is a poem about the shoreline, that liminal space between land and sea that would appear so often in her poetry. As an expatriate American, on the edge of British life; as a bisexual, between sexualities; as an experimental poet, at the cultural margins, she was always at a 'borderline', as the film in which she later appeared with Paul Robeson would be called. In 1921, she would say in a letter to Marianne Moore, 'I can't write unless I'm an outcast'.[122] Louis Martz suggests that 'her poetry and prose, like her own psyche, live at the seething junction of opposite forces' – the reason why 'the active, shifting scene where land and ocean meet' is central to her early poetry.[123] The traveller in this poem has finally reached the safety of the sea-shore ('The hard sand breaks,/and the grains of it/are clear as wine'), yet the sea-shore is, as H.D.'s are so often, a harsh and stormy place:

> Wind rushes
> over the dunes,

> and the coarse, salt-crusted grass
> answers.
>
> Heu,
> it whips round my ankles!

At the beginning of the second part there is a brief moment of respite, associated, as in the original, with a stream:

> Small is
> this white stream,
> flowing below ground
> from the poplar-shaded hill,
> but the water is sweet.

After that, however, the harshness returns. The orchard's apples are 'hard/too small,/too late ripened/by a desperate sun . . . The boughs of the trees/are twisted/by many bafflings'. And yet, all the same, the ending suggests something of a home-coming:

> Hermes, Hermes,
> the great sea foamed,
> gnashed its teeth about me;
> but you have waited,
> where sea-grass tangles with
> shore-grass.[124]

What was this home-coming, buffeted and baffled though it is? I would suggest, as in Pound's 'The Return', Hermes is associated with writing; as Timothy Materer says, Hermes 'symbolizes poetic vision throughout [H.D.'s] poetry'.[125] H.D. had found what Pound would call her 'métier'; she knew now she would be a poet. It would be a struggle, on the margins, but it was her calling. Yet what her next step would be, she did not know. In the poem, Hermes 'of the triple pathways' stands 'Dubious/facing three ways'. In a few weeks, she would leave London to meet up with her parents. Would she ever be back? Even if she had come to a new sense of her aim, she was still doubtful about which path she would be following to achieve it.

V

POUND had, meanwhile, turned to some other prose, reworking the articles on American culture that he had drafted back in the States and that were to appear as 'Patria Mia'. He had asked his father to send those drafts on to him the previous November, but had been in no hurry then to leave the subject of Provençal poetry. Now, just under a year later, after his new engagement with the contemporary world, the moment had come. They appeared weekly in the *New Age* from the beginning of September until mid-November: since they were largely already written, Pound could deliver them with remarkable speed, although there were added references, anecdotes and poetic theories that postdated his American visit. The articles' ostensible subject was a quasi-ethnographic account of present-day America and its in-hospitable climate for the arts; their subtext was a justification of his own presence on this side of the Atlantic, and he was now able to quote Henry James, from their spring meeting, on the inevitability of ex-patriation for the American artist. He recounts fresh experiences, since his return to Britain, of the inanities of American magazine editors, including the rejection of 'Portrait d'une Femme': 'Of course,' he writes, 'art and prosperous magazines are eternally incompatible, for it is the business of the artist to tell the truth whoever mislike it, and it is the business of the magazine editor to maintain his circulation.'[126] This enmity between art and the commercial world would remain a core tenet for Pound, and finding a way of promoting what he saw as art without relying on the market became one of the central drives in his life. What was wrong with the United States, he argued, was not that there was no talent or what he calls 'artistic impulse', but that production was controlled by commercial market forces. Promising poets are told by editors: 'Dear Mr——, Your work, etc., is very interesting, etc., etc., but you will have to pay more attention to conventional form if you want to make a commerical success of it.'[127]

Pound's insistence that good art and commercial success are incompatible, a favourite modernist assertion, is a romantic but dubious one, and Pound's own attitude to the economics of his profession was very contradictory.[128] At the same time as he was denouncing commercialism in the *New Age*, he was writing to his father, explaining that he would soon be receiving a heap of circulars for *Poetry* and instructing him, 'Devote yr. self to booming the same as my screw will depend in part on the circulation.'[129] Shortly he would be writing home to describe his life as 'a few teas, and the old ringaround with wire-pulling concealed'.[130] Pound's preferred source of funding was the support of rich patrons, and later he would be impressively successful in securing these for others, if rarely for himself. In 'Patria Mia' his contention is that the United States is an essentially medieval society, still in the Dark Ages: what it needs is a renaissance, and the Renaissance, of course, had as its economic base the great Italian patrons. When no patron was forthcoming, Pound's alternative method was to rally as many people as possible (again family and friends) to make small contributions to what he thought were good causes (like *Poetry*, for example), rather like the principle Harriet Monroe had used herself. One wonders if his model here (and very possibly that of Monroe) was the funding of missionary societies, which were entirely dependent on the faithful for survival. Missionary societies in Britain and America had vast turnovers in the late nineteenth and early twentieth centuries, and voluntary contributions must have been the foundation for the Italian mission for which Homer and Isabel worked. Pound would have known the method well; perhaps he added to his missionary spirit, missionary economics.

Pound, it should be noticed, is not attacking American mass culture produced by monopoly capitalism, but, as he puts it, 'the appalling fungus of our "better magazines"'.[131] Their editors claim to represent cultured and educated standards, but in reality, according to Pound, favour the bland, the homogenised, the conventional and the out of date. Most, he alleges, judge by the standards of the 1870s, when American poetry was dominated by Boston gentility, and they fear 'the vital and renovating strata of letters more than they would fear beri-beri and the noisesomest pestilences'.[132] Pound's heated polemics make one suspect him of exaggerating, but when one thinks of the bowdlerised form in which Emily Dickinson's verse was published at that time, rhymes and punctuation tidied up, striking images toned down, the whole a travesty, he was perhaps justified. 'There is practically no one in America,' Pound asserts, 'who knows good work from bad – no such person, I mean, who is part of the system for circulation.' Pound was going through a rapid process of what Stephen Greenblatt has taught us to call 'self-fashioning'.[133] The arbiter of taste, in opposition to the craven, tasteless editors, was to be himself, and he would set himself up from now on as the iron judge of artistic merit. These magazine editors had the power to decide what has cultural status, but they promoted 'bad art'. Pound would present the world with what was good. His battle was not with 'the public', but with those in positions of power who had more access to the public than he did. From now on Pound would struggle for a position of authority and control in the literary world. He wanted the power of those editors, he wanted to achieve an artistic *putsch*, to become what we might now think of as a culture Tsar or, given his later hero-worship of Mussolini, a culture Boss: Aldington in his memoirs frequently referred to Pound simply as the *Duce*.

Pound had come to realise – and it was one of the most important lessons of his visit home – that the quality of literature in any place or any period is not simply due to the talent of a number of isolated writers, but that literary works come out of 'the system for circulation', what Pierre Bourdieu would famously describe as a 'field of cultural production'; editors, publishers, critics, agents all play their part in controlling what kind of work is available to read.[134] Given the paucity of patrons, he would have to break into the cultural marketplace and stake out new territory. Hence the number of little magazines that Pound would be associated with over the years in his efforts to change the literary map: *Poetry*, the *New Freewoman*, the *Egoist*, the *Little Review*, the *Dial* and many more. His one-time protégé Eliot would make modernism canonical through his editorship of the *Criterion* and his position at Faber & Faber. Later Pound's disciple James Loughlin would set up the publishing house of New Directions to publish Pound and others of whom Pound approved. Both Pound and Eliot worked tirelessly as critics, and Pound acted as unpaid agent to a host of new writers, and, at one stage, artists. 'Patria Mia' makes explicit that his desire is to seize control of the field of literary production from these despised editors and their errant judgement.

In his assumption, however, that there are absolute standards of good and bad art that admit of no qualification, and that he knows what they are, Pound precisely mirrors the conservative views of the editors he condemns. Many educated people at the time would have agreed, but for most of them these standards were based on the traditional notion of an upper class with a cultured and correct taste. Since the mid-nineteenth century, however, there had been repeated efforts by artists like the Pre-Raphaelites and the aesthetes, or intellectuals like Arnold and Pater, to wrest the arbitration of standards of beauty away from an elite social class to an elite composed of artists, or, in Arnold's terms, from the 'Barbarian' aristocracy and the 'Philistine middle classes' to 'men of culture', who appreciate 'sweetness and light'.[135] Pound displayed little interest in Arnold, yet just as much as Arnold – or the magazine editors – he is sure that he knows what comprises good taste, but like Arnold he thinks the judgements should be made, if not by 'men of culture', by a 'man of culture', viz. himself. Not for nothing would he later produce the uncompromising *Guide to Kultur*.

More radical artists than Pound would soon begin to question the whole category of art. In March of the following year, Marcel Duchamp presented his famous urinal at the Armory Show, throwing the whole notion into question. Peter Bürger has argued that only those who, like Duchamp, subvert the institution of art should be considered avant-garde, in which case Pound, like H.D., Aldington and Eliot, whom they were yet to meet, could never be thought of as avant-garde, for none of them ever gave up their belief in the importance of art. But none of them was solely concerned with aesthetics, with art for art's sake. Pound, as they all did, sees the quality of art and wider social conditions as intimately connected. In 'Patria Mia', when he writes about the coming of an American *Risorgimento*, he does not mean an artistic renaissance alone. 'A Risorgimento,' he writes, 'implies a whole volley of liberations; liberations from ideas, from stupidities, from conditions and from tyrannies of wealth or of army'.[136] Pound believed that censorship of what could and could not be said, the hypocrisy of the cloak of public respectability, corrupted culture, and he was undoubtedly right. One might wish he had been more aware of other of his society's ills, such as social injustice, or that he had been as alert to the impoverishment of factory workers as to that of artists, but the fact remains that he saw an artistic and a social mission as one. That was why he believed it was essential the artist should 'tell the truth whoever mislike it'. He continued to share Orage's view that reviving the arts would produce a better society, though with no clear view of how that would work.

For Pound, the enemy of good art and of the healthy society that would flow from it was chiefly the present literary establishment, in England as well as America, though he blamed the comfortably off middle classes in general. In a footnote he asserts, having condemned the English Poetry Society for making itself 'ridiculous' – he doesn't say how, but no doubt because they had objected to Harold Monro's inclusion of poets like himself in *Poetry Review* – that 'Poetry is not a sort of embroidery, cross-stitch, crochet, for pensionnaires, nor yet a post-prandial soporific for the bourgeoisie. We need the old feud between the artist and the smugger portions of the community revived with some virulence for the welfare of things at large.'[137] If Pound, like other modernists, feared that 'art' as they understood it would be swept away by increasing commercialisation and conformity, it was the 'smugger', well-heeled classes that would be to blame. Yet in the autumn of 1912 he was still optimistic that he could lead the public to accept his judgements, writing to Harriet Monroe that '[his] own belief is that the public is sick of lukewarm praise of the mediocre', though he realises it will take time, as '*Good art can't possibly be palatable all at once*'.[138] Even that limited optimism was to wane.

Pound was putting 'Patria Mia' together with much relish; penning a fiery attack was much more agreeable to him than labouring at careful description, and he decided he could simply recycle the abandoned and unfinished *Gironde* publishing what he had done so far jointly with 'Patria Mia', as 'Studies in Mediaevalism Past and Present'. In fact, the next year he amalgamated 'Patria Mia' with a sequel that appeared in the *New Age* the following summer, 'America: Chances and Remedies', and sent them off to an American publisher, Ralph Fletcher Seymour, a friend of Harriet Monroe, and the publisher of *Poetry* for the first four years of its existence. The manuscript was somehow mislaid, and only turned up again almost forty years later – perhaps appropriately enough, given Pound's by then obsession with economics – in some packages of old accounts.

'Patria Mia' was an immediate success; on 2 October 1912 he wrote to his mother that the editor was saying 'Best stuff on America since . . . etc.'. He was, he said, 'feeling more gay & irresponsible than I have for some months'.[139] By the time Pound had pronounced Aldington and H.D. members of the *cénacle imagiste*, he had become much more hopeful again about his literary career. In his new role of foreign correspondent for *Poetry* he had already achieved a small portion of power in the literary world that he had not possessed earlier in the summer. Imagism was as yet a fledgling school, but *Poetry* would give him a chance to launch his movement. As he gleefully told his mother, the magazine would give him a grip on things for the future. In addition, his place in literary London appeared secure. He was able to give his friend Williams' work a puff in the October American issue of *Poetry Review*, printing seven of the poems which would be included in a collection that he would persuade Elkin Mathews to publish the following year, and writing an introductory note that he described to Dorothy as 'a masterpiece of tactful iniquity'.[140] Yeats was increasingly relying on his companionship as a fellow-poet. (They would have a brief row later in the autumn, when Pound attempted, as he saw it, to improve some of Yeats' poems on their way to Harriet, but it blew over swiftly.) His friendship with Ford had completely recovered from the Geissen episode, and to his great pleasure Ford was now expressing admiration for his more recent poetry. In spite of the equivocal reviews for the Cavalcanti translations, he had a sufficient number of discriminating admirers to claim to be a poet of some standing. And when *Ripostes* was published on 5 October 1912 it attracted, at any rate in some quarters, a better critical reception than *Canzoni*.

Yet if his niche in what Bourdieu calls the field of cultural production carried status, it produced comparatively little income; he had symbolic capital, in Bourdieu's terms, but not economic. Dorothy's parents were certainly unimpressed. Presumably Pound had told them not long after his return of the fall in his fortunes, because in mid-September Olivia wrote him a chillingly frank letter, saying it was now quite impossible for Dorothy to marry him. Pound had already agreed, or perhaps even offered, to see less of her, and Olivia said firmly that once a week was all she would allow. For one thing, she complained, it had been extremely inconvenient keeping two days a week free for Pound's visits the previous winter (a comment which gives an intriguing insight into the arrangements for those visits: Olivia obviously felt she had to be present in the house but must make sure no other guests were). Even more importantly, she wrote, Dorothy must have a chance to meet other people, because it was imperative that she married *somebody*, as Olivia really couldn't bear 'this feminine life practically *à deux* for ever', and needed her out of the way. Should Hope die, she said with unvarnished candour, it would be particularly necessary, because in that case Olivia would probably marry again (did she have her eye on Yeats?) and Dorothy 'wd be very much de trop'. She had nothing against him in himself, she assured him: 'If you had £500 a year I should be delighted for *you* to marry her (no nonsense about waiting 5 years etc.) but as you haven't, I'm obliged to say all this – as her mother I can't see it any other way – I've seen too much of girls wasting their lives on men who can't marry them, & they generally end up by being more or less compromised demivierges.' Dorothy can't, she insists, go about with him 'American fashion – not till she is 35 and has lost her looks'.[141]

Pound was appalled by this mercenary cynicism, as he would soon tell his father, but for now he said nothing to his parents about his problems. At twenty-eight, he must have felt that, as a son-in-law, his gifts should outweigh his lack of wealth; art was more important than money. For now, however, he accepted Olivia's restrictions, though when he passed the edict on to Dorothy, as Olivia had asked him to do, on the grounds that it took a 'surgical operation' to get Dorothy to mention Pound to her, Dorothy simply replied: 'Once a week be hanged – – – Which of many reasons that might be, is given?', a comment which suggests that Pound had not yet mentioned his loss of income to her.[142] Pound did not appear to fret over-much about his restricted access. Perhaps he was having too good a time with Aldington and H.D. to care. One of his epigrams written to entertain Aldington might indeed be thought to indicate a lessening of ardour: 'As a bathtub lined with white porcelain,/When the hot water gives out or goes tepid,/So is the slow cooling of our chivalrous passion,/O my much praised but not-altogether-satisfactory lady'.[143] When Yeats saw this in the American Magazine, the *Smart Set*, in December 1913 he certainly feared that it meant Pound was losing interest in Dorothy, not realising it had been written over a year before. But Pound sent 'The Bath Tub' to Dorothy for her to read, which would have been very tactless even for Pound if he had thought she would take it personally. There is no evidence she did, and Pound's subsequent actions suggest that she had no need to do so.

By the time Dorothy returned to London, probably on 9 October, Pound's financial position had plunged further towards disaster. He had heard Swift & Co. had gone bankrupt; his £100 a year contract was null and void. On the 10th he wrote to his father, telling him that his patron was dead, had in fact been dead for some months, and Swift liquidated. 'None of this bothers *me* much,' he assured him, 'as I can by now look out for myself.' The problem was Dorothy's family, who had insisted they break off the engagement and were planning for Dorothy to be 'sold off in the society fashion'. 'You being a human being,' he told his father, 'would find it hard to understand the Englishness of things. I've been sick of the whole damn crew for some time.'[144] What he suggests is that he bring Dorothy back to the States and that they should live with his parents. He would find something to do, and promised that this time, unlike last, he would stay. Considering that for the last five weeks his articles in the *New Age* had spelt out with some fervour his reasons for refusing to live in America, this was an indication of how desperate he was feeling, though whether he was driven to this point by romantic passion, or sheer outrage at the way the Shakespears were behaving, is hard to gauge. Dorothy, however, anxious to follow the proprieties as best she could even in the circumstances of an elopement, would only agree if Isabel invited her. Homer was to cable either 'Come' or 'Don't', and then both of them were to write to Dorothy care of himself. 'It wont,' he explained 'be any too easy for her to take such a full plunge into the dark – not after the way she has been brought up.'[145] Pound sent a separate letter to his mother, reminding her of the struggle she had had with her genteel family when she first suggested marrying Homer. Isabel ought to understand. They wouldn't be worse off than Isabel and Homer when they first married: 'don't believe you regret it much,' he added.[146]

Homer and Isabel had mixed feelings about this; they were continually trying to persuade Pound to come back, even for a visit, so the possibility of a permanent return must have delighted them. They were, however, thrown by the absence of any reference to marriage, though Pound later reassured his father, a little huffily, that 'Naturally I should have arrived duly and legally united. You needn't have been alarmed on that score.'[147] That was early December. By then, he tells them, 'the situation has cleared', so he would not be returning. The owner of Swift & Co. had been arrested in Tangiers, and it was settled that Pound should have £25 a quarter for the next twelve months, and then a one-off payment of £65.

Although Pound remained on personal good terms with Olivia, the Shakespears' attitude to the marriage probably contributed considerably to a changed attitude to England that begins to emerge in his writing from that autumn. In the place of his very Anglophile sentiments in 1909, he would develop a deep contempt for general English culture, different from, but equal to, that he felt for America. He thought, indeed, as far as marriage arrangements were concerned, that for once American mores were far superior. Had he read Edith Wharton's 1905 novel, *House of Mirth*, which he undoubtedly had not, he would have realised that there were sections of American society where daughters were sold off in much the same fashion, if for a great deal more. As it was, he appears to have had the Shakespears at least partly in mind when in

'Patria Mia' he for once compares American morality favourably with British: 'So far as I can make out,' he wrote there on 31 October, 'there is no morality in England which is not in one way or another a manifestation of the sense of property. A thing is right if it tends to conserve an estate, or to maintain a succession, no matter what servitude or oppression this inflict.' In America, 'Our presumption is that those things are right which give the greatest freedom, the greatest opportunity for individual development to the individual, of whatever age or sex or condition'.[148] Rare praise for his country, which would not often be repeated, though the attacks on England would continue in the new year, when Orage asked him to write a companion series to 'Patria Mia' on England, which Pound entitled 'Through Alien Eyes'. It is worth writing about America, he says there, 'with what *The New Age* calls "moral indignation"', because it might do some good, but he has no such hope of England, with its obsession with ownership, of which the acquisition of its Empire is the apotheosis. 'The Englishman,' he says, 'has the sense of property – of his own property. It has made his empire; made it as fanaticism made the empire of the Crescent . . . The emphasis which the British subject can put on the possessive pronoun strikes us transpontines as at once hateful and barbaric. In the world of flowing phenomena how comes it that this otherwise quiet person can burst into violence with a *my* house, *my* this, *my* that.' In England, he said, he was 'perched on the rotten shell of a crumbling empire'; his little circle of literary friends in 'Kensington and its environs' were

carried on the back of a very large and very sickly elephant . . . London . . . is like Rome of the decadence, so far, at least as letters are concerned. She is a main and vortex drawing strength from the peripheries.

Thus the finest authors . . . are all foreigners.[149]

In illustration, he cites Yeats, James, Hudson and Conrad. No doubt he hoped others might include himself.

VI

In the autumn of 1912, Rabindranath Tagore was another writer who proved to Pound that the decaying heart of the Empire needed to draw strength from its peripheries: he was perhaps responsible for Pound's new consciousness of England as an imperial power, and he gave Pound his first significant contact with non-Western literature. Pound had told Dorothy on 1 October that he was to meet Tagore the next day, reporting with excitement three days later: 'I dined with Tagore on Wed. – discussed metres etc. Spent most of yesterday P.M. (2–6) with him. Discussing prosody, watching [William] Rothenstein paint his portrait, listening to him read & sing . . . He is very fine & makes me feel like a painted pict with a stone war club – Naturally I've done nothing else.'[150] He had arranged, he told her, to send six of Tagore's poems from his forthcoming book to *Poetry*. He had already let Harriet know that he would try to obtain some poems 'by the very great Bengali Rabindranath Tagore' for her: 'They are,' he assured her, 'going to be *the* sensation of the winter'.[151] He was right. The book, entitled *Gitanjali* (Bengali for 'Song-Offerings'), appeared later that month in an expensive and elegantly finished limited edition published by the India Society (750 copies, of which only 250 were for sale at 10s. 6d. each), and was an immediate and phenomenal hit, even though its circulation was comparatively limited. It was published again the next year by Yeats' publisher, Macmillan, and went into several editions. In 1913, Tagore was awarded the Nobel Prize for Literature, and given a knighthood. For Pound, it would be his first significant success in reshaping the cultural marketplace and changing the criteria by which poetry was judged.

The India Society, which first brought Tagore to the notice of the West, was then just two years old, having been founded in 1910 by the artist William Rothenstein, whom Pound had watched painting Tagore's portrait. Rothenstein, the Bradford-born son of Jewish immigrants, later Principal of the Royal College of Art, had developed a passion for Indian drawings, which he says in his memoirs he was able to purchase very cheaply, as they were in general regarded as valueless.[152] The one informed enthusiast for Indian art that he knew well was a remarkable woman artist, Christiana Herringham, then almost sixty, who had organised an expedition to India, largely funded by her own extensive private means, to copy the magnificent Buddhist paintings in the Ajanta caves near Hyderabad.[153] The British administration had no interest in preserving these, and was allowing them to deteriorate; copies were needed so that a record would exist. It may have been Herringham on whom Mrs Moore in *A Passage to India* was based; E.M. Forster certainly knew her and was aware of her sympathy for Indian culture, saying of her copies of the Ajanta paintings, which were exhibited at the Festival of Empire in 1911, that they 'revealed to us marvels of which we were unaware'.[154]

Until then, the usual British view of Indian art was that, whilst there had been, in the dim and distant past of Aryan purity (reckoned to be approximately 900 BC – AD 300), a 'classical period' of Indian architecture that had produced impressive enough art, the racial mix in India had muddied the Aryan inheritance and India had had a steep cultural decline. Although the authorities would admit some charming craft work was carried out, there was now no real art. Considering the high regard among theosophists and occultists for Indian religion and philosophy, it is surprising that such an attitude lasted so long, when Japanese art had been arousing interest for almost half a century and even African art had emerged, albeit as a controversial category, in the late 1890s. British rule in India, however, depended on training its officials to despise the native population, and this blindness to their art perhaps illustrates the pervasive power of the imperial mind-set.

Yet by 1910 change was coming. Rothenstein attended a lecture by Ernest Havell, the former Principal of the School of Art in Calcutta and one of the first British campaigners for Indian art. Havell deplored the British scorn for Indian culture; students in government art schools, he said, were taught European traditions, and learnt to be ashamed of their own, even though art survived throughout India as a part of their traditional culture, intimately bound up with their religious beliefs and everyday life. These government schools aimed to train industrial designers, not artists: as in Britain, industrialisation was destroying art and craftsmanship. Havell, clearly influenced himself by the arts and

crafts movement, argued against the distinction between applied and
fine art, and told his audience that a revival of traditional Indian painting
and sculpture was at last being led by a highly talented former student
of his in Calcutta, Abanindranath Tagore, and his brother
Gaganendranath. Indian art had been sleeping under British rule, but
now was reawakening.

Rothenstein was intrigued, but horrified when the chair of the
meeting, Sir George Birdwood, who had worked all his life on Indian
affairs, fiercely disagreed, insisting that there was no such thing as fine
art in India, intriguingly linking the Indians' decadent imagery with
that of the French symbolists, and saying of their statues of Buddha
that a 'boiled suet pudding would serve equally well as a symbol of
passionless purity and serenity of soul!'[155] It was the blinkered and prejudiced philistinism of those words, Rothenstein later said, which made
him immediately propose the founding of an India Society, to promote
the study and appreciation of Indian art. 'If artists,' he responded, 'had
only realised earlier in their Western art the value of Eastern ideas . . .
Western art would have had an entirely different character.' They could
have learnt from Eastern art that 'reality and realism are not the same
thing, and that the essence of art was reality'.[156] Here he sounds close
to what Roger Fry, whom he knew well, said in 1912 about reality in
Post-Impressionist art. Rothenstein himself was dubious about the Post-
Impressionists, but Fry quickly became fascinated by Indian art and
was one of the first to join the India Society.

The India Society officially came into being in April 1910, and
Rothenstein began to plan a visit to India with Christiana Herringham,
who was returning that autumn to complete her work of copying the
Ajanta cave paintings. His reasons for going caused consternation in the
India Office, where it was feared that an interest in Indian art would
encourage the Nationalists, but he managed to avoid the constraints
they tried to impose on him. He was deeply impressed by the art that
he saw, as well as by the great beauty of the country. Abanindranath
Tagore, Havell's gifted former pupil, had written to him after seeing a
letter he and twelve others sent to *The Times* expressing their admiration for Indian art, and while in Bengal Rothenstein visited the wealthy
and cultured Tagore family's elegant home. There he met their uncle,
Rabindranath, though he did not discover then that he was already a
famous literary figure in Bengal, writing both poetry and novels, as well
as being a fine musician and painter. When Rabrindranath visited
London in 1912, however, he contacted Rothenstein, and showed him

some translations he was making of his own Bengali poems. Rothenstein was impressed, and alerted Yeats, whom he had known since the early 1890s and who rapidly became even more enthusiastic than Rothenstein. Tagore's success in the West was assured.

Tagore was then fifty-one: ten years older than Rothenstein, and four years older than Yeats, a strikingly impressive, handsome and gracious man. Rothenstein did several drawings of him, in which, with his long hair and flowing beard, he looks remarkably like Victorian representations of Christ, no doubt the impression Rothenstein wished to convey. Yeats, with his interest in the occult and theosophy, had always been drawn to the East; at twenty-one he was profoundly and lastingly influenced by another Bengali, Mohini Chatterjee, whom he met through the Dublin Theosophical Society. Chatterjee preached the virtues of a particular variety of Hindu mysticism, Samkara philosophy, whose end was to express 'the supreme in the individual self', an aim which much appealed to the young Yeats.[157] (He was deeply disappointed many years later when he discovered that, after his return to India, Chatterjee had become a rich barrister.) Tagore, for his part, though he was opposed to British imperialism, was very open to the West, for although he wrote in Bengali he knew English well, and was widely read in Western literature.

Most importantly, perhaps, for Yeats, Tagore was a cultural nationalist who wanted to restore the Bengalis' pride in their heritage through his celebration of the country and its traditions, much as Yeats had been doing for the Celts. Yet he, like Yeats, was becoming wary of the political factions among his fellow-nationalists, and both of them had been condemned in their own countries for their refusal to go along with a narrow or reductionist nationalism. Just as Yeats had argued in his 1893 lecture that a national literature should be fed from many sources, Tagore believed the same, and his work blended Eastern and Western traditions. Moreover, Tagore argued that a truly national literature was also a universal one: in 1912 he wrote of Yeats, in an article published in Bengali in India shortly after he had met the Irish poet, that 'In the poetry of Yeats the soul of Ireland has found its expression', and went on to explain that 'the people of any country, be it Ireland, Scotland or any other reflect the light of universal humanity in their own fashion and present hues'. He likened the Irish experience to the Bengali: instead of despising their own language, as the English had taught them do, Bengalis like himself have 'realised that we could have a literature of our own and our own provision to appease the hunger of our minds'.[158]

It is intriguing that Tagore, given his commitment to writing in Bengali rather than English, doesn't mention the fraught question of whether Irish literature should be written in Gaelic or English. Perhaps he was not aware of the issue; it wasn't in any case quite comparable to the Bengali versus English choice, because there was a far smaller percentage of people in Ireland for whom Gaelic was a living language. Nor does he mention the Protestant/Catholic divide, which could have been thought to make Yeats' ability to express all of the Irish soul somewhat problematic. But if there were things about Yeats' position of which Tagore was unaware, he did not reinvent Ireland quite so thoroughly as Yeats reinvented Bengal in his introduction to *Gitanjali*. One of the things that excited Yeats most in what he was told about Tagore was that his songs – he set his poems to music himself – were sung by ordinary people as well as being appreciated by the most cultured. Here in Bengal, he thought, was a culture where all levels of society took its poets seriously, just what had attracted Couchoud to Japan, and Monroe to China. For this modernist moment, non-Western societies represented an idyllic world where art and beauty flourished without the bane of commercialism and utilitarian values. In Yeats' introduction, he reports that an Indian doctor said to him: 'No poet seems to me as famous in Europe as [Tagore] is among us. He is as great in music as in poetry, and his songs are sung from the west of India into Burmah wherever Bengali is spoken.' Yeats comments that

These lyrics – which are in the original, my Indians tell me, full of subtlety of rhythm, of untranslatable delicacies of colour, of metrical invention, display in their thought a world I have dreamed all my life long. The work of a supreme culture, they yet appear as much the growth of the common soil as the grass and the rushes. A tradition, where poetry and religion are the same thing, has passed through the centuries, gathering from learned and unlearned metaphor and emotion, and carried back again to the multitude the thought of the scholar and of the noble. If the civilization of Bengal remains unbroken, if that common mind which – as one divines – runs through all, is not, as with us, broken into a dozen minds that know nothing of each other, something even of what is most subtle in these verses will have come, in a few generations, to the beggar on the roads.[159]

As Richard Ellmann pointed out, this bringing together of 'the metaphors and emotions of unlearned people with those of the learned' was precisely what Yeats had always looked for.[160] For Yeats, Tagore's work achieved a fusion and wholeness impossible in modern culture.

Bengal was in fact a deeply divided society, not just British and Indian, but Hindu and Muslim, high and low caste, rich and poor, extremists and moderates in the struggle against the British. Tagore's family were Brahmin, but not acceptable to other Brahmins, some ancestor having offended tradition, and Tagore believed in a reformed Hinduism, anathema to traditional Hindus. He was, according to Mary Lago, 'somewhat outside the mainstream of community life, a fact of his own life that Rabindranath bore continually in mind'.[161] As a cultural nationalist, his work drew on what was traditional, but it was in an attempt to heal a damaged and divided culture, not something which sprang, as Yeats implied, from an integrated world. For Yeats, art is under threat in the West, because the artists have to battle with a philistine culture, a belief he was at the time impressing strongly on Pound. Western artists wear themselves out in critical attack: 'our minds gradually cease to be creative . . . Four fifths of our energy is spent in the quarrel with bad taste.' In Bengal, poetry is taken seriously; it isn't something left lying on 'ladies' tables', or only read by students who lay it 'aside when the work of life begins'. In the West, he says, 'We write long books where no page perhaps has any quality to make writing a pleasure . . . just as we fight and make money and fill our heads with politics – all dull things in the doing – while Mr Tagore, like the Indian civilization itself, has been content to discover the soul and surrender himself to its spontaneity.'[162] Yeats' enthusiasm for Tagore was very real, but his introduction to these poems was as much an attack on his own culture as a paean to Tagore's.

Yeats praises Tagore for his life-affirming attitudes – he even mentions Nietzsche and Blake in the introduction, those two exemplars of yea-saying for Yeats – but he says very little about Tagore's subject-matter, which draws on Hindu mythology to present the relation between God and the human soul as a love affair between a couple, so his songs could be read as erotically or as spiritually as one pleased. (The reader for Macmillan the next year would suggest that the songs in *Gitanjali* were influenced by the Song of Solomon, which is not the case, but one can see why he thought so.) It is hard to believe that Yeats was not attracted by this fusion of the erotic and spiritual, though he insists on the poet's 'innocence',' simplicity' and childlike closeness to nature.[163] Pound must have seen this as the same fusion of the sexual and the religious as that which lay at the heart of the pagan mysteries that fed into his troubadours' Religion of Love, though his only comment on Tagore's subject-matter is a reference to Dante's sublimated version of this, when he says Tagore's

treatment of love is 'not the Vita Nuova but it is as delicate'.[164] Both he
and Yeats were to associate Tagore with the Provençal poets, since in
his work, like theirs, poem and music are joined, and in Bengali intricately rhymed, as was Provençal poetry. In the English prose translations,
however, Tagore's poems, like the Japanese haiku, perhaps appeared to
offer the combination of directness, simplicity, and exoticism at which
imagism would aim; certainly, according to Pound, in an article he
published on Tagore in *Poetry* that December, the poems had affinities
with both the troubadours and the 'most advanced artists in *vers libre*'.
Tagore's songs, he points out, 'are sung throughout Bengal, more or
less as the troubadours' songs were sung through Europe in the twelfth
century', something a modern Western poet could only yearn for.[165]

Pound's enthusiasm for Tagore was unmistakenly genuine while it
lasted, though, as with Yeats, it was also a weapon with which to castigate the utilitarian West. Pound did not have Yeats' personal investment
in cultural nationalism, but the struggle to produce an art in the face
of the British establishment was one with which he entirely identified.
James Longenbach has suggested that Pound's assertion in *Poetry* that
'world fellowship' would be brought nearer by Tagore is simply absurd
posturing to impress Yeats.[166] But the year before Pound had already
written something very similar to the Japanese poet Yoni Noguchi.
Pound's belief in the power of art should not be underestimated.
Longenbach also finds preposterous Pound's claim that the West's
discovery of Tagore would be for the modern world what the culture
of Greeks from Constantinople had been to the Renaissance; yet eighteen
months later Pound was to assign a similar role to the Chinese. He was
looking for a new renaissance, and was coming more and more to feel
the West needed something from elsewhere, from some older, purer,
more vital tradition to set it in motion. The terms in which Yeats saw
the mercantile modern world in contrast to Tagore's holistic vision
became foundational to his thought. In a longer article on Tagore the
next March in the *Fortnightly Review*, Pound wrote that the humanism
introduced by the Renaissance is largely finished, and he quotes what
he had written in 'Psychology and the Troubadours' about its impact:
'Man is concerned with man and forgets the whole and the flowing.'
Tagore can reintroduce the West to the whole and 'into the emotion of
"the flowing," of harmonic nature, of orderly calm and sequence'.[167] As
he had said in *Poetry*, perhaps another such period is opening up through
this contact with the Bengali, which 'brings to us a pledge of a calm
which we need overmuch in an age of steel and mechanics. It brings a

quiet proclamation of the fellowship between man and the gods; between man and nature.'[168]

Quiet and calm: no wonder Pound came to lose interest in Tagore, if that was how he interpreted his work; such qualities were not for him. (He was wrong of course – if Tagore believed that when 'man realizes the kinship between himself and the universe . . . he sees the whole with the eye of the poet', he also talks of the 'agony of this direct perception of the universal', and the poet's 'inner anguish of realization' which creates 'an affinity between [the poet's] language and the language of ancient melody . . . Each new experience relives the ancient myth' – in fact, much closer to his own thinking than Pound realised.)[169] Another element in Pound's disillusionment was, as with Hulme and Bergson, his dismay the next year at Tagore's growing popularity. But for now he made commendable efforts to understand the form of Tagore's work. He has a very full account of the intricate rhyming system of the Bengali lyrics in the *Fortnightly Review* article, some of which he may have learnt from Tagore himself, and some from Tagore's fellow-Bengali, Kali Mohan Ghose, whom he met through Tagore. Ghose, whom he described as Tagore's 'charming disciple', was persuaded to teach him Bengali (he told his father in December that he was 'struggling with the Bengali alphabet which seems to have about 125 letters that all look exactly alike'), and together they translated some poems into English, like Tagore's lyrics, what one might call spiritual love songs, which were published the next year in the *Modern Review*, an English-language journal in Calcutta.[170] Yet for all Yeats' and Pound's praise of Tagore, even at the height of their enthusiasm they shared an unquestioned assumption that Tagore represented something earlier and older than the modern West, hence in one sense leading to their high estimation of him, but on the other consigning him to what Simon Gikandi has called a 'retrogressive temporality', to a past if better world; they did not recognise him as a contemporary struggling with a different version of the modern condition.[171] (May Sinclair, perhaps more perceptively, describes Tagore as a 'modern, very modern poet', and 'too various to be bound by one tradition'.)[172] Tagore's English was, however, a great deal better than Pound's Bengali ever was; he knew Yeats' work much more fully than Yeats or Pound ever knew his, as so little of his output was translated; he had far more of a handle on their culture than they on his, though it is not likely that this struck either of them. Yeats and Pound were challenging quite powerfully the low esteem in which Indian culture was held by the majority of the British, but one should not be surprised that some of their racist assumptions did not vanish overnight. Even Havell, the great advocate of Indian art, believed it owed its power to the Vedic, that is Aryan, philosophy on which it was based, still implying the racial superiority of the Aryan tradition, while Roger Fry's essays in *Vision and Design* on African and Indian art are full of deeply conventional references to lower and higher races. Still, the steps towards what Pound called 'world fellowship' that people like Pound, Havell and Fry took, making it possible for later generations to move beyond their own limited liberalism, should not be underestimated, even in the case of Pound, who later did so much to support the cause of one particular form of racism, anti-Semitism.

Pound has one other comment on Tagore that is worth noting: towards the end of his article in the *Fortnightly Review*, he wrote: 'He would have, I think, little use for "Art for Art's Sake"'.[173] It is clearly a statement of approval, and I quote it simply because there are still those who believe Pound espoused 'Art for Art's Sake'. Nothing could be further from the truth. Tagore left for America on 19 October, but Ghose remained in England, and Pound continued to see him. Six of Tagore's poems would appear in the December *Poetry*, along with three of Yeats', all solicited and sent in by Pound. He felt very satisfied.

PART IX

FURTHERING THE IMAGIST CAUSE

I

NEITHER H.D. nor Aldington was to meet Tagore. In his memoirs, Aldington says he was not allowed to, as he was 'too profane'. 'But,' he said, 'I could always tell when Ezra had been seeing him, because he was so infernally smug.' 'We had pi-jaw stuff about Tagore for weeks,' he recalled. 'Yeats would read the same things over and over from *Gitanjali*, as if they had been the Book of Common Prayer and we a congregation of fanatical Episcopalians.' Aldington saw the whole thing as a marketing ploy, not unlike certain critics of modernism today: 'The snob appeal was worked with consummate skill, and the first edition of Tagore's book was limited to five hundred expensive copies. May Sinclair gave me one, which was stolen long ago – anyway I didn't want it. But by the time the popular edition was out, all the cliques were chattering Tagore like mad though most of them had never seen a word he had written. Naturally it was a bestseller.'[1] Was H.D. also too profane? She may simply have been too busy packing up to join her parents in Italy, where they were about to arrive for their much delayed visit. A year after they first mentioned the visit, they finally reached Europe in October 1912 for a year-long tour, beginning with Italy. They had spent their honeymoon in Venice; now Charles Doolittle was retired, they wanted to visit it again.

Given the excitement with which H.D. had greeted the art collections of Paris and London, one would have expected her to look forward eagerly to Italy, but that was not the case. 'The Dryad is much depressed at the prospect of returning to its parental bosom,' Pound informed Dorothy in late September.[2] At the time H.D. must have seen this tour as the possible end of her London life. Her parents would expect her to go home to America with them. Her freedom would be over. A few art galleries could not compensate for that. Even if it wasn't the end, attached as she was to her parents, sightseeing with them, observing the proprieties, did not have the same appeal as wandering around a city alone or with her contemporaries. Moreover, as she told Isabel Pound, if she did not mind forgoing the London fogs, it was heart-wrenching leaving her London friends – in particular, perhaps, though she does not mention this to Isabel, leaving Aldington.

Her parents were sailing to Genoa, where H.D. was to meet them. She put off her departure till the last minute, travelling direct, even turning down the offer of the Rummels' guest bedroom in Paris for the night. Dr Snively and his daughter, H.D.'s friend Margaret, had crossed with her parents. Margaret's mother appears to have been dead by this time, though, as she is never mentioned by H.D., perhaps Margaret had been motherless all the time she had known her; in the 1920s, when Mrs Doolittle died, Margaret said that she felt she had lost a second mother. Margaret and Mrs Doolittle were very close, and in some ways Margaret had more in common with her than H.D. had; Margaret was soon to settle happily into domestic life, as Helen Wolle had done, and to occupy herself with her husband and family. Writing to H.D. some forty years later, the greatest tragedy she had to mention was breaking a couple of her favourite plates.

H.D. met up with the four of them on their arrival in Genoa on 14 October.[3] In the very brief 'Autobiographical Notes' that she made for Norman Holmes Pearson's projected biography, she records the event: 'I leave Oct. fog for Genoa, bright green shutters, I have long blue coat and black figured VEIL over largish hat, alone in hotel. Dr S. and M. come with mother and father from big liner. I see tall, grey figure of dad, standing as boat comes slowly in.'[4] They remained in Genoa a day or two, then went to Pisa, and on to Florence by 18 October. H.D.'s mother kept a diary of the tour, though one without many personal details, mainly just where they had been, what she had bought, to whom she had written, or had heard from, only just occasionally, when very excited, saying a little more. She was clearly having a wonderful time. She threw herself into sightseeing – galleries, churches, museums – often with H.D. and Margaret, sometimes just with Margaret, occasionally with Charles, sometimes by herself. Charles appears generally to have gone to sights on his own, or stayed at home reading. On 25 October she bought a dress for H.D. – the first of several on the journey. H.D. was delighted with them. They bought gloves, and looked at rings. H.D., Margaret and Professor Doolittle took Italian lessons in what H.D. recalled as 'a small stuffy upstairs room'.[5] In early December the

Sniveleys left them: Dr Sniveley was going to a position in Nice, presumably at an Episcopalian church there, and he and Margaret remained in Nice till his death two years later. The Doolittles went on to Rome. More sightseeing, more shopping, another dress, or rather the material for one, so visits as well to the dressmaker. According to her mother, H.D. met up a few times with 'English friends'. On 19 December, the entry in Mrs Doolittle's journal reads: 'Richard A. arrived and will be in Rome for a time.'[6]

Aldington apparently had no plans for following H.D. when she first went off. The visit to Paris had already stretched his resources. But he missed her badly, and he had had a stroke of good luck. Since Pound thought highly of Aldington's work and was keen to promote him, he had recommended him to A. R. Orage, editor of the *New Age*, the fairy godmother to so many of the young modernists. Not only did Orage agree to publish some poems, prose poem translations from Renaissance Latin, admittedly without payment, though gratifying none the less, but in addition he offered to commission a paid series of articles if Aldington could find a suitable subject. One wet, foggy morning Aldington had a postcard from H.D. (described simply in his autobiography as 'a friend'). The postcard 'showed a hillside of blossoming almond trees on the Italian Riviera. Underneath was scribbled: "These will be full out in a few weeks"'.[7] By the same post arrived his cheque of $40 from Harriet Monroe for the three poems that had appeared in the November *Poetry*. Aldington went to Orage, and suggested Italy for the series. Orage agreed: Richard bought a ticket for Rome (price £3) and set off.

Aldington was later to claim that at nineteen (he was actually twenty) he did the grand tour of Italy on thirty shillings a week, rather overstating his poverty, as he often did, but it was a spirited act all the same. What the Doolittles thought of Aldington and his friendship with H.D. is not recorded, but the journal entries suggest that they liked him. They invited him to dinner on Christmas Day, met up with him frequently and did not appear to mind that he and H.D. went off by themselves exploring Rome. Aldington was good at charming older women, and he quickly won round Mrs Doolittle. (Fayne Rabb says of the Aldington figure in *Paint it Today*, 'He was very tactful with Mother. Mother adores him.')[8] Aldington's biography furnishes many more examples. Professor Doolittle did not seem to have any qualms either. In February, when Aldington accompanied them further south to Naples, Paestum and Pompeii, H.D. reports that her father was 'very happy and

impressed with temples'.[9] If he had been worried by Aldington's presence that could hardly have been the case. Perhaps after Pound and
Frances Gregg, Aldington was something of a relief. In *Paint it Today*,
in which Aldington appears as Basil, and the Doolittles as the Defreddies,
he is recalled as

the thoughtful, flattering young Englishman who had befriended her against the
Americans in Rome. 'I came to Rome to see Rome and devils and ghosts and the
yellow Tiber,' she had raged at her poor mother, almost in hysteria, one day, 'not
just the very same kind of people we used to have at home, and all those American
School of Excavation idiots.' Basil had rescued her from a tea party. He had not
only rescued her with the utmost tact. He had rescued poor Mrs Defreddie as
well. He had actually taken her to the party in Midget's place and had come back
to the hotel with her and expounded on the party until it really seemed there might
be some grain of truth in his convincing statements. 'Lord, they're alive. You ought
to see the tribe up at the British consulate.'[10]

So perhaps Aldington actually helped soothe any family tensions that
may have arisen – not that Mrs Doolittle's journal gives any hint of
them – and he seems a welcome presence.

Quite apart from anything else, Aldington was probably an excellent
guide: he was very knowledgeable about the classics, and although it
was his own first visit to Italy, he had had Mr Grey's extensive introduction to Italian culture and places and had read, no doubt under Mr
Grey's guidance, all the well-known British homages to Italy (Ruskin,
Browning, Addington Symonds and Berenson are all mentioned in his
New Age articles), and had undertaken strenuous study of his Baedeker.
He must have been an informative as well as lively companion, even if
his information was at times a bit shaky; his *New Age* articles are full
of snippets of vaguely remembered facts that he happily admits may
not be quite accurate. Being Americans and unworldly, the Doolittle
parents probably would not have picked up the subtle signals that hinted
that he was not quite a gentleman, that Virginia Woolf for one sniffed
out so quickly when she met him. Aldington was intelligent, good-
looking, good-natured and very fond of H.D. That appeared to be quite
enough for them.

Mrs Doolittle's diary suggests she, like her husband, was very happy
on that journey south. Her entries become longer, with exclamations of
delight at the beauty of the scenery. The spring weather was lovely, and,
she writes, they 'saw flowers everywhere'. Aldington in his memoir wrote

about that journey that 'In Pompeii the bees hummed softly over the dwarf wild flowers among the ruins, while we rested and looked drowsily at the white smoke ebbing from Vesuvius. At Sorrento there were the freesias under the orange trees of the Coccumella garden . . . At Paestum the mourning asphodel grew profusely and there were tiny wild roses, descendants I like to think of the once famous rose-gardens.'[11] For H.D. and Aldington, 'ardent Hellenists' as Monroe described them, what was most magical about this area of Italy was that it had been settled by the Greeks before the founding of the Roman state, in the fifth or sixth century BC, and was full of Greek remains and associations.[12] Paestum's magnificent, ruined temples (Mrs Doolittle stressed the hawthorn and the narcissi growing round them) made a powerful impact on them all. Aldington wrote a poem about that visit to Paestum:

> Steal out with me
> Over the moss and the daffodils,
> Come to the temple,
> Hung with sprays from untrimmed hedges . . .
>
> Wild roses of Paestum.

It is a love poem, but also, like the asphodel, it is mourning, in this case for the disappearance of a past world and past ecstasies: 'Ghost moths hover over asphodel;/Shades . . . drift past us'.[13] Aldington's poems often evoke this sense of loss, the disappearance from the modern world of the beauty and passion of an earlier time, especially in his poignant evocations of a lost Greek world.

If that Paestum poem is melancholy, Aldington's articles for the *New Age* certainly were not, though they too condemn 'the feebleness of the modern mob' and celebrate the Greek love of beauty.[14] These 'Letters from Italy', as they are entitled, share two of the characteristics of much of British travel writing about Europe at the time: they do not dwell on the major sights, which Baedeker had now been describing in authoritative detail for over seventy years, and they express enormous disdain for tourists, among whom travel writers never included themselves. Edith Wharton, for example, in her 1905 travel book, *Italian Backgrounds*, insists that Italy is 'a foreground and a background. The foreground is the property of the guide-book and of its product, the mechanical sightseer; the background, that of the dawdler, the dreamer and the serious student of Italy', such, of course, as herself.[15] This is very similar to

Aldington, though he is a rather scatty student, notwithstanding his impressive width of reading for a twenty-year-old; yet there's certainly plenty of dawdling and dreaming, and very high spirits into the bargain. In some ways his pieces seem remarkably modern, very much the kind of ego-journalism so much practised today – a great deal about himself, highly opinionated and often extremely rude about the people he meets. Before the end of that first journey he has written off the entire Italian peasantry, on account of their habit of spitting: 'I am a friend of the people; I "hold enlightened views on the franchise"; I never speak of the "hoi polloi" . . . I was once a socialist – but I cannot wholly sympathise with a class whose members have such unpleasant habits.' He has an asterisk by the word 'socialist', linked to an Author's Note at the foot of the page, which reads: 'Since writing this I have become an anarchist.'[16]

Aldington's views are certainly anti-establishment: he is appalled by the behaviour of the Italian soldiers in Rome. 'Militarism,' he exclaims, 'O bilge, O sentiment!'[17] He blatantly refuses to be patriotic – one article in which he describes telling a would-be friendly compatriot in Naples that he hates the English prompted an indignant letter of complaint to the *New Age*. But in other ways he unthinkingly reproduces the prejudices of his day. His jibes against militarism include his scorn for 'ecstasies over darky soldiers from Lybia', and he talks of the way that in England he has been '"fighting the lone hand" against the Jew and the Philistine', apparently equating 'Jew' here unquestioningly with commercialism.[18] And if he dislikes the English, he appears to have nothing but disdain for most other races, especially the Americans, though he does say – perhaps again to be provocative – that the 'pleasantest person' he met on his journey to Rome was a young Bengali friend of Tagore's: 'Odd that one feels such a toad besides these cultured Orientals'.[19] He makes it clear, however, that his programme is an aesthetic rather than political or moral one: 'In spite of Mr Shaw,' he writes, 'who thinks that because he is virtuous there shall be no more cakes and ale, we still dream of the city walled with jasper, where folk, like the ancient Greeks, are more concerned with beauty and the beautiful appearance of things than with any system or work of ethics and conduct.'[20]

These articles give an intriguing insight into this young poetic revolutionary's views on art and literature. Some of his comments are definitely calculated to shock, as, for example, when he writes indignantly, 'What has Dante to do with Florence? That old poker-up of hells, and investigator of vague heavens?'[21] In architecture Aldington rejects everything later than the early Renaissance, and in painting much Renaissance and post-Renaissance work into the bargain. 'Today,' he writes, 'when we have had every degree of photographic vérisme, and the weariness of the artists therewith has shown itself in wave after wave of drastic and sometimes ridiculous revolt, the Chinese, the Byzantines, the Greek vase-painters, stir one far more than all the square miles of canvas between Michelangelo and Courbet.' In fact, although his tone is so often brashly iconoclastic in a typically modernist way, in taste he is quite literally a pre-Raphaelite – Raphael, incidentally, he cannot abide, 'good to sentimentalise over, and . . . meat for the bourgeois'. He dismisses even Michelangelo as 'more madman than mystic, too vague and terrible for anyone but a Blake to worship'. His one 'perfect type of the Renaissance artist' is Leonardo, 'subtle, curious, delicate in technique, seeking all knowledge, beginning everything and completing so little'.[22] Leonardo here is aligned with Sappho and the imagists, as the maker of beautiful fragments.

The works, however, that Aldington praises most on the journey are always Greek; like some bas-reliefs of Bacchic maenads he found in a Rome museum: 'You will not find it in your Baedeker, O earnest student, neither does Cook's conducted take cognisance thereof,' he says, with evident satisfaction.[23] As he walks through the Temple of Poseidon at Paestum, marvelling at the beauty of these 'pre-Periclean Greek things', he says: 'I knew how foolish and trite our "civilisation" is, and that the few who care for beautiful things will not look for them in the twentieth century. What part have we in this loveliness? We have built Balham and Manchester and the new Law Courts as our memorials – and here are these perfect creations, abandoned and silent, with the life that created them lost, but still such a delicate rebuke to our vulgarity.'[24]

The writers whom Aldington commends are as eclectic a bunch as his choices in the visual arts, but they are those who are central to the imagists: he admires Catullus and Ovid; Homer and Shakespeare are quoted *passim*; but the poet he extols most is Theocritus, whom he and H.D. were translating together; he quotes his own translations frequently, but he doesn't mention a companion translator. He pays tribute to 'M. de Régnier's beautiful *vers libre*', and comments that de Régnier must know Theocritus' eclogues by heart, establishing Ancient Greece and contemporary Paris as his main axes.[25] In the period between the Renaissance and the present, he mentions a variety of writers, but there are only two for whom he goes out of his way to signal his affection.

One is that eighteenth-century proto-modernist, or indeed proto-postmodernist, Laurence Sterne, whom he evokes as a model for his own travel-writing, which does indeed have some of the anecdotal, inconsequential style of Sterne's *A Sentimental Journey*. Like Sterne he doesn't stick simply to the English language, but while Sterne introduces the occasional piece of French dialogue, Aldington bestrews his text with French, Latin, Greek and Italian phrases. The other writer he applauds is Swinburne, as he would continue to do long after he fell out of favour with other modernists. In 1950, Aldington would bring out a collection of the aesthetes' writing, in which Swinburne features conspicuously, entitled *The Religion of Beauty*. In 1913, that was very much his own religion, and the same could be said of H.D. The next few months in the peace and beauty of Hellenistic Italy were to be the happiest that H.D. and Aldington would have together.

A few days before H.D. left London, 'Fry's Second Post-Impressionist Exhibition, British, French and Russian Artists' had opened. In spite of Pound's reference to the Post-Impressionists in his preface to Hulme's poems, and although it was phenomenally successful – it had 50,000 visitors and continued to run until January 1913 – he does not appear to have gone. Apart from Whistler and Epstein, Pound was still not taking any great interest in the visual arts, though what with the crisis over Dorothy, and his energetic work on behalf of *Poetry*, perhaps he simply did not find the time. Perhaps Aldington had gone before he left for Italy; he had certainly learnt from somewhere to despise *vérisme*. What was significant about this second exhibition was the inclusion of the British artists: Wyndham Lewis, Duncan Grant, Vanessa Bell, Frederick Etchells and Roger Fry. There was now, in Richard Cork's words, 'an emergent English avant-garde' in the visual arts appearing simultaneously with Pound's new literary movement.[26] Little more than a year later, Pound would be keen that they should join forces, but for now he focused solely on literature.

One poet who did visit that exhibition was John Gould Fletcher, still living a largely lonely and restless life, frequently visiting the continent, and only intermittently in London. He had missed Fry's first Post-Impressionist Exhibition, being on another Italian visit with his sister, Mary. His mother had died earlier in 1910, and his sisters had agreed that instead of the second tranche of $25,000 that they had agreed to give him, they would provide him with an annuity of $3,000, then £600. Given his extravagant tastes and financial impracticality, it was a wise move, though he would repeatedly curse them bitterly while waiting for his next cheque. Fletcher had become interested in the visual arts by late 1910 after meeting the painter Horace Brodzky, who was later a good friend of the sculptor Gaudier-Brzeska and wrote a book about him after his death. For a while Fletcher acted as munificent patron to Brodzky, and wondered if he too should become a painter. They travelled on the continent together, sketching and visiting art galleries, until Fletcher became bored once more and decided to give up patronage. By now his main reading was in French poetry: more Baudelaire, and in addition Emile Verhaeran, Jules Laforgue and Tristan Corbière, people Pound had not yet glanced at. Fletcher's poetry began to change; his subject-matter was now most often, as it was for the French poets, the modern city. In 1912 he made another friend, this time one of whom he would not tire so rapidly: Horace Holley, an American expatriate painter and poet who ran a gallery in Paris. Holley was an ardent supporter of the Post-Impressionists (it was he who published the collection entitled *Postimpressionist Poems* in 1914), and he introduced Fletcher to works by Cézanne, Gauguin and Van Gogh. Deeply impressed, Fletcher wondered once more if he should become a painter, but decided instead to explore similar experiments in poetry. Back in London, enthused by Holley, he went to the Second Post-Impressionist Exhibition, an experience that, he later told Amy Lowell, left all his aesthetic assumptions 'demolished'.[27] Discovering the Post-Impressionists, like his reading of French poets, was moving him towards an increasingly experimental style. Holley was a regular contributor to a feminist journal, the *Freewoman*, which would later evolve first into the *New Freewoman* and then the *Egoist*, and become a crucial vehicle for imagism. It seems likely that it was through Holley that in 1912 Fletcher, who poured scorn on his sisters' support for the suffragettes and wrote in one of his notes, 'woman is purely animal', finally achieved his first publication in this bastion of women's rights.[28]

In the meantime Pound, with the conflict with the Shakespears resolved, had returned once more to fashioning himself as a leader of the avant-garde. He was working, he told his father, on some thoroughly modern poems. In December he was interviewed by a fellow-Philadelphian, John Cournos, who had recently given up his job as art critic of the *Philadelphia Record* to come to London. Cournos summed up the poet's work in what are clearly Pound's own terms, echoing as they do his poem on Whistler in *Poetry*: 'No one need be astonished if, after having passed through the various stages of his wide-ranged development and manifold experiment, he shall achieve something new and distinctly his own, just as in the art of painting a certain distinguished country-man of Pound's succeeded in being Whistler, in spite of Velasquez and the Japanese.'[29] With *Ripostes*, mixed as it is, Pound had begun to find his poetic path. Both Yeats and Ford had found things to praise, which greatly pleased him; it contained some of the best poetry that he had written so far, 'Δώρια', 'The Return', 'The Seafarer' and 'Portrait d'une Femme'. Williams, to whom he had dedicated the collection, wrote what was clearly a long and detailed response to the volume, with which Pound was delighted, telling Williams, 'you've seen a lot that I suppose nobody else will . . . So I suppose you've earned the bloody dedication.'[30]

The reviews of *Ripostes*, however, were a mixed bunch. Pound was beginning to accumulate enemies. The note of 'tactful iniquity' that he had appended to Williams' poems was 'tactful' about Williams' poetry but scarcely so in other respects, for he had included a throwaway note, in which he said that 'considering the tolerance accorded in England to such authors as Mr Noyes, Mr Abercrombie and Mr Figgis, I think there are a number of American works which might be with safety offered to the island market'.[31] As he admitted to Harriet Monroe, 'I make three enemies in a line . . . I raise up for Abercrombie passionate defenders (vid. R. Brooke in the next *Poetry Review*). Even Brooke can find little to say for Noyes, and nothing for Figgis'. He was quite unrepentant: 'Until someone is honest we get nothing clear . . . I'm sick to loathing of people who don't care for the master-work, who set out as artists with no intention of producing it, who make no effort towards the best, who are content with publicity and the praise of reviewers.' He was saying all this as a means of stiffening Monroe's resolve, adding emphatically: 'I think the worst betrayal you could make is to pretend for a moment that you are content with a parochial standard. You're subsidized, you don't have to placate the public at once.'[32] In one sense, it is a highly principled stand, but it presupposes that one's judgements are always right, and that the making of correct poetic judgements justifies cruel and painful attacks. Pound's attitude is, of course, very much tied in to his belief that producing good art is a moral act, a truth-telling process; bad art is a lie. Pound, in fact, had in some ways a similar mind-set to the contemporary Russian revolutionaries, whose hour would come in five years' time. They were convinced that it was essential to destroy the present structure to bring in utopia, even if death, wretchedness and suffering had to be inflicted on the way. A stinging review is, of course, in another league from violent death, but Pound's belief in the necessity of frontal attack was not dissimilar from the Bolsheviks'. It is possible, indeed likely, that he brought about poetic change more rapidly by his *blitzkrieg* tactics (to change the historical analogy), but he would himself – like many of the Russian revolutionaries – pay a heavy price for it. Already he was beginning to recognise this. 'I've got a right to be severe. For one man I strike there are ten to strike back at me. I stand exposed. It hits me in my dinner invitations, in my weekends, in reviews of my own work. Nevertheless it's a good fight.'[33] Aldington's later comment was, 'Unluckily, Ezra had read Whistler's *Gentle Art of Making Enemies*, and practiced it without the "gentle"'.[34] Yet, on the other hand, there are numerous testimonies to his great generosity to other struggling artists. John Cournos, who after that first interview would become friendly with all of Pound's circle, wrote in his autobiography in 1935: 'Ezra . . . was one of the kindest men who ever lived'.[35] And even Aldington admitted that 'when he wants [Ezra] can be a pleasant companion and the most generous of men'.[36]

Pound was to pursue his conflict with Abercrombie further. He had probably been irritated when some of his poems in the February issue of *Poetry Review* were followed by a eulogy to Abercrombie, written by the latter's close friend Wilfrid Wilson Gibson, claiming that 'Since the issue of his first book . . . there has been no doubt in the hearts of those who care most for poetry . . . that Mr Abercrombie's is the most significant voice of our time'.[37] That, Pound doubtless felt, was his own place. When Abercrombie published an article recommending that poets study Wordsworth, Pound was outraged, and challenged him to a duel. He was still indulging in his wild fencing, literally as well as metaphorically. Abercrombie, who heard greatly exaggerated accounts of Pound's fencing skills, suggested that they attack each other with unsold copies of their books, which, as Pound probably had more than Abercrombie, could have been thought of as a generous suggestion. Luckily, however, the event never took place.

When *Ripostes* appeared, with its reference to the Tour Eiffel days and Hulme's five poems, Hulme himself was no longer in London, nor indeed at Cambridge. He had retreated in September to Macclesfield, where his kindly aunt Alice Pattinson lived, and would move on to Germany in November, to flee the wrath of a philosopher acquaintance, Herbert Wildon Carr, who accused him of corrupting his sixteen-year-old daughter, Joan, still a schoolgirl at Roedean. Hulme had tried to seduce her, though unsuccessfully, in spite of the fact she was infatuated with him, but they kept in touch, Hulme writing her letters which could hardly be called love letters in the usual sense, but which apparently (none appear to be extant) introduced her to a range of four-letter words she had failed to learn at Rodean, and described the sexual act to her at length and with clinical exactitude. Anti-romanticism, or anti-pathos, the quality David Trotter ascribes to Hulme and Lewis, could not be taken much further; it is perhaps appropriate that Joan disengaged herself from Hulme's spell by reading Swinburne by candlelight and deciding she preferred his romanticism to Hulme's variety of classicism. She broke off with Hulme, but one of Hulme's letters came to light. Wildon Carr contacted his solicitors and, later, Hulme's Cambridge College, St John's, to which Hulme would never be able to return. He had aborted an academic degree for the second time. He kept the whole thing a secret from his family, who never found out why he had to leave Cambridge once more.

Given Wildon Carr's fury, Hulme might have felt happier if he could have got away sooner from England, in case word spread, but before he left he, or rather Flint, had to complete the translation of a second book, Georges Sorel's *Reflections on Violence*. Flint was resistant at first to pressure to work at greater speed, pointing out he could equally well do overtime at the Post Office, where at least he could rely on payment: but he admired Hulme considerably, and in the end said that he would do it because Hulme was the most intelligent man he knew. Sorel was a socialist of anarcho-syndicalist tendencies, which might make him seem an unlikely choice for a self-proclaimed Tory, but Hulme's idea of a Tory had no more to do with the Conservative Party than his religion had to do with the Anglican Church. Sorel, like himself, was fiercely anti-democratic, and scorned the belief in progress. As an anarchist, like Hulme he rejected philosophic systems and argued that revolutionary action would come about through the direct response to myths or images, rather than reason, an idea with clear analogies to Hulme's Bergsonian view of poetry, and indeed Sorel had been much influenced by Bergson. Sorel was much admired by the Action Française group, as well as by Benito Mussolini, then still a socialist himself. The deadline for the translation was met, but by then Swift & Co., which was publishing the book, had gone bankrupt, and it did not appear until 1916, appropriately enough being reviewed in 1917 by T.S. Eliot, who would later do so much for Hulme's posthumous fame. Eliot admired the book greatly, commenting that 'it expresses that violent and bitter reaction against romanticism which is one of the most interesting phenomena of our time . . . the scepticism of the present, the scepticism of Sorel, is a torturing vacuity which has developed the craving for belief'.[38] This 'violent and bitter' anti-romanticism could well have been what centrally appealed to Hulme. The book finished, Hulme left for Germany, having promised Wildon Carr to stay out of the country for a year. He did in fact return the next May, but the visit to Germany, although involuntary, would bear fruit, introducing Hulme to fresh ideas that offered a new answer to his own tortured scepticism

Like his family, Hulme's London friends were never told of his reasons for leaving the country. The loyal Tancred published another Herrick-like poem in the *Poetry Review* as a send-off, suggesting Hulme was having a well-earned rest:

> Great Hulme! as you by dint of toil have won
> Laurels and cater for your pot, have done
> With fostering verse, lay by Sorél, desist
> From turning your yoked brain-might into grist.[39]

Pound must have missed his conversations with Hulme, but he was seeing more of Ford, spending Christmas with him and Violet in a cottage in which he reported Milton had once lived, not a good omen, as perhaps Pound should have realised; it was damp and dingy, and without enough inkpots to go round, a trying situation for three writers spending a week together. (In fact Milton had lived some miles away; his biographer Max Saunders thinks that Ford was probably romancing again, and Pound a gullible victim.) Ford and Pound would always get on best in briefer encounters. Living together did not go well. Ford knew Elsie's libel suit was in the wings, and he was dreading it; tension was high between himself and Hunt. Being a third party cannot have been easy.

Even without H.D. or Aldington, Pound's life remained busy and sociable in early 1913. As well as meeting up with Yeats, Ford and Plarr, he was seeing more of Flint and Brigit Patmore. He saw Dorothy, though she was out of London for much of the time. Frances Gregg he had continued to see occasionally after H.D.'s departure, sometimes without Louis, for whom he did not care – it was mutual – but she had returned to America at the end of 1912. When not occupied with his own work, he sought out talent for *Poetry*, and, in particular, he applied his mind to furthering the cause of imagism. Three poems of Aldington's had appeared in November, with a note which explained that 'Mr Richard Aldington is a young English poet, one of the "Imagistes", a group of ardent Hellenists who are pursuing interesting experiments in *vers libre*; trying to attain in English certain subtleties of cadence of the kind which

Mallarmé and his followers have studied in French.'[40] Wrong again, as Pound told Alice Corbin Henderson in exasperation: 'The note in *Poetry* is very incorrect. Imagism is concerned solely with *language and present-ation*. Hellenism & vers libre have nothing to do with it . . . There is Imagism in all the *best* poetry of the past.'[41] The notion that imagism was limited to Greek themes must have, however, been reinforced for the readers of *Poetry* that January by the appearance of three of H.D.'s very Hellenistic poems that Pound had sent to Harriet Monroe the previous October. These were published in January and ascribed to 'H.D. Imagiste': 'Hermes of the Ways', 'Priapus: Keeper-of-Orchards' and 'Epigram: After the Greek'. Rather surprisingly, Harriet Monroe had not objected to the title of 'Priapus', nor to its sexually charged content. The former (Priapus is a phallic god of lust) might have been made acceptable by its classicism, and she may not have noticed the latter.[42]

The publication of the sobriquet *imagiste* appears to have taken H.D. somewhat by surprise – apparently she had not realised that Pound's urge to advertise the *imagiste* brand would mean that she would be presented to the world in quite this way. Certainly next time she had poems published she wrote to Harriet Monroe to say that she would prefer that '*imagiste*' be dropped. She would, however, continue to use the name H.D. Some feminist critics claim that she had already decided H.D. was to be her writing name before the day in the British Museum tea-shop, as she had earlier signed a letter to Williams that way. But we have all occasionally used initials as shorthand. It is certainly unlikely she used it to hide her gender, as has also been suggested. Monroe's note on her in that January issue of *Poetry* had stated that she was 'an American lady resident abroad, whose identity is unknown to the editor', and reviews always made clear it was widely known that H.D. was a woman.[43] It was more likely that in the first instance she welcomed the initials because she was always embarrassed by the name 'Doolittle'; after her marriage, she said, the initials ensured that she and Aldington kept their poetic identities separate. Back in January 1913, however, this mysterious H.D.'s poems had been read in Boston by another poet, Amy Lowell, whose first book of poems, *A Dome of Many-Coloured Glass* had been published the previous year. Lowell decided she too was an imagist. It was to be a significant decision for the history of imagism.

III

In the same January issue of *Poetry* as H.D.'s poems was a report by Pound, entitled 'Status Rerum', dated with some precision 'December 10', on 'the state of things here in London . . . as I see it' (a modest qualification which Pound might not have thought of a few years later). In this he announced to the world that he found 'Mr Yeats the only poet worthy of serious study', though he 'would rather talk about poetry with Ford Madox Hueffer than any man in London.' He praised Padraic Colum at some length, and mentioned somewhat non-committally that there are 'a number of men whose names are too well known for it to seem necessary to tell them over' – but then goes on to tell nearly a dozen, from Hardy to Rupert Brooke. He had kind words for some 'little known' others, his friends and former Rhymers Ernest Rhys and Victor Plarr, and also for Wilfrid Scawen Blunt, 'the grandest of old men', whom he was yet to meet. He had a small puff for Aldington: 'Among the very young men there seems to be a gleam of hope in the work of Richard Aldington, but it is too early to make predictions.' He does not mention H.D., but then on 10 December she had not yet been published, so could be said to be not yet part of the state of things. He sums up this list of names by saying that he could mention 'a hundred writers who have given pleasure . . . But it is one thing to take pleasure in a man's work and another to respect him as a great artist'.[44] This is a great deal less glowing than his early eulogies on the subject of the literary scene to Williams, but, although he described it to Dorothy as a 'denunciation of everybody except Yeats & Colum', it is a far cry from Pound's embittered post-war diatribes against the London of this period, though it has to be said that he would comment in a letter to Alice Corbin Henderson, written on 20 January, 'There just IS nothing alive here except W.B.Y. and

Les Imagistes. God I don't want to hide any body from deserved honours BUTTTTTTTTTTT!!!!!!!!!'[45]

The nub of 'Status Rerum' was indeed a passage on imagism. 'The youngest school here that has the nerve to call itself a school is that of the *Imagistes*. To belong to a school does not in the least mean that one writes poetry to a theory. One writes poetry when, where, because, and as one feels like writing it. A school exists when two or three young men agree, more or less, to call certain things good; when they prefer such of their verses as have certain qualities to such of their verses as do not have them.' These disclaiming prevarications can have brought little enlightenment to his readers as to the tenets of *imagisme*, but Pound went on to give one hint of what might be called good by these 'young men', H.D. being again ignored at this point. Explaining that 'space forbids' a proper exposition of the *imagiste* programme, Pound noted that 'one of their watchwords is Precision'. They dislike 'dull and interminable effusions' (it is hard to imagine a poetic school in favour of them), believing that one needs to learn to write a good short poem, or even a good line, before being able to write a long poem. These preferences are in line with the reference to 'life and intensity' in his first letter to Harriet Monroe, but as a poetic programme they are very little changed from that of the Rhymers, who had already reacted against the long Victorian poem, as well as against didacticism, pomposity and verbiage. But in 'Status Rerum' Pound disguises that particular debt. His reference, however, to this still mysterious group of imagists could be relied upon to stir the curiosity of the reader of *Poetry*, in preparation for the next phase of the campaign to establish his new 'school'.

'Schools' was not the way the London literary world so far conceived of itself – clubs were another matter – but Pound saw himself as importing the language of Parisian artistic discipline into the world of London's amateur literati. Over the next few years, as it happened, English poetry would come to be seen by many as a division into two main schools, or at least groupings: on the one hand, the imagists and those later identified as modernists, versus the Georgians, the latter being held up to ridicule or acclaim, depending on the critic's view of modernism. It is not true, however, as has sometimes been suggested, that Pound invented imagism in opposition to the Georgians. In December 1912, neither Pound nor anyone else saw them as taking a distinctive or separate trajectory. Edward Marsh, then Winston Churchill's secretary, a lover of poetry rather than a poet, had just edited *Georgian Poetry 1911–12*, which was published by Harold Monro at the end of 1912. It was not to reach the bookshops until 16 December, although Pound knew of its imminent arrival. The anthology was Rupert Brooke's idea: a collection of modern poems by younger poets, the title merely marking them off historically from the older generations of Victorians and Edwardians. There was no suggestion that the movement would be a refuge for the conventional and staid, as these anthologies were later accused of being. Far from it: they too felt they were rejecting all that was Victorian. Like the imagists, and the Rhymers before them, these poets were opposed to rhetoric and didacticism, and on the whole preferred the brief, lyric form: like the imagists they moved away from poeticised language towards that of everyday. Rupert Brooke saw *Georgian Poetry*, in fact, as 'a volume designed as the herald of a revolutionary dawn',[46] and Monro would later say that it had been Brooke's 'warm contention, indeed, nearly his main principle, that the British public should be shocked'.[47] Pound himself had been asked to contribute to *Georgian Poetry*, and had not done so largely by chance. The two poems Marsh wanted were, firstly, as I mentioned earlier, 'Ballad of the Goodly Fere', which Pound, in his newly sensitive state of embarrassment over his archaisms, refused to let him have on the grounds that it was not modern, and secondly 'Portrait d'une Femme', which Pound wanted for his own collection *Ripostes*. By the time of the second anthology, Marsh had decided only to include British writers, so Pound was not asked again. It is true that he might not have been asked in any case, since his poetry was by then perhaps too modern for Marsh, who liked an element of tradition. Marsh loathed the Futurists, remembered Pound in his memoirs chiefly for his incorrect use of sapphics, and, although he published poems by D.H. Lawrence, chided him gently for his lack of attention to orthodox rhyme. Lawrence, rather less gently, childed him in return with being 'a bit of a policeman in poetry'.[48]

Marsh, public school and Cambridge, was at the heart of the Establishment, even if all his poets were not; in later life, he was a little diffident about this youthful enthusiasm for poetry and said that he felt about his work as an editor 'very much as I should towards having been Captain of Cricket at Westminster'.[49] He remained a bachelor all his life; Brigit Patmore's son Derek suggests he was a repressed homosexual, and says he doubts that he ever had a sexual experience, but he liked to help young literary men, and he idolised the handsome Brooke. As Alan Pryce-Jones has said, 'His outlook . . . was characteristically English. Theorising about art was foreign; announcing aesthetic and critical doctrines was foreign. His approach to artistic problems was pragmatic and amateur. If his formula for an anthology worked, it was good.'[50] It certainly sold. The well-connected Marsh, aided by the also well-connected Brooke, made sure review copies were distributed to the right people on the right papers. The anthology was suitably hyped, albeit with a few caveats about Rupert Brooke's excessive realism, but that probably helped the sales. It was a commercial success from the beginning; seven months later, it was in its sixth edition. In all, Edward Marsh reckoned, 15,000 copies were sold.

Georgian Poetry 1911–12 was the first of five anthologies. Significantly, perhaps, no woman appeared in that first anthology – indeed in the five volumes, only two women ever featured, one of whom was the aristocratic Vita Sackville-West. Marsh had somewhat guiltily tried to find a woman for the third volume; Monro suggested Charlotte Mew, but Walter de la Mare pooh-poohed her and Marsh's courage failed. Marsh's decision to ask British poets only – in practice they were nearly all English, unlike the mainly Celtic Rhymers – did perhaps mark a shift away from what were by then the modernising tendencies, which often came from the Americans in London, and generally from those with a more cosmopolitan outlook. The Georgians looked back to Wordsworth, not across the Channel to Paris. They did not use *vers libre*, nor were there, as one of their admirers put it, any 'carnal influences due to French poetry'.[51] Later Richard Aldington, explaining why he 'thr[e]w in [his] lot with the two Americans' rather than with the English poets, wrote that 'The Georgians were regional in their outlook and in love with littleness. They took a little trip for a little week-end to a little cottage where they wrote a little poem on a little theme. Ezra was a citizen of the world, both mentally and in fact. He went off to Paris or Venice with vastly less fuss than a Georgian affronting the perils of the Cotswolds.'[52] Aldington's view of the Georgians was not entirely fair. A couple of the later volumes, for example, included some of Siegfried Sassoon's bitter and incisive war poetry: nothing little there. T.S. Eliot was equally guilty, as Robert Ross points out, of ignoring the presence of the occasional painfully powerful poem, when he wrote that the main characteristic of the Georgians was 'pleasantness'.[53] The modernist scorn for the Georgians was never shared by the public. The second anthology sold 19,000 copies, something of a record in poetry publishing at the time. But in December 1912, although he was hostile and dismissive, Pound did not realise what the Georgians would come to represent. He reported with some satisfaction to Dorothy that 'The eagle [Yeats] groans that "no one" could read the georgian anthology with pleasure'.[54] He sent off a instant brief review to Harriet, saying 'this collection of verse printed since 1910 will reveal to the American reader about all the younger London points of view in poetry which are likely to be un-represented in my notes . . . Those who have read the *Lyric Year* with interest will peruse this anthology with deepest admiration.'[55] Harriet, perhaps wisely, forbore to publish it.

Georgian Poetry was printed by Harold Monro's Poetry Bookshop, which officially opened in January 1913, bringing the bookshop consid-erable help with its funds, as well as welcome and effective publicity. The arrangement had been that Marsh would guarantee publication costs, but any profits would be divided equally between Monro and the contributors. Marsh himself took nothing, but the royalties, paid approx-imately every six months, were a great solace to indigent poets. The Poetry Bookshop was in Devonshire Street, off the Theobalds Road, an area just south of Bloomsbury, just west of Clerkenwell and just north of Holborn, but not really part of any of them. At the time it was a very poor neighbourhood – a 'slum' is how Flint described it – though para-doxically it was also an area where gold-beaters worked, and the sound of their hammering could be heard all day long. Monro had chosen the neighbourhood because of his desire to take poetry to the people, but, as Flint would later write, 'the people cared nothing for poetry, and the acquaintances he made in Devonshire Street merely regarded him as a possible source of free drinks after the public house had closed'.[56] The littérateurs of London on the other hand poured into his bookshop, came to the readings he organised regularly, and, if without a ready bed, slept upstairs. The Poetry Bookshop became an important publishing house. As well as the phenomenally successful anthologies of *Georgian Poetry* Monro would publish the English edition of *Des Imagistes*, Aldington's first collection, Flint's second, and many other books of poetry.

Monro had ceased to be editor of *Poetry Review* at the end of 1912, though he continued the journal much as he had originally envisaged it under the title of *Poetry and Drama*. The problem with the original *Poetry Review* was that half of it had comprised the *Poets' Chronicle*, the monthly publication of the very conservative Poetry Society, which met in little groups around the better areas of London and the Home Counties. Members of the Poetry Society objected strongly to Monro's choice of contributors and subject-matter (to Rupert Brooke, one should note, as much as to Pound), and *Poetry Review* continued under the

staid editorship of Stephen Phillips, a deeply dull poet who was thought
by the Poetry Society to be a safer pair of hands. Even so, in a late
1913 issue of Phillips' *Poetry Review*, there is a letter of complaint about
the modern poetry that the journal published from none other than
Aldington's father. What must he have thought of his son's work? (The
letter gives evidence that Albert Aldington was not entirely grateful for
his wife's efforts to restore the family fortunes; he disguises the fact
that he lives in an inn by giving his address as the more respectable-
sounding 'Mermaid Club'. Perhaps it was his father who taught
Aldington to be ashamed of his mother.)

During January, Pound gave three lectures in the Mayfair drawing-
room of the well-to-do society hostess and friend of Olivia Shakespear,
Eva Fowler. The lectures covered his various interests in sequence, the
first being on the Provençal troubadours, the second on Tagore, and the
third on *vers libre* and metrics. It was probably in order to give the last
lecture that he read one of the critical books recommended by Flint in
his August article, and already well known to Hulme in 1908, Vildrac
and Duhamel's *Notes sur la technique poètique*, a book which he was soon
to be quoting in discussions of imagism, but, for all his new concern
with the modern, that inclusive lecture sequence perhaps confirmed
that he would never be prepared to proclaim the total superiority of the
present over the past, nor, indeed, that of the West over the East. He
was appalled when Edmund Gosse rebuffed Yeats' efforts to have Tagore
elected to the prestigious Academic Committee of English Letters, and
was still seeing a good deal of the delightful Ghose, but his interest in
the Far East, first aroused by Binyon in 1909, also appeared to be growing,
belatedly following Dorothy's own. Dorothy had recently produced one
of her very few oil paintings, entitled *Landscape: Devil's Cheese Ring*,
which Richard Cork exhibited in his 1974 exhibition, *Vorticism and its
Allies*, describing it as 'her first attempt to break away from the Victorian
water colour tradition and combine an interest in early Cubism (the
boldly simplified foreground trees) with her admiration for Japanese
prints (the mountainous horizon)'.[57] On 4 January 1913, Pound wrote
to tell her that he had 'contemplated mediaeval japanese prints at the
[British Museum] & feel ages older & wiser'.[58] He also reported to both
Dorothy and his father that Binyon had been to the States to see the
Freer collection of Oriental art, and lamented that there was nothing
comparable in Britain. The Far East was, as it happens, in vogue: Pound
had told his father that his lectures would take place in Mrs Fowler's
'new chinese drawing-room'; Dorothy had a new Chinese skirt and

Pound was searching, in Liberty's and elsewhere, to find some matching jade jewellery.[59] But he had also bought a history of 'Hindoostan' for fourpence; India continued to be his main Eastern interest, but only for a few months longer.[60]

Such lectures helped his finances, but Pound was still looking for more ways of promoting imagism. In early January, before the lectures began, he had told Dorothy that Flint was writing 'an intelligent article on me chiefly at my own dictation'.[61] To Alice Corbin Henderson he forbore to mention the dictation, merely saying he was asking Flint to write a note on 'Imagisme': 'I can't very well do it myself,' he explained, 'and he is getting known for his knowledge of contemporary work in France so I thought him the best person to describe the school.'[62] The article would appear in the March *Poetry*, followed by a much longer piece entitled 'A Few Don'ts by an Imagiste', signed by Pound himself and described by him to Dorothy as 'a little kindergarten course in Ars Poetica'.[63] It became one of the most famous imagist documents, and is still required reading on some creative writing courses today. Pound felt the time had come for a manifesto – though it was a manifesto that explicitly denied that imagists had produced a manifesto – and to enlighten, to some extent at least, the readers of *Poetry* as to the nature of this school, following the elusive hints that had been dropped up to then.

According to Patricia Hutchins, who interviewed Flint in the 1950s, the first Flint heard of this article was when Pound arrived at his house with the text of an interview with himself supposedly conducted by Flint. Pound wanted him simply to sign the manuscript. Flint, who was no pliant disciple, something Pound was slow to learn, refused, and reworked it in his own words. Pound insisted on making revisions, slashing away at Flint's text much as he did at his friends' poetry. References to 'Mr Pound' were changed to 'an imagiste', conversation turned into more austere indirect speech, and whole paragraphs removed. Flint's original version was clearer (and funnier) than the final text, but Pound preferred to remain enigmatic yet authoritative. By a neat sleight of hand the article simultaneously claimed and disclaimed avant-garde status. 'The *imagistes* admitted that they were contemporaries of the Post Impressionists and the Futurists; but they had nothing in common with these groups. They had not published a manifesto. They were not a revolutionary school; their only endeavour was to write in accordance with the best tradition, as they found it in the best writers of all time, – in Sappho, Catullus, Villon.'[64] Neither Pound nor the other imagists were in sympathy with the Futurists' uncritical worship of the modern, it is true, though ironically they were to gain some fame in Russian literary circles a couple of years later as the 'English Futurists'. That they simply wrote in 'the best tradition', however, was the position that all four of the present imagists would maintain. Lawrence Rainey interprets this as being straightforwardly anti-avant-garde, but it is surely more complex than that, though it was perhaps a perverse, even a *faux-naïf* line, as they knew perfectly well they appeared 'a revolutionary school', and, in the case at least of Pound and Aldington, very much enjoyed scandalising their readers. Yet Pound, as Eliot was to do later, was always to align himself with his own chosen tradition of the best, and would claim an austere classicism while most rudely upsetting the accepted norms; the article also tells its readers that 'the school musters altogether a most formidable erudition', and that the imagists display 'an earnestness that is amazing to one accustomed to the usual London air of poetic dilettantism'.[65]

The part of Flint's account which would arouse most interest were the three rules that he says the imagists followed. These had been put together by Pound, with his passion for lists:

1 Direct treatment of the 'thing,' whether subjective or objective.
2 To use absolutely no word that did not contribute to the presentation.
3 As regarding rhythm: to compose in sequence of the musical phrase, not in sequence of a metronome.[66]

In those last two rules, Pound had captured two of the most important qualities of the new poetry – its pared-down, elliptical quality, and its shedding of traditional metric forms in favour of more flexible cadences. Pound was later to say that the second was the most important of the three. His phrase 'direct treatment of "the thing"' refers to these poems' freedom from moral comment, explanatory context or narrative elaboration, and has nothing necessarily to do with an attempt at visual exactitude or pictorial clarity, which the name 'imagism' could suggest. Pound, in fact, in 'A Few Don'ts' made it clear that was not his intention: 'Don't be descriptive; remember the painter can describe a landscape much better than you can ... When Shakespeare talks of the "Dawn in russet mantle clad" he presents something which the painter does not present. There is in this line of his nothing one can call description; he presents.'[67]

In Flint's original version the interview continued:

'Surely', I urged, 'these are the rules which every poet worthy of the name has engraved on his heart?' . . . Mr Pound became unprintably voluble for a few minutes. I gathered that in his opinion, there were few poets worthy of the name, and that having judged most contemporary poetry according to his standards, he found it wanting. With this judgment I was inclined to agree; and I thought of the two hundred odd volumes of verse that had passed through my hands during the last few years . . . 'But why Imagistes?' I asked when Mr Pound has [*sic*] recovered his calm.[68]

Pound crossed all this colourful and chatty account out, putting in its place simply 'By these standards they judged all poetry, and found most of it wanting.' He left the next two sentences, the answer to 'why Imagistes?', almost intact: 'They hold a certain "Doctrine of the Image," which they had not committed to writing; they said it did not concern the public, and would provoke useless discussion.'[69] Needless to say this hidden doctrine, even without being committed to writing, has provoked much critical discussion, not all of it useful, it must be granted. The phrase must have been Pound's own, for Flint later suggested it was Pound indulging in mystification, as some later critics have also thought. Pound never offered an actual explanation, but twenty years later he made the suggestive comment that the term 'imagism was formulated almost in order to give emphasis to certain qualities that [H.D.] possessed to the maximum degree: a mytho-poetic sense that was deep, true and of Nature'.[70] The 'Doctrine of the image', one can surmise, referred to this mythopoetic sense, the visionary quality that Pound believed great art should have, the theological term emphasising his belief that art was true religion, and that it connected one with the flows and energies of the universe. As the piece went on to say, the imagists considered that 'Art is all science, all religion, philosophy and metaphysic'.[71]

Pound's set of admonitions, 'A Few Don'ts by an Imagiste', which followed Flint's 'interview' were not all, as he put it, in the 'Mosaic negative'. Much of it, it has to be said, remains very practical advice: 'Use no superfluous word, no adjective, which does not reveal something'; 'Use either no ornament or good ornament'; 'Don't allow "influence" to mean merely that you mop up the particular decorative vocabulary of some one or two poets whom you happen to admire'; 'Don't chop your stuff into separate *iambs*. Don't make each line stop dead at the end, and then begin every next line with a heave.' As well as providing a reading list of exemplary poets, 'Sappho, Catullus, Villon, Heine when he is in the vein, Gautier when he is not too frigid; or . . . seek out the leisurely Chaucer', Pound recommends the practice of translation, the way he had trained himself, and would continue to do. He ends by saying, somewhat sardonically, "'. . . *Mais d'abord il faut être un poète*," as MM. Duhamel and Vildrac have said at the end of their little book, "*Notes sur la Technique Poétique*"; but in an American one takes that at least for granted, otherwise why does one get born upon that august continent?'

The most important part of Pound's 'Don'ts', however, was the beginning, not a 'don't' at all, but his definition of an 'image', which, he says, 'is that which presents an intellectual and emotional complex in an instant of time'. He goes on to explain that he is using "complex" . . . in the technical sense employed by the newer psychologists, such as Hart, though we might not agree absolutely in our application'. Bernard Hart, the 'newer' psychologist referred to here, had described Freud's idea of a complex first in the *Journal of Abnormal Psychology* in 1907, in an issue dedicated to the idea of the subconscious. The issue must have stirred considerable interest, because it was reprinted as a book in 1910. Quite how Pound came across Hart's work he doesn't say, but this was an area in which G.S. Mead and the Quest Society were interested, and Pound was still closely in touch with Mead; his own interest in psychoanalysis at this period, was, as it was for the Quest Society and the Society for Psychical Research, an extension of that mixture of scientific and occult explorations of the nature of the mind that Pound had been led to by Yeats. As I mentioned earlier, H.D. recalled many years later that in 1912 Pound had been very intrigued by psycho-analysis: he knew some American psychoanalysts in Paris, perhaps through Margaret Cravens, whose occult interests, as well as her distressed state of mind, could well have led her in that direction. At the time, H.D. resisted Pound's attempts to persuade her to engage with it, but her own later deep if unorthodox interest in psychoanalysis would blend it, as those pre-First World War psychic investigators did, with her own mystical and esoteric beliefs.

In his article Hart had described the subconscious as 'a sea of unconscious ideas and emotions' on whose 'surface plays the phenomenal consciousness of which we are personally aware'. These unconscious ideas and emotions form 'complexes', fusions which impact on the individual's psyche. They possess, he says, 'both potential and kinetic energy', and can affect consciousness either directly or indirectly, in the latter case through 'symbolisms, word forgetting, disturbance of the association processes, etc.' As he stresses, a 'single idea or image in consciousness' may be the product of a 'multiplicity of unconscious complexes'.[72] In Pound's version of this, the image, for Hart the fusion of the pulsating kinetic energy of these various unconscious complexes, becomes for Pound a complex itself. Hart's unconscious complex has both 'constituent ideas and affect', in other words, both intellectual and emotional elements, as Pound's image has. These two elements, concentration and energy, would be central to Pound's theory of poetry.

Later in the article Hart says that 'the complex may be said to be the psychological analogue of the conception of force in physics', a comparison that surely must have attracted Pound, chiming as it did with his own identification of art with energy by analogy with one form of force or another, electricity or magnetism, or, more broadly, with the physical 'fluid force' of the universe.[73] The 'image' perhaps is connected with the force, not just of the psyche, but for Pound more comprehensively and mystically with the life-force, hence its power. Pound goes on to insist on the visionary impact of 'the image': 'it is the presentation of such a "complex" instantaneously which gives that sense of sudden liberation; that sense of freedom from time limits and space limits – that sense of sudden growth, which we experience in the presence of the greatest works of art'. Yet if, for Pound, this power is a quality of all great art, the terms in which he expresses it are very much of his moment. It is intriguing that 'sudden liberation' was the exact phrase Vanessa Bell used to describe the impact on her of the first Post-Impressionist Exhibition.[74] David Kadlec has pointed out the similarity between the modernist ideas emerging in Pound's thought and those of contemporary anarchists; he links their 'direct action' to the 'direct treatment' of the object, and one could see something similar here in the instanteous liberation given by the impact of the image.[75] Pound shares their urgency and utopianism, even if his aims are very different.

Pound went on to say 'It is better to present one Image in a lifetime than to produce voluminous works.' For the next few years, he would warn against the dangers of over-production, but in producing the 117-odd cantos perhaps he forgot his own advice. There's no doubt he wanted them to fuse as one supremely potent image, but possibly someone should have been brave enough to suggest he revisited them with his 'creative pencil'; if he had ever finished them, he might have done so.

POUND would later say that the three principles on which imagism was based were agreed by H.D., Aldington and himself in 'the spring or early summer of 1912', though he somewhat confusingly places their discussions after the publication of Flint's influential article on French poetry, which he misdates as August 1911 instead of 1912.[76] It was indeed not till after Flint's article that the actual imagist programme began to shape itself, but it is striking that Pound is ready to acknowledge their contribution, and no doubt the debates earlier in 1912 in Kensington and Paris played a part. Now, with Hulme in Germany, and Aldington and H.D. in Italy, in early 1913 Flint was becoming increasingly import-ant to Pound as a literary companion. It was probably on one of the visits to discuss *imagisme* that he decided to apply his pencil in Flint's Highbury dining-room to his poem 'A Swan Song', originally published in *The Net of the Stars*. Pound recalled this as the moment at which Flint saw the light about imagism. Quite what Flint thought at the time is hard to guess. Flint, after all, had already started writing in what he would describe as 'cadences' for Goldring's *Tramp*, and would continue to do so. 'A Swan song' was a very early and still traditional poem, but he had written much more imagist-like poems since. He may well have prickled at Pound's condescension, but the advice on concision and presentation had a noticeable impact on his poetry. Flint's original poem had begun with an evocative description of the swan and the pool on which it floats, but moved on to the poet's own melancholy and suicidal thoughts at some length, the poem being 68 lines in all. Quite apart from anything else, Pound thoroughly disliked such gloominess in poetry, though he realised the lines about the swan on the water itself provided an arresting image. The new version had just 16 lines, each about half the length of the original, and it concentrated on that image, reducing the poem to its most telling phrases. Flint's description of the pool went:

> The fishes quiver in the pool
> Under the lily shadow cool,
> And ripples gilded by the whin,
> Painted, too, with a gloom of green,
> Mingled with lilac blue and mauve,
> Dropped from an overhanging grove;
> White rose of flame the swan beneath the arches.[77]

Those lines in the new version read:

> Under the lily shadow
> and the gold
> and the blue and mauve
> that the whin and the lilac
> pour down on the water,
> the fishes quiver.

The long despondent tail is reduced to just three lines, two of which also draw on that first stanza; the poem in its new version ends:

> Into the dark of the arch the swan floats
> and the black death of my sorrow
> bears a white rose of flame.[78]

In addition to the change from metrics to *vers libre*, from a full description to a few evocative touches, the poem changes from one that overtly describes the poet's feelings at length, to one where a central image is briefly evoked and the poet's mood conveyed through that. 'The Swan' would appear in the July *Poetry*, with three other of Flint's poems described as being in 'unrhymed cadence', and a fourth imagist would be introduced to America.[79]

Meanwhile, Pound was still promoting Tagore, sending several more of his poems to *Poetry* for the May issue. For now he tolerated Tagore's popular success, telling Harriet that 'it serves as illustration of what I said a while back. These fools don't KNOW anything and at the bottom of their wormy souls they know they don't and their name is legion and if once they learn that we do know and that we are "in" first, they'll

come to us to get all their thinking done for them and in the end the
greasy vulgus will be directed by us . . . for that reason we can and must
be strict and INFALLIBLE.'[80] Tagore had written to Pound from the
States, sending him further translations from the Bengali and asking him
in his courtly way to make corrections: 'I do not know the exact value
of your English words,' he explained. 'Some of them may have their
souls worn out by constant use, and some others may not have acquired
their souls yet'. Pound must have written back in alarm saying these
poems were too pious, because Tagore replied that 'in the original there
is nothing that savours of pulpit', but he assured him he would publish
nothing Pound advised against. Pound had sent him a copy of *Personae*,
which Tagore praised through an analogy, surprising for a non-Christian,
but perhaps not for a subject of the British Empire, with the story of
the Garden of Eden. So much modern English poetry, he felt, has 'eaten
the forbidden fruit, lost her simplicity and shamefully become conscious
of her nakedness trying to hide herself in all manner of elaborate garbs
woven of dead and decaying leaves. Your muse . . . has come out, clothed
in her own youthful body, full of life vigour and suggestive of incalcul-
able possibilities of growth.'[81] Pound was no doubt grateful, but his
admiration for Tagore had taken a knock. There would be no point in
his work if it were simply 'more theosophy', he told Harriet.[82] Although
he would still warmly review Tagore's second book that autumn, he no
longer thought Tagore the answer to his renaissance.

Pound's latest poems, a group entitled 'Contemporania', were now
appearing in *Poetry*, making very clear his change of direction:
'Salutation the Second', for example, begins:

> You were praised, my books,
> > because I had just come from the country;
> I was twenty years behind the times
> > so you found an audience ready.
> I do not disown you,
> > do not you disown your progeny.
> Here they stand without quaint devices,
> Here they are with nothing archaic about them.
> Observe the irritation in general:
>
> 'Is this,' they say, 'the nonsense
> > that we expect of poets?'
> 'Where is the Picturesque?'

'Where is the vertigo of emotion?'
'No! his first work was the best.'
'Poor Dear! he has lost his illusions.'[83]

The irony is, of course, that the device he uses, that of the poet addressing his own poems, he derives from Catullus and Cavalcanti, quite quaint and archaic in its own right, however much he had moved towards everyday language: later in the poem he instructs his poems to 'Dance the dance of the phallus/and tell anecdotes of Cybele', still clothing his most shocking pronouncements in classical garb. Pound instinctively removed his poems in one way or another from the quotidian. His very reference to 'coming from the country' seems to relate to another classical tradition, a poet coming from rural simplicity to the sophistication of Rome, though it fits tellingly his twentieth-century experience of expatriation.

Harriet Monroe was not at all sure what to make of these poems. Pound had now decided that art should not only be concerned with what he called 'the cult of beauty', with which he had long been preoccupied, but that there was also a place for 'the delineation of ugliness', the satirical mode that he had learnt from Flaubert and Catullus.[84] Some of these satires she was nervous about printing, and Pound agreed to withhold a couple for now, although he upbraided her sharply for her caution: 'G——d!', he wrote, 'you can't emasculate literature utterly. You can't expect modern work to even look in the direction of Greek drama until we can again treat actual things in a simple and direct manner.'[85] Pound's songs succeeded, as she had feared, in irritating much of the public, though Floyd Dell remained a loyal supporter, writing in the *Chicago Evening Post Literary Review*: 'Ezra Pound . . . Your poems in April *Poetry* are so mockingly, so delicately, so unblushingly beautiful that you seem to have brought back into the world a grace which (probably) never existed, but which we discover by an imaginative process in Horatius and Catullus.'[86] Pound was delighted, writing to Monroe: 'Dell is very consoling. It's clever of him to detect the Latin tone.'[87] Possibly the Latin name for the collection, 'Contemporania', and the title of one of them, 'Pax Saturni', might have given Dell a clue.

Poems like 'Saluation the Second' are entertaining, but they certainly don't have the visionary quality that Pound was implying in his 'doctrine of the Image'. Others in that collection perhaps do, most notably his two-line poem, 'In a Station of the Metro', which he had described to Harriet as his '"Metro" hokku', having belatedly taken up the Tour Eiffel group's interest in Japanese poetry. In *Poetry* it appeared with spaces between the words, presaging his later fascination with the visual impact of Chinese characters.

> The apparition   of these faces   in the crowd   ;
> Petals   on a wet, black   bough   .[88]

Pound told the story of writing this poem in that June's *T.P's Weekly*. One day in Paris, coming out of the Métro, he saw 'in the jostle . . . a beautiful face, and then, turning suddenly, another and another'. He tried desperately to capture this experience in a poem without success. Eventually 'it struck [him]', many months later, 'that in Japan, where a work of art is not estimated by its acreage and where sixteen syllables are counted enough for a poem if you arrange and punctuate them properly, one might make a very little poem', which when it was translated would appear as these brief two lines. And in Japan, he says, 'or in some other very old, very quiet civilisation, some one else might understand the significance'.[89] It is fascinating that again, just as 'The Return' was presented with qualities of a translation from an early Greek masterpiece, this is imagined as a translation from the Japanese, drawing that distant culture in and making possible a creation unachievable in his own. What Seamus Heaney has suggested the imagists took from the haiku was not only an ephiphanic 'evocation of [a] precise instant of perception', but one which like the haiku so often conveys 'a sense of evanescence, of the transitoriness of things, of the stillness behind things into which they eventually pass'.[90] It may have been this poem that encouraged the late Ernest Fenollosa's widow shortly afterwards to ask Pound to deal with her husband's papers on Chinese and Japanese literature, with such important results for the development of Pound's poetry.

At the end of March Dorothy left with her mother and Georgie Hyde-Lees for a visit to Italy, where they stayed in a villa about twenty miles from Rome. They visited Roman remains, guided by their Baedeker, and Dorothy spent a good deal of time sketching. Pound left England shortly after them; he too would visit Italy, though he would not join the Shakespears' party. In the first instance he was heading for a brief visit to Paris, which he wrote up with panache in the *New Age* later that year. He saw Walter, of course, and presumably stayed with him, but this time, unlike the previous year, he was keen to meet French poets. Pound was slowly catching up with contemporary French poetry; to de Gourmont and de Régnier he had now added Pierre-Jean Jouve, whose recent volume *Présences* he had borrowed from Yeats in December, and rapidly reviewed for *Poetry*, referring to its 'modernist' style, using the word for what must be the first time in his published writings.[91] Pound had also discovered the poet Laurent Tailhade, for whose satires he developed a great admiration, and in February he had told his father that he had seen an interesting new book by the *unanimiste* Jules Romains. Having on Flint's recommendation read Charles Vildrac and Georges Duhamel's *Notes sur la technique poétique* (quoted in 'A Few Don'ts'), he had written to Vildrac for a poem for Monroe. He told Alice that the 'new School in France' was 'not quite so vigorous as imagism but very much alive and sound', but he was anxious to meet some of these French poets and find out about their work at first hand.[92]

Pound had travelled to Paris with Yeats, to whom the purpose of Pound's visit must have recalled his own journey to Paris at much the same age to meet Mallarmé and Verlaine; Yeats liked to repeat Verlaine's comment to him on Tennyson's *In Memoriam*, 'he was too noble, too *anglais*, and when he should have been broken-hearted had many reminiscences'.[93] Yeats kept up with French poetry, so he may have been another voice encouraging Pound to extend his knowledge. Pound had, in addition, already claimed to Harriet that he was in touch with the Parisian poets, and he needed to make good that claim. To his great pleasure he met both Vildrac and Duhamel, as well as Jules Romains and another poet, Philippe Arios. When later in the year he described his visit to the basement bar of the Café du Châtelet, it is very clear that he had been entranced by the romance of these sardonic Parisian rebels: 'I found about twenty men in an alcove. They were rather tense and laconic. The brains of tomorrow's Paris were holding a council of war; it was not a plot against the State but only against the general stupidity . . . I think no one of them spoke more than one sentence at a time. Their war against stupidity is a merciless war-to-the-knife . . . for three satiric hours I watched the little flame of free intelligence at strife for its very existence.' The militarism of his language is striking; he does not actually use the term avant-garde, but this is what these 'brains of tomorrow' are. Pound would increasingly construct a polarity between artistic intelligence and conventional stupidity. He was ready to assert that 'Paris is always at least twenty years ahead of all other "worlds of letters" . . . if an original mind appear in any other country he will be driven to Paris to get his recognition'.[94] One piece of information he was not so pleased to be given was that de Régnier was thought to be 'a back number', but he still defended his 'perfect lyric forms', and would say in *Poetry*, in a form of words which embraced both his own admiration and the clamorous Parisian reservations, that the 'work of M. Henri de Régnier has the fineness and the limitations of Greek vase-paintings'.[95]

Pound was not only meeting French poets. He acquired two more Americans for *le mouvemong* on that visit, members, as he told his mother, of 'an interesting and agreeable set of Americans'.[96] One of these was the moody John Gould Fletcher, like Pound only in Paris for a visit. Fletcher was still friendless in London, though he had begun to haunt the Poetry Bookshop since its opening in January, but even there he failed to strike up any kind of acquaintance with Harold Monro, whose habitual lowness of spirits he interpreted as 'iron gruffness and lack of cordiality'.[97] He had taken an expensive flat in a prestigious terrace (Bernard Shaw was one of his neighbours), only to discover it had no kitchen. He would eat alone in restaurants twice a day, overhearing conversations but taking no part in them. As he said in a poem the year before, 'my old soul goes shivering . . . Seeking grey ghosts that resemble me', but he found no soul-mates.[98] In Paris, however, he had his friend Horace Holley, who introduced him to other American and British expatriate painters and poets. Fletcher, apart from his poem in the *Freewoman*, was having no success in getting published, so he had decided to bring out the poems he had written since 1910 in five volumes, with four different publishers, in each case paying for the publication himself, as Pound had done with *A Lume Spento*. In one of Fletcher's innumerable lists with which he obsessively filled his notebooks, when not pouring out turbulent streams of introspection, he notes the dates at which the poems that comprised these volumes were written: *Fire and Wine*, published by Grant Richards, poems from 1910–11; *Fool's Gold*, from 1911–12, and *The Dominant City*, from 1912, both published by Max Goshen (the press run by Douglas Goldring, the one publisher who, Fletcher said, showed some enthusiasm for his work and kindness in his dealings with him); *The Book of Nature*, published by Constable, poems from 1910–12, and finally *Visions of the Evening*, published by Erskine MacDonald, with poems written in early 1913. The poems vary dramatically, from regular metres to free verse, from gloomy self-scrutiny to evocations of urban beauty and squalor. One of the early poems from *Fool's Gold* is almost doggerel, though it shows acute self-understanding. Called 'Discontent', it begins:

> I grumble over life:
> I grumble over meat:
> I carp at everything,
> For I find grumbling sweet.

> Like to a pinch of salt

> To me is bitter strife,
>
> It gives, if nothing else,
>
> A fiery thirst for life.[99]

The more recent poems were very different. There was a strong Baudelairean influence in subject-matter, though written in the freer form of verse that Fletcher had learnt first from Whitman, and then from the later French *vers-libristes*. Fletcher, however, as Pound would complain, had a tendency to loose and expansive verse which had more in common with Whitman than his French models, but what he learnt from them was the use of alliteration and assonance.

In *The Dominant City* the tone is still largely melancholy, even, one might say, morose. A poem that Fletcher wrote in September 1911, for example, 'In the Night', though in the freer metric form, and with much more attention to assonance, with which he would become very skilled, is still almost entirely introspective:

> In the night, the beautiful, bitter night,
>
> I contemplate my perfect loneliness and failure . . .
>
> Desire the inexpressible, long for what I cannot be . . .
>
> I live on, yet a million others die . . .
>
> To the crowd, I am as one of the never born.[100]

Another poem in the same collection, 'In the City of Night', which he wrote in April 1912, this time using an irregular rhyme scheme, works in a much more imagist fashion; still emotionally dark, it projects that emotion on to the city itself:

> Along the dismal, empty streets, stretching endlessly away,
>
> The darkened houses stand, in mournful dull array,
>
> Like wretched starving folk that silently make show
>
> Of asking you for bread:
>
> And their windows pale with starless sky o'erhead
>
> Are as maniac faces white with woe,
>
> And agony of the living dead.[101]

The urban poor appear again and again in these poems, whether as themselves or as imagery, as here. Even if Fletcher was no longer a socialist, he was appalled by the plight of the East End working class. *Visions of the Evening*, the poems from early 1913, are the most clearly

French influenced. The first poem is dedicated 'To the Immortal Memory of Charles Baudelaire', and many of the poems evoke the kind of unexpected images that the symbolists loved to use, his descriptions often suggesting Impressionist, possibly Post-Impressionist paintings of the Paris streets. One, 'Invocation to Evening', evokes the lights flickering and glimmering in the city twilight, though in the end it returns, with Fletcher's customary melancholy, to himself, tellingly continuing the street imagery: 'but do not think, O Evening,/To light one torch within my shuttered heart'.[102] Fletcher had several, mainly very brief reviews; to his discomfiture, the *TLS* thought *The Book of Nature*, his earliest and most conventional book, the most successful, though he was touched by a review by Edward Thomas, who gave a kindly welcome to the new poet, as he had to Pound. Thomas wrote of *The Dominant City*, which he thought the best, that Fletcher was still 'experimenting in technique and in moods, so that his "dominant city," London, might be any city in the presence of a solitary, sensitive questioner. But already his words and his solemn or tortured feelings seem to promise an achievement that would satisfy his readers if not himself.'[103] Fletcher later dismissed these early volumes, as Pound would do his, but they contain some powerful and striking passages, and they show how far he had already moved towards a somewhat similar technique to the one the imagists were evolving.

With publication all arranged, Fletcher left London.[104] He was beginning to think that he should move to Paris, where his one friend lived. Holley had introduced him to his fellow-expatriate Skipwith Cannell, the other American poet that Pound was to meet. Fletcher was largely dismissive of Cannell in *Life Is My Song*, but was probably glad to pass time with him in 1913. Fletcher claims that he persuaded Cannell, who was 'inordinately vain' about his poetry, to give up rhyme; as Cannell's only reading had been Edgar Allan Poe and the Bible, he encouraged him to swap polished Poesian stanzas for the cadences of the Psalms. 'So early was I equipped,' Fletcher asserts, 'not with a literary comrade, but with a disciple.'[105]

He and Cannell were dining together at the Café Closerie de Lilas, opposite the fountains in the Luxembourg Gardens, when another friend of Holley's introduced them to Pound. Fletcher, this young man who at twenty-eight felt himself a 'grey ghost', 'one of the never born', a man with a 'shuttered heart', was mesmerised by the flamboyant and dynamic Pound. He had heard of course of his much-published compatriot, 'having read, with attraction and repulsion almost equally balanced, his own early volumes'.[106] For a short time, he fell entirely under Pound's spell, though he does not quite admit it in the account in his memoir.

In any case this first meeting did not work out quite as he hoped. They fell to discussing *vers libre*, on which Fletcher felt himself to be something of an expert, but Pound took over and dominated the conversation, expounding his theories at length and quoting numerous authorities, 'from Gustave Kahn down to the Italian futurists'. Fletcher, having read none of them, was silenced, but Cannell cheerfully dismissed the theorists and asserted that the best *vers libre* was the Authorized Version. Pound, to Fletcher's chagrin, was impressed, and asked to see Cannell's poems, 'whereat [Fletcher], who knew well how Cannell had simply followed a lead [he] had given him, took refuge in stony silence.'[107]

That cannot have been the whole story, though Fletcher was never one to pass over the slenderest and most unintentional slight. Pound not only enquired about Fletcher's poetry on that visit, but promised to write a review for *Poetry*, and in the event wrote one for publication in England as well. Fletcher was so taken with him that he decided he would return to live in London after all. Pound was pleased to find another enthusiast for French poetry and *vers libre*, and he may have discovered that there was one other influence that they had in common. Fletcher in *Fire and Wine* had included some haiku 'From the Japanese', and some 'From the Chinese'. Pound, having just published his first 'hokku', may have been struck by the convergence. His review of Fletcher's poems in *Poetry*, the only review published of these early books in the States, though rather guarded, recognised how unusual his poetry was. He commended Fletcher for having decided to leave 'the virgin republic of the west as a duckling departs from a hen', and said of his five volumes that there are 'some of them, or at least some parts of them good, and at least one of them important'. The 'important' one, for him, as for Thomas, was *The Dominant City*, but even the others are 'not without their charm, are not without touches of beauty, of mockery and grimness'. What is particularly commendable is that 'Here is an author set to portraying the real; he is contemporary, he has heard of the city of Paris, and even if his book had been written in French it would not have been called old-fashioned.'[108] In return for this praise of his use of his French sources, Fletcher, either in Paris or when they both returned to London, offered to lend Pound some of his books of French poetry, providing Pound with copies of Jules Romains, François Jammes and more Rémy de Gourmont, which he carried off to read, and about which he would soon be writing with all the authority of a recent convert.

V

FLETCHER remained in Paris until June, and was present at the famous first night of the Russian Ballet's performance of Stravinsky's *Rite of Spring*, in which Nijinksy danced to his own choreography in Leon Bakst's colourful and innovative costumes. Fletcher had already seen the Russian Ballet perform in London in what he described as 'the barbaric splendour of *Scheherazade*', and earlier that year in Paris he had visited it several times again, particularly admiring 'Nijinksy's daringly original and nakedly pagan conception of *L'Après-Midi d'un Faune*'. Fletcher writes in his autobiography that 'It seemed to me that in such works as these lay the fusion of all the arts of which Wagner had merely dreamed; that here the conflict between Apollonian restraint and Dionysiac ecstasy that had gone on throughout the nineteenth century had been finally resolved into an art that was Apollonian only in that it expressed itself through the plastic relationship of the dancers' bodies, but was fundamentally and overwhelmingly Dionysiac in general effect.'[109] The last clause applies equally to much of Fletcher's poetry. It is more often despairing than ecstatic, but it never shows Apollonian tranquillity. No wonder the Russian Ballet appealed so much, especially *The Rite of Spring*. Drawing directly on anthropological work on the ancient Slavs, the ballet portrays a solstice festival with the ritual sacrifice of a young woman, torn to pieces by an ecstatic, frenzied crowd. The music's complex, insistent rhythms, its savage dissonances, caused Debussy, who admired it greatly, to describe it as 'une musique nègre'.[110] Like Debussy, Stravinsky saw himself as the transcriber rather than the creator of the music. He believed he was 'tap[ping] some unconscious "folk" memory'.[111] As Christopher Butler has pointed out, the *Rite* has many links with Picasso's *Demoiselles d'Avignon* as an exemplary moment of modernist primitivism. In Picasso's painting, urban prostitution and savagery meet, suggesting the disturbing continuity of savage impulses into the present day that was the constant warning of James Frazer. The *Rite* has the same message though it works differently, drawing the audience into the frenzy through visual and auditory colour. Many in the audience were furious at this assault on their cool rational distance, and began, in a counter-image of the action before them, to shout and scream at the stage. Those in the top balcony, students from the Latin Quarter and no doubt the sardonic young men from the Café du Châtelet, began to shout 'Bravo!' in support; between them the music was drowned, but applause slowly won over the catcalls.

For Fletcher, this experience was a further confirmation that he was on the right path. He wrote in *Life Is My Song*:

This performance of the *Sacre du Printemps* more than anything else that I have ever seen in my life confirmed me in my determination to risk everything to become a modern artist. To be a modern artist involved, I saw, a determination to make and accept every kind of experiment, and not to flinch from any novelty, however strange and uncouth it might seem, or however deeply it aroused the hatred of the mob. If one wished to be a modern artist, one must be prepared alike for one's own isolation and the mob's contempt – as Cézanne and Gauguin and Van Gogh had been prepared, as Nijinsky and Stravinsky were prepared.[112]

The modern artist, he continues, has only one lesson to learn, that taught by Synge, who had said 'that poetry, to be human again, must first learn to be brutal'. This was fundamental to the art of the early twentieth century: 'In revolt against the elaborations of end-of-the-century aestheticism, against the romantic movement faltering in sentimental prettiness, against the genteel tradition in decay, artists everywhere were turning back to the primitively ugly, knowing that in primitiveness alone lay strength.' With hindsight, he adds, 'As yet none saw the pitfall, that in a world given over to the worship of naked and raw force, war was inevitable. Only the man who had in my hearing, cried out on that first night of Stravinsky's ballet, "C'est la musique boche," had, probably unconsciously even to himself, hoisted the danger signal.'[113] Fletcher himself had no apprehension of war; all the same, in another of his lists, this one marking important dates, he records this visit to Paris as the 'last of the gorgeous times'.[114]

Fletcher's attitude to the ballet was in marked contrast to Pound's. Pound had also seen the performance of *L'Après-midi d'un faune*, in London that March, taking, though not paying for, Olivia and Dorothy. The two women were enthusiasts for the ballet, Dorothy particularly admiring Nijinsky, but Pound appears to have regarded it as womanly stuff, too easily enjoyed. Had he seen *The Rite of Spring* he might have felt differently, but by then he was in Italy. After leaving Paris he went to spend a fortnight in Sirmione, planning to meet up later with Aldington and H.D. He had remained in regular correspondence with them both while they journeyed round Italy, and had also no doubt followed Aldington's bouncy and carefree articles about his tour in the *New Age*. They were still in southern Italy, and in no hurry to return. In his articles, Aldington for the most part gave the impression that he was a solitary traveller, though the Doolittles, unnamed, appeared with him on the drive from Amalfi to Sorrento, 'two somnolent elders and a great artist'.[115] That had been in early March, when they were heading, as H.D. notes, for the warm south, on the famous Amalfi drive, which at that time was still by horse and carriage, along a dramatically beautiful road cut into the coastal rock. On 14 March they crossed to Capri. However much the Doolittle parents might have liked Aldington, what happened next is remarkable for 1912. For ten days they were all together on Capri, but after that their paths diverged. Professor and Mrs Doolittle went on to Sicily, and H.D. and Aldington remained in Capri for what Pound was later to describe as their 'unofficial honeymoon', having arranged to rejoin the Doolittle parents later in Venice.[116] They don't appear to have been staying in the same place, so there may have been some element of keeping up appearances, and they were at the quieter end of the island, in Anacapri. ('Laus Deo!' Aldington exclaims in the *New Age*, 'there are but few Americans and English, at least at Anacapri'.)[117] There is no doubt that the Doolittles knew the two were remaining on the island together, for Helen Doolittle records on 25 March that 'Hilda and R. came down to see me off'. The difference between the Doolittles and the Shakespears could not be more striking. The only comment in the journal is: 'Sunday March 23. Made plans. Hilda remains here while we go to Italy.'

Aldington and H.D. were undoubtedly happy to be left alone together, and, in addition, were both probably glad to have a break from the family group. Devoted though she was to them, H.D. always had very ambivalent feelings about her parents, and Aldington, for all his diplomatic charm, was an impatient young man. In his notes from that holiday, as well as some quite erotic and passionate writing there is a poem recalling 'trampling with this girl's stupid mother/ Cursing her senile tears and kind inanities'.[118] Scarcely fair, one feels: Mrs Doolittle was not yet sixty – she would have her sixtieth birthday later in the year – and gives no sign of senility or indeed of stupidity, though possibly that's how Aldington interpreted her love of shopping. Luckily, she appears to have been unaware of this. Yet for both Aldington and H.D. the whole Italian visit was an idyll. Italy always signified for H.D. the time when she and Aldington were in love and rapturously happy, and that springtime in Capri was the jewel. So too for Aldington, who wrote in his memoir, 'In Anacapri, time stood still between Monte Solaro and the blue waves far below. Beside the rocky paths grew white violets, purple anemones, star-of-Bethlehem, cyclamen, and scented jonquils.'[119] In the *New Age* he said: 'one lives in day-long blessed idleness and silence, and . . . one watches the spring growth of orchard and upland manifestly richer each day as the summer sun develops every green thing'.[120] H.D. recalled the time there in her 'Autobiographical Notes': 'C.L.D. leaves, mother joins him in Sicily, I am alone, move from Paradiso [the hotel where she and her parents had stayed] to little room in top of house, in garden, R.A. and work on Greek and walks, R. loses watch, rocks, swallows, etc. Roses, figs, goat-cheese, pear-blossom, iris, Monte Solara, daisies on walls.'[121]

H.D. and Aldington must have spent almost a month in Capri. As H.D. later told Norman Holmes Pearson, it was an important period for her development as a writer. She continued her 'automatic or pseudo-automatic writing', which she had begun the year before, in 'Italy where I spent that winter, Capri especially, where I had some time and space and found the actual geographical Greece, for the first time, Syren isle of the Odyssey'.[122] H.D. does not mention any specific poems that came out of that time on Capri, but she may have kept and reworked what she wrote then; the poems of her 1916 collection, *Sea Garden*, with their flowers and steep cliff paths, may well have had their first drafts there. She and Aldington were continuing their translations of Theocritus, one of H.D.'s first models. Theocritus had lived in Sicily but they associated him with 'the miniature Sicily of Capri – with Vesuvius for Aetna', as Aldington put it, for Theocritus, he said, described a countryside just like Capri's, 'the mingled austerity and richness of these southern rocks in their light garment of flowers'.[123] 'Mingled austerity and richness' precisely describes those *Sea Garden* poems.

H.D., according to her mother's journal, kept in regular touch by letter and postcard, and they were still exchanging letters with Pound, who wrote to Dorothy on 21 April from the Hotel Eden saying that he thought Richard and H.D. had been so 'wholly Hellenized at Capri' that they would be quite out of place in 'bella Venezia'.[124] Dorothy was expressing only moderate enjoyment of her holiday with her mother and Georgie Hyde-Lees near Rome; she had invited H.D. to visit them on her way north, but the visit never happened. Pound, of course, was not offered an invitation, but he seemed entirely cheerful by himself at the shores of Lake Garda. Dorothy said she was pleased he was not 'pining', and although she added that neither was she, clearly she was somewhat worried by this state of affairs.[125] The fact that Pound was at Sirmione without her must have brought home to her the difficulty of achieving a future together. In Sirmione the weather was chilly, unlike the warmth when they were there together, but Pound reported that it was 'cold & grey and full of tears and very wonderful, all the olive grove, and a few more little bits of stone have fallen from the grotte, and your altar is still pink slablet uppermost'.[126] He appeared to be in ebullient spirits, but, though Dorothy's letters were generally as calm and full of cultural activities as ever, she at times let slip signs of unusual depression. She wrote to Pound that 'We don't discuss the Universe much – I used to do so a good deal – lately I have an idea its no use, & that one can only be apathetic & shrug one's shoulders. It makes no odds whether one believes this or that or 'tother – one writes, or paints, or is bored just the same.' At the end of the same letter, after contemplating her plans for when she returned home, she added: 'Any other suggestions for my welfare? Everything needs such a damned lot of application – & it never seems worth the trouble.'[127] Pound paid no attention to this lowness of spirit and continued to fill his letters with his own concerns and his curiosity about Richard and H.D.

Pound reported to Dorothy on 25 April that the 'Theocritan Idyll is, I think still at Anacapri. They've stopped going to Capri for their mail.' He intended to meet up with them in Venice, claiming 'the combination of Richard & Venice' would amuse him.[128] Dorothy was obviously uneasy about his motives for joining them, perhaps all the more so when Pound tactlessly sent her his latest poem, one about a faun, his nickname for Aldington, 'sniffing and snoozling about among my flowers'.[129] (Aldington and H.D. were well aware of this sobriquet, and Aldington would write poems using the persona of a faun, rather enjoying the suggestion of lustiness in the comparison; H.D., in the persona of Hermione in *Asphodel*, recollected seeing with Darrington 'the Naples faun that held the wine jar' on that Italian visit.)[130] There was no doubt Pound was jealous, or at least possessive, and was finding relinquishing his H.D. to Aldington difficult, even though the poem also says, 'But take it, I leave you the garden'. Dorothy must have found these signs of Pound's continued feeling for H.D. painful, but with admirable self-control all she did was point out some of the structural weaknesses in the poem, which Pound accepted with unusual meekness.

Pound duly turned up in Venice, but found that Aldington and H.D. had not yet arrived. 'R & H.,' he told Dorothy, on 3 May, 'appear to be falling in love with each other somewhere en route from Napoli. I suppose I'll have to be ready with a pontifical sanction & then try to soothe their respective progenitors – at least their communications are *very* vague.' But he told her he was very happy to be back in Venice, and found himself, as he put it enigmatically, 'restored to the belief' – belief in himself, his poetry, the imagist cause, the worthwhileness of life? – 'even in the absence of the two people who in all decency ought to regard it as their sole duty to stand present & keep me amused. If not, why have I reared them with such persistent solicitude'.[131] Aldington and H.D. had stopped off in Florence instead of coming straight from Naples to Venice. 'Rebellion,' H.D. wrote in her 'Autobiographical Notes.'[132] Her parents were not happy about it. Aldington wanted to write another article about Florence for the *New Age*, having only touched on it briefly on his journey south; not part of the plans made back in March. H.D. does not explain why the extra delay was thought to be so bad; her mother records receiving a letter from her on 28 April and a postcard on 2 May, so it cannot have been anxiety for her physical safety. Charles Doolittle was due to leave Italy for the States for some weeks on 14 May, so he may have wanted more time with his daughter before he went; but given the depth of the offence H.D. felt she gave, perhaps while the Doolittle parents could shut their eyes to the ambiguity of the couple remaining together in quiet Anacapri, appearing as an unchaperoned pair in a Florence full of American tourists was quite a different thing. Pound reported on 5 May that he had met 'the dryad's family disconsolate on the piazza yesterday afternoon & spent the evening consoling them for the absence of their offspring'.[133] What the Doolittle parents thought of meeting this young man, of whom they had disapproved so much, in such embarrassing circumstances one can only guess; Mrs Doolittle's journal entry gives no hint of anything other than pleasure in seeing him, and H.D. records that when they arrived there was a 'general feeling of disapproval', but that 'Ezra takes on mother and dad', so it sounds as if he took his self-appointed task of soothing the progenitors seriously.[134] He had had dinner with them the two evenings before the prodigals returned, at the first discussing 'the heresy of planetary influences', surely an unwise topic of conversation between the ultra-rationalist astronomer, who had so frowned on his daughter's predilection for the 'sensational' Flammarion, and the confidant of the astrological Yeats?'[135] Later in the week Pound gave a gondola party, he and Mrs Doolittle in one gondola and Richard and H.D. in another; Mrs Doolittle loved it. H.D. took longer to cheer up; guilt about her parents always oppressed her. Pound commented to Dorothy on her arrival that H.D. 'doesn't seem much more in love with [her faun] than when she left london, but her family distresses her & seems to drive her more fawn-wards', but by the next day he was complaining that 'H. & R. are submerged in a hellenism so polubendius and so stupid that I stop in the street about once in every 15 minutes to laugh at them'.[136] He was definitely feeling excluded. He enclosed in the letter a postcard of a church, Santa Maria Miracoli, but doesn't mention that he dragged H.D. through the streets to see it with him, ('in and out of alleys or *calles*, across bridges, narrow passageways, the labyrinth,' as she remembered it.)[137] Ezra remained for another week, leaving probably the same day as Charles Doolittle, having, according to Mrs Doolittle, spent most of his time with them.

After Professor Doolittle and Pound's departure, Aldington, H.D. and Mrs Doolittle stayed on for a couple of weeks before moving on to Verona, and then going to stay a few days at Sirmione on Lake Garda. After Pound's ecstatic praise, a visit had to be made; in *Asphodel* Hermione recalls that 'Darrington had wandered bare-foot under the olives, silver olives, olive silver Sirmio'.[138] Mrs Doolittle was having another dress made for H.D., this time in violet crêpe, and records that H.D. gave her a present of Elinor Glyn's *Halcyone*, rather a racy read for her, one might have thought. June the 6th was Mrs Doolittle's birthday, and her diary entry goes: 'Hilda made birthday very happy – gathered poppies before breakfast – afterwards gave me a lot of pretty crepe things daintily done up. Happy day.' After Richard left, H.D. and her mother visited Innsbruck, and returned to Verona, where Professor Doolittle joined them again on 25 June; 'so so happy,' noted his affectionate wife. The Doolittles were planning to continue their European tour through Germany and Switzerland, but H.D. went off on 6 July to Paris, where Richard would soon join her, to continue their 'unofficial honeymoon', though that cannot be how they put it to H.D.'s parents. Her mother's only comment was: 'I know Hilda will enjoy settling down for a time but we shall miss her.' H.D. corresponded regularly with her mother until her parents joined her in London in early September. H.D. recorded that she had been rather frightened in Paris before Aldington arrived: memories of Margaret and her fate perhaps haunted her. When Aldington arrived it was very different.

One additional pleasure on this visit was that they got to know Henry Slominsky, also visiting Paris from London, a Polish American who had been at Penn with Pound and had just published his doctoral thesis on the pre-Socratic philosophers, Heraclitus and Parmenides. 'He made philosophy as attractive as a Persian tale,' Aldington recalled. 'On a bench under the trees in the Petit Luxembourg, away from the noise and glare of the cafés, we would sit for hours while he talked to us of Hellas and Hellenism, of Pythagoras and Plato . . . of Empedocles and Heraclitus'.[139] Heraclitus, in particular – with his belief that opposites were always interconnected, not rigorously to be distinguished as in modern Western thought – was very much in tune with their generation's understanding of the psyche. H.D. was already meeting such fusions in Sappho, who portrays passion as both fire and ice; such interminglings of opposites would come to be a central element in her poetry.

Pound returned to London to find Dorothy seriously upset with him. Uncomplaining though she generally was, she must have found it extremely galling to have a fiancé whom she was at the best of times only allowed to see once or twice a week in her mother's drawing-room, especially when she was often obliged out of politeness to go on visits to people with whom she had little in common, while Pound swanned around London or Europe with his chosen friends, often attractive women. The Venice episode may have been the last straw. She had mentioned plans to go on a week's sketching course when she returned, though whether or not she did so isn't clear. She wrote rather wearily, 'I suppose I must try to "Career" on my return!' It does not seem to have been an attractive prospect. Their reunion did not go well, and Dorothy was soon saying, 'I wonder if your congé is what *you* want? I wish I knew.' She had earlier consulted him about what prints to put up in her bedroom, newly papered while she was in Rome, but now she wrote: 'As to my room, it is you who can give me an answer, as to whether there is any prospect of my being able to leave it within, say, the next six months? I feel you might have got a job if you had really wanted to, by now . . . I think I have waited very quietly all this Spring for you to have time.' But she hastily wrote again, apologising: 'The boredom was of four square walls – not you. I am feeling better since I decided to have an Archaic Greek frock in sea-green.'[140] Yet two weeks later Dorothy quite uncharacteristically lost her temper with him, when Pound, for his part entirely characteristically, tried to interfere with the guest list for a private concert that Rummel was to give – to Tagore, now back in England, among others – in the Shakespear drawing-room. 'I think you fortify yourself too much against other people,' she told him, '& so do not realise how you hurt them . . . You affect not to care about other people – – – but you try to interfere a good deal with their doings when they affect yourself.' He sent her a reproving poem, in essence suggesting she was behaving not like herself but like 'the cloud of beautiful women who do not concern me', and Dorothy retreated once more.[141] Then, another two weeks later, she wrote:

I cannot marry you. (I can but hope it's not mere cowardice, but a true instinct.)
I am sorry, sorry, sorry, and send my
Love.

Pound simply replied, again enigmatically:

you can not,
you can not,
you can not.[142]

Was that agreement, or protest? Whichever, they were soon reconciled. Dorothy was devoted, unable, perhaps against her better judgement, to make the break.

Pound's letters home reflected none of this. Indeed, he sounded very cheery. He told his mother that Seymour was waiting for the *Patria Mia* manuscript, his reworking in book form of his *New Age* articles, that his translation of Arnaut Daniel was 'about subscribed already', and that the *Quarterly Review*, 'the one venerable & self-respecting organ left', had accepted an article on the troubadours. In one undated letter to his mother, probably early July, he reports that Ford and Violet had had a garden party with 'every one one has ever met', that Katherine Heyman had had a musical party full of countesses and opera rehearsals, that he was being taken to the Oxford and Cambridge cricket match at Lord's, and that he would be going again to the Russian Ballet.[143] Ford's garden party was an act of social defiance, as Pound must have known. Elsie had brought a libel case against the *Throne*, challenging its description of Violet as Mrs Ford Madox Hueffer, and the case had finally been heard that February. As it happened, Ford was staying in Boulogne at the time, and his doctor had written to the court to say he was in too poor a state of health to appear, as he had been suffering from 'neurasthenia' for the past six months or more; but even if he had been well and eager to be there, he would not have been called. Brigit Patmore among others testified in court that Ford and Hunt were widely known as Mr and Mrs Hueffer, but Elsie was, not surprisingly, successful: there was no evidence to prove either a divorce from Elsie or a marriage to Hunt. Violet fled to join Ford in Boulogne, where the other English guests in their hotel refused to speak to them. They moved further away from England, and spent an unhappy few months in the south of France, now scarcely talking to each other. Mrs Clifford, a novelist, who like Violet Hunt belonged to the Committee of Women Writers, a highly respectable body, wrote to say she thought they should stay away for three years: 'I don't think you know *how strong* the feeling about you is, and it would be *impossible* for you to go about and be received without first asking what sort of reception you would get or whether you would get any at all. I would do a good deal for you but I simply should quake if you came here on Sundays, and I believe other people would walk out.'[144] Violet decided she had better resign from the committee, and wrote to May Sinclair to tell her. Sinclair had been very supportive, writing to Ford that 'If it's a question of "volcanoes", I'd rather take a bungalow on the edge of *yours*, than row for five minutes in the same boat with Mrs Elsie Hueffer. I'm sick of the world we live in, with its cowardice & hypocrisy, & abominable, poisonous, sham morality.'[145] But although she said that she personally did not 'care two straws whether your marriage holds good in this country or not (and should *not* care if it had never taken place)', she advised them to stay away for six months.[146]

In the event, they returned in late May because, as Violet told Ford's mother, 'The only thing for Ford & me to do is to wipe the unjustifiable mud Elsie has thrown off our faces, make ourselves presentable & go on as if nothing had happened.'[147] Although Hunt would claim in her memoir that the summer of 1913 was a 'gorgeous season', and that her garden party on 1 July had never been so well attended, by no means everyone came. Douglas Goldring quotes some cutting refusals; he for some reason – it cannot have been disapproval – was unable to go, and surmises that the occasion must have been a flop.[148] It certainly was not that. Those present included Ford's politician friend, Charles Masterman, Yeats (a rare visitor – perhaps Pound persuaded him), Lady Gregory, Cunninghame Graham, Frank and Violet Flint, Epstein and Gaudier-Brzeska: their literary and artistic friends, it appears, largely remained loyal. Though both Ford and Violet hated the scandal, they reacted very differently: Ford never discussed the matter, while Violet wrote endless letters of self-justification to her former society friends. Goldring points out that 'she had inherited and built up at South Lodge a "position in Society" which to a Victorian woman, even one as advanced and emancipated as herself, was of immense importance to her life and happiness. Although she enjoyed the friendship of writers and artists, she was in no sense a Bohemian and dreaded being ostracized by all the solid and respectable people who formed her real background."[149] Her memoir, *The Flurried Years*, published in America with the even more appropriate title, *I Have This to Say*, was her most extended piece of self-justification; in it she steadfastly maintains she believed that she was Ford's wife. Her final attempt to have her name cleared was to ask Goldring to be her literary executor, and then to leave numerous letters tucked away in various books for him to find and, no doubt she hoped, to use as the basis for a convincing defence. Goldring was immensely sympathetic, but it was impossible for him to invent a legal contract that had clearly never existed.

Pound mentions none of this, but a letter from Dorothy at the time of the trial asking 'Is Mrs F.M. Hueffer established?' indicates that he talked to her about it.[150] Hunt had another cause for distress that spring, as Pound probably also knew: Ford's passion for the lovely Brigit Patmore. Patmore always denied that she had had an affair with him, saying in her memoirs that she was not attracted to him. Rebecca West, not attracted to him either, *vide* her famous comparison with the poached egg, was all the same convinced that Brigit and Ford were lovers. Iris Barry, who came to London in 1916, also – without evidence – thought it likely, telling Ford's first biographer, Arthur Mizener, that 'If Violet was jealous of Bridget [*sic*] P., well V. *was* jealous & presumably often with reason & Bridget *was* terribly attractive.'[151] Mizener says Ford claimed that Brigit had given him a ruby cross, which he always wore, even when playing tennis. But Ford is a totally unreliable witness; Brigit denied the story flatly. Given Patmore's admiration for Hunt – and ironically she especially admired her overturning of convention, something that Hunt was mortified to find herself doing at that time – she may have felt that adding to Violet's problems by having an affair with her not-quite husband would be far from kind.

Some time in June, Fletcher returned, and the first person he contacted was Pound. He was invited to call on him in Church Walk, and was shocked by the conditions in which he lived. The entrance to Church Walk was down a narrow alleyway, past the churchyard, now disused, which was full of 'sooty marble gravestones', up a dark staircase to a badly lit room, 'notably barren of comfort'. Shocked by the idea of living in a single room, he was dismayed to find that the first thing one saw was 'a plain white-enamelled bedstead'. Under one of the two windows was a long oak table, lit from the left, 'a concession to Pound's own weak eyesight';

this he used as his desk, 'usually littered deep with manuscripts'.[152] There was a fireplace, which served as a waste-paper basket, another smaller table and two or three chairs, and a very basic iron washstand. With a certain embarrassment, he contrasted this with the comparative luxury in which he lived. When he had moved into his flat, Fletcher had bought Persian rugs, a Jacobean dining table (presumably Victorian Jacobean), a chesterfield and several elegant chairs. Pound was in fact extremely happy back in Church Walk, and had written to his mother on his return from Italy, shortly before Fletcher's visit, to say how delightful his room was, 'full of green trees and sunlight'.[153] Lawrence, one might recall, had thought it 'comfortable and well-furnished'.[154] Fletcher saw none of that. He was perturbed by this poverty, and records that he wondered what he could do to help. Pound would soon have suggestions, but he, for his part, wanted to help Fletcher with his poetry and asked to see 'Irradiations', the series of poems on which Fletcher was working at the time. He read it meticulously and offered detailed criticisms, some of which Fletcher accepted, but most of which he decided to resist. Fletcher is not one of the poets who record their gratitude to Pound's creative pencil.

VI

In July 1913, while Dorothy was in Yorkshire, and Aldington and H.D. in Paris, Pound met the woman who was to snatch the imagist staff from his grasp. Amy Lowell, then thirty-nine, had arrived in London, with an introduction from Harriet Monroe, in search of the leader of the imagists. Having already identified herself as an imagist on first reading H.D.'s poems, she had come to find out more. Pound might be from Philadelphia, but he knew about the Boston Lowells, the nearest thing to royalty the States possessed. Amy Lowell's upbringing in a vast house and grounds with a retinue of servants was in some ways not unlike that of the English monarch's family, though with some significant differences, not least that it was a family with a good deal more intellectual and artistic distinction than the British royal family could muster. Her grandfather's cousin had been the poet James Russell Lowell, a leading man of letters in Boston in the late nineteenth century. (He was much respected in England too. Sir Leslie Stephen asked him to be godfather to his daughter Virginia, and the London Library today still has two shelves of his books, while they have not a single volume by his cousin's grand-daughter and only half a shelf of her great-nephew Robert's.) One of Amy's brothers, Lawrence, was president of Harvard. The other, Percival, had founded the Lowell Observatory in Flagstaff, Arizona, having previously spent ten years in Japan, writing several books about Japan which helped to encourage the interest in Japanese culture which had already filtered through to the Tour Eiffel imagists. He inspired his youngest sister with a love of all things Japanese that would feed into her later poetry. Lafcadio Hearn, mentioned earlier as one of the most influential writers on Japan round the turn of the century, had gone to Japan because he read Percival Lowell's 1888 *Soul of the Far East*. Percival Lowle, as the family name then was, who first reached Massachusetts twenty years after the *Mayflower*, claimed direct descent from William the Conqueror, and if the present Lowell family money came from industry rather than land, that was no diminution of status for a long-established New England family. Amy Lowell had a presence and an air of authority that was not unknown among women of the English aristocracy, but was certainly not common among the women Pound usually met. But Pound liked strong characters, until they crossed him, and their relationship began with great cordiality.

When she was only two, Amy Lowell had persuaded the family coachman to let her hold the reins and drive the carriage to church. Had Pound heard that story he might have been more wary. But Amy, although she was eleven years older than he was, had brought out her first book of verse only the year before, and then to the most tepid reviews. Pound, after all, had by now published six collections of poetry, seven if one counted the Cavalcanti translations, and was foreign correspondent of the leading American poetry magazine. He was prepared to be gracious to this new entry in the field, particularly as she was anxious to learn, and most ready to admit her previous poetic sins. ('When I get through with that girl she'll think she was born in free verse,' he reputedly said.)[155] He was also interested in her money: well handled, this friendship might find him editor of his own review. Unfortunately, Pound, as so often, was not to handle it well. For now, however, they were mutually charmed. Amy was, like himself, a colourful eccentric. She smoked cigars, at a time when few American women even smoked cigarettes; occasionally, she smoked a pipe. In her palatial home, in which she still slept in the bedroom she had had as a child, on a bed with sixteen pillows, she worked all night, getting up at three in the afternoon. She gave numerous dinner parties, but rarely arrived at them until the dessert course, leaving her companion, the beautiful and gracious former actress Ada Russell, to entertain her guests. Aroused, she was formidable. While in London, she discovered that her publishers, Constable, had failed to distribute her book to British booksellers. She stormed into Constable's offices, refusing to leave until her books were located and guaranteed to be on the way out. Although not tall (scarcely five foot) she had imposing bulk. An early account described her as looking as wide as she was tall, but although this description is regularly recycled, photographs show that was scarcely the case. She generally wore well-tailored dark jackets, which of course helped, but next to the late Queen Victoria she could have looked, if still stout, a comparatively compact figure of a woman. But she was certainly ample, and her detractors, who later included Pound, mocked her cruelly for her girth, not always behind her back.

For all Amy Lowell's commanding public persona and strength of purpose, her appearance was a great sorrow to her. A plump little girl, a podgy adolescent, she had become even more overweight as an adult. This was due to a glandular disturbance, though her love of food, particularly puddings, didn't help. Even as a teenager, she wrote in her diary, 'really, you know, I am appaulingly fat'.[156] (She was a clever child, but not a good speller.) Of course, even the most emaciated teenager might write that, and when she came out as a débutante (Boston-style), a photograph shows her as only, by conventional standards, a little too well covered. But she was awkward and plain too. Now, when she travelled she insisted on having all her hotel suite's mirrors swathed in black. She suffered from ill health and depression, in both of which her weight played a part.

It was clear to Amy early on that she was a failure in conventional terms as a woman, 'a great, rough, masculine, strong thing,' as she described herself as a teenager.[157] Yet because she was a woman, she was debarred from the exciting public life her brothers enjoyed. As a child, according to her friend Katie Dana, she had resented being a girl: 'Amy was deeply grieved she was not a boy. She always tried to walk exactly like her brothers Percy and Lawrence, striding along with her head down and her hat crammed over her ears.'[158] She had, Bostonians thought, an unfeminine dislike of authority. The word that best described her, Katie said, was 'obstreperous'. As a teenager, she found dancing lessons and other mixed social events agonies of embarrassment. Young men were never attracted by her, as they were to the other girls. She wrote in her diary with great candour about a young man she idolised: 'It is so silly, but when Paul asks Mabel to walk with him I feel like going off alone somewhere & crying. *This feeling is mixed with a kind of wish to hit Someone.*'[159] As a teenager she felt intensely lonely. She was the youngest of her family: as well as her two distinguished brothers she had two sisters, both now married, leaving her the only child at home. Her elder brother Percival was nineteen when she was born, the younger of her sisters twelve: Percival nicknamed her 'the Postscript', and that was very much how she felt, an addendum who didn't quite belong. Her elderly father was always at work, her mother an invalid. She wrote in her diary, 'What is your idea of happyness?: *To be loved*', and a little later, 'I feel very much in need of a *very* intimate friend.'[160]

As she became an adult she began to feel even more intensely what a misfortune it was to be not just a woman, but an unattractive one. Her débutante season was more enjoyable than she expected: her dancing had improved, her obstreperousness had become high spirits, and she was generally liked. But there was no romance; there was a rumour of a possible engagement, but it appears to have come to nothing. Even the Lowell name and fortune could not find her a husband. What was she to do with her life? She had had a scattered education: an English governess, followed by attendance at a tiny private school set up by cousins, the Cabots, for their own girls and a picked handful of their own class. (The well-known Boston rhyme concludes: 'The Cabots speak only to Lowells/And the Lowells speak only to God'. It didn't work quite like that in the school: Amy talked everyone else down.) Her mother had taught her French, which became excellent in her early twenties when she devoured French novelists and poets, but how was she to use that skill? What she would really have liked to have been was an actress, though it would have caused seismic waves in Boston if a Lowell woman had gone on the stage. But in any case she didn't have the looks.

So in her twenties she went to the theatre; she travelled; she read. She had discovered poetry in her teenage years, finding Leigh Hunt's *Imaginary Conversations* in her father's study, which led her to Keats, the poet who remained her passion, but she did not at this stage think of writing poetry herself. She experimented with novels and plays, for she had been a precocious teller and writer of stories as a child, starting various short-lived mimeographed magazines, written largely by herself, and, at the age of thirteen, with the aid of her mother, producing a book entitled *Dream Drops, or Stories from Fairy Land, by a Dreamer*. She sold this on behalf of Boston's Perkins Institute for the Blind and raised $56, a foreshadowing of her later career as, in Eliot's words, the 'demon saleswoman' of poetry.[161] For now, however, her attempts at prose came to nothing. Her mother died when she was twenty-two, after a painful illness of many years that harrowed Amy, who as the only child at home was the one to bear the emotional brunt of her mother's bitterness and despair. The following year she visited Africa, quite an adventure for a young woman, where she discovered what contemporary women explorers and anthropologists (for example, the British Mary Kingsley or the American Matilda Stevenson and Alice Fletcher) already knew, that white women could have all the pleasures of manly command in a colonial situation. She came back with a taste for power, but her health was impaired, not by any exotic illness, but because she had attempted the Banting diet (nothing but tomatoes and asparagus, preferably, as in her case, while travelling up the Nile). She did not lose much weight, but it made her very ill, and she suffered from a variety of gastric and nervous ailments for several years

It was only after her father died in 1900 that she began to find herself. Her father had lived a frugal, disciplined, narrow existence that had increasingly weighed on Amy. It cannot be a coincidence that the title of her first book of poetry was a quotation from Shelley, the atheist poet whose works her father would not allow in the house. Her late rising, not permitted while he was alive, may have been partly a reaction against her father's mores: he got up every morning in summer at 4 a.m., in winter at 4.30, rather earlier than Amy in 1913 went to bed. Perhaps the death of her parents, and the freedom that gave her to run her own life, was a similar catalyst to that Pound and H.D. found in leaving for Europe. Her father's one passion appears to have been for horticulture, and when Sevenels, the family mansion, was built, he designed magnificent floral gardens, which Amy loved and whose flowers fill her poetry. She bought out her brothers and sisters, and remained in the house. She involved herself with various good works – a wonderful outlet for the restless energies of the Boston upper class, though not always appreciated by those to whom they insisted on doing good – and she began to play a part in Boston voluntary and charitable societies, discovering a talent for public speaking. But she still lacked a sense of direction. Then, in 1902, when she was twenty-eight, she went to see the famous actress Eleanor Duse. She had seen her act a couple of times before, but this time she was electrified. She went home and wrote 'seventy-one lines of blank bad verse'.[162] She realised a poet was what she wanted to be.

The Lowells were not opposed to literary work; after all, her great-great-cousin, James Russell Lowell, had been a famous poet in his day – as a child Amy loyally insisted he was her favourite poet – and she had met Longfellow, another gentleman poet, at the age of five. In that way she was luckier than Edith Wharton, who was born, ten years before Amy, into the best New York society; Wharton writes in her memoir that 'my parents and their group, though they held literature in great esteem, stood in nervous dread of those who produced it . . . On the whole, my mother doubtless thought, it would be simpler if people one might be exposed to meeting would refrain from meddling with literature.'[163] Yet while the Lowells took a much less philistine view when it came to male writers, for a lady to publish was quite another matter. Amy had already caused scandal in the family by speaking in public in the course of her work for good causes; publishing poetry would be even worse.

Amy was not to publish her first poem for another eight years, but from 1902 on she was writing regularly. She transformed Sevenels from the puritan stronghold that it had been under her father's management, turning the front and back parlours into one vast library to house her regular purchases of books, adding wooden panels, built-in bookcases and a safe, camouflaged by dummy books, for the rare manuscripts and books she came to delight in purchasing. She acquired a Whistler and a Constable to hang over the two fireplaces, and later some Japanese wood-blocks. The library doubled as a theatre, and home theatricals became a regular occurrence. She turned the billiard room into an elegant music room, in which piano and song recitals took place. She kept her bedroom suite on the third floor, but repainted it sky blue and hung up dark-blue toned Hiroshiges that Percival had sent her from Japan. Visitors were shown up there, and Amy would entertain them from her vast bed. She installed an outsize tiled bath – her love of bathing was something she would celebrate unashamedly in later poetry. She also installed electricity in the house; it was said, indeed, that she 'electrified it in more ways than one'.[164]

In 1908 Lowell became infatuated with another actress, Lina Abarbanell, whom she had seen in a Boston production of *The Merry Widow*. Abarbanell became a frequent visitor, causing considerable scandal among Boston society by singing risqué songs at a Sunday evening party that Amy gave. Amy was not a whit disconcerted, and continued to see much of her and to shower her with presents. On one occasion Abarbanell brought along a young musician, Carl Engel, who had been trained in France and was working for a Boston music publisher. Carl became an invaluable stimulus and support in the years when she was struggling to become a writer, and she was very attached to him. Amy was undoubtedly bisexual in her desires, and even after Ada Dwyer Russell became her much-loved companion, she retained her penchant for the companionship of handsome young men. Over the years, Engel introduced Amy to modern composers largely unknown in the States, such as Bartók, Stravinsky, Schoenberg and Satie, and gave her advice on her concerts. He encouraged her writing, setting two of her poems to music, and he would later, and most significantly, introduce her to the French *symbolistes*. He was a good friend, though he found Amy at times very emotionally demanding, prone as she was to wild enthusiasms and deep depressions. Amy now knew she wanted to write poetry, but she was full of self-doubt and unsure of her talent, and Engel was admirably patient in his reassurances. Her biographer Jean Gould says

letters that she wrote to Engel suggest she would have liked their relationship to be more than friendship, but he, though an important support
at a crucial stage in her life, had no such intentions. Luckily for them
both, Ada Dwyer Russell came along.

This was in early 1912, at a tense time for Amy, for she was just
about to submit her first book of poems to the solid Boston firm of
Houghton Mifflin. She planned to call it *A Dome of Many-Coloured
Glass*, using the well-known phrase from *Adonais*, Shelley's elegy for
John Keats, to signal her own admiration for Keats' works. She had
attempted publication for the first time in 1910, sending four poems to
the *Atlantic Monthly*, which gratifyingly accepted them instantly. She
had equally little problem in persuading Ferris Greenslet, the editor
with whom she would work for many years at Houghton Mifflin, to
publish her first volume, but she was racked with anxiety beforehand.
She wrote to Carl Engel, who much to her dismay was away in Paris:
'I have been collecting my poems for the book, and they do seem to
me so bad. Barely a half dozen which I like at all. Tonight it seems to
me I should put them all in the fire and take up crocheting. Only of
course I should crochet badly!'[165] She didn't put them in the fire, or
take up crochet, but she remained very nervous. Then in March she
met Ada, an able character actress, whom she had seen on the stage
more than once; this time she was performing in a smash hit by the
name of *The Deep Purple* at a Boston theatre, and was invited to be a
guest speaker at a Boston ladies' lunch club. Amy, still keenly interested
in the theatre, had herself appeared in various amateur productions,
mainly in the Sevenels library, including Wilde's *The Ideal Husband*;
she must have had quite a gift, because people who saw her perform,
Foster Damon tells us, said 'she acted so brilliantly that one quite forgot
her figure'.[166] Jean Gould suggests Amy went to the lunch club, which
she did not often attend, Boston lunchtime being somewhat before her
usual breakfast hour, specifically for acting tips, but Amy was a general
theatre groupie and may mainly have wanted to meet another diva. She
and Ada took to each other immediately. Ada was eleven years older
than Amy, cultured, calm, diplomatic, reassuring. Amy showed her all
her poems and, much to her relief, Ada approved of them all except
one. Amy agreed with her judgement, but decided the offending poem
was necessary to the order of the book, so could not be removed.

Ada went off on tour at the end of March, but she agreed to spend
some of the summer with Amy in Dublin, New Hampshire, in her
country retreat, a house named Broomley Lacey, with 64 acres of ground,

that Amy had bought shortly after her father's death. There, as well as discussing poetry and the theatre, they rode, rowed (Jean Gould says they gardened, but I think that must mean gave instructions to the gardeners) and petted Amy's English sheep-dogs, on whom she was said to lavish affection 'almost to the point of lasciviousness'.[167] It would be just over a year later, in the autumn of 1913, that Ada agreed to live permanently at Sevenels, after her theatrical career had been interrupted by a major illness; she was to help Amy *on a business basis* with her books, and Amy would pay her what she would have earned in the theatre.[168] Amy had finally gained her *'very* intimate friend', who brought her a happiness she had despaired of finding. She had written mournfully to Engel just before she met Ada: 'I wonder why I, with all my natural appetite for love and happiness in a superlative degree, should have managed so badly as to carve out for myself a life made of ashes & fog.'[169] One of the poems in that first book, 'A Fairy Tale', recalls how, as a child, for her the glamour of the fairy tale was always darkened by the fact that 'there was always one unbidden guest/Who cursed the child and left it bitterness'. Now, as an adult, in spite of many advantages, she finds that 'overshadowing all is still the curse/That never shall I be fulfilled by love!/Along the parching highroad of the world/No other soul shall bear mine company.'[170] All that was to change. Her prince, or rather her princess, had arrived.

In the interim, however, back in Boston without Ada, Amy went through a very low period after the publication of *A Dome*, which came out in October 1912. The book, which her first biographer, Foster Damon, describes as 'blighted by proprieties and almost paralysed by despair', received little attention, and what it did was likewarm.[171] Louis Untermeyer, then a young critic, later an admirer of her work, who would write the introduction to her *Complete Poetical Works* in 1955, dismissed these first poems as 'belatedly Tennysonian' and accused Lowell of imagining 'a fatuous, fancied kinship with Keats'.[172] Amy was devastated, and took to her bed with what the doctor called 'nervous exhaustion'; she only recovered by heading after Christmas to Atlantic City to watch Ada on the stage.

Yet, even before the book had appeared, Amy had begun to experiment in less conventional forms. Carl Engel had sent her from Paris a copy of Albert Samain's *Chariot d'or*, thus introducing her to French symbolism and *vers libre*. Samain, who had died in 1900 at the age of forty-two, was highly thought of in the pre-war years; in the anthology that Flint admired so much, *Les Poètes d'aujourd'hui*, his poetry was accorded twice as many pages as Rimbaud's. Amy was deeply impressed by his striking imagery and flexible verse forms, and began to realise the decorous, orderly poetry she had been producing was not the medium for her. One reviewer had said of her book, 'Never do we feel that behind the lines lurks a dynamic personality'.[173] Did that comment give her food for thought? All of Boston knew she had a dynamic personality – why was she not allowing that dynamism into her poetry? The poetry in *A Dome of Many-Coloured Glass* is riddled with poetic clichés, and is, totally unlike the rest of her life, cautiously conventional. She read more symbolist and post-symbolist poets, and began to write her first free-verse poems, as in Flint's early poems, moderating her use of rhyme and regular line lengths rather than abandoning them. She managed to include one of these, 'Before the Altar', as a late addition to the book, where it appears as the opening poem. Like 'A Fairy Tale' it is a dark poem, with strange imagery of self-immolation, a statement perhaps of her desperation and fears as a novice poet: 'Empty and silent . . . On this stone, in this urn/I pour my heart and watch it burn,/My self the sacrifice.'[174] In addition to her original epigraph – one that all her readers would have expected, the lines from Shelley from which her title was taken – she added another from Albert Samain, which, like 'Before the Altar', is full of angst: 'Le silence est si grand que mon coeur frisonne/Seul, le bruit de mes pas sur le pavé resonne'.[175]

In the summer of 1912, Amy, like Pound, had had a letter from Harriet Monroe, who had read her poems in the *Atlantic Monthly*, enclosing a prospectus for *Poetry* and asking her to contribute poetry and help. Amy sent a rather meagre cheque for $25, which did not disappoint Monroe, who did not then know about the Lowell fortune. Indeed, in her autobiography Monroe records having been rather pleased by the thought that 'evidently there was at least one poet with a bank-account'.[176] Amy a little later sent her two of these new poems, which Monroe promptly accepted, though she did not make use of them for some time. So it came about that in January 1913, when Amy was reading hopefully through that month's *Poetry* in search of her own poems, she came across H.D.'s, and made the decision that she was an *imagiste* too.

Shortly after this epiphanic moment, Amy was invited to a dinner in Chicago. Her brother, Lawrence, who had become president of Harvard in 1909, was being given a banquet by the Harvard alumni, male only, as was customary, but a smaller female gathering was planned for his wife. Her sister-in-law, Anna, herself a Lowell and a third cousin, strongly disapproved of Amy's unconventional ways and cannot have been pleased to have found her name on the guest list, but there was nothing to be done. Another of the guests was Harriet Monroe, probably for Anna Lowell a much more congenial dinner companion, as she could always be relied on to observe the proprieties. Harriet recounted the event after Amy's death, explaining that up till then she had had no knowledge of 'Boston genealogies', and no idea that the poet she had contacted came from a leading family there. Amy, of course, was late: 'As we were beginning the dessert, an imposing figure appeared in the remote distance at the top of a half-flight of stairs, and "Oh, there's Amy!" said Mrs Lowell, in a voice which accepted resignedly anything which Amy might do.' Harriet still, she said, did not connect this Amy with the person whose poems she had accepted, and just watched with amazement the way 'the ponderous and regal figure . . . took possession of the occasion, and the company'. She was much taken aback, on being introduced to Amy, to have her turn 'a powerfully reproachful eye on [her] with the query, "Well since you've taken 'em, why don't you print 'em?"'[177] Doubtless the story lost nothing in the telling, and Amy's poems still did not appear until July; Harriet was not easily intimidated.

That spring, Amy was becoming aware of other changes in the arts. Engel returned from France, bringing news of composers so far unknown to Boston, and Amy's concerts now featured the work of Debussy, Fauré and Satie. The Armory show, the inaugurating moment of modernist art in America, came to Boston, and Amy duly visited it, though, if not antagonistic, she was certainly puzzled. She continued to read *Poetry* and was becoming more and more intrigued by the imagists, being fascinated by Pound's list of 'Don'ts' in the March issue. She decided that she must meet these poets, and having prevailed upon Harriet for a letter of introduction to Pound, set sail. Ada was tied up with a theatrical production, so she took as her companion the wife of her favourite nephew, James Roosevelt. Quite what her niece-in-law did in London isn't clear; none of the accounts of Amy's doings there mention her. Perhaps she went shopping, or sightseeing with friends of her own. Presumably she stayed, like Amy, in the suite of rooms at the Berkeley Hotel in Piccadilly, where Amy entertained.

It would be intriguing to know what Monroe's letter of introduction said, but whatever it was, Pound came to dinner at the Berkeley and put himself out to be charming. Lowell was amused by his determination to look the part of the poet, though she must have felt some envy too. There was nothing she could do to make herself look poetical. To Carl Engel she described 'the erratic young poet, Ezra Pound', who dressed like a stage poet, as 'the oddest youth, clever, fearfully conceited, &, at the same time, excessively thin-skinned'.[178] But she told Harriet he had a 'sweep of conversation and youthful enthusiasm which keeps him talking delightfully as many hours as you please', and though she disapproved slightly of his 'chip-on-the-shoulder attitude', said she thought it would disappear in time; how wrong she was.[179] Pound told Harriet he thought Lowell 'pleasingly intelligent', and reported to his mother that 'Miss Lowell gives me hope for the future of America. She says her brother is as intelligent as she is so there may even be some hope for Harvard.'[180] Pound was naturally free with his advice to her, but Amy was an eager pupil. The poems that had eventually come out in *Poetry* that July were still to some extent using conventional forms, even if influenced by *vers libre*, but she had written one free-verse poem, 'In a Garden', which Pound liked, and promised to publish. It was a love poem to Ada, 22 lines long, in irregular stanzas, and the last seven lines went:

> And I wished for night and you.
> I wanted to see you in the swimming pool,
> White and shining in the silver-flecked water,
> While the moon rode over the garden,
> High in the arch of night,
> And the scent of the lilacs was heavy with stillness.
>
> Night and water, and you in your whiteness, bathing![181]

The naked female body bathing became a repeated motif in Lowell's poetry, an erotic image of joyous liberation from the constraints of Bostonian sobriety and starch. The contrast between the sensuous imagery and the stout Boston Brahmin would be cruelly highlighted the next year, but for now Pound was delighted to have a new and rich disciple, though he made no attempts to get her to part with her money as yet. He reported proudly to his parents that she had motored him about 200 miles in one day. 'I am still wind scorched,' he told Dorothy the next day; clearly one of the perils of motoring in 1913.[182]

Pound took Amy to meet Yeats, and to tea with Ford and Hunt at South Lodge. He also introduced her to Fletcher, now back in England, taking him along on another of his visits to the Berkeley. On that occasion Pound monopolised the conversation, declaiming his own poems while Fletcher once again, as so often, sat in stony silence, but as they

left Fletcher plucked up his courage to ask Lowell if he could return
to read some of *his* poetry. Amy agreed warmly, and the reading duly
took place; to Fletcher's delight, Lowell exclaimed, 'Why, my dear boy,
you have genius', something he noted with satisfaction that she had not
said to Pound.[183] They took greatly to each other. When she returned
home she recommended his poems to Harriet, though, as Ben Johnson
points out, rather less fervently than she had to Fletcher's face,
commenting, 'Queer though they are, they seem to show great originality'.[184] She and Fletcher met several times again before she left, and
it may have been on his advice that she visited the Russian Ballet, the
Poetry Bookshop and an exhibition of Post-Impressionist painting. She
gave Fletcher a copy of her book, which he thought 'uniformly stifled,
muffled, conventional, academic, timid, and tame'. She was, he
commented, at the age of forty, 'only beginning to conquer the cramping
conventionalities of her girlhood', and he felt sympathy with her, having
had his own struggle to free himself; he was delighted by 'her attitude
of unabashed eagerness, the entire mental semblance she bore to a mine
of unfettered energy ready to explode and go skyward'.[185] He says that
in London she wrote several of the *vers libre* poems that would be
published the next year, and claims in his 1937 memoir that he thought
she was imitating him. At the time, however, he appears to have been
entirely uncritical of her, and if he thought there were any likenesses,
took them as a compliment. In mid- or late August, Amy returned to
the States. The crossing was extremely hot, and she would escape from
her cabin in the dark to smoke her Manila cigars on deck. Unfortunately,
she was spotted. On the quay as she returned she was met by a flock
of newspaper reporters incredulously demanding if it were true that the
sister of the president of Harvard smoked not just cigarettes but cigars.
Yes, indeed, she said, and the news was splashed all over the next day's
paper. She was getting into practice for her future career as the much-
publicised leader of a revolutionary poetic movement. The issue of
women's smoking was an example of the way in which American society
remained more conservative than British; it is true that even in London
women smoking cigars was unusual, as indeed it still is today, but it was
acceptable for women to smoke in the home if not the street. Causing
scandal in the States Lowell would find delightfully easy.

PART X

DES IMAGISTES

I

ON that London visit Amy may not have stayed long enough to meet
Aldington or H.D., who returned from Paris around the time she went
home, though she certainly learnt that H.D. was one Hilda Doolittle.
More surprisingly there is no mention of her meeting Flint, a frequent
visitor to the Poetry Bookshop, but perhaps he and his family were away
in the country on their annual two-week holiday, always very precious
to him. When Harriet had finally published two of Lowell's poems in
the July *Poetry*, they had followed Flint's four poems 'in unrhymed
cadence'. Lowell would surely have wanted to meet this other imagist,
had he been in London. The four poems included the one for which
Flint became best known, 'London':

> London, my beautiful
> It is not the sunset
> nor the pale green sky
> shimmering through the curtain
> of the silver birch . . .
> that moves me.[1]

Pound would later complain that Flint was an Impressionist rather than
an imagist, by which he appears to mean that his poetry, like Ford's, was
too visual, too descriptive, not sufficiently concentrated. There are visual
elements here, but they are scarcely the point of the poem. The name
'London' instantly evokes its crowds, its buildings, the life of its streets,
but all of that is elided in the opening, as in a Hulme-like way the poet
looks to the sky and the coming of night; the only life on the ground
comes in a reference to 'hopping birds'. Eventually, however, the poem
returns to those inhabitants, to 'the glow' which London, like the moon,

'sheds on men'. It is a compact statement of Flint's aesthetic-political beliefs: ultimately, art and beauty would bring a better world to all. It is a very different picture of London from the evocation of dreary streets in his earlier poems. Flint was now living in Highbury, and the poem reflects a particular aspect of London's charm compared with other capital cities – the large number of houses with gardens even comparatively near the centre; but this new appreciation of the city might owe something to his extensive reading of contemporary French poetry, which so often concentrated on the urban, both its squalor and its beauty.

Much at the same time as he met Amy Lowell, Pound gained access to a second magazine. In the 1950s he remembered that it all started when 'as I recall a very noble, slightly bedraggled probably heroine of Suffragette struggle turned up in Church Walk, . . . working class to school-teacher, to which we owe D.H.L.'[2] The probable heroine had arrived, apparently on Ford and Hunt's advice, to ask Pound if he would care to be literary editor, responsible in the first instance for three columns, of a magazine which had appeared for eleven months as the *Freewoman*, and was about to be relaunched as the *New Freewoman*. He could not recall her name, but it was probably Grace Jardine, a close friend and secretary to the magazine's editor, the tiny, utterly resolute Dora Marsden. According to Rebecca West, then assistant editor, Marsden had 'exquisite beauty . . . the only person I have ever met who could so accurately have been described as flower-like that one could have put it down on her passport': yet, she adds, she also had 'wit and common sense and courage, and each to the point of genius'.[3] This flower-like genius had already been in prison several times, had thrown iron balls into a Liberal party meeting in Manchester, and had climbed on to the roof of the Empire Hall in Southport to denounce Winston Churchill through a porthole while he addressed the faithful. Whether Grace Jardine was 'working class to school-teacher' is not certain, but Dora Marsden certainly was, moving from pupil teacher, to university scholarship, to headmistress by the age of twenty-six. She had been born in a small village at the head of the Colne Valley, the constituency that had elected Victor Grayson, the Marxist so admired by Flint, and while by 1913 she was an anarchist rather than socialist she shared his belief in the necessity of revolutionary change. 'Violent or peaceful,' she said, 'the revolution must come.'[4] She threw up her job to work full time for Christabel Pankhurst's Women's Social and Political Union. The WSPU tried to exert iron discipline over its workers, but failed dismally with Marsden, and they parted acrimoniously in 1911. Marsden had become increasingly critical of WSPU policy, which she felt was wholly mistaken in concentrating solely on the question of the vote. Women's social and sexual oppression needed, she argued, to be radically confronted. Suffrage was not enough.

Later the same year Marsden launched the *Freewoman* as a platform for this wider debate. 'Woman,' she insisted, 'must be taught she is not an adjunct to man.'[5] Dora was backed by Charles Granville, whose company Swift & Co. had given Pound his short-lived contract, and one of the journal's future admirers was to be Floyd Dell, Pound's loyal supporter among American reviewers. In spite of their apparent differences of interest, Pound and Marsden were both recognisably part of a revolutionary tide, and that they should be supported by the same people and eventually join forces was not so surprising. The *Freewoman*, well before Pound in his own poetry attempted any kind of risqué subject-matter, ran articles on monogamy, prostitution, divorce, masturbation, abortion, homosexuality, free love, contraception and venereal disease. The highly respectable feminist Millicent Fawcett was so horrified when she saw a copy of the magazine that she ripped it up into little pieces. It was grist to the mill of the arch anti-suffragist Mrs Humphry Ward, who proclaimed that it revealed 'the dark and dangerous side of the "Woman Movement"' that she had always warned was there.[6] (Dora was so delighted to have outraged Ward she used that quotation regularly as advertising copy along with feminist eulogies and praise from freethinking intellectuals.) Radicals like H.G. Wells and Edward Carpenter admired the magazine wholeheartedly. It was directly responsible, according to Rebecca West, for her change of name: 'I never wrote for *The Freewoman*,' she said later, 'till it had got such a bad name for its candour that I was forbidden to read it by my family, and thus I came to adopt my present pseudonym.'[7]

In September 1912, W. H. Smith banned the *Freewoman*, drastically affecting distribution. Les Garner, Dora Marsden's biographer, suggests that Marsden was probably right when she ascribed the ban not just to horror at the outspoken discussions of sexual matters, but to the fact that the journal was seen as part of a growing revolutionary socialist menace. 'The opposition in the capitalist press,' she commented, 'only broke out when we began to make it clear that the way out of the sex problem was through the door of the economic problem.'[8] As with the Post-Impressionist Exhibition, radical moves in any sphere were instantly associated with the threat of political dissent. The year 1912, with its many strikes and unrest in Ireland, was a troubled one; women like

Dora Marsden unsettling home life as well was too much. The final
blow to the magazine was Granville's disappearance and the liquidation
of Swift & Co., a disaster that simultaneously deprived Pound of £100
per annum. The *Freewoman* closed in October.

Although the *Freewoman* had many socialist and anarchist contributors, it had never been affiliated to any one political party. Even its
commitment to feminism in the usual sense had become increasingly
uncertain. Marsden was becoming unhappy with the very category
'women', questioning the existence of the shared and stereotypical
characteristics the common noun implied, and was moving to a much
more individualistic position. She had come across a recent translation
of a mid-nineteenth-century German book *The Ego and its Own*, by
Max Stirner, unsuccessful in its own day but revived in the wake of the
stir caused by Nietzsche and his rejection of the herd mentality, and
published in an English translation in 1907. Stirner believed in the
uniqueness of the individual, seeing individualistic anarchy as the way
forward, and when the *New Freewoman* opened in June 1913 Dora
Marsden proclaimed in her editorial that the magazine was 'not for the
advance of Woman, but for the empowering of individuals – men and
women'.[9] Pound at that stage would probably have accepted the literary
editorship of any shade of magazine, and would not have been alarmed
had the paper been rabidly suffragist, a position he regarded with
indulgent amusement; but as it was, Marsden's individualism sat
comfortably with his own. When offered the post, he was not required
to show support for women, though he reassured Dora cautiously: 'I
suppose I am an individualist, I believe in the arts as the most efficient
propaganda for a sort of individual liberty that can be developed without
public inconvenience.'[10]

The *New Freewoman* was set up as a limited company, whose largest
shareholder was Harriet Shaw Weaver, honorary secretary to the magazine and later Joyce's chief benefactor. She was known to all as Miss
Weaver, for she would not allow her first name to be used outside her
family, a fact which in itself indicates how unlikely she was as a core
organiser of a journal that had promised to ignore 'all existing tabus'.
Up to that time she had been chiefly concerned with issues of social
deprivation in the East End, for although she came from a solidly
respectable family, by 1912 she was a convinced socialist, believing one
should combine social justice with the promotion of individual freedom.
Like Dora, she was a disillusioned former member of the WSPU and
no longer believed that women's freedom from oppression would

necessarily be achieved by the vote. Dora was once again editor, and Rebecca West, then just twenty, assistant editor.

The magazine's revival was welcomed by its previous feminist supporters, but many soon began to have second thoughts when they realised how far Dora had moved. The first issue, in June 1913, announced that: '"Woman" is doing nothing – she has indeed, no existence. A very limited number of individual women are emphasising the fact that the first thing to be taken into account with regard to them is that they *are* individuals and cannot be lumped together into a class, a sex, or a "movement".'[11] Many present-day feminists would agree entirely that 'Woman' has no existence, even if they might be less sure about the moral claims of egoism, but it was not an idea that went down well at the time. Dora also attacked the Pankhursts viciously, particularly unjustly over the death that month of Emily Wilding Davison, who had thrown herself under the King's horse at the Derby. It was perhaps partly because she was aware that her earlier readers were alarmed, and indeed were defecting, that she agreed with Rebecca West that the magazine's appeal should be increased by the inclusion of a literary section.

The *Freewoman* itself had never neglected literature or the arts. One of its most lively and entertaining regular items had been Rebecca West's own irreverent and controversial weekly reviews; it published occasional poems (the main contributor of verse being John Gould Fletcher's friend, Horace Holley), well-known writers, such as Wells and Galsworthy; promising new ones, like John Rodker, had also written for it. There had been intermittent articles on the visual arts, including a very enthusiastic review of an exhibition of Chinese painting, though they were generally on the Post-Impressionists or Futurists. The readers liked their culture to be as contentious as their social theory. A telling advertisement, nicely gauged for this niche market, had appeared in May 1912 for Florence Farr's marriage question novel, *The Solemnization of Jacklin: Some Adventures on the Search for Reality*. This encouraged readers to ask for the book at their library, adding in bold print: 'Please insist upon getting it, as you will probably find some resistance.' Along with quotations from admiring reviews of the novel was one that read, 'It bears only the resemblance to life that the wildest of Futurist landscapes bears to nature.' Sexually *and* artistically shocking: what could appeal more to their readers! So, if they were to extend this area, who more appropriate than an iconoclastic, avant-gardiste poet for literary editor in the new phase of the magazine? West had met Pound at South Lodge, and liked him, although she had given his *Sonnets and Ballate of Guido Cavalcanti* a very mixed review the previous year, describing Pound as 'a poet of an infuriating and fascinating nature'. She thought most of the translations showed a 'petulant disdain for the English language'. 'Probably in the Elsyian fields,' she wrote, 'Guido Cavalcanti, with his ghostly blood up, is busy translating "The Chansons of Ezra Pound" into Italian. Some great revenge must be brewing.' In only one poem she found 'the very breath of poetry' – significantly, perhaps, not a courtly love poem at all but one about a shepherdess – so charming that she decided that 'Mr Pound's heart is in the right place'.[12] Pound didn't comment on the review, though later he remembered West as an admirer of his work; the reviews of the Cavalcanti book had been so uniformly dire he may have been quite pleased with it.

Pound stipulated that he must have sole jurisdiction over all verse that appeared, to which Dora agreed, if a little anxiously. The *New Freewoman* could not afford to pay contributors, but Pound persuaded John Gould Fletcher to put up the money for payment on his section. Fletcher would later claim he produced the money out of concern for Pound and his fellow-poets' poverty, though he was for now so entranced with Pound he would have agreed to anything. The fact that his first publication had been in the *Freewoman* probably helped to make Fletcher sympathetic to the request, and Pound wrote to Dorothy in high spirits: 'Had tea with J.G.F . . . he gave me some £s wherewith to feed Flint & Cannell & R.A. & such others as I may want to print in The Freewoman, which was, I think, fairly decent of him.'[13] In the early months of this arrangement, Fletcher insisted that nothing by himself should now appear in the journal, in his tortured way fearing to appear to be buying favours for his own work; he soon changed his mind. In any case, as he also changed his mind about Pound, he did not continue to provide the money for very long.

In August 1913, Rebecca West helped Pound launch his page and a half with a puff for *imagisme*. Her article was largely extracts from Flint's *Poetry* interview and Pound's 'A Few Don'ts' (which Dora Marsden's biographer rather appropriately misnames as 'A Few Darts by an Imagiste'), with some introductory sentences in her own unmistakable prose.[14] Pound must surely have been impressed by the accuracy and the panache with which she summed up his principles. She began:

Poetry should be burned to the bone by austere fires and washed white with rains of affliction: the poet should love nakedness and the thought of the skeleton under the flesh. But because the public will not pay for poetry it has become the

occupation of learned persons, given to soft living among veiled things and un-
accustomed to being sacked for talking too much. That is why from the beautiful
stark bride of Blake it has become the idle hussy hung with ornament kept by
Lord Tennyson, handed on to Stephen Phillips [the nineties poet who had become
the staid editor of *Poetry Review* in place of Harold Monro] and now supported
at Devonshire Street by the Georgian school . . . Just as Taylor and Galbraith
want to introduce scientific management into industry so the *imagistes* want to
discover the most puissant way of whirling the scattered star dust of words into
a new star of passion.[15]

West is throwing herself behind this revolutionary movement with
aplomb. It is a tribute to the success of the first *Georgian Poetry* that
the Georgians had after only eight months become identified as a school
of their own, even if here only to be reviled. West's language picks up
on Pound's own imagery, poetry 'closer to the bone', and akin to the
quest of the scientist. West, like Pound and Hulme, is using gendered
imagery when she speaks of poetry, but unlike them she doesn't reject
the feminine. She merely commends the 'beautiful stark bride of Blake'
over the 'idle hussy . . . kept by Lord Tennyson'.

   Pound published seven of his own poems in the 15 August issue, a
selection of the 'Contemporania' that had appeared in *Poetry* in April.
Had she read them, Dora might have approved. She did not bother. 'As
for E.P's poems,' she told Weaver, 'I haven't read 'em. Speak it not. He
is a nice old thing.'[16] Not everyone said that about Pound; perhaps his
niceness at that point was because he was also for the meantime a happy
old thing; he had, quite by chance, secured an English outlet for his
'mouvemong'. For the most part and to most readers, the literary section
appeared to have little in common with the rest of the magazine, and
Pound and his fellow-imagists would complain regularly about Marsden's
convoluted editorials and articles. Yet Marsden was developing a view
of language which at a theoretical level shared much with Pound's, in
particular an opposition to fixed ideas, clichés and abstractions, the ideas
in fact that Pound had expounded in his Osiris articles under Hulme's
influence, and they would also come to share an opposition to democracy and government. But they expressed their ideas very differently
and may never have realised what they had in common, beyond a general
opposition to the status quo. There was, as David Moody puts it, 'no
meeting of these like minds'.[17] Yet, as Bruce Clarke first pointed out,
Marsden's interrogation of Pound on the question of the use of poetry
prompted him to write 'The Serious Artist', the series of articles in

which he developed his view that there was a role in art for social diagnosis as well as the creation of beauty. She may well have contributed, through her very hostility to the idea, to his growing sense of the importance of the arts to cultural well-being.[18]

The good news that Pound would be publishing their poetry in the 1 September issue of the *New Freewoman* greeted Richard and H.D. when they returned to London in the second half of August. They had come back separately, Pound's letters indicate, though only by a day or two. Travelling *à deux* to London could have provoked gossip. When they caught up with the news about Ford and Hunt's turbulent year, H.D. must have thought they had been wise to be discreet; life could still be hard for a woman who stepped out of line. They now both spent much of their time in the British Museum Reading Room, since Aldington was finally eligible for a ticket, having had his twenty-first birthday that July. H.D.'s parents returned to England from Germany in early September, for the final phase of their European tour. The visit had an anxious beginning, for when they reached London by the overnight boat train, H.D.'s father was far from well. The pre-war London tourist trade was buoyant, and H.D. and her mother had to search for a hotel, only managing to secure a room at the third they tried, one close to the British Museum. The next day, H.D.'s father was worse, 'in a wretched condition', her mother says in her diary, clearly deeply worried, and the hotel recommended a doctor from nearby Gordon Square. By 10 September, H.D.'s twenty-seventh birthday, Professor Doolittle was beginning to recover, and they all spent the day together. Two days later, the Doolittles left for Bournemouth so her father could recuperate. From then on, things improved. A week later, 'a beautiful day', her mother recorded, H.D. and Richard came for the day to see them and 'to talk over the future. Such a lovely time and I am happy for them both.' H.D. and Richard caught a train back to London, and Mrs Doolittle went to bed 'happy and peaceful'. Ten days later, on 29 September, the Doolittle parents returned to London, staying again in Bloomsbury, this time off Russell Square, and Mrs Doolittle indulged very happily in an orgy of shopping, most of it for H.D.'s coming marriage. Mrs Doolittle had been in London for less than a week when she noted in her diary that she was 'feeling especially well and at home'.

Pound saw a certain amount of the Doolittle parents, giving them a copy of the 15 August issue of the *New Freewoman* so they could read his 'Contemporania', which, he told Dorothy with some pleasure, they found quite bewildering. H.D. presumably had seen 'Contemporania' before, but she must have been struck by a couple of the articles in that issue on subjects close to her heart. There was one by Edward Carpenter on women in early Greece, which argued that they had a much higher status, particularly in Sparta, than they would have later in history, when a wife became 'a domestic drudge, whose ideal was "to stay at home and mind the house"'.[19] It was a view that must have confirmed the intransigently undomesticated H.D. in her sense that early Greece was her spiritual home. The second article, entitled 'The Earth-Goddess', recommended highly Jane Harrison's work on primitive Greek religion, especially her emphasis on the female principle.

H.D. herself probably showed her parents the *New Freewoman* for 1 September, in which, under the heading of 'The Newer School', her poem 'Sitalkis' appeared along with a selection of poems by her fellow-imagists. One of the images in 'Sitalkis' is of 'Argestes', the Greek autumnal north-west cleansing wind, 'Scattering the broken leaves'; she later recalled writing it after shuffling through the leaves outside the British Museum, presumably the previous autumn.[20] Sitalkis was an avatar of Apollo as an autumn sun god, and the poem refers to the myth that Apollo withdrew for the winter months, this disappearance, like that of Persephone, being a version of the death and rebirth fertility theme that Frazer had made so fascinating to her generation. It is, one guesses, a love poem to Aldington, unusual for her poems of the period in mentioning one of the main Greek gods, though significantly in a little-known guise, and firmly preferred to a 'high god/Who touches us not'. Aldington was represented by 'To Atthis', a translation of one of the recently found Sappho fragments, the original of which H.D. had copied out for him in the British Museum. Pound had tried to persuade Monroe to take it for *Poetry*, but she had shown it to some classicists at the University of Chicago, who thought it too free a translation, and so she refused, though Pound fumed that the text was so mutilated that it was impossible to know exactly what it meant. Lowell's 'In the Garden' appeared, and there were poems by Flint, Skipwith Cannell, in whom Pound was briefly showing an interest, and a poem entitled 'Postlude' by William Carlos Williams, one of the few free verse poems in *The Tempers*, Williams' second book of poems, which Elkin Mathews finally published that September. It was not, incidentally, one of the selection of Williams' poems that Pound had printed the year before in the *Poetry Review*, all of which were in traditional forms.[21] A number of the poems in Williams' volume were influenced by Pound's own earlier enthusiasms –

Provençal subjects and translations from the Spanish – but in just a few, both form and subject were changing. The poem in *The Tempers* that indicated best the way Williams would develop is not 'Postlude', which is a rather languid, classicist piece ('Let there be gold of tarnished masonry/Temples soothed by the sun to ruin/That sleep utterly') but a short poem, called significantly, like Pound's latest poems, 'Contemporania', which begins with the conversational simplicity and quotidian subject-matter that was to be so characteristic of Williams' poetry: 'The corner of a great rain/Steamy with the country/Has fallen upon my garden.'[22] Yet Pound was convinced of Williams' future as a poet, and that December he wrote to say, 'I still think as always that in the end your work will hold.'[23]

II

Now that he had gathered together a reasonable number of practitioners of the 'newer school' in poetry, Pound began to plan an anthology, in which many of the poems included in the 1 September issue would reappear. This anthology has always been presumed, almost certainly correctly, to have been set up by Pound in imitation of, and in rivalry to, *Georgian Poetry*. Certainly this was the rumour going round London: Eddie Marsh had written to Rupert Brooke to say, 'there's a movement for a "Post-Georgian" Anthology, of the Pound-Flint-Hulme school, who don't like being out of *GP* [*Georgian Poetry*], but I don't think it will come off.'[24] When Pound first mentioned the projected anthology in a letter home in early September, he described it as a collection of poems not by imagists but by '*les jeunes*', and in Fletcher's account in his autobiography he mentions that H.D. referred to it at that time as an anthology of 'all the writers who don't belong to the Georgians'.[25] Perhaps that was how it began: certainly not all the writers could be claimed as imagists, although by the title, *Des Imagistes*, Pound was resolutely signalling one more stage in the establishment of his movement. Pound tried to persuade Fletcher to contribute, but Fletcher, although he shared Pound's dislike of the Georgians, was not at all sure he wanted to be labelled an imagist. Pound sent him off to meet Aldington and H.D., in the hope that they would have more luck in drawing him in. Fletcher had already been introduced to Flint ('bespectacled, shy, apologetic') but the two of them never got on particularly well.[26] Fletcher respected Flint's knowledge of French poetry, but their backgrounds were perhaps too different for them to have much mutual sympathy.

Both Flint and Pound had praised H.D.'s poetry highly, Pound telling Fletcher that her work was the best example of what he meant by imagism. Fletcher duly applied himself to reading it, but says that whilst he admired her 'very vivid and keen sense of rhythm', he found himself 'slightly repelled, despite my admiration, by an archaism in choice of subject . . . I was too deeply committed to the task of attempting to deal, as a modern poet, with the life all about me to take much pleasure in H.D.'s Hellenism . . . H.D.'s retreat into the past seemed to me to smack somewhat of an evasion'.[27] It is curious that Fletcher can write this only a few pages after lavishly praising Stravinsky for setting his ballet in 'remote pagan Russia . . . back behind recorded history'.[28] That H.D. also used her remote subject-matter to attain a 'primitive' strength with which to dramatise modern emotions was not something that he recognised until later.

Fletcher was struck by how different H.D. and Aldington were: 'While H.D. was tall, slim, lithe, with a pale oval face framed in masses of dark hair, and a nervous shyness of manner that only emphasized her fragility, Aldington was bluff, hearty, and robust, with the square shoulders of an athlete, the bullet-head of a guardsman, and a general tendency to beefiness which proclaimed his British quality'.[29] Out of sheer nervousness, Fletcher burst into extravagant praise of H.D.'s poetry, while she, equally nervously, told him that 'she was never sure that anything she had ever written had been good. Ezra encouraged her to write and go on writing. She simply wrote as she felt.' Aldington was the only one at ease, and proceeded to lecture Fletcher on his poetic theories. Fletcher thoroughly took against him, and left all the more determined not to join the anthology. Their poetry, he says he told them, was 'remote, refined, and pure, like the Parthenon', his, 'shambling, grotesque, formless, like a primeval monster'. They wouldn't want 'a dinosaur in the Parthenon'.[30]

With Fletcher's uncanny ability for getting the wrong end of any available stick, he went away convinced that it was really Aldington who would be the editor of the projected anthology. He wrote in alarm to Amy Lowell to warn her to have nothing to do with it, as its real aim is 'to boom Aldington'.[31] At this stage, Lowell was very unsure what to make of Fletcher's outbursts, but his warnings may have had some effect. When Pound wrote to her in November to ask whether he could include in the anthology her poem, 'In a Garden', she first agreed, but then changed her mind and refused on the grounds that she too was no longer sure that she was an imagist. She claimed he never replied, though there is extant a letter to her from Pound, saying that it was 'too late to monkey with the Anthology', dated in fact after *Des Imagistes* had appeared in New York, and it is hard to imagine what the context of that letter could have been it was not a reply to the request to withdraw her poem.[32]

Fletcher would spend the next year alternately furious with Pound and under his spell once more. Even in the first flush of admiration that summer, he had brooded on the changes Pound had wanted to make to 'Irradiations', becoming progressively more resentful, but he was grateful to Pound for taking him seriously and making it possible for him to publish his work. When, however, Pound began to bring out his series of articles on French poetry, 'The Approach to Paris', in the *New Age* in mid-August, using among others the books he borrowed from him, Fletcher became incandescent, rebuking Pound bitterly for passing off his (Fletcher's) discoveries as his own. He was furious not to be given an acknowledgement. So, possibly with more justification, was Flint. Pound simply handed Fletcher his books back, and said that even if he wanted no more to do with him he would still like to send his poetry to Harriet Monroe at *Poetry*. Fletcher was so impressed by this disinterested generosity that he became friends once more. He wrote twice to Lowell that autumn saying he was breaking off all contact with Pound and was no longer intending to fund the *New Freewoman*'s literary pages, yet, although by the end of the year he appears to have withdrawn his financial support for the journal, he was still uneasily and moodily on the edges of Pound's circle when Lowell returned the next summer.

Meanwhile, H.D. and Aldington were married on 18 October in Kensington Registry Office. H.D. does not say what she wore, but it may well have been one of the dresses made in Italy, which she records elsewhere as wearing for special occasions. Her parents were present, and so was Pound, but not apparently any of Aldington's family. H.D. never mentions when she was first introduced to Aldington's parents, though she recalled later that his father was the only person she met in England who had heard of the Moravian Brethren. H.D.'s parents do not appear to have had anything like the anxieties over Aldington's income that the Shakespears had over Pound's, even though Aldington's earnings were sparse compared even to Pound's. H.D. had her allowance, about £200 a year, enough for them to get by on. According to Lawrence Rainey, average working-class annual earnings were then £75, and middle-class, £350. Even with their occasional payments for poems and articles, they were scarcely well-off, but money never seems to have worried them. Aldington and she moved from their rooms in Church Walk round the corner to a small flat in Holland Park Chambers. A few days later the Doolittles returned home, H.D. and Aldington seeing them off at the station. It would be the last time H.D. saw her father.

One other person that one might have expected to have attended the Aldingtons' wedding was Brigit Patmore, but as H.D. mentions in her 'Autobiographical Notes', Brigit was having an operation at the time of the wedding. When Pound wrote home in November to say that 'Richard and Hilda were decently married last week, or the week before, as you have doubtless been notified', he added, 'Brigit Patmore is very ill but they have decided to let her live, which is a mercy as there are none too many charming people on the planet'.[33] Violet Hunt and Ford went to see her in her nursing home, after what Violet describes as 'that terrible operation'.[34] Aldington in a later letter to H.D. refers to Brigit's having had an abortion, so that was possibly what 'that terrible operation' was, presumably one that went horribly wrong. Derek Patmore says his mother was unable to have children after his younger brother Michael was born, which may have been as the result of what happened here. An abortion for a married woman begs many questions. Brigit was a devoted mother, who would not, one would think, be likely to resort to an abortion if it were not forced upon her. If Deighton had insisted on it because he knew the baby was not his, it would certainly explain her later bitterness towards him. Of course, Aldington could simply have been jumping to conclusions. It could have been an ectopic pregnancy, which can be extremely dangerous and life-threatening. Violet's comments, it is true, sound as if she is implying that there was a scandal, but as scandal-mongering was her favourite occupation, that is no proof. Perhaps she wondered if it had been Ford's child, as indeed perhaps it was, the origin of his dark hints in later years of his relationship to Derek, a surrogate for the lost baby. But Ford needed no grounds for his fantasies.

Aldington comments on how much energy Brigit lost after this operation, but by early the next year she must have been well recovered, as she would go to stay with Ford and Hunt in their cottage at Selsey on the West Sussex coast, to act as Ford's secretary, and while there Ford dictated the first part of *The Good Soldier* to her. Being secretary to Ford took considerable stamina, as H.D., who took over her role later in the year, would find. According to Aldington (who in due course took over from an exhausted H.D.), Ford produced 6–8,000 words a week, and taking that down in rapid longhand (as amateurs, none of them knew shorthand) was highly stressful. Ford claimed the problem for his secretaries was not just the amount but the intensity of his dictation; he couldn't, he said, resist trying to get a reaction: 'At last you say:

"Damn it all, I *will* make that creature smile. Or have a tear in its eye!" And then you are lost . . . When I was dictating the most tragic portion of my most tragic book to an American poetess [H.D., of course] she fainted several times. One morning she fainted three times. So I had to call in her husband to finish the last pages of the book. He did not faint. But he has never forgiven me.'[35] Yet even if the fragile Brigit was usefully recording Ford's declamations, it is remarkable that Hunt chose to invite the woman she knew Ford loved to stay with them in this intimate setting; perhaps she felt she could control the situation best that way. What is even more curious is that her successor, Stella Bowen, would do exactly the same ten years later when Ford fell in love with Jean Rhys, taking her off on holiday with them, disastrously for all concerned. What was it about Ford that made women act in so self-destructive a way? In neither case did the women Violet Hunt and Stella Bowen feared form a lasting liaison with Ford, but in each case their own relationship with him would never recover, and in a few years end for ever.

Pound, meanwhile, was continuing to supply Harriet with poetry. He had sent the Fletcher poems off to her in mid-August: a selection from 'Irradiations', accompanied by a request to 'use the full sequence', or as much as possible, 'in some way that will establish the tone and in some way present the personality, the force behind this new and amazing state of affairs'.[36] Pound would soon become more guarded in his praise of Fletcher, lamenting his unevenness in a letter to Alice Corbin Henderson soon after. In his letters to Harriet, one should perhaps be careful about accepting at face value his exuberant writing up of poets whom he wanted to promote. He may well have felt that unless he piled on the glowing commendations he would never persuade her to accept the more experimental poets that he sent. In this case, Harriet was won over without difficulty and 'Irradiations' duly appeared in December, with Pound's review of two of Fletcher's volumes of poetry, *The Dominant City* and *Fool's Gold*, in the same issue. During the autumn more poetry by Yeats and another instalment of Pound's 'Contemporania' appeared. Pound mentions in a letter to Alice Corbin Henderson that Frances Gregg, who had been briefly back in London, had done a 'permissible' poem and he had encouraged her to send it in along with anything else she had that was 'decent'.[37] The permissible poem may have been the love poem for H.D. that appeared in *Poetry* later that year, which begins, 'You were all loveliness to me:/Sea Mist, the Spring', and ends with one of H.D.'s own lines, 'spare us from loveliness'.[38] In mid-September Pound sent Harriet some poems by Lawrence, saying grudgingly,

'Lawrence, as you know, gives me no particular pleasure. Nevertheless we are lucky to get him. Hueffer . . . thinks highly of him. I *recognize* certain qualities of his work . . . As a prose writer I grant him first place among the younger men.'[39] Pound was deeply ambivalent about Lawrence. He had written to her earlier in the year, when Lawrence's *Love Poems and Others* was published, 'Lawrence . . . is clever. I don't know whether to send in a review or not . . . Detestable person but needs watching. I think he learnt the proper treatment of modern subjects before I did.'[40] He did in the end review the book, not only in *Poetry* but also in the *New Freewoman*, where he wrote that 'The disagreeable qualities of Mr Lawrence's work are apparent to the most casual reader', but then added, 'let me say without further preamble that Mr Lawrence's book is the most important book of poems of the season'.[41]

Lawrence was in 1913 still living on the continent, though he and Frieda had made a quasi-secret visit back to England for a few weeks that summer, when she had hoped to see her children, while Lawrence arranged for the publication of stories and poems. He did not see Pound on that return visit, though he had been invited to the garden party given by Violet Hunt to which Pound had gone, but received the invitation too late to attend. Since he and Frieda passed as Mr and Mrs Lawrence, with no more foundation than Violet and Ford as Mr and Mrs Hueffer – and for the same reason, Frieda not yet having had her divorce – they would have been particularly appropriate guests. Pound, however, got in touch with Lawrence on that visit, asking him for some stories because 'he had got an American publisher under his wing'.[42] This was Willard Huntington Wright, editor of the *Smart Set* from 1912 until 1914, who had now like Monroe taken up Pound as a quasi-agent for London contacts, though Pound never had the same relation with the *Smart Set* as with *Poetry*. The latter he longed to forge into the most prestigious poetry magazine of the day; the *Smart Set* was a place where he and those he thought worthy of help could be paid a reasonable rate for their work. Pound placed several of Lawrence's stories and poems in the next year in both the *Smart Set* and *Poetry*. Lawrence was, as he put it himself in a letter to Harold Monro, 'woefully poor', so the publications must have been helpful to him – as well as to Pound's reputation as a literary impresario – but it did nothing to encourage either of them to renew their friendship.[43] The poems sent to Monroe appeared in January 1914 – Pound had said they should not go in until after Fletcher's had appeared – and included among others Lawrence's love poem for Frieda, 'Gloire de Dijon', which H.D. admired greatly, a poem to which she alludes in her fictional account of their relationship in her novel, *Bid Me to Live*.

Pound, one might think, would have earned the gratitude of those like Lawrence whose work he promoted, but it was not always so. Pound not only aroused hostility in those whose work he denounced, but he was also regarded with suspicion by some of those he tried to help. Fletcher was a case in point, but the most bitter and resentful recipient of his assistance was Robert Frost, one of whose poems Pound sent off to Monroe at much the same time as Lawrence's. Robert Frost was at that time living in England with his family, and he had made Flint's acquaintance at the January 1913 opening of the Poetry Bookshop, one of his first forays on either side of the Atlantic into the literary world. Flint, as Frost told him later, was the first poet he had ever met. Flint instantly recognised him as an American, and when Frost asked how he did so, laconically replied 'Shoes'. Flint asked him if he knew his countryman Pound, and when told he had never heard of him, replied, 'Well, if you ever meet him, you won't be foolish enough to say that to his face.'[44] Frost's first volume of poetry, *A Boy's Will*, was not yet published, though it had been accepted by a London publisher, David Nutt; Flint promised to review it, and also encouraged him to seek out Pound as a useful contact in the literary world. Frost, for his part, was very taken with Flint, and bought a copy of *In the Net of the Stars*, writing to Flint in warm praise of the poems a few days later and later telling him he had been 'childishly happy in being allowed to make one for a moment in a company in which I hadn't to be ashamed of having written verse. Perhaps it will help you understand my state of mind if I tell you that I have lived for the most part in villages where it were better that a millstone were hanged about your neck than that you should own yourself a minor poet.'[45] How true this was one can't be sure, as Frost was a great mythologiser of his own life, but given the painful lack of interest in the arts in the world in which the young Flint had grown up, his sympathy was instantly engaged. Frost's poems were about the New England countryside, and Flint's about the London streets, Frost used rhymed stanzas, though in very flexible ways, and Flint *vers libre*, but there was much in common in their conversational tone, their interest in the quotidian life and their belief in the importance of cadence in verse, although they approached it very differently. Frost and Flint became good friends for a while, and even thought of writing a joint book on metre and cadence. Lawrance Thompson, in his lengthy biography of Frost, in which Frost is presented as thoroughly disagreeable, suggests he was to some extent making use of Flint as a handy contact, but his letters hardly bear that out.

Flint, with the best of intentions, encouraged Pound to take an interest in Frost, and Pound gave him one of his visiting cards to send to Frost, writing on it the message, 'At home – sometimes'.[46] Frost thought this insultingly casual, but after a month or so grudgingly went to Church Walk to visit Pound, who rebuked him for taking so long to call, and instantly marched him to David Nutt's office to collect an advance copy of Frost's book. On their return, Pound began to read it, expressing his admiration in what Frost felt – or said he felt – were pompous and patronising terms. Frost took the opportunity to fill in the background to his poems of country life by telling Pound quite inaccurate tales about the ill-treatment and harsh financial hardship his family had inflicted on him because he was a poet, and perhaps more accurately about his difficulties in finding magazine editors who would publish his work. Pound sent him home without his book but with a promise that he would review it. He wrote to Alice Corbin Henderson, 'Have just discovered another Amur'kn. VURRY Amur'k'n, with, I think, the seeds of grace', and told Monroe it was their 'second scoop' – the first being Tagore – remarkable in that he had 'only found the man by accident'.[47] As Frost himself would later point out, it had in fact been Flint who discovered him, not Pound, and he would tell Flint that tolerating such claims was another of the ways in which he allowed Pound to exploit him. Flint loyally tried to defend Pound, saying, 'You know I think his bark is much worse than his bite . . . and that much that seems offensive to us externally is merely external and a kind of outer defense – a mask.'[48] It was a perceptive and compassionate comment, and goes a long way to explaining why Flint was so patient for so long under Pound's high-handedness.

Frost was irritated by the review, which described his work as a 'little raw' and 'simple', though also as 'without sham and . . . affectation', and was unreasonably indignant that Pound repeated the story he had told him about his grandfather's disinheriting him because he was 'a useless poet instead of a money getter'. What upset him most, however, was that Pound had seized the opportunity to abuse American editors for not accepting his poetry. He feared it would make it harder for him to make his way in the literary world in the States if he were associated with Pound's vendetta against them. Yet he was also seriously affronted, because, in order to explain the value of folk poetry, which Pound took Frost's to be, he told a story he had heard from Joseph Campbell, one he would repeat in other contexts, about an Irish peasant Campbell had met on 'a desolate waste of bogs', who when asked if he found life there dull replied 'Faith, ye can sit on a midden and dream stars'.[49] Frost thought this shockingly vulgar, and bridled at the comparison between himself and an Irish peasant, as well as between a bog and his farm. Frost's horrified reaction to Campbell's delightful story might seem to prove that Pound was right to think Frost lacked urban sophistication, but Frost was surely right that Pound misunderstood the subtlety and craftsmanship of his work. He was indignant that Pound saw him as a naïve, literary Douanier Rousseau, and by July was complaining that Pound was trying to bully him into writing *vers libre*; he sent Flint a free verse poem attacking Pound, suggesting he was not so much interested in helping Frost's reputation as a poet as his own as a poet-maker.[50] Pound's estimate of Frost's worth was more genuine than he suggests, but it's true the terms in which he described his discovery of Frost to Harriet – 'our second scoop' – echoed the language of the commercial newspaper press, out entirely for their own interests. Many years later Frost would refer to Pound's 'selfish generosity'; in helping new poets, he noted, Pound was also helping himself.[51]

Frost was right: Pound was immeasurably generous in many instances, but he was pursuing his own agenda too. He wanted to wield power and influence in the literary world, and was baffled when his efforts were unappreciated. Pound believed his disinterested goal was the promotion of the best literature, which would in turn produce a better society. If he were at times also aware that he was personally ambitious, it does not seem to have struck him that disinterestedness and ambition might clash. Given his belief in the absolute rightness of his judgements, perhaps there did not appear to him to be a problem. Nor did he realise – and this would be true of several of his fellow-imagists – that those whose careers he helped to launch, grateful though they might be in the beginning, would tire after a while of being treated like pupils and followers, subservient paragraphs in the narrative of Pound's artistic achievements. Yet Pound was often genuinely attached to those he tried to help, and pained when they turned against him; he was like an autocratic father, who cannot understand why his much-loved children reject him when everything he has done, he is convinced, has been for their own good.

One of the most interesting aspects of the story of Pound's dealings with Frost is what it reveals about Flint's attitude at this period. Frost says in one letter to Flint that 'you take Ezra sadly, and I angrily.'[52]

Pound was frequently far from tactful in his dealings with Flint, and Flint's feelings were often bruised. Yet there is no evidence that Flint said anything to Pound at this stage about the way that Pound had reinvented himself as an advocate of French poetry without ever acknowledging how much he had learnt from Flint, and it would only emerge much later that Flint resented the way Pound had taken up the ideas and theories about poetry that he and Hulme had propounded earlier, and drawn on them for his own poetic doctrines, once more, he would come to feel, without due acknowledgement. For now, he was happy for Pound to be the promoter of the new poetry, a role for which he, unlike the diffident Flint, was so extraordinarily well fitted.

III

FLETCHER, that other uneasy recipient of Pound's support, also often took him angrily, but his outburst over the articles on French poetry, and indeed his more surprising reconciliation, may have owed something to the fact that his personal life was in a turbulent state at that period. In the summer of 1913, Fletcher was still a nervous North American virgin, fearful of female sexuality. He had found his visits to Paris particularly disturbing, where the existence of sexual activity and indeed pleasure was so much harder to avoid than in Boston or Little Rock. He writes in his autobiography that when he first came to Europe he invited his sister to join him for a while in order 'to postpone the hour when I would fall victim to some unknown woman'. 'Victim' is a telling word: Fletcher saw women as predatory and dangerous. On the visit to Paris when he met Pound, he had contemplated the possibility of 'physical fulfilment', something he was beginning to feel was almost *de rigueur* for a modern poet, but shrank away once more, recording with relief that there was 'so much for me to see and do, so many impressions crowding into my mind, that I put from me, during the entire time of my stay, all thought of sexual adventure. I was in love now, not with a woman, but with Paris, that combination of masculine rationality and of the eternally feminine which the French genius had conceived.'[53]

It was in England that Fletcher would succumb. He was not an unattractive man, indeed, in a melancholy way, quite handsome, and his wealth, although he never boasted of it, was abundantly clear to the general run of impoverished artists that he met. He was, as he feared, spotted, ambushed and eventually captured. He had made the acquaintance of a gifted photographer, Malcolm Arbuthnot, one of those who, like Stieglitz in New York, wanted photography to be considered as an

art form, and who later exhibited with the Vorticists. Arbuthnot had
gone for a while to Liverpool, and invited Fletcher there to speak at
the opening of a Post-Impressionist exhibition that he had organised.
Fletcher met Arbuthnot's wife Daisy, about ten years older than himself,
a forceful and striking looking woman, who took Fletcher for a walk by
the Mersey, and quite suddenly kissed him. Arbuthnot, as Daisy knew,
had another relationship, but whether she already saw Fletcher as a
possible alternative to her unfaithful husband, or perhaps felt she might
re-engage Arbuthnot's interest if he knew he had a rival, one cannot
tell. Whatever Daisy had in mind, Fletcher was appalled and he left as
soon as possible, deciding once again that life in Paris would be a sounder
idea. He went back to France for a couple of weeks, but by mid-
September he was back, and seeing Daisy again. Nervously, he confessed
all to Arbuthnot, who said immediately, to Fletcher's mixed pleasure
and alarm, that he had no objection to Fletcher having a relationship
with Daisy, and indeed would be happy to divorce her. Fletcher as usual
fluctuated between extremes of emotion, writing on one occasion to his
sisters, 'I am at this moment in Paradise' and on another 'My doom is
sealed'.[54] Daisy at first resisted the divorce, but appears to have had no
intention of letting Fletcher escape. In March 1914 he came to a financial
agreement with Arbuthnot. To enable Arbuthnot to set up a photographic studio in London, Fletcher would agree to make over a third
of his income to Daisy and her two children for the next three years,
and he would move into Daisy's eleven-bedroom Sydenham house,
officially as her lodger. He wrote in his journal that he was burdened
with 'a woman whom I must support for three years and whom I do
not want'.[55] Many years later he would write to a friend, 'My own sexual
state has been curiously morbid and abnormal all my life'; judging from
his journal, simultaneous desire and revulsion appear to have marked
his feelings towards her.[56] Yet, though their relationship would always
be tempestuous, and they seem to have quarrelled most of the time,
something about Daisy held him. He had now a split existence: a stormy
emotional life in the quiet respectability of Sydenham, and a rather
more restful one in Soho cafés and restaurants mixing with avant-garde
poets and artists, none of whom knew about his unorthodox domestic
arrangements.

The articles on contemporary French poetry that had caused
Fletcher such ire had continued in the *New Age* until mid-October
1913, and Pound also published a brief overview of the same topic in
the October *Poetry*. The articles covered a range of poets including

Vildrac, Francis Jammes, Rémy de Gourmont, Henri de Régnier, Corbière and Rimbaud. Pound had started with zest, claiming in one of the early instalments, in an idea he possibly took from Yeats, that: 'For the best part of a thousand years English poets have gone to school to the French, or one might as well say that there were never any English poets until they began to study the French ... The history of English poetic glory is a history of successful steals from the French.'[57] By the final instalment, actually written in early September, his zeal for French poetry was already flagging. There were, he admitted, many other young French poets, but they would 'doubtless receive fitting recognition at the hands of Mr Flint'; he had merely, he said, wanted 'to write in conversational tone of my personal adventure; of such French poetry of today as had seemed of interest to one as easily bored as I am'.[58] As T. S. Eliot was to say of a slightly later article Pound wrote on French poetry, the series read 'like the report of a tourist in French poetry, rather than like the conclusions of a reader who has digested the matter slowly and over a long period of time'.[59] There is no doubt the Parisians had helped Pound find his own *vers libre* form and many of the precepts included in 'A Few Don'ts', and he had certainly learnt from the French poets what Flint would describe as a *stratégie littéraire*; in his case, how to be the leader of an avant-garde school. But for now it was, one suspects, the chutzpah of the sardonic young poets in the basement of the Café du Châtelet that had taken his fancy rather than anything they produced. What had really captured his interest that month were some 'chinese things' in the September *Poetry*, which, he told Dorothy, 'were worth the price of admission'.[60] It was to China that he would now turn.

Dorothy herself was taking her study of Chinese culture increasingly seriously. As well as her interest in the art, she was now applying herself to the language. She had begun to teach herself Chinese in 1901, at the age of fifteen, and she now took it up again, as Pound mentions in a letter to Williams in December 1913.[61] By January 1914 she decided to get a ticket for the British Museum Reading Room so she could study Chinese further, having obviously overcome the inhibitions about going there which had so troubled her when she had been copying out Cavalcanti four years earlier. Pound's hopes for enlightenment from India had now ebbed away, but he still felt he needed to go beyond Europe. Tagore had returned to India in late August 1913, and Pound had attended the farewell dinner. He still liked Tagore personally, but when he said that autumn in a review of Tagore's second book of poems in English that 'Mr Tagore has come and gone', the phrase perhaps indicated more than Tagore's return home. On the surface Pound's praise was still strong, though he was very critical of the way Tagore had been received. 'If his entourage has presented him,' he wrote crossly, 'as a religious teacher rather than an artist, it is much to be lamented . . . Why the good people of this island are unable to honour a fine artist as such; why they are incapable . . . of devising for his honour any better device than that of wrapping his life in cotton wool and parading that about with the effigy of a sanctimonious moralist, remains and will remain with me an unsolvable mystery'. Yet, although Pound claimed that there were verses of 'pure Imagisme' in Tagore's 'Theocritan idylls', Tagore was for him now simply an example of world literature, no longer a pre-eminent one.[62] Pound's enthusiasm for Tagore had lasted less than a year, dampened already after six months by his growing popularity as a religious poet, not least, to Pound's irritation, with his own mother. (It may have been of her he was thinking when he wrote in 1917 that Tagore had 'relapsed into religion and optimism, and was boomed by the pious non-conformists'.)[63] Yet he was certainly delighted that November when Tagore won the Nobel Prize, telling his father he was 'chortling' with delight over it, and that he and Yeats had had much 'gay & unhallowed mirth' at the discomfiture of Gosse and others who had refused to elect Tagore to the Academic Committee.[64] But although he commented on how good the news would be for the reform party in India, an intriguing indication either that anti-imperialism had been part of his support for Tagore, or that he had learnt to be anti-imperialistic through him, poetically and intellectually his interest was moving from India to China.

The Chinese 'things' in *Poetry* were by Allen Upward, an eccentric polymath and traveller aged fifty, with whom Pound struck up a friendship that summer. Upward and Yeats had known each other in the past; they had even attempted to communicate telepathically across the Atlantic, though sadly if predictably they failed, but Pound met him either through the *New Age*, or the *New Freewoman*, with both of which Upward was closely connected. Upward was to be an important influence, though to Pound's lasting indignation his ideas were not taken seriously by many others. Like Edmund Gosse, he was the son of Plymouth Brethren who escaped into free-thought and the intellectual life in adulthood, though, unlike Gosse, he always remained on the radical fringes. He had trained as a barrister, but only practised when short of funds, preferring to be a thorn in the side of the governing classes, producing journalism attacking the great and the good for their oppression of the people's rights, and supporting nationalist movements in Ireland and elsewhere. In about 1900, he met the poet Lancelot Cranmer Byng, who introduced him to Chinese poetry and philosophy, which became one of his main passions; together they established a printing house which they called the Orient Press and launched a series of translations from the Chinese called 'The Wisdom of the East'. He and Cranmer Byng also formed an Order of Genius, which, Michael Sheldon says, was 'for the furtherance of those supremely gifted individuals, like themselves, who felt threatened by the increasing cultural emphasis on mass mediocrity', a way of thinking about the world to which Pound was already inclined, now reinforced by Upward.[65] In 1901, Upward went to Nigeria as an official in the Colonial Office there, and was fascinated by the local customs; he was only there for four months before being invalided home, but he felt himself from then on an expert in 'primitive' ways, and much more authoritative than armchair anthropologists like Frazer. In 1913, just at the time he met Pound, he published (at his own expense) *The Divine Mystery*, an anthropological investigation of the development of religion, in which he suggests that Christ was a genius, 'the ascription of divine fatherhood to Genius [being] a convention of the age'; he also provocatively claimed that those thought of as 'witch-doctors' were also people of genius, prefiguring more recent interpretations of the shaman as poet, priest and healer combined, and an idea on which Pound would seize.[66] Much like Frazer, Upward believed religion to be the prelude to science, though like Pound, but perhaps even more so, his notion of science included every shade of the paranormal and occult investigations of his day. Again like Pound, he had no time for organised Christianity, for which he thought Christ had no responsibility, and he was fiercely hostile to academic philologists, as he made abundantly evident in his 1907 book, *The New Word*.

Pound reviewed *The Divine Mystery* enthusiastically in the November *New Freewoman*, describing it as 'the most fascinating book on folk-lore that I have ever opened'. It is, he points out, 'not a mass of theories', but a 'history told in a series of vivid and precise illustrations', in other words, an exemplum of Pound's method of luminous detail. Upward, he says, 'has traced the growth of religion and superstition from the primitive type of the thunder-maker to the idea of the messiah. He has traced many of the detestable customs of modern life to their roots in superstition . . . Mr Upward has left the charming pastoral figure of Jesus in a more acceptable light than have the advocates of "That religion which the Nazarene has been accused of having founded.'" Though not identical to Pound's synthesis of pagan, Provençal and general mysticism as a counter-religion to established Christianity, it was near enough, and indeed, Pound said, offered 'clues and suggestions for the Provençal love customs of the Middle Ages'; Allen Upward, he says approvingly, is 'one of the devoutest men of the age. He insists that the real God is neither a cad nor an imbecile, and that is, to my mind, a fairly good ground for religion.'[67]

All these different aspects of Upward made him fascinating to Pound, but what was most immediately significant about this new friendship was Upward's conviction of the importance of Chinese thought. Upward's poems in *Poetry* were entitled 'Scented Leaves – from a Chinese Jar'. *Poetry*'s note, as usual slightly wrong, said that these were not translations but paraphrases, but Pound wrote to Harriet to tell her that Upward ('very interesting chap') had told him 'that he made it up out of his head, using a certain amount of Chinese reminiscence'.[68] Their form, in fact, like his own in 'The Return' and his '"Metro" hokku', was the fabricated translation, the evocation of another world. Some people might call such works inauthentic, but to Pound they represented imaginative leaps of crucial aesthetic value. But Upward led Pound to actual translations of Chinese poetry as well. Pound visited him in the Isle of Wight in early October, and it appears to have been then that Upward put him on to Herbert Allen Giles' *History of Chinese Literature*, from which he would adapt some of his most successful short poems.

Upward also introduced him to the works of Confucius, whose philosophy would hold an increasing appeal for Pound. The very story of Confucius' life – a great teacher who never obtained much recognition in his own day, but whose ideas were spread by his disciples – must have fitted with Pound's own idea of the artist struggling for long-awaited recognition. Confucius did not believe in an inherited nobility, but a nobility of the virtuous, just as Pound believed in an aristocracy composed of artists. Like Pound, too, he was deeply religious, whilst being utterly opposed to the way religion was practised in his own day, and he held that it was imperative to use language clearly, just as Pound did. As Pound's own thought became more reactionary, he would increasingly urge the significance of Confucius' stress on order, though it has to be said, in an increasingly disorderly way. There are many references to Confucius (or Kung, as he more often calls him) in the *Cantos*, but Confucius by no means ousted his pagan gods. In Canto 52, Pound asserts that the poles on which his thought turn are 'KUNG and ELEUSIS', though it is not always easy to see how he proposed to reconcile Confucian order with Dionysiac ecstasy and the fertility rituals associated with the Eleusinian mysteries.[69]

As Pound told Dorothy, he was now getting 'orient from all quarters'. He had been to an exhibition of Chinese artefacts, and to a 'new curious and excellent restaurant chinois'. He was, he told her, 'stocked up with K'ung fu Tsze [Confucius] and Men Tsze [Mencius], etc. I suppose they'll keep me calm for a week or so.' In the event, it appears he did not turn his attention to them until later in the winter: for now he was concentrating on Giles, whose account of Chinese poetics immediately suggested parallels with his own. 'I find the chinese stuff far more consoling,' he told Dorothy. 'There is *no* long poem in chinese. They hold if a man can't say what he wants to in 12 lines, he'd better leave it unsaid. THE period was 4th cent. B.C. – Chu Yüan, Imagiste – – – did I tell you all that before???'[70] Zhaoming Qian points out, in his illuminating study of the influence of Chinese poetry and thought on the work of Pound and Williams, that, for all his enthusiasm, Pound only ever referred to half a dozen of the many poets discussed by Giles, and none later than the T'ang period (618–907 A.D.). He suggests Pound picks out those poets most akin to his imagist aesthetic, like Qu Yuan (Pound's Chu Yüan), whom he mentions here, and later the T'ang poets Wang Wei and Li Po (also known as Li Bo, and referred to by Pound by his Japanese name Rihaku). Qu Yuan and his followers, according to Giles, 'indulged in wild and irregular metres which consorted well with their wild irregular thoughts. Their poetry was prose run mad. It was allusive and allegorical to a high degree, and now, but for the commentary, much of it would be quite unintelligible.'[71] (That latter point sounds particularly applicable to the *Cantos*, to most readers, if not all, inexplicable for much of the time if it were not for the work of commentators.) As Qian suggests, Pound was probably most interested in the 'wild, irregular metres', being delighted to discover that the Chinese had their own version of *vers libre*.

Yet more than Giles' comments, it was the poems themselves that made the greatest impact on him. Giles' *History* consists to a large extent of translations, some as prose and some as poetry, produced largely for the scholarly reader rather than the lover of poetry, but, although they have a slight *fin-de-siècle* archaism, they are free of the heavy imposition of Victorian forms and diction in earlier translations of Far Eastern verse. Pound immediately set about making his own

versions, nearly always tighter and more concise than Giles' own. He
was working, perhaps, on the model of the haiku, only a few years earlier
translated in a far more Victorian way than Giles' Chinese translations,
but now presented with such brevity and simplicity. Indeed Pound's
first versions of Giles' translations appear very much like haiku, for
example when he reduced Giles' 10-line translation of Lady Ban's 'Song
of Regret' to a brief three lines. Entitled, 'Fan-Piece, for her Imperial
Lord', Pound's version goes:

> O fan of white silk,
>   clear as frost on the grass-blade,
> You also are laid aside.[72]

This was one of the first he attempted. There would be many more.
Pound may have known that Lady Ban had been called the 'Sappho of
China', and so might have felt this elliptical form especially appropriate
for her poem.[73] Yet for Pound what was most significant was that these
early Chinese poems, like those of Sappho, made it possible for him to
achieve a form of poetry in which, as he had put it earlier in the year,
'an "image" presents an intellectual and emotional complex in an instant
of time'. And, as Heaney suggests, what is conveyed so powerfully is
again the sense of passing and loss.

   Just at the time that Pound was discovering Giles' work, he made what
was perhaps his most significant Oriental contact: 'Dined on monday,'
he told Dorothy on 2 October, 'with Sarojini Niadu and Mrs Fenolosa,
relict of the writer on chinese art, selector of a lot of Freer's stuff etc.'[74]
Sarojini Naidu, whom Pound had probably met through Tagore, was a
Bengali poet who wrote in English, a Nationalist who would become a
supporter of Gandhi. She had published her first book of poems at the
age of nineteen, while a student at Girton. She was taken up by Edmund
Gosse, who in his introduction to her 1912 book of poetry, *The Bird of
Time*, describes how when he first met her he was shocked by how much
she was 'a mocking bird with a vengeance', imitating the British Romantics.
What the British reader wanted from her, he explained, was 'some revelation of the heart of India, some sincere penetrating analysis of native
passion, of the principles of antique religion and of such mysterious inti-
mations as stirred the soul of the East long before the West had begun
to dream that it had a soul'. Naidu duly complied, producing, as Elleke
Boehmer points out, poems once more in 'the tones of the mocking bird
with a vengeance', though this time giving the West the version of the

Eastern soul that it wanted.[75] Her story is reminiscent of Ford's desire for Lawrence to write about the equally unknown and exotic working class; just that month, in fact, Pound would review Lawrence's first book of poems, finding only the dialect poems really admirable.

Mary Fenollosa was an American, widow of Ernest Fenollosa, who had died unexpectedly in 1908, at the age of fifty-five, after thirty years of immersion in the culture of the Far East, seventeen of those years being in Japan. His widow was twelve years younger, forty-eight when she met Pound, and had published several novels and some poetry. Fenollosa, a Harvard graduate, had gone to Japan in 1878 to lecture at the University of Tokyo on European philosophy; Japan was anxious to westernise, and his lectures on Herbert Spencer's evolutionary sociology, and later on Hegel, with their shared assumptions about the inevitability of Western progress, proved very popular, though Fenollosa himself came rapidly to the conclusion that Hegel's dismissive attitude to the Orient was entirely mistaken. He still thought in terms of a Hegelian synthesis, however, and was convinced that the world needed to incorporate both Western and Eastern traditions. Ironically, the Japanese took much more convincing than he did that Hegel had been wrong about their culture; just at the time when Japanese prints were being taken up by Western artists, traditional Japanese art was being abandoned in Japan in favour of Western modes, a curiously similar situation to that of indigenous art in India, though the West had made its impact in quite a different form. Fenollosa began a compaign for the appreciation of Japanese art both in the West and in Japan itself, persuading the authorities there to reintroduce the brush into schools, where children were being taught to use Western pens and ink. He collected Japanese art himself, some of which he sold to Charles Freer, whose famous collection of Far Eastern art and Whistler paintings he gave to the Boston Museum of Fine Arts, where Fenollosa, when he returned home in 1890, would take up a post as Head of the Oriental Wing.

In 1895 Fenollosa was divorced by his first wife and married Mary, then thirty, one of his assistants and very beautiful. Divorce in Boston in 1895 was a major scandal; he resigned his job, left Boston never to return, and they went back to Japan. Things had changed while he had been away; so successful had he been in reviving Japan's pride in its art, that it no longer wanted help with promoting it from a Westerner. He devoted his time now to exploring Japanese Noh plays and Chinese poetry, with the help of several scholars, accumulating information about interpretations, nuances, form and subject-matter. Fenollosa himself knew no Chinese, so with the Chinese he was working at a double remove, but that did not dampen his enthusiasm, and Pound would treat his observations as scriptural truths. The couple returned to New York in 1901, where Fenollosa took up a job at Columbia University, and he began to prepare his manuscripts for publication, a task never completed.

After his death, Mary worked on some of the voluminous notes, translations and incomplete manuscripts he had left, putting together a two-volume work from his research on the visual arts, *Epochs of Chinese and Japanese Art*, which appeared in 1912, published by Heinemann.[76] There still existed much more material, and Mary Fenollosa was looking for someone who would edit the manuscripts from those last five years in Japan on the Japanese Noh plays and Chinese poetry. Whether she had sought out Pound for this task, or was just so taken when she met him with his newly sprung passion for Chinese poetry, it was Pound to whom she offered the manuscripts. Many years later Pound would recall that Mary Fenollosa had said 'that Fenollosa had been in opposition to all the profs and academes, and she had seen some of my stuff and said I was the only person who could finish up these notes as Ernest would have wanted them done. Fenollosa saw what needed to be done but he didn't have time to finish it.'[77] Mary Fenollosa promised that when she returned home she would send him the manuscripts. The next major shift in Pound's literary life was about to begin.

IV

WHILE he awaited the Fenollosa manuscripts, Pound continued to work on the Giles translations. By late November 1913 he had done three and a half poems, he told Dorothy, the half perhaps referring to the brief 'Fan-Piece', or possibly the equally fleeting 'Ts'ai Chi'h': 'The petals fall in the fountain,/the orange-coloured rose-leaves,/Their ochre clings to the stone', not a translation of a single poem, but a drawing together of images from several.[78] It perhaps bears out Qian's contention that one of the qualities of Upward's 'Scented Leaves' that had struck Pound was the way in which he followed the Chinese technique of using colour to evoke a mood. All these translations, as well as 'Scented Leaves', would appear in his anthology of *les jeunes*, for which he found a publisher in early November, through the good offices of John Cournos, the Philadelphian who had interviewed him the previous December. Alfred Kreymborg, a poet and friend of Orrick Johns, whom Pound had met in New York, had just taken over the editing of a magazine called the *Glebe*, and had written to Cournos from New York asking for contributions. Cournos took the letter to Pound, who immediately saw this as an opening. Kreymborg agreed to print the anthology as the February 1914 issue; it was then to appear in March as a book published by Alfred and Charles Boni in Greenwich Village.

John Cournos, who would have a poem in the anthology himself, and later publish nine novels and a volume of verse, was establishing himself in London as a valued friend of the young avant-garde artists and writers. He was not only a fellow would-be writer, but, having been a professional newspaperman for eighteen years, was a highly skilled networker, and ready to use his skills to the advantage of his friends. He was working mainly at the time as a journalist, sending a stream of articles back to America, and was always willing to promote his friends in these, as he had Pound, or to gather subscriptions for their journals, or use his numerous publishing contacts to get their work in print. Flint would write to Amy Lowell in late 1915, after he had been given a contract for a book on French poetry, saying he would never have had it if Cournos had not put him in touch with Constable's reader, and that he was doing similar good turns to half of literary London. Cournos was a remarkable man in many ways, although not everyone would think him such a spreader of good fortune. In the 1920s he had a love affair with Dorothy L. Sayers, and deserted her in a rather heartless fashion, leaving her deeply unhappy for some time, though, as P.D. James pointed out, she got her revenge by putting him into *Strong Poison* as the dastardly Philip Boyes, and giving herself (in the persona of Harriet Vane) 'the satisfaction of killing him off in fiction'.[79] John Cournos was himself apt in later life to wreak vengeance through his own novels on those who had displeased him, making a particular feature of reproducing their letters verbatim. Sayers and her letters appear in *The Devil is an English Gentleman*, and H.D. would eventually also become a victim; both her letters and Richard's are reproduced at length in *Miranda Masters* (1926). But for now Cournos and the Aldingtons were the best of friends, and Flint's warm opinion of Cournos' generosity and geniality was widely shared.

John Cournos had been born Ivan Gregorievitch Korshoon in 1881, near Kiev, in the Ukraine, but his family, who were Hasidic Jews, had, like so many Eastern European Jews of the period, fled abroad to escape the recurrent pogroms, in their case to Philadelphia in 1891. The family lived in great poverty, but at fourteen John managed to get a job as an office boy at the *Philadelphia Record*; by 1912 he was a well-established journalist and the *Record*'s art critic. But he wanted to be a writer, and though he mixed with students from the Pennsylvania Academy of Fine Arts, making sure, as Pound had done before him, that he looked the part – flowing hair, floppy tie and Augustus John black hat – he was convinced he would need to get to Europe to become one. He shared Pound's and H.D.'s reservations about Philadelphia, perhaps with more justification: in his first novel, based on his early life, Cournos describes the way, as a Jew, he was mocked and attacked by gangs of boys in the street; the people of Philadelphia, he said, had 'hearts of stone'.[80] His stepson, Alfred Satterthwaite, says that Cournos was a small, delicate-looking man, with 'a sensitive face dominated by deep-set melting grey eyes and a hawklike nose, hooked and Semitic'. The difficulties of his youth had marked him: 'He always seemed to me,' Satterthwaite writes, 'a man who carried all the centuries of the persecution of his people on his own frail shoulders, not burdensomely, but intrepidly and some- times almost gaily. He seemed somehow to shoulder the sky.'[81] To Aldington and H.D. he was a romantic figure, full of Russian soul and profound depths. Dostoevsky and Chekhov were just making their impact at that time; the Russian Ballet had taken London by storm; being Russian was in style. Cournos was very knowledgeable about the arts, a man of great charm, widely read, and a wonderful conversa- tionalist. Cournos says that it was Aldington who persuaded Pound to include one of his poems in the anthology, and though Aldington says neither he nor H.D. were consulted at all by Pound over its content, he undoubtedly went out of his way to be friendly to Cournos. With his resentment of British snobbery, Aldington was always anxious to befriend those, like Flint and Lawrence, who had had to struggle up from 'the depths', as he put it. Yet Cournos had many friends. On his arrival, he had set about interviewing everyone he could, and rapidly made the acquaintance of most of literary and artistic London. His second novel, *Babel* (1923), is a highly entertaining account of the London in which he arrived in 1912, and its bewildering gamut of literary and artistic movements; in it Hulme and his followers appear as the Intuitionists, and the imagists as the Primitivists, a more appropriate name than many of their later critics have realised. His popularity in these years and his willingness to help his friends is in stark contrast to his later bitterness and at times vindictiveness, but it should not, I think, lead one to think that the early kindliness was false, more that the disappointment and poverty of much of his later life sadly took their toll.

Cournos had another reason for coming to Europe. He had fallen in love in Philadelphia with an art student, Dorothy Arabella Yorke (the first Dorothy in his life, though this one was most often known in the London years as Arabella). Arabella lived with her possessive and deter- mined mother, her father being dead or elsewhere. Mrs Yorke was deeply opposed to the idea of her daughter developing a relationship with a poor Jew like Cournos, not her idea of a good catch for Arabella, but he did not give up hope. In 1911, Arabella and her mother went to Paris, 'where', according to Satterthwaite, 'her mother was seeking her own and her daughter's greater fortune'. Arabella was 'beautiful . . . tall, willowy, jet black hair and dark eyes contrasting with a very white skin, exotic, cryptic', and her mother may have hoped that she would marry well.[82] Cournos, who had sailed to Naples, went straight to visit them in Paris and tried to persuade them to come to London, but without success. Mrs Yorke was hostile; Arabella blew hot and cold. He went on to London by himself.

In his autobiography, Cournos says it was he who introduced Pound to the sculptor Gaudier-Brzeska. It was, in fact, a reintroduction. According to Pound's memoir of Gaudier, he met the sculptor first in July 1913, at the Allied Artists show in London. Pound had gone to the exhibition with Olivia Shakespear, and was engaged in trying to pronounce Brzeska's name when 'a young man came after us, like a well-made young wolf or some soft-moving, bright-eyed wild thing. I noted him carefully because he reminded me a little of my friend William Carlos Williams.' He bounded up to them, explained rapidly in French that it was his name and told them how to say it, and then 'he disappeared like a Greek god in a vision'.[83] Pound is doing a certain amount of mythologising here, but his description is not irreconcilable with Epstein's more down-to-earth comment that Gaudier was 'a picturesque, slight figure with lively eyes, and a sprouting beard. He was very pleasant.'[84] According to Cournos, Gaudier was 'strong, lithe and lean, with a handsome energetic face, live intelligent eyes with a glint of general gayety [sic]. He was simple and lovable. If you were his kind, you were accepted as his friend without the preliminaries of a long acquaintance.'[85] This may be what happened to Pound when John Cournos helped him track down Gaudier again. Pound wrote to Williams: 'I like him very much. He is the only person with whom I can be really "Altaforte".'[86] He had in fact declaimed the belligerent and defiant 'Sestina Altaforte' to Gaudier at Church Walk, the poem which begins, 'Damn it all! all this our South stinks peace', and Gaudier had gone away deeply impressed, reporting to Cournos that he was most excited that Pound dared to include the word 'piss' in a poem. Pound was equally delighted by the story.[87]

In his account of that first meeting at the exhibition, Pound sounds as if his attention was caught more by the sculptor's personality than his work, as perhaps it was, but he was soon to become an advocate of his sculpture as well. Gaudier was '*the* coming sculptor', he told Williams later that year.[88] Given Pound's admiration for Epstein, it is not surprising that Gaudier's sculpture appealed to him; Gaudier, if not exactly a disciple, had learnt from Epstein and worked in a related style. Pound claims that when Gaudier first met Epstein he assured the latter that he worked directly on to the stone as Epstein did, and rushed home to teach himself to do so before Epstein came to see the results. According to Pound, he derived great satisfaction from this method of working:

'He liked to do the "whole thing" from start to finish; to feel as independent as the savage.'[89] Earlier he had been a follower of Rodin, and an admirer of Michelangelo and the Greeks, but now he moved away from realism towards a more abstract use of form, and denounced his former masters with a passion worthy of a Poundian volte-face. Perhaps under the influence of Epstein, he became fascinated by Assyrian and Egyptian art, as well as African and Pacific carvings. Gaudier was himself French, and had come to England to avoid serving in the French Army, which he describes as the 'slaughterers of Arabs'.[90] He lived with Sophie Brzeska, a Polish woman he had met in Paris, twenty years older than himself, who passed as his sister and whose name he had added to his own. Sophie's earlier life had been, it was generally known, full of suffering – Rebecca West described her as 'a veteran in tragedy' – though quite what the tragedy was, no one appears to have discovered. Gaudier adored her, and said she had 'a beauty *à la* Baudelaire – and might have stepped out of *Fleurs du Mal*'.[91] He was extremely poor and worked in a studio under a railway arch in Putney, on pieces of stone allegedly purloined from masonry yards and cemeteries at night. He was then twenty-two. Humphrey Carpenter suggests that Gaudier had few friends, and needed to be taken under Pound's wing, but while that is the impression Pound gives, it is hardly true. Gaudier knew many other artists and intellectuals, Hulme, for whom he made the brass knuckle-dusters mentioned earlier, Lovat Fraser (Grace Crawford's future husband), Nina Hamnett, who also served as a model for him, Epstein, of course, Fletcher's former friend Horace Brodzky, Cournos, the Aldingtons and many others. Most of his friends found Sophie a difficult woman, and she was burningly jealous of them; most preferred to see him without her. Gaudier, Aldington says, had one other disadvantage as an acquaintance: 'He was probably,' he writes in his memoir, 'the dirtiest human being I have ever known, and gave off horrid effluvia in hot weather.'[92] In this too Gaudier may have been following Epstein's example: Pound wrote to his mother that November: 'Epstein is a great sculptor. I wish he would wash, but I believe Michel Angelo NEVER did, so I suppose it is part of the tradition.'[93]

In November 1913 Pound left London to spend three months in the country with Yeats, in a small isolated house called Stone Cottage, near Coleman's Hatch, deep in the Ashdown Forest in Sussex. Yeats wanted to work in peace, but his eyesight was an increasing problem: Pound would write letters for him, act as amanuensis for lectures for another American tour the following January, and read aloud to him after dark.

The sociable Pound did not look forward to this incarceration in the country, telling his mother he thought he would have a perfectly disagreeable time: 'My stay in Stone Cottage will not be in the least profitable, I detest the country. Yeats will amuse me part of the time and bore me to death with psychical research the rest.'[94] Although at one level he was surely delighted to be invited to stay on these intimate terms with the great poet, recreating, as James Longenbach puts it, 'the aspect of the Rhymers' Club that he admired most: the sense of a poetic aristocracy, meeting in private, ignoring the demands of a vastly inferior public', in advance his trepidation appears to have been entirely real.[95]

Pound had originally come to England to find Yeats and to learn from him, but one reason for his doubts about the sojourn at Stone Cottage might have been that more recently other influences had held sway. Since his reconfiguration as a modern poet, Pound had been listening more to Ford. Ford and Yeats had little liking for each other as writers, and did not often mix socially. Ford apparently never went to Yeats' Monday evenings; Yeats was rarely present at the South Lodge events. In 1914, in a review of *Responsibilities*, the volume of poetry that Yeats brought out that year, Ford would, as Foster puts it, 'grudgingly admire the harshness and modernity of this new voice' but in 1913 he was convinced (unfairly it must be said) that Yeats was lost in the Celtic past.[96] He described Yeats, Pound says, as a 'gargoyle, a great poet but a gargoyle'.[97] In August Pound had said to Monroe that '[Ford] and Yeats are the two men in London', but he added, in terms that echo Ford's views, that 'Yeats is already a sort of great dim figure with its associations set in the past'.[98] When Pound sent Monroe an essay by Ford that May, which would later form the introduction to Ford's *Collected Poems*, he insisted it must go in at full length, even if they had to print extra pages, 'as it will be a considerable boost to our prose dept . . . it will be the best prose we've had or are likely to get. Clear the decks for it, s.v.p.'[99] He was incandescent when she did not include it immediately. Ford's arguments in favour of more everyday language had finally begun to make an impact on him: in March, complaining to Monroe about the latest batch of poets in *Poetry*, he wrote: 'Good god! isn't there one of them that can write natural speech without copying clichés out of every Eighteenth Century poet still in the public libraries? God knows I wallowed in archaisms in my vealish years, but these imbeciles don't even take the trouble to get an archaism.'[100] That marks a shift in the three months from the previous December when he was still telling Cournos that he believed in a 'curial' or priestly language for poetry.

Pound had also come to agree with Ford that the artist needed to absorb the modern urban experience, with its disparate traditions, of which Ford had written so eloquently in *The Soul of London*, and he had told Monroe shortly before he left for Stone Cottage that 'all great art is born of the metropolis (or *in* the metropolis). The metropolis is that which accepts all gifts and all heights of excellence, usually the excellence which is *tabu* in its own village. The metropolis is always being accused by the peasant of "being mad after foreign notions".'[101] When he speaks of 'all gifts and all heights of excellence', he may have been thinking particularly of his recent meetings with Indian and Chinese culture through Tagore, Ghose, Upward and Mary Fenollosa, but whatever he had in mind, for someone with such a vivid sense of the cultural excitement of the capital, disappearing into the wastes for three months must have appeared a dispiriting prospect. When he later reported that he was having a good time, he sounded genuinely surprised.

Whatever his misgivings, in addition to the compliment of the invitation, there was the added advantage that it would be much cheaper than living in London. Dorothy knew the house, as she had stayed nearby several times, possibly including the occasion when Yeats found Stone Cottage with Olivia Shakepear. She warned him it could be fearfully wet, and advised thick boots, but also reported that the area was a 'weird place – and possibly faerie', perhaps what had appealed to Yeats.[102] In the event Pound really enjoyed his visit: he wrote to Williams to say 'Yeats is much finer *intime* than seen spasmodically in the midst of the whirl. We are both, I think, very contented in Sussex'.[103] It was a very different story from his time spent with Ford, with whom *intime* visits were never a success. In spite of Pound's growing conviction of Ford's critical acumen, he and Yeats in many ways had much more in common and the time he spent at Stone Cottage with Yeats shaped his future attitudes profoundly. Pound was right about Yeats' contentment: he would write to a friend in January that it had been 'the best winter I have had in years – the only winter in which my evenings have not been a problem & the only winter in which my creative power has been a conscious pleasure'.[104] The house was owned by two sisters, Ellen and Alice Welfare, and Alice looked after them and provided their meals. Yeats went up to London once a week for his Monday evenings and to see his medium, Elizabeth Ratcliffe; Pound went approximately as often to see Dorothy and his friends.

There was of course the matter of his work for *Poetry* and the *New Freewoman*, less easily dealt with in the middle of nowhere, but Pound's zeal for controlling magazines was temporarily slacking. In November he had had one of his periodic outbursts over the quality of work Monroe was publishing, and resigned in dudgeon as foreign correspondent of *Poetry* in favour of Ford; Ford, quick as a flash, resigned immediately in favour of Pound, and Pound grudgingly agreed to go on, 'pending a general improvement of the magazine'.[105] He had just received an unexpected windfall from *Poetry*, which made it hard to refuse. Monroe, on Pound's advice, had given *Poetry*'s annual Guarantors' prize of £50 for the best poem published in the magazine that year to Yeats for 'The Grey Rock', which had appeared in *Poetry* the previous April. Yeats was embarrassed, feeling many of the impecunious poets published in the magazine needed it more than he did; he accepted £10, which he would spend on getting Sturge Moore to design a bookplate for him (Lady Gregory had a very fine one, which may have given him the idea), but asked Monroe to give Pound the other £40. Pound, when he heard that Yeats was returning the money, had first suggested it should be shared between Aldington and Vachel Lindsay, but gave in gracefully. Pound – much, I am sure, to the relief of his correspondents, including Monroe – spent some of the money on a typewriter. He also spent £15 on two statues from Gaudier, very cheap, but, as he said, 'he had next to no market and . . . I . . . next to no income'.[106] Sophie Brzeska thought the amount far too little; it was the first of many grievances she had against Pound, but Pound was, in addition, doing his best to rectify his latest protégé's lack of a market, writing to Dorothy with instructions to put possible purchasers in touch and persuading Olivia Shakespear to buy a very beautiful nude torso that Gaudier had carved, for which Nina Hamnett had been the model. Pound was delighted with his own purchases, and possibly felt more kindly towards the unfortunate editor. Monroe seized the opportunity to soothe his ruffled feathers, announcing in the January *Poetry* that she was delighted to be able to give him the money, 'as it enables her to acknowledge her high appreciation not only of Mr Pound's poetry, but also of his disinterested and valuable service as foreign correspondent of the magazine'.[107]

The *New Freewoman* was a rather different case. Now that Fletcher was no longer providing money to pay contributors, Pound may have found his position there less attractive; cajoling writers to produce work for free was not something he enjoyed. On the other hand, he did not want to lose his influence on the magazine, especially as by now the literary concerns had taken over a good half of its pages. He needed a disciple in place. As it happened, Rebecca West had resigned her position as assistant editor at the *New Freewoman*, and Dora Marsden, presumably on Pound's recommendation, decided that Aldington should be her replacement. He was appointed, at the princely salary of a guinea a week, a position he would keep for almost four years. For a magazine with the name of the *New Freewoman* to have a male assistant editor might seem anomalous, but by the beginning of 1914 Dora's magazine would have changed its name again. For many years the story of the transformation of the *New Freewoman* into the *Egoist* was that the ruthless piratical Pound leapt aboard this barque of feminist sweetness and light and commandeered it for his own ends. Events were not that simple: Pound simply for once had excellent luck, and seized his chance. Rebecca West had suspected that Pound would like to have Richard Aldington in her place, but she herself had made the decision to resign in October. Her resignation was prompted in part, it must be admitted, by her growing irritation at Pound's high-handedness – she was not happy for him to make his own decisions even if Dora was – but Pound (whom she described in retrospect as an *arriviste* poet) was by no means the only or even chief reason. Dora Marsden's new direction was much more the issue. West, like Marsden, had worked for the WSPU (the Women's Social and Political Union), and like her had become critical of the organisation. She too was suspicious of assumptions about women's nature. (She told the story of selling *Votes for Women* as an adolescent along with her sister in Harrogate: 'We offered one to a dear old lady in rustling black silk and widow's bonnet. With superb vigour she raised her umbrella and brought it down on my sister's head, remarking: "Thank God I am a womanly woman!"')[108] West supported the magazine's liberal and free-thinking attitude towards sexuality, very different from that of the WSPU. Christabel Pankhurst had brought out her book on the ravages of syphilis earlier that year; entitled *The Great Scourge and How to End It*, it argued strongly for faithful marriages, urging men to follow the example of women's natural purity, and advocating 'chastity for men and Votes for Women'.[109] Yet in spite of their shared opposition to the WSPU, by now West felt Dora had ceased to face the issues of the practical world in which they lived; some kind of collectivity, she believed, was needed if gender and class oppression were to be overcome. West was a socialist, and even Dora's anarchist supporters were beginning to feel she had gone too far. Her individualistic anarchism was expressed in increasingly philosophical and, West thought, unclear terms: she had behaved much more anarchically as a suffragette. West was, in fact, writing regularly for the much more successful socialist journal, the *Clarion*, and, though she had worked hard to re-establish the *New Freewoman*, she found the *Clarion* a more congenial home. Pound's only comment on her departure, that she 'saw that Egoist [*sic*] was NOT her path to practical success in PAID journalism', may have had some partial truth.[110] And there was also perhaps the fact that her tempestuous affair with H.G. Wells was taking its toll; she was to give up work for the *Clarion* by the end of the year. The following August, she gave birth to Wells' son.

Marsden's appointment of Richard Aldington as West's replacement meant that the imagists' English outlet was secure, or at any rate as secure as the magazine's finances permitted. Pound remained involved as and when it suited him for now, though Dora noted that '"E.P." and the new "sub" spit and scratch at each other', the first hint perhaps of disagreements to come.[111] In November at a directors' meeting it was proposed that the name should be changed to something that did not carry feminist overtones, and Marsden's preference was for the *Egoist*, a title that was much closer to her present philosophical position. Some of the original suffragist supporters who had bought shares were alarmed, but realised, as one put it, that Dora 'would do exactly as she liked'.[112] In December, Pound, Aldington, Allen Upward and two other male contributors wrote a letter published in the journal, throwing their support behind the change to a title 'which will mark the character of your paper as an organ of individualists of both sexes, and of the individualist principle in every department of life'.[113] The letter was a gesture of solidarity with Dora's move, not a cause of her action. Although Harriet Shaw Weaver, many years later, remembered that 'the new masculine element which had allied itself with the paper before long raised objections to the title', it was Marsden's change, not theirs.[114] When Pound returned to London in January, the magazine was appearing under the title of the *Egoist*. Dora for now remained editor in name, though she had gone back to live in Southport, and her main contribution would now be her articles, though Weaver always consulted her over any decisions. Weaver and Aldington both used the offices in Oakley House, Bloomsbury, which was the home of the Blavatsky Institute, set up for the study of Theosophy, Mystical and Occult Philosophy, whose secretary was one of Dora's supporters. The *Egoist*'s most profitable sales were through the Institute's bookshop, as they charged no commission, and theosophist shoppers appeared very happy to mix a little avant-garde writing, calls for free love and a philosophy of individualism with their own occult interests.

Much work meanwhile was being accomplished in Stone Cottage. Yeats always had reservations about Pound as a poet – rather more than Pound ever appears to have realised – but he enjoyed his company. The letter Yeats had written to Harriet recommending him as recipient for the prize makes interesting reading: 'I suggest him to you because, although I do not really like with my whole soul the metrical experiments he has made for you, I think those experiments show a vigorous imaginative mind. He is certainly a creative personality of some sort, though it is too soon yet to say of what sort. His experiments are perhaps errors, I am not certain; but I would always sooner give the laurel to vigorous errors than to any orthodoxy not inspired.'[115] Unqualified praise it was not. Yeats valued Pound more for his advice than his art; he had written earlier in the year to Lady Gregory, saying that Pound 'is full of the middle ages and helps me get back to the definite and concrete away from modern abstractions. To talk over a poem with him is like getting you to put a sentence in dialect. All becomes clear and natural. Yet in his own work he is very uncertain, often very bad though very interesting sometimes. He spoils himself by too many experiments and has more sound principles than taste.'[116] Pound might well have been mortified if he had known of this judgement, but luckily he didn't, though he would report in *Poetry* the next year that Yeats thought the imagists wrote in the 'devil's metres'.[117] In January 1914 he published an editorial in *Poetry* which reads as if it was written as an attempt to convince Yeats of the merits of *vers libre*. Entitled 'The Tradition', it argues that the two most important traditions for lyric poetry are 'that of the Melic Poets [early Greek] and that of Provence', both of whom bring the arts of music and poetry together; in the case of the Melic poets, they even practised a kind of *vers libre*, 'compos[ing] to the feel of the thing, to the cadence, as have all good poets since'.[118]

Yet if Yeats and Pound continued to differ on the question of rhyme and metre, in many other ways that winter together led them each to a greater appreciation of the other. In the first place, although Pound had predicted that he would be bored by Yeats' psychical research, he was in fact fascinated. He had taken with him the first batch of papers from Mary Fenollosa and was working on the Japanese Noh plays, while Yeats was applying himself again to the material he had been working on in Paris two years before, continuing to correlate folk beliefs with contemporary occult practices. Both of them were intrigued by the Noh plays. As Pound would write in 1916, 'These plays are full of ghosts, and the ghost psychology is amazing. The parallels with Western spiritist doctrines are very curious . . . The suspense is the suspense of waiting for a super-natural manifestation – which comes.' He acknowledged that 'Some will be annoyed at a form of psychology which is, in the West, relegated to spiritistic séances', and he added, perhaps a little defensively, 'If the Japanese authors had not combined the psychology of such matters with what is to me a very fine sort of poetry, I should not bother about it.'[119] Pound worked that winter on *Nishikigi*, one of the Noh plays translated by Fenollosa, giving its dialogue a curiously Irish lilting tone, as critics have noticed, a deliberate ploy to make the parallel between Celtic and Far Eastern thought.[120] (T.S. Eliot, for one, strongly objected to the Irish tone when he came to review the volume in which Pound's Noh plays appeared.) In 1918, referring to this play, Pound commented that 'Chinese poetry is full of fairies and fairy lore', 'quite Celtic' in fact, illustrating the point through the similarities between this play and a legend from the Aran isles that Yeats had found.[121] In making this parallel between the Noh and the Aran legends, Pound implies not solely or even primarily likenesses between these two cultures, but, *à la* Frazer, that they echo a universal truth that might be uncovered in numerous places.

That winter with Yeats thrust Pound back again to his earlier concern with mysticism and visions. For most of the year he had concentrated on his satires of one form or another, diagnosing, as he put it in 'The Serious Artist', social diseases. Now he was returning to what he had said was the second kind of poetry: that concerned with the creation of beauty. He wrote in a brief prose poem entitled 'Ikon', published that December, that 'the highest business' of art is 'to create the beautiful image', and these 'images of beauty' will 'furnish the life of our minds with a noble surrounding', so that if, 'as some say, the soul survives the body; if our consciousness is not an intermittent melody of strings that relapse between whiles into silence, . . . [this] abundance of sounds and patterns [will] entertain us in that long dreaming [and] strew our path to Valhalla'.[122] Yeats had been convinced by his medium that the soul survived the body, one reason for his present preoccupation with ghosts. Pound here does not commit himself, but he uses the possibility to add a new dimension to his theory of the image; 'images of beauty' create a certain quality of consciousness, sustaining and enriching. The images become the equivalent of objects buried with the dead by the Egyptians and others to furnish them with all they need in the next world. In other words, images of beauty are potentially what lead the soul to Paradise. It is an idea that would lie behind the structure of the *Cantos*.

V

THAT visit to Stone Cottage was significant in other ways for both Yeats and Pound. James Longenbach argues that while they were there Yeats and Pound mutually reinforced their ideas about an elite and aristocratic art, indifferent to the public, to which Pound now referred regularly as the *vulgo* or the *canaille*. Pound would take on Yeats' causes, echoing him in ever more extravagant terms. Yeats' troubles at the Abbey had already led him to wonder if there would ever be an appreciative audience for art in Ireland, but during 1913 he had been much exercised by another Dublin dispute, which had plunged him into further despair at what he saw as the city's blindness to artistic value. Sir Hugh Lane, Lady Gregory's nephew, had offered to give his collection of Impressionist paintings to the city, if they would be willing to provide an adequate gallery. Such a gallery, however, would be expensive and the Council hesitated. Conditions in Dublin were the worst of any capital in Europe: poverty was rife; the inhabitants of the insanitary Dublin tenements were often half-fed. There were strikes and agitation, and in the background fears about the progress of Home Rule. Ulster was determined to resist its implementation, and a militia of Ulster Volunteers had been formed under the leadership of Sir Edward Carson, famous as the barrister who secured Oscar Wilde's conviction; in the south, in response, Nationalist Volunteers were banding together; civil war was threatening. The money needed to refurbish a large building as an art gallery seemed prohibitive in the economic and political circumstances.

Yet there were others who felt strongly that such a collection would add greatly to the cultural prestige of the new state if and when it came, and the Abbey Theatre, led by Yeats, ardently supported the project, contributing some of the profits from its recent American tour to the cause. Several wealthy figures subscribed, though one of those who considered giving money, Lord Ardilaun, said he would subscribe only if it could be shown that the public wanted the gallery. Yeats was outraged that anyone could think of taking the views of 'the blind and ignorant town', as he put it in one poem, into consideration. Now that the Home Rule for which he had hoped so long appeared imminent, Yeats was beginning to fear that the narrow Catholic philistinism that had greeted Synge's plays was going to be the keynote of the new Ireland, and that a materialist and mercenary country with no feeling for the arts would emerge. 'The intellectual workers in Ireland,' he had said the previous summer, 'see gathering against them all the bigotries – the bigotries of Dublin that have succeeded in keeping "the Golden Treasury" out of the schools, the bigotries of Belfast that have turned Nietzsche out of the public libraries. If Hugh Lane is defeated, hundreds of young men and women all over the country will be discouraged . . . Ireland will for many years become a little huckstering nation, groping for halfpence in a greasy till.'[123] He wrote a series of poems on the issue, one of the best known of which, 'September 1913', springs straight from that speech:

> What need you, being come to sense,
> But fumble in a greasy till
> And add the halfpence to the pence
> And prayer to shivering prayer, until
> You have dried the marrow from the bone;
> For men were born to pray and save:
> Romantic Ireland's dead and gone,
> It's with O'Leary in the grave.[124]

Yeats must have felt his dismissal of the difficult position in which the city found itself needed some justification, for in a note to these poems he said he could have respected the argument about the poverty and the slums, but it was the philistine insults hurled at those who supported the idea of the gallery that horrified him. When Pound later commented on this incident, however, that side of the argument vanished: it became purely an issue of the public's appalling lack of taste. Pound would write in 1915 that 'any new development or even any change in any art has to be pushed down the public throat with a ramrod. The public has always squealed': when 'Sir Hugh Lane tried to give Dublin a collection of pictures, Degas, Corot and Manet, . . . they called him a charlatan and cried out for real pictures "like the lovely paintings which we see reproduced in our city art shops".'[125] The fate of the Dublin poor had entirely disappeared from view.

The Lane controversy, R. F. Foster suggests, led Yeats to believe that the only 'bulwark against middle-class vulgarity' could come from what he described as 'a few educated men & the remnants of an old traditional culture among the poor'.[126] Yeats was moving towards a belief that the aristocrat – literal or spiritual – and the peasant were equally under threat from 'the filthy modern tide', to which they were both far superior. It was a view that received a painful shock that month, when an extract from George Moore's final volume of his autobiography *Hail and Farewell* appeared in the *English Review*; among other gibes at Yeats' and Lady Gregory's expense, Moore affected to be perplexed by Yeats' dislike of the middle classes, since, he said, Yeats was middle class himself. Yeats was stung to the quick; the effect was not to reconcile him to the vulgar middle classes, but to set him out, on the one hand, on a quest over the next few years to establish his family's aristocratic links, and, on the other, to make it clear that terms like 'aristocratic' and 'bourgeois' did not have merely class implications. He said nothing about Moore's insults publicly, but Pound obligingly reproduced Yeats' views in the *Egoist* in pieces purporting to be written by Bastien von Helmholtz, which drew attention to the calumny directed at Yeats by 'One of the boudoir school of journalists'. The journalist, he complains, has misunderstood the meaning of the word bourgeois, which 'is not applied to the middle classes to distinguish them from the aristocracy . . . The bourgeoisie is a state of mind. It is as a term of opprobrium, used by the bohemian, or the artist in contempt of the citizen . . . our journalist . . . has mistaken a term which is the censure of a whole code of morals and of ethics for a term of social snobbery'.[127] In another piece, supposedly on John Synge, who gets little mention, he argues for the celebration of 'great figures' in defiance of the 'cult of mediocrity'. 'There is no truce,' he writes, 'between art and the *vulgo*', although he also asserts, unusually for him, that 'there is a constant and irrefutable alliance between art and the oppressed . . . The oppressed have never set a hand against their artists but the half taught have always done so.'[128] The socially disadvantaged very rarely appear in Pound's thought: it must have been some conversation with Yeats about the downtrodden Irish peasantry that brought this on, but while the oppressed appear to have vanished rapidly from his thought, by April Pound would be arguing strongly that artists were the aristocracy of the future.

It may be because Yeats' mind was running on these things that he suggested a visit to an old friend of Lady Gregory's, Wilfrid Scawen Blunt, who entirely shared his views on the mercenary bourgeoisie of the modern world. Blunt lived not far from Stone Cottage, at his country house, Newbuildings, in Sussex, owned by his aristocratic forebears for generations, where he now bred Arab horses and maintained a pride of peacocks. Blunt was married to the granddaughter of Lord Byron, on whom he modelled his energetic life as a poet, womaniser, and supporter of liberation movements, those of Egypt and India being particularly close to his heart. Yeats had known Blunt for some time, as Blunt had also been a keen supporter of the Irish cause, and in 1888 had been sent to jail for two months for speaking in support of Home Rule. Blunt, now over seventy, had many years earlier had an affair with Lady Gregory – something which Yeats may not have known – but they had remained on the most cordial of terms. Blunt had had a play performed at the Abbey Theatre in 1907, with Florence Farr in the lead, and in 1911 Yeats attempted to get him elected to the Academic Committee, but he was no more successful in that than he was with Tagore.

Blunt, who had published a string of anti-imperialist books, was regarded as a subversive in government circles. He had no truck with any of the new movements in the arts – he has, after all, appeared earlier in this narrative in the context of his outrage at the Post-Impressionist Exhibition, and in connection with his affair with Lady Margaret Sackville, whose very traditional poetry he admired and promoted. Yet, like the young modernists, of whose work in aesthetic terms he disapproved so strongly, he rejected any belief in progress and in the superiority of modern civilisation. He refused to accept the contemporary racial hierarchy of the advanced white races, with non-white humankind descending through gradual steps to the lowly Hottentot, and instead held on to a feudal model, largely regardless of race, having a warm if condescending regard for the peasantry and an admiration for those he saw as the aristocracy in any culture; the new commercial middle classes at home or abroad were those that he could not abide. He wrote of a visit to Algeria that, for

all my love of the French . . . I found my sympathies in Algeria going out wholly to the Arabs . . . The contrast between their noble pastoral life on the one hand, with their camel herds and horses, a life of high tradition filled with the memory of heroic deeds, and on the other hand the ignoble squalor of the Frank settlers, with their wineshops and their swine, was one which could not escape us, or fail to rouse in us an angry sense of the incongruity which has made of these last the lords of the land and of those their servants.[129]

For Blunt, imposing Western modernity only brought degradation and misery. He had considerable admiration for Indian intellectuals and leaders, who he insisted were perfectly capable of self-government, and was shocked by the way the British in India lived their social lives completely segregated from the Indians, though he disturbingly puts forward the idea that relations have deteriorated since the civil service examinations made it possible for the middle classes to become colonial servants. Blunt's admirable resistance to contemporary racial stereotypes was inextricably bound up with his reactionary class attitudes, but that did not in any way make him less attractive to Yeats and Pound.

Blunt appeared to Pound a deeply romantic figure, a Bertrans de Born type, both poet and activist, and he decided that not just a visit, but a tribute must be paid. Shortly before he and Yeats returned from Stone Cottage he set up a committee, to consist of himself, Yeats, Plarr, Sturge Moore, Masefield, Manning, Aldington and Flint, to give a dinner to honour the elderly Blunt. Quite what they were honouring him for even Blunt remained unsure. He had published a considerable amount of poetry, including translations of Arabic poems, but he was much less well known for his poems than for his denunciations of imperial policy, summed up in a pamphlet, *The Shame of the Nineteenth Century*, which he wrote in 1900, in which the 'shame' is the misery and suffering brought by Britain to so much of the world, to India, China, Africa, the 'Pacific Isles', the Maoris and the Australians (i.e. Aborigines).[130] On the Chinese Boxer Rebellion of 1900, which started a Yellow Peril fever in Britain, he wrote in language which, if he read it, must have delighted Pound: 'The Chinese, after a long course of bullying by the Powers, worrying by missionaries, and robbing by merchants and speculators, have risen, and are, very properly, knocking the foreign vermin on the head'.[131] (Incidentally, he also pointed out that 'in the commercial raids on China for the last sixty years it has been always Englishmen who have led the way, and who count now on securing the greater share of the commercial spoils'; the silk painting masterpieces which were 'lost' from the Imperial Palace in Beijing during the rebellion did indeed mysteriously turn up in the possession of the British Museum in 1903: Englishmen, in Blunt's words, once again securing the spoils.)

A letter appeared in *The Times* announcing the committee's forthcoming visit to honour him. Blunt had refused to go to a dinner in London, but invited the committee down to his Sussex 'sixteenth-century defensible grange' to lunch, the meal being retrospectively described as a 'Peacock Dinner', Blunt, at Lady Gregory's suggestion, serving them a peacock in full feathers from the Newbuildings pride. Yeats had hired a motor car to drive over from Stone Cottage, a journey to which Pound had not looked forward; as he told Dorothy, 'if it's as dammmmM cold sunday next as it is now we'll arrive like a box of marrons glacés'.[132] Aldington and Flint came down together by train; Flint was in agonies before the event, convinced his suit would not pass muster, though it looks fine in the group photograph they took. Yeats made a speech saying the occasion was to honour Blunt as a poet, on the grounds that he was the first to use poetry to deal with contemporary issues, freeing it from Victorian abstractions. Only six of the committee of eight poets attended, Masefield's wife, it was alleged, having refused to let him come; Manning too was absent, without explanation, but one might guess his deeply conservative guardian, Galton, had issued a similar veto to him. So the six remaining consisted of three imagists, Pound, Aldington and Flint, and three Rhymers, Yeats, Plarr and Sturge Moore; however, Pound stressed that the idea had not been to narrow the homage to these particular groups. The committee, he said, was 'representative of the present vitality of English verse, although there were, among the younger men, unavoidable omissions, as follows: Mr D.H. Lawrence, who is in Italy; Mr Padraic Colum, now in Ireland; Mr James Joyce, in Austria; and Mr Rupert Brooke, somewhere in the South Pacific'.[133] Blunt met them in the garb of an Arabian sheikh, but, though flattered by their attentions, he was unimpressed by their work. They presented him with a sculpture by Gaudier-Brzeska, which he described in his diary as 'a small marble coffer with an inscription "Homage to W.S. Blunt", and an absurd futurist bas-relief of a naked Egyptian woman the work of a Franco-Pole sculptor coming into fashion'.[134] As soon as they had gone, he turned it face to the wall. Inside the coffer was 'an address signed by the poets in a kind of futurist verse without rhyme or metre or much reason with bits of verse in the handwriting of each'.[135]

The very detailed account of the speeches Aldington reproduced in the *Egoist* – perhaps Flint helped him out with his excellent shorthand – quotes this 'futurist' address, which was a poem by Pound, not one of his best, celebrating Blunt's espousal of individualism and his anti-commercialism, though unfortunately confusing the Egyptian nationalist,

Arabi Pasha, whom Blunt had done much to support, with the well-known Italian patriot, Mazzini, and commending Blunt because he had 'Swung the grand style, not made a trade of art . . . and detested institutions'.[136] Of the 'bits of verse', samples of a poem by each of the others, Blunt somewhat cautiously said, 'I very much appreciate the verses that you have written to me – if they are verses. I could not quite make out whether they were or not. I waited for a rhyme that did not seem to come.'[137] Yet though he thought his visitors 'queer looking young men with shock heads of hair', they were, he decided, 'capital fellows as it turned out, intelligent, and with a great knowledge of literature ancient and modern also some wit and as far as I could judge good hearts'.[138]

Blunt had published no poetry for some years. Later that year he was to bring out his collected poems, but it seems very unlikely this dinner was just about Blunt's poetry. When Pound told Harriet Monroe she should publish some of Blunt's poetry it was for 'the glory of the name' rather than anything to do with the poetry itself.[139] When Pound wrote up the event in *Poetry*, although he quoted one poem, and said Blunt was the last to be 'able to use the . . . "grand style" effectively', perhaps more significantly he praised Blunt because he 'had never ceased to protest against the tyrannies and swindles of the Empire'.[140] For Pound, and in varying degrees for the others, it was the heady mix that Blunt represented that fascinated them: virile, poetic, anti-establishment, anti-Empire and aristocratic. British imperialists were seen in popular culture as the ideal of manliness: Pound wanted to create an alternative masculinity for the artist, and Blunt was an ideal model. Pound's own critique of British imperialism was not particularly deep or systematic, but his experience with the British attitude to Tagore had left him highly indignant that stuffy public school civil servants could think themselves superior to fine artists, merely because they were British and the artists Indian. The full pleasure of the homage to Blunt came when they were told that a Foreign Office official had said he would never speak to any of them again. Pound would remember Blunt in the *Cantos*, associating him with action, nobility and culture:

> But to have done, instead of not doing
> > this is not vanity
>
> To have, with decency, knocked
> That a Blunt should open
> > To have gathered from the air a live tradition

or from a fine old eye the unconquered flame
This is not vanity.[141]

Blunt remained a heroic and romantic figure to Pound, though to others,
including his wife, he was a flawed figure, even if his recognition of the
crimes against humanity perpetrated by the Empire was admirable. In
Blunt's account of the Indians, as in his attitude to Arabi, or to the
Bedouin sheikhs, there is a powerful sense of his acceptance of them as
equals, but it has to be admitted that westernised Jewish financiers were
another matter. Like his friend and fellow anti-imperialist, Hilaire Belloc,
who joined them at Newbuildings for tea, which in his case, according
to Aldington, was a large glass of claret, he was something of an anti-
Semite. Pound does, indeed, suggest that Blunt described the Empire
as 'a Semitic invention of Disraeli's'; anti-Semitism was another way
in which Pound would follow Blunt.[142]

Among the promising young writers who were unable to be present
at the Blunt presentation, Pound had mentioned James Joyce, his first
reference to him in print. Yeats had met Joyce on a couple of occasions,
and thought he was doing new and promising work; since Joyce was
having problems finding a publisher, he offered to help. He told Pound
about the situation, ensuring that help would be provided by the ever
energetic impresario. Pound first wrote to Joyce in general terms, saying
that he knew of him through Yeats and offering to place some of his
work in England, though warning him it was likely to be without pay.
He could also recommend but not guarantee paid publication in the
Smart Set (for short stories) or Poetry (for poems), which at two shillings
a line got 'most of the best people (and one hell of a lot of muck)'. At
this stage Pound told Joyce that he didn't 'in the least know that I can
be of any use to you – or you to me', a revealing, though honest, comment
in itself about Pound's motives.[143] Before Joyce could reply, Yeats had
managed to locate his copy of Joyce's Chamber Music, which Elkin
Mathews had published in 1907, and suggested to Pound that he use
the last poem in that collection for his new anthology. Pound wrote
asking for permission to include it, saying he could pay a guinea immediately, and a share of the profits if there were any, an admirably democratic
arrangement, but Pound did not mind sharing money; only power. Joyce
agreed, also sending Pound some of the manuscript of Portrait of the
Artist as a Young Man, as well as letters he had written to newspapers
about the difficulties that he was having in getting Dubliners published;
he had had two different contracts, the first six years ago, but both

publishers in turn wanted to censor elements of the text, in the first instance on moral grounds, and in the second on political. Joyce had resisted, and the book remained unpublished. Pound immediately printed the story of Joyce's trials over *Dubliners* in the 14 January issue of the *Egoist*, and wrote to Dora Marsden, sending her the first three chapters of *Portrait of the Artist* and asking if they could serialise it. To her credit, she agreed – it was sufficiently subversive and individual-istic to fit the magazine – and the first instalment appeared in the February issue. Pound apologised ruefully for the lack of payment, but he pointed out that 'Appearance in the Egoist may have a slight adver-tising value if you want to keep your name familiar'.[144] That Grant Richards, the first of the publishers who had originally agreed to publish *Dubliners*, finally brought it out that June may have owed something to the *Egoist*'s venture.

Pound would be a loyal supporter of Joyce, and his appreciation of his first novel was very genuine. The tale of the young writer-to-be growing up in an unsympathetic and narrow environment from which he must escape to forge his art must have seemed like the story of his own life. Pound compared Joyce with Flaubert, a direct influence as it happened, but while he admired him as a social critic, a prose stylist, and a writer in whose work he found 'a hardness and gauntness . . . clear statement, no shadow of comment, and behind it a sense of beauty that never relapses into ornament', he never appears to be conscious of Joyce's experiments with different styles of language in his first two novels, apparent even in the *Portrait* with the language moving grad-ually from that of the child to the mature artist; when Pound reviewed *Ulysses* all he commented on was Joyce's use of dialect.[145] Ford was to say, some years later, that because of his lack of interest in prose, Pound, when he did read a novel, was always preoccupied with 'Subject rather than with rendering'.[146] It was perhaps his lack of appreciation of the point of Joyce's 'rendering' that led him later to be so baffled by the emerging *Finnegans Wake* and Joyce's 'blather about the revolution of the word'.[147] Considering, however, how much more appreciative of Joyce he was than so many of his contemporaries, it may be unfair to blame him too much. Trying to get Joyce published would not be an easy busi-ness, however, and the inanity of the public and the publishing world would at times stoke his ire to incandescent fury, further hardening his contempt for the *canaille*.

PART XI

PRELUDE TO WAR

I

ON 22 January 1914, two days after a report of the poets' visit to Blunt appeared in *The Times*, a piece of publicity that Pound relished, he returned to London to speak at the Quest Society, where two years before he had given his talk on 'Psychology and the Troubadaours'. This time he was one of three speakers, as he explained to his mother: 'Hulme lectured at the QUEST last night on futurism and post-impressionism, followed by fervent harangues from Wyndham Lewis and myself'.[1] Pound had not seen much of Hulme since the latter had returned from his Berlin exile the previous May. He sometimes attended Hulme's Tuesdays, but their long discussions of the metaphysics of art had become a thing of the past. Flint, having forgiven Hulme for the delayed payment, seems to have seen him much more frequently. Hulme was now writing art criticism for the *New Age* rather than philosophy, whilst Pound up to this point, in spite of his admiration for Epstein and more recently Gaudier, had taken very little interest in what was happening on the art scene. Nor had Pound seen much of Lewis since their wary first meetings on his first sojourn in London. After the evening at the Quest Society, all that would change.

Lewis had in the last few years achieved much notoriety and just occasional admiration in the art world. Since the 1910 Post-Impressionist Exhibition, experimental work like his own, influenced by European modernist art, had been flourishing in London. In 1911, Lewis joined the Camden Town Group, whose president was his friend Spencer Gore, and exhibited with them, being, he claims, immediately picked out for expressions of special horror by the critics, who would typically write: 'Despite the alarming announcement of the character of this "Group", we find that amongst this band of honest, hardworking young men (with one exception) that good old English conservatism has saved them from excess . . . That one exception is Mr Wyndham Lewis, whose black-guardly, preposterous, putrid etc.' Even Lewis' friend Sturge Moore was dubious about what one critic described as Lewis' 'geometrical experiments'. Yet in the Allied Artists Salon of 1912, held in the Royal Albert Hall, Lewis' large painting, *The Kermesse* (a 'kermesse' being a Breton folk festival), drew the admiration of Roger Fry and Clive Bell, Bell suggesting the painting had the unity of a Beethoven sonata, and Fry commending the 'tense and compact design' as well as the painting's 'Dionysiac energy'. Roger Fry invited Lewis to contribute to the British section of the Second Post-Impressionist Exhibition; Bell made the selection, choosing two large pictures and some illustrations for *Timon of Athens*, the play that centres on the most disillusioned and misan-thropic of Shakespeare's protagonists, whose devastating critique of a money-obsessed society Lewis felt appropriate to the present state of England.[2]

From the start, Lewis' propensity for imagining slights made his rela-tionship with Fry uneasy, but Fry asked him to exhibit with his own Grafton Group in April 1913, and to join the Omega Workshop when it opened in June. It was, as so often with Lewis, a brief collaboration. Lewis walked out in dudgeon in October, suspecting Fry of having cheated him out of a commission. He took several of the other artists with him, including Frederick Etchells, Cuthbert Hamilton and Edward Wadsworth, and they jointly sent a round robin to all likely supporters of the Omega project, denouncing Fry's actions, and adding: 'As to [Omega's] tendencies in Art, they alone would be sufficient to make it very difficult for any vigorous art instinct to remain long under that roof. The Idol is still Prettiness, with its mid-Victorian languish of the neck, and its skin is "greenery-yallery", despite the Post-What-Not fashionableness of its draperies.' They had needed Lewis and his friends to provide the 'rough', 'masculine' art; their own was no more than 'a pleasant tea-party'.[3] Hulme, equally opposed to Fry and his fellow Bloomsbury artists, said in a review in the *New Age* of Fry's Grafton Group exhibition that January that with the departure of Lewis and his friends, the remaining painters (he is referring to Fry and Grant) repre-sented a 'backwater . . . What is living and important in new art must be looked for elsewhere'. In Fry's work, the 'colour is always rather sentimental and pretty. He . . . accomplishes the extraordinary feat of adapting the austere Cézanne into something quite fitted for chocolate boxes.' Fry's painting, he notes, had been described as 'cultured', a word Hulme immediately associates with effete Cambridge dilettantes and 'gentle little Cambridge jokes'; these painters, he says dismissively, have a curious similarity to the Pre-Raphaelites, perhaps because the 'same English aesthetic' lies behind both movements, and 'just as the one ultimately declined into Liberty's, so there is no reason why the other should not find its grave in some emporium which will provide the wives of young and advanced dons with suitable house decoration'.[4] Bloomsbury designs have indeed been used commercially, which one might think wholly appropriate, since Fry's aim in the workshops was, like William Morris, to bring art into the domestic environment. Like Lewis', Hulme's scorn might be seen as typical of the high modernist disdain for the marketplace, the domestic and the feminine, but there is also some class warfare going on here. The Cambridge gentlemanly dilettantes, only capable of producing or appreciating such effeminate works as pretty chocolate box designs, are to be despised for their 'slop and romanticism'; virile art is to be found elsewhere.

The lecture that Hulme gave on 22 January was on 'Modern Art and its Philosophy', and, as he reportedly mumbled it at the time, the present-day reader probably has a much better idea of what he said than did the members of the Quest Society. Pound described it in the *Egoist* as 'almost wholly unintelligible', but he was sitting on the platform, and clearly grasped some of the important points.[5] Hulme was largely paraphrasing the ideas of the art historian and theorist Wilhelm Worringer, whose ground-breaking book, *Abstraction and Empathy*, had excited him tremendously when he discovered it during his time in Germany, providing him with the perfect answer to his fundamental dilemma: how could someone with a desperate desire for absolute solutions cope with a world without certainties or answers? Hulme had made clear, in an article on Epstein the previous December, that he had moved on from his rejection of Romanticism two years before to 'a repugnance' for the world-view of all philosophy since the Renaissance. This philosophy had first taken the form of humanism, then degenerated into a belief in 'Progress', and was now, he averred, disintegrating, and he used Worringer's work to reinforce his argument.[6] For Worringer, there were two fundamentally different forms of art, in Hulme's translation, the geometric and the vital. The latter describes classical Greek art and modern art since the Renaissance; in other words, representational art, the art, Hulme told his audience, they would think natural. The former is the kind of art produced by the Egyptians, Indians and Byzantines, highly stylised, showing, in contrast to the naturalism of vital art, 'what Worringer calls the *tendency to abstraction*'. Hulme attacks the notion, widespread at the time, that geometric art was produced by people who were not skilled enough to work naturalistically; these different forms of art are the outcome, not of difference in skill, but of two very different world-views. Complacent humanism or progressivism, which sees 'a happy pantheistic relation between man and the outside world', produces naturalistic art; geometric art comes from a world-view that, on the contrary, sees a separation between humankind and the rest of the world, such as is found, for example, among 'more primitive people', with their fearful awareness of the 'lack of order and seeming arbitrariness' of things, and also in the other great non-Western cultures: 'No knowledge could damp down the Indian inborn fear of the world, since it stands, not as in the case of primitive man before knowledge, but above it.' Geometric art springs from what Worringer calls a spiritual '"space-shyness" in face of the varied confusion and arbitrariness of existence'. One can hear here an echo of Hulme's own earlier 'space-shyness' when he encountered the 'flat spaces and wide horizons of the Canadian prairie', of his insistent efforts in his poems to make the sky and stars more homely, and his troubled conviction that the world had no meaning or pattern, but was simply a 'chaos' or 'cinderheap'. He is not rejecting the Bergsonian analysis of the world as flux, but he now believes that the creation of geometric shapes offers 'a refuge from the flux and impermanence of outside nature'. Geometric art seeks to transform the changing and uncertain world into something more 'fixed and necessary'.[7]

Worringer had compared this 'space-shyness' to 'the fear which makes certain people unable to cross open spaces', in other words, agoraphobia, a much discussed condition at the time, thought to be exacerbated by modern city spaces, so specifically a very modern, as well as very primitive, fear.[8] Among Hulme's papers is an undated note which says, 'the fright of the mind before the unknown created not only the first gods, but the first art', a sentence translated from Worringer that Herbert Read used as the epigraph for the published version of this lecture.[9] Hulme, who had turned to poetry out of his own 'fright of the mind before the unknown', must have found that Worringer spoke directly to his condition.

Worringer's book was the publication of his Ph.D. thesis, written in 1906. He had worked in the Paris Trocadéro museum, where Picasso at around that very time had discovered African art, but while Worringer was deeply impressed by this non-European art, he was unaware of the impact it was beginning to have on European artists. He writes in the book that, though in his alienated existence in the modern world, 'man is now just as lost and helpless *vis-à-vis* the world picture as primitive man', abstract art is not possible in modern individualistic society.[10] In other words, he believes abstract art is what the modern world needs, but can't achieve. By 1910, when he wrote the preface to the third edition, Worringer had learnt that he had been too pessimistic, and he says there how much pleasure he has had from hearing from practising artists who feel his work is in tune with what they are attempting to do. This is the point that Hulme goes on to make. Not only, he says, are people beginning to appreciate this archaic and Oriental art, but the most significant modern artists are beginning to move towards a similar geometric style. Hulme cites Cézanne as perhaps the most important so far of the artists who show the 'tendency to abstraction', but he also mentions the work of Picasso, Epstein and Wyndham Lewis.

Hulme goes further than Worringer, who advocates a new appreciation of this abstract art but does not explicitly denounce the representational tradition. In Hulme's account, naturalist art becomes dishonest, superficial and banal, abstract art an unflinching confrontation of the true, grim nature of existence. In contrast to art that springs from 'flat and insipid optimism of the belief in progress', this new art may appear 'inhuman, pessimistic'. Its terms of approbation will not be 'graceful, beautiful, etc.', but 'austere, mechanical, clear-cut, and bare'. Although as it develops this new abstract art may be very different from archaic art forms, to start on that road many of these artists first drew on earlier traditions; hence, Hulme said, 'you get the explanation of the fact which may have puzzled some people, that a new and modern art, something which was to culminate in the use of a structural organisation akin to machinery, should have begun by what seemed like a romantic return to barbarous and primitive art, apparently inspired by a kind of nostalgia for the past'.[11] Hulme is rather shamefaced in his concession here that a return to the past is necessary, so very different from his insistence in 1908 on the desirability of the complete destruction of all verse more than twenty years old; one can imagine Pound thinking triumphantly that his own return to the past was vindicated.

Hulme ends by saying he believes this new art presages a change in sensibility and in general outlook, and he could be said to be right. The years ahead would see, at any rate among intellectuals, a widespread loss of faith in progress and the benefits of modernity, and a much darker view of the human condition, a pessimism reinforced and in some cases caused by the disasters of the First World War and its aftermath. The sense of meaninglessness and uncertainty that Hulme identifies has been seen as the result of the collapse of Christian belief and the rapid growth of secularism, but Hulme would not have agreed. He argues that the false optimism of humanism came from the Enlightenment and the Romantic movement, but certainly not from religion. Hulme identified his pessimistic view of the world as the religious one, though his idea of religion was scarcely orthodox Christianity. Of course, the Church agreed with him on Original Sin, but what about Heaven, the forgiveness of sins, the workings of Providence, God's purpose in the world? Hulme ignored them; his view of religion had perhaps more in it of a dark Calvinism, but he would never agree that religious faith could encourage complacency, or, to put it more positively, a sense of security. He was one of the many modernists to put himself in the religious camp, but entirely to reinvent the accepted meaning of religion.

Wyndham Lewis followed after Hulme, speaking equally inaudibly; Pound summed up his talk as saying that 'you could set a loaf of bread in an engine shop and that this would *not* cause said loaf to produce cubist paintings', so presumably he was defending his paintings from the charge that they showed no skill or artistry.[12] Pound came last, to the audience's great relief speaking in tones they could hear, and gave a lively talk, in which he appears to have put forward an idea that had first appeared in 'Psychology and the Troubadours', that the good artist does not just passively receive impressions but actively creates, and he finished by reading some of Hulme's and his own poetry.

The visit to Blunt was written up by Aldington in the *Egoist* for 2 February 1914, and the Quest evening reported on by Pound on the 16th, in a piece entitled 'The New Sculpture'. The two events, though so different, had an underlying link which one might describe as the rejection of the imperial belief in the inevitability and rightness of Western progress, though that was scarcely the language either Pound or Aldington would have used. Pound would be honing his attack on contemporary society in the next few months in blunter and more direct terms. Yeats had ended his address to Blunt by saying, 'Ezra Pound has a desire personally to insult the world', and in Pound's article he made it his business to do just that: 'Modern civilisation has bred a race with brains like those of rabbits and we who are the heirs of the witch-doctor and the voodoo, we artists who have been so long despised are about to take over control'.[13] The presence of witch-doctors there goes back to Allen Upward, but the article takes off from Hulme's critique of humanism and representational art, Pound condemning Greek sculpture out of hand as 'super-fashion plates' that remind 'all rightly constituted young futurists of cake-icing and plaster of Paris', though he does point out, *contra* Hulme's blanket dismissal of Greek culture, that in their tragedy they recognise 'chaos and death and the then inexplicable forces of destiny and nothingness and beyond'. His rejection of humanism is also in rather different terms from Hulme's. Humanism did not, Pound avers, in practice make much impact on society in general, but 'took refuge in the arts'. For a long time artists were humanists trying to save humanity from itself, but the artist today recognises that

the war between him and the world is a war without truce. That his only remedy is slaughter. This is a mild way to say it. Mr Hulme was quite right in saying that the difference between the new art and the old was not a difference in degree but a difference in kind; a difference in intention . . . The artist has no longer any belief or suspicion that the mass, the half-educated simpering general, the semi-connoisseur, the sometimes collector, and still less the readers of the 'Spectator' and the 'English Review' can in any way share his delights or understand his pleasure in forces.

One might call this the Stone Cottage doctrine of the 'blind and ignorant town', though Pound would in practice never cease to try and convince his public of something or other, however much he held to this elitist view of art in theory. Yet he is here elaborating his theory of art in terms of the reactionary politics that he and Yeats were coming to share; the artist 'is born to rule but he has no intention of trying to rule by general franchise . . . he has dabbled in democracy and he is now done with that folly. We turn back, we artists, to the powers of the air, to the djinns who were our allies aforetime . . . It is by them we have ruled and shall rule, and by their connivance that we shall mount again into our hierarchy. The aristocracy of entail and of title has decayed, the aristocracy of commerce is decaying, the aristocracy of the arts is ready again for its service.'[14]

The violence and absolutism of Pound's language in this article is a provocative assertion of the vigour and hardness of the new art; by this time, Gaudier had started work on a carving of Pound's head, which Pound instructed him to make look as virile as possible; Gaudier responded by carving the head as a phallus. Pound, Hulme and Lewis were all intent on inventing themselves as representatives of a new kind of masculinity – brash, authoritarian, contemptuous. In March, Pound published a poem in *Poetry and Drama* defiantly entitled simply, 'Coitus', beginning, 'The gilded phaloi of the crocuses are thrusting at the spring air'.[15] Even the springtime flowers had become plated symbols of an assertive *machismo*. But with a world war about to start in seven months' time, Pound's claim that 'the only remedy is slaughter' now seems a chilling one, and his dismissal of democracy a disturbing presage of his later Fascist views. Pound is undoubtedly partly having fun here, but all the same, the seeds of his future attitudes are disturbingly present.

Pound was now seeing more of Hulme again, and he was greatly taken with Wyndham Lewis, who was fast becoming a vital partner in his '*mouvemong*'; by late February Pound would write to his father, 'The papers are full of Wyndham Lewis' cubist room that he has done for Lady Drogheda. I dont know that I have written of him but he is more or less one of the gang here at least he is the most "advanced" of the painters and very clever and thoroughly enigmatic.'[16] Though Hulme's latest ideas had become crucial for Pound once again, Hulme was not to be characterised as part of anyone's movement but his own. Lewis, it must be said, would later insist that Pound had only been a backward member in *his* personal movement, though, he admitted, a brilliant publicist for it.

Lewis had found a new base in Great Ormond Street from which to work, rented for him by Kate Lechmere. Lechmere, with whom he had earlier had a brief liaison, and who remained a good friend, was an emancipated and independent woman with private means, though with a surprising weakness for misogynist men. Lewis named his atelier the Rebel Art Centre, and he worked there with the others who had broken with Fry, such as Wadsworth, Etchells and Hamilton, as well as attracting some others, Christopher Nevinson, for example, whose sympathies, it would become clear, were really with the Futurists; there were also two women, Jessica Dismorr and Helen Saunders, who were much put upon. Pound was a frequent visitor; Dorothy would later tell Noel Stock that he was the only person that Lewis would allow to see his paintings before they were exhibited, as he kept them locked away in a back room for fear others would steal his ideas. Pound could be trusted, presumably because he had no painterly skill and was therefore incapable of artistic theft, though what he would increasingly emulate was Lewis' paranoia. Lewis organised a series of lectures at the Centre, with speakers including Marinetti, Ford and of course Pound. In April Lewis intended to open as a college, though he had little luck in recruiting students, and he was planning to launch a journal, whose name had already been chosen for maximum ballistic effect: *Blast*.

Pound was still seeing a good deal of Aldington, H.D. and Flint. He continued to promote their poetry, and he had not forgotten the impact of Flint's article on French poetry – that March he held it up to Harriet as an example of how one sufficiently good piece could make a journal's reputation. They for now accepted the extension of the movement to include these sculptors and artists: there are notes extant from H.D. to Flint about visits to a Cubist show and to the Rebel Arts Centre; Aldington was a signatory to the manifesto that appeared in *Blast* and generally joined in the rebel artists' boisterous café life. In mid-1914, there was remarkably, for a brief time, no apparent dissension among Pound's various artistic and literary friends. Aldington mentions Lewis and Gaudier visiting them at their flat, and they were seeing a good deal of Ford. It was at this time that Ford asked H.D. to be his secretary – Brigit must have had enough – and he later dedicated part of *The Good Soldier* to her. In early May, while Aldington and H.D. were staying with Aldington's parents in Rye, Ford came to dinner; Aldington describes the evening in his memoirs:

The food and wine were good, and Ford, ever susceptible to the genial influences of the table and good-fellowship, opened the flood-gates of his discourse and babbled o' green fields – I should say, of celebrities – in his most imaginative strain. A scholarly recluse like my father, with a passion for books and very little acquaintance with writers, was an ideal subject for Ford's experiments. He sensed the virgin sucker at once. So we had the stories about Ruskin, and my uncle Gabriel and my aunt Christina; the Conrad and James stories; the story of the abbé Liszt's concert and how Queen Alexandra took the beautiful infant Ford on her knees and kissed him; the 'old Browning' stories, and the Swinburne stories; gradually working back through the 19th century. My father was swimming in bliss, although once or twice he looked a little puzzled. And then Ford began telling how he met Byron. I saw my father stiffen.[17]

Whether Aldington has further embellished Ford's embellishments must be open to question; interestingly enough, both H.D. and Aldington's mother, the provider of the cheering food and wine, disappear from this tale. Aldington's feelings about Ford would not remain so warm, but when Ford published his long poem 'On Heaven' in *Poetry* that June, Aldington joined Pound in promoting it. He described it in the *Egoist* as better than anything by Yeats, and Pound announced in *Poetry* that it was 'the best poem yet written in the "twentieth-century fashion"'.[18] Presumably they admired its conversational tone, though it is much looser and more wordy than the kind of poetry either of them generally praised, near to *vers libre*, but with jerky, variable line lengths and awkward rhymes. Max Saunders describes it as 'curiously poised between natural speech, effective musical form and the cadences of song, and ironic doggerel', but he also suggests it looks forwad to the kind of modernist narrative poems that Eliot would produce, such as 'The Love Song of J. Alfred Prufrock', which indeed Fletcher later described as 'very, very Huefferish'.[19] Perhaps what Aldington and Pound really admired was its subject-matter, a secular Heaven envisaged as the fulfilment of earthly desire. It was dedicated to Violet Hunt, who had asked Ford to write her a poem about a 'workaday heaven', but she suspected that the love he is imagining consummating is really that for Brigit Patmore, who had been staying with them when he wrote the poem. Max Saunders points out that Ford would later say to an aspiring poet that a poem should be 'a quiet monologue during a summer walk in which one seeks to render oneself beloved to someone one loves'; he read the poem to both of them, but one suspects Violet's suspicions were justified.[20]

There were perhaps hints of differences opening up between Pound and his fellow imagists: Flint was loyal for now, in spite of Frost's attempts to exacerbate his somewhat ambivalent feelings about Pound, but Aldington was becoming readier to criticise Pound, who had been quite shaken earlier in January when Aldington pointed out to him that he had 'used the word delicate 947 times in "Lustra"', as Pound was already calling the poems that he would finally publish in 1916.[21] Pound hastily set about seeking alternatives, but Aldington went on to publish a set of parodies of Pound in the *Egoist*, under the heading of 'Penultimate Poetry: Xenophilometropolitania', using the offending word nine times in 42 lines. He also provided a variation on 'In a Station of the Metro', imitating Pound's typographical gaps:

> The apparition   of these poems   in a crowd:
> White faces   in a black   dead faint.[22]

This parody's evocation of the horror produced by Pound's poems, the shock tactics that amused Aldington so much, is perhaps more affectionate than critical, and Pound assured his father, who was perturbed by Aldington's *lèse-majesté*, that he took them as a compliment. Perhaps a more serious indication that Aldington would follow a different track from Pound and Lewis emerged in an article on 'Anti-Hellenism' in the same issue in which Aldington deplored the fact that Hellenism had become unfashionable, and declared his opposition to the very 'change in sensibility' that Hulme welcomed.[23] Its tone was light-hearted, but the reservations Aldington expressed about this 'unHellenic', 'unhealthy' art went very deep. But for now he enjoyed being part of a rebellious artistic community. The *'mouvemong'* was a performance as much as a programme, and he certainly enjoyed performing. He had no wish yet to dissociate himself from Pound and his projects.

IN the early months of 1914, Pound was writing with manic energy, appearing in the *Egoist* not only as himself, chiefly now as an art critic, but in numerous other guises as well, as Ferrex and Porrex (a reference to Thomas Norton's *Gorboduc*, possibly something else he had been reading with Yeats), Bastien von Helmholtz and his brother Baptiste, and even, parodying Ford, as Hermann Karl Georg Jesus Maria. He was contributing reviews and articles to *Poetry*, and published some poetry in Harold Monro's *Poetry and Drama*. Yeats had left for another American tour, on which Harriet Monroe gave a dinner for him on behalf of *Poetry*. He made a speech at the dinner, which was reported in the magazine, and which included a tribute to Pound, though as ever it was not unequivocal. Speaking of the Rhymers, Yeats had said: 'We rebelled against rhetoric, and now there is a group of younger poets who dare to call us rhetorical. When I returned to London from Ireland, I had a young man go over all my work with me to eliminate the abstract. This was an American poet, Ezra Pound. Much of his work is experimental; his work will come slowly, he will make many an experiment before he comes into his own.'[24] Yeats remained less sure of Pound's skills as a creator than as an editor, though he went on to read to the dinner guests two of Pound's poems that he said had 'permanent value', 'The Ballad of the Goodly Fere' and 'The Return', describing the latter as 'the most beautiful poem that has been written in the free form'. Yeats had, on the other hand, serious reservations about many of the satires Pound was now producing, to say nothing of the tone of his criticism, and was highly disturbed, Pound told Harriet, by his increasingly 'unrestrained language'.[25]

In early 1914, Pound briefly considered the possibility of taking a job in China; Homer had been offered a job in Peking by a Chinese official named F.T. Sung, whom Pound met in London, and who apparently was hopeful of finding a job for Pound as well. Nothing in the end came of it, though he left Pound with the manuscript of a sober assessment of the problems of contemporary China, which, although quite unlike anything else that appeared there, Pound published in the *Egoist* as 'The Causes and Remedies of the Poverty of China', with a prefatory note saying 'At a time when China has replaced Greece in the intellectual life of so many occidentals, it is interesting to see in what way the occidental ideas are percolating into the orient'.[26] Pound decided to settle his future another way. The day before he had appeared at the Quest Society with Hulme and Lewis, he wrote to Dorothy: 'Dearest, I perceive this week will be unduly elongated. I think you'd better perhaps marry me and live in one more room than the dryad.'[27] Surprisingly, despite Pound's evermore ostentatious performance as avant-garde poet, the Shakespears finally agreed. 'Consent appears to be given – with some reluctance,' Dorothy reported some three weeks later.[28] Pound's income was not noticeably better than it had been eighteen months earlier when Olivia had thought the match impossible, but perhaps Dorothy had at last convinced them that she would never marry anyone more suitable, and Pound was their only hope of getting her off their hands. He had indeed been hovering round her for so long that Olivia's fear that gossip about them as a pair would spread may by now have proved only too true. All his close friends knew – H.D., Aldington, Walter, possibly Ford – and others, like Manning, had guessed: it is very unlikely they were all discreet. Yet Eva Fowler, who saw them regularly, was astounded: 'Eva can understand how you might fall in love with me,' Pound reported, 'but – – – marry me – – – well she *might* have done it herself, but she wouldn't have let anybody belonging to her attempt it.'[29] Olivia and Yeats must have talked over the possibility of the match, and Yeats may well have helped to sway Olivia in Pound's favour. Certainly when it was announced he was delighted.

Dorothy's devotion to Pound – in spite of their brief quarrel the previous June – was deep, and for the most part unquestioning. No one doubted that she was marrying him for love. Pound's motives for marrying her, on the other hand, were under suspicion from the start. Frederic Manning's first reaction was, he told Fairfax (they were both put out), that Pound was marrying her for her money ('he is very practical,' he had commented gloomily).[30] Dorothy's allowance of £150 a year was less than H.D.'s, and there must have been plenty of wealthier potential brides, so that seems a most unlikely explanation. It has also been suggested, more plausibly, that Pound saw himself marrying into the literary aristocracy, Dorothy being, if not quite a relation, closely connected with Yeats. Humphrey

Carpenter thinks that Pound was spurred on by opposition, and that he married Dorothy precisely because her parents tried so hard to prevent it. But H.D.'s parents had been almost equally opposed, without the same result. Possibly all those reasons were there somewhere, even if not consciously. But a purely cynical explanation of the marriage would not account for the fact that Pound in one way at least treated his relationship with Dorothy quite differently from any of his many others. He kept Dorothy's letters. H.D., Viola Baxter, Mary Moore, his parents, Margaret Cravens – he burnt all their letters, as he told Margaret Cravens, once he had read them, a kind of scorched earth policy in his emotional life. That in Dorothy's case the letters were preserved has to mean something.

Dorothy was of course, as Yeats told Pound's father, clever as well as beautiful, and when he wrote to Pound himself he mentioned the cleverness again – 'You will have a beautiful & clever wife & that is what few men get'.[31] Pound already relied on Dorothy to be the first critic of most of his poetry, and paid attention to her often shrewd advice. Her letters show her to be full of intellectual curiosity, extremely well read, and always up to date with the arts. Pound's enthusiasm for China undoubtedly owed something to her appreciation of Far Eastern art, and her interest in painting was at least one of the influences leading him to pay serious attention to the visual arts. She was a gifted painter (he had put several of her pictures up in Church Walk), but was always self-deprecating about herself and her talents; she had written to Pound in 1912, when he was working in the Bibliothèque Nationale in preparation for his walking tour: 'You can be scholarly: I'll be surface: I can't be anything else! But nevertheless I am painting quite half-seriously. And I love it very much.'[32] She appears to have been happy to think of herself as an amateur, never questioning the fact that of the two of them, Pound was the artist who counted; she was a helpmeet.[33] Pound liked his women intelligent as well as beautiful, but mainly so that they could be good disciples, and his model of marriage was certainly that the woman's role was to nurture the man – though as far as nurturing on the literal level was concerned, he was quite emancipated – just as well, as Dorothy, who was not of the social class that learnt to cook, made it a condition of marriage that she should not be required to do so; he was a very good cook.[34]

Until their marriage, Pound's relationship with Dorothy had been remarkably troubadour-like. She was guarded closely by her family, a lady in a tower to whom her lover could only sing, in a way none other of Pound's attachments had been, however much his poems might suggest it. No doubt the romance of that appealed to him, though it is not perhaps

a good basis for a happy marriage, and possibly he should have worried
more about the conventionality that had led her to heed her family's prohi-
bitions for so long. It may have been significant that Dorothy's looks were
not unlike Pound's mother's – the same regular features, high forehead
and determined chin; and, like his mother, Dorothy had a great air of
propriety. Iris Barry, who as a hopeful writer was given encouragement
by Pound a couple of years later, wrote of Dorothy that she 'had always
the air of a young Victorian lady out skating'.[35] Other people refer to her
coolness or passivity. Pound himself, if *Asphodel* is to be believed, was
commenting on Dorothy's inhibitions even before their marriage. She had
inherited her gift for painting from her father, though he had given it up
in early life, and she took after him, not her mother, both in features and
personality. Like Hope, John Harwood writes, she was 'reserved, correct
and silent'.[36] Yet for all his noisy flamboyance, Pound was not much better
at speaking of his own emotional life than she was, even if he were unstoppable on his poetic theories.

As I mentioned earlier, Humphrey Carpenter suggests Pound could
well have been a virgin when he married. He bases this partly on a poem
Pound published three years later about one Mr Hecatomb Styrax who
'has married at the age of 28,/ He being at that age a virgin', pointing out
that Pound married at twenty-eight.[37] The poem, of course, proves nothing,
but it is not impossible; respectable young American men at that period
were brought up to be cautious about sexual experience. Eliot appears to
have been a virgin when he married; John Gould Fletcher was a virgin
when he started to live with Daisy. While Pound in his 'Contemporania'
enjoyed shocking his readers by sexual references, his delight in provoking
such a reaction has something of the naughty schoolboy about it, suggesting
perhaps that lack of sexual experience rather than abundance lies behind
it. Another of his poems, 'The Temperaments', precisely makes the point
that talking about sex is no guide as to sexual behaviour. Carpenter goes
on to suggest that sexually the marriage was not a success, indeed he hints
it was unconsummated, as they appear to have slept in separate rooms,
and, even after they had been married ten years, H.D. would note that
Dorothy had not been 'awakened'.[38] A biography of Dorothy is in preparation, compiled from her voluminous papers, which may shed more light
on the marriage. Certainly Dorothy took her role as aid to the great poet
very seriously, whatever reservations she came to have about the man. Of
course, Dorothy had grown up with parents who had had, Olivia told
Yeats, no sexual relations since her conception. It is possible that Pound,
an only child in an era when contraception was not practised by the

respectable, had done the same. He may well have been attracted by someone who shared some of his fears of emotion, loss of control, the piercing of the mask. Much later, in the 1930s, according to Carpenter, Pound said to a friend: 'I fell in love with a beautiful picture that never came alive.'[39] This suggests that Pound thought Dorothy was the problem in the marriage, but it was doubtless more complicated than that; Pound's comment ominously echoes H.D.'s complaint in *Her* that George Lowndes wants to marry a picture out of the Renaissance art book, not a real woman.

If Dorothy's resemblance to his mother was an unconscious draw for Pound, he never, of course, consciously thought her like his mother, or certainly not before marriage; the notion would have horrified him. Dorothy asked him about his mother a few weeks before the wedding – quite late on, one would have thought – because her curiosity was aroused by Isabel's handwriting in a letter she had received welcoming her as a daughter-in-law. Pound replied:

Mother's handwriting??? New York, born 14th St. & second ave. when it was the thing to be born there, porched house, 23rd st, also at the proper time. Uncle's estate on Hudson, reckless rider. Married wild H.L.P. & went to a mining town, returned east to domesticity – traditions, irony, no knowledge of french literature in the original . . . Early painting lessons, penchant for the pretty – horror of all realism in art. Belief in the pleasant. Would like, or would have liked – to see me in the Diplomatic Corps – 'Ambassadour to the Ct. of St. James'. Believes that I should be well clothed. Prude if god ever permitted one to exist.[40]

His mother as he construes her here represents all he felt he was fighting, first in American provincialism and later in European bourgeois respectability; or was it that in fighting American provincialism and European respectability he was really fighting his mother? Something of both. And, of course, where Dorothy did differ from his mother was in her generally ready acceptance of avant-garde and non-realist art, though in March 1914 she was still suspicious of Pound's new alliance with Lewis; she wrote to Pound, 'I am sure BLAST will be horrible. I WON'T have a W. Lewis Lobster picture, anyway. I think they are filthy.'[41] In the event, however, she would be loyally supportive, and was won round to, and even emulated, Lewis' geometric style of drawing.

The first Pound's parents had known of the wedding was a casual message in a letter to his father about the parodies of his poems which Aldington had published in the *Egoist*: 'I suppose I shall get married in April, but you needn't mention the matter. There will be no fuss . . .

You needn't mention the matter to Yeats. I shall write to him in due course.'[42] Pound's parents must have felt very relieved that at least this was going to be somewhat more orthodox than the elopement he had been planning fifteen months earlier, and they soon began mentioning it, if not to Yeats at least to their relations, because letters and presents began to arrive from the States. The warm praise of Dorothy that Yeats sent them must have been immensely reassuring. Homer wrote to Pound to ask for more information about the family and was told: 'Mr Shakespear is "a solicitor" that'd be a "lawyer" in the U.S. Both families are "anglo–indian" (NO, not half breeds.).' With that he had to be content. Isabel sent some jewellery to Dorothy. 'Dorothy seems pleased with the necklaces,' Pound wrote, 'and wore the coral the same evening to the new Shaw play'; her gift of a cross was rather less welcome: 'Christianity and all that thereto appertains is in England so detestable that I don't suppose she will ever use what our dear friend Lower termed "the symbol of your faith"'.[43]

Christianity was rather a sore subject for Pound at this point: the couple were married at St Mary Abbots, Kensington, the church of the offending bells, but only after a brief battle between Pound and Hope Shakespear. Pound had written to him shortly after the reluctant consent was given, on hearing Hope had suggested a church service, to say he would prefer 'the simple and dignified service at the Registry'. He had nothing against Christ, he explained: 'I can not find any trace of Christ's having spoken against the greek gods. He objected, accepting the given documents, to Judaism which is the core of modern "Christianity" . . . I should no more give up my faith in Christ than I should give up my faith in Helios or my respect for the teachings of Confucius.' Pound explained that he counted himself 'much more a priest' than most clergymen, adding: 'It would be intolerable for instance to be put through a religious ceremony by an atheist like Galton, or by a cad like the bishop of London, who are fair examples of the upper sort of clergy'.[44] Considering Galton was an old family friend, this was, even by Pound's standards, very tactless, but in any case the whole drift of the argument made no sense whatsoever to Hope. He sent Pound a somewhat bewildered, unhappy but dignified reply, telling him that:

I shall in no way try to force my views upon her, & if she conscientiously believes it is not right for her to take her vows in a Church I shall say no more of it tho' it will be more distressing to me than perhaps you can understand.

I am a man of few words & keep my views on religious matters between myself & God and it pains me to have to write on such matters.[45]

In a section that he eventually deleted he pointed out that the situation had arisen not because he had gone out of his way to insist on their being married in church, but because it had never occurred to him that anything else would happen. 'Nothing was said as to her wishing to be married otherwise than in the manner in which people in her station in life are usually married', a small reminder to Pound that he was perhaps not quite of the same station.[46] Perhaps Hope crossed that out because he felt the comment too pointed. The couple gave in: one suspects Dorothy took Pound to task quite severely. There is no record of Olivia's view. Olivia loathed Christianity, and claimed either to be Buddhist or agnostic, but she believed in the conventions if not in Christ. She was probably on Hope's side.

The marital home with 'one more room than the dryad' that Pound had proposed was the flat across the corridor from the Aldingtons'. Some people might have wanted more privacy when they started married life, but not Pound. He had spent a good deal of time with the Aldingtons over the last two years or so while his access to Dorothy was limited, and it appeared he had no intention of changing his bachelor ways. Dorothy in her letters to Pound had mentioned going to see the Aldingtons several times since their marriage, and clearly liked them very much, particularly H.D., and she seems to have had no objection to being so near them. Dorothy and Pound would not spend much of their married life *à deux*. In 'Patria Mia' Pound had commented that in America, 'Our family bond is so slight that we collect another family, not bound to us by blood, but by temperament', and Pound always liked a group of friends, or even better, disciples, around.[47] He had not mentioned to the Aldingtons that he was moving in, and H.D. recalled being quite taken aback. 'It was so near,' was her startled comment.[48] One day shortly before the wedding she had noticed the door to the flat immediately opposite theirs was open, and saw Ezra inside. He told her he was looking for a place where he could fence with Yeats. At the time of Pound's marriage, the Aldingtons were out of London, having a holiday at Hindhead, and when they returned Pound and Dorothy were on their honeymoon at Stone Cottage – on which Pound spent his time working on Noh plays – so they may not have found out about their new neighbours for a while. Pound's flat had three rooms; in the largest, which was very dark, he cooked; in the smallest, lighter and memorably triangular in shape, he worked and entertained. Before he was married he had written home to his mother asking for recipes for pancakes, waffles, cream soups and various fries, and said when they came to visit they must bring an American ice-cream maker.

Mrs Langley, his landlady at Church Walk, would, he said, continue to look after him. Ford bought them some 'High Wycombe' chairs as a wedding present – perhaps in memory of the one Pound had broken at South Lodge – and May Sinclair gave them an armchair when she moved to St John's Wood shortly before the wedding, but some of his furniture Pound actually made himself. Yeats gave him money, with which he bought his most treasured item, a clavichord, made by Arnold Dolmetsch, whom Pound got to know later that year, and who had earlier made Florence Farr her psaltery. The clavichord was commissioned in October 1914 after Pound had heard Dolmetsch play his own instruments, and Dolmetsch's enthusiasm for baroque music would exercise a considerable influence on Pound in the years to come.

Before they married, Pound had written to Dorothy in late March to say with some satisfaction '"Anthologie des Imagistes" arrives from U.S.A. so *that's* all right'.[49] English publication followed in April, when it was brought out by Harold Monro, who would a few months later publish the infinitely more profitable *Georgian Poetry 1913–14*. Several of the purchasers of the English edition returned their copies of *Des Imagistes* and demanded their money back, presumably on the grounds that it was not in fact poetry. None of the contributors appear to have been at all disturbed by this. By now, artists in any medium who were attempting something 'modern' would feel they had failed if they were not greeted with some public outrage, and the imagists did get a certain amount of coverage in the press. Aldington wrote with some excitement to Pound, on his honeymoon at Stone Cottage, to say:

You have seen the reviews of the Imagistes? New Age first – malignant squelch. Herald next; working man's natural bewilderment at first being introduced to a gentleman. Morning Post says we are a 'new Via Lactea', 'this slim gracious volume' etcet. Thomas in New Weekly says we are like a marble column and that Flint is the ivy about our base. Fat Ford in the Outlook says he feels like a gargoyle in the midst of the Elgin Marbles . . . Apropos, Remy says we are 'des poétes [*sic*] assez curiex [*sic*]' and that he has 'gouté' us 'avec plaisir'.[50]

It was the first time either he or H.D. had had their poetry appear in a book, and it gave them considerable pleasure. Aldington was somewhat critical of Pound's method of 'just call[ing] on his friends', regardless of any unity of poetic approach, though Pound insisted in an interview in the *Daily News and Leader* on 18 March that all the contributors agreed in avoiding the 'cake-icing on the top of poetry', i.e. 'useless adjectives' and 'unnecessary similes'.[51] Yet when Aldington reviewed the book for the *Egoist* later in the year he very pointedly commented on the fact that the poems of five of the contributors, 'Mr Cournos, Mr Upward, Mr Hueffer, Mr Joyce and Mr Cannell', though he had no objection to them in themselves, were not, strictly speaking, 'Imagiste'.[52] Of these five, the only one who was not Pound's friend was Joyce, and he had been recommended by Pound's friend Yeats. Originally, Aldington and H.D. had both been opposed to the inclusion of Amy Lowell. They only knew her first book of poems, and the still fairly traditional poems that had appeared in *Poetry* in July 1913, and had thought them insipid and conventional, 'fluid, fruity, facile stuff', as Aldington put it.[53] One guesses they suspected Pound was only including her because of her money. When they saw her contribution, 'In the Garden', however, they agreed it was imagistic, and a good poem. The other contributors, besides Pound himself, of course, were Flint, Aldington, H.D. and William Carlos Williams. Aldington had ten poems in the collection, more than anyone else, perhaps what gave Fletcher the idea that he was the central figure; there were six by Pound, 'Δώρια', 'The Return', and the 'three and a half' Chinese poems; H.D. had five, much of her entire published *oeuvre* at that point; Flint five also, including the two that remained his best known, 'London' and 'The Swan'; Allen Upward contributed a selection of his prose poems from 'Scented Leaves from a Chinese Jar', whilst the others were represented by one poem each. In Aldington's review, he singles out H.D.'s poems as the best – 'like nicely carved marble . . . as good a specimen of Imagism as can be found. Hard, direct treatment, absolutely personal rhythm, few and expressive adjectives, no inversion, and a keen emotion presented objectively'.[54] For him, as for Pound, H.D. remained the exemplary imagist.

The various imagist contributors to the anthology provided between them most of the poems published in the *Egoist* during the first half of 1914, generally, one might note, poems that had had their first (paid) publication in *Poetry*. Aldington, H.D., Flint, Amy Lowell and William Carlos Williams (the last with a poem about some strikes in Paterson, an early attempt at the subject of his later modernist epic based on the town) all appeared. Amy Lowell's contribution, five new *vers libre* poems in the February issue, put her conversion to imagism beyond doubt. In addition, there were poems by Fletcher and D.H. Lawrence, who would both later appear in the next three imagist anthologies. Pound was still vigorously promoting the *imagiste* cause, and himself as its leader, though since his association with Lewis and the Rebel Art Centre he was beginning to see it in rather different terms. In the meantime, another journal that would publish the imagists' work was starting up in Chicago. This was the *Little Review*, edited by a young journalist, Margaret Anderson, then twenty-one, who had been working as a reviewer for Floyd Dell, now literary editor of the *Chicago Evening Post* and very supportive of the project. Once she thought of the idea, she recounts in her memoir, 'To me it was already an accomplished fact. I began announcing to everyone that I was about to publish the most interesting magazine that had ever been launched. They found me vague as to why it was going to be so interesting, nebulous as to how it was going to be published, unconcerned about the necessary money, optimistic about manuscripts. Where any sane person would have explained that, sensing the modern literary movement which was about to declare itself, a review to sponsor it was a logical necessity, I only accused them of being unimaginative because they couldn't follow my élan.'[55] Her confidence paid off; she found someone to provide funding, albeit not much, and paying contributors was an impossibility, but the journal was launched that March, and would indeed, as she suggests, help 'the modern literary movement . . . declare itself'.

III

THAT evening at the Quest Society had convinced Pound that what he
was doing in poetry had much in common with the work of Lewis,
Epstein and Gaudier in the visual arts, though it would take him a few
months to find a language to describe their joint programme. In March,
he reviewed an exhibition of their work at the Goupil Gallery in enthusiastic but unusually inarticulate terms, saying of Epstein: 'There is in
his work an austerity, a metaphysics, like that of Egypt – one doesn't
quite know how to say it', though he insists that Epstein's sculptures
are great art 'because they are sufficient to themselves'. Gaudier, he
said, was 'in a formative stage', and his carvings of animals have 'a
"snuggly", comfortable feeling, that might appeal to a child'. Gaudier,
it may be said, was not happy about these comments; by 'snuggly' Pound
was presumably trying to convey what Lewis more aptly described as
the 'soft bluntness' of Gaudier's carvings, but it was a phrase that could
be taken to be patronising. In addition, if Gaudier was undeniably still
at a formative stage, it was tactless to point it out. Pound was equally
tentative in his attempt to discuss the paintings in the exhibition,
complaining that they were even more difficult to write about, but he
offered the advice, in the light of Epstein's comparison of Lewis' pictures
with sculpture, that Cubism should be understood as 'a pattern of
solids'.[56]

Pound had only one noncommittal sentence on Lewis in that March
review, but by June he was expansive in his praise: 'Mr Wyndham Lewis
is one of the greatest masters of design yet born in the occident. Mr
Lewis has in his "Timon" gathered together his age, or at least our age,
our generation, the youth-spirit, or what you will, that moves in the
men who are now between their twenty-fifth and thirty-fifth years.'
Those boundaries included both Lewis, aged thirty-one, and himself,

twenty-eight, but by 'men', Pound does not, he explains, mean 'the man in the street'. 'The rabble and the bureaucracy,' he adds, 'have built a god in their own image and that god is Mediocrity. The great mass of mankind are mediocre . . . If a man have gathered the force of his generation or of his clan, if he has in his "Timon" expressed the sullen fury of intelligence baffled, shut in by the entrenched forces of stupidity, if he have made in "Timon" a type emotion and delivered it in lines and masses and planes, it is proper we should respect him in a way we do not respect men blaring out truisms or doing an endless embroidery of sentiment.'[57] 'Sullen fury' in the face of what he saw as the 'entrenched forces of stupidity' would be increasingly Pound's own posture.

Pound described Lewis in that article as 'a man at war', by which he meant with the forces of mediocrity, but in practice Lewis was more frequently at war with his fellow artists and intellectuals. The short association with Hulme was over. Hulme, reviewing for the *New Age* the same Goupil Gallery exhibition that Pound had written up for the *Egoist*, commented that though he found one of Lewis' drawings, *The Enemy of the Stars*, remarkable, he thought the two paintings failed to cohere: 'In Mr Lewis's work,' he wrote, 'there are always qualities of dash and decision, but it has the defects of these qualities.' He concludes that the 'only really satisfying and complete work in this [Cubist] section is that of Mr Epstein'.[58] Lewis was deeply jealous of this preference for Epstein, but possibly even more searing to his pride was the fact that Hulme had captured the affections of his ex-mistress and patron, Kate Lechmere. The two had first met when Lewis invited Hulme to the Rebel Art Centre, deliberately choosing a day when Lechmere had a luncheon engagement elsewhere. Unfortunately for Lewis it was cancelled, and Hulme and Lechmere met and were immediately attracted. They next saw each other at the Goupil Gallery private view, where Lewis had the galling experience of watching them together at the other side of the room, discussing, and he feared mocking, one of his paintings. Paul O'Keeffe suggests he was mainly afraid that Hulme would encourage Kate to install Epstein in Great Ormond Street in his place, but in spite of his liaison with Lechmere being a thing of the past, he appears also to have greatly resented Hulme's sexual success. Hulme and Lechmere became lovers, though Dollie Kibblewhite – and many of Hulme's friends – never knew. Allegedly, relations between Lewis and Hulme ended when Lewis, after a furious quarrel with Lechmere in a restaurant, rushed to Frith Street and attempted to strangle Hulme. Hulme, the story goes, took Lewis out and hung him upside down by his trouser turn-ups on the railings in Soho Square. Any friendship and co-operation came to an end.

Just before the final rift between the two, however, Lewis was able to call on Hulme to do battle with a common enemy. This was Marinetti's Futurism, to which both Lewis and Hulme were by this time highly opposed; Hulme thought it romantic mess, and Lewis denounced its art as soft, emotional and blurry. Both of them were alarmed at the celebrity status it had achieved in London. Everyone had heard of the Futurists, and in popular parlance the term was used to describe any of the current new art movements, as Pound had done in his February article on 'The New Sculpture', when he had identified with 'all rightly constituted young futurists'. Marinetti had appeared frequently in London since Dorothy had gone to hear him in 1912, and continued to cause a stir, even though he was not always taken very seriously. In December 1913 Aldington had commented on one of Marinetti's readings in the *New Freewoman*, 'London is vaguely alarmed and wondering whether it ought to laugh or not'.[59] Aldington inclined to laughter, and indeed produced a highly entertaining parody, but at that stage he was loath to reject entirely any revolutionary spirit. Monro, ecumenical as ever in his support of poetry, had published a Futurist Manifesto in *Poetry and Drama* in 1913, as well as having Marinetti to read at the Poetry Bookshop in November that year, and in May 1914 throwing a dinner for him, at which Aldington and Flint were present, though Pound was still on his honeymoon in Stone Cottage. Aldington took Monro and Marinetti after the dinner to meet Yeats, an event he described to Pound with relish:

You missed some hell by being away. Yeats read his Helen and divers things in best Dublin fashion, and Marinetti said it was 'tres beau, il déclame bien, vous voyez'. And Marinetti recited the Motor-car and yelled the siege of Adrianople, and Bill Butler bowed his bleedin ead an said in Stately manner '*Very* impressive, very interesting'. Naturellement, considering that it was 1 a.m. and that the place rocked and boiled in tourbillons of noise.[60]

In the version of this episode which appears in *Life for Life's Sake* (in which he mistakenly says Pound was present), Aldington adds that eventually Yeats had to ask Marinetti to stop as 'neighbours were knocking in protest on the floor, ceiling, and party walls'.[61] Yeats, who had declined an invitation to the dinner, may not have been best pleased.

To Aldington, Marinetti was now definitely a joke, but to Lewis he had become an arch-rival, whose position as the most *avant* of the avant-garde he was determined to usurp. When Lewis had first left the Omega Workshop, the previous autumn, though never a follower of Marinetti, he had been happy to be known as an admirer, largely because Fry was deeply opposed to him, and he and his friends organised a celebration dinner for Marinetti at the Florence restaurant, a noisy event at which the Italian had recited his poem about the siege of Adrianople at the top of his voice, accompanied, one observer said, 'with various kinds of onomatopoeic noises and crashes in free verse, while all the time a band downstairs played, "You made me love you, I didn't want to do it"'.[62] By June 1914, however, Lewis wanted to proclaim his movement's independence, and to arrogate Marinetti's place as the most talked about artist in London. (Pound, until his recent close association with Lewis, had taken little interest in Marinetti one way or the other.) The crunch came when, to Lewis' intense chagrin, one of his rebel artists, Christopher Nevinson, who had always been influenced by the Futurists, defected to the Marinetti camp. He and Marinetti published in the *Observer* for 7 June a joint 'Futurist Manifesto; Vital English Art', claiming that among the Futurist artists were Epstein, Lewis, and most of his Rebel Art Centre associates, including Etchells and Wadsworth. When Marinetti and Nevinson shared a platform at the Doré Galleries on 12 June to present their manifesto, Lewis, Hulme and about eight others went along to disrupt proceedings. According to Lewis' *Blasting and Bombardiering*, an entrancing read but not necessarily a reliable factual record, they met in a Soho restaurant. 'After a hearty meal,' he recalled, 'we shuffled bellicosely round to the Doré Gallery.'[63] Their interventions were much helped by Gaudier, who was, Lewis notes, very good at the '*parlez-vous*', quite naturally, being French, and who argued vociferously with Marinetti. Until now Lewis and his group had generally been described as the English Cubists, but during the evening it was Nevinson who mentioned in public for the first time the joint name that would designate the literary and artistic movements that Pound had recently described separately as 'Imagisme and Cubism'. They would now both be covered by the name of Vorticism.

On 13 June, the day after the Marinetti/Nevinson event, a report in the *Manchester Guardian* mentioned the 'new Seceders from the Marinetti group, Messrs. Wyndham Lewis and Co., who now call themselves the Vorticists'; on the same day it was announced in the *Spectator* that *Blast* would contain a Manifesto for Vorticism, though the public had to wait until the periodical appeared for any explanation of what that term might mean.[64] *Blast*, now with the subtitle, *A Review of the Great English Vortex*, finally came out on 2 July, appropriately a day of violent thunderstorms, much to Pound and Lewis' delight. As Stock points out, the subtitle had not appeared in the advertisement for the magazine in the *Egoist* in April (though it did challengingly proclaim 'End of the Christian Era'); it had earlier been described simply as a 'Discussion of Cubism, Futurism, Imagisme and All Vital Forces of Modern Art'.[65] *Blast* carried the date of 20 June, its publication having been delayed because the publisher, John Lane, decided at the last minute that three lines in a poem by Pound must be deleted (the word 'testicles' appeared in one, and the other two contained a distinctly unerotic reference to orgasm). The two women members of Lewis' Rebel Art Centre, Helen Saunders and Jessica Dismorr, were given the job of blacking out the lines before publication was allowed, though as in fact they could still be read, it only served to draw attention to them, much to Lewis' pleasure.

Pound, whose marketing skills were as sharp as ever, had of course produced the new name, which allowed Lewis to proclaim himself the leader of an entirely separate school from either Marinetti's Futurism or Picasso's Cubism. As Richard Cork points out, some people have found it an oddly inappropriate name for the kind of art the Vorticists produced: 'the visual image of a vortex, bound up as it is with the curvilinear and gyrating rings of a whirlpool, flatly contradicts the rigid, angular, diagonally orientated language with which the movement is associated'.[66] Timothy Materer, for one, however, insists that the vortex motif and spiral forms appear in Lewis' paintings from 1912, and it is certainly true that the idea of the vortex worked on many levels for Pound. As well as the art itself, the image suggests the atmosphere out of which the art came, the turbulent energies of the metropolis, which Pound had described as 'the Vortex' in a letter to Williams the previous December.[67] After three months in Stone Cottage out of the metropolitan 'whirl', as he himself put it, Pound was no doubt very conscious on his return of the surging vitality of artistic production in the capital. But Pound had earlier thought of a vortex in more personal terms, as the building up of energy that could sweep him into a burst of creativity. He had explained this to Dorothy the previous September, when they had had a quarrel over her liking for embroidery, which Pound always figuratively condemned in poetry, and which even in a literal form he despised. It would, he told her, never generate the right sort of energy for her painting:

Energy depends on ones ability to make a vortex – genius *même*. Chess, Tennis, fencing all help. They demand complete attention . . . in chess, reason; in tennis, physics, in fencing, to a great extent psychology, i.e. in thinking the other mans thought & muscular coordination, The foils are perhaps the most concentrative – you probably need to be 'more awake', more versatile in shifting from one apprehension to another . . . Anything that demands only partial attention is useless for developing a vortex.[68]

One other source of the idea, if not the term, may have been Allen Upward, who, as several critics have pointed out, denied the distinction between force and matter and said the fundamental essence of the universe consisted of whirling energies.[69] Yet for Pound, just as there was a secret doctrine of the image, there was a mystical dimension to Vorticism. He had used the word 'vortex' as early as in *A Lume Spento* to suggest the fundamental flowing energies of the universe, in a sonnet entitled 'Plotinus'. As the title suggests, the image came out of Pound's Neoplatonist interests, but two notes on the original typescript link the idea to both yogic and Hindu sources. Pound's mysticism was a typical turn-of the-century fusion of multiple traditions; though the traditions he was interested in changed over time, both his religious and his artistic creed always depended on a sense of rushing energies, the artist at one with what he had called in 1912 the 'fluid force' of the 'germinal' or 'vital universe'.[70] That element would not be part of Lewis' view of Vorticism; he would later say, to the indignation of his fellow-artists, in a brief statement, bespattered with commas, so it sounds like a sharp volley of shots, 'Vorticism, in fact, was what I, personally, did, and said, at a certain period.'[71]

Blast, as reviewers rapidly pointed out, owed much to the Futurists, including its bold black typography and explosive style. Its format was unusually large for a periodical – twelve and a half by nine and a half inches – partly no doubt for effect, but probably mainly for the very practical reason that the many reproductions of Vorticist drawings would have lost too much detail on a smaller page.[72] Lewis would say later that in shape it looked rather like a telephone directory. '*BLAST*' was written in 'huge block capitals', as Goldring described them, diagonally across each cover, variously described in the numerous reviews as 'purple', 'chill flannelette pink', 'cerise' and, in the *Little Review*, as 'something between magenta and lavender, about the colour of a sick headache'.[73] Goldring himself called it 'puce'. Its techniques of visual presentation were closer to contemporary newspaper headlines and advertisements than to most intellectual journals, indeed rather bolder than most of the comparatively sober advertisements of 1914; it strikingly prefigured the experimental typography of the Russian Futurists.

Blast borrowed an idea from Apollinaire, who had published a 'Futurist Anti-Tradition' manifesto in 1913 with lists entitled respectively *merde à* and *rose à* (intriguingly, the only English figure in the *rose* category was Roger Fry). This format had been used rather unimaginatively by Marinetti and Nevinson in their 'Vital English Art' manifesto as 'Against' and 'We Want', but it appeared in *Blast* as lists of things to Bless or Blast.[74] These had been compiled at a tea party for all interested supporters, described by Goldring in *South Lodge*, over which Lewis and Pound presided and at which Jessica Dismorr was instructed to make the tea; luckily she was only a rebel artist, not a rebellious feminist, so she complied. The items are random and frequently inexplicable; even though W.C. Wees has studiously identified most of them, it is by no means clear why they are there.[75] The inclusion of the vicar of St Mary's – 'Rev. Pennyfeathers (Bells)' – among the blasted must have come from Pound. Among the blessed was 'Bridget', i.e. Brigit Patmore; Aldington would later tell her that he had suggested her. The blasted included Tagore, while among the blessed was Allen Upward's friend and fellow Chinese enthusiast Cranmer Byng, indicating firmly Pound's switching of sympathy from the subcontinent to the Far East.

Goldring points out how many of the blessed were music-hall artists; also blessed were four boxers, three aviators and one cricketer (the brilliant bowler, George Hirst, a Yorkshire man and a professional – the dashing amateur C.B. Fry was among the blasted).[76] The idea that this branch of the modernist avant-garde ignored popular culture is far from the truth. Much of the periodical was made up of pieces the length of newspaper articles, not journal-length pieces at all. Indeed, as W.C. Wees points out, like Marinetti's Futurists, this apparently elitist avant-garde movement had a symbiotic relationship with the mass-market press, which covered their escapades with strong disapproval. The way the avant-garde functioned was in fact, he suggests, dictated by the newspaper's desire for speed of turnover and 'shock value', and its demands for leaders, followers, splits, defections, then new leaders, new followers and yet more splits. 'The metaphorical implications of "avant-garde",' Wees says, 'turned art movements into battles, advances and retreats, victories and defeats', and artists 'were expected to "fight for" some ism that could be reduced to a simple common denominator like the "cube" or the "Vortex" . . . The popular press helped create the public image of the avant-garde movement as we know it today (no such image existed until there *was* a popular press) . . . The Futurists, who were most adept at exploiting the mass media of the day, paved the way for the Vorticists, who got instant publicity by publicly attacking Futurism. Under headlines like "FUTURIST SQUABBLES", "THE FUTURIST SPLIT", "REBELS IN ART," and, simply, "VORTICISM," the Vorticists' emergence on the avant-garde scene was suitably announced to the public.'[77] James Joyce sent Pound a cutting from an Italian newspaper, in which an article on them appeared entitled 'I VORTICISTI SORPASSANO IN AUDACIA I FUTURISTI', so they were achieving, if not global media coverage, at least international.[78] Lewis himself acknowledged that *Blast*'s 'portentous dimensions and violent tint did more than would a score of exhibitions to make the public feel that something was happening'.[79] If Pound's imagism could be described as both pro- and anti-avant-garde at one and the same time, Vorticism was surely both populist and anti-populist.

The contents of *Blast* were as varied and lively as its typefaces. Ford published an early section of *The Good Soldier*; Rebecca West contributed a brilliant short story, 'Indissoluble Matrimony', which the *English Review* had refused to publish. Wadsworth provided a review and extracts from the English translation of Kandinsky's *Concerning the Spiritual in Art*, emphasising Kandinsky's belief that colour and form have, and can convey, direct emotional significance, an idea with which Pound was very taken, realising immediately the links with his own poetic theories. Lewis wrote the first two manifestos, a series of short pieces with the overall title of 'Vortices and Notes', an appreciation of his friend Spencer Gore, who had died that March, and an extraordinary piece, *The Enemy of the Stars*, which announced itself as a play, but which in fact is more like something between a story, a film script and a long imagist poem; Paul Edwards suggests it is an Expressionist 'elemental psychodrama'.[80] The 'play' is full of violence, bleakness and fear, and the setting grim, with lines such as 'The stars shone madly on the archaic blank wilderness of the universe, machines of prey', and 'The night plunged gleaming nervous arms down into the wood, to wrench it up by the roots.'[81] Its atmosphere fitted well with the numerous reproductions of Vorticist paintings and drawings, including Lewis' own drawing with the same name as the quasi-play, *Enemy of the Stars*, which Hulme had grudgingly admired in his piece on the Goupil Gallery. As many of these paintings later disappeared, *Blast* remains an important record of the movement. Indeed, Wees suggested that *Blast* itself should be considered the most successful work of art that the movement produced. Pound, as well as a number of poems, contributed his own manifesto, in which he cited H.D.'s 'Oread', published in the *Egoist* that February, as a touchstone of Vorticist poetry:

> Whirl up sea –
> Whirl your pointed pines,
> Splash your great pines
> On our rocks,
> Hurl your green over us,
> Cover us with your pools of fir.[82]

Lawrence Rainey has argued that *Blast* did not cause anything like the stir Pound had predicted, but if the suaver reviewers like A.R. Orage and J.C. Squire signalled their disapproval by affecting to yawn over its assault on the conventions, while Aldington excitedly exaggerated its pariah status in claiming there was 'a dismal howl of protest' from reviewers, it did eventually produce enemies for Pound and Lewis.[83]

Aldington himself hailed the magazine in a brief, exuberant announcement in the *Egoist* on 1 July:

There is no time for detailed criticism, but from a hasty glance through the manifestoes and some of the contributions I can declare that this is the most amazing, energised, stimulating production that I have ever seen. Death to the English Review! Death to the 'Times'! Death warrant of tedious amorphous hangers-on from past eras! (I have caught the manner!)[84]

Aldington would later qualify his enthusiasm, but in its violent attack on the status quo *Blast* was in tune with the times. Among the blessed are figures from the three groups that George Dangerfield argues were already in the process of destroying the British Liberal establishment before the war began: the Ulster rebels, the suffragettes and the trade unionists. As Ulster Unionists were generally supported by those to the right of the Liberal Party, and the trade unions by those to its left, whilst the suffragettes had enemies everywhere, *Blast*'s politics were in maverick opposition to the liberal mainstream, and in general support of the widespread social – and, in the case of Ulster, potentially military

Harriet Monroe in Chinese dress with a citation for
'further[ing] the cause of modern poetry'. *Vanity Fair*,
New York, August 1920. Monroe had visited China in
1911 just before founding *Poetry: A Magazine of Verse*,
and like Pound, she was a great admirer of Chinese poetry

Alice Corbin Henderson, a poet herself and Monroe's associate editor at *Poetry*
in the years when Pound was foreign correspondent. Pound later said (most unfairly)
she was the 'only means of getting an idea into dear ole 'Arriet's hickory block'

A CORNER FOR POETS, PAST AND PRESENT.

Mr. Harold Monro, the former editor of the " Poetry Review," has embarked upon a new enterprise, which should bring hope to the heart
of the minor poet. He has taken an eighteenth century house near Theobald's Road and converted it into a bookshop for the sale of the verses
of all poets. Poems popular and unpopular will be found on the shelves of the shop, which, it is hoped, will encourage the young versifier. The
picture on the right shows a purchaser sampling the wares in the poetry shop, and on the left a view of the exterior is given.

Publicity for Harold Monro's Poetry Bookshop in Devonshire Street, opened in 1913.
The model for the visiting poet may have been Arundel del Re, Monro's young Italian
assistant, who deeply offended Pound by his criticisms of his Cavalcanti translations

The diminutive but intrepid Dora Marsden, in one of her frequent brushes with the police during her suffragette years

Ezra Pound in October 1913, in his dressing gown at 10 Church Walk, photographed by Alvin Langdon Coburn, with whom he later developed the 'Vortograph'

The photo to commemorate the Peacock Dinner, given to honour Wilfrid Scawen Blunt at his country house, Newbuildings, in Sussex in January 1914. From left to right: Victor Plarr, Thomas Sturge Moore, W.B. Yeats, Blunt, Ezra Pound, Richard Aldington and F.S. Flint

Wyndham Lewis, in 1914, when he founded the Rebel Art Centre and launched *Blast*, 'the most "advanced" of the painters', Pound said, and 'very clever and thoroughly enigmatic'

Horace Brodzky's cartoon 'The Lewis-Brzeska-Pound Troupe. Blasting their own trumpets before the wall of Jericho', accompanying Aldington's review of *Blast* in the *Egoist* in July 1914

Blast, which appeared on 2 July 1914, its cover being described variously as 'purple', 'chill flannelette pink', 'cerise' and 'puce'

Page 6 of *Blast*, denouncing the entire Victorian era

6

BLAST

years **1837** to **1900**

Curse abysmal inexcusable middle-clas (also Aristocracy and Proletariat).

BLAST

pasty shadow cast by gigantic **Boehm**
(imagined at introduction of **BOURGEOIS VICTORIA VISTAS).**

WRING THE NECK OF all sick inventions born that progressive white wake.

BLAST their weeping whiskers—hirsute
RHETORIC of EUNUCH and STYLIST—
**SENTIMENTAL HYGIENICS
ROUSSEAUISMS** (wild Nature crank
**FRATERNIZING WITH MONKEY
DIABOLICS**—raptures and roses
of the erotic bookshelve
culminating in
**PURGATORY OF
PUTNEY.**

13

Self-portrait by Henri Gaudier-Brzeska, the young sculptor of whom Pound said,
'I like him very much. He is the only person with whom I can be really "Altaforte"'

The advertisement for Amy Lowell's second volume
of poetry that enraged Pound so much

T.S. Eliot with an admiring sister in 1910. Pound met him in 1914

Catholic Anthology 1914-1915, edited by Pound, cover designed by Dorothy;
Pound said that his chief pleasure in publishing the anthology was to have
Eliot's poems appear in a book for the first time

Blast war number, with Lewis's sombre black on off-white cover, a Vorticist depiction of soldiers and guns

T.E. Hulme in 1914

D.H. Lawrence in 1915, when he was living near the Aldingtons in Hampstead

Amy Lowell, whom Margaret Anderson of the *Little Review* described as 'among the most charming people I have known', though she also noted that Lowell's nose was 'like a Roman emperor's and her manner somewhat more masterful'. This photo is from 1916, the year of the second of the post-Pound anthologies of imagist poetry

John Gould Fletcher (left) with the ex-Philadelphian art critic and novelist John Cournos (right), whom Fletcher met in 1917

Wyndham Lewis's war painting *Officers and Signallers*, one of his moving depictions
of the 'hideous desert known as "the Line" in Flanders and France'

H.D. during the war years

Richard Aldington in army uniform

Ezra Pound, drawn by Lewis in 1920

– insurrection that faced the authorities in 1914. Between January and July there were 937 strikes, and over the summer miners, railwaymen and port workers were preparing for a general strike, though the war intervened before their plans materialised.[85] The suffragettes were increasingly militant, and their support was growing; the WSPU's income had risen from £2,700 in 1907 to £36,500 in 1914, and *Votes for Women* sold 30,000 copies an issue.[86] In the first seven months of 1914, the suffragettes set no fewer than 107 buildings on fire, and completely destroyed several churches. They attacked a number of works of art, including the Rokeby *Venus*, slashed that March in the National Gallery by one suffragette; another slashed Sargent's portrait of Henry James. Bombings and window-smashing went on unabated. Hunger strikes continued in prison, and a débutante shocked the court by demanding loudly that the King put an end to force-feeding. Pound, under the pseudonym Bastien von Helmholtz, contributed an article entitled 'Suffragettes' to the *Egoist*, a piece which dismissed the vote as a useless shadow, though one to which the suffragettes, if they wanted it, had a perfect right. 'As for their actions of late,' he adds, 'it is rot to say "we deplore violence"; we all like violence so long as they don't smash our own windows. We all like to see big headlines. We like the papers to have racy bits of news in 'em. We like to read of bombs and explosions. The undergraduate in all of us survives up to that extent – unless we have property and interests in danger.'[87] He did, as it happened, think they went too far in attacking Sargent's portrait of his hero James, and when *Blast* expressed admiration for the suffragettes, in particularly large type, promising to make them a present of their votes, it asked them to leave works of art alone, because 'you might some day destroy a good picture by accident'.[88] Suffragettes had already attacked two works in the Doré Galleries, where the Vorticists frequently exhibited, so their unease was understandable. Pound, however, was very aware of the spiritual affinities of Vorticism and the suffragettes. When he had written to tell his mother that *Blast* was coming out ('delicate, sensitive work' is how he described it), he added 'Suffragetttes are blowing up most everything else'.[89] The most significant violent act of the summer, however, happened on the continent. On 28 June, while Dismorr and Saunders were busy blocking out the word 'testicles' from Lewis' weapon of artistic mass destruction, the Archduke Franz Ferdinand, heir to the Austro-Hungarian Empire, was assassinated in Sarajevo.

None of the Vorticists or their associates, any more than most of their fellow-citizens, appears to have worried about that distant death. Nor did they concern themselves with the political difficulties of those who ran the country. 'The *Male* mind,' Pound had written in that article, 'does not want to be bothered with Asquith or Wright or their kind. Politics is unfit for men, it may be good enough for women, we doubt it. The male mind does not want a state run by women, or "old women".'[90] Much of *Blast* was the creation of Lewis, and reflected his concerns rather than Pound's, but in this aim they were agreed. *Blast* was undoubtedly projecting itself as a product of what Pound calls 'the *Male* mind', in its blunt and aggressive typography, its harsh angular art, and the violent militarism of its language. The Vorticists were, they proclaimed, 'Primitive Mercenaries in the Modern World' (though just exactly who was paying them?) and would 'fight first on one side and then on the other' to purge England of its manifold blemishes. These included luxury, sport, 'the idée fixe of Class, producing the most intense snobbery in the world', the latter aim admirable enough, though elsewhere snobbery is, perhaps predictably, defined as the 'disease of femininity'. Though England was thoroughly blasted on many counts, Lewis was putting Vorticism forward as a specifically English, northern avant-garde movement, associated with the male domain of industry. He dismissed the Futurists' romantic cult of the machine, but claimed that 'our industries, and the Will that determined, face to face with its needs, the direction of the modern world, has reared up steel trees where the green ones were lacking . . . and found wilder intricacies than those of Nature'. The English, whose country was the home of the industrial revolution, are surrounded by factories and machines, which 'inspire them more forcibly and directly. They are the inventors of this bareness and harshness, and should be the great enemies of Romance'.[91] Paul O'Keeffe has pointed out that a curious motif that appeared several times in the pages of *Blast*, a cone on a vertical axis, was adapted from a coastguard's signal for a gale coming from the north; as he puts it, 'a blast from the north. It was the English avant-garde's answer to the Futurist invasion of London from the Latin south.'[92]

THE day after *Blast* appeared, the London *Standard* announced a very different invasion: the arrival of Amy Lowell at the Berkeley Hotel. Great Britain's declaration of war on Germany would come only a month and a day later, though Lowell had no intimation on her arrival of that imminent cataclysm. In the wake of the Archduke's assassination, which had happened while Amy was still at sea, Austria-Hungary had immediately begun to plan reprisals against Serbia; its close ally, Germany, had the task of making sure that Russia did not mobilise in Serbia's defence, and that Russia's ally, France, remained neutral. Russia's third ally, Britain, was not thought likely to take much interest. Things would not work out to plan, but in the meantime Kaiser Wilhelm left for his annual cruise on 6 July; on the 23rd, Lloyd George assured the House that relations with Germany were at their best for years. The London that greeted Amy was unconcerned. This year she was accompanied by Ada Russell, a maid, and her maroon Pierce-Arrow motor car with a maroon-liveried chauffeur to match. She arrived with letters of introduction to, among others, Thomas Hardy and Mrs Havelock Ellis. The Russian Ballet was back in London, and she and Ada went several times with great excitement; Lowell, like Fletcher – and perhaps influenced by him – immediately decided that *The Rite of Spring* was a masterpiece. Her main impulse in coming was, however, to meet up again with Pound and reconnect with the imagist movement. She arrived with much-improved credentials as an imagist poet. As well as the five *vers libre* poems that had appeared in the *Egoist* in February, she had had another set of eight poems in the April *Poetry*, only one of which was in a traditional metre, and seven more *vers libre* would appear in the August *Egoist*. Her second collection was due out with Macmillan in the USA in September, and a few days after she arrived they agreed to bring out an English edition. Pound had been in touch with her earlier in the year; having given her advice on her poetry, he now turned his attention to her money, urging her to take over the *Egoist*, whose American correspondent she appears to have suggested earlier she would like to become. Pound gave her a quite erroneously rosy picture of its finances – he may well have honestly believed it was doing better than it was – and urged her to think of paying contributors and selling in America, possibly installing himself and Ford as paid staff. 'My flair,' he added, 'is also at the service of anybody. That may be a drawback.'[93]

That was in mid-March, but a week later he had written to say that the *Egoist* had had an anonymous donation of £250 (it was of course from Harriet Shaw Weaver) and so was not available for takeover. Dora Marsden, who disliked the patrician, capitalist Lowell intensely, was most relieved. When she had heard of Pound's negotiations, she wrote to Weaver to say she feared that '*The Egoist* spark of intelligence' would 'be extinguished under Miss Lowell's respectable bulk'.[94] It was at that point that she had begged Weaver to take over the editorship, while she herself would remain as a contributing editor, still writing her 'Views and Comment' and other articles. Pound, however, now suggested Lowell set up a quarterly, to be staffed by himself, Ford, Joyce, Lawrence and Flint on, as he put it 'this side', and by herself and anyone she liked on the other.[95] (Had Pound consulted any of his suggested collaborators? Unlikely, but the mention of Flint shows he still thought highly of him.) Amy did not bite, though she did send him a wedding present; how large is not recorded. According to a letter she wrote to Monroe that September, Pound came to see her as soon as she arrived in London, wanting her to take over and guarantee the *Mercure de France* with himself as a salaried editor. Amy did not reject the idea out of hand, but having worked out the minimum cost as $5,000 a year, decided she could not afford it. Pound did not believe her, and it must be true that, had she chosen to, she could have found the money – fewer sheep-dogs, fewer cigars, fewer dinner parties, fewer private theatricals, staying somewhere less grand than the suite at the Berkeley, a smaller car, only one chauffeur – there were all kinds of minor economies she could have made which would certainly have released the necessary sum, but such a notion was inconceivable to her. She felt Pound exaggerated her wealth: 'Like many people of no income,' she said to Harriet, 'Ezra does not know the difference between thousands and millions, and thinks that anyone who knows where to look for next week's dinners, is a millionaire, and therefore lost his temper with me completely, although he never told me why, and he accused me of being unwilling to give money towards art.'[96]

Amy was not used to people losing their temper with her, and she felt maligned by Pound's accusation, but for now relations continued in a reasonably civil fashion. Pound may have been cross that she would not fall in with his plans, but he still found her, as he told Alice Corbin Henderson some years later, a 'charmer', and in any case he may have hoped there might be other ways of encouraging her to spend the Lowell fortune on his projects.[97] What happened next is more in doubt. There were two dinners in mid-July, and both became the stuff of legend; although there are multiple accounts of these dinners, they by no means agree, and what actually went on is to a certain extent a matter of conjecture. Peter Brooker has written a brilliant summary of the confusingly varied versions of these dinners, pointing out that sometimes not only do names of guests and topics of conversation differ strikingly, but even the venue shifts.[98] One thing one can be sure of, in fact, is that these two dinners were at the very smart Dieudonné restaurant; one can also be sure that the first dinner, on 15 July, for which guests paid 10s. 6d. (though some versions reduce the price to ten shillings) was to celebrate the publication of *Blast*, and the second, two days later, at which Amy was hostess, was to celebrate *Des Imagistes*. But it was not true, as has been alleged, that Amy gave her dinner because she was mocked at the first; she might have been mocked on that occasion, but she had started planning the second dinner before the first took place, and Pound had drafted in Richard Aldington to help her with the organisation.

Pound himself complained to his parents that he had been left to do all the work setting up the *Blast* dinner as Lewis had gone off to Paris, which perhaps explains some of the eccentricities of the guest list, which included not only Amy and Ada, but also Arthur Symons, recovered somewhat from his mental breakdown and occasionally visiting London. Gaudier-Brzeska came, giving Pound a small carving in lieu of his 10s. 6d.; Wyndham Lewis as editor was of course there, as was Kate Lechmere, whose money had partially supported *Blast* (the rest came from Lewis' mother), and an American novelist, Mary Borden Turner, with whom Lewis was having an affair. Presumably some of the other contributors to *Blast*, or those who signed the manifesto, attended; Ford appears to have been there, though apparently neither of the Aldingtons, nor Flint. In William Roberts' painting entitled *The Vorticists at the Tour Eiffel: Spring 1915*, which depicts what must have been a dinner for *Blast*'s second and last number, which appeared in June 1915 (although the copy of *Blast* that appears in the painting is the first), the guests depicted – in addition to Pound and Lewis, there is Roberts himself, Cuthbert Hamilton, Frederick Etchells, Edward Wadsworth, Jessica Dismorr and Helen Saunders – were all members of or associated with the Rebel Art Centre and are quite likely to have been at the first dinner at the Dieudonné.

It has generally been assumed that Amy Lowell was immediately horrified by Vorticism; certainly before she returned to the States she would speak critically of it and of *Blast* to Harriet Monroe, but not till later that month, and much had happened by then. Lowell, with her admiration for imagism, for contemporary French music and poetry, and even for the controversial *Rite of Spring*, took readily to certain aspects of the avant-garde. She would later refuse to see any good in either Eliot or Joyce, but that was after the rift with Pound and may well have been because they were his protégés; nor did she care for Gertrude Stein, but perhaps they were too alike, as her biographer Jean Gould has suggested – born in the same month, large, imperious and charismatic – and she also drew the line at certain writers she thought too violent or too crude. Possibly she thought from the start that this latest movement came into this category. But there is no evidence. Fletcher had already taken against Lewis, but not so much on artistic grounds as because he resented the way that Lewis, when Pound introduced him, had treated him as a disciple of Pound's who could be immediately commandeered for the Rebel Art Centre. On the other hand, Fletcher admired Epstein and very much liked Gaudier, whom he memorably described as 'looking like a combination of a faun and medieval Christ' – as he would have known, Gaudier was described by his friends as the 'savage messiah' because of his love of what was then thought of as 'primitive art'.[99] But Lowell was always ready to give anything new a go. According to Foster Damon she visited Gaudier in his studio under the railway arch, and had a 'very jolly picnic luncheon' with her fellow-contributor to *Des Imagistes*, Allen Upward, whose views on conventional religion probably accorded well with her own.[100]

On the day of the Vorticist dinner, Aldington's full review of *Blast* appeared in the *Egoist*. Aldington had been, as he puts it, one of those who 'gleefully' put their names to *Blast*'s manifestos, though, perhaps significantly, neither H.D. nor Flint had done so, and his review was, as W.C. Wees points out, the most positive the magazine received. Yet all the same, in it the signs of a crack between Pound and his fellow-imagists begin to appear. Aldington began by lambasting the generality of English fiction and poetry before welcoming *Blast* as a periodical 'designed to be the organ for new, vigorous art in England'. 'This purely English art', he says, is 'naturally . . . energetic, tremendously energetic, but with frequent British grins, and rather religious'. He praises Lewis's 'Enemy of the Stars', which he says 'stirs one up like a red-hot poker'; he likes its 'sudden clear *images* – flashes of lightning suddenly displaying forms above the dark abysmal conflict . . . It seems to me that this hard telegraphic language expresses pretty well one side of our modern life . . . when we want to get to the crux of the matter, the intensity of emotion, as quickly as possible, the telegraphic method seems to me to have very serious recommendations . . . Mr Lewis' play solves it in one way; I think the best of the Imagiste poems do so, too.' Gaudier comes in for some affectionate though teasing praise:

Mr Gaudier Brzeska is really a wild, unkempt barbarian, with a love of form and a very clear knowledge of the comparative history of sculpture. He is the sort of person who would dye his statues in the gore of goats if he thought it would give them a more virile appearance . . . Fortunately . . . his worst crimes consist in the abuse of all Greek sculpture whatsoever, and of everything which is not tremendously virile and cannibalistic and geometric . . . He is perhaps the most promising artist we have. If he ever becomes civilised he will lick creation.

Aldington's appreciation of this Vorticist art, however, does not, he adds, 'in the least spoil [his] old literary love for such terribly over-suave, over-sweet, over-graceful productions such as Tanagra statuettes and Japanese prints', and he thinks the 'one danger of the thing' is the 'religious part': 'Some people like religion; I don't. And it seems to me that the profound intellectuality, the love of abstract design, of abstract colour, the serious revolt against the Renaissance and all sensuousness – all of which I agree is perfectly and truthfully English – gives to this movement something that I can only call religious.' What he sees there – and this is, I think, perceptive – is a puritanism lurking underneath Hulme and Lewis' anti-pathos; it is present in Pound as well, Aldington points out, in a fairly damning dismissal of the poems Pound published here:

As the uncleanness of his language increases to an almost laughable point the moral sentiment of his writing becomes more and more marked . . . It is not my business to abuse Mr Pound – he gets enough of it from other people – and I shall probably be called all kinds of sad names if I say that his contributions to 'Blast' are quite unworthy of their author . . . Mr Pound cannot write satire. Mr Pound is one of the gentlest, most modest, bashful, kind creatures who ever walked this earth; so I cannot help thinking that all this enormous arrogance and petulance and fierceness are a pose. And it is a wearisome pose.[101]

This is of course tongue in cheek: modest and bashful are risible epithets to apply to Pound. The schoolboy rudeness of the poems can be weari-some, but whether it is precisely a pose is more doubtful: Hugh Kenner sees 'Salutation the Third', for example, as a failed attempt to emulate Lewis' bitingly satiric tone, likening it to the 'impotent vituperation' of Pound's wartime broadcasts; one might also compare it with the passages of paranoid fury in the *Cantos*.[102] Pound has assumed yet another persona; like his troubadours, this persona is unsuccessful yet undefeated, but instead of Cino or Marvoil's cheery insouciance, the speaker is bitter, contemptuous, resentful and, unusually at this stage, but as would regu-larly be the case in those later instances, anti-Semitic. In 'Salutation the Third' Pound wishes death on a hostile reviewer, whom he describes as 'You slut-bellied obstructionist,/You sworn foe to free speech and good letters,/You fungus, you continuous gangrene'. He accuses such people of driving artists to madness or death, and insists 'I will not go mad to please you./I will not FLATTER you with an early death./OH, NO! I will stick it out,/I will feel your hates wriggling about my feet,/And I will laugh at you and mock you.'[103] David Trotter in his book, *Paranoid Modernism*, reminds us that, according to Freud, paranoia springs from repressed desire – in Freud's view repressed homosexual desire. Trotter quotes Freud's summing up of the psychic mechanism involved: '"*I* (a man) *love him* (a man)" becomes "I do not *love* him – I *hate* him", which in turn becomes by projection, "I do not *love* him, I *hate* him, because he persecutes me"'. 'By this account,' Trotter adds, 'the paranoiac attrib-utes the hatred he has unconsciously made of his love to someone else.'[104] I think in Pound's case this psychic pattern is suggestive, though I would argue that what is repressed is not homosexual desire, but the desire for success and fame. Pound desperately craved public success, as earlier he had to some extent acknowledged, but now he was repressing that insuf-ficiently satisfied craving, masking it by his proclaimed belief in the serious artist inevitably unappreciated by the vulgar *canaille*. At least persecution would show some interest, and Pound – like Lewis – is courting persecution here; but I think Kenner is right to suggest that while paranoia honed Lewis' art, it caused Pound's to disintegrate. These *Blast* poems mark a new and disturbing strand in Pound's work, and one can sympathise with Aldington's alarm. Whether or not he was 'called all kinds of sad names' by Pound as a result of these comments, they cannot have gone down well. Lewis, on the other hand, must have liked the review; a copy of that issue of the *Egoist* was found by Patricia Hutchins in his empty flat after his death.

Whatever the variations in detail, most accounts suggest that the atmosphere at the Vorticists' dinner was as spiky as their paintings. Lewis quarrelled with Mary Borden Turner, and Foster Damon reports that Lowell had a disagreement with Ford over 'literary principles', something Ford himself alleges in an account he gave in 1919, though one which appears to scramble the two dinner parties, while the time and place he mentions fits neither.[105] He describes being at a dinner hosted by a woman, a 'Neutral', who was a 'monstrously fat, monstrously monied, disagreeably intelligent coward' – coward, the suggestion is, because she wanted to get away from the war, which, at the time of the Dieudonné dinners, was for most people still unimaginable.[106] When rebuked by Flint for such a cruel description, Ford pleaded that he had written that under the effects of shell-shock; he claimed he had been thinking of someone quite different, certainly not Lowell, about whom he would never have said such things. Even in the unlikely case of that being true, his words could be an unconsciously accurate account of his instinctive feelings towards her. For both Pound and Ford, creativity in a beautiful and sexually attractive woman was permissible, but not in a plain, fat one. Hunt, H.D. and Dorothy passed the test; Amy did not. Ford was not in a strong position to accuse other people of being overweight, but in his and Pound's view, 'Fat Ford', as Pound and Aldington called him, could be both stout and a poet; Amy, as a woman, had to endure the humiliation of the sobriquet 'hippopoetess', as Pound liked to call her.[107] What is intriguing in Ford's description is his comment that she was 'disagreeably intelligent'. Amy was indeed very sharp, and it sounds as if she perhaps worsted him in their dispute, if they had one.

Leaving aside Ford's malign account, whichever dinner it refers to – or rather whichever it embroiders – the two main versions we have of the dinner hosted by Lowell are from Fletcher and Cournos. Written over twenty years after the event, they both suggest it was less than a happy occasion for Amy. Fletcher, who took along his copy of *Des Imagistes* and asked all the diners to sign it, then keeping it for the rest of his life, can probably be relied upon for an accurate guest list. Present were, he said, in addition to their hostess and Ada Russell,

Pound and Dorothy, Ford and Violet Hunt, himself, the Aldingtons, Allen Upward, John Cournos, Flint and Gaudier. (Jean Gould says Amy 'could not abide' Gaudier, but gives no evidence, and there is simply no reason why she should have invited him if she disliked him.)[108] According to Fletcher, along with the coffee there was a series of speeches, mainly about the impossibility of defining imagism, and there was an argument between Aldington and Gaudier about the value of Hellenic sculpture – Pound referred later to their 'perpetual, acrimonious, and fundamentally amical dispute as to whether Greek art and civilization were worthy of serious consideration'.[109] Pound meanwhile had left the room, and returned with a tin bathtub on his head, deposited it on the floor and then announced that there was to be a new school, 'no longer called the "imagiste" but the "nageiste" school', and the bathtub would be its symbol. The school had been inaugurated by Miss Lowell with her poem 'In the Garden', whose last line Pound quoted, 'Night, and the water, and you in your whiteness bathing'. Here, Fletcher says, everybody laughed; Amy took it all good-naturedly, and the 'evening ended in a general display of high spirits, a great deal of it at Ezra's own expense . . . Ezra's squib had fizzled out, after all. Every one felt as I did, that we now owed homage to the gallant spirit of this woman who had brought us together, and who maintained her position with unruffled dignity under the most difficult circumstances.'[110]

Cournos' account is very different; he loathed Amy, perhaps because she represented the wealthy American elite who, Cournos felt sure, despised poor immigrants like himself, though in actual fact she was very impressed by his Russian credentials. There was, he says, at the dinner 'an undercurrent of hostility, and if not hostility, then condescension towards the hostess'. In his version, only Allen Upward makes a speech, there is no bathtub, but Upward took 'as his text' that same poem, and 'pictured the poet bathing in the moonlight, and he did so in such a way as to perturb and vex her puritanic soul'. Again, everyone laughs, but Cournos says he could not help feeling sorry for her as 'the butt of the excruciatingly witty if cruel jest'.[111]

Clearly the subject-matter of Amy's poem was evoked by someone, and the 'nageiste' school does sound very like Pound; Fletcher was not strong on jokes, and it seems unlikely he could have invented it. Whether Pound actually found a tin bathtub is more open to doubt; Damon records him juggling with some waiters' trays. But the story is intriguing. Fletcher says that Amy's response was to say that 'for her part, she was sure that, whether as "imagiste" or in Ezra's newly discovered "nageiste," the new

movement in poetry would go on'.[112] And, of course, it would, and under
Amy's aegis, not as something inaugurated, but certainly continued, by
her. But Pound – unless it was Upward – had picked on the element in
her poetry which would cause most consternation in the future: her motif
of the female body bathing. Cournos suggests she had a 'puritanic soul'
but it was her critics' narrow prejudice that was at issue, not hers. It was
simply unthinkable to connect a woman of her bulk with erotic feelings.
Amy was breaking a taboo that went further than either these revolutionaries, or the conservative American public, could stomach. In this
particular poem, the body is in fact not hers, but that appears to have
gone unnoticed. The response is deeply misogynistic; whether it was
homophobic as well is harder to gauge. Possibly H.D. would have recognised it as a lesbian love poem, but no one else at the time appears to
have done so. Lowell was able to exploit the lack of gender specificity
in the imagist 'I'; when she wrote love poems to Ada, most of her listeners
assumed she was speaking though a male persona.

Lowell, acutely sensitive about her appearance, was deeply wounded
by this mockery, even though she carried it off so well. In August two
poems of hers entitled 'Miscast' appeared in the *Egoist*. In the first, the
miscasting is social, and the poem shows more projective imagination
than the Boston capitalist has always been given credit for, but the
contrast between the appearance and the inner life is also the one she
had experienced herself:

> I have whetted my blade until it is like a Damascus blade,
> So keen that it nicks off the floating fringes of passers-by,
> So sharp that air would turn its edge
> Were it to be twisted in flight.
> Licking passions have bitten their arabesques into it,
> And the mark of them lies, in and out,
> Worm-like,
> With the beauty of corroded copper patterning white steel.
> My brain is curved like a scimitar,
> And sighs at its cutting
> Like a sickle mowing grass.
>
> But of what use is all this to me!
> I, who am set to crack stones
> In a country lane![113]

It was one of a fine group of poems, which helped her establish her place with the Aldingtons and Flint, even if Pound was now cooling towards her.

Amy's reason for offering the second dinner was most likely that she felt that if a magazine to which she had not contributed was having a dinner to celebrate its launch, the anthology in which she had appeared deserved no less, but a more sinister motive has often been suggested: a determination to seize control of imagism now Pound had loosened his grasp, the desire to transform it into what Pound would call 'Amygism', which he saw as a deliberate effort to dilute his pure concepts. Certainly Amy preferred instinctively to lead, rather than to be led, and without question in hosting the dinner she was moving herself from a peripheral position as minor contributor and latecomer to a central pos- ition within the imagist project. She had no thoughts as yet, however, of parting ways with Pound. If she had thought of sponsoring the next anthology, she had not yet mentioned it; certainly not to Pound. Fletcher's later assertion that Lowell arrived in England ready to conduct 'a carefully planned and long-sustained literary campaign' is dubious.[114] In the account Amy gave to Harriet, she says the idea of the anthology came to her in the wake of Pound's accusation that she would give no money to the arts, as a way in which she could do just that, while, she admitted, engagingly honestly, helping her own career at the same time. But she only appears to have suggested this some time after the dinners.

Yet if in mid-July Amy had not yet planned her dawn raid on the imagist movement, it is also incorrect to say, as is frequently done, that Pound had lost interest in imagism. Had he done so, the fight with Amy would not have been so bitter. When Pound published an essay on 'Vorticism' in the *Fortnightly Review* on 1 September, he made it very clear that imagism was the poetic arm of the Vorticist movement, and still his chief preoccupation; indeed he spends most of the article talking about imagism, before finally getting on to the question of its relation- ship to Vorticism in painting. His explanation of imagism, it is true, has changed a little. He repeats the three main tenets, and still believes the image should make an instantaneous impact, but now he is drawing on the model provided by Kandinsky rather than Freud or Bergson. Following Kandinsky's theory that certain colours and forms can directly convey particular emotions, he writes, 'The image is the poet's pigment.' This immediacy of impact is for Pound one of the things that Vorticist painting and sculpture share with imagism. His language is much less provocative than in his account of the vortex in *Blast*, but as there he puts great emphasis on intensity, something that had been central to him since his walking tour in France, and that he had recognised anew during the winter that he shared with Yeats. 'Vorticism,' he says, 'is an intensive art . . . The image is not an idea. It is a radiant node or cluster; it is what I can, and must perforce, call a VORTEX, from which, and through which, and into which, ideas are constantly rushing.'

To this dynamic, energised theory, he adds one more element: what he calls 'super-position', the technique of the haiku, 'one idea,' as he puts it, 'set on top of another'. He may already have taken this idea from the Chinese pictogram, which he would use to illustrate it later, but it was precisely the idea that Hulme had put forward in Bergsonian terms in 1908, and it may have been lying dormant with him from the Tour Eiffel days; it is perhaps significant that the first haiku he mentions is the same as the one Flint had quoted in the *New Age*, in Pound's version: 'The fallen blossom flies back to its branch: A butterfly.' He quotes his poem 'In a Station of the Metro', as an example of this '*hokku*-like' super-position, but adds a footnote to say, 'Mr Flint and Mr Rodker have made longer poems depending on a similar presentation of matter. So also have Richard Aldington, in his *In Via Sestina*, and "H.D." in her *Oread*, which latter poems express much stronger emotions than my lines here.' So he was far from repudiating his fellow-imagists at this time. Imagism, he says, is the kind of poetry 'where painting or sculpture seems as if it were "just coming out into speech"', which again echoes Hulme's 1908 insistence that modern poetry should resemble sculpture.[115] Throughout the article he emphasises that he is an *imagiste*, something that is not negated by the fact that 'vorticism' is the overarching term that includes '*Imagisme*' in poetry. Pound probably wrote this piece in July, so it is a fair assumption that at the time of the July imagist dinner he had no intention of dropping imagism, any more than Amy had any idea of imagism continuing without Pound.

V

POUND did not see much of Lowell in the later part of July, as his parents came to London shortly after the dinner; they stayed in 48 Langham Street, where he had lodged when he first came to London, as had H.D. and the Greggs. Ever since Pound had returned to Europe in February 1911, his parents had been begging him to return home or suggesting they paid a visit. Finally, they had made it. In terms of world events, with a world war only a fortnight away, it was most unfortunate timing, but they were delighted to meet Dorothy. Amy was, meanwhile, seeing a good deal of the Aldingtons; she would tell Harriet Monroe that 'The great thing which my summer has done for me is bringing me the intimacy of the Aldingtons. They are a perfectly charming young couple.'[116] They, for their part, were charmed by her 'vivacious intelligence', as Richard described it.[117] She had also been very pleased to meet Flint, whose expertise in French poetry greatly impressed her. Flint kept, as one might put it, as *au courant* as ever with French poetry; in June, Aldington had written in the *Egoist* of the 'amazing energy' with which he applied himself to it:

Whenever I meet Mr Flint, I say to him, 'Well, I've read the latest thing from Paris you told me to read the other day,' and he says, 'My dear child, did I tell you to read *that* old-fashioned book? However, I am afraid I can't stop now, because I have six new Fantaisiste authors, two volumes of Apollinaire and thirty-two other books by representatives of sixteen different schools to review by Saturday.'[118]

Lowell and Flint struck up a warm friendship, which never seemed disturbed by the gulf between their political views, and she was delighted too to renew her acquaintance with Fletcher. They all came frequently to the Berkeley. Amy would recall later:

What evenings we used to have in London in the old days, before the war! All of us sitting round a big box of candied fruit . . . glancing lightly over the literature and history of the world, cracking jokes, unmercifully criticising each other's poems, and every now and then stooping to watch the moon cutting through the purple night outside the window.[119]

In the meantime, Amy was bending her mind to the future of imagism. By the second half of July she had indeed begun to work on the idea of a second anthology, but not on the rather random structure of the first. Foster Damon suggests she had been indignant at having been represented by only one poem, and that she wanted an anthology that would make clear that she was an equal partner. There may have been something in that; she certainly proposed a new format, whereby each poet should have equal space, choosing their own poems. But perhaps more significantly, she believed that an audience could be found for the new poetry; she had no wish for it to languish in exquisite obscurity. Already that April, she had told Pound that it was 'necessary to create a public which shall no longer be bound by the Victorian tradition. That can be done . . . if one can only get an ear'.[120] Hence she believed it was essential to find a more mainstream publisher for the imagists; and she would take it upon herself to find a publisher of 'reputable standing', as she would put it to Harriet Monroe that September, and if necessary pay for the publication. Lowell did not aim in the first place to take imagism away from Pound, only to make sure it operated more successfully. At that stage she was thinking of publishing the anthology for five consecutive years, which, she pointed out, 'would enable us, by constant iteration, to make some impression on the reading public . . . it is a method which the editors of the "Georgian anthology" have found most satisfactory'.[121]

Aldington, H.D. and Flint thought it was an excellent plan. Pound, on the other hand was furious, accusing Amy, not entirely unjustly, of trying to usurp his place as editor. He said that he would only come in if Amy promised to give $200 a year to an impecunious poet. It was Amy's turn to be indignant; she always deeply resented other people telling her how to spend her money, and regarded Pound's ploy as a piece of blackmail: 'I told him,' she explained, 'that the $200 a year might be managed should anyone in stress of circumstances need such a sum, but that I absolutely refused to be intimidated into buying anything, or to buy his poems at the expense of my self-respect. I also told him that I would not have suggested "The Anthology" had I known that he would not like the idea, and that it was intended to benefit him, quite as much as the rest of us.'[122] Pound told the Aldingtons, according to Lowell, that they had to choose between Amy and himself, but they assured him that it was not a question of personalities but of principle. They liked the idea of selecting their own poems, and sharing equal space. Pound's patronage, though so helpful two years before, was now, it appears, beginning to feel a rather irksome tyranny, as Aldington's own account bears out. Amy, he says:

proposed a Boston Tea Party for Ezra, the immediate abolition of his despotism and the substitution of a pure democracy. There was to be no more of the Duce business, with arbitrary inclusions and exclusions and a capricious censorship. We were to publish quietly and modestly as a little group of friends with similar tendencies, rather than water-tight dogmatic principles . . . To preserve democratic equality names would appear in alphabetical order . . . On these terms Ezra was invited to contribute, but refused.[123]

While Pound was still resentfully mulling this over, Amy proposed another dinner party. There was one other of *les jeunes* that she was anxious to meet: D.H. Lawrence. When Pound had written to her about the projected quarterly earlier in the year, and mentioned Lawrence and Joyce as well as Ford and himself for staff, she wrote back to say: 'I don't know who Joyce is. You say he and Lawrence are the best among the younger men. I quite agree with you as to Lawrence.'[124] Those who thought Amy had a 'puritanic soul' might have been surprised; Pound himself found Lawrence's prose distastefully 'heavy with sex'.[125] Lawrence and Frieda had returned to England from Italy shortly before Amy arrived. Frieda's divorce was now through, and they were going to get married. While in England Frieda hoped to see her children, and Lawrence to secure a contract for his next novel, currently called 'The Wedding Ring', later to be rewritten as both *The Rainbow* and *Women in Love*. He was also arranging the publication in book form of some of his short stories, which would eventually appear as *The Prussian Officer and Other Stories*. They expected to stay three months at the most, and then return to Italy, much better for Lawrence's health, much cheaper, and where he felt happier than in England. Within a few days of his arrival he had been promised an advance of £300 for the novel, a gratifyingly substantial amount. In addition, Duckworth agreed to publish the short stories; it looked as if he were assured of a successful future. His relationship with Frieda was already tempestuous, but they

had no doubt that they wanted to be together. On 7 July, he wrote to
a friend: 'Your most vital necessity in this life is that you shall love your
wife completely and implicitly and in entire nakedness of body and
spirit.'[126] On 13 July they were married in Kensington Registry Office;
according to Lawrence, 'a very decent and dignified performance'.[127]

How Amy contacted Lawrence is not clear. Harold Monro, whose
Poetry Bookshop she visited again, to hear an inaudible poetry reading
by Rupert Brooke, may have told her how to reach him. (It is remarkable how many of these impassioned artists were incapable of projecting
their voices.) She invited Lawrence for dinner on 30 July, along with
the Aldingtons.[128] Aldington later wrote, 'It was the end of a sunny tranquil July day and, if we had been able to see into the future, the end
of tranquillity in Europe for many a long and bitter year'.[129] Austria had
issued a final ultimatum to Serbia on 23 July; on the 24th, Sir Edward
Grey warned the cabinet for the first time that there could be trouble
ahead; on 28 July Austria declared war on Serbia; Russia began to
mobilise, though most people still thought of it all, as Aldington put it,
as one of 'these senseless European squabbles'. But the posters on the
news-stand at the other side of Piccadilly had flaring and ominous headlines, which Aldington remembered as 'Germany and Russia at War,
Official' (if they said that, it was premature by two days), and 'British
Army Mobilised'. When Lawrence arrived, 'a tall slim young man, with
bright red hair and the most brilliant blue eyes . . . with a lithe, springing
step', he said to them all, even before the introductions, 'I say, I've just
been talking to Eddie Marsh, and he's most depressing. He says we
shall be in the war.'[130] Marsh, as Winston Churchill's secretary, was in
a position to know, but according to Aldington, dinner began and they
forgot all about the threat. Lawrence wrote to Harriet Monroe the next
day, 'I was at dinner with Miss Lowell and the Aldingtons last night,
and we had some poetry.' He complained ruefully about the fact that
Monroe was proving difficult about publishing his 'Ballad of Another
Ophelia', and talked of the effort and suffering in writing poetry, ending
up by saying 'Mrs Aldington has a few good poems.'[131] He said nothing
about the possibility of war.

When H.D. wrote about her first meeting with Lawrence at this
dinner in *Bid Me to Live*, she suggests the war had already begun. They
were all in

that great drawing room, overlooking Green Park. There were Elsa, Rafe, Mary
Dowell of Boston and her friend Mrs Potter. Mary had collected them, was editing

an anthology, a fabulously rich and gifted woman from Boston. Taking the whole top floor of the Berkeley, with the corner balcony overlooking Green Park. The window had been open. It was early August. The war was not a week old. 'Don't you know, don't you realise this is *poetry*?' said Frederick, edging her away toward the far end of the room. He held the pages she had brought Mary Dowell for her anthology.

'Don't you realise this is poetry?'[132]

That meeting was the beginning of a strong bond of sympathy between them.

The next day, Amy left London to pay a visit to Thomas Hardy in Dorchester. Even her vast motor car moved slowly, and she and Ada spent a night *en route* at Salisbury, where they were shocked to see the marketplace full of cannon, and soldiers everywhere. A waiter at the hotel assured them it was only manoeuvres, but the chauffeur, who talked to some of the soldiers, had had hints of something more ominous. When they reached Hardy's house, they found him deeply gloomy about the prospect of war, yet, in spite of his anxious state of mind, he and Amy immediately took to each other. Hardy, by then seventy-four, was delighted to discover that Lowell was an admirer of his poetry, for which he was much less well known than his novels, even though he had published four books of poetry since his final novel, *Jude the Obscure* had appeared in 1895; *Satires of Circumstance*, which included the poems of 1912–13 mourning the death of his love for his first wife and which had been published that year, is now considered his finest poetry. Of course, the main reason for turning to poetry had been the comparative freedom it gave, just because it was so much less read. As he had said himself, if Galileo had expressed his views in poetry, the Inquisition would never have troubled him.

Ada and Amy spent two days in Bath, returning to London on Monday, 3 August. Lowell described the situation there later that year in the *Little Review*, the order in which she lists the tell-tale signs of war telling one much about her priorities. The economic evidence comes first: petrol had gone up to five shillings a can, and in addition there was no money to be obtained. Then there was the fact that Americans were pouring in from the continent, 'Without their trunks, naturally. There was no-one to handle trunks at the stations in Paris. The refugees were all somewhat hysterical.' Later that night, 'A great crowd of people with flags marched down Piccadilly, shouting: "We want war! We want war!" They sang the Marseillaise, and it sounded savage, abominable.

The blood-lust was coming back, which we had hoped was gone forever from civilised races.'[133]

War, however, had not yet been declared by Britain, but when Amy got back to the Berkeley she found a declaration of hostilities awaiting her from Pound. He had written on 1 August stating his views on the proposed anthology. He might give them permission, he said, to bring out an 'Imagiste' anthology, as long as it was made entirely clear that he had nothing to do with it. But he would then be deprived of his 'machinery for gathering stray good poems . . . or poems which could not be presented to the public in other ways, poems that would be lost in magazines. As for example, "H.D.'s" would have been for some years at least.' After all, he points out, the 'present machinery was largely or wholly my making. I ordered "the public" (i.e. a few hundred people and a few reviewers) to take note of certain poems.' It is a curious way of conceiving of editorship, and certainly suggests that Aldington's analogy with the 'Duce' was not without justification. Amy has promised to find a 'better publisher', he wrote indignantly, 'if I abrogate my privileges, if I give way to, or saddle myself with, a dam'd contentious, probably incompetent committee. If I tacitly, tacitly to say the least of it, accept a certain number of people as my critical and creative equals, and publish the acceptance.' Her proposition would, he added, mean that 'Imagisme' would lose its meaning: 'It stands, or I should like it to stand for hard light, clear edges. I can not trust any democratized committee to maintain that standard. Some will be splay footed and some sentimental.' He suggests that what she is really saying is she is going ahead with the plan and he 'could come in or go hang', but then modifies what even he must have realised sounded very peevish. 'At least that was my impression which may have been inexact. We may both have rushed at unnecessary conclusions.'[134]

Pound's letter is a curious mixture of arrogance, conviction and pain. Here are these people whom he has nurtured biting the hand that fed them. He was angry at the loss of power, but there is no doubt that he sincerely believed he could use that power for artistic good. This was the first time since he reinvented himself in August 1912 that his movement appeared to be slipping from his control. Yet it was perhaps inevitable. As Herbert Read would comment later, Pound 'was not made for compromise or cooperation, two qualities essential for any literary or artistic "movement".'[135] On the eve of the First World War, Pound was about to be worsted in literary battle.

PART XII

WAR

I

'THE season of 1914,' wrote Douglas Goldring, 'was a positive frenzy of gaiety. Long before there was any shadow of war, I remember feeling that it couldn't go on, that something *had* to happen. Something certainly did!'[1] Goldring is one of many memoir writers of the period to chronicle the abrupt passing of what came to be seen in retrospect as a golden, halcyon age: 'With the outbreak of war,' he recalls, 'the nineteenth century ended with dramatic suddenness.'[2] At a stroke, there vanished the security and stability which they assumed existed under merely superficial tremors of industrial unrest and artistic protest. August 4, 1914, was the end of an era, an era, as most of the rebel artists and radical thinkers had agreed before the war, of commercialisation, hypocrisy and injustice, when plutocrats and philistines held sway. But it had also been an era when those with modest incomes, secure in the metropolitan heart of the British Empire, could live lives of peaceful privilege.

Pound, Aldington and H.D. would all look back at the years 1912 to 1914 as their happiest. They were not unaware of the brutalities that had kept that privilege intact: exploitation abroad, deprivation at home, violence inflicted on the colonised in the Empire, on strikers and suffragettes in Britain itself. Yet none of that impinged very closely on their personal sense of freedom and possibility. And nobody was prepared for the carnage of the next four years, for a generation of young men who would be killed, maimed, traumatised or brutalised by trench warfare. 'War was a fiend that stopped our clocks/Although we met him grim and gay,' wrote Siegfried Sassoon. For almost a hundred years, it had been largely in the colonies that the British Army fought its battles, and there on the whole, for all the occasional spectacular defeat like that of Gordon of Khartoum, they could be sure that their superior arms would ensure victory. ('Whatever happens, we have got/The Maxim Gun, and they have not,' as the marauding Captain Blood says as he faces a group of unruly natives in Hilaire Belloc's anti-imperialist satire, *The Modern Traveller*.)[3] Now two massive forces could achieve little but mutual destruction: the devastation that the European powers had inflicted on so many areas of Africa in the hectic scramble for resources and possessions they would now mete out to each other on European soil.

Few people had been prepared for the outbreak of hostilities. The papers immediately before the war had been full of the troubles in Ireland. The British soldiers, who had refused to move against the Protestant Ulster Volunteers, turning a blind eye to their acquisition of 30,000 rifles, had opened fire in Dublin at a demonstration of unarmed Nationalist sympathisers, killing three. Fury swept the nationalist community, and civil war was feared to be imminent. The papers talked of little else. The *Egoist* was no exception. The 1 August number had an editorial by Dora Marsden on the Ulster Rebellion, while Aldington began a review of a book on Conrad with the comment: 'The artists of today are its true religious. There is more acrimonious feeling between two artists of opposing theories than there is between a Catholic Nationalist and a Protestant Orangeman.'[4] No hint that a world war would begin in three days' time. Only in the last 48 hours were there rumours everywhere. Germany had declared war on Russia on 1 August, and on France on 3 August, threatening to invade France through Belgium; Belgium appealed to Britain for help. Britain asked Germany to send its promise to respect Belgian neutrality by 11 p.m. on 4 August. Crowds gathered in front of Buckingham Palace waiting for an announcement. The Aldingtons and John Cournos were there when the proclamation of war was made. Until that minute, Cournos says, people had been standing in silence; when the news came, they danced in the streets, singing 'Rule Britiannia', or chanting anti-German insults: 'Orgiastic hysteria had taken hold of the people,' he wrote; it 'swept them into the holocaust of destruction and self-destruction'.[5]

H.D. was appalled by the deadly frenzy of patriotism, and fearful of what lay in store. In *Paint it Today*, she writes of the coming of war, 'Time had them by the throat. Time had the world by the throat, shaking and shaking, evil and vicious.'[6] There was as yet no conscription, but just six days after war was declared, Aldington, in spite of his erstwhile pacifism, went with Hulme, characteristically eager to join combat, to enlist with the Honourable Artillery Company. Hulme was immediately

accepted, but Aldington was turned down, on account of the hernia
operation that he had had as a teenager. The burly Hulme consoled him
for his rejection by saying, somewhat patronisingly: 'War is not for sensitive men.' Aldington commented later: 'He thought he was tough. He
was, I think.'[7] Aldington felt humiliated, though Hulme was right.
Aldington was a sensitive man, but in 1914 sensitivity and manliness
were hard to reconcile, and Aldington definitely wanted to be thought
manly. He doesn't mention Hulme's comment in his memoirs, but he
does record that at the interview he was 'told contemptuously that there
wasn't the slightest chance of [his] ever getting into the army'. He got
lost on the way out, and wandered into the armoury, where he was
arrested on suspicion of being a German spy because of his 'small beard'
and 'French jacket'.[8]

According to Jean Gould, even though Amy's elder brother Percival,
also in London at the time for an astronomers meeting, wanted her to
leave immediately with him, her only fear was that her car might be
commandeered; she sent that on ahead along with the chauffeur, deciding
to wait for the publication of her second book, *Sword Blades and Poppy
Seed*. The faithful Ada, and presumably the maid, remained with her.[9]
Amy was having far too good a time to leave, though the American
writer Robert McAlmon, who met her at that juncture, remembered
her storming up and down her suite at the Berkeley, complaining: 'My
book is supposed to come out! A lot of attention it will get now with a
war on! What's the matter with England? Why don't they just stop the
war?' She offered her help to Herbert Hoover, who was organising both
the Belgian War Relief and the repatriation of stranded US citizens,
and joined his committee. Not only did she donate $10,000 to the work
(Amy could be generous when she thought it right) but she also met
the trains coming in from the continent at Victoria station, with a large
placard hanging in front of her imposing bosom which read, 'American
Citizens Apply Here'.[10]

She had not, however, been distracted from her plans for the new imagist
anthology. She saw more of the Aldingtons, and had long discussions about
modern French poetry with Flint, who recalled their meetings in 1916 in
a review of her *Six French Poets*, a book which she acknowledged owed
much to these conversations with him:

Through the long French window open in the corner could be seen the length of
Piccadilly, its great electric globes, its shiny roadway, and on the left, the tops of
the trees of Green Park, dark grey in the moonlight; the noise of the motor-buses

and of taxis reached us in a muted murmur, and at the corner of the park opposite, beneath a streetlamp, stood a newsboy, whose headlines we strained our eyes from time to time to catch. It was in this tenseness created by the expectation of news that Miss Lowell read Paul Fort or Henri de Régnier to us (she reads French beautifully).[11]

When Amy read this, she wrote to Flint immediately:

How I wish we could resume those happy evenings at the Hotel Berkeley! I never enjoyed anything so much, nor found anything so stimulating. That they left upon you such a happy impression is not the least of the satisfactions of your review to me. Do you realize that we only saw each other for seven weeks? And yet those seven weeks have left a bond which only grows stronger. You and Richard and Hilda seem to me a part of myself, and we are all banded together against a common enemy.[12]

Who was the common enemy? For Pound it would have been the respectable bourgeoisie, but it is hard to imagine Amy would think in quite those terms; probably it was more generally a philistine culture with no time for poetry and the arts – though she could just conceivably by 1916 have been referring to Pound himself. But not in August 1914; she was still anxious to settle her quarrel with Pound amicably. She must have sent a soothing letter in reply to his invective of 1 August, because he wrote again on the 12th, centainly not going so far as agreeing to contribute, but saying he thought the anthology in itself a good idea, though he would prefer it to be called *Vers Libre*, because he wanted imagism 'associated with a certain clarity and intensity'. He did not, he said, want to prevent anyone else joining in with her, and in fact rather generously said he would refrain from publishing another anthology in America before 1916, because he realised that the Aldingtons were keen to be published by Macmillan, with whom Amy was then in negotiation. He ended by suggesting that if she wanted to 'drag in the word Imagisme', she should have a subtitle which said '"an anthology devoted to Imagisme, vers libre and modern movements in verse" or something of that sort. I think that will be perfectly fair to everyone'.[13] That does seem quite reasonable, though Amy could have pointed out that *Des Imagistes* contained a number of poems which could hardly be called imagist, but that had not stopped Pound from using the title. Her reply to Pound has not survived, but it was presumably placatory once more, because he and Dorothy came to the dinner, and they passed a cordial evening. But she was not giving way to any great degree. She had decided they should call the anthology 'Some *Imagiste* Poets', so that Pound could publish another *Des Imagistes* if he wished, but she was not going to drop the word altogether. Amy still hoped that Pound would relent and join them, if not in this anthology, then a later one. One can be sure that at that stage she genuinely would have preferred to include Pound, if only because she would have calculated he would have been good for sales. But when he would not join forces on her terms, she swept on regardless. When Harold Monro told her the anthology would fail without Pound, she brushed his comment aside.

In her remaining weeks in London, Amy also saw more of Lawrence. It is a testimony to how little credence he had given Marsh's warning of a coming war that he had left London immediately after their dinner for a week's walking tour in Westmorland, but he was back in London with Frieda by 8 August, making contact again with the Aldingtons and Amy. Now faced with the actuality of war, Lawrence was appalled by the prospect. Writing to Lowell on the 9th, he said to her, 'we are so miserable about the war. My wife is German, so you may imagine – her father was an army officer. Everything seems gone to pieces.'[14] Anti-German feeling was everywhere, and Frieda had found herself suddenly surrounded by hostility and suspicion. When they went round to dinner with David Garnett in his father's Chelsea flat shortly after Lawrence's return, Garnett had three visits from the police in the following week, having been, he was told, one of hundreds each day reported by vigilant neighbours on suspicion of being German spies. One of the other guests had been heard jocularly calling *Auf Wiedersehen* to Frieda on the stairs.[15]

Luckily no one had the temerity to investigate Amy when she invited Frieda and Lawrence to dinner at the Berkeley. Lawrence had just heard that Methuen had, after all, rejected his novel. He would spend the next six months rewriting it, making it less overtly erotic, but it was a depressing intimation of the difficulties his work would have from now on, and of the money problems that would ensue. When Lowell attempted to persuade him to contribute to the anthology, she met little resistance. He insisted he wasn't an imagist, and indeed, according to Damon, regarded imagism as an advertising scheme.[16] Lowell, he told Glenn Hughes, tried to convince him that he was an imagist by quoting his lines, 'The morning breaks like a pomegranate/In a shining crack of red'.[17] As he was financially completely dependent on his writing, he would probably have agreed at that moment to any paying publishing venture. He was also, of course, publishing with the Georgian anthologies, but Amy was unconcerned about that. It being impossible to return to Italy for the present, he and Frieda moved out of London to a cottage at Chesham in Buckinghamshire in an attempt to save money, and possibly also to get away from prying eyes. When he sent Amy his selection of poems for the anthology, he invited her warmly to visit them there, saying it would all be 'perfectly rural and idyllic'.[18] She and Ada went on 27 August, taking the Aldingtons with them, as usual in a motor car, though it cannot have been the maroon Pierce-Arrow, by then safely back in the States. Lawrence had written to Edward Marsh just a couple of days earlier: 'The war is just hell for me. I don't see why I should be so disturbed – but I am. I can't get away from it for a minute: live in a sort of coma, like one of those nightmares when you can't move. I hate it – everything.'[19] Yet in spite of that underlying nightmare, the day was a great success, Amy's exuberance temporarily banishing Lawrence's gloom. H.D. recollected that they met Katherine Mansfield there and also the painter Mark Gertler, whom Lawrence later so cruelly depicted as Loerke in *Women in Love*. By then, however, Amy had regretfully decided that she should return to America, as she had heard that the British publication of her book had been delayed, whilst the American edition would appear in the States in September. By the time she and Ada sailed, the manuscript of the new anthology was near completion.

The Pound parents had also been caught in England. Homer Pound, who had to return to work, left at much the same time as Amy, though not, like her, travelling first-class, and suffered abominably from seasickness. Eventually Isabel, clearly fully approving of Dorothy as a wife for her adored son, reluctantly tore herself away and returned to Philadelphia at the end of October. No one yet thought the war would imperil civilian shipping. Fletcher, who with characteristic bad timing had left for a holiday in Switzerland at the beginning of August, had had a difficult journey back to London, though one on which, he told Amy Lowell, in spite of suffering 'a great deal of inconvenience and anxiety', he was never in any real danger.[20] With some aplomb he had visited the British consul in Geneva posing as a British aristocrat, obtained a British passport, and made it back through Paris, complaining bitterly about the lack of taxis and porters. He joined Daisy in Cornwall, where she was on holiday with her children and Malcolm. To the children, Fletcher was only the lodger, so there had been no question of his accompanying them solo, originally the reason that he had taken his holiday abroad. How comfortable a party they were Fletcher does not reveal, though as he always appeared to get on much better with Malcolm than Daisy, he at least may quite have enjoyed it. Fletcher, Daisy and the children then returned to Sydenham once more, but he soon decided to head back across the Atlantic, giving as his reason to Amy, perhaps in case she thought it was fear, a new and portentous sense of an American mission. 'The war and the resulting utter confusion of intellect and intelligence that it has brought about over here,' he told her, 'has increased my desire to revisit my country. This is certainly America's opportunity to prove herself fit to carry on the great traditions of literature and the arts. She has now her unique chance to do original and vital work. Whether she will avail herself of it remains to be seen.'[21] He told Daisy that he would be back within three months, but he had already decided he would not return to her unless she obtained a divorce. He sailed back to New York on 14 November.

Neither Pound nor H.D. appears to have contemplated a return to America, and in spite of the contentious anthology, the Pounds and the Aldingtons for now remained on reasonably good terms, though Aldington's earlier admiration was certainly dinted. On 21 September he reported to Amy, with whom both he and H.D. would now be in regular correspondence, that Pound was unwell, lying on a couch and telling everyone that he had 'cerebral gout'. 'Poor devil,' he added, 'I wonder if Fat Hueffer was right? Perhaps Ezra is a little cracked. He doesn't seem able to talk of anything except himself and his work.'[22] Pound's obsessions would certainly grow during the war years, but he wasn't totally self-absorbed. He was still on the lookout for new talent; on 22 September, the day after Aldington's letter, he met another young American expatriate, T.S. Eliot, at that stage studying philosophy and apparently on the way to brilliant academic success. Eliot was also, however, a poet, though his only publications so far were as a student at Harvard, including the Class Ode that he had recited at his graduation. A week after their first meeting, he sent Pound a copy of 'The Love Song of J. Alfred Prufrock'. Pound was enormously impressed; whether he compared the poem's ironic, witty yet compassionate treatment of its indecisive anti-hero with his own less poised attempts at modern satire, he did not say, but Eliot was one of the few fellow-writers he would come to treat as an equal. Pound sent the poem immediately to Harriet, telling her that Eliot had 'actually trained himself *and* modernised himself *on his own*. The rest of the *promising young* have done one or the other but never both (most of the swine have done neither). It is such a comfort to meet a man and not have to tell him to wash his face, wipe his feet, and remember the date (1914) on the calendar.'[23]

The language of the nursery perhaps indicates Pound's own childish excitement, though Eliot might have been in two minds about being thus patronised. For his part, Eliot was far from impressed by Pound's poetry at the time, though admittedly he had only read some of the earlier poetry, and the poems in *Blast*: if he had seen *Ripostes* or Pound's contributions to *Des Imagistes* he might have thought differently. He had been two months in London before he got round to introducing himself to Pound, though his Harvard friend Conrad Aiken, who had just published his own first book of poetry, had been pressing him to do so from the start. Eliot's background was rather grander than Pound's, if not quite as grand as Lowell's. He came from the American *haute bourgeoisie*: one Andrew Eliot had come to New England in the seventeenth century, from East Coker in Somerset, but the original Eliots had, it was said, come to England with the Norman invasion. (As I noted earlier, the Lowells, going one better, actually claimed to be descended from William the Conqueror himself.)[24] Eliot had been brought up in St Louis, his grandfather having gone there from Boston as a Unitarian missionary to the largely French Catholic frontier city. His family were cultured and highly respectable, with a deep work ethic and ingrained puritanism, but the young Eliot, as the descendant of New Englanders, felt out of place in St Louis, and, as a student at Harvard, found that his Midwestern upbringing made him feel equally alien in Boston. At Harvard he had discovered the poetry of the 1890s and had read Symons' *The Symbolist Movement in Literature*, so discovered Baudelaire and Jules Laforgue several years before Pound had done so; their ironic urban poetry was an important model for the poetry he had shown to Pound. Eliot was quiet, courteous, and would rapidly be accepted as an honorary English gentleman, a feat Pound never achieved, nor indeed wished to. But at first Pound had to struggle to get Eliot's work into print, and it was some months before Monroe agreed to print the poem, which she found perplexing and un-American; Pound's letters on the subject grew increasingly acrimonious.

Eliot, on a travelling scholarship from Harvard, and due to spend a year at Merton College, Oxford, had been on a summer philosophy course in Marburg in Germany when news of the imminent war broke, and he hurriedly returned to England. He was one of a number of English and American students abandoning German universities in haste to return home. Another was Alec Randall, Aldington's University College friend, who had been studying for a postgraduate degree in German literature at the University of Tübingen. Back in England, he and his wife Amy and the Aldingtons saw each other frequently, and Randall would write articles on German writers for the *Egoist*. Nearly all Aldington's acquaintances, in fact, appear to have been required to produce copy; as the work was unpaid, it was clearly easier to ask friends. Aldington himself, as well as being assistant editor at the *Egoist*, was now acting as secretary to Ford, having taken over from the traumatised H.D. Ford had been recruited (on his own insistence in an honorary capacity) by his friend Masterman, who, having lost his parliamentary seat at the last election, had been put in charge of a secret department dedicated to combating German propaganda in America. Ford was to write anti-German propaganda, a curious task for a comparatively recent applicant for German nationality, but, although Ford as a good European was profoundly grieved by an inter-European war, his loyalties were solely to the southern Germans; he already loathed the Prussians and was able to turn his ire on them.

Aldington was asked to extend his duties from dictation to researching Prussian history for Ford, and his friend Alec Randall was also recruited for his German expertise, in his case the experience setting him on the path to a distinguished diplomatic career. They had to find evidence for Ford's argument that, unhappily for Europe, Germany had become dominated by Prussia, whose culture was in his view (as Max Saunders summarises it) 'materialist, egoistic, philological, and militarist'.[25] For Ford, the war was a battle for the cause of creativity, the imagination and freedom, against academicism, instrumentalism and regimentation; it was another version of his Pre-Raphaelite forebears' campaign for arts and crafts instead of industrialism, or the aesthetes' opposition to a materialist and philistine bourgeoisie. In his first propaganda book, *When Blood is their Argument: An Analysis of Prussian Culture*, he particularly attacks the Prussian educational system, giving an account of its dehumanising schooling that could well, one suspects, owe something to Pound's hatred of Germanic scholarship. Ford, not having been to university, and with no experience of a philological training in literature, had less first-hand knowledge of the matter than Pound and is unlikely to have lighted on the study of philology as the expression of an autocratic and martial spirit without some prompting. Pound was delighted, writing to his mother that 'The book is very good. I trust the faculty of my rotten University will read and digest it. The preface contains a number of statements similar to those which I have made repeatedly any time for the last ten years.'[26]

Aldington himself appears to have been convinced by Ford's arguments, denouncing the Prussians in the *Egoist* and describing the war
to Lowell with some passion as one 'of democracy against autocracy, of
the individual against the state, of the Anglo–Latin civilisation against
the Prussian, of even vers libre against academic metres!'[27] The British
generals would have been startled by that last point. His letters to Lowell
included frequent news of the deaths of young French writers, which
he also reported in the *Egoist*, an increasingly grim and ominous tally
that he feared might presage his own demise. He was unable to write
any poetry, he told her, only journalism and translations, though that
must have been true only fairly briefly, for he went on producing poetry
regularly throughout the war, even in the trenches. He was working
frenetically, contributing articles to almost every issue of the *Egoist* that
autumn, yet at times even journalism was hard; as he wrote that
November, 'when the most bloody battles of the world are taking place
a few miles away, it needs a certain amount of phlegm – which I frankly
don't possess – to be able to write precisely and dogmatically on the
latest Anglo–American literary productions'.[28]

H.D. also wrote to Amy in October saying he felt 'every swing of this
war pendulum so keenly!' The same was undoubtedly true of herself.
H.D. was pregnant, having discovered the news, Barbara Guest suggests,
on the day the war was declared.[29] Whilst that date has symbolic appeal,
it doesn't fit the biological facts; the earliest she could have known would
have been some weeks later, though the baby must have been conceived
very near the outbreak of war. The war was a dark cloud over this pregnancy. H.D. was apprehensive from the start: a war was the wrong time
to have a baby; Aldington might have to fight, and in any case, even if
he didn't have to enlist, H.D.'s £200 allowance and their meagre literary
earnings would scarcely provide lavishly for family life. H.D. was
completely undomesticated. She must have wondered if she was capable
of looking after a baby without the services of a nanny, and indeed it is
most unlikely that she would have been; when eventually she did become
a mother, full of maternal love though she was, and rapturous about
motherhood at an exalted level, she took no part in the physical care of
her child. But in addition to those more practical worries, she must have
been fearful that a child might put an end to her recently launched poetic
career. The successful women writers she knew, like Violet Hunt and May
Sinclair, were childless, as had been the best-known women writers of
the previous century, Jane Austen, the Brontës, Elizabeth Barrett
Browning, George Eliot, Emily Dickinson and Christina Rossetti. Rebecca

West was now a mother and carrying on with her writing, but her illegitimate son was a well-kept secret, and H.D. would have had no inkling of
his existence. Pregnancy, *Asphodel* suggests, made her feel drained of all
creativity: 'her mind glued down, broken, and held back like a wild bird
caught in bird-lime . . . months and months when her flaming mind beat
up and she found she was caught, her mind not taking her as usual like
a wild bird but her mind-wings beating, beating, and her feet caught,
glued like a wild-bird in bird-lime'.[30] H.D. recorded that the woman
doctor whom she consulted pressed her to have the baby, implying, though
she does not say so directly, that she wondered about termination. As
abortion was both illegal and dangerous at that time, that she even contemplated such a course indicates the panic that pregnancy induced in her.
If Brigit's near-fatal operation had been an abortion, it is even more
remarkable, but H.D., who always lived somewhat on the edge of breakdown, was already under great nervous strain. Like Lawrence, she would
experience the war as an ongoing nightmare, which the events of her
personal life would only make darker.

II

THE beginning of the First World War, five days after Lowell's dinner in the Berkeley Hotel, might be said to mark, among many other things, the end of the second major stage in the history of imagism. The Tour Eiffel period, as I suggested earlier, was the first, proto-imagist stage, with many of the ideas and techniques that appeared in later imagism already there – simplicity, directness, *vers libre*, brevity, imagistic intensity – but still a somewhat diffuse set of theories that did not immediately result in any clear change of poetic direction, though Hulme, Flint, Campbell and even Pound, who at that stage had paid so little attention to the theories, were moving at different paces to a sharper, sparer form of *vers libre*. The years 1912–14 saw those ideas both gain a critical mass, and, with a name and what Lewis would call a *chef de bande*, emerge as enough of a coherent programme, to say nothing of publicity stunt, to make a small but striking intervention in traditional poetic practice, much in the way Fry's 1910 exhibition intervened in the practice of art in Britain. The Post-Impressionist Exhibition of 1910, of course, presented works from abroad in a bid to revolutionise British art.[31] *Des Imagistes* might at first sight seem to be rather different, the work of a group of Anglo-American poets (and one Irishman) who presented their own English-language poetry, bar the sprinkling of foreign titles. Yet in a sense they too were presenting works from elsewhere to revolutionise indigenous practices, but through the medium of translation: Greek, Japanese, Chinese, Latin and French originals or forms stand behind the poems in this book.

Where that 1910 exhibition was very different from the 1914 *Des Imagistes* was in the size of its impact, the crowds that it drew to the Grafton Galleries, and the heated and highly politicised debates that it provoked in the papers. *Des Imagistes* caused a ripple in some poetry-reading circles; it had a certain amount of press coverage, but it did not sell well and its immediate influence was more on individual writers than on the wider public. It was in retrospect that it would come to be seen as a milestone in the development of modernist Anglo-American poetry. Vorticism made much more of a public impact: an advantage of joining up with the visual artists, and one which cannot have escaped Pound's notice, was that post-1910 modern painting and sculpture had established a presence in the press. It could command much more immediate newspaper attention; often coverage was more denunciation than praise but it would be welcome all the same. 'The Press,' as Lewis pointed out, 'in 1914 had no Cinema, no Radio, and no Politics: so the painter could really become a "star".'[32] *Blast* had produced a noisy stir; and Pound through association with these painters had achieved a much higher profile – and greater opprobrium – with *Blast* than with *Des Imagistes*, even though the latter contained some of his best early poems, and the former some of his worst. But as far as poetry was concerned Vorticism was for Pound at the time more a new name than a new school: after all, his finest example of a Vorticist poem had been H.D.'s 'Oread', which would appear in the 1915 *Some Imagist Poets*.

Now, however, the third and final stage of imagism was beginning; Pound was no longer undisputed leader. Indeed, the imagism that would soon be attracting attention was one independent of Pound. Pound dismissed this version of his movement as Amygism, and complained that the high standards that he had instituted had vanished. Certainly not every poem in the later imagist anthologies would be entirely successful nor entirely in keeping with imagist precepts, though, as already pointed out, one could say that of the poetry that Pound had published in *Des Imagistes*. But Lowell was determined to make her imagist anthologies reach a wider audience than *Des Imagistes* had done, and she would succeed spectacularly. In the meantime, back in the States, her own book appeared on 22 September and, unlike her first, immediately attracted considerable attention. Like Pound's *Ripostes*, it was a transitional work. Although the book included some of her earlier more conventional work, she had added several of her new *vers libre* poems as well as four prose poems, including one of quite daring subject-matter for her Boston neighbours, 'The Forsaken', about an unmarried pregnant woman contemplating suicide. She used as epigraph for the book an extract from Henri de Régnier's 'Médailles d'argile', by now something of a touchstone for the imagists, and in her introduction acknowledged her debt to the French, and defended her use of *vers libre*, or as she says she prefers to call it, drawing on Flint's phrase, 'unrhymed cadence'. 'Henley,' she says, 'speaks of "those unrhyming rhythms in which I have tried to quintessentialise, as (I believe) one can scarce do in rhyme". The desire to "quintessentialise," to head-up an emotion until it burns white-hot, seems to be an integral part of the modern temper, and certainly "unrhymed cadence" is unique in its power of expressing this.'[33] The book was widely reviewed, and received both praise and criticism; she would never go unnoticed again. Many of the free verse poems had been published in the *Egoist*, where Aldington reviewed it in November, dismissing the Keatsian rhymed narratives out of hand but giving warm praise to her most recent work: 'Miss Lowell's short vers libre poems,' he wrote, 'are sometimes extremely good. She has – besides her Gallic training – a natural gift of eloquence, a sense of rhythm, a sensitive appreciation of beauty, irony, and a facility for coining new images'.[34] Yet of the fifteen reviews mentioned by Lowell's biographer, Damon, Aldington's was the only English one. Amy's impact was very much in the States, as imagism's would be. Five hundred copies of the book would be sold by Christmas in America, but only four in Britain, though sales there must have been, as she feared, affected by the war. The poetry that was selling in Britain that autumn was, judging from the reviews, hackneyed but soothingly patriotic war poetry.

Thomas Hardy, to whom Amy had sent a copy, wrote a warm letter, not giving an overall judgement but tactfully mentioning poems that he particularly liked, including three of the *vers libre* poems, incidentally picking out some of the most sexually evocative, 'The Captured Goddess,' 'The Tree of Scarlet Berries' and 'Clear with Light'. About those, however, he commented: 'Whether I should have liked them still better rhymed, I do not know.'[35] H.D. and Flint wrote praising her prose poems, as Aldington had also done, though Flint, like Aldington, was ready to point out faults as well as successes, being particularly critical of the regular metres in her narrative poems. Lowell, however, had already abandoned these. The prose poems, full of movement, colour and sound, she would continue to develop, contributing one entitled 'The Bombardment' to a special war issue of *Poetry* that November. This was a dramatic, not to say histrionic description of a town under attack, focusing more on the terror and destruction of houses than any actual blood, its emphasis being on the collapse of civilisation and culture that war brings. It featured repeated 'BOOMS', and later, when she gave readings, as she increasingly would of her poetry, she would get her musician friend Carl Engel to stand behind the curtains and dramatically sound a gong as she spoke the word: shades of Marinetti. The *Poetry* war issue as a whole was not, it must be said, overall an especially successful number. Joseph Campbell, Aldington and a young unknown called Wallace Stevens also contributed, but not their best work; perhaps it was too soon after the shock of the onset of war to expect an adequate response. When Lawrence received his copy of the November *Poetry*, he wrote to Harriet, condemning it out of hand, but picking out for particular contempt Amy's references to the breaking of Bohemian glass, which he regarded as frivolous in the face of the mangling of human flesh that was taking place. Aldington, on the other hand, told Amy that he found the poem very moving in its depiction of the 'horror and sadness' of war. But he added, expressing a view that had some currency at the time: 'I think perhaps we over-civilised ones are apt to think too highly of mere life; and I feel sometimes that perhaps after all a long peace becomes a disease which only war can remedy.'[36] He would not think this way for long.

The success of *Sword Blades and Poppy Seed* gave Amy a new confidence in her poetic career, but, like Pound, she was anxious not just to be published herself but also to promote the work of those she admired. She had brought with her not only the manuscript for the imagist anthology, but also that of Fletcher's *Irradiations: Sand and Spray*, and the British edition of Frost's *North of Boston*, for which she was anxious to secure an American publisher. The latter she did not have to worry about, because Frost had found one for himself, and all she could contribute was a long and warm review. Lawrence wrote reminding her that she had promised to visit the publisher Mitchell Kennerley, who had brought out the American edition of *Sons and Lovers*, for which Lawrence was still owed £10, and who had in his possession a copy of the manuscript of the proto-*Rainbow*, which Lawrence was anxious to retrieve to offer to a more reliable publisher. Lawrence sounded wretchedly miserable, and was clearly very hard up. Not only did Amy contact Kennerley, but she also wrote at once to Harriet, whom she knew had some poems from Lawrence, begging her to publish them as soon as possible, and saying she herself didn't want to insult him by offering him money (though later she would make such an offer several times, and Lawrence would accept gratefully, finding no insult at all). Casting about for what she could do to help, she decided to send him a typewriter that she claimed to be discarding. Lawrence was delighted with the typewriter, though suspicious of her story. It was a splendid typewriter, he said, and he was sure she had really wanted to keep it.

He was by then sounding much more cheerful; since he had written before, he had had a grant of £50 from the Royal Literary Fund, which, though he disparaged, was obviously very useful, and £8 from Harriet, who published the poems in the December issue, though probably only because she was intending to do so in any case, not at Amy's bidding.

Amy had also sent the Lawrences a copy of *Sword Blades and Poppy Seed*, and when she wrote to say it would be arriving, Lawrence promised that she would see him 'prowling through your verses like a beast of prey: and oh, the hyena howl I shall send up when I seize on a lameness'.[37] In the event, though not as savage as this suggests, he delivered a candid verdict that was more incisive and perceptive about her faults than either Aldington or Flint. Like Aldington, he admired the short free verse poems, but not her 'story-poems', which he thought that she spoilt 'with a sort of vulgar, artificial "flourish of ink"'. 'I like *you* in your poetry,' he told her. 'I don't believe in affecting France . . . Why don't you always be yourself . . . If it doesn't come out of your heart, real Amy Lowell, it is no good, however many colours it may have. I wish one saw more of your genuine strong, sound self in this book, full of common-sense and kindness and the restrained, almost bitter, Puritan passion. Why do you deny the bitterness in your nature, when you write poetry? . . . Why do you take a pose? It causes you to shirk your issues.'[38] Lawrence was right that the more conventional narrative poems were still hampered by Bostonian gentility. Lowell's most successful poems were arguably her more personal ones, as Jean Gould contends, especially on the one hand her love poems, and on the other those on the miscasts in life, powerful poems where the bitterness that Lawrence wanted certainly appears. One of the most admired poems in the volume, 'The Taxi', picked out by both Aldington and Lawrence, as well as by several other reviewers, brings together both love and bitterness:

> When I go away from you
> The world beats dead
> Like a slackened drum.
> I call out for you against the jutted stars.
> And shout into the ridges of wind.
> Streets coming fast,
> One after the other,
> Wedge you away from me,

And the lamps of the city prick my eyes
So that I can no longer see your face.
Why should I leave you,
To wound myself upon the sharp edges of the night![39]

Lawrence described it as 'very clever and futuristic – and good'. His final summing up of the volume was to say that he liked the poems 'because after all they have a lot of you in them – but how much nicer, finer, bigger you are, intrinsically, than your poetry is', a verdict about which Amy must have had ambivalent feelings.[40] In the 'democratic' system of imagism that Amy was to set up, the tensions caused by the poets' criticism of each other's poetry would prove the most tricky to overcome, but if Amy were put out by Lawrence's comments, she did not hold them against him.

Since Lowell's return to Boston, Aldington and H.D. had been waiting to hear how her plans for the next anthology were materialising. Pound was still keeping his distance from the venture, but luckily, for now, also his peace. That rapidly changed some six weeks after Lowell had left England. On 5 October she saw an advertisement for her book, which described her as the 'foremost member of the "Imagists" – a group of poets that includes William Butler Yeats, Ezra Pound, Ford Madox Hueffer'.[41] She realised immediately this would enrage Pound, and cabled Aldington to warn him, as well as writing a letter of protest to her publishers. Aldington replied that he wasn't quite sure from the cable what the 'crime' was, but guessed it was that 'your publishers have advertised you as American founder or leader of the imagists'. He had shown her wire to Pound, who, he said, had taken it quite calmly at the time, while H.D. had said that she would 'far rather have [Amy] as leader than anyone else'.[42] The advertisement only appeared in the American press, not the British, but if nowhere else Pound would undoubtedly have seen it when it appeared in the October *Poetry*. Pound wrote a furious letter to Lowell on 19 October, though curiously enough, he had already written to Monroe a week before, saying he didn't suppose that Lowell herself was much to blame and venting his anger on that 'lying grocer' Macmillan, and on Monroe herself for accepting the advertisement just because it would earn *Poetry* some much-needed dollars.[43] In the event, he had plenty of spleen left for Lowell, and she cannot have guessed that he did not think her to blame. He pasted the offending advertisement on the first page of his letter, and then thundered: 'In view of the above arrant charlatanism on the part of your publishers,

I think you must now admit that I was quite right in refusing to join you in any scheme for turning Les Imagistes into an uncritical democracy with you as intermediary between it and the printers.' This seems a somewhat illogical response, since the publishers' offence was precisely going against the idea of a democracy by making Amy the leader. Pound, however, told her that she had better cease to call herself an *imagiste*, arguing that the *Dome* was not imagist, something of course Amy would never have claimed, and she could have pointed out that neither was *Canzoni*. Yeats, he said, was 'more amused than delighted' at being identified as an imagist; if her publishers, who she had claimed were 'of good standing', had tried to sell cement or soap in that way they would be sued. He concluded caustically: 'Blessed are they who have enterprise, for theirs is the magazine public.'[44] Pound must understandably have found it galling to be proclaimed in the States as a mere follower in the movement that he had launched, and to be seen as coming second to this woman to whom he had taught so much. Yet perhaps he also found it disturbing that Macmillan clearly thought the new poetry would indeed find an audience. The advertisement said that Amy Lowell 'had won wide recognition for her writing in new and free forms of poetical expression', and that *Sword Blades and Poppy Seed* was 'an unusual book. It contains much that will arouse criticism, but it is a new note in American poetry. Miss Lowell has broken away from academic traditions and written, out of her own time, real singing poetry, free, full of new effects and subtleties.'[45] Pound would always remain in a double-bind towards the public. He was angry when it refused to accept his judgements, yet he felt that the fact that the crass public was unable to appreciate work that he promoted was proof of that work's artistic merit. Success would mean standards had been lowered. When he later wrote of Walter Savage Landor that 'Landor has not been a popular author', that was significant praise.[46] If Lowell was going to be a success, it was a cause for simultaneous envy and scorn.

Aldington, when he heard about the letter, told Lowell not to worry: 'If I were you, I would just have a smoke and a read and forget it'.[47] Lowell, however, had already written apologising, pointing out she had done all she could to correct Macmillan's errors. Calling her the 'foremost member' was 'undoubtedly due to an underling's error in the office. I told Macmillan last spring that inclusion of those two names was foolish, as neither Yeats nor Hueffer were Imagistes.' The names were there simply to 'boom the book', a common American practice. One wonders if this recalled to Pound his earlier demands that his father 'boom' his work; a month later, he would be telling Alice Corbin Henderson he used the *Egoist* as a vehicle for 'booming' his favourite writers, and wondering if he should ask her to 'boom' his latest idea, a College of Arts.[48] Amy was, perhaps, simply more honest about the fact that writing was, as we might now put it, a cultural industry, and that attention had to be paid to marketing. Whilst in her preface she had, as she pointed out, said that she belonged to no school, she thought that Pound could hardly object to her being known as an *imagiste*, having included her – against her wishes – in the *Des Imagistes* anthology: 'Having been given the name of Imagiste I shall certainly not repudiate it,' she told him. She had every right to be called one of the foremost members of the group, both because of the amount she had published and the attention it had gained. 'You have only yourself to blame,' she added, 'for including me in the group, and it is not agreeable to feel that you only wished the inclusion as long as I could be kept obscure and insignificant.' As for suing, she pointed out that 'even in cement and soap you would have to get out a patent in order to sue anyone'; as the name had not been patented, it could not be done. She might be on shaky grounds there under modern intellectual copyright law, but she added cheerfully that she would be delighted if he sued, 'as they would then put new jackets on the book which I should greatly prefer. Also, it would be a good advertisement.'[49]

Much has been made in recent years of the modernists' bad faith over their professed scorn for the marketplace; Lowell was engagingly straightforward in her approach. Pound had added a postscript to the letter, saying it was a pity Macmillan had not mentioned some of the lesser known members of the group, which at least would have helped to promote them. Amy's reply on this point perhaps illustrates the difference between their ideas of how to 'boom', a practice, even if Pound was not admiting it at that moment, to which they both paid acute attention. It was unrealistic, she argued, to expect the publishers not to use names 'of world-wide reputation' (Pound should have felt something of a warm glow from that, since he was one of them). Amy took a pragmatic approach to the publishing world, sometimes rather too pragmatic, her fellow-imagists felt, but on the whole they were grateful to her for her business sense. Pound found compromise impossible; he wanted control, everything done his way, and found it hard to distinguish between his principles and his prejudices. Though, through his use of patrons and little magazines, he succeeded in promoting a range of highly gifted writers and artists, with greater tact he might have helped them even more. Lowell was able to point out that in this instance her methods would aid the others most in the end. In the anthology, she reminded him, their names would be in alphabetical order, so she would come last. 'Far from wishing to keep the other members of the group insignificant and unknown I have given a very handsome tribute to Richard and Flint in an article I wrote from London to "The Little Review".'[50] She was as concerned as he was to boost them, she implied, and possibly would be more successful. Pound was not mollified.

H.D. was unhappy at the dissension in their ranks. She was always ambivalent – understandably – about Pound, but she did not want a rift. It was an added upset at a difficult time. She thought Pound was being unreasonable, but she still hoped for peace on that front at least. Lowell's productivity and energy she much admired, but she could not help contrasting it with her own anxious, enervated state. 'Mine seems to be a most tenuous shoot of this Imagist Tree of Life!' she wrote to her.[51] Mentioning her pregnancy was, of course, out of the question, but she could refer to the wartime tensions. Yet she was continuing to write poetry, poems not overtly connected with the hostilities, but certainly suggestive of the lacerating climate of the time: 'each leaf is rent like split wood,' she wrote in a poem entitled simply 'Storm', 'You burden the trees/with black drops,/you swirl and crash'.[52]

H.D., as always, wrote soothingly to Lowell, and was probably talking soothingly to Pound. Aldington, whilst he agreed Pound was unreasonable, less tactfully expressed his irritation at the way the American arm of Macmillan had behaved. 'Macmillan's advertisement over here is perfectly correct and calm,' he wrote to Amy, 'but Ezra should have known that in America advertisement is a different thing . . . We are out to write poetry not advertisements. And is poetry a fine art or a jar of pickles? (I can't help girding at American commercialism; it is hell, and strangles art absolutely.)'[53] Aldington was an idealist, constantly disappointed and angered by the modern commercial world. In his next letter he said to Amy: 'It is a matter of great regret to me that Ezra should have been so "uncultured" in the English sense, as to write the idiotic letters he did. For after all, our little group was a small and efficient organism for the fostering of such remnants of "culture" as are left in this industrial world. It was Ezra's business, as it is the business of all of us, to care primarily for the art rather than for notoriety, and to work for the benefit of others rather than for his own.' In spite of this high-mindedness, however, he was obviously exasperated by Pound's 'peculiar irritable vanity', which he rather thoughtlessly described to

Amy as a 'form of exaggerated Americanism'. He also complained about Ford, whom he was seeing almost every day: 'He is incurably vain and self-satisfied. He repeatedly tells me that he is "the only poet there has been during the last three hundred years" and "the greatest intellect in England". And about a fortnight ago he said that he was after all the only real Imagist. So I shan't be sorry when I am through with this job. I could tell you lots more about him and lots more about Ezra and his present position but I had rather not write it. Perhaps I shall see you soon and we can talk these noble tragedies over.'

Aldington's own irritable frame of mind was probably caused as much by the war as by the foibles of his friends. He had told Amy earlier in that letter that he thought he would have to join up after Christmas, because he doubted if his work for the *Egoist* and Ford would go on much longer, and he would need to earn money; 'the king's shilling,' he said dourly, 'would at least settle the matter temporally – perhaps permanently'.[54] Although he does not mention it, a further problem must have been that the war had affected the exchange rate; there were now $7 to a pound instead of $5, so H.D.'s allowance was worth less. Aldington dreaded the prospect of joining the army. He loathed militarism, and, at twenty-two with a pregnant wife, must have found the thought of risking injury and death a profoundly depressing, not to say terrifying prospect. Even if he had found Dover College so alien, he had imbibed too much of the British public school spirit to admit in his letters to fear, but his poetry makes it increasingly apparent that he was living with dread. The next May he would write a poem about his tortured response to the loveliness of spring in time of war:

> A pear-tree, a broken white pyramid
> In a dingy garden, troubles me
> with ecstasy . . .
>
> And I am tormented,
> Obsessed,
> Among all this beauty,
> With a vision of ruins,
> Of walls crumbling into clay.[55]

His 'religion of beauty' was powerless to save him from the horror he saw ahead.

III

IF Pound had pointed out the evils of German philology to Ford, in other ways he remained as yet uninfected by the current war fever. He may have been influenced by Yeats, who was maintaining a stance of wary neutrality. Yeats wanted to endorse neither British patriotism nor Irish nationalist anti-recruiting agitation. Pound was not interested in the Irish dilemma, but he certainly followed Yeats for now in his role as the artist who remained above partisan nationalistic squabbles. When he wrote to Harriet in November, he did his best to sound disengaged: 'Ricketts,' he told her, 'has made the one mot of the war, the last flare of the 90's: "What depresses me most is the horrible fact that they can't *all* of them be beaten."'[56] Like many in late 1914, Pound saw the war as a temporary interruption, and was busy reviving an idea, which he had earlier expounded in 'Patria Mia', of a College of Arts, about which he would write to Alice Corbin Henderson. This was, he told Harriet, a 'scheme to enable things to keep on here in spite of the war-strain and (what will be more dangerous) the war back-wash and post bellum slump'.[57] The prospectus would be published in the *Egoist* in early November; the College of Arts, aimed at visiting Americans, would be doing something quite different from the formal courses given in conventional universities: 'We aim,' the prospectus said boldly, 'at an intellectual status no lower than that attained by the courts of the Italian Renaissance . . . This instruction is offered to anyone who wants it, not merely to those holding philological degrees. A knowledge of morphology is not essential to the appreciation of literature, even the literature of a forgotten age or decade.'[58] The names attached were, of course, Pound and his friends, including Wyndham Lewis, Edward Wadsworth, Arnold Dolmetsch, Katherine Heyman (clearly still around, though Pound did not appear to see much of her), Alvin Langdon Coburn (a photographer with whom Pound would later evolve an abstract form of photography which they called a 'vortograph') and John Cournos. For Americans seeking European culture, Britain was now one of the few safe destinations; it could have brought in useful money, but this was not so much a Mother-Courage-like attempt to cash in on the disaster, as Pound seizing an opportunity to instigate his own alternative form of education, as he would do some decades later in Rapallo. It could potentially have been a wonderful crucible of artistic innovation, but nothing appears to have come of it; by the next year, when the Germans had started torpedoing civilian shipping and sending Zeppelins to bomb London, Britain joined the rest of Europe as an unattractive destination for all but the most determined American students of the arts.

The war frustrated other of Pound's efforts to further his artistic projects. His essay on the Noh theatre came out in the *Quarterly Review*, but its editor, G.W. Prothero, told him, when he offered another piece, that he could not open the journal to anyone associated with *Blast*; he had given his word on the Noh article earlier in the year, so that had to go ahead, but there would be no sequel. It was an ill omen; the press would revert to a sturdy conservatism under the pressures of war, and Pound's irreverent cocking of snooks, tolerated indulgently before the war, became increasingly unwelcome in the climate of hysterical patriotism. The other troublemakers, as George Dangerfield points out, the suffragettes, the trade unionists and even for now the Irish, had immediately reverted to being loyal and law-abiding citizens; the rebellious artists, London thought, should do the same. Before the war, being shocked by the latest artistic innovation was an agreeable pastime. Lewis was probably not so wrong when he suggested that it had been to some extent a mutually enjoyable game: '"Kill John Bull with Art!" I shouted. And John and Mrs Bull leapt for joy, in a cynical convulsion. For they felt as safe as houses. So did I.' But now, even though, as Lewis says, 'a bigger *Blast* than mine had rather taken the wind out of my sails', that small artistic explosion appeared worryingly part of the conflagration.[59] Like Lawrence, Pound would find his earnings plummeting during the course of the war.

Pound did not reply to Lowell's letter about the advertisement, and she continued undeterred with her efforts to place the anthology. Macmillan had appeared enthusiastic, but she discovered that Pound, as well as writing to her, had sent a stinging letter to them, which had the result of making them decide, in spite of the success of Amy's own book, that they would rather not be involved with the new anthology. So she went back to Ferris Greenslet, the editor who had accepted her first book, to ask if Houghton Mifflin would be interested, and was so successful in convincing him that the new poetry was *la nouvelle vague* that he agreed to launch a whole new series devoted to the new poetry. Two of the first would be the anthology and Fletcher's *Irradiations*; two of the others a volume of Binyon's poetry, and some translations from the Japanese selected from the works of Lafcardio Hearn. Greenslet would publish eight volumes in this series in 1915, nine in 1916 and one in 1917. In November it was agreed that Amy would pay for the publication of the anthology, and Houghton Mifflin for advertising. There was, however, a stipulation. They would take it on only if Ford's poem 'On Heaven', which earlier that year Pound and Aldington had both so extravagantly praised, were dropped, as they considered it blasphemous. 'You know what the Puritan temper is,' Amy wrote. 'Orthodox religion has a strong hold over here, stronger than I, who live so far away from it, had realised.'[60] She wanted Aldington to ask Ford to submit some other work, but Ford, not unnaturally, would have nothing more to do with the venture.

Aldington was furious, and wrote Amy a long and impassioned letter, which he told her also expressed H.D.'s and Flint's views. He appeared to have quite forgotten his recent attack on 'the incurably vain and self-satisfied' Ford, when all he had admitted in Ford's favour was that he was 'a good critic – when not blinded by prejudice or *interest* – a good poet in a few of his poems'. Now he claimed that 'On Heaven' was 'their chief glory'. What would these 'imbeciles' object to next? he asks: 'Do you think there is a probability of them censoring me and Hilda for being Hellenically "irreligious"? The last book contained a poem called "Lesbia" by me and one called "Priapus" by Hilda, as you know; would these religious gentleman censor them?'[61] He asked her to remonstrate again with the publishers, but there was no suggestion that the other imagists would refuse to be published if her arguments failed. They were grateful to her for paying for the publication, and very happy that it looked like going ahead.

Houghton Mifflin remained resolutely opposed to 'On Heaven', though they said there was a possibility it might go in a later volume. Lowell in any case thought Ford's style somewhat *passé*, but she refrained from saying so to her fellow-imagists, instead defending the firm on the grounds that it was purely a commercial decision, not a justification that can have impressed Aldington. A mixture of irritation and gratitude would characterise the Aldingtons' relation with Amy: irritation less at her own actions than at her businesslike acceptance of the mores of American publishing. When Aldington told her the previous month that he had heard Rémy de Gourmont was sick and in penury, he was delighted when she immediately sent $200, saying it was 'a very small sum to pay for the inspiration and knowledge I have derived from his writings. Through him I can pay off a little of my immense debt to his nation.'[62] He was also grateful when she persuaded the recently launched *New Republic*, whose editor, Herbert Croly, was a friend of hers, to publish six articles by de Gourmont, which Aldington would translate. But there would soon be trouble.

The appearance of the *New Republic* had been welcomed in the *Egoist* (by Baptiste von Helmholtz, alias Pound) as a possible American equivalent to itself, because, like the *Egoist*, it promised to 'respect no taboos', though Pound had been dubious of such a claim by an American publication, citing the 'male hen' at the *Atlantic Review* and abusing the 'little old ladies, male and female, of those aged editorial offices' more generally.[63] Pound's misogynistic rhetoric was regrettable, but his suspicions turned out to be justified. The editor explained to Lowell that 'no taboos' only referred to political matters: he had heard Rémy de Gourmont's books were 'very French', and he stipulated that there must be 'nothing too French for their readers'.[64] Unfortunately de Gourmont was not able to purge his Frenchness to their satisfaction; they then claimed the articles were not up to their standards, which Aldington refused to believe, though Lowell defended Croly by saying that once de Gourmont had had to remove his 'Gallicisms' he was not left with enough to say.[65] Aldington was outraged, and wrote an insulting letter to Herbert Croly, no longer extant, but Aldington's comment on it to Amy suggests the flavour: 'I am still sufficiently a goddam Englishman to do & say exactly as I please & to have a profound contempt for all things American.'[66] Amy, put out at his treatment of Croly, especially as she wished to go on publishing in the *New Republic* herself, rebuked Aldington in her most Boston manner for his lack of restraint and insularity, but with Ferris Greenslet's help persuaded the *Boston Evening Transcript* to take the whole series, so there was a happy ending. De Gourmont sent her some manuscripts for her collection, and wrote to say: 'In brief, I am shipwrecked, and I shall never forget that you came nobly to my rescue, you who know me only through my writings.'[67] Poor man, he did not have long to remember it; he died in September 1915.

For now Pound was not making difficulties, though Aldington told

Amy he was worryingly 'unctuous', and feared he was 'meditating some devilry'.[68] Pound was in fact very preoccupied with his work on the Fenollosa papers, having moved on from the Japanese material to the Chinese. He was making translations, or rather, adaptations of translations, from Li Po, the poems which would appear the next year as *Cathay*, and rushed into the Aldingtons' flat four or five times a day to show them his latest, which H.D. thought very beautiful; indeed their simplicity and tautness may have owed something to her example. In spite of Pound's outbursts and Aldington's suspicions, they were still friends. Ford and Violet Hunt invited H.D. to stay with them in their cottage at Selsey for a while, and when she returned Pound reported to his mother, with what seems affectionate solicitude, that she was now looking more robust. The Aldingtons were, however, becoming closer to Flint, whom they now knew as Frank or Frankie. H.D. would refer to Flint as a brother (the Pre-Raphaelite Brotherhood appears to be the reference, though there may also have been memories of the extended family of her youth), and even talked of little Ianthe, to whom she was much attached, as her niece. Flint was by now even more darkly suspicious of Pound than Aldington. When his friends quarrelled, Flint always felt he had to take sides, and he had no doubt sided with Hulme against Lewis, and hence against Vorticism, and increasingly Pound.

In late December, the climate suddenly changed again. Pound was working on two new articles on imagism, and realising afresh how important it was to him. The first was in the *New Age*, in a series entitled 'Affirmations', mainly promoting the Vorticist artists and sculptors, though one article dealt with imagism in poetry. He reminded his readers firmly that it was he who had named the movement: 'Imagisme', he says, 'has been taken by some to mean Hellenism; by others the word is used most carelessly, to designate any sort of poem in vers libre. Having omitted to copyright the word at its birth I cannot prevent its misuse. I can only say what I meant by the word when I made it.' He won't, however, 'guarantee that [his] thoughts about it will remain absolutely stationary'. He insists, as before, that 'the Image is more than an idea. It is a vortex or cluster of fused ideas and is endowed with energy', but in other ways his definition has shifted somewhat again. He refers back to his earlier article in the same series on Vorticism, in which he had emphasised that the different arts have different 'primary pigments', but that all forms of Vorticism, of which imagism is one, have in common a reliance on 'the creative faculty as opposed to the mimetic'. These points re-emerge ('pigment' has rather engagingly turned into 'figment'), and he also repeats his conviction that energy or 'intense emotion' creates form. As he had explained by way of analogy in the 'Vorticism' article, 'if you clap a strong magnet beneath a plateful of iron filings, the energies of the magnet will proceed to organise form', and it is, he says, 'emotional force [that] gives the image'.[69]

The second article was for *T.P.'s Weekly*. In it, Pound makes clear that his ideas have moved on yet again, for he now insists that imagism exemplifies all that excited him about the Chinese, through which he had recently found a new model for his poetics. The imagists, he says, have 'sought the force of Chinese ideographs *without knowing it*'. It is the first expression of his conviction, which would remain central to his thought, that poetry should emulate what he believed to be the directness and simultaneity of the Chinese characters, his latest version of the poet's Adamic language. English, 'being the strongest and least inflected of the European languages', is, he says, according to 'the late Ernest Fenollosa, sometime Imperial Commissioner of Art in Tokyo', the best language to 'render the force and concision of the uninflected Chinese'. Imagism was not new, a point all the imagists repeatedly make, and to prove it he quotes from a range of authors from the poet of 'The Seafarer' to Swinburne, 'the most uneven of the Victorian poets and the most splendid', ending unexpectedly with Lionel Johnson – nothing, Pound claimed, could be more Chinese than his line, 'Clear lie the fields, and fade into blue air'.[70]

With this renewed consciousness of imagism's significance, Pound began to complain again about the fact that the anthology was to have the word 'imagist' in the title. H.D., still hoping for peace, wrote to Lowell, begging her to change the name. It would be, she said, 'much nicer not to be an –ism in any case. Weren't the Pre-Raphaelites "The Seven" or possibly "The Nine"?' Perhaps they should be 'The Six'. H.D. would have greatly preferred to drop the contentious term; it meant a great deal to her to be one of a group of poets working together, but she hated being labelled. She added a postscript underlining twice that Aldington had said '*in no event can we now appear under the direct title Imagiste*'.[71] Lowell cabled back that she would talk to the publishers.

Aldington wrote himself a few days later, urging Lowell again to drop the word. Having spoken to the publishers, however, she was reluctant to do so. Ferris Greenslet had suggested, drawing on her quotation from Henley in her preface to *Sword Blades and Poppy Seed*, that 'Quintessentialists' might actually fit them better, but he was in no doubt that imagism had, in today's terms, market appeal. Amy wrote on 19 January 1915 (having said she had bankrupted herself on cables) to make the point:

'Imagiste' has come to have a certain meaning among lovers of poetry, and although Ezra is known to have invented it, it has swung far beyond him and really become a word to designate a certain kind of poetry. For that reason it has a commercial value, as people interested in our sort of poetry know that they are getting it when they see the word 'Imagiste' on the cover. Ezra knows that very well or he would not be so anxious to hang on to the word because, mind you, Ezra is thoroughly American in his understanding of the value of advertisement.[72]

There is no doubt that Lowell was correct in that last statement (I have indeed quoted it earlier), and the same applied to herself; she and Pound were much more alike than either of them would ever be happy to admit. Yet whatever else one might think of her actions, it has to be granted that she took her promise of democracy seriously. Aldington – and therefore one presumes H.D. – reluctantly agreed, but Lowell would not go ahead without Flint's support. He wrote her a letter, with his usual sardonic wit, which gave her more reassurance than she had ever hoped for:

Richard tells me that you have been disturbing the herrings in the pond with the multiplicity and plexity of your cablegrams. And that you want my permission to do something or other. Do it by all means; I leave everything to you on the spot. But don't issue us into the world as the Quintessentialists or anything else high falutin' and fantastic. Please don't do that. Before you decide on anything: ask yourself: Would Boston do it? If yes, don't. Perhaps you had better stick to the old title of Some Imagists or whatever it was. Never mind about Ezra. He no more invented imagism than he invented the moon. I have all the documents in proof. He got all his ideas about Imagisme from the little cénacle which used to meet at the Tour Eiffel, off Tottenham Court Road. He was a late comer to those meetings – much later than I said in my review of his Ripostes, where, in the preface to Hulme's Complete Poetical Works, he refers to our jousts. There Hulme, the leading and combining spirit talked of Images, and so forth, as we all did, and produced the first Imagiste poems . . . All Ezra did therefore was to run about talking about the things which existed as though it was the thing that he had made. I thought his phrase in the preface . . . to the effect that the future was in the keeping of the Imagists was in jest at the expense of Hulme & co. Be all that as it may – Imagisme be damned! I don't want to be called an Imagiste at all. I entered the whole thing as a joke, – une mystification littéraire – stratégie littéraire si vous voulez. That Ezra would strut about as the inventor of a real new live aesthetic afterwards did not occur to me. There is nothing new in Imagisme: and if I write its history it will be seen that Ezra's part in it was very little more than the – very American – one of advertising agent; and he has done his work so badly that everyone has taken the thing as a silly joke.[73]

Lowell was delighted, and it was decided that the anthology would be entitled *Some Imagist Poets*, eschewing Pound's Gallicisms. Fletcher had also written to corroborate Flint's version, saying that although he had not been part of the earlier group, he had been invited to join its meetings in 'some dirty little Italian restaurant somewhere', and recalled reading Pound's statement in *Ripostes* to the effect that the *imagistes* were the descendants of this same *Ecole des Images*.[74] For now, resolution was at last achieved, and the anthology went to press.

IV

ONE has to sympathise with Pound. Even if there is much in what Flint says about the fact that Pound did not invent a new aesthetic, he gave the movement direction, manifestos, drive and, most importantly, a name. He had constantly revisited it, suggesting new metaphors and analogies by which those original ideas could be understood. On the one hand, for him it had come to have a visionary significance. On the other, he had invented a brand, one with 'commercial value', as Amy said, and even if Pound would not have wished to make his protest in those terms he was conscious of what its loss would mean. He considered himself the major poetic talent of the imagist movement, and most literary critics would still agree, though some might now argue the case for H.D. or, if one includes him among the imagists, Williams, but at the time Pound was an established poet in the way none of the others were. It is hard to gauge his inner feelings; if, as Williams had noticed a decade earlier, he rarely even as a young man gave away any hint of his vulnerabilities, one has glimpses of them in his letters to Margaret and occasionally to Dorothy, and in the notes on his walking tour. The letters by this stage are largely public performances, full of fireworks and bravado. Yet Pound was without doubt deeply hurt by what he felt was a betrayal, though he responded by demonising Lowell cruelly and unrelentingly; her reputation is only just beginning to recover from his malign denunciations.

Yet, in addition, Pound must also have felt a crisis of identity; two years earlier he had reinvented himself as a leader of a movement, and now that movement was in disarray. What made things even worse was that, if Amy were edging imagism out of Pound's grasp, there were already ominous signs that Vorticism would not survive the war; Pound's efforts to prolong it would grow more and more frenzied. The Rebel Arts Centre had dissolved after Lewis and Lechmere fell out bitterly, shortly after the *Blast* dinner. Within a fortnight, the Great Ormond Street premises had been vacated. In happier circumstances, alternative accommodation might have been found, but the war began a week later and the painters went their separate ways. Richard Cork has suggested that, apart from Lewis, they were in any case always restive under the collective name of Vorticists, which they felt Lewis and Pound had sprung on them. Even Lewis and Pound had rather different views of what Vorticism was, although Pound at least does not seem to have realised this, certainly not at the time. One of Lewis' several manifestos in *Blast* proclaimed, 'Our vortex is not afraid of the Past: it has forgotten it's [*sic*] existence'.[75] (Lewis' misuse of the apostrophe rivals even that of most present-day undergraduates.) Lewis in particular blasted the years 1837–1900, while Pound quoted both Pater and Whistler as ancestors; he did not repudiate everything between 1837 and 1900. In Pound's manifesto he wrote that 'All experience rushes into this vortex. All the energized past, all the past that is living and worthy to live'. With Vorticism as with imagism, Pound argues that the best art of the past followed similar precepts. 'Music,' he insisted, 'was vorticist in the Bach–Mozart period, before it went off into romance and sentiment and description.'[76] Lewis in the 1920s would assert that Pound was at heart a *passéiste*, and that the literary side of the movement always had lagged behind the visual, but at the time he tolerated Pound's continued interest in the past; making the best of it, he would describe him in the second issue of *Blast* as a 'Demon pantechnicon driver, busy with removal of old world into new quarters. In his steel net of impeccable technique, he has lately caught Li Po. Energy of a discriminating Element.'[77] It was a description that delighted Pound.

There were other differences between the two. Whilst Pound wanted to emphasise the energy and fluid force of the Vortex, Lewis, anxious to distance himself from the Futurists' love of speed and movement, stressed its still centre. According to Douglas Goldring, Lewis would explain the Vortex to all and sundry thus: 'You think at once of a whirlpool . . . At the heart of the whirlpool is a great silent place where all the energy is concentrated. And there, at the point of concentration, is the Vorticist.' Goldring's comment on this definition was simply: 'Whatever else the Vorticists may have been, they were certainly not silent.'[78] Noisiness was something Pound shared with Lewis, but Lewis' insistence that the machine and the industrial are the proper subject of Vorticist art found little echo in Pound. His example of a Vorticist poem had been H.D.'s 'Oread', whose sea, pines and rocks could not be more different from the subject-matter advocated by Lewis. When Lewis changed his mind about the machine, he would distance himself from Vorticism for reasons Pound appears never to have grasped.

Lewis did not reject the past completely, but he saw it very differently from Pound; like Hulme, Lewis asserted the kinship of this new geometric art with that of archaic and non-Western peoples. 'The Art-Instinct,' he wrote in *Blast*, 'is permanently primitive.'[79] Like Worringer, the German art historian who had so influenced Hulme, he saw geometric form, wherever it appeared, as a defence against the fearful chaos of existence. The Vorticists, with what he described as their 'egoistic hardening', their concentration, their eschewal of the softness of the humanistic, representational tradition, their rejection of the messiness of everyday life for the abstractions of art, are in tune with those archaic and non-Western people: he praised an exhibition of German woodcuts because the 'black, nervous fluid of existence flows and forms into hard stagnant masses in this white luminous body . . . It is African black . . . disciplined, blunt, thick and brutal'.[80] As with Hulme, one is left with the paradox that an aggressively masculine stance comes out of a fearful core. The belligerence of Vorticism is a response to what Lewis saw as a violent and predatory world. If, like Lewis, one thinks the cultured surface of bourgeois life a sham, and sees a society of embattled desires and hostile forces, an industrial world of competition and ruthless disregard for the weak, the metropolis as an 'iron jungle', as *Blast* 2 would put it, the world is a dangerous and cruel place.[81] All one can do is to fight aggressively to be one of those who win. Lewis' vision of the world in 1914 has at base much in common with that of his Marxist contemporaries, though while they would condemn the way the strong oppressed the weak, Lewis takes it as a fact of life. Pound's version of primitivism was very different; he loved the periods when art forms were young and new, simple yet intense, and his values were more purely bound up with his belief in the importance of art, an aestheticism for which Lewis would later castigate him.

Lewis' differences with Pound would gradually become clear to him, but for now they were on the barricades together. In 1914, they both had immensely high hopes for the movement they called Vorticism. Under the antics and the quarrels they had been deadly serious; the showmanship was, they believed, simply a necessary tactic. At the imagists' dinner, Pound, Lowell reported, quite openly described *Blast* as advertising, and he would write in 1915 that *Blast*'s 'large type and the flaring cover are merely bright plumage. They are the gay petals which lure.'[82] But this did not mean that he and Lewis did not believe in the Vorticist mission, even if they thought it meant different things. As Lewis would write later of himself: 'He thought the time had come to shatter the visible world to bits, and build it nearer to the heart's desire; and he really was persuaded that this *absolute* transformation was imminent . . . The War looked to him like an episode at first – rather proving his contentions than otherwise.'[83] Perhaps it was a *folie à deux*, but they had really believed they were going to change the world, and their disappointment would be bitter. Pound was still writing in January 1915, 'are we, as one likes to suppose, on the brink of another really great awakening, when the creative or art vortices shall be strong enough, when the people who care will be well enough organised to set the fine fashion, to impose it, to make the great age?'[84] His use of the word 'impose' is characteristic, and emblematic of his misunderstanding of how artistic changes come about, or, at any rate, worthwhile artistic changes – in two decades' time, the Nazis and the Stalinists would certainly be imposing artistic styles by decree. Yet Pound's question mark itself perhaps indicated that doubt was already setting in. As Lewis later wrote: '*We are the first men of a Future that has not materialised. We belong to a "great age" that has not come off.*'[85] Ultimately, as far as the world of the arts and of literature was concerned, those pre-war artistic experiments did indeed make an impact, but the next few years would prove dark and discouraging.

One after another, many of the rebel artists and their supporters left for the war. By the autumn of 1914, Hulme and Gaudier were already at the front, Gaudier having like Hulme immediately enlisted, in his case in the French Army. Initially, he found this a problematic venture, having deserted the army some time before; for a while he was in danger of being court-martialled rather than sent to the trenches, but he was finally accepted. Epstein recalled in his autobiography seeing him off at Charing Cross station: 'The turmoil was terrible. Troops were departing and Sophie was in a state of hysterics and collapse. Gaudier's friends, including Hulme, Richard Aldington, Tancred and Ethel Kibblewhite, were there to see him off, and Gaudier himself, terribly pale and shaken by Sophie's loud sobs, said good-bye to us.'[86] Aldington later recalled that they sang the Marseillaise as Gaudier left, adding even more to the noisiness of the scene.[87] Lewis would be around for a while; he was suffering from severe gonorrhoea that had turned into septicaemia, which made enlisting out of the question for now, but Pound reported to Harriet Monroe that 'Wadsworth, along with

Augustus John and nearly everybody, is drilling in the courtyard of the Royal Academy'.[88]

Those of the *Blast* group who were left out of uniform were moving in different directions. Lewis and Epstein had quarrelled, much to Pound's dismay, though as Epstein was very much Hulme's protégé and friend, it was not surprising that once Hulme and Lewis had become enemies, Epstein would take Hulme's side. In addition, *Blast* looked a very different production in the autumn from the way it had appeared in June. Even some of those who had enjoyed its rebellious energy in June began, once the war was under way, to find the aesthetics and antics of those that Aldington described as the Blastites disturbingly akin to the bombardments on the front. Aldington, who had already decided he wanted no more truck with Lewis, reported to Amy: 'I met Epstein the other day and he told me he had also determined to have nothing to do with Lewis . . . I said Lewis was a charlatan, and he said yes, but he wasn't even a decent charlatan, he was ungenerous.'[89] It might seem a volte-face on Aldington's part, but the world had changed. In June 1914, *Blast*'s aggression was a delightful joke. By the end of the year, the bleak message behind what Pound had called the 'bright plumage' and 'gay petals', that the world was engulfed in a hard, violent, mechanised conflict, felt terrifyingly like the glorification of a grim truth.

Judgement of the movement depended, perhaps, on whether one thought of the Vorticist vision as diagnosis or programme; in the later war years, to most people, even to Lewis himself, it began to look more like the latter. Yet Lewis had earlier argued in *Blast* that 'an Art must be organic with its Time', and Ford, in full agreement with this doctrine, had defended the Vorticists as recorders of the modern world when he had reviewed that first issue: 'Nowadays, ten times a day we are whirled at incredible speeds through gloom, amidst clamour. And the business of the young artist of to-day is to render those glooms, those clamours, those iron boxes, those explosions, those voices from the metal-horns of talking machines and hooters.'[90] From the longer perspective, many critics would agree with Ford that the power of Vorticism came from its diagnosis of the time. Paul Overy has written of the movement that at 'their best the Vorticists achieved a strong visualisation of the head-long flight of Europe into mechanical barbarity, an awareness of the brutalisation of man by his irresponsible control of his environment that is lacking in the idealised art of Cubism and the romanticized art of Futurism.'[91] Such a diagnosis is what Jacob Epstein himself said he offered in his famous carving of the *Rock Drill*, which he would exhibit the following spring. Epstein remained deeply opposed to Lewis, and in no way considered himself a Vorticist, but Richard Cork suggests that this work, which had originally appeared mounted on a mechanical drill, is 'the most unequivocal and haunting sculptural expression of the Vorticists' dual concern with the machine and with dehumanised destruction'.[92] Epstein himself in his autobiography describes it as 'the armed, sinister figure of today and tomorrow. No humanity, only the terrible Frankenstein's monster we have made ourselves into.'[93] The Jewish Epstein was by then looking back after the horrors of the Second as well as the First World War, and in retrospect he saw his work as a prophetic and terrible warning, but even at the time it may have been his horror at the deadly and destructive modern machines of war, of which news came from the front daily, that had made him so suspicious of Lewis. When Epstein exhibited the piece again in 1916, he had removed the drill, cut off the driller's legs, making his work, according to Cork, 'a victim of the machine age . . . his eyes look pitiful under their metal hood as they peer into the distance with no hope'.[94]

In spite of these departures and dissensions, Vorticism hung on. Ford had given Lewis a commission to do up his study, 'transforming it,' as Richard Cork puts it, 'into a crimson Vorticist showpiece', not perhaps very restful for a study, but then Ford was not a resting man.[95] The next year Lewis with Helen Saunders' help would decorate a Vorticist room at the Tour Eiffel restaurant. Lewis and Pound were planning another issue of *Blast*, though they would not be able to produce it until the following July; 1915 would also see the first and only Vorticist Exhibition. Pound was coming to think that the war climate was inimical to good art. He wrote to Monroe in November 1914 to say there was a Rodin exhibit at the South Kensington Museum (it had been the Victoria & Albert for some time, but no one appears to have used the name), 'good of its kind but it does look like muck after one has got one's eye in on Epstein's Babylonian austerity'. An exhibition of Modern Spanish Art – with no Picassos – was also 'MUCK', this time in capitals.[96] The violence of Pound's judgements was steadily increasing; under criticism from others, he was becoming more and more locked into his persona of the authoritarian arbiter of artistic excellence, the ruthless denouncer of all sham art, the lonely but fearless battler against the forces of philistinism.

War damage was taking its toll on London's literary world and in one way or another openings for the 'newer' poets were closing. The *New Age* took up a patriotic pro-war position, and was notably less sympathetic to artistic and poetic experimentation than it had been; it

still continued to publish the young avant-garde, but denounced them
more and more belligerently.[97] Monro's *Poetry and Drama* would cease
publication at the end of 1915, largely on account of paper shortages,
and the *Egoist* was shaky. The latter had a tiny circulation, and never
made money, as it attracted little advertising. Even the *Freewoman* had
carried more, with regular advertisements for women's clothes from
places like Debenham and Freebody's, but those had all gone. During
1914, the magazine brought in £37, but had cost £337 to bring out,
and was in fact being funded by anonymous donations from Harriet
Shaw Weaver herself. Pound suggested they suspended publication until
after the war, but Weaver was not one to give in easily. She wrote to
Amy in November asking her to buy the literary section of the magazine for £300 a year. Amy thought London was too far away for her to
have the control she would have liked; in any case she loathed Dora
Marsden's articles, and felt she would be too out of sympathy with that
side of the paper. Dora Marsden was increasingly opposed to democracy, which she saw as a sham that offered the illusion that the people
had some say in their government, whilst in fact it was controlled by
vested interests. Like Pound at this stage, in the war she saw little difference between the sides. All this shocked Lowell, but Dora Marsden was
equally opposed to Lowell. That she had reluctantly agreed to approach
Lowell again is a measure of her anxiety about the paper's financial
health. In the event Harriet Shaw Weaver managed to keep it going by
herself. She cut the size of each issue to 16 pages, changed it from fortnightly to monthly, and cut the editorial salaries, and, of course, put in
some more of her own money. The *Egoist* would outlast the war.

V

Now that Lowell had Ada Russell living with her permanently, she was settling down to a very comfortable way of life in her vast house in Brooklyn. Ada Russell was housekeeper, critic, adviser and friend. She organised the household, which she made sure carried on its business as silently as possible until Amy rose at three in the afternoon. Ada would always be available to read and comment on Lowell's latest poem, playing such a vital role in sustaining Lowell's efforts and advising on them, to say nothing of being the inspiration of much of her writing, that Lowell suggested she should put a sign over the front door saying 'Lowell & Russell, Makers of Fine Poems'.[98] What would Pound, or even Aldington, have said about this shameless analogy between poetry and trade? Ada also arranged Amy's frequent dinner parties, entertaining the guests until the hostess appeared late in the meal, accompanied by her sheep-dogs. After dinner, they would move to the library, and Lowell would sit and talk vivaciously to her guests, while cigarettes, cigars, coffee and liqueurs were passed round. Guests were provided with towels for their laps, in case the sheep-dogs wanted to sit on them. The evening would finish sharply at 12.05, and guests would depart to catch the last car to Boston at 12.15. Amy would then start work, with a cold supper tray laid out for her in case she felt hungry during the night. In the morning her two secretaries, whom she began to employ after her return from London, would type up the previous night's work – new poems, corrected drafts, articles and lectures. After three they would be summoned to the bedroom to take dictation, mainly of Amy's voluminous correspondence. They kept carbons of all her letters, which means that copies still exist of letters that never reached her English recipients because the top copies had gone on ships that were torpedoed *en route*.

In early December, John Gould Fletcher came to stay for a week. He had written to Amy before he left England, saying he would be staying in New York, but wouldn't be able to afford the trip to Boston. Somehow he managed it. Lowell was apprehensive about the visit, writing to Aldington that 'I am a good deal worried over Fletcher's arriving as I can see no future for him with his inability to put himself in harness and his untactful manner with people.'[99] In the event, the visit was a great success, with Lowell reporting that Fletcher was much improved, a 'most delightful companion' and 'a thoroughly nice fellow'.[100] There was one difficult scene, when Fletcher was taken out to dinner by Carl Engel and another musician, and, in a fit of irritation, was extremely rude to them both and stormed out of the restaurant. Amy, he said later, rebuked him fiercely and he burst into tears, whereupon she became sweetness and light, calmed him down, and appears not to have held the incident against him. Fletcher was full of admiration for her work, praising her poetry and telling her that her prose poems, which he named 'polyphonic prose', were something absolutely new in poetry, as new, in fact, as Chaucer had been. Fletcher was right that Lowell's polyphonic prose was strikingly innovative, and if, like all her poetry, it was neglected for many years, it has recently been much praised for its rich and musical synaesthetic evocation of the sounds, colours and smells of city life, a new kind of poetry responding to modern urban experience.[101] Lowell enjoyed Fletcher's praise, and she felt that, being American and on hand, he was a particular ally. His views coincided with her own on many points, including their shared loathing for Pound. More positively, they both wanted to develop a new poetry in America, but not one that rejected outside influences. Commenting on an article that she had just published in *Poetry* on 'Nationalism in Art', he said he too was quite sure that 'there *is* an American note, and it is to be found precisely in those works which carry on and develop further the elements of the universal art-tradition, not in those who try to be "barbaric yawps" and nothing else'.[102] At this point he saw Lowell very much as a comrade. Poets must free themselves, he told her, from the kind of internecine artistic bickering that goes on in London: 'It is time for artists to become a new army and to make some sort of a stand against the encroaching bourgeoisie, instead of wasting time in sharp-shooting among themselves'.[103] Unfortunately, Fletcher would prove incapable of eschewing sharp-shooting for very long, but he was on his best behaviour for now.

Fletcher went on to Chicago, a two-day train journey though blizzards, but he was rewarded by a wonderful view of the Niagara Falls, with all the surrounding trees coated in ice from the spray, and, he noted approvingly, free from tourists. He had gone to meet Harriet Monroe, who accepted an article from him on Lowell's poetry. At once his resolution against artistic infighting was sorely tested: he told Amy he had had 'to talk about nothing but Lindsay and Pound since I arrived. I am sick of those two worthies'. He assured her, however, that he had been polite, though he did acknowledge that he probably 'hadn't made a hit'. He also called in to meet the editor of the *Little Review*, Margaret Anderson, whom he scornfully described as a 'Vassar sophomore . . . Giggles, enthusiasm, blind confidence, utter lack of knowledge', by which latter trait he appears to mean that she had never heard of him.[104] He was introduced to Edgar Lee Masters, of whom he had never heard. Masters, whose *Spoon River Anthology* was about to be an instant success, translated into seventy languages, became in Monroe's eyes the third figure in the Chicago renaissance, joining Carl Sandburg and Vachel Lindsay as exemplars of Middle Western poetic vigour. Even Pound admired Masters for a while, saying at one stage he thought he and Eliot were the two most promising American poets, but he soon lost his enthusiasm; he had probably genuinely changed his mind, but he could not have brought himself to admire a bestseller. It is just possible Pound's description of Masters in the January 1915 *Egoist* as the first poet discovered by the American press was an oblique way of pointing out that in his view Amy was not a real poet, since the American press had discovered her some time earlier. Aldington certainly thought that was Pound's aim.

Fletcher never even briefly admired the Chicago triumvirate. He told Lowell that Monroe had wanted him to meet Lindsay and Sandburg, but he had managed to avoid them. He tried to persuade Harriet not to accept a 'neurasthenic' war poem by Lawrence, and tactlessly told Amy that Lawrence had sent the letter criticising 'The Bombardment' for its frivolity, which Harriet had unwisely shown him. Monroe also let him read Eliot's 'Prufrock', to get his opinion of Pound's latest discovery. She had written to Pound complaining that it was 'too much like "Henry James carried to the Nth degree"', part of its strength, one might argue. Fletcher thought it rather good. 'It has an excellent beginning – a description of a London fog (Eliot is in London somewhere) and is called "The Love Song of J. Alfred Prufrock," being an attempt to put down the state of mind of a man who is so well bred as to be incapable of affirming his love for anyone on earth.'[105] Fletcher's biographer suggests that he recognised Prufrock's problem so sharply because it was so very much his own. He thought the poem went off towards the end, a judgement which led Monroe to attempt to get Eliot at least to rewrite the conclusion before she published it; she predictably received an incandescent letter from Pound: 'a portrait satire on futility can't end by turning that quintessence of futility, Mr P. into a reformed character breathing out fire and ozone'. And he added: 'Fletcher is no great judge of anything. He has a lawless and uncontrolled ability to catch certain effects, mostly of colour, but no finishing sense', a comment that has a certain validity.[106] 'Lawless and uncontrolled' was true of Fletcher's personality as well as his poetry. Fletcher, however, became a great admirer of Eliot's poetry.

From Chicago, Fletcher returned home to Arkansas, finding it very dull. He had only gone there in order to dun his sisters for money to return to live in Boston, but it would be some months before he could persuade them to give him enough to get back. His sisters, he told Amy, took no interest in his poetry. He mooned around the house by himself, brooding over his relationship with Daisy and his past. Yet while he was there, he wrote his moving sequence, 'The Ghosts of an Old House', recalling his childhood there. He starts with his father's bedroom:

> The clump of jessamine
> Softly beneath the rain
> Rocks its golden flowers
>
> In this room my father died:
> His bed is in the corner.
> No one has slept in it
> Since the morning when he wakened
> To meet death's hands at his heart.
> I cannot go into this room,
> Without feeling something big and angry
> Waiting for me
> To throw me on the bed,
> And press its thumbs in my throat.[107]

The jessamine tenderly rocking its flowers, the dark terrors the father in death still inspires: the longings and agonising fears of his childhood are simultaneously evoked here. The sequence is one of Fletcher's most powerful and poignant works.

One reason for Fletcher's visit to the *Little Review* had been to report to Lowell on whether it might be a good investment for her. Although she had turned down the *Egoist* offer, owning a portion of a magazine still appealed to her. Fletcher gloomily warned against it, saying it was bound to fail, as the only things behind it were 'girlish enthusiasm and complete ignorance'. Lowell would have trouble 'restraining Miss Anderson's exuberance', and Harriet Monroe would undoubtedly become jealous.[108] Anderson, he added, was too much under the influence of people like the anarchist Emma Goldman, and poets like Vachel Lindsay and Rupert Brooke – an extraordinarily diverse set of influences – and Fletcher was suspicious of her printer, apparently on the grounds that he was Jewish; since he published the *Little Review* for free because his wife liked the magazine, he sounded ideal. Lowell was not to be deterred. After all, Anderson had been a keen supporter of the imagist cause from the start, in July 1914 reprinting some of the original *Des Imagistes*, including Lowell's 'In a Garden'. Amy travelled to Chicago in January 1915, partly to see Harriet Monroe, who threw a poets' party for her, but also to meet Margaret Anderson.

Anderson recounted the episode in her memoir, *My Thirty Years' War*: 'Harriet Monroe,' she recalled, 'appeared at the door of 917 one morning with a visitor – a large and important visitor whom I have always considered among the most charming people I have known.' She had already spoken to Lowell on the telephone, and from her voice had imagined her 'a slender and imperious blonde'. Well, imperious was right. 'Culture and good taste were stamped upon her. She was brunette, her voice was contralto, her nose like a Roman emperor's and her manner somewhat more masterful.' Lowell's proposition was that for $150 a month (slightly more than the *Egoist* had been asking) she would direct the poetry department. She introduced this offer in a way that delighted Anderson: 'I've had a fight with Ezra Pound,' she began. 'When I was in London . . . I offered to join his group and put the Imagists on the map. Ezra refused. All right, my dear chap, I said, we'll see who's who in this business. I'll go back to America and advertise myself so extensively that you'll wish you had come in with me.' Having control of poetry at the *Little Review* would enable her to support the cause of modern poetry, and she assured Anderson that she could count on her 'never to dictate'. Anderson thought otherwise: 'No clairvoyance was needed to know that Amy Lowell would dictate, uniquely and majestically, any adventure in which she had a part.'[109] She turned her down, though she would continue regularly to publish her work, as well as that of the Aldingtons, Flint and Fletcher. It's a highly entertaining story, but was Anderson's assessment of Lowell's character right? In fact, Lowell never precisely dictated to her fellow imagists – they would have taken it very ill – though it has to be said, as with the issue of the anthology's title, they would often come round to her point of view in the end. Perhaps it was her charm as much as her purposefulness, though one should not ignore the fact that publication of the anthology depended on her money. The flaw in Lowell's view of poetic democracy was the same as that in her very American understanding of political freedom: she would never recognise that those who set out with money were more equal than those without.

In the meantime, Lowell had had a much more cheerful letter from Aldington. In December, he and H.D. had moved to a larger flat in Hampstead, with, as he told Amy, 'a real bathroom & kitchen'. Both of them preferred the country to the city, but Hampstead, living as they did in Christchurch Place close to the heath, was in some ways the best of both worlds. They were much happier out there, Aldington reported: 'I surprise my useless American wife with my skill & accuracy in cooking potatoes & mending chairs – they are admirable avocations for clearing one's mind in this cleaner atmosphere, away from Kensington squabbles.' Aldington said optimistically that the anthology would bring them 'fame, if not fortune'. Unlike Lowell, he did not anticipate wide sales. Aldington had been schooled by Pound to distrust the public; contrary to Anderson's view, he thought Lowell too democratic, and upbraided her for it: 'You still believe in the people! My dear Amy, that is because your means allow you to ignore the people. If you wish accurate accounts of the people, apply to Lawrence, Flint & co, who have risen from the deep.'[110]

Whether H.D. still went to the British Museum during the remainder of her pregnancy is hard to guess. She and Aldington kept in touch with their Kensington friends – in spite of Aldington's disparaging comments on Kensington squabbles – and Aldington went regularly to Bloomsbury to the *Egoist* office. But the British Museum Reading Room was at the best of times a male-dominated place, and she may have felt self-conscious going there as a pregnant woman. One indication – not conclusive, of course – is that her poems during that period were no longer translations, on which she generally worked there, though she would return to these later in the year. Aldington claimed the two of them were happier, but walks on the heath, even the coming of spring, could not banish the war. Rereading her early poems many years later

H.D. was struck by how sad they were, and recalled that at this time an 'iron-curtain' fell between her and her secure upbringing, with her 'somewhat – well – not hot-house, but in a way, very comfortable surroundings' and her 'very petted and spoiled American life'.[111] She was now in a bleak and menacing world, vulnerable and afraid. One poem she wrote that spring was entitled 'Midday', in which emotional exhaustion and debilitating strain are suggested through the enervating, corrosive heat of a too hot noon:

> The light beats upon me.
> I am startled –
> A split leaf rushes on the paved floor
>
> I am anguished – defeated.
>
> A slight wind shakes the seed-pods.
> My thoughts are spent as the black seeds.
>
> My thoughts tear me.
> I dread their fever.
> I am scattered in its whirl.
> I am scattered like hot shrivelled seeds.
>
> The shrivelled seeds are spilt on the path.
> The grass bends with dust.
> The grape slips under its crackled leaf.[112]

Paradoxically, she had created a powerful poem about the loss of creativity, evoking a sense of the barren, anguished, diminished existence experienced by so many civilians at the time, torn by constant anxiety about the war.

The Aldingtons did not move in order to put distance between themselves and Pound, but given the tensions it may have been an added bonus. Pound and Dorothy were in any case out of London for January and February 1915, having gone to Stone Cottage with Yeats at the end of December. One might think this an odd experience for a new wife, but Dorothy appears to have accepted it with good grace. She was used to spending time in country houses. Yeats reported that she was doing the housekeeping, but that must only have meant that she was giving Alice Welfare the orders for meals. Dorothy, of course, did not cook.

She was an avid reader, and she was doing more painting, in particular designing a Vorticist cover for a new edition of *Ripostes* that Mathews was to bring out later in the year. Yeats wrote to Mabel Beardsley that Pound's 'charming young wife' looked 'as if her face was made out of Dresden China. I look at her in perpetual wonder. It is so hard to believe she is real; & yet she spends all her daylight hours drawing the most monstrous cubist pictures.'[13] For all three, it was something of a relief to get away from the talk of the war, from the troops passing through London on their way to the front, from the newspapers full of loud patriotism and dark news. Yet on one occasion they had a blackout imposed – an unheard of thing at that time, though something to which the country would get rapidly accustomed. Soldiers were constantly manoeuvring all around them; one day, Pound told his mother, a regiment descended on them and drank all their cider. In addition, as James Longenbach points out in *Stone Cottage*, Pound was hearing regular reports from Gaudier in the trenches, and Yeats news from Maud Gonne, who was nursing the wounded and dying in France. Even in their country retreat, the war could not be kept at bay.

Pound's main task as Yeats' secretary, as the year before, was to read to him in the evenings, to save further damage to Yeats' eyes. That winter, as well as a wide variety of poetry, he read aloud to Yeats a strange travel book, for which they both professed great admiration. This was C.L. Doughty's long *Arabia Deserta*, little read when it was first published in 1888, written in strangely convoluted and archaicised English, so that the desert Arabs appear distanced in time as well as space, and the language itself gives the impression that they still live in biblical days. Longenbach suggests the experience of reading Doughty encouraged both poets further in their belief that they should speak only to an elite audience. He quotes what Pound wrote in 1917 in the *New Age*: 'the number of people who can read Doughty's "Arabia Deserta" is decently and respectfully limited; so much so that the readers of that work tend to form an almost secret society, a cellule at least of an actual, if almost imperceptible, aristocracy'.[14] Yet, Pound was also attracted by Doughty's acounts of the *djinn*, the spirits of the dead that speak through living people, in whom Allen Upward had already aroused his interest, the artist's 'allies aforetime', as he had called them in his article on 'The New Sculpture' the previous February. Longenbach suggests the *djinn* must have recalled to Pound his intense experience of the presence of the troubadours on his walking tour, for in March he published a poem, entitled 'Provincia Deserta', full of memories of the places he passed through then, recalling the fascination with the light in the mountains that he had recorded in his diary: 'I have lain in Rocafixada,/level with sunset,/Have seen the copper come down/tingeing the mountains,/I have seen the fields, pale, clear as an emerald,/Sharp peaks, high spurs, distant castles'. He ends simply: 'I have walked over those roads;/I have thought of them living.'[115] 'Provincia Deserta' has the direct, conversational tone of the free verse he had written on the walking tour itself. It is a poem of memories, a Proustian recall of the past emotions reawoken in the present, and some of these memories would become a key element in the *Cantos*, on which he would start work that year. Since he had taken on his role of leader of the newest literary school, his love of the troubadours had been in temporary eclipse, but they were too important for him to be dropped for long.

Yet in spite of this reawakening of his affection for the troubadours, China remained dominant. Pound was correcting the proofs for *Cathay*, and continuing to study Fenollosa's observations on Chinese characters. In *Poetry* that February he argued that if poets used the Chinese as a model, the American renaissance for which he hoped would come: 'The first step of a renaissance, or awakening,' he said, 'is the importation of models for painting, sculpture or writing . . . The romantic awakening dates from the production of *Ossian*. The last century rediscovered the middle ages. It is possible that this century may find a new Greece in China.' Pound had taken this idea of the need for fresh, little-known models from Rémy de Gourmont, whose views on tradition Aldington had translated for the *Egoist* the previous July. De Gourmont made a distinction between a 'continuous tradition', which he regards as stultifying, and the 'renewed tradition. They must not be confounded. The seventeenth century believed it was renewing the bond with antiquity. The Romanticists believed they had rediscovered the Middle Ages. These discontinued traditions are more fertile when the period being renewed is distant and unknown.'[116] Pound could draw on the distant – such as his troubadours or eighth-century China – and still claim to be making a break with conventions of his day. Yet in practice, the imagists had worked by using imported models from the start – Japanese, Gaelic, Greek and indeed Chinese; as so often, the theory was simply catching up.

For his renaissance to succeed, however, Pound still believed that patrons were vital. If the best art could only be appreciated by a tiny handful, an aristocratic 'cellule', there was no alternative. Much of his quarrel with Lowell was over her insistence on being an artist rather than a patron: 'Too bad about Amy,' he had written to Harriet in January, 'why can't she conceive of herself as a Renaissance figure instead of a spiritual chief, which she ain't.'[117] (The situation is very different, but there is an echo of his insensitivity to Margaret Cravens' artistic hopes.) But for Pound and Lowell the question of audience went to the heart of their dispute. Amy believed not only that it was it possible to educate readers to appreciate modernist verse, but that it was essential to let more people know, appreciate and be liberated by this new poetry, a continuation, in another form, of her earlier good works. Jane Marcus has suggested that 'Amy Lowell's American imagism for the people . . . was a direct threat to the Eliot/Pound European modernist mode of the cult of genius', a shrewd observation, and even if to say Amy was hoping to reach the 'people' is perhaps an overstatement, she was much more optimistic than Pound about her likely audience.[118] Whilst it cannot be denied that she enjoyed self-promotion as much as Pound, and though the democracy she had introduced into the imagist group had its inbuilt limitations, it was quite different from Pound's desired autocracy as presiding genius. Pound wrote that January 1915 to Monroe:

In the Imagist book I made it possible for a few poets who were not over-producing to reach an audience. That delicate operation was managed by the most rigorous suppression of what I considered faults.

Obviously, such a method and movement are incompatible with effusion, with flooding magazines with all sorts of wish-wash and imitation and the near-good. If I had acceded to A.L's proposal to turn 'Imagism' into a democratic beer-garden, I should have undone what little good I had managed to do by setting up a critical standard.[119]

Pound wanted desperately to be acknowledged as leader of the poetic avant-garde, and not solely because of personal ambition; it was only he, he was convinced, who had the artistic judgement to advance the cause. 'My problem,' he told Harriet, 'is to keep alive a certain group of advancing poets, to set the arts in their rightful place as the acknow-ledged guide and lamp of civilization.' That has a certain heroism, if tinged with megalomania, but keeping the advancing poets under his control was to become more and more difficult.

Yet good news was in the offing: a possible patron for his renaissance was about to emerge. He was back in touch with John Quinn, the lawyer whom he had met along with Yeats' father in New York in 1910. In January

1915 he had published an article on Jacob Epstein in the *New Age*, lamenting the fact that American collectors would not buy works like his, but only 'autograph MSS of William Morris, faked Rembrandts and faked Vandykes'.[120] John Quinn, who had bought Morris manuscripts in the past, took this to be a personal attack, and wrote to Pound to say that he had given up buying manuscripts and was now buying modern art – Picasso, Matisse and Derain; and he had – as Yeats had told Pound after the article was published – even bought an Epstein; he was now interested in buying work by Gaudier-Brzeska. Pound was delighted, and in March replied at length, apologising for apparently attacking Quinn so unjustly and assuring him he had not had him in mind. (He might equally well, he said, have mentioned those who bought Keats manuscripts, in this case undoubtedly with Amy in his sights.) He promised to find out what Gaudier might have to sell: 'My whole drive,' he told Quinn, 'is that if a patron buys from an artist who needs money (needs money to buy tools, time and food), the patron then makes himself equal to the artist: he is building art into the world; he creates.' With just a few patrons who 'back their own flair' and 'buy from unrecognised men' there could soon be a renaissance in the arts.[121] John Quinn was going to play the role in which Lowell had so conspicuously failed. He and Pound would work together over the next few years, Pound as adviser, Quinn as investor, supporting in one way or another, among others, Lewis, Joyce and the *Little Review*.

Pound also proclaimed a new renaissance in the *New Age*, this time with no suggestion it would be a specifically American *Risorgimento*, though again China would play a central role. His article on Jacob Epstein had been one of a series, entitled 'Affirmations', defending Vorticism and his related current enthusiasms. Another, titled 'Analysis of this Decade', had argued that a few men, mainly the Vorticists, were introducing some innovative ideas that would bring 'a new focus' to the age. Pound mentions Ford's '*mot juste*', Lewis's 'sense of emotion in abstract design', and his own 'qualitative analysis in literature'. He also more controversially claimed he had introduced the notion of the 'Image': one would have thought that as Mathews was republishing *Ripostes* at much the same time, including his preface to Hulme's poems and his tribute to the 'School of Images', he would have had some qualms about making such claim to sole authorship of this idea. Yet what Pound emphasises most in this article are the outside sources from which these new forms of art sprang: his own concern for 'world-poetry', Gaudier's 'feeling of masses in relation', practised by 'Epstein and

countless "primitives" outside the Hellenic, quasi-Renaissance tradition', and, of course, 'Fenollosa's finds in China and Japan': 'these
new masses of unexplored arts and facts are pouring into the vortex of
London,' he writes. 'They cannot help but bring about changes as great
as the Renaissance changes . . . The Renaissance sought for a lost reality,
a lost freedom. We seek for a lost reality and a lost intensity'.[122] In China,
he believed, they would find it.

VI

BACK in Boston, Lowell was delivering lectures on French poetry to the Bostonians. The six poets she had chosen were Henri de Régnier, Rémy de Gourmont, Albert Samain, Paul Fort, Emile Verhaeren and Francis Jammes. In his review of the published lectures, Flint would recount how he had tried to persuade her over the Berkeley dinner table to drop Albert Samain, as not of sufficient significance, and to include instead Stuart Merrill and Francis Vielé-Griffin, both Americans who wrote in French and played a central role in the development of a revivified French poetry: 'But she only motioned the waiter to fill my glass with champagne, and what can a man do against such argument and such a will?'[123] Amy worked frantically on these lectures, up to fifteen hours a day; each lecture would be 40 typed pages, and one of her secretaries would hand her the final pages as she stepped into her car on the way to the lecture. She was a superb performer, and the lectures were a great success. She was particularly pleased at the last lecture when her reading of one of Paul Fort's poems, in the original French, moved her audience to tears.

Lowell's enthusiastic review of Robert Frost's *North of Boston* was published in the *New Republic* on 20 February 1915. Frost arrived back from England a couple of days later, and by chance bought a copy of the *New Republic* while walking into New York from the wharf. Frost, as might have been predicted, felt Amy misunderstood him quite as much as did Pound, but he was pleased by her warm praise, and would tell her later that he had felt that he was being welcomed back to his native land. When he came to Boston shortly after his return, he rang to thank her for her support, and she invited him to dinner. He accepted, refraining from telling her that when Pound had offered to introduce him to her in the summer of 1913, he had refused, saying he 'knew the president of Harvard, and therefore had no desire to meet the president's sister'.[124] It was the beginning of what Amy thought was a pleasant friendship, but Frost, though outwardly agreeable, would become increasingly hostile, if not to her, at any rate to her poetry. Whether Frost and Lowell discussed Flint, one can only guess. Frost had seen little of him since the end of 1913, feeling he was too much of Pound's camp, and had made his friends among the Georgians, with whose poetic aims he had more sympathy. He had written to Flint just before he sailed back from Liverpool, saying, with a typical mixture of aggrievedness and appreciation: 'I ought to know by the length of your silence that you don't want to write to me any more – cor silicis [i.e. heart of flint]. And if you don't I ought to have pride enough not to ask you to. But no matter, I must at least say goodbye to the man who opened England to me. You are good.'[125] One hopes Flint was touched.

Fletcher was also present at this dinner, having returned to Boston via Chicago, and liked Frost's 'quiet unworldliness, his serene detachment of manner', qualities so unlike his own.[126] Fletcher was not staying with Amy on this second and longer visit, but living in a boarding-house in the centre of Boston, though visiting Sevenels regularly, and was always on hand to discuss the latest tactics in their poetic campaign, on which Amy was now focusing. She had rather been neglecting the imagist cause in the whirl of her lecture series, but when Aldington wrote to her in February 1915 to say that to promote the anthology he was planning a special imagist number of the *Egoist* for May, when it was due to appear in England, she decided she must play her part. In preparation for the American publication of *Some Imagist Poets* in April, Lowell decided to visit the Poetry Society of America, which met in New York, and to which Pound had gone briefly some four years earlier, and asked if she could read for five minutes. She caused a near riot. According to the secretary Jessie Rittenhouse, she set out to court controversy: her account of the imagist principles 'bristled with so much provocative dicta that the right wing was stirred to action and primed for reply'.[127] She then read two of her poems, 'Venus Transiens' and 'Spring Day'. The former was one of her most evocative love poems for Ada:

> Tell me,
> Was Venus more beautiful
> Than you are,
> When she topped

The crinkled waves,
Drifting shoreward
On her plaited shell?
Was Botticelli's vision
Fairer than mine . . .'[128]

The Poetry Society disliked its form, but appear to have had no quarrel with the subject-matter. One might have thought that to read a lesbian love poem in public would have caused a stir, but Lowell was so eminently respectable that it never apparently occurred to her audience that that was what it was. As so often, they took it that she was writing in the persona of a man. 'Spring Day' was another matter. This was in her polyphonic prose, and consisted of five scenes from her day, the first entitled 'Bath'. This was the one that caused the trouble, just as 'In the Garden' had made trouble for her in England; reading a poem about lying naked in the bath seemed truly scandalous, especially when the naked body in question was so very large. 'Bath' mainly concentrates on the sunlight reflected in the water, but that didn't seem to help: 'I lie back and laugh, and let the green-white water, the sun-flawed beryl water, flow over me. The day is almost too bright to bear; the green water covers me from the too bright day. I will lie here awhile and play with the water and the sun spots.'[129] She read a couple more poems by other imagists, including H.D.'s 'Oread', and sat down, to receive a barrage of hostile comments and angry denunciations. There was a club rule that poetry read by guests, such as Amy Lowell, could not be discussed, but nobody paid any attention to it. Lowell appears to have rather enjoyed the sensation she was causing, and she certainly succeeded in drawing attention to the anthology. When it was published on 17 April, the same day, as it happens, as John Gould Fletcher's *Irradiations: Sand and Spray*, of the 750 copies published, 481 had been ordered in advance.

Before then, however, in England, on 6 April, Pound's *Cathay* was published; it would prove to be his most widely admired book of poems so far, however much he was coming to conceive of himself as a poetic pariah. Even Amy wrote to Harriet to say that 'Ezra's new book "Cathay" is full of the most beautiful things. What a pity the boy does not confine himself to working and leave strictures on other people's work alone.'[130] William Carlos Williams wrote to Harriet Monroe: 'I suppose you've seen [Pound's] "Cathay" the Chinese things are perhaps a few of the greatest poems written.'[131] The collection contained some of his most

moving poems, in one way or another very much in tune with the mood
of the time; they deal with departure, loss, loneliness and exile, while
some are directly concerned with warfare. Some critics indeed, like
Hugh Kenner, have seen them all as war poems, which might be said
to be true if one thinks about them as *wartime* poems, that is, about the
emotions experienced in time of war, by civilians as well as soldiers.
Ronald Bush has pointed out that originally Pound was going to include
four poems that in no way bore on the war climate, but at quite a late
stage he substituted four much more explicitly concerned with warfare,
an indication of his growing realisation of the seriousness of the war.
Pound, who had commented in the January *Egoist* that 'you have to go
back to Rihoku to find a man telling the truth about warfare', earlier
sent some of them to Gaudier in the trenches, who had said that 'the
poems depict our situation in a wonderful way'.[32] 'Lament of the
Frontier Guards', one of those included at a late stage, must have struck
many as movingly applicable to that particular moment in 1915:

> There is no wall left to this village.
> Bones white with a thousand frosts,
> High heaps, covered with trees and grass;
> Who brought this to pass?
> Who has brought the flaming imperial anger?
> Who has brought the army with drums and with kettle-drums?
> Barbarous kings.
> A gracious spring, turned to blood-ravenous autumn,
> A turmoil of wars – men, spread over the middle kingdom . . .
> Sorrow to go, and sorrow, sorrow returning.[133]

Ford captured the sense Pound evokes of a hitherto unknown but
instantly comprehended world when he described the book as being
'like a door in a wall, opening suddenly upon fields of an extreme beauty,
and upon a landscape made real by the intensity of human emotions'.[134]
This, he points out, is in spite of their being translations of poems
written over a thousand years ago; on this occasion Pound had proved
to him that emotions felt around them in the modern world could sometimes be best conveyed by a parallel from another time.

Pound reprinted 'The Seafarer' as a companion piece to a poem
called 'The Exile's Letter', and would later say that these two, along
with *Homage to Sextus Propertius*, which he would write in 1917,
were his most important personae. Ronald Bush has pointed out that

Pound has shifted the emphasis of the original of the 'Exile's Letter', which is a lament for separation from a particular friend, to the loss of a close band of friends, who 'made nothing of sea-crossing or of mountain crossing,/If only they could be of that fellowship,/And we all spoke out our hearts and minds, and without regret'.[135] The exile's sorrow over that parting 'is like the flowers falling at Spring's end/Confused, whirled in a tangle./What is the use of talking, and there is no end of talking,/There is no end of things in the heart.'[136] Both the seafarer and the exile are lonely figures, but in different ways. The seafarer has chosen his path across the sea, leaving the burghers and prosperous men in order to pursue his passion. But the Chinese exile has known rewarding friendship, now gone; only what Pound would in other contexts call his *métier*, his calling as a poet, drives him on. From Pound's return to England in 1911 until the outbreak of war, he might have done battle with the public, but he had done so with good friends on his side. What with the war, and what with quarrels, his circle was breaking up.

Pound had, of course, wanted to be acknowledged as superior in his artistic community; in 1913, he had written in warm praise of the editor of the *Smart Set* for having 'the good sense to divide all of the poets here [in London] into two classes; Yeats and I in one class, and everybody else in the other'.[137] His complaint to Amy Lowell about her plan for the new anthology had been that he would have to accept his fellow-poets as his equals. Yet when Aldington complained that Pound wanted them as disciples, not friends, he was not quite right.[138] Pound wanted them as disciples *and* friends, if friends who knew their place. Lewis would later conclude that Pound was an inherently gentle character, who constructed for himself an antithetical persona as the authoritarian maestro. There is much in that, though Pound should not be thought only superficially authoritarian; the need for mastery was as much part of him as his frequent warmth and kindliness. Lewis was perhaps closer to the mark when he identified Pound as having a 'tragic fracture' in his nature.[139] Pound lived his life by a set of doctrines which inevitably made him enemies, when temperamentally, as Williams had realised when he was a student, he would much rather have been liked. His frustration at his failure to achieve much-desired fame, and his talent for provoking hostile reactions, instead of what he really wanted, friendship and praise, was making him paranoid and bitter. There is in the *Cathay* poems a compassion for the human condition and a perceptive and sympathetic understanding of human pain that, as Lewis pointed

out, seems the voice of a different person from the hectoring and vituperative Pound that was beginning to emerge in many of his letters, and
in some of the *Blast* poems: at this stage as the violent scourge of poet-
asters and magazine editors, later as the coruscating flail of bankers and
usurers. Neither the embittered speaker of 'Salutation the Third' nor
the melancholy exile is giving up hope, but these are two very different
'masks of the self', two starkly contrasting developments from Pound's
Provençal poets, cheerfully picking themselves up again after rejection.
The strange mixture in the *Cantos* of angry denunciation and warm
memories of friends (there are of course many other things too) was
part of that sad and strange dislocation of his personality.

During April came the news of Rupert Brooke's death. The loss of
this handsome young poet was widely covered in the press, and his
patriotism praised by a range of establishment figures. Dean Inge quoted
one of his poems in a sermon at St Paul's. Winston Churchill wrote to
The Times, portraying him as the ideal poet-soldier, writer of a 'few
incomparable war sonnets', who loved his country beyond his life:
'Joyous, fearless, versatile, deeply instructed, with classic symmetry of
mind and body, ruled by high undoubting purpose, he was all that one
would wish England's noblest sons to be.'[140] Thus was the legend
endorsed by the government itself. That Brooke had seen himself as an
opponent of convention and a poetic revolutionary was forgotten. He
became in the public eye the model of the young patriot, upholder of
all that was best in England. Hence the popularity after his death of his
poem that begins: 'If I should die, think only this of me:/That there's
some corner of a foreign field/That is for ever England.'[141] The public
backlash against the avant-garde in both literature and the visual arts
increased. The *New Age*, with its growing conviction that modernist
experiment was suspiciously foreign and unpatriotic, had already in
February, much to Pound's indignation, unexpectedly terminated
'Affirmations', his series promoting his fellow avant-garde artists.[142] After
Brooke's death had been seized on as propaganda for the war effort,
things grew steadily worse.

PART XIII

BATTLES AND DIVISIONS

ALDINGTON, meanwhile, was continuing to work on the imagist number of the *Egoist*, only viable because someone had anonymously given the magazine £50. The donation, he told Lowell incredulously, had come because the donor '*admired D. Marsden*'.[1] Although pleased they could go ahead, he was dismayed by this boost for Marsden; he had been trying to persuade Harriet Shaw Weaver to break with her, which she now could not do. As the anonymous donor was very likely Weaver herself, she had perhaps chosen an astute way to protect her friend without offending Aldington. Flint was writing a history of the movement for the issue, along the lines that he had sketched in his letter to Lowell, and Aldington had asked Monro, who had written a warm review of *Des Imagistes* the year before, to review the anthology. The imagists would each contribute one poem, and there would be a series of articles about them individually, largely by each other. Aldington had asked Pound to send a poem too but he had not replied: 'really *absurd*,' he complained to Amy, 'considering how long & how intimately I have known him . . . he imagines I want his poem because of his "great reputation."'[2] He had also asked him to get one from William Carlos Williams, but there was no word on that, although May Sinclair contributed one, on her time in Belgium with the Red Cross in the first weeks of the war; it was something of a coup, not because it was a particularly powerful poem, but the signal that this prestigious and well-established writer was throwing in her lot with the imagists was invaluable. Marianne Moore, then an unknown at the beginning of her career, had sent in some unsolicited poems, already in the accomplished syllabic verse for which she would be famous; some had appeared in April, and one would be included in the May imagist number. This latter, a wry elegant poem, 'To William Butler Yeats on Tagore', commended his belief that 'it pays,/To cut gems even in these conscience-less days', an insistence that art still mattered that Aldington was happy to print.[3] H.D. wrote to Marianne Moore to say she remembered her from Bryn Mawr, and told her how much she and Aldington admired her poetry. She urged her to come to London. 'I know, more or less, what you are up against, though I escaped some five years ago!'[4] One wonders what Marianne Moore replied, but she stayed in the States. By 1915, the literary and artistic scene in America had changed considerably since H.D. left in 1911, and Moore had no wish for the expatriate life.

The May *Egoist*, when it appeared, was not altogether successful as promotion for the imagist cause. When Harold Monro's review of the anthology came in, it was disappointingly negative. Monro was deeply opposed to the log-rolling habits of the London literary press; one reason for his falling out with the Poetry Society was his refusal to praise its members' poetry uncritically; and perhaps the very fact that he was a good friend of Aldington and Flint made him all the more determined to prove his impartiality. He was also in low spirits, upset especially by Brooke's death. The imagists' emphasis on technique, and their lack of concern, as he saw it, for social and political questions, appalled him in the present circumstances. When he had met up with Pound in the early days of the war, he had felt him to be, according to his biographer Dominic Hibberd, 'almost contemptibly irrelevant, a long-haired dilettante chattering among the teacups'.[5] The tone of his review conveys a similar irritation: it rebuked the imagists for their 'fixed principles of not admitting their obligations', describing them as 'one of the latest groups in the forward movement of English poetry – not the only one'; the preface's statement that imagism was now a household word was, he pointed out, a 'vain exaggeration'. All very true. The imagists, he asserted, in their determination to cut out cliché, to pare down their work, had scarcely left themselves with anything to say or with the means to say it. H.D.'s 'Oread', so admired by Pound, he describes as 'petty poetry', 'minutely small'. He calls her the 'truest "Imagist" of the group', but it is clear that that is not a compliment. 'Her poems,' he says, 'have a slight flavour of brine; they are as fragile as sea-shells. If I came too near them I should be afraid of crushing them into the sand with my clumsy feet.' He had slightly kinder words for Flint and Aldington, but Lowell he dismissed as prose, but then she had greatly upset him by some unkind comments on the Poetry Bookshop in the *Little Review* the year before. He ended by saying the imagists' chief fault was pretension: they 'labour to appear skilful'.[6]

The issue also included articles on each of them, generally by a fellow-imagist, and these were far more sympathetic, though in the case of Fletcher's article on Lowell too much so. He sent in a gushing eulogy that Aldington felt obliged to tone down, much to Fletcher and Lowell's annoyance. All the others avoided unqualified praise. Aldington wrote warmly though not uncritically on Flint, and in mixed terms on Pound, an article included at the last minute; he had earlier thought to ignore him altogether. In the end he gave Pound both considerable praise and some mockery, identifying him as a Romantic poet, about which, as he knew, Pound would not be happy. Flint wrote a tribute to H.D., quoting Aldington's description of her work as 'an accurate mystery', justifying this appropriation by saying, 'I could not find a better phrase, for in detail it has the precision of goldsmith's work, in ultimate effect it is mysterious and only to be comprehended by the imagination'.[7] Ferris Greenslet, the editor from Houghton Mifflin, supplied a judicious piece on Fletcher; he had visited London earlier in the year and met Aldington; presumably he had spoken well of *Irradiations*, which he had then just accepted for publication, giving Aldington the idea of asking him. The mutual congratulation, even though it was laced with qualifications, rather backfired; Eliot's friend Conrad Aiken attacked them in the *New Republic* and accused them of simply giving each other undeserved puffs, and the accusation of being a self-promoting coterie would return to haunt them. Yet the attacks the imagist *Egoist* provoked, like those on the anthology itself, usefully played their part in increasing its notoriety and its sales. The issue itself sold many more copies than usual, 1,000 rather than the average 750.

Aldington had arranged for 150 extra copies of the May *Egoist* to be printed for distribution by Lowell to American bookshops, to promote the anthology there. When they reached her, however, she was horrified: Dora Marsden's opening article would, she was convinced, prevent most from looking further and, if they did, Monro's caustic review, 'in which', as she put it to Aldington, 'he pitches into us all and the movement in general with the most delightful impartiality', would be appalling for their reputations.[8] Quite what she had against this particular Marsden article is hard to know, though Marsden's cumbersome style and tendency to argue in the most abstract of terms – ironic in light of the fact that her main theme at that period was the danger of abstractions – made her philosophical pieces far from lively reading. As she was writing in that May article about the power of images in the mind, it was curiously appropriate for the imagist issue. Lowell, however, was also horrified by Lawrence's war poem, which 'for farfetched indecency beats anything' that she had ever seen. 'Sometimes,' she added, 'I think his condition is almost pathological, and that he has a kind of erotic mania.'[9] Lawrence's poem was called, 'Eloi, Eloi, Lama Sabachthani?', that is, 'My God, My God, why hast thou forsaken me?', Christ's words from the cross. It is spoken through the persona of a soldier recalling the act of bayoneting, with the killing of the enemy coming to represent some perverted sexual rite:

> Like a bride he took my bayonet, wanting it,
> Like a virgin the blade of my bayonet, wanting it,
> And it sank to rest from me in him,
> And I the lover, am consummate,
> And he is the bride, I have sown him with the seed
> And planted and fertilized him.[10]

It is a powerful and disturbing depiction of the perversions of emotion that war produces. We are now familiar with the idea that in war sexual and aggressive drives become strangely and dangerously mixed; not so Amy Lowell and the people of Boston in 1915. It would, she said, 'do us immeasurable harm to be associated with such an outpouring'.[11] She refused to distribute the copies, but sent Harriet Shaw Weaver the $15 that she should have made on commission, only mentioning Dora Marsden's prominence (a gibe she was happy to make) as the reason. Lowell often admired Lawrence's eroticism, but she liked eroticism to be about happy love, not connected with the darker emotions.

Sexuality is never a topic raised in Amy's voluminous correspondence, or not in any I have read, though she did talk about its portrayal in literature in a letter to Margaret Anderson, reminding her of a conversation they had had about the difference between love and lust, when they had both agreed, according to Lowell, that 'love on the purely mental side is apt to be as dry and brittle as a withered leaf; but love on the purely physical side is as unpleasant as raw beef steak. It is the combination of the two which is perfection.'[12] What comes out of Lowell's own love poetry is indeed a combination of warm affection and delight in sensuous, sexual response. She often thought Lawrence achieved that perfect combination: in 1918, she would say of him in a lecture given at the Brooklyn Institute, 'Other poets have given us sensuous images; other poets have spoken of love as chiefly desire; but in no other poet does desire seem so surely "the outward and visible form of an inward and spiritual grace" . . . Mr Lawrence has been spoken of as an erotic poet, and that is true, but it is only one half of the truth. For his eroticism leans always to the mystic something of which it is an evidence.'[13] Amy was also an erotic writer, expressing the 'outward and visible form of an inward and spiritual grace' through the dapple of light and shade, the bright colours and movement of flowers. Yet she could only accept eroticism in the context of love, something that placed a distance between herself and most of the modernist male, and some female, writers of the period. Amy could be open about so many things that it is always a surprise when suddenly she bangs the door closed; one might hazard a guess that she felt so strongly that her own feelings for Ada were not perverse, however others might perceive them, that she found the imputation of perversity to any kind of eroticism deeply disturbing. Ada had helped her escape from a place of darkness and pain, to which she never wanted to return.

Luckily, however, notices began to appear of the anthology, most of them unsympathetic, but it was unmistakably creating a stir. Amy was delighted at the sensation they were causing, and forgot her criticisms of the *Egoist*. What Pound thought of *Some Imagist Poets* when it appeared in 1915 he never said. He would later tell Aldington that he never read any D.H. Lawrence after 1914, so, if that is true, perhaps he did not look at any of the rival anthologies, in which case his continued strictures about the dilutions introduced by Amy remained largely theoretical, though he must have seen the various imagists' poems that appeared in either *Poetry* or the *Egoist*. Several of the poems in this 1915 volume had indeed been published in *Poetry* on his own recommendation. The new anthology contained many of H.D.'s finest early poems, and was arguably a more cohesive and even volume than *Des Imagistes*. Lowell's poems included 'Venus Transiens', and among Lawrence's was his fine early poem, 'Ballad of Another Ophelia', as well as 'Green', another poem that Lowell might have used to point to his affinities with imagist poetry:

> The sky was apple-green,
> The sky was green wine held up in the sun,
> The moon was a golden petal between.
>
> She opened her eyes, and green
> They shone, clear like flowers undone,
> For the first time, now for the first time seen.[14]

The preface, written by Aldington and edited by Lowell, who removed a conciliatory mention of Pound, followed the original imagist precepts fairly closely, though without mention of a doctrine of the image; however, 'the language of common speech', 'the *exact word*', 'new rhythms', 'poetry that is hard and clear' and the presentation of 'images' are all mentioned. There is no reference to the French *vers libre* as such, but the preface claims that 'We do not insist upon "free-verse" as the only method of writing poetry. We fight for it as a principle of liberty. We believe that the individuality of the poet may often be better expressed in free-verse than in conventional forms. In poetry, a new cadence is a new idea.' This emphasis on individualism and liberty, while not necessarily inconsistent with Pound's poetic doctrines at this stage (he had after all insisted that Vorticism was a movement of individuals) places a weight on freedom that he would increasingly prefer to place on technique and control. Michael Levenson in *The Genealogy of Modernism* uses this preface as an example of what he sees as early libertarian modernism in contrast to the more authoritarian and prescriptive position to which Pound was moving, exemplary, he argues, of high modernism. The preface's final point is intriguing: 'most of us believe concentration is of the very essence of poetry'.[15] Which ones did not? Lawrence almost certainly, and possibly Fletcher. Fletcher still did not really feel at ease with the imagist programme; writing to Daisy that March, he had said he was only in the anthology because Lowell had been very 'decent' to him, and he 'wanted to get back at that wretched little viper, Pound'.[16] Yet it could be argued that whilst Fletcher, unless he disciplined his work, rapidly lost focus among a riot of effects, Lawrence was moving towards an open and flowing form of poetry, which had considerable power, without conceding to the imperative that Pound decreed to achieve concentration. It is a pity Pound never read the later Lawrence; perhaps he would have acknowledged that a poem like 'The Ship of Death' achieved its own power by other means – or perhaps he would indeed have thought that the development of the ongoing image of the ship of death gave the poem concentration and intensity after all.

Although *Some Imagist Poets* had appeared at its due date in April in the States, the May publication in England was delayed because of troubles with shipping. What did come to London in April 1915 were the German Zeppelins. They had first been sighted over the coast on 29 December 1914: now they reached the capital, adding to the growing hysteria and fear. By the scale of the Second World War, bombing from the air did comparatively little damage, though in the 1914–18 war 1,127 civilians were killed in England, enough for the air raids to be a powerful psychological weapon in spreading dismay and anxiety. From then on in the war, the imagination of Londoners would be dominated by the air raids, at first curiously exciting as well as terrifying, as Shaw so graphically suggests when, at the end of *Heartbreak House* after a Zeppelin raid, which the characters have watched in rapturous terror, Mrs Hushabye and Ellie fervently hope they will be back the next night. Lawrence greeted his first sight of a Zeppelin raid as a cosmic Apocalypse, the bringing in of 'a new heaven and a new earth, a clearer eternal moon above, and a clean world below'.[17] But the mixture of thrill and fear soon gave way to steady, draining dread. People who had children, like Flint, found the raids unbearable from the start; the better off, as he later told Amy, would send their families to the countryside for the duration, but that was not an option for him.

The war was intensifying in other ways. Germany introduced gas into warfare and in early May sank the liner *Lusitania*: 1,200 of its civilian passengers were drowned. (One was Hugh Lane, who had offered his Impressionist pictures to Dublin; Yeats and Lady Gregory would be closely involved in the wrangling over whether his will left the paintings to Ireland or England.) The manufactured atrocity stories, such a feature of First World War propaganda, reached a new level with the account in *The Times* on 10 May of the crucifixion of a Canadian soldier by the Germans.[18] There was rigorous censorship, and war correspondents were kept well away from the front, but the bellicose press improvised relentlessly, and its endless stream of horrors – a kind of verbal bayonet practice designed to dehumanise, indeed demonise, the enemy – intensified the ever-present nightmare of war. In a story H.D. wrote in 1930, 'Kora and Ka', she depicted the mind of a man, John Helforth, suffering a nervous breakdown precipitated by the war, in which he had been too young to take part; what he cannot get out of his mind, as Trudi Tate has pointed out, are the atrocity stories he has read, systematic propaganda to inculcate murderous war fever:

we were trained to blood-lust and hatred. We were sent out, iron shod to quell an enemy who had made life horrible. That enemy roasted children, boiled down the fat of pregnant women to grease cannon wheels . . . His men raped nuns, cut off the hands of children, boiled down the entrails of old men, nailed Canadians against barn doors . . . and all this we heard mornings with the Daily Newsgraph and evenings with the Evening Warscript. The Newsgraph and the Warscript fed out

belching mothers, who belched out in return, fire and carnage in the name of Rule
Britannia.[19]

Yet the fervid patriotism in the press could not disguise the fact that
the war was going badly. Gallipoli, where an Anglo–French offensive
had begun in April, had not produced the rapid defeat of the Turks that
had been expected. Three battles were lost in France, and it was becoming
apparent to many that Kitchener as Secretary of War was running the
campaign disastrously. Many of the Liberal leaders resisted the move
to something nearer the command economy essential in a modern war;
in particular, the army was desperately short of shells, as Kitchener
refused to use any but a limited number of established firms, and was
unwilling to spend the necessary money. In early 1915, the Germans
were producing 250,000 shells a day, France 100,000, and Britain only
22,000. Soldiers on leave told of their lack of supplies and of the misery
of trench warfare. Hulme, who had been in the trenches on the Belgian
border, not far from Ypres, farming country that at first reminded him
of his native Staffordshire, though shells and mud rapidly eliminated
the resemblance, was invalided back that April with a wound in his arm,
and gave a vivid account of the British lack of supplies to Pound, who
visited him in St Mark's College Hospital in Chelsea. Countless other
soldiers must have been telling similar stories. Northcliffe, proprietor
of both *The Times* and the *Daily Mail*, got wind of the shell shortage
and prepared to launch a campaign exposing the scandal, but before he
did so the Liberal Government gave way to a coalition, still with Asquith
as Prime Minister and Kitchener as Secretary of War, but with Lloyd
George in the newly created post of Minister of Munitions. By the end
of the next year, he would be Prime Minister.

It was against this backdrop that H.D went into a nursing home to
have her baby. She gave birth on 21 May to a little girl, who was stillborn.
Aldington wrote to Amy Lowell that 'the nurse said it was a beautiful
child & they can't think why it didn't live. It was very sturdy but wouldn't
breathe. Poor Hilda is very distressed, but is recovering physically. I
don't think there is any danger.'[20] In *Tribute to Freud* H.D. wrote that
she lost the baby 'from shock and repercussions of war news broken to
me in a rather brutal fashion.'[21] In a later unpublished manuscript, she
says more: using the names she would ascribe to Aldington and herself
in *Bid Me to Live*, she wrote, 'Rafe Ashton . . . destroyed the unborn,
the child Amor, when a few days before it was due, he burst in upon
Julia . . . with "don't you realise what this means? Don't you feel

anything? *The Lusitania has gone down.*'" But she added a marginal note, 'But this never happened. Surely this was fantasy.'[22] H.D. certainly felt that the death of the baby was in some way connected with the war strain she was experiencing, exacerbated by the militaristic, jingoistic atmosphere; Charles Doyle says that Aldington was curiously elated by the sinking of the *Lusitania*, hoping, like many, that it would bring the Americans into the war, so there may be something behind H.D.'s memory. In *Asphodel* she says simply, 'Khaki killed it.'[23] Perhaps the fantasy memory of Aldington destroying the child Amor with news of the war fuses two facts: first, that their marriage never recovered its closeness after the loss of this baby, and secondly, that their relationship would be finally destroyed by the changes brought to Aldington's personality, and perhaps to her own, by the war. The war would kill their 'Amor', as it had the baby.

The nursing home was, Aldington told Amy, considered a good one, but even the nurses seemed brutalised by the war atmosphere. In *Asphodel*, they certainly could be said to breathe 'fire and carnage in the name of Rule Britannia', as they callously discuss stories of atrocities: 'they stood at the end of my bed, and told me about the crucified –', Hermione begins to say to Darrington, who won't let her finish. In the novel, the baby is actually born during an air raid, and Hermione thinks of the nurses as 'Good old ecstatic baby-killers – killers like the Huns up there'. They make her suffer for being the wife of a young and healthy-looking non-combatant: 'how *lucky* for *you*,' they say, 'to have your husband when poor Mrs Rawlton's husband is actually now lying wounded . . . Why isn't Mr Darrington in Khaki? . . . *Why isn't Mr Darrington in khaki?*'[24] Aldington was well aware of their attitude, which they made plain to him too, and he realised how they added to H.D.'s unhappiness; he wrote to Amy five days after the stillbirth, 'I wish to God you were here – these English people are awful; they haven't the faintest idea how to treat a fine mind like Hilda's.'[25] H.D. had to remain in the nursing home, however, for another two or three weeks, after which Richard took her to stay in the country, Brigit having lent them her car for the journey.

While she was in the nursing home, friends rallied round. In her 'Autobiographical Notes', H.D. writes: '1915. Spring, confinement. Mrs Fowler brings iris, May Sinclair, strawberries; Mrs Wadsworth comes [Fanny Wadsworth, the Vorticist Edward Wadsworth's wife]. Brigit in beautiful summer dresses, blue hydrangia [*sic*]. Flint comes, nurse is surprised when he rises and opens door for her . . . I have phobias of khaki, fear the street and soldiers. I get back into the dark blue skirt and coat that mother had made for me in Rome, it is a beautiful costume; R. brings huge bunch of violets; the whole nursing-home had looked askance at me, as R. is not in uniform.'[26] She would tell Amy Lowell next January that her 'nerves' had been 'shattered' for months after the stillbirth. In both the war period of *Asphodel* and the whole of *Bid Me to Live*, the narrative emphasises the half-suppressed hysteria, near-breakdown of the H.D./Hermione/Julia figure. Trudi Tate has argued convincingly that H.D. was by now in a state of 'war neurosis', a condition doctors at the time were beginning to realise was experienced by civilians, as well as soldiers.[27] In *Asphodel*, Darrington is tender, kind, distressed at Hermione's unhappiness, but Hermione feels very alone in her grief: '"But don't you care?"' Hermione asks him, and Darrington replies '"Darling. You – know – I – do." . . . Tea steamed into her face and she drank the tea like some drug fiend, the scent of drug. Tea smelt of far sweet hours, of afternoons of all the happy little times they'd had together. Darrington had made the tea while she lay listening. He was nice, did nice things. She supposed he really did care, had been sorry. It's so hard for a man to say such things. He knew it hurt her to talk about the baby. She supposed he had cared.'[28] Communication between them was no longer as easy as it had been.

That was not all. H.D. was told she ought not to have another baby until after the war – she never says on what grounds, but perhaps the doctor agreed with her view that the war strain had killed the baby. Birth control does not appear to have been an option; it is not clear whether her sexual relationship with Aldington ceased altogether for the meantime, but it was undoubtedly problematic for them both. In *Bid Me to Live*, Julia thinks:

Then 1915 and her death, or rather the death of her child. Three weeks in that ghastly nursing-home and then coming back to the same Rafe. Herself different. How could she blithely face what he called love, with that prospect looming ahead and the matron, in her harsh voice, laying a curse on whatever might have been. 'You know you must not have another baby until after the war is over.' Meaning in her language, you must keep away from your husband, keep him away from you. When he was all she had, was country, family, friends.[29]

Aldington was deeply distressed by the loss of the child, but only able to express his grief repackaged as concern for H.D., and he had the additional dread, always in his mind, of being sent to the front. H.D.

understood and sympathised with those fears, but their different traumas would have the effect, as for many others in the war, of pushing them apart rather than together. What had seemed to their friends a perfect marriage would become increasingly strained.

II

THE visit to the country was to stay with well-to-do friends, James Whittall and his wife, in their house at Vale End in Kent. Whittall, of Philadelphian Quaker origin, had no pretensions to bohemian or avant-garde credentials; he says in his memoirs that he had feared, when he first met the Aldingtons, that his 'having enough money to live on comfortably would always prevent anything but a casual relationship' with the Aldingtons, but this proved not to be the case.[30] The Aldingtons were grateful for Whittall's invitations to his agreeable sequestered country house – he had a home in London as well – which Aldington described that summer as 'looking over wide stretches of fertile Kentish land and surrounded by a brilliantly coloured sea of large poppies, scented lupins, carnations, roses, foxgloves and many other flowers'.[31] Whittall for his part was encouraged by their keen interest in his work as a translator; H.D. helped when his publisher asked him to put into *vers libre* the translations he was making of Judith Gautier's *Le Livre de jade*, translations in turn of Chinese poetry, first published in 1867 and greatly admired in France; some of the resulting *vers libre* appeared in the *Egoist*.[32]

Whittall comments, as so many of those who met them did, on how very different the Aldingtons were, though he describes them both as 'irresistible'. H.D., he says, 'was tall, slender, strangely beautiful, sensitive, possessed of a gift for making one feel important and for the moment absorbingly interesting to her'. She lived much of the time in another world 'near the shores of the Aegean', yet she would return to the present world with delight: 'Her sudden entries into our talk and her effortless domination of it filled us with elation because she brought with her such disarming enthusiasm and delivered herself with such amazing speed and clarity on any subject that might be uppermost.'

Richard, on the other hand, appeared thoroughly of the here and now, and, although he affected a black cloak and long hair, was far from being a languid aesthete: 'His energy of brain and body was like a fresh, strong wind which invigorated without whipping skirts about or blowing off hats . . . his speech was alive with the true accents of the young innovator, passionately opposed to all comfortable mediocrity. He hated publishers, successful authors, critics, Americans and Quakers, but he had friends among them all, consistency being a trait seldom possessed by a dangerously charming person.'[33] Whittall's account indicates that in spite of the war and the loss of the baby, the Aldingtons could still be lively and entertaining companions, who continued to get much out of life together.

Amy had written Richard a warm note of sympathy on hearing of the stillbirth, urging them to ask if they needed help with any extra expense, and offering to pay their fares if they would like to visit her to give H.D. a change of scene. She sent them a bunch of newspaper clippings, some about the anthology, others more generally about the new poetry, for the imagists were already producing followers, some of whom alarmed her considerably. Kreymborg, whose magazine the *Glebe* had only survived a few issues, had invited her to contribute to his next one, this time to be called *Others*, dedicated to those who have 'died to make verse free'. Aldington would describe it as 'a small periodical which publishes nothing but vers libre, of which its choice is catholic though perhaps not apostolic'.[34] Amy was at first delighted and eagerly sent off a contribution, and she was no doubt pleased that when *Others* first appeared in July, an article in the *New York Tribune* pointed to the prominence in the new poetry movement of women, and commented that 'Two, at least, of the best known leaders are women, Miss Amy Lowell and Miss Monroe.'[35] But now she wondered, she told Aldington, if she had made a mistake to ally herself to these newcomers, because it seemed that 'all the questionable and pornographic poets' were trying to sail under the imagist flag. That Amy herself was a questionable poet in many people's eyes, and that she used her *vers libre* to express quite unacceptable lesbian desire was something that did not seem to occur to her. The immediate association that the papers were making or implying between 'free verse' and 'free love' bothered her, even though, or perhaps because, it had so much truth; Lowell was, she told Aldington, particularly worried about an article from the *New York Call*, presumably the one by Emanuel Julius, 'This Summer's Style in Poetry, or the Elimination of Corsets in Versifying', which had appeared on 16 May.[36]

Again, the analogy between the fashion for freedom in underwear and in poetic metre undeniably carried a social truth about the period; notwithstanding Lowell's expressed disapproval, it must have made an impact on her, because she would draw on that image for her most popular poem, 'Patterns', which she published later in the year. Poor Amy, she was too large to abandon corsets in real life: another reason the article may have struck such a chord of alarm, though perhaps what really perturbed her about Julius' article was that he had rather wittily coined the phrase, the 'vers libertines'.

Lowell would wax hot and cold about *Others*, whose contributors would include William Carlos Williams (at one stage editor), Marianne Moore, Wallace Stevens, H.D., Pound, Lowell, Frances Gregg and Mina Loy. Lowell, like Monroe and indeed Pound, was always uneasy about the Greenwich Village scene, but it may have been its politics rather than its sexual mores that she really found most uncongenial. A contemporary described the Village as 'a spiritual geography. It is bounded on the North by the Feminist Movement, on the East by the Old World Bohemia . . . on the South by the Artistic temperament and on the West by the I.W.W. [Industrial Workers of the World].'[37] It was undoubtedly the latter that she found the most alarming; in spite of her admiration for the anarchist-inclined de Gourmont, Amy was a thoroughgoing capitalist.

Aldington wrote to thank Amy for sending the cuttings, which he assured her had cheered H.D. up. May Sinclair had written a sturdy defence of the imagists in the June *Egoist*, first taking issue with Monro's attack on H.D. and then giving one of the most illuminating contemporary accounts of their poetics. H.D.'s poetry, she writes, '*proves* the power of the clean, naked, sensuous image to carry the emotion without rhyme – *not*, I think, without rhythm; the best Imagist poems have a very subtle and beautiful rhythm – and always without decoration'. She goes on to search for a definition of the 'Image', which, she insists, 'is not a substitute; it does not stand for anything but itself. Presentation not Representation is the watchword of the school. The Image, I take it, is form. But it is not pure form. It is form and substance.' For all poets, she says, poetry is a sacramental act, like the mass, but whilst the Victorians were Protestants, offering symbols of a reality to be found elsewhere, the imagists were Catholics, creating a reality themselves. May Sinclair was herself becoming deeply involved with psychoanalysis at this period, and, when she wrote here that 'what the Imagists are "out for" is direct naked contact with reality', she is perhaps, like Pound in 1913, making an analogy with the contact with the repressed truth of the unconscious that analysis claimed to give.[38] Yet Sinclair's comparison with the mass was an apt one for the imagists; like the sacrament, for them the poem was a means to salvation, to a fuller and better life. Walter Benjamin would argue in the 1930s that in the age of mechanical reproduction the visual work of art has lost its 'aura', but for the imagists their poetry should, at any rate at its best, maintain a sacramental power. This article was the first of many that Sinclair wrote on behalf of the new poetry: defences of Flint, Aldington, Pound, Eliot, as well as more support for H.D. would all be provided over the next few years. They had a good friend in May Sinclair.

The Aldingtons do not seem to have been in touch with Pound since he refused to send a poem for the May *Egoist*. Pound was not one of those who visited H.D. in the nursing home, though he heard the news. He wrote to his mother two days after the stillbirth: 'Hilda's infant died, so dont send it a christening spoon, or embarrass Mrs Doolittle with enquiries. Hilda is, I believe recovering quite nicely.'[39] It sounds callous, but was not necessarily so. When Aunt Frank, of whom he was very fond, had died in 1913, all he could say to his mother was, 'Yes, I suppose A.F. was at about the end of her tether.'[40] Pound could not handle his or others' personal grief in any direct way. Although he had been greatly angered by Flint's history in the May *Egoist*, he said nothing for now, possibly because even he realised it was not a good moment for a row. In addition, in spite of his irritation with Amy, he may have felt unwilling to fall out with his erstwhile good friends; he still thought highly of H.D.'s work, and he remained fond of her. He was busy with his other ploys too, continuing to supply Monroe with poets, and to remonstrate with her when she didn't take his advice; he sent a more than usually vitriolic letter that May condemning the contents of the latest *Poetry*, though he was mollified when she finally printed 'Prufrock' in June. He was also in frequent contact with H.L. Mencken, who had now taken over from Wright as editor of the *Smart Set*. Pound had had hopes of acquiring his own weekly, but his efforts to raise funds were fruitless, though his endeavours to secure Joyce some money from the Royal Literary Fund would be, thanks to Yeats' intervention with Edmund Gosse, more successful, in spite of the fact, as he told Joyce with some delight, that Gosse complained that 'neither you nor W.B.Y. have given any definite statement of loyalty to the allies'.[41] He was also preparing three more Noh plays from the Fenollosa papers for publication, sending them off in early July to the Chicago magazine *Drama*; and in June the first and only London Vorticist exhibition in Pound's lifetime took place.[42]

The exhibition opened in the Doré Galleries on 10 June 1915; Dismorr, Etchells, Gaudier, Roberts, Saunders, Wadsworth and Wyndham Lewis formed the main group of Vorticists, though there was a subsection of non-Vorticists who had been invited to contribute, including, surprisingly, the Bloomsbury painter, Duncan Grant. The catalogue proclaimed that 'by Vorticism we mean a) ACTIVITY as opposed to the tasteful PASSIVITY of Picasso; b) SIGNIFICANCE as opposed to the dull or anecdotal character to which the Naturalist is condemned; c) ESSENTIAL MOVEMENT and ACTIVITY (such as the energy of a mind) as opposed to the imitative cinematography, the fuss and hysterics of the Futurists'.[43] Such a negative way of defining a programme, by its opposition to other movements, was perhaps an indication of an uncertainty within the movement about its future direction. It was much surer of what it disliked than what it wanted, and though more information about Vorticism was promised in the second issue of *Blast*, the promise, as W. C. Wees points out, was not kept. To nobody's surprise, the reviews were largely antagonistic, and the works attacked as a celebration of mechanical barbarity. In an article in the *New Age* that January Pound had tried to counteract the widespread perception of Vorticism as violent and anarchic, writing there that the 'political world is confronted with a great war, a species of insanity. The art world is confronted with a species of quiet and sober sanity called Vorticism'.[44] He convinced very few, possibly not even himself.

In early June, Pound wrote to his father saying, 'Gaudier is getting very tired of the trenches its time someone came in and hurried matters.'[45] He would soon learn that Gaudier had escaped trench warfare for ever. Though the news did not come through until later in the month, he had been killed, while leading a charge, by a German bullet, said to be direct to the head, at Neuville Saint-Vaast, five days before the exhibition opened. His death changed Pound's whole attitude to the war, and left its mark on his later politics. Charles Olson, after talking to Pound in 1946, suggested that Gaudier's death was 'the source of his hate for contemporary England and America' and 'in 1915, his attack on democracy got mixed up with Gaudier's death, and all his turn since has been revenge for the boy's death'.[46] Not everyone would agree. Even at the time there were those who questioned Pound's sincerity. Aldington, who was very upset himself, told Amy that

Hueffer and Ezra are writing the most awful bosh about [Gaudier] . . . I am really angry about this, for all Gaudier's real friends, Nina Hammet, Cournos, Brodzky, Hulme etc, have been pushed by, while these Vorticist cuistres who have never cared a cent for him, go about writing in the papers, making capital out of his death. Ezra wrote a ridiculous article in the Westminster Gazette and Cournos wrote to the paper and frankly told him he was a liar and was 'making capital out of Gaudier's death'.[47]

Pound, to do him justice, told Harriet he felt like a ghoul for getting paid for writing on Gaudier, especially as it was the only paid work he could find at that moment. He was wounded to the quick by Cournos' comment, telling Alice Corbin Henderson, 'I have found it necessary to eliminate Cournos . . . from my list of acquaintance (re/Brzeska's death, not on a point of style or literary activity).'[48] Yet though Aldington was surely right that there were others closer to Gaudier, that does not mean Pound's outrage at this loss was insincere. Humphrey Carpenter, suspicious like Aldington of Pound's reaction, suggests he was not much disturbed by the news, basing this on the fact that his reporting of Gaudier's death to his father is fairly matter-of-fact: 'Brzeska has been killed, which is pretty disgusting, though I suppose it is a marvel it hasn't happened before'.[49] But that was a typical Pound response, and one would not expect more revelation of feeling from most sons to their fathers in 1915. It is surely significant that in almost every one of his letters to his parents during those first ten months of the war Pound had passed on news of Gaudier. In May, when a cheque for their first wedding anniversary arrived, he promptly used it to pay off some of his debt to the sculptor, this at a time when, as he told Joyce, he was making his own furniture because they could not afford to buy any. One of the first people to whom he wrote about Gaudier's death was his old professor, Felix Schelling, the pioneer of the philological method, in the University of Philadelphia, whom he had last seen by chance in the British Museum in October 1913. Schelling had generously, in view of their past differences, written to congratulate him on *Cathay*; in his reply, Pound referred to Gaudier, doubtless completely unknown to Schelling. 'Gaudier-Brzeska has been killed . . . and we have lost the best of young sculptors and the most promising. The arts will incur no worse loss from the war than this is. One is rather obsessed with it. P.S. Have you seen Hueffer's *When Blood is Their Argument*?'[50] Pound felt strongly – as he had already told his mother – that Ford's linkage of philology and militarism was something that Schelling and the Penn faculty needed to register. Pound wrote to others about Gaudier's death, including Joyce, but if he was genuinely appalled by this death, which he called the 'worst calamity of the war', it was perhaps not only because of the loss of the man but, as he put it to an American friend Milton Bronner, because of the 'loss to art'.[51] And this particular loss to art was inevitably a blow to his movement, to his own artistic mission; one can understand why Gaudier's close friends, in mourning for a charming and immensely talented young man, full of vitality and zest for life, suspected there was an element of something self-interested in Pound's response. Yet his grief was no less bitter for the fact this death threatened his own hopes for the new world that Vorticism was meant to bring.

Pound's later hatred of capitalists and espousal of Social Credit was fuelled by his belief that bankers and financiers were responsible for the war; they starved artists in peacetime, and killed them in war. After Gaudier's death, from being unconcerned about American support for the conflict, he became ever more angry that they were failing to assist the Allies. He wrote an article later that year about 'The Net American Loss', the loss, that is, that America had incurred in failing to enter the war; in it he abuses the United States for being preoccupied with usury and neglecting to protect civilisation against the 'Prussian empire and its philology'.[52] Pound's obsessions were developing apace; he sent the article to John Quinn, asking him to get it published, but perhaps it's not surprising that no one could be persuaded. But he was now convinced that the serious artist's role was to demonstrate what was wrong with the world, and he was certain his political analyses were as correct as his aesthetic judgements.

Hulme had remained in hospital till June, scandalising the nurses by his insistence on reading German philosophy (probably Husserl, his latest discovery), an activity they considered exceptionally unpatriotic. He would not return to the front until May 1917; he had originally enlisted as a private, doubtless because of his dislike of the English upper classes, but being given orders when he thought he knew better did not appeal to him. After his convalescence he set about trying to obtain a commission, and training as an officer took time. He too was saddened by Gaudier's death, but he never appears to have had second thoughts about returning to the front himself; his letters home from the trenches were published after his death, and although they by no means suggest he was insensitive to the carnage about him, Aldington's assessment of him as a tough man appears justified. Indeed, he even seems to have achieved a certain calm that had not been there earlier.

Both Karen Csengeri, who edited his *Collected Works*, and his biographer, Robert Ferguson, compare his descriptions of the front with the world he describes in 'Cinders'. Ferguson suggests that perhaps the reason that he accepted trench warfare so stoically was 'he had already seen it before, "all the mud, endless"', in his bleak vision of a meaningless world in those early notes.[53] The prairies had spoken to him of the limitations of human understanding, Worringer's 'spiritual dread of space' of the alienation and disorientation of modernity, but the front, which made literal those existential fears of an absurd universe, was in a strange way something of a solace. It was not that he denied that it was 'a fearful place'; 'really like a kind of nightmare, in which you are in the middle of an enormous saucer of mud with explosions & shots going off all around the edge, a sort of fringe of palm trees made of fireworks all around it'; as on the prairies, he discovers, 'there is nothing certain or fixed.'[54] Yet, unlike most of his contemporaries, Hulme does not seem to have been surprised and shocked by the advent of war. It chimed with the view of the world he had always had; humanity for him was limited and flawed, progress a myth, and the imposition of order and compulsion always necessary. The war was simply a melancholy necessity. That it was incompetently organised he constantly pointed out, but that in no way affected his conviction that it was right to fight the Germans. Even the right-wing Hulme was beginning to praise democracy, at least when defined in his own terms, over German despotism.

Hulme was the person who organised breaking the news of Gaudier's death to Sophie, though deputising the task to the Polish wife of a friend, and he later tried to help Sophie gather together Gaudier's work for sale. She was not an easy person to assist, as she grew increasingly suspicious and paranoid. In French law she cannot have had any right to Gaudier's estate, and Hulme appears to have been a go-between with the family, who strongly disapproved of her. Pound was also hovering, buying up works for John Quinn and placing some in museums. Sophie kept a diary, written to Gaudier, in which she vigorously complained about both of them. Pound, she reported to Gaudier, was more assiduous in his help than Hulme, but only because it served his own interests. Whether Hulme and Pound actually quarrelled over Gaudier's remains isn't clear, but a rift definitely emerged. Hulme, according to Kate Lechmere, now 'took a great dislike to Pound', though 'he always loved Gaudier'.[55] Over the years, Hulme had grown more irritated by Pound: when asked what he thought of him, Epstein alleges that he said he knew exactly when he would kick him downstairs.[56] He never appears to have done so. Pound, for his part, reported rather regretfully to John Quinn that dealing with Gaudier's estate had ended six years' friendship between himself and Hulme. He blamed Sophie, but it may have been that Hulme, like Aldington, had been thoroughly exasperated by Pound's proprietorial attitude to Gaudier.

LEWIS, meanwhile, with Helen Saunders' help, was carrying out his next commission, painting three abstract panels for a Vorticist room at the Tour Eiffel restaurant, which he frequented at the time (he lived at no. 4 Percy Street, and it was no. 1). It was now a more expensive restaurant than it had been in 1909, but Stulik liked Lewis, and his eating there was subsidised. Possibly he was paid for the decoration in free meals, which was what Stulik had given William Roberts for some earlier painting. In July, the second issue of *Blast* was finally published. Entitled *War Issue*, with a powerful Vorticist drawing by Lewis on the cover, it lacked, scarcely surprisingly, the ebullience of the first. Pound wrote defensively that *Blast* 'alone has dared to show modernity its face in an honest glass . . . to present the actual discords of modern "civilization", DISCORDS now only too apparent in the open conflict between teutonic atavism and unsatisfactory Democracy'.[57] Yet the editorial, written by Lewis, who was responsible for over half of the issue, was almost apologetic: 'BLAST finds itself surrounded by a multitude of other Blasts of all sizes and description. This puce-coloured cockleshell will, however, try and brave the waves of blood, for the serious mission it has on the other side of World-War'.[58] This must have been written before Lewis decided to produce this issue in a sober black and off-white cover; it had been due out in December 1914, and Lewis appears to have done little to revise the contents. Even the sentiments here seem outdated; few people now saw the war as a temporary blip in a generally calm world. Nor did many feel the confidence Lewis displays later in the issue that 'Life after the War will be the same brilliant life as it was before'.[59]

Apart from Lewis' contributions, in which he attempted to associate the Vorticists with the war effort, claiming that the Kaiser has 'declared murderous war on Cubism and Expressionism', *Blast 2* contained poetry by Dismorr, Saunders, Ford, Eliot and Pound.[60] Eliot had originally offered some of the rather schoolboyish scurrilous verse that he was apt to circulate, but Lewis, after the trouble with Pound's 'testicles' the year before, rather wisely turned it down. Instead he published some of Eliot's 'Preludes' and his 'Rhapsody on a Windy Night', all poems from his Parisian days, and by far the most impressive contributions to the issue. Pound's poems were among his weakest, and he caused a furore with a poem about Rupert Brooke's sexual escapades in the Pacific. Brooke, now a national hero, was not admissible as the butt of ribald jokes. Pound was apologetic, saying he thought Brooke the best of the Georgians and pointing out that the issue had after all been meant to come out the previous year; he blamed Lewis, and indeed a more careful editor might have thought to remove the poem. (Pound republished the poem in his 1926 collection, which suggests his penitence was not deep.) Also reproduced was a drawing by Dorothy entitled 'Snow Scene', and her design for the cover of *Ripostes*, along with an advertisement from Elkin Mathews for Pound's books.

Perhaps what was most disturbing were some notes sent by Gaudier from the trenches:

This war is a great remedy.

In the individual it kills arrogance, self esteem, pride.

It takes away from the masses numbers upon numbers of unimportant units, whose economic activities become notorious as the recent trade crises have shown us.

He admits he had found a Mauser rifle, which seemed to him an 'IMAGE of brutality', and had cut off the butt to carve something with 'a gentler order of feeling', but adds, 'I WILL EMPHASIZE that MY DESIGN *got its effect* (just as the gun had) FROM A VERY SIMPLE COMPOSITION OF LINES AND PLANES.' Yet, though Gaudier says, 'My views on sculpture remain absolutely the same', those notes were written when he had been fighting only two months, probably no later than December 1914.[61] As would soon become public knowledge, by the time of his death he had changed his mind, and planned a piece for the third issue of *Blast* in which he would announce his return to organic sculpture. One by one, as they became painfully aware of the brutal horror of the war machine, the Vorticists would return to more representational art, natural rather than mechanical form, though often an inventive and arresting fusion of the two. The *War Issue* published some fine drawings, but for all the high artistic achievements of Vorticism, it was a doomed movement. Gaudier's statement was followed, as if symbolically, by the announcement of his death, 'MORT POUR LA PATRIE', one last-minute change that Lewis, who, like Pound, saw Gaudier's death as a tragic loss, took the trouble to make.

Among the poems Pound contributed was one beginning, 'I cling to the spar', which vividly demonstrated how his sense of persecution was escalating. The seafarer is now shipwrecked, 'Washed with the cold salt ice' and 'Insidious modern waves'. He is threatened by 'cowardly editors', who tell him he must not say what he thinks, utter his hates or his loves, praise people like Lewis, Epstein and Brzeska, nor 'spit out the later Rodin', or 'they will have my guts;/they will cut down my wage, force me to sing their cant . . . be before all a model of literary decorum./Merde!' Abandoning the watery image with which it begins, the poem ends up in a Dantean forest, on the way, presumably, to explore Hell:

> Friends fall off at the pinch, the loveliest die.
> That is the path of life, this is my forest.[62]

One might have expected the warm reception of *Cathay* to have led Pound to feel less beleaguered, though it is likely he had written this poem some months before that appeared, when the *New Age* had refused to let him finish his series, 'Affirmations'; the hates and loves he mentions here are a good summary of the topics he covered then. Yet the aggressive stance of the poem itself, the emphasis on hatred, and swearing at the world in general, hardly add up to the best way to promote your friends. It was true that much of the press was nervous, conservative and wary of anything that did not support the status quo: there were few prosecutions of literary works under the Defence of the Realm Act, brought in at the beginning of the war, and since then made more draconian, but editors were wary. Pound's income was indeed affected; he would calculate that November that he had only earned £42 10s. during the last twelve months, considerably less than a working man's wages, though Dorothy had her £150 a year to help him out. While it was a wild exaggeration to suggest that editors like Orage or Prothero had any specific designs on his guts (Orage would continue to publish him for the rest of the war, albeit towards the end largely under pseudonyms), some people in London literary circles had always disliked

Pound, though in the past not enough, in numbers or intensity, for him to notice. The balance was shifting. Wyndham Lewis – not entirely a reliable witness – later described the aversion of some of those who met Pound in 1910 to what they saw as 'a bogus personage' who was a 'tiresome and flourishing, pretentious aspirant to poetic eminence'.[63] Then Pound had been happily unaware of any adverse impact he had; by 1915, he was indignantly answering charges of charlatanry in the daily papers. Visitors to Yeats' Monday evenings, which he continued to dominate, took against him in increasing numbers, as he continued to be, as R.F. Foster puts it, as 'energetically offensive' as ever.[64] Yet years later, Aldington would write in Pound's defence: 'He is sensitive, highly-strung, and irascible. All this throwing down of fire-irons and sputtering of four-letter words is merely Ezra's defence against a none too considerate world. I should say Ezra has had to put up with far worse annoyances from other people than they ever have from him.'[65] All very true, yet Pound remained intent on provoking vilification. And if in 1913 he had been delighted when he was attacked in the same week in the *New Age* and the *New Freewoman*, now the attacks ate into him.[66]

Significantly missing from his poem, in the list of those to whom he is offering support, are Pound's former protégés, H.D. and Aldington. One suspects they may be included among the 'friends' who 'fall off at the pinch'. Yet it was only after *Blast* was out in July that Pound decided to take issue with the May *Egoist*. He had by no means lost interest in imagism, nor shed his sense of ownership, and the long work he was beginning to plan he saw as a long imagist poem, something that he had referred to as a possibility in his article on Vorticism in the *Fortnightly Review* the year before, and which he mentioned again when discussing the Noh plays in *Drama* that June. The *Cantos* would be structured round a series of repeated images, or linked analogies, that build a pattern rather than form a narrative, a structure he described earlier in the year as 'pattern units'. Pound was looking for ways of creating a poem that would bring together the present and the past, the social and mystical, his personal life and public order, hellish depths and paradisal light. In August he wrote to Henderson, 'I am working on a long poem that will resemble the Divina Commedia in length but in no other manner. It is a huge, I was going to say, gamble, but shan't, it will prevent my making any money for the next forty years, perhaps.'[67] In that latter point, he would largely be correct. Some critics suggest that the *Cantos*' form was influenced by the repeated motifs in Vorticist drawings, but it was more crucially a product of what Pound called the 'mytho-poetical' quality of imagism; at its core is a series of mythic references, a form of Eliot's 'mythical method', still owing much to Frazer.[68] For Pound in 1915, if this 'huge gamble' was to be a long imagist poem, he needed to assert his pre-eminent right to the movement. At the end of June he did so.

Aldington wrote to Amy on 8 July 1915, the day after they had arrived back from H.D.'s convalescence in the country, reporting crossly that 'Ezra has been annoying Franky [i.e. Flint] and me with absurd and abusive letters about the Imagist number of the Egoist. Franky sent him a fairly crushing retort, I have taken no notice.' In fact, Pound was not attacking the issue in general, but venting his ire on Flint's 'History.' 'After deliberate consideration,' Pound's letter to Flint said firmly, he remained of the opinion that Flint's article was 'BULLSHIT'.[69] Flint's 'History' had been similar to – though more detailed and more neutral in tone than – the one that he had given to Lowell, and on factual grounds it would be hard to fault. The meetings at the Tour Eiffel, the group's experimentation with forms, the interest in *vers libre*, the influence of French symbolist and Japanese poetry are not in question. Hulme was, Flint had said, the leader of the group, insisting on direct and unelaborated presentation; encouraged by Storer in particular, the idea of the image was much discussed and practised. Again, it was a simple account of the facts. Pound, Flint pointed out, only joined the group a month after they began to meet; he had then no interest in French poetry later than the Middle Ages: 'he was very full of his *troubadours*; but I do not remember that he did more than attempt to illustrate (or refute) our theories occasionally with their example'. It was, Flint added, with total accuracy, only in 1912 that Pound began to take some interest in this intellectual debate. He recalled that Pound had included, at the end of *Ripostes*, the complete poetical works of T. E. Hulme, and had there described the *imagistes* as 'the descendants of the forgotten . . . "School of Images"'. 'In that year,' Flint continued, 'Pound had become interested in modern French poetry; he had broken away from his old manner; and he invented the term "Imagisme", to designate the aesthetic of "Les Imagistes"'. Pound set out the four 'cardinal principles of "Imagisme"' in the 'interview' in *Poetry*, and edited the anthology *Des Imagistes*, 'which, though it did not set the Thames, seems to have set America, on fire'. He made no mention of the latest anthology. Flint had begun by quoting Hulme's 'Autumn' as one of the first imagist poems, and quoted from Storer's *Mirrors of Illusion* as the first book of imagist poetry; Storer then believed in a form of poetry which Flint himself had described, he reminded his readers, as 'a form of expression, like the Japanese, in which an image is the resonant heart of an exquisite moment'. The very first poem in that collection, he noted, was entitled 'Image'. Flint ended his article by asserting – and this he must have known would be contentious – that 'there is no difference, except that which springs from difference of temperament and talent, between an imagist poem of today and those written by Edward Storer and T.E. Hulme'.[70]

Although Flint does not say in this history, as he had to Lowell, that Pound was only imagism's 'advertising agent', that is certainly what he implies; his tone, however, is scrupulously dispassionate and he makes no explicit attack on Pound. Of course, the very fact of pointing out that Pound, who had presented himself as such a knowledgeable advocate of modern French poetry, had so recently discovered it, must have been galling in itself. Yet, as Christopher Middleton first pointed out, there is a much more virulent draft among Flint's papers; he had considerably tempered the language of his final account, if not its thrust. In the draft he makes clear that he thinks Pound simply stole the ideas of the Tour Eiffel group and presented them as his own: and whilst he does not say this in so many words in the published version, it could be deduced. Pound began his counter-attack on Flint's article, not with the treatment of his part in the story but by demanding that Flint acknowledge that 'the whole drive towards simple current speech etc. comes from F.M.H. [Ford Madox Hueffer], and that it was never decently considered by the group of 1909'. Flint pointed out in his reply, which he sent the next day ('I hasten to acknowledge your bolt from Olympus'), that many others had advocated this besides Ford: 'The whole drive towards simple current speech does not come from F.M.H. He was one of the generals of division in an army composed of many divisions. No doubt his operations seem of paramount importance to you because you were enrolled under him.'[71] Certainly Pound was on weak ground there: if the Tour Eiffel poets, who had indeed tended to use 'simple current speech', did not talk much about it, neither did Pound in his early definitions of imagism; the first public imagist statement to speak of the 'language of common speech' was in fact the recent preface to *Some Imagist Poets*, with which Pound had had nothing to do. Pound, however, was also angry about the reference to Storer: 'it is ridiculous', he wrote, 'to pretend that the Hellenic hardness of H.D.'s poems is in any way traceable to his custard.' Poor Storer! what a noun – evoking the soft, the sweet, the cowardly, the bland; in a word, the despised feminine, as opposed to H.D.'s paradoxically masculinised hardness. Yet 'hardness' was not a quality mentioned in the first imagist manifestos, though it had been evoked by Pound elsewhere since early 1912. Flint responded by explaining that he wasn't saying H.D.'s poetry was 'traceable' to Storer, merely that Storer's poetry at that stage had certain imagist qualities, including 'direct speech, or simple current speech'. In any case, he added, he wasn't sure the word 'hardness' conveyed very much as far as poetry was concerned.[72]

Only half-way through his letter did Pound mention his real grievance: 'As to the energy, the organising faculty, the whole formulation of Imagism, and the effort that went to making it what it is, i.e., the dominant force in contemporary english and american verse, oO, la la! We will leave that unimportant factor out of the case.' Flint's reply was:

You deserve all the credit for what you have done, and occupy therefor [sic] a proportionate place in . . . The History of Imagism. But where you have failed, my dear Ezra . . . is in your personal relationships . . . You had the energy, you had the talents (obscured by a certain American mushiness), you might have been generalissimo in a compact onslaught: and you spoiled everything by some native incapacity for walking square with your fellows. You have not been a good comrade, voilà![73]

In what way had Pound not walked square? Pound could bully, and he could patronise, but perhaps Flint had in mind actions like Pound's cavalier take-over of his own expertise on French poetry without due acknowledgement, for which he was belatedly taking his revenge; in the draft he shows he had not forgiven Pound for this, emphasising that it was only in August 1912 that Pound 'was led to discover the "Approach to Paris" . . . which I had made for him'.[74] Most centrally, however, Flint was angry about what he saw as Pound's passing off as his own the ideas of the Tour Eiffel group, in particular those of Hulme: in the unpublished draft, he had written that Pound 'added nothing of any value to the discussion. Most of the members of the group were pretty widely acquainted with . . . French theory, and Mr Pound had nothing to teach them; but he took very much. He took away the whole doctrine . . . of what he later on called Imagisme.'[75] In his reply to Pound, Flint wrote, 'You don't pretend that there is anything particularly original or revelatory to me, a student of French theory and practice, in your Donts of an Imagist . . . My dear chap, think again!'[76] Flint was pouring out all the resentment that he had built up over the years towards Pound, and was no longer inclined to make the allowances that he had in 1913.

Flint's anger with Pound had increased even since he had written to Lowell in January, his indignation having been fuelled in February by Pound's claim in his 'Analysis of this Decade' that he was the originator of the concept of 'the Image'. Had Hulme himself been around in early 1915, and not, as Flint put it, 'read[ing] German philosophy in the trenches', he might well have taken it ill that Pound was appropriating ownership of his earlier ideas. Flint, who visited Hulme in hospital, perhaps told him, another reason for Hulme's growing dislike of Pound. Flint had written in another draft for the history, 'Mr Pound, in *The New Age*, has been claiming "The Image" as his own peculiar contribution to the aesthetic of the past decade. His claim, however . . . does not hold water.' His reply to Pound ended up being quite as abusive as Pound's letter to him. He accused Pound of being 'entangled in the charlatantry of Vorticism', said he was probably not even an imagist poet himself, and added that there were faults in Pound's work which were of 'equal and greater avoirdupois' than Storer's.[77]

On 7 July Pound wrote back once more, ignoring these *ad hominem* remarks, and insisting that 'when, on a certain evening in, I think, 1912, I coined the word Imagisme, I certainly intended it to mean something which was the poetry of H.D, and most emphatically NOT the poetry of friend Storer'. He went on to emphasise that 'in that definition the other two original imagists most certainly concurred', as if to make the point that Flint was in this instance a later comer, as Flint had said that Pound himself was at the Tour Eiffel. (Pound describes Flint nonchalantly as the 'fourth or fifth' imagist, though undoubtedly he was the fourth.) In reply to Flint's comment on the imprecision of the term 'hardness', which may have hit home, as Pound's use of the word is so obviously rhetorical *machismo*, he said peevishly that the advantage of a 'precise' term was that it made it 'unnecessary to discuss with every Frank, John and Amy, whether "hardness" for example is or is not a virtue in itself'.[78] Refusal to admit discussion, dogmatic statement, a conviction that his own views were entirely right, and the belief that he was being unfairly and cruelly attacked for his attempts to shed light were becoming default positions for Pound.

Flint pointed out to Pound that, 'in my History, I was tracing Imagism to no particular person . . . Imagism, like all other literary movements, was a general movement, a product and impulse of the time.'[79] In this, he was surely correct, and indeed one of my aims in writing this book has been to show how right he was. Yet Pound's panache and energy galvanised the currents that were already flowing and gave a focus and intensity to the changing aesthetic climate; even finding a name was not a negligible contribution. Another way of saying Pound was the movement's advertising agent would be to say he brought it to public attention; he created the spectacle of imagism; he performed flamboyantly the role of leader of the imagist avant-garde; he accelerated the forces for change that were already in motion, and channelled them so they became a powerful stream. It was of course to Flint he owed his first understanding of how continental avant-garde movements worked, but his years as a Whistlerian genius had been an excellent training. Pound's energetic formation of the movement and fiery framing of its creed was the vortex into which the numerous ideas of the time poured. As Michael Levenson has said, 'Pound willed [imagism] into being, wrote it into doctrine, and publicized it into prominence.'[80] The lines from 'Portrait d'une Femme', that I earlier suggested could be read as a comment on his poetry, could equally apply to his shaping of imagism: 'No! there is nothing! In the whole and all./Nothing that's quite your own./Yet this is you'.[81] Nothing in imagism was singular to him, or originated with him, but it still bore his stamp.

As far as the ideas were concerned, however, Flint was understandably angry to have Pound tell him that 'the light fell on' him when Pound explicated to him the theories to which he had been endeavouring to get Pound to listen for the previous four years. As he said in his draft, Pound only came to accept these ideas after repeated 'indoctrinations', and did not have his own first 'illumination' until the spring of 1912, presumably when Flint introduced him to the work of de Gourmont and de Régnier.[82] Yet Pound was able to communicate those ideas dramatically and concisely in a way Flint could never have done. Where they differed was that, to Flint, imagism was an aesthetic theory, to Pound, a religious doctrine; to Flint, imagism was a practice, to Pound an essence; Flint wanted to argue that H.D. simply wrote better poems than Storer, Pound that they were of a different species. Pound himself accused Flint of confusing *imagisme* and Impressionism, the latter being for Pound passive and descriptive, whilst the former, as he had argued in the *New Age*, was actively creative, the product of 'intense emotion' which causes 'pattern to arise in the mind'.[83] Pound was aware that he had made the most of the glitter and razzmatazz of leading an avant-garde '*mouvemong*', but he also believed that he had produced something new, his particular version of the image, with its visionary intensity. It is true that Hulme's Bergsonian

images, whose conjunction sparked the intuitional insight into the nature
of reality, the ever-flowing flux of duration, were closely allied to Pound's
'cluster of fused ideas . . . endowed with energy'. Whether his definition
of the image as 'an intellectual and emotional complex in an instance of
time', or more recently as a 'radiant node or cluster; . . . a VORTEX,
from which, and through which, and into which, ideas are constantly
rushing', was in fact so different in nature from Hulme's is a matter for
debate, but it is more memorably put.

One can sympathise with both Flint's and Pound's viewpoints. In
fact, they were not so far apart. Even in Pound's second letter, he had
written that if Flint would allow that there was a difference in form and
style between Storer and H.D., they could come close to agreeing. In
1921, the two of them would work on a sketch for the history of imagism
which would not differ in essence greatly from Flint's 1915 version,
though it carried the story on further, and in that version Pound promin-
ently acknowledged Hulme's introduction of the idea of the image and
the importance of Flint's article on French poetry. But for now, Flint
and Pound remained furious with each other, and both were left bruised.
Flint had ended his letter to Pound by saying, 'life has made a mess of
the job that was in front of her when she created the lot of us'.[84] It
appears to be about this time that Flint began to write his melancholy
autobiographical novel, *Failure*, never apparently completed and certainly
never published, but it may have been his sense that Pound had cheated
him out of success that turned him back to look at the way that his
childhood had undermined his self-belief. He wrote there that it was
from his mother that he 'inherited that artistic instinct and lack of self-
assertion which in a queer ravelled thread of gold and grey had twisted
round and strangled what might otherwise have been a commonplace,
successful life'.[85] Artistic instinct he certainly had, and if in this correspondence he had for once been self-assertive, he was badly bruised as
a result. Unlike Pound, he did not find it easy to pick himself up after
a blow.

IV

IF Flint's 'History' has had an unfortunate afterlife as a bone much chewed upon by critical dogs in the dispute over whether Ford or Hulme should be seen as the Ur-imagist, Flint's strong sense that Hulme's contribution deserved acknowledgement had nothing to do with his personal feelings about Ford. Though he admired Hulme's intelligence greatly, his relationship with him was always uneasy, whilst he and Ford responded warmly to each other. Indeed, his one concession to Pound was to say that 'it was an omission on my part not to have mentioned [Ford's] influence on you: it shall be repaired'. Ford had a strong sense of Flint's worth – he later told Glenn Hughes that he was 'one of the greatest men and one of the most beautiful spirits of the country' – and he refused to be drawn into Pound's quarrel with him. Flint had retained his friendship with Ford, in spite of Aldington's grumbles about him, though as he said rather poignantly to Pound, 'I wish I had more leisure, lived nearer, and could see him oftener'.[86] Ford generally did his best to keep out of the disputes between *les jeunes* – after all, in spite of Pound's opposition, he had been willing to go into *Some Imagist Poets* until turned down by Houghton Mifflin, while at the same time he had loyally continued to lend his name to Pound's movement. It was doubtless the inclusion in *Blast* of his poem, 'Antwerp', which Eliot would describe in 1917 as 'the only good poem I have met with on the subject of the war', that had led Aldington to identify him as one of the 'Vorticist cuistres', though he himself was well aware his work was very different.[87] Ford later claimed that Lewis had denounced his writing, insisting that he was 'Finished! Exploded! Done for! Blasted in fact! . . . What is the sense of you and Conrad and Impressionism?'[88] And, indeed, while Pound valued Ford's support, his conversation and those of his critical views that agreed with his own, he rarely appears to have appreciated

Ford's own artistic achievements. Apart from 'On Heaven', he was lukewarm about his poetry, which like Lewis he complained was impressionist, and if he admired Ford's wartime propaganda, he took little interest in his fiction. *The Good Soldier*, the novel which is generally agreed to be Ford's finest, and indeed one of the finest of the period, had been published that March, but though the early sections had appeared in the first *Blast*, Pound appears to have ignored it. At the time, it didn't get a good deal of coverage – the war saw to that – but it had admirers, among them Rebecca West, May Sinclair and H.G. Wells. But most critics thought it immoral, and were shocked that in the middle of this patriotic war the title turned out to describe an adulterer. Much of Ford's self-division and unhappiness had gone into the book; he was still in love with Brigit and increasingly unhappy with Hunt, who, according to Aldington, feared Ashburnham's suicide at the end of the novel might prefigure Ford's. Ford, however, chose another way out of his predicament. He dramatically renounced literature (that of course did not last), and joined the army, using his influential political friends to get him a commission. He would later claim it was Gaudier's death that convinced him that he should join up, writing plangently about his memories of the sculptor, as usual highly reinvented in ways that infuriated Aldington. Max Saunders, however, suggests that the assertion had a certain displaced truth: he 'had identified Prussia . . . with commercialism', and joining the war against those who killed artists like Gaudier was 'his only means left to express his rage at a largely indifferent public, and against hostile critics and publishers'.[89] But escape from Violet Hunt, including his financial dependence on her, was surely the central motive. At the end of July 1915 he joined the Welch Regiment. He was forty-one, and his health had not been good – the cause was diagnosed as 'neurasthenia', a fashionable category which included all kinds of nervous ailments and psychological stress. Two months later, according to Pound, he looked twenty years younger.

Aldington and H.D. had unequivocally taken Flint's side in the quarrel with Pound. 'Don't – don't worry about that beastly letter from E.P.,' H.D. had written from Surrey on 5 July, before their return home. 'He sent a copy to R. and that, you see, is the reason I know about it'.[90] Pound had perhaps hoped to quarrel only with Flint, and to maintain the links with the Aldingtons. Although Aldington seems to imply to Lowell that Pound had written abusively to himself as well as Flint, no letter to Aldington on the issue is extant. Pound had used H.D. in his letter to Flint as the exemplum of imagism, and had also drawn a clear distinction between Flint's history and Aldington's article on himself: 'Richard and Hilda both detest a certain part or phase of my work. I may not agree about "romanticism" etc. but it is obvious to any one that R. has been even meticulously careful to say nothing in his article that he does not sincerely believe to be true.'[91] Yet if Pound thought he could drive a wedge between the Aldingtons and Flint, he was mistaken. They were horrified by what they saw as his bullying tactics, and for the next two years would have little to do with him. By August Pound was writing to Alice Corbin Henderson, 'I am very much displeased with Richard, more displeased with Flint'. He and Aldington, he told her, were no longer 'on terms'; he considered him poetically 'dead stuck', and insisted that all Aldington's ideas, save a 'feeble Hellenism', were taken from himself or Ford.[92] On the other hand, in September he was still including H.D. in a list of American poets who could put the English to shame.[93] Yet he was now personally estranged from two of those he himself insisted were the three original imagists, and in America imagism would soon be much more readily associated with Amy Lowell than himself. He wrote to Harriet Monroe two months after the exchange with Flint, 'Since the latest manifestation, I scarcely know whether to repudiate all connection, or whether to attempt to continue the movement on the basis of the common sense of the original program. I don't suppose that either way it will matter a tuppenny d– –n!'[94] Harriet read this out to Fletcher, who was once more visiting her Chicago office, and he reported it back with unkind glee to Amy Lowell. Pound would in fact tell Henderson the next year (in the context of one of his regular tirades against Lowell) that he had thought in 1914 of declaring the imagist movement over after the appearance of *Des Imagistes*, and much regretted that he had not done so.[95] If this is true, it must have been a notion he swiftly discarded, because he battled hard and long to keep his position as leader and controller of the imagists.

Pound was not the only one to take issue with Flint's 'History.' In the June issue of the *Egoist* was a letter from his friend Allen Upward, in the form of a poem called 'The Discarded Imagist', protesting that he had become an imagist through quite a different route from that Flint described:

In the year nineteen hundred a poet named Cranmer Byng brought to my attic
in Whitehall Gardens a book of Chinese Gems by Professor Giles,

Eastern butterflies coming into my attic there beside the Stygian Thames,
And read me one of them – willows, forsaken young wife, spring.

Immediately my soul kissed the soul of immemorial China:
I perceived that all we in the West were indeed barbarians and foreign devils,
And that we knew scarcely anything about poetry.

I set to work and wrote little poems . . .
Then I hid them away for ten or twelve years,
Scented leaves in a Chinese jar

The poem goes on to recount how Ezra Pound 'the generous' had pronounced him an imagist ('I had no idea what he meant'), but how astonished he had been to discover, the previous month, that imagism had been started by Hulme and Storer.[96] Whether Upward could really be described as an imagist is debatable, though it has to be said this particular poem is the most effective of his that I have read, and whilst in one way his poem might seem to be questioning Flint's history, by pointing another path into imagism, more importantly he is reinforcing Flint's argument that imagism could not be ascribed to the influence of any one person. In his portrayal of imagism as a moment of recognition of the inadequacy of Western traditions he is evoking one of its constant features.

If imagism was moving out of Pound's control, perhaps what added to the bitterness with which he attacked Flint was that the Vorticist cause was in further danger. There were those who were now pointing out in the press that Gaudier, one of the three central Vorticists, was in the process of abandoning it when he was dispatched by a German rifle. When John Middleton Murry, in an article in the *Westminster Gazette* on 22 July 1915, referred to Vorticism as 'a passing phase' of Gaudier's work, Pound sent in an indignant refutation, saying Gaudier had shown no sign of 'recantation' when he had written to him two days before his death.[97] Murry's response to Pound's reproach added fuel to his paranoia: 'the term "Vorticism",' he said, 'has, since its promulgation, come to signal extravagance and *fumisterie* in art. Because of that, I was anxious that readers of the *Westminster Gazette* should not be prejudiced against a sculptor who had genius, merely because his fellow-Vorticists had none.' In August, Roger Fry wrote in the *Burlington Magazine* that when Gaudier died he had been on the point of giving up Vorticism and returning to organic forms, emphasising that even in his most Vorticist sculpture, 'the general principles of organic form are adhered to, the plasticity is rounded with peculiar bluntness and yet sweetness of form, but remains sensitive and full of life'.[98] Fry's assertion is corroborated by Aldington, who in his memoirs recalled that before Gaudier returned to the front for the last time he had said that he intended to go back to Greek models. John Cournos wrote an article on Gaudier's sculpture for the September *Egoist* ignoring Vorticisim.[99] To prove that Gaudier had not defected from Vorticism became for Pound an urgent task.

Pound persuaded John Lane to let him bring out a memorial volume about Gaudier, which he produced at lightning speed, assembling Gaudier's contributions to *Blast*, an article from the *Egoist*, his letters from the front to himself, Wadsworth and Olivia Shakespear, reproductions of his work, Pound's own article on Vorticism, and two of the 'Affirmations' series, 'Gaudier-Brzeska' and the contentious 'Analysis of this Decade', to which he added some linking narrative; the job was done in about a month. The result was a book that remains a fascinating document in the history of modernist art, and one that profoundly influenced, among others, Henry Moore, but Pound's account of Gaudier's work has been repeatedly questioned. Both Jacob Epstein and Horace Brodzky, who would later himself write a book on Gaudier, thought Pound saw the sculpture too much through the prism of literature and did not really understand what Gaudier was trying to do. Levenson suggests Pound's object was 'as much to legitimise Vorticism as . . . to memorialise Gaudier-Brzeska', and points out that in the last pages he 'virtually disappears from the text': it is certainly true that in that section Whistler is mentioned much more frequently than Gaudier.[100]

One striking, though unsurprising, omission in the book is that Pound refuses to acknowledge that Gaudier had never been solely within the Vorticist camp. As Timothy Materer has pointed out, Gaudier had had contacts with the Omega group, and continued to carry out commissions for them after his involvement with the Vorticists. He had also had dealings with Middleton Murry, and had done drawings for his magazine *Rhythm*. Fry and Murry in their comments may have aimed to damage Vorticism, but they may well have been drawing on firsthand knowledge of Gaudier's thoughts in order to do so. Lewis himself, much as he admired Gaudier, would later say that he was 'a good man on the soft side', and that he was not 'one of us'.[101] In fact Gaudier's work, as Fry had commented, had rarely been purely abstract; he had never shared Lewis' Vorticist passion for the machine, though like Lewis he had a keen interest in ancient or so-called primitive art. In his 'Vortex', in the first issue of *Blast*, Gaudier had rejected a 'derivative' 'petrified' culture like that of the Greeks, and placed the origins of his work and those like him (such, he says, as Epstein, Brancusi and Modigliani) in palaeolithic cave painting, in ancient Egyptian sculpture, in Assyrian, Chinese, and African and Pacific art, the last two of which he admired particularly for the centrality of sexuality in their work.[102] Gaudier was fascinated by this non-mimetic art's exploration of expressive form, but he makes no mention of the modern industrial world, and, unlike Lewis, he was primarily interested in art that depicts animal life, like that of the Dordogne cave-dwellers, or the Assyrians with their man-headed bulls. By the time of his death, he was moving away from formalism: in April 1915 he wrote to Olivia Shakespear, to whom he had promised a sculpture of her cat Max, 'I am getting convinced it is not much use going further in the research of planes, forms, etc. If I ever come back I shall do more "Mlles G . . ." in marble.' Pound printed this letter in the book, but he added a footnote: '"Mlle G . . ." is the nickname of a naturalistic torse . . . He had repeatedly stigmatised it as insincere. However, this passage is all I can find about the "renunciation" so vaunted by our enemies.'[103] Pound did not even include a photograph of 'Mlle. G.' in the book, so deep was his disapproval, and though he does acknowledge that Gaudier was planning an essay on the 'Need of Organic Forms in Sculpture', he did not admit the possibility that his fellow-Vorticist was rethinking his position. He told Henderson that the 'present attacks have taken the form of defining "vorticism" to suit the attackers' taste and then saying that Brzeska, or I Am, are, was, *not* vorticists, etc. ad infinitum'.[104]

It was not only in England that Pound felt unappreciated. In August, he wrote a furious letter to the editor of the *Boston Evening Transcript* accusing their '(?negro) reviewer', William Stanley Braithwaite, who had earlier savaged *Provença*, of being a liar for saying that 'my friend Robert Frost has done what no other American poet has done in this generation ". . . that is, unheralded, unintroduced, untrumpeted, he won the acceptance of an English publisher on his own terms"'. Not only had he, Pound, been published in just that way rather earlier, but 'Frost was a bloated capitalist when he struck this island, in comparison to yours truly'. He recounted the story of his own dealings with Mathews, and went on to ascribe Frost's success largely to being launched by himself, adding, 'Of course, from the beginning, in my pushing Frost's work, I have known that he would ultimately be boomed in America by fifty energetic young men who would use any club to beat me; that was well in my calculation when I prophesied his success with the American public and especially with the American reviews.'[105] Frost, who had so feared Pound would damn him in American eyes, must have been amused to discover Pound thought his American success was due to Pound's own endeavours, but Harriet Monroe wrote to Pound to remonstrate, pointing out the letter was simply taken as indicating that Pound was jealous of Frost, which at some unadmitted level he no doubt was.

There were other blows in store for Pound. Earlier that year, he had begun to plan a new anthology as a rival production to Lowell's, his to be called the *Catholic Anthology* to indicate that he was now above sectarian schools. In the event, when it came out in late 1915, the title caused offence to the pious, who took it to be a blasphemous reference to the Catholic Church, and bookshops were unwilling to sell it. To Pound's disappointment, very few copies were bought, and Noel Stock says that there were still copies available in 1936 at the original price of 3s. 6d.[106] It was in fact a rather fine anthology, with poems by Yeats, Eliot, Williams and Pound himself, some of the Georgians, such as Douglas Goldring and Harold Monro, some of the Chicago poets, including Carl Sandburg, Edgar Lee Masters, Harriet Monroe and a striking poem by Alice Corbin Henderson, other *Egoist* regulars, like John Rodker and Allen Upward, and two of the New York poets connected with *Others*, Orrick Johns and Alfred Kreymborg. Aldington was highly amused when he heard that Pound was including poems by Monro, about whom he was usually totally scornful, but in fact one of the four Monro poems for the anthology was the wonderful 'Milk for the Cat', for which he is probably best remembered as a poet:

> The children eat and giggle and laugh;
> The two old ladies stroke their silk:
> But the cat is small and thin with desire,
> Transformed to a creeping lust for milk.[107]

Monro would complain later, when it appeared with great regularity in anthologies for schools, that it was an adult poem, not for children: what, he demanded, would they understand by 'a creeping lust'? Pound, however, said that his chief pleasure in publishing the anthology was to have Eliot's poems appear in a book, just as earlier he had conceived *Des Imagistes* to give book publication to Aldington and H.D. 'Prufrock' and 'Portrait of a Lady', the latter having appeared in *Others* in

September, were both included along with three shorter poems. Pound was still not convinced that Eliot was of the stature of Lewis or Joyce, to whom he referred in a letter that summer to Alice Corbin Henderson as 'the two men of genius', Eliot appearing solely as 'a quaint mind full of intelligence'.[108] Yet when writing publicly, he was already promoting Eliot as a leading figure. He had managed to include a reference to Eliot in the Gaudier memoir: Whistler, he wrote,

> was almost the first man, at least the first painter of the last century to suggest that intelligent and not wholly ignorant and uncultivated men had a right to art . . . After an intolerable generation we find again this awakening . . . Lewis, Brzeska, James Joyce, T.S. Eliot all proving independently and sporadically that the possession of a certain measure of intellect, education, enlightenment does not absolutely unfit a man for artistic composition.
>
> In this awakening I find very great comfort.[109]

By the next year Eliot would unquestionably be fêted by Pound on equal terms with Lewis, Joyce and himself, and Lewis would later immortalise the four of them as 'the men of 1914', ignoring with his usual insouciance the fact that Eliot was not published until 1915.

Pound was now seeing more of Eliot, who had given up his postgraduate studies at Oxford. In many ways the two of them were very different, Pound too loud and precipitate, Eliot too cautious and contained. Pound had no social skills; Eliot had impeccably good manners. Pound was always a maverick and outsider; Eliot assimilated into the most respectable English society. Pound eschewed logic and relied on intuitive convictions; Eliot could have been a professional philosopher, and was always, even after his conversion to Anglicanism, of a deeply sceptical turn of mind. Yet, as Peter Ackroyd points out in his persuasive biography of Eliot, they also had important experiences in common, both finding that American society could not nourish their desire for the arts and literature, and feeling impelled to make their creative lives abroad.[110] In addition, however, they were both academics *manqués*, deeply disapproving of contemporary university education, yet eventually having a considerable impact on it. Both were extraordinarily literary writers, drawing repeatedly on earlier writers' work to make their own. Both would write intensely personal poetry – what Eliot would call in the case of Pound 'reticent autobiography' – while claiming to be producing something quite impersonal.[111] Both wanted to remake the canon of great works, to reconstruct the great tradition, and to establish themselves as arbiters of taste. In the last aim, Eliot would be much more overtly successful, although Pound's influence – often through Eliot – would be far from negligible.

That June, Eliot had impulsively married a young, well-connected Englishwoman, Vivien Haigh-Wood, an abandonment of his usual caution that he would long regret, for it was to be a disastrous marriage for them both. Eliot was a virgin when he married, obsessed with and repulsed by sexual matters. He had spent a year studying in Paris in 1910, and like Fletcher had found the overt sexuality of the city nightmarish rather than appealing, as the disturbing, menacing yet pathetic and tawdry female presences suggest in the 'Rhapsody on a Windy Night' that he had written there.[112] Vivien, it appears, found sexual relations equally distressing. Her brother Maurice, according to Ackroyd, said that the only person with whom Eliot ever discussed the sexual failure of his marriage was Pound, an astonishing claim, given Pound's dislike of 'personal tosh'. Yet, although there is so much less evidence about Pound's married life, if, as Humphrey Carpenter surmises, Pound's own marriage was also sexually unsuccessful, perhaps they did – I am sure in the most inhibited way – hint at their shared marital problems. Yet their situations were scarcely comparable; Pound was not entirely free of American puritan inhibitions, but his drives went elsewhere: into his work, of course, but also into his search for fame, for literary power, for leadership of the band of advancing poets. It was when he was frustrated there that pain and bitterness ensued. Eliot's much deeper fear of the destructive consuming power of female sexuality appears in many of his poems, including one he contributed to the *Catholic Anthology* tellingly called 'Hysteria', as well as in *The Waste Land*. Yet one would guess that Pound, Eliot and Fletcher were all, to differing degrees, in emotional terms sexually dysfunctional; American puritanism took a heavy toll, though, of course, Hulme and Lewis, with their inability to bring affection and sexuality together, could be seen as emotionally dysfunctional in a very English mode.

At the time of his marriage, Eliot asked Pound to write to break the news to his father that he had married an Englishwoman, given up his studies, and now intended to make his way as a writer. It is possible Pound had been trying to persuade Eliot to abandon the academic world as he himself had done, and Eliot felt that the least Pound could do was present his arguments to his father. Pound told Henry Ware Eliot (prophetically) that his son would have a much easier time making his way in England than he himself had done. Eliot fitted in as he would never do. Yet, as Ackroyd points out, although Eliot was grateful for Pound's help, and saw a certain amount of him over the next few years, he actually felt more at ease with the writers of the Bloomsbury group, who, for all their overthrowing of some conventions, were much closer to the world of well-bred English gentry to which Eliot was drawn. Pound despised the Bloomsbury group, no doubt encouraged to do so by Lewis. He never appears even to have met Virginia Woolf. One wonders what they would have made of each other. The limitation of Pound's form of modernism is perhaps no more keenly illustrated than in his failure to appreciate the contribution to modern literature made by writers like Woolf.

V

BACK in Boston, Fletcher's burst of enthusiasm for Lowell was rapidly waning. By the time Aldington had excised his most gushing and extravagant comments on her work in his article for the imagist issue, doubts had already set in. He was alternately mesmerised by her energy and drive, and terrified that he would be swept along in her wake and fail to make his mark. He resented the way she was achieving public success, and her charismatic performances made him all the more aware of his awkward diffidence. He was put out that the reviews of *Irradiations: Sand and Spray*, though more numerous than they would been because of the book's simultaneous appearance with the anthology, read his poems as an extension of the imagist programme, while in fact he had written them before he first met Pound. Fletcher was intensely interested in producing rich musical effects (at the time he was writing a series of poems he described as 'symphonies') and exotic evocations of colour, but his poems had none of the chiselled directness espoused by the imagists. He had become friendly with Eliot's Harvard acquaintance, Conrad Aiken, a Southern poet like himself, and now also back in Boston. When Aiken had attacked the imagists in May, he exempted Fletcher from his critique and gave warm praise to *Irradiations*, balm to Fletcher's ever tormented soul, made even sweeter when Aiken followed his example in writing poetic 'symphonies'. Together they went to concerts, and Aiken encouraged him in his deepening passion for Japanese and Chinese forms. In Chicago Fletcher had visited an exhibition of Japanese prints, an experience that led him to write a series of poems, not precisely haiku but influenced by the haiku's clear imagery and minimalism; with typical impetuousity he wrote the first drafts of some fifty poems at the exhibition itself. He had been attracted to Far Eastern art since his time at Harvard, when he had visited the Oriental wing of the Boston Museum of Fine Arts, the collection that owed so much to Fenollosa; in London he had read some of Lafcadio Hearn's writings on Japan, Giles' *A History of Chinese Literature*, and Judith Gautier's *Le Livre de jade*, but what had most immediately stimulated his interest again had been the present from Pound the previous year – before the bad blood – of an 1862 French translation of Chinese poetry. So the fact that Fletcher was working on these poems at the same time as Pound's *Cathay* was going through the press was not coincidental. The poems themselves are taut and evocative, more disciplined than *Irradiations*, some hinting at a mood, others at a narrative. One, called 'Scene from a Drama', went:

> The daimyo and the courtesan
> Compliment each other.

> He invites her to walk out through the maples,
> She half refuses, hiding fear in her heart.

> Far in the shadow
> The daimyo's attendant waits,
> Nervously fingering his sword.[113]

What is the story? Has the courtesan been unfaithful, and is she facing summary punishment? Fletcher's sense of sexuality as a dangerous punitive force is perhaps imaged there. These poems would be published in 1918 as a collection entitled *Japanese Prints*, although individual ones appeared earlier. Later Fletcher talked of there being two strands of imagists: those influenced by France and Japan, Pound, Lowell and himself, and those influenced more by Greece, such as the two Aldingtons. For Fletcher, the example of the Far Eastern forms encouraged a restraint and simplicity that usefully tempered his tendency, in Pound's word, to 'splutter', and for a while he toyed with Zen Buddhism as a way of finding a calmer relation to his surrounding world, not something he would achieve for very long. Yet the Far East was not his only enthusiasm. Later in the year he made another visit to the south-west, where he was much moved by the Native American traditions he found there, though he appears to have had rather more interest in their past and their ancient ruins than in the present inhabitants. Yet he pared his verse to match the bareness of the landscape, and, though in a very different style from the Japanese poems, produced understated yet resonant poems, one of which, 'Arizona', he would include in the 1916 anthology. He returned to Boston later in the year and visited Sevenels regularly, where Lowell remained convinced he was her close poetic comrade, whilst behind her back he grumbled about her in person to Aiken, and in letters to Daisy, whose divorce was now a matter of time; the prospect of returning to marry her appears to have filled him with a mixture of dread and longing.

While in England, Fletcher had always treated the Aldingtons with suspicion, but from the other side of the Atlantic he was beginning to feel more sympathetic towards them. Slightly surprisingly, given his usual self-absorption, he was most distressed to hear about the stillborn baby and told Daisy he had tried to write them a letter of condolence, but that was the sort of thing he couldn't manage, so they can have had no idea of his genuinely compassionate response. He exchanged letters with them occasionally, but Lowell was on the whole the one who maintained the transatlantic link. The imagist – or at any rate contributor to the imagist anthologies – with whom the Aldingtons' acquaintance grew during the autumn of 1915 was Lawrence. On 4 August, exactly one year after the outbreak of war, the Lawrences moved from Sussex, where they had been living since January, to a flat in Hampstead at 1 Byron Villas, not far from the Aldingtons in Christchurch Place. Frieda's children were living in London, and she desperately wanted to see them, though for the most part that only meant catching an occasional glimpse of them on the way to school. While living in Sussex she and Lawrence had been quarrelling bitterly, Frieda deeply unhappy at the separation from her children and resentful of her pariah status as a German in wartime England. Their relationship was always stormy, and the stress had told on them both; at one point Frieda threatened to move out. Lawrence continued to find the war nightmarish, writing in a letter that April: 'hell is slow and creeping and viscous, and insect-teeming: as is this Europe now – this England'.[14] Like H.D., he hated the jingoistic patriotism and febrile atmosphere; his health was bad, his spirits bitter, and he was desperately jealous of Frieda's longing for her children. John Helforth, the non-combatant traumatised by the war in H.D.'s story 'Kora and Ka', also quarrels with the woman with whom he lives because she misses her children. Helforth is, perhaps, partly based on Lawrence. Lawrence shared Helforth's loathing of papers like the 'Daily Newsgraph' and the 'Evening Warscript'; and the violence of language that Helforth uses suggests Lawrence's own wartime letters. Certainly the tormented state of mind described in that story was something both

Lawrence and H.D. endured, even if the war would not produce in H.D. the overt extremities of anger and loathing that Lawrence directed against the world.

Now that he was unable to return to Italy, Lawrence's hatred of England grew, or rather, hatred of what he felt England had become. Since the Aldingtons had last seen him the previous August, he had been taken up by a number of upper-class and well-known figures, but his relationships with them were for the most part uneasy, and tended to fuel his conviction that English society was corrupt and abhorrent. Class differences were too deeply ingrained at that period ever to be quite forgotten, and though Lawrence was drawn to cultured aristo-crats, he nearly always felt, resentfully, if probably correctly, that he was the object of condescension, or, even worse, simply a pastime for them, an exotic, intriguing object of entertainment. In 1915 he and Frieda were in frequent contact with the hostess, Lady Ottoline Morrell, one of those he would turn against, though for now, whilst at times critical of her, he rather enjoyed the civilised ambience she created, and loved her sixteenth-century Garsington Manor. Frieda and Ottoline, however, were always enemies; Frieda resented Ottoline's absorption in Lawrence and lack of interest in herself, and Ottoline would later blame Frieda for poisoning Lawrence against her, convinced that the egregious Hermione Roddice in *Women in Love* was really her creation. Eliot would also be taken up by Ottoline, but that would be a much smoother encounter.

Earlier in the year Lawrence had met another aristocrat and intel-lectual: Bertrand Russell, then in his early forties, a lecturer in mathematics at Cambridge and Ottoline's lover. Lawrence and he were at first immensely taken with each other, but not for long. Lawrence, like Hulme, despised the Cambridge–Bloomsbury nexus he met through Russell, partly through class antagonism, but also because he was disgusted that so many were homosexual – 'horrible little frowsty people, men lovers of men, they give me such a sense of corruption, almost putrescence, that I dream of beetles'.[115] Lawrence's hysterical homophobia, even more pronounced than Aldington's, is sometimes ascribed to guilt about his own homoerotic desires, but whilst those undoubtedly existed, the extremity of his feelings may be linked with his fraught anxiety about his own manhood. Sickly, thin, a writer not a doer, lower class without any redeeming physical strength or manly occupation, Lawrence would always want to define himself against a woman, his alterity from her being his only sure claim to the elusive power of masculinity. Lawrence wrote to Russell about E. M. Forster, 'Why can't he take a woman and fight clear to his own basic, primal being?'[116] That, Lawrence says, is what he himself does, but even the 'ordinary [i.e. heterosexual] Englishman of the educated class goes to a woman now to masturbate himself,' and then moves on to 'Sodomy . . . a nearer form of masturbation'.[117] Lawrence, the implication is, was much more truly masculine.

In spite of disliking Russell's world, Lawrence continued to think for a while that the two of them could work together to transform society. They began to plan a lecture series, but by July the incompatibility of their views became apparent; Lawrence returned the lecture notes Russell had sent him covered with indignant 'NOs' and accompanied by a furious letter in which he said that Russell should drop democracy and relinquish his belief in 'the people', telling him that there 'must be an aristocracy of people who have wisdom, and there must be a Ruler: a Kaiser: no Presidents and democracies'.[118] There is a certain irony in the son of a coal-miner lecturing a future earl in those terms, but the idea of joint lectures was dropped. In September, relations broke down badly when Lawrence described Russell's stand as a pacifist, for which he would eventually lose his Cambridge post and be sent to prison, as 'perverted, mental blood-lust'. 'What you want,' he told him, 'is to jab and strike, like a soldier with a bayonet, only you are sublimated into words'.[119] Lawrence was totally against the war, and thought it should never have been started, but he despised conscientious objectors. Lawrence, who got over his rages swiftly, tried to start the friendship again, assuring Russell that his outbursts were 'largely a quarrelling with something in *myself*', but Russell was further alienated when Lawrence wrote to him in December, in great excitement over an idea he had gleaned from James Frazer's *Totemism and Exogamy* – certainly not an idea that Frazer had meant to recommend – that there was something called 'blood-consciousness' as well as 'mental consciousness', telling Russell that 'the tragedy of this our life, and of your life, is that the mental and nerve consciousness exerts a tyranny over the blood-consciousness, and that your will has gone completely over to the mental consciousness, and is engaged in the destruction of your blood-being or blood-consciousness'.[120] Russell was appalled by what he saw as this embrace of irrationality, asserting in later life that Lawrence's 'mystical philosophy of blood-consciousness "led straight to Auschwitz"'.[121]

By September 1915, Russell had taken up Eliot: like Ottoline, he found him a more amenable protégé and moved him, along with Vivien, into his London flat. Russell can be forgiven for thinking from Lawrence's tirades that he was simply a dangerous proto-Fascist, yet Lawrence was, for all his intemperate language, looking for a way of finding a holistic balance between the conscious and unconscious, the mind and the flesh, the individual human being and what he would call 'the circumambient universe'. As he would later put it: 'the whole life-effort of man was to get his life into direct contact with the elemental life of the cosmos, mountain-life, cloud-life, thunder-life, air-life, earth-life, sun-life. To come into immediately *felt* contact, and so derive energy, power, and a dark sort of joy.' He is close here to Pound's wish in 'Psychology and Troubadours' to be in touch with the 'universe of fluid force' and 'the germinal universe of wood alive, of stone alive', as well as to the passionate, elemental, chthonic world of H.D.'s imagist poetry.[122]

Although Lawrence's spirits rose briefly when he first arrived in London, and he enjoyed making their tiny flat home-like, buying second-hand furniture in the Caledonian Road and Camden High Street, he was soon even more wretched there than in the Sussex countryside. There were soldiers everywhere, recruits, as he recalled in *Kangaroo*, drilling in Parliament Hill Fields, wounded soldiers on Hampstead Heath, 'bright blue soldiers with their red cotton neck-ties, sitting together like macaws, pale and different from other people'.[123] Conscription had still not been brought in – the Liberals were resisting it to the last – but under Lloyd George's increasing influence a new push was made in a propaganda offensive on recruitment. Posters were increasingly aimed at women: 'Is your "best boy" wearing Khaki? . . . If your young man neglects his duty to his King and Country, the time may come when he will NEGLECT YOU!'[124] Lawrence would later write:

It was in 1915 the old world ended. In the winter 1915–1916 the spirit of old London collapsed; the city, in some way, perished, perished from being a heart of the world, and became a vortex of broken passions, lusts, hopes, fears and horrors. The integrity of London collapsed, and the genuine debasement began, the unspeakable baseness of the press and the public voice, the reign of that bloated ignominy, *John Bull*.[125]

This 'vortex of broken passions' is a very different one from Pound's, a whirlpool of despair, not creativity. *John Bull*, a viciously xenophobic publication, was edited by Horatio Bottomley, who was later imprisoned for fraud, though not for the fraudulent copy he was then regularly publishing on the government's behalf. Lawrence had spent much of September and October trying to launch a journal called *The Signature*, which he worked on with his friends – though it was, as so often with Lawrence, an uneasy friendship – Middleton Murry and Katherine Mansfield, who were then living in St John's Wood. He had high hopes for this new venture, telling Lady Cynthia Asquith, the Prime Minister's daughter-in-law and one of the few of her class he did not come to distrust, that he would use it to preach 'beliefs by which one can reconstruct the world'. 'I think my papers are very beautiful and very good,' he told her. 'I feel if only people, decent people, would read them, somehow a new era might set in'.[126] It was not to be, or at least not through the work of the *Signature*, which had to close after three issues, with Lawrence's essay, 'The Crown', which he was publishing in it serially, only half-way through. That 'very beautiful and very good' message would not reach the world in full until 1925.[127]

The Rainbow, whose rewriting Lawrence had completed by March, was published on 30 September, shortly before he and the Aldingtons met up again in early October. Aldington reported to Amy that Lawrence now had 'a vast red beard and is very cantankerous and anti-war . . . He is dying of consumption, of course. His last novel has created less stir than one would have thought, but the war is an awkward competitor.'[128] He spoke too soon. The novel was about to cause a stir, but not the kind he meant. It had none of the widespread praise that *Sons and Lovers* had received, but it soon attracted almost universal and vociferous condemnation. The *Sphere* described it as an 'orgy of sexiness', and the *Daily Mail* as 'a monstrous wilderness of phallicism'. The review in the *Star* was a stark example of the way the tide had turned against any kind of questioning of conventions: 'Art,' it said, 'is a public thing. It is a dweller in the clean homes and swept streets of life. It must conform to the ordered laws that govern human society. If it refuse to do so, it must pay the penalty. The sanitary inspector of literature must notify it and call for its isolation.'[129]

Even Lawrence's usual supporters disliked the novel: Edward Garnett, who had done so much to help Lawrence in the past, did not care for it, Edward Marsh found it distasteful, and Murry bewildering. The denunciations of the book often hinted at Lawrence's German sympathies; he was known to have a German wife and to be against the war, and he had in addition defiantly dedicated the novel to Frieda's sister Else. It might have proved even more problematic if he had been allowed to present the dedication in the way he had wanted to, as '*zu Else*', printed in German Gothic script.[130] The *Star* contrasted the Brangwen family with the soldiers at the front: 'The young men who are dying for liberty are moral beings. They are the living repudiation of such impious denials of life as *The Rainbow*. The life they lay down is a lofty thing. It is not the thing that creeps and crawls in this.'[131]

In early November, an even bitterer blow than unsympathetic reviews fell on Lawrence. All copies of *The Rainbow* were seized on the grounds of obscenity, and burnt by the public hangman. The suppression embittered Lawrence still further towards the English and plunged him into poverty for the rest of the war. He not only lost his royalties on *The Rainbow*, but for the next few years found it difficult to publish any more fiction. Although he finished *Women in Love* in 1916, he would not be able to bring it out until 1921. Sir Philip Morrell, Ottoline's husband, asked questions in the House, but to no avail; Eddie Marsh tried to use his influence, those people from Bloomsbury whom Lawrence despised so much tried to help, though only because of their dislike of censorship, not liking for the book.[132] The irreproachable May Sinclair did admire it, writing that 'the suppression of this book was a crime, the murder of a beautiful thing', but failed to get her words into print.[133] Protest was fruitless.

The Aldingtons were outraged by the seizure of the book, which Richard always maintained was because of Lawrence's opposition to the war. They saw quite a bit of the Lawrences that autumn; both the Aldingtons thought highly of *The Rainbow*, and Lawrence must have been glad to find an oasis of support. H.D. told Lowell it was a 'magnificent' book: with her own turbulent psychic life, she was perhaps readier than some to appreciate Lawrence's portrayal of his characters' stormy, vital desires, and the character of Ursula, finding her own freedom, must have struck her forcefully; Lawrence had described the book the previous year as the story of a 'woman becoming individual, self-responsible, taking her own initiative', and the blurb on the original dust jacket (thought to be written by Lawrence) says the book 'ends with Ursula, the leading-shoot of the restless, fearless family, waiting at the advance post of our time to blaze a path into the future.'[134] Ursula was a woman who had struck out, and, unlike Joan of Arc or Margaret Cravens, had not been defeated.

Reports of *The Rainbow*'s suppression soon reached America; Lowell, a keen admirer of *Sons and Lovers*, was alarmed by the graphic denunciations she read, and wrote to ask if his presence would harm the anthology. Aldington replied bracingly that the reports about the book had been 'exaggerated and distorted' and that it had been suppressed under 'some practically obsolete law which enables any puritanic clergyman or other damnable scoundrel to apply to a magistrate to have a book suppressed'.[135] Aldington at that stage had hopes of the order being reversed in a higher court, which was not to happen, but he was horrified at the idea of leaving Lawrence out on such grounds. Now that Lawrence was being persecuted by the philistines, Aldington was fiercely determined to support him. The second *Georgian Poetry*, he told Amy, in which Lawrence had several poems, had come out a few days after the seizure of the book and had sold out on its first day, with Lawrence's poems being 'favourably noticed'. In any case, he argued, 'the eroticism people make so much fuss about is no more than that of a dozen continental authors of world-wide reputation'. It was in fact, he warned, going to be hard to persuade Lawrence to come in for the second year, for he was rather cross with Amy because she had not yet sent him his share of the royalties. They must not lose 'the fine artist that Lawrence is'; he 'must be written to, cosseted, and not criticised'. Lawrence was, Aldington now insisted, only 'petulant' because he was ill.[136]

As it happened, this letter crossed with one from Amy, who had spoken to Ferris Greenslet. He had not 'the faintest objection to having Lawrence, in spite of the public executioner', and she was no longer anxious about his inclusion. On the question of the delayed royalties, she wrote back very contritely, having cabled them to Lawrence with a long and friendly message, regarding the expense as her punishment. She had been meaning to find a moment to send him a proper letter, and somehow it hadn't come. Now, however, she had written 'a long letter . . . of the most cossety kind I can think of', asking him for poems, and begging Aldington to follow this up.[137] There was no need, however. Lawrence wrote back at once with poems, though he told Amy they were not imagist poems, and he wouldn't mind if she turned them down. Amy agreed that they were not imagist, she told Aldington, but felt she couldn't turn them down with 'this row about Lawrence in England'. In any case, they 'have none of the objections his work sometimes has', though they were, she thought, 'a bit vague and cosmic':[138] Lawrence was much preoccupied at this time, no longer with a moral revolution in society in general, something of which he now despaired, but with the need for the elite few to go through some form of spiritual death and resurrection. Perhaps this notion of spiritual rebirth was what appeared cosmic vagueness to the down-to-earth Amy: Lawrence's poem, 'In Trouble and Shame', which would appear in the next anthology, is on this theme, with vivid imagery, if perhaps not imagistic. In it Lawrence writes that he wants to go through the 'swaling sunset',

> Through the red doors where I could put off
>> My shame like shoes in the porch
>> My pain like garments,
> And leave my flesh discarded lying
> Like luggage of some departed traveller
>> Gone one knows not whither.

Then, he says, he 'would laugh with joy'.[139] Lawrence's plan now was to move to some remote spot to set up a community with a small chosen band of his most valued friends. He called this projected community Ranamin, from the Hebrew word 'Ra'ananim' meaning 'green, fresh or flourishing' that he had learnt from his Russian Jewish friend, S. S. Koteliansky.[140] He and Frieda hoped that autumn to go with two friends to Florida, where they had been promised the use of a cottage. Under recent legislation, however, Lawrence had to gain military exemption in order to leave the country. H.D. reported to Amy, 'Poor Lawrence waited for hours in a queue to get his "medically misfit". – But it rained on him & hundreds of others for hours – literally – and he was so horribly unhappy about the whole thing – that he flew home without his "misfit" and has been in bed ever since!'[141] Leaving the country was for the present impossible, and he and Frieda decided to go to Cornwall for a while. Yet now he was planning to form Ranamin, he had renewed hope; in September he had written to Lady Cynthia, 'The sight of the people of London strikes me into a dumb fury. The persistent nothingness of the war makes me feel like a paralytic convulsed with rage.' Now he told her: 'We want to make a new life in common – not a thing just for ourselves, a new life in common, a new birth in a new spirit . . . I am going to be happy – really really happy – we all are'.[142]

VI

DURING those autumn months of 1915, a bond grew between H.D. and Lawrence. Although Lawrence was in a dark mood much of the year, he had another side. His sudden bursts of optimism made him sunny and kind, as that letter to Lady Cynthia shows, and his misanthropy could give way to gentleness and concern. Lawrence was perceptive about other people's states of mind, and realised something of the psychic anguish that H.D. was experiencing. He called in occasionally to talk while Aldington was in Bloomsbury in the *Egoist* office, and was aware that she was still very distressed over the stillborn child; she would write, in *Bid Me to Live*, that Rico, the Lawrence figure, 'was the only one who seemed remotely to understand what I felt when I was so ill – well – it was long ago, I know. But he understood that.'[143] As John Worthen puts it, 'they had a special tenderness for each other thereafter'.[144]

Like Lawrence, H.D. was discovering that the war had made her into an object of derision, with the widespread anti-Americanism that came with growing resentment at their non-participation. (Pound, incidentally, had feared the *Catholic Anthology* would be attacked for containing too many Americans, and indeed it was.) H.D. wrote to Lowell that November: 'You don't know how stodgy, how awful the war has made the average – no, not only the average English person! The most broadminded – they have all re-iron-coated their shells – and just the word America – American – and there is an inevitable burst of laughter and a "too proud to fight" . . . – It gets worse, every, every day.'[145] Living in this hostile, envenomed environment, she was acutely aware of how gruelling Frieda and Lawrence found the lurid, ever increasing hatred of all things German. That April, several days of anti-German rioting had broken out in the East End; in May, there were three days of anti-German riots in Liverpool. Deep prejudice was faced by anyone who sounded German; shops owned, or thought to be owned, by Germans, were sacked. Names were hastily changed: the royal family dropped Saxe-Coburg-Gotha in favour of Windsor; before joining the army, Ford changed his middle name from Hermann to Madox; and the Bechstein Hall became the Wigmore. German men who had lived in Britain, sometimes for years, like the artist husband of H.D.'s friend, Lilian Sauter, were interned; Lawrence and Frieda feared that it might be German women next.

As a healthy twenty-three-year-old non-combatant, Aldington also knew what it was to experience hostility; in May he had published a misanthropic, bitter poem, 'In the Tube', in which he finds himself being watched by a 'row of eyes,/Eyes of greed, of pitiful blankness, of plethoric complacency,/Immobile':

> Antagonism
> Disgust,
> Immediate antipathy,
> Cut my brain, as a sharp dry reed
> Cuts a finger.

> I surprise the same thought
> In the brasslike eyes:

> *'What right have you to live?'*[146]

Yet though Aldington was shocked by the way Lawrence was treated by the authorities, notwithstanding his sturdy defence to Amy he remained ambivalent about him. He wrote later that Lawrence's 'psychological insight enables him to flatter women into bubbling sympathy and to irritate men into sharp hostility. Like most geniuses, he prefers women because they have been trained not to contradict and will not puncture his assertions with argument and fact.'[147] Possibly that was the pattern of the Aldingtons' relationship with Lawrence that autumn. In retrospect, Aldington would write warmly of the sympathy between Lawrence and H.D., saying that 'when we were all young together, it was obvious that there was a poetic kinship between them'.[148] When they first met in 1914, according to *Bid Me to Live*, Lawrence particularly admired her flower poems for their 'bite and sting', especially 'Sea Iris', which is 'scented and stinging . . . sweet and salt', its colour presenting a miraculous blaze in a harsh world:

Do your roots drag up colour
from the sand?
Have they slipped gold under you;
rivets of gold?

Band of iris-flowers
above the waves,
You are painted blue,
painted like a fresh prow
stained among the salt weeds.[149]

By the time they met up again in the autumn of 1915, Lawrence had developed a keen interest in the Greeks, something which may also have played a part in their growing friendship. In July 1915 he had read a book by John Burnet, entitled *Early Greek Philosophy*, lent to him, incidentally, by Russell, which deeply impressed him. 'Those early Greeks have clarified my soul. I must drop all about God,' he told Russell. 'I am rid of all my christian religiosity. It was only a muddiness.'[150] Paul Delany suggests that Lawrence was particularly impressed by Heraclitus, about whom H.D. had learnt from the pre-Socratic scholar and mesmerising talker, Henry Slominsky, on that Paris visit on the way home from Italy. In place of the Judaeo-Christian dualisms on which Lawrence had relied so far, such as 'Love and Law, Body and Spirit, God and the Devil', Heraclitus' belief 'that a constant intermingling of opposites constitutes the world' meant that 'to distinguish between, for example, good and evil was meaningless, and that to deplore violence and war was to deny life itself.'[151] Burnet may have given him a new and deeper sympathy with H.D.'s poems, with their intermingling opposites, their liminal settings, between sea and land, their fascination with what like the sea iris is both 'scented and stinging', 'sweet and salt'.

H.D. was probably not yet aware of Lawrence's developing views on the need for male dominance, as from *The Rainbow* she had seen him as someone sympathetic to women's need for independence and freedom. She might have been more wary of the exchange of poems they began had she known what he had written in late 1915 to the writer Catherine Carswell. He criticised Carswell's poems for their lack of passion, telling her she needed to give herself more to the poem if she were to write something worthwhile, but then added: 'I'm not sure I want you to – there is something tragic and displeasing about a woman who writes – but I suppose Sapho [*sic*] is as inevitable and right as Shelley – but you must burn, to be Sapho – burn at the stake. And Sapho is the only woman poet.'[152] The imagery is curious – burning with passion is one thing; being burnt as a heretic is quite another. Did he think that in a woman writer the one might imply the other? It links up strikingly with what H.D. would write in *Asphodel*, when Hermione thinks with horror of the fate of Joan of Arc, emblematic of the woman artist: 'I don't want to be burnt, to be crucified just because I "see" things.'[153] Lawrence, like Pound, preferred women to be disciples rather than fellow–artists. On the other hand, H.D.'s poetry has a Sappho-like intensity, which was perhaps why he admired it. Aldington suggests persuasively that Lawrence was influenced at the time by the spare, direct form of H.D.'s poetry.[154] Another letter that Lawrence wrote to Catherine Carswell around that time gives an indication of how close he was at this juncture to the imagist aesthetic:

The grave-yard poem is *very* good. I *do* wish, however, you didn't use metre and rhyme. It is verse which in spirit bursts all the old world, and yet goes corseted in rhymed scansion. Do leave it free . . . break the rhyme rather than the stony direct-ness of speech.

The essence of poetry with us in this age of stark and unlovely actualities is a stark directness, without a shadow of a lie, or a shadow of deflection anywhere. Everything can go, but this stark, bare rocky directness of statement, this alone makes poetry, today.[155]

The 'stark, bare rocky directness' of H.D.'s poetry could well have been in his mind. When writing to Dollie Radford in January 1916 from Cornwall, Lawrence referred to H.D. as 'Mrs Aldington', so there was still some formality in their friendship, but he also expressed pleasure that Dollie had liked H.D., and asked her to try to persuade the Aldingtons to move to Cornwall too.[156] H.D. was not yet on his list of people to join Ranamin, but she soon would be.

That autumn, Aldington had kept himself busy with his work for the *Egoist*, to which he still regularly contributed reviews, articles and poetry. In addition, he had launched a Poets' Translation series, the *Egoist*'s first book publishing venture, for which he himself translated Anyte of Tegea, because, he told Lowell, she was the poet who had suggested two of H.D.'s first poems, including 'Hermes of the Ways', and he thought that would make the work of interest to supporters of the imagists. He also translated some Renaissance Latin poets, and agreed to publish a rather laboured translation of Sappho by Edward

Storer, who to Pound's disgust was back in touch with the other imagists. James Whittall, the Aldingtons' Philadelphian friend, was persuaded to provide a translation of Leonidas of Tarentum, one of the most prolific of the poets in the Greek Anthology, though scarcely a household name; it is hard to escape the conclusion that the series was set up to demonstrate the group's recondite erudition as much as anything else. Aldington had been introduced by Flint to the bookstalls on the Farringdon Road, where Flint himself had first discovered Keats, and where it was possible to buy leather-bound classics at twopence each. Aldington was delighted when he found the copy of a particularly obscure and previously untranslated work, the *Mosella*, by a Latin writer, Ausonias, which he proceeded to get Flint to translate. H.D. had translated some choruses from Euripides' rather better known *Iphigenia in Aulis*, the prequel to the play in which she saw Pound some ten years previously. Her translations, direct yet powerful, were much praised; Yeats expressed his admiration at the time, and Eliot would later say how superior he thought them to Gilbert Murray's more authoritative, but also more florid, work. In *Bid Me to Live*, Rico, the Lawrence figure, also says he prefers Julia's 'Greek renderings' to Gilbert Murray.[157] There is a description in the novel of how Julia works on such a translation:

It would take her for ever to get what she wanted, to hew and chisel those lines, to maintain or suggest some cold artistry . . . She brooded over each word, as if to hatch it. Then she tried to forget each word, for 'translations' enough existed and she was no scholar. She did not want to 'know' Greek in that sense. She was like one blind, reading the texture of incised letters, rejoicing like one blind who knows an inner light, a reality that the outer eye cannot grasp. She was arrogant and she was intrinsically humble before this discovery. Her own.

Anyone can translate the meaning of the word. She wanted the shape, the feel of it, the character of it, as if it had been freshly minted. She felt the old manner of approach was as towards hoarded treasure, but treasure that had passed through too many hands, had been too carefully assessed by the grammarians. She wanted to coin new words.[158]

It is an account which works, like her poems, though the paradoxical linking of opposites. Although the language is so different from anything Pound would have used, she shares with him the combination of the emphasis on crafting the work like sculpture, 'hewing' and chiselling', with the visionary, intuitive insight, the 'inner light'. What is different is that wonderful image of her 'brooding' over the translations, 'hatching' them, the poet as mother, not, as increasingly with Pound, a figure of phallic power. The first chorus, spoken by the women of Chalkis, describes their dazzled admiration of the Greek fleet leaving before the Trojan War:

> If a god should stand here
> He could not speak
> At the sight of ships
> Circled with ships.
>
> This beauty is too much
> For any woman.
> It is burnt across my eyes . . .
>
> These are Achilles' ships.
> On the prow of each
> A goddess sheds gold.[159]

Euripides' caustic view of the deceptive glamour of war, the godlike heroes setting out to pain, humiliation and death, was intensely topical. H.D. would write a few years later that Euripides was 'caught in a mesh of political and social upheaval' that could be compared with 'a modern great-war period', and his anti-war protest was as brave and unpopular a gesture as writing against the present war. 'How would 1917 London have acclaimed such anti-war propaganda? Work that out,' she says, 'and you will have some idea of the power and detachment of the Attic dramatist.'[160] This translation was the first time H.D. had used her poetry to attack war, but it would not be the last. According to Flint, the warm review that the Poets' Translation series received in *The Times*, which particularly commended H.D., was by none other than the scholar J. W. Mackail, the editor of *Select Epigrams from the Greek Anthology*, one of the imagists' sacred texts.

Six of these pamphlets – which was really what they were, rather than books – had appeared by February 1916. Aldington was very happy with them, and also delighted that Harold Monro, in spite of his antagonistic review of *Some Imagist Poets*, had agreed to publish a book of poems each by himself and Flint under the Poetry Bookshop imprint, entitled respectively *Images* and *Cadences*. They came out in late 1915, and Flint wrote to Amy with some satisfaction in early January 1916 to say they had each already sold 250 to 300 copies, a good number for poetry; by June he reported that sales were continuing neck and neck, both volumes being almost sold out. There is a copy of *Cadences* in the Beinecke Library, inscribed 'To Richard & Hilda Aldington quos amo plus quam me ipsum' ('whom I love more than myself'). It is signed F.S. Flint and dated Christmas 1915. Lowell, helpful as ever, found an American publisher for Aldington's *Images*. H.D. found it hard to start to write poetry again after the loss of the baby, her first and only publication in 1915 after 'Midday' being the Euripides translation in November. Perhaps that released her; she began to write again, further encouraged by being given the third prize in 1915 by *Poetry* for the five poems that had appeared the previous March. It was for £10, and she celebrated the event with Aldington and Flint, according to the latter with plentiful red wine. Like them, she had put together poems for a collection, but she does not appear to have offered hers to Monro, whose attack on her poetry she had taken to heart – Monro thought most unreasonably so – but whilst she was the last of the imagists to have a volume published, she gained a rather more prestigious, or at any rate more mainstream, contract with Constable for the book that she would call *Sea Garden*, which appeared in the autumn of 1916.

Lowell herself had been as prolific as ever, in spite of bouts of serious illness. Her *Six French Poets*, the book version of her lecture series, was published in America in the autumn of 1915, though copies would not reach the British market until early 1916. Like the original lectures, the book proved very popular in America, half its first edition being sold out in the first three weeks, and it was well reviewed; it sold well in Britain too, although Middleton Murry and Lytton Strachey gave it somewhat cutting notices. The essays are highly readable and engagingly enthusiastic, although Lowell had neither the extensive knowledge of French literature nor the critical sharpness that these English critics demanded. Flint gave her a kind review, which, since she had warmly thanked him in the preface, was perhaps all he could do. Amy did not, as Pound was apt to do, bludgeon readers into a state of guilt for not knowing these authors, but simply gave the impression that reading these poets was an intensely pleasurable occupation and also, she managed to imply, something of a rebellious act. The new poetry, which refused the conventional in verse, went hand in hand, her message was, with the refusal of the conventional in life. None of her six chosen poets exemplified this more than Rémy de Gourmont, and she quotes at length from his 'Preface' to the *Livre des masques*:

'What does *Symbolisme* mean? . . . it means: individualism in literature, liberty of art, abandonment of existing forms, a tending toward what is new, strange, and even bizarre . . . for poets, *Symbolisme* seems associated with *vers libre* . . . The capital crime for a writer is conformity, imitation, the submission to rules and teaching . . . The sole excuse which a man can have for writing is to write down himself, to unveil for others the sort of world which mirrors itself in his individual glass; his only excuse is to be original; he should say things not yet said, and say them in a form not yet formulated . . . Admit then that *Symbolisme* is, even though excessive, even though tempestuous, the expression of individualism in art.'

She would quote de Gourmont's preface again in the introduction to the 1916 *Some Imagist Poets*. For her, his beliefs were central to imagism. As Amy sums it up here, 'Individualism, not only in art, but in everything else, has been his creed'.[161] This was the message that appealed to her young American readers, weary of the provincial propriety that had so exasperated Pound and H.D. It was also the message of her most popular poem, 'Patterns', which she had published the previous August in the *Little Review*, and which, in spite of being reprinted numerous times in the intervening nine months, was included in the 1916 *Some Imagist Poets*.

'Patterns' was a development of one of her constant themes, the person 'miscast', living in circumstances that stifle and confine. The speaker is an eighteenth-century aristocratic young woman, walking in her formal 'patterned garden', contrasting the daffodils and 'bright blue squills' that flutter in the breeze with her imprisonment in her 'stiff, brocaded gown'. 'With my powdered hair and jewelled fan,/I too am a rare/Pattern . . . not a softness anywhere about me,/Only whalebone and brocade'. She longs to bathe in the fountain, and imagines her lover near at hand watching her:

> What is Summer in a fine brocaded gown!
> I should like to see it lying in a heap on the ground.
> All the pink and silver crumpled up on the ground.
>
> I would be the pink and silver as I ran along the paths,
> And he would stumble after.

She fantasises about the chase, and her lover's embrace, 'aching, melting, unafraid', and then suddenly pulls back into the suffocating present: 'I am very like to swoon/ With the weight of this brocade,/For the sun sifts through the shade.' Then it emerges that she has heard just that morning that her lover is dead, killed in the war. Totally self-controlled, her only outward response is to walk in the garden: 'Held rigid to the pattern/By the stiffness of my gown./Up and down I walked,/Up and down'. The poem ends:

> I shall go
> Up and down,
> In my gown.
> Gorgeously arrayed,
> Boned and stayed.
> And the softness of my body will be guarded from embrace
> By each button, hook, and lace.
> For the man who should loose me is dead,
> Fighting with the Duke in Flanders,
> In a pattern called war.
> Christ! What are patterns for?[162]

To young people, chafing against the conformity and prudishness of American middle-class life at the period, it was an image of their condition, cut off from vitality and life by the stultifying patterns of convention. This was the generation that a few years later, in the early 1920s, would challenge their parents' sexual mores, become the Bright Young Things, and herald the Jazz Age. Take Margaret Mead, for example, who by 1928 would achieve fame, while still in her twenties, with her controversial book, *Coming of Age in Samoa*, whose underlying message was the need for greater sexual freedom for American adolescents; fieldwork in Samoa was only the vehicle. 'Patterns' was her favourite poem, as it was of her friend, lover and fellow-anthropologist, Ruth Benedict, whose book, *Patterns of Culture*, it inspired. Mead had found breaking away from the values of her home painful but necessary, and both she and Benedict saw cultures as imposing patterns of behaviour on their members, patterns that might work well for some, but for others would be oppressive and restricting. 'Patterns' had a particular appeal for women, always more the victims of propriety than the men. When Amy visited Wellesley College, the famous women's college just outside Boston, in 1918, Robert Frost's daughter, who heard her read, said that every girl there knew 'Patterns' by heart. Amy Lowell herself was such a mixture of conformity and rebellion that she understood only too well the problems of breaking out. Her wealth let her ignore certain rules, but though she often defied Boston, she was very aware of pressures it exerted. She expected 'Patterns' to be considered quite risqué – what with a naked woman, the pursuing lover, and the blasphemous last line – and she sent it to the *Little Review*, which was proud of the fact that it carried work no other American publication would touch, rather than to one of the commercial magazines now willing to publish her. But the climate was changing more rapidly than she had realised. Everyone wanted it. It was, one might note, and perhaps this was the reason it was so successful, in some ways more conventional than her poetry often was – the sprinkling of rhymes, the heterosexual plot, the costume drama – though the impulse to write it actually came from one of her weeks of misery when Ada had gone off to visit her daughter. But it was the poem that in those years cemented her reputation as an advocate of new freedoms in verse and in life.

PART XIV

DISPERSAL

I

THE Gallipoli campaign ended in ignominious failure in January 1916, another portent of continuing stalemate in an ever more bloody war. Compulsory conscription for unmarried men began, introduced, not because more soldiers were needed, but because the government needed to be seen to act in the face of bad news from the front. It was munitions, not men, that remained in short supply. The Liberals, including Asquith, still Prime Minister, who until then had been deeply opposed to conscription, reluctantly gave way. As far as Aldington was concerned, the government's reasons were immaterial. It was clear that compulsory conscription would soon be brought in for married men. In September the requirements had been changed, and his hernia would no longer grant him total exemption. He knew he would not for long evade the horrors of the front; the death and mutilation across the Channel haunted him. A poem that appeared in the 1916 anthology suggests his dread:

> The white body of evening
> Is torn into scarlet,
> Slashed and gouged and seared
> Into crimson,
> And hung ironically
> With garlands of mist.
>
> And the wind
> Blowing over London from Flanders
> Has a bitter taste.[1]

White bodies slashed and gouged, youth and beauty destroyed by the forces of war; grotesque violence and the pathetic vulnerability of the soldiers – it is an angry but despairing protest against their, and potentially his own, fate.

Traditionally, British liberals had been opposed to conscription, denouncing it as an infringement of an Englishman's rights. Now opinion in the country rapidly changed to wholehearted support, with intense antagonism being directed against conscientious objectors. This posed little problem to most of the artists and writers associated with Pound, who joined up voluntarily. Besides Gaudier and Hulme, the Futurist Nevinson was an early volunteer; in 1915, not only Ford but Pound's first writer friend in England, Frederic Manning, enlisted, the latter in spite of his asthma; the Vorticists Edward Wadsworth and William Roberts enlisted in 1916, as did Lewis, who joined the Royal Garrison Artillery that March. Pound himself would make several attempts to join up once America had entered the war. Many of the Bloomsbury figures, however, whom Lewis and Hulme had earlier denounced for their effete, dilettante art, were, like Bertrand Russell, pacifists and ready to defy the call to military service, a position which demanded at least equal if different courage. Aldington, in spite of his earlier attempt to enlist, took an uneasy middle position between the Vorticist and Bloomsbury camps, leaning strongly to pacifism, and yet feeling a duty to fight; for now, he was uneasily debating his next move.

Hulme, still in London awaiting his officer's training, took up the debate under the pseudonym of 'North Staffs', in a series of articles published in the *New Age* between November 1915 and March 1916. These 'War Notes', as they were entitled, were remarkable pieces, maverick as always, but marking yet another stage in his development. Though convinced of the German threat to civil liberties, Hulme was far from conventionally patriotic. He castigated the inept running of the war, and denounced the elderly generals and staff officers whose incompetent tactics and inadequate provision of supplies were sending young men to their deaths; but he also poured scorn on the pacifists, especially those from Bloomsbury. Such liberals, he asserted, thought that the Europe they had known would never greatly change, failing to recognise it had always been, and was now dangerously, in flux. They had a naïve belief in Progress, a facile optimism that democracy would inevitably triumph and their safe world survive; in other words, they were still enmired in the Rousseauesque humanism that Hulme had been denouncing since 1912. He granted their irritation with those who saw the combatants in terms of white and black, but, he argued, the fact that England was distinctively grey did not detract from the fact that Germany was 'a very much blacker grey'; the difference was not due to any essential national characteristics, but to their respective histories. The war had to be fought, not for any 'great *liberation* of mankind, or for any great jump forward', but 'merely in order that bad may not get worse'.[2] The two figures with whom he took issue most were Clive Bell and Bertrand Russell. Bell as an art critic was 'a particularly foolish specimen of the aesthete . . . best known as a pup of Mr Roger Fry', any knowledge he had being acquired simply because he had the wealth to travel. He was, Hulme said, 'a contemptible ass', whose pro-peace pamphlets with their 'disgusting whining' were insufferably condescending; Bell as one of the leisured rich had the gall to tell the poor what to think, and lacked the 'generosity of mind' which drove many to enlist rather than leave others to suffer on their behalf. As example, Hulme mentions Gaudier-Brzeska, and adds, 'It is sickening to think that a man like this who showed promise of becoming a considerable artist should be killed, while this wretched artistic pimp still survives.'[3]

Reading this now, Hulme's contemptuous scorn for Bell's unearned affluence reminds one that this was less than two years before the Russian revolution; impatience with inherited privilege took many forms, but it was becoming world-wide. Hulme is more temperate about Russell himself, 'the only man of any real distinction among the pacifists', but equally dismissive of his views. For Russell the ultimate value is human life, but Hulme asserts that there are objective and absolute ethical values which are above life, 'more heroic or tragic', that justify the sacrifice of life. This conviction of an objective truth, among the 'flux' (he still uses the Bergsonian word) of human history, is what he had been looking for all his life. Intuition is still central, what he calls here the 'logique du coeur', the reasons of the heart (a reference to Pascal, who had become deeply important to him), but intuition no longer gives access only to the inner life, but to the apprehension of absolute values.[4] Hulme was, in fact, simultaneously expounding these new views in more philosophical terms under his own name, or at least his initials, again in the *New Age*, in a series called 'A Notebook'; reading them now, the two series seem very closely intertwined, but there is no indication that anyone at the time, except Orage, who commissioned both, realised the connection.

Hulme's 'War Notes', according to Herbert Read, riled both militarists and pacifists, and Russell publicly took issue with 'North Staffs'. Yet Hulme's identification of the war as a melancholy duty must have chimed with the feelings of many, like Aldington, reluctantly facing

conscription. H.D. was sympathetic to pacifism, though she was ready
to support Aldington in whatever stand he decided to take. Like him,
in early 1916, she was unhappy and overwrought, telling Amy, 'I cannot
write you what I think, feel & know about this terrible war. I want you
to get this letter without delay.' She had the censors in mind – censorship of foreign cables and correspondence had been introduced at the
beginning of war – and indeed the next couple of sentences are scratched
out. All that is left is the comment that 'We are all weakened by this
continual strain'.[5] In mid-January, she had an additional anxiety. Two
months of her allowance had failed to arrive. Her parents were away on
holiday in the Pacific, and couldn't be contacted. She wrote in some
desperation to Amy for an emergency loan, saying Richard did not know
about her request; she wasn't well, she had never recovered from the
trauma of the previous year, and could not take this added anxiety. The
next day, she heard the delay was only a bank error, and the money was
on the way. She cabled the news, but Amy sent £40 all the same, on
the grounds that H.D. had only said that the money was coming, 'and
coming is not come'. Amy was touched to be treated as a surrogate
relation, and told H.D. that she thought

it was very nice of you to give me an opportunity to chip in a little bit. That is
what I call being really friendly, and I am perfectly delighted that you should have
written to me. It is a wonder to me that your remittances from home ever come,
with mails in the state they are, and there must have been lots of mail lost when
various vessels have been sunk . . . Please do not think anything about it, and do
not dream of paying it back. Take it as the most natural thing in the world as I do.

She was concerned about H.D., whose unhappiness recalled her own
years of misery in the pre-Ada days: 'You see, my Dear Girl,' she wrote,
'I know what it is to have shattered nerves, I had nervous prostration
for seven years once, and it is not a nice condition; so you mustn't have
anything to worry about.' She pressed her to ask again if she was in
any trouble, adding, 'I am most anxious to do everything I can "for
the cause" and if you and Richard are not "the cause" I don't know
what is.'[6]

   In spite of everything, the next imagist anthology was nearing completion; by the end of January, Amy had only to worry about the preface.
Fletcher had sent her a draft, but it was 'so violent and militant' that
she was rewriting it in a more 'conciliatory' tone.[7] Both Aldington and
Fletcher had wanted to bring in other poets, Aldington suggesting

William Carlos Williams and Marianne Moore, while Fletcher wanted
T.S. Eliot, and also Wallace Stevens, whose poems were beginning to
appear in *Poetry* and *Others*. Amy resisted – a great shame, because it
could have been a superb and historic collection of poets. Aldington
also suggested their friend John Cournos, perhaps more out of affection than anything else, but Cournos never forgave Amy for not accepting
him. Putting this issue together had been more problematic than the
first. Amy and Fletcher did not like two of Aldington's poems, Aldington
and H.D. did not like two of Amy's, and Amy very much disliked one
of Flint's. Irritation was in the air; the anxiety under which they lived
lacerated taut nerves and spread depression. H.D. did her best to smooth
things over. The only sticking point in the end was Flint's poem 'Evil',
about a man being drawn to visit a prostitute, which ends as he
approaches her door; the title remains unexplained – is it the woman's
allure or the man's desire that is evil? Lowell was appalled, quite why
she didn't say. It is a somewhat clichéd and unconvincing poem, and a
feminist critique of the poem for its stereotyping of the figure of the
prostitute could be and has been made, but Lowell's reaction seems
extreme: one suspects it was yet again the notion of sex as evil that
disturbed her. H.D. finally wrote to her:

About Flint – take out the poem you don't like, if it really matters. Say I said you
were to if there is any fuss, as he is terribly touchy and over-strained just now. He
is ill, he has extra hours at the Post Office without any extra pay, and a new extra
baby. I really don't think I ever knew anyone quite so hard pushed, and trying all
the time to do his own work. He has started a very valuable book, an order from
a publisher which he cannot finish because of the long hours at the post office.
But you knew all this before. We have been working to try and get him a job in
the Ministry of Munitions with the same pay and his evenings free.[8]

The baby was a boy, Oliver, though H.D. would generally refer to him
as Nero, which suggests that he may have been a demanding child.
Aldington's father was working at the Ministry of Munitions, and they
hoped to use his influence, but they had no luck finding Flint a job.
Flint was never to write the book, the one on contemporary French
poetry for which Cournos helped secure the contract: it proved to be
one of the many casualties of war. Any spare time he had was taken up
with translation work, quicker and more enjoyable if not in the long
run better paid than his clerical work. In fact, from 1911 until the end
of the First World War, having completed his full day at the Post Office,

he worked virtually every evening on something or other. In 1917, he would do extra work at weekends as well on the war loan for the Bank of England; in 1918, when he was told he would be called up – though he never had to leave the country – he spent until late each evening teaching himself telegraphing so that he could qualify for the Signal Section of the Royal Engineers. But his poetry, written in spite of these pressures that would surely have defeated most people, was the work that was most precious to him. He was angered by Lowell's refusal to publish 'Evil', his ire exacerbated by the fact that she included in the preface to the anthology a sentence of praise for *Poetry* and Harriet Monroe, who had recently turned down some of his poems. For a brief period he tried to persuade H.D. and Aldington to renounce their friendship with Lowell, surely another sign of frayed nerves, for he was essentially very fond of her, and soon forgave the slight; he was further mollified when shortly afterwards she persuaded Monroe to publish some of his poems. In the meantime, H.D. begged him: 'Do not row Amy please as it is too late anyhow & it will only react on us!'[9] Flint's increasing tendency under his many stresses to burst out in sudden fury was something she would now regularly try to contain.

Lowell, however, had good news to give them. The 1915 anthology was continuing to sell well and there was a new payment of royalties, some $73 between the two Aldingtons, pro rata for Flint and Lawrence. Amy was anxious that the second anthology should be even better than the first: the novelty appeal, she warned them, would have worn off. While most critics had been hostile they were at least given plenty of coverage, but critics might no longer feel they were so newsworthy, and the imagists would 'miss the interest and the antagonism that [they had] enjoyed'.[10] Amy had had a recent chance to enjoy such mixed reactions when she revisited the Poetry Society of America in late November, this time not just to speak for five minutes but to read some imagist poetry and to give a lecture on 'New Metres and the Poets who Write Them'. Some three or four hundred people were there, and, as she told Aldington, 'we had a most lively time. The Society is extremely reactionary and the evening turned into a sort of gladiator fight and wild beast show with thumbs down and I impersonating the early Christians'.[11] All the same, they were increasingly making an impact. Louis Untermeyer, the critic who had been so hostile to them to start with, now defended them, and his wife Jean Starr, Amy reported, was herself writing 'some really nice *vers libre* poems'. Jessie Rittenhouse, the secretary of the Poetry Society and earlier as reactionary as any, was coming round, and included their poetry in some lectures on modern poetry that she gave at Columbia University.

Amy had developed a fresh argument about the new poetry's relation to earlier American literature, and, now being in much demand as a speaker, expounded it to audiences in Boston and New York. Poets like Longfellow, Emerson, Whittier and Bryant were really English provincial poets, she maintained, in the puritan Protestant tradition. The first truly American poets were the pagan Whitman, Poe and Dickinson, and the new poets – also opposed to puritan moralising – were their heirs. What they have to say is

different from . . . any English poet . . . Our environment is no longer exclusively English. Our immense immigration is at last beginning to be felt. We of the pure Anglo-Saxon stock are constantly coming into contact with people of other nationalities, and consciously or unconsciously we are being modified by them. We may not realise it, but slowly before our eyes, the American race is being born. And one of the evidences of it is that we are beginning to hew new pathways for ourselves in this most intimate thing, Poetry, and to free ourselves from the tutelage of another nation . . . the New Poetry is blazing a trail towards Nationality far more subtle and intense than any settlement houses and waving the American flag in schools can ever achieve. I might say with perfect truth that the most national things we have are skyscrapers, ice water, and the New Poetry.[12]

It was in many ways a remarkable statement from a member of the Boston upper class, generally more inclined to fear and despise the immigrants than to see them as enriching the American race. Yet in welcoming a new American national art, Lowell was not alone. Though some American artists and intellectuals, like Pound, Eliot and H.D., still felt it imperative to flee to European civilisation, there was emerging a new indigenous modernism in the arts, of which poets like William Carlos Williams and the painter Charles Sheeler would be leading examples. It was after all Harriet Monroe's aim for *Poetry* to bring a specifically American poetry to the fore, and the idea that imagism was an American poetic form, indeed *the* American poetic form, was a doctrine that *Poetry* would soon be promoting.

IF Pound was for now out of touch with the Amygists, he was alert to news about them, passing on with glee to Monroe a quite erroneous rumour that Lowell and Fletcher were to be married. He and Dorothy were again spending the winter with Yeats at Stone Cottage; they arrived in December 1915 and remained there, apart from the occasional London visit, until March 1916. Yeats was glad to get away from the Zeppelins, though Pound always claimed to be quite unworried by them, only expressing the hope that they would destroy the Reverend Pennyfeather's bells (they did not). As before, however, retreat to the country did not mean escape from the impact of war, and the visit brought home to them once more how different a place England had become since 1914. A. J. P. Taylor has argued that one of the greatest changes the war brought to Britain was the vastly increased degree of state control: before the war there were no passports, no immigration restrictions, no limitation on changing sterling for foreign currency, no conscription, few taxes.[13] Over the course of the nineteenth century, Factory Acts had limited manufacturers' freedom to disregard their workers' safety, and Education Acts had made schooling compulsory until the age of thirteen; since 1906, the Liberal government had, against deep opposition, brought in tiny pensions for the elderly poor, and some state insurance for sickness and unemployment. But overall, regulation was minimal. Pound had not been obliged in any way to take cognisance of the British state: he had to ask no one's permission to come to England, or to leave it again; there were no restrictions on his working there, or to his movements around the country. No wonder so many Russian revolutionaries found Britain a haven. After August 1914, all this changed. Censorship had been introduced, passports became necessary for foreign travel, and, even at home, the movements of anyone who was not a British citizen (and some who were) were closely watched. The Pounds were greatly taken aback, some six weeks after they had returned to Coleman's Hatch, by the arrival of a policeman at the door of Stone Cottage to demand that Pound and Dorothy, as foreigners (in the eyes of the law, as his wife she was an American), report to the local police station, as they were 'Aliens in a Prohibited Area'. Pound should, he discovered, have reported to the police as soon as he arrived; for a while he was deeply worried in case he were prosecuted; with his growing sense of persecution he was convinced that as an artist he would have no chance of escaping conviction. Yeats and he solicited help from various acquaintances, sending urgent letters asking them to guarantee that Pound was Yeats' secretary and a respected poet. That helped not at all; Pound returned to London to collect a passport from the American embassy that he could show to the police, and Ford's friend Masterman, who had met Pound at South Lodge, persuaded the authorities that Pound and his wife were not in fact a danger.

Apart from that alarm, however, the Pounds and Yeats placidly continued their routine of the previous year: work for most of the day, though Pound and Yeats would always fence for an hour or so at some stage, and in the evenings Pound would read to Yeats. They continued to be obsessed by ghosts, possibly even more than before; Longenbach suggests their earlier fascination may have taken on a new dimension with the horrors of mass death across the Channel; Pound, he notes, had written an early draft of a canto that autumn about Gaudier's ghost. Pound was also back working on Fenollosa's translations of the ghost-filled Noh plays, which he was planning to issue in book form, and Yeats, who had taken an increasing interest in his work on the Noh, wrote the introduction. Yeats was intrigued by these esoteric and aristocratic dramas, which wove together words, music, dance and exotic costumes, and began to adapt elements of these plays to Irish themes; his first play in that vein, *At the Hawk's Well*, dedicated to Pound, was written at Stone Cottage that winter. Yeats had known about Noh theatre before, as it had been performed in London on several occasions from the 1870s onwards, most recently at the immensely popular Japanese-British Exhibition in 1910, which Pound had missed as he was out of the country. Yeats had already suggested in 1911, before Pound discovered Fenollosa, that as 'a writer of poetic drama, and of tragic drama, desiring always pattern and convention, I would like to keep to suggestion, to symbolism, to pattern like the Japanese'.[14] Yet Pound's fascination with these plays played a significant part in alerting Yeats to the possibility of drawing on their example to produce a new form of poetic drama, what Pound would describe as Yeats's 'Celtic Noh' plays.

Pound was also able to introduce Yeats to an ideal performer. The previous October, he had had some translations of Japanese dance poems performed by a talented Japanese dancer, Michio Ito, whose evocative dancing interpreted their elliptical and suggestive words for the audience. Ito was an intriguingly postmodern figure, who had arrived in England with almost no knowledge of Noh drama – he had last seen it performed when he was seven – but with an excellent training in European dance, having been inspired by Nijinksy and the Russian Ballet in Paris, and spending several years training at the Dalcroze Institute in Germany. (He would later dance with Martha Graham in New York, probably more to his liking.)[15] Pound took to him immensely, telling Harriet Monroe, 'I am very fond of him, though I mostly detest the Japs, i.e., the moon-faced thin-minded sort. This man is a samurai, more like an American Indian to look at, the long face you see in some of the old prints.'[16]

Ito had come to London at the outbreak of war, and was taken up first by Lady Ottoline Morrell and then by Lady Cunard, who persuaded him to dance for their guests. When he discovered that Pound wanted Noh, he read it up in books and obligingly reinvented himself as a traditional Noh dancer. No one questioned his credentials, and Yeats was very taken with his talent, asking him to dance the role of the Guardian of the Well in his new play; they went together to the London Zoo to study the movement of hawks. Ito was extremely handsome, and by all accounts a wonderful dancer, though R. F. Foster suggests it was not so much his dubious expertise in the Noh as his familiarity with the aesthetics of the late nineteenth century – he was an admirer of Mallarmé, Maeterlinck, Debussy and Oscar Wilde – that enabled him to interpret Yeats' work so well. The painter and illustrator Edmund Dulac had painted a portrait of Ito in November 1915, dressed in the traditional medieval costume of a Noh dancer (though once again, how traditional is perhaps in question, as the costume was designed by Dulac himself and the painter Charles Ricketts). Yeats felt he had found the perfect combination of talents. Dulac created the backdrop, properties and costumes, including some striking masks, and eventually arranged the music as well. The play had its première in Lady Cunard's drawing-room on 2 April 1916, with a small audience drawn from the avant-garde and high society. The press were excluded. Two days later the play was performed again, this time in Lady Islington's house, on that occasion to raise money for a war charity (tickets at a guinea each). Queen Alexandra, Princess Victoria, Margot Asquith and Lady Randolph Churchill were among the 300-strong audience, composed, Pound reported with some hyperbole, 'exclusively of crowned heads and divorcées'.[17]

With these select audiences, Yeats was freed from the battles he had had with the public in Ireland. 'No press, no photographs in the paper, no crowds,' he wrote to John Quinn. 'I shall be happier than Sophocles'.[18] Even the charity performance he regarded as inferior to the smaller but more culturally informed gathering at Lady Cunard's. When Pound published his book on the Noh, significantly entitled *Certain Noble Plays of Japan*, he made much of its exclusivity, its elevated status, its subtlety and complexity. 'The Noh,' he says, 'is unquestionably one of the great arts of the world, and it is quite possibly one of the most recondite . . . It is not, like our theatre, a place where every fineness . . . of word or of word-cadence is sacrificed to the "broad effect"; where the paint must be put on with a broom. It is a stage where subsidiary art is bent precisely on holding the faintest shade of a difference; where the poet may even be silent while the gestures consecrated by four centuries of usage show meaning."[19] Pound's own interest in Japanese art would have faded a year later, by which time he had decided that 'China is fundamental, Japan is not', but he was becoming ever more convinced that, as with the Noh, only the elite few would appreciate his own recondite, complex art.[20] Pound had taken Eliot, definitely one of the elite, along to Lady Cunard's; Eliot, who up to then had thought Yeats 'a minor survivor of the '90s', recalled, in an article in 1946, that 'thereafter one saw Yeats rather as a more eminent contemporary than an elder'. The qualities which Pound and Eliot would soon be insisting should be found in what Eliot called 'the modern movement in poetry' were defined through that encounter with the Noh; it would be esoteric, erudite, elitist, returning to the past in order to speak of the present.[21] That performance could be seen as marking the transition from what Michael Levenson sees as early to high modernism for Pound and Eliot, though such terminology is, many would now agree, misleading in that it suggests there is only one story about the development of modernism.[22] There were in fact numerous other modernisms – H.D.'s, Fletcher's, Lowell's, Woolf's, to name but a few. But Eliot's and Pound's would become the dominant form in the inter-war years, and for decades would ensure the neglect of those others. And whilst Yeats and Pound would never co-operate so closely again, Yeats had put his stamp on the kind of artistic movement that Pound and Eliot would espouse.

Already by May, Pound's friendship with Yeats was cooling a little: he wrote to Alice Corbin Henderson, saying that while there had been no actual breach between them, their time together in the country had left him feeling 'tired of a lot of dead ideas'.[23] Yeats and he would not return to Stone Cottage again. Pound did not tell Henderson which particular 'dead ideas' he objected to, but they certainly disagreed over Vorticism, for which Yeats had little sympathy. In March Pound was writing to John Quinn, enthusing about the Lewis drawings he was sending him for a New York Vorticist exhibition Quinn had agreed to mount, and exclaiming: 'Blake, that W.B.Y. is always going on about!!!! . . . [Lewis] has got Blake scotched to a finish.'[24] Meanwhile, Yeats was writing to his father about his dislike of Lewis' use of a machine-like abstraction incompatible with the rhythms of natural life. They had clearly clashed. Yeats was out of sympathy with the kind of tactics embraced by *Blast*; he had included some biting satires in *Responsibilities*, but the blatancy of Pound's efforts to 'insult the world' was not his style. In the letter to his father, Yeats significantly referred to Lewis as a Cubist, suggesting he was refusing even to admit the existence of Vorticism. Pound's understanding of Vorticist form was, as Materer has argued, steeped in the kind of occult symbolism he and Yeats had explored together, but Yeats certainly did not see it that way.[25] Yeats and Lewis represented two different strands of Pound's development, on the one hand the visionary, on the other the iconoclastic. Both the visionary and the iconoclastic would remain part of Pound's work and of his personality, but his relations with Lewis and Yeats themselves, ironically in both cases at their most intimate at this period, would become more strained.

Pound continued to act as foreign editor for *Poetry*, though he was deeply put out when that spring Alice Corbin Henderson was diagnosed with consumption, and was sent on medical advice to the warmer climate of New Mexico. Without her as buffer, his relations with Harriet Monroe would deteriorate steadily over the next three years. He kept in touch with Henderson, who developed a passionate interest in Native American poetry, which she vainly tried to persuade Pound to take up, wanting him to do for it what he had done for the Chinese. He ignored that – perhaps it reminded him too much of his American roots – but continued to write and give her news of the literary scene, and to vent his frustrations with Monroe. His letters to Monroe herself continued to be a steady stream of invective. He was now, however, back in touch with Harriet Shaw Weaver and was much more of a presence again in the *Egoist* in 1916 than in 1915, both in his own contributions – in March he even appeared on the same page as Amy Lowell, which cannot have pleased either of them – and with copy from others. He had written to the Aldingtons in early 1916, expressing concern that Richard might be conscripted. H.D., perhaps unfairly, suspected that, with the likelihood growing daily that Aldington would have to fight, he had his eye on the assistant editorship. Whether or not that was the case, Weaver appears to have been grateful for Pound's input, perhaps especially because Dora Marsden was ill and did not appear in the magazine for the first half of 1916.

Pound was working hard to promote Lewis and Joyce, and persuaded Weaver to serialise Lewis' first novel, *Tarr*; and, since no regular publisher would touch it, to bring out Joyce's *Portrait of the Artist as a Young Man* in book form now that Aldington's Poets' Translation series had established the Egoist Press as an independent imprint; in the event he was able to secure a double publication with the American publisher Huebsch. Pound himself would have a productive year. His *Gaudier-Brzeska* appeared in spring 1916, and was widely reviewed. *Certain Noble Plays of Japan* was published by the Cuala Press, which had been set up by Yeats' sisters, and a longer version by Macmillan as *'Noh', or Accomplishment* appeared in early 1917, the latter attracting a warm review in *The Times* (two columns long, Pound pointed out with satisfaction to Henderson). In return for Yeats' preface to the Noh plays, Pound wrote one for a Cuala Press edition of Yeats' father's letters in 1917, which he then glowingly reviewed himself.[26] In September 1916, after much wrangling, his next book of poetry appeared, his ninth, including the translations; not an insubstantial achievement for a thirty-year-old. This was *Lustra*, which contained most of the poetry that he had written since *Ripostes*, including 'Contemporania', the poems from the two *Blasts*, the poems published in *Cathay* as well as other Chinese translations, and his recent meditative free-flowing Provençal poems, like 'Provincia Deserta' and another entitled 'Near Perigord'; in all, a remarkable range of styles, some evocative and beautiful, some witty and mischievous, some clumsy and ineptly striving to give offence. In spite of the ineptness, offence was duly taken: Elkin Mathews had agreed to publish the collection without reading it through, but when the printer came to set it up, he was horrified. Mathews read it hastily and agreed. It would take some months for the matter to be resolved. In the end, there were two editions, a private one of 200 copies, and a general one, which left out several poems, and even in the private edition Mathews insisted on some changes. Pound and Mathews' relationship would never be the same again. The collection was dedicated to Brigit Patmore, as Vail de Lencour, the Provençal name Pound had given her. Brigit had moved out of London with her sons to avoid the Zeppelins, but she was based on the south coast and came back frequently; she had tactfully maintained her friendship with both the Aldingtons and Pound, and was in close touch with them all.

In spite of the quarrel over the history of imagism, Pound was still taking an interest in the Aldingtons' work, having largely recovered from his crossness with Richard, though he would take longer to forgive Flint. He had been furious that the *Poetry* prize for 1915 had gone not to Eliot but to Lindsay; the only 'sop to the intelligent', he told Harriet, was that H.D. had had third prize, and he complained indignantly that *Poetry* ought to have had 'that incomprehensible thing of H.D.'s in the March *Egoist*' as well as the 'two decent things by R.A. in the *Poetry Journal*'.[27] H.D.'s 'incomprehensible thing' was entitled 'The Last Gift'; her poems were now once more appearing regularly in the *Egoist*, 'The Cliff Temple' in January, 'The Helmsman' in April, and 'Sea Gods' in June, rather longer poems than most of hers had been until then, though equally concentrated and powerful. Their imagery possibly springs from Jane Harrison's idea that art first emerged from ancient rituals, by which Lawrence had also been impressed, and which he and H.D. may well have discussed. Although Lawrence had moved down to Cornwall in late December, they were corresponding regularly, as they would continue to do over the next two years. Just as his work at that period reflects something of her influence, hers reflects his. 'The Last Gift', though very much in H.D.'s own terms, is concerned with the possibility of a spiritual rebirth like the one Lawrence felt was so urgently needed in the wartime maelstrom. The poem is about the rejection of a too easy beauty, 'oversweet', 'over-painted, over-lovely', for the ardent pursuit of a more austere, mystic vision:

> another life holds what this lacks,
> a sea unmoving, quiet . . .
> a stretch of sand,
> no garden beyond, strangling
> with its myrrh-lilies –

a hill, not set with black violets
but stones, stones, bare rocks,
dwarf-trees, twisted

The war is never mentioned, but H.D. seems to be searching for an aesthetic commensurate with the bleakness and desperation of the present moment. In the poem, the speaker compares this 'tortured, intense' quest to that of the initiates of a cult seeking some ecstatic revelation through their 'inmost rites'. H.D. later used a similar comparison in *Bid Me to Live*, where she writes that during the war, 'the constant flayed nerves and constant brutality of the present' produced a sense of purification and intensity like that attained 'in temples, Yogi, Tibet, Eleusinian Mysteries'.[28] The Greek world H.D. conjures up in these poems is very much, in the famous distinction Nietzsche makes in *The Birth of Tragedy*, a Dionysian rather than an Apollonian one, intense, extreme, tempestuous, a way of being he too associates with the Eleusinian Mysteries.

Aldington remained as dedicated an admirer of H.D.'s work as ever, but one wonders if it was beginning to strike him that what had appeared to be their shared enthusiasm for the classical world masked deeply divergent approaches to the Greeks, and beyond that to life in general. He saw the Greeks as Apollonian, serene and harmonious, a view that Pater, drawing on the work of the eighteenth-century connoisseur Winckelmann, had influentially expounded in *The Renaissance*, and still very much the received wisdom.[29] When Aldington had written in the defence of Hellenic art in the *Egoist* in 1914, he had praised their 'blitheness' (one of Pater's words), and their love of the simple things, 'health and beauty and youth in the midst of friends'.[30] H.D.'s Greeks are very different: they are full of passion, suffering, joy, desire, intoxication; there can be calm oases, rich beauty, moments after the storm dies down, but they are less common. Perhaps it's significant that H.D. was more interested in Greek drama than Aldington, for the tragedies, as Nietzsche says, make the Pater/Winckelmann theory of Greek serenity hard to maintain – a point even Pound had made in the face of Hulme's 1914 onslaught on Greek art. Freud's view of Greek myth, also drawn from the tragedies – the torments of Oedipus, and the dark secrets of the psyche dramatised in his story – accords much more closely with H.D.'s than Pater's, as she would realise in later life. Aldington, on the other hand, would continue to hold on to his idealisation of the Greeks' simple, happy, uncomplicated existence; he was already growing bitter at the way the modern world denied him the beauty and calm that he felt was owed to him. May Sinclair, always very fond of Aldington, said of him in 1921:

To be born at the end of the nineteenth century and to be young in the youth of the twentieth must be counted as misfortune to a poet like Richard Aldington. For there is no mistaking his modernity. One half of him is not Greek, and it brings into his poetry an element which is not Greek, a pain, a dissatisfaction, a sadness that the purely Greek soul did not know . . . Richard Aldington brings his sad modernity into the heart of the Greek world. His joy in beauty which was pure joy to the ancient Greek who had to do with beauty unadulterated and unstained, his joy has in it a deep incurable dissatisfaction. Beauty hurts him as it did not and could not hurt the Greek; because he sees that its position in the modern world is dangerous and impermanent.[31]

That was an acute analysis of Aldington's painful sense of the split in his life between the unhappy, fraught present and his dream of Greek unsullied joy. Yet for H.D., the whole point of Greek myth was that it mapped the same conflicts, desires and pains that the modern age experienced. It was a means to understand and explore the present, not an escape from it; in *Asphodel* Hermione thinks, 'Greece is a thing of rocks that jag into you, every Greek line of poetry breaks you, jags into you . . . *hurting*.'[32] Nothing serene and harmonious there. H.D. recreates the Greek world, much in the way Jane Harrison had done; instead of the Victorians' masculine citadel of Homeric heroes or Athenian repose, it becomes an earlier, more elemental place where the struggles of the female psyche can be played out. H.D.'s Greeks belong to the archaic world that was being evoked by Epstein in his statues. No longer the originators of Western rationalism, they represent a non-Western intensity and passion through which she can present her own psychic turmoil. Both she and Aldington would continue to believe, in the words Pater quotes from Winckelmann, that 'by no people . . . has beauty been so highly esteemed as by the Greeks'.[33] Yet in other ways they were moving apart.

III

In May, the second imagist anthology appeared. It was widely reviewed, even occasionally in complimentary terms, and again sold well. Amy had already written in February to say that *vers libre* was being much discussed in all the papers, and in June she told Aldington that 'Imagism is fast ceasing to be a freak subject over here and is beginning to be treated with respect; people are fast getting inoculated; and I think in a few more years we can feel we have really succeeded.' By July she was saying, 'It is extraordinary how the movement is progressing . . . One can hardly take up a paper that does not mention some of us; in fact it is becoming a country-wide movement on this side of the Atlantic, and it is astonishing to think that a little handful of perfectly unknown poets have done this thing.'[34] When she had lectured that March in Chicago on 'The New Poetry, with a Particular Inquiry into Imagism', a hundred people were turned away. Her 'Spring-Day' with its description of her bath continued to be controversial, but 500 of the 1,000 copies of the anthology were sold in the first month, and sales of the first anthology had reached 1,301. A drop in the ocean by *Georgian Poetry* standards, but excellent compared with most volumes of poetry. Amy had cautiously predicted the previous November that the 'storm of abuse' which had greeted the 1915 volume would be turned by that of 1916 into 'reluctant praise', and she was proved right.[35]

Lawrence wrote to Lowell from Cornwall later that month, to thank her for his copies, saying it 'looks very nice, as usual, the book. And I think it *quite* up to the mark, don't you? It should make a considerable impression', though he would later say to a former colleague from Croydon that his and H.D.'s were the only good poems.[36] The Aldingtons also wrote to acknowledge theirs; over the last few months neither of them had written with any frequency to Amy, as she plaintively pointed out. Their lives, though she did not know it, were in some turmoil. They had not taken up Lawrence's suggestion that they should join him and Frieda in Cornwall. H.D. was tempted, but Richard, despite his admiration for Lawrence as a writer, saw he could be a difficult neighbour, as indeed Murry and Mansfield, whom he succeeded in enticing down, were to find. The idea of escaping London, the Zeppelins and the winter fog had, however, been immensely appealing, and in addition, according to Aldington's biographer, Charles Doyle, they were told it was advisable for the sake of H.D.'s health. John Cournos, of whom they had been seeing a good deal, suggested that they went to north Devon, to a village called Martinhoe by the coast, near which lived two of his writer friends, Carl Fallas and John Mills Whitham. Cournos had shared lodgings in London for a while with Fallas, and thought highly of him as a short story writer; although Fallas never became well known, in 1955 Winston Churchill unexpectedly awarded him the first Prime Minister's Annual Literary Award, as Aldington noted in a letter to H.D. at the time. Fallas had a young wife, Flo, like him from Manchester, and a baby; they had little money, and in London the three of them had all lived together in one room. Fallas was unfailingly cheerful and 'happy-go-lucky': Flo, Cournos said, was 'very good-looking, fully a head taller than Carl; charmingly simple, a country-girl in spirit'.[37] Whitham was a novelist, according to Aldington writing Hardyesque 'rural tragedies which terrified the subscription libraries'. He had 'cast off puritan doctrine but retained the puritan temperament', and although he had 'prodigious ideals, was often as melancholy as a gib cat'.[38] It was Flo who found the Aldingtons a cottage, or rather half a cottage. Pound reported to his mother in late February that he had heard that they were going to Devon for a while, and they probably went in early March. Cournos promised that he would come and join them as soon as possible, but it took him time, as an American, to get the necessary permit. The Aldingtons tried to persuade Flint to give up his job and to bring his family to join them, but he lived too near real poverty to do anything so reckless. In any case, working in the Post Office was still a reserved occupation – that would later change – and while he remained there he would not be called up, even if – or rather, as they well knew, when – married men's conscription was introduced. Aldington was still undecided what he would do in that eventuality. H.D. told Flint that he was wondering about going to prison rather than fighting. Neither prospect was appealing.

Devon was a welcome respite. Aldington wrote in his memoir: 'I got to like that valley. In front of the cottage ran one of those rocky Devonshire trout streams, "warty" as Herrick calls them. Across a meadow there began a wooded hillside, and about a mile and half down the valley was the sea.' Until spring finally came – there had been six inches of snow when they arrived – he spent much of his time cutting wood to burn. With the warmer weather there were walks, beach parties and sea bathing, and they 'recaptured the good fellowship and gaiety which had vanished from London'.[39] Even so, John Cournos records, when he came to join them, 'our little colony lived in a state of perpetual apprehension . . . A terrible war was on, and in its repercussions our nerves were badly jangled.' He shared the Aldingtons' house, Carl and Flo Fallas lived half a mile, and Whitham two miles away. They were all, with the apparent exception of Flo, spending much of their time writing, though she was sometimes employed by one or other of them as a typist. Cournos himself was working on his first novel, based on his early childhood in Russia and his subsequent move to Philadelphia, but they all met three or four times a week, for meals, or long walks. Cournos comments somewhat mysteriously that they suffered from 'abnormal moods needing abnormal outlets', though the examples he gives do not seem particularly strange. Their bathing was naked, but that had become quite the fashion among young intellectuals. He also mentions that they discovered that the local inn had quantities of German wine in the cellar that the landlord was unable to sell to the patriotic inhabitants of Devon; to this they applied themselves merrily – presumably, since they were all hard up, at a very cheap price – and 'like souls possessed, danced and capered up and down the Devon Hills, and scintillated with a wit which but rarely sprang from sober tongue'.[40] None of this sounds very abnormal, but perhaps Cournos was hinting here at another kind of taboo-breaking and excess that he could not mention in a memoir: Aldington had an affair with Flo Fallas.

Aldington had been immediately attracted to Flo, as he wrote to tell Flint in March, although at that time he dismissed the idea of an affair, as he felt it would be too hurtful to H.D. Some commentators have suggested that the Aldingtons had agreed to have an open marriage, as George Winterbourne and his wife Elizabeth do in Aldington's 1929 novel, *Death of a Hero*. In the book, they both have other relationships from the beginning of their marriage, but there is no reason to suppose that this was true of Aldington and H.D. Aldington's letter to Flint does not suggest that he expected H.D. to be anything but deeply unhappy about his infidelity. It was certainly true, however, that they distinguished

their marriage from the conventional bourgeois tie. They held theoretic-
ally to the de Gourmont view of individualism and liberty, but that
does not mean they ever expected it to apply to their relationship.
Aldington's anti-bourgeois precepts had emerged strongly in a review
he had written the previous June of a book by Anna Wickham, an
Australian poet married (unhappily) to an English solicitor; she was in
rebellion against conventional marriage, and he commended her opinions thoroughly, if not always her verse. (Under her married name of
Mrs Hepburn she had, incidentally, been blessed in the first *Blast*.)
'Anna Wickham's book,' Aldington had written, 'is a chunk of life. She
makes me think of those punching machines on Folkestone pier; you
hit a leather projection, and a dial registers the force of the blow. Life
hits Anna Wickham and she registers a poem . . . She wants to know
what the devil women are to do with their lives.' Her poems, he says,
are the 'protest of a sane woman observing the insane things which are
exacted from her sex by bourgeois rules . . . Her misfortune is to be
clear-sighted among the blind, vital among the insipid, natural among
the affected, sane among the stupid.' He quotes one poem that begins,
'I have been so misused by chaste men with one wife/That I would live
with satyrs all my life', and another called 'The Tired Man', whose
second verse goes:

> I am a quiet gentleman,
>> And I would sit and think;
>> But my wife is walking the whirlwind
>>> Through night as black as ink.

Her book 'registers', Aldington concludes, 'the revolt of a human mind
from the exasperating restrictions and limitations of English middle-
class life. It is not a work of art; it is a series of cartels.'[41] The Aldingtons
had come to know Anna Wickham, who lived near them in Hampstead,
and though they liked her, began to understand something of her
husband's desire for a quieter life. In her 'Autobiographical Notes', H.D.
writes of their time there, 'Anna Wickham is rather wearing.'[42] Yet
Aldington's somewhat vague condemnation of middle-class mores here
did not necessarily mean very much in practice. Aldington and H.D.'s
time together in Paris and Capri had certainly been a gesture of defiance to the conventional world, but up to this point they appear to have
been a devoted couple. Richard and Brigit would flirt, but Brigit appears
to have flirted a good deal, and she was devoted to H.D.; although H.D.

would much later come to wonder if they had had an affair in those years, it seems clear from Aldington's extant letters to Brigit that they had not. By 1918 Aldington was certainly putting forward the theory that he and H.D. could both have other relationships without damaging their essential closeness, but this does not seem to have been an idea that he thought H.D. would be happy with in 1916. H.D. undoubtedly had told him about Pound's multiple 'engagements', and he must have been well aware of how she would react to betrayal by himself. Aldington's instinct was always to protect H.D. from the world; she had felt safe with him, but he would hurt her bitterly all the same.

Flint, his wife and their two children came to visit at Easter. Whether Aldington talked over his feelings about Flo with Flint, there is no record, but one presumes he did. Flint, whose unpublished writings suggest both that he was deeply attached to Violet, but also worn by the strains of a poverty-stricken domestic life and resentful that he could not live in a freer, more expansive way, may have encouraged him. Easter was late that year; Easter Monday was 24 April, the day on which what became known as the Easter Rising took place in Dublin. Aldington had never shown any great interest in the Irish question, and he probably never knew that the uprising sealed his fate. In March, the first bill had been passed in Parliament paving the way for legislation to conscript married men, but it was not until May that such conscription – universal military service up to the age of forty-one – began. Asquith's government was riven in two over the issue and he was afraid to pursue the bill, but news of the Dublin rebellion produced a surge of support in Parliament for the measure, and on Tuesday, 25 April he was able to get it through.

The rising itself was put down in a few days, but the scars left by the heavy-handed English response soured relationships between England and Ireland for decades. The English authorities had been taken off their guard. Just as at the beginning of the war, everyone had been looking at Ireland instead of Europe, now, with all eyes on the Great War, they had forgotten the possibility of trouble there. Even Yeats, Pound told his parents, had been taken by surprise. Pound probably would not have known at this stage that his erstwhile fellow Tour Eiffel poet, Desmond FitzGerald, had been involved. Joseph Campbell, with whom FitzGerald hid for a few days that week, had stayed with Pound as recently as late 1914, and Nancy kept in touch with Dorothy, so Pound would certainly have been aware that there was deep anger at the failure to implement Home Rule. The leaders of the Easter Rising, many of whom Yeats knew, were executed, transformed instantly into martyrs, and memorialised in Yeats' great poem on the rising in which he declares 'a terrible beauty is born'. Roger Casement, who had been knighted in 1911 for exposing the abuses inflicted on workers in the rubber industries in the Congo and the Amazon, was hanged for treason in August for his attempts to get German support, though only after diaries relating his homosexual activities had been used to besmirch his name. (John Quinn, the nearest thing in Pound's life to a Renaissance prince, tried to plead for Casement, and was one of the few of those who, on being shown selected pages from the diary, did not desist.) Yeats wrote to Asquith on Casement's behalf; Wilfrid Scawen Blunt was both heart-broken at Casement's death and somewhat envious of his martyrdom; Joseph Campbell, who had never forgotten Casement's earlier kindness, wrote a tribute to him as one of a line of Irish heroes. Pound had at first treated the uprising fairly flippantly, having by now been trained by Yeats and Joyce to despise Irish nationalism (though this incident would change Yeats' attitude), but even he realised the British government was bungling things. In any case, he, like them, remained deeply critical of the British Empire; he told the young aspiring writer, Iris Barry, who contacted him for advice that year, that the only comparable decadence had been that of the late Roman Empire, and the British treatment of the rebels seemed another example of both this decadence and ineptitude.[43]

How much the Aldingtons heard of the rising in Devon is hard to know. Brigit, who was corresponding with H.D. and still a keen Irish nationalist, would undoubtedly have written to her about it, and even the *Egoist* mentioned it, so they cannot have missed it altogether. Probably, like Lawrence, who wrote indignantly about the events to Ottoline Morrell, they saw the executions as more evidence of English militaristic barbarity, but they must have been much more exercised by the news about conscription. Whitham decided he would be a conscientious objector, prison or no, and indeed to prison he went, though he was out by early September. Cournos, as an American, was exempt from military service. Carl and Aldington decided to enlist together in late May; if they did so voluntarily, they could choose their battalion and stay together. It was finally in May, too, it appears, that Aldington and Flo briefly became lovers. Presumably Fallas, who according to Cournos prided himself on the docility of his wife, knew nothing about it, though one wonders at the logistics. Aldington described to Flint his panic when the postman knocked on the door of the Fallas cottage when he and Flo were in bed together. But where, one wonders, was Carl? And where was the baby? Aldington was taking a risk with his own marriage and with Flo's, but with the thought of war service ahead the future carried few guarantees for him. The affair was perhaps as much an escape from fear of life, or worse, of death, at the front, as anything else, a desperate effort to seize, if only temporarily, the simple, uncomplicated joy espoused by his Greeks that the world denied him.

Whether Aldington told H.D. or not about the affair, and he seems not to have done at the time, she was aware of it. In her 'Autobiographical Notes' many years later, she recalled of that time: 'R. goes much to the Fallas cottage'.[44] John Cournos became her confidant, as Flint was Aldington's. She tried to be calm and reasonable. She knew the strain that Aldington was under. Though she was emotionally very dependent on him, their sexual life must have been at best attenuated at this period. In *Bid Me to Live*, Julia says she had lived in fear of Rafe's 'over-physical sensuality' since 'the ordeal in the nursing home'.[45] Aldington was behaving like many a Victorian husband, though he would have been aghast at the thought; when the next year H.D. would hint at a comparison with the womanising Deighton Patmore, whom he despised, he was appalled. Aldington was deeply romantic, as well as highly sexed, and, in a somewhat naïve though not uncommon fashion, always held to the idea that his sexual liaisons were in themselves good and beautiful expressions of the human spirit, no matter what devastation they caused. And H.D. was certainly devastated. But her feelings were all the more confused because Aldington almost immediately had to enlist. The person who had hurt and betrayed her was now one who needed all the love, support, warmth and encouragement that she could give him.

Government regulations, Richard told Amy, allowed them five weeks from enlisting to put their affairs in order. He went off for army training on 24 June, and H.D. was left both anguished and concerned. Aldington hated army life, as he was sure he would. He had enlisted as a private; he had some hopes that his father's connections through the Ministry of Munitions might get him a commission, but his father was as unsuccessful as he had been in his attempts to find Flint a position there. Even before he joined up, Aldington had dreaded, as he told Amy, 'ceas[ing] to exist as an individual' once he had entered the military machine.[46] 'My number on the form,' he told her, 'is 61, so that in a fortnight I cease to be "Richard Aldington, the celebrated Imagist poet" (vide Dramas ad!) and become Private R. Aldington, 61, 6th Devonshire

Regiment.'[47] Once there, it was even more of a 'soul–destroying mechanism', as he describes it, than he had feared.[48] He found himself revolted
by the tasks he had to carry out. Aldington wrote bitterly to Flint and
Cournos of the degradation he had to endure. For the Officers' Mess
Fatigue, he was given tasks generally done by female domestic servants:
Aldington, free though he thought he was of class prejudice, found, as
an ex-public-school boy, working as a kitchen maid intensely galling.

H.D. stayed on in Martinhoe for about a month, and Cournos stayed
with her. He commented later, somewhat harshly, for by then much had
gone wrong between them, that 'H.D. was dreadfully upset by Richard's
departure, though she had had ample time to prepare for it.'[49] At the
time, he was more sympathetic, saying to her, when she told him of the
affair, that he felt responsible for her unhappiness over Flo, as he had
introduced them to the Fallases; H.D. would tell him in early September
that during that month he had saved her life, doubtless an exaggeration, but one she probably believed. Cournos had become a close friend
to both the Aldingtons. Although, ever since he had come to Europe,
he had hoped eventually to persuade Arabella, the beautiful Philadelphian
art student whom he had followed to Paris, to marry him, and had made
intermittent though unsuccessful attempts to renew his suit, he was by
now in love with H.D.; H.D., in her distraught state, saw him as her
only support. 'Psychically wrought up, immediately after [Richard's]
departure,' Cournos says, 'she impetuously walked over to me in the
sitting room we all jointly occupied and kissed me.' Was this true? He
is clearly hinting that this was a sexual advance, and continues ambiguously, 'This revelation of confidence and its implication of the two of
us being left to maintain the thinning thread of spirit in growing chaos,
touched me, and I resolved to help her breach the emptiness of the days
immediately before her', a course of action which his readers could
interpret either as disinterested kindliness or an affair, though it appears
not to have been quite either.[50] H.D.'s letters to Cournos suggest that
he was the one who declared his love for her, 'absolute and terrible and
hopeless love', as she puts it in one letter, while she, though both grateful
and anxious to hold on to his affection and sympathy, told him that,
fond of him as she was, she cared for Aldington in a way she did not
for him.[51] The letters H.D. wrote to Cournos over the next few months
are almost frighteningly intense; she writes like someone living on the
very edge of complete breakdown, but, although she speaks obsessively
of Aldington, of her anxieties about what he is enduring in the 'hell of
soldiering', and of her desperate unhappiness about Flo, one cannot

really blame Cournos – as she begs him repeatedly to continue writing and pours out her gratitude and affection – for being confused about her attitude towards him. One critic has referred to these letters as flirtatious, a word that with its connotations of fun and light-hearted dalliance suggests a different universe from the fevered torment that the letters convey.[52] But that H.D. was eager to keep the sustaining emotional bond between them is very clear.

Cournos, whatever his feelings for H.D., was anxious to remain in the role of faithful friend to Richard. Two days after Aldington left, sitting with H.D. in the cottage sitting-room, he recounts that they both heard Aldington's voice calling him 'Korshoon', his original Russian name by which Richard and H.D. knew him.[53] H.D.'s letters repeatedly tell Cournos how fond Richard is of him, and how much his letters meant to him. Aldington, for his part, as well as trying desperately to convince H.D. that he still loved her, was attempting to prevent her from realising how much he loathed the army. His unhappy letters to Flint and Cournos include repeated instructions not to tell H.D. of his misery, though she appears to have been well aware of it. On his weekend leaves, surprisingly frequent, he was desperate to reassure H.D. of his devotion. She ceaselessly encouraged their friends to write to him. Indeed, both of them tried, in a somewhat frenzied, but not necessarily insincere, way, to prove how devoted they were to each other.

Amy Lowell was one of those H.D. begged to write, a more complicated matter than she had realised. Her letter to Amy giving the camp address was returned by the censors, as the location of camps was not to be revealed to foreign nationals. Lowell had to write to the *Egoist*, which forwarded her letters. Amy had been much dismayed for them both when she heard Aldington was in the army, writing to him in late June to say 'I cannot bear to have your brains and beautiful imagination knocked here and there in the rough duties of a private soldier's life', though adding a trifle bracingly that poets must be 'virile' and that the war might be 'a splendid experience, which will enlarge not only your outlook on life but your suggestions for poetry'. She added with some embarrassment that she must sound 'sententious', but didn't seem to recognise that Aldington feared he might soon no longer have a life on which to have an outlook.[54] There is no extant comment from Aldington on that particular letter, but he would grow increasingly irritated by Lowell's upbeat exhortations. He was grateful for the generosity with which she worked to help him continue to publish while at the front; from the time she returned in 1914 she had been assiduous in placing poems by both Aldington and H.D. in the American press, acting as unpaid agent, but she now redoubled her efforts. Yet when she wrote saying she almost wished that she too could be at the front, Aldington furiously condemned her hypocrisy in making such statements from her 'fat Boston sitting room'.[55] Her 'almost' wish was, however, probably genuine. Part of her always wanted to be able to do the things that in Boston were restricted to men. It is not surprising that in her letters and lectures she applies the word 'virile' to poetry with almost as much zest as Hulme had done. But she would never have wanted to be a private; a general would have been much more to her taste.

I V

A month after Aldington joined the army, H.D. moved to Corfe Castle in Dorset, to be near his camp at Wareham. John Cournos returned to London, where he was put up by Richard's friend Alec Randall and his wife Amy, both of whom now contributed to the *Egoist*. Flo and the baby went to stay with her parents back in Manchester, where Carl went to see her on leave in September. The Fallases were desperately short of money, and H.D., in spite of everything, tried to help. The £40 that Amy had earlier sent her when her allowance was late she had refused to keep for herself, but with Amy's agreement gave it away to various writers even more hard-up than themselves; some of the money went to the Fallas family, a generous gesture in the circumstances. H.D. was determined to be civilised. As she recalled later in life, thinking over this period, the 'impulse to fling plates, à la Lawrences, has been discreetly suppressed in me . . . I can feel the old insufficiency and frustration but I never flared out at Richard or at the earlier Ezra with his relay or chorus.'[56] H.D. did, it must be said, resist a suggestion that Flo should come and stay with her in Corfe Castle so that she too could be near her husband; there were limits to her generosity, though she wavered even on that. But having moved there, what with the beauty of the place and the fact that she could see something of Aldington, at least her anxieties moved to her husband's misery in the army. When she first arrived at Corfe Castle, she told Cournos later, 'I was so intense in my prayer for Richard's mere physical safety, that I could not complicate it with other things. I came to him as if nothing had ever happened. I think we were happy together.' In late August she was saying to Cournos that she 'hope[d] to soon be [her]self again'.

She had, as well, other things to think about. On 1 June, a notice had appeared in the *Egoist*, informing readers that Aldington had been called up and that the assistant editorship would be taken over in his absence by '"H.D." (Mrs Richard Aldington)'. She had to turn her mind to soliciting copy, and to writing it herself. Her first review appeared in August, of Marianne Moore's poetry, an indication of how much she admired her former fellow-student's work, as Moore's first book was not published until 1921, and reviews of uncollected poems are rare. 'Miss Moore,' she wrote, 'turns her perfect craft as the perfect craftsman must inevitably do, to some direct presentation of beauty, clear, cut in flowing lines, but so delicately that the very screen she carves seems to stand only in that serene palace of her own world of inspiration – frail, yet as all beautiful things are, absolutely hard – and destined to endure longer, far longer than the toppling sky-scrapers, and the world of shrapnel and machine-guns in which we live.'[57] H.D. was developing her own poetic doctrines, which share elements with both Hulme and Pound's but are in other ways very different. Like them, H.D. sees beauty in what is 'hard', but, unlike them, in what is simultaneously frail. She uses the analogy of carving, as Pound does, though he generally thinks of sculpting stone, and she is talking of delicate wood fretwork; she evokes qualities like those Hulme recommended for modern art, which he thought should be 'austere', 'bare', 'clear cut'. But Hulme had added the word 'mechanical', and like both Yeats and Lawrence, she is wary of that; the machine for her, as for them, is inevitably connected with the machinery of war.

What H.D. says of Moore's poetry could be read as an oblique manifesto for her own collection, *Sea Garden*, which came out in September, and which also presents an imagined world which is 'frail, yet as all beautiful things are, absolutely hard'. *Sea Garden* was, overall, a supremely impressive first volume, restrained yet intense, passionate yet disciplined. Like *Cathay*, the poems evoke the wartime atmosphere; for all their beauty, they are bleak, stoical and stark. In the flower poems, such as 'Sea Rose', with which she opens the volume, emblems of love and femininity are transformed into stony but delicate, battered though enduring, images of the time. Some of the poems predate the war, though even they are uncannily appropriate to its dark atmosphere. 'The Last Gift', after all, which reappeared here, with its 'bare rocks/dwarf-trees, twisted', recalls the landscape of her first published poem, 'Hermes of the Ways'.[58] They are, in Pound's word mythopoetic, visionary poems, some evoking Pater's image of the return of the gods that Pound had drawn on in 'The Return', and which became an urgent wartime theme for H.D., representing to her the need in 'the world of shrapnel and machine-guns in which we live' for the artist to make possible the imaginative recreation of a more humane and worthwhile world. As a whole, the volume makes clear that her rejection in 'The Last Gift' of an 'over-sweet', 'over-painted' beauty was the rejection of a conventionally feminine traditional verse for one that can speak to the tortured intensity of the present, her own version of the modernist revolution; in 'Sheltered Garden', for example, she writes:

> I want wind to break,
> scatter these pink-stalks,
> snap off their spiced heads,
> fling them about with dead leaves . . .
> O to blot out this garden
> to forget, to find a new beauty
> in some terrible
> wind-tortured place.[59]

What she seeks is a vision and a poetry that can endure and transcend the buffetings and violence of the times. *Sea Garden* is a version – an unusual version – of the pastoral, like the sea iris, stinging as well as scented, salt as well as sweet; it ends with the poem 'Cities', which had appeared in the July *Egoist* and which returns the reader to the metropolitan world, evoking the oppressive here and now, but with new hope and insight, the traditional end of the pastoral.

Sea Garden had few reviews in England, though H.D. told Amy that it had found some appreciative readers. Fletcher, now back in England, would give it a warm review in *Poetry* (why, Pound demanded of Alice Corbin Henderson, had it not been sent to the foreign correspondent?). When Lowell had written to Aldington in June, she asked if they had yet seen Fletcher, to whom she had regretfully said goodbye in late May. Only earlier that month, she had been telling them what a solace he was to her, and how well settled in Boston, so he must have left it to the last moment to break the news that he was definitely going. He had told her about Daisy in late 1915, but vacillated for months about returning. He was as ambivalent and changeable as ever about the marriage, and, even when he decided he wanted to be with Daisy, was appalled by the thought that he might be conscripted if he returned to England. He had written as one of his 'symphony' poems a long nightmarish meditation on an earth 'sown with dead', entitled 'Poppies of the Red Year: a Symphony in Scarlet', vividly evoking the horror of the battlefield. The third section imagines the carnage:

> Scarlet tossing poppies
> Flutter their wind-slashed edges,
> On which gorged black flies poise and sway in drunken sleep.
> The black flies hang
> Above the tangled trampled grasses,
> Grey, crumpled bundles lie in them:
> They sprawl,
> Heave faintly;
> And between their stiffened fingers,
> Run out clogged crimson trickles,
> Spattering the poppies and standing in beads on the grass.[60]

No illusions about the glamour of warfare there, but added to this sharp fear of being sent to the front was the fact that Lowell endeavoured to persuade him that it would be ruinous for his poetic career to return to England. He was slowly building up his reputation in America, she said; in England he would be forgotten and dismissed as an expatriate. She could have given as warning the contrast between Frost and Pound. If Frost had stayed away and allowed himself to be promoted as one of Pound's 'American literary refugees', he would never have been taken up in his home country. Now, safely back, he was a bestseller; Pound's admirers were still little more than a handful. In April Fletcher's *Goblins and Pagodas* had appeared, containing what was perhaps the most successful and moving poem he ever wrote, his long poem of childhood memories, 'The Ghosts of an Old House', which he had written on that first miserable return home. The volume had been due to come out at the same time as the 1916 *Some Imagist Poets*, but the anthology was delayed, so he at least had the pleasure of separate reviews; they were mixed, but the book was certainly noticed.

Fletcher was, however, a good deal more worried about being overshadowed by Lowell in America than of being forgotten when he left. He remained in many ways under the spell of her powerful personality, and was well aware she could be a useful influence with publishers, but, as her success grew, so did his rancour; when Daisy said she thought Amy plagiarised him, he was delighted to agree. While he rarely, if ever up to this point, appears to have criticised Lowell to her face – she thought him her most sympathetic literary contact – his letters about her to Daisy had become vituperative. One letter written in January 1916 lists a range of slights and ill-deeds – some clearly imaginary – chief among his complaints being her suggestion to Aldington, whom he now described as 'very decent and upright', that he should become editor of an American *Mercure de France*, a project she then decided she couldn't afford to set up.[61] Fletcher felt he had been compromised because he had written to encourage Aldington to accept. In fact Aldington, though he liked the idea, had been well aware that, given the likelihood of conscription, he would not have been allowed to leave England, and was much less perturbed than Fletcher was on his behalf. As Fletcher's biographer suggests, his real grouse was probably that Lowell had not asked him to be editor. Fletcher was now full of good will – temporarily at any rate – towards the Aldingtons; he talked with sympathy about their lack of funds, H.D.'s delicacy and Aldington's anxiety about leaving her if he were called up. Ever since the stillbirth, his attitude to them had markedly changed. In April 1916, he wrote a sympathetic review of Aldington's *Images* for *Poetry*, praising its 'simplicity and restraint' in contrast to much American verse, which was 'hectic, disorganised, lacking in reflective judgment'.[62] When he returned to England, he was ready to be friendly, and H.D. and Aldington to welcome him. Fletcher had sent 'The Ghosts of an Old House' to the *Egoist* the year before, where it appeared in instalments; Aldington was deeply impressed by it, and, with his own memories of childhood unhappiness, had come to feel a new sympathy as well as respect for Fletcher. It would be some months, however, before they met up.

Fletcher arrived in England on 8 June, just three days after Lord Kitchener drowned when the vessel that he was on struck a mine. It was a blow to the country's prestige, and there was a clamour for further internment of Germans living in Britain as the rumour went round, Fletcher told Lowell, that Kitchener had lost his life as the result of information passed on by a German spy. Fletcher was amazed by the surface calm. There were notices everywhere, warning people not to discuss military and naval matters, and most people avoided the subject of the war altogether, venting their anxieties by complaining about the high prices, double, he estimated, those of 1914. (By the end of the war, the pound would be worth a third of what it had been pre-war.) Half the bus conductors were now women, London swarmed with soldiers, and the fashionable ladies of the pre-war era had largely disappeared. A notice by the Trafalgar Square lions read: 'To dress extravagantly in war time is worse than bad form. It is unpatriotic.' Fletcher described all this in a letter written to Amy within three days of his arrival, and signed 'yours affectionately', so he was not yet making any very decisive break. He wrote again later in the month, saying he was appalled by the feebleness of the poetry that was emerging during the war, ascribing this to the fact that no one 'wants to think of the tragic side, and everyone is trying to be as cheerful as possible . . . a lot of the old Puritan morality has been swept overboard at a stroke. The amount of immorality that goes on in munitions factories, etc., is staggering.'[63] Presumably the latter information he had from the papers, as he had no contact with munitions factories, and outrage at loose wartime morals was a favourite topic in the press. He had seen no one he knew, bar of course Daisy; he had called in at the Poetry Bookshop, but found that Harold Monro was engaged in anti-aircraft work, having joined the army just that same month. One would not have expected him to seek out Pound or Lewis, and indeed Lewis was no longer in London, but training for the army in Dorset, though in frequent communication with Pound over the progress of negotiations for selling his work to John Quinn. Fletcher, however, exchanged letters with the Aldingtons. Amy had secured a position for Aldington as foreign correspondent for a new journal that was about to be launched by William Stanley Braithwaite, who had come to admire Lowell, but now Aldington was in the army he could no longer do it, and Fletcher offered his own services in his place; they were not taken up, yet another grievance.

Fletcher and Daisy were married on 5 July. Poor Amy! Carl Engel married the same month, so she lost the attentions of the two friends that she had leant on most, always of course excepting the rock-like Ada (Lowell would frequently call her Peter, in tribute to that quality). In early August, Fletcher wrote to Lowell, after a honeymoon in Cornwall, sounding depressed, saying now he had been back for two months he found himself thinking constantly of the war. Horrific numbers of wounded soldiers arrived back daily at Charing Cross, to be greeted by women who threw flowers into the ambulances, while the soldiers appeared pitifully indifferent to their heroes' welcome. He made no comment on married life, but his unhappy tone suggests he was already uncertain that he had done the right thing. He spent the month of August with Daisy and her children at Ramsgate, so he was not back in Sydenham until September. In the meantime, Aldington, who had expected to be sent abroad that month, had a reprieve. He may have hated army life, but he was a hard worker, highly competent at whatever he did, as well as strong and muscular. Dover College would have been gratified to know that his superiors soon decided that he had the makings of a leader. His physical appearance, in any case, fitted him for officer class; few working-class privates had his height and build. H.D. told Cournos that 'R. looks so much a "gentleman" that from a distance approaching Tommies prepare to salute. It is a great joke – they are so surprised when they find R. one of themselves.' By early September he was promoted to non-commissioned officer, which meant he would not have to go to France for another three months. His adjutant had even asked him if he would like a commission, but he had said not yet. H.D. does not explain why; one might surmise that even though he had earlier hoped his father would obtain one for him, his dislike of what he saw as the snobbish distinction accorded to the officer class made him hesitate, though later in the war he agreed to become a lieutenant. Almost immediately, however, that he learnt of his delayed departure, there was a further crisis in his relationship with H.D. With the imminent threat of danger to his life removed, her other fears returned: she came across in the *Poetry Review of America* two poems by Aldington, clearly written about Flo, with whom she was now convinced Aldington was passionately in love. 'I have lived through hours of torture,' she wrote to Cournos, 'beside which those in which you saw me were paradise.'

She poured out her despair, anger and pain in a series of long poems, very different from the brief, highly charged and honed work that she had published in *Sea Garden*. These poems are, as Louis Martz, the editor of her *Collected Poems*, has commented, much more personal, and mark a new stage in her writing, as if imagist control could not withstand the flood of psychic pain; they are driven, anguished, much more explicit about the human situation from which they arise.[64] They remain Sappho-like in their intensity and conflicting range of emotions; the Greek frame is still there, but there is a new dramatic urgency and directness. She saved three of these poems, 'Amaranth', 'Eros' and 'Envy', keeping them in a folder marked 'Corfe Castle, 1917'. That was the wrong year; she would no longer be in Corfe Castle in 1917, but Aldington would betray her even more disastrously in that year; as she would later learn to say, it was a Freudian slip. She never published these in full in her lifetime, though she printed some extracts from them in the 1920s, describing them as 'Fragments from Sappho' and making changes to disguise the personal source. The first section of 'Envy' begins:

> I envy you your chance of death,
> how I envy you this.
> I am more covetous of him
> even than of your glance . . .

After a powerful personification of death, who even if he 'pierce me
with his lust/iron, fever and dust' cannot hurt her as much as her faithless lover, she asks,

> What is left after this?
> what can death loose in me
> after your embrace?
> your touch,
> your limbs are more terrible
> to do me hurt.
>
> What can death mar in me
> that you have not?[65]

For all the pain, there is an extraordinary fire and energy in these poems;
as she said to Cournos, 'the hurt has freed my song'.

H.D. described the poems that she wrote at Corfe Castle to Cournos
as 'a series that all runs on continuously but can be read as single poems.
I feel it will be very, very far ahead of all my other work if I find strength
to go on with it . . . These poems seem absolutely dictated from without.
I am burning all the time like an early Christian, like a mad fanatic in
the desert, well, like a poet.' The imagery of burning is reminiscent of
what Lawrence had said of Sappho to Catherine Carswell; as he was
writing regularly to H.D. at the time, he may well have said it to her
too. It is an image that runs through all the letters to Cournos, where
she uses it both of her writing and of her feelings about Aldington, her
passion for him and the pain he caused her. Explaining to Cournos why
she had not accepted the relationship he offered, she said that, though
she might have found some consolation with him, it would not have
been so productive for her writing: 'I love Richard with a searing, burning
intensity. I love him and I have come to this torture of my free will. I
could have forgotten my pride broken and my beauty as it were, unappreciated. I could have found peace with you. But of my own will, I
have come to this Hell. But beauty is never Hell. I believe this flame is
my very Daemon driving me to write. I want to write.' Both Aldington

and Brigit would in later life comment – disapprovingly – on what they saw as H.D.'s puritanism and her embrace of suffering: neither of them was in favour of mad fanatics in the desert nor of early Christians in general. But for H.D., if this extremity led to art, that was enough.

Though H.D. expresses misery in her letters to Cournos, she is scrupulously and strikingly uncomplaining and uncritical of Aldington. At times, she attempts to be almost superhumanly unselfish: 'if Flo loves R, there is nothing I would not do for her and for R . . . She may be a great help, a great influence in R.'s life. If so, I will always be tender and grateful to her.' At other times she blames herself: 'I feel myself such worthless trash somehow. No personal consideration should count in the stark face of death – and the idea of death, I know, is with R. so much of the time: – But I feel *chained* at times to a tortured ego and my fear is that I give only pain. Yet the ego *is* in a sense, pain . . . I am neurotic – a wreck – really unfitted for life. At times, I feel a sort of beautiful serenety [*sic*] – and poof – a breath, and I am prisoned by that miserable, hyper-sensitive, nerve-cracked, self-centered self!' Yet in the letters the anger and indignation that she expresses in the poetry are never allowed to appear. In 'Amaranth' she writes

> But I,
> how I hate you for this,
> how I despise and hate,
> was my beauty so slight a gift,
> so soon, so soon forgot?

Only later in the poem she adds, 'Turn, for I love you yet'.[66] In the letters the hate is never acknowledged, only the love.

H.D. still tried to live, certainly in her relationship with Aldington, by the standards of unselfish womanly goodness and kindliness she had learnt from her Moravian mother, though her religion was now that of beauty. She and Aldington idealised each other, and they both tried desperately to live up to each other's view. Because they were artists, with a mission to bring beauty back to the world, sordid emotions like jealousy and possessiveness were not for them. Aldington, she knew, saw her as high-minded, spiritual, beauty-loving, sensitive, delicate; all true of course, but when he aroused in her emotions that didn't fit that image, she was thrown into mental anguish. While she was agonising in Devon, Aldington was writing to Amy, 'H.D. has been truly wonderful; her affection and unselfish devotion have been the prop of my existence.

There is a general idea prevalent in England that American girls are selfish; it is a silly lie, for no one could ever have a more unselfish wife than my American one! I think she will come to stay near here in a couple of weeks, so that I can see her on Sat & Sunday afternoons. That will be fine, won't it?'[67] Knowing he thought that, and one can be sure he said the same to H.D. herself, how could she acknowledge, even to herself, the fury she felt about Flo? She could admit to being neurotic and nerve-cracked, but certainly not – outside the poetry – to bitterness and resentment.

V

IN early September, in the midst of the crisis over Flo, Flint, Violet and
the family took their annual holiday to Swanage, not far from Corfe
Castle, specifically to be near the Aldingtons and see something of them
again. Flint still regarded them as his best friends, and he had missed
them greatly in London that year, especially now Ford and Monro, his
closest other literary companions, were also in the army. Both Aldington
and H.D. corresponded with him frequently, well aware of his frequent
bouts of depression, and of what Aldington described as his 'almost
imbecile modesty'; they tried to build up his belief in himself, but he
still felt isolated and low.[68] Violet and the children had come ahead to
the seaside some time before they were joined by Flint, so he must have
been lonelier than ever. H.D. saw the Flints several times, and they came
to see Richard on his weekend leave. But the tensions in the air made
the visit a less happy one than everyone had hoped. Flint and H.D. each
managed briefly to upset the other. Flint wanted to come across to see
Richard again for a second weekend; Richard, who was working very
long hours, had found the influx rather overwhelming – at least according
to H.D. – and for her part she was anxious to talk to him about Flo, not
something she felt she could tell Flint. So she suggested it would be
better if they didn't come. Flint, always super-sensitive, was shocked and
hurt, as it was entirely out of keeping with the way the Aldingtons usually
behaved towards him. Feeling aggrieved, he responded by saying to H.D.
words to the effect that the fuss she was making about Aldington really
didn't help him. H.D. was deeply wounded, partly because she wondered
if he were right. She wrote to Cournos: 'I am often unhappy to think
that my complicated nature has led R. to think I am unhappy. That was
why Frank's remark hurt me to the heart. I think of it and wonder if
perhaps it would be best for me to leave England as R first begged me

to do. I wonder if I am not causing him pain by staying here.' H.D. and Flint made it up, but she did not feel quite the same about him after that, and perhaps he too had new reservations about her. When Flint mentioned the visit to Amy, he pointedly emphasised that he had gone to see Richard specifically, not both of the Aldingtons: he and Richard 'had some good hours together – far too short'. Aldington was looking very well, he told her, but 'it is a heartbreaking thing to consider the purpose to which all that physical splendour must be put'.[69] Flint wrote a poem the next year, dedicated to Aldington, recalling the Easter visit, 'the days/ we climbed the Devon hills together', and expressing his desolation that Aldington was in France: 'I sit here at my table,/holding back my tears,/with my jaw set and my teeth clenched'.[70] From now on Flint would be Richard's friend first and foremost.

Aldington and H.D had a brief visit to London in the second half of September, when they met up with Cournos and Flint and finally saw Fletcher again, who was now back in Sydenham. The bitter quarrels with Daisy had started again, and he was glad to have an escape route to his former literary contacts. They all had dinner in Soho; Fletcher, like Flint, was struck by how well Aldington looked, as he told Lowell, adding that 'you would scarcely know he is the same, so completely has the army changed him. I find him much more human than he used to be, and much more modest.' H.D., on the other hand, looked very strained: 'she is dreadfully thin,' Fletcher commented, 'and I think the whole business of R's going into the army, etc., has had a very bad effect on her. When I saw her first I was shocked at the change; she looked so absolutely frail and wasted that I was afraid she would not be long for this world.'[71] He added, however, that the ordeal had improved her poetry.

Flint, who, Fletcher said, somewhat enigmatically, had not changed at all, also mentioned this dinner to Lowell when he wrote to thank her for his latest royalties (£8, which, although not princely, must have helped his meagre finances). It was, he pointed out, 'the most comprehensive gathering of the clan that has yet happened . . . the absent ones being yourself on the bay where the tea was spoiled and Lawrence on some little bay in Cornwall'. For Flint, that was clearly a moment of cheer in a largely depressing existence. He had started the letter by saying, 'I'm pretty down in the mouth at present, and have been sick enough of everything during the past few months.' He ends by pointing out that less than 48 hours after the dinner Richard had returned to camp, and added bleakly, 'it's a rotten mad world'.[72]

H.D. had agreed at the dinner to collect together everyone's poems for the anthology by the beginning of November. She was the person, Fletcher told Lowell, who was in touch with Lawrence, and would be responsible for soliciting poems from him. Although she wrote to Lawrence regularly, it seems unlikely that H.D. would have told him more of her personal trauma than that Richard had joined up, though in *Bid Me to Live* Julia says that she sent to Rico, the Lawrence figure, poems that she had not shown to Rafe; if that were the case with H.D., he may have gathered something of what she was going through. His letters back did not offer unqualified cheer. H.D. mentions Lawrence and his coruscating letters (although she doesn't give a name, it is clearly him) when writing to Cournos at the end of October. She has started to see people as colours, she says: Cournos is lapis-lazuli blue, and Richard wine-red; then she abruptly adds, 'But there is another now . . . There is a yellow flame, bright, hard, clear, terrible, cruel: . . . There is a power in this person to kill me. I mean literally. For the spiritual vision, his thoughts, his distant passion has given me, I thank God . . . But . . . there is yet another side – if he comes too near I am afraid for myself . . . You, no doubt, know in your heart of whom I write as a cruel-fire! I do not want that person to die. He has a great gift. He is ill. But I must be protected'.

Lawrence was in low spirits, intensely lonely in Cornwall yet unable to face a return to wartime London. He continued to think the war 'utterly wrong, stupid, monstrous and contemptible', and though he was coming to the end of *Women in Love*, which he told Dollie Radford he thought a masterpiece, he was convinced, rightly, that he would find it impossible to publish it in England during the war.[73] He poured out his anger with the human race in his letters. To E.M. Forster, at the time in Alexandria, which in itself Lawrence, imprisoned in the Cornish damp, must have found galling, he said: 'I am in a black fury with the world, as usual. One writes, one works, one gives one's hand to other people. And the swine are rats, they bite one's hand. They are rats, sewer-rats, with all the foul courage of death and corruption, darkness and sewers.'[74] People, he said to Catherine Carswell, '*are* a destructive force. They are like acid, which can only corrode and dissolve. One *must shun* them.'[75] Probably he was saying similar things to H.D. Yet her comments to Cournos suggest Lawrence was also directly attacking her, as indeed, in the fictional account in *Bid Me to Live*, Rico castigates Julia. Julia recalls Rico's letters: 'He had written about love, about her frozen altars. "Kick over your tiresome house of life," he had said, he had jeered, "frozen lily of virtue," he had said, "our languid lily of virtue nods perilously near the pit"'. All the same, the novel says, 'when it came to one, any one of her broken stark metres, he had no criticism to make'.[76] Lawrence's letters in 1916 and 1917 refer several times to how much he admires H.D.'s poetry, so it is unlikely that the 'frozen altars' are an attack on her poetry, more on her attitude to art and to life in general. Indeed, perhaps he was struck, as one is today by reading those letters to Cournos, by the disjuncture between the emotional charge and range of her poetry, and the strained high-mindedness that she strove to cling to in the version of herself she admitted to the world. She and Lawrence sometimes clashed as well over their attitudes to poetry. Lawrence had written to Lowell that August: 'Hilda Aldington says to me, why don't I write hymns to fire, why am I not in love with a tree. But my fire is a pyre, and the tree is the Tree of Knowledge.'[77] Yet in other ways they had much in common: they shared the sense of the need for a rebirth, a new beginning, one of the themes, according to Lawrence, of *Women in Love*, as it had been of *Sea Garden*. He said of the novel to Catherine Carswell that 'The book frightens me: it is so end-of-the-world. But it is, it must be, the beginning of a new world too.'[78] His denunciation of all humankind except the tiny handful that he wished to take to Ranamin (which now included H.D.) was on the grounds that they prevented this rebirth: 'one is so few and so fragile,' he told Carswell, 'in one's own small, subtle air of life. *How* one must cherish the frail, precious buds of unknown life in one's soul. They are the unborn children of one's hope and living happiness, and one is so frail to bring them forth.'[79] If he wrote in those terms to H.D., she must have felt that they were very much in tune: the frail, precious flowers of *Sea Garden* endured their buffeting world with equal difficulty. But there is nothing in her work like Lawrence's appalling tirades against swinish or rat-like humanity; no wonder at times she found him terrifying.

Ever since Fletcher's return, Amy Lowell had been pressing him to find out how the Lawrences were. Fletcher was generally unhelpful, but H.D., whom she had also asked, wrote to say that she knew that Lawrence had been 'ill and had a miserable, shattering experience before he was exempted from the army', a humiliating encounter with the authorities that Lawrence would describe in *Kangaroo*.[80] Although he had managed to bring out two books that year, another volume of poetry, *Amores*, which H.D. particularly admired, and his first book of travel writing, *Twilight in Italy*, she was sure they were hard up, but it was impossible to ask directly what their financial position was. As it happened, Frieda, knowing nothing of this, wrote without Lawrence's knowledge to Lowell, asking for help, and Lowell instantly responded with £60. Lawrence was immensely grateful. The money had arrived about the same time as a copy of Lowell's latest collection, *Men, Women and Ghosts*, which Lawrence told her he preferred to *Sword Blades*. This book was a collection of narrative poems, opening with 'Patterns', the majority in free verse or polyphonic prose; it was the latter Lawrence picked out, admiring their swirling evocation of the random sounds and colours in the modern city, what he called in her work 'the shock and clipping of the physico-mechanical world'.[81] How much he really liked her poetry overall is hard to say; he told another correspondent shortly after that she was not a good poet, though a very good friend, but he had a fascinating analysis of the American nature of the poetry she and H.D. wrote. 'It is very surprising to me,' he told her,

now I have come to understand you Americans a little, to realise how much older you are than us, how much further you and your art are . . . [in] apprehension of the physico-sensational world . . . of things non-human, not conceptual. We still see with concepts. But you, in the last stages of return, have gone beyond tragedy and emotion, even beyond irony, and have come to the pure mechanical stage of physical apprehension, the *human* unit almost lost, the primary elemental forces, kinetic, dynamic – prismatic, tonic, the great massive, active, *inorganic* world, elemental, never softened by life, that hard universe of Matter and Force where life is not known, come to pass again. It is strange and wonderful. I find it only in you and H.D. in English.[82]

One can see how this relates particularly to *Sea Garden*, where the gods are elemental, associated with sea and rock and wind – the only named god in the collection is Hermes of the Ways, the chthonic herm stone; otherwise only dryads, nereids, nymphs and undifferentiated gods appear, the pre-Homeric forces quasi-immanent in the natural world; as one critic puts it, 'unnamed daimonic presences compelling responses both erotic and fearful'.[83] Lawrence's analysis in some ways suggests Williams' later, very American doctrine of 'no ideas but in things'.[84] The general thesis was one Lawrence was elaborating much more generally about American culture and literature. He had been reading American novels, Melville, Cooper, Richard Henry Dana and others with passionate interest, and wrote a series of articles on them which were published in the *English Review* in

1918 and 1919, and then in a revised version as the now famous *Studies in Classic American Literature*.

By October, Aldington appears to have convinced H.D. that the affair with Flo had been a passing fancy; he had written to say: 'Hang Flo & damn Carl . . . For God's sake, love your Faun', and she eventually managed to take his advice.[85] If she were less distressed about Aldington's infidelity, however, she was still living under extreme strain. She said to Cournos in early October, about her outpouring of work: 'Everything burns me – everything seems to become significant – the most sordid, mud-dragged leaf has its meaning. This is wonderful, this life for me – but I am torn and burnt physically.' The quelling of one anxiety again only served to offer space for another, and she began to agonise over the war; everything seemed 'worthless, futile in the face of this world-calamity'. The battle of the Somme was drawing to its indecisive end, and the horrific loss of life on both sides appalled many besides H.D. This was the war that Aldington would have to join. Yet she was continuing with her work for the *Egoist*. In September she wrote a warm review of *The Farmer's Bride* by May Sinclair's friend, Charlotte Mew, which had been brought out by the Poetry Bookshop. This was doubtless partly a favour to Sinclair, who recommended it to every editor she knew; H.D. was one of the few to oblige. When Pound saw her reviews, he commented that she shouldn't be allowed to write criticism; a surprising judgement, as they seem entirely cogent. Perhaps he was put out that she had praised Mew's gifts as a dramatic lyricist in the Browning tradition, without mentioning his.

In the October *Egoist*, H.D. included a poem by Williams, entitled 'March', about the desperate longing for spring induced by the drawn-out East Coast winters, the same idea that would lie behind his 1920 prose poems, *Kora in Hell*. She had made some changes, and Williams was outraged to see it appear in a 'purified form', 'thanks', he says, 'to her own and her husband's friendly attentions'. H.D. had written to him to say she had removed the 'flippancies' which to her mind spoilt the beauty of the poem: 'I don't know what you think but I consider this business of writing a very sacred thing!' Williams was furious at this aesthetic piety, writing two years later, when he recounted this story: 'There is nothing sacred about literature, it is damned from one end to the other. There is nothing in literature but change and change is mockery. I'll write whatever I damn please and as I damn please and it'll be good if the authentic spirit of change is on it.' He believed, he said, in the 'inventive imagination' which gives 'deliverance from every other misfortune as from the desolation of a flat Hellenic perfection of style'.[86] Williams' anger is understandable, though he did admit that what H.D. had excised had been derivative, but without knowing the original version it is hard to judge if she was being blinkered or showing good editorial sense. Williams passed on the story to Pound, who commended him for refusing to write 'Alexandrine greek bunk, to conform to the ideas of that refined, charming, and utterly narrow minded she-bard "H.D."'[87] Improving other people's verses was his prerogative. H.D.'s boldness in seizing the editorial pencil possibly increased Pound's desire to move back into a position of influence at the *Egoist*. As he had said to Flint, he was well aware that both the Aldingtons were entirely out of sympathy with what Yeats described as his 'violent' poems, but if they were beginning to censor his friends he must do something about it.

By October, Fletcher's warmth of feeling for his fellow imagists had waned once more, and he wrote to Lowell, sending his contributions for the 1917 anthology but simultaneously saying he hoped it would not appear; the other four's contributions were hopeless, and in any case he wasn't an imagist: 'I do not believe a poem should present an "image", I believe it should present an emotion. I do not believe in "clear, hard and definite presentation". I believe in complete, that is to say, shifting and fluid presentation.' In that last point, most modernist novelists would be in tune with him, and one can only applaud when he says he does not believe that the 'exact word' is possible. He is, he says, a 'Rhythmist or a Symbolist, not an Imagist.'[88] Intriguingly enough, an appreciation of his poetry appeared in the November *Egoist* making these very points, and describing him as 'amongst the most important of modern writers in English'. It was by one R. Herdman Pender, surprisingly for the middle of the war, from Ruhleben in Germany. One might even wonder if it could be Fletcher under a pseudonym, but he told Glenn Hughes later that Pender was a civilian prisoner of war and publisher, who had written to ask for his books; Fletcher must have replied in similar terms to those he used to Lowell.[89] But for now he told Amy that she had no need to publish as one of a set of poets who produced such poor stuff: she should bury imagism and start a new American group if she wanted to lead a movement. He continued to protest his loyalty to her, though implying pointedly that the others did not appreciate her. There is no doubt Fletcher's misanthropic bile would help to fissure the group, but Lowell was already aware she no longer needed her fellow-imagists. *Men, Women and Ghosts* had sold all but 300 of the 1,250 copies of its first edition by the time of publication, and within a couple of months was in its third, and her lecturing career was going from strength to strength. Despite her affection for the Aldingtons, she felt acutely their coolness towards some of her poetry; Aldington had now taken against her polyphonic prose, and she felt that H.D thought much of her narrative poetry insufficiently imagistic. She brooded over the effusiveness of H.D.'s review of Marianne Moore, which she obscurely felt was a rebuke to herself. All the same, she felt deeply concerned for them and had no wish to distress them further; she had said she would support the anthologies for three years, and she would honour her word.

Although Fletcher had been so admiring of *Sea Garden*, he now announced that he considered H.D.'s new long poem, 'The Tribute,' of which Aldington had written glowingly to Lowell, a sad falling away. 'The Tribute' (published in the November *Egoist*) is more explicitly concerned with the war than H.D.'s other poems, though perhaps less successful for that; it is more insistent on its message, an attempt to write more directly about the political world, which so far she had paradoxically attempted only in her translations from Euripides. Louis Martz sees this and her poem 'Cities' as her first move towards a prophetic voice, which would be so important in her later poetry. The subject-matter is still not directly contemporary, but the implications are clear. In 'The Tribute', the city has been gripped by the 'squalor' of war frenzy; all the old gods are banished save one, a phallic war-god. The young men have gone to war, 'the songs withered black on their lips'; only a few of those left, including the speaker of the poem, would not 'sing to the god of the lance', but instead search for a god of healing to return to the city. Like Pound, the poem associates war-mongering with the marketplace, with 'the haggling, the beggar, the cheat', but in the end asserts that beauty can never 'be done to death'.[90] It may have been of poems like 'The Tribute' and 'Cities' that Pound was thinking the next year, when he told Margaret Anderson that, although H.D. was still doing work as good as the early poems that he had admired so much, she had also 'let loose dilutions and repetitions, so that she has spoiled the "few but perfect" position which she might have held on to'.[91] He of course blames the 'flow-contamination' of Lowell and Fletcher, but I think Martz is right that it was a first move towards a different form of writing, which would make possible poems like her powerful Second World War *Trilogy* and the later *Helen in Egypt*.

H.D. must have had doubts about the poem herself; having sent it

to Lowell for inclusion in the 1917 anthology, she then very firmly withdrew it, but its insistence that it was the duty of the artist to preserve
what was of value to the human spirit in this destructive wartime world
was increasingly important to her; it was, perhaps, the point she had
tried to make to Williams, though he took it so ill. During the autumn
of 1916 she wrote a number of prose pieces embodying her feelings
about the war, some of which she sent to Aldington or Cournos; they
remained unpublished at the time, though one in particular she thought
of publishing in the *Egoist* unsigned. This may well have been a remarkable short review-essay, in the end only published posthumously, about
Yeats' *Responsibilities* (presumably not the 1914 edition, but the extended
version published in 1916). Like the review of Moore's poetry, it is an
indirect manifesto for her own poetic mission: in it she outlines her
belief that art and the artist must stand against the forces of war and
destruction, and struggle to find a transformative vision of a more
humane and healing world. H.D. had never in the past shared Pound's
admiration for Yeats, and she begins by saying she had been wary of
what she describes as the 'misty transient beauty' of Yeats' earlier poetry.
In *Reponsibilities*, however, 'there are poems of another mood of a greater,
sterner intensity'. It is a change comparable to her own sense of the
need to reject the 'over-sweet' and seek 'a new beauty/in some
terrible/wind-tortured place'.

Yeats, H.D. says in this review, tells his readers he is almost forty-nine,
but he speaks to her generation, with their world changed irrevocably by the war. Some are dead, others at the front may yet return,
she hopes 'not broken by the bitterness of their experience', but in spite
of it 'taut and aflame for the creation of beauty'. Those few who are
left at home are 'crouched as in a third line of battered trenches . . .
hanging on against all odds, in the wavering belief that we are the link,
the torch-bearers'. The enemy her generation battles against is not, as
in the 1890s, 'the so-called middle-classes', but 'a more treacherous
force . . . the great overwhelming mechanical daemon, the devil of
machinery, of which we can hardly repeat too often, the war is the
hideous offspring'. Worst of all, 'inasmuch as its cubes and angles seem
a sort of incantation, a symbol for the forces that brought this world
calamity, her 'generation did not stand against the enemy – it *was* the
enemy . . . The black magic of triangles and broken arcs has conquered
and we who are helpless before this force of destruction can only hope
for some more powerful magic, some subtle and more potent daemon
to set it right.' Her generation must 'wait, endure, confess the past was

all a mistake', and 'chastened with old calamities, redefine and reconstruct boundaries and barriers, and reinvoke some golden city, sterner
than the dream-cities, and wrought more firm to endure those riveted
of steel and bleak with iron girders'.[92]

H.D. may not have published this because it was too direct a critique
of the Vorticists, their erstwhile allies, now mainly at the front themselves, and in the case of Gaudier, dead. After all, 'Oread' had been
picked out as the exemplary Vorticist poem by Pound, who would
certainly have been infuriated, and indeed, given his disagreement earlier
that year with Yeats over Lewis' machine-like art, might have found her
analysis of Yeats' opposition to Vorticism most disagreeably perceptive.
But if H.D. was sparing Pound's feelings, he had no such compunction
about blasting Amy's imagism, which he had described that April in
Poetry, perhaps as spoiling copy for the May anthology, as having gone
'off into froth', its 'chief defects' being 'sloppiness, lack of cohesion . . .
rhetoric, a conventional form of language . . . and in some cases a
tendency more than slight towards the futurist's cinematographic
fluidity'. But that was largely aimed at Lowell and Fletcher; he picks
H.D. out in the same piece as one of the best of contemporary American
poets.[93]

What H.D.'s review-article does perhaps reveal is how, though so
near breakdown for much of the war, she survived its lacerations; she
positions herself not as a victim, but an artist with a 'task', as she puts
it in 'Cities', that of 'recall[ing] the old splendour' and awaiting 'the
new beauty of cities'.[94] She and Pound differed over Vorticism, but the
war had led both of them to a belief in the role that the artist must play
in restoring a broken society. Perhaps this sense of a mission, even if
in this war not so clearly worked through as in her *Trilogy* during the
next, was one reason why she was so reluctant to leave England, as
Aldington was pressing her to do. He wanted her to return home for
the duration of the war, for though crossing the Atlantic was becoming
more dangerous, with the number of ships going down soon to be one
in four, once home she could escape the strains of wartime London,
and live surrounded by the comfort and affection of her family. For a
while she agreed, feeling she ought to reduce his worries, but one can
imagine that the thought of giving up her freedom horrified her. She
went as far as booking her passage for mid-November but changed her
mind at the last moment, telling Amy, who was deeply disappointed,
that she wasn't coming because Richard's transfer to France had been
delayed, and she didn't want to leave the country while he was still

there. When Aldington wrote to Lowell about it he said she was having too good a time to leave: scarcely the case, but he was probably right to guess it was more than just devotion to him. Flint, incidentally, strongly advised her not to go; he could see it would have been disastrous for her. Aldington eventually left for France on 21 December 1916; he had been training in the north of England, and was now a lance-corporal. He was sent straight from the training camp without a final leave, but H.D., who had now moved back to London, went to Waterloo to see him off. He would not be back until the middle of 1917.

1916 had been a year of stalemate and mutual carnage at the front, and of increasing pessimism at home. In early December, Lloyd George manoeuvred the gentlemanly but ineffectual Asquith into resignation, and became Prime Minister in his stead. Lawrence wrote gloomily to Amy that at least there had been some 'old English *decency*' in Asquith. Lloyd George, on the other hand, was 'a clever little Welsh *rat*, absolutely dead at the core, sterile, barren, mechanical'.[95] There was no immediate improvement in Britain's fortunes; for civilians 1917 would be the worst year of the war, with increasing shortages of fuel and food as the German blockade began to bite, and, for those in London, a steep rise in the number of air raids. In those terms, H.D.'s return to London was badly timed, but it was where she wanted to be.

H.D. had taken a room in a large Bloomsbury house, 44 Mecklenburgh Square, owned by a Miss James, a Fabian, supporter of the suffrage movement and a woman of immense respectability. She lived on the premises and expected her lodgers to behave with sober propriety, an expectation doomed to disappointment when renting out a number of rooms to independent young people in the later years of the war. H.D.'s room on the second floor was spacious, with three long windows; John Cournos had had a smaller room near the top of the house for some time. H.D. and Aldington corresponded frequently, the delivery of post to and from the front being extremely good; Aldington was stationed near Cambrai in northern France, for the most part away from the main action, so he suffered more from discomfort, dirt and boredom than danger and was able to do a certain amount of writing. Some gruelling action came in the late spring; in *Death of a Hero* we are told of George that since 'Arras (April '17) he had lived on his nerves', and that by then he was 'a bit off his head, as nearly all the troops are after six months in the line'.[96] The only extant letters of H.D.'s in these months are to Amy; mainly about the placing of poems and the anthology, they give little of her feelings away. Lawrence, however, commented in a letter that she was 'very sad and suppressed'.[97] She continued to hate the air raids – on one occasion the house next door was struck – but she fell in love with the cinema, much frequented by soldiers on leave, who like her gladly lost themselves in the vicarious terrors of filmic melodrama. In *Bid Me to Live*, she describes one visit. Watching a car careering round hairpin bends, Julia thinks: 'the old Greek *katharsis* was at work here, as in the stone-ledged theatre benches of fifth-century Greece; so here, a thousand doomed, the dead were watching destruction, Oedipus or Orestes in a slim car, dashing to destruction . . . She was part of this. She swerved and veered with a thousand men in khaki, toward destruction.' But the car reaches its destination. A beautiful woman comes out: 'Venus . . . Persephone in Enna, Primavera . . . Beauty was not dead. It emerged unexpectedly in the midst of this frantic maelstrom.'[98] Both Pound and Aldington despised the cinema and its audiences, but for H.D. it was a mythic medium, speaking a universal language.

H.D. was continuing to write and to work as assistant editor at the *Egoist*, and she saw much of her friends. She was back in touch with Olivia Shakespear, and occasionally saw Pound, and Brigit when she was in London. Flint and his wife she saw regularly, and every one or two weeks she and Cournos met up with Fletcher, who was feeling more warmly again towards his fellow-imagists. In the December 1916 *Egoist*, he had written a review of Lawrence's *Amores*, not wholly uncritical but commenting perceptively that Lawrence was 'quite free from any suspicion of posing, and nakedly honest with himself and the world'; he had also contributed an article on war poetry, which was, surprisingly, given his recent rant to Lowell, a defence of imagism. In the same issue, H.D. had written an appreciative review of *Goblins and Pagodas*, commending his 'moving, whirling, drifting' poetry. With her love of film she was much more appreciative of his cinematic-like techniques than Pound was, her comments no doubt irritating Pound once more, though reassuring Fletcher.[99] One might have imagined that Fletcher would be feeling more confident about his poetry, as he had been awarded the $100 *Poetry* prize that November for his Arizona poems, but he had been so depressed that at first he turned it down, though he changed his mind two days later. He had been deeply upset that Lowell's ally, William S. Braithwaite, had described her in the *Boston Evening*

Transcript as the only worthwhile imagist; he was sure the slight to him was her doing, and was outraged when he discovered that Houghton Mifflin had turned down a collection of despairing and intemperate love poems that he had submitted to them because, when asked, Lowell had found herself unable to say that they were his best work. For the first time he attacked her directly and angrily, and whilst it would not be the end of their relationship – he would wax hot and cold several more times – it was never the same. Amy herself had had a difficult autumn; she had been seriously ill and in great pain for two months, as the result of a hernia that would eventually prove fatal, and when her beloved elder brother Percival died in November, had been too weak to be told for several days. Fletcher's bitter and unjustified complaints upset her greatly. She wrote, remonstrating against his unfairness but offering to pay for the book's publication. Fletcher did not take the offer up, but he was somewhat mollified by the fact that Lowell was working on some lectures, later to be published as a book, *Tendencies in American Poetry*, on six contemporary American poets, including himself and H.D. She wrote to each asking for anecdotes about their youth, and Fletcher replied expansively, though H.D. said her life was without incident. The resourceful Amy wrote to her mother instead, who was more obliging.

Given Fletcher's stormy anguish over Amy and Daisy, both women he in very different ways needed desperately and resented bitterly, the meetings with H.D. and Cournos were a lifeline. Daisy became jealous of H.D. – not conducive to domestic harmony should it ever have existed – but if Fletcher was enamoured of anyone it was Cournos, whom he adulated. Just before he left the States Fletcher had fallen briefly under the spell of a young poet called Edward O'Brian, as he had much earlier at Harvard of his fellow student Lyman Rogers, who had introduced him to aestheticism and Nietzsche. Now he hero-worshipped Cournos, entranced by his gentle charm and brilliant conversation. Fletcher's biographer suggests that it was Cournos who 'encouraged the evolution from the aesthetic Impressionism dominant in his early London work to the mythic Romanticism' of his later writing.[100] Fletcher's career is often described in two stages, his imagist period, which Pound would have agreed was really impressionist, and then the later period when he became identified with the politically conservative and backward looking Southern Agrarian school in the States. But Fletcher was never really part of anyone else's movement.

What Cournos undoubtedly fostered in Fletcher were the anti-industrialist convictions that had always been there, earlier expressed in his short-lived Ruskinian and socialist phases, and later making him sympathetic to the Agrarians' rejection of modern industrial society. Cournos himself divided modern artists into two classes: those for and those against the machine. He writes in his autobiography that 'there was, on the one hand, the art of men like Cézanne, Matisse, Van Gogh and Gauguin, which rebelled against the Machine and the culture it invoked; and on the other, the chaotic art of the Futurists and the methodical, mechanical art of the school of Picasso, both wholeheart-edly, in their own way, accepting the Machine and what the Machine implies in the culture of our time'.[101] When Fletcher wrote a book on Gauguin a couple of years later, it would be in this spirit. Perhaps Cournos had influenced H.D. in her rejection of the Vorticists' 'black magic of triangles and broken arcs'; she certainly later credited him with being one of her 'initiators', the male figures who had taken her through crucial stages in her artistic development, and who included Pound, Aldington and Lawrence. But perhaps she influenced him. Be that as it may, Cournos, Fletcher and H.D. found they agreed in their opposition to what they saw as the machine's dehumanising force, the apotheosis of which was what Lawrence described as 'the huge obscene machine they call the war'.[102] It was in fact an attitude that all the 'Amygists', with the possible exception of Amy herself, shared. Self-consciously modern though they were, in this they remained heirs to the Romantics and the Pre-Raphaelites, and felt the distance growing between them-selves and Pound, with his continued association with Lewis and Vorticism and his mounting tendency to present, however misleadingly, his poetics as a break with the Romantic past. Mechanised modernity was less of an overt concern for Lowell than the others; her family wealth came from the New England cotton-mills, so she had a literal investment in modern industry and remained a stout defender of capi-talism. She could write exuberantly about the noise and clamour of modern cities, yet her poetry is repeatedly concerned, as for example in 'The Captured Goddess', with bringing the transcendent and the vibrant back into the urban scene; two of the poets she admired most were Romantics: Coleridge (she saw his influence on Poe as crucial for the development of the line of American poetry that led to work like her own) and Keats, whose biography she would soon start to write.

H.D. may have kept her own criticisms of the Vorticists to herself, but she encouraged Cournos to write a piece about the artist Christopher Nevinson, who before the war had so eagerly embraced Marinetti's Futurism; whether or not she had realised he would also set his sights on Vorticism, she let it appear in the January 1917 *Egoist*. In it Cournos praised a recent exhibition of paintings by Nevinson, who had relinquished Futurism after experiencing life at the front and had returned to more representational work, which, Cournos says, 'preserves just enough of the geometric touch to give poignancy to the mechanical nature of our age and to the machine-like qualities of our armies'. The article was entitled 'The Death of Futurism', but not only does he say that Futurism is dead as an art form, he insists that so is 'Vorticism and all those "brother arts", whose masculomaniac spokesmen spoke glibly in their green-red-yellow-becushioned boudoirs of "the glory of war" and "contempt for women"'.[103] That is not entirely fair to the Vorticists who, aggressive though they were, did not glorify war, but the point he also makes that their art could now appear prophetic of the war was true enough, as even Lewis would later agree.

Nevinson was not alone in retreating from abstract forms. Gaudier's return to more organic forms had been followed by Epstein and Wadsworth, the latter also after experiencing life at the front, whilst Epstein's work had begun to change even before he was conscripted. The same would happen to Lewis soon after he reached the war zone later that year. The dehumanisation and destruction of the war prompted what he described as an instinctual revulsion from the mechanical and the abstract; in his memoir, *Rude Assignment*, he writes that when he was in the 'hideous desert known as "the Line" in Flanders and France . . . subject matter so consonant with the austerity of that "abstract" vision', valued by the Vorticists, he found himself impelled to bring humanity back to it: 'when Mars with his mailed finger showed me a shell crater and a skeleton with a couple of shivered tree stumps behind it, I was still in my "abstract" element. And before I knew quite what I was doing I was drawing with loving care a signaller corporal to plant upon the lip of the shell crater.'[104] Like Nevinson, Lewis never returned to a straightforward realism, but, as in his later powerful portraits of Pound and Eliot, developed a highly stylised, geometric fashion of drawing. In fact, of course, few even of his most Vorticist drawings had been entirely abstract; as he had written in the first *Blast*, 'The finest Art is not pure Abstraction, nor is it unorganised life.'[105]

Both Pound and Hulme had been dismayed by these defections; it is a pity they had fallen out or they might have consoled each other. In 1916, Pound had begun to plan a book on Lewis, and Hulme one on Epstein; neither was ever written. Ferguson suggests that Hulme – usually a rapid writer – could not make progress because he was too disturbed by Epstein's move away from abstraction, which Hulme was still advocating as the true modern art. Given Pound's earlier distress over rumours of Gaudier's retreat from Vorticism, he may well have abandoned his book on Lewis for similar reasons; though he was not without praise for Lewis' later work, he firmly expressed his preference for his more abstract style. If, between the wars, Lewis was to criticise Pound as a *passéiste*, Pound saw Lewis as an artistic backslider. Other artists in Europe, of course, went on pursuing abstract forms after the war (Pound especially admired Brancusi and Picabia), but it was perhaps because the Vorticist rhetoric had so much implied that abstraction, brutality, the machine and aggression were all intimately bound up, that when the bigger Blasts, as Lewis called them, began, and all the horrors of modern mechanical warfare became apparent, abstraction seemed to be on the side of death and carnage. Possibly the very fact that Pound had ignored the praise of the machine meant that for him Vorticism and abstract art had no such connotations. Yet the stylised, geometric quasi-realism to which the Vorticists moved produced some fine works of art, which owed much to the earlier experiments with abstraction, even if they did not fit Pound and Hulme's theories. And although Cournos was right that Futurism would die in Britain, it would survive on the continent, and be closely linked with the growing Fascist movement. Nor was Vorticism yet entirely dead; John Quinn had put on the exhibition in New York, even if it stirred little interest, or at least not among those who could afford to buy. And Pound had, along with the photographer Alvin Langdon Coburn, developed a form of abstract Vorticist photography, shown in an exhibition of 'Vortographs' that February, at the opening of which, Pound told Henderson, 'Arbuthnot, Fletcher's friend, made a few intelligent remarks'.[106] Those were, however, Vorticism's last rites: Cournos' assertion that Vorticism was over had a considerable measure of truth, but that cannot have endeared the piece to Pound, and it is surely no coincidence that around this time he began to plan to remove the assistant editorship from H.D., and transfer it to T.S. Eliot.

Reading Cournos' article now, however, what stands out most is his rejection of 'contempt for women' and 'masculomania' (his own inventive coinage), a very different stance from that of most of the male artists H.D. knew, perhaps one reason why he was so important to her at the time. As a Philadelphian Jew, Cournos, like her, knew what it was to be treated as a second-class citizen; the belligerent assertion of masculine authority was not for him. Otto Weininger's enormously popular book of 1903, *Sex and Character*, reprinted numerous times, had argued that Jews, like women, are inferior to true men, and cannot be treated as truly masculine. It was a widespread view, of which Cournos was undoubtedly well aware. Not that he was free of the macho modernists' penchant for feminising their opponents, as his reference to the Vorticists' 'becushioned boudoirs' indicates, but he was less aggressively assertive in other ways. In later life, H.D. would recall how in these early days she had to struggle to keep her poetic talents from being overwhelmed by the powerful male artistic egos around her, whether Pound, Aldington or Lawrence. Cournos never posed the same threat. Yet he had his own masculine pride, and was growing more and more resentful that H.D. appeared to see him as a lesser man than Aldington. He finally tried to persuade her to go to bed with him; she rejected him indignantly, saying he should know their relationship was a purely spiritual one. Cournos was deeply humiliated; though H.D. thought their friendship went on as before, he would never forgive her.[107]

When Lowell wrote to H.D. in mid-February 1917 with the half-yearly royalties, she was able to tell her that the 1915 anthology was now in its third edition, and the 1916 one in its second: imagism had made its mark. The 1916 anthology had even had an enthusiastic review that January in the *Times Literary Supplement*, of all places, which had begun, 'Imagist poetry fills us with hope'. And in America, there appeared for the first time the suggestion, which would be eagerly taken up, that imagism was really an indigenous American form. In February 1917, *Poetry* had published an issue devoted to Native American poetry; or rather, largely poems by white poets 'interpreting' Indian traditions. The passionate interest that Alice Corbin Henderson had developed in the south-west in their culture was shared by Harriet Monroe, who contributed an editorial that showed remarkable if eclectic knowledge of the translations of Indian songs and rituals published by the Bureau of American Ethnology, and made an eloquent plea for the preservation of their way of life, in particular their 'beautiful primitive poetry'. The Native Americans, especially the Pueblos of the south-west, were now seen by many of America's intelligentsia as having a culture, albeit now under threat, that fostered artistic creation, unlike theirs, which Lawrence, making the same contrast, described as 'mechanical America'. But it was Carl Sandburg who made the crucial comparison with imagism. Writing about the translations of Indian songs made by the ethnomusicologist Frances Densmore – which did indeed look like brief, imagistic poems on the page – he commented: 'Suspicion arises definitely that the Red Man and his children committed direct plagiarisms on the modern imagists and vorticists.' It was an idea that was taken up by others. The next year Henderson would write: 'Whether it is due to the spirit of the land reacting upon our poets to make them like the earlier owners of soil and sky, or whether it is due to some other cause, certain it is that those Indian poems are very similar in spirit and method to the poetry of our most modern American poets.' She compared them with Chinese poetry, thinking of Pound's *Cathay*, 'the same realism, the same concrete simplicity, and acceptance of the commonplace experience'.[108]

This Native American issue of *Poetry* indicated a radical change in attitude to this culture, comparable indeed to the earlier discovery of the Japanese haiku, early Chinese poetry and Tagore's Bengali lyrics, and to Hulme and the Vorticists' embrace of non-Western art forms, an opening up to the possibility of artistic work beyond the bounds of European culture. Native Americans did possess rich mythic and poetic literary traditions, and if the comparison with the imagists was based on scant knowledge, misapprehensions and the dubious self-deluding desire to claim an authentic American heritage, it was none the less significant as part of the modernist reappraisal of the value of Western society in relation to other world traditions. Indeed, a good part of the appeal of imagist poetry had always been to the inherent primitivism that was so much part of modernism; its pared-down simplicity had suggested something elemental, a direct apprehension of a deeper truth that had more validity and power than what were now often felt to be the superficial elaborations of modern culture. When another admirer of Native American culture, Mary Austin, argued in 1919 that *vers libre* and imagism were 'primitive' forms, she meant it as significant praise; she too insisted that whether written by Native Americans or her Euro-American contemporaries they were 'generically American forms, forms instinctively created by people living in America and freed from outside influence'.[109] Given the plethora of influences from which Pound and H.D. evolved their imagism, that was hardly a defensible position, yet H.D. was the poet whose Greek-inflected work was picked as most comparable to the Native American. Harriet Monroe, for example, would later suggest that in carrying English poetry back to the Greeks, who 'like all singers of primitive races, were never indoors', she produced work that was more 'akin to our aborigines than it is the Elizabethans or Victorians'.[110]

The imagist most intrigued by Native American culture was Fletcher;

he had been thrilled by the February issue of *Poetry*, and must have been delighted two years later that when Henderson reviewed an anthology of translations and 'interpretations' of Native American poetry, with the Navajo-derived title of *The Path on the Rainbow*, she expressed regret that Fletcher's poems on Native American themes had not been included. In spite of all Henderson's attempts to draw a response from him, Pound never commented on the Native American issue; for him, imagism was poetry, drawing on world literature, and never solely American. Yet this claim that imagism was indigenous was just one indication of its wide acceptance among educated readers in America. Reviewing the 1917 *Some Imagist Poets*, Henderson would comment: 'Nowadays everyone is writing imagist *vers libre*, or what the writers conceive as such, particularly those who at the beginning made the most outcry against it. Free verse is now accepted in good society, where rhymed verse is even considered a little shabby and old-fashioned.'[111] If the same could not be said for England, the fact remains that the third *Georgian Poetry* anthology, when it came out later in 1918, had a far less warm review in the *TLS* than the imagists had had; its conservatism was now seen as a matter for regret, though in fact the best of the poets that volume published, Isaac Rosenberg and Siegfried Sassoon, were writing verse whose vigour and stinging power the new poetic climate had helped make possible.

Yet if an avant-garde school started to be praised by the *TLS*, perhaps it was time to shut up shop. And this the imagists did. The 1917 anthology appeared in the States on 14 April, but eight days earlier America had joined the war on the side of the Allies. Poetry sales slumped, and even the 'demon saleswoman' of poetry, Lowell, was unable to create the same level of interest as there had been in the early volumes. It was a slightly briefer collection, and overall uneven, though Flint had some of his strongest work there, in poems that came out of his Devon visit and wartime London, and the poems that H.D. had eventually chosen for the volume were all impressive, particularly 'Eurydice', a powerful, driven persona poem in the mode that she had developed in her Devon anguish. Disappointingly, by August it had sold just 430 copies. Indeed, only a few copies can have reached England before the end of the war, as in March it had been announced that consignments of books could no longer be imported into Britain. Houghton Mifflin sent plates to be printed on the spot, but the ship went down, and by the time they heard the news, a ban had been placed on printers' plates as well. Only individual copies could be sent.

Amy decided the time had come to call a halt to the anthologies. She hesitated to break the news to her fellow-imagists, but when Flint wrote to her in June to ask if there would be an anthology in 1918, she had to confess. She wrote individually to Flint and H.D. on 14 July, and then to Richard on the 20th. To Flint, she said that the third anthology had not done as well as the first two, though his poem 'Zeppelins' and Fletcher's 'Lincoln' had been much praised. The fact that the anthology had made less impact, she was sure, was nothing to do with the quality of the poetry; America's entry into the war meant that cultural matters were now neglected. All the same, she added,

I think myself that the anthology has done its work and done it remarkably well. I think it has given us all a wider audience than we should have had without it, but I think its time as a collection has passed, and it would be better for us now to depend upon our own books. Everybody knows what Imagism is, and Imagistic work has become (here in America) a test stone for a certain kind of writing, which is what we desired . . . Certainly the soil is tilled and ready, and it is up to us to get a harvest out of it. These 'Anthologies' have been the plough, and our own books must be the sowing of the seed.[112]

But, as she said in her letter to H.D., she was also finding the imagist path too narrow: 'I know you people do not follow me in all my experiments, but I suppose that is inevitable, as we become more individual we shall each depart more and more from the group ideal. Still, I feel that we shall all be more in sympathy with each other than with any other.'[113]

H.D., as it happened, never received this. Though written on the same day as the one to Flint, they must have left the States by different boats. H.D.'s went down, while Flint's arrived safely. Aldington passed on the news to H.D., who wrote to thank Amy for all her work; she told her how grateful she was for the experience of working as a family of poets, as it had felt to her, but agreed it was right they should move on in their different directions. She and Fletcher, she said, were both in transitional phases, and, aware that Amy felt she censured her less imagist work, added tactfully how admirably Lowell's work was broadening. Flint was the most disappointed of the group; he told Amy in October that he was 'melancholy at the thought that the blooming old (it has reached that stage) anthology is to cease'.[114] With his pressured life, the co-operative activity of the anthology helped to keep him in touch with his fellow-writers in a way he found invaluable. Fletcher had no such regrets; he was entirely ready to repudiate his imagist years. Lawrence would doubtless have contributed to a fourth anthology if asked, but, never having been convinced that he was an imagist, or indeed that there was really a style that could be isolated as imagism, was unconcerned with the movement's demise. Imagism would continue to be praised, censured and debated for some time, but the imagist group were rapidly to go their separate ways.

VII

WITH Amy bowing out, Pound lost interest, at any rate for now – he would periodically return to the charge – in claiming the movement. The three writers that he was now bent on promoting were Joyce, Lewis and Eliot: none of them had been imagists, even if Joyce had had one poem in *Des Imagistes* and Eliot's most famous poem, *The Waste Land*, can be read as a series of imagist poems. In the latter half of 1917, Pound, with Eliot's help, commenced a campaign against what he saw as the excesses of *vers libre*. Eliot contributed an elegant dismissal of the form, deploring its ubiquity but paradoxically insisting that '*Vers Libre* does not exist . . . there is no freedom in art . . . *vers libre* which is good is anything but "free"'.[115] Pound summed up their rearguard action many years later, explaining that:

at a particular date in a particular room, two authors, neither engaged in picking the other's pocket, decided that the dilutation of *vers libre*, Amygism, Lee Masterism, general floppiness had gone too far and that some counter-current must be set going. Parallel situation centuries ago in China. Remedy prescribed 'Émaux et Camées' (or the Bay State Hymn Book). Rhyme and regular strophes.[116]

The result of this application of 'rhyme and regular strophes' would be, on his part, *Hugh Selwyn Mauberley*, published in 1920, Pound's farewell to London and to lyric poetry. From then on in his own writing he would concentrate on his major work, the *Cantos*, neither rhymed nor in strophe, and owing much to his earlier experiments with both *vers libre* and his persona poems. Although he moaned in the *Egoist* that July that 'it is too late to prevent vers libre', one can only try to 'improve it', he acknowledged that if he criticised the 'versi libristi', the 'anti-versilibristi' were worse. He stressed, as always, attention to music, and all the imagists would have concurred with the advice he quoted from the composer Couperin on the need to remember the superiority of cadence over measure: 'Cadence is properly the spirit, the soul that must be added.'[117] In Pound's development, 1917 was important not so much for his attack on Amygism as for the publication of the first three cantos in *Poetry*, though they would be radically rewritten by the time that version appeared in print, and many times again. Those ur-*Cantos* are full of his memories of all that had happened to him since he came to Europe, particularly that walking tour, when he felt the presence of the troubadours so powerfully; 'Ghosts move around me/Patched with histories,' he writes, recalling his experience on Salisbury Plain, which he links again with the Provençal poets, as he had in his letter to Flint, and he thinks of 'olive Sirmio', one of the places where 'Gods float in the azure air', and of his time in Venice. Although he would not be satisfied with those versions, they contain, as Ronald Bush has argued, many elements that would remain.[118] In addition, 1917 was the year of his ebullient quasi-translation, *Homage to Sextus Propertius*, also in *vers libre*. He persuaded John Quinn to fund an American edition of *Lustra*, a great deal less censored than the English one, in itself an interesting indication of the dramatic speed with which American metropolitan culture was changing; he had Eliot write a pamphlet, entitled *Ezra Pound: His Metric and Poetry*, which stressed the technical excellence of his work, so the reader could contrast his discipline and professionalism with what Pound called 'Amy's gush and Fletcher's squibbs'.[119] (It was published anonymously at the time – Pound was promoting Eliot so busily in so many arenas, it would not have looked good if it were known that Eliot was in turn promoting him.) Eliot himself produced some well-turned stanzaic poems, ironic and polished, such as 'The Hippopotamus', 'Whispers of Immortality' and the now notorious 'Burbank with a Baedeker: Bleistein with a cigar' ('The rats are underneath the piles./The Jew is underneath the lot'); at the time, no one appears to have noticed the anti-Semitism.[120] Eliot had always, however, moved between stanzaic, rhymed forms and *vers libre*, and would continue to do so. Even his last poems, the *Four Quartets*, use both forms. As he said in early 1917, it is the 'contrast between fixity and flux' which is 'the very life of verse', adding, in the magisterial style he was so rapidly perfecting, 'the division between Conservative verse and *vers libre* does not exist, for there is only good verse, bad verse and chaos'.[121] In Eliot's career 1917 was significant for the publication of his first book of poetry, *Prufrock and Other Observations*, which Pound had worked hard to get brought out. He had failed with Elkin Mathews, with whom his influence was waning in the wake of the *Lustra* débâcle, but generous Miss Weaver agreed to publish it with the Egoist Press.

Pound in 1917 was himself earning little: in spite of his productivity, few of his ventures paid well, yet over the next couple of years he was perhaps in the most powerful position that he would ever acquire as a shaper of the modern scene. He was acting as unpaid art dealer for John Quinn, aiding several careers and reputations. He was still foreign correspondent for *Poetry*, and in addition developed a link with Margaret Anderson's *Little Review*, now based in New York but in financial straits. He persuaded Quinn to underwrite it, with himself as foreign editor, controlling a certain number of pages where he could publish himself, Joyce, Lewis, Eliot and others, paying for their work with money direct from Quinn. According to H.D., when the *Little Review* started in 1914 Pound had been rather scornful about it, and he had written somewhat condescendingly to Monroe that it would be a 'jolly place for people who aren't quite up to our level', though in fact they frequently published the same writers.[122] The *Little Review*, however, unlike *Poetry*, had no money with which to pay contributors, possibly the reason Pound himself did not send any contributions until 1916. Yet he cannot have failed to notice that Anderson was a much bolder editor than Monroe, no doubt why he decided to home in on her magazine. His new position was announced in the issue for April 1917, and almost at once he was able to send the *Little Review* some Yeats poems. Henderson and Monroe felt betrayed that Pound, still officially *Poetry*'s foreign editor, should make this new arrangement without letting them know, and disparaging *Poetry* to boot in his first contribution to their rival: it was the end of Henderson's warm relationship with him. Pound was undeterred. Lewis contributed a short story, 'Cantelman's Spring-mate', to the October *Little Review*, which was immediately seized and suppressed for offending public morality – as Lewis loved to do – but the most controversial and significant work Pound obtained for the *Little Review* was *Ulysses*, which they serialised; four of the issues in which episodes appeared were seized and burnt, for Anderson, a badge of honour.

In June Pound succeeded in moving T.S. Eliot into the assistant editorship of the *Egoist*, with John Quinn paying him £9 a quarter, so he now had considerable influence over three different outlets. Pound had had intermittent discussions with Weaver for some time, raising the matter again in January at the time of Cournos' onslaught, and there is no doubt he was keen to bring the *Egoist* back on message. In the end, however, the change was probably negotiated with H.D. and Aldington rather than a take-over. Although their old intimacy had not revived, they were for now once more on reasonably friendly terms, which would scarcely have been the case if they felt he had shoehorned H.D. out. Richard had a piece in the June issue, and H.D. a poem in July. Pound was delighted when Aldington came back on leave in June, and appeared to take a personal pride in the fact that he had been recommended for a commission; Aldington was equally pleased to see him, their quarrel no longer seeming of much importance after his experiences at the front. Pound took the Aldingtons out for a celebratory dinner, and at one of his parties they for the first time met T.S. Eliot, whom H.D. very much liked, finding his quiet courteous manners a marked contrast to Pound's noisy ebullience. She treated Pound with rather more caution than her husband did. Perhaps he had started to make love to her again; Humphrey Carpenter suggests that 1917 was the year in which Pound had a 'sexual awakening' and embarked on a series of affairs, and he may well have hoped H.D. would be one of them.[123] What did rather shock her, as she told Lowell, was that unlike the rest of them Pound appeared singularly unaffected by the horrors of the war, something on which Monro and Eliot also commented at different times. Was Pound really so indifferent? The poems in *Cathay* two years earlier had suggested not. Perhaps the relentless impresario activity was partly an effort to escape from the wartime anxieties; if he worked tirelessly for a future for writing, everything else would sort itself out. His latest persona, Petronius in the *Homage*, is portrayed refusing cavalierly to write imperial war epics instead of love poetry, but Pound insisted that here he was making a serious political point, drawing attention to the shared 'infinite and ineffable imbecility' of the British and Roman empires.[124] Yet he may also at some level have been refusing to acknowledge uncongenial events around him, as he would do so disturbingly in the build-up to the Second World War, in his uncritical admiration of Mussolini's Fascism.

At the time, H.D. was disturbed and baffled by his seeming indifference, but many years later, in 1948, after Pound had been indicted for treason and had begun the years of incarceration in St Elizabeths Hospital, when she came to see him as a tragic, misguided figure, she tried to understand what had happened. She wondered if the beginning of his 'down-curve' (personal and political down-curve, she meant, not as a writer) dated back to the war years. Many have thought the same, but H.D. linked it, not to Gaudier's death or just to the war itself, though 'being there and not IN it' she felt contributed, but to his pain at the hostility he was provoking in London in those years. Being 'made much of' by the leading writers in pre-war London (she mentions Ford, Rhys, Stuart Moore, Hewlett and Yeats) had given him intense pleasure and self-belief after his Philadelphian ostracism; the wartime attacks now took him straight back, she suggests, to the desolation he had felt then, the despair he had felt before he first went to Europe.[125] Pound himself later seems to have recognised that time as a watershed. There is a letter to H.D. written in the late 1950s, after she had sent him the manuscripts of *End to Torment* and of the poem she wrote for him, *Winter Love*, both of which entranced him, where Pound talks of his '2000 memories' of their early friendship, 'ten years of beauty' which 'the Gods can envy'.[126] Perhaps those were the years 1905 to 1915, after which their friendship and so much else fell apart.

News that Pound cannot have entirely ignored came in September: T.E. Hulme, the founder of the School of Images, who had returned to France in April, was killed by a direct hit from a shell. All the notes for the still unwritten Epstein book disappeared with him, and, according to Pound's *Cantos*, several London Library books. Apart from the translations of Bergson's *Introduction to Metaphysics* and of Sorel's *Reflections on Violence*, nothing of his had appeared in his lifetime in book form. Eliot may also have noticed this death, having reviewed the Sorel appreciatively that year.[127] He would come to greatly admire some of Hulme's later, more 'reactionary' writing – 'reactionary' being Eliot's adjective, and for him a term of praise – and would do much to establish his reputation after Herbert Read brought out a collection of Hulme's writing with the title of *Speculations* in 1924.[128] Hulme's opposition to the idea of progress, his conviction of humanity's limitations, his rejection of Romanticism, all played a part in the kind of modernism that Eliot would evolve.

As it happened, two of the other members of the Tour Eiffel group resurfaced in print that year. Joseph Campbell brought out his last and most powerful collection, *Earth of Cualann*, which was reviewed in the *Egoist* for December 1917, the review, unsigned but undoubtedly by Pound himself, reiterating once again his admiration for the Tour Eiffel poet who had most influenced him in those early days: 'Mr Campbell is one of the half-dozen or so of writers who are responsible for there being any contemporary poetry. He has established his own style of *vers libre* . . . The stuff is Irish, with a peculiar bitter flavour, a dourness, of Mr Campbell's own. He uses Gaelic names with effect, but none of the poems is simply a whoop from the peat-bog . . . It is the best of recent books of verse.'[129] In addition, Flint's friend Desmond FitzGerald, at that time in prison for his part in the Easter Rising, achieved what seems to have been his first publication of his poetry in the *New Age* in late 1917 and early 1918, love poems, written in the *vers libre* he had treated with such caution before. Later that year, while still in prison, he would be elected a Sinn Fein MP. FitzGerald had a play put on at the Abbey Theatre in 1919, but, like Hulme, he would never have a book of his poems published. Quite why is not clear, because Campbell's Dublin publishers Maunsell agreed in 1918 to publish a collection, but it never materialised. FitzGerald wrote to Storer in 1922 saying he had written nothing since 1919, and the years from 1922 to 1925, of civil war and uneasy peace, cannot have allowed much time for poetry; but he eventually had a volume of poems privately printed in France in 1925. It was entitled *La Vie quotidienne* – a reference to a line by Jules Laforgue, 'Ah! que la vie est quotidienne', the title of one of the poems – and was only circulated to his friends.[130] Some poems had been previously published, including those that had appeared in the *New Age*. They must, one presumes, have been written before his jail sentence, or during it, though perhaps surprisingly, even though he was so immersed in nationalist politics, FitzGerald no longer attempted to use Irish forms or themes as he had done in his early, deeply gloomy play. Many of the poems are still melancholy, but they deserved more general circulation. Yet that this poet was in prison must have seemed to Pound in 1917 further confirmation of the 'infinite and ineffable imbecility' of the British Empire.

The Aldingtons, of course, only knew of the Tour Eiffel meetings by repute, and they had in any case other things on their minds. After a brief period of leave in London, Aldington had been dispatched for further training at Lichfield in Staffordshire, and H.D. went to stay nearby. Her room in 44 Mecklenburgh Square was taken in her absence by Arabella Yorke, Cournos' earlier love, back in London after some time in Paris, and looking more kindly at Cournos than before. He was less impoverished than when he had known her earlier, having recently acquired a well-paid part-time post translating cables from Russian for Marconi, and was much more established as a journalist. Cournos was still bruised by his rejection by H.D., but his passion for Arabella, as strikingly attractive as ever, quickly revived. He had, however, already agreed to go in October as a translator for the Anglo-Russian mission to Petrograd; after the February revolution and the Tsar's abdication, a broad-based Provisional government had been established, which was still fighting on the Allies' side, but the British were rightly anxious to ensure their continuing support. The country was known to be unstable and the mission possibly dangerous, but none of the members of the party, or the Foreign Office who sent them, seems to have anticipated the Bolshevik revolution, which took place not long after they arrived. Cournos had written to H.D. before he left asking her to look after Arabella, who moved up to his room, H.D.'s now being taken by the Lawrences, who had been forced to leave Cornwall under suspicion of being spies. H.D., 'like an angel', as Lawrence put it to Lowell, gave them refuge, until she and Aldington returned in late November, when the Lawrences moved into a flat in Earls Court owned by the mother of a young musician friend, Cecil Gray, who had been in Cornwall with them and returned with them to London.[131] He might well have felt he ought to help them, as it was his playing of Hebridean folk melodies that finally convinced the neighbourhood that they were spies.

While the Aldingtons were in Lichfield, Amy sent H.D. a copy of the chapter she had written on her in *Tendencies in American Poetry*, which came out that autumn. Like Lowell's other books it sold well, though she was rightly criticised by *Poetry* for excluding Pound and Vachel Lindsay, and mocked by Pound for comparing Fletcher favourably to Rimbaud. She had much to say in praise of H.D., in slightly embarrassingly high-flown terms, though the chapter did much to establish H.D.'s reputation in the States. She described her as a 'great artist', and employed her own favourite image to describe her poetry, saying that though some thought her poetry cold, 'let me liken "H.D." 's poetry to the cool flesh of a woman bathing in a fountain – cool to the sight, cool to the touch, but within is a warm, beating heart.' But she also had some criticisms: H.D.'s poetry, she said, was 'a narrow art, it has no scope, it neither digs deeply nor spreads widely', perhaps revenge at some level for what she saw as the Aldingtons' critical attitude towards her range of modes. But most hurtful of all was her comment that H.D. 'seems quite unaffected by the world around her'.[132] Harriet Monroe wrote in similar terms, probably only a month or so later than this when H.D. was back in London, rebuking her for not getting into 'life' or 'the rhythm of our times'. As H.D. recalled in 1937, in a letter to Norman Holmes Pearson explaining when and why she wrote her poems, the letter had been waiting for her in Mecklenburgh Square when she 'had staggered home' one day from an air raid, 'exhausted and half-asphixiated. (I and my companion had been shoved off the pavements, protesting to a special policeman that we would rather be killed on the pavement than suffocated in the underground.)' To explain her poetry, she said to Pearson, she would have to 'drag in a whole deracinated epoch', and she goes on: 'Perhaps specifically, I might say that the house next door was struck another night. We came home and simply waded through glass, while wind from now unshuttered windows, made the house a barn, an unprotected dug-out. What does that sort of shock do to the mind, the imagination – not solely of myself, but of an epoch?'[133] For H.D., her poetry was precisely an attempt to find a way of expressing the rhythm – the fissures and explosions – of her time, and she was distressed that Monroe, who first published her poetry, and Lowell, to whose promotion she owed much, could not see this.

Aldington loyally told her to ignore Lowell's comments, but in other ways things were less good between them. When he had first returned, Aldington had been delighted to see England and his friends again, but his good spirits did not last. In particular, his reunion with H.D., for which they had both longed, had proved an uneasy one. Inevitably, they had both changed. Aldington, like many returning soldiers, quickly came to feel that civilians were almost another species, incapable of under-standing the world that existed at the front; in his memoir he recalls writing to Lawrence during the war, 'There are two kinds of men, those who have been to the front and those who haven't'.[134] Women, with no threat of war service, were exponentially distant from the soldier's world. He grew increasingly bitter, angry with the establishment that had led them into war, and impatient with the self-interested machinations of the literary world that carried on back home. Like George Winterbourne in *Death of a Hero*, he resented the fact that when 'life might in its brief passing be so lovely and so divine', as a soldier he had 'nothing but oppo-sition, and betrayal and hatred and death forced upon [him] . . . born for the slaughter like a calf or pig'.[135] The war news was bleak; the sector of the front where he had been stationed was now involved in the long-drawn-out battle of Passchendaele, and there was constant news of casu-alties. It was to such carnage Aldington could expect to return. He tried to protect H.D., not telling her how traumatised he was by his army expe-rience, yet was simultaneously angry with her because she could not know what it was like. H.D. herself was worn, anxious, over-wrought; Aldington tried to be sympathetic, but traces of irritation undoubtedly appeared. Civilian strain, he now felt, was so much less than his; what were the air raids she dreaded compared to shelling at the front? If their sexual rela-tionship had been going well, that might have helped, but the picture H.D. gives in *Bid Me to Live* suggests she had retreated even further into her inner, burning world, and found herself shrinking away from this 'great, over-sexed officer on leave', whose moods were becoming ever more violent.[136] It can't have been easy for either of them, and, once back in London in the febrile atmosphere of 44 Mecklenburgh Square, Aldington and Arabella started an affair.

This affair was a much more open, not to say more blatant one than that with Flo. Aldington's relationship with Arabella was physically passionate and consuming, only too apparent to the other inhabitants of number 44, including their outraged landlady, Miss James, but he had no wish to give up his marriage to H.D. As he wrote in a letter to her, 'I love you, I desire *l'autre*'.[137] In *Bid Me to Live*, Bella, the Arabella figure, says to Julia, 'You tyrannize his soul . . . he loves my body, but he isn't all there, half of him is somewhere else.'[138] But the distinction between loving and desiring is not perhaps so clear-cut as Aldington tried to persuade H.D. to think, and certainly Arabella was very much in love with him. It was, as he acknowledged, a mess. H.D. felt she could not interfere or remonstrate; that would have been against all her principles and instincts, but she felt lacerated living in the same house as her husband and his mistress, who sometimes made love in Arabella's room, sometimes in hers, Aldington once more blindly seeking the carefree Greek happiness he felt was his due. In *Bid Me to Live*, Rafe says to Julia, 'I won't come back, you might allow me a little fun . . . I want Bella. Bella makes me forget. You make me remember.' But then, at other times, he says: 'I'll go mad, I am torn to pieces, I love you.'[139]

As before, H.D.'s pain drove her to write, but what came out must have shocked her with its extremity, because she destroyed it all, some 10,000 words, much to Aldington's dismay, who thought it 'fine & vivid & inevitable, though bitter'.[140] There was no Cournos this time to whom to turn; H.D. still corresponded with him, but Arabella's defection was not news she could pass on. The other solace – though it was also a scourge – that she had had during the previous affair was her intense and highly charged correspondence with Lawrence. They had built up a powerful bond through their letters, one which H.D. called 'cerebral' and Lawrence 'ecstatic subtly-intellectual'. They didn't always see eye to eye; H.D. had been disappointed with *Women in Love*, which Lawrence had sent her to read in manuscript, so much more bitter and male-supremacist than *The Rainbow*. When H.D. sent him a sequence of Orpheus and Eurydice poems, he was appalled that she had attempted a male persona; as Rico says in *Bid Me to Love*, 'How can you know what Orpheus feels? . . . Stick to the woman-consciousness, it is the intuitive woman-mood that matters': Julia is deeply irritated by his 'man-is-man, woman-is-woman' attitude, and thinks indignantly of his own lack of inhibition in depicting women.[141]

But like Julia, H.D. knew Lawrence thought highly of her poetic gifts, and that he valued her as a person. After all, she was included in the select group going to Ranamin; she must have some worth. She saw the Lawrences several times over the next few weeks; both of them had got to like Arabella while they were living in the same house, and Lawrence, in spite of his regard for H.D., disconcertingly appeared to have approved of Richard's affair, certainly a more sexually fulfilling relationship than the Aldingtons' intense but strained devotion. Aldington said Arabella had earthy passions like himself; she could give him what he needed then. Frieda, who was, or was thinking of having an affair with Cecil Gray, and who, although she liked and admired H.D., disapproved strongly of Lawrence's subli-mated, spiritually intense attitude to her (and his similar attitude to another young American, Esther Andrews), regarding it as unhealthy if not perverted, suggested, possibly mischievously, that Lawrence and H.D. should pair off to give her more time with Gray. Nothing came of it, for all H.D. and Lawrence's mutual embrace of the 'flame and the fire, the burning, the believing' in their letters.[142] In the fictional version, Rico says, 'You are there for all eternity, our love is written in blood', but when Julia puts a hand on Rico's sleeve, he shrinks back, 'like a hurt jaguar'; '*noli me tangere* (his own expression),' she adds, in a reference to Lawrence's late story, *The Man Who Died*.[143] Their relationship was not to be of that kind, but, given H.D.'s isolation and pain, it would soon not be of any other.

Frieda and Gray's putative flirtation or *tendresse* also evaporated, and Cecil Gray, like everyone else well aware of the Arabella-Aldington liaison, began to show solicitude for H.D.'s desolate state. He was only twenty-three, courteous and undemanding: as a composer, he was an artist in the musical realm that meant so much to H.D. He came along with the Lawrences on several occasions to 44 Mecklenburgh Square; Christmas was approaching, and if everyone was on edge, and hysteria in the air, it was overlaid by feverish gaiety. They had several parties: Lawrence and Frieda, Gray, the Aldingtons, Arabella, Brigit and her latest lover, Captain Jack White, a supporter of the Irish revolutionaries. At one, which they all remembered indelibly (it is described in both *Bid Me to Live* and *Aaron's Rod*), Lawrence organised charades; they acted out the creation myth – H.D. was told to be the Tree of Life (did Lawrence know Pound called her Dryad?), Richard and Arabella were Adam and Eve, Frieda the serpent, Gray the angel at the gate – with an umbrella for his flaming sword – and Lawrence, naturally, God Almighty. Was it an allegory of their situation? Richard and Arabella, the eternal, ur-couple, Lawrence judging and deciding events, Frieda as temptress – and of course, the

Tree of Life and the angel left together after the Fall, just as H.D. and Gray were, though still under God's, i.e. Lawrence's, watchful eye.

Early in 1918, with Aldington back at his officer's training but returning regularly for weekends spent largely in bed with Arabella, Gray, who had a slight heart condition that had saved him from conscription, began to beg H.D. to go back with him to Cornwall, where he had a largish house near the sea, with a respectable full-time housekeeper who could act as chaperon. He returned there in January, and after some hesitation she joined him in March. As H.D. writes in *Bid Me to Live*, 'Given normal civilised peace-time conditions of course, all this could never have happened, or it would have happened in sections, so that one could deal with one problem after another, in due sequence . . . Changing partners, changing hands, dancing round, in a Bacchic orgy of war-time love and death'.[144] Aldington was quite relieved to have her find some consolation, but Lawrence, according to H.D., was deeply disapproving, perhaps because H.D., while grateful to Gray, who was quiet, civilised and soothing, as well as reassuringly admiring of her beauty and gifts, was clearly not in love with him. H.D. was very aware of male exploitation of women, but, as she herself would recognise later, there could be said to be something exploitative in the way she used the admiration and indeed adoration of men like Cournos and Gray, for whom she might have liking but not love. Perhaps that is what Lawrence thought, and he must have recognised too that given the price the social world could still make a woman pay for loss of reputation, it could have seemed a terrible risk to take if not for passion, but it was an indication of her anguished need to escape. Lawrence and H.D. would not meet up again, but that was probably largely chance; his references to her in later letters are for the most part compassionate and concerned, and she would never forget the impact he had on her and her writing. Lawrence's descriptions of Cornwall had made her long to see it, and when she got there, she loved it, an ancient world with a landscape of rocks and crags like that in *Sea Garden*. As well as translations and poems, she began a novel, the story of those years, which would take so many different forms, *Paint it Today*, *Her*, *Asphodel*, and finally *Bid Me to Live*. She had gone to Cornwall, Aldington told Lowell slightly tetchily, to get away from the bombing, which although in his opinion not particularly heavy, was difficult for one of her nervous temperament to cope with. He mentioned neither Gray nor Arabella in his letters. Nor did H.D.

VIII

JOHN Cournos arrived back in April, after a long and hazardous journey home, getting away shortly before Russia, to the dismay of the other Allies, signed an armistice with Germany, and escaping the civil war that then broke out. He quickly learnt that Arabella was Aldington's lover and no longer had any interest in himself. He was furious with both the Aldingtons: openly yet briefly with Richard, but, though he said nothing to her, much more lastingly and bitterly with H.D. He had decided that the reason she had refused to sleep with him was that she had a morbid fear of pregnancy, and seized on the idea that she had in effect pandered Arabella to escape from her husband's sexual attentions. It is true that H.D. does suggest in *Bid Me to Live* that the one consolation for all the pain Julia feels is that it relieves her of the fear of Rafe's 'over-physical sensuality', but H.D. would not have engineered such immolation as a way of achieving this. Before she went to Cornwall they even seem to have had some sort of sexual reconciliation, because Richard wrote to her from the front that he wished she had loved him passionately *before* the relationship with Arabella started, rather than only after. But that move to Cornwall presaged the breakdown of their marriage, and the final dispersal of the imagists.

When H.D. had left London, although the joint venture of the imagist anthologies was over, her closest friends were all in one way or another linked with her imagist years. Despite her readiness to abandon the imagist label, which she had never wanted in the first place, she had loved working with a group of fellow-writers, the 'brother-ship' as she had put it to Amy. For much of the last few years H.D. had been the lynchpin of the imagists, gathering the poems, soothing Amy, placating Flint, corresponding with Lawrence, encouraging Fletcher and keeping her soldier husband in touch with the world of poetry. Now, the direction of her life was about to change. If when she came to London an iron curtain had cut her off from her comfortable American life, now a ravine would open up that would separate her from her imagist years. In August, H.D. wrote to Aldington, who had been back at the front since April, to say she thought she was pregnant; Aldington, though he insisted he still loved her, became increasingly despairing about any future together. He could not bear the thought of this new child in the place of his dead daughter, and wrote H.D. near-hysterical letters, unable to see what to do about her or Arabella; the shell shock – as it was called then – from which he was suffering as the war came to an end, was already taking its toll.

Gray went back to London, probably to evade a threat of conscription, apparently without knowing about the pregnancy. H.D. left Cornwall shortly afterwards, but not before she had been visited by a twenty-four-year-old admirer of the imagists, Winifred Ellerman, who had already published a pamphlet of lyrical praise for Amy Lowell, and who knew H.D.'s *Sea Garden* by heart. Bryher, as she preferred to be known, was the daughter of a shipping millionaire, Sir John Ellerman, reputed to be the richest man in England, and a major shareholder in *The Times* and other publications. Bryher was determined to be a writer and was working on her first novel: highly intelligent, rebellious, unhappy and disturbed, she immediately fell in love with H.D., who she thought looked like a Greek goddess. H.D. was touched by her enthusiasm for imagism, and gave her advice about her writing, but their friendship remained formal for some months. H.D. said nothing of the problems with the marriage, and in fact put Bryher in touch with Aldington, as a second literary adviser.

When the war ended – almost as unexpectedly, for most of those involved, as it began – the question of whether H.D. and Aldington would stay together still hung in the balance. H.D. spent the autumn and winter in a cottage in Buckinghamshire with her childhood friend Margaret Snively, now Pratt, herself already a mother. Significantly, she never told Margaret, and indeed hardly anyone else, that the child was not Aldington's; she was terrified of becoming the subject of a scandal, like poor Violet Hunt. She and Aldington corresponded regularly, though mainly, at her insistence, about his plans for a new series of Poets' Translations, and Bryher came to see her several times. H.D. continued to act as literary mentor and adviser; but by now she must have been aware of Bryher's feelings about her, and was discovering something of Bryher's own inner turmoil at that time: her misery at not being a boy, her impatience with the constraints of her upbringing, her near-suicidal depression. H.D. had other painful shocks as well. Her brother Gilbert had been killed in the last month of the war, and the following March her father died; of grief, she thought. Kind and practical Brigit – who knew about Aldington and Arabella, and, being devoted to H.D. (and highly critical of contemporary male mores), very much took her side – arranged for the birth to be in 'the decorous St Faith's Nursing Home, in Ealing'. While staying in a rented room nearby as the confinement approached, H.D. contracted Spanish influenza in the post-war epidemic that killed more people than the war itself. It turned to pneumonia and, as she recalled in *End to Torment*, it was thought impossible that both she and the child would live. Bryher visited her one day, to be asked by a surly landlady if she would pay the funeral expenses when H.D. died. Shocked and appalled, she immediately arranged for H.D. to be admitted to the home early, promising her, to persuade her to hang on to life, that she would take her to Greece after the baby was born. Aldington visited H.D. in the home, and so did Ezra. Pound clearly knew the father was not Aldington; as H.D. recalled the visit later: 'Beard, black soft hat, ebony stick – something unbelievably operatic – directoire overcoat, Verdi . . . He seemed to beat with the ebony stick like a baton . . . pounding, pounding (*Pounding*) . . . "But" he said, "My only real criticism is that this is not my child".'[145]

The baby was safely born on 31 March and named Frances Perdita, after Frances Gregg and the lost daughter from *The Winter's Tale*, since the baby had arrived, as Bryher would put it, 'with

> the daffodils.
> That come before the swallows dare, and take
> The winds of March with beauty

just in time to earn her Shakespearean name'.[146] Aldington for a while appeared to be ready to resume the marriage, and he and H.D. moved into a hotel in Soho, Perdita having been, reluctantly on H.D.'s part, installed in a nursery. The story now is somewhat confused but it seems that after a day or two Aldington had a violent outbreak of rage, evidently in a state of breakdown, and threatened H.D. with prison if she put his name on the birth certificate. H.D. was terrified, fearing for the baby's future. Aldington rang Bryher and told her to take H.D. away, and their lifelong companionship began. H.D.'s feelings about Bryher at that stage were a mixture of gratitude and concern. Bryher, she felt, had saved her life and Perdita's, and she was able to save Bryher from her suicidal impulses. Her relationship with Bryher would only ever be comparatively briefly that of lovers, and there was none of the burning passion that she had felt for Pound or Frances Gregg, but they remained close all their lives, with many shared interests, not only literature, but film, psychoanalysis and gossip. H.D.'s letters to Bryher (they wrote copiously to each other when apart) are funny, self-probing, full of interest in the world; they can express all kinds of pain and self-doubt, but they are free of the intense and self-lacerating high-mindedness of the letters to Cournos. Bryher helped invaluably in bringing up Perdita, whom H.D. adored but had no idea how to look after, and, most importantly, Bryher recognised and protected the centrality of writing in H.D.'s life. Though H.D. would have other relationships, mainly with men, Bryher remained a devoted friend and, though she too would have other attachments, gave H.D. a fundamental loyalty that Aldington and Pound – and indeed Gregg – had never shown.

But this would be her post-imagist life, beyond the scope of this book. For the next decade, to her deep regret, H.D. saw little of her fellow-imagists, though on a visit to America in 1921 she met up again with Lowell, Williams and Marianne Moore. Her life was mainly divided between Switzerland and London, and she travelled a good deal, making the promised visit to Greece. She occasionally saw Pound, who was much disliked by Bryher (it was mutual). She saw Brigit regularly until the mid-1920s, when Brigit's own marriage finally collapsed, but Bryher also disliked Brigit, and the friendship lapsed. She met Frances again, now divorced and with two children, but Bryher, perhaps more understandably, regarded her with suspicion too.

In 1930 the imagists would come together, at least within the covers of a book, to publish one last anthology, with the support of a keen young West Coast scholar, Glenn Hughes, who published the first book on the group, *Imagism and the Imagists*, in 1931. Aldington, who took up the idea, wrote to H.D. to ask her to help solicit poems (back to her old role) from those who had contributed to *Des Imagistes* or *Some Imagist Poets*. He had got back in touch with her the previous year, having just left Arabella for Brigit. During the 1920s Aldington had had a highly successful journalistic career, the kind that Pound had earlier dreamt of, set on his way by Bryher, whose father used his influence to have him made the French specialist on the *Times Literary Supplement*, and his writing was soon widely in demand. He was Eliot's assistant at the *Criterion*, so at the centre of the literary world. But mentally he had been through considerable anguish, post-traumatic stress as we would know it now; physically, he never recovered from the effects of gas poisoning during the war, nor did the bitterness towards the literary world that he had developed in his time in the army disappear. In 1929, as well as leaving Arabella, he left England and began a new career as a novelist; his loosely autobiographical novel about the war, *Death of a Hero*, came out that year and was a best-seller. Reading it now, it feels almost mawkishly self-justifying; George, the hero, is a thoroughly decent chap in a corrupt and cynical artistic milieu, much put upon by the women in his life; his men at the front are, on the other hand, the salt of the earth (though George never seems to find out their names): for years the book was promoted in the Soviet Union as an outstanding analysis of the decadent capitalist system. But at the time, for many people who had been through the war, it captured their sense of how their elders had betrayed them. The novel had not yet appeared when Aldington and H.D. met up in Paris, and when, obliging as always, she agreed to do her best to help with the anthology.

Amy Lowell, who had done so much to establish the imagist name, was, alas, dead, having died of a stroke in 1925, after publishing several more highly successful collections, *Can Grande's Castle* and *Pictures of the Floating World* among them. Pound's friend and mentor Allen Upward was also dead; he committed suicide in 1926, a victim, Pound felt, of the ignorance and apathy of the general public who refused to recognise his gifts. But James Joyce, now famous or infamous as the author of *Ulysses*, contributed an extract from what would become *Finnegans Wake*, actually rather more imagistic than the somewhat overwrought poem that he had contributed to *Des Imagistes*. Flint sent Aldington a short play; though he had continued to write criticism and do a wealth of translation, he had for the most part stopped writing poetry since he published his collection *Otherworld* in 1920, the year that Violet died in childbirth along with their third child. H.D. had written a very feeling letter of condolence to him, which he kept, but did not answer. Aldington told Lowell that Flint had a kind of breakdown after Violet's death and wouldn't contact anyone for a while. H.D., to her sadness, never heard from him again. Flint saw Aldington regularly, and perhaps felt he could not be in touch with them both (he told Violet Hunt he had decided after the break-up of her relationship with Ford that he could not see her because he was still a friend of Ford's, but she would have none of it). Yet Flint sometimes made references to his admiration for H.D.'s poetry in the reviewing he continued to do. Before Violet's death, his talents had at last been recognised at work: he was given a much better paid job in the civil service and eventually reached a senior position in the Ministry of Labour, becoming an expert on international labour statistics. He had married one of Violet's sisters not long after Violet's death, probably desperate to have a carer for the children, who were only eleven and five, but it was an unhappy mistake. Yet as well as seeing Aldington, he remained friendly with Ford and Monro, and found another congenial literary circle, the so-called *Criterion* club, those who were associated with Eliot's prestigious magazine, which had first appeared in 1922.

John Gould Fletcher readily contributed to the anthology; he was still publishing prolifically and still, for now, though not for much longer, living unhappily with Daisy. Like Flint he was a contributor to the *Criterion*, and regularly escaped from Sydenham to the *Criterion* club lunches and dinners, developing a surprisingly good if somewhat formal relationship with Eliot himself. A couple of years earlier, after a decade of hero-worship, he had finally fallen out with Cournos, who was now married to Helen Satterthwaite, a detective-story writer who used the pseudonym of Sybil Norton. Cournos himself had by then published several novels, but he would be disappointed to know that today, since his fiction mostly consists of thinly disguised accounts of himself and his literary friends, it is mainly read by literary historians hoping for colourful vignettes. Cournos agreed immediately to contribute to the anthology, in spite of his earlier brush with the Aldingtons, but Lawrence, by now very ill (he died before the anthology appeared), acceded to H.D.'s request only in the most churlish of terms. Poor H.D.! She felt that his unfriendly letter was a rebuke to herself, but it was undoubtedly much more one to Aldington, with whom he and Frieda had just had a holiday, along with both Arabella and Brigit; Lawrence, though he always liked Brigit, who on this occasion helped with his nursing with particular kindness, had fallen out acrimoniously with Aldington over his treatment of Arabella. Aldington felt Lawrence resented his rude health, which he undoubtedly did, but in addition, as John Worthen points out, for someone to whom sexual relationships had been so central, to be surrounded, in his frail and impotent state, by the others' swirling desires, must have been hard to bear without a bitter sense of loss. Yet he sent some poems none the less.

No one seems to have located Fletcher's erstwhile Parisian acquaintance, Skipwell Cannell, but H.D. wrote to Ford, who obliged with both a poem and a highly amusing if fantastic introduction, in which he suggested that imagism had emerged out of Vorticism and was entirely dependent on his own ideas. Ford had spent most of the 1920s with the Australian painter, Stella Bowen, moving to Paris in 1922 after another unsuccessful attempt at the simple life, this time as a pig farmer. There he founded the avant-garde and international journal the *Transatlantic Review*, which brought out new, fledgling and established writers, and published his tetralogy, *Parade's End*; now often regarded as his masterpiece, at the time it did little to improve his shaky finances. By 1930, when the anthology appeared, he was beginning the final and most happy relationship of his life, with the painter Janice Biala, born a Polish Jew, but American by upbringing. Under her influence he moved left in his political sympathies and in particular campaigned against anti-Semitism over the next few years, something that did not endear him to Pound. Pound, in fact, from whom Aldington had been hoping for a canto, gave the one unequivocal refusal. Both Aldington and H.D. saw Pound when they met up in Paris, and he had been extremely friendly, so they were disappointed, if scarcely surprised.

In 1920 Pound had rejected England, where he felt unappreciated, for Paris, leaving Eliot, for whose work he had done so much, to move into the position of literary leadership he had so much wanted for himself. By 1925 he had become dissatisfied with Paris, and moved his home to Rapallo, in Italy, ardently supporting Mussolini and dividing his life between the violinist Olga Rudge, who bore him a daughter that year, and the long-suffering Dorothy, who had a son the next. In his terms, his refusal was understandable enough. In spite of his recent friendly meetings with both Aldington and H.D., for him to agree to appear, with so many writers he continued to feel were his inferiors, and certainly never imagist, would be to forgive retrospectively and indeed condone Amy's usurpation of his role as leading imagist. Aldington told H.D. not to worry. He had earlier written to her when the idea was mooted, '[Pound] may have invented "Imagism", but, after all, you wrote the poems.'[147] Perhaps 1930 was an appropriate year for the commemorative anthology to appear. If imagism had been, as H.D. suggested to Ford, the 'curtain-raiser' to the dazzling show of modernist and experimental writing that followed, 1930 is the year often seen as the end of its most vibrant phase. The world would rapidly darken once more. Many of the former young iconoclasts – Pound, Eliot, Fletcher, Lewis, and indeed the slightly older Yeats – were moving, like the political revolutionaries in Russia, and as revolutionaries so often do, to embrace authoritarianism and the demand for order, albeit in their case on the right rather than the left. For many years that was seen as the narrative of modernism, but it was not the only pattern for the writers of this generation; it was not true of H.D., nor of many other women writers, nor of Ford, nor of Joyce. But that again is another story. Aldington and H.D. were not in touch with each other or Pound again for many years, but after the war, when Aldington had disastrously run off with Brigit's daughter-in-law, who then left him and their daughter, he and H.D. became regular and warm correspondents, and while they were appalled by Pound's Fascist sympathies, they both got back in touch with him by letter at various points, and he with them. In fact, his occasional late letters to H.D. are some of his most moving. They all looked back to their friendship before the war as, in Aldington's words, those 'magical early years in London', the period that H.D. felt had made her who she was, and to which she would return so repeatedly in her writing.[148] Pound wrote sadly to her in the 1950s saying that never since the four of them, himself, Richard, H.D. and Brigit, had been together in those early years, 'has there been any harmony around me'.[149]

Was imagism a poetic school? An advertising stunt? A name plucked from the air to promote a group of varied and disparate talents? A primitivist escape from the elaborations of convention in search of something more elemental and profound? A breakthrough to a strikingly modern way of writing, with its spare syntax, its juxtapositions, its unexpected twists? A response to the rich heterogeneity, cultural difference and multiple sensations of the modern world? A rebellious protest at the status quo? It was all of these. Those involved came from extraordinarily different backgrounds, and they developed in very different ways, but none of them would forget those years, which had a profound impact on them all, and on the course of Anglo-American writing. It has been fashionable, among some critics, to see modernism as proto-Fascist from the start. Yet imagism, a product of the pre-war libertarian years, was as subversive of the cultural power structure as the heterogeneous radicals who published alongside this group of poets. Its aim, after all, was the epiphanic 'sense of sudden liberation . . . which we experience in the presence of the greatest works of art', and if some of those who formed the movement might later harden their views, and if the war had darkened all their hopes, it had been, for a while at least, personally and artistically liberating for the imagists, and for many of their readers.

ACKNOWLEDGEMENTS

This book has been many years in the writing, and I have many debts of gratitude. Firstly, to Philippa Brewster, pearl among editors, for her patience, insight, blue pencil and constant support; to my colleagues at Goldsmiths, University of London, especially Chris Baldick, Maura Dooley, Bill McCormick, Blake Morrison and Maria Macdonald in my own department, and the late and much missed Ben Pimlott, with whom I had many conversations about the art of biography; to my students, for their constant stimulation and fresh thinking: to Laura Marcus, Andrew Thacker and Michael Doolan, who read parts of the book as it was in progress; to the British Academy, the Leverhulme Trust and Goldsmiths for grants that supported this project, and to Isobel Armstrong, Gillian Beer and Rachel Bowlby for supporting my applications for these, and for much intellectual enrichment besides; to the members of the London Modernist Seminar and the Ezra Pound Cantos Reading Group; to many other fellow scholars with whom I have talked over aspects of this work, including Rebecca Beasley, Vicky Bertram, Peter Brooker, Ron Bush, Rod Edmond, Lucy McDiarmid, Peter Nicholls, Suzanne Raitt, Nigel Rigby, Nick Selby; many thanks also to Sarah Barnsley, Sarah Martin and Emily Carr for brilliant assistance in the final delivery of the manuscript; and to my immensely supportive editorial team at Jonathan Cape: Dan Franklin, Alex Bowler and Sarah Thomas; as well as my agent, Bill Hamilton. I also owe particular thanks to Christopher Middleton, who talked to me in Austin about F.S. Flint, to Ethel Simpson in Fayetteville, for discussions about John Gould Fletcher, and to Dr Garret FitzGerald, his daughter Mary and niece Jennifer, for information, warm hospitality and generous assistance when I visited Dublin to learn more about Desmond FitzGerald. My warm thanks also to the research libraries I have used, for all their assistance, and for permission to quote from unpublished manuscripts: the Beinecke Rare Book and Manuscript Library, Yale University; the Houghton Library, Harvard University; the Harry Ransom Humanities Research Center, University of Texas at Austin; Special Collections, University of Arkansas Libraries, Fayetteville; the Special Collections Research Center, Morris Library, Southern Illinois University, Carbondale; the UCD Archives, James Joyce Library, University College Dublin; and most of all the British Library, where I have spent so many happily engrossed hours over the years. My thanks as well to the staff of the London Library, Senate House Library, Cambridge University Library and not least Goldsmiths Library, especially Ann Alridge for her help with interlibrary loans. And very special thanks to all my long-suffering family, particularly to Ben and Emily for all their support and encouragement, and most of all to Tony, always my first reader and critic.

Grateful acknowledgement to Linda Flint for permission to quote from the works of F.S. Flint, to Polly Bird, copyright holder and literary executor, for permission to quote from the works of Douglas Goldring, and to Garret FitzGerald for permission to quote from Desmond FitzGerald's unpublished papers and his own. Many thanks to Catherine Aldington for her good wishes for the book; extracts from Richard Aldington's published and unpublished work (held at the Beinecke Rare Book and Manuscript Library, Yale University; the Houghton Library, Harvard University; and the Special Collections Research Center, Morris Library, Southern Illinois University, Carbondale), all © copyright the Estate of Richard Aldington, reproduced by kind permission of the Estate of Richard Aldington c/o Rosica Colin Limited, London. Extracts from *The Letters of D.H. Lawrence*, Vols. 1–3, reproduced by kind permission of the Estate of Frieda Lawrence Ravagli and Pollinger Ltd. Extracts from *Ford Madox Ford: A Dual Life*, Vol. 1 (1996) by Max Saunders, and *The Complete Works of T.E. Hulme* (1994) edited by Karen Csengeri, reproduced by permission of Oxford University Press. Extracts from the work of W.B. Yeats by permission of A.P. Watt on behalf of Gráinne Yeats.

Grateful acknowledgment to Faber & Faber Ltd for permission to reproduce various extracts from Humphrey Carpenter, *A Serious Character: the Life of Ezra Pound*; 'The Love Song of J. Alfred Prufrock', 'Burbank with a Baedeker: Bleistein with a cigar' in T.S. Eliot, *Collected Poems: 1909–1935*; *Selected Prose of T.S. Eliot*, ed. Frank Kermode; *Selected Essays of T.S. Eliot*, Faber & Faber, quoted in Robert Crawford,

The Savage and the City in the Work of T.S. Eliot, Oxford: Clarendon Press.

Grateful acknowledgment to Faber & Faber Ltd and to New Directions Publishing Corporation for permission to reproduce various extracts from *Ezra Pound and Dorothy Shakespear: Their Letters: 1909–1914*, copyright ©1984 by the Trustees of the Ezra Pound Literary Trust; *Letters of Ezra Pound, 1907–1941*, copyright © 1950 by Ezra Pound; 'Histerion', 'Alba Beningalis', 'Piccadilly', 'The White Stag', 'Planh', 'Blandula, Tenulla, Vagula', 'Und Drang', 'To Hulme (T.E.) and FitzGerald (a Certain)', 'Redondillas', and 'Shallot' in *Collected Early Poems of Ezra Pound*, copyright © 1976 by the Trustees of the Ezra Pound Literary Property Trust; Cantos 1, 77, 80, 81, 87, 115 in *Cantos of Ezra Pound*, copyright ©1975 by the Trustees of the Ezra Pound Literary Property Trust; *Literary Essays of Ezra Pound*, copyright © 1954 by Ezra Pound; *Selected Prose: 1909–1965*, copyright © 1973 by Ezra Pound; *Polite Essays*, copyright ©1937 by Ezra Pound; *The Translations of Ezra Pound*, copyright © 1953 by Ezra Pound; *Pound/Ford: The Story of a Literary Friendship*, copyright © 1971, 1972, 1973, 1982 by the Trustees of the Ezra Pound Literary Property Trust; *Pound/Joyce: The Letters of Ezra Pound to James Joyce*, copyright © 1967 by Ezra Pound; *Pound/Lewis: The Letters of Ezra Pound and Wyndham Lewis*, copyright © 1985 by the Trustees of the Ezra Pound Literary Property Trust; *Pound/The Little Review: The Letters of Ezra Pound to Margaret Anderson*, copyright © 1988 by the Trustees of the Ezra Pound Literary Property Trust; *Pound/Williams: Selected Letters of Ezra Pound and William Carlos Williams*, copyright © 1996 by the Trustees of the Ezra Pound Literary Property Trust; *A Lume Spento and Other Poems*, copyright © 1965 by Ezra Pound; 'The Tree', 'Cino', 'Praise of Ysoult', 'In Durance', 'Sestina: Altaforte', 'Ballad of the Goodly Fere', 'Portrait d'une Femme', 'The Seafarer', 'Δώρια', 'The Return', 'The Garden', 'Salutation the Second', 'The Bath Tub', 'Fan-Piece for her Imperial Lord', 'Ts'ai Chi'h', 'Coitus', 'The Tea Shop', 'Provincia Deserta', 'Lament of the Frontier Guards', 'Exile's Letter', 'Mœurs Contemporaines', *Hugh Selwyn Mauberley*, 'Three Cantos, 1917', 'Salutation the Third' in *Personae: the Shorter Poems of Ezra Pound* (rev. edn., ed. Lea Baechler and A. Walton Litz) copyright © 1926, 1935, 1971 by Ezra Pound.

Grateful acknowledgment to New Directions for permission to reproduce various extracts from *A Walking Tour in Southern France: Ezra Pound among the Troubadours*, copyright © 1992 by the Trustees of the Ezra Pound Literary Property Trust; *The Spirit of Romance*, copyright

Perdita Schaffner; *Her*, copyright © 1981 by the Estate of Hilda Doolittle; *Asphodel*, copyright © 1992 by Perdita Schaffner; *Bid Me to Live: A Madrigal*, copyright © 1960 by Norman Holmes Pearson; *Paint it Today*, copyright © 1992 by Perdita Schaffner; *Tribute to Freud*, copyright © 1956, 1974 by Norman Holmes Pearson; *The Gift: the Complete Text*, copyright © 1969, 1982 by the Estate of Hilda Doolittle, copyright © 1998 by Perdita Schaffner; *The Cantos of Ezra Pound*, ed. Ernest Heminway et al., copyright by Hilda Doolittle, 1933; also from H.D.'s work in periodicals, in the *Egoist*, including extracts from 'Mid-day', 'Choruses from *Iphigenia in Aulis*' and 'Oread', and in *Contemporary Literature* and *Agenda*; and previously unpublished extracts from H.D.'s unpublished work and correspondence held at the Beinecke Rare Books and Manuscript Library at Yale University, the Harry Ransom Center, University of Texas, Austin and the Houghton Library, Harvard University. All copyright © by the Estate of Hilda Doolittle.

Grateful acknowledgment to New Directions Publishing Corporation for permission to reproduce various extracts from the writing of William Carlos Williams: 'A Sort of Song', *Selected Poems*, copyright © 1955, 1956, 1957, 1959, 1960, 1961 and 1962 by William Carlos Williams; 'Prologue (1918)', *Kora in Hell*, in *Imaginations*, copyright © 1960, 1970 by Florence H. Williams; 'A Street Market, N.Y., 1908', *Poems*, copyright © 1909 by William Carlos Williams; 'Postlude' and 'Contemporania', *The Tempers*, copyright © 1913 by William Carlos Williams; *Selected Letters of William Carlos Williams*, copyright © 1957 by William Carlos Williams; *The Autobiography of William Carlos Williams*, copyright © 1951 by William Carlos Williams; *I wanted to write a poem: the autobiography of the works of a poet*, copyright © 1958 by William Carlos Williams; and in Zhaoming Qian, *Orientalism and Modernism: the Legacy of China in Pound and Williams*, copyright © 1995 by William Eric Williams and Paul H. Williams.

While every effort has been made to obtain permission from holders of copyright material produced herein, the publishers would like to apologise for any omissions and will be pleased to incorporate missing acknowledgements in any further editions.

ABBREVIATIONS

Books

ALAM   Adrienne Munich and Melissa Bradshaw (eds), *Amy Lowell: American Modern*, New Brunswick: Rutgers University Press, 2004

AMY   Jean Gould, *Amy: The World of Amy Lowell and the Imagist Movement*, New York: Dodd, Mead & Co., 1975

ASPH   H.D., *Asphodel*, ed. Robert Spoo, Durham, NC: Duke University Press, 1992

BB   Wyndham Lewis, *Blasting and Bombardiering*, London: Eyre & Spottiswoode, 1937

BID   H.D., *Bid Me to Live: A Madrigal*, New York: Grove Press, 1960

BP   Brigit Patmore, *My Friends When Young: The Memoirs of Brigit Patmore*, edited with an introduction by Derek Patmore, London: Heinemann, 1968

CEP   *Collected Early Poems of Ezra Pound*, London: Faber & Faber, 1977

CH   Eric Homberger (ed.), *Ezra Pound: The Critical Heritage*, London: Routledge & Kegan Paul, 1972

CPRA   *The Complete Poems of Richard Aldington*, London: Allan Wingate, 1948

CZ   Caroline Zilboorg (ed.), *Richard Aldington & H.D.: The Early Years in Letters*, Bloomington: Indiana University Press, 1992

CZ2   Caroline Zilboorg (ed.), *Richard Aldington & H.D.: The Later Years in Letters*, Manchester: Manchester University Press, 1995

DC   John Gould Fletcher, *The Dominant City*, London: Max Goschen, 1913

DH   Richard Aldington, *Death of a Hero* [1929], London: Chatto & Windus, 1930

DHLL1   *The Letters of D.H. Lawrence*: Vol. 1, *September 1901–May 1913*, ed. James T. Boulton, Cambridge: Cambridge University Press, 1979

DHLL2   *The Letters of D.H. Lawrence*: Vol. 2, *June 1913–October 1916*, ed. George J. Zytarak and James T. Boulton, Cambridge: Cambridge University Press, 1981

DHLL3   *The Letters of D.H. Lawrence*: Vol. 3, *October 1916–June 1921*, ed James T. Boulton and Andrew Robertson, Cambridge: Cambridge University Press, 1984

DRE   Donald Read, *England 1868–1914: The Age of Urban Democracy*, London: Longman, 1979

END   H.D., *End to Torment: A Memoir of Ezra Pound*, ed. Norman Holmes Pearson and Michael King, New York: New Directions, 1979

EPC   *The Cantos of Ezra Pound*, London: Faber & Faber, 1973

EP/DS   *Ezra Pound and Dorothy Shakespear: Their Letters: 1909–1914*, ed. Omar Pound and A. Walton Litz, London: Faber & Faber, 1984

EPK   Patricia Hutchins, *Ezra Pound's Kensington: An Exploration 1885–1913*, London: Faber & Faber, 1965

EPL   *Letters of Ezra Pound, 1907–41*, ed. D.D. Paige [1950], London: Faber & Faber, 1951

EP/MC   *Ezra Pound and Margaret Cravens: A Tragic Friendship*, ed. Omar Pound and Robert Spoo, Durham, NC: Duke University Press, 1988

EPP   Noel Stock, *Ezra Pound's Pennsylvania*, Toledo: Friends of the University of Toledo Libraries, 1976

EPP&P1 *Ezra Pound's Poetry and Prose: Contributions to Periodicals*, Vol. 1, *1902–1914*, prefaced and arranged by Lea Baechler, A. Walton Litz and James Longenbach, New York: Garland Publishing, 1991

EPP&P2 *Ezra Pound's Poetry and Prose: Contributions to Periodicals*, Vol. 2, *1915–1917*, prefaced and arranged by Lea Baechler, A. Walton Litz and James Longenbach, New York: Garland Publishing, 1991

EPP&P7 *Ezra Pound's Poetry and Prose: Contributions to Periodicals*, Vol. 7, *1936–9*, prefaced and arranged by Lea Baechler, A. Walton Litz and James Longenbach, New York: Garland Publishing, 1991

EPT   *The Translations of Ezra Pound*, London: Faber & Faber, 1970

FG	John Gould Fletcher, *Fool's Gold*, London: Max Goschen, 1913
FORD	Max Saunders, *Ford Madox Ford: A Dual Life*: Vol. 1, *The World before the War*, Oxford: Oxford University Press, 1996
FY	Violet Hunt, *The Flurried Years*, London: Hurst & Blackett, 1926
GB	Ezra Pound, *Gaudier-Brzeska: A Memoir*, London: John Lane, 1916
GIFT	H.D., *The Gift: the Complete Text*, ed. and annotated by Jane Augustine, Gainesville, Florida: University of Florida Press, 1998
GIFT2	H.D., *The Gift*, ed. Griselda Ohanessian, London: Virago, 1984
HC	Humphrey Carpenter, *A Serious Character: The Life of Ezra Pound*, London: Faber & Faber, 1988
HD	H.D., *Hermetic Definition*, New York: New Directions, 1972
HDCP	H.D., *Collected Poems, 1912–44*, ed. Louis L. Martz, New York: New Directions, 1983
HER	H.D., *Her*, London: Virago, 1984
HULME	Karen Csengeri, *The Collected Writings of T.E. Hulme*, Oxford: Clarendon Press, 1994
IND	Ezra Pound, *Indiscretions, or, Une revue de deux mondes*, Paris: Three Mountains Press, 1923. *Indiscretions* first appeared in twelve parts in the *New Age* in 1920, and was published in book form in 1923. It was republished in *Pavannes and Divagations*, Peter Owen, 1960
JGF	Ben F. Johnson III, *Fierce Solitude: A Life of John Gould Fletcher*, Fayetteville: University of Arkansas Press, 1994
JGFL	*Selected Letters of John Gould Fletcher*, ed. Leighton Rudolph, Lucas Carpenter and Ethel C. Simpson, Fayetteville: University of Arkansas Press, 1996
JGFP	*Selected Poems of John Gould Fletcher*, ed. Lucas Carpenter and Leighton Rudolph, Fayetteville: University of Arkansas Press, 1988
LE	Ezra Pound, *Literary Essays*, London: Faber & Faber, 1954
LL	Richard Aldington, *Life for Life's Sake*, New York: Viking, 1941
LMS	John Gould Fletcher, *Life is My Song: the Autobiography of John Gould Fletcher*, New York: Farrar & Rinehart, 1937
ML	Frances Gregg, *The Mystic Leeway*, ed. Ben Jones, Ottawa: Carleton University, Press, 1995

NS   Noel Stock, *The Life of Ezra Pound* [1970], Harmondsworth: Penguin, 1974

P/ACH   *The Letters of Ezra Pound to Alice Corbin Henderson*, ed. Ira B. Nadel, Austin: University of Texas Press, 1993

PER   *Personae: The Shorter Poems of Ezra Pound*, rev. edn, ed. Lea Baechler and A. Walton Litz, New York: New Directions, 1990

P/F   *Pound/Ford: The Story of a Literary Friendship. The Correspondence between Ezra Pound and Ford Madox Ford and their Writings about Each Other*, ed. Brita Lindbergh-Seyersted, London: Faber & Faber, 1982

PIT   H.D., *Paint it Today*, ed. Cassandra Laity, New York: New York University Press, 1992

P/J   *Pound/Joyce: The Letters of Ezra Pound to James Joyce, with Pound's Essays on Joyce*, ed. Forrest Read, London: Faber & Faber, 1968

P/L   *Pound/Lewis: The Letters of Ezra Pound and Wyndham Lewis*, ed. Timothy Materer, London: Faber & Faber, 1985

P/LR   *Pound/The Little Review: The Letters of Ezra Pound to Margaret Anderson*, ed. Thomas L. Scott, Melvin J. Friedman and Jackson R. Bryer, New York: New Directions, 1988

PM   Ezra Pound, *Patria Mia*, Chicago; Ralph Fletcher Seymour, 1950. (Slightly reworked version dating from 1913 of the series 'Patria Mia' [1912] and 'America: Chances and Remedies' [1913] which appeared in the *New Age*.)

P/Q   *The Selected Letters of Ezra Pound to John Quinn 1915–1924*, ed. Timothy Materer, Durham, NC: Duke University Press, 1991

P/W   *Pound/Williams: Selected Letters of Ezra Pound and William Carlos Williams*, ed. Hugh Witemeyer, New York: New Directions, 1996

RA   Wyndham Lewis, *Rude Assignment: an Intellectual Auto-biography* [1950], ed. Toby Foshay, Santa Rosa: Black Sparrow Press, 1984

RIP   Ezra Pound, *Ripostes*, London: Elkin Mathews, 1912

RTY   Ford Madox Ford, *Return to Yesterday*, London: Victor Gollancz, 1931

SC   James Longenbach, *Stone Cottage: Pound, Yeats and Modernism*, Oxford: Oxford University Press, 1988

SFD   Samuel Foster Damon, *Amy Lowell: A Chronicle, with Extracts from her Correspondence*, Boston: Houghton Mifflin, 1935

SL Douglas Goldring, *South Lodge: Reminiscences of Violet Hunt, Ford Madox Ford and the English Review*, London: Constable, 1943

SP Ezra Pound, *Selected Prose 1909–1965*, ed. William Cookson, London: Faber & Faber, 1973

SR Ezra Pound, *The Spirit of Romance: An Attempt to Define Somewhat the Charm of the Pre-Renaissance Literature of Latin Europe*, London: Dent, 1910

SR2 Ezra Pound, *The Spirit of Romance*, rev. edn including the 1912 lecture 'Psychology and the Troubadours', New York: New Directions, 1968

TRIB H.D., *Tribute to Freud*, rev. ed. Manchester: Carcanet, 1985

VE John Gould Fletcher, *Visions of the Evening*, London: Erskine MacDonald, 1913

WBY R.F. Foster, *W.B. Yeats: A Life*: Vol. 1, *The Apprentice Mage, 1865–1914*, Oxford: Oxford University Press, 1998

WBY2 R.F. Foster, *W.B. Yeats: A Life*: Vol. 2, *The Arch-Poet, 1915–1939*, Oxford: Oxford University Press, 2003

WBYCP W.B. Yeats, *The Poems: a New Edition*, ed. Richard J. Finneran, London: Macmillan, 1983

WT *A Walking Tour in Southern France: Ezra Pound among the Troubadours*, edited and introduced by Richard Sieburth, New York: New Directions, 1992

Journals

EG *The Egoist*

ER *English Review*

JIL *Journal of Irish Literature*, 8/3, September 1979, Joseph Campbell number

NA *The New Age*

NFW *The New Freewoman*

PMV *Poetry: A Magazine of Verse*

PR *Poetry Review*

Manuscripts

AN H.D., 'Autobiographical Notes', Beinecke Rare Book and Manuscript Library, Yale University, YCAL 24 Box 47/1183

BL Patricia Hutchins papers at the British Library

HFL John Gould Fletcher's letters to Amy Lowell at the Houghton Library, Harvard University

HFLL   F.S. Flint's letters to Amy Lowell at the Houghton Library, Harvard University

HHDL   H.D.'s letters to Amy Lowell at the Houghton Library, Harvard University

HLF   Amy Lowell's letters to John Gould Fletcher at the Houghton Library, Harvard University

HLFL   Amy Lowell's letters to F.S. Flint at the Houghton Library, Harvard University

HLHD   Amy Lowell's letters to H.D. at the Houghton Library, Harvard University

HLP   Amy Lowell's letters to Ezra Pound at the Houghton Library, Harvard University

HLRA   Amy Lowell's letters to Richard Aldington at the Houghton Library, Harvard University

HRAL   Richard Aldington's letters to Amy Lowell at the Houghton Library, Harvard University

SIU   Richard Aldington's papers at the Special Collections Research Center, Morris Library, Southern Illinois University, Carbondale

UAF   John Gould Fletcher's papers at the Special Collections, University of Arkansas Libraries at Fayetteville

UCD   Desmond FitzGerald's papers at UCD Archives, James Joyce Library, University College, Dublin.

UTA   F. S. Flint's papers at the Harry Ransom Humanities Research Center, University of Texas at Austin

YB   Bryher's papers in the Beinecke Rare Book and Manuscript Library, Yale University, YCAL 97

YHD   H.D.'s papers in the Beinecke Rare Book and Manuscript Library, Yale University, YCAL 24

YP   Ezra Pound's papers in the Beinecke Rare Book and Manuscript Library, Yale University, YCAL 43

NOTES

Prologue

1 END 18
2 T.S. Eliot, 'American Literature and the American Language', in *To Criticize the Critic and Other Writings*, London: Faber & Faber, 1965, p. 58
3 Ezra Pound, 'The Later Yeats', PMV 4/2, May 1914, p. 65
4 Aldington used the phrase in his introduction to his *Complete Poems*: CPRA 13
5 Christopher Middleton, 'Documents on Imagism from the Papers of F.S. Flint', *The Review*, 15, 1965, p. 43
6 LL 121

Part One: American Beginnings

1 H.D. in *The Cantos of Ezra Pound: Some Testimonies*, Ernest Hemingway et al., New York, Farrar & Rinehart, 1933, p. 17. Pound in fact didn't go to Tunis, though he did visit Tangiers
2 END 3
3 H.D. in *The Cantos of Ezra Pound*, p. 17
4 All quotations from Henry James in this chapter are from Chapter IX, 'Philadelphia', in *The American Scene* [1907], Harmondsworth: Penguin, 1994, pp. 202–223
5 EPP 8
6 IND 14
7 END 22
8 IND 21
9 END 22
10 Lincoln Steffens, *The Shame of the Cities*, London: Heinemann, 1904, p. 193
11 LE 327
12 IND 54
13 HC 26
14 BP 59
15 RTY 388
16 According to Humphrey Carpenter he eventually reached the height of 5' 10", though whether or not that includes the piles of red-gold curls he doesn't say
17 YP 59/2647. Pound's letters to his parents are largely undated, though often a date is suggested in what appears to be Homer's handwriting. Sometimes this seems to have been added in retrospect, though sometimes the date given seems to be the date when the letter arrived. This letter is in fact dated 'Jan 18', though unusually no one has added a year date.

I will generally not give dates for these letters, but cite the folder in which they are kept in the Beinecke Rare Books and Manuscript Library, Yale University

18 HC 34

19 A. David Moody suggests in his recent book that Pound did not get to Tangiers until his next visit with Aunt Frank in 1902: see *Ezra Pound: Poet. A Portrait of the Man and his Work*: Vol. 1, *The Young Genius 1885–1920*, Oxford: Oxford University Press, 2007, p. 10

20 END 14

21 NS 23

22 HER 65

23 CEP 34

24 LE 320

25 EPL 146, Dedication to *A Lume Spento*

26 It taught such skills as textile design, illustration, ceramics, metalwork and interior decoration, as well as offering classes in drawing, painting and sculpture. Over 1,000 students enrolled in 1901–2; in 1910 the figure for the University of Pennsylvania was 697. Carol Troyen and Erica Hirshler, *Charles Sheeler: Paintings and Drawings*, Boston: Little, Brown, 1987, p. 3

27 EPP 33

28 Walter Pater, *The Renaissance: Studies in Art and Poetry* [1875], London: Macmillan, 1902, pp. 237–239

29 Ronald Bush sees him as being under Pater's influence until 1915, and visionary moments remain important right to the end of the *Cantos*: see Ronald Bush, *The Genesis of Ezra Pound's Cantos*, Princeton: Princeton University Press, 1976

30 END 13–14

31 These letters are reproduced in James J. Wilhelm, 'The Letters of William Brooke Smith', *Paideuma*, 19/1 & 2, 1990, pp. 163–168

32 END 15

33 Wilhelm, 'The Letters of William Brooke Smith', p. 168

34 Ernest Earnest, *S. Weir Mitchell: Novelist and Physician*, Philadelphia: University of Pennsylvania Press, 1950, pp. 180 & 178

35 Nathan Hale, *Freud in America: The Beginnings of Psychoanalysis in the United States, 1876–1917*, New York: Oxford University Press, 1971, p. 44

36 EPL 229

37 Emily Mitchell Wallace, 'Youthful Days and Costly Hours', in Daniel Hoffman, ed., *Ezra Pound & William Carlos Williams: The University of Pennsylvania Conference Papers*, Philadelphia: University of Pennsylvania Press, 1983, p. 27

38 AMY 117

39 William Carlos Williams, *I wanted to write a poem: the autobiography of the works of a poet*, reported and edited by Edith Heal, Boston: Beacon Press, 1958, p. 5

40 David Frail, *The Early Politics and Poetics of William Carlos Williams*, Ann Arbor: UMI Research Press, 1987, p. 29

41 Williams, *I wanted to write a poem*, p. 5

42 Ibid., p. 7

43 Paul Mariani, *William Carlos Williams: A New World Naked*, New York: McGraw-Hill, 1982, pp. 101 & 109 on Pound and *The Tempers*

44 William Carlos Williams, *The Autobiography of William Carlos Williams*, New York: Random House, 1951, p. 58

45 YP 59/2648. Here the letter in which the phrase 'delighted . . .' comes is dated 11 June, and someone (I think Homer) has added 1903. The letter from which 'or be out . . .' comes is dated by Pound 'Monday night' and the other hand has added 'Sept 20'

46 YP 59/2649, 29 April (1904)

47 YP 59/2651

48 Ibid.

49 YP 59/2652

50 YP 59/2651

51 'Introduction' to *Oxford Book of Modern Verse: 1892–1935*, ed. W.B. Yeats, Oxford: Oxford University Press, 1936, p. xi

52 Pater, *The Renaissance*, p. 2

53 Roy Harvey Pearce, *The Continuity of American Poetry*, Princeton: Princeton University Press, 1961

54 SR viii

55 Faubion Bowers, 'Memoir within Memoir', *Paideuma*, 2/1, 1973. Her father was a well-known German Jewish violinist, though as her mother was gentile, she was technically right to say that she was not Jewish

56 YP 59/2650

57 EPL 146–7

58 'Scriptor Ignotus', CEP 24–6

59 Quoted in Leon Surette, *The Birth of Modernism: Ezra Pound, T.S. Eliot, W.B. Yeats and the Occult*, Montreal: McGill-Queen's University Press, 1993, p. 13. Surette is one who has argued strongly for the importance of the occult for many modernists. See also Timothy Materer, *Modernist Alchemy: Poetry and the Occult*, Ithaca: Cornell University Press, 1995

60 Elizabeth Butler Cullingford, 'At the Feet of the Goddess: Yeats's Love Poetry and the Feminist Occult', in *Yeats and Women*, ed. Deirdre Toomey, Basingstoke: Macmillan, 1997, pp. 55–6

61 Wassily Kandinsky, *Concerning the Spiritual in Art*, trans. M.T.H. Sadler [German original, 1911, trans. 1914], New York: Dover, 1977, p. 13

62 See Demetres P. Tryphonopoulos, '"That Great Year Epic": Ezra Pound, Katherine Ruth Heyman and H.D.', in Jacqueline Kaye, ed., *Ezra Pound & America*, Basingstoke: Macmillan, 1992

63 Williams, *Autobiography*, pp. 56–7

64 YB 16/612. Letter to Bryher, 17 October 1948

65 YP 59/2650

66 John L. Brown, writing in 1932, quoted in E. Fuller Torrey, *The Roots of Treason: Ezra Pound and the Secret of St Elizabeths*, London: Sidgwick & Jackson, 1984, p. 29

67 P/W 6

68 Charles Norman, *Ezra Pound*, rev. edn, London: Macdonald, 1969, p. 13

69 EPP 35

70 CEP 91

71 LE 367

72 CEP 46

73 Hugh Witemeyer, *The Poetry of Ezra Pound: Forms and Renewals, 1908–1920*, Berkeley: University of California Press, 1969, p. 47. He argues that 'Motif' draws particularly on Fiona Macleod's 'The Unknown Wind'

74 'The Renaissance: 1', PMV 5/5, February 1915, p. 228

75 TRIB 32

76 GIFT 37

77 GIFT2 xi

78 GIFT 94

79 TRIB 187

80 GIFT 41

81 GIFT 89

82 GIFT 47–8

83 GIFT 112

84 GIFT 101

85 GIFT 90, TRIB 121

86 TRIB 28, 33

87 TRIB 124 (final ellipsis H.D.'s)

88 GIFT 96, 98

89 TRIB 33, 121

90 Williams, *Autobiography*, p. 68

91 PIT 5

92 TRIB 132

93 *To the Lighthouse* [1927], Oxford: Oxford University Press, 2006, p. 9

94 PIT 8

95 Emily Mitchell Wallace, 'Hilda Doolittle at Friends' Central School in 1905', *H.D. Newsletter*, 1/1, Spring 1987, pp. 17–28; pp. 18 & 22

96 Ibid. p. 18

97 TRIB x

98 Emily Wallace suggests H.D. must have been exceptional to be allowed to take the examination in 1904, but there is no evidence that it was seen this way

99 PIT 5

100 END 12

101 END 50

102 ASPH 39

103 See Williams, *I wanted to write a poem*, p. 7. According to Emily Wallace, Bryn Mawr did let their students study Greek, but H.D. was never given the chance

104 Williams, *Autobiography*, p. 57

105 Barbara Guest, *Herself Defined: The Poet H.D. and her World* [1984], London: Collins, 1985, p. 20

106 John C. Thirwall, ed., *The Selected Letters of William Carlos Williams*, New York: McDowell, Obolensky, 1957, pp. 8–9

107 Wallace, 'Youthful Days and Costly Hours', p. 14

108 Williams, *Autobiography*, p. 68

109 Ibid.

110 Emily Wallace, 'Afterword: the House of the Father's Science and the Mother's Art', *William Carlos Williams Newsletter*, 2/2, Fall 1976, p. 5

111 William Carlos Williams, 'A Letter from William Carlos Williams to Norman Holmes Pearson Concerning Hilda Doolittle and Her Mother and Father' (11 July 1955), *William Carlos Williams Newsletter*, 2/2, Fall 1976, p. 3

112 Letter from H.D. to William Carlos Williams, quoted in Frail, *The Early Politics and Poetics of William Carlos Williams*, p. 44

113 Williams, 'A Letter', p. 2

114 END 22–3

115 Glenn Hughes, *Imagism & the Imagists: A Study in Modern Poetry*, California: Stanford University Press, 1931, p. 110

116 James McNeill Whistler, 'The Ten O'Clock Lecture', in *Mr Whistler's 'Ten o'Clock' together with Mr Swinburne's Comment and Mr Whistler's Reply*, Chicago: Old Dominion Shop, 1904, p. 3

117 LE 367

118 END 23

119 END 70

120 EP/MC 41

121 HD 88

122 END 3–4

123 END 12

124 Ibid.

125 Ibid.

126 William Carlos Williams, *Imaginations*, New York: New Directions, 1970, p. 12

127 Ibid.

128 SP 41

129 Williams, *I wanted to write a poem*, p. 4

130 Williams, *Autobiography*, p. 52

131 Pater, *The Renaissance*, p. 12

132 SR 83–4

133 Pater, *The Renaissance*, p. 13

134 Hughes, *Imagism & the Imagists*, p. 110

135 Ibid.

136 YP 59/2650

137 SR2 48, SR 58

138 EPP 58

139 'Burgos: A Dream City of Old Castile', *Book News Monthly*, 25/2, October 1906, pp 91–94 in EPP&PI, 11

140 'Raphaelite Latin', *Book News Monthly*, 25/1, September 1906, pp. 31–34, in EPP&PI, 5

141 Pater, *The Renaissance*, xx–xxi

142 He later irritated Pound considerably by asking at one point for free copies of his books, although by then he, unlike Pound, was a rich man, which may explain Pound's refusal to acknowledge what he learnt from him. See LE 367

143 See, for example, Cornelius Weygandt, *Tuesday at Ten: A Garnering from the Talks of Thirty Years*, Philadelphia: University of Pennsylvania Press, 1928 and *The Time of Yeats: English Poetry of To-day against an American Background*, New York: D. Appleton-Century, 1937

144 Susan Stanford Friedman, ed., *Analyzing Freud: Letters of H.D., Bryher and their Circle*, New York: New Directions, 2002, p. 213

145 Ibid., pp. 212–3

146 HER 5

147 TRIB x

148 END 15

149 Hale, *Freud in America*, p. 85

150 Wallace, 'Youthful Days and Costly Hours', p. 27

151 END ix, 18–19

152 Williams, 'A Letter', p. 2

153 'Toward the Piraeus,' HDCP 177

154 END 17

155 Ibid.

156 HER 85, 174

157 'Toward the Piraeus', HDCP 179

158 HER 172–3

159 HC 70

160 YP 59/2654

161 PER 19–20

162 W.B. Yeats, *Ideas of Good and Evil*, London: Macmillan, 1903, pp. 168, 178

163 Ezra Pound, 'Letters to Viola Baxter Jordan', ed. with commentary by Donald Gallup, *Paideuma*, 1, 1972, p. 109

164 PER 3, WBYCP 81. See Witemeyer, *Poetry of Ezra Pound*, p. 48

165 END 84, 73

166 HER 42, 82, 83

167 SR2 92

168 Witemeyer, *Poetry of Ezra Pound*, p. 24

169 On Pound and Browning, see Mary Ellis Gibson, *Epic Re-Invented: Ezra Pound and the Victorians*, Ithaca: Cornell University Press, 1995

170 Pound, 'Letters to Viola Baxter Jordan', p. 107

171 P/W 7 (In quoting from this text, I silently omit the editor's use of '*sic*', which is not inserted in most editions of Pound's correspondence, though in EPL his spelling is tidied)

172 Pater, *The Renaissance*, p. 171

173 Pound, 'Letters to Viola Baxter Jordan', p. 109

174 DHLL2 183

175 T.S. Eliot, 'The Love Song of J. Alfred Prufrock', *Collected Poems: 1909–1935*, London: Faber & Faber, p. 12

176 GB 98

177 'The Truth of Masks' was one of the essays in Oscar Wilde's 1891 volume, *Intentions*

178 PER 6–8

179 'Letters to Violet Baxter Jordan', p. 110

180 PM 81

181 Pound's letters to Mary Moore are held in the University of Pennsylvania archives

182 HC 77

183 END 15–16

184 YP 59/2655

185 END 14

186 NS 55

187 PER 240

188 END ix

189 Barbara Guest, *Herself Defined: The Poet H.D. and her World*, London: Collins, 1985, p. 6

190 YB 16/612 (Letter to Bryher, 13 October 1948)

191 END 15

192 END 35; 'Toward the Piraeus', HDCP 176

193 END 47

194 YHD 13/466, 24 June 1959

Part Two: Entry into Europe

1   EPK 40

2   YP 59/2555

3   NS 57

4   YP 59/2664

5   YP 59/2655

6   Phyllis Bottome, *From the Life*, London: Faber & Faber, 1944, p. 76

7   YP 59/2555 (Pound's ellipsis)

8   Ibid.

9   YP 59/2656

10 Ibid.

11 Ibid.

12 YP 59/2665

13 HLRA (19 January 1915)

14 CEP 9–10 (Pound's ellipses)

15 CEP 8

16 CEP 5

17 HC 95
18 CEP 322 (the editor suggests 'is' could be 'was', and 'intensity' may be 'intensifying')
19 Williams, *I wanted to write a poem*, p. 18
20 CEP 322
21 Walter Pater, *The Renaissance: Studies in Art and Poetry* [1873], London: Macmillan, 1902, pp. 239, 189–190. See Herbert Sussman, *Victorian Masculinities: Manhood and Masculine Poetics in Early Victorian Literature and Art*, Cambridge: Cambridge University Press, 1995
22 CEP 252
23 CEP 320. The quotation is not actually reproduced in CEP, but I presume Pound used the Authorized Version, as here
24 YP 59/2655
25 Ibid.
26 YP 59/2657
27 HC 107
28 YP 59/2658
29 YP 59/2657
30 Ibid.
31 CEP 71
32 Thomas H. Jackson, *The Early Poetry of Ezra Pound*, Cambridge, MA: Harvard University Press, 1968
33 'Verse', *The New Age*, 6 January 1910
34 David Leverenz, *Manhood and the American Renaissance*, Ithaca: Cornell University Press, 1989
35 Sussman, *Victorian Masculinities*, p. 168
36 HC 113
37 SL, 46
38 Ernest Rhys, *Everyman Remembers*, London: Dent, 1931, p. 114
39 James G. Nelson, *Elkin Mathews: Publisher to Yeats, Joyce, Pound*, Madison: University of Wisconsin Press, 1989, p. 7. My thanks to Chris Baldick for introducing me to this fascinating book, as to many others
40 Owen Seaman, *The Battle of the Bays*, London: John Lane, Bodley Head, 1896, p. 24
41 Richard Le Gallienne, *The Romantic '90s* [1926], London: Robin Clark, 1993, p. 98
42 Nelson, *Elkin Mathews*, p. 16, EPK 58
43 Nelson, *Elkin Mathews*, p. 252, n. 30
44 Ibid., p. 16
45 Quoted in R.K.R. Thornton, ed., *Poetry of the Nineties*, Harmondsworth: Penguin, 1970, p. 26
46 Nelson, *Elkin Mathews*, p. 134
47 See P/W 7–11, from which the all following quotations come
48 See David Moody's perceptive analyses of Pound's early poems, particularly his early experiments with metrics and cadence. A. David Moody, *Ezra Pound: Poet. A Portrait of the Man and His Work*: Vol. 1, *The Young Genius 1885–1920*, Oxford: Oxford University Press, 2007
49 Pater, *The Renaissance*, p. xix
50 James Griffyth Fairfax, *The Gates of Sleep, and Other Poems*, Vigo Cabinet Series no. 38, London: Elkin Mathews, 1906
51 YP 59/2661
52 EP/DS 3
53 YP 59/2659. Carpenter and Qian say Mathews in fact introduced them
54 Laurence Binyon, 'For the Fallen', *The Winnowing-Fan: Poems on the Great War*, London: Elkin Mathews, 1914, p. 29
55 YP 59/2659
56 EPC 572

57   YP 59/2660
58   Zhaoming Qian, *Orientalism and Modernism: The Legacy of China in Pound and Williams*, Durham, NC: Duke University Press, 1995
59   Rhys, *Everyman Remembers*, pp. 252, 105, 255
60   YP 59/2661
61   Rhys, *Everyman Remembers*, p. 93
62   YP 59/2659
63   Ibid.
64   Ibid.
65   P/W 13
66   William Carlos Williams, 'A Street Market, N.Y., 1908', *Poems*, privately printed by Reid Howell, Rutherford, 1909, p. 15
67   P/W 14–15
68   See WBY 259, 337
69   'Impressionism – Some Speculations: II', PMV 2/6, September 1913, p. 220
70   ER I, December 1908, p. 2
71   FORD 243
72   Jessie Chambers, *D.H. Lawrence: A Personal Record*, London: Jonathan Cape, 1935, p. 156
73   FY 19–20
74   END 9–10
75   RTY 371
76   In January 1910, a letter to his mother says that Ford was reading Pound extracts from his novel *The Simple Life Limited*, but that is all. At this stage Pound read little prose, certainly not modern fiction
77   'Impressionism – Some Speculations: II', p. 217
78   FORD 28
79   FY 141
80   SL 39
81   FORD 42
82   'Ford Madox Hueffer', NFW, 15 December 1913, p. 251
83   BP 54
84   SL 9
85   Alan G. Hill, 'Introduction' to Ford Madox Ford, *The Soul of London: A Survey of a Modern City* [1905], London: Dent, 1995, p. xxi
86   Guy de Maupassant, *Pierre and Jean*, London: Heinemann, 1890, pp. 12, 14, 15–16
87   FORD 388
88   Ford Madox Ford, 'English Literature Today', ER 3, October 1909, p. 488
89   RTY 389
90   See *Stories from de Maupassant*, trans. E.M. (Elsie Martindale), preface by Ford Madox Hueffer, London: Duckworth, 1903. One person who has looked at this is R. G. Hampson in '"Experiments in Modernity": Ford and Pound', in *Pound in Multiple Perspective*, ed. Andrew Gibson, Basingstoke: Macmillan, 1993
91   David Garnett, *The Golden Echo*, London: Chatto & Windus, 1953, p. 118
92   FY 57
93   SL 89
94   SL 42
95   BP 50, 52
96   Garnett, *Golden Echo*, p. 183
97   SL 135
98   Wyndham Lewis, *Rude Assignment*, London: Hutchinson, 1950, p. 122, FORD 368
99   FY 41

100 FORD 28. Judith Soskice, *Chapters from Childhood: Reminiscences of an Artist's Grand-daughter*, London: Selwyn & Blount, 1921, pp. 1–2, 3–4, 10; FORD 46

101 Soskice, *Chapters from Childhood*, pp. 1–2, 3–4, 10

102 Ford, *Soul of London*, pp. 12–13

103 Douglas Goldring, *Odd Man Out: The Autobiography of a 'Propaganda Novelist'*, London: Chapman & Hall, 1935, p. 121

104 Ford, *Soul of London*, p. 13

105 RTY 370, 388

106 Attempts have been made to date their meeting to a party on 4 April, but that depends on yet another colourful anecdotal memoir, David Garnett's *The Golden Echo*, not necessarily a wholly reliable source

Part Three: The School of Images at the Tour Eiffel

1 YP 59/2659

2 Douglas Goldring, *Odd Man Out: The Autobiography of a 'Propaganda Novelist'*, London: Chapman & Hall, 1935, p. 120

3 Later still, when that area north of Oxford Street became known as Fitzrovia, the Tour Eiffel, by then in other hands and known as the White Tower, became a favourite drinking place for Dylan Thomas and his writer friends

4 Robert Ferguson, *The Short Sharp Life of T.E. Hulme*, London: Allen Lane, 2002, p. 30

5 It was perhaps a sign of the times that while the Rhymers' Club, which had met at the Cheshire Cheese pub in Fleet Street, was entirely male, fifteen years later the Poets' Club admitted women, and women poets several times gained their annual prize for the best poem of the year

6 F.S. Flint, 'Book of the Week: Recent Verse', NA, 11 February 1909

7 T.E. Hulme, 'Belated Romanticism', NA, 18 February 1909

8 'A History of Imagism', EG 2, 1 May 1915, p. 70; WBY 43; Ferguson, *T.E. Hulme*, p. 43

9 Ferguson, *T.E. Hulme*, pp. 20–21

10 HULME 49

11 J.C. Squire, *The Honeysuckle and the Bee*, London: Heinemann, 1937, p. 155

12 HULME 3

13 There is extant a letter from his college's director of music alleging that Hulme was 'ruining . . . one of the choral-scholars' morals by day and night', but although later Hulme was to cultivate an image as a womaniser, this is the only hint of sexual scandal for now, though that would be the central issue when he was sent down from Cambridge for a second time in 1912. Ferguson, *T.E. Hulme*, p. 29

14 Ferguson, *T.E. Hulme*, p. 27

15 J.B. Harmer, *Victory in Limbo: Imagism 1908–1917*, London: Secker & Warburg, 1975, p. 18

16 Alun R. Jones, *The Life and Opinions of T.E. Hulme*, London: Victor Gollancz, 1960, p. 22; Ferguson, *T.E. Hulme*, p. 34

17 HULME 22

18 Herbert Read, who brought out the first book-length collection of Hulme's writings, suggested they were meant to be a set of aphorisms, held together by an allegory, on the model of Nietzsche's *Thus Spake Zarathustra*; there is a reference to a mysterious Aphra at one point, whom Read identifies as the potential Zarathustra figure, but if that were Hulme's plan, it was left in embryo

19 HULME 86

20 HULME 87

21 HULME 53

22 HULME 10–11, 9, 11

23 HULME 8

24 HULME 50

25 UCD Every Day Diary, 3–9 July 1930, P80/1202 (7)

26 'History of Imagism', p. 71

27 BB 111

28 LL 154

29 BL ADD 57725, marginal note by Pound on Patricia Hutchins' draft of 'Ezra Pound in Kensington', p. 7

30 David Garnett, *The Golden Echo*, London: Chatto & Windus, 1953, p. 237

31 HULME 15, 13

32 See Maud Ellmann, *The Poetics of Impersonality: T.S. Eliot and Ezra Pound*, Brighton: Harvester Press, 1987

33 David Trotter, *Paranoid Modernism: Literary Experiment, Psychosis, and the Professionalization of English Society*, Oxford: Oxford University Press, 2001

34 HULME 233

35 Hulme has often been attacked as a contradictory and muddled thinker, but that has largely been because his work was originally published undated and confusingly arranged. In the first collection of Hulme's writings to appear, edited by Herbert Read under the title of *Speculations* in 1924, and for a long time the only available source of most of Hulme's work, the essays are almost precisely in reverse chronological order. The publication of *Further Speculations* in 1954 did nothing to clarify the chronology, which has only recently been established. As Hulme's ideas changed significantly about 1912, trying to read what was written before and afterwards as a coherent philosophical stance was certainly problematic

36 HULME 3

37 Dominic Hibberd, *Harold Monro: Poet of the New Age*, London: Palgrave, 2001, p. 104

38 All unattributed quotations in this chapter are from Flint's unpublished papers in the Harry Ransom Humanities Research Center, University of Texas at Austin (UTA)

39 See Flint's obituary by H.B. Grimsditch, reprinted in *The Fourth Imagist: Selected Poems of F.S. Flint*, ed. Michael Copp, Madison: Fairleigh Dickinson University Press, 2007, p. 141

40 At this stage he was probably not yet reading Nietzsche in German, as in 1909 there are lists of German vocabulary in one of his notebooks, suggesting that he was only working on it then. Certainly by 1911, he was quoting Nietzsche in German and complaining that he was badly translated. Perhaps he learnt German so that he could read Nietzsche in the original

41 Flint gives this passage the date 1868, the date of its first appearance in Pater's essay on William Morris; both that essay and the conclusion of the first edition of *The Renaissance* use the phrase 'art for art's sake'. Pater dropped the conclusion altogether for the second edition, and when he restored it for the third edition modified the phrase to 'art for its own sake'

42 This final quotation comes from the essay on Winckelmann in Walter Pater, *The Renaissance: Studies in Art and Poetry* [1873], London: Macmillan, 1902, p. 188

43 Foreword to J.B. Hobman, ed., *David Eder: Memoirs of a Modern Pioneer*, London: Victor Gollancz, 1945, p. 9. The book's appearance must have been delayed by the war; Freud died in 1939

44 Wallace Martin, *'The New Age' under Orage: Chapters in English Cultural History*, Manchester: Manchester University Press, 1967, p. 140

45 Hobman, *David Eder*, p. 21

46 'Unreality', NA, 2 December 1907

47 Quoted in Martin, *'The New Age'*, p. 19

48 Samuel Hynes, *Edwardian Occasions: Essays on English Writing in the Early Twentieth Century*, London: Routledge & Kegan Paul, 1972, p. 41

49 Ibid. pp. 42–43

50 Martin, *'The New Age'*, p. 41

51 Hynes, *Edwardian Occasions*, p. 44

52 EPK 104

53 Hynes, *Edwardian Occasions*, p. 42

54 Ibid.

55 NA, 6 June 1907

56 See Martin, '*The New Age*', p. 91

57 EPK 106. Pound did not appear in the *New Age* for most of 1914, as will become apparent

58 Wallace Martin, ed., *Orage as Critic*, London: Routledge & Kegan Paul, 1974, pp. 135, 143, 138

59 Ann Ardis in particular has rightly argued that recent accounts have too glibly seen the *New Age* as a modernist journal, but I think she overstates its hostility to the avant-garde; it is true that from about 1913 onwards the avant-garde would often be attacked in its pages, but it generally went on publishing their work. See Ann Ardis, *Modernism and Cultural Conflict: 1880–1922*, Cambridge: Cambridge University Press, 2002

60 'Women and Men 4: Average People', *Little Review*, 6/1, May 1918, p. 59

61 'Palinode', NA, 18 January 1908

62 These articles appeared in the journal *Les Lettres* but were later collected in Paul-Louis Couchoud, *Sages et poètes d'Asie*, Paris: Calmann-Lévy, 1916. This phrase appears on p. 7

63 'Recent Verse', NA, 11 July 1908

64 Edward Storer, *Mirrors of Illusion*, London: Sisley's, 1908, pp. 80, 81

65 'Recent Verse', NA, 28 November 1908

66 EPC 518 (Canto 81)

67 Storer, *Mirrors of Illusion*, pp. 26, 71

68 Hulme 53, 51, 50–1. This time he gave the assemblage no overall name, though it has since been published as 'Notes on Language and Style'

69 HULME 16

70 HULME 44

71 On Pound and de Gourmont, see Richard Sieburth, *Instigations: Ezra Pound and Rémy de Gourmont*, Cambridge, MA: Harvard University Press, 1978

72 Richard Aldington, ed., *Selections from Rémy de Gourmont* [1928], London: Chatto & Windus, 1932, p. 21

73 Ibid., p. 109

74 HULME 27, 31, 51

75 HULME 87

76 Henri Bergson, *An Introduction to Metaphysics* (first published in French in 1903), trans. T.E. Hulme (first published in 1912), Indianapolis/Cambridge: Hackett 1999, pp. 27–28

77 HULME 54

78 HULME 3

79 HULME 21

80 HULME 51

81 Harmer, *Victory in Limbo*, p. 21

82 UCD Letter from D. Fitzgerald to Mabel McConnell, 1910 or 1911, P80/1496(3)

83 'Looking Backwards: 1879–1900', JIL, p. 60

84 Ibid., p. 66

85 Ibid.

86 Ibid., pp. 66–67 (second two sets of ellipses his)

87 'The Turn of the Century', JIL, p. 79

88 Austin Clarke, ed., *The Poems of Joseph Campbell*, Dublin: Allen Figgis, 1963, p. 1

89 'Persons, Plays and Songs', JIL, pp. 94–95

90 Norah Saunders and A.A. Kelly, *Joseph Campbell, Poet and Nationalist: A Critical Biography*, Dublin: Wolfhound, 1988, p. 32

91 Austin Clarke, 'Joseph Campbell: A Personal Sketch and a Critical Assessment', JIL., p. 21

92 Joseph Campbell, *The Rushlight*, Dublin: Maunsel, 1906, p. 7

93 'This Hulme Business', *The Townsman*, 11/5, January 1939, reprinted in EPP&P7 417

94 Clarke, 'Joseph Campbell', 22

95 W.B. Yeats, *Uncollected Prose, 1886–1896*, Vol. 1, ed. John P. Frayne, London: Macmillan, 1970, pp. 272, 274

96 Ibid. See also WBY 131

97 Clarke, 'Joseph Campbell', p. 22

98 WBY 306

99 Clifford Bax, ed., *Florence Farr, Bernard Shaw, W.B. Yeats: Letters*, London: Home & Van Thal, 1946, p. v

100 Ibid., p. ix

101 Ibid., p. 33 (from a letter to Edward Dowden)

102 Ibid., p. 54

103 Ibid., p. 33

104 Josephine Johnson, *Florence Farr: Bernard Shaw's 'New Woman'*, Gerrards Cross: Colin Smythe, 1975, p. 144

105 Bax, *Florence Farr*, pp. 13, 34

106 Mary K. Greer, *Women of the Golden Dawn: Rebels and Priestesses*, Rochester, Vermont: Park Street Press, 1993, p. 85; Johnson, *Florence Farr*, p. 157

107 *The Music of Speech, containing the words of poets, thinkers and musicmakers regarding the practice of the bardic art, together with fragments of verse set to its own melody by F. Farr*, London: Elkin Mathews, 1909, p. 10. On Farr's influence on the group, see Ronald Schuchard, '"As Regarding Rhythm": Yeats and the Imagists', in *Yeats: an Annual of Critical and Textual Studies*, 2, 1984

108 BL ADD 57725, Ezra Pound to Patricia Hutchins 7 November, 1957

109 UCD Introductory section of an account of his political awakening, p 80/1382

110 Garret FitzGerald, *All in a Life: An Autobiography*, Dublin: Gill & Macmillan, 1991, p. 3

111 Ibid., p. 5

112 In later life he displayed a deep knowledge of French literature and philosophy, an interest that perhaps began with his friendship with Flint. In the 1930s he was for a while a professor of philosophy at Notre Dame University in the United States. By that time he was concerned with French Catholic philosophers like Jacques Maritain, but in his more radical younger days his philosophical bent apparently led him elsewhere

113 Garret FitzGerald, personal communication

114 HULME 217

115 *The Shanachie, an Irish Miscellany*, Vol. 6, Winter 1907

116 UCD P80/1382

117 Vincent J. Cheng, *Joyce, Race and Empire*, Cambridge: Cambridge University Press, 1995, pp. 19, 33, 37–38; Desmond FitzGerald, *Memoirs, 1913–16*, London: Routledge, & Kegan Paul, 1968, p. 21. My grateful thanks to W.J. McCormack for telling me the poet and the politician were the same person, and for putting me in touch with his son

118 Garret FitzGerald, unpublished papers detailing family history. My warm thanks to Garret FitzGerald for letting me see these, and for all his help and kindness

119 UCD. Written on a spare space of a letter from Langdon Everard, dated 1908, on *Labour Leader* writing paper, P80/1156. It may of course have been written later, perhaps when coming across a letter whose date (Everard had written in ignorance of his bereavement) reminded him of his father's death: yet even if later, it is revealing

120 UCD

121 CEP 214–215

122 UCD 27 February 1914 from Co. Kerry P80/1224(1)

123 F.W. Tancred, *Poems*, Edinburgh: William Blackwood, 1907 (no page number)

124 Ibid.

125 F.S. Flint, 'A History of Imagism', EG 2, 1 May 1915, p. 71. On Tancred see Harmer, *Victory in Limbo*, pp. 22–4

126 Ezra Pound's 'Harold Monro', *Polite Essays*, London: Faber & Faber, 1937, p. 8

127 'A History of Imagism', p. 71

128 Arthur Symons, *The Symbolist Movement in Literature* [1899], New York: AMS Press, 1980, p. 9

129 F.S. Flint, 'Verse', NA, 9 December, 1909. This is also quoted in Wallace Martin, '"The Forgotten School of 1909" and the Origins of Imagism', in J. Howard Woolmer, *A Catalogue of Imagist Poets with Essays by Wallace Martin and Ian Fletcher*, New York: J. Howard Woolmer, 1966

130 The tanka is a slightly longer poem than the haiku, with 31 syllables rather than 17

131 Algernon Swinburne, in James McNeill Whistler, *Mr Whistler's 'Ten O'Clock Lecture' together with Mr Swinburne's Comment and Mr Whistler's Reply*, Chicago: Old Dominion Shop, 1904, pp. 34, 52

132 Earl Miner, *The Japanese Tradition in British and American Literature*, Princeton: Princeton University Press, 1958, p. 74

133 In France, Judith Gautier's translations of Chinese poems, *Le Livre du jade*, had been published to great acclaim in 1867, though none of her poems were translated into English until selections appeared in the *Egoist* in 1915. Judith Gautier's French versions, however, made no attempt to convey anything of the Chinese form. She also published versions (adapted from literal translations) of Japanese tanka in 1885, also conventionally rhymed, as *Poèmes de la libellule*, but at the time these did not cause the same stir

134 Basil Hall Chamberlain, *The Classical Poetry of the Japanese*, London: Kegan Paul, Trench, Trübner, 1880, p. 117 (Japanese poem is attributed to Anon.)

135 Basil Hall Chamberlain, *Japanese Poetry*, London: John Murray, 1911, pp. 4–5, 19–20

136 Chamberlain, *Japanese Poetry*, pp. 149–150, 150–151. Paul-Louis Couchoud had read Chamberlain's article when it was first published, and it had helped arouse his interest in the form

137 Carl Dawson uses Ronald Barthes' phrase 'fictive nation' to describe Hearn's picture of Japan in his book, *Lafcadio Hearn and the Vision of Japan*, Baltimore: Johns Hopkins University Press, 1992

138 See Helen Carr, 'Imagism and Empire', in *Modernism and Empire*, ed. Howard Booth and Nigel Rigby, Manchester: Manchester University Press, 2000, for a discussion of the influence of the haiku

139 Colin Rhodes, *Primitivism and Modern Art*, London: Thames & Hudson, p. 24

140 Translation mine, Couchoud, *Sages et poètes*, p. 8

141 F.S Flint, '*Ripostes* by Ezra Pound', *Poetry and Drama* 1, March 1913, pp. 60–62; Pound, 'Harold Monro', p. 8

142 HULME 3

143 Joseph Campbell, *The Mountainy Singer*, Dublin: Maunsel, 1909, p. 50

144 HDCP 55 'Darkness', *The Mountainy Singer*, p. 3

145 *In the Net of the Stars*, London: Elkin Mathews, 1909, p. 4

146 'A History of Imagism', p. 71

147 Edward Storer, *Mirrors of Illusion*, London: Sisley's, 1908, p. 101

148 'A History of Imagism', p. 71. Ronsard was a sixteenth-century poet

149 PER 26–8. This troubadour is more often known as 'Bertran', but Pound uses the form 'Bertrans', so I follow him

150 YP 59/2660

151 *The Gilly of Christ*, Dublin: Maunsel, 1907, pp. 2–3

152   PER 31

153   YP 59/2660

154   See 'How I Began', *T.P.'s Weekly*, 6 June 1913, in EPP&P1 147. Pound does not mention his debt to Campbell. The figure of 150 cancelled subscriptions is given by Pound to his father; it may well have been an exaggeration

155   YP 59/2663

156   CEP 217

157   Robert R. Ross, *The Georgian Revolt: Rise and Fall of a Poetic Ideal, 1910–22*, London: Faber & Faber, 1967, p. 122

Part Four: Suddenly Somewhat of a Success

1   YP 59/2660

2   Ibid.

3   YP 59/2661

4   YP 59/2662

5   WBY 438

6   WBY 400

7   WBY 388

8   WBYCP 93.

9   P/W 14

10   SL 49

11   CH 60

12   NS 82

13   CH 6

14   YP 59/2660.

15   'Verse', NA, 27 May 1909

16   CH 58–59

17   HC 391

18   PER 15–16

19   CH 55–57

20   CH 59

21   SP 115–116

22   PER 90: Peter Russell, ed., *Ezra Pound: A Collection of Essays to be Presented to Pound on his Sixty-fifth Birthday*, London: Peter Nevill, 1950, p. 262

23   EPK 68

24   YP 59/2661

25   SL 47

26   FY 108

27   FORD 367

28   SL 49

29   FY 108

30   Derek Stanford, 'Introduction', and Oscar Wilde, 'The English Renaissance of Art', in Derek Stanford, ed., *Writing of the Nineties: From Wilde to Beerbohm*, London: Dent, 1971, pp. xvii, 19

31   Ibid., p. 4

32   YP 59/2657.

33   SR2 9

34   YP 59/2663

35   YP 59/2664

36   YP 59/2662

37   NS 93

38   CH 61

39   ER 4, December 1909, pp. 160–161. David Moody suggests this review was by Flint, but it
     sounds far more Ford's style than Flint's, and Flint reviewed *Exultations* in quite different
     terms in the *New Age*. A. David Moody, *Ezra Pound: Poet. A Portrait of the Man and his
     Work*: Vol. I, *The Young Genius 1885–1920*, Oxford: Oxford University Press, 2007, p. 109

40   'Verse', NA, 6 January 1910

41   CEP 121

42   CH 66

43   NS 95

44   SR2 67

45   ER 4, December 1909, p. 161

46   F.S. Flint, *In the Net of the Stars*, London: Elkin Mathews, 1909, p. 11

47   EP/DS 8

48   CEP 126

49   END 15, 54

50   EP/DS 42, CEP 98

51   ASPH 98

52   HC 396

53   Grace Lovat Fraser, *In the Days of My Youth*, London: Cassell, 1970, p. 3

54   Grace in her memoirs says September but Pound mentioned the visit in a letter home on
     30 July

55   Fraser, *In the Days of My Youth*, p. 124

56   Ibid., p. 125

57   Ronald Schuchard, '"As Regarding Rhythm": Yeats and the Imagists', in *Yeats: An Annual
     of Critical and Textual Studies*, Vol. 2, 1984, p. 210

58   Fraser, *In the Days of My Youth*, pp. 127–128

59   JGF 6

60   John Gould Fletcher, *Arkansas*, Chapel Hill: University of North Carolina Press, 1947, p. 130

61   Ibid., pp. 118–119

62   JGF 7

63   LMS 7

64   Ibid., JGF 10

65   JGFP 90–91

66   JGFP 90

67   Michael North, *The Dialectic of Modernism: Race, Language & Twentieth-Century Literature*,
     New York: Oxford University Press, 1994, p. 78

68   JGF 19

69   LMS 21

70   JGF 20

71   LMS 22

72   LMS 19

73   JGF 21

74   JGF 27

75   UAF Box 1, File 17

76   LMS 11

77   LMS 23

78   LMS 8

79   LMS 5

80   LMS 25

81   JGF 29

82 Quoted in LE 364

83 UAF Box 2, file 25, 'Inventory', 1910 p. 16

84 LMS 26

85 LMS 31

86 UAF Box 2, diary for 2 June, 1909

87 Ibid. Box 2, file 25, 'Inventory', 1910, pp. 17, 29

88 Arthur Symons, *The Symbolist Movement in Literature* [1899], New York: AMS Press, 1980, p. 8

89 DHLL1 144

90 DHLL1 145

91 Ibid.

92 DHLL2 132–3

93 D.H. Lawrence, 'Autobiographical Sketch', in *Phoenix II: Uncollected, Unpublished and Other Prose Works by D.H. Lawrence*, ed. Warren Roberts and Harry T. Moore, London: Heinemann, 1968, pp. 593–594

94 Glenn Hughes, *Imagism & the Imagists: A Study in Modern Poetry*, California: Stanford University Press, 1931, p.170

95 Jessie Chambers (E.T.), *D.H. Lawrence: A Personal Record*, London: Jonathan Cape, 1935, pp. 164, 170–174, RTY 96, 97

96 Edward Nehls, ed., *D.H. Lawrence: A Composite Biography*: Vol. 1, *1885–1919*, Madison: University of Wisconsin Press, 1957, p. 142

97 BP 81

98 Chambers, *D.H. Lawrence*, p. 57

99 John Worthen, *D.H. Lawrence: The Early Years 1885–1912* [1991], Cambridge: Cambridge University Press, 1992, p. 222

100 Russell, *Ezra Pound*, pp. 258–259

101 Chambers, *D.H. Lawrence*, p. 96

102 RTY 392

103 Worthen, *D.H. Lawrence: The Early Years* p. 171. Lawrence and his friends were, however, probably given more space to discuss such subversive ideas in the Eastwood Debating Society, run by the Socialist Willie Hopkin, than in the Chapel

104 Fraser, *In the Days of My Youth*, p. 137. CH 63

105 Ibid., pp. 137, 143, 144

106 Phyllis Bottome, *From the Life*, London: Faber & Faber, 1944, p. 76

107 EP/DS 15

108 Fraser, *In the Days of My Youth*, p. 134

109 In *Blasting and Bombardiering* (BB 278), Lewis dated his meeting with Pound to 1910, but it was probably the year before

110 SL 40

111 FORD 247

112 FORD 279

113 Jeffrey Meyers, *The Enemy: A Biography of Wyndham Lewis*, London: Routledge & Kegan Paul, 1980, p. 1

114 Quoted in Gill Perry, 'Primitivism and the Modern', in Charles Harrison, Francis Frascina and Gill Perry, *Primitivism, Abstraction, Cubism*, New Haven: Yale University Press, 1993, p. 8

115 Meyers, *The Enemy*, pp. 23–24

116 Paul Edwards, *Wyndham Lewis, Painter and Writer*, New Haven: Yale University Press, 2000

117 Michael Holroyd, *Augustus John: The New Biography* [1996], London: Vintage, 1997, p. 259

118 Meyers, *The Enemy*, p. 23

119 *Tarr: The 1918 Version*, ed. Paul O'Keeffe, Santa Rosa: Black Sparrow Press, 1990, pp. 30, 31, 29, 60

120 BB 281
121 Ibid.
122 EPC 507 (Canto 80)
123 SL 39
124 BB 279
125 BB 280
126 Russell, *Ezra Pound*, pp. 257–258
127 *Criterion*, April 1935, p. 436
128 HC 140
129 YP 59/2663
130 Verna Coleman, *The Last Exquisite: A Portrait of Frederic Manning*, Melbourne: Melbourne University Press, 1990, p. 7
131 P/F 6
132 Manning's poem published ER 4, December 1909, p. 6, Pound's ER 4, January 1910, p. 193
133 James George Frazer, *The Golden Bough: A Study in Magic and Religion: A New Abridgement from the Second and Third Editions*, ed. Robert Fraser, Oxford: Oxford University Press, p. 405
134 Robert Fraser, ed., *Sir James Frazer and the Literary Imagination*, London: Macmillan, 1990, p. 121
135 LE 32
136 Frazer, *Golden Bough*, p. xx
137 Ibid., pp. 53–54
138 T.S. Eliot, '*Ulysses*, Order and Myth', in *Selected Prose of T.S. Eliot*, ed. Frank Kermode, London: Faber & Faber, 1975, p. 178
139 Wilde, 'The English Renaissance of Art', p. 9
140 EPL 246
141 LE 194

Part Five: American Interlude

1   BL ADD 57726, letter from Lucy Masterman to Patricia Hutchins, 9 February, 1965
2   CEP 98
3   YP 59/2664
4   Robert Ackerman, *J.G. Frazer: His Life and Work*, Cambridge: Cambridge University Press, 1987, p. 213
5   DRE 468
6   Ibid.
7   YP 59/2660
8   YP 59/2665
9   Ibid.
10 SR 13
11 YP 59/2664
12 YP 59/2665
13 EPC 471 (Canto 77). This is a reference to Swinburne's poem, 'Dolores', whose subtitle is the Virgin Mary's title of 'Notre Dame de Sept Douleurs'
14 EP/MC 17
15 EP/MC 10, 11, 12, 31, 20
16 SR 239
17 YP 59/2665. This is a letter addressed to 'Dear H' which Noel Stock takes to be H.D. Possibly because it refers to the beauty of the place so eloquently, H.D. may have passed it on to his parents, hence its survival
18 EP/MC 31

19   Sirmione as the home of the gods reappears in Pound's early versions of the *Cantos* in 1917

20   SR 97

21   P/J 57

22   SR 51

23   EP/DS 19

24   EP/DS 33–34

25   NS 86

26   CEP 150

27   EP/DS 8

28   YP 59/2661

29   CEP 322

30   BL ADD 57726, letter from Lucy Masterman to Patricia Hutchins, 9 February, 1965

31   EP/DS 23

32   EP/DS 24

33   DHLLI 165–166

34   EP/DS 26

35   END 15

36   PIT 7

37   HER 57

38   In what follows I shall make clear when I am drawing on the fiction, and readers can judge for themselves

39   PIT 39

40   William Carlos Williams, 'A Letter from William Carlos Williams to Norman Holmes Pearson Concerning Hilda Doolittle and Her Mother and Father' (11 July 1955) *William Carlos Williams Newsletter*, 2/2, Fall 1976, p. 2

41   PIT 7

42   END 48

43   This collection was probably the 1608 anthology collected by Ranulus Gherus, on which Pound had written in the *Book News Monthly* before he left the States, and from which he translated at least one poem while in Crawfordsville. See CEP, p. 299

44   AN 1

45   TRIB 153

46   END 8

47   PIT 8

48   Ibid.

49   Oliver Marlow Wilkinson, ed., *The Letters of John Cowper Powys to Frances Gregg*, Vol. 1, London: Cecil Woolf, 1994, p. xv

50   'Van Ness' was John Cowper Powys' spelling: Oliver Wilkinson, Frances' son, spells it 'Vanness'.

51   Louis Umbreville Wilkinson, ed., *Letters of John Cowper Powys to Louis Wilkinson 1935–1956*, London: Macdonald, 1958, p. 385

52   Frances Gregg, 'Male and Female', in *That Kind of Woman: Stories from the Left Bank and Beyond*, ed. Bronte Adam and Trudi Tate, London: Virago, 1991, p. 210

53   PIT 9, 16, 21

54   Richard Perceval Graves, *The Brothers Powys*, London: Routledge & Kegan Paul, 1983, p. 88

55   ASPH 50

56   Graves, *Brothers Powys*, p. 88

57   Oliver Wilkinson, *Letters*, p. xvi

58   Graves, *Brothers Powys*, p. 88

59   Ibid., pp. 89–90

60 TRIB 151

61 HDCP 5

62 Oliver Wilkinson, *Letters*, p. xvii

63 Graves, *Brothers Powys*, p. 94

64 'The Unknown Face', in *The Second American Caravan*, ed. Alfred Kreymborg et al., New York: Macaulay, 1928

65 HER 178

66 See Rita Felski, *The Gender of Modernity*, Cambridge, MA: Harvard University Press, 1995. Gregg confessed in her memoir she used the role to pass on, according to her feelings about her listener, 'whatever was wise and good, or kind, or unkind and malicious', but was disconcerted by the way her predictions so often came true. When later she admitted this to Yeats, for whom she once acted as medium, she was disconcerted to have him tell her that even though she thought she was cheating, she could not know what powers were speaking through her. ML 90–91

67 Quoted in Susan Stanford Friedman and Rachel Blau Duplessis, '"I had two loves separate": The Sexualities of H.D.'s *Her*', in *Signets: Reading H.D.*, ed. Susan Stanford Friedman and Rachel Blau Duplessis, Madison: University of Wisconsin Press, 1990, p. 228

68 Perdita Schaffner, 'Afterword', HER 237

69 PIT 11

70 PIT 11–12

71 END 36

72 HER 161–162

73 HER 145–146

74 HER 57–58

75 END 35–36

76 HER 58, 61

77 HER 58

78 ML 81

79 HER 95

80 HER 3, 15

81 ASPH 53

82 HER 202

83 HER 203 (H.D.'s ellipsis)

84 Oliver Wilkinson, *Letters*, p. xviii

85 Diane Chisholm, *H.D.'s Freudian Poetics: Psychoanalysis in Translation*, Ithaca: Cornell University Press, 1992. Chisholm, like several other H.D. scholars, takes the *Her* Freudian uncle as literal

86 EP/MC 42

87 Jonathan Culler, 'Introduction,' in Charles Baudelaire, *The Flowers of Evil*, ed. and trans. Jerome McGowan, Oxford: Oxford University Press, 1993, p. xv

88 Algernon Charles Swinburne, 'Charles Baudelaire' [1862], in *Poems and Ballads: Atalanta in Calydon*, ed. Morse Peckham, Indianapolis: Bobbs-Merrill, 1970, pp. 309–310

89 Baudelaire, who wrote a poem about Sappho entitled 'Lesbos', was, according to Jonathan Culler, the first nineteenth-century author to depict Sappho as a lesbian.

90 Swinburne, 'Notes on Poems and Reviews' [1866], in *Poems and Ballads*, ed. Peckham, p. 328

91 AN 1

92 Oliver Wilkinson, quoted in Barbara Guest, *Herself Defined: The Poet H.D. and her World*, London: Collins, 1985, p. 24

93 END 12, HER 167

94 END 53

95   END 35–36
96   HER 149
97   Baudelaire, *Flowers of Evil*, ed. McGowan, p. xiv
98   Robert Crawford, *The Savage and the City in the Work of T.S. Eliot*, Oxford: Clarendon Press, 1987, p. 183
99   EP/MC 40
100 EP/MC 48
101 PM 55
102 EP/MC 41
103 EP/MC 41–42
104 SR2 97
105 EP/MC
106 WBY 434
107 CEP 96, SR vi
108 Friedrich Nietzsche, *Twilight of the Idols/The Anti-Christ*, trans. R.J. Hollingdale, Harmondsworth: Penguin, 1990, p. 93
109 YP 59/2664
110 HER 133
111 SR2 9
112 SR v
113 CH 67
114 SR 165, 234
115 She particularly liked the Dante chapter, which is perhaps why *The Spirit of Romance* appears as this 'book on Dante' in *Her*
116 SR 10
117 SR2 19. This last comment only appears in the revised version
118 SR 177
119 EP/MC 52
120 HER 30
121 HER 99
122 Gregg, 'Male and Female', p. 214
123 PM 27
124 EP/DS 38
125 HC 150
126 ASPH 34
127 Gregg, 'Male and Female', p. 210
128 PIT 32
129 She added, 'Nothing has ever happened that bore any relation to that first kiss. Mr Pound . . . you had something – in those first kisses you scattered so widely like stars upon a cerulean field of flowering maidens'. ML 92
130 Gregg, 'Male and Female', p. 220
131 Ibid., pp. 217, 216
132 Quoted in Guest, *Herself Defined*, p. 26
133 H.D was at number 4
134 AN 1
135 Oliver Wilkinson, *Letters*, p. 163
136 EP/MC 93
137 YP 64/2777
138 PIT 37
139 Alyse Gregory, *The Day is Done*, New York: E.P. Dutton, 1948
140 PM 27

141 PM 27, 33

142 Douglas Tallack, *Twentieth-Century America: The Intellectual and Cultural Context*, Harlow: Longman, 1991, pp. 83–85

143 PM 41

144 PM 37

145 Ibid.

146 EP/MC 60, 51

147 EP/MC 93

148 David Frail, *The Early Politics and Poetics of William Carlos Williams*, Ann Arbor: UMI Research Press, 1987, p. 57

149 David Frail takes it that he did meet the Stieglitz group there, and wonders why he did not introduce them to Williams, but it is clear he did not make their acquaintance on this visit

150 PM 21 (This is the 1913 wording; it was slightly different in 1912)

151 Max Eastman, *Enjoyment of Living: Autobiographical Reminiscences*, New York: Harper, 1948, p. 409

152 CH 76

153 EP/MC 55, 57–58

154 YP 59/2664

155 Frail, *The Early Politics and Poetics of William Carlos Williams*, p. 51

156 EP/MC 63

157 CH 75

158 CH 70–72

159 Quoted in G. Thomas Tanselle, 'Two Early Letters of Ezra Pound', *American Literature*, 34, 1962, 117, 116, 118

160 CH 73

161 EP/MC 63, 64, 65

162 Jessie B. Rittenhouse, *My House of Life: An Autobiography*, Boston: Houghton Mifflin, 1934, p. 268

163 YP 59/2666

164 Marius de Zayas, 'The New Art in Paris', *The Forum*, 45, February 1911, pp. 187–188

165 EP/MC 64

166 AN 1

167 EP/MC 67

168 Ibid.

169 Michael Ingham, writing on 'Ezra Pound and Music' in *The Cambridge Companion to Ezra Pound*, ed. Ira Nadel, Cambridge: Cambridge University Press, 1999, is rather dismissive of Rummel as a composer, describing his work as being in 'the rather sloppy emotional style appropriate to the Parisian salon' (p. 242), but he was highly thought of by Pound and others at the time

170 *Monthly Musical Record*, November 1911, quoted in EP/MC 153

171 EP/MC 154

172 EP/MC 67

173 EP/MC 153–154

174 Tanselle, 'Two Early Letters of Ezra Pound', p. 116

175 EP/MC 67

176 WBY 439

177 'The Science of Poetry,' *Book News Monthly*, 29/4 (December 1910), 282–283, in EPP&P1 40–41

178 EPT 18. On Pound and science, see Ian Bell, *Critic as Scientist: The Modernist Poetics of Ezra Pound*, London: Methuen, 1981. Bell is undoubtedly right that Pound took more from Maxim than he liked to admit, even if he rejected his nineteenth-century materialist basis

179 YP 59/2666

180 The letter in which Pound mentions the Salon Indépendant says Yeats has left, so must be late May or early June, though it is dated earlier by the Beinecke. See Rebecca Beasley for a more detailed discussion of his interest in the visual arts, though she suggests rather warmer interest at this stage than I find he evinces: *Ezra Pound and the Visual Culture of Modernism*, Cambridge: Cambridge University Press, 2007

181 YP 59/2666

182 HC 390

183 EP/DS 37–38

184 EP/DS 39, CEP 215. A 'redondilla' is an eight-syllable quatrain, much used by Lope da Vega, though only intermittently appearing here – much of it isn't even, as the subtitle suggests, 'Something of the Sort'

185 CEP 169, 168, 170

186 CEP 305

187 EP/DS 34

188 Ezra Pound, 'Paris Letter', *Dial*, 74, 1923, p. 89. See EPC 448 (Canto 74) and 480 (Canto 78)

189 YP 59/2667

Part Six: H.D. Comes to Europe

1 William Carlos Williams, 'A Letter from William Carlos Williams to Norman Holmes Pearson Concerning Hilda Doolittle and Her Mother and Father' (11 July 1955), *William Carlos Williams Newsletter*, 2/2, Fall 1976 p. 3

2 ML 107

3 Barbara Guest, *Herself Defined: The Poet H.D. and her World*, London: Collins, 1985, p. 27. Barbara Guest gives few sources for her facts. Where I am quoting something from her book which I have not found corroborated elsewhere, I shall indicate that she provides the only evidence. She did quite a few interviews, so may be adding new information, but sometimes her interpretations seem strained

4 YHD 17/584 (all postcards to her mother catalogued under this)

5 AN 1

6 *Blast*, 1914, p. 132

7 LL 101

8 YP 59/2666

9 END 50

10 ASPH 31

11 ASPH 29–30

12 ASPH 30

13 END 3–4

14 ASPH 39

15 ASPH 35

16 Quoted in Stefan Jarocinski, *Debussy: Impressionism and Symbolism* [1966], trans. Rollo Mymes, London: Eulenberg Books, 1976, p. 95

17 AN 1

18 YHD 17/584

19 PIT 73

20 Nigel Jones, *Rupert Brooke: Life, Death & Myth*, London: Richard Cohen, 1999. See also Paul Delany, *The Neo-Pagans: Friendship and Love in the Rupert Brooke Circle*, London: Macmillan, 1987

21 PIT 14–15

22 PIT 15–16

23 HDCP 8, 25

24 PIT 17

25 ASPH 4

26 Date ascertained from a postcard to her mother

27 FORD 306

28 Richard M. Ludvig, ed., *Letters of Ford Madox Ford*, Princeton: Princeton University Press, 1965, p. 48

29 P/F 8; YP 59/2667

30 SP 431–432

31 Humphrey Carpenter says the poem was written there, though I have not been able to find independent proof for that myself. But given the high level of accuracy in Carpenter's work, and the appropriateness of the poem to that period of decision-making about his future that Pound experienced during the 1911 visit to Sirmione, I have accepted the dating. HC 156

32 PER 60–61

33 G. Thomas Tanselle, 'Two Early Letters of Ezra Pound', *American Literature*, 34, 1962, p. 116

34 PER 63

35 PER 61–62. See Peter Brooker, *A Student's Guide to the Selected Poems of Ezra Pound*, London: Faber & Faber, 1979, p. 69

36 YP 59/2666

37 EPC 3 (Canto 1)

38 CH 179

39 CH 78, 81, 83–84

40 EP/DS 46

41 EP/MC 85

42 EP/DS 49

43 Ibid.

44 EP/DS 47

45 EP/DS 55

46 PER 64. The link between this letter and the poem has also been made by A. David Moody: see his *Ezra Pound: Poet. A Portrait of the Man and his Work*: Vol 1, *The Young Genius 1885–1920*, Oxford: Oxford University Press, 2007, p. 162

47 EP/MC 89. Sapphics are a complex mixture of dactyls and spondees in a regular four-line stanza, of which three lines have five feet and the final one has two

48 EP/DS 63–64

49 'Imagisme', PMV 1/6, March 1913, p. 199

50 EP/MC 88

51 EP/MC 101

52 CEP 174

53 Quoted in DRE 402

54 George Dangerfield, *The Strange Death of Liberal England* [1935], London: McGibbon & Kee, 1966, p. 191. See DRE 498–499 on the role of syndicalists after 1912

55 Virginia Woolf, 'Mr Bennett and Mrs Brown', in *A Woman's Essays: Selected Essays, Volume One*, ed. Rachel Bowlby, Harmondsworth: Penguin, 1991, pp. 70–71

56 Douglas Goldring, *Odd Man Out: The Autobiography of a 'Propaganda Novelist,'* London: Chapman & Hall, 1935 p. 126

57 See E. J. Hobsbawn, *The Age of Empire, 1875–1914* [1987], London: Cardinal, 1989

58 Valerie Steele, *Fashion and Eroticism: Ideals of Beauty from the Victorian Era to the Jazz Age*, Oxford: Oxford University Press, 1985, p. 227. ASPH 49

59 Frances Spalding, *British Art since 1900*, London: Thames & Hudson, 1986, p. 37

60 Quoted in DRE 432 (the comment appeared on 7 November 1910)

61   J.B. Bullen, ed., *Post-Impressionists in England*, London: Routledge, 1988, pp. 109–110

62   Peter Stansky, *On or About December 1910: Early Bloomsbury and its Intimate World*, Cambridge, MA: Harvard University Press, 1996, p. 181

63   Paul O'Keeffe, *Some Sort of Genius: A Life of Wyndham Lewis*, London: Jonathan Cape, 2000, p. 101. James Beechey, 'Defining Modernism', in *The Art of Bloomsbury*, ed. Richard Shone, Tate Gallery, 1999, p. 40

64   Wilfrid Scawen Blunt, *My Diaries: Being a Personal Narrative of Events, 1888–1914*, London: Martin Secker, 1919, p. 343

65   Stansky, *On or About December 1910*, p. 7

66   Frances Spalding, *Vanessa Bell*, London: Weidenfeld & Nicolson, 1983, p. 91

67   'Post-Savages', NA, 29 December 1910

68   Roger Fry, 'Retrospect', in *Vision and Design*, London: Chatto & Windus, 1920, p. 193. In Paris, there were considerable links between some avant-garde artists and political anarchists: see Mark Antliff, *Inventing Bergson: Cultural Politics and the Parisian Avant-garde*, Princeton: Princeton University Press, 1993

69   In *Nation*, 19 November 1910, quoted in Stansky, *On or About December 1910*, pp. 201–202

70   Spalding, *Vanessa Bell*, p. 92

71   'Picasso', NA, 30 November 1911

72   EP/MC 95

73   EP/DS 44

74   Yoko Chiba, 'Ezra Pound's Versions of Fenollosa's Noh Manuscripts and Yeats's Unpublished "Suggestions and Corrections"', *Yeats Annual*, 4, ed. Warwick Gould, Basingstoke: Macmillan, 1984, p. 122

75   AN 2

76   EP/DS 71

77   EP/DS 72. Actually from the draft in Hope's office files; this was not a letter Pound kept

78   YP 59/2668

79   Ibid.

80   EP/DS 72, 75

81   YP 59/2668

82   EP/MC 101

83   END 9–10; Suzanne Raitt, *May Sinclair: A Modern Victorian*, Oxford: Oxford University Press, 2000, pp. 93–96

84   YP 64/2777

85   ML 145; Raitt, *May Sinclair*, p. 193

86   YP 64/2777

87   NS 194

88   James Gindin, *John Galsworthy's Life and Art: An Alien Fortress*, London: Macmillan, 1987, p. 50

89   YP 64/2777

90   YHD 17/584; ML 151

91   ASPH 52, 53

92   ASPH 57

93   EP/MC 97

94   EP/MC 94

95   PIT 18, 20–21

96   PIT 18

97   YP 59/2668

98   The Greek Anthology is a collection of 4,000 poems, ranging from seventh century BC to the sixth century AD, assembled by Byzantine scholars. H.D. used J. W. Mackail's 1890 selection, *Select Epigrams from the Greek Anthology*, the last edition of which appeared in 1911,

which includes the original poems as well as prose translations and a lengthy introduction

99 END 30 (H.D.'s ellipses). In A. David Moody, *Ezra Pound: Poet. A Portrait of the Man and his Work*: Vol. I, *The Young Genius 1885–1920*, Oxford: Oxford University Press, 2007, p. 446, Moody suggests that when she wrote *End to Torment*, H.D. misremembered Pound's renewal of his love-making in London, and says he knows of no independent evidence for it. But H.D. had recalled it long before in correspondence with Bryher; Pound's attentions to her are confirmed by Gregg's quite independent memoir. In the late 1950s Pound himself read the manuscript of *End to Torment*, much of which he thought had great beauty; he quibbles about some of her speculations towards the end about what was happening in his life at that period, but said there was nothing to question in the earlier part of the book, from which this recollection comes. So it is confirmed by Pound himself (Letter 6 November 1959, YHD 14/489)

100 ASPH 73

101 YHD 17/584; YP 64/2777

102 ASPH 71, 74

103 ASPH 71

104 YP 64/2777

105 YP 59/2668

106 EP/MC 97–98

107 PER 190

108 Ronald Schuchard, '"As Regarding Rhythm": Yeats and the Imagists', in *Yeats: An Annual of Critical and Textual Studies*, 2, 1984

109 Norah Saunders and A.A. Kelly, *Joseph Campbell, Poet and Nationalist: A Critical Biography*, Dublin: Wolfhound, 1988, p. 49

110 Ibid.

111 Ibid., p. 50

112 Ibid., p. 47

113 Ibid., p. 50

114 Ibid., p. 50. EP/DS 80

115 'Affirmations VII: the Non-Existence of Ireland', NA, 25 February 1915

116 Information from Garret FitzGerald, *All in a Life: An Autobiography*, Dublin: Gill and Macmillan, 1991, and personal communication from the author

117 EP/DS 166–167

118 Edward Storer, *William Cowper*, London: Herbert & Daniel, 1912, p. vii

119 Florence Farr, *A Calendar of Philosophy*, London: Frank Palmer, 1910, p. 15. Those quoted included Montaigne, Lao Tzu, Blake, Yeats, Nietzsche, Douglas Jerrold, Goethe, Wagner, Mallarmé, Verlaine, Bergson and many more

120 HULME 158 from NA, 2 November 1911 (signed Thomas Gratton)

121 LE 162

122 Ford Madox Ford, *The Critical Attitude*, London: Duckworth, 1911, p. 190

123 CEP 218

124 Robert Ferguson, *The Short Sharp Life of T.E. Hulme*, London: Allen Lane, 2002, p. 143

125 J.C. Squire, *The Honeysuckle and the Bee*, London: Heinemann, 1937, p. 156

126 EP/MC 98

127 The three previous volumes had come out earlier in the year, the two-volume *The Magic Art and the Evolution of Kings* in March, and *Taboo and the Perils of the Soul* in May

128 PER 185

129 LE 159

130 EP/MC 101

131 See Gail McDonald, *Learning to be Modern: Pound, Eliot and the American University*, Oxford: Clarendon Press, 1993

132 YP 59/2668

133 EP/MC 102

134 YP 60/2699

135 Some Hulme scholars have suggested it was only the former, but even if that were the case, Pound no doubt heard Hulme's views in conversation as well, and he was also following his articles in the *New Age*

136 HULME 189

137 The point about Burke is made by Sanford Schwarz, 'Bergson and the Politics of Vitalism', in *The Crisis in Modernism: Bergson and the Vitalist Controversy*, ed. Frederick Burwick and Paul Douglas, Cambridge: Cambridge University Press, 1992, p. 296

138 'I Gather the Limbs of Osiris: II; A Rather Dull Introduction', NA, 7 December 1911. These articles, without the translations, are republished in SP 21–43

139 SR v

140 EP/DS 71; 'I Gather the Limbs of Osiris: II'

141 'I Gather the Limbs of Osiris: II'

142 HULME 201

143 'I Gather the Limbs of Osiris: II'

144 'Modern Fiction', in *The Essays of Virginia Woolf*, Volume IV, 1925–1928, London: Hogarth, 1994, p. 159. Many years later, in captivity in 1946, Pound would read Arnold Bennett for the first time, and bitterly regret he had denounced him earlier out of sheer ignorance. Bennett's novels were a revelation, he said: 'as good as the French – my damned snobbery deprived me of knowing it in 1910': Robert Spoo and Omar Pound, *Ezra and Dorothy Pound: Letters in Captivity, 1945–46*, Oxford: Oxford University Press, 1999, p. 27

145 HULME 201

146 For Hulme, this is linked to his belief, again a crucial idea for Pound, that the artist does not create so much as *discover* a truth about the nature of reality, which has to be conveyed with precision and exactitude. Pound would write a couple of years later that a poet has to be more like a scientist than 'an advertising agent for a new soap': 'the scientist does not expect to be acclaimed as a great scientist until he has *discovered* something.' 'A Few Don'ts by an Imagiste,' PMV 1/6, March 1913, pp. 203–204. Later Pound would come to emphasise the need for the exact word in social, political and moral contexts as well, not just psychological

147 HULME 192

148 HULME 200

149 'I Gather the Limbs of Osiris: IX: On Technique', NA, 25 January 1912

150 'I Gather the Limbs of Osiris: XI', NA, 15 February 1912

151 Samuel Beckett is an example of a writer who shared Hulme's view of the inadequacy of language without giving up writing: 'you must go on. I can't go on. I'll go on,' as he famously wrote at the end of *The Unnamable*. Samuel Beckett, *The Unnamable* (1958), London: Calder & Boyars, 1975, p. 132

152 'I Gather the Limbs of Osiris: IX'. Many of these ideas Hulme had taken from Rémy de Gourmont's *Le Problème du style*, which has led some critics to suggest Pound was already reading that for himself: however, this must have been written in late 1911, and it was not till the second half of February 1912 that he discovered de Gourmont for the first time, and then at first only his poetry and his anthology of medieval Latin poetry. When he first wrote about de Gourmont in September 1913 he didn't mention *Le Problème*, and that was an article he had difficulty making long enough; if he knew it then he would surely have mentioned it (see EP/DS 245). Later de Gourmont's criticism would be immensely important to him. See Richard Sieburth, *Instigations: Ezra Pound and Rémy de Gourmont*, Cambridge, MA: Harvard University Press, 1978

153 'I Gather the Limbs of Osiris: VI: On Virtue', 4 January 1912

154 'I Gather the Limbs of Osiris: XI'. The twelfth part consisted of three Arnaut Daniel *canzoni*

155 See Andrzej Sosnowski, 'Pound's Imagism & Emanuel Swedenborg', *Paideuma*, 20/3, 1991, pp. 31–38

156 Pound's starting point here was probably Blake and Yeats again; on the idea of Adamic language see Robert Essick, *William Blake and the Language of Adam*, Oxford: Clarendon Press, 1989, and Robert Kern, *Orientalism, Modernism, and the American Poem*, Cambridge: Cambridge University Press, 1996. Farr, according to Mary Greer, was intrigued by similar ideas

157 'I Gather the Limbs of Osiris: XI'

158 HULME 61

159 HULME 62

160 HULME 66

161 HULME 55

162 'I Gather the Limbs of Osiris: XI'

163 '*Nel mezzo del cammin*' is a quotation from the opening of Dante's *Commedia*, 'in the middle of the road (of his life)', i.e. in middle age

164 'Prologomena', PR 1/2, February 1912, pp. 72–76 (reprinted as 'Prolegomena' in LE 8–9)

Part Seven: The Future Imagists Assemble

1 YP 64/2777

2 H.D., '*Responsibilities*', unpublished review, written *c.* 1916, *Agenda*, 25, 3/4, 1988, pp. 51–52

3 Barbara Belford, *Violet: The Story of the Irrepressible Violet Hunt and Her Circle of Lovers and Friends – Ford Madox Ford, H.G. Wells, Somerset Maugham, and Henry James*, New York: Simon & Schuster, 1990, p. 185. But see FORD 354–5, which suggests that if there was a ceremony it was probably in Paris in September, or in October in Trier

4 DHLL1 315

5 DHLL1 339

6 DHLL1 362

7 DHLL1 363–364

8 DHLL1 335; YP 59/2668

9 EP/MC 98

10 EP/MC 100; NS 136

11 YP 60/2672

12 SL 68

13 FY 215

14 FY 216

15 BP 51

16 BP 48

17 BP 47

18 Derek Patmore, *Private History: An Autobiography*, London: Jonathan Cape, 1960, p. 16

19 BP 9

20 Patmore, *Private History*, p. 52

21 Ibid., pp. 16, 17

22 Ibid., p. 17. Barbara Guest suggests H.D. learnt Olivia was Yeats's 'Diana Vernon' in the late 1930s, and quotes her comment on this to Aldington in 1961. See Barbara Guest, *Herself Defined: The Poet H.D. and her World*, London: Collins, 1985, p. 248

23 BP 58, 63.

24 END 4

25 BP 60

26 BP 59

27 BP 110

28 HC 336

29 AN 15

30 BP 64

31 BP 65

32 Ibid.

33 BP 66

34 SL 17

35 Douglas Goldring, *Odd Man Out: The Autobiography of a 'Propaganda Novelist'*, London: Chapman & Hall, 1935, p. 105

36 UTA (Letter from T.S. Eliot to Flint dated 12 June 1925)

37 *The Tramp*, September 1910, p. 556

38 *The Tramp*. November 1910, p. 183; *Cadences*, p. 3 (in that version the punctuation is slightly different, and only the first lines of each short stanza begin with a capital letter)

39 Peter Jones, ed., *Imagist Poetry*, Harmondsworth: Penguin, 1972, p. 76

40 'Prologomena', PR 1/2, February 1912, p. 72

41 EPC 433 C74

42 EP/MC 105

43 *The Letters of Maurice Hewlett*, ed. Laurence Binyon, London: Methuen, 1926, p. 118

44 EP/MC 105; EP/DS 82

45 BP 60

46 ASPH 70, 68

47 BL ADD 57725 Letter, 11 April 1958. Patricia Hutchins' extensive correspondence with Pound and his friends, which was the basis of her book, *Ezra Pound's Kensington: An Exploration, 1885–1915*, London: Faber & Faber, 1965, is now lodged at the British Library

48 HRAL, 20 November 1917. He does say in his letter that his father's novel had 'some measure of success', but it seems most improbable

49 ASPH 63

50 Albert Aldington, *The Queen's Preferment*, London: Digby, Long & Co., 1896, p. 227

51 Charles Doyle, *Richard Aldington: A Biography*, Basingstoke: Macmillan, 1989, p. 4

52 DH 15

53 DH 151

54 LL 56

55 DH 87

56 DH 159

57 CPRA 57

58 CPRA 56

59 LL 35

60 LL 37–38

61 LL 39

62 DH 77

63 HRAL (20 November 1917)

64 LL 45, 46

65 LL 46, 47

66 LL 54

67 LL 84; Norman T. Gates, *The Poetry of Richard Aldington: A Critical Evaluation and an Anthology of Uncollected Poems*, University Park: Pennsylvania State University Press, 1974, pp. 228, 227

68 LL 57

69 LL 61

70 LL 63

71 LL 65

72 Alister Kershaw and Frédéric Jacques Temple, eds, *Richard Aldington: An Intimate Portrait*, Carbondale: Southern Illinois University Press, 1965, p. 112

73 CZ 3

74 CZ2 90

75 LL 96

76 Ibid.

77 HRAL (20 November 1917)

78 CZ 43

79 CZ 8

80 YHD 1/22 (16 December 1950)

81 Dominic Hibberd, *Harold Monro: Poet of the New Age*, London: Palgrave, 2001, p.11

82 Ibid., p. 3

83 'Preface', PR 1/1, January 1912, p. 3

84 Alida Monro, ed., *The Collected Poems of Harold Monro*, London: Cobden-Sanderson, 1933, pp. viii–ix

85 Hibberd, *Harold Monro*, p. 91

86 Ibid., p. 94

87 Ibid., p. 3

88 '*Canzoni*. By Ezra Pound', PR 1/1, January 1912, pp. 28–29

89 UTA. Flint, according to *Poetry* in 1913, had published in the *Nation*, so something may have appeared there

90 YP 64/2777

91 Ibid.

92 A letter to Bryher many years later also places Walter's revelation of the engagement that spring, and while again memories may play false, most evidence points to a date in March; the diary H.D. kept in Paris that summer suggests that she had known by April

93 PR 1/1, January 1912, p. 25

94 ER 9, October 1911, pp. 361–362

95 Quoted in Robert B. Ross, *The Georgian Revolt: Rise and Fall of a Poetic Ideal, 1910–1922*, London: Faber & Faber, 1967, p. 52

96 HRAL (20 November 1917)

97 Norman T. Gates, ed., *Richard Aldington: A Biography in Letters*, University Park: Pennsylvania State University Press, 1992, p. 7

98 'Prologomena', p. 72

99 EP/DS 351

100 YP 60/2669

101 EP/DS 61

102 SR2 87

103 SR2 91, 90, 95, 96. Peire Vidal is how Pound spells it here, though he also has a poem, 'Piere Vidal Old', PER 28–30

104 EP/DS 61

105 SR2 94

106 'Translator's Postscript' (dated 21 June 1921) to *The Natural Philosophy of Love*, by Rémy de Gourmont, trans. Ezra Pound, London: Casanova Press, 1920, p. 169

107 Richard Ellmann, *Eminent Domain*, Oxford: Oxford University Press, 1967, p. 83

108 SR2 92–93, 95

109 LE 295

110 PM 33

111 LE 315. As Ronald Bush points out, Pound said he had adopted the style of the late Henry James for his quasi-autobiographical *Indiscretions*, and Bush suggests he may also have used

late James as a narrative model for the Cantos: see Ronald Bush, *The Genesis of Ezra Pound's Cantos*, Princeton: Princeton University Press, 1976, pp. 176–180

112 PER 85

113 EP/DS 87

114 EP/DS 90

115 EP/DS 89

116 Quoted in EP/DS 90

117 Lawrence Rainey, *Institutions of Modernism: Literary Elites and Public Culture*, New Haven: Yale University Press, 1998

118 LL 121

119 'Prologomena', pp. 75, 73–74

120 According to Flint (in his review of *Ripostes* in *Poetry and Drama* in March 1913), Epstein came along sometimes to the Tour Eiffel group, but Pound may not have met him, and certainly didn't seem to see his work then

121 YP 60/2669

122 Ibid.

123 'Approach to Paris: II', NA, 11 November 1913

124 'Copper-coloured rose, more fraudulent than our joys, copper-coloured rose, embalm us in your lies, hypocritical flower, flower of silence./Rose, with your face painted like a whore, rose with a prostitute's heart, you pretend to be pitiable, hypocritical flower, flower of silence' (my translation)

125 HDCP 25

126 'Psychology and the Troubadours', *The Quest: A Quarterly Review*, 4/1, October 1912

127 René Taupin, *The Influence of French Symbolism on Modern American Poetry* [first published in French 1929], trans. William Pratt and Anne Rich Pratt, New York: AMS Press, 1985, p. 128

128 SR2 90

129 'Then I said: Here are flutes and baskets; Bite into the fruit . . . I said again: Listen' (my translation). 'Les Médailles d'argile' from Henri de Régnier, *Les Médailles d'argile*, Paris: Société du Mercure de France, 1890, p. 2. See also the discussion of this poem and the de Régnier poem in William Pratt, '"To Have Gathered from the Air a Live Tradition": Pound's Poetic Legacy', in *Ezra Pound and Poetic Influence*, ed. Helen M. Dennis, Amsterdam: Rodopi, 2000

130 PER 70

131 He would also compare it to Gaudier-Brzeska's 'Boy with Coney', which he said looked like an ancient Chinese work

132 'Introduction' to *Oxford Book of Modern Verse: 1892–1935*, ed. W.B. Yeats, Oxford: Oxford University Press, 1936

133 'Vorticism', *Fortnightly Review* 96 (NS) 1 September 1914, p. 404. GIFT 84

134 BP 66

135 DH 125

136 END 18

137 END 17

138 ASPH 96

139 ASPH 74

140 END 8

141 PIT 32

142 There were actually two other Powys brothers, and three sisters, but these three were the writers and the friends of Louis

143 Brenda Humfrey, ed., *Recollections of the Powys Brothers: Llewelyn, Theodore and John Cowper*, London: Peter Owen, 1980, p. 21

144 Oliver Marlow Wilkinson, 'Introduction' to *Seven Friends*, by Louis Marlow, Thame: Mandrake Press, 1991, p. 10

145 Quoted in Humfrey, *Recollections*, p. 174

146 Kenneth Hopkins, *The Powys Brothers: A Biographical Appreciation* [1967], Southrepps, Norfolk: Warren House Press, 1972, p. 28

147 *Others: An Anthology of the New Verse*, ed. Alfred Kreymborg, New York: Knopf, 1916, p. 45

148 Louis Umfreville Wilkinson, *The Buffoon*, New York: Knopf, 1916, p. 211

149 Janet Beer and Katherine Joslin, 'Diseases of the Body Politic: White Slavery in Jane Addams' *A New Conscience and an Ancient Evil* and Selected Stories by Charlotte Perkins Gilman', *Journal of American Studies*, 33/1, 1999, p. 4

150 Louis Marlow (the name under which most of Louis Wilkinson's books appeared), *Swan's Milk*, London: Faber & Faber, 1934, p. 316

151 John Cowper Powys, *Autobiography* [1934], London: Picador, 1967, p. 266

152 Oliver Marlow Wilkinson, ed., *Letters of John Cowper Powys to Frances Gregg*, Vol. 1, London: Cecil Woolf, 1994 p. xxvii

153 See Oliver Marlow Wilkinson, 'A Rival to Jack', in *Recollections of the Powys Brothers*, pp. 180–187

154 Marlow, *Swan's Milk*, p. 318; Richard Perceval Graves, *The Brothers Powys*, London: Routledge & Kegan Paul, 1985

155 AN 2

156 END 8–9 (First ellipsis H.D.'s)

157 END 9

158 AN 2

159 PIT, 9, 35

160 Powys, *Autobiography*, pp. 266, 406, 410, 411

161 Ibid., p. 406

162 Louis Marlow, *Seven Friends*, London: Richards Press, 1953, pp. 67–68

163 EP/DS 94

164 YHD 47/1197. All quotations in this section from the diary are located here

165 ASPH 98, 97

166 H.D., 'Letter to Norman Pearson, 1937 ("A Note on Poetry")' (first published in 1937, re-edited for this publication by Diana Collecott), *Agenda*, 25/3&4, Autumn/Winter 1987/1988, p. 73

167 PIT 60

168 EP/MC 135

169 PIT 59

170 YP 60/2669

171 Ibid.

172 WT xi

173 YP 60/2669

174 EP/MC 111. Pound had already left Poitiers, so the letter was returned

175 EP/MC 117

176 EP/MC 114

177 EP/MC 117

178 ASPH 9

179 EP/MC 3

180 EP/MC 127

181 EP/MC 2

182 EP/MC 131

183 EP/MC 118–119. In an early letter, Pound did write to her, 'As one artist to another, my

congratulations,' but even there he is referring to her as an artist in the way she handles her patronage, not her music. EP/MC 23

184 ASPH 103, 105
185 EP/DS 108; EP/MC 119
186 EP/DS 109
187 EP/MC 118
188 H.D. in *The Cantos of Ezra Pound: Some Testimonies*, Ernest Hemingway et al, New York: Farrar & Rinehart, 1933, p. 19
189 EP/DS 118
190 YHD 14/489 (6 November 1959)
191 EP/DS 113

Part Eight: *Imagisme* is Born

1 WT 35
2 WT 3
3 In this letter words are occasionally illegible, but the drift is clear
4 YP 17/743. As far as I am aware, no Pound scholars have commented on this letter, which is misdated in the Beinecke, being put in a folder marked 1928–1960
5 See, for example, May McKisack, *The Oxford History of England: The Fourteenth Century, 1307–1399*, Oxford: Oxford University Press, 1959, pp. 138–140
6 EPC 515 (Canto 80)
7 WT 84
8 SR v
9 EPC 510, C80. Pound visited Excideuil again in 1919 with T.S. Eliot, as he recalls in Canto 29, though there he identifies it only by the wave pattern (EPC 145)
10 WT xvi, xi
11 For example, when speaking of adventures, he comments that 'the kind that make good telling are usually very fatiguing & uncomfortable while they last, & even then, if one plays anything like a role, a laudable role, this modern, false modern self consciousness keeps one from boasting of it'. WT 48
12 Eric Hobsbawm, *The Age of Empire: 1875–1914* [1987], London: Cardinal, 1989, pp. 226–227
13 WT 31
14 WT 22
15 WT 53
16 WT 26
17 WT 30
18 YHD 47/1196
19 EP/DS 131
20 WT 57 (words in fact deleted)
21 EP/DS 131
22 EP/DS 116
23 WT 39
24 YP 60/2670
25 WT 48, 50
26 WT 38
27 WT 48, 50, 51, 52
28 EPC 794, C115
29 WT 50
30 WT 53
31 WT 58 (Pound's ellipsis)

32 WT 60–61

33 Ibid.

34 EP/DS 131

35 EP/DS 137

36 EP/DS 136

37 EP/DS 137

38 EP/DS 103, 104

39 George Dangerfield, *The Strange Death of Liberal England* [1935], London: McGibbon & Kee, 1966, p. 249

40 DRE 496

41 EP/DS 111

42 Richard Cork, *Art Beyond the Gallery: In 20th Century England*, New Haven: Yale University Press, 1985, p. 61

43 Paul O'Keeffe, *Some Sort of Genius: A Life of Wyndham Lewis*, London: Jonathan Cape, 2000, p. 112

44 'Imaginary Letters', *Little Review*, 6/1, May 1918, p. 55

45 EP/DS 136

46 WBY 476–477

47 WT 61

48 Josephine Johnson, 'Florence Farr: Letters to W.B. Yeats, 1912–17', in Deirdre Toomey, ed., *Yeats and Women* [1992], Basingstoke: Macmillan, 1997, p. 295

49 Johnson, 'Florence Farr', pp. 300–301

50 Harrison's warm review of Farr's performance in *Hippolytus* in 1904 was republished in *The Music of Speech, containing the words of poets, thinkers and musicmakers regarding the practice of the bardic art, together with fragments of verse set to its own melody by F. Farr*, London: Elkin Mathews, 1909

51 Johnson, 'Florence Farr', p. 293

52 EP/DS 130

53 PER 57–58

54 YP 60/2670

55 LE 32

56 PM 77

57 'The Serious Artist', NFW 1/9, 15 October 1913, p. 162, reprinted LE 45. 'Prologomena', PR 1/2, February 1912, p. 76

58 PER 89

59 By 1917 he also belonged to the London Library: much more convenient given his long hours, as he could borrow the books. Whether he did in 1912 I am not sure

60 See Cyrena N. Pondrom, ed., *The Road from Paris: French Influence on English Poetry, 1900–1920*, Cambridge: Cambridge University Press, 1974, p. 22

61 Ibid., p. 74 (my translation)

62 Michael Levenson, ed., *The Cambridge Companion to Modernism*, Cambridge: Cambridge University Press, 1999, p. 2

63 '*Les aînés*', as Flint called them, had had some limited coverage, mainly in the *New Age*, but not much interest was provoked: see Pondrom, *Road from Paris*, p. 18

64 Le Roy C. Breunig, 'F.S. Flint, Imagism's "Maître d'Ecole"', *Comparative Literature*, 4, 1952, p. 133

65 'Contemporary French Poetry', PR 1/8, August 1912, p. 355; Pondrom, *The Road to Paris*, p. 84

66 Ibid., p. 357

67 Ibid., pp. 357–358

68 Ibid., p. 358. Flint's argument that imagism is the continuation of symbolism is the central theme of Frank Kermode's *Romantic Image* [1957], London: Fontana, 1971

69   LE 12

70   'Contemporary French Poetry', p. 360

71   Breunig, 'F.S. Flint', p. 134

72   EP/DS 161

73   SP 340

74   EP/DS 142

75   HULME 201, 200

76   HULME 198, 196

77   HULME 95, 201.

78   P/LR 155

79   PMV 11/5, February 1918, p. 273. Harriet Monroe, *A Poet's Life: Seventy Years in a Changing World*, London: Macmillan, 1938, p. 222

80   Ibid., p. 223

81   Ibid., p. 234

82   Ibid., p. 239

83   Harriet Monroe, *Poets and their Art* [1926], New York: Macmillan (enlarged edn), 1932, pp. 14, 13

84   EP/MC 132

85   P/ACH 2

86   EP/MC 133

87   See the discussion by Cyrena N. Pondrom in 'H.D. and the Origins of Imagism,' in *Signets: Reading H.D.*, ed. Susan Stanford Friedman and Rachel Blau Duplessis, Madison: University of Wisconsin Press, 1990

88   All quotations from this letter EPL 43–44

89   PM 50, 51

90   'To Whistler, American', PMV 1/1, October 1912, p. 7

91   EP/DS 161

92   EP/DS 155

93   EP/DS 142

94   PER 266

95   J.B. Harmer, *Victory in Limbo: Imagism 1908–1917*, London: Secker & Warburg, 1975, p. 17

96   'A Few Don'ts by an Imagiste', PMV 1/6, March 1913, pp. 202–203

97   YP 60/2670. Paul Selver, another occasional visitor, describes the manuscript as the 'proof sheets'; very likely true, as the poems would be published in October. Paul Selver, *Private Life*, London: Jarrolds, 1929

98   EP/DS 155

99   PER 120

100 *A Lume Spento and Other Early Poems*, New York: New Directions, 1965, p. 7

101 LL 122

102 LL 123, 121, 122

103 END 18

104 END 40

105 TRIB xi

106 YHD 38/1012; 'Compassionate Friendship', pp. 24, 23

107 Pondrom, 'H.D. and the Origins of Imagism'

108 Monroe, *A Poet's Life*, p. 267

109 EPL 45

110 T.S. Eliot, 'Hamlet and his Problems', in *The Sacred Wood* [1920], London: Methuen, 1960, p. 100

111 Pound's letter to Monroe is simply dated October, without specifying a day, but as he refers in it to a letter dated 13 October, it must be after then

112 LL 125

113 'Choricos', PMV 1/2, November 1912, pp. 40–41

114 'Notes and Announcements', PMV 1/1, October 1912, p. 31

115 There is a slightly ambiguous comment in Norman Holmes Pearson's 1969 interview about this, which could be taken to imply that she published some poems in New York in 1910–11 as well as the short stories, but nothing has to my knowledge come to light, and all H.D.'s own comments suggest this was her first publication: see 'Norman Holmes Pearson on H.D.: an Interview', *Contemporary Literature*, 10/4, 1969, p. 437

116 See note 98 in Part 6

117 In J. W. Mackail's translation, the poem goes: 'I, Hermes, stand here by the windy orchard in the cross-ways nigh the grey sea-shore, giving rest on the way to wearied men; and the fountain wells forth cold stainless water'. *Select Epigrams from the Greek Anthology*, London: Longmans, Green, 1890, p. 193. By the time Anyte wrote in the third century BC, the epigram may not have literally been an inscription, but 'epideictic', written as if it were an inscription. See *The Greek Anthology and Other Ancient Epigrams* [1973], ed. Peter Jay, Harmondsworth: Penguin, 1981, p. 13

118 'Norman Holmes Pearson on H.D.: an Interview', p. 441

119 W.B. Yeats, *Essays & Introductions*, London: Macmillan, 1961, p. 509

120 Jane Ellen Harrison, *The Religion of the Ancient Greeks*, London: Archibald Constable, 1905, pp. 18, 19

121 Jane Ellen Harrison, *Prolegomena to the Study of Greek Religion*, Cambridge: Cambridge University Press, 1903, p. 630

122 Quoted in Susan Stanford Friedman, *Penelope's Web: Gender, Modernity, H.D.'s Fiction*, Cambridge: Cambridge University Press, 1990, p. 219

123 HDCP xi

124 HDCP 37–39. In the original *Poetry* version every line begins with a capital letter, but these had vanished by the time of the poem's republication in 1916

125 Timothy Materer, *Modernist Alchemy: Poetry and the Occult*, Ithaca: Cornell University Press, 1995, p. 89

126 PM 44

127 PM 42, 43

128 There has been much critical work now on modernist marketing, the most influential being Lawrence Rainey, *Institutions of Modernism: Literary Elites and Public Culture*, New Haven: Yale University Press, 1998

129 YP 60/2670

130 Ibid.

131 PM 38

132 PM 82

133 See Stephen J. Greenblatt, *Renaissance Self-Fashioning: From More to Shakespeare*, Chicago: University of Chicago Press, 1980, PM 43.

134 See Pierre Bourdieu, *The Field of Cultural Production: Essays on Art and Literature*, ed. Randal Johnson, Oxford: Polity Press, 1993

135 Matthew Arnold, *Culture and Anarchy* [1869], in *Selected Prose*, Harmondsworth: Penguin, 1970, *passim*, but see for example, pp. 215–216

136 See Peter Bürger, *Theory of the Avant-Garde*, trans. Michael Shaw, Minneapolis: University of Minnesota, 1984. PM 42

137 'Patria Mia: V', NA, 3 October 1912. This footnote was cut from the book version.

138 EPL 46–47

139 YP 60/2670

140 EP/DS 145

141 EP/DS 154

142 EP/DS 153, 157

143 PER 101

144 YP 60/2670

145 Ibid.

146 Ibid.

147 Ibid.

148 PM 54 (NA, 31 October, 1912)

149 'Through Alien Eyes: 1', NA, 16 January 1913, 'Through Alien Eyes: 2', NA, 23 January 1913, and 'Through Alien Eyes: 3', NA, 30 January 1913

150 EP/DS 162–163

151 EPL 44

152 His interest in Indian art, it is said, stemmed from the time as a young man in Paris when he saw a statue of Hindu goddess Apsaras in Degas' studio

153 She had previously, in 1903, provided the money that launched the National Art Collections Fund, one of whose early purchases was the Rokeby *Venus*

154 Mary Lago, *Christiana Herringham and the Edwardian Art Scene*, London: Lund Humphries, 1996, p. 228

155 Mary Lago, ed., *Imperfect Encounter: Letters of William Rothenstein and Rabindranath Tagore, 1911–1914*, Cambridge, MA: Harvard University Press, 1972, p. 5

156 Ibid., p. 5. See also William Rothenstein, *Men and Memories: Recollections*: Vol. 2, *1900–1922*, London: Faber & Faber, 1932

157 WBY 48

158 Rabindranath Tagore, 'W. B. Yeats', in *Rabindranath Tagore and William Butler Yeats: The Story of a Literary Friendship*, Delhi: Department of Modern Indian Languages, University of Delhi, 1965, pp. 2, 5

159 W.B. Yeats in Rabindranath Tagore, *Gitanjali (Song Offerings): A Collection of Prose Translations made by the Author*, London: Macmillan, 1913, pp. viii–xi

160 Richard Ellmann, *Eminent Domain*, New York: Oxford University Press, 1967, p. 63

161 Lago, *Imperfect Encounter*, p. 15

162 Tagore, *Gitanjali*, pp. x, xi, xii, xiv

163 Ibid., p. xv

164 NFW, 1 November, 1913, pp. 187–188

165 'Tagore's Poems', PMV 1/3, December 1912, pp. 92, 93

166 SC 25

167 SR2 94. 'Rabindranath Tagore', *Fortnightly Review*, 93 (N.S.), 1 March 1913, pp. 571–579

168 'Tagore's Poems', p. 93

169 Tagore, 'W.B. Yeats', p. 4

170 YP 60/2670

171 Simon Gikandi, 'Race and the Modernist Aesthetic', in *Writing and Race*, ed. Tim Youngs, London: Longman, 1997, p. 155

172 Suzanne Raitt, *May Sinclair: A Modern Victorian*, Oxford: Oxford University Press, 2000, p. 194

173 'Rabindranath Tagore', p. 577

Part Nine: Furthering the Imagist Cause

1 LL 99

2 EP/DS 161

3 According to Caroline Zilboorg (CZ 12), H.D. had had a short holiday in Paris, where Pound also was briefly staying, on her journey to Genoa, but it seems most unlikely that Pound could have spared the time to be there. He was sending frequent advice and poems to Harriet

Monroe, meeting Tagore, organising Walter Rummel to come to London to play Debussy to Tagore, and writing articles for *New Age* and reviews for *Poetry*. I think Zilboorg is misled by Barbara Guest, who displaces the whole May–July visit to October.

4   AN 3
5   Ibid.
6   YHD 48/1202. All quotations from this diary are located here. The English friends probably included Phyllis Bottome, actually half-American and a writer acquaintance of Pound's, whom she describes very entertainingly in her book *From the Life*, London: Faber & Faber, 1944
7   LL 110–111
8   PIT 28
9   AN 2
10 PIT 58–59
11 LL 116–117
12 'Notes and Announcements', PMV 1/2, November 1912, p. 65
13 CPRA 40
14 'Letters from Italy: III. – Rome: First Days', NA, 27 February 1913, p. 404
15 Edith Wharton, *Italian Backgrounds*, London: Macmillan, 1905, p. 177
16 'Letters from Italy: I – En Route', NA, 13 February 1913, p. 356
17 'Letters from Italy: III'
18 Ibid., p. 404, and 'Letter from Italy: VIII – A Sentimental Letter', NA, 3 April 1913, p. 531
19 'Letters from Italy: I', p. 355
20 'Letters from Italy: V – "Is of nothing, and of nothing worth"', NA, 13 March 1913, p. 454
21 'Letters from Italy: II – Firenze', NA, 20 February 1913, p. 386
22 'Letters from Italy: XXII – Old Painters in Florence', NA, 10 July 1913, p. 296
23 'Letters from Italy: IV – Two Classic Beauties', NA, 6 March 1913, p. 430
24 'Letters from Italy: XII – Cava–Corro di Cava–Paestum', NA, 1 May 1913, p. 14
25 'Letters from Italy: XVI – Sorrento', NA, 22 May 1913, p. 87, and 'Letters from Italy: XVIII – Theocritus on Capri', NA, 12 June 1913, p. 176
26 Richard Cork, *Vorticism and its Allies*, London: Arts Council of Great Britain, 1974, p 7
27 JGFL 47
28 UAF Box 2, file 25, 'Inventory', 1910, p. 29
29 NS 163–164
30 P/W 19
31 'A Selection from *The Tempers*. By William Carlos Williams [Introductory Note by Ezra Pound]', PR 1/10, October 1912, p. 481
32 EPL 46
33 EPL 47
34 LL 96
35 John Cournos, *Autobiography*, New York: G.P. Putnam's Sons, 1935, p. 235
36 LL 95
37 'Reviews', PR 1/2, February 1912, p. 82
38 HULME xxviii. The review appeared in a philosophical journal called *The Monist*
39 'To T.E. Hulme', PR 1/12, December 1912, p. 537
40 PMV 1/2, November 1912, p. 65
41 P/ACH 4
42 'Priapus' may have been Pound's title. When this poem came out later in book form, in *Sea Garden*, H.D. would simply call it 'Orchard'
43 PMV 1/4, January 1913
44 Ibid., pp. 123–127
45 EP/DS 161, P/ACH 17–18

46	Robert H. Ross, *The Georgian Revolt: Rise and Fall of a Poetic Ideal, 1910–22*, London: Faber & Faber, 1965, p. 119

47	Hibberd, *Harold Monro*, p. 97

48	DHLL2 104

49	Quoted in James Reeves, ed., *Georgian Poetry*, Harmondsworth: Penguin, 1962, p. xiv

50	Derek Patmore, *Private History: An Autobiography*, London: Jonathan Cape, 1960, p. 181. Alan Pryce-Jones quoted in Ross, *The Georgian Revolt*, p. 108

51	Herbert Palmer, *Post-Victorian Poetry*, London: Dent, 1938, p. 77

52	LL 100

53	Ross, *The Georgian Revolt*, p. 181

54	EP/DS 167

55	EP/DS 168

56	Alida Monro, ed., *The Collected Poems of Harold Monro*, London: Cobden-Sanderson, 1933, p. xi

57	Richard Cork, *Vorticism and its Allies*, London: Arts Council of Great Britain, 1974, p. 41

58	EP/DS 177

59	EP/DS 178

60	EP/DS 180

61	EP/DS 179

62	P/ACH 18

63	EP/DS 182

64	'Imagisme', PMV 1/6, March 1913, pp. 198–199. The content here is all Flint's, though the wording is made more impersonal

65	Lawrence Rainey, *Institutions of Modernism: Literary Elites and Public Culture*, New Haven: Yale University Press, 1998. 'Imagisme', p. 200

66	'Imagisme', p. 199

67	'A Few Don'ts by an Imagiste', PMV 1/6, March 1913, p. 203

68	Christopher Middleton, 'Documents on Imagism from the Papers of F.S. Flint', *The Review*, 15, 1965, p. 37. Flint had 'we' instead of 'they', and 'cause' instead of 'provoke'

69	'Imagisme', p. 199

70	EP/DS 343. See the discussion of H.D.'s 'mytho-poetic' writing in A. D. Moody's 'H.D., "Imagiste": An Elemental Mind', *Agenda*, 25/3–4, 1987/88, pp. 77–96

71	'Imagisme', p. 200

72	Bernard Hart, 'Chapter Six: The Conception of the Subconscious', in Hugo Münsterberg et al., *Subconscious Phenomena*, London: Rebman, 1911, pp. 129–130

73	Ibid., p. 133

74	Frances Spalding, *Vanessa Bell*, London: Weidenfeld & Nicholson, 1983, p. 92. This quotation appears here in Part Six, p. 368

75	David Kadlec, *Mosaic Modernism: Anarchism, Pragmatism, Culture*, Baltimore: Johns Hopkins University Press, 2000

76	LE 3

77	F.S. Flint, *In the Net of the Stars*, London: Elkin Mathews, 1909

78	PMV 2/4, July 1913, p. 138

79	Ibid., pp. 136–139

80	EPL 52

81	YP 51/2309

82	EPL 55

83	PER 86–87

84	'The Serious Artist: 1', NFW 1/9, 15 October 1913, p. 162

85	EPL 54

86	CH 98–99

87 EPL 55

88 EPL 53. PMV 2/1, April 1913, p. 12

89 'How I Began', *T.P.'s Weekly*, London 21/552, 6 June 1913, p. 707, reprinted EPP&P1 147. The original experience must have been in 1911, because he refers to going on to Italy. In a second account, he says that six months later he wrote a 30-line poem about this experience, but rejected it as of 'second intensity'. GB 86–9

90 Seamus Heaney, 'The Pathos of Things', *The Guardian*, 24 November 2007, reprinted from *Our Shared Japan*, ed. Irene de Angelis and Joseph Woods, Dublin: Dedalus, 2007

91 PMV 1/5, February 1913, pp. 165

92 P/ACH 22

93 WBY 139

94 'The Approach to Paris: 1', NA, 4 September 1913

95 'The Approach to Paris: V', NA, 2 October 1913; 'Paris', PMV 3/1, October 1913, pp. 26–30

96 YP 60/2671

97 LMS 50

98 'The Evening Clouds', DC 11

99 FG 14

100 DC 31

101 DC 23

102 VE 3

103 LMS 56. This is what Fletcher says; the review by Edward Thomas in *Poetry & Drama* 1, September 1913, pp. 363–364, though also very sympathetic, doesn't use these words – perhaps he reviewed it elsewhere as well. Thomas also wrote to Fletcher after reviewing his work, so this quotation may be from the letter

104 Fletcher says in his autobiography he went to Paris in May, but it must have been earlier, or he would not then have met Pound

105 LMS 57. Fletcher remembered him as a fellow-Southerner, but Pound describes Cannell as a Philadelphian (EPL 57). In *Poetry*, he is described as having been born in Philadelphia, but educated at the University of Virginia (PMV 2/5, 1913 p. 190)

106 LMS 59

107 LMS 60

108 PMV 3/3, December 1913, p. 111–112

109 LMS 65

110 Christopher Butler, *Early Modernism: Literature, Music, Painting in Europe, 1900–1916*, Oxford: Oxford University Press, 1994, p. 117

111 Ibid., p. 116

112 LMS 68

113 Ibid.

114 UAF Box 3, file 38, p. 193

115 'Letters from Italy: XV – Sorrento', NA, 22 May 1913 (misnumbered in the original as XVI), p. 87

116 END 5

117 'Letters from Italy: XVI – Capri', NA, 29 May 1913, p. 117

118 SIU Box 9/5

119 LL 117

120 'Letters from Italy: XVIII – Theocritus on Capri', 12 June 1913, p. 176

121 AN 5

122 H.D., 'Letter to Norman Pearson, 1937 ("A Note on Poetry")' [first published in 1937, re-edited for this publication by Diana Collecott], *Agenda*, 25, 3&4, Autumn/Winter 1987/1988, p. 73

123 'Theocritus in Capri', in *Literary Studies and Reviews*, London: George Allen & Unwin, 1924, p. 242

124   EP/DS 207

125   EP/DS 208

126   EP/DS 199

127   EP/DS 204–205

128   EP/DS 211, 207

129   EP/DS 213

130   ASPH 125

131   EP/DS 217

132   AN 5

133   EP/DS 220

134   AN 3, 5

135   EP/DS 220

136   EP/DS 224, 226

137   END 5–6

138   ASPH 125

139   LL 108. Aldington inaccurately calls him 'Slonimski'. He also implies they met him in 1912 but H.D. places it on this visit as 1913

140   EP/DS 230, 231

141   EP/DS 232–233

142   EP/DS 235

143   YP 60/2671

144   FORD 376

145   Suzanne Raitt, *May Sinclair: A Modern Victorian*, Oxford: Oxford University Press, 2000, p. 147

146   FORD 377

147   FORD 376

148   FY 243

149   SL 106–107

150   EP/DS 190

151   FORD 382

152   LMS 70

153   YP 60/2671

154   DHLL1 145

155   Harriet Monroe, *A Poet's Life: Seventy Years in a Changing World*, London: Macmillan, 1938, p. 275

156   SFD 96

157   AMY 41

158   SFD 65

159   AMY 43

160   AMY 40, 41

161   Peter Russell, ed., *Ezra Pound: A Collection of Essays to be Presented to Pound on his Sixty-fifth Birthday*, London: Peter Nevill, 1950, p. 29

162   AMY 79

163   Edith Wharton, *A Backward Glance* [1934], London: Constable, 1972, p. 68

164   AMY 76

165   AMY 92

166   SFD 64–65

167   AMY 94

168   AMY 123

169   AMY 92

170   Amy Lowell, *A Dome of Many-Coloured Glass*, Boston: Houghton Mifflin, 1912

171 SFD 190

172 AMY 109

173 SFD 192

174 Lowell, *A Dome*, p. 6

175 'The silence is so great that my heart shivers/only the noise of my footsteps sounds on the pavement' (my translation)

176 Monroe, *A Poet's Life*, p. 254

177 'Memories of Amy Lowell', PMV 26/4, July 1925, p. 209

178 AMY 117

179 NS 176

180 EPL 58, YP 60/2672

181 NFW 1/6, 1 September 1913, p. 114

182 EP/DS 245

183 LMS 91

184 JGF 58

185 LMS 99

Part Ten: *Des Imagistes*

1 PMV 2/4, July 1913, p. 136

2 BL ADD 57725, Ezra Pound to Patricia Hutchins, September 14, 1953

3 Jane Marcus, ed., *The Young Rebecca: Writings of Rebecca West 1911–17*, Bloomington: Indiana University Press, 1982, pp. 4–5

4 Les Garner, *A Brave and Beautiful Spirit: Dora Marsden, 1882–1960*, Aldershot: Avebury, 1990, p. 79

5 Ibid., p. 56

6 Ibid., p. 60

7 Marcus, *Young Rebecca*, p. 5

8 Garner, *Brave and Beautiful Spirit*, p. 77

9 Ibid., p. 103

10 Ibid., p. 115

11 'Views and Comments', NFW 1/1, 15 June 1913, p. 5

12 The *Freewoman*, 5 September 1912, pp. 306–307

13 EP/DS 238

14 Garner, *Brave and Beautiful Spirit*, p. 115

15 'Imagisme', NFW 1/5, 15 August 1913, p. 86

16 Garner, *Brave and Beautiful Spirit*, p. 115

17 A. David Moody, *Ezra Pound: Poet. A Portrait of the Man and his Work*: Vol. I, *The Young Genius 1885–1920*, Oxford: Oxford University Press, 2007, p. 221

18 On likenesses between their thought, see Andrew Thacker, 'Dora Marsden and *The Egoist*: "Our War is with Words"', *English Literature in Transition, 1880–1920*, 36, 1993 for one of the first discussions of the similarities. Some critics have argued for a more consciously shared programme. See Bruce Clarke, *Dora Marsden and Early Modernism: Gender, Individualism, Science*, Ann Arbor: University of Michigan Press, 1996, and Rebecca Beasley, *Ezra Pound and the Visual Culture of Modernism*, Cambridge: Cambridge University Press, 2007.

19 Edward Carpenter, 'The Status of Women in Early Greek Times', NFW 1/5, 15 August 1913, p. 68

20 Sitalkis is, according to Eileen Gregory, a version of Apollo as protector of the corn (see Eileen Gregory, *H.D. and Hellenism: Classic Lines*, Cambridge: Cambridge University Press, 1997, pp. 237–238), though H.D. herself many years later told Norman Holmes Pearson she

had thought Sitalkis an autumn sun god – not incompatible, of course: Apollo was the sun
god, and by autumn the corn has been harvested

21 Pound reviewed Williams' book in the *New Freewoman* that December

22 William Carlos Williams, *The Tempers*, London: Elkin Mathews, 1913, p. 31

23 P/W 23

24 Robert Ferguson, *The Short Sharp Life of T.E. Hulme*, London: Allen Lane, 2002, p. 147

25 LMS 80

26 LMS 76

27 LMS 78

28 LMS 65

29 LMS 79

30 LMS 79–81

31 JGFL 3

32 EPL 70

33 YP 60/2672

34 FY 245

35 FORD 472

36 EPL 59

37 EPL 60

38 PMV 3

39 EPL 59

40 EPL 52

41 'In Metre', NFW 1/6, 1 September 1913, p. 113

42 DHLL2 26

43 DHLL2 53

44 Lawrance Thompson, *Robert Frost: The Early Years, 1874–1915*, New York: Holt, Rinehart,
1966, p. 407

45 Ibid., p. 408

46 Ibid., p. 410

47 EPL 49–50, 51–52

48 Thompson, *Robert Frost: The Early Years*, p. 423

49 PMV 2/2, May 1913, pp. 72–4

50 Thompson, *Robert Frost: The Early Years*, p. 422

51 Lawrance Thompson, *Robert Frost: The Later Years, 1938–1963*, New York: Holt, Rinehart,
1976, p. 49

52 UTA

53 LMS 46, JGF 46, LMS 58

54 JGF 61

55 JGF 267

56 JGFL 131

57 'Approach to Paris II', NA, 11 September 1913

58 'Approach to Paris VII', NA, 16 October 1913

59 Peter Russell, ed., *Ezra Pound: A Collection of Essays to be Presented to Pound on his Sixty-
fifth Birthday*, London: Peter Nevill, 1950, p. 31

60 EP/DS 256

61 Zhaoming Qian, *Orientalism and Modernism: The Legacy of China in Pound and Williams*,
Durham, NC: Duke University Press, 1995, p. 57

62 'Rabindranath Tagore: His Second Book into English', NFW 1/10, 1 November 1913, pp.
187–188

63 Harold Hurwitz, 'Ezra Pound and Rabindranath Tagore', *American Literature*, 38, 1964, p. 58

64 YP 60/2672

65 Michael Sheldon, 'Allen Upward: Some Biographical Notes', *Agenda*, 16/3–4, Autumn/Winter 1978–79, p. 114

66 Kenneth Cox, 'Allen Upward', *Agenda*, 16/3–4, Autumn/Winter, 1978–79, p. 92

67 'The Divine Mystery', NFW 1/11, 15 November 1913, pp. 207–208

68 EPL 59

69 EPL 258

70 EP/DS 264, 267

71 Qian, *Orientalism and Modernism*, p. 27

72 PER 111

73 Qian points out that Pound saw further likenesses between the Greeks and the Chinese. Qian, *Orientalism and Modernism*, p. 45

74 EP/DS 264 (Pound misspells both names)

75 Elleke Boehmer, 'East is East and South is South', *Women: A Cultural Review*, 11/1–2, p. 62

76 Pound mentioned this work when he told his parents about meeting Mary Fenollosa. Whether he actually read it or not he does not say, but there is in the first volume a very striking photograph entitled 'A heap of broken statues found by Ernest Fenollosa'; possibly the origin of his famous phrase in *Hugh Selwyn Mauberley*, 'two gross of broken statues'

77 Donald Hall, 'Ezra Pound', *Writers at Work: The Paris Review Interviews*, ed. George Plimpton [1963], Harmondsworth: Penguin, 1977, p. 49

78 PER 111

79 P.D. James, 'Preface', *The Letters of Dorothy L. Sayers: 1899–1936: The Making of a Detective Novelist*, ed. Barbara Reynolds, London: Hodder & Stoughton, 1995, p. xv

80 John Cournos, *The Mask*, London: Methuen, 1919, p. 111

81 Alfred Satterthwaite, 'John Cournos and "H.D."' *Twentieth-Century Literature*, 22, 1976, pp. 397, 396

82 Satterthwaite, 'John Cournos and "H.D"', pp. 397, 398

83 GB 45, 46

84 Jacob Epstein, *An Autobiography*, London: Hulton Press, 1955, p. 44

85 John Cournos, *Autobiography*, New York: G.P. Putnam's Sons, 1935, p. 257

86 EPL 65

87 Cournos, *Autobiography*, p. 260

88 EPL 65

89 GB 38

90 Timothy Materer, *Vortex: Pound, Eliot and Lewis*, Ithaca: Cornell University Press, 1979, p. 68

91 Ibid., p. 67

92 LL 151

93 YP 60/2672

94 Ibid.

95 SC 26

96 WBY 521

97 'This Hulme Business', *Townsman*, 2/5, January 1939, reproduced in EPP&P7 418. Pound's parallel association with them both, playing tennis with Ford in the day and attending Yeats' evenings, prefigures in a strange way his two-stranded domestic arrangements in Rapallo in the late 1930s, when he spent the days with Dorothy and the evenings with Olga Rudge

98 EPL 58

99 EPL 57

100 EPL 50

101 EPL 62

102 EP/DS 250

103   SC 37
104   WBY 506–507
105   EPL 64
106   GB 46
107   PMV 3/4, January 1914
108   Marcus, *Young Rebecca*, p. 162
109   Garner, *Brave and Beautiful Spirit*, p. 109
110   BL ADD 57725 Ezra Pound to Patricia Hutchins, 19 September 1933
111   Garner, *Brave and Beautiful Spirit*, p. 116
112   Ibid., p. 117
113   'Views and Comment', NFW 1/7, 15 December, 1913, p. 244
114   Garner, *Brave and Beautiful Spirit*, pp. 117–118
115   NS 182–183
116   WBY 476
117   'The Later Yeats', PMV 4/2, May 1914, p. 65
118   'The Tradition' PMV 3/4, January 1914, p. 137. The ideas about tradition he puts forward are probably taken from Rémy de Gourmont's *Le Problème du style*. Aldington would publish a translation of the relevant sections the following year in the *Egoist*. Pound must have read the book since his September article on de Gourmont when he says nothing about the book. See Part Six, note 152
119   EPT 222, 236
120   The translation was first published in *Poetry* in May 1914
121   Quoted in Hugh Witemeyer, *The Poetry of Ezra Pound: Forms and Renewals, 1908–1920*, Berkeley: University of California Press, 1969, p. 148
122   EP/DS 277–278. Published in the *Cerebralist*, of which there was only one issue. 'Ikon' is described in the NFW advertisement as a brief note
123   WBY 494
124   WBYCP 108
125   'Affirmations II: Vorticism', NA, 14 January 1915
126   WBY 501
127   'The Bourgeois', EG 1, 2 February 1914, p. 53
128   'John Synge and the Habit of Criticism', EG 1, 2 February 1914, p. 54
129   Wilfrid Scawen Blunt, *The Secret History of the English Occupation of Egypt*, London: Fisher Unwin, 1907, p. 5.
130   Wilfrid Scawen Blunt, *The Shame of the Nineteenth Century. A Letter addressed to the 'Times', December 24, 1900*, London: no publisher, 1901, p. 3
131   Elizabeth Longford, *A Pilgrimage of Passion: The Life of Wilfrid Scawen Blunt*, London: Weidenfeld & Nicolson, 1979, p. 343
132   EP/DS 297
133   'Homage to Wilfrid Blunt', PMV 3/6, March 1914, p. 222
134   Longford, *A Pilgrimage of Passion* p. 394
135   Ibid.
136   Flint would also write a report on the visit for *Poetry & Drama*
137   'Presentation to Mr W.S. Blunt', EG 1, 2 February 1914, pp. 56–57
138   Longford, *A Pilgrimage of Passion*, p. 394
139   EPL 73
140   'Homage to Wilfrid Blunt', p. 221
141   EPC 522 C81
142   'Homage to Wilfrid Blunt', p. 222
143   P/J 18
144   Ibid.

145 'Affirmations VII: The Non-existence of Ireland', NA, 25 February 1915

146 P/F 44

147 SP 425

Part Eleven: Prelude to War

1 YP 60/2673

2 Paul O'Keeffe, *Some Sort of Genius: A Life of Wyndham Lewis*, London: Jonathan Cape, 2000, pp. 106, 109, 115

3 Paul Edwards suggests Lewis was probably also attracted by Timon's profligate generosity in the first part of the play. Paul Edwards, *Wyndham Lewis, Painter and Writer*, New Haven: Yale University Press, 2000, pp. 86, 98. Most accounts of this incident defend Fry, but Edwards thinks Lewis was in the right

4 HULME 264, 266, 267. Hulme says he will not discuss Picasso, André Derain and others who were also exhibited there, as they are not part of the group. He also singles out Gaudier-Brzeska and William Roberts, also there, as doing good work

5 'The New Sculpture', EG 1, 16 February 1914

6 HULME 257. Worringer's book, whose title in English is *Abstraction and Empathy: A Contribution to the Psychology of Style*, was published in 1908 and was already in its third edition

7 HULME 273–275

8 HULME 273

9 T.E. Hulme, *Speculations*, ed. Herbert Read [1924], London: Routledge & Kegan Paul, 1960, p. 73. This is in fact a translation from Worringer

10 Wilhelm Worringer, *Abstraction and Empathy: A Contribution to the Psychology of Style* [1908], trans. Michael Bullock, London: Routledge & Kegan Paul, 1953, p. 18

11 HULME 277–280

12 'The New Sculpture', p. 67

13 'Presentation to Mr W.S. Blunt', EG 1, 2 February 1914, p. 57; 'The New Sculpture', p. 68

14 'The New Sculpture', pp. 67–68

15 *Poetry & Drama* 2/1, March 1914, p. 21

16 YP 60/2673

17 LL 137

18 'Mr Hueffer and the Prose Tradition in Verse', PMV 4/3, June 1914, p. 114

19 FORD 398, JGFL 19

20 Richard M. Ludwig, ed., *The Letters of Ford Madox Ford*, Princeton: Princeton University Press, 1965, p. 88; FORD 397

21 EP/DS 293

22 EG 1, 15 January 1914, p. 36

23 'Anti-Hellenism: A Note on Some Modern Art', EG 1, 15 January 1914, p. 35

24 '*Poetry*'s Banquet', PMV 4/1, April 1914, p. 27

25 SC 70

26 EG 1, 16 March 1914 p. 105

27 EP/DS 304

28 EP/DS 306

29 EP/DS 310

30 John Harwood, *Olivia Shakespear and W.B. Yeats: After Long Silence*, Basingstoke: Macmillan, 1989, p. 151

31 EP/DS 332

32 EP/DS 99

33 Interestingly, however, Richard Cork points out that, when she exhibited, it was as Dorothy Shakespear. Richard Cork, *Vorticism and its Allies*, London: Arts Council of Great Britain, 1974, p. 33

34 Hugh Kenner, 'D.F.P. Remembered', *Paideuma*, 2/3, 1973, pp. 485–493

35 Iris Barry, 'The Ezra Pound Period', *The Bookman* (New York), 74/2, October 1931, p. 165

36 Harwood, *Olivia Shakespear*, p. 146

37 PER 176

38 HC 239

39 HC 241

40 EP/DS 337

41 EP/DS 333

42 YP 60/2673

43 Ibid.

44 EP/DS 307

45 EP/DS 309

46 EP/DS 308

47 PM 56

48 END 5

49 EP/DS 337

50 YP 1/22: only dated Sunday

51 LL 123, EP/DS 325

52 'Modern Poetry and the Imagists', EG 1, 1 June 1914, p. 202

53 LL 124

54 'Modern Poetry and the Imagists', pp. 202–203

55 Margaret Anderson, *My Thirty Years' War: An Autobiography*, New York: Covici, Friede, 1930, p. 36

56 'Exhibition at the Goupil Gallery', EG 1, 16 March 1914, p. 109

57 'Wyndham Lewis', EG 1, 15 June 1914, p. 233

58 HULME 296

59 'M. Marinetti's Lectures', NFW 1/12, 1 December 1913, p. 226

60 YP 1/22. This is the same letter as that about the reviews of *Des Imagistes*

61 LL 98

62 Christopher Nevinson, quoted in Cork, *Vorticism and its Allies*, p. 8

63 BB 36

64 Richard Cork, *Vorticism and Abstract Art in the First Machine Age*: Vol. 1, *Origins and Development*, London: Gordon Fraser Gallery, 1976, p. 235

65 Richard Cork, the chief historian of the movement, points out that nearly all the references to Vorticism are at the front or the end of the magazine

66 Cork, *Vorticism and its Allies*, p. 5

67 P/W 23

68 EP/DS 251

69 See Timothy Materer, *Vortex: Pound, Eliot and Lewis*, Ithaca: Cornell University Press, 1979, pp. 15–16, 134

70 SR2 92–3

71 Cork, *Vorticism and its Allies*, p. 5. Paul Edwards does however see a Gnostic element in Lewis' play, *The Enemy of the Stars*, so perhaps he would have had some sympathy with Pound's approach. See Edwards, *Wyndham Lewis*, pp. 143–144

72 30.5 by 24cm, in metric

73 SL 67; O'Keeffe, *Some Sort of Genius*, p. 157

74 Cork, *Vorticism and its Allies*, p. 20

75 See William C. Wees, *Vorticism and the English Avant-Garde*, Manchester: Manchester University Press, 1972

76 Paul O'Keeffe intriguingly suggests the latter was really cover for 'Chocolate Box Fry', i.e. the despised Roger Fry

77 Wees, *Vorticism*, p. 40

78 GB 53

79 RA 135

80 See his chapter 'The Modernism of *The Enemy of the Stars*', in his book *Wyndham Lewis* (this quotation p. 142)

81 *Blast*, pp. 64, 67

82 *Blast*, p. 154

83 'Blast', EG 1, 14 July 1914, p. 272

84 EG 1, 1 July 1914, p. 248

85 DRE 317

86 DRE 206

87 'Suffragettes', EG 1, 1 July 1914, p. 255. This article has been interpreted as showing Pound in sympathy with the anarchist left (though his reference to 'the undergraduate' in itself seems to tell against that), but I would argue that Pound's anti-democratic stance was consistently elitist. See David Kadlec, *Mosaic Modernism: Anarchism, Pragmatism, Culture*, Baltimore: Johns Hopkins University Press, 2000, p. 2

88 *Blast*, p. 151

89 YP 60/2674

90 'Suffragettes', p. 256

91 *Blast*, pp. 30, 32, 15, 36, 41

92 O'Keeffe, *Some Sort of Genius*, p. 157

93 EPL 72

94 Les Garner, *A Brave and Beautiful Spirit: Dora Marsden, 1882–1960*, Aldershot: Avebury, 1990, p. 132

95 EPL 73

96 SFD 237

97 P/ACH 138. ('Charmer' is actually Henderson's word, but Pound agrees she has 'charm')

98 See Peter Brooker, *Bohemia in London: The Social Scene of Early Modernism*, Basingstoke: Palgrave Macmillan, 2004

99 LMS 84

100 SFD 231

101 'Blast', pp. 272–273

102 Hugh Kenner, *The Pound Era* [1971], London: Pimlico, 1991, p. 243

103 *Blast*, p. 45. Pound very slightly revised this later: see PER 75–76

104 David Trotter, *Paranoid Modernism: Literary Experiment, Psychosis, and the Professionalization of English Society*, Oxford: Oxford University Press, 2001, p. 54

105 SFD 232

106 'Henri Gaudier', ER 29, 1919, pp. 297–304

107 In fact first used by Witter Bynner. See Melissa Bradshaw, 'Remembering Amy Lowell', ALAM, p. 171

108 AMY 127

109 GB 22–23

110 LMS 151

111 John Cournos, *Autobiography*, New York: G.P. Putnam's Sons, 1935, p. 271

112 LMS 151

113 'Miscast I', EG 1, 1 August 1914, p. 288. Lowell's unhappiness after these dinners and her

changed attitude, towards Allen Upward for example, emerges in a letter dated 20 July 1914 to Harriet Monroe, quoted in Ellen Williams, *Harriet Monroe and the Poetic Renaissance: The First Ten Years of Poetry, 1912–1922*, Urbana: University of Illinois Press, 1977. Williams has a very hostile account of Lowell, as often at that period

114   LMS 145

115   'Vorticism', *Fortnightly Review*, 96, September 1914, pp. 461–471

116   SFD 240

117   LL 124

118   'Some Recent French Poets', EG 1, 15 June, 1914, p. 221

119   SFD 236

120   Jayne E. Marek, 'Amy Lowell and the Context of the New Poetry', ALAM, p. 157

121   SFD 238

122   Ibid.

123   LL 127

124   SFD 223

125   'Affirmations, VII. The Non-existence of Ireland,' NA, 25 February 1915

126   DHLL2 191

127   DHLL2 196

128   Aldington says Fletcher was there, but Lawrence was not to meet Fletcher until 1917

129   LL 127–128

130   LL 128

131   DHLL2 203

132   BID 140. Frieda (Elsa) does not in fact seem to have been at that first dinner; nor had the war actually begun

133   SFD 242; *Little Review* 1, 6–9 October 1914

134   EPL 77–78

135   NS 280

Part Twelve: War

1   Douglas Goldring, *Odd Man Out: The Autobiography of a 'Propaganda Novelist'*, London: Chapman & Hall, 1935, p. 127

2   Ibid., p. 134

3   Siegfried Sassoon, 'Songbooks of the War', *Georgian Poetry 1918–1919*, London: Poetry Bookshop, 1919, p. 135. Hilaire Belloc, *The Modern Traveller*, London: Edward Arnold, 1898

4   Dora Marsden, 'Views and Comment', and Richard Aldington, 'In the Arena', EG 1, 1 August 1914, pp. 284 & 287

5   John Cournos, *Autobiography*, New York: G.P. Putnam's Sons, 1935, p. 276

6   PIT 45

7   Robert Ferguson, *The Short Sharp Life of T.E. Hulme*, London: Allen Lane, 2002, p. 183

8   LL 148

9   Damon says there were no liner tickets available, but it surely is inconceivable that a Lowell could not have got one if she desired

10   AMY 136; LL 129

11   'Six French Poets', EG 3, 1 January 1916, pp. 9–10

12   HLFL (29 December, 1915)

13   EPL 78–79

14   DHLL2 206. The collected correspondence of Lawrence and Lowell has been published in *The Letters of D. H. Lawrence and Amy Lowell 1914–1925*, Santa Barbara: Black Sparrow Press, 1985

15   David Garnett, *The Flowers of the Forest*, London: Chatto & Windus, 1955, p. 4

16 SFD 246
17 Glenn Hughes, *Imagism & the Imagists: A Study in Modern Poetry*, California: Stanford University Press, 1931, p. 169
18 DHLL2 210
19 DHLL2 211
20 HFL (24 September, 1914)
21 Ibid.
22 HRAL (21 September 1914)
23 EPL 80
24 AMY 8
25 FORD 471
26 P/F 28
27 HRAL (7 December 1914)
28 'Two Poets', EG 1, 16 November 1914, p. 422
29 HHDL (23 November, 1914). Barbara Guest, *Herself Defined: The Poet H.D. and her World*, London: Collins, 1985, p. 72
30 ASPH 113
31 London-based artists (the future Vorticists Wyndham Lewis and Frederick Etchells, and the Bloomsbury artists, Vanessa Bell, Duncan Grant and Roger Fry) were included in the 1912 exhibition
32 BB 39
33 Amy Lowell, *Sword Blades and Poppy Seed*, London: Macmillan, 1914, p. ix
34 'Two Poets', EG 1, 16 November 1914, p. 423
35 SFD 262
36 HRAL (21 October 1914)
37 DHLL2 223
38 DHLL2 234
39 AMY 144. Amy Lowell, *Sword Blades and Poppy Seed*, London: Macmillan, 1914 (earlier published as 'Poems', EG 1, 1 August 1914, p. 288)
40 DHLL2 235
41 The advertisement does not appear in the bound copies of *Poetry* that I have seen, but an example can be found in the *Little Review*, 1/7, October 1914, p. 59, and it also can be seen on the online version of *Poetry* provided by the Modernist Journals Project on the Brown University website: http://dl.lib.brown.edu:8081exist/mjp/show_issue.xq?id= 1201882375609375/ (PMV 5/1, no page number but would be 55)
42 HRAL (8 October 1914)
43 EPL 84
44 EPL 84–85
45 *Little Review*, 1/7, October 1914, p. 59
46 SP 354
47 HRAL (6 November 1914)
48 P/ACH 89, 91
49 HLP (3 November 1914)
50 Ibid.
51 HHDL (23 November 1914)
52 HDCP 36
53 HRAL (12 November 1914)
54 HRAL (21 December 1914)
55 'London (May, 1915)', in *Images*, London: Poetry Bookshop, 1915, p. 30
56 EPL 88
57 Ibid.

58   'Preliminary Announcement of the College of Arts', EG 1, 2 November 1914, p. 413

59   George Dangerfield, *The Strange Death of Liberal England* [1935], London: McGibbon & Kee, 1966. BB 40

60   HLRA (25 November 1914)

61   HRAL (7 December 1914)

62   HLRA (6 November 1914), SFD 275–276

63   'Those American Publications', EG 1, 15, October 1914, p. 390

64   HLRA (11 November 1914), SFD 276

65   HLRA (24 December 1914), SFD 283

66   HRAL (1 February 1915)

67   SFD 287

68   HRAL (14 December 1914)

69   'Affirmations IV: As for Imagisme', NA, 28 January 1915 'Affirmations II: Vorticism', NA, 14 January 1915

70   'Imagisme and England: A Vindication and an Anthology', *T.P.'s Weekly* 25, 20 February 1915, p. 641, reproduced in EPP&P2 19

71   HHDL (17 December 1914)

72   HLRA (19 January 1915)

73   HFLL (24 January 1915)

74   JGFL 24

75   *Blast*, p. 147

76   *Blast*, p. 153. 'Vorticism', *Fortnightly Review*, 96 (NS), 1 September 1914, p. 471

77   *Blast*, 2, p. 82

78   SL 65

79   *Blast*, p. 33

80   Ibid., pp. 134, 136

81   *Blast*, 2, p. 9

82   'Affirmations, V: Gaudier-Brzeska', NA, 4 February 1915

83   Timothy Materer, *Vortex: Pound, Eliot and Lewis*, Ithaca: Cornell University Press, 1979, p. 31

84   'Affirmations I: Arnold Dolmetsch', NA, 7 January 1915

85   BB 258

86   Jacob Epstein, *An Autobiography*, London: Hulton, 1955, p. 46

87   HRAL (3 September 1915)

88   EPL 89

89   HRAL (3 October 1914)

90   *Blast*, p. 34; Ford, quoted in William C. Wees, *Vorticism and the English Avant-Garde*, Manchester: Manchester University Press, 1972, p. 195

91   Paul Overy, 'Vorticism', in *Concepts of Modern Art*, ed. Nikos Stangos, London: Thames & Hudson, rev. edn, 1981, p. 109

92   Richard Cork, *Vorticism and its Allies*, London: Arts Council of Great Britain, 1974, p. 24

93   Epstein, *Autobiography*, p. 57

94   Cork, *Vorticism and its Allies*, p. 74

95   Ibid., p. 24

96   EPL 86

97   The *New Age* had been moving in this direction for a while; significantly their previous art critic, Huntly Carter, who had welcomed Fry's First Post-Impressionist Exhibition, had moved to the *New Freewoman* and was replaced by the much more reactionary Anthony Ludovici, witheringly denounced in his turn by Hulme: see Rebecca Beasley, *Ezra Pound and the Visual Culture of Modernism*, Cambridge: Cambridge University Press, 2007

98   AMY 152

99   HLRA (25 November 1914)

100 HLRA (24 December 1914)

101 See Andrew Thacker, 'Unrelated Beauty: Lowell, Polyphonic Prose and the Imagist City', in ALAM.

102 JGFL 14

103 JGFL 15.

104 JGFL 17 (16 December 1914)

105 JGFL 19

106 EPL 95

107 JGFP 89

108 JGFL 17

109 Margaret Anderson, *My Thirty Years' War: An Autobiography*, New York: Covici, Friede, 1930, pp. 60–61

110 HRAL (1 February 1915)

111 YHD 1012; 'Compassionate Friendship', p. 12

112 EG 2, May 1915, p. 74

113 WBY2 6

114 SC 146

115 PER 126–127

116 Ezra Pound, 'The Renaissance: 1. The Palette', PMV 5/5, p. 228. Rémy de Gourmont, 'Tradition and Other Things', trans. Richard Aldington, EG 1, 15 July 1914, p. 261

117 EPL 94

118 Jane Marcus, 'Amy Lowell: Body and Sou-ell', in ALAM, p. 192

119 EPL 92

120 'Affirmations III: Jacob Epstein', NA, 21 January 1915

121 EPL 99

122 'Affirmations VI: Analysis of this Decade', NA, 11 February 1915

123 'Six French Poets', *Little Review*, January/February 1916, pp. 16–17

124 Lawrance Thompson, *Robert Frost: The Years of Triumph, 1915–1938*, New York: Holt, Rinehart & Winston, 1970, p. 18

125 Lawrance Thompson, *Robert Frost: The Early Years, 1874–1915*, New York: Holt, Rinehart & Winston, 1966, p. 474

126 JGF 84

127 SFD 292

128 *Some Imagist Poets*, Boston: Houghton Mifflin, 1915, p. 81

129 'Poems', EG 2, 1 May 1915, p. 78

130 SFD 312

131 Zhaoming Qian, *Orientalism and Modernism: The Legacy of China in Pound and Williams*, Durham, NC: Duke University Press, 1995, p. 114

132 Hugh Kenner, *The Pound Era* [1971], London: Pimlico, 1991, p. 202. Ronald Bush, 'Pound and Li Po: What Becomes a Man', in G. Bornstein, ed., *Ezra Pound among the Poets*, Chicago: University of Chicago Press, 1985 pp. 42–43. 'Webster Ford', EG 2, 1 January 1915, p. 11; GB 63

133 PER 136–137

134 CH 109

135 PER 137

136 PER 139

137 SC 21

138 CZ2 46

139 P/L xiv

140 Robert H. Ross, *The Georgian Revolt: Rise and Fall of a Poetic Ideal, 1910–22*, London: Faber & Faber, 1965, p. 162

141 'The Soldier', PMV 6/1, April 1915, p. 19

142 The final piece was to be on Masters (it was the advocacy of his free verse to which Orage objected), and was in fact published in May in St Louis, by the paper that had originally printed the poems, so Pound's effort was not wasted

Part Thirteen: Battles and Divisions

1   HRAL (4 April 1915)

2   Ibid.

3   'Poems', EG 2, 1 May 1915, p. 77. She would first be published in *Poetry* that same month

4   H.D., 'Letters to Marianne Moore', in *The Gender of Modernism*, ed. Bonnie Kime Scott, Bloomington: Indiana University Press, 1990, p. 137

5   Dominic Hibberd, *Harold Monro: Poet of the New Age*, London: Palgrave, 2001, p. 148

6   'The Imagists Discussed', EG 2, 1 May 1915, pp. 77–80

7   'The Poetry of H.D.', EG 2, 1 May 1915, p. 72

8   SFD 307–308

9   Ibid.

10 'Poems', EG 2, 1 May 1915, p. 75

11 SFD 307–308

12 SFD 348

13 AMY 243

14 *Some Imagist Poets: An Anthology*, Boston: Houghton Mifflin, 1915, p. 78

15 Ibid., p. vii. Michael Levenson, *A Genealogy of Modernism: A Study of English Literary Doctrine, 1908–1922*, Cambridge: Cambridge University Press, 1984

16 JGF 80

17 DHLL2 390

18 Trudi Tate, *Modernism, History and the First World War*, Manchester: Manchester University Press, 1998, p. 43

19 H.D., *Kora and Ka, with Mira-Mare* [1934], New York: New Directions, 1996, p. 36. Robert Spoo in the introduction notes that a correction by H.D. of the original published text changed 'fed out belching mothers' to 'fed our' (p. xv)

20 HRAL (21 May 1915)

21 TRIB 40

22 Susan Stanford Friedman, *Psyche Reborn: The Emergence of H.D.*, Bloomington: Indiana University Press, 1981, pp. 29, 301

23 ASPH 108

24 ASPH 107–109

25 HRAL (26 May 1915)

26 AN 5

27 Tate, *Modernism, History and the First World War*, pp. 10–40

28 ASPH 113

29 BID 24–25

30 James Whitall, *English Years*, London: Jonathan Cape, 1936, p. 55

31 Richard Aldington, 'The Poetry of Amy Lowell', EG 2, 1 July 1915, p. 110

32 'Chinese Poems', EG 2, 2 August 1915, p. 122

33 Whitall, *English Years*, pp. 55–57

34 'Young America', EG 2, 1 November 1915, p. 177

35 Suzanne W. Churchill, 'Making Space for *Others*', *Journal of Modern Literature*, 22/1, 1998, p. 63

36 Ibid., p. 48

37 Ibid., p. 54

38   'Two Notes', EG, 1 June 1915, p. 88

39   YP 60/2676

40   YP 60/2672

41   P/J 42

42   There had been a Vorticist section in the earlier London Group exhibition that March, in which Epstein's *Rock Drill* was included, and there would be a Vorticist exhibition in New York in 1917, but London would have to wait until the 1974 *Vorticism and its Allies* exhibition to see their work brought together again, and by then much of it was lost

43   Richard Cork, *Vorticism and its Allies*, London: Arts Council of Great Britain, 1974, p. 25

44   'Affirmations II. Vorticism', NA, 14 January 1915

45   YP 60/2676

46   HC 280

47   HRAL (9 September 1915). 'Cuistre' can mean 'prig' or 'pedant', or alternatively 'lout' or boor'; perhaps Aldington was intending to convey both meanings

48   P/ACH 118

49   YP 60/2676

50   EPL 108

51   NS 228

52   'The Net American Loss' [written 1915], in '"Ezra Pound On America and World War I", presented by Timothy Materer', *Paideuma*, 18/1&2, 1989, pp. 208–209

53   Robert Ferguson, *The Short Sharp Life of T.E. Hulme*, London: Allen Lane, 2002, p. 211

54   'Diary from the Trenches' (1914–15), in HULME 313, 319, 326

55   Ferguson, *Short, Sharp Life*, p. 214

56   Jacob Epstein, *An Autobiography*, London: Hulton, 1955, pp. 59–60

57   *Blast*, 2, pp. 85–86

58   *Blast*, 2, p. 5

59   *Blast*, 2, p. 24

60   *Blast*, 2, p. 9

61   *Blast*, 2, pp. 33–34

62   'Et Faim Saillir le Loup des Boys', *Blast*, 2, p. 22

63   BB 281

64   WBY2 5

65   LL 95

66   EP/DS 260. Orage had in fact been very critical of his 1913 'Approach to Paris' articles. It seems unlikely that this was because they promoted the French, as has been suggested – the *New Age* had done so for many years – more perhaps the manner in which they promoted the French by insulting the English, and also because of their support for *vers libre*, of which Orage disapproved, the reason why the Masters piece was cut. Orage's dislike of the 'Approach to Paris' articles may have been why Pound did not publish at all in the *New Age* in 1914, but he might just have been too busy launching Vorticism

67   P/ACH 129

68   Reed Way Dasenbrock, *The Literary Vorticism of Ezra Pound and Wyndham Lewis: Towards the Condition of Painting*, Baltimore: Johns Hopkins University Press, 1985, and Ronald Bush, *The Genesis of Ezra Pound's Cantos*, Princeton: Princeton University Press, 1976. Ronald Bush argues both for the influence of Vorticist form and for Pound's mythopoetic vision

69   HRAL. Both the letters of Pound I quote from here are held with Flint's papers at the University of Texas at Austin

70   F. S. Flint, 'A History of Imagism', EG,2, 1 May 1915, pp. 70–71

71   Christopher Middleton, 'Documents on Imagism from the Papers of F.S. Flint', *The Review*, 15 April 1965, p. 41. Middleton's article paraphrases Pound's letters. In this chapter I quote direct from the letters at UTA

72   Ibid., p. 42

73   Ibid.

74   Ibid., p. 39

75   Ibid., p. 40

76   Ibid., p. 43

77   Ibid., p. 44

78   The first of Pound's letters is dated 2 July, the second 7 July

79   Middleton, 'Documents', p. 43

80   Levenson, *A Genealogy of Modernism*, p. 137

81   PER 58

82   Middleton, 'Documents', p. 39

83   'Affirmations IV: As for Imagisme', NA, 28 January 1915

84   Middleton, 'Documents', p. 43

85   UTA

86   Glenn Hughes, *Imagism & the Imagists: A Study in Modern Poetry*, California: Stanford
     University Press, 1931, p. 166. Middleton, 'Documents', p. 41

87   FORD 473

88   RTY 418

89   FORD 484

90   Cyrena N. Pondrom, ed., 'Selected Letters from H.D. to F.S. Flint: A Commentary on the
     Imagist Period', *Contemporary Literature*, 10/4, 1969, p. 563

91   UTA

92   P/ACH 118–119

93   NS 230

94   JGFL 30

95   P/ACH 142

96   'The Discarded Imagist', EG 2, 1 June 1915, p. 98

97   Timothy Materer, *Vortex: Pound, Eliot and Lewis*, Ithaca: Cornell University Press, 1979,
     p. 26. Whether Gaudier did write to Pound so near his death is uncertain; Pound was anxious
     to claim this, but the letter was in fact dated a month earlier; according to Pound, this was
     in error

98   Materer, *Vortex*, p. 26. For Gaudier's links with Murry and Fry, see also Paul O'Keeffe,
     Gaudier-Brzeska: An Absolute Case of Genius, London: Allen Lane, 2004

99   'Gaudier-Brzeska's Art', EG 2, September 1915, pp. 137–138

100 Levenson, *Genealogy of Modernism*, pp. 141–142

101 RA 138

102 As Timothy Materer, who writes perceptively about the relationship between Pound and
     Gaudier, observes, in this way Gaudier is very different from Hulme and Lewis who, like
     Worringer, saw fear as the constitutive emotion behind such art; see his chapter 'Gaudier-
     Brzeska Vortex' in Materer, *Vortex*.

103 GB 75

104 P/ACH 120

105 EPL 109–110

106 NS 239

107 *Catholic Anthology 1914–1915*, London: Elkin Mathews, 1915, p. 60

108 P/ACH 120

109 GB 151

110 Peter Ackroyd, *T.S. Eliot* [1984], London: Cardinal, 1988, p. 24. For his comment on Eliot
     and Bloomsbury, see p. 74

111 Ronald Bush, *The Genesis of Ezra Pound's Cantos*, Princeton: Princeton University Press,
     1976, p. 5

112 T.S. Eliot, *Collected Poems, 1909–1935*, London: Faber & Faber, 1936, p. 26

113 JGFP 127

114 DHLL2 331

115 DHLL2 323

116 DHLL2 283

117 DHLL2 285

118 DHLL2 365

119 DHLL2 392

120 DHLL2 442, 470

121 Miranda Seymour, *Lady Ottoline Morell: Life on a Grand Scale* [1992], London: Sceptre, 1998, p. 299

122 SR2 92

123 D.H. Lawrence, *Kangaroo* [1923], Harmondsworth: Penguin, 1950, p. 240

124 Harry T. Moore, *The Priest of Love: A Life of D.H. Lawrence* [1974], Harmondsworth: Penguin, 1976, p. 311

125 Lawrence, *Kangaroo*, p. 240

126 DHLL2 386, 405

127 Lawrence published a revised version of 'The Crown' essays in *Reflections on the Death of a Porcupine* in 1925

128 HRAL (29 October 1915)

129 Moore, *The Priest of Love*, p. 306; Paul Delany, *D.H. Lawrence's Nightmare: The Writer and his Circle in the Years of the Great War*, Hassocks: Harvester Press, 1979, p. 156

130 DHLL2 349

131 Keith Sagar, *The Life of D.H. Lawrence*, London: Eyre Methuen, 1980, p. 90

132 John Worthen, *D.H. Lawrence: The Life of an Outsider*, London: Allen Lane, 2005, p. 164

133 Suzanne Raitt, *May Sinclair: A Modern Victorian*, Oxford: Oxford University Press, 2000, p. 141

134 HHDL (4 October 1915, though mistakenly ascribed by Houghton to 1916); Sagar, *Life of D.H. Lawrence*, illustrated opposite p. 128

135 HRAL (29 November 1915, in H.D.'s handwriting and filed with her letters)

136 HRAL (29 November 1915)

137 HLRA (23 November 1915)

138 HLRA (30 December 1915)

139 'In Trouble and Shame', in *Some Imagist Poets, 1916: An Annual Anthology*, Boston: Houghton Mifflin, 1916, p. 73

140 Sagar, *Life of D.H. Lawrence*, p. 75

141 HHDL (7 November 1915)

142 DHLL2 386, 486

143 BID 65

144 Worthen, *D.H. Lawrence*, p. 163

145 HHDL (7 November 1914)

146 'In the Tube', EG 2, 1 May 1915, p. 74

147 Richard Aldington, *D.H. Lawrence*, London: Chatto & Windus, 1930, p. 17

148 SIU Unpublished lecture on 'H.D. and Lawrence' given in the USA in 1939, Box 19/6

149 BID 66; *Some Imagist Poets, 1916*, pp. 25–26 (HDCP 36–37)

150 DHLL2 364–365

151 Delany, *D.H. Lawrence's Nightmare*, p. 119

152 DHLL2 493

153 ASPH 10

154 LL 127

155 DHLL2 502–503. Dollie Radford, a poet and wife of the former Rhymer, Ernest Radford, was then in her fifties; she and her husband were always supportive of Lawrence

156 DHLL2 541

157 BID 66

158 BID 162–163

159 'Choruses from *Iphigenia in Aulis*', EG 2, 171, 1 November 1915, and HDCP 73–74

160 'Euripides', pp. 2, 3 (one of some largely unpublished essays on Greek writers), YHD 43/1116

161 Amy Lowell, *Six French Poets: Studies in Contemporary Literature*, New York: Macmillan, 1915, pp. 120–121

162 Amy Lowell, *Men, Women and Ghosts*, New York: Macmillan, 1916, pp. 3–9. *Some Imagist Poets, 1916*, pp. 77–81

Part Fourteen: Dispersal

1   'Sunsets', in *Some Imagist Poets, 1916: An Annual Anthology*, Boston: Houghton Mifflin, 1916, p. 10

2   HULME 350, 397

3   HULME 375, 376, 377, 380

4   HULME 392, 411, 332, 414

5   HHDL (February 1916)

6   HLHD (6 February 1916)

7   HLHD (12 January 1916)

8   HHDL (24 January 1916)

9   Cyrena N. Pondrom, ed., 'Selected Letters from H.D. to F.S. Flint: a Commentary on the Imagist Period', *Contemporary Literature* 10/4, 1969, p. 566

10 HLHD (12 January 1916)

11 HLRA (15 December 1915)

12 SFD 339, 341

13 A. J. P. Taylor, *English History, 1914–1945*, Oxford: Clarendon Press, 1965, p. 1

14 SC 197

15 WBY2 39

16 EPL 110

17 WBY2 39

18 WBY2 41

19 EPT 213–214

20 P/Q 94

21 Peter Russell, ed., *Ezra Pound: A Collection of Essays to be Presented to Pound on his Sixty-fifth Birthday*, London: Peter Nevill, 1950, pp. 25, 29

22 See Michael Levenson, *A Genealogy of Modernism: A Study of English Literary Doctrine, 1908–1922*, Cambridge: Cambridge University Press, 1984, p. 29

23 P/ACH 140

24 P/Q 66

25 See the chapter on 'Daemonic Images' in Timothy Materer, *Modernist Alchemy: Poetry and the Occult*, Ithaca: Cornell University Press, 1995

26 He also published a book of translations of the poet, Jean de Bosschère, one of the many Belgian refugees in London, who had translated the work of the imagists for the *Mercure de France*. (Jean de Bosschère is not much remembered now, but Flint also translated his poems, and Conrad Aiken said that he thought de Bosschère was an important influence on T.S. Eliot.) Pound had also written an account of contemporary literature, to be called 'This Generation', but that was never published; he generously withdrew it from its

American publisher so that they would publish Joyce's *Portrait* instead, but they published neither

27 EPL 114, 118

28 'The Last Gift', EG3, March 1916, p. 35, HDCP 18. BID 41–42. The ancient Eleusinian Mysteries were associated with the mother and daughter goddesses, Demeter and Persephone, and also with the cult of Dionysus, the dark god of ecstasy and wine

29 Walter Pater, *The Renaissance: Studies in Art and Poetry* (1873), London: MacMillan, 1902

30 Richard Aldington, 'Anti-Hellenism', EG 1, 15 January 1914

31 'The Poems of Richard Aldington', ER 32, May 1921, pp. 400–401

32 ASPH 169

33 Pater, *The Renaissance*, p. 207

34 SFD 364–365

35 HLHD (23 November 1915)

36 DHLL2 610

37 John Cournos, *Autobiography*, New York: G.P. Putnam's Sons, 1935, p. 249

38 LL 161

39 LL 160

40 Cournos, *Autobiography*, pp. 288–289

41 EG 2, 1 June 1915

42 AN 5

43 Pound had, however, no sympathy with Casement and came near to quarrelling with Quinn over whether or not he was a traitor, and is likely to have argued about this with Yeats

44 AN 6

45 BID 58

46 HRAL (6 May 1916)

47 HRAL (11 June 1916)

48 CZ 24

49 Cournos, *Autobiography*, p. 289

50 Ibid.

51 YHD 17/581–583. All quotations in the letters from H.D. to Cournos come from here

52 CZ 22

53 H.D. would spell it 'Korshune'

54 HLRA (28 June 1916)

55 CZ 116

56 YHD 38/1012. 'Compassionate Friendship', pp. 72, 74

57 EG 3, August 1916, p. 118

58 In *Sea Garden*, 'The Last Gift' appears as 'The Gift'

59 HDCP 20–21

60 JGFP 116

61 JGFL 35

62 'Mr Aldington's Images', PMV 8/1 April 1916, pp. 49, 5

63 JGFL 41, 43

64 HDCP xviii–xix

65 HDCP 319–320

66 HDCP 314

67 HRAL (August 1916)

68 Glenn Hughes, *Imagism & the Imagists: A Study in Modern Poetry*, California: Stanford University Press, 1931, p. 165

69 HFLL (8 October 1916)

70   'Soldiers', in *Some Imagist Poets 1917: An Annual Anthology*, Boston: Houghton Mifflin, 1917, pp. 61–62

71   JGFL 48

72   HFLL (8 October 1916)

73   DHLL3 37

74   DHLL3 21

75   DHLL3 24

76   BID 138, 80

77   DHLL2 645

78   DHLL3 25–26

79   DHLL3 24

80   HHDL (14 August 1916)

81   DHLL3 32

82   DHLL3 30–31

83   Eileen Gregory, *H.D. and Hellenism: Classic Lines*, Cambridge: Cambridge University Press, 1997, p. 112

84   William Carlos Williams, 'A Sort of Song', *Selected Poems*, New York: New Directions, 1968, p. 109. It appears in the poem as 'No ideas/but in things'

85   H.D. quotes this in a letter to Cournos

86   William Carlos Williams, 'Prologue' (1918), *Kora in Hell*, in *Imaginations*, ed. Webster Schott, New York: New Directions, 1970, pp. 12–13

87   P/W 37

88   JGFL 50. He knew the 'Rhythmist' painter J.D. Fergusson through his friend Horace Holley

89   R. Herdman Pender, 'John Gould Fletcher', EG 3, November 1916, pp. 173–174

90   HDCP 59–68

91   EPL 169

92   H.D., 'Responsibilities', *Agenda*, 25/3–4, Autumn & Winter, 1987/88, pp. 51–3

93   'Status Rerum – The Second', PMV 8/1, April 1916, pp. 39–40

94   HDCP 41

95   DHLL3 48

96   DH 18

97   DHLL3 105

98   BID 123–126. H.D. in the 1930s took a keen interest in the Mass Observation project, which was dedicated to learning more about the experiences of ordinary people: see Georgina Taylor, *H.D. and the Public Sphere of Modernist Women Writers 1913–1946*, Oxford: Clarendon Press, 2001, p. 149

99   John Gould Fletcher, '"Amores" by D.H. Lawrence', and H.D., 'Goblins and Pagodas', EG 3, December 1916, pp. 182, 183

100 JGF 108

101 Cournos, *Autobiography*, p. 211

102 D.H. Lawrence, *Aaron's Rod* [1922], Harmondsworth: Penguin, 1950, p. 143

103 'The Death of Futurism', EG 4, January 1917, p. 6

104 RA 138. See also the discussion in Timothy Materer, *Vortex: Pound, Eliot and Lewis*, Ithaca: Cornell University Press, 1979, pp. 117–118

105 *Blast*, p. 134

106 P/ACH 187

107 See Alfred Satterthwaite, 'John Cournos and "H.D."', *Twentieth-Century Literature*, 22, 1976

108 'Aboriginal Poetry, 1 & 2', PMV 9/5, February 1917, pp. 251, 255. 'Poetry of the North American Indian', PMV 14/1, April 1919, pp. 2, 46

109 Michael Castro, *Interpreting the Indian: Twentieth-Century American Poets and the Native American*, Albuquerque: University of New Mexico Press, 1983, p. 240

110 Harriet Monroe, *Poets and their Art* [1926], New York: Macmillan (enlarged ed.), 1932, p. 93. Even Jonathan Cape, when it published H.D.'s *Heliodora and Other Poems* in 1924, advertised it with the comment: 'Her work blends European suavity with a kind of red-Indian terseness, nerve and barbarity of phrase.' Barbara Guest, *Herself Defined: The Poet H.D. and her World*, London: Collins, 1985, p. 168

111 PMV 11/6, March 1918, p. 339

112 HLFL (14 July 1917)

113 HLHD (14 July 1917)

114 HFLL (4 October 1917)

115 T.S. Eliot, 'Reflections on *Vers Libre*' [first published *New Statesman*, 3 March 1917], in *Selected Prose*, ed. Frank Kermode, London: Faber & Faber, 1975, pp. 31, 32, 36

116 'Harold Monro', *Polite Essays*, London: Faber & Faber, 1937, p. 14

117 'Vers Libre and Arnold Dolmetsch', EG 4, July 1917, pp. 90–91

118 PER 229, 232

119 P/ACH 206

120 T.S. Eliot, *Collected Poems, 1909–1935*, London: Faber & Faber, 1936, p. 41

121 'Reflections on *Vers Libre*', pp. 33, 36

122 P/LR xxiv

123 HC 333

124 EPL 231

125 YB 16/612. Letter to Bryher, 13 October 1948

126 YHD 14/489 (13 November 1959)

127 HULME xxviii

128 Flint was asked to do so first, but refused

129 'Short Reviews', EG 4, December 1917, pp. 172–173

130 As far as one can tell, these poems were all written rather later than the Tour Eiffel period, as they have much more flexible forms than the early poems, though they probably date from before 1919. None of those preserved in manuscripts with his London address are included, and in both style and subject-matter the poems in the book are more finished and mature than those early ones

131 According to the Western dates, the February Revolution took place in March, just as what we know as the October revolution occurred in November. DHLL3190

132 Amy Lowell, *Tendencies in American Poetry*, New York: Houghton Mifflin, 1917, pp. 276, 279, 275

133 H.D., Letter to Norman Pearson, 1937 ('A Note on Poetry'), [first published in 1937, re-edited for this publication by Diana Collecott] *Agenda*, 25, 3&4, Autumn/Winter 1987/1988, pp. 73, 71–72

134 LL 197

135 DH 297

136 BID 47

137 These words appear in one of Aldington's letters (20 May 1918): 'The truth is: I love you & I desire – l'autre', CZ 57, BID 56;

138 BID 102

139 BID 49, 71

140 CZ 89

141 BID 51, 62

142 DHLL3 180. BID 52

143 BID 78, 81

144 BID 139, 140

145   END 5–6
146   Bryher, *The Heart to Artemis: A Writer's Memoirs*, London: Collins, 1963, p. 193
147   CZ2 17
148   YHD 1/22, 16 December 1950
149   YHD 14/489, 8 September 1959

INDEX

EP = Ezra Pound; H.D. = Hilda Doolittle; *q.v./qq.v* = 'see entry'